Microsoft® Windows NT® Secrets®, Option Pack Edition

Microsoft® Windows NT® Secrets®, Option Pack Edition

Harry M. Brelsford

IDG Books Worldwide, Inc.
An International Data Group Company

Foster City, CA ♦ Chicago, IL ♦ Indianapolis, IN ♦ New York, NY

Microsoft® Windows NT® Secrets®, Option Pack Edition

Published by
IDG Books Worldwide, Inc.
An International Data Group Company
919 E. Hillsdale Blvd., Suite 400
Foster City, CA 94404
www.idgbooks.com (IDG Books Worldwide Web site)

Copyright © 1999 IDG Books Worldwide, Inc. All rights reserved. No part of this book, including interior design, cover design, and icons, may be reproduced or transmitted in any form, by any means (electronic, photocopying, recording, or otherwise) without the prior written permission of the publisher.

Library of Congress Cataloging -in-Publication Data

Brelsford, Harry M., 1961–
   NT secrets, option pack editiion   /   Harry M. Brelsford
      p.   cm.
   Includes index.
   ISBN: 0-7645-3130-1 (alk. paper)
    1. Microsoft Windows NT.   2. Operating systems (computers)
  I. Title.
QA76.76.063B7415   1999   99-19196
005.4'4769--dc21   CIP

Printed in the United States of America

10 9 8 7 6 5 4 3 2 1

1B/QV/QV/ZZ/FC

Distributed in the United States by IDG Books Worldwide, Inc.

Distributed by CDG Books Canada Inc. for Canada; by Transworld Publishers Limited in the United Kingdom; by IDG Norge Books for Norway; by IDG Sweden Books for Sweden; by IDG Books Australia Publishing Corporation Pty. Ltd. for Australia and New Zealand; by TransQuest Publishers Pte Ltd. for Singapore, Malaysia, Thailand, Indonesia, and Hong Kong; by Gotop Information Inc. for Taiwan; by ICG Muse, Inc. for Japan; by Norma Comunicaciones S.A. for Colombia; by Intersoft for South Africa; by Le Monde en Tique for France; by International Thomson Publishing for Germany, Austria and Switzerland; by Distribuidora Cuspide for Argentina; by Livraria Cultura for Brazil; by Ediciones ZETA S.C.R. Ltda. for Peru; by WS Computer Publishing Corporation, Inc., for the Philippines; by Contemporanea de Ediciones for Venezuela; by Express Computer Distributors for the Caribbean and West Indies; by Micronesia Media Distributor, Inc. for Micronesia; by Grupo Editorial Norma S.A. for Guatemala; by Chips Computadoras S.A. de C.V. for Mexico; by Editorial Norma de Panama S.A. for Panama; by American Bookshops for Finland. Authorized Sales Agent: Anthony Rudkin Associates for the Middle East and North Africa.For general information on IDG Books Worldwide's books in the U.S., please call our Consumer Customer Service department at 800-762-2974. For reseller information, including discounts and premium sales, please call our Reseller Customer Service department at 800-434-3422.

For information on where to purchase IDG Books Worldwide's books outside the U.S., please contact our International Sales department at 317-596-5530 or fax 317-596-5692.

For consumer information on foreign language translations, please contact our Customer Service department at 800-434-3422, fax 317-596-5692, or e-mail rights@idgbooks.com.

For information on licensing foreign or domestic rights, please phone +1-650-655-3109.

For sales inquiries and special prices for bulk quantities, please contact our Sales department at 650-655-3200 or write to the address above.

For information on using IDG Books Worldwide's books in the classroom or for ordering examination copies, please contact our Educational Sales department at 800-434-2086 or fax 317-596-5499.

For press review copies, author interviews, or other publicity information, please contact our Public Relations department at 650-655-3000 or fax 650-655-3299.

For authorization to photocopy items for corporate, personal, or educational use, please contact Copyright Clearance Center, 222 Rosewood Drive, Danvers, MA 01923, or fax 978-750-4470.

> **LIMIT OF LIABILITY/DISCLAIMER OF WARRANTY**: THE PUBLISHER AND AUTHOR HAVE USED THEIR BEST EFFORTS IN PREPARING THIS BOOK. THE PUBLISHER AND AUTHOR MAKE NO REPRESENTATIONS OR WARRANTIES WITH RESPECT TO THE ACCURACY OR COMPLETENESS OF THE CONTENTS OF THIS BOOK AND SPECIFICALLY DISCLAIM ANY IMPLIED WARRANTIES OF MERCHANTABILITY OR FITNESS FOR A PARTICULAR PURPOSE. THERE ARE NO WARRANTIES WHICH EXTEND BEYOND THE DESCRIPTIONS CONTAINED IN THIS PARAGRAPH. NO WARRANTY MAY BE CREATED OR EXTENDED BY SALES REPRESENTATIVES OR WRITTEN SALES MATERIALS. THE ACCURACY AND COMPLETENESS OF THE INFORMATION PROVIDED HEREIN AND THE OPINIONS STATED HEREIN ARE NOT GUARANTEED OR WARRANTED TO PRODUCE ANY PARTICULAR RESULTS, AND THE ADVICE AND STRATEGIES CONTAINED HEREIN MAY NOT BE SUITABLE FOR EVERY INDIVIDUAL. NEITHER THE PUBLISHER NOR AUTHOR SHALL BE LIABLE FOR ANY LOSS OF PROFIT OR ANY OTHER COMMERCIAL DAMAGES, INCLUDING BUT NOT LIMITED TO SPECIAL, INCIDENTAL, CONSEQUENTIAL, OR OTHER DAMAGES.

Trademarks: All brand names and product names used in this book are trade names, service marks, trademarks, or registered trademarks of their respective owners. IDG Books Worldwide is not associated with any product or vendor mentioned in this book.

 is a registered trademark or trademark under exclusive license to IDG Books Worldwide, Inc. from International Data Group, Inc. in the United States and/or other countries

ABOUT IDG BOOKS WORLDWIDE

Welcome to the world of IDG Books Worldwide.

IDG Books Worldwide, Inc., is a subsidiary of International Data Group, the world's largest publisher of computer-related information and the leading global provider of information services on information technology. IDG was founded more than 30 years ago by Patrick J. McGovern and now employs more than 9,000 people worldwide. IDG publishes more than 290 computer publications in over 75 countries. More than 90 million people read one or more IDG publications each month.

Launched in 1990, IDG Books Worldwide is today the #1 publisher of best-selling computer books in the United States. We are proud to have received eight awards from the Computer Press Association in recognition of editorial excellence and three from Computer Currents' First Annual Readers' Choice Awards. Our best-selling ...For Dummies® series has more than 50 million copies in print with translations in 31 languages. IDG Books Worldwide, through a joint venture with IDG's Hi-Tech Beijing, became the first U.S. publisher to publish a computer book in the People's Republic of China. In record time, IDG Books Worldwide has become the first choice for millions of readers around the world who want to learn how to better manage their businesses.

Our mission is simple: Every one of our books is designed to bring extra value and skill-building instructions to the reader. Our books are written by experts who understand and care about our readers. The knowledge base of our editorial staff comes from years of experience in publishing, education, and journalism — experience we use to produce books to carry us into the new millennium. In short, we care about books, so we attract the best people. We devote special attention to details such as audience, interior design, use of icons, and illustrations. And because we use an efficient process of authoring, editing, and desktop publishing our books electronically, we can spend more time ensuring superior content and less time on the technicalities of making books.

You can count on our commitment to deliver high-quality books at competitive prices on topics you want to read about. At IDG Books Worldwide, we continue in the IDG tradition of delivering quality for more than 30 years. You'll find no better book on a subject than one from IDG Books Worldwide.

John Kilcullen
Chairman and CEO
IDG Books Worldwide, Inc.

Steven Berkowitz
President and Publisher
IDG Books Worldwide, Inc.

Eighth Annual
Computer Press
Awards ≥1992

Ninth Annual
Computer Press
Awards ≥1993

Tenth Annual
Computer Press
Awards ≥1994

Eleventh Annual
Computer Press
Awards ≥1995

IDG is the world's leading IT media, research and exposition company. Founded in 1964, IDG had 1997 revenues of $2.05 billion and has more than 9,000 employees worldwide. IDG offers the widest range of media options that reach IT buyers in 75 countries representing 95% of worldwide IT spending. IDG's diverse product and services portfolio spans six key areas including print publishing, online publishing, expositions and conferences, market research, education and training, and global marketing services. More than 90 million people read one or more of IDG's 290 magazines and newspapers, including IDG's leading global brands — Computerworld, PC World, Network World, Macworld and the Channel World family of publications. IDG Books Worldwide is one of the fastest-growing computer book publishers in the world, with more than 700 titles in 36 languages. The "...For Dummies®" series alone has more than 50 million copies in print. IDG offers online users the largest network of technology-specific Web sites around the world through IDG.net (http://www.idg.net), which comprises more than 225 targeted Web sites in 55 countries worldwide. International Data Corporation (IDC) is the world's largest provider of information technology data, analysis and consulting, with research centers in over 41 countries and more than 400 research analysts worldwide. IDG World Expo is a leading producer of more than 168 globally branded conferences and expositions in 35 countries including E3 (Electronic Entertainment Expo), Macworld Expo, ComNet, Windows World Expo, ICE (Internet Commerce Expo), Agenda, DEMO, and Spotlight. IDG's training subsidiary, ExecuTrain, is the world's largest computer training company, with more than 230 locations worldwide and 785 training courses. IDG Marketing Services helps industry-leading IT companies build international brand recognition by developing global integrated marketing programs via IDG's print, online and exposition products worldwide. Further information about the company can be found at www.idg.com.

1/24/99

Credits

Acquisitions Editors
Tracy Thomsic
John Read

Development Editors
Lisa Donohoe
Jennifer Rowe

Technical Editor
James R. Kiniry, Jr.

Copy Editors
Robert Campbell
Larisa North

Production
IDG Books Worldwide Production

Proofreading and Indexing
York Production Services

About the Author

Harry M. Brelsford, MCSE, MCT, CNE, CLSE, CNP, MBA is a contributing editor for *Microsoft Certified Professional Magazine*, for which he pens the regular column, "Professionally Speaking." He is the network consulting manager for CN Consulting (a Microsoft Certified Solution Provider and a subsidiary of Clark Nuber PS) in the Seattle, Washington area, where he specializes in Microsoft BackOffice projects. Harry is an instructor in the evening MCSE program at Seattle Pacific University, a Microsoft AATP. He has published over 100 technology and business articles in numerous magazines, and is a founding member of the BackOffice Professionals Association (BOPA) in Redmond, WA. When time allows, Harry enjoys cross-country skiing and sailing with his family in the Pacific Northwest. You can contact him at harry@nwlink.com.

To Kristen, my wife and the mother of our Geoffrey Sailor and Harry Skier! You were truly there, whether you knew it or not, typing each key, writing each page, and reviewing each draft with me. You made contributions to this book in a million ways.

Foreword

What happens after you make the decision to install Windows NT?

If you're a network professional responsible for deploying, supporting, and maintaining this complex product, you know that inserting that first CD is just the beginning. What comes after that is a huge need for knowledge — far beyond what's available from Microsoft sources.

Harry Brelsford knows what it means to sit in front of a server and install the product, and then support and maintain it for demanding customers after the fact. His expertise as a consultant and his years of in-the-field experience as a practicing Windows NT professional are reflected in this book.

I've worked with Harry since shortly after the launch of *Microsoft Certified Professional Magazine* in early 1995, so I know that he's been out there in the trenches right along with the rest of you. He's both a Contributing Editor to the magazine and an MCSE — further proof that he understands Microsoft technology in general and Windows NT in particular.

The title of the book says it all. The "secrets" about Windows NT inserted throughout the book are truly that: little-known tips and tricks for saving time and increasing productivity, tested by someone who has used the product for years.

If you need further proof of Harry's real-world expertise, take a look at the table of contents. Only someone who really understands Windows NT knows that you won't get far without a solid knowledge of TCP/IP — hence the inclusion of Part II. And only someone who has done plenty of NT installations, troubleshooting, and support calls would include extensive information on third-party tools useful in many Windows NT installations. If you're not using some of these tools now, perhaps that section will be an eye-opener for what's out there that can save you time and hassle. You can bet that Harry has used all of them in his own projects. If you're running NT now or planning to, you'll also want to take a look at his coverage of optimization and troubleshooting — much of it is information I haven't seen anywhere else.

If you're not familiar with Windows NT yet, but are eyeing it with interest, this is a perfect book to show you the richness and complexity of the product from someone who enjoys working with it. You won't find marketing spiels or product apologies here. Instead, you'll get useful, professional information on NT, all of it written in Harry's inimitable style. And if you're thinking of moving to Windows 2000 eventually, or want to make sure you're prepared, Harry gives you information about that as well.

I have no doubt this book is timely. In fact, as I read through the diverse topics covered, I thought over and over, "What a great article idea for the magazine!" Harry's been brightening the pages of *MCP Magazine* for years with his knowledge, insights, and wit. Spend some time with this book and let him give you a true insider's coaching on Windows NT.

Linda Briggs
Editor-in-Chief, *Microsoft Certified Professional Magazine*
February 1999

Preface

Welcome! *Microsoft Windows NT Secrets, Option Pack Edition* is a book based on Microsoft's successful network operating system and its latest enhancements, such as the Option Pack. It is a book unlike many others on the shelf. It is a collection of secrets gathered in the trenches from my 10+ years of experience as a computer professional. This book is about having "been there and done that" with Windows NT Server. And with its quippy delivery, it is both a reference book and a summer-vacation-at-the-beach kind of read. But more on all that in a moment.

Why use this book? Isn't Windows NT Server 4.0 going to be retired soon, giving way to Windows 2000 Server? I can give you at least a half-dozen reasons to purchase this book today, in anticipation of tomorrow:

- **Windows 2000 Server transition and planning**. The old adage "proper planning prevents poor performance" clearly applies to Windows NT Server today, with a knowing wink toward Windows 2000 Server tomorrow. By getting your Windows NT Server house in order now, you'll have more success when you upgrade to Windows 2000 Server later. This is a recurring theme that spans my entire effort, but is discussed most thoroughly in Chapter 26, "Defining and Planning for Windows 2000 Server."

- **Option Pack and Service Pack 4.** The Option Pack was a significant addition to the core Windows NT Server operating system, not only extending its functionality, but also providing an early look at what life will be like in the forthcoming Windows 2000 Server world. Service Pack 4 provides the maturity that many of us, especially those with significant networking experience, needed to convince both ourselves and our stakeholders that Windows NT Server 4.0 is now ready for mission-critical use in the enterprise. Working with the Option Pack and Service Pack 4 is a step you can take to prepare for Windows 2000 Server.

- **MCSE Certification Tips.** This book is written by a practicing MCSE. Hey, I've taken those demanding exams (sometimes more than once). May my well-placed MCSE insights enable you to pass your exams sooner rather than later.

- **TCP/IP.** This is a timeless topic that you can never get enough of. Mastering TCP/IP is one of the fastest ways to achieve greatness in the Windows NT Server community, regardless of the product release version. I am especially proud of my discussion on DNS in Chapter 8. DNS is an area I highly recommend you master immediately, because it assumes a core role in the upcoming Windows 2000 Server release. TCP/IP is covered from cradle to grave in Part II, "TCP/IP."

- **Performance Analysis.** Like TCP/IP, this topic doesn't have an expiration date. In fact, the more experienced you become with Windows NT Server, the more important performance analysis becomes. Too often, you learn performance analysis in a crisis, but hopefully you'll read Part VI, "Optimizing and Troubleshooting Windows NT Server 4.0" before that day arrives. Truth be told, I initially wrote this section for my own benefit because I just could not find another Windows NT Server book on the market that adequately addressed performance analysis issues, such as PerfMon logging and Network Monitor packet analysis. I hope you will benefit from my efforts in this area.

- **Third-party solutions, Terminal Server, and Small Business Server.** Another motivating factor in writing this book was my use of the Microsoft Official Curriculum (MOC) as a practicing MCT. The MOC is a great first step for getting certified. But the MOC has not and will probably never highlight third-party solutions that we experienced Windows NT Server professionals like to use (and often must use) to keep our networks humming and our stakeholders singing. In that spirit, I serve up deft discussions on the use of third-party applications, utilities, and tools such as NessSoft's PingPlotter, Seagate's Backup Exec, Computer Associate's Inoculan, Hewlett Packard's JetDirect card, and so on. Let's face it—too many books are written myopically about Windows NT Server in a vacuum. Most of us, however, supplement Windows NT Server with a variety of third-party applications, utilities, and tools. My book reflects this real-world paradigm.

And because I couldn't find abundant reference works on Terminal Server and Small Business Server, I assumed you couldn't either. So, I took the bull by the horns and included these topics, based on my work experience, in this book. For Terminal Server, see Chapter 19; for Small Business Server, see Chapter 20.

Are You Ready for This Book?

To fully enjoy this book, you must, at a minimum, have a keen interest in Windows NT Server. Add computer-related work experience, network certifications, degrees, and training, and you'll get even more benefit from reading and using this book. In short, you will derive from this book what you put into it. Those with less Windows NT Server experience may be the ones to utter "wow" and "cool" the loudest and longest. Those who are gurus can always benefit from revisiting many tried-and-true Windows NT Server management methods presented herein. And I think the gurus will benefit greatly from my inclusion of several real-world, third-party matters, such as non-Microsoft tools that extended the reach of Windows NT Server.

How This Book Is Organized

I have organized the book into seven parts, as follows:

- **Part I: Introduction, Planning, Setup, and Implementation.** It is here that I present, in a sincere and honorable way, the steps for installing Windows NT Server. I say "sincere and honorable" because here, as throughout the book, I go to great lengths to avoid recasting the user manuals that shipped with Windows NT Server. Rather, in addition to providing the installation basics you must follow, I offer supplemental secrets at every installation and implementation turn in the road.

- **Part II: TCP/IP.** Enough said. This important topic is, of course, worthy of its own book, but I strive to integrate core TCP/IP topics into the discussion of Windows NT Server. I think you will especially enjoy the DNS, troubleshooting, and Internet discussions. And no, I don't recount for you the history of the Internet, starting with the Department of Defense (I'm sure you already have books that do that).

- **Part III: Windows NT Server Administration.** This section could have been titled "Real-World, Day-to-Day Windows NT Server." I took my own experiences, validated by a group of peers, and created a list of the 12 most likely Windows NT Server-related tasks you will perform each day. The result? See Chapter 11, "The Daily Dozen." Monthly and annual matters are covered in Chapter 12, which offers compelling insights into network vision creation.

- **Part IV: Service Pack 4.0 and the Windows NT Server Option Pack.** It is for this section that this edition of Windows NT Server Secrets was released. The use of the Option Pack and implementation of Service Pack 4 are so important that four significant chapters were dedicated to these topics. This section offers more step-by-step guidance than other sections so you can properly install and implement both the Option Pack and Service Pack 4.

- **Part V: The Four Flavors of Windows NT Server 4.0.** Windows NT Server isn't just good old build 1381 anymore. There are now several flavors of Windows NT Server. Regular Windows NT Server, which most of us are familiar with, is revisited in Chapter 17. The Enterprise Edition of Windows NT Server is discussed in Chapter 18. Terminal Server, a real treat, is covered extensively in Chapter 19, and Small Business Server is covered from A to Z in Chapter 20.

- **Part VI: Optimizing and Troubleshooting Windows NT Server 4.0.** Here, you will find the secrets to improving the performance of your Windows NT Server network. Topics include the basic quantitative analysis (MBA-style), Performance Monitor, and the basic and advanced use of Network Monitor. You will also greatly benefit from the secrets and insights into Windows NT Server troubleshooting. Troubleshooting topics include troubleshooting hands-on approaches, methodologies, tools, and resources. If some of my tips save you even just one hour of network downtime, might I suggest this book has more than paid back the price you bought it for.

- **Part VII: Preparing for Windows 2000.** This section not only defines what Windows 2000 Server is, but also what it will mean to you. Indeed, there are steps and precautions you can take today to ensure that you will soon enjoy a smoother and more successful upgrade experience with Windows 2000 Server!

There are four CD-ROMs at the back of the book. Many of the third-party applications discussed in the book are available, in trial version, on the companion CD-ROM 1.

Conventions Used in This Book

I use two icons throughout this book. You should know their meaning before proceeding:

Secret

The Secrets icon underscores why we're here. Secrets are the foundation of this book; they are little-known timesavers, productivity gainers, and other proprietary Swiss Army knife-like workarounds you might like to know as a Windows NT Server professional.

Note

Notes are more widely known tidbits of information, factoids, trivia, and the like. I also use notes in a very serious manner, to warn you of danger!

Tell Us What You Think

A book about Windows NT Server necessarily assumes some of the "behaviors" of Windows NT Server, right? By that, I mean that you've probably thought of ways in which Windows NT Server could be improved. Likewise, as you read and refer to this book, you'll undoubtedly think of ways in which this book could be improved.

That said, both IDG Books Worldwide and I want to hear from you. Please register your book online at the IDG Books Worldwide Web site (at my2cents.idgbooks.com) and give us your feedback. If you are interested in communicating with me directly, send e-mail to harryb@nwlink.com. Bear with me, I'll try to answer your e-mails within a few business days. Hey — when you're a practicing Windows NT Server professional, things sometimes get a little crazy!

Acknowledgments

No author is an island, although many of us live on 'em. Behind the title and author's name on the cover, there is a supporting cast that contributed to the effort of producing this book.

First and foremost are the contributing writers who assisted with bits and pieces of this book. They are Larry Youngquist, Pat Newton, John Smith, Dave Marsh, Peter Henley, Joe Paulino, and Dawn Casey. And of course there is the wonderful Jim Kiniry, the technical editor for this work.

Second is the support team at IDG Books Worldwide, who worked double-time to get this book out on the market for your benefit. Thanks in particular to Tracy Thomsic, Jennifer Rowe, and Lisa Donohoe. (Needless to say, there are many other cast members at IDG Books who I've overlooked — thanks again!).

Third, kindly join me in acknowledging my portfolio of consulting clients who have provided unlimited contributions to this book. Without them, I would be secretless in Seattle, and this book would have suffered greatly as a result.

Fourth, please recognize those rare and special individuals we all have in our lives. For me, that includes not only my extended family on both sides, but also a whole host of mentors who have largely paved my road in life. To Eric Wohlforth, the municipal bond counsel who, more than 20 years ago, encouraged me to master the business purpose of computer technology (and to communicate it all in English). He said that if I did that, everything would work out fine. (He was right.) To Mark Levine, the Denver-based super-lawyer in real estate syndications and taxation, author, and professor to me at the University of Denver. To Richard Brandenburg of Seattle, who took me under his wing when I arrived on these shores ten years ago with only his business card and the cash in my hip pocket. And to countless others (including George Sedlock, for the printer to print my manuscript drafts, Ralph Kester, Bob Nuber, yadda yadda yadda).

Whew! Enjoy the book!!!

Contents at a Glance

Foreword ix

Part I: Introduction, Planning, Setup, and Implementation 1
Chapter 1: Another Look at Windows NT Server 3
Chapter 2: Windows NT Server 4.0 Planning, Setup, and Installation 11
Chapter 3: Windows NT Server 4.0 Implementation 53

Part II: TCP/IP 105
Chapter 4: TCP/IP Secrets 107
Chapter 5: TCP/IP Implementations 143
Chapter 6: Installing and Configuring TCP/IP 167
Chapter 7: Troubleshooting TCP/IP 211
Chapter 8: DNS, DHCP, WINS 253
Chapter 9: Advanced TCP/IP Secrets 333
Chapter 10: Internet Secrets 349

Part III: Windows NT Server Administration 385
Chapter 11: The Daily Dozen 387
Chapter 12: Monthly and Annual Windows NT Server Activities 425

Part IV: Service Pack 4.0 and the Windows NT Server Option Pack 447
Chapter 13: Windows NT 4.0 Option Pack 449
Chapter 14: History and Role of Service Packs 533
Chapter 15: Service Pack 4 Fixes 549
Chapter 16: Service Pack 4 Additions and Miscellaneous 561

Part V: The Four Flavors of Windows NT Server 4.0 597
Chapter 17: "Regular" Windows NT Server 599
Chapter 18: Windows NT Server — Enterprise Edition 615
Chapter 19: Microsoft NT Server — Terminal Edition 629
Chapter 20: Windows NT Server — Small Business Server 649

Part VI: Optimizing and Troubleshooting Windows NT Server 4.0 729

Chapter 21: Analyzing and Boosting Performance 731
Chapter 22: Performance Monitor 757
Chapter 23: Network Monitor Secrets 803
Chapter 24: Task Manager and Other Neat Tricks 851
Chapter 25: Troubleshooting Secrets 907

Part VII: Preparing for Windows 2000 961

Chapter 26: Defining and Planning for Windows 2000 Server 963

Appendix A 987

Appendix B 1023

Appendix C 1045

Appendix D 1047

Appendix E 1061

Index 1073

End-User License Agreement 1118

CD-ROM Installation Instructions 1122

Contents

Foreword ix

Preface xi

Acknowledgments xv

Part I: Introduction, Planning, Setup, and Implementation 1

Chapter 1: Another Look at Windows NT Server 3
Aged to Perfection 3
What Is Windows NT Server 4.0? 4
    Enterprise Edition 5
    Terminal Server 6
    Small Business Server 6
TCP/IP Paradigm Shift 6
Internet Paradigm Shift 7
Option Pack and Service Pack 4 7
The MCSE 8
Preparing for Windows 2000 Server 8

Chapter 2: Windows NT Server 4.0 Planning, Setup, and Installation 11
Planning 11
    Physical site 11
    System components 14
    Loose ends 23
Setting Up Windows NT Server 27
    Things to know before you begin setup 28
    Running Setup 33
    Graphical setup 38
Alternate Setup Methods 41
    Installing Windows NT Server from a network share 41
    Installing Windows NT Server over other operating systems 43
    Dual-booting 44
Installation Secrets 44
    Putting the NT source files on the server's hard disk 44
    Editing boot.ini to shorten the OS startup delay 46
    Establishing a real "boot partition" for your boot files 48

Chapter 3: Windows NT Server 4.0 Implementation 53
Tools of the Trade 54
    User Manager for Domains 54

  Creating a new user 54
  Deleting users 56
  Managing accounts 57
  Delegate administrators 59
  Domains 59
  Domain trust relationships 59
  Global and local groups 62
  Security identifiers (SIDs) 62
  Users, global, local, rights (UGLR) 62
Delivering User Services 62
  Adding printers to your server 63
  File sharing with Windows NT Server 63
Securing Your Network 68
  Logon security 69
  NT File System permissions 70
  Share permissions 71
  User profiles 74
  System policies 76
Getting Your Users Connected: Logon Scripts 78
  Logon script functions 81
  Logon script requirements 82
  Logon script tips and useful tidbits 83
Protecting Your Data with Backups 84
  Backup strategies 85
  Off-site storage 86
Protecting Your Network from Viruses 90
  Infection points 91
  The virus-warning virus 91
  Don't poor-boy virus protection! 92
Remote Access 92
  Remote Access Service 95
  PCAnywhere 95
Microsoft Mail 97
 98

Part II: TCP/IP 105

Chapter 4: TCP/IP Secrets 107

About TCP/IP 108
  The standard-bearer 108
  By committee: Requests for Comments (RFCs) 109
  It's a suite, not just a protocol 112
  Comparing TCP/IP to operating systems 114
A Look at the Protocols 114
  Transmission Control Protocol (TCP) 116
  User Datagram Protocol (UDP) 117
  Internet Protocol (IP) 118
  Address Resolution Protocol (ARP) 119
  Internet Control Message Protocol (ICMP) 121
  Internet Group Management Protocol (IGMP) 121
  Simple Network Management Protocol (SNMP) 123
What Is the Microsoft TCP/IP Protocol Suite in Windows NT Server 4.0? 123

The TCP/IP Settings in Windows NT Server 126
A Day in the Life of a TCP/IP Packet 129
    IP 129
    TCP 133
Internetworking with TCP/IP 136
    Breeder networks 137
    Heterogeneous Networks 137
    Windows Sockets 138
    Third-party TCP/IP software support 138
    Simple routing 140
A Word about Research 142

Chapter 5: TCP/IP Implementations 143

Internet Addressing 143
    IP addresses 144
    Subnet masks 148
    Default gateways 152
Understanding IP Routing 161
Routing Tables 163

Chapter 6: Installing and Configuring TCP/IP 167

TCP/IP Installation Preparations 167
Installing TCP/IP on Windows NT Server 169
    At setup 170
    On an existing Windows NT server 171
    Supporting roving users with TCP/IP 198
Installing and Configuring Simple Network Management Protocol (SNMP) 199
    Planning for SNMP 200
    Installing SNMP service 201
    Configuring the SNMP agent 202
    Configuring SNMP communities and traps 204
    Configuring SNMP security 206
TCP/IP-Related Services 208

Chapter 7: Troubleshooting TCP/IP 211

TCP/IP Troubleshooting Basics 211
First Step: Ask the Basic Questions 213
Second Step: Define the Tools 213
Third Step: Use the Tools 215
    IPConfig 216
    PING 219
    ARP 223
    NBTSTAT 226
    Route 228
    Netstat 228
    Tracert 231
    Hostname 232
    FTP 232
    TFTP 234
    Telnet 235

                RCP 238
                RSH 239
                REXEC 239
                Finger 239
                Microsoft Internet Explorer 239
            Other TCP/IP Troubleshooting Angles 240
                Troubleshooting TCP/IP Database Files 240
                Reinstalling TCP/IP 247
            TCP/IP Q & A 249
            Additional TCP/IP Troubleshooting Resources 251

Chapter 8: DNS, DHCP, WINS 253

    Be Resolved 253
        NetBIOS name resolution 253
        Host name resolution 254
    DNS 255
        How DNS really works 257
        DNS benefits 261
        DNS details and definitions 262
        Name resolution — how it works 262
        Zone transfer 271
        Installing DNS 272
        Configuring DNS 273
        DNS standard and revisions 273
        Final DNS musings 285
    DHCP 286
        Benefits and overview of DHCP 287
        How does DHCP really work? 287
        Installing the DHCP Server service 289
        Creating DHCP scopes 297
        Using DHCP Manager 300
        Configuring DHCP options 302
        DHCP and DNS 306
        Managing DHCP database files 318
        Troubleshooting DHCP servers 319
    WINS 319
        How WINS Works 320
        Installing WINS servers 321
        Configuring WINS servers 322
        Configuring WINS clients 323
        Using WINS Manager 326
    WINS and DNS Integration 327
    Dynamic DNS 330

Chapter 9: Advanced TCP/IP Secrets 333

    The Fine Art of Subnetting 333
    What Subnetting Is 333
        Easier administration 334
        IP address conservation 334
        Improved security 334
        Another name for switching? 335

Bottom line? 335
What Subnetting Isn't 336
Code Breaking 101 336

Chapter 10: Internet Secrets 349

Dial-Up Connection 349
    Configuring Dial-Up Networking 352
    Dial-Up Networking dialog box 359
    Dialing The Internet 368
    Dial-Up Networking Monitor 369
    Dial-Up Networking with ISDN modems 370
Digital and Wide Area Network Internet Connections 370
    Scenario 1: ISDN Router 370
    Scenario 2: ISDN and WAN combination 373
    Scenario 3: Direct Frame Relay Connection 374
    Scenario 4: WAN Connection 374
    Scenario 5: WAN over Internet (VPN) 375
Point-To-Point Tunneling Protocol (PPTP) 376
    Defining PPTP 377
    Installing PPTP 377
Internet Explorer Secrets 380
Internet Information Server 383

Part III: Windows NT Server Administration 385

Chapter 11: The Daily Dozen 387

Step 1: The Windows NT/MCSE Toolkit 388
    User Manager for Domains 388
    Server Manager 389
    Event Viewer 390
    Performance Monitor 390
    Administrative Wizards 392
    Third-party administration tools 393
    The MCSE toolkit 394
Step 2: End User Support 399
    Remember your manners 399
    Educate the user 400
    Document your solutions 400
Step 3: Server Troubleshooting 400
    Documentation 401
    Logical deduction and process of elimination 401
    Microsoft TechNet 402
    Internet support groups 403
Step 4: Tape Backups 404
    Defining a backup schedule 404
    Checking backup logs 405
    Performing test restores 405
Step 5: Virus Protection 405
    Testing your antivirus software 406
    Updating data files 406
    Centralizing virus protection 407

Step 6: Free Disk Space 408
    Successful storage techniques 408
    More detail on weekly disk space monitoring 409
Step 7: Event Logs 410
Step 8: Verification of Servers and Applications 413
    First: Check on the servers and services 414
    Second: Check applications and databases 414
Step 9: Verification of LAN and WAN Connectivity 415
Step 10: New Hardware 417
    Preparing for installation 418
    Installing the hardware 418
    Installing and configuring drivers 419
Step 11: Documentation and Sharing Procedures 419
Step 12: Working and Happy Users 420
    Protect the users 421
    Keep the users informed 421
    Keep the help desk informed 422
    Strive for 100 percent uptime 422

Chapter 12: Monthly and Annual Windows NT Server Activities 425

Auditing Your Network 426
Reviewing Security 427
Baselining and Monitoring Performance 428
The Monthly Reboot 428
Mapping Disk Space on Servers 431
    The manual method 431
    The "automatic" method 431
    A real-world war story 432
Recovering from Disaster 433
    Third-party solutions 433
    Identical spare servers 434
    Reciprocity agreements/hot sites 435
    Why bother? 435
    Annual drill 435
Implementing Service Packs and Hotfixes 436
    Hotfixes 437
    Be conservative 438
Upgrading and Removing Applications 438
Creating Backup Archives 438
Budgeting for Your Network 439
    Zero-based budgeting 439
    Linear percent growth 440
    Percent of revenue 440
    Windows NT Server on $5 a day 441
Creating a Technology Committee 442
Evaluating Systems on the Horizon 444
    The case of Windows 2000 Server 444
    Two real-world examples 445
Remembering the Annual Planning Retreat 446

Part IV: Service Pack 4.0 and the Windows NT Server Option Pack 447

Chapter 13: Windows NT 4.0 Option Pack 449

Introduction to the Windows NT Option Pack 449
Installation and Troubleshooting 450
Internet Applications 455
    Internet Information Server (IIS) 4.0 455
    Certificate Server 1.0 485
    Index Server 2.0 494
Administration and Management 506
    Microsoft Management Console (MMC) 1.0 506
    Site Server Express 2.0 510
    Windows Scripting Host (WSH) 521
Transaction Processing 522
    Microsoft Transaction Server (MTS) 2.0 522
    Microsoft Message Queue Server (MSMQ) 1.0 523
Miscellaneous Components 529
    Microsoft Data Access Components (MDAC) 529
    Microsoft Script Debugger 530

Chapter 14: History and Role of Service Packs 533

Service Packs and HotFixes 533
The Service Pack 2 Fiasco 534
Service Pack 3 and Post Hotfixes 535
    SP3 installation 535
    SP3 troubleshooting 540
    Post-SP3 hotfixes 542
Service Pack 4 544
    Preinstallation requirements 545
    The installation process 545
    40-Bit versus 128-Bit encryption 546
    Uninstallation 548

Chapter 15: Service Pack 4 Fixes 549

Year 2000 (Y2K) Fixes 550
Internet Explorer 4.01 Service Pack 1 (SP1) 552
Option Pack Fixes 552
    Certificate Server 552
    Internet Information Server 4.0 553
    Message Queue (MSMQ) for Windows NT 553
    Microsoft Transaction Server (MTS) 555
    Simple Mail Transport Protocol (SMTP), Network News Transport Protocol (NNTP) 555
Networking and OS Fixes 555
    Dynamic Host Configuration Protocol (DHCP), Domain Name Server (DNS), Windows Internet Naming Service (WINS) 556
    Routing Information Protocol (RIP) Listener, Microsoft Routing and Remote Access Service (RRAS), and Point-to-Point Tunneling Protocol (PPTP) 557
    Event Log Service 559
    Other fixes 560

Chapter 16: Service Pack 4 Additions and Miscellaneous 561

- Security Configuration Editor (SCE) 561
  - Installing SCE 562
  - Template components 564
  - Configuring and analyzing 571
  - Command line configuration and analysis 573
  - Conclusion 574
- NetShow Services 3.0 574
  - NetShow terminology 575
  - Installation 576
  - NetShow service administration 577
- Site Server Express 3.0 588
- Miscellaneous SP4 Components 590
- Windows NT Services for UNIX 592

Part V: The Four Flavors of Windows NT Server 4.0 597

Chapter 17: "Regular" Windows NT Server 599

- Plain Old Windows NT Server 599
  - A 32-bit network operating system 600
  - The NT operating system model 600
  - Features of NT Server 4.0, build 1381 602
- Server versus Workstation: The Right Tool for the Job 607
  - Tuning issues 608
  - Processors 610
  - Clustering 610
  - RAS connections 610
  - Client connections 610
  - Security 611
  - File system support 611
  - Requirements 611
  - Fault tolerance 611
  - Internet Server services 612
- Using Windows NT Server as a User Workstation 612

Chapter 18: Windows NT Server — Enterprise Edition 615

- Microsoft's Great Challenge — The Enterprise 616
- Defining the Enterprise Edition 617
  - Key Differences from "Regular" Edition 617
  - What's in the Option Pack? 617
  - When to use Enterprise Edition 618
  - Design challenges 618
  - Technologies 619

Chapter 19: Microsoft NT Server — Terminal Edition 629

- History 629
- Environment 631
- Features 633

Remote control	634
Multisession	635
Centralized management	635
Lower costs	635
Components	635
Operating system	636
Remote Desktop Protocol	636
Terminal Server clients	636
Implementation	638
Hardware	639
Software	639
A Terminal Server Session	640
MetaFrame	641
Compare and Contrast	642
Terminal Server Downfalls	646

Chapter 20: Windows NT Server — Small Business Server 649

Defining Small Business Server	650
SBS version 4.0a	652
Windows NT Server 4.0	655
Microsoft Exchange Server 5.0	658
SQL Server 6.5	664
Microsoft Proxy Server 1.0 and 2.0	666
Microsoft Internet Information Server	668
Microsoft Fax Server 1.0	669
Microsoft Modem Sharing Server 1.0	672
Microsoft Index Server 1.1	673
Crystal Reports 4.5	674
SBS console	675
Client-side components	676
The Small Business Model	679
Small business server philosophy	679
Who are the SBS customers?	682
Looks can be deceiving	682
SBS architecture	682
SBS server-side setup	683
SBS workstation-side setup	698
SBS Administration	720
SBS Troubleshooting	724
Do your software vendors support SBS?	725
Modem sharing	725
HP network printers	728
Be careful changing passwords	728
Implementing Proxy 2.0	728
Harmless event logs errors	729
Revisiting SBS security	729
Virus detection	731
The Future of SBS	731

… xxvii

Part VI: Optimizing and Troubleshooting Windows NT Server 4.0 729

Chapter 21: Analyzing and Boosting Performance 731

Performance Analysis 732
    Built-in performance analysis tools 733
    More quantitative tools 736
    Qualitative tools too! 741
    Data = information 743
Are You Being "Outperformed"? 743
    Performance Monitor 743
    Network Monitor 744
    Task Manager 744
Conceptual Steps in Performance Analysis 744
Troubleshooting via Performance Analysis 745
The Big Four Areas to Monitor 746
    Memory 746
    Processor 747
    Disk subsystem 747
    Network subsystem 748
Why Performance Declines 752
Lying with Performance Analysis 754
Performance Benchmarks 755

Chapter 22: Performance Monitor 757

The Power of Performance Monitor 757
    Comparing Performance Monitor to NetWare MONITOR.NLM ... 759
    Performance Monitor basics 760
    Six quick steps to using Performance Monitor 761
The Four Faces of Performance Monitor 765
    Chart 765
    Alert 766
    Log 772
    Report 773
Data Collection and Interpretation 773
    Collecting data 774
    Interpreting your data 778
Performing In-Depth Analysis 783
    Memory bottlenecks 783
    Processor bottlenecks 787
    Disk bottlenecks 790
    Network bottlenecks 791
    Analyzing protocols 792
Analysis in Different Computing Environments 793
    File and print server environment analysis 794
    Application server environment system performance 795
Making Better Use of Performance Monitor 796
    Relogging 796
    Running multiple Performance Monitors 797

Removing clutter 799
Next steps 800

Chapter 23: Network Monitor Secrets 803

Initial Network Monitoring 803
    Network Monitor basics 804
    Capture window components 805
    Capturing frames 807
    Required hardware 808
    Analysis 809
Ongoing Network Monitoring 811
    Using the capture trigger 811
    Larger capture sessions 812
    Capture buffer size 813
    Frame size setting 813
    Capture filters 814
    Display filter 818
    Differences between capture filter
      and display filter? 822
    Password protection 824
    Watching you watch me 825
    The name game 825
It's All in the Patterns 829
Timing Is Everything 831
Artificial Intelligence Arrives
  in Network Monitor 831
I Want to Learn More! 832
    Paid support incidents 832
    Microsoft Solution Provider Program 833
    Official Microsoft Certification Training 833
    Display Filter Box—protocol definitions 834
    Microsoft TechNet CD-ROM 835
    Internet-based research 838
    Hardware devices 839
    Books 840
    Comparing Network Monitors:
      SMS versus NT Server 4.0 841

Chapter 24: Task Manager and Other Neat Tricks 851

Introducing Task Manager 852
    Configuring Task Manager—Applications view 855
    Configuring Task Manager—Performance view 856
    Configuring Task Manager—Processes view 859
    Multiple processors 872
WinMSD Is a Winner! 874
    Version tab sheet 875
    System tab sheet 876
    Display tab sheet 878
    Drives tab sheet 878
    Resources tab sheet 881
    Environment tab sheet 882
    Network tab sheet 883

Memory and Services tab sheets	886
Reporting meaningful system information	887
System Properties Sheet	888
General	889
Performance	889
Environment	890
Startup/shutdown	891
Hardware profiles	893
User profiles	895
SQL Trace	895
SQL Server ODBCPING and Exchange RPING	896
Event Logs	897
Microsoft Office — Microsoft System Information	898
Last but Not Least — Dr. Watson.	905

Chapter 25: Troubleshooting Secrets 907

Troubleshooting Steps	908
Defining Troubleshooting	910
A methodology	911
The one-hour rule	915
The value of downtime	917
The Troubleshooting Quilt	918
A troubleshooting map	919
Learning curve analysis	919
Avoiding box canyons	920
So much troubleshooting, so little time	921
Hardware versus Software — What a Paradox!	922
Let's Get Technical!	923
BOOT.INI switches	924
Four phases of booting	925
How to Get Out of Trouble	938
Expanding your way out of trouble — the case of the missing system files	938
Hot-wiring NT so the it will start: The NT boot disk	941
911 — The emergency repair process	942
Double 911 — Keep a current emergency repair disk	945
Examining Stop Screens	947
So what to do with stop screens?	949
Important debugging terms	950
Debuggers du jour	950
Interpreting dump files	953
Troubleshooting via the Registry	953
Troubleshooting Resources	953
The Internet: The Web and Newsgroups	954
Books to help you	955
Microsoft TechNet	956
Training and education	957
Professional resources	957
From the Backroom to the Boardroom	959

Part VII: Preparing for Windows 2000 961

Chapter 26: Defining and Planning for Windows 2000 Server 963
The Transition Chapter 964
Expectation Management 964
    Buy today/install today 964
    Feature short 965
    Unstable 965
Microsoft's Position on
  Windows 2000 Server 966
    File servers 966
    Print servers 966
    Web servers 966
    Applications servers 966
    Infrastructure servers 967
    Communications servers 967
Introducing Windows 2000 Server 967
    General 967
    Networking 970
    Internet 981
    Active Directory 981
    Change and configuration management 982
    Security 983
Planning for Windows 2000 Server 984

Appendix A 987

Appendix B 1023

Appendix C 1045

Appendix D 1047

Appendix E 1061

Index 1073

End-User License Agreement 1118

CD-ROM Installation Instructions 1122

Part I
Introduction, Planning, Setup, and Implementation

Chapter 1: Another Look at Windows NT Server

Chapter 2: Windows NT Server 4.0 Planning, Setup, and Installation

Chapter 3: Windows NT Server 4.0 Implementation

Chapter 1

Another Look at Windows NT Server

In This Chapter

▶ The Windows NT Server enhancements and optimizations

▶ Advantages of Windows NT Server 4.0

▶ Additions and enhancements to Windows NT Server 4.0: Option Pack and Service Pack

▶ Windows NT Server 4.0 and future releases of Windows 2000 Server

Many network professionals know never to use a network operating system (NOS) before its time. You may recall that those professionals familiar with NOSes didn't touch the original release of Windows NT Advanced Server 3.1 or Windows NT Server 3.5. In fact, wise network professionals didn't fully implement Windows NT Server in the enterprise until Service Pack 5 appeared for Windows NT Server 3.51. Not until that time did they trust Windows NT Server enough to take it seriously. Such is the feeling today with Windows NT Server 4.0 with the Option Pack and Service Pack 4.0. Now even the most conservative network professionals believe that Windows NT Server 4.0 with the Option Pack and Service Pack 4 is fully ready for use as the backbone for a company's network.

Windows NT Server 4.0 deserves another look with the release of the Option Pack and Service Pack 4.0 because, taken together, this "version" of Windows NT Server 4.0 represents your transition path to Windows 2000 Advanced Server. In fact, reading this book and implementing the Option Pack and Service Pack 4.0 on your Windows NT 4.0 network today are perhaps the best steps that you can take in order to prepare for Windows 2000 Advanced Server.

Aged to Perfection

With the release of the Windows NT Server Option Pack and Service Pack 4, network professionals not only feel confidence in Windows NT Server 4.0 as an NOS today but also know that they are well positioned to upgrade to Windows 2000 Advanced Server tomorrow. The smart money knows that Windows NT Server 4.0 will remain in service as the company's workhorse NOS for a long time, well after the introduction of Windows 2000 Server.

Note

It is important to remember that, like beef and fine wine, an NOS should be aged to perfection before use. Using an NOS before its time is certainly not recommended and would be considered foolish among qualified and experienced network professionals. One of my earliest experiences with Windows NT Server 4.0 was, unfortunately, a learning experience. So eager to deploy Windows NT Server 4.0 after only its first service pack (SP1) had been released, I successfully convinced a client not to deploy Windows NT Server 3.51 with its Service Pack 5 (SP5). Needless to say, this mistake was serious in a real production environment. Early releases of Windows NT Server 4.0 were just that: early. Perhaps I was seduced more by the attractive interface and less by the stability of its predecessor at the SP5 level. If I had it to do over again, I would have taken a more conservative approach in the early days of Windows NT Server 4.0 and deployed Windows NT Server 3.51 (SP5) first.

Clearly, if you haven't deployed Windows NT Server 4.0 on a production server yet, now is the time. If you are already running Windows NT Server 4.0 in a production environment, you will greatly benefit from the bug fixes within Service Pack 4 (SP4) and the additional features and functionality from the option pack. Be sure to see Appendix D for a detailed list of fixes in Windows NT Server 4.0 SP4. All NT professionals, both new and experienced, can benefit from the guidance this book provides in planning for the Windows 2000 Server.

What Is Windows NT Server 4.0?

Microsoft has positioned Windows NT Server 4.0 as a robust, reliable, and secure network server operating system, with an emphasis on running applications. It is a 32-bit operating system that participates in a "true" server scenario, that of the domain security model. And don't overlook its easy-to-use Windows 98–like graphical user interface (GUI). That interface is something seasoned NetWare administrators have greatly appreciated!

Beneath the pretty face, Windows NT Server is a huge, powerful network operating system. In fact, in many ways Windows NT Server is too big for any one individual to completely master, and at the enterprise level, it is common to see job classes divided so that one person is responsible for managing only part of the Windows NT Server.

Because many of you know the basics of Windows NT Server 4.0, I defer that discussion to Chapter 17, "Regular Windows NT Server." You may refer to that chapter as necessary.

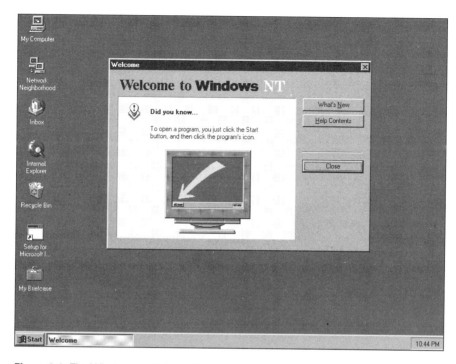

Figure 1-1: The Windows NT 4.0 desktop

The basic understanding of Windows NT Server started to change about halfway through its history. Historically, Windows NT Server was known as a single version of a network operating system; there weren't "other" types of Windows NT Sever. At that time (circa 1997), variations of "regular" Windows NT Server such as the Enterprise Edition, Terminal Server, and Small Business Server were introduced.

Such stratification within the Windows NT Server line had never occurred prior to the introduction of these "other" Windows NT Server 4.0 variations.

Enterprise Edition

The Enterprise Edition of Windows NT Server represents Microsoft's foothold in the enterprise. It is here the hard-fought battles to displace UNIX and the mid-range and mainframe computers will occur. In other words, the day your community hospital terminates its use of clustered UNIX servers in favor of the Enterprise Edition of Windows NT Server or Windows 2000 Server, you'll know the battle for the enterprise has been won by Microsoft. See Chapter 18, "Windows NT Server — Enterprise Edition," for more discussion.

Terminal Server

Many Windows NT Server professionals have tried and been disappointed with Remote Access Services (RAS) in Windows NT Server 4.0. The promise was that users could connect remotely to their Windows NT Server network from a remote location to check e-mail, transfer files, and even print their work! Because of both the disappointment in RAS and the success of third-party remote communications applications such as WinFrame and PCAnywhere, Microsoft recently introduced Terminal Server. Terminal Server is built on the foundation of Windows NT Server 4.0 with the features and functionality of WinFrame (a Microsoft acquisition). Terminal Server is discussed in Chapter 19, "Windows NT Server — Terminal Edition."

Small Business Server

My favorite variation in the Windows NT Server 4.0 family is the Small Business Server (SBS). With SBS, Microsoft addressed the huge small business market with an "all in one" networking solution. The services and functionality in SBS rest on a trimmed version of Windows NT Server 4.0. With great pleasure, SBS is presented in Chapter 20.

TCP/IP Paradigm Shift

Clearly, Windows NT Server 4.0 extends the use of the TCP/IP protocol suite "paradigm shift" that started with Windows NT Server 3.51. Microsoft, at last, has embraced the de facto standard for network protocols: TCP/IP. That is, TCP/IP is *the* protocol of the Internet. The paradigm shift I speak of relates to Microsoft using TCP/IP because of its worldwide acceptance, its open standards (something lacking in IPX/SPX) and its routable nature (something that's missing in NetBEUI). And since the Internet uses the TCP/IP protocol suite, Microsoft's TCP/IP paradigm shift was also Microsoft's Internet paradigm shift — but more on that in a moment.

Now the default network protocol in Windows NT Server 4.0, TCP/IP is automatically installed when you set up Windows NT Server (as discussed in Chapters 2 and 3). And while you may continue using other network protocols such as NetBEUI and IPX/SPX, you have fewer and fewer reasons to do so.

With the TCP/IP protocol suite, Windows NT allows you to have a true network server that conforms to the conventional thinking of the Internet. In order for you to exploit the vast resources of the Internet on your Windows NT Server network, it is critical that you use the TCP/IP protocol suite. By reading the chapters in Part II, "TCP/IP," you will have the opportunity to master this protocol. The information in Part II may be the most important part of this book. But whatever your motivations and viewpoint, to master TCP/IP is a smart move on your climb to Windows NT Server guru status.

Internet Paradigm Shift

Early in the history of Windows NT Server 4.0, Microsoft refocused its business mission from its traditional LAN and desktop view of computing to the Internet. Many of the improvements that Microsoft made to Windows NT Server 4.0 during its life have focused not only on bug fixes but also on increasing Internet functionality. Nowhere is this more apparent than in the consistent improvements to Internet Explorer that are a deeply engrained part of Windows NT Server 4.0. Equally, if not more, important is the Option Pack's implementation of Internet Information Server (IIS) 4.0 on top of Windows NT Server 4.0.

Option Pack and Service Pack 4

The information in this book will allow you to take advantage of the Windows NT Server Option Pack and Service Pack 4. Detailed questions about what is included in the Option Pack and Service Pack 4 are answered in Part IV, "Service Pack 4.0 and the Windows NT Server Option Pack."

Briefly, the Option Pack includes:

- IIS 4.0
- Internet Explorer 4.01
- Certificate Server v1.0
- Index Server 2.0
- Internet Connection Services for RAS
- Management Console (MMC) 1.0
- Site Server Express 2.0
- Windows Scripting Host
- Transaction Server 2.0
- Message Queue Server 1.0
- Data Access Components
- Numerous development tools (Visual InterDev, Script Debugger)

Option Pack and SP4 make Windows NT Server 4.0 rock solid. This NOS is now palatable to all network professionals, even skeptics of Windows NT Server. Don't forget that it will take at least a couple of years for Windows 2000 Server to achieve the same level of stability that Windows NT Server 4.0 enjoys today. Accordingly, many people won't fully implement Windows 2000 Server until several hot fixes and service packs have been released. It works that way every time a new version of a network operating system is released.

The MCSE

Many readers are pursuing their Microsoft Certified Professional designation known as the Microsoft Certified Systems Engineer (MCSE). As a practicing MCSE, I know the journey you are on. In general, I have emphasized topics such as TCP/IP and performance analysis that benefit MCSE candidates seeking to pass the grueling certification exams. Where possible, I offer secrets that are MCSE exam specific. I've been there and done that. I hope I can help you get there too!

The dramatic increase in the popularity of the MCSE designation occurred after Windows NT Server 4.0's appearance, but a few of us started and obtained our MCSEs during the Windows NT Server 3.*x* era. Many friends have joined us during the Windows NT Server 4.0 era. And it's a good thing! Designing, installing, implementing, and managing Windows NT Server 4.0 are enough work for everyone. And mastering such tasks is not only a key aspect of the MCSE program but also the underlying emphasis of this book.

This book is not necessarily written for the newly arrived NT professional. In fact, it is assumed you have worked with Windows NT Server before and are seeking to improve your Windows NT Server–specific skill set. Hence the numerous notes, tips, and (of course) secrets. I will revisit this theme throughout the text in order to answer your questions along the way. Simply stated, this is not a rewrite of the user manual or the resource kit. I believe you will welcome and appreciate this approach.

Preparing for Windows 2000 Server

Last and certainly not least, you must prepare for the next major release of Windows NT Server. Known as Windows 2000 Server (a.k.a. Windows NT Server 5.0), this release is a major redesign of Windows NT Server as we know it. By planning now, you will ensure that your migration to Windows 2000 Server will be not only more efficient but also more effective.

Interestingly, it is likely you will actually run both Windows NT Server 4.0 and Windows 2000 Server on the same network for many of the reasons cited earlier in this chapter. When Windows 2000 Server ships in its retail form, I for one will not be implementing it live on production servers at client sites. Rather, I will be launching test scenarios involving Windows 2000 Server. These scenarios, running on test (not production) networks, will allow myself and others to confirm that mission-critical applications will not only run well but run well under heavy load conditions on Windows 2000 Server. In fact, it will probably be a year, well into two or three service pack releases, before my clients run production servers with Windows 2000 Server. Until that time, most of these sites will continue to run Windows NT Server 4.0 with the Option Pack and SP4. In a strange way, one might say, "Long live Windows NT Server 4.0!"

With that said, enjoy *Microsoft Windows NT Secrets, Option Pack Edition*.

Summary

In this chapter, we have covered these topics:
- How Windows NT Server has been enhanced and optimized for your network
- Advantages of Windows NT Server 4.0
- Additions and enhancements to Windows NT Server 4.0: the Option Pack and Service Pack
- Windows NT Server 4.0 and future releases of Windows 2000 Server

Chapter 2

Windows NT Server 4.0 Planning, Setup, and Installation

In This Chapter

- Planning for Windows NT Server 4.0 in your organization
- Preparing hardware and components
- Installing Windows NT Server
- Postinstallation secrets

Getting it right the first time is key to installing Windows NT Server 4.0 properly. A proper installation involves more than just three setup disks and the I386 subdirectory on the Windows NT Server 4.0 CD-ROM. If the setup was that easy, this chapter would be short, referring you to the "skinny" user manual that ships with Windows NT Server.

As a Windows NT Server consultant and practicing MCSE, I find that many of the hours devoted to a Windows NT Server build don't actually relate to the "three-floppy swap," as the setup routine is affectionately known in many circles. Rather, many hours go into upfront planning to "get it right."

Planning

Planning your Windows NT Server implementation has several dimensions, some of which you may not have considered. You may be aware of several of these points but not others. We'll start with the physical site and end with the people.

Physical site

Too often, Windows NT Server specialists give belated attention to the physical site at which they'll be installing the Windows NT server. I've been stuck at 11 p.m. on a Sunday evening unable to move an attorney's large oak desk, counting the hours until the Monday morning stampede. I had overlooked a basic feature of the physical site, and that mistake was costly. As you implement Windows NT Server, you'll need to give attention not only to the technical infrastructure and hardware and software resources, but also to the physical layout of the site.

Media infrastructure

Before you begin installation, ask whether the cabling is in place or whether both the cabling and the installation service have been ordered. Have you "tested" the cabling if you are using existing cabling on your Windows NT Server network? A simple handheld cable tester will save you a little of the pain and agony that I've suffered from seemingly ideal cabling that in reality is faulty.

O.K., so you don't have a $5,000 Fluke cable tester handy. You can easily test a cable run for basic "fitness" with a hub, a laptop with a network adapter, and cabling. Having a buddy and two cheap walkie-talkie handheld radios will help as well. First, set up the hub in the wiring or server closet/storage area and attach it to the patch panel via patch cables. Second, hit the floor with a live laptop and a network adapter (typically in the form of a dongle hanging from a PC card). Test each and every LAN wall jack to make sure that you are "green lighting" back at the hub. You have now completed a very basic cabling test at the physical level. Oh, and put the buddy and walkie-talkies to work so that you don't need to run back and forth between laptop and hub too many times when performing this test.

As-builts

Before assuming responsibility for a site or performing a server conversion (typically from NetWare to Windows NT Server these days!), insist on completing a computer system as-built of the site (see Figure 2-1). If you know something about the construction industry, you are certainly no stranger to the term *as-built*. But if you are, an as-built in real estate is a drawing that show everything at a site: building, fixtures, improvements, and so on. An as-built is also similar to an x-ray at the doctor's office. An x-ray shows everything you have. A computer system as-built drawing likewise provides a snapshot view of your existing hardware and software resources.

An as-built drawing is akin to a set of x-rays used by a doctor. The doctor relies on the x-rays as a here-and-now view of your "system" in order to make the correct medical decisions. You should do the same with your computer system prior to implementing Windows NT Server. How do I create the as-built drawings? I simply perform a technical walkthrough of the site armed with a handheld dictaphone. Later, at the office, I transcribe my notes, much as a doctor does, to create my as-built drawing using Visio (a popular network diagramming product).

Chapter 2: Windows NT Server 4.0 Planning, Setup, and Installation

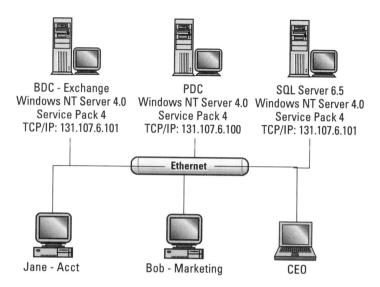

Figure 2-1: A sample computer network as-built drawing

By insisting on creating a computer system as-built as an early planning step for Windows NT Server implementations, you can avoid the typical problem of missing a few details along the way, such as not having a Jet Direct card for the HP printer you plan to reuse. In part because of my up-front reliance on as-built drawings, I've served up more competitive Windows NT Server installation project bids, but more important, I've done a better job of managing my client's expectations. That's resulted in higher client satisfaction survey results!

Physical infrastructure

Consider the condition of the physical plant in which the network will reside. Is it newer office space with few concerns about dust, heat, and other basics? Or is this a working environment such as a front office/manufacturing facility combination? Different environments will necessitate different strategies. The physical infrastructure may determine what type of machines you place on the network. I'm seeing manufacturing sites readily accept Windows Terminal Server vis-a-vis Windows NT Server 4.0 as a low-cost and durable computing solution for less than ideal conditions. And the physical infrastructure can determine how I treat the implementation from a personal comfort perspective. At the downtown legal firm in the glass tower I wear nothing but suits and ties. A visit to the Windows NT Server network at the construction company means golf shirt and shorts.

Secret

Trust me when I say this: Be sure that all surface spaces such as table tops, desks, and shelving are at least 12" away from the wall or could be easily moved if necessary. I've stopped entire Windows NT Server conversions because the immovable objects stood between myself, the server, and power outlets. That gets expensive at $125 per hour!

Be sure to use that last preinstallation walk-through to establish that sufficient power outlets are available for all of the components associated with your Windows NT Server, including spare outlets for plugging in your laptop for performing CD-ROM-based research. It's funny how an installation of Windows NT Server can suddenly compel you to find answers via your Microsoft TechNet CDs. Also, it's not a bad idea to confirm that a telephone jack (without PBX dial-out restrictions) exists near the server. Even if you don't plan to use the server to manage communications, it's a good idea to have a free telephone line for the modem on your laptop or to plug in a telephone so that you can call vendor product support lines.

Ensure that you have adequate ventilation so that both you and the server don't overheat. One of my secrets for surviving summer is to spend lots of time in air-conditioned server rooms. In large enterprise-level installations, things like sufficient power, telephone jacks, and ventilation are givens.

With the conclusion of your walk-through, you've now concluded your site survey and are armed to make the best purchasing decisions possible.

Secret

Remember that your as-builts, site surveys, and walk-throughs should allow you to right-size your Windows NT Server installation. From this exercise, you create your Windows NT Server purchase specifications. Purchasing too much — that is, buying your way out of trouble — is as great an IS management sin as purchasing too little or forgetting critical components.

System components

Network professionals and MCSE-types working with Windows NT Server enjoy working with technology from two dimensions: hardware and software. Conversely, developers and MCSD-types are typically concerned only with the software side. This additional dimension is what makes "getting it right the first time" with Windows NT Server such a challenge. And don't overlook the service providers and people you will need to implement your Windows NT Server–based network. I haven't, and I discuss these critical team players in several pages.

Let's discuss hardware first. Your commitment to hardware is up front (that is, early in the life cycle of your Windows NT Server network). It is important to make good decisions in the beginning because the hardware is going to be with you for some time. It's certainly no fun to go back to the boss and ask for more. With hardware purchases, you typically get just one chance to ask for what you want.

Server hardware

The actual server that will run Windows NT Server should, of course, be a server-class machine if at all possible. We're primarily concerned with five areas when right-sizing a server for a Windows NT Server installation: processor, memory, network subsystem, server internals, and disk storage.

Processor

Beware of Intel advertisements in trade journals that might give you a bad case of processor envy. Yes, the processor is very important. But right-sizing your Windows NT Server environment means that you understand how the file server will be used. Plain old file and print server–type environments aren't as dependent on processor power as client/server environments. Saving a document to a network shared storage area is very different from running one or more Microsoft BackOffice components on your Windows NT Server machine. If you don't believe me, run this very basic processor utilization test if you'd like to observe at first hand the differences between a Windows NT Server that behaves as a file and print server and one that behaves as an application server. First, right-click the Windows NT Server taskbar so that the secondary menu is displayed (see Figure 2-2). Then, with the Performance tab sheet selected in Task Manager, observe the graphical display of the processor utilization rate (see Figure 2-3).

Interestingly, if you're not running BackOffice or similar major applications on this Windows NT server machine, you will probably see what I see: a processor utilization rate in the single digits or low teens. Thus, it may not be wise to spend your funds on a super-expensive four-way processor solution such as the high-end Compaq servers. Next, if you have any major client/server or server-based applications installed on your machine, launch these applications and create user activity. You should observe a significant increase in the processor activity as displayed by Task Manager. If this second set of conditions, running busy server applications, is the world you live in, then you are really running an applications server and you may benefit from additional processing power.

Note that I discuss Task Manager and a range of performance measures later in Part VI of this book, "Optimizing and Troubleshooting Windows NT Server 4.0."

That said, of course you should strive to purchase the best processor (Pentium II class) that you can afford. If anything, purchasing the best processor you can today will help extend the useful life of your server 48, 60, or even 72 months from now, when you implement demanding server-based applications that need power beyond your immediate needs today.

Part I: Installation, Planning, Setup, and Implementation

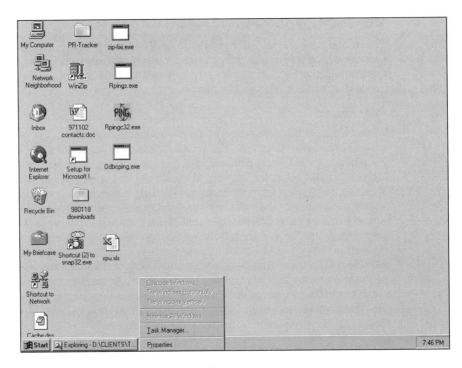

Figure 2-2: The Windows NT Server desktop

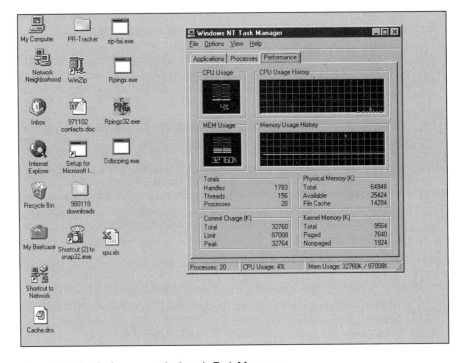

Figure 2-3: The Performance tab sheet in Task Manager

Chapter 2: Windows NT Server 4.0 Planning, Setup, and Installation

In fact, I'm right-sizing my smaller and medium-sized Windows NT Server client sites with dual-processor Dell PowerEdge servers at or near the $5,000 price point (as of late 1998). Why dual-processor motherboards? By purchasing this motherboard architecture today, even with a single processor, I have "engineered" the future into this Windows NT Server machine. By adding a second processor at a future date, be it to accommodate new applications or for some other reason, we dramatically extend the life of this server and improve its performance for a relatively small outlay of funds (a second server-class top-of-the-line Intel processor can typically be purchased for under $1,000). Why am I favoring Dell in this discussion? Because at that same price point, it has been my experience that Compaq only offers a single processor–capable motherboard.

Secret

Purchasing a dual processor–capable server today with a single processor on board allows you to do one other thing: Ride the processor price yield curve. The law of technology is that processing power doubles every 18 months, and processor prices decrease in relationship to this law. So by deferring for several months the outlay of funds needed to double the processing power of your computer, you effectively ride the processor pricing yield curve. That means you could take advantage of a lower total price to double your system power at a future date. That's smart IT management.

The option of adding a second processor at a future date has been a very compelling component of my presentation to Windows NT Server clients. I'm typically working with business decision makers who need to hear the "business case" for purchasing name brand server-class machines (ones that are dual processor–capable).

Another argument allows me to prevail at this planning stage. By looking more closely at the needs of my client, I can often easily see that Windows NT Server is being introduced into the organization to allow introduction of some "killer" business application that, more likely than not, is based on Microsoft SQL Server.

A prime example of this is Great Plains Dynamics — SQL version. Such a high-powered accounting application enables management to get information via reports that they've never had before. Great Plains Dynamics only runs on Windows NT Server (and only on the Intel platform version of Windows NT Server). My typical Windows NT Server installation for a Great Plains Dynamics customer includes a dual-processor server such as one in the Dell PowerEdge line. Because the introduction of Windows NT Server into these organizations affects several other "systems" (for instance, it affords the opportunity to convert from Word Perfect to Microsoft Office 97), the Great Plains Dynamics installation usually follows two to three months after the Windows NT Server machine has been built. That is because organizations like to get the Windows NT Server network up and running with everyone happy prior to introducing Great Plains Dynamics. It's a smart move.

That three-month delay allows my clients to enjoy a price reduction of $100 to $200 on the second processor. When working with small and medium Windows NT Server sites, that's the kind of good news that I want to deliver. It's also another example of riding the processor pricing yield curve!

Memory

The more memory, the better (of course!). Here there is, in my humble opinion, a one-to-one return for each dollar spent on RAM. Windows NT Server loves RAM. So if you're faced with hardware trade-offs, RAM is one option that you should trade up. Doubling your RAM on a Windows NT server will noticeably improve performance, especially when you are running memory-intensive applications at the server such as Microsoft SQL Server. You will recall that this is, in part, because RAM acts as primary memory on the machine. It's very fast. Hard disk–based storage acts as secondary memory, which is slower. And even though we can fool Windows NT Server into thinking life is good and that we have much more RAM than we really do (via a large paging file), there's nothing like an abundance of real RAM.

Secret

Be sure to consult a bona fide hardware technician as you consider what type of memory to add to your Windows NT Server machine. I've made the mistake of ordering the wrong type of RAM memory for older machines, clones, and the like. To the naked eye, parity and nonparity RAM chips look very much alike. The same is true of DRAM and SRAM memory. Be aware of these issues in your planning stage.

Network subsystem

Of course a 100MB network card using the PCI architecture is preferable to a 10MB ISA-based card. The rule here is clearly to implement the fastest network components possible. No-brainer.

Secret

The "hidden cost" that I've confronted head-on with clients seeking counsel on the choice of 100MB versus 10MB isn't the explicit cost of the network adapter card. Heck, a 10/100 PCI-based network adapter card from 3COM can be had for under $100.

The real cost of going to 100MB, in my experience, has involved other network components, such as a 100MB hub, a 10/100 dual-speed hub, or a switch. Whereas I can purchase a 10MB hub for pennies (say an eight-port hub for under $100), a 100MB hub may cost more than three times that amount. For smaller clients, the ones who gripe over $20 backup tapes, the additional network speed isn't considered valuable.

Want to be a true hero at a relatively low cost? Then consider adding a second NIC card to boost network subsystem performance. Remember that the job of the network adapter card is essentially to convert the parallel electronic data stream from the internal bus architecture of the computer to a serial format that is placed onto network media (which may consist of twisted pair cabling). Talk about an obvious bottleneck — reducing data from a parallel form to a serial form!

Adding a second network adapter card will be most beneficial in file servers. Here I am thinking of large file transfers such as of 20MB AutoCAD files. That's a lot of information be sent as serial data! A second network adapter card works wonders here.

Chapter 2: Windows NT Server 4.0 Planning, Setup, and Installation

Server Internals

You may or may not be a strong hardware person. Perhaps you are and you've purchased this book to learn more about the software side of Windows NT Server 4.0 (if so, you've come to the right place). But remember that the network equation is easily 50 percent hardware and 50 percent software. It takes the two to tango on the Ethernet. That said, how can you hope to make the most appropriate decisions regarding the server's internal architecture?

Secret

To cut to the chase and learn the difference between ISA, EISA, and SCSI (and its various forms), I suggest that you select the Networking Essentials MCSE certification text from IDG Books Worldwide. The book, *Networking Essentials MCSE Study Guide* by Jason Nash (ISBN: 0-7645-3177-8) is over 500 pages of good stuff relating to networking fundamentals. Specifically, you can sharpen your understanding of server "internals."

Disk storage

Essentially disk storage implementations can be poor, adequate, or superior.

- **Poor Design.** Poor design takes two forms.
  - The first involves single hard drives in a machine. In my experience, this occurs when an older machine is being used as a Windows NT server, and that machine only has one hard drive. Perhaps the machine dates back to an era when storage space was relatively expensive, resulting in a generation of single hard drive machines. Another case is when off-the-shelf workstations are used as Windows NT Server machines. Your average Dell or Gateway workstation is designed for the end user and typically ships with a single hard disk (although it will typically have multiple partitions). A single hard drive implementation has no fault tolerance.

  - The second scenario that I call poor design relates to spanned hard drives. Here again, this most likely involves an older machine that has been converted from an older version of NetWare or a desktop operating system into a machine running Windows NT Server. Because storage is cheap, many network administrators take the path of least resistance and simply daisy-chain additional storage devices to the server to satisfy increased space needs. A spanned drive implementation has no fault tolerance.

    Either of the two examples just offered suggest poor planning, and perhaps the parties involved are saving a few dollars today, but in a foolhardy manner.

  - **Adequate Design.** Adequate storage solutions include mirroring and duplexing. Here, one hard disk is an exact copy of the other. If these two hard disks share the same controller card, the solution is known as *mirroring*. If the two hard disks have separate controllers, the solution is known as *duplexing* (which is technically better than mirroring, although hard disk controllers fail far less often than hard disks). This is a common solution but expensive. In order to have 10GB of usable storage space, you would need to purchase two hard disks of 10GB each (for a total purchase of 20GB). The result is a 50 percent utilization ratio, which is costly.

- **Superior Design.** A superior storage design is RAID-based. Here, a redundant array of inexpensive disks (RAID) work as a team to provide maximum performance and usable space at the lowest possible costs. A RAID solution using RAID 5 (which is the RAID solution spoken of most often) requires at least three hard disks (and most often five or more). Each disk both stores data and includes a parity or recalculation zone area. The parity zone maintains just enough information about the other disks so that if one of the disks fails, the missing data from the failed member can be rebuilt according to information provided by other RAID member disks. The total storage available is much higher than with mirroring. For example, if you had a five-disk RAID array totaling 10GB of space, then 8GB would be usable. Here, one-fifth of the total storage is dedicated to the parity zone.

Secret

To find the space used by the parity zone in a RAID scenario, just take the inverted fraction of the number of disks. For example, a five-disk RAID array may be expressed as 5 / 1 = 5. Thus, the parity area is 1 / 5 = .20 or 20 percent. Further, that means that 80 percent of the disk space is usable for storing data. This information might be useful as you prepare for the Networking Essentials exam as part of the MCSE track.

Note

A hardware-based RAID solution managed by the server is greatly preferred over having Windows NT Server managing the RAID solution. That's because you take advantage of the "smart" disk subsystem by allowing it to manage the RAID function. You avoid taxing the Windows NT Server operating system with additional RAID management overhead.

A RAID-based storage solution is only slightly more expensive than mirroring. Add to that higher performance with read activity in which the server employs multiple read head I/O, and RAID appears to be a very attractive storage solution. The next time you are pricing storage, get bids for both mirroring and RAID and see for yourself.

Name brands versus clones

One final comment on planning your hardware: Remember that you are probably asking Windows NT Server to act as the foundation for your company's information infrastructure. And like any foundation, if it is off-center, everyone that follows will have to "shim" their layer to make it fit, much as shims are used on windows in a house when the foundation isn't level.

The kind of hardware that you purchase will make a difference in how your network infrastructure performs in the long run. Name brands such as Compaq, Dell, and IBM tend to be rock solid and reliable. These machines typically have better plumbing than cheaper clones from your uncle's computer shop. Better "plumbing" might take the form of larger fans or two power supplies. And the organizations that support your server tend to be more reliable when trouble strikes. Support is certainly IBM's historical claim to fame.

Clones, on the other hand, will typically run Windows NT Server with few problems initially. But more than one client who insisted on saving a few dollars and purchasing a clone PC to use as a Windows NT Server machine has called a year later looking for Joe, the clone maker. Needless to say, one year later Joe has found the love of his life and moved to Bora Bora.

At the enterprise level, it has been my experience that clones aren't consider in the server farm mix. In fact, many name brands are eliminated from consideration for two reasons (although I'm sure there are more). First, name brands such as IBM, Compaq, and Dell have superior server hardware management applications that other name brands don't. With Compaq, this includes the SmartStart and Insight Manager applications. These management applications not only assist in the configuration of your servers during setup, but more important, they mitigate server down time in a crisis by directing your efforts to failed server components. This management capability is rarely available in clones, or even in some of the name brands you might think would know better. So server hardware management applications are a huge reason for selecting well-known name brand servers over other alternatives.

The second criterion for many firms when deciding on a server is the hardware manufacturer's support network, something I hinted at two paragraphs ago. Take a well-known Western U.S. auto parts retailer with 110 stores in locations both large and small. Few hardware manufacturers can support all of these locations within a four-hour callback period. In fact, the only organization that I've seen consistently provide this level of support is IBM. Not the cheapest server solution perhaps, but for organizations with far-flung operations, perhaps the best.

So for what it's worth, don't save a few dollars and mistakenly purchase the cheapest clone on the market as your Windows NT Server machine. In fact, my firm has been known to turn down business because a client didn't want to purchase a name brand server. That alone has proven to be an early warning sign of problems ahead.

Software

We now get to one of my favorite topics: software. As I explain the "greatness" of Windows NT Server to business decision makers (the ones who write the checks), the inevitable line of questioning comparing Windows NT Server to other network operating systems starts early. The debate can actually be cut short if you think smart. Businesses are really implementing one network solution or another because of the applications that they need to run. In fact, such thinking is often part of the Introduction to Computers lecture at any college. First you find the applications that you need. Then you find a computer and operation system that will run the applications.

If this rule holds true for you, then you want to heed the underlying trend present today in the business software market. ISVs are beating a path to the Windows NT community. In fact, many businesses are now finding that the next release of their favorite business software is only available on the Windows NT Server platform. The often uttered phrase "We no longer support our product on NetWare" is the sound of money to this MCSE!

It's the software, stupid! Don't forget, this paradigm not only drives Windows NT's growth but is a fundamental tenet of successful technology implementations.

Service providers

Any successful Windows NT Server deployment requires the involvement of others. These parties are listed here in the order that you should consider contacting them (based on observed delays such as service delivery).

1. **Telco.** Clearly you can never order your telephone company–related service(s) too early. Even an extra business telephone line can take weeks to arrive. And if you're implementing a WAN, sometimes the service requests are measured in months. Make the telco your first call.

2. **ISP.** Internet service providers (ISPs) need sufficient lead time to order your domain name or switch your domain name.

3. **Cabling.** Although the cabling team may complete their work in a day or two, depending on the size of your network, these critical players are often scheduled weeks in advanced. An early call is necessary so that you can book your work dates.

4. **Outside subject matter experts.** Although we consultants believe we can respond rapidly to your call, such is not always the case. The more time we have to work with you on a project, the better job we can do, because we'll be less rushed, have more time to prepare and conduct research, and ultimately charge you less.

5. **Hardware/software resellers.** Don't wait until the last moment to order your hardware and software.

As of this writing, in late 1998, hardware resellers such as Dell are experiencing backlogs on servers averaging two weeks. I predict this backlog will grow in 1999 as the Year 2000 approaches and many businesses upgrade their systems to eliminate motherboard BIOS problems.

People

Don't forget the people involved as you plan for a successful Windows NT Server implementation. At least three groups need your attention: managers, administrators, and users. Maintaining contact with the people in all these groups is essential for a smooth implementation. Management should be kept informed and happy at all times. They write the checks for your project! Who are the administrators and how much do they need to know? Remember to make the membership of this club (administrators) exclusive. It is a very powerful group. Keeping the users satisfied will ultimately make or break a successful Windows NT Server implementation. Make sure your users can print, save files, use e-mail, and generally trust the system.

Secret

The planning phase of the project is the best time to arrange for end user training on the new Windows NT Server–based network. And take my advice. Have a real trainer perform the training at your organization. We MCSE-types sometimes look foolish trying to train end users on networking basics (logons, printing, saving) and e-mail (Outlook).

Key contact list

As part of your planning activities, be sure to create a list of key contacts (telephone numbers, e-mail addresses). Allow up to six telephone numbers per key contact for main office, private office, home, cellular, pager, and fax.

Loose ends

I've grouped everything in this section as planning loose ends to consider addressing as you implement Windows NT Server in your organization.

General

Even experienced network professionals need to "stick to the knitting" when implementing a Windows NT Server network. That includes reviewing the following points and, as necessary, completing the tasks called for. Admittedly, creating drive mappings isn't terribly exciting or difficult, but the failure to do so is extremely embarrassing. For that reason, I share the following general points:

- **Drive mappings.** Try to create your drive mappings in advance, and get end user sign-offs for the drives. Why? Some vendors want to use specific drive letters. Other vendors cannot use UNC naming for drives and need a drive letter assigned.

- **The ISVs' unique needs.** Anything is possible in this category. Some accounting software vendors can only use TCP/IP and not IPX/SPX. Other accounting software vendors require Registry modifications (Great Plains). Some ISVs will provide you with lengthy network installation manuals that you should peruse in advance (Timberline's 60-pager is a record in my book).

- **User security.** Out of the box, Windows NT Server tends to grant very generous rights (for instance, full control on new shares). Use a whiteboard to create a security map showing what users have what rights. And how do you enforce security: logon, shares, NTFS-based security, or other ways (logon machine and hour restrictions)?

- **Naming conventions.** Plan for machine names, share names, printer names, and user names in advance. Don't find yourself installing Windows NT Server before you think of the basics. Otherwise you're bound to overlook something, resulting in a substandard network.

Secret

Keep names as short as possible and avoid using separators. When you are referring to a shared resource or mapping a drive, a short name is always preferred to a long name. Shorter names are, at a minimum, easier to spell.

- **Keep it simple starting (KISS).** Use the fewest Windows NT Server domains possible, not only to simplify the management of your network but to assist your efforts to migrate to Windows 2000 Server (the fewer domains the better!). Many inexperienced people working with Windows NT Server create far too many domains because MCSE textbooks taught them to do so! Closely related to fewer domains is the idea that you should minimize the trust relationships that you have on a network.

- **Reseat cards.** When building the server, look under the hood and reseat the interface cards (modem, network adapter, sound, hard disk controller). These cards may have come loose on the long journey from the computer manufacturing facility. Avoid the mistakes I made, such as when I found an unseated network adapter card only after I'd nearly completed a Windows NT Server installation (reaching the point when you specify the network adapter driver).

- **Create the utility partition.** Sometimes when looking at the work of others, I've seen name brand servers such as Compaq lacking the hidden utility partition that you should create during server setup. With Compaq, the SmartStart tool allows you to access useful drivers, run system tests, and register cards. Be sure to create the hidden utility partition before you start installing Windows NT Server. Each server vendor has its own utilities (for instance, Dell's is called Server Assistant).

- **Decide on partitions.** Several schools of thought exist in the networking profession about how to handle partitions in Windows NT Server. At a minimum, I have two partitions: one for the Windows NT Server operating system that I prefer to keep formatted as FAT (so I can always get to it) and a data partition for the user's applications and data (which I format as NTFS for maximum security and performance). But I refer you to the Microsoft MCSE course 922, "Supporting Microsoft Windows NT Server 4.0 Core Technologies," which illustrates a small system partition in FAT format holding several Windows NT Server startup files such as NTLDR and a boot partition containing the Windows NT Server operating system in the %systemroot% directory. The boot partition is formatted as NTFS. The partition names, which indeed sound backward, are fair game on the MCSE exams.

Existing networks

If you are introducing Windows NT Server into an existing network, you should consider the following points:

- **Existing Windows NT Server domains.** If you plan to add a Windows NT Server to an existing domain, you will need to make it a backup domain controller or a member server. It cannot be a primary domain controller for an existing domain during its setup, because the existing domain already has a primary domain controller.

   If you are creating a second domain, be sure to point the workstation clients to the new domain by modifying their network properties. With Windows NT Workstation, you will need to register the workstation NetBIOS name with the newly created primary domain controller in the new domain via Server Manager.

- **NetWare.** This venerable operating system is frequently converted to Windows NT Server. Several issues exist regarding conversions from NetWare and NT/NetWare coexistence.

- **Gateway Services for NetWare (GSNW).** This service is necessary to "see" a NetWare server and use the Migration Tool for NetWare. GSNW provides client-side connectivity that allows you to attach and be authenticated on a NetWare server from the Windows NT Server machine. It also provides existing clients on your Windows NT Server network that have no NetWare client to see and use the NetWare server via the "gateway" function of GSNW.

- **Macintosh.** The Macintosh community has embraced Windows NT Server as a file and print server, but not as an application server. That's because Services for Macintosh, when installed on Windows NT Server, provides robust file sharing and printer support.

- **UNIX.** Out-of-the-box support for UNIX connectivity to Windows NT Server is typically fortified by third-party enhancements such as NFS clients. Natively, Windows NT Server doesn't have strong UNIX support.

Secret

I would recommend caution when using the GSNW, as each user going through the GSNW gateway is assigned the broader share-level permission for a single NetWare logon account when you map to NetWare resources (such as the SYS volume). Users accessing a NetWare resource via GSNW cannot be assigned individual rights, so this scenario tends to be overly generous with rights to the NetWare server. I learned this fact the hard way at a manufacturing concern when we discovered that all users accessing the NetWare server via GSNW were able to see the HR (human resources) directory. The problem was that some GSNW-enabled users need to access the HR directory, but others did not. But access to GSNW is managed at the share level with just one account (the single account used to log onto the NetWare server). Thus there was no way to distinguish between users when it came to managing the HR directory on the NetWare server. Big problem!

NetWare

The Migration Tool for NetWare application is great for migrating users and data from a NetWare 3.x environment to Windows NT Server 4.0. Note that if you are using NetWare 4.x, this tool will interact with your existing environment via NetWare 3.x–type bindery emulation (GSNW does not have native NetWare 4.x support). The migration tool is very robust and has a trial migration feature that allows you to make a test run before committing to the actual migration. Mistakes discovered during the test are logged, allowing you to "fix" these mistakes before bringing the real data and users over. Such mistakes tend to focus on users and groups with the same names as existing Windows NT Server users and groups. File-related mistakes tend to focus on NetWare permissions that are supported natively by Windows NT Server 4.0, such as the hidden right. Leave no doubt about it, the Migration Tool for NetWare is great when needed, and I've found it to be much more powerful with its server-to-server direct communications.

Services for NetWare is a special add-on that must be purchased to run on your Windows NT Server. It contains File and Print Services for NetWare (FPNW). FPNW is a service that creates and maintains a NetWare 3.x environment on a Windows NT server. More important, it allows an NTFS partition to be seen as a NetWare partition. That way, NetWare clients without an installed Windows NT Server–based network client may interact with the Windows NT server. It actually works as advertised, providing NetWare 3.x emulation. However, it has one large problem: performance. Like all forms of emulation, massive "conversions" between native Windows NT Server activity and emulated NetWare 3.x activity are constantly occurring. Thus, when I deployed FPNW in a real 500-user environment, it worked as advertised from the server side. But from the end user side, the performance was unbearable. Saving a large AutoCAD data file from a user's workstation took three minutes! A bad deal to say the least.

Another NetWare issue to consider involves introducing Windows NT Server on a routed network of existing NetWare servers. This lesson learned comes from the school bus company, where a fatal NetWare server crash caused the network administrator to dive headlong into that long-delayed conversion to Windows NT Server. He rebuilt his server as Windows NT Server and actually had his 30 users functional again in two business days. That was an impressive, albeit ad hoc, accomplishment. But everything was not as it appeared. Soon, offices scattered across town reported they couldn't see his server any longer. A closer inspection revealed that he hadn't enabled NWLink IPX/SPX to propagate Type 20 broadcasts on his network. This means that the IPX/SPX protocol stack used with Windows NT Server is slightly different than the native IPX/SPX protocol stack used with NetWare. Thus, the Windows NT Server IPX-based packets weren't routed to the other business offices at the bus company. The solution? Install the RIP for NWLink IPX service under the Services tab sheet in the Network applet in Control Panel and answer Yes when asked if you want to enable NetBIOS Broadcast Propagation. My friend at the bus company did this, and presto, he could see the other business offices!

Finally, issues arise regarding the file storage space requirements for data migrating from a NetWare partition to an NTFS or FAT partition. When you migrate data from a NetWare partition to a FAT partition, I've noticed, you may need twice as much space on the FAT partition to accommodate the newly migrated data. That's because FAT is a weak file format scheme that simply doesn't handle data as efficiently as a NetWare partition. But if you are migrating data from a NetWare partition to an NTFS partition, no such issues exist. If you have 4GB of data on a NetWare partition and migrated it to a NTFS partition, it will take 4GB.

Macintosh

Macintosh support in Windows NT Server is actually very robust. By installing Services for Macintosh on an NTFS partition, you allow Windows NT Server to provide basic logon, file, and print capabilities for Macintosh clients. Note however that the Windows NT Server does not support native Macintosh application support. That is, you may not run Macintosh applications on a Windows NT server using Services for Macintosh. However, I've used Services for Macintosh on several Windows NT servers connected by a WAN and I was favorably impressed. I was able to store and retrieve, in a secure fashion, large data files on the Windows NT server. I was able to print from my Macintosh client to printers such as HP LaserJets that were managed by the Windows NT Server. In short, Services for Macintosh, once you clearly understand what services are and are not provided, is a winner.

UNIX

UNIX support is limited with Windows NT Server 4.0. Properly configured, a UNIX host and a Windows NT server may ping and FTP each other when communicating via the TCP/IP protocol suite. However, more robust connectivity between a UNIX host and a Windows NT server requires a third-party NFS application such as the UNIX/NT gateway products from ISVs like NetManage, WRQ, Wall Data, and Attachmate. Note the MCSE exams hold you responsible for basic UNIX/Windows NT Server interaction. Favorite questions center on Line Printer Remote (LPR) and Line Printer Daemon (LPD). Be sure to educate yourself before taking the Windows NT Server 4.0 Core Technologies exam.

Setting Up Windows NT Server

Setting up Windows NT Server is of course more difficult than it appears. Perhaps you have been seduced by NT folklore that it's easy because it involves just three floppy disks and one CD-ROM. I guess if you came from the NetWare 2.*x* generation (where swapping more than 20 setup floppy disks was the order of the day), then you really would find this easy. But most of the time you commit to setting up Windows NT Server will not be in the form of disk swapping. That's just the physical act. There are the logical acts of gathering system information, planning, and testing your server after setup.

Part I: Installation, Planning, Setup, and Implementation

This section begins by telling you the things you need to know in advance of setup and the actual "act" of running setup.

Things to know before you begin setup

During the setup process, you're asked to make many decisions and supply a lot of information about your server's hardware and the operating system's configuration. Installation will be much easier if you have the following items prepared beforehand:

- Small Computer System Interface (SCSI) or Integrated Drive Electronics (IDE) hard drive controller information and/or drivers
- Network adapter information and/or drivers
- A check of the NT 4.0 Hardware Compatibility List (HCL) to ensure your server's hardware will be supported
- The server's planned role in your domain or organization
- The Computer Name
- The Domain Name, if you are creating a new domain by installing Windows NT Server as a Primary Domain Controller
- The Licensing Mode you'll choose (Per Server or Per Seat)
- The file system you intend to install (FAT or NTFS)
- An Administrator account password for the new server or domain

It's also helpful to have a disk available to use as an Emergency Repair Disk, as Setup will ask you whether you'd like to create this disk during the setup process. Let's address these items one by one.

SCSI or IDE hard drive controller

It is essential that Windows NT Setup detect your hard drive, or that you manually configure your hard drive, in order for the operating system to install correctly. This seems fairly obvious — if Setup can't find a drive, it can't install any files. Be absolutely sure that your hard drive controller's driver is included with the built-in driver list Setup uses, or that you have drivers available on a separate floppy disk so that you can manually configure it during the setup process. If you don't have the proper drivers available, your NT installation will come to a grinding halt in a hurry.

Secret

Remember, just because your hard drive controller or SCSI controller may be included in the NT 4.0 Hardware Compatibility List (HCL), that doesn't necessarily mean it will be automatically detected by Setup.

Network adapter

This is another biggie: For Windows NT Setup to detect your network adapter, you must have the proper drivers and hardware settings available. This isn't such an issue now that most servers use PCI network cards, but if you have older hardware or a funky hardware setup, you'll need to know the interrupt and memory address that you want the adapter to use. Also, have the proper drivers available if you are not absolutely sure that your adapter will be identified automatically.

Secret

If you have network adapter drivers on a floppy that contains multiple directories, make sure you know exactly where the proper oemsetup.inf file is on the disk, because there is no "Browse" function when you click Have Disk during the NIC setup — you have to provide the correct path yourself. If you don't know exactly where the oemsetup.inf file is located, you'll need to take the floppy to another machine and look for it. At a client site, this has the potential to be rather embarrassing and can delay your setup significantly if you don't have another computer handy.

The hardware compatibility list

When Microsoft releases a new operating system, they also release a list of hardware they have tested and found to work successfully with the system. This list is called a Hardware Compatibility List or HCL, and the Windows NT 4.0 version (in booklet form) is shipped with the installation CD. A more up-to-date version can be found on the company's Internet site. If you're using FTP, look for the HCL at .

If you prefer to browse the Web using HTTP, go to http://www.microsoft.com/hwtest/hcl/.

If your server has older hardware or specialized hardware, or even if it's a new system, it's always a good policy to find each component on the HCL, to save yourself some hardware-related headaches later.

Server role

Windows NT servers can be set up as Primary Domain Controllers, Backup Domain Controllers, domain member servers, or stand-alone servers. I'll explain these roles briefly:

- **Primary Domain Controllers, or PDCs.** These contain the master copy of the domain's security accounts database, also called the SAM database. They process logon requests from users, and they inform other servers as to which global and/or local security groups users are members of. PDCs also replicate the SAM database periodically to Backup Domain Controllers, or BDCs.

- **Backup Domain Controllers, or BDCs.** BDCs also handle logon requests, both to take load off the PDC and to act as (appropriately enough) a backup logon server should the PDC fail. BDCs receive replicated copies of the SAM database at an interval set by administrators.

- **Member servers.** These are members of a domain but do not process logon requests and do not receive replicated copies of the SAM database. Member servers do have access to the database, and domain users and groups can be granted permission to access resources located on member servers.

- **Stand-alone servers** are not members of a domain and must rely on their own local accounts list to handle local logon requests and manage permissions.

You'll want to install your server according to which of these roles fits its intended use.

Secret

It's very important to remember that member or stand-alone servers cannot be "upgraded" or "promoted" to be domain controllers, and vice-versa. Once NT Server has been installed as a domain controller or nondomain controller, it remains so until Windows NT is reinstalled. This is one of those facts that bright-eyed MCSE students can recite over and over, but it can slip one's mind when it's long since dark outside and you're working on your fifth double latte.

If you think you might want to use the server as a domain controller later, you might as well install it as a BDC now.

Computer name

Many newer administrators, and some veterans as well, like to get "cutesy" with computer and device names. Resist the temptation! At one company I worked at, somebody thought it would be a great idea to categorize all the printer names in each building: bird names in one building, car names in another, tree names in a third, and so on. What do you think happened a year or so down the road? You guessed it: So many printers had been installed in each building that the list of common names was exhausted, and the administrators had to consult the encyclopedia each time they wanted to add a new printer. Meanwhile, the company's poor Help Desk support techs were sentenced to spending days walking users through hooking up to printers with names like PILEATED_WOODPK.

So don't mess with fancy names. Keep it simple, to the point, and as descriptive of the server's true job as possible. There's nothing wrong with a name like ACCTG_PRINT. Also, don't put spaces in server names. Sure it's aesthetically pleasing and most of the time won't cause too many problems, but it creates headaches such as having to use quotation marks every time you want to specify a UNC path.

Secret

Be advised that your computer name will affect other Microsoft BackOffice applications. For example, the hyphen ("-") character is an illegal character in a machine name when working with SQL Server, but such a character isn't illegal natively inside of Windows NT Server. Computer names that contain a hyphen and run SQL Server will not be able to participate in replication or multiserver operations.

In fact, Boeing, a large U.S. aerospace conglomerate, made the exact mistake I just mentioned regarding names with hyphens. Boeing was responsible for a SQL Server fix that allows alias machine names (thus, it is known as the "Boeing fix"). This fix is the sp_addserver stored procedure. It is discussed at length in Knowledge Base article Q158450 found at the support site on

Basically, computer names should be straightforward, 15 characters or less, and absolutely unique; they cannot be the same as any other computer or domain on the network. And as mentioned earlier, the shorter, the better.

Domain name

If you are installing NT Server as a Primary Domain Controller and creating a new domain, it's important to remember that the new domain name also must be unique; it cannot match any computer or domain name that currently exists on your network, including the computer name of the PDC you're installing. Give some thought to selecting an appropriate domain name; depending on the size and complexity of your network, changing it later may not be a simple task.

Licensing mode

Windows NT Server supports two licensing modes: Per Seat and Per Server. If you install Per Server licensing, you only buy as many licenses as you'll have *concurrent* users of the server. For example, if there are 25 people in your office but five of them work the night shift, you can safely buy 20 licenses, because no more than 20 people will be connected to the server at any one time, theoretically. However, if the company grows, you will need to add new licenses in a hurry. If the number of people connected exceeds the number of Per Server licenses, new users who try to connect will be unable to log on — they'll receive a message indicating the server is out of licenses.

Per Seat licensing, on the other hand, is an absolute licensing mode; that is, you buy a license for each desktop that will be connecting to the server. In the preceding example, the network administrator would purchase 25 licenses, one for each employee. Some of these licenses might sit idle while the employees are away, but they will never be met by an "Unable to log on — server out of licenses" message.

Secret

It's very important to remember that simply holding a license for a client operating system such as Windows for Workgroups, Windows 95, or Windows NT Workstation does not automatically allow an administrator to connect those client PCs to the NT server. An appropriate number of NT Server Client Access Licenses must also be purchased. The number of CALs you purchase is influenced by your decision to go with Per Server or Per Seat licensing, so consider this decision carefully.

Most sites I've worked with at small and medium-sized companies just go with Per Seat licensing so that anyone can log on at any time, no questions asked. This is discussed in more detail in Chapter 20, "Windows NT Server – Small Business Server."

File system

When installing Windows NT Server 4.0, you have the choice of using the FAT (file allocation table) or NTFS file system. Both have advantages and disadvantages; I'll try to cover the major points here.

- **FAT (file allocation table) advantages.** The FAT file system has been around since DOS days and is still the most widely used file system in PCs. It has a proven record of compatibility with many operating systems and can be accessed by computers running DOS, OS/2, and any version of Windows. If you're dual-booting your server with another non–Windows NT operating system and you'd like that operating system to be able to access files on the NT partition, FAT will be your file system of choice.

- **FAT disadvantages.** FAT doesn't have any kind of security built in, so share permissions are your only method for selectively granting access to server resources. DOS can also see FAT partitions, so anyone with a DOS boot floppy and physical access to your server can get to your vital company files. In addition, FAT lacks many of the fail-safe and performance enhancements that NTFS provides, and it does not support connections from Macintosh clients across the network.

- **NTFS advantages.** The NT file system is much more robust and reliable than FAT, and it has several fail-safe and recovery features that help prevent data loss in the event of an unexpected shutdown. NTFS also supports file and directory permissions, so administrators can restrict access to sensitive files on the server. Additionally, if you want Macintosh clients to be able to access NT Server files across the network, NTFS is required.

- **NTFS disadvantages.** NTFS is a lot more complex than FAT and is not visible to non–Windows NT operating systems, except across the network. For example, a copy of Windows 95 installed on the server in a dual-boot situation would not be able to see or access any of the NTFS partitions.

It's important to remember that although you can convert FAT partitions to NTFS without data loss using the CONVERT.EXE utility, the only way to convert an NTFS partition back to FAT is to begin Windows NT Setup, format the partition back to FAT and reinstall NT, and then restore all the data from backups.

Microsoft dropped support for the old High Performance File System (HPFS) when they released Windows NT 4.0. If you are running HPFS on an earlier version of NT and intend to upgrade, you'll need to choose between FAT and

NTFS when you do so. And note that the HPFS support question has been known to appear on the Windows NT Server Core Technology MCSE exam.

Administrator password

If you intend to install this server as a Primary Domain Controller, the administrator password will apply to the entire domain. Otherwise, it will be the local administrator password for that particular NT server, except in the case of BDCs, which use the domain SAM. In any case, the administrator password can be a very dangerous thing and a very useful thing at the same time. On the one hand, you don't want anyone to have access to the password or be able to guess it, so you'll want to make it something difficult. On the other hand, when it's crunch time, you don't want to be struggling for two hours to remember the combination of alpha, numeric, and symbolic characters. Only you can determine the proper compromise between security and practicality for your network, but here are a few good ground rules regarding administrator passwords:

1. Try not to use a simple word, no matter what language it's in. This practice can make your server vulnerable to dictionary-based password attacks. Instead, insert a couple of numeric or special characters into the word, and also change case if possible. If this sounds a little paranoid for your small network, remember that even though not every administrator works for the Department of Defense, most CEOs consider their company data at least that important.

2. Keep the administrator password somewhere safe, not written on a slip of paper in your unlocked desk drawer. Remember, most experienced hackers will try the easy way in first — why break down the door if it's already unlocked?

3. Change the administrator password periodically, especially when employees who have the password leave the company. This may sound obvious, but some companies don't follow this practice unless the employee leaves on bad terms. Save yourself some headaches later — change the password when your admins move on, no matter what the circumstances.

Now that your planning phase is done and all your documentation, driver disks, and such are spread out before you, you're ready to run Windows NT Server 4.0 Setup!

Running Setup

You have completed all your network testing and surveys, the server has been physically built and placed in its proper location, you've eaten most of your club sandwich, and it's time to actually install the operating system. Many networking professionals have installed NT 4.0 so many times they've lost count, but for those of you who haven't, here's how it goes.

Two-stage setup

Just as NT 3.51 did, Windows NT 4.0 installs in two stages — a text-based, or "blue screen," stage and a graphical stage. The first stage consists of four main tasks:

1. Identifying your server's disk controller hardware, either by allowing NT to detect disk controllers or by specifying them yourself using vendor-supplied driver disks.

2. Creating or deleting hard disk partitions, then choosing which partition the operating system should be installed onto.

3. Specifying the file system to be used on that partition (NTFS or FAT) as well as the directory where NT Server should be installed.

4. Copying "essential" files to the hard disk so that the Setup program can reboot the machine and run a full version of NT in the Windows-based graphical mode.

This graphical second stage allows you to install networking, specify passwords, determine which role the server will play in the domain, and complete a host of other tasks to ready the server for its first "real" boot. More on that later.

Note

This section covers in detail the "three-floppy and CD" setup procedure. For more information about alternate setup methods, see the end of this chapter.

Beginning the setup process

The first step in Windows NT Server 4.0 setup is booting the machine with the three setup boot disks supplied along with the NT CD-ROM. These disks contain a miniature version of the NT operating system that loads and allows the server to run through the text-based portion of Setup.

Secret

Lose your setup disks? Have no fear — simply pop the NT Server CD into a running Windows machine, change to the proper directory (i386, Alpha, or MIPS, and type **WINNT /OX** (on DOS, Windows 3.1, and Windows 9x) or **WINNT32 /OX** (on NT). This will allow you to create new setup disks from the CD. NT seems to be rather finicky about the disks it will write to, so make sure your disks are freshly formatted.

Upon booting with the first disk, you will be prompted for Disk 2 as follows:

```
Please insert the disk labeled
Windows NT Server Setup Disk #2
into Drive A:
* Press ENTER when ready.
ENTER = Continue      F3=Exit
```

Pressing Enter continues the setup process, and a short time later you will arrive at the Welcome screen, which appears with the following text:

```
Welcome to Setup.
```

Chapter 2: Windows NT Server 4.0 Planning, Setup, and Installation

```
The Setup program for the Microsoft(R) Windows NT(TM) operaing system
version 4.0 prepares Windows NT to run on your computer.
*  To learn more about Windows NT Setup before continuing, press F1.
*  To set up Windows NT now, press ENTER.
*  To repair a damaged Windows NT version 4.0 installation, press R.
*  To quit Setup without installing Windows NT, press F3.
EMTER=Continue    R=Repair   F1=Help   F3=Exit
```

At this point, you will most likely select Enter to continue the setup process, but if you were attempting to repair a damaged installation of Windows NT Server from the Emergency Repair Disk (ERD), you would select "R" for the repair option. Selecting F1 for help is always a viable option if you have questions. And of course, if you want to terminate the Windows NT Server setup, you may select F3 to exit.

Secret

Once again, remember to have your hard drive controller and network adapter drivers handy! On more than one occasion, I've been forced to stop in the middle of an NT installation because I didn't remember which model the ancient ISA network card was. I had to open up the server (a test server in this case), do the "penlight shuffle" to try to find some kind of model number, and then conduct a long Web search in order to find the right driver before starting the setup process over again. This is bad enough on a test server during the workday with a LAN connection to the Web available, and it's that much worse late at night at a client's office, where your trusty laptop and PC Card modem might be your only link to the outside world.

Disk controller detection

Once you proceed past the welcome screen, you are into NT setup in earnest. The first step is NT's detection of your disk controllers or drive arrays. At this point, you can allow Setup to do its thing and see if it finds your hardware by selecting Enter, or you may press S to choose your disk controllers from a list, or from a vendor's driver disk.

During this process, Setup requests the third NT setup disk, as that one contains all of the built-in disk controller drivers. The screen that asks you to insert Disk Three is similar to the following screen:

```
Please insert the disk labeled
Windows NT Server Setup Disk #3
into Drive A:
* Press ENTER when ready.
ENTER = Continue        F3=Exit
```

If you elected to autodetect disk controllers earlier, the list of detected devices will come up at the top of the screen. When this is finished, Setup again offers you the chance to specify hardware manually.

When you're finished with the drive controller identification phase, pressing Enter will allow Setup to load some necessary drivers and then will bring you to the end user license agreement. After you read the agreement and accept it by pressing F8, Setup will proceed to search for previous versions of NT on the machine. If it finds one, you will be offered three choices:

1. Upgrade the existing NT version by pressing Enter.

2. Repair a damaged NT installation by pressing R. The Emergency Repair process is covered in detail elsewhere in this book.

3. Install a fresh copy of Windows NT, either over the top of the existing install or in a different directory, by pressing N.

If you choose to upgrade, Setup will proceed to copying files at this point. If you choose to install a fresh copy, you'll be met with the same screen you'd get if you were installing NT "clean." This screen gives you a brief readout of the keyboard, mouse, disk controller, and video components it detected in your server, and it allows you to change these if necessary. If not, press Enter and Setup will proceed.

Partition "magic"

The next screen of Setup allows you to choose the disk partition you'd like to install NT on. You can also create partitions from unpartitioned space on the disk, or delete partitions that already exist:

```
The list below shows existing partitions and spaces available for
creating new partitions.
Use UP and DOWN ARROW keys to move the highlight to an item in the
list.
* To install Windows NT on the highlighted partition or unpartitioned
space, press ENTER.
* To create a partition in the unpartitioned space, press C.
* To delete the highlighted partition, press D.

| 11119 MB Disk 0 at Id 0 on bus 0 on atapi               |
|    Unpartitioned space                       11118 MB   |
|                                                         |
|                                                         |
|                                                         |
|                                                         |
|                                                         |
|                                                         |

ENTER=Install    C=Create Partition    F1=Help   F3=Exit
```

Secret

In many cases, this screen is the only place where you can delete an NTFS partition. Deleting NTFS partitions, even inactive ones, often does not work from NT's Disk Administrator program—you obviously cannot delete the partition that contains the copy of NT you're running, and even trying to delete other NTFS partitions from Disk Administrator may return errors indicating files are in use. Don't try your trusty old DOS boot disk, either—FDISK can't delete partitions it can't see!

Chapter 2: Windows NT Server 4.0 Planning, Setup, and Installation

Many network administrators recommend the use of a true "boot partition": a small FAT partition that contains only the core files necessary for NT boot: NTLDR, BOOT.INI, NTDETECT.COM, BOOTSECT.DOS (if you're dual-booting with a DOS-based system), and NTBOOTDD.SYS (for small computer system interface (SCSI) disks not using a SCSI BIOS). The BOOT.INI file in this partition points to a separate partition where the operating system is actually installed. That way, if any of these critical files are damaged, it's a simple matter of booting to DOS and replacing them, rather than having to reinstall NT. This technique will be discussed in more detail later, but now's the time to create that partition, so devote a couple of megs of your disk array to it.

Once you have all your partitions created, highlight the one where you'd like to install NT, and press Enter. The next screen appears as shown here:

```
The partition you have chosen is newly created and thus unformatted.
Setup will now format the partition.
Select a file system for the partition from the list below.
Use the UP and DOWN ARROW keys to move the highlight to the file
system you want and then press ENTER.
If you want to select a different partition for Windows NT, press ESC.
   Format the partition using the FAT file system.
   Format the partition using the NTFS file system.
```

This screen offers you the chance to format the partition with FAT or NTFS, or to leave the current file system intact. If you choose NTFS, Setup will actually format the partition with FAT initially and then will run CONVERT.EXE when the system reboots at the very end of Setup. The partition will be converted to NTFS during the next boot process. When you have selected a formatting option, press Enter.

Next, you will be asked which directory you'd like to install Windows NT Server into. The default is WINNT, but you may want to change this, if you're dual-booting, for example. If you don't have a compelling reason to change the install directory, however, make life easier for yourself and leave it set to WINNT. Press Enter when you're finished.

Secret

Be advised that there are "legacy" or poorly developed applications that expect the directory that actually contains Windows NT Server 4.0 to be named WINNT. I can think of a construction accounting program that did this. You would also want to avoid naming the directory with the version name of the operating system. Microsoft did this prior to the release of Windows NT Server 4.0. For example, with Windows NT Server 3.50, the default directory name was WINNT35. This directory name looks silly today for machines that have been upgraded to Windows NT Server 4.0, yet because of the upgrade process and the need to retain existing Registry settings, the original Windows NT Server 3.50 default directory name of WINNT35 was retained. Silly indeed, and it allows you to see at a glance that this machine has been upgraded from previous versions of Windows NT Server.

File copying

The text-based portion of Windows NT Setup is almost finished at this point. Setup will run CHKDSK on your hard drive and then will copy over all the essential files Windows NT needs to finish setup in its graphical, "Full NT" mode. When file copying is complete, Setup will prompt you to remove the floppy disk and then reboot the machine. The text-based portion is over, and you can go back to the mouse now!

Graphical setup

The graphical portion of Setup consists of three parts:

- Gathering information about your computer
- Installing Windows NT Networking
- Finishing Setup

Gathering information

During the first part, Setup gathers more information from you than from your computer. It needs your name and organization, the CD key from your NT Server CD, the licensing mode you want, and the password you'd like to assign for the local Administrator account. Once you have entered those choices, Setup will also ask if you would like to create an Emergency Repair Disk. ERDs are the safety net of server administration — they contain (or point to) all the vital files that will save your administrative bacon if the server crashes. However, these disks are only good if you update them on a regular basis. Further detail on Emergency Repair Disks will be provided later on, but for now it's a good idea to create the disk and keep it in a safe place, such as a lock box in the server room.

Installing Windows NT Networking

Networking is Windows NT Server's raison d'etre, its purpose in life. The operating system is designed so that multiple users can access resources on the server across the network, and in this section of Setup, you give the server the ability to talk to that network.

The first question you're asked is whether your server will be wired to the network or will use dial-up networking to connect. I've never personally seen someone install NT Server with only dial-up connectivity, but I'm sure it's been done. If you choose that option, NT will help you set up a modem before it proceeds with the rest of networking setup.

Network adapter detection and setup

If you choose to have your server wired to the network, as most of us do, the first step is for NT to determine what type of network adapter(s) are in the server, or for you to provide that information to Setup.

If Setup does not detect your network card and you know it should, you might have a hardware problem — either the card is bad, or the BIOS simply didn't detect it properly when you started the server. This is more common with PC clone-based servers than with name brand hardware. In this case, you can manually install the driver and deal with the hardware later, or you can exit Setup, fix the hardware problem, and then boot the server to begin the graphical portion of NT Server setup again.

Optional network services and protocols

Once the NIC driver has been installed, Setup will tell you which network services it is installing by default and ask which optional services you'd like to install, such as RAS, Network Monitor Agent, Microsoft TCP/IP printing, and others (see Figure 2-4). If you'd like to install these services now, click Select from List and pick the services you want.

Figure 2-4: Selecting services

After you've chosen the proper services, Setup asks what network protocols should be installed. TCP/IP is chosen by default, and you can also choose NWLink IPX/SPX Compatible Protocol and/or NetBEUI. TCP/IP is the protocol of the Internet and is becoming the de facto standard for most networks these days, but if your NT server is going to need connectivity with older NetWare servers, or if some clients will need to talk to NT via IPX, you'll want to install that protocol as well. NetBEUI, on the other hand, is optimized for small networks — it is simple and fast but will not work across routers. Also, if the server or network will be connected to the Internet in the future, it's a good idea to install TCP/IP along with or rather than NetBEUI so that you won't have to spend time reconfiguring later.

When you have finished telling Setup which services and protocols you want to use, it will raise dialog boxes and ask for configuration information for each. For instance, TCP/IP will ask whether you want to use a DHCP client configuration (uncommon with servers) or manually configure TCP/IP, RAS will prompt you to install a modem, and so on. Next, Setup will allow you to modify the binding order for the services and protocols, should you wish to do so. When you're done, Setup will attempt to start the NT network.

Starting the network

Once the network starts, Setup will move on and ask for domain information. (Here's where you'll want to make sure you have a good connection to the rest of your network.) If the server is being installed as a domain controller, you will be given a chance to specify the computer name again, as well as the domain name. Remember, neither the computer name nor the domain name (if you're creating a new domain by installing NT Server as a PDC) may be the same as any other computers or domains your network is connected to. When you press Enter on this screen, Setup checks for duplicate names on the network; if it finds one, it will ask you for a different computer name or domain name, depending on which is duplicated.

If Setup freezes while trying to start the network, it's generally indicative of a hardware or driver problem. Any of the following might be happening:

- You might have installed the wrong driver for your network adapter.
- The adapter might be using a different interrupt or memory address than you specified.
- The network might not be functioning properly; check for "green light" at the card and the hub, and for ThinNet (10Base2) networks, check for proper termination.

Secret

On Ethernet 10BaseT networks, it's easy to isolate network faults to the adapter or network. Simply unplug the RJ-45 connector from your network card, and the network should start if the adapter is configured properly. A "hot" network connection is not necessary at this point; the network will start if NT can talk to the network adapter. If networking will not start, then a hardware or driver problem exists.

When Setup is satisfied that it's talking to your network and the naming choices you have specified are appropriate, it will move on to the third and final portion of graphical setup.

Finishing Setup

In this brief section, you provide Setup with your date and time settings. Setup also brings up the Display configuration window, defaulted to VGA settings of 640 × 480, 16 colors, and prompts you to test this setup. If you wish, you can change your display adapter settings at this point, provided your video adapter's drivers can be found on the NT setup CD or on a floppy disk. Once you have chosen and tested the adapter and settings you wish, Setup will proceed to final configuration and file copying, and it will then prompt you to remove floppy disks and reboot the computer. When the reboot is complete, your system will boot into NT Server for the first time. Congratulations! Your new server is now up and running!

Alternate Setup Methods

We've covered the "three-floppy and CD" method of NT Setup in detail, but many administrators find other Setup techniques to work as well or better than this one. Let's touch on some of those methods.

Installing Windows NT Server from a network share

One of most efficient ways to install NT is across the network. In addition to improving speed, network installs allow administrators to do some neat tricks involving load balancing of file copy operations, such as using more than one share point as a file source.

To install Windows from a network share point, simply connect to that share point in one of two ways:

- If the machine does not have an existing operating system, use a network boot floppy that boots DOS, loads networking, and connects to the share.
- Connect to the share with the machine's existing operating system.

  Once connected to the share, start a command prompt, change to the proper directory for your hardware platform, and execute the WINNT or WINNT32 command. WINNT is run from 16-bit operating systems such as DOS and Windows 3.1. WINNT32, on the other hand, will be your choice if you're currently running a 32-bit OS such as Windows 95/98 or an earlier version of NT and you wish to install Windows NT Server over the top of, or in addition to, the existing operating system.

Both of these commands support several command line switches, described in Table 2-1.

Table 2-1 WINNT32.EXE and WINNT.EXE Command Line Options

Option	Description	Available with WINNT.EXE, WINNNT32.EXE, or Both
/s: sourcepath	Specifies the source location of the Windows NT files. Must be a full path of the form x:\ [path] or .	Both
/t: tempdrive	Specifies a drive to contain temporary setup files. If none is specified, Setup will attempt to locate a drive for you.	Both
/I: inffile	Specifies the filename (no path) of the setup information file. The default is DOSNET.INF.	Both
/ox	Creates boot floppies for CD-ROM-based installation.	Both
/x	Specifies that Setup should not create the boot floppies but still should ask for them (when you already have a set of floppies, for example).	Both
/f	Does not verify files as they are copied to the boot floppies.	WINNT.EXE
/c	Skips the free-space check on the boot floppies you provide.	WINNT.EXE
/b	"Floppyless operation" — setup files are copied to the hard drive, so the user does not have to load or eject boot floppies.	Both
/u: scriptfile	Unattended installation using the specified script file.	Both
/u	Unattended upgrade of a previous NT version.	WINNT32.EXE
/r	Installs one or more additional directories in the directory tree where Windows NT is being loaded.	Both
/e	Specifies a command to be executed when installation is complete.	Both

Secret

It is possible to specify up to three additional source paths when running WINNT or WINNT32 with the /S switch. Simply add them in one by one when you type the command. This accomplishes some "load balancing" — Setup will copy each file from whichever path is least busy.

For instance, let's say your network had four software installation servers: INSTALL1, INSTALL2, INSTALL3, and INSTALL4. If you wanted to specify all of them, you would connect to INSTALL1 initially, and then run the following command utilizing UNC naming conventions:

```
WINNT /S
```

This command will pull files from each of those servers while it's copying.

Installing Windows NT Server over other operating systems

Many administrators may want to upgrade existing systems that run DOS, Windows 95/98, or an earlier version of NT. This is a fairly straightforward process—let's take a look at how it works.

Upgrading from DOS

A DOS upgrade is very simple—Windows NT will be installed into the directory you choose, but DOS will remain on the machine so that you can boot back into it if you like.

Upgrading from Windows 95/98

This "upgrade" is not quite as easy, because no upgrade support is available for those systems in Windows NT 4.0 due to differences between the Windows 95/98 Registry and NT's Registry. In order to install NT over 95, you'll need to back up any vital data on the machine, install NT, and then reload all of your applications and restore the data.

Upgrading from a previous version of Windows NT

This method is even simpler—just run WINNT32.EXE /u, and it will run an unattended upgrade from the existing installation to Windows NT Server 4.0. Configuration information is copied from your previous installation, and you don't have to answer any questions. The preserved configuration includes the following items:

- Control Panel settings including custom desktop settings
- Custom program groups you created under the earlier NT version
- Custom Registry settings
- Network settings including hardware settings, protocols, and services such as RAS
- The local security accounts database

Dual-booting

It is possible to run Windows NT 4.0 on systems that also run other operating systems, and NT Setup will configure the boot.ini file so that you can still get to your existing OS. For instance, a machine currently running Windows 95 can be set up with Windows NT Server as well—you will have the choice of either operating system at boot time. This is due to the presence of the BOOTSECT.DOS file, which keeps track of the additional system's boot record.

To make dual-booting work, just be sure to install Windows NT into a different directory than the current operating system is installed in. For Windows 3.*x* and Windows 9*x*, this isn't difficult, because the default directory for those systems is WINDOWS and the default for NT is WINNT.

Remember, any applications that are visible to you in previous versions of Windows will not be visible in Windows NT until you reinstall them while running NT. You can install them into the same directories they occupy under other versions of Windows—Windows NT just needs the install routine to update its own Registry settings for the application.

Installation Secrets

Every NT administrator worth his salt knows that the Windows NT Setup process doesn't end the first time you log on—not by a long shot. There are many other things to do—some covered in the manual, some that just come with time and experience. I'll try to share a few of the latter type with you now.

Putting the NT source files on the server's hard disk

Once your server is up and stabilized, one of the first things you'll want to do is copy the Windows NT source files to the hard disk. As you add and remove server software components over the server's lifetime, you'll frequently be asked for these source files, so that Windows may add the required components (DLL and EXE files, for example) to the current installation. Every NT administrator has, in one crunch time situation or another, found himself or herself scurrying around searching for the NT installation CD. Who needs this hassle? We've got enough to deal with. If the source files are on the hard disk, you won't have to look around for the original CD; you'll just confirm the location of the files on the hard disk, and away she'll go.

In order for this process to work, you must complete two tasks: Copy the source files from the CD to the hard drive, and then edit the Registry so that NT is aware of the new location. Let's take this in two steps.

Copying the files across

The first task is easy enough; most administrators like to copy the proper files for their installation of Windows NT, such as i386, Alpha, or MIPS, to the root of their system partition, You can do this by dragging and dropping, or by running XCOPY /S from a command prompt.

For instance, if the CD-ROM drive is E and you want to copy the NT source files for Intel-based systems to the C drive, the command would be:

XCOPY /S E:\I386 C:\I386

If you installed NT from a network share, simply substitute the UNC pathname for the E: in the preceding example.

Editing the Registry to point to the new location

As always, exercise care when editing your Registry. Microsoft recommends making a full backup of your Registry before making any changes.

Once the files are in place, you must tell NT where they are so that you don't have to retype the path each time it needs a source file. In order to do this, you must edit the following Registry key:

HKEY_LOCAL_MACHINE\SOFTWARE\Microsoft\Windows NT\CurrentVersion\SourcePath

To do so, run regedit or regedt32, whichever you prefer, from the Start menu. Drill down in the Registry to find the proper key. This key is of type REG_SZ (see Figure 2-5) and probably reads D:\i386 or something similar, if you installed NT from the CD-ROM. Change the string to reflect the new location of the source files, which would be C:\i386 in our previous example.

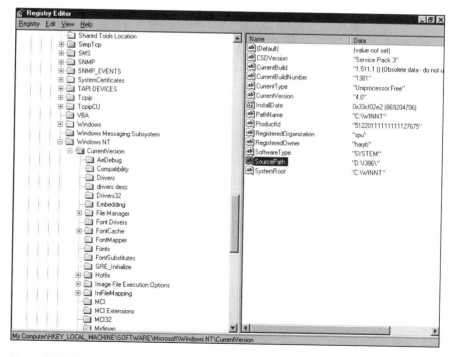

Figure 2-5: Changing the SourcePath key in Registry Editor

After you've completed this procedure, exit Registry Editor. Now try adding a service or component to Windows NT, and check out the new process!

Editing boot.ini to shorten the OS startup delay

One of my favorite tweaks is changing the timeout parameter in boot.ini so that the server will boot more quickly when it's unattended. Sure, if you're standing right there you can just hit a key at the bootup selection screen, but if you reboot a server remotely, your users will experience an unnecessary delay before they're able to connect again. And I've had clients who incorrectly complained that the server was slow when in reality, the problem was a long delay in BOOT.INI, not the machine itself performing badly.

To change this parameter, you can choose one of two methods: the feel-good GUI method or the hardcore geek command line method.

The GUI method

The OS startup delay parameter can be found in the System Properties sheet, accessed by right-clicking My Computer and choosing Properties. Once in the sheet, select the Startup/Shutdown tab, and you'll see your target, as shown in Figure 2-6.

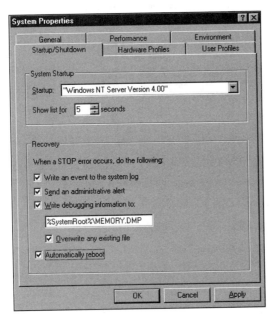

Figure 2-6: The Startup/Shutdown tab in the System Properties sheet

Simply change the timeout value to reflect your current preference (I like 10 seconds, myself) and click OK. Windows will modify boot.ini in the background, and the timeout delay will be changed the next time you reboot the server.

The geek method

Boot.ini is nothing more than an ordinary text file with some special file attributes to prevent tampering by overzealous users and administrators (like us!). Sure, it contains ARC names which take some doing to understand, but we're not going to worry about that here. All you're concerned with at this point is changing the timeout=XX parameter.

Note

Unless you have explicit understanding of all the parameters in the boot.ini file, do not change anything within the file except the single parameter we're discussing here. Doing so could render your system unbootable, and if the partition is formatted with NTFS, the only recovery option will be to perform the Emergency Repair process.

Before you can change anything about the boot.ini file, you must remove its read-only file attribute. You can do this by first right-clicking the file in Windows NT Explorer and selecting Properties and then unchecking the read-only box on the Properties sheet, or you can do the same thing from a command prompt by typing **attrib –s –r boot.ini** while in the root of your system partition. (The –s removes the system attribute, which is necessary to remove the read-only attribute from a command line.)

Once the read-only attribute is removed, you may proceed with editing the file (see Figure 2-7). Open it in your favorite text editor (it will default to Notepad if double-clicked in Explorer) and change the timeout= parameter to whatever you like. Save the file, put back the system and read-only attributes if you removed them, and voila! Your bootup delay is just the way you like it.

Figure 2-7: Editing the boot.ini file

Establishing a real "boot partition" for your boot files

Every battle-scarred NT administrator has gone through the following headache at least once: You're minding your own business, rebooting a server for one reason or another, and suddenly the server will not boot. Instead, you receive a friendly message indicating "Boot: Cannot find NTLDR." Yikes! Suddenly, a typical operation has just turned into a disaster, and you're scrambling for a way to get the server back up.

The reasons for problems with system bootups are many and varied; they can include missing files, misconfigured files (such as a bad boot.ini), or Registry problems. Most often, however, there's a problem with one of the server's crucial boot files. "That's easy to fix," you say to yourself, "I'll just boot up with a DOS floppy and replace the files." Nope! If your partition is formatted with NTFS, that solution ain't gonna fly — you're heading for the land of Emergency Repair.

At first glance, it would seem that you're stuck between two less-than-ideal options: using the FAT file system on all your servers so that you can access the boot files from a DOS boot floppy, or having to go through Emergency Repair anytime one of these files becomes corrupted. Luckily, there is a happy medium if you have an Intel x86-based system. You can place the boot files on a small FAT partition and then manually modify the boot.ini file to point back to the NTFS partition that contains the actual NT system files.

Before exploring the rest of this tip, some basic explanation of the NT boot process is in order. Windows NT Server uses several files while booting the system, and all of those files must be found on the server's active partition, that is, the partition it looks to at boot time. These files include

- NTLDR, which begins the boot process and loads boot.ini
- BOOT.INI, which tells the system which disk partition the OS is located on
- NTDETECT.COM, which builds a hardware listing after you select which operating system to boot
- BOOTSECT.DOS, which is only present if a DOS-based (that is, non-NT) OS is present on the machine. This file contains the boot record for those systems.
- NTBOOTDD.SYS, which is only present if the system contains a SCSI controller that is not visible to the system BIOS

Let's look at the process for moving these files to a small boot partition and then making that partition "active" so that the server will boot from it.

Formatting the partition with a FAT

Remember that small two-megabyte partition we created during the DOS-based portion of NT Setup? Well, this is its day in the sun. The first step is to format this partition using the FAT file system. To do so, boot into NT and start the Disk Administrator program, found in the Administrative Tools section of the Start menu (see Figure 2-8).

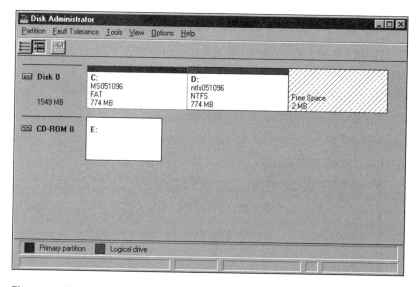

Figure 2-8: Disk Administrator

Click on the small partition to select it, and then choose Tools ⇨ Format. Format the partition with FAT, and then assign it a drive letter of your choosing. You might want to make it an uncommon letter, such as T or U.

Copying the boot files to the new FAT partition

When the format is complete, exit Disk Administrator and open a window containing the original boot files, for example C:. In order to see all of them, you may have to change your View options to show hidden files. To do this, click View ⇨ Options and then select the View tab, as shown in Figure 2-9. Choose the Show All Files radio button and then click OK. You should now be able to see all the files in the root of your C drive.

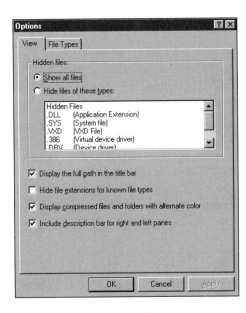

Figure 2-9: Enabling hidden file access

Copy all of the critical boot files mentioned to the new partition. Once this is complete, you must edit the boot.ini file to reflect the partition number where the operating system files are stored. Such a path is based on the ARC naming path and appears as

```
multi(0)disk(0)rdisk(1)partition(2)
```

The ARC naming path can be interpreted from Table 2-2.

Table 2-2 ARC Naming Conventions

Term	Description
multi / scsi (x)	This identifies the type of hardware adapter (or controller).
	multi: includes all disk adapters/controllers (including, ironically, SCSI disk controllers with the BIOS enabled).
	scsi: includes SCSI controllers when the SCSI BIOS isn't enabled.
	(x): is the ordinal number of the disk adapter/controller.
disk (y)	This is the SCSI bus number (this value is always "0" for multi).
rdisk (z)	This is the ordinal number of the disk (this is ignored for SCSI disk adapters/controllers).
partition (a)	This is the ordinal number of the partition.

Run Disk Administrator again. Click the partition to select it, and then choose Partition ⇨ Mark Active from the menu. Close Disk Administrator and reboot, and your system will boot from the small FAT partition.

Why did I do this again? If one of your boot files becomes corrupted and your system will not boot, you can now boot from a DOS floppy and replace the file(s) in question without having to go through the Emergency Repair process. You also can keep your Windows NT system files and data on one or more NTFS partitions, thus retaining the peace of mind that NTFS security provides.

Summary

You have now created the foundation of your Windows NT Server network. Properly set up, your Windows NT Server 4.0 server machine will make it easy to introduce additional server features, services, BackOffice applications, and yes, even third-party applications with confidence. Improperly set up, your server will always face you with Windows NT Server foundation issues such as badly behaved hardware drivers causing crashes ("blue screens"). I've been there and done that, an experience set that only compounds my belief that this chapter, with its secrets, tips, and notes, is one of the most important chapters in the book. In this chapter, we

▶ Surveyed and optimized the existing network before installation.

▶ Planned for a successful installation of Windows NT Server 4.0.

▶ Selected proper server hardware.

- Implemented Windows NT Server and explained how to install it from the network.
- Completed some essential postinstallation tasks to make administration easier down the road.

Chapter 3
Windows NT Server 4.0 Implementation

In This Chapter

- Setting up and maintaining user accounts and groups
- Delivering file and print services with Windows NT Server 4.0
- Securing your network using NT's built-in security tools
- Connecting users to their data using logon scripts
- Implementing server and network backups
- Protecting your network from viruses
- Implementing remote communications
- Setting up basic e-mail

Congratulations if you've successfully set up your Windows NT Server network after studying Chapter 2. This chapter is about post-installation tasks that need to be performed before you throw caution to the wind and let the end users in. These eight postimplementation tasks, listed at the start of this chapter, could be considered necessities to both a network administrator and an end user: to have a network that is functional and allows logons in a secure environment where one can save and retrieve files, print, know that data is backed up, gain remote access, and send and receive basic e-mail in a virus-free environment. Consider it your Windows NT Server network mission statement!

Contrary to what you may be expecting, this chapter will not be a step-by-step explanation of User Manager, Server Manager, and other administration tools. This book is written by working NT administrators, for working NT administrators. If you're reading this book, you've probably been working in the Windows NT world for a while. Simply stated, I have too much respect for you, the reader, to give you a rehash of every single button and check box you'll ever use while maintaining your network. For that type of feature review, you should start with the Windows NT Server user manuals and on-line help.

Rather, this chapter offers tips, secrets, and techniques gleaned from day-to-day experience with Windows NT Server in different environments — "Best Practices," if you will. We will briefly touch on the basics of Windows NT Server administration, but most of this chapter will be devoted to techniques that hopefully will assist you in running your networks better tomorrow than you did yesterday.

Tools of the Trade

While I was in college, I worked summers and breaks at an automobile service station. During that time, I found that professional mechanics have a large cache of tools on hand, many of them specialized for certain tasks. However, those specialized tools spent much of the time idle — the mechanics usually came back to just a handful of tools that they used for most jobs. These were the ones that were well worn from years of battle with spark plugs, brake pads, and water pumps.

The tools of the trade in this section include User Manager for Domains and how to add, delete, and manage user accounts. The use of domains in your network is discussed, as are groups and security identifiers (SIDs).

User Manager for Domains

For Windows NT Server administrators, User Manager for Domains is one of those often-used tools that's usually found running on the admin's desktop during the workday.

Stand-alone and member servers have the User Manager tool that enables administrators to manage local accounts for those particular servers. If you're working with a domain, this tool is called User Manager for Domains (see Figure 3-1). Both tools do the same thing: They enable you to add and delete users, as well as modify user properties such as group membership, passwords, logon restrictions, and the like.

Creating a new user

To create a new user, start up User Manager for Domains, found in the Administrative Tools group under the Start menu. Once into User Manager for Domains, click User ⇨ New User in the menu, and you'll be presented with the New User dialog box (see Figure 3-2).

Chapter 3: Windows NT Server 4.0 Implementation

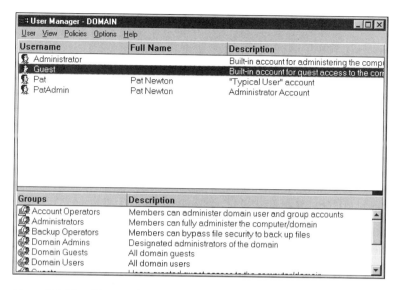

Figure 3-1: User Manager for Domains

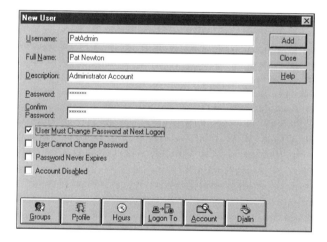

Figure 3-2: Creating a new user in User Manager for Domains

Once you've filled in the required fields, click the Groups button to add the user to any groups you may want, or click Profile to specify a roaming or mandatory profile for the user (see Figure 3-3). More on user profiles appears later in this chapter. You may also want to modify the user's logon attributes or dial-in privileges. Information on those operations is available in the User Manager Help file.

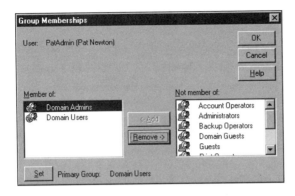

Figure 3-3: Adding a user to groups

When you're all done, click Add and the user is off and running!

Secret

This is an appropriate time to discuss administrative account policies. One "best practice" I've found is to minimize use of the actual Administrator account on a server or domain. Instead, put the Administrator password away for safekeeping and set up other accounts with administrative rights that you or other administrators may use while maintaining the server or network.

It is also a very good idea to set up separate administrative and "typical user" accounts for yourself, because you're probably only in "admin mode" some of the time. Set up one account with normal user access that you'll use most of the time, and an administrative account to log onto when you need to add or delete users, change permissions, or do other tasks that require high-level access. Make this administrative account a member of the Administrators or Domain Admins group (more on groups in a few pages), and you will have the access you need. You may find that typical user rights allow you to perform many of your day-to-day tasks without any trouble. Also, minimizing your time in "admin mode" minimizes the chance for problems caused by human error.

This type of account arrangement with the appropriate use of administrator and user is especially efficient in a multiuser NT environment such as Citrix WinFrame or Windows NT 4.0 Terminal Server Edition. An administrator can be logged onto his or her local workstation with "normal user" access and simply fire up a WinFrame or Terminal Server session to log on via the admin account when administrator-level access is needed.

Deleting users

Deleting a user is even simpler than creating one. Simply start up User Manager for Domains, highlight the user in the list, and hit the Delete key on your keyboard. Remember our discussion a few pages ago, however: Make sure you're deleting the correct person or computer, because if you have to replace a mistakenly deleted account, it will be assigned a new SID.

For example, let's say an administrator receives a request to delete the account of Sally Richards, an accountant who left the company. By a slip of the fingers, the well-meaning admin actually deletes Sally Romano, the company's CEO. Oops! Even if he creates another account immediately with Sally Romano's user name, she will not have the same access, because her new SID is different. Time for some fancy footwork.

Tip

With that in mind, I offer this tip. Rather than deleting users outright, it's a good idea to just disable their accounts initially and then delete the accounts when it becomes completely clear that their access is no longer needed. You can do this by checking the "Account Disabled" box in User Manager for Domains. Often, former managers will want to get into the user's files, network home directories, or e-mail, and the simplest way to do this is to keep the account around in case it's needed. Also, I've been bitten by the "occasional temp worker" situation more than once. A temp leaves the company, you delete his or her account, and after three weeks the same worker is back and needs a logon again. I find that it's more efficient to keep these accounts around until you're absolutely sure the temp is gone for good.

I have also been guilty of deleting a terminated user who planned to return the following week, with management's blessing, to clean out her desk and remove personal data files and e-mail messages. Here, I should have disabled the account for a reasonable period of time after the employee's termination. Deleting the account proved to be a mistake on my part.

Secret

One note about disabling accounts: Be absolutely sure to inform your help desk of the situation. In a large company where users' comings and goings are not widely known, a well-meaning tech support person could give the former employees their access back in response to a help desk phone call.

Managing accounts

First, let's understand when you might rename an existing account, copy an existing account, or create a new account when you need to add a user to your Windows NT Server network. In truth, I don't remember the last time I created a new account on my network. Ninety-five percent of the time, I just copy an existing user's account and affix a new user name to it. In fact, the security form we receive from hiring managers has a space asking which existing account we should model the new user after. The necessity of user copying definitely depends on your environment. Friends who work in small companies and have only 25–30 users have told me they usually create new accounts and add them to domain groups manually. That's a good way to go in a small shop, where the administrator probably knows by heart all the groups a new sales manager should be in, for instance.

However, in the world of medium-sized businesses, with anywhere from 100 employees on up, creating a new user can be more problematic. If a request comes in for an account to be created for the new marketing intern and you are responsible for its creation, it's doubtful that you will know all the proper groups, restrictions, and such off the top of your head. If you choose to create a new account, you'll have to consult documentation and manually add the new user to all the proper groups, configure his or her access, and so on. Now don't get me wrong; documentation of your domain groups and how each type of user fits in is an excellent thing to have and is essential to good network administration. However, creating a new user each time is an inefficient way of accomplishing a simple task. In large enterprises, with hundreds or thousands of users, simply creating a new user with correct access the first time around may be impossible.

Instead, you should bring up another marketing intern's account, use the Copy function in User Manager for Domain's User menu, and assign a new user name and password. Then the task is complete.

Secret

Some shops, in fact, use "template" accounts for different job functions and copy new users from those templates. I recommend that you create generic accounts for different staff positions. Then simply copy the generic account to create a real user account that fits a certain situation. For example, a low-level bookkeeper may hold the title GSA1. Assuming Robert McKay is hired as a new GSA1 at the firm, simply copy the generic account you've created called GSA1 to Robert McKay, and you're well on your way to making Robert a valid and secure user on your Windows NT Server network.

But enough war stories for now. As shown in Figure 3-4, you can simply take a tried-and-true user account and apply it safely to a new network user.

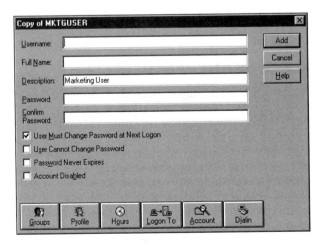

Figure 3-4: Copying a new user from a template account

Renaming users is also a useful technique for efficient system administration. If a particular person is leaving the business and a replacement has been designated, it's often better to rename the old user's account with the replacement's user name and assign a new password; the new employee is then ready to go. This often works well with temporary employees, who can come and go unpredictably. Just be sure the temp who's leaving isn't going to return soon!

Delegate administrators

Here's another valuable gleaning: Only give your delegate administrators the access they absolutely need. For instance, if your shop has a help desk group that only needs to reset passwords and work with accounts, limiting their admin access to that of the NT Account Operators group is a wise choice. A war story illustrates this thought well.

A few years ago, I was a member of a help desk team in a large enterprise. The group had administrative access for certain tasks we had to perform on a regular basis. We could have gotten by with Server Operator access, but instead we were members of the Domain Admins group. When things got slow at the help desk, as they sometimes did on Friday afternoons, a popular group pastime was playing hacky-sack among the cubes. One week, disaster was narrowly averted during a particularly energetic hacky-sack game, when a teammate pulled off an impressive move — a "jester," I believe it was — and the hacky found its way to another teammate's keyboard. He had Server Manager running, and by the time the bouncing stopped, the hacky-sack was one confirmation box away from removing the company's main Exchange server from the domain. As Dave Barry so eloquently puts it, I am not making this up. When the NT administrators got wind of that one, you can bet they cleaned up our access immediately. The moral of the story: Don't give users more administrative privileges than they need.

Domains

Groups of Windows NT computers that share the same account database are called *domains*. Windows NT domains allow users to access resources on many different computers through a single logon. Once the user is authenticated on the domain, he or she can access information contained on servers within the domain, because the servers share information about who's who within the domain, and what resources they should have access to.

Domain trust relationships

In a multiple-domain environment, it is possible to configure "trust relationships" so that users from one domain may access resources on another domain. This enables you to adhere to Windows NT Server's one user–one account law. Furthermore, some BackOffice applications such as Proxy Server, SQL Server, and Microsoft Exchange participate in the Windows NT Server domain directory services security model, relying on this "one account" to function.

For example, if users in the Sales domain need to access data on servers in the Engineering domain, it's essential that Engineering "trust" Sales, that is, the Engineering server's security subsystem can determine "Oh yeah, this guy is from Sales — we trust them."

Setting up trust relationships is fairly straightforward. It's done from User Manager for Domains, by clicking Policies ⇨ Trust Relationships from the menu. To establish a trust, you must first ensure that a network physically connects the two domains, and then determine a trust password. Click the appropriate Add button (see Figure 3-5), depending on whether you want to add a *trusted* domain or a *trusting* domain. Enter the domain name and the trust password, and click OK. Perform the converse procedure on the other domain, or have your counterpart do so, and the trust is established.

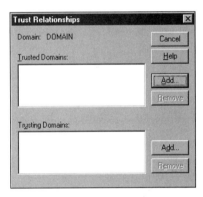

Figure 3-5: Preparing to add a trust relationship

Once the trust is in place, users from the *trusted* domain can access resources such as files, printers, and applications on the *trusting* domain.

One-way and "two-way" trusts

Trusts like the one just described are called one-way trusts, because one domain trusts the other. Two-way trusts are where each domain trusts the other — they're actually just two one-way trusts that are mirror images of each other.

Note: Remember that trust relationships are not transitive in Windows NT Server 4.0. That Domain A trusts Domain B and Domain B trusts Domain C doesn't necessarily mean that Domain A trusts Domain C. That third trust must be specifically set up.

So why the heck would you want to set up all these complicated trusts? Here's an example from a large IT shop I worked in. This company had 3,000 users and several thousand computers spread out over 14 states. In order to keep all of these resources straight, they decided to place all the users into one domain and all the computers and resources into other domains called resource domains. Because the users all logged onto their user domain, the resource domains had to trust that user domain, or the users wouldn't have been able to access them.

Trust models

Windows NT Server uses four types of trust models: single, single master, multiple master, and complete. Note that you need to honor these models today with Windows NT Server 4.0, but in Windows 2000 Server (a.k.a. Windows NT Server 5.0), the directory services tree known as Active Directory will largely render these models moot. Let's quickly review the Windows NT Server domain models:

- **Single domain model.** Only one domain

- **Single master domain model.** One domain for accounts (master) and any number of resource domains

- **Multiple master domain model.** More than one master account domain and any number of resource domains. This model is very popular in large corporations such as Boeing.

- **Complete trust domain model.** Two one-way trusts connecting every domain in the Windows NT Server network. Ironically, this model is typically used when no one trusts each other.

In other words, consider the following when using domains: The type of trust in which all the users are located in one domain and other domains trust that one is called the single master domain model. Networks with users located in more than one domain, where the users need to access resources located in many domains, use the multiple master domain model. The simplest, of course, is the single domain model. This is appropriate for smaller networks, or any network with no specific need for multiple domains. Single domains are by far the easiest to manage, because trust relationships are not necessary. Remember, "Keep it simple, stupid!" is a motto that's been proven successful in network design and maintenance.

Note

That last statement is very important. Most people overdesign the Windows NT Server trust model. Your migration to Windows 2000 Server will be much easier with fewer domains. This book does not spend a great deal of time discussing domains for many of the reasons already stated. For more information on domains, you are advised to attend Microsoft's "Supporting Microsoft's Windows NT Server 4.0 Enterprise Technologies" course (MOC #689).

Global and local groups

In a Windows NT domain, user accounts can be gathered together in two kinds of groups: *global* and *local*. Table 3-1 presents the key differences between global and local groups.

Table 3-1   Differences Between Global and Local Groups

Global	Local
Contain users from the domain in which they were created.	Contain both users from their own domain and global groups from their own or a trusted domain.
Are visible across domains; i.e., global groups from one domain can be added to a local group on another domain.	Are visible only in their own domain; they cannot be seen by trusting domains.
Have no built-in "rights": Log On Locally, Shut Down Server, etc.	Are predefined in NT and have certain preset user rights.

Security identifiers (SIDs)

Windows NT keeps track of all users, computers, and even domains themselves by assigning each resource a unique Security Identifier, or SID. This SID is the main tool NT's security system uses to keep track of who's who and what's what on its network. A new SID is created each time an administrator adds a user, computer, or domain to the network, regardless of whether the user name, computer name, or domain name previously existed on the network. (Of course, the system won't let you add a duplicate name if the name still exists on the network.)

A SID looks similar to:

```
S-1-5-21-1181630594-508303197-1458450816-500
```

It's important to note the fact that a unique SID value is created for each new user, computer, or domain, because all permissions, group memberships, and such are tracked by SID rather than user name. And as mentioned previously in "Deleting users," if an account is deleted by mistake, simply adding the account back under the same username will not give the user access to everything he or she had before.

Users, global, local, rights (UGLR)

Anyone who's ever attended a Microsoft Official Curriculum (MOC) NT administration class knows the mantra: "Users are put into global groups, global groups, into local groups, and rights are assigned to local groups."

This is known as UGLR. In fact, when an NT professional is studying for the Windows NT Server in the Enterprise certification exam, even his or her spouse gets to know this by heart.

This method makes good sense for large networks where users and resources are spread out across domains and trust relationships must work properly. But do you really need such complexity in a single-domain network of 25, 50, even 200 people? I don't think so. In a Windows NT domain, it's just as easy to assign individual users to local groups that you create, thus eliminating the global group step altogether.

For example, in the network at my workplace, we create groups by resource, with a specific group for each printer, network share, primary directory on our file servers, and so on. Until recently, my firm had one global group and one local group for each resource; the global groups contained the users, and the local groups contained only that particular global group. Permissions were then assigned to the global group.

Finally, our network manager noted that we didn't need this unnecessary hassle. Why not just move the users to the local groups, and eliminate the global groups altogether? This method has worked well for us. It may not fit every environment or security strategy, but you might want to consider it if you're looking for a way to simplify your network.

Delivering User Services

Now that you've created all your user accounts and organized them into tidy groups, you need to set up resources. Because every Windows NT network administrator knows that the first call you'll receive from end users is an "I can't print," I start with that first. Printing is often not as it seems, so I discuss not only using the Add Printer Wizard but how to interact with a third-party print component such as the HP JetDirect card. And if you don't hear from your users about printing, you're likely to hear about folders, files, and data. This section doesn't let you down on that front. See the discussion on file sharing later in this chapter.

Adding printers to your server

In the early days of network computing, one of the main reasons a small business would install a network was so that multiple users could share the same printer. Users were tired of employing "Sneakernets" when they wanted to print something (that is, saving the document to a floppy disk, walking over to the computer that had a printer attached, and printing the document there). Users wanted the ability to print from their desks, anytime, with their feet up. Thus, the concept of network printers was born.

Windows NT Server supports many different kinds of printer connections, and once a printer is hooked up to the server you can share it out to users anywhere on your network, including those across WAN links. Before we get into printer sharing, however, let's discuss some of the ways you can connect a printer to a Windows NT Server.

Printer connections

Many network administrators confront the inevitable issue of how to connect a printer to the network. Do you want a local connection at either the server or local machine? Or would you prefer higher-performing network-connected printers using the HP JetDirect card, an Intel print server, or some other third-party network printing solution? For answers, look no further than the next few pages.

Local ports

Most LAN administrators are familiar with the Add Printer Wizard in Windows 95 and 98. The Add Printer Wizard in Windows NT Server 4.0 looks and functions very much like the one in these systems. When you begin to add a printer via the Add Printer Wizard, NT asks you if the printer is connected to the local server ("My Computer") or to another network print server. As shown in Figure 3-6, we want to connect the printer locally so that the server can become the print server. Once you choose to connect the printer locally, the wizard asks which port the printer is connected to. If the printer is connected to a truly local port like LPT1 or COM1, great, you can proceed with the printer installation. If not, you may need to choose the Add Port button to add another type of port.

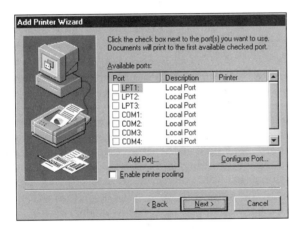

Figure 3-6: The port choice screen in the Add Printer Wizard

HP JetDirect–connected printers

One of the prevailing trends in network printing has been the advent of printers that connect directly to the network. That is, these printers act as network nodes. The benefits of such printers are obvious. First, these printers interact with the clients much faster than printers connected via a parallel interface. In fact, a parallel port operates at approximately 256Kb/sec, whereas a printer that is directly connected to network may receive data at up to 10Mb/sec, or up to 40 times faster. And that large number only increases exponentially if you are using one of the new 100Mb/sec network interface cards on a 100Mb/sec network.

Chapter 3: Windows NT Server 4.0 Implementation

Network printer solutions include offerings from Intel, Digital, and Hewlett-Packard (HP). I'll take a few moments to discuss HP's JetDirect solution. JetDirect cards are placed inside an HP laser printer, whereas the external JetDirect device enables you to attach both HP and non-HP printers, so the external JetDirect device may be a better fit if you have non-HP printers.

The key to successfully setting up your HP JetDirect device is twofold. First, it is essential that you install the HP JetDirect port on the Windows NT Server that will act as the printer server (see Figure 3-7).

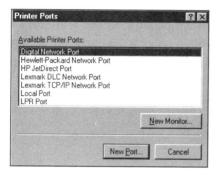

Figure 3-7: The HP Jet Direct port

STEPS:
To install the HP JetDirect port

Step 1. Open the Printers applet in Control Panel. Note this is the same as the Printers folder access from other points in Windows NT Server (Windows NT explorer, My Computer, and so on).

Step 2. Launch the Add Printer Wizard.

Step 3. Select the My Computer radio button. Even though the printer utilizing the JetDirect device isn't physically connected to the Windows NT Server at which you are performing these commands, this server is acting as the printer server that will queue and manage the printer and print jobs. Click Next.

Step 4. The Available Ports screen, you will notice, has no way to trap the network-connected printer or the HP JetDirect card (in this example). Only "traditional" ports such as LPT1, COM1, and the like are shown. We need to add the HP JetDirect port by clicking Add Port.

Step 5. The Printer Port dialog box appears sans any reference to any HP JetDirect card. Only built-in printer ports (such as the Digital Network port) that ship with Windows NT Server are displayed. Click the New Monitor button so that you can add the HP JetDirect port.

Continued

STEPS
To install the HP JetDirect port *(continued)*

Step 6. The Installing Print Monitor dialog box appears. You are asked to provide the path from which to copy the appropriate printer monitor files (.inf files). At this point, insert your HP JetDirect CD-ROM and direct the path to the Windows NT Server subdirectory (\winnt) on that CD-ROM. Assuming your CD-ROM is drive d:\, the path would appear as d:\winnt. Click OK.

Step 7. The HP JetDirect Port will now appear in the Printer Ports dialog box as shown in Figure 3-7. Select the HP JetDirect Port and click New Port.

Step 8. You will configure the HP JetDirect device via the Add HP JetDirect Port Wizard. It is here that you supply the network printer name or static TCP/IP address to assist the Port Wizard in "trapping" the port.

On comment regarding the use of TCP/IP with HP JetDirect devices: I recommend that you consider assigning static IP addresses in this area, as I've found the dynamic address assignment approach used by HP JetDirect devices (BOOTP) to be both bothersome and unreliable.

After you have installed, trapped, and configured the HP JetDirect port, proceed to install and share the printer. These steps are provided next.

Note
The point in step 3 regarding the My Computer radio button is important. I and others have selected the Network Printer Server radio button in the past when trying to install a HP JetDirect card or some other form of network-connected printer solution. In part, that is because the network printer cards and devices often say "printer server" right on the box they were shipped in. It is also a function of misguided logic. A laser printer directly connected to the network would appear to be a network printer server at first take. Such is not the case. By selecting My Computer when implementing a network-connected printer, you are in effect declaring that "this" Windows NT Server is the point of administration for that printer. Again, such administration includes printer management, document management, print job spooling, and queuing.

Installing and sharing the printer

Once you have told Windows what port the printer is connected to, the Add Printer Wizard will ask you to specify the manufacturer and model of the printer, as shown in Figure 3-8. If you have updated driver disks, you should click the Have Disk button; otherwise, choose the proper make and model from the list.

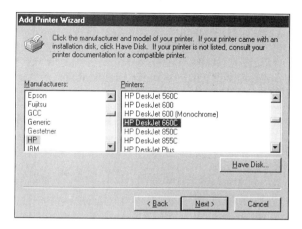

Figure 3-8: Choosing the proper print driver

After the driver is specified, the wizard will move on to the printer sharing screen, seen in Figure 3-9. It asks what local name you'd like to assign to the printer, and whether you'd like to share it. If you choose to share the printer, NT also asks which other operating systems will be using the printer over the network, so it can install the proper drivers for "Point and Print" operation. In Point and Print, when a user connects the network printer to his or her computer, the appropriate drivers are automatically downloaded from the print server.

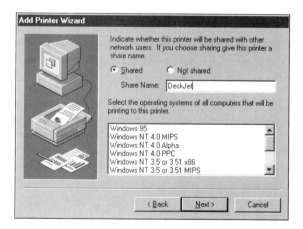

Figure 3-9: Sharing the printer on the network

Once you have filled in all these fields, click Next to proceed to the test page screen, choose whether or not you'd like a test page, and then click Finish; the printer is set up!

Tip

Be careful with your choice of printer name. Make sure the name is as clear as possible and somehow defines the location or task of the printer. For example, in a small company with one printer in the Marketing department, naming the printer MKTG would be perfectly appropriate. In any case, make sure you label the printer itself with its name, the print server it's connected to, and its IPX or IP network address, if applicable.

As always, a shorter name is preferred to a longer name when sharing resources on a Windows NT Server network.

File sharing with Windows NT Server

File sharing is the other service just about all Windows users demand, and it's easy to set up on NT Server. Windows NT supports many simultaneous connections, or as many as you have licenses for if you chose to use "Per Server" licensing when you set up your server. Let's look at how to set up file sharing so that users can get to shared data.

Setting up the shares

The first step, of course, will be to set up an appropriate directory structure on your server so that your users will have a starting point for their data. Once you determine the top-level folders you'd like to share, simply right-click them in Windows Explorer UserData Properties and choose Sharing from the context menu (see Figure 3-10).

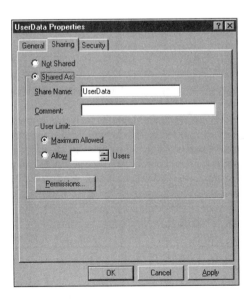

Figure 3-10: Sharing a directory called UserData

In the Sharing tab of the property sheet, click Shared As and choose a share name. If you wish to restrict access to the share, you can click the Permissions button in this sheet; otherwise, click OK and the share will be created, thus enabling users to see it in Network Neighborhood. Repeat this procedure for all the directories you'd like to share on the network.

Secret

If you place a dollar sign ($) at the end of a share name in the Sharing properties box, the share will be hidden, meaning it won't be visible to users browsing the network. This can be useful for keeping prying eyes away from sensitive data when users get the urge to wander through Network Neighborhood. This approach enables you to create the equivalent of a hidden attribute from the Novell NetWare community. Not having a native hidden attribute has to be considered a Windows NT Server weakness.

Connecting users to the shares

Users can connect to the server's shares in several ways. They may browse for the share in Network Neighborhood or File Manager. They may have the share automatically mapped to a drive letter by a network logon script. (Logon scripting will be discussed further in this chapter.) They may connect a drive letter to the share from their workstation using the Tools ⇨ Map Network Drive menu choice in Windows Explorer (see Figure 3-11). The syntax is \\servername\sharename. For example, if your server is called SERVER1 (creative!) and the share is called DATA, the "network path" would be \\SERVER1\DATA.

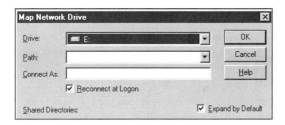

Figure 3-11: Mapping a network drive from Windows NT Workstation

Once the users are connected to the share, they can use the data just as if it were located on their own computer.

Securing Your Network

One of the biggest challenges any systems engineer or administrator faces is security. Two interests are always at work: system protection and user convenience. On the one hand, you want to make sure your system is bulletproof and protected from the prying eyes and fingers of unauthorized users. On the other hand, you don't want to lock the system down so tightly it becomes difficult to use. Balance is the key.

Most networks I've been in contact with blend a fairly decent mix of these factors; security is preserved and yet it's easy for users to get to the data they need. These are examples of well-thought-out networks. Windows NT engineers or administrators face a daunting task when implementing a security model for their networks, but Windows NT offers a variety of security tools, each with a different purpose and each useful in keeping your network safe.

In this section, we discuss the five basic forms of Windows NT Server–based security:

- Logon security
- NTFS-based security
- Share-level security
- Profiles
- Policies

Add to this list on of my favorites, that of physical security. Because today's servers are smaller than their predecessors, it's critical that you physically secure the server by locking it in a closet or computer room. Note that this section does not discuss physical security or other security approaches such as SQL Server's mixed security model or the firewall protection provided by Microsoft Proxy Server. While important, these additional topics are beyond the scope of this book. You are encourage to visit IDG Books Worldwide's Web page () for information on books that address these and other network security issues.

Logon security

In a Windows NT domain environment, each client computer must log onto the domain before the user is able to access resources such as files, directories, and printers on the network. If not successfully authenticated, the user will be limited to the files on his or her own PC and will not be able to access anything outside of that PC. Even if the permissions on a network resource are wide open, only authenticated users have access to the resources protected by those permissions. If you haven't been authenticated, you're not getting anywhere.

This system works well for two reasons. First, it makes life tough for hackers or unauthorized users, because they are shut out from all network resources if they cannot log on. Second, once an authorized user is logged onto the domain, that user can get to every network resource he or she has permission to, after entering one password. In my experience with corporate users, the fewer passwords, the better.

Tip

If at all possible, store all important data on the network, rather than on individual PCs. Trusting vital company data or even an individual's files to a PC hard disk is unwise, in my opinion. Too many users become unreasonable when their hard disk dies and takes their e-mail and documents along with it. I once worked for a company that didn't have an organized network storage system; some data was on the servers and thus was backed up each night, but some vital company data was actually stored on individuals' hard drives and was never backed up. This is less than prudent.

If users are running Windows NT Workstation PCs, the operating system is even more secure; without a valid logon, the users cannot even get to data on the PC they're sitting at. With Windows NT, there's no way to cancel through the logon process as there is with Windows 95/98 or Windows for Workgroups. Unless the user is validated, the operating system will not let him or her in, and the computer might as well be a large, beige toaster.

Note

If an NT Workstation's hard drive is formatted with the FAT file system, an unauthorized user could still get to the data on that drive by booting up from a DOS boot floppy. The "hacker" wouldn't have access to the operating system but would be able to read, change, and copy some files from DOS itself. If you're concerned about this type of use, format your workstations' hard disks with NTFS.

NT File System permissions

One great advantage of the Windows NT File System (NTFS) is that it offers complete file and directory security. An administrator can specify exactly which users have access to data, and which folders and files those users can see. Using file-level NTFS permissions, admins can even determine whether a certain user or group of users can execute a file or just view the file.

Planning

The first step in implementing NTFS security is to formulate a security plan. A well-thought-out security plan is essential to the success and smooth operation of your network, especially if you share administrative duties with other people. Without a plan, your network can quickly become a twisted hodgepodge of file and directory permissions that gets out of control as administrators grant, revoke, and change security settings while fighting daily fires. Even in modest networks, correcting this problem can take person-weeks. In larger networks, it may be nearly impossible.

The cardinal rule of design

I'm a big fan of the K.I.S.S. (Keep it simple, stupid) method of network design. One way to apply this principle to NT security is to decide between two security defaults: wide open or locked down. This will vary by organization; a small software development company might take the "wide-open" path, so that all departments can share information freely. An organization like the

Department of Defense, on the other hand, would likely use the "locked-down" scenario, because most of its data is very sensitive and should only be available to a select few users.

Once you decide on one of these paths, stick to it. This is fairly easy to do; if you decide on the wide-open network, you have a minimum number of permissions to maintain. If you opt for a locked-down network, your default is either very limited or no access for most users, and access only when needed. In either case, the number of permissions that must be maintained on the network is kept to a minimum, and so administration time is minimized as well.

Document your network security

I can't emphasize this step enough; it's absolutely essential to keep records of NTFS permissions: record which directories and files have which permissions, and more important, make notes on why. While a spreadsheet is sufficient for this type of work, creating a database is a much better idea. A simple Access database will suffice, or you can make the database as feature-rich as you like. Once your network security information is in a database, you can create all sorts of queries that will assist in running your systems smoothly.

Tip

One tool that will assist your efforts to document the security configuration of your Windows NT Server network is the SHOWACLS.EXE application on the CD-ROM that accompanies the Windows NT Server 4.0 Resource Kit. This program, in character-based form, displays NTFS permissions for files, folders, and directory trees for the directory that SHOWACLS.EXE is launched from.

Also, keeping the security documentation up to date is just as essential for long-term success. When you make changes to NTFS permissions, take a couple of moments to record them in your spreadsheet or database. Make sure you train all of your administrators to do the same. This way, you'll always have a living record of your network's security, which is helpful for current employees and also simplifies the task of training new administrators who may come on board.

Implementing NTFS permissions

Setting up your permissions structure is fairly simple in Windows NT Server 4.0. Instead of being a separate item in File Manager as in NT 3.51, permissions and other security information are integrated into the Properties sheets for files and directories on NTFS partitions. To get to this information, right-click a file or directory in Windows Explorer or a desktop window, choose Properties, and then select the Security tab (see Figure 3-12).

Chapter 3: Windows NT Server 4.0 Implementation

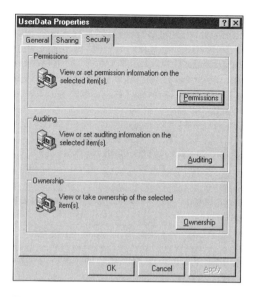

Figure 3-12: The Security tab of a directory's Properties sheet

To get to the NTFS Permissions screen, click the Permissions button at this tab. You'll then see the screen shown in Figure 3-13, which enables you to grant or revoke permissions for users or groups, or change the permission level, to control access to NTFS files or directories. Shown are the default permissions that are in place when Windows NT Server is installed; all directories except certain subdirectories of WINNT\System32 have these permissions by default.

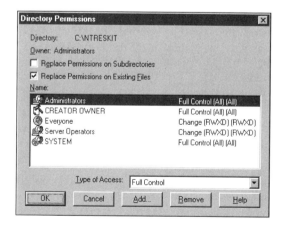

Figure 3-13: The Directory Permissions window

If you want to grant permission to additional users or groups, click the Add button, and the system will display a list of groups on the server or domain and enable you to display the list of users if you wish. Choose the users or groups you wish to grant access to, then choose the type of access, and click OK. See Table 3-2 for an explanation of user rights and the different types of access. To delete a user or group's access to a resource, simply click that user or group, and then click Remove.

Table 3-2   NTFS Access Types and Associated Rights

Type of Access	User Rights
No Access	Users cannot get into file or directory and will receive an "access denied" message.
List	Users can see listing of files or directories but cannot open them.
Read	Users can open and execute existing files or directories but cannot change them or add anything new.
Add	Users can add and execute new files or directories but cannot read or change existing files or directories.
Add & Read	Users can open and execute existing files or directories as well as add new files or directories but cannot change any existing data.
Change	Users can add, read, change, delete, and execute files or directories.
Full Control	In addition to Change rights, users can take ownership of files or directories and change permissions for those files and directories.

Tip

It's important to remember that the No Access permission setting supersedes all others. For example, let's say Joe User is a member of the Finance group as well as the Sales group. Joe would like to use a particular directory in the Finance area on your server, but you have set the permissions to No Access for all groups other than Finance, because the directory contains sensitive payroll information. Because Joe is also a member of the Sales group, which has No Access to the directory, he will be locked out, even though he's also a member of the Finance group and that group has Change access.

For this reason, use the No Access setting sparingly. There are probably other ways to accomplish what you're trying to do, such as removing all permissions from that directory except the Finance group's Change permission.

Share permissions

Another way to secure your network is through the use of share permissions. Share permissions can be used in addition to or instead of NTFS permissions, but they don't offer many of the features that NTFS does, such as file-level permission control. However, share permissions are simpler to administer and might be all you need to secure your network to your satisfaction.

Share permissions, as the name implies, control access to network shares on Windows NT servers and workstations. They are helpful for keeping curious users out of shares where they don't belong. Share permissions are both similar to and simpler than NTFS permissions; they only offer four choices:

- No Access
- Read
- Change
- Full Control

It is critical you understand that, in general, the default share-level permissions are much too generous in Windows NT Server. When you create a share, the default permission is for everyone to have full control. This can be problematic if you do not proactively take steps to change this at share creation time. It is also easy to forget that this occurs, so when you create shares, you "forget" to restrict the share-level permissions, leaving everyone with full control by default.

Share permissions can be set up at the time a resource is shared or thereafter. To administer share permissions when you set up a share, click the Permissions button in the Share Properties box to see the screen shown in Figure 3-14.

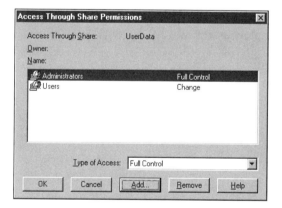

Figure 3-14: Administering share permissions

Just as with NTFS, you can add, remove, or change permissions from this screen. Just select the users or groups you want, and grant them the permissions level you want.

Tip: When designing your network's security setup, decide whether you are going to use NTFS security, share security, or both to protect your data. Be consistent about this; protecting some resources with NTFS and some with share permissions will create an environment that is confusing and hard to maintain.

User profiles

One of the distinct advantages to having Windows NT Workstation on your organization's desktops is the ability to use mandatory user profiles for user environment control. When mandatory profiles are implemented, users cannot make unauthorized changes to their desktop and many other user settings. Before we get into a discussion of mandatory profiles, however, a brief refresher on profiles is in order.

When each new user logs onto a workstation, Windows NT builds a "user profile" for that user consisting of desktop settings, application preferences, printer connections, and other settings. You've probably noticed this before; when you are logging onto an NT workstation or server you haven't used before, the system will bring up the default profile with basic desktop and application settings and will launch the Windows NT "welcome" screen.

In addition to being stored on the local Windows NT computer, these profiles can also be stored on the network. When they are stored on the network, profiles come in two flavors: "roaming" and "mandatory" profiles.

Roaming profiles

Many offices these days employ a "first-come, first served" method of desk assignment. When employees arrive at the beginning of a business day, they take whichever desk is available at that time; there's no consistency from day to day. Roaming profiles are perfect for this sort of environment, because they are stored on the network and thus allow users to have the same desktop appearances and settings no matter what computer they log onto. Roaming profiles also work well in any environment where users change workstations frequently and need to retain their desktop and application settings. The users may change or customize their environments during the workday, and when they log out those changes will be saved to the roaming profile location on the network. Roaming profiles are generally saved to the %systemroot%\Profiles\<username> directory on a domain controller or Windows NT server, but can be saved anywhere the administrator sees fit. The location is specified in User Manager for Domains by opening a user's account window and clicking the Profile button. You'll see the User Profile Path in the User Environment Profile window, as shown in Figure 3-15.

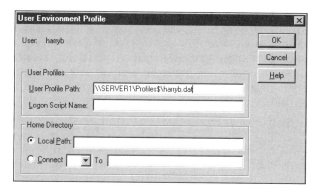

Figure 3-15: A roaming profile in User Manager

Mandatory profiles

Mandatory profiles work essentially the same as roaming profiles, except that any changes the user makes are not saved to the network. Mandatory profiles are designated by the filename *username*.man rather than *username*.dat (where *username* is the user's logon name on the domain). Just as with roaming profiles, mandatory profile locations are specified in User Manager for Domains.

Mandatory profiles are well suited for larger environments where users need to be "reined in" as far as PC customization goes. Keeping your organization's PC environment consistent is a great help to the help desk and on-site support staff, because they know what to expect. When I worked on a large enterprise's help desk, I always preferred calls from users with mandatory profiles, because many of the typical troubleshooting questions I would ask were already answered.

Mandatory profiles for user convenience

In most environments I've worked in, all but the "hard-core" power users have liked mandatory profiles, for the convenience factor. These users know that each day when they log on, their PC's working environment will be consistent; it will look the same as it did the day before, even if they spent part of that day "messing up" their desktop with icons and such. In addition, administrators can set popular application settings in the mandatory profile, such as the default location Word saves documents to. For example, let's say every user has a home directory on the network which is mapped to drive letter F. You want users to save files to this location rather than their Personal folder, so you change the setting in Word. Once this profile is copied to the network and designated as a mandatory profile, all users will have this setting, and their default file saving location will be F.

System policies

In many applications, mandatory profiles are the best way to customize your users' desktop setups without having to visit each desktop. However, Windows NT offers another, more powerful tool for "locking down" your desktops: *system policies*. System policies are an incredibly powerful, infinitely customizable way for administrators to secure their networks and ensure that users don't tamper with files or settings when they shouldn't. Basically, system policies are files stored on the network that contain information about settings in the HKEY_CURRENT_USER and HKEY_LOCAL_MACHINE Registry hives. Once they are set up, these files are downloaded each time a user logs onto an NT workstation or server or Windows 9*x* computer, and the settings in the policy file override those on the user's PC.

Using system policies, you can customize desktops in several ways, including:

- Locking users out of certain Control Panel applets, or out of Control Panel altogether
- Removing the "Run" or "Shut Down" option on the Start menu
- Limiting users to certain approved programs, and forbidding access to other programs
- Limiting or removing access to Network Neighborhood
- Hiding some or all desktop icons
- Designating a custom wallpaper
- Creating custom groups in the Start menu which will appear on all desktops

As you can see, system policies can be a boon to administrators in large networks, because they can control just about every aspect of the user's desktop.

Practical uses for system policies

As I said earlier, system policies are perfect for large organizations with many "task-oriented" users, that is, users who need only limited access to their PCs in order to do their jobs. Here's an example of that type of setup.

In a former position, another administrator and I were given the task of "locking down the desktop" for a large group of customer service representatives. Management was becoming concerned about productivity problems caused by users messing around with their PCs, playing games, and so forth, and called upon the IS department to assist. We decided system policies would be a perfect solution to these problems.

This group of people needed three specific applications to perform their job duties, and nothing else. They were so task oriented, in fact, that they didn't even use Microsoft Office applications in their jobs and thus didn't have a need for file storage locally or on the network. My fellow administrator and I created several system policies, which gave these users varying levels of access depending on their job function, more specifically their membership in certain domain groups. The basic customer service reps ended up with a desktop that was standardized in every way:

- All desktop icons were hidden.

- All PCs had the same desktop wallpaper, and users were not given access to Display properties.

- The users' Start menus consisted of the Shut Down option, Help, the Documents menu, and a custom Programs group that contained only their three core business applications.

- The Run, Find, and Control Panel options were removed from the Start menu.

As you can imagine, this setup was received with mixed emotions, but after they got used to it, many users really enjoyed the new setup because of its simplicity. This is another advantage of locking down the desktop: The user's view is simplified and the chance that "computer-illiterate" users will get lost is drastically reduced.

Setting up system policies

To set up system policies, an administrator runs the System Policy Editor program, found in the Administrative Tools group on Windows NT Server 4.0. By default, the System Policy Editor loads up two policy templates, winnt.adm and common.adm. These templates contain the Registry information for each option that will appear in the policy file. When you create a new policy file by clicking File ⇨ New in the menu, two options come up: Default Computer and Default User.

Default Computer

The settings under Default Computer will be applied to every computer in your domain, once the policy file is saved. For this reason, it's very important to be careful when making any changes to this item, or you may want to delete it from the policy file altogether. To do so, simply click the Default Computer icon and press your Delete key.

Default User

I offer similar advice when dealing with the Default User section of the policy file. Any changes you make to this will be applied across the domain, so be very careful. You may well want to apply some changes to all users, but again, be careful; these settings apply to *all* users, administrators or not. If you don't have any global settings to apply, delete the Default User icon.

I usually find that assigning settings by domain group is the most effective way of implementing system policies. In order to add a group, click the Add

Group button in the System Policy Editor toolbar, or select New Group from the Edit menu. Policy Editor will prompt you to select a group or groups to be governed by this policy.

When you have added that group to your policy file, double-click the group's icon. A screen will appear similar the one in Figure 3-16.

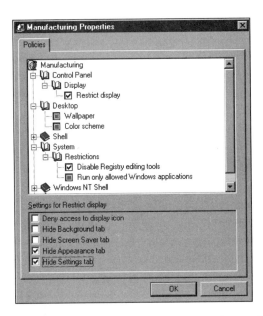

Figure 3-16: Editing desktop settings in the System Policy Editor

System policies are set very simply: by the use of check boxes. However, these check boxes are slightly different from those in the rest of Windows; they have three states:

- Checked boxes indicate that the policy will be implemented for this group of users or computers. This means that the policy will overwrite the particular Registry setting that controls the item in question on the local computer.

- Unchecked boxes mean the local Registry setting will still be overwritten, but access to the setting will be guaranteed, regardless of any existing settings on the local system.

- A shaded box indicates that the policy file will have no effect; the local computer's Registry setting will be maintained.

It's important to remember the differences between these check box states, because an unchecked box is definitely not the same as a shaded box. Some items have subitems or filename requirements, which will appear at the bottom of the screen if necessary. Once you have selected all the options you wish to set for this group of users, click OK to return to the main System Policy Editor screen, shown in Figure 3-17.

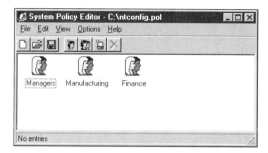

Figure 3-17: A system policy file with several groups added

At this point, you can change settings for another group of users or save the policy file. At logon time, Windows NT 4.0 looks for policy files in the NETLOGON share of the domain controller the user authenticated on. For this reason, you'll want to save the policy file in that share on the PDC, so that it may be replicated across the domain controllers. By default, the NETLOGON location is %winroot%\system32\repl\import\scripts, so you'll want to save the policy file in the %winroot%\system32\repl\export\scripts directory on the primary domain controller.

The policy file's name also is important. If it is to be read by Windows NT computers, it should be saved as ntconfig.pol.

Once these files are saved, any members of the specified groups will download the policy settings at logon time.

Note

If your experience with System Policy Editor is anything like mine, you'll find yourself wishing there were many more settings and check boxes than are provided in the winnt.adm and common.adm policy template files. Fear not — Microsoft anticipated this need and includes several more template files in its Zero Administration Kit for Windows. Also, it's fairly simple to create your own custom policy templates that will enable you to set darn near anything in HKEY_CURRENT_USER and HKEY_LOCAL_MACHINE. Information on how to do so can be found on the Web or in industry magazines.

You also may control Windows 9x clients with system policies. To do so, create those policies with the System Policy Editor that comes on the Windows 9x CD, and then save the file in the NETLOGON share of your PDC with the name config.pol.

Getting Your Users Connected: Logon Scripts

In a network environment, it's the administrator's job to connect the users with their data and other resources, in addition to setting those resources up. One of the best ways to accomplish this goal is through the use of *logon scripts,* batch files or programs that run automatically whenever the user logs on. Logon scripts make life much easier from the user's perspective, because they don't have to worry about how their PC is connected to the network—it just works.

Working with logon scripts requires that you understand:

- How logon scripts function: how they connect to network shares and printers, push updated software, and set environmental variables and the time
- What requirements logon scripts have
- How logon scripts work most effectively

Logon script functions

What's the magic behind logon scripts? Well, it can be as simple or as complex as the particular administrator likes: anything from simple DOS-type batch files to more complicated, feature-rich programs that run as services on the network. Before we get into the different types of logon scripts, let's take a quick look at what these programs do for the users.

Connection to network shares

Most administrators who implement logon scripts include network drive connections as a primary function. After all, if the users can't get to their network data, they can't do business. Also, automatic drive mappings via logon scripts are much easier to deal with in terms of support than persistent drive mappings on Windows 9x or Windows NT Workstation machines. The NET USE command in a logon script can accomplish this for you.

Connection to network printers

Logon scripts also can automatically connect users to their printers via NET USE commands in batch files, or other techniques in third-party solutions. This can be very valuable, as printer connection problems can cause lengthy help desk calls. If the printer is connected each time the user logs on, these calls are reduced.

Automatic update of data files or software

Logon scripts can be configured to execute programs that reside on the network in order to copy updated data files (for example, virus protection data files) or run "silent" upgrades to existing software on client PCs.

Note

If you intend to upgrade client PCs over the network using entries in the logon script, make sure laptop users won't be connecting to the network via RAS when the upgrade is set to occur. Nothing makes remote users angrier than waiting for a several-megabyte update to come across their phone line!

Setting environment variables

Logon scripts can also be invaluable in setting environment variables, particularly the PATH variable, that installed software needs to run. The script can update any other variable you'd like, as well.

Setting time on the client PC

Keeping PCs' time consistent across machines is easily done from a logon script with the NET TIME command. Inserting such a command into your logon script will ensure that all PCs on the network have the same time of day set.

Tip

If you're going to include a NET TIME command in your script and your company has offices in more than one time zone, make sure you understand the headache you might create for yourself if you specify a particular server in the statement. Basically, all PC clocks will be set to the time that server reports, even if they are in other time zones. For example, I implemented a NET TIME statement in a logon script a while ago, and before the staff knew it, all of the PCs in my company's Honolulu office were reporting the time as in the Pacific time zone. Oops! They were not amused. A better approach would be to use the variable %logonserver% rather than a particular server name; that way the PCs will get the time off their local BDC.

Logon script requirements

In Windows NT networks, three things must be present in order for logon scripts to work. First, the network must be set up as a Windows NT domain. Logon scripts will not work properly in a workgroup setup. Second, the script itself must be present in the NETLOGON share of whatever domain controller the user authenticates on. As mentioned earlier, this directory is %winroot%\system32\repl\import\scripts. If you want to implement a logon script and you have replication set up among your domain controllers, save the script in the %winroot%\system32\export\scripts directory on the PDC, and it will be replicated across. Third, the user's account on the domain must have the logon script specified in User Manager for Domains, as shown in Figure 3-18.

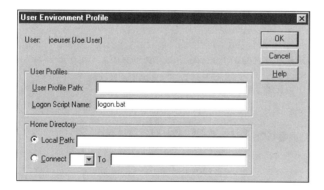

Figure 3-18: Specifying a logon script name

When all three of these conditions are met, the Microsoft redirector on the client's PC will download and process the script, thus connecting drives and printers, setting variables, and running programs as you've specified on the script.

Logon script tips and useful tidbits

Longtime Windows NT Server professionals know that, regretably, the built-in logon scripting capabilities of Windows NT Server 4.0 truly come up short. In fact, many of us use third-party tools to make logon scripts really work! I will now discuss several of these tools.

PUTINENV

In many networks, a user's home directory is shared with the username as the share name. Obviously any logon script worth its salt should connect the user to his or her home directory, but non–Windows NT machines don't store the variable %username%, so what's an admin to do with all those Windows 95/98 clients?

To the rescue comes a neat little utility called PUTINENV. This freeware utility, which can be found on the Web, enables you to grab many LAN Manager variables (including user name) and import them into a machine's DOS networking system. Then you can use the program's partner in crime, WINSET, to actually set the variable so that it will be recognized in Windows. You can install these programs on client PCs, or you can place them in the NETLOGON shares on the network; we chose the latter option for my network.

I've seen these two tools at work in several places, and they're really slick. Windows 9x users on the network enjoy the same logon features that are available to Windows NT, which keeps much better track of network-related variables. Check the Web for more information; just do a search on "PUTINENV."

Kixtart

Although most logon scripts are simple DOS batch files, other script interpreters exist that are more feature-rich and offer better branch processing. One of these is called Kixtart, an early version of which is located on the Windows NT 4.0 Resource Kit CD. Kixtart has several impressive features that set it apart from normal logon scripts, such as the ability to customize the window a user sees when the script is running. More information about Kixtart can be found on the Resource Kit CD or the World Wide Web.

Group membership determination

One popular application for logon scripts is to map drives to different network paths based on group membership. This proved to be a challenge in my network; we didn't know of any tools available that would help with this job. My manager came up with a great solution. Here's how it works.

The first step in the logon script is to map a drive (we use X:) to a share on our network. Inside that share are folders containing a simple text file: a flag file. We created a folder for each domain group that was significant for logon script purposes and then set the NTFS permissions so that only members of that group have any access to that directory. So basically, if a user can see his or her group's flag.txt file (which we determine through an if exist command), then that user must be a member of that group, because nobody else has access. We then can proceed with drive mappings based on that group membership and disconnect the X: drive mapping at the end of the script.

To give you an idea of what logon scripts look like, here is a very basic script listing for Windows NT clients in a small office environment:

```
REM Logon script to map user's drives and printers and add to PATH
statement
REM Proceed with drive mappings- H to home dir, G to shared dir
NET USE H:
NET USE G:
REM Map client to shared printer
NET USE LPT1: \\SERVER1\DeskJet
REM Set path variable to add G:\Apps\MSApps to existing path value
SET PATH=%path%;G:\Apps\MSApps
EXIT
```

As you can see, even the simplest logon scripts can save a ton of administration and help desk time by automatically connecting your users to their data. More elaborate logon scripts can silently, automatically perform many other functions that would normally require a visit to the desktop.

Tip

And now, back to the law firm. I was providing consulting assistance for a small law firm that had the policy of allowing (and encouraging) anyone to use any personal computer at any time to accomplish his or her work. That meant a file clerk could log on and use a law partner's machine if need be. When this site was a NetWare 3.x environment, such a policy was easy to enforce because NetWare has powerful system and individual logon scripts. Such is not the case natively with Windows NT Server. However, by deftly creating a batch file with extensive use of the NET USE command (and other tricks described previously) to map individual drive mappings, I was in effect able to create powerful logon scripts for the law firm, now happily running Windows NT Server. Anyone at the law firm was then able to log on at any workstation and receive individual drive mappings. All's well that ended well.

Protecting Your Data with Backups

Every experienced network administrator knows that a good data backup solution is the cornerstone of a well-run network. Backups are essential for several reasons: First, valuable data is bound to be lost sometime, either through human error (users deleting files they shouldn't have) software problems, or hardware problems. In addition to these items, disasters also threaten your data; earthquakes, fires, floods, or other disasters can take out entire networks and all the data contained in them. No matter how many RAID arrays you have or how securely you've locked down your server room, something will happen sooner or later that will require backup copies of your data to be restored.

Backup strategies

The first step in implementing a backup system is deciding what kind of backup protection you need. For small networks, a tape plugged into the server at the end of the day may be sufficient. For larger networks, a fully automated and scheduled client/server backup solution may be necessary. Here are some needs to consider when selecting a backup program:

- How often will backups be run?
- How often will files need to be restored?
- How many servers will need to be backed up?
- In case of disaster, how much downtime will be acceptable to management?
- Are there special backup requirements, such as the ability to back up open files or online databases like the Microsoft Exchange Information Store?

As I said before, different networks will require different levels of backup protection. At a minimum, you should consider the grandfather/father/child backup approach:

1. **Grandfather.** A monthly full backup tape that is created on the last Friday of the month. It is typically stored off-site.
2. **Father.** A full backup run on the first three Fridays of the month
3. **Child.** A tape backup job run each evening from Monday through Thursday. I recommend that each child tape be a full backup, but others believe that it may be a differential backup (changed files since the last full backup are backed up to the tape) or incremental (changed files since the last full or differential backup are backed up to tape).

If I can't make a full backup, I'll settle for a differential backup. I never make incremental backups because it would be a waste of time (and pain) to go back and find which incremental tape contains a file that I'm looking for.

Windows NT Backup

Good old NTBACKUP is the free backup application in Windows NT Server 4.0 (see Figure 3-19). This program, while basic, provides the functionality necessary for basic backup services. NT Backup enables you to back up and restore files or directories, span multiple tapes, and schedule backups to happen automatically using a command line batch file and the AT command scheduler in Windows NT. Although NT Backup will do the job, I don't know of too many shops with more than 30 users that utilize this tool (it is used

Chapter 3: Windows NT Server 4.0 Implementation

extensively with small businesses that utilize Microsoft BackOffice Small Business Server — see Chapter 20). If you are from the NetWare community, note that NTBACKUP is the functional equivalent of NBACKUP or SBACKUP (two NetWare backup applications that were widely disregarded).

Windows NT Backup enables you to select all files or just the files your want to back up. When you are performing a full backup, all files are selected, as shown in Figure 3-19. If you were to perform only a partial backup, only the selected check boxes would be chosen.

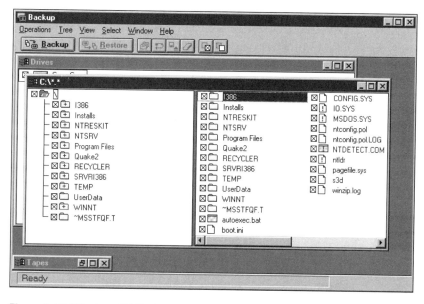

Figure 3-19: Windows NT Backup

Note that you may run NTBACKUP with a "timer" to run unattended backup jobs.

STEPS:

To run timed backups with NTBACKUP

Step 1. Make sure the Schedule service is running. Set this service to start automatically.

Step 2. Create the following command file in Notepad and save it at the server as c:\mybackup.cmd:

```
c:\winnt\system32\ntbackup.exe backup c: /v /d "My Backup Files" /b /hc:on /L "c:\backup.log"
```

Continued

STEPS
To run timed backups with NTBACKUP *(continued)*

Yes, it is a command file that assumes you only have a c:\ drive on your server that needs to be backed up.

Step 3. Next, execute the following AT command to schedule the job for each workday evening (Monday through Friday) at 11 P.M. The "interactive" switch enables you to interact with the backup routine at the server if necessary (insert tape, and so forth). This command is executed at the command prompt of the server:

```
c:\> AT 23:00 /every:M,T,W,Th,F c:\mybackup.cmd /interactive
```

If you own the Windows NT Server or Workstation resource kit, you may copy the winat.exe file from the utilities CD-ROM to a directory on the server and then launch the file to give you a GUI-based "AT" scheduler that faithful performs the commands just listed. Note that Windows 2000 Server will natively offer a GUI-based AT-like task scheduler that is much more robust than the winat.exe solution today.

The unattended backup using the "timer" method just described will not back up the Microsoft Exchange Directory Services (DS) or the Information Store (IS), assuming you have Microsoft Exchange installed on your Windows NT Server machine. To back up the Microsoft Exchange DS and IS, you must manually run a backup job in NTBACKUP where you have selected these components in the Exchange backup window. Failure to do so may result in a server that has backed up data but still loses its all important e-mail. Note that the third-party backup solutions discussed later address this weakness.

Another weakness of NTBACKUP is how it treats SQL Server information. As you know, SQL Server is a popular Microsoft BackOffice application that runs on top of Windows NT Server 4.0. Because SQL Server is a robust, enterprise-wide relational database solution, it typically runs 7×24 or nonstop. Thus, if you run NTBACKUP on a machine hosting SQL Server, you will notice that SQL Server's *.DAT files are not backed up (these are the database devices that house the actual databases). In short, you haven't protected your SQL Server's data. That's unacceptable. The reason that this occurs is that NTBACKUP does not have a native SQL Server backup agent to turn off and restart key SQL Server services, allowing a successful backup of SQL Server data. The best solution is to use one of the third-party backup applications discussed later and implement the SQL Server backup agent for each respective product.

Tip

However, if you insist on using NTBACKUP in an environment with SQL Server, here is how you would successfully back up your critical SQL Server–based data. First, use SQL Server's Daily Maintenance Wizard to perform a "backup" to the server hard disk of your critical devices (and databases). These "backups" might include the SQL Server devices and databases for your accounting software and so on. It is critical that you also use the Daily Maintenance Wizard to back up the master device. Without the master device and database, your other devices will not be easily restored.

I recommend that you have SQL Server's Daily Maintenance Wizard perform these backups in the late evening, say 10:30 P.M. Then have NTBACKUP run at, say, 1:00 A.M., well after the Daily Maintenance Wizard has completed its backup. You will now have backed up the *.DAT files of your choice.

Because of the limitations of NTBACKUP, let's look at some products that may better meet your network's backup needs.

Seagate Software BackupExec

One of the leading third-party backup applications in the Windows NT Server community is Seagate's Backup Exec for Windows NT Server. This application enables you to create multiple jobs that may be scheduled to run unattended. Jobs may be configured to properly back up your data, Microsoft Exchange and SQL Server.

Much of the configuration duties performed with Backup Exec may be performed by its assistant (see Figure 3-20). As you can see, Backup Exec is much more robust than the NTBACKUP program provided in Windows NT Server.

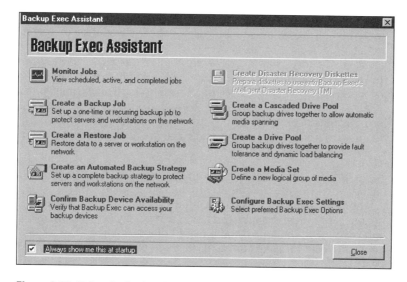

Figure 3-20: Using the Backup Exec Assistant

Cheyenne ARCServe

Long a favorite of the NetWare community, ARCServe is available for Windows NT Server 4.0. It provides similar functionality as Backup Exec, but it is newer (and thus less mature). I've found that Backup Exec holds the edge today between the two tools. Cheyenne ARCServe is developed by Computer Associates.

IBM ADSTAR Distributed Storage Manager (ADSM)

This is the product used on my network. ADSM for Windows NT is a perfect example of a heavy-duty backup solution. Tremendously complex and tremendously powerful, ADSM can be made to do just about anything you'd like it to do, using batch files and a proprietary macro language. The program is based on one server, which contacts ADSM "clients" (servers to be backed up) over the network. The "client" servers do not have local tape drives; the ADSM system uses tape magazines attached to the ADSM server for storage. ADSM uses "backup pools" to store backed up data, and the most recent backups can be kept in a disk pool: a hard disk array that also is attached to the ADSM server. Restoring files from this disk pool is much faster than restoring from tape.

ADSM's macro language also enables administrators to easily make month-end and quarterly backups for storage off site, and it includes automatic disaster recovery support. All in all, it's a very powerful system, but it takes quite a while to master and may be more than your network needs.

Off-site storage

Implementing a safe off-site storage location is also very important when setting up a backup strategy for your network. Even the most scrupulously maintained backups are worthless if they're destroyed in the same disaster that takes out your company's online data, such as a fire or earthquake. At my workplace, we rotate three daily backup tape magazines: one is in the office, and two are at our off-site storage location. We also send all month-end backups off site as soon as they are completed. That way, if something happens to our building, we can restore the network and be up and running again at an alternate site.

When considering an off-site storage provider, make sure you tour their facility and evaluate their ability to survive a major disaster such as an earthquake. Many regions of the country, including many leading high-tech regions, are in "earthquake territory." Especially if you work in a large enterprise with millions or billions of dollars riding on the protection of your data, you want to make sure that data will come through the disaster unscathed.

In any case, make sure you plan for and implement a sound data backup solution, and do it now. You never know when the CEO's going to accidentally delete that important file, or when disaster might strike.

Protecting Your Network from Viruses

An unfortunate reality of system administration in the late 1990s is the proliferation of computer viruses. As a veteran of several corporate virus infections when I worked on an enterprise-level help desk, I can tell you that these infections create incredible amounts of work for phone support personnel and hands-on technicians, greatly increasing the expense involved with owning and supporting PCs. Luckily, the viruses I dealt with were of the fairly benign "annoyance" type, as opposed to viruses that cause real damage.

Infection points

Every week, networking and IT trade magazines detail accounts of new viruses that have arrived on the scene. In order to choose the best protection from these critters, you need to think about the routes viruses use to get into the network itself.

E-mail

Most often, viruses first enter corporate networks via electronic mail carried on the Internet. I don't think I've ever seen a user who doesn't use their e-mail access for personal purposes some of the time, and friends on the Internet are constantly exchanging postcard messages and holiday applications that fill the desktop with ghosts, pumpkins, turkeys, snowflakes, you name it. Many of these e-mail attachments are executables, and 99 percent of users open them without even thinking about the chance that a virus might be attached. Even though most corporate e-mail programs warn the user that it's dangerous to open executable files, many people open these files anyway.

Because of this, protecting your corporate e-mail system from viruses is very important. A virus protection program that runs on your Internet mail gateway as well as a mail/groupware server such as Microsoft Exchange or Lotus Notes is essential for guarding your network and can drastically reduce the instances of new virus infections. In fact, since we installed virus protection on the Exchange server at my office, we haven't had a single new virus identified on the network.

Web browsers

Virus infection via the Web is a relatively new challenge for systems engineers and administrators, but the threat is growing. Several security holes in various Web browsers have been reported in the last few months, and unscrupulous Web site administrators can use these holes to introduce viruses into your network when the user visits their site. Virus protection vendors offer products that help prevent these stealth attacks, so look into one if you believe this to be a threat to your network. Also, browser developers are generally excellent at fixing these holes once they're found, and patches are often available within a few days. Watch for these patches to become available, and make sure you update all the browsers on your network, either through desktop visits or through automatic means such as logon scripts.

Floppy disks

Virus infection by disk is becoming a less common occurrence these days, but it's still something to think about. Users will occasionally bring files from home on floppy disk and install them on their corporate machines. This may be in violation of the company's desktop standards, but it happens anyway. The best method of protection from this threat, as well as virus threats in general, is to install a good virus protection program on each client PC and keep those programs updated with the latest antivirus data from the program vendor. In networks larger than 30 users or so, some form of automatic virus data distribution is recommended, because desktop visits every month or two months are an unrealistic goal.

The virus-warning virus

Any engineer or administrator who's been in the business for any length of time has undoubtedly seen some of the countless "VIRUS WARNING!" e-mail messages that come across from the Internet and online services. While these messages are obviously harmless, they are terribly annoying and reduce the productivity of every user who receives them. Moreover, these messages create a paranoiac sense that viruses are everywhere and can be distributed simply by opening e-mail messages. If these "warnings" make it to senior management and those managers are not tech-savvy, you may find yourself directed to spend a week making sure your network is not infected by the "Good Times" virus.

Responses to this sort of thing are touchy; while you want to dispel the users' worries, you don't want them to forget about the threat of real viruses. I suggest a gentle message to all users reminding them that 99.9 percent of the time, just opening an e-mail message cannot infect their computer with any virus. Also let the users know about the virus protection measures that are in place, and tell them the network administration group is always on the lookout for new viruses and will issue warnings if a real threat comes up. This may not eliminate the problem, but it will hopefully minimize the impact these bogus virus warnings have on your users.

Don't poor-boy virus protection!

I've seen people try to save money when it comes to virus protection by using a variety of stunts including using the "free" McAfee VirusScan software that ships with new Dell and other leading computers. The McAfee VirusScan

Chapter 3: Windows NT Server 4.0 Implementation

CD-ROM included with new Dell will not work with Windows NT Server. If you try to install it, you will receive the error message shown in Figure 3-21.

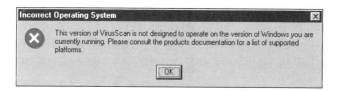

Figure 3-21: A McAfee VirusScan error message

Note

In another approach using the Windows 9x version of McAfee VirusScan, some crafty Windows NT Server administrators map a drive from Windows 9x workstation back to the root drive(s) of the Windows NT Server and then scan those mapped drives for viruses. This will actually work but provides only static virus protection. Such a method doesn't provide dynamic virus scanning required for e-mail attachments and real-time protection. In order to run McAfee VirusScan on Windows NT Server, you should purchase the full server version of this product.

A more robust and real-time virus scanning solution is Cheyenne's InocuLAN for Windows NT. This product, shown in Figure 3-22, provides an ongoing and constant server-based monitor for viruses. This means that incoming and outgoing files are scanned as shown in Figure 3-23.

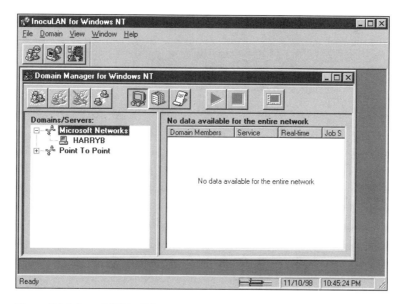

Figure 3-22: InocuLAN for Windows NT

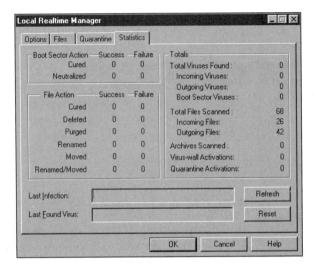

Figure 3-23: InocuLAN's realtime virus scanning

One of the best features found in InocuLAN and other high-end dedicated server-based virus scanning applications is the ability to "phone home." On a scheduled basis, InocuLAN will use the Internet to retrieve its most recent virus signature file. This updated virus signature file assures you that the latest viruses are being sought after and discovered on your Windows NT Server network. The "phone home" function in InocuLAN is managed by the AutoDownload Manager as shown in Figure 3-24.

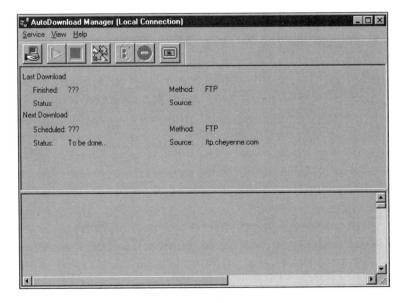

Figure 3-24: InocuLAN's Phone Home function

Remote Access

Another postinstallation task to address is remote access. Once a Windows NT Server network is up and running, users very quickly want additional features such as remote access. In fact, the users may not consider the network to be "complete" until they can dial in from home or the hotel room to check e-mail and transfer files.

Three remote access approaches are discussed in this book. This section presents Windows NT Server's Remote Access Service (RAS) and Symantec's PCAnywhere. In Chapter 19, you will find discussion of Windows NT Server — Terminal Edition.

Remote Access Service

Many of us have used the Remote Access Service (RAS) at one time or another. Perhaps you've had good luck with RAS, a freebie included in Windows NT Server 4.0. However, it is equally likely that you've tried RAS and been disappointed. Unfortunately, I have become disenchanted with RAS, but the only way that I grew to that understanding was to actively use RAS and discover both its strengths and its weaknesses. I suggest you consider doing the same, so I will first discuss RAS.

Just a few more final RAS configurations remain to select. You will be asked questions depending on which network protocols you have installed. For example, you may be asked whether a machine dialing in from a remote location using the NetBEUI protocol is allowed access to the entire network. Note this is more than a simple yes or no question depending on how you have your network configured. For example, suppose you are running TCP/IP on your internal Windows NT Server LAN and your dial-in clients call in using IPX (perhaps to also access a NetWare server). In this scenario, RAS will actually act as a gateway and translate NetBEUI traffic into TCP/IP traffic. This is a little-known feature that when appropriate is wonderful. I've used it at a large mental health organization running Windows NT Server, NetWare, and UNIX. It's the type of approach that you will use when you know you need to. For more information on using RAS as a gateway, I would encourage you to consult the texts for MOC Course #922 — Supporting Microsoft Windows NT Server 4.0 Core Technologies.

Note

What the dial-out options in RAS do not provide is the ability for network users to dial out, via the Windows NT Server, to external sites such as BBSs or the Internet. Such a capability is called modem pooling and is provided via third-party modem pooling applications such as SAPS in a Windows NT Server 4.0 environment. You will note with interest that Small Business Server (SBS), discussed in Chapter 20, has such a modem pooling solution called Microsoft Modem Sharing Server 1.0.

However, it is a common misperception that Windows NT Server 4.0 has modem pooling capabilities via RAS. Be aware of this type of question on the MCSE exams.

STEPS:

To install Remote Access Service (RAS)

Step 1. Make sure you are logged onto the Windows NT Server machine as a member of the Administrators group.

Step 2. Select the Network applet from Control Panel.

Step 3. Select the Services tab sheet in the Network dialog box.

Step 4. Click the Add button and select the Remote Access Service in the Select Network Service dialog box as shown in Figure 3-25.

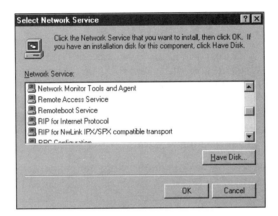

Figure 3-25: Remote Access Service in the Select Network Service dialog box

Step 5. Provide the path to the Windows NT Server source files when requested.

Step 6. Configure RAS via the Remote Access Setup dialog box (Figure 3-26).

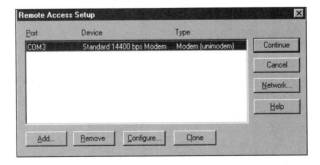

Figure 3-26: Configuring port usage

After the basic RAS service has been configured, you may monitor RAS activity and assign remote access rights to users via the Remote Access Admin application found in the Administrative Tools (Common) program group.

Tip

To be brutally honest, RAS is a huge disappointment when it comes to user remote access to the Window NT server and network. It is unreliable in my humble opinion. It seems that the modem won't pick up whenever the CEO is overseas trying to check e-mail. The modem won't hang up on occasion. I've made special trips to reboot the Windows NT server at a site to restart the RAS service properly. In short, RAS has cost myself and my clients time and money.

PCAnywhere

Today wherever possible I recommend remote control solutions for ease of use and reliability reasons. One of my favorites is the ever popular PCAnywhere application from Symantec (see Figure 3-27). Another remote control solution that I've fallen in love with is Terminal Server (discussed in Chapter 19).

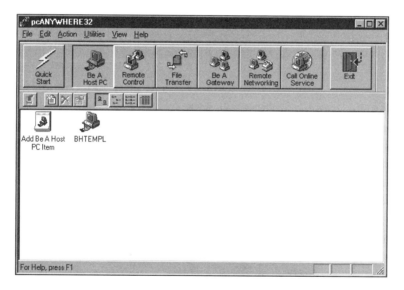

Figure 3-27: PCAnywhere

PCAnywhere, running on a "regular" workstation such as Windows 95/98, is a proven solution for allowing users the ability to check their e-mail, transfer files, and run applications (such as business accounting applications). PCAnywhere provides logon security to prevent hackers from abusing the network. However, it is critical to understand that you must not run PCAnywhere on the Windows NT Server machine. Because the typical PCAnywhere configuration is to have the host reboot at the end of a session to refresh the computer and enforce security, it is unacceptable to have PCAnywhere running on your Windows NT Server machine. As stated at the top of this paragraph, PCAnywhere should run on a workstation.

Microsoft Mail

No network today can be considered fully implemented until basic e-mail services are provided. For most Windows NT Server networks, that means robust e-mail capabilities provided by Microsoft Exchange Server. It means Internet e-mail. But for other Windows NT Server networks, it might mean simple workgroup post office–level e-mail. Such "simple" e-mail capabilities are built into Windows NT Server. That may be something you didn't previously know about.

This simple e-mail system is known as Microsoft Mail (Workgroup Post Office version). By implementing this e-mail system initially, you can get the e-mail ball rolling and then perhaps convert to Microsoft Exchange Server at a future date. The good news it that Microsoft Exchange Server will import the Microsoft Mail post office information, so when you convert, you won't lose your e-mail (and the e-mail of your users).

STEPS:
To install Microsoft Mail

Step 1. Make sure that you are logged on as a member of the Administrators group on the Windows NT Server.

Step 2. Select the Add/Remove Programs applet in Control Panel.

Step 3. Select the Windows NT Setup tab sheet.

Step 4. Select the Windows Messaging option and when the Windows Messaging dialog box appears (see Figure 3-28), select the Microsoft Mail and Windows Messaging options. Note that Microsoft Mail requires Windows Messaging.

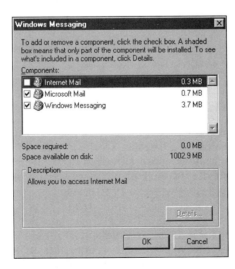

Figure 3-28: The Windows Messaging dialog box

Step 5. Click OK.

Step 6. Provide the path to the Windows NT Server source files when requested.

STEPS:
To configure Microsoft Mail

Step 1. Select the Microsoft Mail Postoffice application in Control Panel.

Step 2. Select the Create a New Workgroup Postoffice radio button in the Microsoft Workgroup Postoffice Admin Wizard (Figure 3-29).

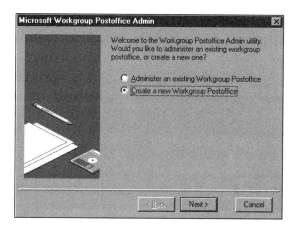

Figure 3-29: The Microsoft Workgroup Postoffice Admin Wizard

Step 3. Specify where the new workgroup postoffice should be located when asked to provide the postoffice location (Figure 3-30). Click Next.

Continued

STEPS

To configure Microsoft Mail (continued)

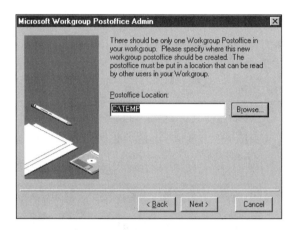

Figure 3-30: Specifying a Postoffice location

Step 4. Confirm the workgroup postoffice location (Figure 3-31). Click Next.

Figure 3-31: Confirming a workgroup postoffice location

Step 5. Provide the Administrator account details when asked via the Enter Your Administrator Account Details dialog box (see Figure 3-32).

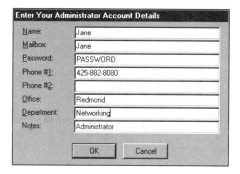

Figure 3-32: Administrator account details

Step 6. Be sure to honor the Mail warning regarding the need to share the workgroup postoffice folder (see Figure 3-33). Click OK and you have completed setup of your workgroup postoffice.

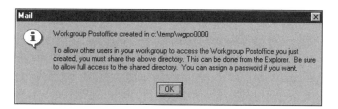

Figure 3-33: A warning to share the workgroup postoffice subdirectory

STEPS:

To add users to Microsoft Mail

Step 1. Assuming you have set up the workgroup postoffice with the preceding steps, select the Microsoft Mail Postoffice application in Control Panel.

Step 2. Select the Administer an Existing Workgroup Postoffice radio button in the Microsoft Workgroup Postoffice Admin Wizard. Click Next.

Step 3. Confirm the postoffice location. Click Next.

Step 4. Log on as the administrator of the Microsoft Mail workgroup postoffice. Click Next.

Continued

STEPS

To add users to Microsoft Mail *(continued)*

Step 5. Click the Add User button in the Postoffice Manager dialog box (see Figure 3-34).

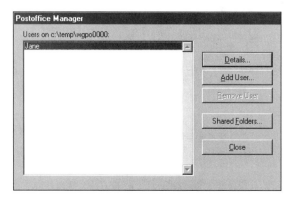

Figure 3-34: Postoffice Manager

Step 6. Complete the Add User dialog box for each user that you want to add to your Microsoft Mail workgroup postoffice.

Step 7. Click the Close button on the Postoffice Manager dialog box when you have completed adding users in step 6.

To complete the configuration of your e-mail system, go to each user's workstation and configure the Microsoft Exchange Inbox or Microsoft Outlook to use your newly created Microsoft Mail workgroup postoffice. Enjoy!

Summary

Successfully implementing Windows NT Server in your organization involves many different tasks beyond simply installing the operating system onto a server. This chapter showed you how to:

▶ Set up and maintain user accounts and groups.
▶ Deliver file and print services with Windows NT Server 4.0.
▶ Secure your network using NT's built-in security tools.
▶ Connect users to their data using logon scripts.

- Implement server and network backups.
- Protect your network from viruses.
- Implement remote communications.
- Set up basic e-mail.

Part II
TCP/IP

Chapter 4: TCP/IP Secrets

Chapter 5: TCP/IP Implementations

Chapter 6: Installing and Configuring TCP/IP

Chapter 7: Troubleshooting TCP/IP

Chapter 8: DNS, DHCP, WINS

Chapter 9: Advanced TCP/IP Secrets

Chapter 10: Internet Secrets

Chapter 4

TCP/IP Secrets

In This Chapter

- Defining TCP/IP
- Microsoft's implementation of TCP/IP
- A detailed analysis of TCP
- A detailed analysis of IP
- Windows Sockets — definition and application
- Windows NT Server basic routing

Did you ever wonder what the payoff was from years of US military expenditures? Was it $200 wrenches and other doo-dads publicly highlighted by former Senator William Proxmire and his "Golden Fleece" awards? No, two of the great payoffs from the huge military buildup that spanned generations were Transmission Control Protocol/Internet Protocol (TCP/IP) and the Internet itself. Not only has TCP/IP become a de facto standard for internetworking, it is also the default protocol for Windows NT Server.

As I prepared this chapter, I promised myself that I wouldn't drone on about the history of the Internet, Request for Comments, and other historical hooey that have been covered in far too many books. In fact, I made two assumptions in designing this chapter. First, that you are not a newbie, you know the definition of TCP/IP and have other thicker and more technical resources dedicated specifically to TCP/IP. Second, that perhaps like I, you have trouble sitting still when the going gets boring, so if the presentation of TCP/IP (which can be very dry) isn't exciting, then you will drift away and miss the finer points about TCP/IP that are important to catch. Call it attention deficit disorder, but you have my assurance that I'll cut to the chase and tell you what you need to know about using TCP/IP with Windows NT Server 4.0. That said, may I take just a few pages to set the foundation for our TCP/IP discussion?

About TCP/IP

Although TCP/IP's popularity can in part be traced to darn good publicity, it is also an efficient routable protocol robust enough to perform well on large corporate networks. Network engineers now favor TCP/IP because it is scalable from the smallest node (a single workstation running TCP/IP for dial-up Internet access) to a LAN and even a worldwide enterprise WAN. Developers know that TCP/IP has an important role in their lives as they develop client/server WinSock-compliant applications at the upper layers of the OSI model.

Remember the golden rule of TCP/IP: It's a good fit and truly you could say one size fits all when discussing protocols.

So important is TCP/IP area that a grassroots movement has arisen within the MCSE certification community to have it included as a "core" exam for the MCSE track. And with good reason. Perhaps no greater paradigm shift has occurred in network computing than the early/mid-90s shift to the Internet and use of the TCP/IP protocol. Not only did the move to the Internet catch many (including Microsoft) off guard, but the rapid acceptance of the TCP/IP protocol left more than one from the Novell camp (and the IPX world) briefly concerned about their job prospects.

The standard-bearer

Transmission Control Protocol/Internet Protocol (TCP/IP) has emerged as the standard protocol for not only networked personal computers but also stand-alone computers that access the Internet. Close to celebrating its thirtieth birthday, TCP/IP was developed in 1969 at the height of the antiwar protests by the Department of the Defense. It was part of the experiment that created ARPANET, which became the Internet as we know it.

Tip

The key point to remember about TCP/IP is that it is routable, is scalable, connects unlike systems via FTP and Telnet, and was designed for use with wide area networks (or internets). Equally important today, don't forget that TCP/IP was designed for use with the Internet.

Additionally, TCP/IP is an "enabling" or foundation technology that not only supports Internet connectivity but also Point to Point Protocol (PPP), Point to Point Tunneling Protocol (PPTP) and Windows Sockets. PPP and PPTP will be discussed later in this section of the book.

Note

Uppercase "Internet" refers to the global Internet that millions use and enjoy. Lowercase "internet" refers to a private wide area network connected via routers.

Developers can rejoice because Microsoft's implementation of TCP/IP supports the Windows Sockets interface, a Windows-based implementation of the Berkeley Sockets interface for network programming (a widely used standard). Thus, developers (in general) find Microsoft's TCP/IP to be a robust, scalable cross-platform client/server framework that they can achieve success with.

By committee: Requests for Comments (RFCs)

A popular moniker in professional basketball in the late 1990s is to say "we win by committee." That is, everyone contributed to the effort. Well, you could say everyone contributed to the effort to develop the TCP/IP protocol suite, but more important, everyone has contributed to effort to maintain it. These contributions come in the form of Requests for Comments (RFCs). These documents go a long way toward helping both developers and network engineers alike understand both the TCP/IP protocol suite and the Internet itself. Indeed, unlike the media shy, those of us that spend significant time in the TCP/IP community are very interested in "comments" related to implementing TCP/IP.

The standards setting process is managed by the Internet Activities Board (IAB). This is a committee that is responsible for not only setting Internet standards but controlling the publication of RFCs. Two groups are governed by the IAB: the Internet Engineering Task Force (IETF) and the Internet Research Task Force (IRTF). Whereas the IRTF coordinates all TCP/IP research projects and the like, the IETF focuses on Internet problems and solutions. RFCs are officially published by the IETF with input from the parent organization (IAB), the IRTF, and contributors like you and me.

In fact, anyone in the networking and development communities can contribute to the TCP/IP standard-making process. Just submit a document as an RFC to the Internet Engineering Task Force (IETF). Crazy? You bet. But it's true. The RFC that you submit might just cut the mustard and become "published" after extensive editorial review, testing, and consensus among the powers that be.

Secret

Many companies in the software and technology field contribute significant resources to having their implementations of protocols and other networking and developer features adapted as standards by industry boards like the IETF. Although it is "possible" to contribute to the TCP/IP RFC process, in reality, this is the world of corporate-level software engineers from companies like HP, IBM, and Microsoft. Standards implemented via the consensus method in place for TCP/IP RFCs have survived a very political process (and not necessarily of the Justice Department variety).

Likewise, a manufacturer may elect to implement certain RFCs and ignore others. Table 4-1 shows the full set of RFCs that make up the Microsoft's implementation of the TCP/IP protocol suite.

Table 4-1 Request for Comment Supported by Microsoft's TCP/IP Protocol Stack

RFC	Title
768	User Datagram Protocol (UDP)
783	Trivial File Transfer Protocol (TFTP)
791	Internet Protocol (IP)
792	Internet Control Message Protocol (ICMP)
793	Transmission Control Protocol (TCP)
826	Address Resolution Protocol (ARP)
854	Telnet Protocol (TELNET)
862	Echo Protocol (ECHO)
863	Discard Protocol (DISCARD)
864	Character Generator Protocol (CHARGEN)
865	Quote of the Day Protocol (QUOTE)
867	Daytime Protocol (DAYTIME)
894	IP over Ethernet
919, 922	IP Broadcast Datagrams (broadcasting with subnets)
959	File Transfer Protocol (FTP)
1001, 1002	NetBIOS Service Protocols
1034, 1035	Domain Name System (DNS)
1042	IP over Token Ring
1055	Transmission of IP over Serial Lines (IP-SLIP)
1112	Internet Group Management Protocol (IGMP)
1122, 1123	Host Requirements (communications and applications)
1134	Point to Point Protocol (PPP)
1144	Compressing TCP/IP Headers for Low-Speed Serial Links
1157	Simple Network Management Protocol (SNMP)
1179	Line Printer Daemon Protocol
1188	IP over FDDI
1191	Path MTU Discovery
1201	IP over ARCNET
1231	IEEE 802.5 Token Ring MIB (MIB-II)
1332	PPP Internet Protocol Control Protocol (IPCP)

RFC	Title
1333	PPP Authentication Protocol
1533	DHCP Options and BOOTP Vendor Extensions
1534	Interoperations between DHCP and BOOTP
1541	Dynamic Host Configuration Protocol (DHCP)
1542	Clarifications and Extensions for the Bootstrap Protocol
1547	Requirements for Point to Point Protocol (PPP)
1548	Point to Point Protocol (PPP)
1549	PPP in High-Level Data Link Control (HDLC) Framing
1552	PPP Internetwork Packet Exchange Control Protocol (IPXCP)
1553	IPX Header Compression
1570	Link Control Protocol (LCP) Extensions

Tip

If you want to track RFC activity in the TCP/IP and Internet communities, point your browser to to review the IAB-published quarterly memo titled "IAB Official Protocol Standard." Here you will receive the current RFC status for each "protocol" in the TCP/IP protocol suite. You may also download the RFCs from this site.

Note that the IAB home page () is now housed within the School of Engineering at the University of Southern California (see Figure 4-1). To be honest, those who are newer to Windows NT Server may not be as interested in RFC and visiting the IAB home page as those who have worked in the industry for longer periods of time. Why? My observation is that the longer you've been working with networks, the more interested you are in expanding your horizons beyond just the Windows NT Server NOS. If that is true, then RFCs are a great place to start that expansion.

To obtain RFCs via FTP or e-mail, send an e-mail message to with the subject "getting rfcs" and the message body "help: ways_to_get_rfcs." You may also obtain RFCs via FTP at the following FTP sites:

NIS.NSF.NET

NISC.JVNC.NET

VENERA.ISI.EDU

WUARCHIVE.WUSTL.EDU

SRC.DOC.IC.AC.UK

DS.INTERNIC.NET

NIC.DDN.MIL

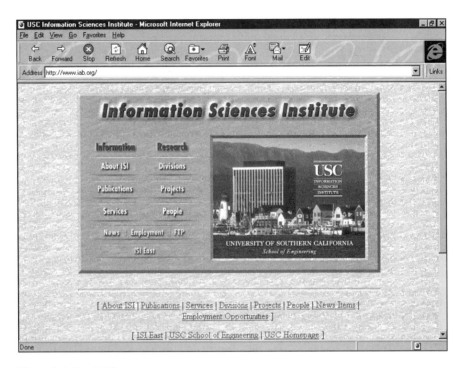

Figure 4-1: The IAB home page

It's a suite, not just a protocol

It's essential to understand that TCP/IP is a protocol suite that spans several layers of the OSI model. It is incorrect to think of TCP/IP as a protocol in a singular sense; for example, it's not just a networking layer protocol. In fact, TCP/IP doesn't even map well to the OSI model; it's based on an alternate networking model called the DOD model (that's for Department of Defense). It is also known as the Internet Protocol Suite. Whereas the OSI model has seven layers, the DOD model has four layers that map to the seven layers of the OSI model as shown in Figure 4-2.

It is interesting to note that:

- The DOD application layer maps to the upper three layers of the OSI model (application, presentation, session). This is where you find TCP/IP applications such as Telnet. It is also the home of Windows Sockets and NetBIOS.

- The transport layer is simple. The DOD model and the OSI model map directly to each other. Here is where TCP and UDP reside. *Tip:* Remember that TCP is connection-oriented and guaranteed. UDP is connectionless and doesn't guarantee delivery.

- The DOD "Internet" layer maps directly to the OSI network layer. Here you find IP, ARP, ICMP, and so on.
- At the bottom of the DOD model, we have the network interface. This layer maps to the OSI's data link and physical layers.

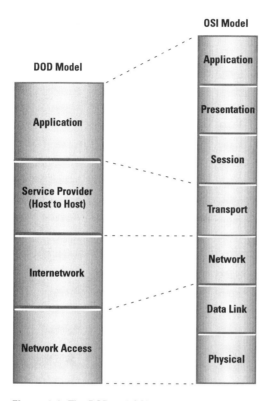

Figure 4-2: The DOD and OSI protocol models

The DOD model provides a comparative framework for understanding TCP/IP in other contexts than the OSI model. That is clearly understood from the points just covered. But, as an MCT instructor, I still enjoy the predictable question of "How does it apply to me" from my MCSE students. Granted, certification students quickly lose interest in a subject if they can't see its relevance. Regarding the DOD discussion, you can see that TCP/IP packets captured on a Windows NT Server network reference the DOD model (see the Ethernet Type line in Figure 4-3).

Basically it is important to understand the underlying models that can be used to describe the TCP/IP protocol suite and how it is implemented. When working with peers from the Windows NT Server community, you will find that it is assumed you know this stuff. If you don't at least understand the basics, you'll quickly be lost in the proverbial ether.

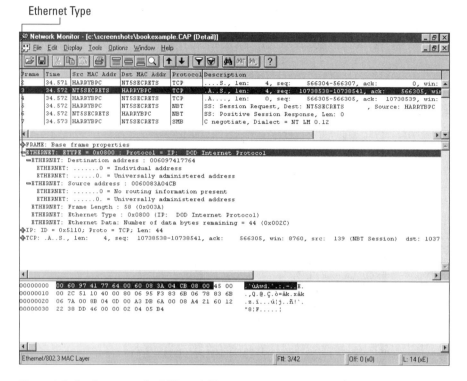

Figure 4-3: A reference to the DOD model in a packet capture

Comparing TCP/IP to operating systems

Unfortunately, one thing neither the OSI or DOD model will do for you is conceptually map TCP/IP to the underlying operating system on your computer. That is because both the OSI and DOD models are oriented toward explaining communications models via a layering approach. A ring model describes the world of operating systems starting basically with the Kernel (see Figure 4-4).

With the operating system "ring" model, note that the Kernel is in Ring 0 and applications run in Ring 3. Do you know what the difference between running code in Ring 0 and Ring 3 is? Hint: Ring 3 has protected memory space for applications; Ring 0 is very fast!

A Look at the Protocols

Like a large American farm family, every member or protocol in the TCP/IP protocol suite has a job. These family members contribute to the greater whole; that being the communication between hosts on a network. And like a large family, each protocol lives on a certain floor in the house. That was shown previously when the TCP/IP protocol suite was mapped to both the OSI model and the DOD Model. At each layer of the DOD model (see Figure 4-5), we treat our data differently, similar to the OSI model.

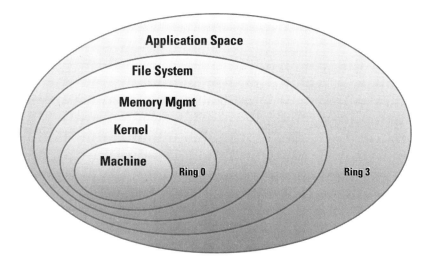

Figure 4-4: The operating system ring model

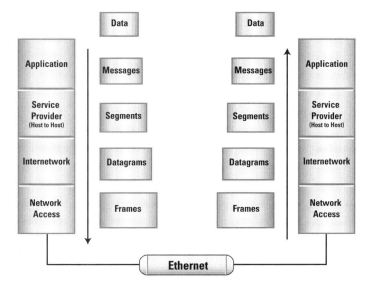

Figure 4-5: DOD layering and communications

Transmission Control Protocol (TCP)

The most common protocol used today at the transportation level, TCP provides a reliable, connection-oriented delivery service on top of IP. TCP not only guarantees the delivery of packets but goes so far as to ensure the proper order of packets. A checksum feature assures that the packet header and data are accurate. If these are not accurate or a packet is otherwise faulty or lost, TCP assumes responsibility for retransmitting the packet. Because of TCP's orientation toward reliability, it is a good upper-level member of the TCP/IP protocol suite to use for client/server applications and important or critical services such as messaging. In short, TCP is the transport layer protocol of choice for session-oriented transmissions. In Figure 4-6, frames 2–4 show the three-way handshake that is the signature of ACK-based communications involving TCP. Packet 3 is both a response and an acknowledgment. Packet 4 is an acknowledgment that acknowledges packet 3. So many packets, so little bandwidth!

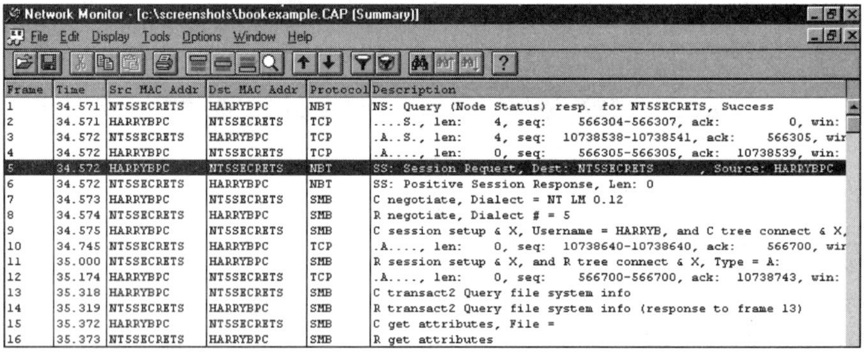

Figure 4-6: TCP/IP frame capture

As in life, using TCP results in tradeoffs. The primary tradeoff from implementing TCP is the increased network traffic the acknowledgment process generates. Think of it as active listening in a group counseling scenario. Each participant tells his or her story; someone in the group is responsible for repeating the information shared by the participants back to the group. If you've been in a group counseling scenario, you know what I mean. Well, that form of acknowledgment in a counseling group certainly slows down the overall speed of communications but arguably increases the quality of the communication (the repetition exercise is a form of acknowledgment). On the network, these acknowledgments (ACKs) effectively slow down the network but, of course, increase reliability.

User Datagram Protocol (UDP)

Meet TCP's evil brother. Unreliable to say the least. UDP, which operates at the transport layer in the DOD model like TCP, offers connectionless-oriented service that makes no delivery or sequencing guarantees.

Secret

This has long been a favorite method for transporting multimedia information such as video and sound. Think about it. If you are using CUSEEME on the Internet and an occasional frame is dropped, it's really not a big deal (it would have the effect of appearing to lower your video frame capture rate). The video might look a little bumpy but otherwise would be fine.

However, don't despair about UDP. The application using UDP may be handling the error correction and reliability issues. Thus you might achieve the best of both worlds: higher network data transfer speeds because ACKs are not required, at least as far as UDP is concerned; high-level applications enforcing acknowledgments. An optional UDP checksum value can also validate header and data integrity.

Tip

To see this checksum value setting, see the "UDP Checksum" field under the UDP header when viewing UDP-related packets in Network Monitor.

The default value for the UDP Checksum is 0 or not active (see Figure 4-7), as shown via the Display Filter of Network Monitor. Of course if the checksum capability isn't implemented, it is of little use.

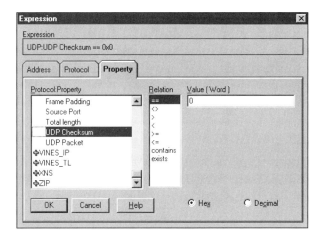

Figure 4-7: The default value for the UDP checksum

In Figure 4-8, UDP is being used and the checksum value is 0XBE91. This checksum value will vary from packet to packet — it is packet unique. A checksum may be your best ally when attempting to debug a network communication issue surrounding UDP.

Internet Protocol (IP)

Essentially IP provides packet delivery for all of the other protocols within the TCP/IP protocol suite. Computer data under the auspices of IP communications is treated to a best-effort, connectionless delivery system. There is no guarantee that IP packets will arrive at their destination or in order. The checksum feature, shown in Figure 4-9, relates only to the integrity of the IP header.

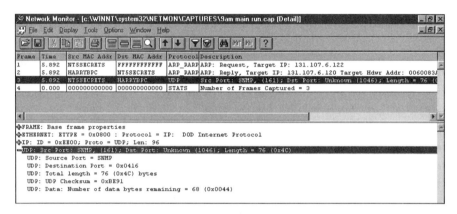

Figure 4-8: The UDP checksum value

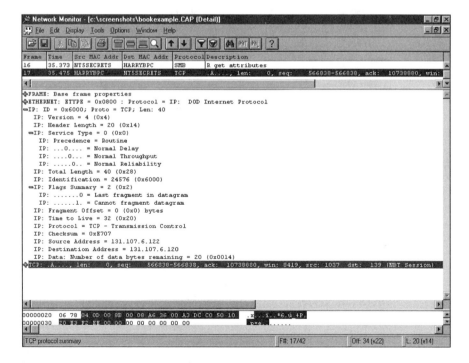

Figure 4-9: The IP section of a data packet on a network

So what, you ask, is the connection between IP and TCP? Well, TCP is providing the guarantee; IP offers us the world in terms of addressing. IP provides the routing information necessary so that data may be passed from one host to another. IP also assists in the fragmentation and reassembly of packets. This is accomplished by imposing rules that routers adhere to.

Address Resolution Protocol (ARP)

Although not directly tied to the transport of data, ARP could be thought of as a maintenance protocol that, although not seen by users and applications, is important in its support of the TCP/IP protocol suite. Basically, the sending host must somehow map the destination IP address to its respective MAC address (physical hardware address). That's because network communications, at the physical level, look like the diagram in Figure 4-10.

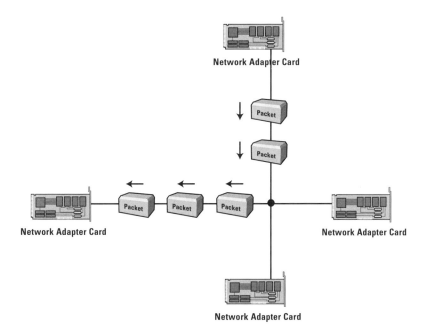

Figure 4-10: A packet travelling between network adapters

This physical address is acquired by IP via the broadcast of a special inquiry packet (ARP request packet). This is a broadcast packet, so it is evaluated by all ARP-enabled system on the local IP subnet. The node that "owns" the IP address being queried replies and reports its MAC address to the original sender in an ARP reply packet. This sequence is shown in Figure 4-11.

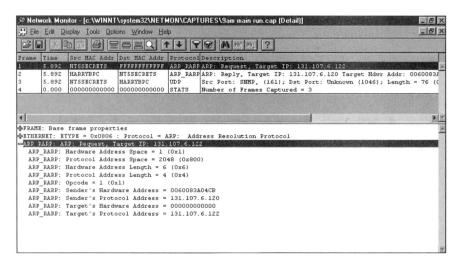

Figure 4-11: The ARP request packet

Frame 1 shows the initiation of the ARP polling process. Notice the Target's Hardware Address is empty but the Target's Protocol Address is displayed as 131.107.6.122. Remember that you are trying to resolve the target's hardware address to its IP address. This is the first step in that process.

Frame 2 (see Figure 4-12) presents the ARP reply packet. Here the target of frame 1 (just described) becomes the sender and reports its MAC address as 06097417764, thus resolving the IP address of 131.107.6.122. This information is returned to the computer that was the sender in frame 1 and is the target in frame 2.

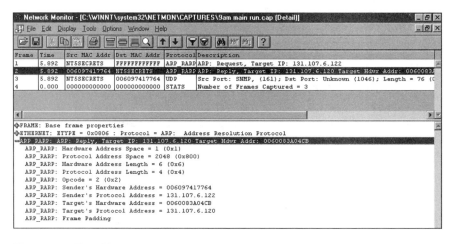

Figure 4-12: The ARP reply packet

Don't forget that each system maintains an ARP table that caches the type of resolution information just detailed. You may use the arp utility to view the ARP tables. The correct syntax for this is:

```
C:>arp -a
```

Internet Control Message Protocol (ICMP)

ICMP is a bread and butter "maintenance" protocol. Two nodes on a network may share status and error information via ICMP. Look no further than the ping utility to see ICMP in action. Ping uses the ICMP-based echo request and echo reply packets to detect if a specific IP-based network node is functioning. Thus, while ping is really important in managing your network or routers, it's safe to say that ICMP is even more so.

The ICMP packet (packet 5) shown in Figure 4-13 initiates the echo command from IP address 131.107.2.214 to 131.107.2.216.

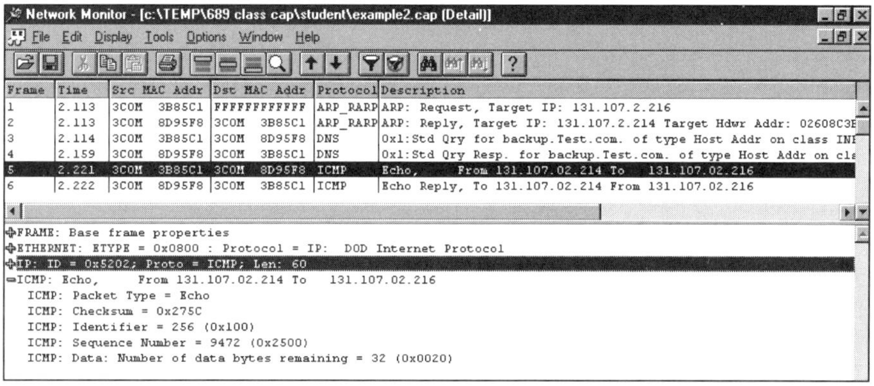

Figure 4-13: The ICMP packet 5

The ICMP packet (packet 6) shown in Figure 4-14 shows the echo reply from IP address 131.107.2.216 to 131.107.2.214.

Secret

ICMP is required in each and every IP network implementation.

Internet Group Management Protocol (IGMP)

Yet another "maintenance" protocol, IGMP is similar to ICMP in that it provides a method dictating how devices can share and report status information on an IP network. Interestingly, IGMP uses multicasting (a form of broadcasting) to communicate with all devices contained in the membership of a multicast group. This group is displayed in the group address field shown in Figure 4-15. Notice the group address option displays the NetBIOS name of all machines detected on the subnet.

Part II: TCP/IP

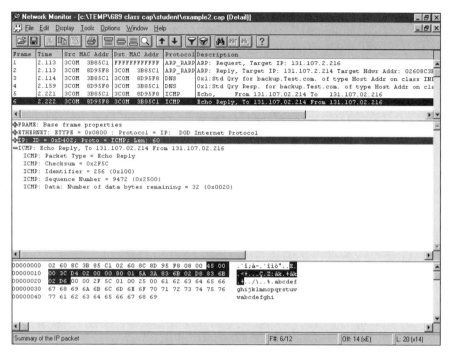

Figure 4-14: The ICMP packet 6

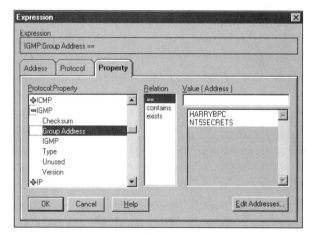

Figure 4-15: IGMP protocol properties

Secret

Your router must be configured to allow multicasting to permit IGMP-based packets to pass through.

Simple Network Management Protocol (SNMP)

SNMP is a management protocol that facilitates the exchange of information from SNMP devices on the network. Routers, hubs, and bridges can all be SNMP devices depending on the device you are using.

Secret

Be careful about paying the SNMP tax unless you really need this functionality. The SNMP tax is that incremental cash outlay you will incur to purchase a device that is SNMP enabled rather than not. A perfect example is a DSU. There the SNMP tax can amount to several hundred dollars or more depending on the DSU model. Note that Windows NT Server really has limited SNMP management capabilities that are available via Management Information File (MIF) interpretation in System Management Server (SMS), a Microsoft BackOffice component. You will typically use a specific SNMP management device, such as a high-end HP Open View–based solution.

What Is the Microsoft TCP/IP Protocol Suite in Windows NT Server 4.0?

Earlier I said that even Microsoft missed the early signs of the TCP/IP revolution. This is true. Those of us who rushed out to purchase and install Windows NT Advanced Server 3.1 will recall that the default protocol was NetBEUI. That changed with the Windows NT Server 3.5x releases where first IPX and then TCP/IP became the default protocol for Windows NT Server. As many say about Microsoft, they got it right on the third try.

Another sign of Microsoft's late arrival to the TCP/IP party was its zero presence in the early days of the commerce use of the Internet. Early arrivals to the Internet were using such things as FTP, Gopher, and Mosaic browsers. Microsoft didn't have a contribution until around late 1995 when Bill Gates issued an internal memo on Pearl Harbor Day that year proclaiming Microsoft as the new Internet company. And they haven't missed a beat since. In fact, as you shall see, the TCP/IP protocol suite included with Windows NT Server 4.0 includes several features that improve both its performance and its reliability.

Specifically, the TCP/IP protocol stack included with Windows NT Server 4.0 has the following features:

- **Core TCP/IP.** Support for core TCP/IP protocols, including TCP, IP, User Datagram Protocol (UDP), Address Resolution Protocol (ARP), and Internet Control Message Protocol (ICMP). This TCP/IP protocol suite implementation dictates how computers communicate and how networks interconnect.

- **Network programming support.** Support for network programming interfaces such as Windows Sockets, remote procedure calls (RPC), NetBIOS, and network dynamic data exchange (Net DDE).

Part II: TCP/IP

- **TCP/IP connectivity utilities.** Basic connectivity utilities found in Microsoft's TCP/IP protocol suite that enable Windows NT users to interact with different systems such as UNIX.
- **LPR.** The "server" side of TCP/IP printing for UNIX clients. Prints a file to a host running the Lpdsvc service. Note that "lpd" is line printer daemon in the UNIX community.
- **FINGER.** Can obtain system information from a remote computer that supports the TCP/IP Finger server.
- **FTP.** Allows bidirectional transfer of files between a Windows NT computer and another host running FTP server software.
- **RCP.** Remote Copy Protocol. Copies files between a Windows NT computer and a host server running the RCP service (which is a UNIX utility).
- **REXEC.** Remote Execution. Runs a process on a remote computer.
- **RSH.** Remote Shell. Runs commands on a server running the RSH service (which is a UNIX utility).
- **Telnet.** Provides terminal emulation to a TCP/IP host running Telnet server software.

Tip

Telnet is your best friend in the TCP/IP world when working with WANs. There is perhaps no better test than to Telnet into a distant server and check e-mail. Telnet is a better test than a simple ping because Telnet runs more as an application. For example, just because you can ping a distant location doesn't mean that you can Telnet into the site. As you will discover, Telnet is incredibly valuable for managing your routers and DSUs.

- **Tftp.** Provides bidirectional file transfers between a Windows NT computer and a TCP/IP host running TFTP server software. Communicates via messaging using UDP instead of TCP.
- **Diagnostic utilities.** TCP/IP diagnostic utilities to detect, resolve, and prevent TCP/IP networking problems.
- **Arp.** Resolves hardware or MAC addresses to IP addresses.
- **Hostname.** Returns the computer host name for authentication by the RCP, RSH, and REXEC utilities.
- **Ipconfig.** This is similar to winipfg in Windows 95/98 but, quite frankly, is not as robust. Part of the problem is that ipconfig is still character based and its reports are somewhat limited. By contrast, winipcfg is GUI-based and more pleasant to work with.
- **Lpq.** Obtains status of print queue on a host running LPD service.
- **Nbtstat.** Returns a list of NetBIOS computer names that have been resolved to IP addresses.
- **Netstat.** Returns TCP/IP protocol session information.
- **Ping.** Tests connectivity and verifies configurations.
- **Route.** Modifies or returns the local routing table.

Chapter 4: TCP/IP Secrets

Secret

This can be used to set up a static route. A static route is extremely valuable in certain conditions. If you are working with multiple subnets and multiple routers, it's likely you will learn this command.

- **Tracert.** Displays the path taken by a packet to its destination host. Here again, you will use this utility extensively in your TCP/IP travels. Tracert is frequently employed when resolving possible WAN failures or router configuration errors.

- **Internet support.** Support for Internet, internet, and intranet-based computers. This support includes:

  - **Internet Information Server.** Used for Web publishing and administration

  - **Dynamic Host Configuration Protocol (DHCP).** For automatically configuring TCP/IP network nodes

  - **Windows Internet Naming Service (WINS).** For dynamically registering and querying NetBIOS computer names

  - **Domain Name System (DNS).** A service for registering and querying DNS domain names

  - **TCP/IP printing.** For accessing UNIX-defined printers or network printers directly connected via a network adapter card (such as HP's JetDirect card, which now uses TCP/IP printing — as an aside, HP's JetDirect card used the DLC protocol almost exclusively back in the "old days")

Tip

It is a common mistake for Window NT Server newbies to overload the services required to effectively manage and optimize their network. TCP/IP printing services are often loaded without any reason. I suspect this occurs during setup because it looks like the kind of service you should "just load." Know your services and don't overload your Windows NT Server unnecessarily.

  - **Simple Network Management Protocol (SNMP) agent.** Remote management of your Windows NT computer is possible by loading this service and using a management tool such as HP Open View. SNMP support is also included for DHCP and WINS servers with Microsoft's TCP/IP protocol stack.

  - **Simple Protocols.** Simple protocols to respond to simple requests — Microsoft's TCP/IP protocol suite allows Windows NT to respond to computers that request and support the following:

    Character Generator

    Daytime

    Discard

    Echo

    Quote of the Day

- **Path MTU Discovery.** Provides the capability to determine the datagram size for all routers between Windows NT–based computers and other computers on the WAN.
- **Internet Group Management Protocol (IGMP).** Microsoft TCP/IP supports IGMP. It is typically used by workgroup software products at the upper layers of the OSI model.

Many of these TCP/IP utilities and commands are discussed at length in Chapter 7, "Troubleshooting TCP/IP."

The TCP/IP Settings in Windows NT Server

Where are the Windows NT TCP/IP settings stored? In the Windows NT Registry, of course! Typically modified via GUI-based applications such as the Network property sheet — Protocol tab sheet, basic TCP/IP configuration parameters are fairly straightforward. However, what about modifying parameters such as Time to Live (TTL)? The TTL value is 32 seconds or 32 hops, whichever comes first (see Figure 4-16). It is effectively the number of routers that a packet may pass through before being discarded.

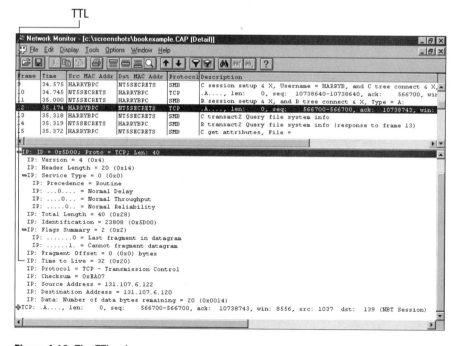

Figure 4-16: The TTL value

Many TCP/IP parameters may only be modified via the Registry. Quite frankly, most parameters are configured under the Parameters key. The Parameters subkey (see Figure 4-17) houses most of the important TCP/IP configuration parameters that you should be concerned with.

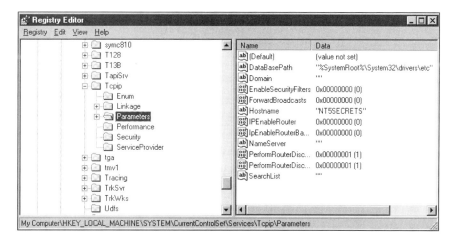

Figure 4-17: The Parameters subkey

Here are important existing values within the Parameters subkey:

- **DataBasePath.** Used by the Windows Sockets interface, this specifies the path to such standard Internet database files as HOSTS, LMHOSTS, networks, and protocols.

- **Domain.** This is the domain entry you make in the TCP/IP Protocol Properties dialog box on the DNS tab sheet (see Figure 4-18). This value is used by the Windows Socket interface. The Domain is the name of the Internet domain that your computer belongs to. As you know, a domain is nothing more than a group name that has computers associated with it.

- **EnableSecurityFilters.** If the entry value is 1, Windows NT Server filters all incoming UDP datagrams, raw IP datagrams, and TCP SYNs (connection requests). Accepted values may be defined via these keys: UdpAllowedPorts, TCPAllowedPorts, and RawIpAllowedProtocols. Interestingly, incoming packets are filtered with respect to the local computers. Packets destined for other computers are not filtered.

- **ForwardBroadcasts.** This entry specifies if broadcasts should be forwarded between two or more adapters. The enabled state has visible broadcasts forwarded.

Secret

The ForwardBroadcasts value entry is not supported in Windows NT Server 4.0. It may be safely removed. In any event, the system ignores it.

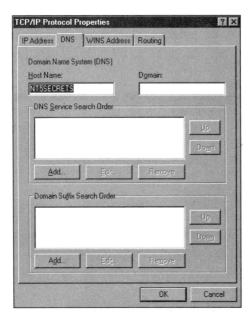

Figure 4-18: The DNS tab sheet

- **Hostname.** This is the name entered in the Host Name field in the TCP/IP Protocol Properties dialog box on the DNS tab sheet. It is the DNS host name of the system. Whenever a Windows Sockets application issues the hostname command, this name will be returned.

- **IPEnableRouter.** A value of "1" indicates that the system can route IP packets between networks that is it connected to. Packets are not routed if the value is 0.

- **NameServer.** Lists the DNS servers that will resolve names when queried by Windows Sockets.

Secret

This value overrides the value in the DhcpNameServer value field (a value supplied to DHCP clients via a scope).

- **SearchList.** Lists domain name suffixes to try when an unsuffixed name cannot be resolved by using DNS. This information is used by the Windows Sockets interface.

- **Adding Registry Values.** Other values that you may add to HKEY_LOCAL _MACHINE\SYSTEM\CurrentControlSet\Services\Tcpip\Parameters are:

  - **ArpCacheLife.** Specifies how long entries will remain in the ARP cache table. An entry remains in the ARP table until it expires or the table entry is reused.

  - **DefaultTTL.** Is the default Time to Live (TTL) value found in the header of outgoing IP packets. TTL is the number of seconds that an IP packet can live on a network without reaching its destination.

- **KeepAliveInterval.** Calculates the interval between keep-alive retransmissions until a received response. Basically calculates the wait until the next keep-alive transmission. After the number of transmissions specified in TcpMaxDataRetransmissions are unanswered, the connection will abort.

- **KeepAliveTime.** Specifies the interval that TCP sends a keep-alive packet to verify a connect is still intact.

- **TcpMaxConnectRetransmissions.** Is the number of times that TCP retransmits a connect request before aborting its attempts. Interestingly, this value is doubled with each attempt from its default three seconds.

- **TcpMaxDataRetransmissions.** Is the number of times that a data segment will be retransmitted by TCP before aborting.

- **TcpNumConnections.** Is the maximum number of open TCP connections that can occur simultaneously.

- **TcpTimedWaitDelay.** Determines how long a connection stays in a wait state known as TIME_WAIT before being closed.

- **TcpUseRFC1122UrgentPointer.** Defines how TCP defines urgent. "1" is based on RFC 1122. "0" or no entry in the Registry uses the "mode" from Berkeley-derived BSD systems.

A Day in the Life of a TCP/IP Packet

Remember the famous photo essay book *A Day in the Life of America*, which showed a snapshot of life in America? It was interesting and introspective. I thought you might enjoy getting into the details of a day in the life of a packet in a similar manner. As stated in RFC 791, which relates to the IP portion of the packet:

"The implementation of a protocol must be robust. Each implementation must expect to interoperate with others created by different individuals. While the goal of this specification is to be explicit about the protocol there is the possibility of differing interpretations. In general, an implementation must be conservative in its sending behavior, and liberal in its receiving behavior. That is, it must be careful to send well-formed datagrams, but must accept any datagram that it can interpret."

When you get down to packet analysis, you are often left thinking that it's amazing this stuff works as well as it does. That said, many have asked over the years just how do you "read" a TCP/IP packet. Well, this is how you do it!

IP

First, examine the IP portion of the TCP/IP network packet, because it comes first in the packet (see Figure 4-19).

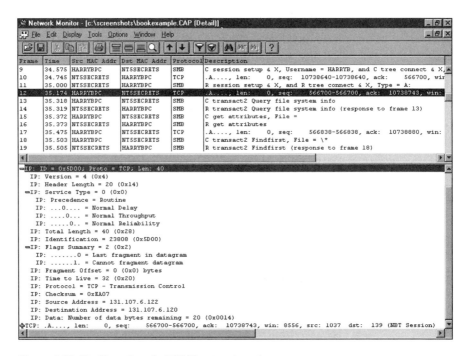

Figure 4-19: The IP portion of a TCP/IP network packet

Version: 4 bits

The Version field indicates the format of the internet header. As you can see in Figure 4-19, this is version 4.

Internet Header Length (IHL): 4 bits

Internet Header Length is the length of the internet header in 32-bit words and points to the beginning of the data. The minimum value for a correct header is 5.

Type of Service: 8 bits

The Type of Service provides an indication of the abstract parameters of the quality of service desired. These parameters are used to guide the selection of the actual service parameters when transmitting a datagram through a particular network. Several networks offer service precedence, which treats high-precedence traffic as more important than other traffic (generally by accepting only traffic above a certain precedence at times of high load). An example of this might be some of the newer networking technologies such as ATM that enable you to set priorities for different traffic. The major choice is a three-way tradeoff between low delay, high reliability, and high throughput.

The information in Table 4-2 is shown as subcategories underneath the IP:Service Type = 0 (0X0) field.

Table 4-2 IP Service Type Information

Bit	Description
Bits 0-2:	Precedence
Bit 3:	0 = normal delay, 1 = low delay
Bits 4:	0 = normal throughput, 1 = high throughput
Bits 5:	0 = normal reliability, 1 = high reliability
Bit 6-7:	Reserved for future use

The use of the delay, throughput, and reliability indications may increase the cost (in some sense) of the service. In many networks, better performance for one of these parameters is coupled with worse performance for another.

Precedence

The type of service is used to specify the treatment of the datagram during its transmission through the internet system. Example mappings of the internet type of service to the actual service provided on networks such as AUTODIN II, ARPANET, SATNET, and PRNET is given in "Service Mappings." Our sample packet shows "Routine." Table 4-3 provides the list of precedence options.

Table 4-3 Precedence Values

Value	Description
111	Network Control
110	Internetwork Control
101	CRITIC/ECP
100	Flash Override
011	Flash
010	Immediate
001	Priority
000	Routine

The Network Control precedence designation is intended to be used within a network only. The actual use and control of that designation is up to each network. The Internetwork Control designation is intended for use by gateway control originators only. If the actual use of these precedence designations is of concern to a particular network, it is the responsibility of that network to control the access to, and use of, those precedence designations.

Total Length: 16 bits

Total Length is the length of the datagram, measured in octets, including internet header and data. This field allows the length of a datagram to be up to 65,535 octets. Such long datagrams are impractical for most hosts and networks. All hosts must be prepared to accept datagrams of up to 576 octets (whether they arrive whole or in fragments). It is recommended that hosts only send datagrams larger than 576 octets if they have assurance that the destination is prepared to accept the larger datagrams.

The number 576 is selected to allow a reasonable-sized data block to be transmitted in addition to the required header information. For example, this size allows a data block of 512 octets plus 64 header octets to fit in a datagram. The maximal internet header is 60 octets, and a typical internet header is 20 octets, allowing a margin for headers of higher-level protocols.

Identification: 16 bits

This is an identifying value assigned by the sender to aid in assembling the fragments of a datagram.

Flags: 3 bits

In our same packet, the settings are "Last fragment in datagram" and "Cannot fragment datagram." Here are the possible flag settings.

> Bit 0–5: reserved, must be zero
>
> Bit 6: (DF) 0 = May Fragment, 1 = Don't Fragment.
>
> Bit 7: (MF) 0 = Last Fragment, 1 = More Fragments.

Fragment Offset: 13 bits

This field indicates where in the datagram this fragment belongs. The fragment offset is measured in units of eight octets (64 bits). The first fragment has offset zero.

Time to Live: 8 bits

This field indicates the maximum time the datagram is allowed to remain in the internet system. If this field contains the value zero, then the datagram must be destroyed. This field is modified in internet header processing. The time is measured in units of seconds, but given that every module that processes a datagram must decrease the TTL by at least one even if it processes the datagram in less than a second, the TTL must be thought of only as an upper bound on the time a datagram may exist. The intention is to cause undeliverable datagrams to be discarded, and to bound the maximum datagram lifetime.

Protocol: 8 bits

This field indicates the next-level protocol used in the data portion of the internet datagram.

Header Checksum: 16 bits

This is a checksum on the header only. Because some header fields change (as does Time to Live), this is recomputed and verified at each point that the internet header is processed.

The checksum algorithm is: The checksum field is the 16-bit one's complement of the one's complement sum of all 16 bit words in the header. In English, it's a calculated value similar to a cyclical redundancy check to ensure that the data packet has "integrity."

Source Address: 32 bits

This is the source address.

Destination Address: 32 bits

This is the destination address.

Options: variable

The options may appear or not in datagrams. As you can see, none appear in our sample data packet. They must be implemented by all IP modules (host and gateways). What is optional is their transmission in any particular datagram, not their implementation.

Padding: variable

The internet header padding is used to ensure that the internet header ends on a 32-bit boundary. The padding is zero.

TCP

Now for the details about TCP. TCP is that part of the TCP/IP protocol suite that reside in the middle OSI layers. Its primary responsibilities include assuring reliable delivery by maintaining a connection-oriented session between sender and receiver (see Figure 4-20).

Source Port: 16 bits

The source port number is the port value of the sender.

Destination Port: 16 bits

The destination port number is the port value of the receiver.

Sequence Number: 32 bits

This is the sequence number of the first data octet in this segment (except when SYN is present). If SYN is present, the sequence number is the initial sequence number (ISN) and the first data octet is ISN + 1.

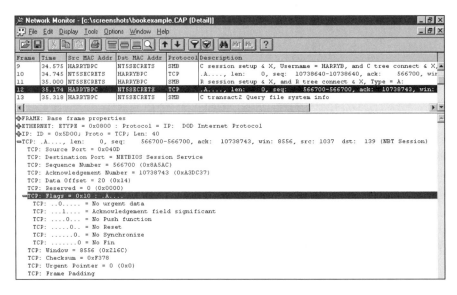

Figure 4-20: The TCP portion of our sample data frame

Acknowledgment Number: 32 bits

If the ACK control bit is set, this field contains the value of the next sequence number the sender of the segment is expecting to receive. Once a connection is established, this is always sent.

Data Offset: 4 bits

This is the number of 32-bit words in the TCP header. This indicates where the data begins. The TCP header (even one including options) is an integral number 32 bits long.

Reserved: 6 bits

Reserved for future use, this must be zero. This is exactly the type of field that a software developer, seeking an edge for its technology, might use to fundamentally modify TCP for its own purposes.

Flags: 6 bits (from left to right):

This is officially known as Control Bits in RFC 791.

URG: Urgent Pointer field significant

ACK: Acknowledgment field significant

PSH: Push Function

RST: Reset the connection

SYN: Synchronize sequence numbers

FIN: No more data from sender

Our sample data packet in Figure 4-20 has these settings:

- No urgent data
- Acknowledgement field significant
- No Push function
- No Reset
- No Synchronize sequence numbers
- No Fin

Window: 16 bits

This is the number of data octets beginning with the one indicated in the acknowledgment field that the sender of this segment is willing to accept.

Checksum: 16 bits

The checksum field is the 16-bit one's complement of the one's complement sum of all 16-bit words in the header and text. If a segment contains an odd number of header and text octets to be checksummed, the last octet is padded on the right with zeros to form a 16-bit word for checksum purposes. The pad is not transmitted as part of the segment. While computing the checksum, the checksum field itself is replaced with zeros.

The checksum also covers a 96-bit pseudoheader conceptually prefixed to the TCP header. This pseudoheader contains the Source Address, the Destination Address, the Protocol, and TCP length. This gives the TCP protection against misrouted segments. This information is carried in the Internet Protocol and is transferred across the TCP/Network interface in the arguments or results of calls by the TCP on the IP.

Urgent Pointer: 16 bits

This field communicates the current value of the urgent pointer as a positive offset from the sequence number in this segment. The urgent pointer points to the sequence number of the octet following the urgent data. This field is only be interpreted in segments with the URG ("urgent") control bit set.

Options: variable

Options may occupy space at the end of the TCP header and are a multiple of eight bits in length. All options are included in the checksum. An option may begin on any octet boundary. There are two cases for the format of an option:

- **Case 1.** A single octet of option-kind
- **Case 2.** An octet of option-kind, an octet of option-length, and the actual option-data octets

The option-length counts the two octets of option-kind and option-length as well as the option-data octets.

Note that the list of options may be shorter than the data offset field might imply. The content of the header beyond End-of-Option must be header padding (that is, zero).

When adhering the to strict RFC, TCP must implement all options. When not adhering to the RFC, software developers may elect not to implement all TCP options. Currently defined options are included in Table 4-4 (kind indicated in octal).

Table 4-4 TCP Options

Kind	Length	Meaning
0	—	End of option list
1	—	No-Operation
2	4	Maximum Segment Size

Here are the specific option definitions for Table 4-4 to assist your understanding of each possible selection:

- **Kind = 0 "End of Option List."** This option code indicates the end of the option list. This might not coincide with the end of the TCP header according to the Data Offset field. This is used at the end of all options, not the end of each option, and need only be used if the end of the options would not otherwise coincide with the end of the TCP header.

- **Kind = 1 "No-Operation."** This option code may be used between options, for example, to align the beginning of a subsequent option on a word boundary. There is no guarantee that senders will use this option, so receivers must be prepared to process options even if they do not begin on a word boundary.

- **Kind = 2 Length = 4 "Maximum Segment Size."** Maximum Segment Size Option Data: 16 bits. If this option is present, then it communicates the maximum receive segment size at the TCP that sends this segment. This field must only be sent in the initial connection request (that is, in segments with the SYN control bit set). If this option is not used, any segment size is allowed.

Padding: variable

The TCP header padding is used to ensure that the TCP header ends and data begins on a 32-bit boundary. The padding is composed of zeros.

Internetworking with TCP/IP

TCP/IP is especially well suited to take advantage of Windows NT Server 4.0's new "paradigm" of being the digital nervous system for an enterprise.

Because of its scalability, TCP/IP can easily provide a solution for a peer-to-peer network or a global wide area network for a Fortune 500 corporation.

Out of the box, Microsoft has released its TCP/IP stack for:

- Windows NT Server
- Windows NT Workstation
- Microsoft TCP/IP-32 for Windows for Workgroups
- Microsoft LAN Manager

Breeder networks

One thing you can count on today in the networking profession is the proliferation of subnets once you deploy a networking solution in your organization. Inevitably you will find your company opening a new branch office that must be connected to the central site. Or perhaps you will eat or be eaten by a rival. Whatever the case may be, you're bound to see your network group (or "breed") once deployed. Plan for it in advance, even when it seems like the remotest of possibilities.

Heterogeneous Networks

Perhaps the coolest thing about TCP/IP is its ability to communicate with foreign hosts in a way that no other protocol I'm aware of can. These foreign hosts include:

- Host systems on the Internet
- UNIX-based host systems
- Apple Macintoshes running TCP/IP protocol stacks such as MacTCP.

Note that an Apple Macintosh can communicate and interact with a Windows NT server if Services for Macintosh are installed on an NTFS partition. In that scenario, the Macintosh and Windows NT Server would be running AppleTalk as the common transport protocol.

- IBM-based mainframes
- Open VMS systems
- Printers with network adapters cards such as the HP JetDirect card

Although TCP/IP is obviously the preferred and recommended transport protocol, don't forget that other transport protocols are supported that allow Windows NT Server to be a good citizen on diverse and heterogeneous networks:

- IPX/SPX
- NetBEUI

- AppleTalk
- Third-party protocol stacks such as DECnet are supported.

Windows Sockets

Just as Microsoft has selected TCP/IP as its default protocol to ensure wide support and acceptance in the networking community, the Windows Sockets applications programming interface (API) exists to provide a "standard framework" for developing applications. No doubt this API-based standard framework is provided to enable third-party developers to write network-based applications that will run well on Microsoft-based networks using Microsoft's TCP/IP protocol stack. And thank god for it. Could you imagine the state of affairs on Windows NT Server–based networks if such an API weren't provided for developers to hook into underlying services? It wouldn't be pleasant, to say the least.

So what exactly is WinSock, as the Windows Socket API is known as? If you were on the proverbial 90-second elevator ride and had to explain it to a layperson, well, you couldn't. But that said, Microsoft refers to it as ". . . an interface and a communications infrastructure . . . not a protocol." Technically, it is an open specification derived from Berkeley Software Distribution (BSD) UNIX 4.3 sockets API for TCP/IP. Starting with the original WinSock 1.1 specification, which was created in early 1993, WinSock has now matured to version 2.0 and is now known as WinSock2. WinSock2 was originally introduced in late 1995 and shipped with Windows NT Server 4.0. It is the version that ships with Windows NT Server 4.0. WinSock2 is completely backward compatible with applications developed under previous WinSock specifications.

Beyond providing robust backward compatibility, WinSock2 introduced:

- **Better performance capabilities.** Underlying architectural changes to WinSock2 have taken the original WinSock subsystem and divided it into two layers. One layer is the DLLs providing the Windows Sockets APIs. The second layer is the service providers residing below the DLLs — these interact with upper-layer services via the Service Provider Interface (SPI).
- **Name resolution.** Basically, developers can write applications that access directory services such as DNS, NDS from Novell, and X.500.
- **Concurrent access to multiple network transports.** By writing to the SPI, developers can write once and use twice. That is, an application can utilize both TCP/IP and IPX/SPX under WinSock2.

Third-party TCP/IP software support

Obviously, TCP/IP as an entity doesn't live in a static vacuum. In fact, just the opposite is the case. The design goals from the founding fathers of TCP/IP were to create an open and extensible protocol suite for use by the masses.

That key tenet has not only resulted in the widespread acceptance of TCP/IP but has also spurred tremendous advances in TCP/IP tools, applications, and utilities. Developers, knowing that no one company explicitly owns TCP/IP, are emboldened to devote their best and brightest development resources on projects that extend the features, functionality, and manageability of TCP/IP. In this section, I profile a few third-party solutions that extend TCP/IP beyond its native capabilities in Windows NT Server 4.0.

Secret

It's a fact: Even in Windows NT Server 4.0, Microsoft's TCP/IP protocol suite is incomplete and lacks certain connectivity utilities and server services (daemons) that are supplied by third-party software vendors such as NetManage with its Chameleon TCP/IP protocol stack product line. One such service that is lacking is support for NFS or Network File System. In order to communicate with a Sun Workstation and a computer running Windows NT 4.0 (either Server or Workstation), you must have NFS — Network File System — connectivity between the two dissimilar systems (otherwise you're doomed to ping or Telnet connectivity).

NetManage's Chameleon UNIX Link97 (see Figure 4-21) provides NFS-based connectivity between UNIX systems and Windows NT. Chameleon is known in particular for its speed; it is considered a very robust and fast NFS client.

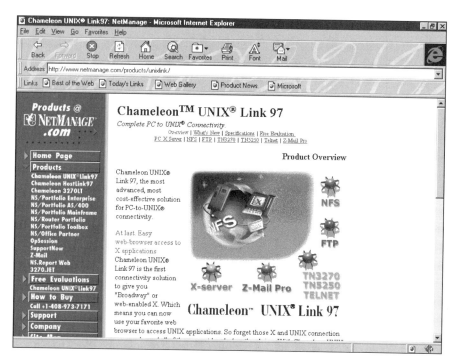

Figure 4-21: NetManage Chameleon UNIX Link97

Seattle-based WRQ supplements Microsoft's TCP/IP protocol stack with its connectivity solutions for connecting disparate systems. In particular, WRQ

Reflection products are basically terminal emulation applications for HP, Digital, UNIX, IBM, and X systems hosts and Windows-based clients. Reflection NFS Connection (see Figure 4-22) works with Windows NT Network Neighborhood and Windows Explorer.

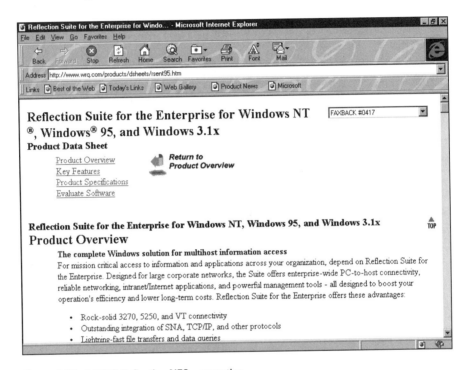

Figure 4-22: A WRQ Reflection NFS connection

Simple routing

By definition, an internetwork needs some form of OSI layer 3 routing capabilities to connect its subnets. Without routing each subnet would live in a vacuum and not communicate fully with the other subnets. However, this discussion in the context of TCP/IP and internetworking is about the "out of the box" routing capabilities of Windows NT Server. I would highly recommend that you educate yourself on hardware-based routing solutions for vendors such as Cisco and even Microsoft's robust software-based routing solution found in its Steelhead application.

Secret

When you hear term "multihomed" do you think of the well-to-do with homes both in the city and the country? The term actually refers to Microsoft TCP/IP's support for IP routing. You can use these built-in IP routing capabilities in systems with multiple network adapters attached to distinct and separate networks.

Implementing the multiple network adapter card–based routing capabilities of Windows NT Server 4.0 is easy. This election is made under the routing tab in the TCP/IP Protocol properties dialog box (see Figure 4-23). After making this change, you will need to reboot the machine.

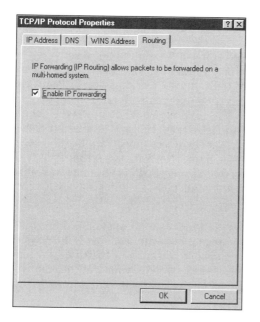

Figure 4-23: The Routing tab sheet

Secret

There are risks associated with the Enable IP Forwarding option. For example, if your Windows NT server is connected directly to the Internet, then enabling this option is akin to leaving the barn door open. Don't forget that IP routing is a two-way street; keep a high awareness that you are potentially inviting unwelcome guests to enjoy your network. This is even a problem in misconfigured implementations of Microsoft Proxy Server. Affectionately called the "poor man's firewall," Proxy Server uses a dual network adapter card to create the physical separation between your network and the Internet. However, if you accidentally have selected the "Enable IP Forwarding" option, you have effectively defeated and overridden the firewall built by Proxy Server. Take this problem seriously; I've seen this mistake made numerous times, and unfortunately, the Proxy Server documentation makes assumptions that you know this problem could occur.

Don't be fooled that Windows NT Server–based IP routing is the same as configuring and utilizing a traditional hardware-based router such as a Cisco 4500. It is not. The IP routing capabilities found in Windows NT Server 4.0 merely forward packets between physically separate subnets. No intelligent decisions are made with respect to IP filtering or cost-based path analysis.

A Word about Research

So we end this chapter on TCP/IP secrets. In the spirit of my next secret (research), I've placed it at the end. That's because far too many of us have conducted our research too late in a project or implementation to save us, or else, more likely, the implementation itself was ultimately "chalked up" to research.

How often have you pursued a possible solution but discovered later that more research would have prevented mistakes? Certainly an overused phrase but no where is it more appropriate that working with TCP/IP. One fledgling ISP shared with me an experience that came about from inadequate research. After it was too late, this ISP discovered what has been well documented in the trade press and other published resources: Windows NT Server provides adequate or better solutions for those seeking an application server, file server, and Internet server all in one; NetWare is a stronger file server than either an application or Internet server; UNIX is about as friendly as a junk-yard dog. The lesson learned by this ISP was, don't make your server into something that it is not.

Tip

And a final thought regarding TCP/IP. A simple system is more trouble free. That's an absolute true statement. Start with a simple TCP/IP system and work your way up to the more complex. If you are new to TCP/IP, it's mandatory that you start simple and progressively work your way into more complex TCP/IP implementations. Breaking this rule will most assuredly result in your getting in over your head far too quickly.

Summary

The intense TCP/IP definitions shared with you in this chapter round out the TCP/IP foundational knowledge to assist you in working with TCP/IP and in reading the next several chapters devoted to TCP/IP. From here on, you are ready to grow as both a Windows NT Server professional and TCP/IP practitioner. This chapter covered the following:

- TCP/IP definitions
- Microsoft's implementation of TCP/IP
- Detailed analysis of TCP
- Detailed analysis of IP
- Windows Sockets — definition and application
- Windows NT Server basic routing

Chapter 5

TCP/IP Implementations

In This Chapter

▶ Understanding the three parts to Internet addressing: IP address, subnet mask, default gateway

▶ Understanding basic routing and routing tables

Let's break down the elements of TCP/IP and discover a few secrets along the way. By revisiting the fundamentals, you're bound to be stronger. You have at least three reasons for being attentive to basic TCP/IP issues and definitions. The first reason is technical. If you don't understand the basic components used in implementing TCP/IP, you may well create a network that doesn't work. An example of this might be having the wrong subnet mask class associated with a specific range of IP addresses. If you do that, some of your older routers, being the unforgiving devices that they are, won't work properly. Second, a weakness with respect to TCP/IP fundamentals may well cause you to make a tactical error. Here the possibilities are endless but include humiliating yourself in front of other network professionals who know TCP/IP. Think of it as native English speakers finding humor in a nonnative English speaker's attempt to hold a fluent conversation. Third, you might very well make life harder on yourself. By not understanding the fundamentals of TCP/IP, you risk having to take the TCP/IP certification exam several times instead of once. All three cases just described can be avoided if you simply take the time, in this chapter, to master the TCP/IP fundamentals.

Internet Addressing

We've got to get the packet from here to there. That is the role of TCP/IP addressing. Remember that there are three components to a TCP/IP address: IP address, subnet mask, and default gateway. I encourage you to draw analogies from other "worlds" to appreciate the importance of the three components just listed. If this were the U.S. mail, you might think of the street address as the IP address, the city as the subnet mask, and the zip code as the router. Take a moment to challenge yourself to think "outside" of the TCP/IP box and draw analogies to other parts of your life to better define the IP address, subnet mask, and default gateway (hint: try thinking out how telephone numbers are organized with area code, prefix, and telephone number).

IP addresses

The IP address is a 32-bit value that is used to correctly identify a source and destination address in packet-based network communications. An IP address typically reads something like 204.107.2.100. The address can be broken down into four positions of eight bits each and can also be represented in binary form. These positions are called octet positions and are each eight bits in length.

Tip

Make sure you commit to memory Table 5-1, which shows these octet positions. You will inevitably find yourself in a planning meeting or be on a telephone call when others drop into what could be called TCP/IP shorthand. You'll hear terms like "dot one hundred in the fourth octet position" thrown around freely. You will be expected to keep up.

Table 5-1 IP Address Components for Sample Address 204.107.2.100

Value	Octet Position	Standard Alpha Variable Notation*
204	First Octet	W
107	Second Octet	X
2	Third Octet	Y
100	Fourth Octet	Z

*This is how IP models typical refer to the octet position when referenced via alpha characters. This is conceptually similar to the study of algebra when we refer to discrete items as either A, B, C or X, Y, Z.

To represent an address in binary format, let's revisit what binary counting is all about. Binary represents values by a one or a zero. It's the classic on-off mentality of digital computing that we've all grown up with and love. Table 5-2 is a simple binary conversion table to help you translate a dotted decimal value to its binary form.

Tip

Note we are assuming that we are reading left to right, as this sentence is being read. So for the binary representation 11001100, which is the number 204, we would say the first bit position of the octet is a one ("1"). While it may seem incredibly obvious to say we read from left to right, it is necessary to communicate this point correctly because some areas in the TCP/IP and Internet worlds actually read right to left. For example, Internet domain names are technically read from right to left. Thus the addresses is first evaluated as a commercial or "com" domain.

Table 5-2 Simple Binary to Decimal Conversion Table for Converting Octet Value 204 to Binary Value 11001100

Octet Position	Decimal Notation	Binary Value
1st Bit*	128	1
2nd Bit	64	1
3rd Bit	32	0
4th Bit	16	0
5th Bit	8	1
6th Bit	4	1
7th Bit	2	0
8th Bit	1	0

Thus the IP address of 204.107.2.100 would translate to the binary representation shown in Table 5-3.

Table 5-3 Translation of IP Address to Binary Values

Octet Bit Position	1st	2nd	3rd	4th	5th	6th	7th	8th
Octet Value\Dotted Decimal Notation	128	64	32	16	8	4	2	1
204 (First Octet)	1	1	0	0	1	1	0	0
107 (Second Octet)	0	1	1	0	1	0	1	1
2 (Third Octet)	0	0	0	0	0	0	1	0
100 (Fourth Octet)	0	1	1	0	0	1	0	0

Stated another way, 204.107.2.100 translates to zeros and ones, organized by octets in a column format, as shown in Table 5-4. Table 5-4 is presented to help you understand how a specific IP address appears when organized by octet.

Table 5-4 Alternative View: Binary to IP Address Conversion

First Octet	Second Octet	Third Octet	Fourth Octet
11001100	01101011	00000010	01100100
204	107	2	100

Tip
Don't forget that an IP address should be thought of as a unique address on a TCP/IP network. Stated again, every node on a TCP/IP network must have a unique IP address. If two nodes on your TCP/IP network have the exact same IP addresses, you will see the following messages.

Figure 5-1 shows the error message that would be displayed by the Windows NT Server that was first to participate on the TCP/IP network before the second host appeared with a duplicate address. This first host will continue to operate without incident. In short, the first computer obtained the specific IP address in question and doesn't have to give it up just because a second host wants it.

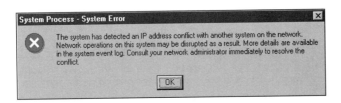
Figure 5-1: An IP address conflict error message

The message shown in Figure 5-2 indicates that the computer operator has attempted to assign the same network using an IP address that already exists. The resulting error message means that all networking functionality has been disabled because of the duplicate address conflict. In short, the second host simply can't have the same IP address being used by the first host.

Figure 5-2: A second host IP address error message

Secret
Getting around a duplicate IP address scenario is actually quite easy. If you have a second transport protocol loaded and bound to your network adapter, you will be automatically authenticated as a network citizen using the second valid protocol. Of course I'm assuming the Windows NT server you are trying to attach to is also running this second protocol. Remember that in a nonrouted scenario, the NetBEUI protocol would be a fine selection. In a routed scenario, you would need to consider using NWLink (IPX/SPX), which is routable.

My discussion so far relates to IP addressing issues on a LAN or a WAN that is not participating on the Internet via a full-time connection. When connected to the Internet, the rules possibly change, depending on your situation. The basic rule applies that any node on the Internet must have a unique address.

Tip

Remember, you must be especially careful that computers that are directly connected to the Internet and do not route through a proxy server to use an authentic Internet IP address use the correct address that has been assigned by the Internet Network Information Center (InterNIC). Given the architecture of TCP/IP and how it is implemented on the Internet, it is essential that we have unique IP addresses for nodes with direct Internet connections.

To receive a valid Internet address and connect to the Internet, contact:

Network Solutions
InterNIC Registration Services
505 Huntmar Park Drive
Herndon, VA 22070
`www.internic.net`

The IP "green movement"

Let's face it, TCP/IP addressing is not as easy as it looks, and with a finite supply of IP addresses on the Internet, it is essential that you consider an alternate IP address strategy that allows your internal network nodes to have unique IP addresses yet fully participate and take advantage of the Internet. Think of this as the green strategy, as you'll find you're doing your part to save IP address, much as many good-hearted souls are out trying to save the world's trees from harvest.

Secret

Although you can contact the organization just mentioned to get your unique Internet address (a.k.a. netid), I have a better idea.

There is one way to use both phony and real Internet IP Addresses on the same network. This situation requires the use of Microsoft Proxy Server, wherein the internal LAN may have "phony" addresses such as 131.107.2.100 to .200 and yet the organization may only have one real Internet IP address such as 204.222.104.2 for its "real" Internet connection. This is a perfectly legitimate way to connect to the Internet from the desktop and has the added benefit of helping save real Internet IP addresses (an endangered species). Proxy Server, with its routing and filtering capabilities, in effect converts the phony internal IP addresses to route to the Internet via the valid Internet IP address.

Mysteriously misappropriated Internet domain names

While writing this book, I twice observed situations in which domain names were "switched" to different Internet IP addresses (something unknown to all network parties that had a need to know), so I thought it was worth mentioning. Perhaps the mere telling of these stories will prevent you from suffering a similar situation. In each case, these clients noticed that their Internet e-mail service seemed to be failing. Both were running Windows NT Server as their network operating system and Microsoft Exchange 5.*x* as their e-mail application.

One day, client 1 (a small software developer) noticed that while the internal Exchange e-mail continued to operate as expected, the externally routed e-mail to the Internet, both internal and external, was failing. Of course a round of network troubleshooting commenced: routers were tested, Telco services were looped back, and Exchange services were analyzed. Many billable hours later the discovery was made that the Marketing Director had apparently taken advantage of, and been taken advantage of by, a discount Web hosting firm that offered not only to develop your Web site but host it as well. There was only one catch to this great deal. The Web hosting firm would take control of your domain name and the IP address assigned to your organization and repoint it to its location. Well, that caused fits with the Exchange-based Internet e-mail service. Once corrected, that is, once the domain name and IP address were pointed back to the client's original location, the Exchange-based Internet e-mail worked just fine. The moral? This is a classic case of the marketing department not communicating with the networking engineers. It sounds like the classic MBA lecture where marketing and engineering don't speak to each other.

The second time I encountered such a domain name and IP address reassignment was again a situation where a management team member, the Chief Financial Officer (CFO), contracted with a bargain Web hosting firm to develop and host the firm's Web site. Here again, the sun rose one day and the Exchange-based Internet e-mail failed, although not completely — it was somewhat random at first, working for a few hours and then failing. Several hours of troubleshooting, including the threat to FDISK the Exchange Server machine and start from ground zero, resulted in the discovery that the Web hosting firm had contacted InterNIC and pointed the client's domain name and corresponding IP address away from the client's original location. Once said domain name and IP address were restored to their proper locations, Exchange again worked just fine.

So beware of low-cost Web hosting solutions. More important, beware of other stakeholders in your organization accepting such offers on your behalf.

Caution

Just as with the preceding examples of low-cost Web hosting firms reassigning domain names and IP addresses inappropriately, be advised that a disturbing trend on the Internet involves unethical bulk e-mailing organizations. Apparently these organizations are having InterNIC reassign legitimate domain names to their illegitimate sites. Next, a flood of annoying bulk e-mailings are launched and the replies are gathered for several hours or days until the domain name assignment is discovered and cured.

Subnet masks

The subnet mask is used to mask or distinguish the network portion of the address from the host or node portion of the address. The subnet mask provides information about how an address should be read.

The subnet mask is extremely valuable in helping organize IP address assignments on the Internet into classes. Ingeniously, we have Class A, Class B, and Class C. Important reasons exist for using address classes to manage all of the TCP/IP madness on the Internet. Although we are only concerned with Classes A, B, and C (shown in Table 5-5) as networking professionals, there are two other classes. Class D is used for multicasting to a special group of nodes in a land where we mere mortals don't participate. Class E is reserved for future use and growth (thank goodness — we're going to need this class considering the incredible growth of Internet nodes).

Table 5-5 Internet Address Classes Using the 204.107.2.100 Sample IP Address

Class	Network Address	Host Address	Bit Position That Separates Network and Host Address*	Standard Subnet Mask Value
A	204	107.2.100	8th	255.0.0.0
B	204.107.	2.100	16th	255.255.0.0
C	204.107.2.	100	24th	255.255.255.0

*Remember that an IP address is expressed as a 32-bit value. The division points between octets occur at the 8th, 16th, and 24th bits.

Secret

The Microsoft Official Curriculum (MOC) for several Microsoft Certified Systems Engineer (MCSE) courses provides some damaging misinformation for the student who is new to TCP/IP implementations. Let's play what's wrong with this picture. This is the actual configuration taken from the MOC instructor's manual for several courses that I have delivered: Implementing and Supporting Windows 95, Supporting Windows NT Server 4.0 – Core Technologies, Supporting Windows NT Server 4.0 – Enterprise Technologies, Supporting Microsoft Internet Information Server, and Supporting Proxy Server:

```
IP Addresses: 131.107.2.100−.200
Subnet Mask: 255.255.255.0
```

So I ask you – what's wrong with this picture? Challenge yourself to find what is fundamentally flawed here. If you can do so immediately, my compliments to you. If you can't, read on, as the following text might enlighten you further as to the fundamentals of TCP/IP and enable you to see what is wrong with this IP address and subnet mask combination.

The IP has an invalid beginning and ending private Internet network address range given the standard subnet mask value that is being used. While not a problem on a single subnetted internal private network, this can wreck havoc when you work with "real" routers such as the hardware-based Cisco offerings that may or may not expect your addressing to conform exactly to the known valid private Internet network address ranges.

Although it is essential that you be able to identify the potential problems with this configuration, it's more important that you don't apply this misinformation to your future TCP/IP implementations. Oh yes, it's also important that you don't incorrectly answer MCSE examination questions based on this misunderstanding. That perhaps is the worst consequence of this goof, given it was delivered in the context of an MCSE certification course!

Table 5-6 shows valid private Internet network address ranges, enabling you to arrive at the correct answer to the previous riddle. Remember that we are talking about the network portion of the IP address. As we shall see in a few moments, the subnet mask helps us distinguish what portion of the IP address is defined as the network address and what portion of the address is defined as the host address.

Table 5-6   Valid Private Internet Network Address Ranges

Class	Start of Address Range in First Octet	End of Address Range in First Octet
Class A	001	126
Class B	128	191
Class C	192	223

First octet values above 223 (starting with 224) are reserved and may not be used. Don't forget that:

- All network addresses must be unique. This statement holds true whether you are on the Internet or your own internetwork. This is a good rule to adhere to.

- Remember that a network address cannot begin with 127 (the reserved address for internal loopback testing).

- You may not have all zeros in the first octet of a network address. If all bits are set to zero, that indicates a local address and prevents routing.

- You may not have 255 in the first octet of a network address. If all bits are set to one (which equals 255), this acts as a broadcast.

Host addresses

Regarding the host portion of an IP address, you will find the following points vital in mastering the fundamentals of TCP/IP:

Tip

Note the word "host" is interchangeable with the term "node" within the technical community. That is, the two terms essentially have the same meaning, assuming correct usage.

- Host addresses must be unique on a given network. This is a truism. Think about it. Each node on a network must have a unique address, and thus the host portion of the IP address must be unique. Table 5-7 shows valid host portion addresses within an IP address.

- All "1" bits are not allowed as the host address. If this is the case, the address is interpreted to be a broadcast address, not a host address.

- Likewise, all "0" bits may not be used as the host address. Doing so would communicate "this network only."

Table 5-7   Valid Host Portion Addresses

Class	Start	End
Class A	w.0.0.1	w.255.255.255
Class B	w.x.0.1	w.x.255.255
Class C	w.x.y.1	w.x.y.254

Caste classes

Let's discuss Classes A, B, and C. Perhaps you'll agree that TCP/IP has such clear class distinctions that it might better be thought of as a "caste" society. However, all joking aside, very important technical reasons exist for having classes. This separation enables you to better organize your network to achieve a best fit given the size of your network. If you are connected to the Internet, the class designation is even more important and is perhaps the most important way in which order is ultimately maintained on the wild and free wide-open world of the Internet.

Class A

Class A assignments are very rare and are for only the largest networks. Theoretically only 127 Class A networks can exist on the Internet because the network portion of the 32-bit address is on seven of the first eight bits in the first octet. If all eight bits were used in this octet, the number of networks possible would be 128. The unused bit in the octet is referred to as the high-order bit and is reserved. But let's not stop there. Because the number 127 in the first octet is a reserved number, there can really only be 126 Class A networks.

Secret

The number 127 is reserved in the first octet position to facilitate such features as internal loopback testing. To perform an internal loopback test in TCP/IP using the ping command, type **Ping 127.0.0.1**.

The number of nodes possible on a Class A network is approximately 17 million (actually, it's 16,777,214 nodes). An example of a Class A network is the original Internet, which at first was called ARPANET and managed by the Department of Defense.

Class B

Class B assignments are for medium-sized networks. This network address is 16 bits long and consumes the first two octet positions. Because two high-order bit positions are set to 1 and 0 respectively, there can only be 16,383 networks. But each network may have 65,534 nodes.

Class C

Class C allows for 2,097,151 networks and up to 254 nodes per network. Not surprisingly, this class is best suited for smaller networks. In fact, most of us work with Class C networks in the Internet. This class of license is by far the most popular address class. Three high-order bits have Class C addresses (set to 1-1-0 respectively).

Why only 254 nodes? Because 255 is a reserved number with TCP/IP addressing that is typical employed for network- and internetwork-level broadcasting. Such a reservation is necessary for TCP/IP network management purposes.

Table 5-8 summarizes these network classes and nodes.

Table 5-8 Summary of Class A, B, and C Networks and Nodes

Class	Actual Number of Networks Possible	Actual Number of Nodes Possible
A	126	16,777,214
B	16,384	65534
C	2,097,151	254

Default gateways

Default gateways are important, providing a place for IP hosts to seek help when trying to communicate with distant IP hosts on another IP network. In essence, the default gateway address points or instructs the host to use another node to handle its routing needs. The goal of default gateways is to make IP routing efficient. In fact, individual hosts (say workstations) use default gateways extensively to avoid being burdened with address resolution.

On a larger network with hardware-based routers, this entry field will typically be the IP address of your router. On smaller networks using the IP forwarding capabilities of Windows NT Server, this would be the address of the server. In either case, the default gateway maintains current and detailed knowledge of network IDs of other networks on an "internetwork" (that is, a network of networks).

Chapter 5: TCP/IP Implementations   **153**

Tip

In fact, if you are new to TCP/IP and don't know a lot about the network you are working with, just put the IP address of the Windows NT server in the default gateway field until you are able to better understand what the appropriate value for your network should be. (Of course this sage advice pertains to a smaller network — on a larger network, you should hire a Microsoft Certified Professional networking consultant to assist with your TCP/IP implementation.)

As shown in Figure 5-3, the default gateway is defined on the IP Address tab sheet on the TCP/IP Protocol Properties property sheet in Windows NT Server 4.0.

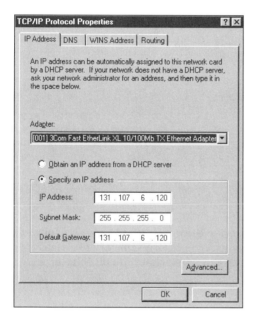

Figure 5-3: The default gateway

Secret

On the Networking Essentials certification exam that must be passed to earn your MCSE designation, remember that the default gateway value is an optional entry in a TCP/IP scenario. The IP address and subnet mask are required.

That said, what are some situations that you might not enter a default gateway? One is a small LAN where all nodes reside on one subnet. Before reading my second observation on not using a default gateway, take a moment to think about situations in your networking experience where you didn't use a default gateway entry.

A second situation in which we would be sans default gateway is a network that, while containing different "segments," doesn't use a router to route packets. Perhaps such a network uses a switch. Remember that switches reside at layer two of the OSI model (the data-link layer) and don't require the kind of addressing information that packets do at OSI model layer three (the network layer).

What are the mechanics of a default gateway and how is such a beast used on your Windows NT Server network? Suppose you have a network with a node called Host 100 and a node called Host 200. Note that Host 100 is located on Network 1 and Host 200 is located on Network 2. Assume that Host 100 addresses and sends a packet to Host 200. After Host 100 checks its local routing tables and is unable to resolve the "path" to Host 200, it forwards the packet to the default gateway.

A Windows NT computer builds the local routing table automatically, making one entry per route. This is obviously important for routing and resolution purposes. The local routing table can be displayed via the ROUTE PRINT command:

```
C:> route print
Active Routes:

Network Address   Netmask           Gateway Address  Interface      Metric
0.0.0.0           0.0.0.0           131.076.120      131.107.6.120     1
127.0.0.0         255.0.0.0         127.0.0.1        127.0.0.1         1
131.107.6.0       255.255.255.0     131.107.6.120    131.107.6.120     1
131.107.6.120     255.255.255.255   127.0.0.1        127.0.0.1         1
131.107.255.255   255.255.255.255   131.107.6.120    131.107.6.120     1
224.0.0.0         224.0.0.0         131.107.6.120    131.107.6.120     1
255.255.255.255   255.255.255.255   131.107.6.120    131.107.6.120     1
```

The following sections describe these columns that are displayed when we use the route print command. Such descriptions are necessary, as the table, viewed alone, is both boring and somewhat difficult to interpret.

Network address

The first column is where the network address is searched for. Possibilities include 0.0.0.0, a value that refers to "this network" (the current network that originated the packet). At the other end of the scale, we have 255.255.255.255, a value that includes all networks; this means all hosts on all networks that could receive limited broadcast traffic. Typically, the 255.255.255.255 address is implemented when the default gateway proves unresponsive, initiating a broadcast to all hosts on all networks.

Netmask

The netmask is the second column. The entry found here represents the subnet mask that is associated with the network address.

Secret

A netmask of 255.255.255.255, which is all "ones" when displayed in binary format, tells us that this is the host entry; the network address and the IP address are exactly the same and so refer to one and the same machine (the local host).

Gateway address

The gateway address is the default IP address used by the local host to resolve network address (the address of the IP router used to forward IP packets to other IP networks).

Interface

The interface is the IP address of the local network adapter card on the machine. This network adapter card address will be used when forwarding IP packets to the network.

Metric

This is the number of hops required to travel to the IP destination. A hop count is conceptually similar to the hop count discussion you might have encountered when mastering Messaging Transfer Agents (MTA) in Microsoft Exchange or Microsoft Mail.

You can interpret the local routing table according to the entries in the Network Address column of Table 5-9. Note the information displayed in this example reflects a Windows NT server that has its own IP address as the default gateway. As discussed earlier, it is common to put the Windows NT server's IP address in the default gateway column on LANs that have no subnets or routers.

Table 5-9 Detailed "Route" Information

Network Address	Description
0.0.0.0	Default Gateway address line. See the Gateway Address column (third column in the preceding list) for the correct default gateway address entry. In this case, that value is 131.107.6.120.
127.0.0.0	Loopback address
131.107.6.0	Local network
131.107.6.120	Host IP address
131.107.255.255	Network-level broadcast
224.0.0.0	Multicast address
255.255.255.255	Internetwork-level broadcast

Addresses are added to the local routing table via the ROUTE ADD command. This command once initiated IP-based WAN communications between two cities for a client when nothing else would. For example, imagine you have a situation in which you cannot successfully ping across a router. Now consider the following command:

```
C:>route add 204.107.3.0 mask 255.255.255.0 204.107.2.199 -p
```

So what's going on here? Challenge yourself to answer that simple question by considering this router command in the light of Figure 5-4. Hopefully you, like me, enjoy an occasional analytical exercise to solve. If you can quickly see the main point (hint: make a persistent route), I again applaud your understanding of TCP/IP fundamentals and encourage you to strongly consider taking the Microsoft TCP/IP certification exam if you haven't already done so.

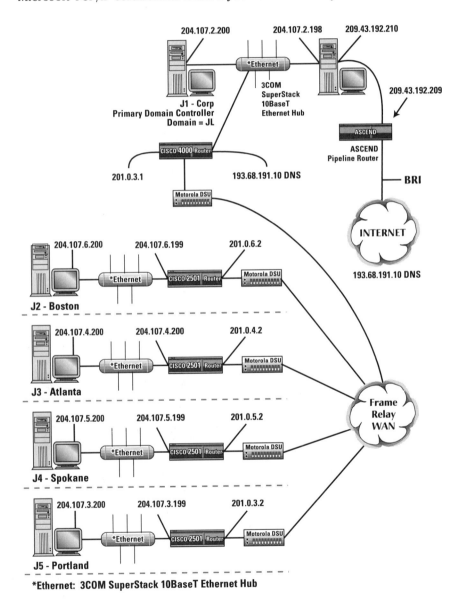

Figure 5-4: A network with routers

The preceding route add command explicitly states that to get to the 204.107.3.0 subnet with a mask of 255.255.255.0, use gateway 204.107.2.199 and make this a static of persistent route by writing it to the Registry (-r).

This persistent route is written to HKEY_LOCAL_MACHINE\SYSTEM\CurrentControl\Set\Services\Tcpip\Parameters\PersistentRoutes. Shown in Figure 5-5, this is significant because it allows the persistent static route to survive the expiration of the current computing session. That is, when the Windows NT Server is rebooted, the persistent route will be recreated on the basis of the Registry entries displayed in Figure 5-5. By analogy, think of a congressional bill that survives between two different sessions of the U.S. Congress with the same number.

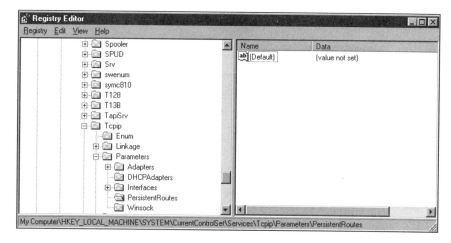

Figure 5-5: HKEY_LOCAL_MACHINE\SYSTEM\CurrentControlSet\Services\Tcpip\Parameters\PersistentRoutes

Multiple default gateways

Many people are confused about the use of multiple gateways in Windows NT Server. Multiple gateways are entered on the Advanced IP Addressing property sheet. Figure 5-6 shows where multiple gateway addresses are added. You may also elevate one gateway address over another using the up- and down-arrow keys. Elevating a gateway address causes it to be evaluated sooner than the gateway address listed immediately below it.

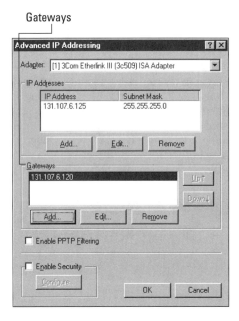

Figure 5-6: Adding multiple gateway addresses

The common misconception is that you would add multiple gateway values to connect disparate networks. For instance, a corporate private WAN connected via Cisco routers could be connected to the Internet at some point via an ISDN router (and an entirely different subnet).

In Figure 5-7, notice the private WAN for this company is connected via Cisco routers. The Internet connection, via a 7 × 24 ISDN connection, is an entirely different network.

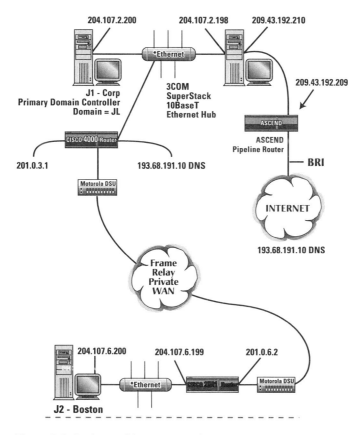

Figure 5-7: A private wide area network

It would be a mistake to make the entry shown in the Gateways field in Figure 5-8 to account for both the Cisco router and the ISDN router at the Corporate location. In the figure, notice that the Cisco router and ISDN router addresses have been entered as gateways on this Windows NT server (located at Corporate in Figure 5-7). This is an incorrect way to try to connect two disparate networks that have multiple routers.

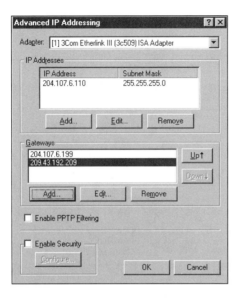

Figure 5-8: Router addresses on a Windows NT server

Tip

The real purpose of the multiple gateway entries is not to account for the multiple routers at the Corporate site in the preceding example, but to provide a backup route for WAN traffic routing should the "default" gateway fail or go down. Stated another way, only the default gateway is used. If it is down (by that, I mean it is physically unavailable and not just unable to resolve an address), the second gateway entry is employed to get the packet from Point A to Point B.

Here is a correct use of multiple gateway address. In this scenario, we have a "backup" WAN link between two sites via RAS. Should the regular WAN link, via the Cisco routers, fail, then we are rerouted and reconnected via the WAN connections. Note that this second gateway entry value would point to the dial-up adapter. As shown in Figure 5-9, the second gateway address relates to our second or backup WAN connection.

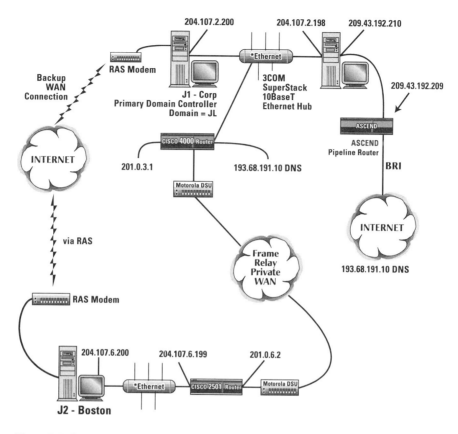

Figure 5-9: A second gateway address

Understanding IP Routing

We technical types often remember back to our college days with both glee over the meaty technical courses we eagerly excelled in and the required liberal arts courses we suffered through. One such unmemorable course for many may well have been Communications 101. In that course, you learned about something called an S/R model. The basic S/R model, showing communications based on a sender and a receiver, appears in Figure 5-10.

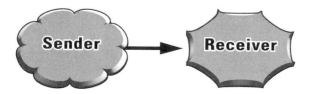

Figure 5-10: A basic S/R model

Likewise, the Communications 101 instructor probably told you that someday you would appreciate the lecture being delivered. Guess what! The instructor was right. Not only is the S/R model the foundation of network communications, it is also the underlying theory behind routing. Think about it. Routing is nothing more then connecting two parties that want to communicate but need a helping hand because of some barrier, such as separate subnets. Thus routing is used to get the data packets, in this case, IP datagrams, from sender to receiver. In an IP routing scenario, we are basically concerned with two addresses, the destination address and the origination (or sender's) address.

Secret

Truth be told, routing is considered by many to be the primary function of IP. With IP routing, we're living at layer three (the network layer) of the OSI model. Basically, the IP-related services evaluate each packet by examining the destination host address. The address is compared against the local routing table and evaluated to determine if any forwarding is necessary. If the destination address can be found on the local subnet, the packet is not forwarded. If the opposite is true, that is, the destination address is located on a distant and (for our purposes) physically separate network, then IP services undertake the appropriate forwarding steps. These include having the first router, which has evaluated the packet destined for a distant subnet, forward the packet to the other router, which is associated with that distant subnet.

Many of you know (but a surprisingly huge number of Windows NT Server professionals do not) that routers only forward information from router to router. See Microsoft's *Network Essentials* (Microsoft Press, ISBN 1-55615-806-8) for a quick review of this basic but often overlooked concept.

Officially, according to Microsoft, IP routers "use two or more network connection interfaces to attach and interconnect between each physically separate IP network for which they are enabled to forward packets between." And don't forget we use IP routing (and routing in general) to filter as much as we do to forward. For example, IP routers are by default configured not to forward broadcast packets beyond their native subnets. With respect to hardware-based routing solutions, it's best to think of these beasties as positive check-off devices. You must positively elect to have certain packet types flow through the system; with most routers, the default state is not to pass any packet through unless it is specially instructed to do so. So out of the box, the average router is probably skewed more toward filtering than forwarding.

Conversely, a negative check-off is analogous to joining a mail-order Record of the Month Club. That is, until you explicitly tell the record company not send you monthly recordings, you receive monthly music in perpetuity. That's a negative check-off because you are forced to explicitly stop a certain activity. This is more akin to lower OSI-level devices such as switches. Typically, a switch will forward everything until told different (that is, if you have a "smart" switch that can be instructed to perform limited filtering).

Now let's focus on common characteristics of IP routers. First, routers are multihomed hosts. That means a router has at least two network interfaces.

This can be a Windows NT server with two network adapter cards or a hardware-based router with an internal LAN network interface port and an external network adapter port. These interfaces provide the connection between the two separate networks, as shown in Figure 5-11.

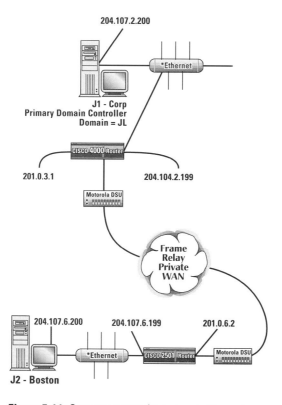

Figure 5-11: Separate networks connected by routers

Another of the functions performed by IP routers is to forward packets for TCP/IP hosts. At a minimum, the IP router must be able to forward IP-based packets to other networks. And of course more often than not, you are interested in some level of filtering.

Finally, routers can be hardware based or "out-of-the-box" implementations provided by such vendors as Cisco, Bay, and HP. Software-based routing solutions included Microsoft's Steelhead routing technology and RAS.

Routing Tables

Routers depend on routing tables to figure it all out. Routing tables exist to store addressing information about IP networks and hosts. Here is how routing tables are put into action via a three-step approach that always has the underlying goal of getting the packet to where it belongs.

- Step 1: The computer sends a packet. It inserts its own source IP address and destination address into the IP header (see Figure 5-12).

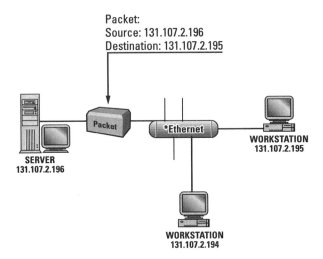

Figure 5-12: Step 1: The computer sends a packet.

- Step 2: The destination address is examined by the computer and compared against the local routing table. Three possible actions follow depending on what the computer found in its local routing table (see Figure 5-13).

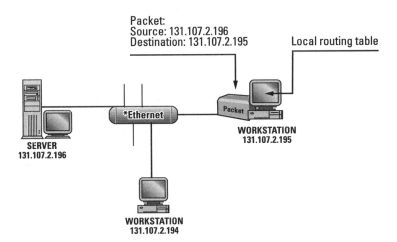

Figure 5-13: Step 2: The destination address is examined by the computer and compared against the local routing table.

Chapter 5: TCP/IP Implementations   **165**

- Step 3a: The packet can be forwarded up to a higher protocol layer in the OSI model if the destination address is the same as the machine performing the packet evaluation. This packet has already arrived at its destination (see Figure 5-14).

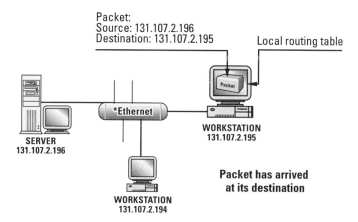

Figure 5-14: Step 3a: The packet can be forwarded up to a higher protocol layer.

- Step 3b: The packet can be forwarded to another computer (or in the case of RAS, an attached dial-up adapter). See Figure 5-15.

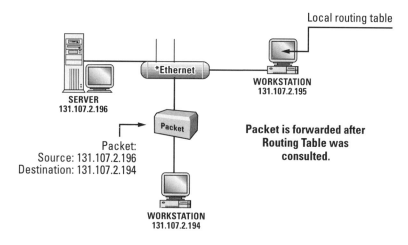

Figure 5-15: Step 3b: The packet can be forwarded to another computer.

Part II: TCP/IP

- Step 3c: If appropriate, the packet can be killed then and there (see Figure 5-16). This is referred to as discarding.

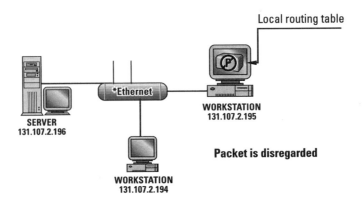

Figure 5-16: Step 3c: If appropriate, the packet can be killed.

So by following these steps, a packet ultimately gets to where it belongs on a routed network. That is in large part why many of us, as network professionals, are here: to get the packet from point A to point B. Consider it the equivalent of the old saying about "making the trains run on time."

With that, you now know the finer points of TCP/IP implementations and a few of the pitfalls to be avoided. Godspeed to you as you start implementing TCP/IP-based networks using Windows NT Server.

Summary

This chapter presented the following:

▶ Three parts to Internet addressing: IP address, subnet mask, default gateway

▶ Basic routing and routing tables

Chapter 6

Installing and Configuring TCP/IP

In This Chapter
- Installing TCP/IP
- Configuring TCP/IP
- Configuring additional TCP/IP services

This chapter provides all that you need to know to install TCP/IP and its related services for Windows NT. TCP/IP protocol configuration is also explained. It is essential that you correctly install and configure the TCP/IP protocol if indeed you intend to utilize this protocol on your Windows NT Server network. Why? Remember at the end of Chapter 2 when I discussed the initial setup of Windows NT Server as a foundational issue that will forever mark how your network performs? The same can be said about TCP/IP and its foundation-level role on your network. Simply stated, if you are not completely successful in installing and configuring TCP/IP when you mean to be, TCP/IP misconfigurations will come back to haunt you for the life of your network. Got it?

TCP/IP Installation Preparations

The good news is that the past TCP/IP chapters have prepared you for this moment: installing TCP/IP. Be advised that many problems on a network (including failed installations) can be traced to defective network protocol installations. That is, TCP/IP was installed, but important TCP/IP-related information was incorrect or missing. And while these topics have been touched on in the prior TCP/IP chapters, this is the chapter where the hands meet the keyboard.

A plain TCP/IP protocol installation in Windows NT requires a certain level of manual configuration. A few planning steps up front may dramatically lessen the opportunity for failure. To manually configure TCP/IP with Windows NT Server, you need to consider the following.

Will the computer function as a Dynamic Host Configuration Protocol (DHCP) server or will it act as a DHCP client (obtaining its TCP/IP configuration information from another DHCP server on the network)?

Tip

It has been my experience that you should manually configure TCP/IP on Windows NT Server and have true client workstations such as Windows NT Workstation and Windows 95/98 act as DHCP clients, if for no other reason than that a clear demarcation line is drawn between server and client. Plus it seems that you're always modifying the TCP/IP configuration on a server but not necessarily the client workstation.

Determine whether you want this Windows NT Server to act as Windows Internet Name Service (WINS) server. In a single-server environment, the answer is typically yes because WINS aids greatly in resolving NetBIOS names to TCP/IP addresses.

Secret

Windows 2000 Server will support WINS for backward compatibility reasons. Be advised the preferred method of name resolution in Windows 2000 Server will become Dynamic DNS. Advance information on this topic is already circulating on both the Web sites and the newsgroups at www.microsoft.com.

So assuming that you are going to manually configure TCP/IP on your Windows NT server and not receive your configuration from an existing DHCP server, let's revisit the "necessities" to configure TCP/IP (of course I'm assuming that you've read the earlier TCP/IP chapters and have a basic understanding of TCP/IP configurations). Map out the following information in advance of the TCP/IP installation process (see the sample as-built network diagram in Figure 6-1):

- The IP address and subnet mask for each network adapter card installed inside the machine

- The IP address and subnet mask for any PPP connection you will make from the machine. This is typically modem-specific TCP/IP configuration information stored on a per-dialer basis under Dial-Up Networking (nested inside the Accessories menu selection from Programs). You will make this type of manual TCP/IP configuration when attempting to connect to the Internet via Dial-Up Networking from your machine.

- The IP address for the default gateway on the local subnet. Unless you are truly using routing (for instance with a Cisco router), this value is typically one of the Windows NT servers on your subnet. It may even be the IP address of the Windows NT server that you are configuring TCP/IP on as part of this exercise.

- The IP address(es) and DNS domain name(s) of the DNS servers on your network/internetwork. Depending on whether you are connected to the Internet, these values will vary. I'll discuss this more in a moment.

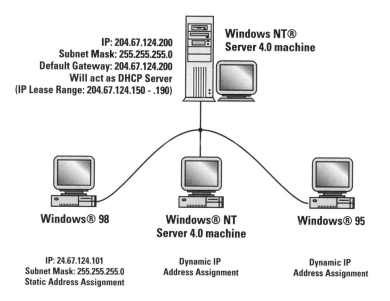

Figure 6-1: TCP/IP Configuration on a Small Network

Tip I strongly recommend that you consider creating a LAN/WAN plan as part of the as-built drawing process discussed in Chapter 2. There's nothing like a map to guide your TCP/IP configuration efforts.

Installing TCP/IP on Windows NT Server

The TCP/IP protocol is implemented by default when you are installing Windows NT Server 4.0. TCP/IP is thus known as the default protocol. Because Windows NT Server only allows the custom installation option during setup, you will have the opportunity to add other protocols and even remove TCP/IP. On that last point, I wouldn't recommend removing TCP/IP because it provides such great networking functionality in a Windows NT Server environment (like supporting robust direct Internet connections!).

Secret Did you know that the TCP/IP protocol became the default installation protocol commencing with Windows NT Server 3.51 and higher? Prior to that, the default protocol was NWLink IPX/SPX for Windows NT Server 3.50 and NetBEUI for Windows NT Advanced Server 3.1. Just a little trivia I thought you might enjoy.

At setup

Assuming you allow the installation of TCP/IP during the Windows NT Server setup, here are some issues to address.

First make sure that, indeed, TCP/IP is selected as at least one of the protocols that will be installed. It's OK to install other protocols, but always revisit the reasons for installing additional protocols. For example, if you are using an older HP JetDirect card, perhaps you will need to install the DLC protocol. NWLink IPX/SPX is a good protocol installation choice if you have NetWare servers present.

Second, make sure that the correct network adapter card has been detected. This is one of the few opportunities to actually watch Windows NT Server 4.0 perform autodetection. And regrettably, the detection, while on target for known network adapters with drivers found in the \i386 setup subdirectory, comes up short (as expected) for newer network adapter cards shipped after the Windows NT Server 4.0 build you are working with. Be sure to keep that network adapter driver disk handy that shipped with your new network adapter card!

Finally, minimize the number of TCP/IP-related services that are installed during the setup of your Windows NT server.

Even if you installed TCP/IP as part of the Windows NT Server setup, I recommend that you continue and read the next section discussing how to install TCP/IP. I call this my snow day strategy. In my hometown of Seattle, Washington, whenever we receive snowfall, the city literally shuts down because of the hilly terrain. I've made a pact with myself that on these days, when I'm unable to get to work, I will trot down to my basement office and review my old BackOffice manuals again, even though I probably have BackOffice (including Windows NT Server) running just the way I want it. Well, given that we only receive snow once or twice a year, this forced review of BackOffice setups and administration via the user manuals always results in my remembering something simple, something I could be doing better, or perhaps something I should stop doing. So by reviewing the TCP/IP setup section next, perhaps you can benefit from my snow day strategy.

Secret

I've seen too many TCP/IP services installed at start-up spoil the whole apple cart. One example is the SNMP service, which is often installed only to enhance the number of object: counters available in Performance Monitor. Why else would SNMP be installed on a Windows NT Server when the network doesn't even utilize SNMP-aware devices or management applications? That said, under these scenarios, you can get start-up event errors that not only populate the System Log in the Event Viewer but can cause other BackOffice applications to fail, such as Microsoft Exchange and Proxy Server. Be advised.

On an existing Windows NT server

Perhaps you have valid reasons to install the TCP/IP protocol at a later date, or as suggested in my "Troubleshooting TCP/IP" chapter that follows, you need to reinstall the TCP/IP protocol. Here is how you do it. It is important to understand that whether you install TCP/IP during the setup of your server machine or you add TCP/IP to an existing Windows NT Server, the "end" is still the same: a properly functioning TCP/IP protocol suite. Granted, the "means" are slightly different. For information on how to install TCP/IP during setup, kindly review the discussion in the section "Setting Up Windows NT Server" of Chapter 2, "Windows NT Server 4.0 Planning, Setup, and Installation." To install TCP/IP on an existing Windows NT Server, perform the steps that follow.

STEPS:
To install Microsoft TCP/IP

Step 1.   Log on as an administrator or member of the Administrators group at the Windows NT Server machine at which you will be installing or reinstalling the TCP/IP protocol.

Step 2.   Launch the Network applet one of two ways: from Control Panel or using the secondary menu from Network Neighborhood (see Figure 6-2).

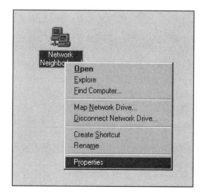

Figure 6-2: The Network Neighborhood secondary menu

Because the Network applet is a commonly used tool, you might consider creating a desktop shortcut from the Network applet in Control Panel, as shown in Figure 6-3. To do this, simply right-click the Network applet when Control Panel is displayed and select the Create Shortcut option. This selection will only allow you to place the shortcut on the desktop.

Continued

STEPS

To install Microsoft TCP/IP *(continued)*

Figure 6-3: Creating a Network Applet shortcut

Step 3. In the Network dialog box shown in Figure 6-4, select the Protocols tab sheet.

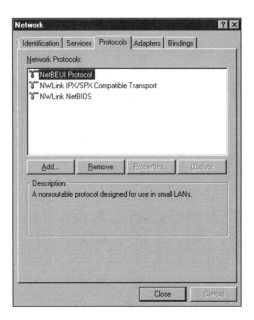

Figure 6-4: The Protocols tab sheet in the Network dialog box

Step 4. Click the Add button. The Select Network Protocol dialog box appears, as shown in Figure 6-5.

Step 5. Select the TCP/IP Protocol from the list of Network Protocols and then click the OK button.

Chapter 6: Installing and Configuring TCP/IP

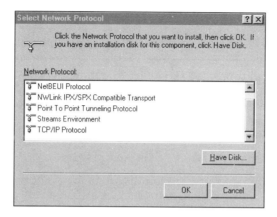

Figure 6-5: The Select Network Protocol Dialog Box

Step 6. Reply to the TCP/IP Setup message that allows you to configure TCP/IP via DHCP or manually (see Figure 6-6). As a server, you are more likely to configure the TCP/IP settings manually, suggesting you would reply "No" to the dialog box. You will note that "No" is the default answer because it has the "focus."

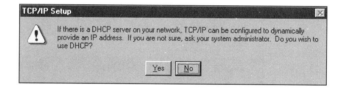

Figure 6-6: A TCP/IP Setup message relating to DHCP configuration

Step 7. Windows NT Server Setup will next ask you to provide the full path to the Windows NT Server distribution files. The default path for your source files will be original install path that contained the \i386 subdirectory during the installation of Windows NT Server. Accept this entry or type the full path and click Continue. Remember from Chapter 2, "Windows NT Server 4.0 Planning, Setup, and Installation," that you should at your earliest convenience (and for your continued convenience) copy the contents from the \i386 subdirectory on the Windows NT Server 4.0 CD-ROM to a like-named subdirectory on your hard disk.

Continued

STEPS

To install Microsoft TCP/IP *(continued)*

Secret

If you copied your \i386 setup files from the original Windows NT Server 4.0 CD-ROM to your server's hard disk, then you should change the source file path so that each time you add a service, adapter, or what not, your default source file location will point to your file server's hard disk. This change may be made via the regedit utility on the "SourcePath" value name found at:

`HKEY_LOCAL_MACHINE\SOFTWARE\Microsoft\Windows NT\CurrentVersion`

You may specify a path to a floppy disk drive, a CD-ROM drive, a network share point such as a shared network directory, or a network resource accessible via the Universal Naming Convention (UNC) path name. An example of a UNC name is `\\SPRINGER01\CABS`, where `SPRINGER01` is the NetBIOS machine name and `CABS` is the directory share name. At this point, the installation program copies all necessary files to the your hard disk.

Because Windows NT Server 4.0 is no longer installed from floppy disks, it's highly unlikely you would ever specify a floppy disk as the path in the dialog box shown in Figure 6-7. To be honest, the last time I installed Windows NT Server from floppy disks was Windows NT Advanced Server 3.1. But be advised, it is just this type of trick question that has been known to appear on MCSE exams!

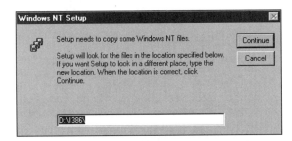

Figure 6-7: Specifying a path to the Windows NT Setup files

Secret

Assuming you are working with an existing Windows NT Server installation and merely adding the TCP/IP protocol to your machine, you can go find your Windows NT Server setup files in the \i386 subdirectory if you've changed what drive this subdirectory is located on.

Here is what I mean. Today drives are divided into many partitions because of the sheer size of hard disks and your preference to organize information by partition. Add a CD-ROM tower or two to your Windows NT Server machine, and you've quickly created a long list of local drive letters. Given this real-world scenario, it's common to forget the path to your CD-ROM-based \i386 subdirectory. Don't laugh! I've done it.

Chapter 6: Installing and Configuring TCP/IP 175

The solution to this forgetfulness? Simply hold the Ctrl+Esc simultaneously so that the Windows NT Server taskbar appears. From the Start button on the taskbar, simply launch Windows NT Explorer from the Programs group and go fish for your \i386 subdirectory. If only the dialog box in Figure 6-7 had a Browse button!

If you are unlucky, you may receive an error message resulting from a failed read from missing or bad media similar to the copy error shown in Figure 6-8.

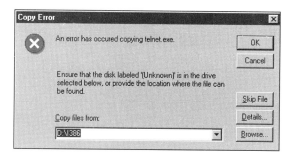

Figure 6-8: A Copy error

This message has appeared under two circumstances. Either the CD-ROM disc containing the \i386 subdirectory has a surface dimple or scratch and is thus defective or you have forgotten to place the CD-ROM disc in the CD-ROM drive. I've seen it both ways.

Step 8. After the TCP/IP protocol files finish copying from the Windows NT Server Setup source directory, click Close at the bottom of the Network properties dialog box. This will cause the TCP/IP protocol stack to bind to the existing network adapter card(s).

Tip

Failure to click the Close button at this stage and any attempt to configure the TCP/IP protocol (either by double-clicking the TCP/IP listing under the Protocols tab sheet or highlighting the TCP/IP protocol and then clicking the Properties button) will result in an error message. This error message will communicate that the TCP/IP protocol is not bound to any adapter and further configuration isn't possible. This problem is solved by simply clicking the Close button as described.

Step 9. Depending on whether you earlier chose to configure TCP/IP manually or to have a DHCP server automatically configure your Windows NT Server machine, you will select one of two forks in the road.

At this point, the easiest path is clearly automatic configuration via the DHCP server. End of story here. Windows NT Server will automatically complete all of the TCP/IP configuration settings.

Continued

STEPS

To install Microsoft TCP/IP *(continued)*

If you decided to manually configure the TCP/IP protocol, you are now presented with the Microsoft TCP/IP Properties dialog box.

Secret

The TCP/IP binding process actually stops at midpoint if you have elected to manually configure TCP/IP.

TCP/IP reaches its midpoint binding juncture as shown in Figure 6-9.

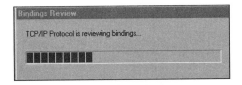

Figure 6-9: The TCP/IP binding midpoint stop

You are then presented with the Microsoft TCP/IP Properties dialog box shown in Figure 6-10.

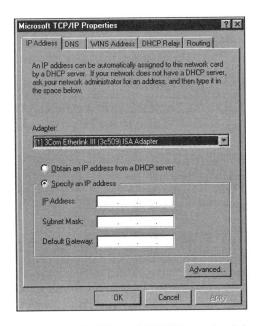

Figure 6-10: The Microsoft TCP/IP Properties dialog box

Configuring TCP/IP

Remember that two cases arise in which you would configure TCP/IP manually on a Windows NT server. First, the server may be a DHCP server, requiring a static IP address. The second (you guessed it) is when you do not acquire your TCP/IP configuration information from a DHCP server. These points are fair game on the Windows NT MCSE exams.

Tip

Because you are now implementing manual TCP/IP configurations, be sure to revisit your network plan or as-built drawings so that you avoid duplicate IP addresses on the same network.

Duplicate addresses will result in the error message shown in Figure 6-11, and you will see unpredictable or downright weird behavior on your network. Typically, the host that had the IP address originally is unimpeded. However, the second host that attempts to assume the same IP address will have no network functionality. The rule regarding duplicate IP addresses? In general, the first host wins and all other hosts trying to use the same IP address lose.

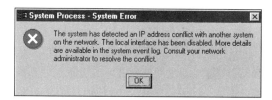

Figure 6-11: The Duplicate IP address error message

STEPS:
To configure TCP/IP manually

Step 1. The Microsoft TCP/IP Properties dialog box (Figure 6-10) is the starting point for manually configuring TCP/IP. As shown previously, this dialog box will automatically appear in a manual configuration scenario when you are installing TCP/IP.

You may also access this dialog box from the Network dialog box (see Figure 6-12). One way to access the Network dialog box is to right-click Network Neighborhood and select Properties. Select Protocols and then select the TCP/IP Protocol listing.

Continued

STEPS

To configure TCP/IP manually (continued)

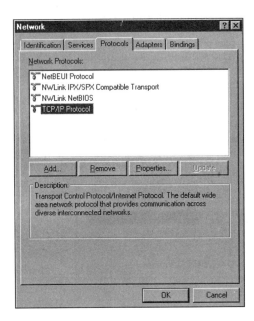

Figure 6-12: The Microsoft TCP/IP protocol in the Network dialog box

Step 2. Either double-click the TCP/IP Protocol listing or select the Properties button when the TCP/IP Protocol listing is selected.

Step 3. Select the IP Address tab sheet (this is the default tab sheet when you open the Microsoft TCP/IP Properties dialog box, regardless of which tab sheet you worked with in a prior session for this dialog box). Select the network adapter that you want to assign IP addresses from the Adapter drop-down list (see Figure 6-13).

All adapters that are "bound" to TCP/IP will appear in the Adapter list. So, you ask, how do you get a newly added network adapter card on an existing Windows NT Server to appear on this list if you haven't yet bound TCP/IP to this new card? Simple. Follow these steps.

First, add the network adapter under the Adapters tab sheet on the Network dialog box. Click the Add button to display the Select Network Adapter dialog box (see Figure 6-14).

Chapter 6: Installing and Configuring TCP/IP

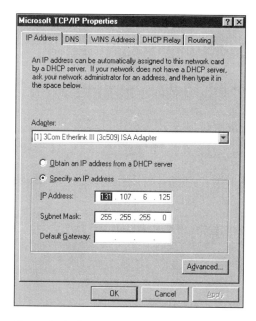

Figure 6-13: Adapter selection in the TCP/IP Properties dialog box

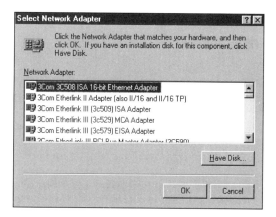

Figure 6-14: Adding an adapter

After providing the obligatory Windows NT Setup source path information, the adapter appears as one of the network adapters (see Figure 6-15). In this case, it is adapter (2) 3Com Fast Etherlink XL Adapter (3C905).

Continued

STEPS

To configure TCP/IP manually *(continued)*

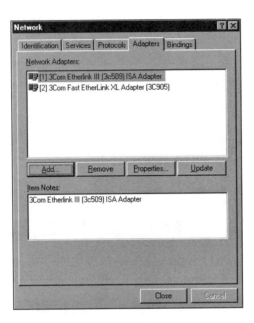

Figure 6-15: Adding an adapter

However, at this point, if you go to the Protocol tab sheet and observe the TCP/IP Properties, you will note that only one adapter appears under the Adapter list. That is because the newly installed adapter hasn't been "bound" to the TCP/IP protocol. This occurs when you select the Close button on the Network dialog box. Once binding occurs, the installed network protocols are bound to the newly installed network adapter card. For TCP/IP, you will be presented with the Microsoft TCP/IP Properties dialog box (Figure 6-13) requesting configuration information.

Step 4. You must set unique IP address information for each bound adapter. Type that value in the IP Address field.

Step 5. You must provide the information required in the Subnet Mask field. As discussed at length in Chapter 5, "TCP/IP Implementations," this information may be any of the items in Table 6-1.

Chapter 6: Installing and Configuring TCP/IP   **181**

Table 6-1   Possible Subnet Mask Values

Class	Value
Class A	255.0.0.0
Class B	255.255.0.0
Class C	255.255.255.0
Other	Appropriate Subnet Mask based on your subnetting scenario (e.g., 255.255.255.240)

Tip

Note for automatic TCP/IP configuration via a DHCP server, you would select the Obtain an IP Address from a DHCP Server radio button in the TCP/IP Properties dialog box.

Step 6. You may or may not provide an IP address value for the Default Gateway field depending on your situation. Here again, it's like tax law: everyone's situation is typically unique. If you are on a single subnet, this is not a required value.

Secret

On the MCSE exams, understand that the Default Gateway value is an optional entry on nonrouted networks.

Single subnet scenarios will typically leave this value blank or insert the IP address value of one of the Windows NT servers. Multiple subnet or "routed" scenarios will typically insert the value of the actual router (for instance, a Cisco router).

Secret

Leaving the Default Gateway value blank doesn't mean that your subnet doesn't participating in a routed network scenario. Routing may occur in other ways: RAS, Microsoft Proxy Server, or the Windows NT Server routing table (via the route command).

Properly configured, RAS can act as a router to the other networks including the Internet. RAS can also do this while acting as a gateway that translates network-based communications between different types of protocols. RAS can even transport data from a fundamentally nonroutable network based on NetBEUI (a nonroutable protocol) to another network such as TCP/IP based on its ability to act as both a router and a gateway. These RAS capabilities were previously discussed in Chapter 3, "Windows NT Server 4.0 Implementation."

Another routing scenario on a Windows NT Server network when the Default Gateway field is left blank occurs when Microsoft Proxy Server is part of the picture. This occurs in two ways. First, when the WinSock Proxy (WSP) client is installed on a client, all Windows Sockets activity or calls are redirected to Microsoft Proxy Server. In English, that means you can leave your default gateway field blank on a client yet have your Internet Explorer browser correctly find a resource on the Internet via Microsoft Proxy Server and a valid Internet connection. In essence, Microsoft Proxy Server is acting as the default gateway via the WSP client configuration and the Proxy Server declaration you make on the Connection tab sheet of Internet Explorer.

A second Microsoft Proxy Server routing scenario relates to the use of the IPX protocol for a client on your internal network and the TCP/IP protocol for your connection to the Internet. Properly configured (be darn sure to read the README and RELEASE NOTES files that ship with Microsoft Proxy Server to correctly implement an IPX client. Trust Me!!!), the IPX-based client directs its Internet communications through Microsoft Proxy Server to the TCP/IP-based Internet. Bingo — routing and gateway functionality all in one.

The route command allows for routing when the Default Gateway field is left blank by enabling you to create static routes between networks. This was discussed previously in Chapter 5, "TCP/IP Implementations."

Secret

Static routes created by the route utility always override the default gateways.

Advanced TCP/IP configurations

Clicking the Advanced button on the Microsoft TCP/IP Properties dialog box will spawn the Advanced IP Addressing dialog box (see Figure 6-16).

Adding IP addresses

This is your opportunity to add multiple IP addresses to an adapter. Truth be told, I've learned the hard way that this is never more than an interim solution or workaround to a specific problem (such as the three I describe later). Regrettably I've found that this feature exposes some of the fundamental weaknesses in the TCP/IP protocol stack in Windows NT Server 4.0. Adding multiple IP addresses to a single adapter "kinda" works but never works as well as adding multiple adapters to the same Windows NT server, each with its own unique IP address. Stated another way, I'd rather have three network adapter cards with three unique IP addresses than one network adapter with three IP addresses assigned to it.

Chapter 6: Installing and Configuring TCP/IP 183

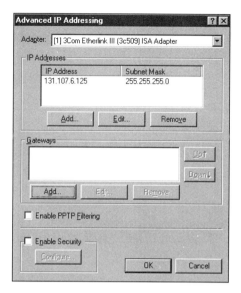

Figure 6-16: Advanced IP addressing

The types of errors that I've encountered when assigning multiple IP addresses to a single adapter range from intermittent network failures such as the inability of clients to access a distributed database that replies heavily on TCP/IP-based communications (such as Windows NT implementations of the Progress database application and its use of the HOSTS file) to the popular refrain "No Domain Controller Found."

Secret

This is a known gotcha on the MCSE exams. Spend an extra few moments in this section understanding why you would or wouldn't assign multiple IP addresses to a single network adapter card.

Why would we ever assign multiple IP addresses to a single network adapter card? For several reasons, all based on TCP/IP encounters that I've had over the years.

Scenario one involves a client that was underengineered and underserved by the previous Internet consultant. Not allowing for growth, the client received a small range of real IP addresses from the consultant. Later, the firm experienced growth and had a second but separate range of real Internet addresses assigned to the site. In order for all of the workstations to see and utilize the Windows NT Server machine, a second IP address from this new range of IP addresses was assigned and bound to the single adapter inside the server (see Figures 6-17 and 6-18).

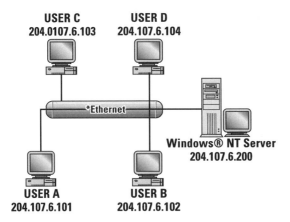

Figure 6-17: A small Windows NT Server network with a single IP address assigned to the server network adapter card

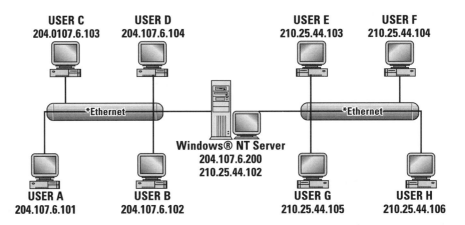

Figure 6-18: A small Windows NT Server network with two IP addresses assigned to the server network adapter card

It didn't work. No sooner was this second address range implemented on the network than I (the newly hired consultant) started to receive service-related calls that User A couldn't browse the Internet, User B's Internet e-mail didn't work, and the Point-of-Sale machine (User H) couldn't write to the Progress database on the Windows NT Server machine. One $80 network adapter later (plus my labor, which of course exceed the price of the network adapter), each subnet had a specific network adapter inside the Windows NT Server machine. And each of these network adapters had only one IP address. Life was good! (Note that I did turn on routing under the Routing tab sheet under TCP/IP Protocol properties. I discuss this feature shortly.)

A follow-up comment to scenario one (just described): Several months later, for a variety of reasons, an effort was made to clean up the split IP address layout. A new ISP was selected that acquired an Internet IP address range that was more than sufficient to accommodate the present and future IP addressing needs for this firm. That allowed the Windows NT Server machine to operate with just one network adapter. Life was really good then!

Scenario two for having multiple IP addresses assigned to the same network adapter card involves network rework. Here a client had a network that, while not incorrectly configured, wasn't (shall we say) optimally configured. This firm had designed a network right out of the Microsoft Official Curriculum (MOC) with "classroom" IP addresses of 131.107.2.2*xx* with a Class C subnet (255.255.255.0). It basically worked until the Cisco router engineer voiced objections to having a Class B range of host addresses associated with a Class C subnet mask. Fair enough. But because I couldn't get to each client machine instantaneously to change its IP address (even via lease assignments with DHCP), I had to "temporarily" assign a second IP address (perhaps 204.107.2.200) to the network adapter inside the Windows NT Server machine.

It worked fine and allowed the clients to log onto the network under either the old IP address range (131.107.2.2*xx*) or the new IP address range (204.107.2.2*xx*). This "temporary" fix of having two IP addresses assigned to the same network adapter on the server was kept in place for just a few days. At that point, the network adapter card inside the Windows NT Server machine assumed just the new IP address. Problem solved, resulting in a happy client and a happy Cisco router engineer.

Scenario three is similar to scenario two. Often, a client will proceed with a TCP/IP-based network installation prior to receiving its "real" IP address assignment from the InterNIC. There are typically compelling business reasons to move ahead without regard for what IP addressing is being used. These reasons, of course, typically involve money, such as an expiring support agreement on an old AS-400 that the client (a) doesn't want to renew and (b) wants to convert to Windows NT Server and the BackOffice applications pronto! In these cases, I've used the dummy IP address range of 10.0.0.*x* while awaiting an IP address assignment (typically Class C) and domain registration from the InterNIC.

Once the real IP address range arrived, I briefly had to support the phony IP address range (10.0.0.*x*) and the real IP address range until each client machine could be properly reconfigured. Again, similar to scenario two, this real-world example underscores the appropriate use of multiple IP addresses assigned to a single network adapter.

To add multiple IP addresses, simply click the Add button and enter the IP address on the screen shown in Figure 6-19.

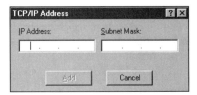

Figure 6-19: Adding TCP/IP addresses

Secret

Clicking anywhere on the Subnet Mask field will automatically populate this entry for you. Thus, you do not need to manually enter the required Subnet Mask value if you are conforming to the traditional Classes A, B, and C host range rules. For example if you entered a 204.107.6.165 as an additional IP address and clicked Add, the Subnet Mask column would already be populated with 255.255.255.0 (the Class C Subnet Mask value). Beware of using unusual combinations of IP address and Subnet Mask values and relying on the automatic Subnet Mask field populate feature. For example, if you were an ardent MCSE student and set up your network exactly like that found in classrooms using the MOC, you would be trouble with the automatic Subnet Mask field populate feature. That's because the MOC setup of 131.107.6.x is a Class B host value but the MOC uses a Class C subnet mask value. Bad news when using the automatic Subnet Mask field populate feature. In this example, you would need to overwrite the default subnet mask value of 255.255.0.0 and insert 255.255.255.0 to truly conform to the MOC class setup guidelines.

I successfully added one dozen TCP/IP values to one network adapter before tiring of the exercise. You can actually add up to 255 IP address to a single network adapter.

However, understand that Microsoft's official position with respect to assigning multiple IP addresses to a single network adapter is useful for a computer connected to one physical network that contains multiple logical IP networks. Enough said.

Multiple gateways

Hang on to your hat. This field isn't even what you think it is. Perhaps you thought this was the holy grail for having a Windows NT Server machine participate on two internetworks simultaneously. This is an increasingly common scenario, illustrated in Figure 6-20, when the corporate LAN may be connected via a Frame Relay–based WAN and the Internet connection is via an ISDN or ADSL/DSL connection from the corporate headquarters.

However, the Gateways field isn't designed to accommodate this routing need. It is designed to create redundant routes on the same internetwork. Thus, defining multiple gateways would be useful for a corporate network that rightfully needs robust WAN connectivity between its sites and is willing to pay for it! The proper use of multiple gateways is shown in Figure 6-21.

Chapter 6: Installing and Configuring TCP/IP **187**

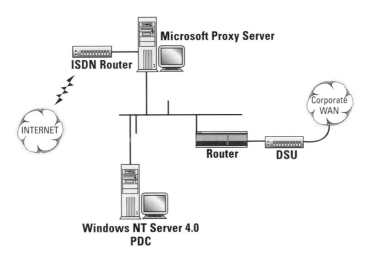

Figure 6-20: Corporate WAN and ISDN Internet connection

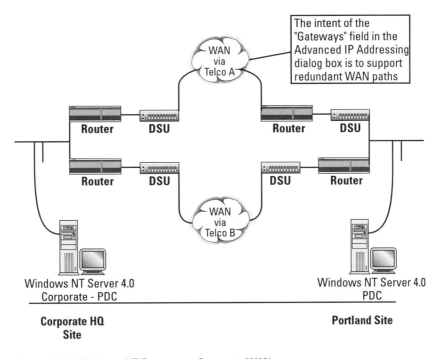

Figure 6-21: Windows NT Server on a Corporate WAN

188   Part II: TCP/IP

Tip

By the way, the solution for the multiple internetwork scenario presented in Figure 6-20 is to create multiple static routes via the route utility. And be sure to make those routes persistent with the –p command line switch (or else you will have to enter the static routes again when you reboot the Windows NT Server machine).

The bottom line on multiple gateways? Properly configured, internetworking communications capabilities are maintained even when transmission problems are occurring because the system will try other routers in the internetwork configuration to ensure success.

Tip

If you use multiple gateway entries, be sure to make use of the Up and Down buttons so that the most appropriate gateway value is evaluated first.

Enable PPTP filtering

Point-to-Point Tunneling Protocol (PPTP) filtering is enabled via this check box on the Advanced IP Addressing dialog box. That means that all other protocols bound to the network adapter are effectively disabled. Only PPTP traffic is allowed. PPTP is discussed in detail in Chapter 10, "Internet Secrets."

Enable security

The TCP/IP Security dialog box enables TCP/IP security (see Figure 6-22). Basically you may further lock down your network by specifying ports that are allowed to pass. Remember that upper-range port values (between 1,024 and 65,536) are available to you for private use and in creating secure sessions. The problem is, similar to a CB radio conversation between two truckers occurring on upper CB channels, all parties participating on your network using TCP/IP security must agree to the specific port values that will be allowed. Be careful here. Although TCP/IP security enables you to control the type of traffic (typically Internet) that actually reaches the network adapter card of your Windows NT server, if these values are incorrectly set, your network can suffer from great havoc!

Other configuration issues

Several additional tab sheets on the Microsoft TCP/IP Properties dialog box need configuring to fully implement the TCP/IP protocol stack.

DNS

DNS, of source, offers robust name resolution for TCP/IP hosts. This lengthy topic is discussed in Chapter 8, "DNS, DHCP, WINS." You should use DNS to better interact with non-Windows network computers such as UNIX and Internet hosts.

Chapter 6: Installing and Configuring TCP/IP

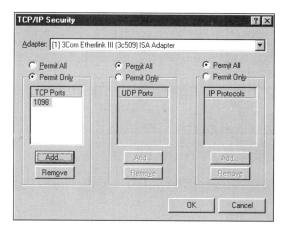

Figure 6-22: Enabling TCP/IP security

Tip

The DNS configurations made on the DNS tab sheet are global. These modifications are not made on a per-network adapter basis, but rather a per-machine basis. The entries that you make here affect all network adapters on your Windows NT Server machine.

STEPS:
To configure TCP/IP DNS connectivity

Step 1. Assuming you have the Network properties dialog box displayed (accessible via Control Panel), Click the Protocols tab sheet and display the properties for the TCP/IP Protocol.

Step 2. In the Microsoft TCP/IP Properties dialog box, select the DNS tab sheet. As shown in Figure 6-23, the DNS dialog box appears.

Step 3. In the DNS dialog box, you may enter the computer name in the Host Name field. This is an optional entry and may be any name you like as long as illegal characters aren't used. To be brutally honest, this is by default the NetBIOS name of the computer, but it can be any name consisting of letters A–Z, numbers 0–9, the hyphen (-), and the period (.). Several utilities, such as HOSTNAME, use this entry in addition to being used by DNS servers that resolve host names to IP addresses.

Continued

STEPS

To configure TCP/IP DNS connectivity (continued)

Figure 6-23: The DNS configuration dialog box

Step 4. You are highly encouraged to make an entry in the Domain field although it is optional for basic LAN operations. However, if you connect to the Internet with your Windows NT Server, this is a critical entry.

Secret

Failure to correctly complete the Domain field will cause the Internet Mail Service (IMS) to fail upon startup in Microsoft Exchange 5.x.

Microsoft Exchange will write out Error #4067 to the Application log in Event Viewer (see Figure 6-24). But you'll probably learn of this "misconfiguration" another way, from the users who complain they don't have Internet e-mail. It seems that users are always your best error log.

Step 5. DNS Service Provider Search Order is a critical field to populate when you are properly implementing your Windows NT Server–based Internet connection. At least two of the entries that you make here will be for DNS servers used by your Internet service provider (ISP). The ISP will provide these values for you, typically in the form of a FAQ on its Web site or an account configuration worksheet.

Chapter 6: Installing and Configuring TCP/IP

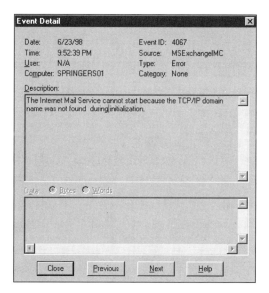

Figure 6-24: A missing TCP/IP domain name error generated by Microsoft Exchange

Secret

You might also make a third entry, for your ISP's SMTP mail server, if you plan to use DNS resolution with the Microsoft Exchange IMS and the SMTP server is separate from the other DNS servers maintained by the ISP. Failing to make the correct entry in the DNS Service Search Order field and electing to use DNS with the IMS may result in message delivery failure to the Internet. In English, get it right and it will work.

> Although Microsoft Exchange is a BackOffice application and Windows NT Server 4.0 is an operating system, this example does serve to demonstrate how BackOffice applications are integrated with the underlying Windows NT Server 4.0 operating system. Figure 6-25 shows one form of such integration with the selection of DNS being used by Microsoft Exchange's IMS.

Step 6. Domain Suffix Search Order is a little-used entry when configuring TCP/IP. You may add up to six domain suffixes such as .com, .edu, .net to aid in name resolution. This is an optional field.

Continued

STEPS

To configure TCP/IP DNS connectivity (continued)

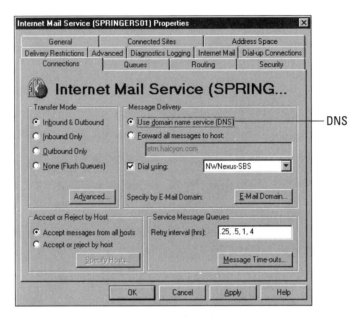

Figure 6-25: The Microsoft Exchange IMS configured to use DNS for message delivery

Finally, with respect to the DNS tab sheet, it is important to recognize that you are merely configuring the DNS client-side to interact with DNS servers. DNS servers are configured differently if they are Windows NT Server–based (through the DNS Service discussed in Chapter 8, "DNS, DHCP, WINS").

WINS addresses

The WINS Addresses tab sheet offers a client-side configuration to allow the machine you are configuring to point to one or more WINS servers. You may make two elections that can dramatically impact how names are resolved. The implicit assumption prior to performing the configurations on this tab sheet is that a WINS server exists on your network.

Chapter 6: Installing and Configuring TCP/IP

STEPS:
To configure or reconfigure TCP/IP to use WINS

Step 1. From the Network dialog box (accessed via Control Panel), click the Protocols tab sheet and select the properties for the TCP/IP Protocol. The Microsoft TCP/IP Properties dialog box will appear.

Step 2. Select the WINS Address tab sheet. The WINS Address dialog box appears as shown in Figure 6-26. Select the adapter card you wish to configure from the Adapter drop-down selection field.

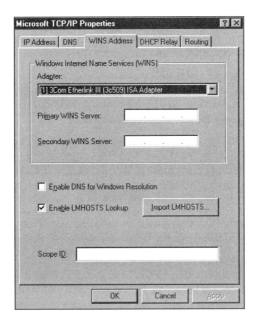

Figure 6-26: The WINS Address dialog box

Step 3. Populate the Primary and Secondary WINS Server fields with the IP addresses for the appropriate WINS servers on your network. Note that having a secondary WINS server typically suggests that you are working with an Enterprise or large-scale Windows NT Server installation.

In the absence of specified addresses for WINS servers, Windows NT Server uses name query broadcast (NetBIOS over TCP/IP b-node mode) and the entries in the local LMHOSTS file to resolve computer names to IP addresses. This causes several issues to surface:

- The names discovered via broadcasts are cached and can be displayed via the nbtstat command (discussed extensively in Chapter 7, "Troubleshooting TCP/IP").

Continued

STEPS

To configure or reconfigure TCP/IP to use WINS *(continued)*

- Windows NT Server cannot broadcast beyond the local network, requiring the use of WINS proxy agents. This is discussed shortly.

- Entries in the LMHOSTS file can be preloaded into the name resolution cache via the #PRE statement. This results in much faster name resolutions because this information is maintained in primary storage (cached in RAM memory) instead of requiring an access to secondary storage (the LMHOSTS file stored on the local hard disk).

- When in doubt, with any name resolution dilemma, by all means feel free to reboot the Windows NT server to update the cached IP to name mappings. A reboot forces a refresh.

- WINS works great in Windows NT Server 4.0 for Microsoft-friendly clients (machines using NetBIOS names) but falls far short in its support for foreign client environments such as Macintosh clients on a Windows NT Server–based network.

- WINS will be supported in Windows 2000 Server for backward compatibility purposes, but the future of IP-to-NetBIOS name resolution rests squarely with Dynamic DNS, one of the new features in Windows 2000 Server. Dynamic DNS is discussed more in Part VII, "Preparing for Windows 2000 Server."

Step 4. To use DNS resolution on your network for name resolution, select the Enable DNS for Windows Resolution check box.

Make sure that you have correctly configured the DNS settings on the DNS tab sheet prior to selecting this command. It is assumed you have correctly identified the DNS servers you intend to use if you select this command. These DNS settings on the DNS tab sheet were discussed previously in this chapter.

In Windows 2000 Server, this type of selection will be the de facto resolution method. That is because Microsoft has signaled the networking community rather strongly via seminars, conferences, white papers, and beta releases that DNS resolution will rule in Windows 2000 Server.

The Enable DNS for Windows Resolution check box can be an extremely dangerous selection to make if you have a direct Internet connection and have configured your DNS tab sheet with the IP addresses for the DNS servers at your ISP.

Here's why: Suppose that you have multiple Exchange servers spanning two or more Windows NT Server domains in your organization. As you may know, Microsoft Exchange makes heavy use of Remote Procedure Calls (RPCs) to communicate between its servers. In order to establish a sessions between two or more Microsoft Exchange servers and commence communications, these servers must find each other.

If you have selected the Enable DNS for Windows Resolution check box, that means one of the name resolution search methods will potentially be to query your ISP's DNS servers for name resolutions. And of course the ISP's DNS servers, unable to resolve the names, turn into DNS forwarders to send the name resolution request up the Internet DNS resolution hierarchy. Well, when this happened to me, I kept running into nasty Exchange RPC session establishment timeout conditions. In English, the Exchange servers never did talk to each other to establish a session. Now admittedly I was working with a dicey connection between my Exchange servers to begin with (for reasons I never did determine), but once I deselected the Enable DNS for Windows Resolution check box and pursued the use of the LMHOSTS file, I was able to eliminate those session establishment timeout conditions and get my Exchange servers talking to each other, which (lest we forget) was the ultimate goal of this exercise.

Step 5. To use the LMHOSTS file, select the Enable LMHOSTS Lookup check box. This is selected by default in Windows NT Server 4.0 when the TCP/IP protocol stack is installed. By default, Windows NT Server uses the LMHOSTS file maintained in the \WINNT\SYSTEM32\DRIVERS\ETC sub-directory. The LMHOSTS file is discussed at length in Chapter 7, "Troubleshooting TCP/IP." Alternate LMHOSTS file locations may be specified via the Import LMHOSTS button.

Step 6. Scope ID. Type the computer's scope identifier if required. To communicate, all computers on a TCP/IP internetwork must have an identical scope ID. The Scope ID identifies information to use if a DNS server is not found for name resolution. If you did not define a scope ID for your internetwork, leave this value blank.

Step 7. Not surprisingly, after you have completed configuring WINS, you will need to reboot your Windows NT Server machine for these changes to be implemented.

DHCP relay

Windows NT Server doesn't officially support the Bootstrap protocol (BOOTP) derived from our brethren in the UNIX community. Instead, Windows NT Server supports DHCP, which is based on BOOTP. While it is interesting to know that BOOTP was originally created for diskless workstations, that discussion is beyond the scope of this book.

Secret

Some third-party vendors interact with Windows NT Server's DHCP implementation as if it were BOOTP. The best example of this is the HP JetDirect card used in HP laser printers. If you want to have an IP address assigned to your HP laser printer automatically, just select the BOOTP option in the TCP/IP configuration section of the robust LCD-based configuration menu on your HP laser printer. Restart the HP laser printer and it will acquire an IP address from the Windows NT server that is running the DHCP Server service on your subnet. Interesting.

In general terms, a Windows NT server running the DHCP Server service may provide IP addresses to clients on distant subnets if the router connecting the subnets is able to act as an RFC 1542 (BOOTP) relay agent. If such is not the case, that is, if your routers don't support this function, then each subnet must have its own DHCP server. It is important to understand that the RFC 1542 functionality must be embedded in your router, as it is not native to Windows NT Server.

Tip

I'll discuss this more in Chapter 8, "DNS, DHCP, WINS," but you'll never go wrong if you adhere to the rule of one DHCP server per subnet.

However, Windows NT Server, lacking the RFC 1542 support discussed, does offer an alternative. It can act as a DHCP relay agent. A DHCP relay agent resides on a client's subnet and captures DHCP/BOOTP broadcasts and forwards these to DHCP servers. This occurs even if these messages are crossing IP routers. In other words, a DHCP relay agent acts as a local proxy for remote DHCP servers.

STEPS:
To configure/reconfigure a DHCP relay agent

Step 1. From the Network dialog box (accessed via Control Panel), click the Protocols tab sheet and select the properties for the TCP/IP Protocol. The Microsoft TCP/IP Properties dialog box will appear.

Step 2. Select the DHCP Relay tab. The DHCP Relay dialog box similar to that shown in Figure 6-27 appears.

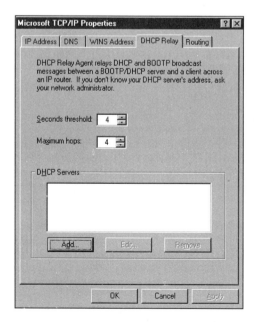

Figure 6-27: The DHCP Relay dialog box

Three settings may be configured in the dialog box:

- **Seconds Threshold.** When the relay agent receives a client message, the relay agent compares the value of the seconds field in the message to the seconds threshold value to determine whether or not the message should be relayed. If the seconds field is greater than or equal to the seconds threshold, the relay agent forwards the message.
- **Maximum Hops.** When the relay agent receive a client message, the relay agent compares the value of the hops field in the message with the maximum hops value to determine whether or not to forward the message. If the hops field is less than or equal to the maximum hops, the relay agent relays the message. By definition, a relay agent is not allowed to relay a message whose hops field exceeds a value of 16.
- **DHCP Servers.** This parameter identifies the server or servers to which you want to relay DHCP/BOOTP messages.

Step 3. To change the value in the Seconds threshold box, select it and type in a new value or click the arrows to select a new value. The default value is 4.

Step 4. To change the value in the Maximum Hops box, select it and type in a new value or click the arrows to select a new value. The default value is 4.

Step 5. Click Add under DHCP Server. The DHCP Relay Agent dialog box appears. In the Domain Server box, type the IP address of a server to which you want to forward DHCP/BOOTP messages. Next, click Add to populate the DHCP Servers list. Repeat the process for any additional server addresses.

Step 6. When you are done modifying DHCP relay options, click OK. If you have not already installed the BOOTP (DHCP) Relay Agent service, you will be prompted to do so now. Otherwise when the Network dialog box reappears, click Close. I highly recommend that you restart your computer for the changes to take effect (remember, always restart Windows NT Server after making significant changes).

Routing

So innocent, so inviting, so seductive. There you sit with a multihomed Windows NT server (contains two or more network adapters each TCP/IP configured to participate on separate subnets) thinking that you've beat Cisco by not having to purchase a bona fide hardware-based router. To some extent you are correct. Having two or more network adapters in a Windows NT server on separate subnets with the Enable IP Forwarding check box selected (see Figure 6-28) will indeed allow you to forward and receive IP packets between the different subnets. In fact, this offers internal routing capabilities very similar to what those of us from the NetWare community enjoyed for years (remember the router command at the NetWare command prompt?).

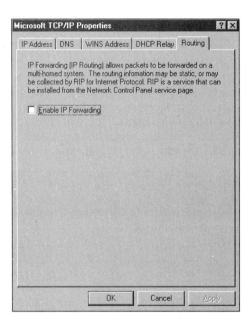

Figure 6-28: The Routing dialog box

Secret

But looks are deceptive. Selecting the Enable IP Forwarding check box may expose you to the comings and going of the Internet. Of course I'm assuming that you have a connection to the Internet from your Windows NT Server machine, an increasingly common configuration.

Here is the danger I speak of. Let's assume that you've correctly installed Microsoft Proxy Server on your Windows NT Server machine and you have two network adapters to create a physical separation zone. Your firewall protection via Microsoft Proxy Server is largely a function of keeping a squeaky clean Local Address Table (LAT) that prevents intruders from penetrating your LAN. However, it is a common configuration error that I've observed at sites running Microsoft Proxy Server to have the Enable IP Forwarding check box selected. That defeats the whole purpose of the LAT-based firewall in Proxy Server. The firewall now has a large hole in it with IP forwarding enabled. What goes out can come back in. Don't be careless with the Enable IP Forwarding check box.

Supporting roving users with TCP/IP

A client showed me this problem that actually applies to the Windows 95 and Windows 98 Registry. He was faced with using real IP addresses at a half dozen athletic clubs that he oversaw. Each athletic club had its own subnet.

One problem was that, because of an older database, static IP addresses (referenced in a HOSTS file) made DHCP addressing impossible. And several managers carried laptops running Windows 95 between the clubs. These static IP addresses resulted in a "No Domain Server Available" message when a user traveled to a distant club with a different subnet and attempted to log on. The solution?

Secret

My client created a *.reg file for each of the six athletic clubs and placed these "reg" files on each user's desktop. The files had names that corresponded to club names, such as ctc.reg and jbc.reg. The contents of the ctc.reg file are:

```
[HKEY_LOCAL_MACHINE\System\CurrentControlSet\Services\Class\
NetTrans\0001
"IPAddress" = "209.34.123.156"
"DefaultGateway" = "209.34.123.145"
"IPMask" = "255.255.255.240"
```

Each user, by double-clicking the appropriate *.reg file, changes the IP address information on the Windows 95 laptop and so is able to participate fully on the club's network. Again, the Registry entry, via the *.reg file approach, applies to Windows 95 and Windows 98. But in reality, it's an issue that you will confront when managing TCP/IP on your Windows NT Server network.

Installing and Configuring Simple Network Management Protocol (SNMP)

One of the reasons I so enjoy my interactions with business people is that they, in the course of our conversations, help keep me grounded in reality. Whereas I'm most excited about some of the advanced and powerful features of Windows NT Server 4.0, my business brethren view technology simply as a tool. The average business person just wants to run his business better. If I can help him do so with my tool set, including Windows NT Server 4.0, so much the better.

For your part, you might view SNMP as a tool to help you run your network better. In fact, you might not be concerned about the finer points of SNMP but more interested in its management reporting capabilities. Most likely, you just want to know when something is wrong with your network. For you, SNMP is a great place to start.

In the real world, SNMP has become the accepted standard for managing network devices. HP Open View, CA UniCenter TNG, and other management system tools rely on SNMP not only to gather network device information but also to manage and configure these devices. The bottom line on SNMP in general: its power and flexibility to monitor and control networks. This is accomplished by its distributed architecture with basically two components, the management system (like the third-party products mentioned previously) and agents.

The bottom line on SNMP with Windows NT Server 4.0: loser. Natively, Windows NT Server 4.0 doesn't utilize SNMP at any great level of depth. The only thing a Windows NT server may do running the SNMP service (without any enhancements) is to report its status to an SNMP management system on a TCP/IP network.

Secret

In other words, the Windows NT Server SNMP service is merely an SNMP agent. SNMP agents may only initiate trap operations. You may or may not know that a trap operation alerts management systems to events such as logon failure due to password violations. Microsoft's SNMP service is not natively an SNMP management system. To be one, it would have to be running SNMP management software (such as HP Open View).

This disappointment extends even to Microsoft System Management Server (SMS), a network management application that is included as part of Microsoft BackOffice (SMS is a popular management tool for Enterprise-level implementations of Windows NT Server). In fact, if you've taken the MCSE course on SMS, you will recall that SMS doesn't even use SNMP to gather network information. It is the one Microsoft application that you would expect to do so. Nope! SMS gathers network information via SMS agents that run on end user workstations (including Macintosh) and other servers.

The only interaction between SMS and SNMP is at the Management Information Base (MIB) level. The configuration information from SNMP-compliant hosts running SNMP agents can be displayed via the "Event to Trap Translator" in SMS. That is, you may, in a read-only fashion, view SNMP agent configuration information on your TCP/IP network. You may not actually manage the SNMP nodes from either SMS or Windows NT Server 4.0 itself.

The only thing SNMP is really good for out of the box is to provide, as I've mentioned in passing previously, additional TCP/IP-related object:counters in Performance Monitor. Its value increases greatly when used in conjunction with third-party solutions such as HP Open View and CA UniCenter. But alone, SNMP on Windows NT Server 4.0 isn't much to write home about.

Architecturally speaking, the SNMP service runs at the application layer of the OSI model. Descending through Windows Sockets, the SNMP service uses UDP, not TCP, as its transport layer protocol (you will recall that UDP is a connectionless, nonguaranteed connection mechanism).

Secret

If you are interested in developing for SNMP in Windows NT Server, you are best advised to contact the Microsoft Developer's Resource Group at netman@microsoft.com.

Planning for SNMP

Make sure that you've covered these three areas prior to installing the SNMP service:

1. Have the IP addresses or host names for all hosts that will send SNMP traps.

Chapter 6: Installing and Configuring TCP/IP **201**

2. Be sure that the Windows NT Server name resolution methods you are utilizing have the IP/host name mappings for all SNMP hosts on your network. For example, if you were using the LMHOSTS file, you would manually make these name resolution mapping entries.

3. Select an SNMP management system. To properly utilize the Microsoft SNMP service, you must have at least one SNMP management system.

Installing SNMP service

Installing the Simple Network Management Protocol (SNMP) service is very simple. It is installed, as are other services, via the Network Applet Services tab. To successfully install the SNMP service, you will need to be logged on as a member of the Administrators group.

STEPS:
To install SNMP

Step 1. Launch the Network applet from Control Panel or Properties on the Network Neighborhood secondary menu.

Step 2. Select the Service tab in the Network dialog box. Click Add to display the Select Network Service dialog box, shown in Figure 6-29.

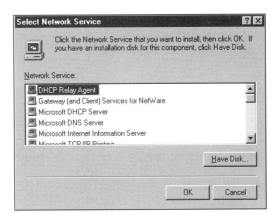

Figure 6-29: The Select Network Service dialog box

Continued

STEPS

To install SNMP *(continued)*

Step 3. Select SNMP Service under Network Services and click OK.

Step 4. When Windows NT Setup requests the full path to the Windows NT distribution files, provide this information and click Continue. The necessary files are copied to your hard disk, and the Microsoft SNMP Properties dialog box is displayed.

Configuring the SNMP agent

First you are asked to provide user contact and physical location information when presented with the default Agent tab sheet view of the Microsoft SNMP Properties dialog box. You will also elect what types of services may be reported based on the computer's SNMP Agent configuration.

Remember that as you manage your Windows NT Server–based network, you will have plenty of opportunities to provide user and location information. Aside from the SNMP Agent configuration, you will have the chance to provide similar information when creating a user in Microsoft Exchange and when Microsoft System Management Server performs a hardware inventory at a client machine (and creates an MIF file).

The reason I share this observation is that one of the underlying principles of database management is the creation and maintenance of a single table for certain data types. Just something to think about as you complete the SNMP Agent configuration.

The SNMP configuration information identifies communities and trap destinations:

- Community name. Much as the name implies, an SNMP community is a grouping of hosts running the SNMP service. Not surprisingly, communities are identified by a community name. An SNMP community is akin to a domain in Windows NT Server, an organization in Microsoft Exchange, or a site in SMS. And like local security in SQL Server, an SNMP community name provides basic security and context checking for agents and management systems that receive requests/initiate traps and initiate requests/receive traps respectively. The community name is embedded in the SNMP packet when the trap is sent.

- When the SNMP service receives a request for information that does not contain the correct community name and does not match an accepted host name for the service, the SNMP service can send a trap to the trap destination(s), indicating that the request failed authentication.

- Trap destinations are the names or IP addresses of hosts to which you want the SNMP service to send traps with the selected community name.

Chapter 6: Installing and Configuring TCP/IP

You might want to use SNMP for statistics but may not care about identifying communities or traps. In this case, you can specify the "public" community name when you configure the SNMP service.

STEPS:
To configure SNMP agent information

Step 1. In the Microsoft SNMP Properties dialog box, choose the Agent tab (see Figure 6-30).

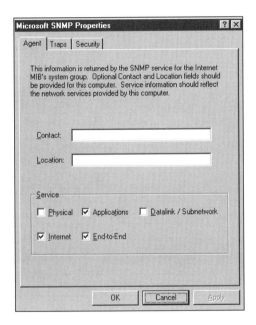

Figure 6-30: The Agent dialog box

Step 2. Type the computer user's name in the Contact box and the computer's physical location in the Location box. These comments are treated as text and are optional.

Step 3. Set the services options as described in Table 6-2. Check all the boxes that indicate network capabilities provided by your Windows NT computer. SNMP must have this information to manage enabled services.

If you have installed additional TCP/IP network devices, such as a switch or a router, you should consult RFC 1213 for additional information, as these configurations are beyond the scope of this book.

Continued

STEPS

To configure SNMP agent information *(continued)*

Step 4. Go on to configure SNMP Traps and Security information and after you complete all procedures, choose the OK button. There are several SNMP-specific services to select as seen in Table 6-2. When the Network Services dialog box reappears, choose the Close button. The SNMP service and SNMP security are ready to start without rebooting the computer, but don't you believe that for a moment. When making such changes to the underlying network service, always reboot your Windows NT Server computer to ensure proper binding.

Table 6-2 SNMP Services

Option	Description
Physical	Select this option if this Windows NT computer manages any physical TCP/IP device, such as a repeater.
Applications	Select this option if this Windows NT computer includes any applications that use TCP/IP, such as electronic mail. This option should be selected for all Windows NT installations.
Datalink/Subnetwork	Select this option if this Windows NT computer manages a TCP/IP subnetwork or datalink, such as a bridge.
Internet	Select this option if this Windows NT computer acts as an IP gateway.
End-to-end	Select this option if this Windows NT computer acts as an IP host. This option should be selected for all Windows NT installations.

Configuring SNMP communities and traps

Two necessary configurations for the SNMP service are community names and traps. Both of these configurations are set with the Traps tab sheet, as the next several steps will show you.

Chapter 6: Installing and Configuring TCP/IP

STEPS:

To Configure SNMP traps

Step 1. In the Microsoft SNMP Properties dialog box, choose the Traps tab. The Traps dialog box appears, as shown in Figure 6-31.

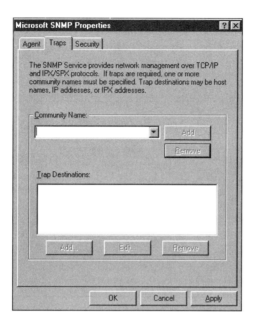

Figure 6-31: The Traps dialog box

Step 2. To identify each community to which you want this computer to send traps, enter the name in the Community Name box. After typing each name, choose the Add button to move the name to the Send Trap with Community Name list.

Typically all hosts belong to public, which is the common name of all hosts. To delete an entry in the list, select it and choose the Remove button.

Secret

An SNMP agent may be a member of multiple communities simultaneously allowing communications with SNMP managers from different communities. Note that community names are case sensitive.

Continued

> **STEPS:**
>
> To Configure SNMP traps *(continued)*
>
> **Step 3.** To specify hosts for each community to which you send traps, after you have added the community and while it is still highlighted, click Add under the Trap Destinations box. The Service Configuration dialog box appears. Enter a host name, its IP address, or its IPX address in the IP Host or IP Address field. Then choose the Add button to move the host name or IP address to the Trap Destination for the Selected Community list.

Configuring SNMP security

SNMP security allows you to specify the communities and hosts from which a computer accepts requests and to specify whether to send an authentication trap when an unauthorized community or host requests information.

> **STEPS:**
>
> To configure SNMP security
>
> **Step 1.** In the Microsoft SNMP Properties dialog box, choose the Securities tab. The SNMP Security dialog box appears as shown in Figure 6-32.
>
> **Step 2.** If you want to send a trap for failed authentication, select the Send Authentication Trap check box.
>
> **Step 3.** In the Accepted Community Names box, click the Add button. The Security Configuration dialog box appears. Type the community name you want to accept requests from. Click Add to move the name to the Accepted Community Names list.
>
> A host must belong to a community that appears on this list for the SNMP service to accept its requests. Typically, all hosts belong to public, which is the standard name for the common community of all hosts. To delete an entry in the list, select it and choose the Remove button.

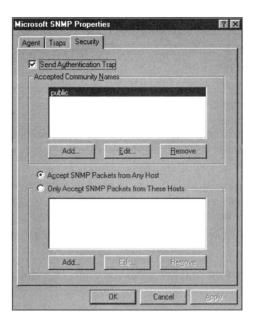

Figure 6-32: The Security dialog box

Step 4. Specify whether to accept SNMP packets from any host or from only specified hosts.

- If the Accept SNMP Packets from Any Host option is selected, no SNMP packets are rejected on the basis of source host ID. The list of hosts under Only Accept SNMP Packets from These Hosts has no effect.

- If the Only Accept SNMP Packets from These Hosts option is selected, SNMP packets are accepted only from the hosts listed. Click Add to display the IP Host or IPX Address dialog box. Then type the host names, IP addresses, or IPX addresses of the hosts from which you want to accept requests. Next choose the Add button to move each host name or IP address to the list box. To delete an entry in the list, select it and choose the Remove button.

Step 5. Choose the OK button. The Network Properties box reappears.

Step 6. When the Network dialog box reappears, choose the Close button. The SNMP service and SNMP security are ready to go at this point without rebooting; however, it is highly recommended that you reboot nonetheless.

TCP/IP-Related Services

This chapter ends with a quick review of TCP/IP-related services that may be installed via Network applet. Having read this chapter and installed and worked with TCP/IP, you're now ready to add more services as needed.

Tip

However, remember that you should never add more services than necessary. Not only do unnecessary services take up precious RAM but it has been my personal experience that, poorly implemented, additional Windows NT Server services can lead to poor performance and even unexplained blue screens. Use only what you need!

The way to extend and take advantage of all that TCP/IP has to offer isn't necessarily to type IP addresses into a dialog box all day. Rather, you extend TCP/IP on your Windows NT Server network by considering whether the services listed in Table 6-3 enable you to run your network better.

Table 6-3   TCP/IP-Related Services

Service	Description
Microsoft Internet Information Server	Microsoft Internet Information Server 3.0 is a BackOffice application that provides Web connectivity and Web page hosting, managing other features. This is considered a must-add in that the management of Internet and intranet Web sites is now standard operating procedure with Windows NT Server.
DHCP Relay Agent	The DHCP relay agent passes DHCP packets from one subnet to another. See Chapter 8, "DNS, DHCP, WINS," for more information. Conforms to the RFC 1542 specification.
Microsoft DHCP Server	Automatically configures TCP/IP on clients including Windows NT, Windows 95/98, Windows for Workgroups, and Windows 3.11.
Windows Internet Name Service (WINS)	Used for dynamically registering and querying NetBIOS computer names on an internetwork.
Microsoft DNS Server	Domain Name Service (DNS) registers and queries DNS domain names on an internetwork.
Microsoft TCP/IP Printing	Implements the LPD printing service for accessing printers connected to UNIX-based computers. Note that this option must be installed if you want to use the Lpdsvr service so that UNIX computers can print to Windows NT printers. Note that discussion of this service has appeared on MCSE certification exams.
RIP for Internet Protocol	This service is necessary to enable routing via the TCP/IP protocol (found under TCP/IP Properties on the Network applet). Routing was discussed earlier in this chapter.

Service	Description
Simple TCP/IP Services	Provides the client software for the Character Generator, Daytime Discard, Echo, and Quote of the Day services. Select this option to allow this computer to respond to requests from other systems that support these protocols.
SNMP Service	As discussed in this chapter, this service for the Simple Network Management Protocol installs SNMP agent software on the local Windows NT Server. SNMP Service also adds several robust TCP/IP object:counters visible under Performance Monitor.

Summary

In this chapter, TCP/IP was installed and configured for use on a Windows NT Server network. The following were covered:

- Installing TCP/IP
- Configuring TCP/IP
- Configuring additional TCP/IP services

Chapter 7
Troubleshooting TCP/IP

In This Chapter

- Troubleshooting TCP/IP in Windows NT Server 4.0
- TCP/IP troubleshooting steps
- Defining which is the best TCP/IP troubleshooting tool to solve your problem
- Mastering basic TCP/IP utilities

Troubleshooting is, it seems, an exercise in matrix mathematics. That is, we use a variety of approaches and influences to successfully solve our problems. These approaches may include structured methodologies, inductive and deductive reasoning, common sense, experience, and luck. And this is what troubleshooting is made of.

Troubleshooting TCP/IP problems is really no different from troubleshooting other Windows NT Server 4.0 problems. Needless to say, Windows NT Server 4.0 offers several TCP/IP-related tools and utilities to assist us, but more on the specifics in a moment.

TCP/IP Troubleshooting Basics

The goal in TCP/IP troubleshooting is very simple: fix the problem. Too often, it is easy to become overly concerned about why something happened instead of just fixing the problem. And by fixing the problem, I mean cost effectively.

1. **Be cost-effective.** Don't forget that several hours of MCSE-level consulting time can more than pay for the additional bandwidth that may easily solve your TCP/IP WAN-related problem. Don't overlook such an easy fix when struggling to make a WAN connection between sites utilizing Windows NT Server 4.0. Too little bandwidth is typically the result of thinking pennywise and pound foolish. Oh, it also causes nasty timeout conditions that can wreak havoc on your TCP/IP-based network.

2. **Experience is the best teacher.** One of the more challenging corporate training assignments I frequently face is when I'm asked to deliver, over a few days, a custom TCP/IP and Windows NT Server 4.0 troubleshooting

session. The challenge is this: I'm not sure I can teach troubleshooting. It's really just something you do and you're ultimately skilled at or not. The good news is that TCP/IP troubleshooting is heavily experienced-based. The more time on the keyboard you put in ("stick time"), the better you will do.

3. **Use inductive reasoning.** Microsoft officially recommends pursuing a TCP/IP troubleshooting strategy of working from the bottom up. This is so that you may isolate a problem. Such an approach is also known as induction or inductive reasoning, which *Webster's New World Dictionary* defines as "a bringing forward of separate facts or instances, esp. so as to prove a general statement." This mindset is largely the basis for this chapter, as individual tools and utilities will be discussed that in reality would be used independently to solve a larger TCP/IP-related problem.

   In contrast, deductive reasoning is really better suited for the Windows NT server developers in feature-set brainstorming sessions where the whole idea is to come up with great new features and then work down to the implementation specifics. *Webster's* defines deduction as "Logic — the act or process of deducing; reasoning from a known principle to an unknown, from a general to the specific."

4. **Use the in-house help.** Many wonderful tools are included in Windows NT Server 4.0 for use in your TCP/IP troubleshooting efforts. These include native commands and utilities such as IPConfig and ping that will be reviewed in this chapter. And given that Windows NT Server 4.0 is often bundled with the full version of BackOffice, don't forget the full-featured version of Network Monitor included in Microsoft Systems Management Server (SMS). You will recall that tools such as Network Monitor were discussed at length in Part VI of this book, "Optimizing and Troubleshooting Windows NT Server 4.0."

5. **Don't forget third-party tools.** Not surprisingly, a wide range of third-party TCP/IP troubleshooting tools are available to assist you. One favorite that will be discussed in Chapter 11, "The Daily Dozen," is Ping Plotter, a low-cost shareware application from Richard Ness at Nessoft (). This application tests ping connectivity and measures ping performance across WAN hops.

6. **Always reboot.** Last and certainly not least, you must always reboot when modifying anything related to the TCP/IP protocol stack in Windows NT Server 4.0. Even though the "stack" has improved dramatically, I still inherently don't trust it completely. In my eyes, there is nothing like a complete reboot where you shut the computer down for 15 seconds after you've modified any TCP/IP protocol settings. And it's an easy lesson to overlook! Here's why. Let's assume you switch your IP address from a dynamic DHCP-assigned address to a static IP address. So far so good. But if at this moment, you run the IPConfig command that reports basic TCP/IP configuration information (discussed later in this chapter), you will note that the TCP/IP configuration information reports the new, updated IP address as if it were properly bound to the network adapter. Don't you believe it for a minute! Always reboot.

Secret

In fact, if you want my $59.95 advice, I'd highly recommend you follow Step Zero and that is to completely cold-reboot your Windows NT Server prior to concluding you have any problems with TCP/IP. Don't ask me why, but I've seen many Windows NT Server 4.0 TCP/IP-related gremlins disappear this way. And that's something you won't read about in the official MCSE study guides. Trust me.

First Step: Ask the Basic Questions

So where do you go from here? Remember that troubleshooting any problem is a function of asking enough questions. Here is a short list of questions you can start your TCP/IP troubleshooting journey with. It is by no means inclusive:

- What's working?
- What's not working?
- What is the relationship between those things that work and those things that don't work? Is there any such relationship?
- Did the things that now do not work *ever* work on this computer or network?
- If the answer is yes, what has changed since they last worked?

You can ask more specific questions in your quest to resolve your TCP/IP problems. These questions are presented and answered at the end of the chapter.

Second Step: Define the Tools

Having completed this first step, you're ready to begin troubleshooting TCP/IP in Windows NT Server 4.0. Table 7-1 provides a list of TCP/IP diagnostic utilities and troubleshooting tools, many of which will be discussed further in this chapter.

Table 7-1 Windows NT Server 4.0 TCP/IP Troubleshooting Tools and Utilities

Utility/Tool	Description
ARP	Address Resolution Protocol. Enables you to view local computer ARP table entries to detect invalid entries.
Hostname	Typing this at the command line returns the current host name of the local computer.
IPConfig	Current TCP/IP information is displayed. Command line switches enable you to release and/or renew your IP address.

Continued

Table 7-1 *(continued)*

Utility/Tool	Description
Nbtstat	Connections using NetBIOS over TCP/IP and protocol statistics are displayed. The LMHOSTS cache is updated (purged and reloaded).
Netstat	Active TCP/IP connections are displayed in addition to TCP/IP statistics.
Nslookup	Internet domain name servers are queried and record, domain host aliases, domain host services, and operating system information is returned.
Ping	Packet Internet Gopher. Tests connections and verifies configurations.
Route	Displays, prints, or modifies a local routing table.
Tracert	Checks the route from the local to a remote system.
FTP	File Transfer Protocol. This tool is used for two-way file transfers between hosts.
TFTP	Trivial File Transfer Protocol. Provides another form of two-way file transfer between hosts. Typically used when one host demands TFTP. I've used this in conjunction with router configuration and troubleshooting scenarios.
Telnet	Is a basic terminal emulation program that establishes a session with another TCP/IP host running a Telnet host.
RCP	Remote Copy Protocol. Enables you to copy files between TCP/IP-based hosts.
RSH	Remote Shell. Enables you to be authenticated by and run UNIX commands on a remote UNIX host.
REXEC	Enables you to be authenticated by and run processes on a remote computer.
Finger	System information is retrieved from a remote computer running TCP/IP and supporting the Finger command.
Microsoft Internet Explorer	The browser is used for locating information and retrieving resources from the Internet.

Two important TCP/IP-related "tools" that are missing in Windows NT Server 4.0 are native NFS client support and the whois command. For NFS client support, as discussed in Part VI of this book, "Optimizing and Troubleshooting Windows NT Server 4.0," check with NetManage or WRQ, two independent software vendors that provider NFS client solutions for Windows NT Server 4.0.

Typing **whois** at the Windows NT Server 4.0 command line results in the following error message:

```
'whois' is not recognized as an internal or external command, operable
program or batch file.
```

In a moment, in the Telnet discussion, I will share a secret for using the whois command with Windows NT Server 4.0.

Before going any further, it is important to establish your troubleshooting paradigm. Consider the following as you work with TCP/IP and read the remainder of this chapter. These are considered TCP/IP diagnostic commands: arp, hostname, IPConfig, nbtstat, netstat, ping, route, and tracert. These are considered connectivity commands: Finger, FTP, rcp, rexec, rsh, Telnet, and TFTP.

Secret

Did you know that FTP, rexec, and Telnet not only use but rely on clear-text passwords in a Windows NT scenario? That's a huge departure from Windows NT Server's basic reliance on encrypted password–based security. Be sure to think about this little fact the next time you use these tools.

Third Step: Use the Tools

Now the details. Having read of the TCP/IP troubleshooting tools and utilities found in Windows NT Server 4.0, you're now ready to learn the finer points. This section includes an array of TCP/IP tools including:

- IPConfig
- ping
- arp
- nbtstat
- route
- netstat
- tracert
- hostname
- FTP
- TFTP
- Telnet
- rcp
- rsh
- rexec
- Finger
- Microsoft Internet Explorer

But before using the tools, I want to spend a moment discussing how to "learn" the variables, command line entries, and switches associated with each tool.

Secret

The next several pages detail each of the suggested TCP/IP tools and utilities you may use in your troubleshooting efforts. Don't forget that you may "capture" any command line details in Windows NT Server 4.0 by redirecting the screen output to a text file. This is accomplished by appending your command line statement with the pipe or mathematical greater than sign (>). Observe:

```
C:\> dir >foo.txt
```

This command would direct the directory contents listing to the file foo.txt. That is a file that could easily be read in Notepad or another text editor. And be sure to use a filename without spaces when you redirect screen output to a text file. If you took the preceding example and directed the output to the filename "foo one.txt," unfortunately it would be stored under Windows NT Server 4.0 as "foo" with no additional attributes such as the ".txt" extension. That's problematic when you've created output with similar names such as "foo.txt" and "foo one.txt." Later when you try to open your important output with Notepad or WordPad, the filenames look nearly identical.

Be careful when naming your output files from the command line. Be sure to use contiguous filenames such as "fooone.txt" to distinguish your filenames. Otherwise, as shown in Figure 7-1, the filenames are difficult to separate.

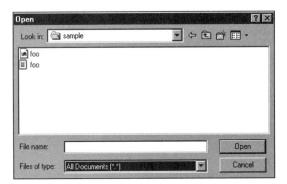

Figure 7-1: Incorrect naming of output files

IPConfig

The IPConfig command line utility provides a baseline view of where your system is at with respect to TCP/IP. Host TCP/IP connection parameters are verified, and you may observe whether the TCP/IP configuration has properly initialized. It is a good first step to take because it enables us to check the TCP/IP configuration on the computer having the alleged problem.

Chapter 7: Troubleshooting TCP/IP

There are several variations of the IPConfig command. These are implemented as command line switches:

```
Windows NT IP Configuration
USAGE:     ipconfig [/? | /all | /release [adapter] | /renew
[adapter]]     adapter    Full name or pattern with '*' and '?' to
'match',                  * matches any character, ? matches one
character.
Options
/?       Display this help message.
/all     Display full configuration information.
/release Release the IP address for the specified adapter.
/renew   Renew the IP address for the specified adapter.
/flushdns Purges the DNS Resolver cache.
```

The default is to display only the IP address, subnet mask, and default gateway for each adapter bound to TCP/IP. For Release and Renew, if no adapter name is specified, then the IP address leases for all adapters bound to TCP/IP will be released or renewed:

```
Examples:
> ipconfig                          ... Show information.
> ipconfig /all                     ... Show detailed information
> ipconfig /renew                   ... renew all adapters
> ipconfig /renew EL*               ... renew adapters named EL....
> ipconfig /release *ELINK?21*      ... release all matching adapters,
               eg. ELINK-21, myELELINKi21adapter.
```

Tip

The most robust view of IPConfig is with the /all switch. Information for each physically bound network adapter card, modem connections, and even virtual bindings are displayed:

```
Windows NT IP Configuration
    Node Type . . . . . . . . . : Broadcast
    IP Routing Enabled. . . . . : No
    WINS Proxy Enabled. . . . . : No
PPP adapter NDISWANIPIN:
    Host Name . . . . . . . . . : SECRETS2
    DNS Servers . . . . . . . . :
    Description . . . . . . . . : WAN (PPP/SLIP) Interfacet
    Physical Address. . . . . . : 00-53-45-00-00-00
    DHCP Enabled. . . . . . . . : No
    Autoconfiguration Enabled . : Yes
    IP Address. . . . . . . . . : 0.0.0.0
    Subnet Mask . . . . . . . . : 255.255.255.255
    Default Gateway . . . . . . :
PPP adapter NDISWANIPOUT{50DA9B43-18E3-11D2-AFF9-EFE843E45279}:
    Host Name . . . . . . . . . : SECRETS2
    DNS Servers . . . . . . . . :
    Description . . . . . . . . : WAN (PPP/SLIP) Interface
    Physical Address. . . . . . : 00-53-45-00-00-00
    DHCP Enabled. . . . . . . . : No
    Autoconfiguration Enabled . : Yes
    IP Address. . . . . . . . . : 0.0.0.0
```

```
        Subnet Mask . . . . . . . . : 255.255.255.255
        Default Gateway . . . . . . :
PPP adapter NDISWANIPOUT{50DA9B44-18E3-11D2-AFF9-EFE843E45279}:
        Host Name . . . . . . . . . : SECRETS2
        DNS Servers . . . . . . . . :
        Description . . . . . . . . : WAN (PPP/SLIP) Interface
        Physical Address. . . . . . : 00-53-45-00-00-00
        DHCP Enabled. . . . . . . . : No
        Autoconfiguration Enabled . : Yes
        IP Address. . . . . . . . . : 0.0.0.0
        Subnet Mask . . . . . . . . : 255.255.255.255
        Default Gateway . . . . . . :
PPP adapter NDISWANIPOUT{50DA9B45-18E3-11D2-AFF9-EFE843E45279}:
        Host Name . . . . . . . . . : SECRETS2
        DNS Servers . . . . . . . . :
        Description . . . . . . . . : WAN (PPP/SLIP) Interfacet
        Physical Address. . . . . . : 00-53-45-00-00-00
        DHCP Enabled. . . . . . . . : No
        Autoconfiguration Enabled . : Yes
        IP Address. . . . . . . . . : 0.0.0.0
        Subnet Mask . . . . . . . . : 0.0.0.0
        Default Gateway . . . . . . :
Ethernet adapter Local Area Connection(2):
        Host Name . . . . . . . . . : SECRETS2
        DNS Servers . . . . . . . . :
        Description . . . . . . . . : ELNK3 Ethernet Adapter
        Physical Address. . . . . . : 00-60-97-BF-A1-23
        DHCP Enabled. . . . . . . . : No
        Autoconfiguration Enabled . : Yes
        IP Address. . . . . . . . . : 131.107.6.171
        Subnet Mask . . . . . . . . : 255.255.255.0
        Default Gateway . . . . . . :
Ethernet adapter Local Area Connection:
        Host Name . . . . . . . . . : SECRETS2
        DNS Servers . . . . . . . . :
        Description . . . . . . . . : 3Com 3C90x Ethernet Adapter
        Physical Address. . . . . . : 00-60-08-3A-04-CB
        DHCP Enabled. . . . . . . . : No
        Autoconfiguration Enabled . : Yes
        IP Address. . . . . . . . . : 10.0.0.2
        Subnet Mask . . . . . . . . : 255.0.0.0
        Default Gateway . . . . . . :
```

When interpreting this IPConfig output, you can decipher whether a duplicate IP address has been configured. If the subnet mask appears as 0.0.0.0 for a particular IP address, that indicates that said address is a duplicate IP address. Likewise, if you dynamically assign IP addresses to your network via DHCP, you can determine if your network adapter was unable to obtain an IP address. This is observed when the IP address appears as 0.0.0.0.

Take that last point to heart. Most problems I can recall having with TCP/IP on a Windows NT network center on the duplicate or unobtainable IP addresses. Hopefully, you can avoid such a fate.

Chapter 7: Troubleshooting TCP/IP   219

Tip

Don't forget to make use of "|more" when executing the IPConfig command at the Windows NT Server 4.0 command line. Otherwise the TCP/IP information will rapidly scroll past without stopping, causing you to miskey TCP/IP configuration information. This command is especially critical when the /all switch is used with the IPConfig command and lots and lots of important TCP/IP configuration information is displayed.

If your system reports appropriate TCP/IP configuration and connection information, such as that displayed previously, proceed to using the ping command.

Tip

Remember that Windows 95/98 uses the winipcfg command in place of the IPConfig command. That distinction is important for both the MCSE certification exams and working with client and server operating systems in the field.

PING

Assuming you've successfully executed and interpreted the preceding IPConfig command, you're ready to employ the ping command. Ping is my friend. It's a low-level command that anyone can execute, and thus it's a command that I ask clients to try while I'm performing over-the-telephone diagnosis. The answer to whether you have ping connectivity is either yes or no.

In layperson's terms, ping is used to diagnose connection-related failures. By executing the ping command, you can determine whether a particular TCP/IP-based host is available and responding in a nondysfunctional manner.

Technically, the ping command is transmitting Internet Control Message Protocol (ICMP) packets between two TCP/IP-based hosts. Remember that ICMP relates to session management and special communications between hosts. With ICMP, messages and errors regarding packet delivery are reported. Great stuff!

The ping command has several command line switches that increase its functionality. These switches, listed here, may be observed by typing **ping /?** at the command line:

```
Usage: ping [-t] [-a] [-n count] [-l size] [-f] [-i TTL] [-v TOS]
            [-r count] [-s count] [[-j host-list] | [-k host-list]]
            [-w timeout] destination-list
Options:
    -t             Ping the specified host until stopped.
                   To see statistics and continue - type Control-
Break;
                   To stop - type Control-C.
    -a             Resolve addresses to hostnames.
    -n count       Number of echo requests to send.
    -l size        Send buffer size.
    -f             Set Don't Fragment flag in packet.
    -i TTL         Time To Live.
    -v TOS         Type Of Service.
    -r count       Record route for count hops.
```

```
-s count      Timestamp for count hops.
-j host-list  Loose source route along host-list.
-k host-list  Strict source route along host-list.
-w timeout    Timeout in milliseconds to wait for each reply.
```

Typing the basic ping command followed by a host IP address results in the following information, which indicates that basic, low-level TCP/IP connectivity has been established:

```
Pinging 131.107.6.123 with 32 bytes of data:
Reply from 131.107.6.123: bytes=32 time=10ms TTL=60
Reply from 131.107.6.123: bytes=32 time<10ms TTL=60
Reply from 131.107.6.123: bytes=32 time<10ms TTL=60
Reply from 131.107.6.123: bytes=32 time<10ms TTL=60
```

If the host is unreachable, the ping command fails, as shown by:

```
Pinging 131.107.6.199 with 32 bytes of data:
Request timed out.
Request timed out.
Request timed out.
Request timed out.
```

For MCSE exam and other official purposes, follow the traditional six-step ping command food chain and its relationship to IPConfig (see Figure 7-2). I call this phenomenon of IPConfig and ping working together as being reunited!

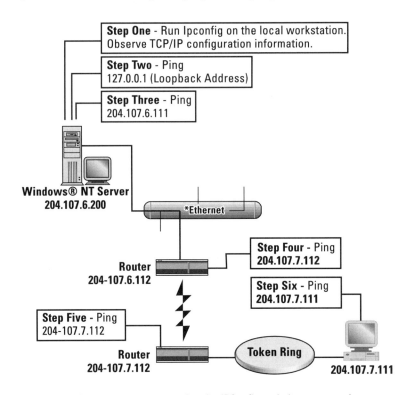

Figure 7-2: Six steps to success using the IPConfig and ping commands

Chapter 7: Troubleshooting TCP/IP **221**

STEPS:
To use the IPConfig and PING commands

Step 1. Run the IPConfig command on the local workstation and observe the TCP/IP configuration information.

Step 2. Ping the internal loopback address to verify that TCP/IP is installed and configured correctly on the local host computer. This address is 127.0.0.1, a reserved address that can't be used as a real IP address on a network. See Chapter 9 for more information.

Step 3. Ping the address of the local host computer to ensure that TCP/IP is working correctly. Here we are typically pinging the network adapter card(s).

Step 4. Ping the IP address of the router or default gateway so that you know and may verify that the router/default gateway are functioning correctly. This also ensures that you have a functional infrastructure in place to communicate with a local host on the local network or subnet.

Step 5. Ping the distant router across a WAN link if appropriate. This is a step I've added to the traditional scenario that you may or may not see in the MCSE texts or exams. However, this is based on real-world experience. Often you can ping a remote router yet are unable to ping the desired remote host. That's because something as simple as a return route may not be programmed (see the route command discussion later in this chapter and in Chapter 5, "TCP/IP Implementations").

Step 6. Ping the IP address of the remote host. Success at this stage establishes that you can communicate through the remote router and that the remote host is functional.

Typically, I use the ping command in a bankruptcy law fashion. What do I mean by that? I mean I work backward (remember that in U.S. Bankruptcy law, one starts with chapter 11 and progresses backward to chapter 7 . . . get it?). So I first ping the remote host (Step 6) and work backward. This approach better maps the real-world need to communicate with another workstation/server/host somewhere. If that doesn't work, I back up and ultimately try to find the source of failure.

Secret

The ping command is a great command for testing your implementation of IP security in Windows NT Server 4.0. If you've correctly implemented IP security, even the ping command will fail between two hosts that are not allowed to speak with each other. See more discussion on IP security in Chapter 6 of this book.

For a real good time, use the ping command to test the Windows Sockets–based name resolution on your network. This is accomplished by pinging a host name. For example, on the Internet, I might ping the domain name of my ISP with the following command:

```
ping nwlink.com
```

If I enjoy successful replies, then I know there is no problem with address resolution or the network connection. However, if the ping command using a host name isn't successful but the ping command using the IP address is, then I know that I only have an address resolution problem, not a network connection problem.

A few general steps to consider when the ping command doesn't work include:

- Reboot the computer after TCP/IP was installed or modified (see my comments earlier under "Always reboot" in the "TCP/IP Troubleshooting Basics" section).
- Check that the local host's address is valid as displayed in Internet Protocol (TCP/IP) Properties tab sheet under the Local Area Connection Properties, found under Network Connections if it is a static IP address (see Figure 7-3).

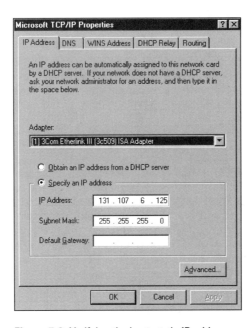

Figure 7-3: Verifying the host static IP address

- If necessary, make sure Windows NT Server–based routing is operational and a link exists between routers. In other words, perhaps you're having a Telco-related communications problem.

ARP

The Address Resolution Protocol (ARP) cache is composed of both dynamic and static addresses. In reality, ARP is used several ways, but fundamentally, ARP maps an IP address to a hardware address. This role is defined in RFC 826. The hardware address is the Media Access Control (MAC) or physical address. This hardware address can best be obtained by viewing the "Physical Address" entry returned by the IPConfig command.

Tip

Other ways to obtain physical hardware addresses include using the install utility on the driver disk that comes with your network adapter card or trapping packets with Network Monitor. The former approach is good for workstations that might be running IPX/SPX or NetBEUI, and the latter is good for nonmainstream workstation implementations in a Windows NT Server 4.0 environment such as Macintosh clients. See Chapters 23 and 25 for further discussion of these techniques.

The bottom line on network communications is that hosts must ultimately know each other's physical addresses to communicate on a network. Address resolution via ARP is the act of converting the host's IP address to its physical address. In that context, ARP is responsible for gathering the hardware addresses on broadcast-based networks. When operating in a dynamic discovery mode, this is accomplished by ARP issuing a local broadcast of the remote IP address to discover the physical address of this remote host. Having obtained the physical address, it adds it to the ARP cache. In fact, for a given host, both the IP address and the physical address are stored as one entry in the ARP table such as:

```
Interface: 10.0.0.2 on Interface 0x2
  Internet Address       Physical Address        Type
  10.0.0.3               00-aa-62-c6-08-00       static
Interface: 131.107.6.171 on Interface 0x3
  Internet Address       Physical Address        Type
  131.107.6.88           00-60-97-ba-f1-25       static
```

The ARP cache is always read for an IP–physical address mapping before any ARP-related request broadcasts are initiated. Dynamic ARP table entries are maintained for 10 minutes. This ensures the freshest ARP resolution information at all times. Static ARP table entries are maintained until the machine is rebooted. Remember that caching allows ARP to operate efficiently. If you did not have any ARP caching, your network would have far too many ARP-type broadcasts (such as shown in Figure 7-4) travelling to resolve IP addresses to physical addresses. Not a wise way to manage a network.

ARP broadcasts appear as shown in Figure 7-4 when viewed by Network Monitor.

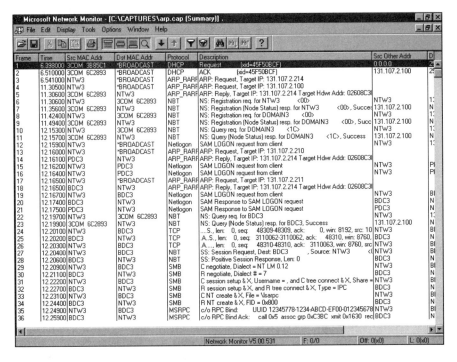

Figure 7-4: ARP broadcasting

Tip

Remember that Windows NT Server makes heavy use of address caching in its TCP/IP implementation. That's a helpful hint to keep in mind when things aren't going smoothly and you decided to reboot the server to refresh the address cache.

So how does ARP resolve an IP address? Before I get to the steps that ARP undertakes, remember that the IP addresses for any two hosts must be "resolved" before a communications session may be established.

1. Any time one host tries to communicate with another, an ARP request is initiated. An example of such a communication would be the ping command. If the IP address to physical address entry exists in the local table, then the address is resolved. End of story.

2. However, if no entry exists in the ARP table that resolves the IP address to a physical address, ARP starts asking questions in the form of a broadcast packet (such as the packet traffic displayed in Figure 7-4).

3. Every host on the local network evaluates the broadcast and determines whether the IP address in the ARP packet is the same as its IP address.

4. When a match is found, the destination host sends an ARP reply packet back to the source host. Again, this is akin to the traffic shown in Figure 7-4.

5. Routers in scenarios that span multiple subnets participate in ARP-related events in the following manner (also outlined in Figure 7-5): The ARP broadcast is forwarded to the default gateway for evaluation. The ARP broadcast packet is forwarded yet again to a remote router if necessary. Once a session is established with the remote router, the source host sends the ICMP-based request (such as a ping) to the remote router. The remote router resolves the request by sending the ping command to the destination host.

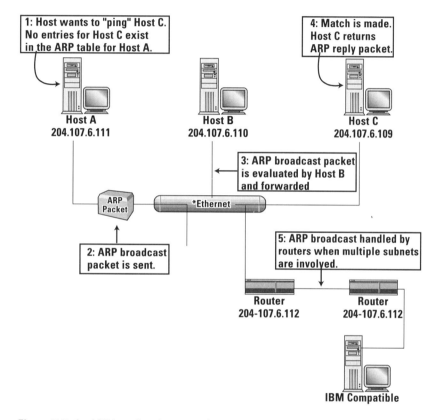

Figure 7-5: An ARP broadcasting scenario

Common ARP-related problems

Two common problem areas are associated with ARP.

First is the problem of duplicate addresses. ARP operates with the FIFO principle. That means ARP table entries are made on a first come, first served basis. Thus it is possible that if duplicate IP addresses accidentally exist on the network, the wrong IP-based host may reply and cause an incorrect IP address–physical address entry to be added to the ARP table. See my ARP case study in a moment that incorporates elements of this ARP problem.

Second, broadcast storms strike when subnet masks are invalid and countless ARP broadcasts are sent in vain on the network looking for a host. In essence, the numerous broadcast packets being sent are the storm. You and your users know the outcome as decreased network performance.

ARP case study

The is the case of the naughty ISDN router. Malcontent as it was, this ISDN router at the headquarters of an athletic club chain in the greater Seattle area was incorrectly causing duplicate IP address errors on the network irrespective of the IP addresses we assigned to the hosts. We'd receive "duplicate IP address" errors at the Windows 95 workstation whether we assigned the IP address to the workstation dynamically or statically. What gives, we pondered? We were only dealing with two dozen or so workstations and, by all accounts, didn't have duplicate IP addresses.

Finally, a breakthrough arrived. Using the ARP command, we were able to resolve the "bogus" IP address (and there were a bunch of 'em) back to the ISDN router's MAC address. In short, one MAC address was mapped to several IP addresses. Whenever a Windows 95 workstation attempted to acquire what should have been a valid IP address, it of course got the duplicate IP address error. ARP bailed us out that day and got us a new, correctly functioning router for the athletic club.

Microsoft's position on ARP

Microsoft's position on TCP/IP troubleshooting is this: After running IPConfig and ping, you should then test IP-to-MAC address resolution using ARP. The bottom line? If two hosts can't ping each other, try running ARP commands to see if the host computers have the correct MAC addresses.

NBTSTAT

One of the apparent dilemmas in a Microsoft Windows NT environment is the resolution of NetBIOS names to IP addresses. This is handled several ways including Dynamic DNS, WINS server queries, local cache resolution, broadcasts, and LMHOSTS and HOSTS lookup. If you want to drop under the hood, you have the nbtstat command. In addition to acting as a name resolution troubleshooting tool, it enables you to correct or remove preloaded name entries.

Options for the nbtstat command are:

```
NBTSTAT [ [-a RemoteName] [-A IP address] [-c] [-n]
        [-r] [-R] [-RR] [-s] [-S] [interval] ]
   -a   (adapter status) Lists the remote machine's name table given its name
   -A   (Adapter status) Lists the remote machine's name table given its
                         IP address.
   -c   (cache)          Lists NBT's cache of remote [machine] names and their IP addresses
```

Chapter 7: Troubleshooting TCP/IP

```
   -n   (names)           Lists local NetBIOS names. That is, names are
displayed that were registered locally by the on the system by the
server and redirector services.
   -r   (resolved)        Lists names resolved by broadcast and via WINS
   -R   (Reload)          Purges and reloads the remote cache name table
(LMHOSTS)
   -S   (Sessions)        Lists sessions table with the destination IP
addresses
   -s   (sessions)        Lists sessions table converting destination IP
                          addresses to computer NETBIOS names.
   -RR  (ReleaseRefresh)  Sends Name Release packets to WINs and then,
starts Refr
esh
   RemoteName   Remote host machine name.
   IP address   Dotted decimal representation of the IP address.
   interval     Redisplays selected statistics, pausing interval
seconds
                between each display. Press Ctrl+C to stop redisplaying
                statistics.
```

In the following nbtstat example, I run the command with the -S switch to list the current NetBIOS sessions, complete with status and statistics:

```
\Device\NetBT->Tcpip->Local Area Connection:
Node IpAddress: [10.0.0.2] Scope Id: []
                    NetBIOS Connection Table
    Local Name           State     In/Out  Remote Host
Input   Output
    ─────────────────────────────────────────────
    SECRETS2        <03>  Listening
    ADMINISTRATOR   <03>  Listening
\Device\NetBT->Tcpip->Local Area Connection(2):
Node IpAddress: [131.107.6.171] Scope Id: []
                    NetBIOS Connection Table
    Local Name           State     In/Out  Remote Host
Input   Output
    ─────────────────────────────────────────────
    SECRETS2        <03>  Listening
    ADMINISTRATOR   <03>  Listening
\Device\NetBT_Tcpip_NdisWanIpOut{50DA9B45-18E3-11D2-AFF9-
EFE843E45279}:
Node IpAddress: [0.0.0.0] Scope Id: []
    No Connections
\Device\NetBT_Tcpip_NdisWanIpOut{50DA9B44-18E3-11D2-AFF9-
EFE843E45279}:
Node IpAddress: [0.0.0.0] Scope Id: []
    No Connections
\Device\NetBT_Tcpip_NdisWanIpOut{50DA9B43-18E3-11D2-AFF9-
EFE843E45279}:
Node IpAddress: [0.0.0.0] Scope Id: []
    No Connections
\Device\NetBT_Tcpip_NdisWanIpIn:
Node IpAddress: [0.0.0.0] Scope Id: []
    No Connections
```

Secret

A trick you may use to ensure that you're using a fresh local name cache is the nbtstat -r command. This command updates the local name cache immediately from such sources as the LMHOSTS file.

Route

The route command is discussed extensively in Chapter 5, "TCP/IP Implementations," in the context of IP gateways. However, a quick review is in order. Using the route command, you may view or modify the route table. The route table lists all current IP routes seen by the host. This includes routes that Windows NT Server creates automatically and routes learned by running the router information protocol (RIP). Common options for the route command are shown in Table 7-2.

Table 7-2   Common Options for the Route Command

Command	Function
Route print	Displays all current IP routes known by the host.
Route add	Used to add persistent and nonpersistent routes to the table. It is necessary to use the -p command line option with route add to create a persistent route. Otherwise, the route is lost when the machine is rebooted.
Route delete	Deletes routes from the table.

Netstat

This command displays the current TCP/IP connections and protocol statistics. Options for the netstat command include:

```
NETSTAT [-a] [-e] [-n] [-s] [-p proto] [-r] [interval]
  -a             Displays all connections and listening ports.
  -e             Displays Ethernet statistics. This may be combined with the -s
                 option.
  -n             Displays addresses and port numbers in numerical form.
  -p proto       Shows connections for the protocol specified by proto;
proto
                 may be TCP or UDP.  If used with the -s option to
display
                 per-protocol statistics, proto may be TCP, UDP, or IP.
  -r             Displays the routing table.
  -s             Displays per-protocol statistics.  By default,
statistics are
                 shown for TCP, UDP and IP; the -p option may be used
to specify
                 a subset of the default.
  interval       Redisplays selected statistics, pausing interval
seconds
```

Chapter 7: Troubleshooting TCP/IP

```
                        between each display.  Press CTRL+C to stop
redisplaying
                        statistics.  If omitted, netstat will print the
current
                        configuration information once.
```

Here is sample output from the netstat command using both the -e (Ethernet statistics), -a (all connections and listening ports), -r (route table), and -s (per-protocol statistics) command line options:

netstat -e

```
Interface Statistics
                             Received               Sent
Bytes                        291244                 107280
Unicast packets              0                      0
Non-unicast packets          1509                   758
Discards                     0                      0
Errors                       0                      0
Unknown protocols            1128
```

netstat -a

```
Active Connections
   Proto   Local Address           Foreign Address         State
   TCP     SECRETS2:echo           SECRETS2:0              LISTENING
   TCP     SECRETS2:discard        SECRETS2:0              LISTENING
   TCP     SECRETS2:daytime        SECRETS2:0              LISTENING
   TCP     SECRETS2:qotd           SECRETS2:0              LISTENING
   TCP     SECRETS2:chargen        SECRETS2:0              LISTENING
   TCP     SECRETS2:ftp            SECRETS2:0              LISTENING
   TCP     SECRETS2:name           SECRETS2:0              LISTENING
   TCP     SECRETS2:domain         SECRETS2:0              LISTENING
   TCP     SECRETS2:80             SECRETS2:0              LISTENING
   TCP     SECRETS2:135            SECRETS2:0              LISTENING
   TCP     SECRETS2:443            SECRETS2:0              LISTENING
   TCP     SECRETS2:445            SECRETS2:0              LISTENING
   TCP     SECRETS2:printer        SECRETS2:0              LISTENING
   TCP     SECRETS2:548            SECRETS2:0              LISTENING
   TCP     SECRETS2:1025           SECRETS2:0              LISTENING
   TCP     SECRETS2:1026           SECRETS2:0              LISTENING
   TCP     SECRETS2:1028           SECRETS2:0              LISTENING
   TCP     SECRETS2:1031           SECRETS2:0              LISTENING
   TCP     SECRETS2:1034           SECRETS2:0              LISTENING
   TCP     SECRETS2:1035           SECRETS2:0              LISTENING
   TCP     SECRETS2:3389           SECRETS2:0              LISTENING
   TCP     SECRETS2:5162           SECRETS2:0              LISTENING
   TCP     SECRETS2:nbsession      SECRETS2:0              LISTENING
   TCP     SECRETS2:1027           SECRETS2:0              LISTENING
   TCP     SECRETS2:nbsession      SECRETS2:0              LISTENING
   UDP     SECRETS2:echo           *:*
   UDP     SECRETS2:discard        *:*
   UDP     SECRETS2:daytime        *:*
   UDP     SECRETS2:qotd           *:*
   UDP     SECRETS2:chargen        *:*
   UDP     SECRETS2:name           *:*
   UDP     SECRETS2:135            *:*
```

```
UDP     SECRETS2:snmp           *:*
UDP     SECRETS2:445            *:*
UDP     SECRETS2:1030           *:*
UDP     SECRETS2:1032           *:*
UDP     SECRETS2:1033           *:*
UDP     SECRETS2:9987           *:*
UDP     SECRETS2:domain         *:*
UDP     SECRETS2:bootp          *:*
UDP     SECRETS2:68             *:*
UDP     SECRETS2:nbname         *:*
UDP     SECRETS2:nbdatagram     *:*
UDP     SECRETS2:1029           *:*
UDP     SECRETS2:domain         *:*
UDP     SECRETS2:bootp          *:*
UDP     SECRETS2:68             *:*
UDP     SECRETS2:nbname         *:*
UDP     SECRETS2:nbdatagram     *:*
```

netstat -r

```
===========================================================================
Interface List
0x1 ........................... MS TCP Loopback interface
0x2 ...00 60 08 3a 04 cb ...... 3Com 3C90x Ethernet Adapter
0x3 ...00 60 97 bf a1 23 ...... ELNK3 Ethernet Adapter
0x4 ...00 53 45 00 00 00 ...... WAN (PPP/SLIP) Interface
0x5 ...00 53 45 00 00 00 ...... WAN (PPP/SLIP) Interface
0x6 ...00 53 45 00 00 00 ...... WAN (PPP/SLIP) Interface
0x7 ...00 53 45 00 00 00 ...... WAN (PPP/SLIP) Interface
===========================================================================
===========================================================================
Active Routes:
Network Destination        Netmask          Gateway         Interface    Metric
          10.0.0.0        255.0.0.0         10.0.0.2         10.0.0.2       1
          10.0.0.2  255.255.255.255        127.0.0.1        127.0.0.1       1
    10.255.255.255  255.255.255.255         10.0.0.2         10.0.0.2       1
         127.0.0.0        255.0.0.0        127.0.0.1        127.0.0.1       1
       131.107.6.0    255.255.255.0    131.107.6.171    131.107.6.171       1
     131.107.6.171  255.255.255.255        127.0.0.1        127.0.0.1       1
   131.107.255.255  255.255.255.255    131.107.6.171    131.107.6.171       1
         224.0.0.0        224.0.0.0         10.0.0.2         10.0.0.2       1
         224.0.0.0        224.0.0.0    131.107.6.171    131.107.6.171       1
   255.255.255.255  255.255.255.255         10.0.0.2         10.0.0.2       1
===========================================================================
Route Table
Active Connections
  Proto  Local Address          Foreign Address        State
```

netstat -s

```
IP Statistics
  Packets Received                   = 1646
```

```
  Received Header Errors          = 0
  Received Address Errors         = 685
  Datagrams Forwarded             = 0
  Unknown Protocols Received      = 0
  Received Packets Discarded      = 0
  Received Packets Delivered      = 997
  Output Requests                 = 748
  Routing Discards                = 0
  Discarded Output Packets        = 0
  Output Packet No Route          = 0
  Reassembly Required             = 0
  Reassembly Successful           = 0
  Reassembly Failures             = 0
  Datagrams Successfully Fragmented = 0
  Datagrams Failing Fragmentation = 0
  Fragments Created               = 0
ICMP Statistics
                              Received      Sent
  Messages                       12           6
  Errors                          0           0
  Destination Unreachable         0           0
  Time Exceeded                   0           0
  Parameter Problems              0           0
  Source Quenchs                  0           0
  Redirects                       0           0
  Echos                           0           0
  Echo Replies                    0           0
  Timestamps                      0           0
  Timestamp Replies               0           0
  Address Masks                   0           0
  Address Mask Replies            0           0
TCP Statistics
  Active Opens                    = 0
  Passive Opens                   = 0
  Failed Connection Attempts      = 0
  Reset Connections               = 0
  Current Connections             = 0
  Segments Received               = 0
  Segments Sent                   = 0
  Segments Retransmitted          = 0
UDP Statistics
  Datagrams Received     = 963
  No Ports               = 34
  Receive Errors         = 0
  Datagrams Sent         = 729
```

Tracert

A route tracing utility, tracert utilizes the IP TTL field and ICMP error messages to discover host-to-host routes through the network. Options for the tracert command include:

```
Usage: tracert [-d] [-h maximum_hops] [-j host-list] [-w timeout]
target_name
```

```
Options:
    -d                  Do not resolve addresses to hostnames.
    -h maximum_hops     Maximum number of hops to search for target.
    -j host-list        Loose source route along host-list.
    -w timeout          Wait timeout milliseconds for each reply.
```

Here is sample output from the tracert command:

```
Tracing route to SECRETS2 [131.107.6.171]
over a maximum of 30 hops:
  1    <10 ms    <10 ms    <10 ms   SECRETS2 [131.107.6.171]
Trace complete.
```

Hostname

This is a very simple but useful command. It returns the NetBIOS computer name for the machine on which the command was executed.

Tip

The hostname command is a quick and dirty way to find out (or remember!) what machine you are working on. This command line utility eliminates the need to find similar information via the MMC. It's a favorite command of mine in part because of its simplicity.

The hostname command and its output appear as

```
C:\>hostname
SECRETS2
```

where SECRETS2 is the actual host name.

Secret

You may not change the host name via the hostname command. The -s option is not supported in Windows NT Server 4.0. You must use the Network applet in Control Panel to change the host name followed by a reboot.

FTP

This command remains very popular with Windows NT Server 4.0 users. This is an important point because other TCP/IP processes from the same era (such as Gopher) have faded. Using Port 21, FTP is the basic command for transferring information from one Internet host to another. There are several "variations" of this command, three of which I will show you. First, there is the command line version contained within Windows NT Server 4.0, which provides very basic, character-based two-way file transfer capabilities. Here is sample output with the FTP command using the fully qualified domain name:

```
C:\>ftp secrets2
Connect to SECRETS2.
220 SECRETS2 Microsoft FTP Service (Version 4.0)
User (SECRETS2:(none)): anonymous
331 Anonymous access allowed, send identity (e-mail name) as password.
Password:
230 Anonymous user logged in.
ftp>
```

Note that this session could have been initiated by using the IP address for SECRETS2 (e.g. 10.0.0.2).

Tip

The return codes listed in the preceding FTP session, along with all of the other FTP return codes, may be found at http://andrew2.andrew.cmu.edu/rfc/rfc640.html.

Table 7-3 shows the commands that may be used during an FTP session such as the one just displayed. Note these commands are listed by typing "?" at the FTP prompt. You will note that most of these commands reveal their UNIX heritage openly.

Table 7-3 Commands for Use in an FTP Session

!	debug	ls	put	status
?	dir	mdelete	pwd	trace
append	disconnect	mdir	quit	type
ascii	get	mget	quote	user
bell	glob	mkdir	recv	verbose
bye	hash	mls	remotehelp	
cd	help	mput	rename	
close	lcd	open	rmdir	
delete	literal	prompt	send	

Table 7-4 provides explanations of the more common FTP commands.

Table 7-4 Common FTP Commands

Command	Description
!	Spawns an MS-DOS shell but FTP remains active. Typing exit returns the user to the FTP prompt.
!command	Executes an MS-DOS command inside the FTP session on the local computer.
Bye	Terminates or ends the FTP session.
Delete	With appropriate permissions, files are deleted on the remote computer.
Dir	Lists the remote directory's files and subdirectories.
Get	Copies a file to the local computer from a remote computer.
Help	Displays FTP command descriptions.
Put	Copies files from the local computer to the remote computer.
Mkdir	With appropriate permissions, enables you to create a directory on a remote computer.

Secret

The key to using the command-line FTP command in Windows NT Server 4.0 is that the host you are "ftp-ing" to will accept your request and initiate a session. FTP management is configured via the FTP service in Microsoft Internet Information Server (IIS), which is included with Windows NT Server 4.0. Note that changing the default TCP port value used by FTP is one way to create a more secure FTP server site. Both hosts must agree to use the same TCP port value to initiate a session. Using a nondefault TCP port can thwart intruders.

Also consider is how you might really use this tool. Basically, I've used FTP for low-level file transfers when I don't have an NFS-based solution to communicate with true UNIX hosts and Windows NT Server. Specifically, I once used FTP to transfer files from Sun workstations to a Windows NT Server for storage and printing. The FTP service in Microsoft Internet Information Server (IIS) is shown in Figure 7-6.

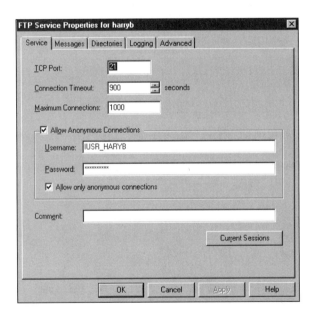

Figure 7-6: Managing the FTP service via the Internet Information Server application

TFTP

Operating on Port 69 by default, Trivial File Transfer Protocol is a variation of FTP that is used to transfer files to and from a remote computer. I've used TFTP to transfer files from a Windows NT Server machine to a Cisco router. Whatever works! here are the TFTP commands available to you:

```
TFTP [-i] host [GET | PUT] source [destination]
   -i            Specifies binary image transfer mode (also called
                 octet). In binary image mode the file is moved
                 literally, byte by byte. Use this mode when
```

```
                        transferring binary files.
host                    Specifies the local or remote host.
GET                     Transfers the file destination on the remote host to
                        the file source on the local host.
PUT                     Transfers the file source on the local host to
                        the file destination on the remote host.
source                  Specifies the file to transfer.
destination             Specifies where to transfer the file.
```

Telnet

Telnet is of course a basic terminal emulation feature that enables you to establish a terminal-mode session with another host. You might, for instance, use Telnet to establish a session with your Windows NT Server over the Internet. Another valid use is programming a router, either internally or externally via the Internet.

Tip

When executing the Telnet command, you may save an extra step by appending the Telnet command with the IP address or host name of the server you intend to log onto. Such a command would appear as:

C:> telnet nwlink.com

Note that nwlink.com is the host name.

Telnet is used each and every day. Honest. When I'm at a remote site that is connected to the Internet, I like to Telnet back to my ISP to check my e-mail. Such a session involves issuing the Telnet command with the fully qualified domain name of my ISP and then launching pine, a character-based e-mail program that is hosted by my ISP (see Figures 7-7 and 7-8).

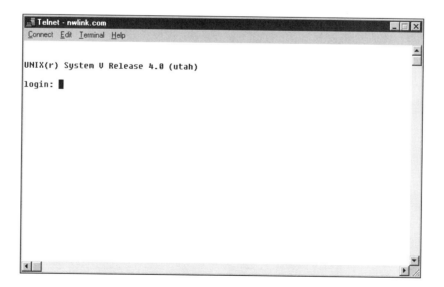

Figure 7-7: Using the Telnet utility to access an ISP from a remote location

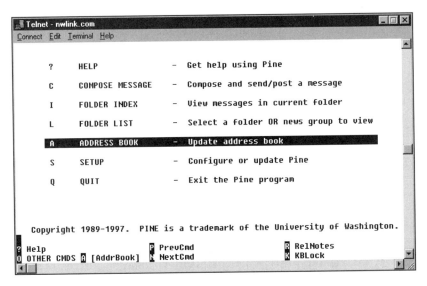

Figure 7-8: Remote access of e-mail via Telnet and other e-mail applications

Because Windows NT Server doesn't natively support the whois command, you should use the following trick to add this powerful command to your arsenal. Telnet to a bonafide UNIX server on the Internet. Your ISP should be your first choice. Next, issue the whois command at the UNIX command prompt as described next.

Why use the whois command? To spy on thine Internet neighbor of course! Just kidding, but the whois command enables you to see who sent that junk mail by performing the whois command against the e-mail's Internet domain name to the right of the "@" symbol. More important, ISP customer service reps and perhaps you can use the whois command (see Figure 7-9) to see if a specific Internet domain name has been taken already (a.k.a. "registered"). At a minimum, the whois command returns important Internet domain registration information (see Figure 7-10). Note the whois command applies only to second-level (such as `idgbooks.com`), not third-level (`springers.nwnexus.com`), domain names.

Chapter 7: Troubleshooting TCP/IP 237

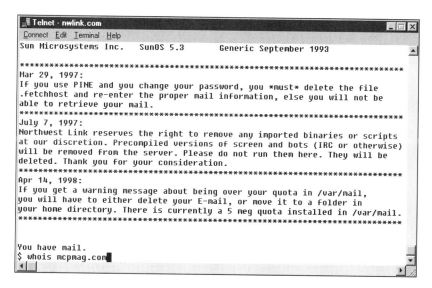

Figure 7-9: The whois command at the UNIX command prompt

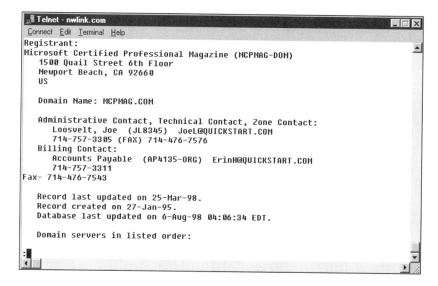

Figure 7-10: Valuable Internet domain name registration information

Note that in Windows NT Server 4.0, the Telnet screen, with its limited size, requires two screens to display the full Internet domain name registration information. Figure 7-11 shows the second screen.

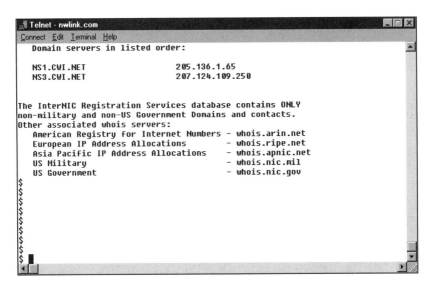

Figure 7-11: The Windows NT Server second Telnet screen

RCP

The Remote Copy Protocol (RCP) enables you to copy files between TCP/IP-based hosts. Settings for this command include:

```
RCP [-a | -b] [-h] [-r] [host][.user:]source [host][.user:]
path\destination
   -a               Specifies ASCII transfer mode. This mode converts
                    the EOL characters to a carriage return for UNIX
                    and a carriage
                    return/line feed for personal computers. This is
                    the default transfer mode.
   -b               Specifies binary image transfer mode.
   -h               Transfers hidden files.
   -r               Copies the contents of all subdirectories;
                    destination must be a directory.
   host             Specifies the local or remote host. If host is
                    specified as an IP address OR if host name
contains
                    dots, you must specify the user.
   .user:           Specifies a user name to use, rather than the
                    current user name.
   source           Specifies the files to copy.
   path\destination Specifies the path relative to the logon
directory
                    on the remote host. Use the escape characters
                    (\ , ", or ') in remote paths to use wildcard
                    characters on the remote host.
```

RSH

This command launches a remote shell on a UNIX host. Settings for this command include:

```
RSH host [-l username] [-n] command
  host            Specifies the remote host on which to run command.
  -l username     Specifies the user name to use on the remote host.
If
                  omitted, the logged on user name is used.
  -n              Redirects the input of RSH to NULL.
  command         Specifies the command to run.
```

REXEC

This command enables you to run commands on remote hosts running the REXEC service. Rexec authenticates the user name on the remote host before executing the specified command. Settings for this command include:

```
REXEC host [-l username] [-n] command
  host            Specifies the remote host on which to run command.
  -l username     Specifies the user name on the remote host.
  -n              Redirects the input of REXEC to NULL.
  command         Specifies the command to run.
```

Finger

This command displays information about a user on a specified system running the Finger service. Output varies based on the remote system. Settings for this command include:

```
FINGER [-l] [user]@host [...]
  -l       Displays information in long list format.
  user     Specifies the user you want information about. Omit the
user
           parameter to display information about all users on the
           specified host.
  @host    Specifies the server on the remote system whose users you
           want information about.
```

Microsoft Internet Explorer

Even though I tout the benefits of a robust Internet browser such as Internet Explorer (IE) several times in this book, it's worth repeating here. The "official" Microsoft party line is that IE is very much of a troubleshooting tool for the TCP/IP protocol in Windows NT Server 4.0. That's because IE increasingly supports TCP/IP protocol suite utilities such as FTP. This is a capability beyond the original browser, which basically has Hypertext Transfer Protocol (HTTP) support. In reality, I use IE every day to go up on the Internet and download resources to optimize my Windows NT Server 4.0 installations.

Other TCP/IP Troubleshooting Angles

Having reviewed the primary utilities that "ship" as part of the TCP/IP protocol suite in Windows NT Server 4.0, let's explore a few other time-tested TCP/IP troubleshooting tricks.

Troubleshooting TCP/IP Database Files

This section is written for the MCSE candidate in mind. In the real world, you and I rely on the GUI-interface presentation of TCP/IP information in Windows NT Server 4.0. However, if you're an old timer in the industry or you're trying to pass the demanding TCP/IP exams on the MCSE tracks, the files shown in Table 7-5 contain critical TCP/IP information. Everyone else can benefit by observing the file descriptions and contents.

Table 7-5 Windows NT Server UNIX-style Database Files

File Name	Description
HOSTS	Provides host name–to–IP address resolution for applications that are Windows Sockets–compliant.
LMHOSTS	Provides NetBIOS name–to–IP address resolution for Windows-based networking.
Networks	Provides network name–to–network ID resolution for TCP/IP management.
Protocol	Provides protocol name–to–protocol ID resolution for Windows Sockets applications.
Services	Provides service name–to–port ID resolution for Windows Sockets applications.

Sample output from the HOSTS file contained at \%systemroot%\system32\drivers\etc is:

```
# Copyright (c) 1993-1995 Microsoft Corp.
#
# This is a sample HOSTS file used by Microsoft TCP/IP for Windows NT.
#
# This file contains the mappings of IP addresses to host names. Each
# entry should be kept on an individual line. The IP address should
# be placed in the first column followed by the corresponding host
  name.
```

```
# The IP address and the host name should be separated by at least one
# space.
#
# Additionally, comments (such as these) may be inserted on individual
# lines or following the machine name denoted by a '#' symbol.
#
# For example:
#
#      102.54.94.97        rhino.acme.com          # source server
#       38.25.63.10        x.acme.com              # x client host
127.0.0.1        localhost
```

Sample output from the LMHOSTS (lmhosts.sam) file contained at \%systemroot% \system32\drivers\etc is:

```
# Copyright (c) 1993-1995 Microsoft Corp.
#
# This is a sample LMHOSTS file used by the Microsoft TCP/IP for Windows
# NT.
#
# This file contains the mappings of IP addresses to NT computer names
# (NetBIOS) names.  Each entry should be kept on an individual line.
# The IP address should be placed in the first column followed by the
# corresponding computer name. The address and the computer name
# should be separated by at least one space or tab. The "#" character
# is generally used to denote the start of a comment (see the exceptions
# below).
#
# This file is compatible with Microsoft LAN Manager 2.x TCP/IP lmhosts
# files and offers the following extensions:
#
#       #PRE
#       #DOM:<domain>
#       #INCLUDE <filename>
#       #BEGIN_ALTERNATE
#       #END_ALTERNATE
#       \0xnn (non-printing character support)
#
# Following any entry in the file with the characters "#PRE" will cause
# the entry to be preloaded into the name cache. By default, entries are
# not preloaded, but are parsed only after dynamic name resolution fails.
#
# Following an entry with the "#DOM:<domain>" tag will associate the
# entry with the domain specified by <domain>. This affects how the
# browser and logon services behave in TCP/IP environments. To preload
# the host name associated with #DOM entry, it is necessary to also add a
```

```
# #PRE to the line. The <domain> is always preloaded although it will not
# be shown when the name cache is viewed.
#
# Specifying "#INCLUDE <filename>" will force the RFC NetBIOS (NBT)
# software to seek the specified <filename> and parse it as if it were
# local. <filename> is generally a UNC-based name, allowing a
# centralized lmhosts file to be maintained on a server.
# It is ALWAYS necessary to provide a mapping for the IP address of the
# server prior to the #INCLUDE. This mapping must use the #PRE directive.
# In addition the share "public" in the example below must be in the
# LanManServer list of "NullSessionShares" in order for client machines to
# be able to read the lmhosts file successfully. This key is under
# \machine\system\currentcontrolset\services\lanmanserver\parameters\nullsessionshares
# in the registry. Simply add "public" to the list found there.
#
# The #BEGIN_ and #END_ALTERNATE keywords allow multiple #INCLUDE
# statements to be grouped together. Any single successful include
# will cause the group to succeed.
#
# Finally, non-printing characters can be embedded in mappings by
# first surrounding the NetBIOS name in quotations, then using the
# \0xnn notation to specify a hex value for a non-printing character.
#
# The following example illustrates all of these extensions:
#
# 102.54.94.97     rhino            #PRE #DOM:networking   #net group's DC
# 102.54.94.102    "appname \0x14"                         #special app server
# 102.54.94.123    popular          #PRE                   #source server
# 102.54.94.117    localsrv         #PRE                   #needed for the include
#
# #BEGIN_ALTERNATE
# #INCLUDE \\localsrv\public\lmhosts
# #INCLUDE \\rhino\public\lmhosts
# #END_ALTERNATE
#
# In the above example, the "appname" server contains a special
# character in its name, the "popular" and "localsrv" server names are
# preloaded, and the "rhino" server name is specified so it can be used
# to later #INCLUDE a centrally maintained lmhosts file if the "localsrv"
# system is unavailable.
#
# Note that the whole file is parsed including comments on each lookup,
```

Chapter 7: Troubleshooting TCP/IP   243

```
# so keeping the number of comments to a minimum will improve
performance.
# Therefore it is not advisable to simply add lmhosts file entries
onto the
# end of this file.
```

Secret

I've highlighted in bold the two most valuable lines from this sample file. First the line **102.54.94.97 rhino #PRE #DOM:networking** is an entry type that I've used to solve pesky resolution problems. Sometimes preloading the entry (the #PRE statement) and forcing a domain name for the host (#DOM) will solve nasty timeout conditions over slow WAN links. Been there and done that.

The other interesting entry is the **102.54.94.102 "appname \0x14"** line. What is occurring here, in English, is that the full 15 positions of the host name are being filled out or padded. This is necessary in some resolution scenarios. Most likely you will be working with Microsoft Technical Support when you get to the point that this becomes necessary. As stated in the preceding sample file, the \0x14 represents nonprinting characters.

In fact, one time that I can recall where I worked extensively with the LMHOSTS file was when I was troubleshooting the dickens out of a Microsoft Exchange performance problem across two domains. Upon reflection years later, I now see that this was an exercise in using TPC/IP tools to troubleshoot an integration problem between a Microsoft BackOffice component and the underlying Windows NT Server operating system. Such lofty insights, garnered from bumps, bruises, and general maturity with Windows NT Server, have made me a more effective network professional. I'm sure you will enjoy the same positive results from ascending both the Windows NT Server and TCP/IP learning curves.

Tip

If you want to convert the lmhosts.sam file from being a sample file to acting as your real lmhosts file, you will need to remove the .sam file extension.

Sample output from the Networks file contained at \%systemroot% \system32\drivers\etc is:

```
# Copyright (c) 1993-1995 Microsoft Corp.
#
# This file contains network name/network number mappings for
# local networks. Network numbers are recognized in dotted decimal
form.
#
# Format:
#
# <network name>    <network number>      [aliases...]  [#<comment>]
#
# For example:
#
#     loopback      127
#     campus        284.122.107
#     london        284.122.108
```

```
loopback                127
```

Sample output from the Protocol file contained at \%systemroot%\system32\drivers\etc is:

```
# Copyright (c) 1993-1995 Microsoft Corp.
#
# This file contains the Internet protocols as defined by RFC 1060
# (Assigned Numbers).
#
# Format:
#
# <protocol name>  <assigned number>  [aliases...]   [#<comment>]
ip        0     IP       # Internet protocol
icmp      1     ICMP     # Internet control message protocol
ggp       3     GGP      # Gateway-gateway protocol
tcp       6     TCP      # Transmission control protocol
egp       8     EGP      # Exterior gateway protocol
pup       12    PUP      # PARC universal packet protocol
udp       17    UDP      # User datagram protocol
hmp       20    HMP      # Host monitoring protocol
xns-idp   22    XNS-IDP  # Xerox NS IDP
rdp       27    RDP      # "reliable datagram" protocol
rvd       66    RVD      # MIT remote virtual disk
```

Sample output from the Services file contained at \%systemroot%\system32\drivers\etc is:

```
# Copyright (c) 1993-1995 Microsoft Corp.
#
# This file contains port numbers for well-known services as defined by
# RFC 1060 (Assigned Numbers).
#
# Format:
#
# <service name>   <port number>/<protocol>   [aliases...]   [#<comment>]
#
echo            7/tcp
echo            7/udp
discard         9/tcp      sink null
discard         9/udp      sink null
systat          11/tcp
systat          11/tcp     users
daytime         13/tcp
daytime         13/udp
netstat         15/tcp
qotd            17/tcp     quote
qotd            17/udp     quote
chargen         19/tcp     ttytst source
chargen         19/udp     ttytst source
ftp-data        20/tcp
ftp             21/tcp
```

```
telnet              23/tcp
smtp                25/tcp      mail
time                37/tcp      timeserver
time                37/udp      timeserver
rlp                 39/udp      resource        # resource location
name                42/tcp      nameserver
name                42/udp      nameserver
whois               43/tcp      nicname         # usually to sri-nic
domain              53/tcp      nameserver      # name-domain server
domain              53/udp      nameserver
nameserver          53/tcp      domain          # name-domain server
nameserver          53/udp      domain
mtp                 57/tcp                      # deprecated
bootp               67/udp                      # boot program server
tftp                69/udp
rje                 77/tcp      netrjs
finger              79/tcp
link                87/tcp      ttylink
supdup              95/tcp
hostnames          101/tcp      hostname        # usually from sri-nic
iso-tsap           102/tcp
dictionary         103/tcp      webster
x400               103/tcp                      # ISO Mail
x400-snd           104/tcp
csnet-ns           105/tcp
pop                109/tcp      postoffice
pop2               109/tcp                      # Post Office
pop3               110/tcp      postoffice
portmap            111/tcp
portmap            111/udp
sunrpc             111/tcp
sunrpc             111/udp
auth               113/tcp      authentication
sftp               115/tcp
path               117/tcp
uucp-path          117/tcp
nntp               119/tcp      usenet          # Network News Transfer
ntp                123/udp      ntpd ntp        # network time protocol
(exp)
nbname             137/udp
nbdatagram         138/udp
nbsession          139/tcp
NeWS               144/tcp      news
sgmp               153/udp      sgmp
tcprepo            158/tcp      repository      # PCMAIL
snmp               161/udp      snmp
snmp-trap          162/udp      snmp
print-srv          170/tcp                      # network PostScript
vmnet              175/tcp
load               315/udp
vmnet0             400/tcp
sytek              500/udp
biff               512/udp      comsat
```

```
exec              512/tcp
login             513/tcp
who               513/udp    whod
shell             514/tcp    cmd                  # no passwords used
syslog            514/udp
printer           515/tcp    spooler              # line printer spooler
talk              517/udp
ntalk             518/udp
efs               520/tcp                         # for LucasFilm
route             520/udp    router routed
timed             525/udp    timeserver
tempo             526/tcp    newdate
courier           530/tcp    rpc
conference        531/tcp    chat
rvd-control       531/udp    MIT disk
netnews           532/tcp    readnews
netwall           533/udp                         # -for emergency broadcasts
uucp              540/tcp    uucpd                # uucp daemon
klogin            543/tcp                         # Kerberos authenticated
rlogin
kshell            544/tcp    cmd                  # and remote shell
new-rwho          550/udp    new-who              # experimental
remotefs          556/tcp    rfs_server rfs# Brunhoff remote
filesystem
rmonitor          560/udp    rmonitord            # experimental
monitor           561/udp                         # experimental
garcon            600/tcp
maitrd            601/tcp
busboy            602/tcp
acctmaster        700/udp
acctslave         701/udp
acct              702/udp
acctlogin         703/udp
acctprinter       704/udp
elcsd             704/udp                         # errlog
acctinfo          705/udp
acctslave2        706/udp
acctdisk          707/udp
kerberos          750/tcp    kdc                  # Kerberos authentication-
tcp
kerberos          750/udp    kdc                  # Kerberos authentication-
udp
kerberos_master   751/tcp                         # Kerberos authentication
kerberos_master   751/udp                         # Kerberos authentication
passwd_server     752/udp                         # Kerberos passwd server
userreg_server    753/udp                         # Kerberos userreg server
krb_prop          754/tcp                         # Kerberos slave
propagation
erlogin           888/tcp                         # Login and environment
passing
kpop              1109/tcp                        # Pop with Kerberos
phone             1167/udp
ingreslock        1524/tcp
```

Chapter 7: Troubleshooting TCP/IP

```
maze            1666/udp
nfs             2049/udp                # sun nfs
knetd           2053/tcp                # Kerberos de-multiplexor
eklogin         2105/tcp                # Kerberos encrypted rlogin
rmt             5555/tcp    rmtd
mtb             5556/tcp    mtbd        # mtb backup
man             9535/tcp                # remote man server
w               9536/tcp
mantst          9537/tcp                # remote man server,
testing
bnews           10000/tcp
rscs0           10000/udp
queue           10001/tcp
rscs1           10001/udp
poker           10002/tcp
rscs2           10002/udp
gateway         10003/tcp
rscs3           10003/udp
remp            10004/tcp
rscs4           10004/udp
rscs5           10005/udp
rscs6           10006/udp
rscs7           10007/udp
rscs8           10008/udp
rscs9           10009/udp
rscsa           10010/udp
rscsb           10011/udp
qmaster         10012/tcp
qmaster         10012/udp
```

Secret

For all the hoopla surrounding Internet connectivity in Windows NT Server 4.0, it is interesting to discover that the Services file does not register HTTP at Port 80. I just thought you might like to know.

Reinstalling TCP/IP

Clearly one trick that is always available is to deinstall and reinstall the TCP/IP protocol suite in Windows NT Server 4.0. Something I've said before, that the Microsoft TCP/IP protocol stack is a weaker stack, unfortunately holds true in the heat of battle on occasion (and it always seems to be at the Enterprise level, not my home basement lab!).

So let's assume that you've tried just about every TCP/IP troubleshooting approach mentioned in this chapter and nothing, absolutely nothing, is solving your problem. Time for drastic action. Simply stated, remove and reinstall the TCP/IP protocol stack. Correctly done, this approach will work wonders.

But of course it isn't that simple. When reinstalling the TCP/IP protocol suite, it's entirely plausible that you will receive an error message that indicates "The Registry Subkey Already Exists." The fix is obvious. To fully remove

TCP/IP, you must remove the "embedded" Registry entries the protocol suite made during installation.

Tip

Experienced Microsoft Exchange users will immediately recognize what's going on here. To completely remove Microsoft Exchange from a Windows NT server, you must manually remove its related Registry entries. The same can be said for TCP/IP.

The TCP/IP protocol suite and related services entries that should be removed from the Registry are:

Connectivity utilities

Assuming you have removed the TCP/IP protocol "component," then you must remove:

```
HKEY_LOCAL_MACHINE\Software\Microsoft\NetBT
HKEY_LOCAL_MACHINE\Software\Microsoft\Tcpip
HKEY_LOCAL_MACHINE\Software\Microsoft\TcpipCU
HKEY_LOCAL_MACHINE\SYSTEM\CCS\Services\DHCP
HKEY_LOCAL_MACHINE\SYSTEM\CCS\Services\LMHosts
HKEY_LOCAL_MACHINE\SYSTEM\CCS\Services\'NetDriver'\Parameters\Tcpip
HKEY_LOCAL_MACHINE\SYSTEM\CCS\Services\NetBT
```

SNMP service

Assuming you have removed the SNMP service, you must remove:

```
HKEY_LOCAL_MACHINE\Software\Microsoft\RFC1156Agent
HKEY_LOCAL_MACHINE\Software\Microsoft\Snmp
HKEY_LOCAL_MACHINE\SYSTEM\CCS\Services\Snmp
```

TCP/IP network printing support

These entries relate to the LPDSVC line printer components. You must remove:

```
HKEY_LOCAL_MACHINE\Software\Microsoft\Lpdsvc
HKEY_LOCAL_MACHINE\Software\Microsoft\TcpPrint
HKEY_LOCAL_MACHINE\SYSTEM\CCS\Services\LpdsvcSimple TCP\IP Services
```

The next two entries related to the simple TCP/IP service. You must remove:

```
HKEY_LOCAL_MACHINE\Software\Microsoft\SimpTcp
HKEY_LOCAL_MACHINE\SYSTEM\CCS\Services\SimTcp
```

DHCP Server service

Assuming you have removed the HCP Server service, you must remove:

```
HKEY_LOCAL_MACHINE\Software\Microsoft\DhcpMibAgent
HKEY_LOCAL_MACHINE\Software\Microsoft\DhcpServer
HKEY_LOCAL_MACHINE\SYSTEM\CCS\Services\DhcpServer
```

WINS Server service

```
HKEY_LOCAL_MACHINE\Software\Microsoft\Wins
HKEY_LOCAL_MACHINE\Software\Microsoft\WinsMibAgent
HKEY_LOCAL_MACHINE\SYSTEM\CCS\Services\Wins
```

DNS Server service

Assuming you have removed the DNS Server service, you must remove:

```
HKEY_LOCAL_MACHINE\Software\Microsoft\Dns
HKEY_LOCAL_MACHINE\Software\Microsoft\WinsMibAgent
HKEY_LOCAL_MACHINE\SYSTEM\CCS\Services\Wins
```

Tip Few Windows NT Server professionals know about the required TCP/IP-related Registry housekeeping just detailed (removing Registry entries, and so on). By following the preceding suggestions, you've set yourself apart from the NT pack!

TCP/IP Q & A

As promised, here are more specific TCP/IP troubleshooting–related questions and answers.

Is TCP/IP correctly installed on my Windows NT Server?

This question isn't as easy to answer as you might think given the possibilities of corrupt TCP/IP protocol stack components that won't easily reveal themselves during a moment of need. However, you can always stick to a few basics. First, ping the loopback address of 127.0.0.1. Assuming this worked and a reply occurred, you're possibly home free. If it failed, however, observe the event logs and see what types of TCP/IP-related information were recorded in the system log. Second, ping another address (a host machine, another workstation, or such) and see if you receive a reply. If so, yet another TCP/IP-related hurdle has been passed.

I receive Error 53 when connecting to a server. What is it?

When host name resolution fails, Error 53 is returned. That's the bottom line. Possible resolution paths include confirming that the host name is spelled correctly (such as in the UNC format) when you attempt resolution (this assumes of course that the other computer is running TCP/IP). The preceding advice is valid for a remote host located on the same or a different subnet. However, if you are crossing to another subnet, the resolution scenario becomes more complex. For mixed Windows NT Server networks, you might also check that the WINS database contains the same type of name–to–IP address mappings. Heck, if you're really old fashioned, it wouldn't hurt to see if the LMHOSTS file contains the appropriate name–to–IP address mapping entries.

I'm relying on the LMHOSTS file for resolution. I've added a new name mapping, but I'm experiencing long connect times or timeout conditions. Why?

Supposing you have a large LMHOSTS file (of course this would only occur at the enterprise level), your new entries may be too far down the list for speedy name resolution. Therefore, it behooves you to preload the entry with the #PRE command. This and other LMHOST file goodies were discussed previously in the LMHOSTS discussion. You may also place your mapping higher in the LMHOSTS file.

I am having a difficult time connecting to a specific server. What gives?

Run the nbtstat -n to determine without doubt what names, including the server you are seeking, are registered on the network. See the nbtstat discussion earlier in the chapter for more information.

I cannot connect to a foreign host when using host names, but I can connect with IP addresses. Why?

Simply stated, you're having problems with DNS-related resolution. Check that the DNS Server setup for the TCP/IP protocol is correct. Make sure that the DNS addresses are correct and in the proper order. If you are using the HOSTS file, make sure that the remote computer name is spelled correctly with proper capitalization.

I'm communicating with a remote host, and the TCP/IP connection appears hung. I've confirmed this by observing TCP/IP-related errors in my error log. Why?

Using the netstat -a command, you can observe the port activity for TCP and UDP. A good TCP connection typically has 0 bytes in the send/receive queues. Blocked data will reveal itself as a connection problem. If this is not the case, then you're experiencing application delays or network problems. Don't overlook the possibilities of application delay. There's nothing like a client/server database suffering from contention problems that are disguised and appear as TCP/IP connection problems. If you're an experienced network professional, you probably have similar epic stories.

When using Telnet, the banner on the title bar isn't correct but I'm sure I've specified the correct IP address. Why?

It's important to verify that the DNS name and HOSTS table are current. Also, verify that no two computers have the same IP addresses on the same network. Imposter problems such as this are among the most difficult to track down and resolve. Using the arp -g command, you will see mapping from the ARP cache. This will display the Ethernet (MAC) address for the particular remote computer, possibly allowing you to delete the import entry with arp -d if you know the erroneous MAC address. After undertaking these steps, try pinging the remote host address, an action that forces an ARP. Finally, check the arp table again with arp -g.

I've received a message "Your default gateway does not belong to one of the configured interfaces." How can I solve this?

Basically, the default gateway doesn't appear to be on the same logical network as the computer's network adapter. This can be determined, and resolved, by comparing the network ID portion of the default gateway's IP address with the network ID(s) of any of the computer's network adapters.

I can't ping across a router when using TCP/IP as a RAS client.

The RAS Phonebook is the culprit here. If you have selected "Use default gateway on remote network" under the TCP/IP settings in the RAS Phonebook, you will have this problem. The resolution is this: Using the route add command, add the route of the subnet you're attempting to connect to.

Additional TCP/IP Troubleshooting Resources

Just a short note to wrap up TCP/IP troubleshooting. Remember that the event logs such as System and Application will assist your troubleshooting efforts, as will Microsoft TechNet, the online Microsoft Knowledge Base found at www.microsoft.com, Microsoft Technical Support, and Performance Monitor. If you use Performance Monitor, make sure that you've installed the SNMP service on your Windows NT Server so that you have the full suite of TPC/IP-related object:counters.

Summary

This chapter explored all the important topics of troubleshooting TCP/IP:

- Learning how to troubleshoot TCP/IP
- Understanding TCP/IP troubleshooting steps
- Understanding TCP/IP utilities and tools used for troubleshooting
- Selecting the best tool to solve your TCP/IP-related problem.

Chapter 8
DNS, DHCP, WINS

In This Chapter

- Learning DNS
- Learning DHCP
- Learning WINS
- Comparing and contrasting DNS, DHCP, and WINS
- Learning about integrating WINS and DNS
- Learning about the forthcoming Dynamic DNS

Three big topics and only one chapter available to cover them. Each topic, Domain Name System (or Domain Name Service, DNS), Dynamic Host Configuration Protocol (DHCP), and Windows Internet Name Service (WINS), are worthy of individual books. However, by studying these topics together, you may see how each has different yet integrated roles. In essence, Microsoft has implemented DNS, DHCP, and WINS so that they complement each other when used on the same network. Observe the following:

- **DNS.** Using DNS, clients can locate non-WINS supporting resources via static mappings maintained in the DNS database. In addition, any non-WINS-aware client that uses DNS to resolve names and has a static mapping to the DNS service can locate a WINS client, provided you configure the Microsoft DNS server to use a WINS server for additional names resolution.

- **DHCP.** The DHCP service enables you to allocate dynamic IP addresses automatically to DHCP clients that move between subnets.

- **WINS.** Using WINS, clients register their computer name and IP address automatically, every time they start up their computer. If the computer moves between subnets, this information is updated automatically as well.

Be Resolved

First, a review of name resolution. And I'm not talking about the pop '90s therapy where you deal with your resentments and make amends. This is network-based name resolution in which computer identifiers (typically hardware or IP addresses) are resolved to some form of name that is meaningful (computer name). "Names" on a computer network are really the following:

NetBIOS Name (for instance, SPRINGERS01)

TCP/IP Address (121.133.2.44)

Host Name (Abbey)

Media Access Control (MAC) — this is the network adapter hardware address

Note that these are four generally accepted naming conventions used on a Windows NT Server network (I've omitted the cursing-based names sometimes uttered by end users at misbehaving machines!).

NetBIOS name resolution

As you know, these names must be resolved so that you can find someone or something on the network to interact with. For NetBIOS names (such as those called from UNC commands) Microsoft uses a six-step resolution approach, as shown in Figure 8-1.

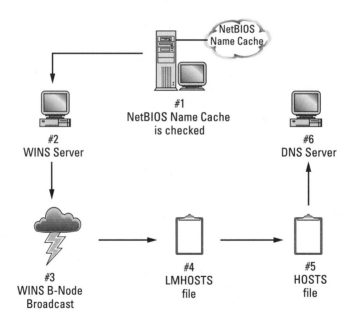

Figure 8-1: The Microsoft method for resolving NetBIOS names

STEPS:
To resolve NetBIOS names

Step 1. Check the cache. The NetBIOS name cache, built by the computer browser, is checked for the NetBIOS name/IP address mapping. If found, the resolution is complete.

Step 2. If the name isn't resolved from Step 1, the first of three attempts is made to contact the WINS server (if one is present). If the name is resolved, the IP address is returned to the source host. If the three attempts are unsuccessful, the resolution process continues.

Step 3. If the name is not resolved by the WINS server, three b-node broadcasts are sent on the local network by the client. If the proper NetBIOS name is found on the local network, the resolution to the IP address is complete.

Step 4. Next, the LMHOSTS file is consulted. Here again, if resolution is reached, the name resolution process terminates.

Step 5. The HOSTS file is consulted, assuming none of the previous steps have worked.

Step 6. Finally, as a final name resolution step, the source host sends a request to its respective domain name server, which resolves the host name to an IP address if successful.

Host name resolution

A similar, six-step name resolution approach is used for host name resolution in Windows NT Server (see Figure 8-2):

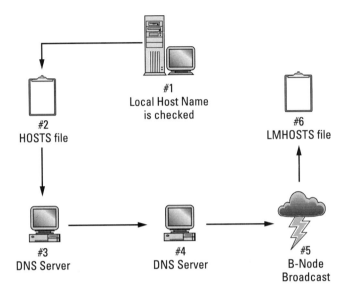

Figure 8-2: The Microsoft method for resolving host names

STEPS:

To resolve host names

Step 1. The host name typed by the user is compared to the local host name. If the two names match, resolution occurs without generating any network activity.

Step 2. Next, the HOSTS file is checked if the user-typed host name and the local name are not the same. Address resolution occurs if the user-typed host name is found in the HOSTS file. The host name is mapped to an IP address.

Step 3. If the host name is still unresolved, the source hosts sends a request to the domain name server. If the host name is resolved by a DNS, an IP address is mapped to it. If resolution doesn't occur initially, more attempts are made on the DNS at 5, 10, 20, and 40 second intervals.

Step 4. Assuming name resolution hasn't occurred, the local NetBIOS name cache is checked next followed by three attempts to contact and achieve resolution via configured WINS servers.

Step 5. The local host initiates three b-node broadcasts if name resolution still hasn't occurred.

Step 6. Last, the local LMHOSTS file is checked.

If all six steps fail and you are unable to resolve a host name to an IP address, then darn it, you're stuck with contacting the remote host via IP address (not host name). And most likely, a round of troubleshooting will follow.

Tip

One sign that DNS has been unsuccessful is when it has a timeout condition.

This typically results in some form of error message being returned to the user's terminal (see Figure 8-3). Resolution failure may be the result of hardware or software configuration errors. Determining what might be causing your resolution failure is the ongoing DNS challenge.

Figure 8-3: Host name resolution failure

Secret

DNS tries to resolve names by making resolution attempts at 5, 10, 20, and 40-second intervals.

DNS

At the most basic level, the Domain Name System (DNS) is a group of protocols and services widely used over the Internet and TCP/IP-based networks. Why? Because DNS provides name registration and name to address resolution capabilities. And DNS drastically lowers the need to remember numeric IP addresses when accessing hosts on the Internet or any other TCP/IP-based network. As an example, instead of typing **ping 131.107.6.200** to ping a specific host, you could type **ping harryb.com**, which is much easier (of course my example assumes that 131.107.6.200 maps to the host name harryb.com). This user-friendly functionality of DNS can be employed on your private Windows NT Server network by running DNS locally. That of course is the purpose of this section and the DNS installation section in Chapter 6, "Installing and Configuring TCP/IP."

So hopefully, it is clear that DNS enables you to interact with your computer, its network, and the Internet using street or "friendly" names while, largely in the background, these "friendly" names are resolved to an address. Likewise, addresses may be reverse-engineered back to a friendly name. This reverse-engineering is akin to this example involving cars. Suppose a car driving alongside you is of interest. Perhaps you would like to purchase the car. But at 70 miles per hour on the freeway, you are only able to write down the license number. Once home, you "reverse engineer" the license number to its owner by scanning the Department of Motor Vehicles car registration lists. This is a real-world example of reverse-engineering an "address" or numeric value back to a friendly name. Of course, in most states, motor vehicle records are confidential and unavailable (but early in my computing career, I did have occasion to legally purchase a computer database of car owners in Alaska that was used for marketing purposes).

DNS is well-suited for the enterprise given its method of managing host names and other name resolution information via a distributed system of replicated and delegated names databases. Based on specifications RFC 1034 and RFC 1035, DNS is based on the hierarchical and logical tree structure known as the domain name space. The top of the tree is the Internet Network Information Center (InterNIC), which can be accessed at `www.ds.internic.net`. InterNIC could truly be thought of as the Internet God in its role of performing domain registration and administration tasks. Once entered into the master database at InterNIC, domain names are replicated and managed through the use of distributed databases. These databases reside on numerous name servers located across the Internet. Each name server maintains a zone file that contains pertinent database information for its use, given its position in the tree hierarchy.

Microsoft's DNS service is something that separates Windows NT Server from other popular networking alternatives such as Novell's NetWare, Artisoft's LANtastic, and Macintosh. Those other NOSes historically have not provided the same level of DNS support out of the box. And that's something to consider as networks become increasingly Internet-centric.

Before DNS, the practice of mapping friendly host or computer names to IP addresses was handled via host files. Host files are easy to understand. These are static ASCII text files that simply map a host name to an IP address in a table-like format. Windows NT Server 4.0 ships with a HOSTS file in the \winnt\system32\drivers\etc subdirectory. The Windows NT Server HOSTS file is discussed at length in Chapter 7, "Troubleshooting TCP/IP."

The fundamental problem with the host files was that these files were labor intensive. A host file is manually modified, and it is typically centrally administrated. What a pain as your network grows, especially if your network is the Internet! Much of that pain and agony has disappeared because DNS is a much more distributed and automated approach.

Today, while not implemented perfectly in Windows NT Server 4.0, DNS is a huge step in the right direction. By electing to use the DNS service in Windows NT Server 4.0, you are well positioned to upgrade to Windows 2000 Server. Why not perfect today? Because DNS as we know it still has a nasty time lag when propagating changes. It seems that whenever I assist a client in moving their domain from one Internet service provider (ISP) to another, the changes do not fully take effect for 24 hours! That often means that I make a return site visit to the client site to fully test their system after the DNS-related propagation has completed. It's not perfect.

Secret

When using the WHOIS command (which was discussed in Chapter 7, "Troubleshooting TCP/IP"), you will note that every Internet domain registered with the InterNIC has at least two DNS servers associated with the domain name. Why? Believe it or not, this Internet-related feature is a US Department of Defense design feature. According to my good friend, a highly placed source who has worked in government and academic computing communities since the Eisenhower era, this design paradigm stems from the cold war. In the event of a thermonuclear war, the Internet as we know it would survive, in part due to its inherent redundancy. Having two separate DNS servers tied to each domain account is part of this redundancy.

Be sure that you verify that two DNS servers are associated with your Internet domain name (see Figure 8-4). The dual DNS server requirement is your responsibility and is in place to ensure that your Internet domain name is properly resolved on the Internet. Clearly, that is to your benefit. And if you're involved in electronic commerce, it is essential. Could you imagine customers not being able to find your store front? Not having two DNS servers associated with your Internet domain name places you at a risk of exactly this: lost sales because customers can't successfully find and use your Web site.

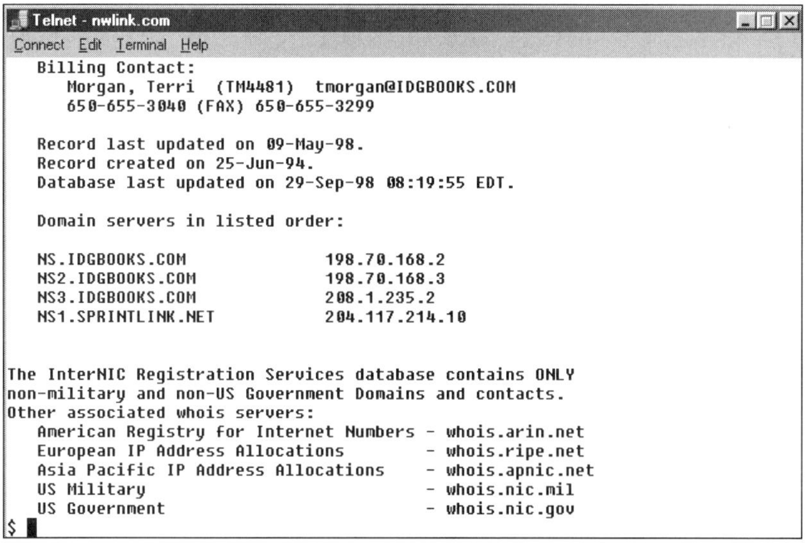

Figure 8-4: The DNS servers for idgbooks.com

As a Windows NT professional, you will have the opportunity to work with a wide range of applications that, being TCP/IP based, depend on DNS properly functioning. One example is a small law firm that I advise. This law firm uses WestMate, an application from WestLaw for its legal research. Older versions of this application used modem dial-up connections to a local telephone

Part II: TCP/IP

number or CompuServe. A later version, version 7.x, uses a Winsock-based connection to the law firm's existing Internet service to operate correctly. More specifically, the application uses FTP port 23 to communicate over the Internet. This application depends heavily on DNS properly operating because it is connecting to the site `westmate.westmate.com` when it launches and attempts to log on and authenticate the research-minded attorney. If DNS is somehow not working, the application fails, the lawyers are researchless, and I receive a call to "fix it."

As another example, observe how Internet Explorer, Microsoft's Web browser, works. When you type in the uniform resource locator (URL), that name is resolved via DNS. So typing `www.idgbooks.com` triggers a series of events that connects you and your browser with the distant site on the Internet.

Finally, you may use DNS with your Microsoft Exchange application. A common configuration with the Internet Mail Service (IMS) in Microsoft Exchange is to have DNS perform the outgoing mail resolution. And even if you don't explicitly have DNS selected, providing a mail host name such as `smtp.nwnexus.com` when configuring the IMS assumes you have DNS capabilities that can resolve this street-friendly host name.

Note

Exceptions to the rule of generally connecting to any Internet site you desire include little-known sites that are literally located in distant lands; these sites can be too many hops away. An example of this includes sites such as the far reaches of Alaska (if you are located in the 48 contiguous states). Perhaps these sites haven't had their domain names replicated across the DNS databases of the world. So when you attempt to access this site, and the domain name can't be easily resolved, your browser may return a "host not found" error. In reality, the host exists but can't be resolved within the time window your browser supports. I typically refer to this problem as a host that is too many hops away.

The preceding problem has two solutions. First, request that the remote site mirror or publish its Web page to another server somewhere else in the world. This is what Microsoft, Novell, and other vendors do with the well-traveled Web pages. These large sites mirror their sites to other servers not for resolution purposes but for load balancing and reliability. When you have a popular Web site, you may need to use mirror servers just to keep up with the traffic demands. Just ask Microsoft and Novell. The second solution is my next secret, so read on.

Secret

One possible way to get around the problem of finding a site that is too many hops away and by all account appears unbrowsable is to use a search engine for your name resolution tasks and then click the hot link from the search engine hit list. Search engines to consider include Yahoo! (`www.yahoo.com`), Alta Vista (`www.altavista.com`), or Infoseek (`www.infoseek.com`). As you know, these search engines may be selected via the search button on the taskbar of your browser. Ideally, this would provide you another pathway to that faraway site. And the domain name resolution would have occurred differently, that is, via the search engine. By the way, do you want to know my favorite search engine? For a single search engine, I prefer Infoseek for reasons I fully explain (such as robust drill down) in Part VI, "Optimizing and Troubleshooting Windows NT Server 4.0." But here, where I want to find a little-known domain name or Web site, I want to cast as wide a net as possible, so I typically perform these "domain seeking" searches from a site that is a "clearing house" for search engines. This site is www.dogpile.com. Dogpile is a search engine of search engines. By executing your search here, you effectively search all the other engines.

How DNS really works

So by now you can appreciate that Windows NT Server administrators can (and should!) use DNS to manage domain names.

DNS uses a client/server model in which the DNS server maintains a static database of domain names mapped to IP addresses. The DNS client, known as the resolver, perform queries against the DNS servers. The bottom line? DNS resolves domain names to IP address using these steps (see Figure 8-5):

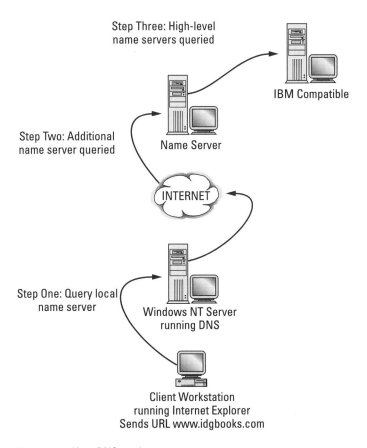

Figure 8-5: How DNS works

> **STEPS:**
> To resolve domain names to an IP address with DNS
>
> **Step 1.** A client (or "resolver") passes its request to its local name server. For example, the URL term www.idgbooks.com typed into Internet Explorer is passed to the DNS server identified in the client TCP/IP configuration. This DNS server is known as the local name server.
>
> **Step 2.** If, as often happens, the local name server is unable to resolve the request, other name servers are queried so that the resolver may be satisfied.
>
> **Step 3.** If all else fails, the request is passed to more and more, higher-level name servers until the query resolution process starts with far-right term (for instance, com) or at the top of the DNS tree with root name servers.

DNS benefits

Several benefits accrue to those Windows NT Server administrators who elect to employ DNS in their networks:

- DNS provides a head start on managing your network for the forthcoming Windows 2000 Server.
- Computer users may connect to UNIX systems via friendly names.
- Users may fully exploit the Internet via Internet naming conventions such as URLs (for instance, www.idgbooks.com).
- Enterprises can maintain a consistent naming structure for both external Internet resources and internal network resources.

DNS details and definitions

I will use the next several pages to get into the details of DNS, now that you've considered DNS from several vantage points.

Defining domain name space

The DNS database is known as the domain name space and assumes a tree form. Each position in the tree is called a *domain*. Just as a tree can have branches shooting out from its trunk, a domain may have subdomains. The main thing to remember is that entries in the domain name space must adhere to the accepted DNS naming conventions. These conventions are quite simple. At each level, a period (.) is used to separate each child domain (or subdomain) from its parent.

Defining domains

Domains contain both hosts and other domains. A domain has five components, all of which may be present in any given domain name space, but not all five components (such as the subdomain name component) are always present in smaller domain name spaces.

The domain root

Considered to be the root node of the DNS tree, the domain root is known as the unnamed or null entry. You might see this referred as the trailing period, which is typically not listed when displaying a domain name.

However, to display a fully qualified domain name (FQDN) requires this period (".") as the last term displayed on the far right of the domain name.

The top-level domain

In reality, the top-level domain is the far-right term in a typical Internet domain name as displayed. This domain level is specifically managed by InterNIC and is divided into three areas:

1. **Organizational.** This is the three-character code any network professional or Internet surfer is familiar with (these are listed in Table 8-1).

2. **Geographical.** Based on ISO-3166 (a standard) these are typically country designations (such as .nz for New Zealand). Perhaps you've encountered these top-level domain designations in e-mail messages you've received from overseas, for instance.

3. **In-addr.arpa.** This is the least known of the three top-level domains. It is a special reserved domain used for IP-address-to-name mappings, also known as reverse lookups.

Did you know the United States has a geographic top-level domain of "us"? It does! Perhaps you haven't encountered this form, because it is seldom used.

Table 8-1 provides a list of top-level domain names in a DNS tree. The number of these names continues to grow, however.

Table 8-1 Top-Level DNS Domain Names

Domain Name	Designation
COM	Commercial (businesses, corporations)
EDU	Education (schools, universities)
GOV	Government (local, state, federal)
INT	International, such as the United Nations
MIL	Military, such as the Navy and the Army
NET	Internet service providers (for instance, ibm.net)
ORG	Nonprofit organizations, such as mssociety.org

Second-level domains

Second-level domains are the names most familiar to network professionals, Internet surfers, and even the general audience. Such a name typically consists of a company name or a product name that is meaningful, useful, and memorable. For example, the publisher of this book, IDG Books Worldwide, has registered the second-level domain name idgbooks.com with the InterNIC. Not surprisingly, second-level domain names are indeed managed by the InterNIC in order to ensure that each name is unique.

Second-level domains are causing lots of fun and litigation in the business community right now! Speculators are registering trademark names (with InterNIC) prior to the trademark holders doing so. Often, the company that holds the trademark will then "purchase" the second-level domain registration from the speculator, who typically makes a handsome profit on his or her $50 InterNIC domain registration fee (although some trademark holders are suing, rather than paying to recover trademark names being used as domain names). All in a day's work for some, but for others the implicit message should be to register your second-level domain names as soon as possible before someone else does! By analogy, yesterday's mad rush to acquire 1-800 telephone numbers is today's rush to acquire the second-level domain name of your choice.

Third-level domain names (subdomains)

The third-level domain name is an optional term in DNS. Typically it is used to append or further subdivide the "regular" domain name. For example, perhaps you want to subdivide functional departments at the imaginary company Springers Unlimited. If the "regular" domain name known to all is springers.com and you want to further subdivide the domain name to better reflect your organization, you might have domain names such as marketing.springers.com and legal.springers.com. Another use of subdomains is to create distinctions by location. Following my example, if you further subdivided springers.com by locations, you might have a third-level domain titled west.springers.com. You get the picture.

You will note that Microsoft makes extensive use of third-level domain names appended to its regular domain name of microsoft.com to distinguish different departments, programs, promotions, and such.

Third-level domain names are managed by you, the network administrator, and not the InterNIC. You may, in theory, append as many third-level domain names to your regular or second-level domain name as you wish! In effect, all the employees in your organization could have their own domain names. Such names mean that name resolution will occur locally on your server designated to handle second-level domain name activity after the path has been correctly resolved by DNS servers on the Internet that deliver the session communications. This process is shown in the Figure 8-6, where traffic destined for springers.com from the Internet is further subdivided internally according to, in this example, departments.

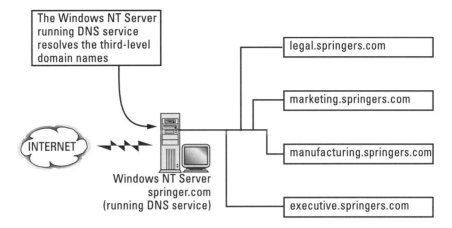

Figure 8-6: Using third-level domain names on your network

In the preceding example, having the local Windows NT server perform the third-level domain name resolution would require that the DNS service be installed and fully functional on the local Windows NT server.

One place you most assuredly will use third-level domain names is when you run the Internet Connection Wizard in Small Business Server (see Chapter 20, "Windows NT Server — Small Business Server"). Here, the Internet Connection Wizard automatically creates a third-level domain name when you open an account with an SBS-compliant Internet service provider (ISP). Thus if I had registered Springers Unlimited with Northwest Nexus (a Pacific Northwest ISP), the third-level domain address that would automatically be created for me might be `springers.nwnexus-sbs.com`.

In reality the use of third-level domain names is still rare in the business community. Blame it on the marketing departments of companies across the land, but second-level domain names are in and third-level domain names look both cheap and kind of weird. The business community, which has no shortage of egos and public relations specialists, very much demands second-level domain names because image is everything. You are more likely to see a company use a second-level domain name and a virtual directory.

Make darn sure you understand the difference between a subdomain and a virtual directory. The key point is that subdomains are a way to divide your domain name space, and virtual directories point to storage areas on your server's hard drive. A virtual subdirectory is typically displayed as a forward slash after the top-level domain term (for instance, `/harryb`), and a subdomain name is displayed as a term to the left of the second-level domain name (as discussed previously).

It is not uncommon to see both a subdomain and a virtual directory displayed in a URL on the Internet. For example, `springers.nwnexus-sbs.com/~dawgs` shows the subdomain name `springers` and the virtual directory `~dawgs`.

Note virtual directories are discussed in Chapter 10, "Internet Secrets."

Host names

Host names are entered in the TCP/IP Properties box of the Network applet in the Control Panel in Windows NT Server. In DNS, the host name appears to the left of the top-level and second-level domain names. This is similar to how third-level domain names appear.

As an example, the host name `harryb` in the domain `springers.com` would appear as: `harryb.springers.com`. Note that the host name resolution would be performed by a Windows NT server on your network similar to the process discussed previously in relation to Figure 8-2.

Evaluating domain names

Evaluating a domain name is different from other activities you are probably used to performing. It is not like reading the printed page, such as this, where you read from left to right. It is not like finding a position on a map, where you use a column and row grid. It is not like finding your physical location with a Global Positioning System (GPS) device, where you rely on high-altitude satellites.

Tip

You read a fully qualified domain name from right to left. A second-level domain name such as `idgbooks.com` would be evaluated first as a commercial top-level domain and then as the second domain term `idgbooks`. A third-level domain name might appear as `springers.nwnexus-sbs.com`: And once again, if you didn't notice, a period is used to divide each domain name level.

To assist you in your efforts to better interpret domain names, Table 8-2 breaks down a sample Internet domain name into each domain level.

Table 8-2   Evaluating a Third-Level Domain Name

Domain Name Level	Term	Comments
Top-level domain name	com	Designates a commercial entity.
Second-level domain name	nwnexus-sbs	Would be registered with InterNIC (the Internet domain registration authority).
Third-level domain name	springers	Not registered with InterNIC. Typically the holder of the second-level domain name will create the as many third-level domain names as necessary. Third-level domain names are typically resolved by DNS running on a Windows NT server on the local network (although this configuration isn't required).

Note

Under Windows NT Server, the DNS host name defaults to the same name as the NetBIOS computer name. You can change this if you need separate names. Also be advised that the term "domain" in the context of DNS relates to Internet domains, not Windows NT Server domains.

Take a moment to analyze your own Internet domain name if you have one. Does the preceding discussion help you to better understand how your domain name?

Secret

DNS names that do not conclude with a trailing period (such as ".com.") are not fully qualified domain names (FQDN).

Zones

In my MCSE lectures that I deliver as an MCT, I often refer to Windows NT Server domains as administrative units. In the language of DNS, *zones* can also be thought of as administrative units. Database records relating to a particular portion of the domain name space, a zone, are saved in a file known as a *zone file*.

Understand that a zone can consist of a single domain (DNS-style, not Windows NT) or a domain with subdomains. A single DNS server can be configured to manage one or more zone files. Each zone is anchored by a discrete domain node (known as a zone's *root domain*).

Let's take a moment to make a distinction between a zone and a DNS-style domain. A domain refers to a single node and all of its child nodes. A zone is a full and complete set of resource records that is delegated to a specific name server. Another take on the matter is this: Domains represent a logical, hierarchical organization of name space. Zones represent the physical arrangement of how names and resource data are distributed or delegated to name servers.

Files used by DNS

Remember this as you master DNS with Windows NT Server: The underlying files in a DNS system are text files. The good news is that with Windows NT Server, you will enjoy using its graphical user interface-based DNS tool set to edit and manage the DNS zone files.

Zone files

A database file or "zone file" is a file of resource records (RRs) for the portion of the domain for which the zone is granted responsibility. A resource record could be defined as an individual data entry containing a domain name and other information related to this named domain or host. Note that resource records may be either of these:

- **Record type.** Type is used to indicate the type of data stored by each record. Type defines the format or individual field structures for each particular resource record. In other words, different types of records occur in zone files, and you may elect to query for only one type of record.

- **Record class.** Class is used to indicate the class of network or type of software that this record supports. In most cases, the only class used for DNS data that is stored and used in most TCP/IP networks is the Internet Class (IC).

I've defined the important zone files, ranging from Start of Authority (SOA) to Canonical Name (CNAME), that you need to know in Table 8-4, "Zone Record Definitions," in the section "Configuring DNS."

Cache files

Cache files contains host names and addresses of root name servers. You can observe the default cache file (cache.dns) provided by the DNS server in Windows NT Server.

```
Cache file:
.                           2163095040 IN    NS    A.ROOT-SERVERS.NET.
A.ROOT-SERVERS.NET.         2163095040 IN    A     198.41.0.4
.                           2163095040 IN    NS    B.ROOT-SERVERS.NET.
B.ROOT-SERVERS.NET.         2163095040 IN    A     128.9.0.107
.                           2163095040 IN    NS    C.ROOT-SERVERS.NET.
C.ROOT-SERVERS.NET.         2163095040 IN    A     192.33.4.12
.                           2163095040 IN    NS    D.ROOT-SERVERS.NET.
D.ROOT-SERVERS.NET.         2163095040 IN    A     128.8.10.90
.                           2163095040 IN    NS    E.ROOT-SERVERS.NET.
E.ROOT-SERVERS.NET.         2163095040 IN    A     192.203.230.10
.                           2163095040 IN    NS    F.ROOT-SERVERS.NET.
F.ROOT-SERVERS.NET.         2163095040 IN    A     39.13.229.241
.                           2163095040 IN    NS    G.ROOT-SERVERS.NET.
G.ROOT-SERVERS.NET.         2163095040 IN    A     192.112.36.4
.                           2163095040 IN    NS    H.ROOT-SERVERS.NET.
H.ROOT-SERVERS.NET.         2163095040 IN    A     128.63.2.53
.                           2163095040 IN    NS    I.ROOT-SERVERS.NET.
I.ROOT-SERVERS.NET.         2163095040 IN    A     192.36.148.17
```

For DNS installations not connected to the Internet, this file may be replaced or modified. If you are managing your own domain name space privately, you should include host records for root name servers within your private network that can be contacted to authoritatively resolve names not managed by the server's zone files.

Note

To see the current Internet cache files for the worldwide Internet, go to ftp://rs.internic.net/domain/named.cache on the Internet.

Reverse lookup files

As the name implies, reverse lookup files are the files consulted when a reverse lookup is undertaken in the in-addr.arpa domain. A reverse lookup is performed when you supply the IP address and the computer, via a reverse lookup, returns the matching domain host name. The key point about reverse lookup files is that some applications depend on these types of reverse resolutions. One application area that takes advantage of them consists of NFS clients.

Boot files

Boot files are used to configure the startup environment of DNS servers that use Berkeley Internet Name Domain (BIND). However, Microsoft DNS does not have complete BIND conformance, and thus boot files are present to support migrations from other BIND environments. The boot file contained at c:\winnt\system32\dns appears as:

```
The DNS Server is now booting from the registry.
New zones or changes to zone information made through the DNS Manager,
require the DNS server to boot from information stored in the
registry.
Further changes to zone configuration MUST be made through the DNS
Manager,
as the boot file is no longer being read.
The previous boot file has been moved to the backup directory.
If you must return to using a boot file, use the registry editor to
open
HKEY_LOCAL_MACHINE\SYSTEM\CurrentControlSet\Services\DNS\Parameters
and delete
the value EnableRegistryBoot.  Then replace your desired boot file in
the
system32\dns directory.  Note, however, that ALL changes to zone
information,
including new zones, made through the DNS Manager will be lost.
```

Name servers

Simply stated, a *name server* is any server that retains and stores information about the domain name space. Known on the network as DNS servers, these machines run vendor-specific DNS implementations such as the DNS service in Windows NT Server.

It is important that you understand that name servers have one or more zones that they are responsible for. To respond affirmatively to a name query, a name server must have the authority to do so for the zone in which the queried name resides. This authority is handled by the start of authority (SOA) record at the top of the zone file. SOA is discussed later, in Table 8-4 (see the section "Configuring DNS").

Three types of name servers

When building your DNS environment, you may implement three type of name servers. These servers are primary, secondary, and caching. Most of us working in smaller and medium-sized organizations would use a primary domain server. However, if you work at the enterprise level (especially with geographical dispersed operations), you will not only benefit from but seek to use secondary and caching servers. The number and types of name servers you use are directly correlated to the size of your network.

Primary servers

A primary server is a single server for each zone that contains the master database files (resource records for all subdomains and hostnames, and so on) for the zone it is allowed to service. This server retrieves its resolution information or zone data locally, and likewise, changes are made locally.

Secondary servers

If I were discussing Microsoft System Management Server (SMS), I would be referring to "helper" servers. That's what secondary servers are for DNS: helper servers. Secondary servers have a copy of the appropriate domain name space data from another name server on the network. The server that provided the "copy" had the authority to do so and is known as an authoritative server. The mechanism for copying the information to the secondary server? Replication. The replication process occurs via a regular zone transfer from the other name server.

Three important reasons exist for having secondary servers in the enterprise:

- **Load reduction.** Having secondary servers reduces the load on the primary name servers.

- **Distant locations.** Secondary servers, similar to BDCs in the context of Windows NT Server, should be placed at remote locations that have significant client activity. This avoids having clients suffer from slow WAN links when trying to query DNS.

- **Redundancy.** It is necessary to have at least two DNS servers for each zone. One server is the primary; the other(s) is/are secondary. Typically these machines are placed on separate networks for sake of fault tolerance.

Caching-only servers

The caching-only type of name server doesn't contain any active database files and isn't associated with any specific DNS zone. It relies on other name servers for its knowledge of the DNS domain structure. Every time a caching-only server queries a name server, the information it receives back is stored in its name cache.

Forwarders and slaves

Suppose the DNS server on your Windows NT network is unable to resolve the name query? In this case, additional DNS servers are consulted to satisfy the name query. Assuming you've correctly configured your internal DNS servers to use forwarders, then other servers on the Internet are typically consulted, resulting in name resolution.

Remember that specific DNS servers, via the DNS Manager (discussed later in this chapter), are configured to use forwarders. And only forwarders may contact Internet-based DNS name servers.

Slaves are configured to use forwarders and return error messages if a request fails.

Resolvers

You can think of resolvers as client services that execute name queries against name servers. More specifically, resolvers are typically part of the client's operating system (such as the TCP/IP DNS configuration information in Windows 95/98) that:

- Oversees and manages communications between TCP/IP client programs using DNS and name servers.
- Formats the DNS query packets that are sent to name servers.
- Caches previous DNS query replies to speed future name resolutions.

Resolver programs perform the following three functions on behalf of the DNS client:

- **General lookup function.** Involves finding records with a specific name, type, or class.
- **Address-to-name translation.** This is reverse name resolution. When presented with a 32-bit IP address, the program returns a host name.
- **Name-to-address translation.** When given a host or domain name, the program locates the appropriate 32-bit IP address. This is the most common use of DNS.

Name resolution — how it works

By now you certainly understand that the key point to DNS is name resolution. Users provide friendly names that are resolved to IP addresses. The IP addresses are necessary for many programs, such as your browser (for instance, Internet Explorer), to operate. In the next few sections, I discuss four types of name resolution: recursion, iteration, caching, and reverse lookup.

Recursion

First, your DNS name server must be configured to support recursive forwarding of name queries. In this scenario, your name server assumes responsibility for forwarding unresolved name queries until it receives either a positive or negative response. Stated another way, when a recursion-compliant DNS server is contacted, it contacts other name servers until a clear and definitive answer for the original name query is received.

The default condition for the DNS service in Windows NT Server is that recursive requests are allowed.

Iteration

In the case of iteration, a name server responds to a resolver based on its most complete or "best knowledge" of the data being queried. That's it. A best effort. With iteration, the name server may provide the address of another name server for the resolver to use if the best efforts weren't good enough.

It is worth noting that clients are typically configured, via the client's TCP/IP setup, to use other DNS servers if the first DNS server can't resolve the name query.

Caching

The concept of caching is easily understood. As local name servers perform name queries for resolvers on a network, these servers build a name cache based on their findings. In effect, these local name servers learn along the way. Once name resolution information is stored in cache memory of the local name server, this information may be quickly accessed again when the local name server receives other name queries. Simply stated, the name cache, a very fast resolution approach, is consulted for the benefit of the resolvers.

Note that a Time to Live (TTL) value applies to records that are cached. That way, older records that may not be relevant or readily accessed again are deleted from cache memory. This benefits name server performance.

The contents of the cache.dns file found on Windows NT Server is loaded into cache memory when a Windows NT server running DNS is started. The file cache.dns was displayed several pages ago.

Reverse lookup

Most lookups via DNS are "forward lookups," where a "friendly" name is resolved to an IP address. But what about this scenario: Suppose on the information superhighway you see the following graffiti at a road stop: "for a good time visit 131.107.6.200." Being the curious Windows NT Server engineer that you are, you decide to see just who 131.107.6.200 is before finding out whether a good time can really be had. A reverse lookup, presented to the special domain `in-addr.arpa`, will reveal the identity of this address. It's as if you found a telephone number and wanted to know who it belonged to. (In fact, for a brief period in the 1980s when I was living in Alaska, a reverse telephone book was published before privacy concerns quashed it.)

Zone transfer

Zone transfers are transmissions of name space information among DNS servers. Historically, this occurred when, periodically, the entire zone file from one name server was transferred to another name server. This is now also done by the incremental zone transfer method. Here, just the delta (or changed) information is transferred. Incremental zone transfer is discussed in RFC 1995.

Chapter 8: DNS, DHCP, WINS

Note: Zone transfers between name servers are what we MCSE-types in the real world view as propagation delays when implementing domain name transfers, starting new domain names, and such.

Installing DNS

Installing DNS is relatively simple. Configuring it is more difficult. In this discussion, a quick review of installing DNS will be followed by the more complex discussion of configuring DNS.

STEPS:
To install DNS services

Step 1. Make sure that you are logged on as a member of the Administrators group.

Step 2. Select the Network applet from Control Panel.

Step 3. Select the Services tab sheet and click the Add button. You will recall that these three steps are remarkably similar to the network-related configuration steps shown in Chapter 6, "Installing and Configuring TCP/IP."

Step 4. Select Microsoft DNS Server from the Select Network Service dialog box and click OK. When prompted, provide the directory path for the Windows NT Server source files.

Step 5. Finally, click OK on the Network dialog box and reboot the computer.

Once correctly installed, the DNS service will appear in Windows NT Server in three ways. First, it will appear as a Network Service under the Services tab in the Network applet. Second, it will appear as "Microsoft DNS Server" in the Services applet accessed via Control Panel. Finally, you will utilize the DNS Manager application found in Administrative Tools [Common]. This is the tool that I will discuss next.

Configuring DNS

DNS Manager, shown in Figure 8-7, has as its primary function the configuration of DNS objects. Each object has a discrete set of manageable properties. DNS Manager is a visual interface or GUI-based tool used to configure the DNS objects. Table 8-3 shows Common DNS Manager objects that you will likely find yourself configuring.

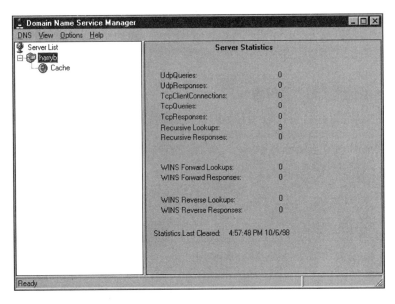

Figure 8-7: DNS Manager

Table 8-3 Common DNS Objects Needing Configuration

Object	Description
DNS Resource Record (RR)	This is the principle object in DNS. It is the component that contains the information managed by DNS. Three DNS properties common to all RR types are owner, class, TTL (Time to Live).
RR — Owner	This identifies the RR's DNS domain or host.
RR — Class	This identifies a defined group of RR types. Most common today is the "IN" class for Internet class.
RR — TTL	Time to Live reflects duration that RR information is valid.
DNS Domain	This is a discrete node in the DNS tree. It encompasses the resource records for that domain.
DNS Zone	This is a DNS database subtree that is administered as a single entity. This might be a single domain or a rich domain structure of a domain with subdomains.
DNS Server	This administers one or more DNS zones.
Server List	This is a list of DNS servers that are eligible to be managed by DNS Manager. You may add DNS servers as necessary to this list.

STEPS:

To configure DNS services

Step 1. Plan what you are attempting to accomplish with the DNS service. Admittedly, with some areas of Windows NT Server 4.0, you can wing it and not plan exactly why you are doing something. The DNS service isn't one of those areas, and in fact, poorly planned and implemented, the DNS service can wreak havoc on your network.

Step 2. Launch the DNS Manager from the Administrative Tools [Common] group found under the Programs menu option when you click the Start button.

Step 3. To create a zone, right-click on the server (for instance, harryb) listed in the left pane of DNS Manager. Select New Zone (note you will also see this menu option under the DNS drop-down menu in DNA Manager).

Step 4. Select either Primary or Secondary zone in the Creating New Zone dialog box, as shown in Figure 8-8. Click Next.

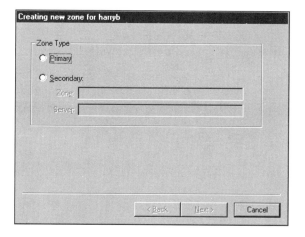

Figure 8-8: Select primary or secondary zone.

Step 5. Type in a Zone Name. Tab to the Zone File tab sheet (see Figure 8-9).

Continued

STEPS

To configure DNS services *(continued)*

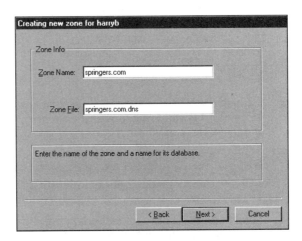

Figure 8-9: Provide a Zone Name and a Zone File.

Note

The Zone File name is automatically created for you. Essentially, the Zone File name is the same as your Zone Name with ".dns" appended to it.

Step 6. Finish the zone creation process by clicking the Finish button on the last screen of the Creating New Zone Wizard. The zone is listed on the left pane of DNS Manager. In this case, the zone is springers.com (see Figure 8-10). The right pane provides detailed zone information.

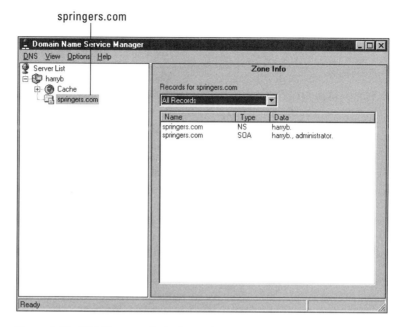

Figure 8-10: DNS Manager displaying springers.com

Notice in the right pane, Zone Info, there is a drop-down menu for different types of records. The additional records are defined in Table 8-4.

Table 8-4 Zone Record Definitions

Record Type	Definition
Host (A)	Maps host name to IP address in a DNS zone. Has three fields: Domain, Host Name, Host IP Address.
Aliases (CNAME)	Canonical name resource record that creates an alias for a host name. CNAME records are typically used to hide implementation details from clients. Fields include: Domain, Alias Name, For Host DNS Name.
Nameservers (NS)	Identifies the DNS name servers in the DNS domain. NS records appear in all DNS zones and reverse zones. Fields include: Domain, Name Server DNS Name.

Continued

Table 8-4 *(continued)*

Record Type	Definition
Pointer (PTR)	Maps IP address to host name in a DNS reverse zone. Fields include: IP Address, Host DNS Name.
Mail Exchange (MX)	Specifies a mail exchange server for a DNS domain name. Note that the term "exchange" does not refer to Microsoft Exchange, a BackOffice e-mail application. However, to connect Microsoft Exchange to the Internet via the Internet Mail Server (IMS), the MX record must be correctly configured by your ISP. A mail exchange server is a host that will either process or forward mail for the DNS domain name. Processing the mail means either delivering it to the addressee or passing it to a different type of mail transport. Forwarding the mail means sending it to its final destination server, sending it using Simple Mail Transfer Protocol to another mail server that is closer to the final destination, or queuing it for a specified amount of time. Fields include: Domain, Host Name (Optional), Mail Exchange Server DNS Name, Preference Number.
Host Information (HINFO)	Identifies a host's hardware type and operating system. The CPU Type and Operating System identifiers should come from the MACHINE NAMES and SYSTEM NAMES listed in RFC 1700 (Assigned Numbers). Fields include: Domain, Host Name, CPU Type, Operating System.
Text (TXT)	Associates text with an item in the DNS database. For example, a use might be to communicate a computer location such as Build 10, Room 1a. The Text string is limited to 256 characters. Fields include: Domain, Host Name (Optional), Text.
Well Known Services (WKS)	Describes the services provided by a particular protocol on a particular interface. Typically this is the TCP or UDP protocol, but it can be any protocol listed in the PROTOCOLS file (located at \winnt\system32\drivers\etc). The services are services specifically below Port 256 from the SERVICES file (located at \winnt\system32\drivers\etc). Fields include: Domain, Host Name, Host IP Address, Available Services, Available Protocol.

Record Type	Definition
Responsible Person (RP)	This indicates who is responsible for the DNS domain or host. Multiple RP records may be specified for a single DNS domain. The record is divided into two parts: electronic mail address and a DNS domain name that points to additional information about the contact. Fields include: Domain, Host Name (Optional), Responsible Person Mailbox DNS Name, DNS Name for TXT Reference.
AFS Database (AFSDB)	Provides the location of either an AFS (Andrew File System) cell database server or a DCE (Distributed Computing Environment) cell's authenticated name server. Transac's AFS is a network file system, similar to NFS, but designed for WANs.
	The AFS system uses DNS to map a DNS domain name to the name of an AFS cell database server. The Open Software Foundation's DCE Naming Service uses DNS for a similar function, mapping the DNS domain name of a DCS cell to authenticated name servers for that cell.
	Fields include: Domain, Host Name (Optional), Server DNS Name, Server Type.
X.25 (X25)	A variation of the A record, the X25 record maps the host name to an X.121 address. Fields include: Domain, Host Name (Optional), X.121 PSDN Address.
ISDN (ISDN)	Maps the host name to an ISDN address instead of an IP address. Fields include: domain, Host Name (Optional), ISDN Phone Number (and DDI), ISDN Subaddress (Optional).
AAAA (IPNG)	Known as the address resource record, this maps a host name to an Ipv6 address. This record will assume greater importance as the next generations of IP are implemented. Fields include: Domain, Host Name, IPv6 Address.

Additional zone configuration options are presented when you right-click the zone name (see Figure 8-11).

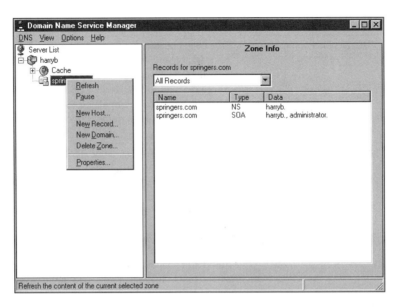

Figure 8-11: Secondary menu options for zone name

The significant secondary menu options include:

- **New Host.** Adds a host at this node level, in this case, springers.com (see Figure 8-12).

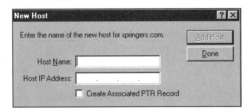

Figure 8-12: New Host

- **New Record.** Creates a new record at this node (see Figure 8-13).

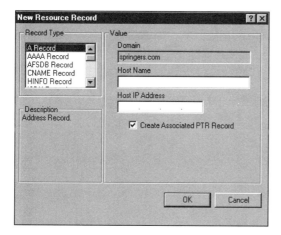

Figure 8-13: New Resource Record displaying A record setup

Tip

This menu option is extremely powerful, as it exposes you to the inner workings of the DNS service in Windows NT Server. It is here that you would provide the detailed configurations for your zone. Configurations made involve the records defined in Table 8-4 plus these others:

- Mailbox Name (MB)
- Mail Group (MG)
- Mailbox Information (MINFO)
- Renamed Mailbox (MR)
- Route-Through Information (RT)

Note that selecting different records in the left scroll window will change the fields displayed on the right side of the New Resource Record dialog box under the value box. For example, Figure 8-14 shows the fields displayed when the MINFO record type is selected.

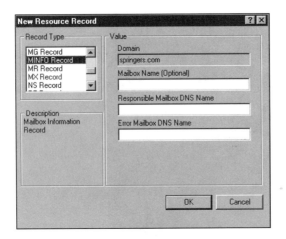

Figure 8-14: MINFO record setup

- **New Domain.** Creates a new domain at this node, as shown in Figure 8-15.

Figure 8-15: New Domain

- **Properties.** The zone properties selection enables you to configure the four separate tab sheets shown in Figure 8-16.
- **General tab sheet.** This tab sheet (see Figure 8-16) enables you to modify the Zone File Name and Zone Type (Primary or Secondary).
- **SOA tab sheet.** This relates to the Start of Authority record. One of the settings that may be modified is the minimum default setting for Time to Live (TTL). Note that the TTL setting may be modified for seconds, minutes, hours, days, weeks, months, years (see Figure 8-17).

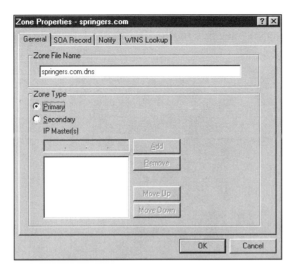

Figure 8-16: Zone Properties showing the General tab sheet

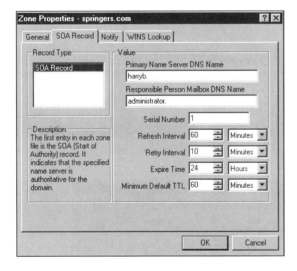

Figure 8-17: Zone Properties showing the SOA tab sheet

- **Notify tab sheet.** This sheet, shown in Figure 8-18, enables you to list IP addresses for secondary DNS name servers that are notified when changes occur to the primary DNS name server. When the changes occur, the primary name server sends DNS change notification messages to all secondary servers on the list. When notified, the secondary name server(s) can request a zone transfer immediately without waiting for the Refresh Interval specified in the SOA record (see Figure 8-17) to expire.

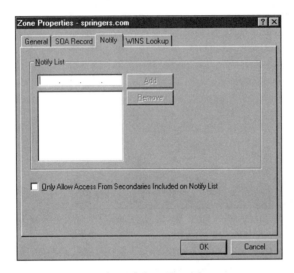

Figure 8-18: Zone Properties showing the Notify tab sheet

- **WINS Lookup tab sheet.** This is a critical dialog box to configure if you want to integrate DNS and WINS on your Windows NT server. This topic is discussed later in this chapter. If you select the Use WINS Resolution check box shown in Figure 8-19, you will be required to enter the IP address of the WINS server on your network. For smaller networks, this IP address is typically the same server, and thus same IP address, as the DNS server.

Figure 8-19: Zone Properties showing the WINS Lookup tab sheet

Final DNS Manager configurations include modifying the Preferences dialog box found under the Options menu of DNS Manager (see Figure 8-20).

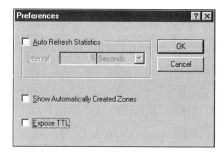

Figure 8-20: DNS Manager preferences

- **Auto Refresh Statistics.** Enables you to set how often DNS Manager periodically updates the server statistics display.

Selecting this option will cause additional DNS-related traffic on the network. This would be a concern at the enterprise level, where packet traffic management is always a concern.

- **Show Automatically Created Zones.** This check box, as the name implies, causes automatically created zones to be displayed in DNS Manager.
- **Expose TTL.** Species whether DNS Manager displays and lets you change the minimum default Time to Live (TTL) interval when you view resource record properties.

And finally, remember that DNS servers require a static IP address. This fact is fair game on the MCSE exams.

DNS standard and revisions

Not surprisingly, additional DNS-related resources such as the RFC-type standards are available for you to continue your DNS education. Table 8-5 provides a list of DNS-related RFCs.

Table 8-5   DNS RFC Standards

RFC	Title
1034	Domain Names — Concepts and Facilities
1035	Domain Names — Implementation and Specification
1101	DNS Encoding of Network Names and Other Types

Continued

Table 8-5	(continued)
RFC	**Title**
1464	Using the Domain Name System to Store Arbitrary Strong Attributes
1536	Common DNS Implementation Errors and Suggested Fixes
1591	Domain Name System Structure and Delegation
1664	Using The Internet DNS to Distribute Mail Address Mapping Tables
1706	DNS NSAP Resource Records
1712	DNS Encoding of Geographical Location
1713	Tools for DNS Debugging
1794	DNS Support for Load Balancing
1886	DNS Extensions to Support IP version 6
1912	Common DNS Operational and Configuration Errors
1995	Incremental Zone Transfer in DNS
1996	A Mechanism for Prompt Notification of Zone Changes
2052	A DNS RR for Specifying the Location of Services
2065	Domain Name System Security Extensions
2136	Dynamic Updates in the Domain Name System (DNS UPDATE)
2137	Secure Domain Name System Dynamic Update

Secret

The last RFC (2137) in Table 8-5 relates to Dynamic DNS, a feature that will be introduced in Windows 2000 Server.

Final DNS musings

To finish the discussion of DNS, Table 8-6 provides the definitions of the DNS Server statistics displayed when you click a server name in the left panel of DNS Manager.

Table 8-6	DNS Server Statistics
Statistics	**Definition**
UdpQueries	Number of UDP queries received by this DNS server
UdpResponses	Number of UDP responses to queries that were sent from this DNS server
TcpClientConnections	Number of TCP connections from clients or other DNS servers

Statistics	Definition
TcpQueries	Number of TCP queries received
TcpResponses	Number of TCP messages sent in response to queries. This number includes zone transfer responses.
Recursive Lookups	Number of queries sent to other DNS servers
Recursive Responses	Number of responses from other DNS servers
WINS Forward Lookups	Number of queries sent to WINS servers
WINS Forward Responses	Number of responses from WINS servers
WINS Reverse Lookups	Number of NetBT node status queries sent by this server
WINS Reverse Responses	Number of NetBT node status responses received by this server

DHCP

As you know, computers running TCP/IP must identify themselves via specific information that is unique on the network on which it resides. Such identification includes having a unique host name and a unique IP address. In this section of the book, you have already learned that the IP address for the computer may be assigned either manually (or statically) or dynamically via DHCP services in Windows NT Server. This part of Chapter 8 will discuss configuring DHCP and using DHCP Manager.

Benefits and overview of DHCP

Historically, TCP/IP environments have been difficult to configure. That is because you, as the network administrator and engineer, had to manage pesky TPC/IP configuration details that were easy to misconfigure. Have you ever transposed TCP/IP address value when fatigued late at night? Of course you have!

Enter the Dynamic Host Configuration Protocol (DHCP) approach that reduces, but does not eliminate, the configuration effort needed when using the TCP/IP protocol suite. DHCP is defined in RFCs 1533, 1534, 1541, and 1542. At the 50,000 foot level, you could view DHCP as centralizing TCP/IP configuration information and automatically assigning IP addresses to client systems configured to use DHCP.

DHCP is used by two types of systems:

- **DHCP servers.** To use DHCP on you Windows NT Server-based network, you must have at least one Windows NT server running the Microsoft DHCP service. This server will need to have a DHCP scope defined that specifies TCP/IP configurations and a pool of IP addresses that may be assigned to DHCP-compliant clients.

This is accomplished by the DHCP server responding to a request from the DHCP client for an IP address lease. The DHCP server then selects from its address pool an unused address that it may lease out to the client. Typically, the DHCP server also provides additional TCP/IP configuration information for the client (which I discuss more in this section).

- **DHCP clients.** When installing TCP/IP on a DHCP client (such as Windows 95/98 or Windows for Workgroups), you can invoke the ability to have IP addresses assigned automatically by properly configuring the client. For example, in Windows 98 (see Figure 8-21), this is accomplished by selecting the Obtain an IP Address Automatically radio button from the IP Address tab sheet for TCP/IP Properties.

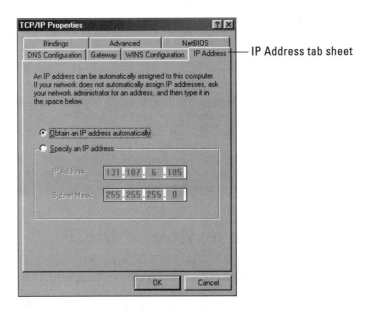

Figure 8-21: Enabling a DHCP client

Upon reboot of the Windows 98 client machine, you have created a DHCP client. Note that for Windows for Workgroups, this type of configuration requires that TCP/IP 32 be installed and that you manually configure several *.INI files.

As long as a DHCP server on the same network as the client responds with an IP address to lease, then the DHCP server fully loads the TCP/IP configuration information on the client and uses TCP/IP to communicate. Typically no additional configuration information is supplied by the administrator or user, but there are exceptions. The biggest exception that I've seen involves people who haven't taken advantage of DHCP's rich configuration capabilities. For example, when the system is properly configured, you can supply DNS server information to the DHCP client automatically. But alas, I often see DHCP used only to assign IP addresses; rarely do I see it fully exploited with rich configuration information being supplied to the client.

So the benefits of using DHCP on your network are really twofold:

- The administrator can centrally define global and local subnet TCP/IP parameters for the entire internetwork or just the local LAN segment.
- Client computers do not require manual TCP/IP configuration. When a client computer crosses subnets, it can be easily reconfigured.

Note

Whereas the DHCP server service may be started and stopped via the Services applet in Control Panel, such is not the case with DHCP clients. To stop the DHCP client service in Windows 98, you must first disable the DHCP client capabilities by selecting the Specify an IP Address radio button shown in Figure 8-21 and restart the computer.

How does DHCP really work?

In the beginning there was the Bootstrap Protocol (BOOTP), based on RFC 951 and later modified to RFC 1542. In a layperson's terms, you may think of BOOTP as both the predecessor to DHCP and sort of a DHCP for UNIX systems. In fact, Microsoft had significant influence in the development of RFC 1542 (that incorporates DHCP). You would not be incorrect if you thought of Microsoft as a founding father of DHCP.

The major advantage to having DHCP use the same message format as BOOTP is that an existing router may act as an RFC 1542 (BOOTP) relay agent to relay DHCP messages between subnets. But note that the operative term "may" is critical to understanding this concept. Not all routers support RFC 1542, and the older routers are the worst offenders. Newer router models released by Bay, Cisco, and others do not have this problem. So if you have a router that is 1542-compliant, it is possible to have a single DHCP server provide IP addresses and configuration information on both subnets in a two-subnet scenario.

This section is also familiar territory if you have taken the MCSE plunge and attended the MOC-687 or MOC-922 Microsoft Windows NT Server 4.0 Core Technologies course, where DHCP is covered in great detail.

Leasing an IP address

To obtain an IP address from a DHCP server, DHCP clients pass through a series of states, as shown in Figure 8-22.

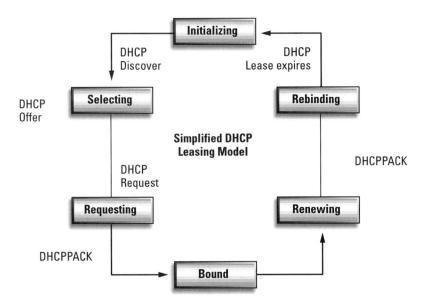

Figure 8-22: The DHCP client leasing model

- **Initializing state.** When a DHCP client boots, TCP/IP initially loads and initializes with a NULL IP address so that it can communicate with the DHCP server on the network via TCP/IP. The DHCP client then broadcasts a DHCPDISCOVER message to its subnet. The DHCPDISCOVER message contains the DHCP client's media access control (MAC) address and computer name. This type of message, known as a packet, is discussed and displayed in Chapter 23, "Network Monitor." If the DHCP client has successfully received an IP address from a specific DHCP server before, the DHCP client includes the previous IP address in the DHCPDISCOVER message to try to lease the same IP address.

A Windows NT–based DHCP client (such as Windows NT Workstation) stores its leased IP address in the Registry. Each time the client system boots and sends out a DHCPDISCOVER message, it requests the IP address stored in the Registry.

Interestingly, the DHCP leased address list on the DHCP server is stored in a Microsoft Access–format (*.mdb) file. More on that later in the chapter.

Because the DHCP client does not yet have an IP address and does not know the IP address of any DHCP servers, the source IP address for the DHCPDISCOVER broadcast is 0.0.0.0 and the destination address is 255.255.255.255.

- **Selecting state.** Any DHCP server that receives a DHCPDISCOVER message and has a valid configuration for the DHCP client responds with a DHCPOFFER message. The DHCP servers send their DHCPOFFER messages via broadcast because the DHCP client does not yet have an IP address. This message contains the following components:

- The DHCP client's MAC address
- An offered IP address
- An appropriate subnet mask
- A server identifier (the IP address of the offering DHCP server)
- Length of the lease

When a DHCP server sends a DHCPOFFER message offering an IP address, the DHCP server reserves the IP address so that it cannot offer the same address to another DHCP client. In other words, no double assignments of the same IP address are allowed (otherwise you would have a network with two identical IP addresses).

If a DHCP client does not receive a DHCPOFFER message from a DHCP server on startup, it first notifies you that a DHCP server as unavailable (see Figure 8-23).

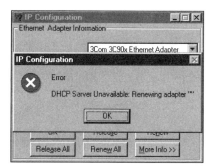

Figure 8-23: A client reporting no DHCP server located

Then the DHCP client attempts its request for an IP address four more times every five minutes at four-, six-, eight-, and sixteen-second intervals.

The DHCP client accepts the DHCPOFFER under the following conditions:

- The client receives the requested IP address.
- The client is willing to accept any IP address.
- The client has tried to accept an IP address two or more times unsuccessfully.

- **Requesting state.** The DHCP client collects all of the DHCPOFFER messages, selects an offer — usually the first offer received — and sends a DHCPREQUEST message to the DHCP server. The DHPREQUEST message indicates that the DHCP client accepts the offered IP address. It includes at a minimum the server identifier from the accepted DHCPOFFER and may also include a request for any additional configuration information that the DHCP client requires, such as a default gateway and the IP address of a WINS server.

Note that even at this stage, the TCP/IP protocol is still not fully initialized on the DHCP client, so the DHCPREQUEST message is sent via broadcast. Broadcasting the message ensures that the same DHCP servers that received the initial DHCPDISCOVER message also receive this message. Because the server identifier is included in the DHCPREQUEST, any other DHCP servers that offered the DHCP client an IP address basically withdraw the offer and return the offered IP address to their pool of available IP addresses.

- **Bound state.** The DHCP server responds to the DHCPREQUEST message with a DHCPACK (DHCP acknowledgment) message that contains a valid lease for the negotiated IP address as well as any configuration parameters. Here again, the DHCP server sends the DHCPACK message via broadcast because the DHCP client doesn't yet have an IP address. On receipt of the DHCPACK message, the DHCP client completes the TCP/IP binding and the client workstation can use TCP/IP to communicate over the network.

Renewing IP leases

As you know, DHCP clients lease their IP addresses from DHCP servers. When this lease expires, that IP address can no longer be utilized by the DHCP client. For that reason, DHCP client must periodically renew their IP address leases, preferably before the lease has expired or is about to expire.

Secret

I also like to have DCHP clients frequently renew their IP address leases for other reasons. Often, when configuring a Windows NT Server network, I'll lease a "phony" set of IP address such as 10.0.0.x while I wait for final ID address configurations to be approved by both the client and the WAN engineer. Or while waiting for the ISP to provide my sites real Internet IP addresses, I'll need to use phony IP addresses in the interim. Once I'm ready to implement a new IP addressing schema, it's nice that the DCHP clients will automatically seek to renew their IP addresses and receive a "new" IP address from the properly configured DHCP server.

Referring to Figure 8-22, the DHCP client passes through the renewing and rebinding states to renew its IP address lease.

- **Renewing state.** The DHCP client first attempts to renew its lease when 50 percent of the lease time has expired. To renew its lease, the DHCP client sends a directed DHCPREQUEST message to the DHCP server that provided the original lease. If renewal is allowed, the DHCP server automatically renews the lease by responding with a DHCPACK message. This new IP address lease contains not only the original IP address if still available (or another IP address otherwise) but any TCP/IP client configuration information.

- **Rebinding state.** If, for whatever reason, the DHCP client is not able to communicate with the original DHCP server the executed its lease, it attempts another approach called *rebinding*. Here the DHCP client attempts to contact any available DHCP server when 87.5 percent of the lease time has expired. The leasing process is akin to that detailed over the last several pages.

Additional DHCP messages

You should be aware of a few additional DHCP messages that haven't been discussed yet:

- **DHCPDECLINE.** The DHCP client sends a DHCPDECLINE message to a DHCP server if the configuration parameter sent by the DHCP server is invalid.

- **DHCPNAK.** A DHCP server sends a DHCPNAK message to a DHCP client to notify the DHCP client that it has incorrect configuration information.

- **DHCPRELEASE.** A DHCP client sends a DHCPRELEASE message to a DHCP server to release its IP address and cancel its lease on the IP address.

Manually releasing and renewing the IP address in a DHCP Client scenario is accomplished in one of two ways, depending on the workstation operation system that you are using. For Windows NT (both Server and Workstation), you would enter **ipconfig/release** and **ipconfig/renew** at the command line. For Windows 98/95, you would type **winipcfg** at the command line and select the release and renew buttons respectively that appear in the IP Configuration dialog box shown in Figure 8-24.

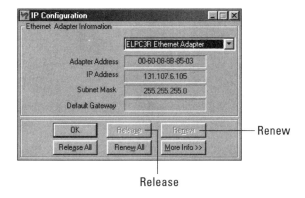

Figure 8-24: The IP Configuration dialog box

Planning for DHCP servers

The decision to deploy a Windows NT Server–based DHCP server on your network should not be taken lightly. You should honor several considerations prior to installing the DHCP Server service on Windows NT Server and configuring your workstations to act as DHCP clients.

On paper, having a DHCP server is a great idea. Who wouldn't welcome centralized network management at the protocol-level? For Small Business Server (SBS), the default network configuration is to have the Windows NT server act as a DHCP server. And it works reasonably well (be sure to read more on this in Chapter 20, "Windows NT Server — Small Business Server").

Another opportunity to effectively deploy a DHCP server is on a network that may be changing. Perhaps you are still learning Windows NT Server, or you haven't finalized the network design. When your network has a large delta factor (high propensity for change), having a DHCP server is great because you can change the TCP/IP configuration in a centralized manner at the Windows NT server without having to "touch" each workstation out on the floor.

But at times I've noticed that DHCP may not be the best choice. Understand that, like tax law, these observations may or may not apply to your situation.

In enterprise-wide networks, it may go both ways. Many enterprises successfully use DHCP Server and enjoy the great benefits of reduced IT-specific management of the TCP/IP configuration area. But I'd be remiss if I didn't share this observation about a North Seattle hospital. Administrators tried and tried to perfect the use of DHCP Server in their Windows NT Server environment, and regrettably they returned to using static IP addresses for workstations. The bottom line? Trying to make the DHCP server work flawlessly was taking more time than having the computer technicians just go out on the floor and "touch" each workstation. They concluded that, for whatever reason, DHCP just wasn't ready for prime time.

Other situations that didn't work for DHCP have included the athletic club that needed static IP addresses at workstations, defined on the Windows NT server in the HOSTS file, so that its Progress database could work properly. And organizations that want to assign a permanent IP address to a workstation to facilitate an Internet video conference (for instance, CUSEEME) often bypass using DHCP Server. That's because workstations that use CUSEEME or another video conference solution need a fixed, real Internet-registered IP address. When using video conferencing, such an address is necessary so that you may "call" the destination host using the IP address as something of a telephone number.

Otherwise, you should honor the traditional planning steps of a network implementation when rolling out DHCP Server and its services (design the network, run a pilot test, and so on). General planning topics are covered in Part I, "Introduction, Planning, Setup and Implementation," of this book.

Implementing DHCP servers in a small LAN

If you have a smaller LAN without routers and subnetting, a single DHCP server will work just fine. Be sure to map out which computers can immediately become DHCP clients, which computers should retain static IP addresses, and what TCP/IP configurations should you create and invoke via DHCP Server (see Figure 8-25).

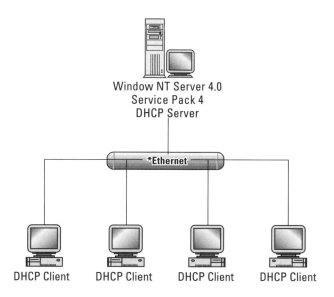

Figure 8-25: A small LAN with a single DHCP server

Implementing DHCP servers in a large LAN

Using DHCP servers on a large LAN elevates you to an entirely different league in the Windows NT Server community. It isn't as easy as it appears.

Large networks typically use routers and relay agents so that DHCP servers on one node of an internetwork may respond to TCP/IP configuration requests from distant remote nodes. The relay agent forwards requests from local DHCP clients to the DHCP server and subsequently relays responses back to the DHCP clients. Besides the issues mentioned regarding a small LAN, additional planning issues for the large enterprise network include:

- **Compatibility with hardware and software routers with DHCP.** Routers must support RFCs 1532, 1533, and 1541. These RFCs speak toward the forwarding of packets required by the DHCP service. As mentioned earlier in this chapter, a correlation exists between the age of the router and support for these RFCs: newer routers tend to support these RFCs; older routers do not.

- **Physical subnetting of the network and relative placement of DHCP servers.** This includes planning for the placement of DHCP (and WINS, which is discussed later in this chapter) Place servers on subnets in a way that reduces b-node broadcasts across routers. You should note that b-node resolves names using broadcast messages (see the name resolution discussion early in this chapter).
- **The DHCP option types and their values defined per scope for the DHCP clients.** This may include planning for separate scopes to meet the needs of specific user groups. An example is mobile users with laptops who likely have different TCP/IP configuration requirements as they move from branch office to branch office. You might also have more advanced TCP/IP configuration needs on a large WAN with multiple subnets. You get the picture.
- **Multiple DHCP servers.** If you are planning to implement multiple DHCP servers (which is a good way to distribute the load on a large network), each DHCP server must (of course) have a static IP address. Be darn sure to exclude these "used" IP addresses from your DHCP scope(s).
- **Static IP addresses.** Just as described in the preceding point, you must exclude static IP addresses that you need from the DHCP scope(s). These might include:
  - DHCP servers
  - Non-DHCP computers such as workstations connected directly to the Internet via "real" static IP addresses
  - Routers
  - Non-Microsoft Remote Access Service (RAS) clients that are using Point-to-Point Protocol (PPP) to connect to the network

  If you forget to make such exclusions, you can count on name/address conflicts occurring. Obviously such conflicts will prevent your clients from communicating on the network and might even lead to network crashes (such as router failures).
- **DHCP Server database replication.** This feature doesn't exist in the current release of Windows NT Server 4.0, so if you install multiple DHCP servers on a single subnet (say for load balancing), it is necessary to split the DHCP scope into distinct IP ranges.
- **DHCP Server database backup.** Because the DHCP database contains all of the DHCP scopes for the DHCP server and the network's TCP/IP configuration parameters, it is a good idea to implement a backup policy. Typically a well-designed complete Windows NT server will back up the *.mdb files in the SYSTEMROOT\SYSTEM32\DHCP subdirectory. But as

Chapter 8: DNS, DHCP, WINS

with any mission-critical backup scenario, you should consider manually backing up this subdirectory above and beyond the normal tape backups that you perform on your Windows NT server. The DHCP database files will be discussed at length in a few pages.

Installing the DHCP Server service

Installing the DHCP Server service is very simple and akin to install most Windows NT Server 4.0 services. You may elect to install the DHCP Server service when you install TCP/IP as part of the Windows NT Server setup or at a future date. The step-by-step instructions that follow assume that Windows NT Server and TCP/IP have been previously installed.

Caution

Also check that it is permissible to install the DHCP Server service on your Windows NT server. More than once, at my own job, I and other nameless co-conspirators have inadvertently built "test" Windows NT servers and SBS servers running the DHCP Server service to test-drive the latest BackOffice applications, Great Plains Accounting software releases, and so on. No sooner than we cross that line, that is, bring our test servers on line than our IS Director across the floor starts getting user complaints. Why? Our test servers dish out IP addresses to our firm's regular users as they log on. And guess what! Our test IP addressing layout is far different from that of our corporate network. Bottom line? Real users are unable to work because there are (inadvertently of course) multiple DHCP servers, providing very different TCP/IP configurations, on the same network.

You must log on as a member of the Administrators group for the Windows NT server which you are installing or administering as a DHCP server.

STEPS:
To install DHCP Server

Step 1. Start the Network applet in Control Panel. When the Network dialog box appears, click the Services tab to display the Network Services dialog box as show in Figure 8-26.

Continued

STEPS
To install DHCP Server *(continued)*

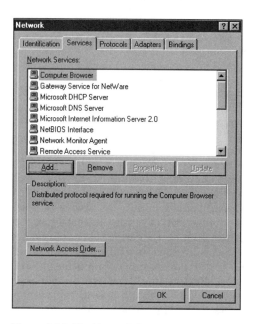

Figure 8-26: The Network Services dialog box

Step 2. Click the Add button. In the Network Services list, select Microsoft DHCP Server, and then click OK.

Step 3. When requested by Windows NT Setup, provide the full path to the Windows NT Server distribution files and choose the Continue button. All necessary files are copied to your hard disk.

Step 4. Complete all of the necessary steps for manually configuring TCP/IP as described in Chapter 6, "Installing and Configuring TCP/IP." Granted, you may have already manually configured TCP/IP on this machine. At this point, all of the appropriate TCP/IP and DHCP software is ready for use after you reboot the computer.

Note

If the DHCP server is multihomed (has multiple adapters configured and bound to the operating system), you will be required to use the Advanced Microsoft TCP/IP Configuration dialog box to specify IP addresses and other configuration information for each adapter (assuming that you have not previously done this). Refer to Chapter 6, "Installing and Configuring TCP/IP."

If any adapter on the Windows NT server that you have just installed DHCP Server is connected to another subnet that you do not want this server to support, you must disable the bindings to that subnet for the particular adapter.

STEPS:

To disable bindings

Step 1. Choose the Network applet in Control Panel. Then select the Bindings tab sheet in the Network dialog box. The Network Bindings dialog box appears as shown in Figure 8-27.

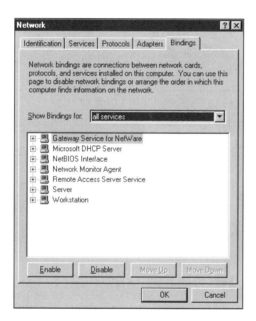

Figure 8-27: The Network Bindings dialog box

Step 2. Disable the related binding by highlighting it in the Bindings list box.

It is not possible for you to use DHCP to "automatically" configure a new DHCP server because a computer may not act as a DHCP client and DHCP server simultaneously. Configuring a DHCP server is still a manual process.

STEPS:
To pause the DHCP Server service

Step 1. In the Control Panel, select the Services icon. You may also choose Services from the Computer menu in Server Manager.

Step 2. In the Services dialog box, select Microsoft DHCP Server service.

Step 3. Select the Pause button and then select the Close button.

You may also start, stop, and pause the DHCP Server service at the command line with the commands shown in Table 8-7.

Table 8-7   DHCP Server Service Command Line Commands

Command	Function
net start dhcpserver	Start the DHCP Server service.
net stop dhcpserver	Stop the DHCP Server service.
net pause dhcpserver	Pause the DHCP Server service.

Tip

Once the DHCP Server service is installed, you must reboot the Windows NT Server computer (even though it's technically not required). Note that the DHCP Server service automatically starts during system setup. You should pause the DHCP Server service while configuring scope the first time.

Creating DHCP scopes

A DHCP scope may be defined as an administrative unit or grouping of DHCP clients. Typically you create a scope for each subnet on the network to facilitate TCP/IP configurations for that subnet.

These properties are common to all scopes:

- A subnet mask to determine the subnet related to a given IP address. Note that a scope may have the same subnet mask and different IP address ranges. But the rule of thumb is to have one scope per subnet (and the subnet mask provides this distinction).
- A scope name
- Lease durations to be used by DHCP clients with dynamic addresses

Chapter 8: DNS, DHCP, WINS 301

Larger networks will want to have two or more online DHCP servers so that a DHCP client may always obtain valid TCP/IP configuration information. This is just another form of redundancy and load balancing that you should consider on your network.

Caution

Not only will DHCP clients fail if their IP address leases expire and cannot be renewed, but TCP/IP will not be properly configured and initialized by the DHCP client if there are no DHCP servers available. If TCP/IP is not properly configured and initialized on a DHCP client, that workstation will not be able to communicate on the network using TCP/IP (either another network protocol will need to be used, or network communications will fail).

One law regarding multiple DHCP servers on the network is to avoid overlapping scopes. The DHCP servers do not communicate with each other to adjudicate such issues. Duplicate IP addresses would be a very real possibility.

Tip

Another consideration regarding DHCP servers is that each subnet must have its own DHCP server. This is a general rule that will keep you safe on the Windows NT Server 4.0 MCSE exam, but there are variations to this rule.

Variation one is one DHCP server per subnet with support for all subnets by any DHCP server. Here each subnet has its own DHCP server, and the subnets are connected by a router supporting RFC 1542 (BOOTP) relay agents. An RFC 1542–compliant router modifies DHCP messages to indicate which subnet originated the broadcast. This action allows DHCP Server to lease an IP address from the scope that applies to the DHCP client requesting the configuration.

Variation two is recognition that you do not need to have a DHCP server on each subnet. An RFC 1542–compliant router will forward DHCP requests across subnets.

If you already haven't done so, take a moment to sketch out how you are using your existing DHCP scopes, or if you are just implementing a Windows NT Server–based network, how you might best use DHCP scopes. A few moments of planning now is certain to yield tremendous dividends later.

Note

Suppose you are on a true LAN with little need for a real router (such as Cisco) between subnets. You can, of course, configure a multihomed Windows NT server to act as a router. Thus, a Windows NT server running the DHCP Server service with two or more network adapters (and the TCP/IP configuration "Enable IP Routing" enabled) would allow, in this case, one DHCP server to serve multiple subnets. Be advised this isn't an ideal situation given my mixed experience with the IP routing function of Windows NT Server. It's the old "you get what you pay for." If you're serious about having one DHCP server for multiple subnets, purchase an RFC 5142–compliant router and do it right.

Using DHCP Manager

The DHCP Manager application is found in the Administrative Tools (Common) group under Programs from the Start menu. DHCP Manager is use to complete the following tasks:

- Create DHCP scopes.

- Define DHCP scope properties including lease duration, and valid and excluded IP address ranges.

- Establish default TCP/IP configuration information such as default gateway, DNS servers, and WINS servers to be provided to DHCP clients.

- Provide additional custom options.

STEPS:
To start DHCP Manager

Step 1. As mentioned, you may select the DHCP Manager (see Figure 8-28) from the Administrative Tools (Common) group. You may also start DHCP Manager with the following command line: dhcpadmin.

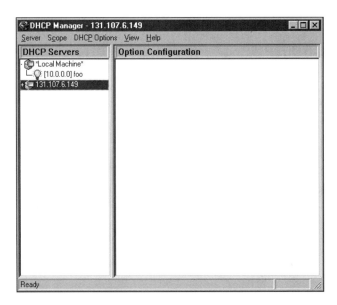

Figure 8-28: DHCP Manager

Chapter 8: DNS, DHCP, WINS

Step 2. When DHCP Manager is run for the first time, only the "local computer" option is displayed in the left pane. After you've created a scope for the local computer (the existing computer that is running the DHCP Server service), the scope is displayed in the left pane when you click the plus sign ("+").

Note

DHCP Manager may be used to manage other DHCP servers on your network. If you elect to do this, the additional DHCP servers are displayed in the left pane of DHCP Manager as well.

STEPS:
To connect to a DHCP server

Step 1. From the Server menu, choose the Add command.

Step 2. In the Add DHCP Server to Server List dialog box (see Figure 8-29), type the IP address or NetBIOS name of the DHCP server that you want to connect. Select the OK button.

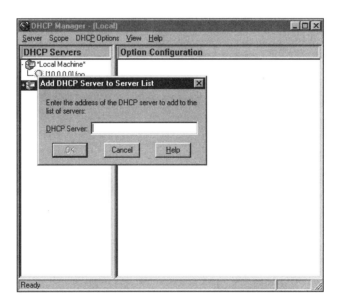

Figure 8-29: The Add DHCP Server to Server List dialog box

304   Part II: TCP/IP

STEPS:
To disconnect from a DHCP server

Step 1.   Select the DHCP server listing in the left pane of DHCP Manager.

Step 2.   From the Server menu, select Remove. You may also press the Del key when the DHCP Server listing is highlighted.

Creating scopes

You must use DHCP Manager to create, manage, or remove scopes.

STEPS:
To create a new DHCP scope

Step 1.   In the DHCP Servers list in the left pane of DHCP Manager, select the server that you intend to create a scope for.

Step 2.   From the Scope menu, select Create. The Scope Properties dialog box appears similar to that shown in Figure 8-30.

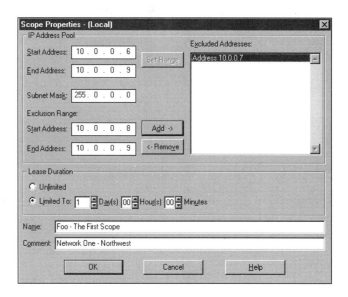

Figure 8-30: The Scope Properties dialog box

Step 3. Define the Start and End IP addresses for this scope. This information is necessary to activate the scope.

Step 4. Type in the value for the subnet mask in the Subnet Mask field.

Step 5. Exclude IP addresses as necessary. Type in the start and end of the IP address exclusion range. A single IP address that is being excluded has the same start and end IP address.

Secret

It is highly recommended that you always create at least a small IP address range that is excluded from the IP address pool that may be leased to DHCP clients. This exclusion range is useful in several situations, including badly behaved workstations that never successfully operate as DHCP clients. Another use for excluded IP addresses is for printers that are connected directly to the network, such as HP LaserJet printers and the HP JetDirect card. I've found that the JetDirect card scenario still considers dynamic IP address assignments to be via BOOTP, not Microsoft DHCP. Thus, I've encountered dynamic IP address assignment failures when it comes to JetDirect-based printer scenarios. When such is the case, I simply revert back to a static IP address, taken from the IP address exclusion range defined in my DHCP scope, to attach my HP LaserJet printer to the network.

Note that other uses for excluded IP addresses beyond badly behaved workstations and HP JetDirect cards include:

- Other DHCP servers that need a static IP address
- Non-DCHP clients on your network (such as Macintosh computers)
- Diskless workstations
- RAS and PPP clients

Step 6. Specify the lease duration to apply to the IP addresses in this scope. You may either select Unlimited or Limited To. You may limit leases to the days, hours, and minutes that you select.

Step 7. Type the scope name in the Name box. This is a meaningful field that appears as part of the scope identification in the left pane of DHCP Manager. It may be up to 128 characters in length, so I would recommend that you consider using a friendly title.

Step 8. Likewise, you may add a comment in the Comment field. I recommend that you do so to further define this use of the scope in a way that its name is unable to do. For example, I've used the field to mention a geographic location such as "Northwest."

Step 9. Select the OK button to create the scope creation process.

Continued

STEPS

To create a new DHCP scope *(continued)*

Step 10. You will be asked via a DHCP Manager message to activate the scope. Typically you answer Yes to the question, but be advised that you usually don't activate a DHCP scope until after you have defined the DHCP options for this scope (see "Configuring DHCP Options" later in this chapter). The activation dialog box is shown in Figure 8-31.

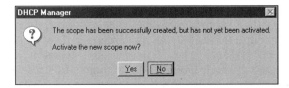

Figure 8-31: A scope activation request

Assuming you have not activated the scope so that you can make additional DHCP configurations, you may activate the DHCP scope at a later time by choosing the Activate command from the Scope menu.

Changing scope properties

You may elect to make changes to your scope at a future date. To do so, select the scope that you want to modify. Select Properties from the Scope menu. You must select OK after making changes to the scope.

Removing a scope

To remove a scope that you no longer need, select the scope in the left pane of DHCP Manager and press the Del key. You may also select the Delete command from the Scope menu.

You typically deactivate a scope for a reasonable period of time before you delete it. This behavior is analogous to deactivating a user account before deleting it.

Configuring DHCP options

DHCP Manager is used to create rich TCP/IP configurations that a DHCP server assigns to a DHCP client. These configuration options are largely based on RFC 1542 (BOOTP) standard parameters. The DHCP Option menu offers the following three selections:

- **Scope.** Edits the configuration options for the selected scope.
- **Global.** Edits global DHCP client options that will apply to all scopes.
- **Default.** Defines and maintains default TCP/IP configuration values and option types.

STEPS:
To create and assign DHCP configuration options

Step 1. Select the scopes that you want to configure in the left pane of the DHCP Manager window. This assumes that you have previously created scopes.

Step 2. Select either Global or Scope commands depending on whether you want to make global changes that apply to all scopes or changes that apply to a specific scope. The DHCP Options: Global dialog box appears in Figure 8-32.

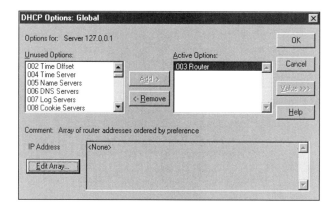

Figure 8-32: The DHCP Options: Global dialog box

Step 3. Select the option you want to configure in the Unused Options list (left side) and click the Add button to move the option to the Active Options list (right side).

Continued

STEPS

To create and assign DHCP configuration options *(continued)*

Step 4. Defining a value for the active option is easy. Simply select the option in the Active Options list and click the Values button. Then edit the value by selecting the Edit (or some variation of Edit) button. Create, modify, or edit the information via the IP Address Array Editor dialog box (see Figure 8-33). This dialog box presents a simple, GUI-based interface for entering IP addresses, values, and strings. The type of information you enter will depend on the option selected.

- For IP addresses, enter the address to the selected options.
- For numbers, type the appropriate decimal or hexadecimal value for this option.
- For strings, type an appropriate ASCII string containing letters and numbers.

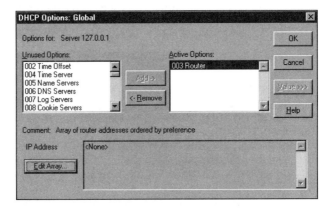

Figure 8-33: Editing DHCP configuration options

Step 5. Select the OK button after you have completed your changes.

DHCP Server provides a robust list of DHCP Client configuration options based on RFC 1533. Table 8-8 lists these predefined configuration options.

Table 8-8 DHCP Client Configuration Options

Code	Option Name	Description	Configuration Category
2	Time offset	Specifies Universal Coordinated Time (UCT) offset in seconds.	Basic
3	Router	Specifies a list of IP addresses for routers on the client's subnet.	Basic
4	Time Server	Specifies a list of IP addresses for time servers available to the client. Ordered by preference.	Basic
5	Name Servers	Specifies a list of IP address for name servers available to the client. Ordered by preference.	Basic
6	DNS Servers	Specifies a list of IP addresses for DNS name servers available to the client. Ordered by preference.	Basic
7	Log Servers	Specifies a list of IP addresses for MIT_LCS User Datagram Protocol (UDP) log servers available to the client.	Basic
8	Cookie Servers	Specifies a list of IP addresses for RFC 865 cookie servers available to the client. Ordered by preference.	Basic
9	LPR Servers	Specifies a list of IP addresses for RFC 1179 line printer servers available to the client. Ordered by preference.	Basic
10	Impress Servers	Specifies a list of IP addresses for Imagen Impress servers available to the client.	Basic
11	Resource Location Servers	Specifies a list of RFC 887 Resource Location servers available to the client.	Basic
12	Host Name	Specifies the host name for a client adhering to the RFC 1035 character set. The name may be 63 characters long.	Basic
13	Boot File Size	Specifies the size of the default client boot image file in 512-octet blocks.	Basic

Continued

Table 8-8 *(continued)*

Code	Option Name	Description	Configuration Category
14	Merit Dump File	Specifies the path name for the crash dump file.	Basic
15	Domain Name	Specifies the DNS domain name that the client should use for DNS name resolution.	Basic
16	Swap Server	Specifies the IP address of the client's swap server.	Basic
17	Root Path	Specifies the path name for the client's root disk character set NVT ASCII.	Basic
18	Extensions Path	TTPT file for option extensions. Specifies a file that is retrievable via TFTP and contains information interpreted the same as the end or extension field in the BOOTP response, except the file length is unconstrained and references to Tag 18 in the file are ignored.	Basic
19	IP Layer Forwarding	Enables or disables IP packet forwarding on the client.	IP Layer Parameters per Host
20	Non-local Source Routing	Enables or disables nonlocal datagrams.	IP Layer Parameters per Host
21	Policy Filter Masks	Specifies policy filters that consist of a list of pairs of IP addresses and masks specifying destination/mask pairs for filtering nonlocal source routes. Any source routed datagram whose next hop address does not match a filter is discarded by the client.	IP Layer Parameters per Host
22	Max DG Reassembly Size	Specifies a maximum size of datagram for reassembly by a client. Maximum size is 56 characters.	IP Layer Parameters per Host
23	Default Time-To-Live	Is the default Time to Live (TTL) the client uses on outgoing datagrams. Value may be between 1 and 255.	IP Layer Parameters per Host

Code	Option Name	Description	Configuration Category
24	Path MTU Aging Timeout	Is the timeout in seconds for aging Path MTU values. Based on RFC 1191.	IP Layer Parameters per Host
25	Path MTU Plateau Table	Is a table of MTU discovery sizes to use when performing Path MTU Discoveries as defined in RFC 1191. Table is sorted in size from the largest to the smallest. Minimum MTU size is 68.	IP Layer Parameters per Host
26	MTU Option	Sets the MTU discovery size for this interface. Minimum MTU value is 68.	IP Parameters per Interface
27	All subnets are local	Specifies whether the client assumes that all subnets of the client's internetwork use the same MTU as the local subnet where the client is connected. "1" indicates that all subnets share the same MTU. "0" indicates that the client should assume some subnets may have smaller MTUs.	IP Parameters per Interface
28	Broadcast Address	Specifies the broadcast IP address used on the client's subnet.	IP Parameters per Interface
29	Perform Mask Discovery	Specifies whether the client should use ICMP for subnet mask discovery. "1" indicates the client should perform mask discovery. "0" indicates the client should not.	IP Parameters per Interface
30	Mask Supplier Option	Determines whether the client should respond to subnet mask requests via ICMP. "1" indicates the client should respond. "0" indicates the client should not.	IP Parameters per Interface
31	Perform Router Discovery	Determines whether the client should solicit routers using RFC 1256. "1" indicates the client should perform router discovery. "0" indicates the client should not use it.	IP Parameters per Interface
32	Router Solicitation Address	Specifies the IP address to which the client submits router solicitation requests.	IP Parameters per Interface

Continued

Table 8-8 *(continued)*

Code	Option Name	Description	Configuration Category
33	Static Route Option	Specifies a list of IP address pairs that indicate the static routes the client should install in its routing cache. Any multiple routes to the same destination are listed in descending order of priority. The routes are destination/router address pairs.	IP Parameters per Interface
34	Trailer Encapsulation	Specifies whether the client should negotiate use of trailers (RFC 983) when using the ARP protocol. "1" indicates the client should attempt to use trailers. "0" indicates the client should not use trailers.	Link Layer Parameters per Interface
35	ARP Cache Timeout	Specifies the timeout in seconds for ARP cache entries.	Link Layer Parameters per Interface
36	Ethernet Encapsulation	Specifies whether the client should use IEEE 802.3 (RFC 1042) or Ethernet v.2 (RFC 894) encapsulation if the interface is Ethernet. "1" indicates the client should use RFC 1042 encapsulation. "0" indicates the client should use RFC 894 encapsulation.	Link Layer Parameters per Interface
37	Default TTL Option	This is the default Time to Live option. Specifies the default TTL that the client should use when sending TCP segments. The minimum value of the octet is 1.	TCP Parameters
38	Keepalive Interval	Is the keepalive interval in seconds. A value of "0" indicates the client should not send keepalive messages on connections unless specifically requested by an application.	TCP Parameters
39	Keepalive garbage	Specifies whether the client should send TCP keepalive messages with an octet of garbage data for compatibility with older implementations. "1" indicates a garbage octet should be sent. "0" indicates it should not be sent.	TCP Parameters

Code	Option Name	Description	Configuration Category
40	NIS Domain Name	Is the name of the Network Information Service domain.	Application Layer Parameters
41	NIS Servers	Gives addresses of NIS servers on client's subnet.	Application Layer Parameters
42	NTP Servers	Gives addresses of Network Time Protocol servers.	Application Layer Parameters
43	Vendor Specific Info	Supplies binary information that clients and servers use to exchange vendor-specific information. Servers not equipped to interpret the information ignore it. Clients that don't receive the information attempt to operate without it.	Vendor-specific Information
44	WINS/NBNS Servers	Specifies a list of IP addresses for NetBIOS name servers (NBNS).	Vendor-specific Information
45	NetBIOS over TCP/IP NBDD	Specifies a list of IP addresses for NetBIOS datagram distribution servers (NBDD).	Vendor-specific Information
46	WINS/NBT node type	Allows configurable NetBIOS over TCP/IP clients to be configured as described in RFC 1001/1002, where "1" is b-node, "2" is p-node, "4" is m-node, and "8" is h-node.	Vendor-specific Information
47	NetBIOS Scope ID	Specifies a string that is the NetBIOS over TCP/IP scope ID for the client, as specified in RFC 1001/1002.	Vendor-specific Information
48	X Window System Font	Specifies a list of IP addresses for X Window font servers available to the client.	Vendor-specific Information
49	X Windows System Display	Specifies a list of IP addresses for X Window System Display Manager servers available to the client.	Vendor-specific Information
64	NIS+ Domain Name	Is the name of the client's NIS+ domain.	Vendor-specific Information
65	NIS+ Servers	Is a list of IP addresses indicating NIS+ servers.	Vendor-specific Information
66	Boot Server Host Name	Is the TFTP boot server host name.	Vendor-specific Information
67	Bootfile Name	Specifies the bootfile name.	Vendor-specific Information

Continued

Table 8-8 *(continued)*

Code	Option Name	Description	Configuration Category
68	Mobile IP Home Agents	Gives mobile IP home agents in priority order.	Vendor-specific Information

The category configurations are defined as:

- **Basic.** Represents basic configuration options.
- **IP Layer Parameters per Host.** Specifies IP parameters on a per-host basis.
- **IP Parameters per Interface.** Represents IP parameters that affect the operation of the IP layer on a per-interface basis. A client may issue multiple requests, one per interface, to configure interfaces with their specific parameters.
- **Link Layer Parameters per Interface.** Represents link layer parameters per interface. These options affect the operation of the data link layer on a per-interface basis.
- **TCP Parameters.** Represents TCP/IP parameters that affect the operation of the TCP layer on a per-interface basis.
- **Application Layer Parameters.** Represents application layer parameters that are used to configure applications and services.
- **Vendor-specific information.** Represents options for vendor-specific information.

If you are using DHCP to configure WINS clients, be sure to set options 44, WINS Servers, and option 46, Node Type (from Table 8-8). These options allow DHCP clients to find and use a WINS server automatically.

Managing client leases

You can view important lease information via DHCP Manager. You can thus determine what machine has what IP address.

Being able to determine what machine has what IP address is often important when you are troubleshooting problems on your network.

STEPS:
To view client lease information

Step 1. In the DHCP Server list (left pane) of DHCP Manager, select the server that you want to observe lease information for.

Step 2. Either double-click the selected scope or, from the Scope menu, select Active Leases. The Active Leases dialog box appears as shown in Figure 8-34.

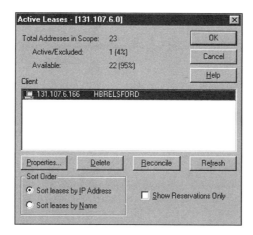

Figure 8-34: The Active Leases dialog box

Note

You may delete the DHCP configuration information for a DHCP client by selecting the Delete button. This is useful when you have removed a machine from the network but the client's DHCP Client configuration is still displayed in the Active Leases dialog box. In effect, this enables you to clean the DHCP database before the removed client's expiration period arrives. It is analogous to running DBCLEAN in SQL Server.

Note that deleting a client's DHCP configuration has the same effect as if the client's DHCP lease had expired. Be advised that deleting an active client could result in duplicate IP addresses on the network. That's because the active client that was inadvertently deleted from the DHCP database still retains its dynamically assigned IP address for its remaining lease duration. However, DHCP Server believes said IP address is again available for dynamic assignment. The result? Duplicate IP addresses on the same subnet. Ouch!

Continued

> **STEPS**
> **To view client lease information** *(continued)*
>
> **Step 3.** Select the computer in the Active Leases dialog box whose lease you want to view. Choose the Properties button to view detailed lease information (see Figure 8-35). If you want to see clients using reserved IP addresses, check the Show Reservations Only box.

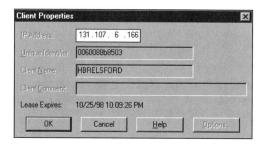

Figure 8-35: The Client Properties dialog box

Note It is possible to edit the Name Identifies and Comments fields that are maintained in the DHCP database.

Managing client reservations

Specific IP addresses may be reserved for a client. Typically, this is undertaken for the following reasons:

- For domain controllers if the network also uses LMHOSTS files that define IP addresses for domain controllers
- For clients that use IP addresses that were assigned using another method for TCP/IP configurations
- For assignment by RAS to non-DHCP clients
- For DNS servers

It is important to note that if multiple DHCP servers are providing the same scope addresses, each DHCP server must maintain the same client reservations (or else the DHCP reserved client potentially receives different IP addresses).

Note The IP address and static name specified in WINS will "win" or take precedence over the IP address assigned by the DHCP server. For such clients, create client reservations with the IP address that is defined in the WINS database.

STEPS:

To add a reservation for a client

Step 1. From the Scope menu, choose Add Reservations. The Add Reserved Clients dialog box appears as shown in Figure 8-36.

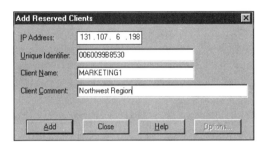

Figure 8-36: The Add Reserved Clients dialog box

Step 2. In the Add Reserved Clients dialog box, type information to identify a reserved client.

- The IP Address field specifies an address from the reserved address pool.

- The Unique Identifier field specifies the MAC address for the client's network adapter. To see the MAC address for your Windows 95/98 computer, type **winipcfg** at the command line. The dialog box shown in Figure 8-37 will appear.

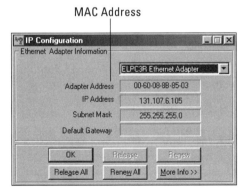

Figure 8-37: The IP Configuration dialog box displaying the Adapter Address (MAC address)

Continued

STEPS

To add a reservation for a client *(continued)*

Step 3. To see the MAC address on a Windows NT machine (either server or workstation), type **net config workstation** at the command line (see Figure 8-38).

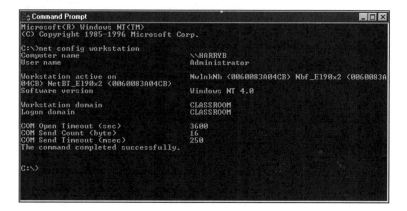

Figure 8-38: The net config workstation command

- The Client Name field specifies the computer name for the client.
- The Client Comment field is optional text that you may enter.

DHCP and DNS

Here is a favorite interview question of mine when I'm interviewing a technical professional: "Given your choice, which would you use on a network, DNS or DHCP?" Of course the answer is my favorite tax law response of "it depends." I then probe further into why my perspective employee might use only DNS on network, make use of DHCP, or more likely than not, use both DNS and DHCP on the network. Of course I am still speaking of a Windows NT Server–based network, because if I'm discussing a UNIX-based network and my candidate mentions DHCP, he or she is out the door (remember that the UNIX community uses BOOTP, not DHCP). Let's explore the relationship between DNS and DHCP.

Tip

Although you can use DNS to provide names for network resources, remember that a DNS configuration is static, and that can create problems. With DHCP, a host can easily have a different IP address if its lease expires.

But no standard exists for updating DNS servers dynamically when IP address information changes in Windows NT Server 4.0. Note this will change in Windows 2000 Server when Dynamic DNS is introduced (this topic is discussed at the end of this chapter). So in Windows NT Server 4.0, DNS naming conflicts may occur if you use DHCP for dynamic allocation of IP addresses.

This problem primarily affects systems that participate on internetworks such as WANs and the Internet. For example, a server acting as a Web server may require users to connect to it using DNS names. In such cases, such clients should have reserved leases with an unlimited duration.

Managing DHCP database files

The following list of files represents the DHCP-related database files on Windows NT Server 4.0. These files are stored in the \%systemroot%\SYSTEM32\DHCP directory on the DHCP server. Note the *.MDB files are Microsoft Access data files:

- DHCP.MDB is the DHCP database file.
- DHCP.TMP is a temporary file that DHCP Server creates for temporary database information.
- JET.LOG and the JET*.LOG files contain logs of all transactions done with the database. These files are used by DHCP to recover data if necessary.
- SYSTEM.MDB is used by DHCP for holding information about the structure of its database.

It is important that you not tamper or remove the files listed. Note that the DHCP database and accompanying Registry entries are automatically backed up at a regular interval (the default interval is every 15 minutes) to the \%systemroot%\SYSTEM32\DHCP\BACKUP directory.

Secret

Starting with Windows NT Server 4.0, it is no longer necessary to run a Microsoft Access–related utility called JETPACK.EXE. This application was used in Windows NT Server 3.51 and earlier to compress and optimize the DHCP database files (*.MDB). Such interaction on your behalf is no longer necessary because, starting in Windows NT Server 4.0, the DHCP database files are automatically compressed and optimized.

Troubleshooting DHCP servers

Before leaving the DHCP discussion, here are several DHCP-related troubleshooting topics.

Routers used as RFC 1542 (BOOTP) relay agents

Many older routers do not function as RFC 1542 (BOOTP) relay agents with DHCP. That's because Microsoft DHCP contains new and modified fields that these older routers simple can't deal with. Thus, make sure that your routers support RFC 1541 and RFC 1542 before you assume that these routers will function properly as BOOTP relay agents.

DHCP server problems

These error conditions indicate that you are having problems with your DHCP server:

- **The RPC server is unavailable** or **Error 1753: The DHCP Server service is not running on the target systems.** When DHCP Manager attempts to connect to a DHCP server, the DHCP Manager application may return one of these error messages. Both of these errors are indications that the Microsoft DHCP Server service isn't running on the system that the DHCP Manager is attempting to connect to.

- **The DHCP Client couldn't obtain an IP address** or **The DHCP Client couldn't renew the IP address lease.** A DHCP client may see one of these messages. Both error messages indicate that the DHCP Client system was unable to communicate with a DHCP server. This may occur for a variety of reasons ranging from the DHCP Server service not running on the target Windows NT server to the DHCP client's connection to the network not functioning for some reason. The "DHCP Client couldn't obtain an IP address" error message can also be generated if the DHCP server has no more IP addresses available to lease.

If your network develops any of these problems, the first task is to make sure that the DHCP Server service is running on your Windows NT server.

Secret

In reality, I've found this message to reflect some fundamental weaknesses with Microsoft TCP/IP protocol stack. And given that time is of the essence when serving in my role as a network consultant, I have (regrettably) had to take some Windows NT Server sites back to static IP addresses (having never resolved to my satisfaction why the DHCP Server–related process was acting up).

WINS

Successfully maintaining a Windows NT Server–based network means using every tool that you have on your shelf. In the world of Windows NT Server 4.0, Windows Internet Naming Service (WINS) is one of those tools. Note that WINS will be displaced by Dynamic DNS in Windows 2000 Server, so in reality, you could say that WINS is on its way out of favor. And although Windows 2000 Server will support WINS for backward compatibility reasons, at this point in the Windows NT Server 4.0 life cycle, you are advised to plan for DNS-based network name resolution and to deemphasize your reliance on WINS.

That said, this section will provide you with what you need to know about WINS. It will provide little more given WINS' impending exit from the Windows NT community. And although you certainly need to know WINS basics, be advised that your time is better spent mastering the first two topics of this chapter (DNS, DHCP).

WINS was designed to eliminate broadcasts and maintain a dynamic database providing computer name–to–IP address mappings.

Note

The key point with WINS is its "dynamic" paradigm. Its database is updated dynamically or on the fly. By contrast, DNS maintains a static database of addresses that may only be upgraded by receiving a propagated delta DNS database periodically.

A WINS system has two components: servers and clients.

- **WINS servers.** WINS servers maintain the database that maps a WINS Client IP address to its NetBIOS computer name. Broadcasts for NetBIOS-type name resolutions are eliminated (or at least reduced) because the database on the WINS server may be consulted for immediate name resolution.

- **WINS clients.** A WINS client is a workstation that is configured with the WINS server(s) IP address(es). At system startup, the WINS client registers its name and IP address with the WINS server. When a WINS client needs a name resolved, the WINS server and its database are consulted. This results in fast and efficient name resolution.

At the enterprise level, a network typically has one or more WINS servers that a WINS client may contact for name resolution. In fact, WINS servers may be configured on a given network so that they replicate all computer names to IP address mappings to each other's respective databases.

Implementing WINS Server on your Windows NT Server network results in the following benefits:

- Reduced broadcast network traffic
- No need for an LMHOSTS file
- Dynamic name registration
- No duplicate computer names
- No specific need for a DNS server (although dispensing with one is not recommended!)

How WINS Works

Out of the box, when you configure a Windows NT Server–based network to use WINS for its name registration, it adheres to the h-node broadcasting methodology. You will recall the h-node refers to one of the NetBIOS over

TCP/IP modes that defines how NBT identifies and accesses resources on a network.

During name resolution, the WINS client:

- Checks to see if it is the local machine name.
- Looks at its cache of remote names. Any name that is resolved is placed in a cache, where it remains for 10-minutes.
- Attempts to contact the WINS server.
- Attempts broadcasting.
- Checks the LMHOSTS file (if it is configured to use and check the LMHOSTS file).
- Last, tries the HOSTS file and then DNS (if appropriately configured).

You will recall that this process was previously discussed early in the chapter in the "Be Resolved" section.

If a DHCP client has been configured to use m-node name resolution, the client first attempts to broadcast. The WINS server is consulted second.

When a WINS client boots, a Name Registration Request packet is sent to the WINS server so that the client computer name may be registered. As many Name Registration Request packets are sent as necessary to register names. Not surprisingly, these packets contain the WINS client's IP address and name.

Installing WINS servers

You may elect install a WINS server when you are initially setting up your Windows NT server or at a future date. In order to set up a WINS server, you must be logged on as a member of the Administrator group.

STEPS:
To install a WINS server

Step 1. Choose the Network applet in Control Panel. The Network dialog box appears.

Step 2. Select the Services tab sheet in the Network dialog box.

Step 3. Click the Add button. The Select Network Service dialog box appears.

Step 4. Select Windows Internet Name Service in the Select Network Service dialog box.

Step 5. Windows NT Server displays the Windows NT Setup dialog box asking for the complete path to the Windows NT Server distribution. Type in the correct path and click Continue.

Step 6. Observe that the Windows Internet Name Service appears as one of the Network Services listed on the Service tab sheet of the Network dialog box. Click Close.

Step 7. Restart the computer. When the computer restarts, the WINS server is ready to receive name registrations and resolve name requests.

Note that the WINS service will be configured to start automatically. It may be stopped via the Services applet in Control Panel.

Configuring WINS servers

You will use the WINS Manager located in the Administrator Tools (Common) program group to configure your local and remote WINS servers on your network (see Figure 8-39).

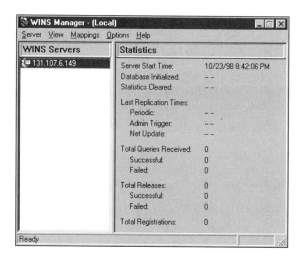

Figure 8-39: WINS Manager

The left pane of WINS Manager displays the WINS servers visible on your network. Typically these are shown as IP addresses, but it is entirely possible that the WINS server list will display NetBIOS names (if that is what the specific server supplied). If indeed a computer name is supplied, then WINS Manager establishes a connection to the WINS server via named pipes.

STEPS:

To configure a WINS server

Step 1. Select the Configuration command from the Server menu (see Figure 8-40).

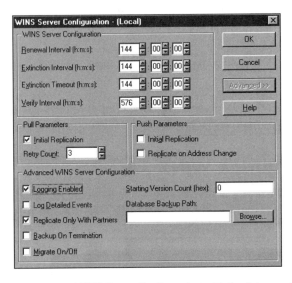

Figure 8-40: WINS Server Configuration with the Advanced button selected

Step 2. Click the Advanced button to expand the WINS Server Configuration dialog box.

Step 3. Configure the WINS Server Configuration dialog box options according to Table 8-9.

Table 8-9 WINS Server Configuration Options

Option	Definition
Renewal Interval (h:m:s)	Defines how often a client reregisters it names. Default is five hours.
Extinction Interval (h:m:s)	Defines the interval between when an entry is marked as released and when it is marked as extinct. The default is four times the renewal interval.

Option	Definition
Extinction Timeout (h:m:s)	Defines the interval between when an entry is marked extinct and when the entry is finally scavenged from the database. The default is dependent on the renewal interval and, if the WINS server has replication partners, on the maximum replications time interval.
Verify Interval	Defines the interval after which the WINS server must verify that old names it does not own are still active. The default is dependent on the extinction interval. The minimum allowable value is 24 days.
Pull Parameters	**Initial Replication.** Defines whether this WINS server pulls replicas from known partners whenever the system is initialized or whenever a replication-related parameter is changed. For example, this might be when a partner is added or deleted or a parameter specific to a partner is changed. **Retry Count.** Defines the number of times that the server should attempt to connect (in case of failure) with a partner for pulling replicas. Retries are attempted in accordance with the value for the Replication Interval specified in the Preferences dialog box. After a specified number of retries, the server stops momentarily before retrying again. The interval for this time is about three times the Replication Interval.
Push Parameters	Governs how the server pushes replicas from its partners. **Initial Replication.** Defines that this server will inform pull partners of the database status when the system is initialized. **Replicate on Address Change.** Defines that this server will inform pull partners of the database status when an address changes in the mapping record.
Logging Enabled	Specifies whether to log database changes in the JET.LOG file.
Log Detailed Events	Specifies that event logs include detailed information. This requires considerable system resources and should be turned off if you are tuning for performance.
Replicate Only with Partners	Specifies that replication will be done only with WINS pull or push partners. If this option is not checked, an administrator can ask a WINS server to pull or push from or to a nonlisted WINS Server partner.
Backup on Termination	Specifies that the database will be backed up automatically when the WINS Service is stopped, except when the system is being shut down.

Continued

Table 8-9 *(continued)*

Option	Definition
Migrate On/Off	Specifies that static unique and multihomed records in the database are treated as dynamic when they conflict with a new registration or replica. This means that if they are no longer valid, they will be overwritten by the new registration or replica. Select this option if you are upgrading non–Windows NT systems to Windows NT. By default, this option is not selected.
Starting Version Count	Specifies the version ID number for the database. Change this value to a higher number if the database becomes corrupted and needs to start fresh. In such a case, set this value to a number higher than the version number counter that appears for replications of this WINS server's records on all its remote partners. WINS may adjust the value you specify to a higher one to ensure that database records are quickly replicated to other WINS servers. This value appears in the View Database dialog box in WINS Manager.
Database Backup Path	Specifies the path to the folder where backup copies of the database are stored. If you specify a backup path, WINS automatically performs a full backup of its database to this folder every three hours. ***Do not*** specify a network drive as the backup location, as it may not be available in the future.

Note that advanced WINS configuration topics such as configuring replication partners are considered to be beyond the scope of this book given WINS' limited life before the release of Windows 2000 Server and its Dynamic DNS solution. If you are interested in advanced WINS configuration topics, I recommend that you consult the Windows NT Server 4.0 Resource Kit or Microsoft TechNet.

Configuring WINS clients

If a client workstation has TCP/IP installed, it may be configured to use a WINS server to perform its computer name–to–IP address resolution. This is accomplished when the client workstation is configured with the IP addresses of the primary and secondary WINS servers.

WINS Server on Windows NT Server 4.0 can support the following WINS clients:

- Windows NT Server 4.0
- Windows NT Workstation 4.0
- Windows 98

- Windows 95
- Windows for Workgroups 3.11 (WFW) with the Microsoft 32-bit TCP/IP VxD installed.

WFW is one of the clients supported on the Windows NT Server 4.0 CD-ROM in the \i386\clients\msclient directory. This is also one of the clients that is supported and configured via the Network Client Administrator application found in the Administrative Tools (Common) program group. Note this client support also extends to the next two clients (Microsoft Network Client for MS-DOS and LAN Manager for MS-DOS 2.2c).

- Microsoft Network Client for MS-DOS with real-mode TCP/IP driver
- LAN Manager for MS-DOS 2.2c

If a DHCP server is used to supply TCP/IP configuration information to DHCP clients, such TCP/IP configuration may contain the following WINS configuration information:

- 044 WINS/NBNS servers configured with an IP address of one or more WINS servers
- 046 WINS/NBT Node Type set to 0x1 (b-node), 0x2 (p-node), 0x4 (m-node), or 0x8 (h-node). For detailed information on node types, you should consult the Windows NT Server Resource Kit or Microsoft TechNet.

Using WINS Manager

The great thing about WINS Manager is that after its initial configuration, it becomes a reporting tool for you to observe WINS server–related name resolution activity. This service essentially runs itself. The statistics in Table 8-10 are displayed in the Statistics pane in WINS Manager.

Table 8-10   Statistics in WINS Manager

Statistic	Description
Database Initialized	Displays the last time that static mappings were imported into the WINS database.
Statistics Cleared	Displays the last time that statistics for the WINS server were cleared with the Clear Statistics command from the View menu.
Last Replication Times	The last time the WINS database was replicated.
	Periodic. The last time the WINS database was replicated based on the replication interval specified in the Preferences dialog box.

Continued

Table 8-10 *(continued)*

Statistic	Description
	Admin Trigger. The last time the WINS database was replicated because the Administrator selected the Replicate Now button in the Replication Partners dialog box.
	Net Update. The last time the WINS database was replicated as a result of a network request, which was a push notification message requesting propagation.
Total Queries Received	The number of name queries (name query request messages) received by this WINS server. Successful indicates how many names were successfully matched in the database, and Failed indicates how many names this WINS server could not resolve.
Total Releases	The number of messages received that indicate a NetBIOS application has shut itself down. Successful indicates how many names were successfully released. Failed indicates how many names this WINS server could not release.
Total Registrations	The number of messages received that indicate name registrations for clients.

To see detailed information about the current WINS server, select Detailed Information from the Server menu. The Detailed Information dialog box shown in Figure 8-41 appears. Select the Close button to dismiss the Detailed Information dialog box.

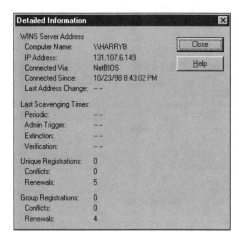

Figure 8-41: Detailed Information dialog box

Since in all likelihood you and I are both going to be living with Windows NT Server 4.0 for the foreseeable future either as the primary NOS or as a background NOS to Windows 2000 Server, it is prudent to drop down to the WINS engineering level and educated ourselves on the detailed statistics that are reported back from WINS (see Table 8-11).

Table 8-11   Detailed Information Statistics

Statistic	Description
WINS Server Address	**Computer Name.** Identifies the computer on the Windows NT network.
	IP Address. Is the unique four-octet address assigned to this computer.
	Connected Via. Shows the network protocol for the connection.
	Connected Since. Shows how long this computer has been on-line.
	Last Address Change. Indicates the time at which the last WINS database change was replicated.
Last Scavenging Times	**Periodic.** Indicates when the database was cleaned based on the renewal interval specific in the WINS Server Configuration dialog box.
	Admin Trigger. Indicates when the database was last changed because the administrator selected Initiate Scavenging.
	Extinction. Indicates when the database was last cleared based on the Extinction interval specified in the WINS Server Configuration dialog box.
	Verification. Indicates when the database was last cleared based on the Verify Interval specified in the WINS Server Configuration dialog box.
Unique Registrations	Indicates the number of name registration requests that have been accepted by this WINS server.
	Unique Conflicts. Shows the number of conflicts encountered during registration of unique names owned by this WINS server.
	Unique Renewals. Shows the number of renewals received for unique names.
Group Registrations	Indicates the number of registration requests that have been accepted by this WINS server.
	Group Conflicts. Shows the number of conflicts encountered during registration of group names.
	Group Renewals. Shows the number of renewals received for group names.

WINS and DNS Integration

The Windows NT Server DNS service integrates with the WINS Server service to provide name resolution for client computers running Windows 95/98 or Windows NT. An example of this involves a scenario with a UNIX computer seeking to connect to a computer that has a WINS name and a dynamic IP address. Here, you would configure the UNIX computer's resolver to use the Windows NT Server machine running the DNS service. You would also make sure that the Windows NT server running the DNS service has a correctly configured WINS Server service. Next, decided in which Internet-style domain the WINS names should reside. As an example, you might decide that springers.com is the name space that all WINS computers are named. The expectation is that the WINS lookup will handle queries for p100.springers.com when looking for the p100 machine.

Windows NT servers that run DNS and also provide WINS lookup should not be configured to use DNS for Windows Resolution (this is check box on the WINS Address tab sheet in the Network applet found in Control Panel).

STEPS:
To provide WINS names through the DNS service

Step 1. Use any text editor (such as Notepad) to edit the PLACE.DNS file found in the \%systemroot%\SYSTEM32\DNS\SAMPLES directory.

Step 2. Find the Start of Authority (SOA) record for the domain in which you want to use WINS names. The SOA record points to the computer that is the best source of computer name information in the domain.

Step 3. Create a new line under this line, consisting of the strong $WINS. This must be on a line by itself and start in column 1. Do not put the $WINS line in the reverse-lookup (IN-ADDR.ARPA) domains.

Step 4. Save the file to the \%systemroot%\SYSTEM32\DNS directory.

For more information on integrating WINS and DNS, you should consult the Windows NT Server Resource Kit or Microsoft TechNet.

Dynamic DNS

Imagine merging DNS and WINS together and using a best-of-breed name resolution tool. That is exactly what Windows 2000 Server will do with the introduction of Dynamic DNS. Dynamic DNS, based on RFC 2136, is a means for providing dynamic updates of zone data on a zone's primary server when an authorized server requests an update.

Clearly, Dynamic DNS has several advantages over old-fashioned DNS. One such advantage is that updates are not limited to manual edits of a zone's resource records. This is handled by a new message type for formatting DNS update requests. My advice? Learn DNS inside and out while working with Windows NT Server 4.0 today and you'll be ready to exploit Dynamic DNS in the forthcoming Windows 2000 Server!

Summary

This chapter described DNS, DHCP, and WINS. These are three critical TCP/IP areas on a Windows NT Server network. The following were emphasized:

- Learning DNS.
- Learning DHCP.
- Learning WINS.
- Comparing and contrasting DNS, DHCP, and WINS.
- Learning about integrating WINS and DNS.
- Learning about the forthcoming Dynamic DNS.

Chapter 9

Advanced TCP/IP Secrets

In This Chapter

▶ Learning what subnetting is
▶ Learning what subnetting isn't
▶ Determining subnetting requirements
▶ Mastering subnet-related calculations

TCP/IP is, of course, a study in itself. Mastering the TCP/IP protocol suite in Windows NT Server 4.0 is much more than understanding what an IP address, a subnet mask, and a Default Gateway are. Mastering TCP/IP is akin to mastering mathematics. That is, while you might be hired as a Windows NT Server network administrator, having mastered TCP/IP will enable you to be successful when troubleshooting and tackling those network issues that simply aren't covered in the books.

The Fine Art of Subnetting

Learning the fine art of subnet masking is akin to learning how to operate a sailboat. What? How can that be? Here's how. Sailing has best been described as an endeavor that requires only common sense to be successful. Subnetting is very much the same as sailing: not terribly difficult but makes heavy use of our common-sense skills. So here we go!

What Subnetting Is

Subnetting is really the implementation of the divide and conquer strategy in the TCP/IP community. Routers are used to divide, or subnet, networks into multiple physical segments. So what the conquering part? First on the list is simplification. Whenever confronted with a tough problem or a complex area, something that subnetting certainly is, a tried and true troubleshooting strategy is to divide the problem into smaller elements that can be managed, solved and conquered if you will. Thus, by subdividing a large network into smaller subnets, you conquer the network in your battles, not vice-versa. So why would you do this? There are several benefits to subnetting, including ease of administration, conservation of limited IP addresses, tighter and improved security, and more efficient use of our networking resources via traffic management.

Easier administration

Administration is potentially made easier by subnetting because a large network can be subdivided logically and physically by routers. A clean network is a happy network. The use of subnetting, properly done, enables you to "organize" your networks. And don't overlook the harsh reality of corporate politics on your network. Analogous to the complete trust model used in multiple-domain Windows NT Server 4.*x* and prior networks, subnetting enables you to potentially divided your enterprise-wide network along political boundaries. How? Remember the complete trust domain model was typically implemented when no one trusted each other and every little kingdom of users and resources had to be accommodated? With subnetting, you can create little LANs that reflect different groupings of users, resources, and in the language of the forthcoming Windows 2000 Server, objects.

Subnetting enables you to make network planning decisions without regard for the single LAN cable if you so desire. Whereas many of us old timers in the industry have "traditionally" thought of a network segment or subnet as a physical cable run, with subnetting, you have the opportunity to think much more logically. Multiple TCP/IP subnets can exist with ease on a cable segment, allowing you to divide your network into small networks for any conceivable reason. Likewise, you may also join unlike IEEE standards and media into a single subnet. Thus, users on a Token Ring network can communicate with users on an Ethernet network. These users would be joined together on a single, logical IP network using subnetting.

IP address conservation

In other sections of this book, I tout Microsoft Proxy Server as a way to save precious IP addresses. Properly implemented, IP subnetting allows one "real" or Internet-registered address to be partitioned into numerous internal network addresses. Here the router correctly routes packets between the external network or Internet and the internal or subnetted network. IP address conservation should be a fundamental guiding principle in your Windows NT Server network design and planning efforts.

Improved security

Properly implemented, subnetting can improve your network's security from external intruders. That's because, as implied, the router will route between the visible external network and the invisible networks in your organization.

And while we consider justice to be blind in America, in networking we know that peace is maintained to the degree that we can make our internal networks invisible to external intruders. But don't get me wrong. This form of security in no way substitutes for a real firewall, but this discussion may prompt you to think from a security perspective when considering the design of your network.

Another name for switching?

What happens if ten WAN engineers get together to create a subnetting plan for a network? Inevitably, the discussion becomes one of routers versus switches. Properly implemented, you can direct traffic to its location efficiently without its having to be evaluated by computers all across the network. In effect, you can use subnetting to create smaller networks that are "logically" designed to keep traffic within the neighborhood (see Figure 9-1). You can also use subnetting to reduce broadcasts in a similar manner.

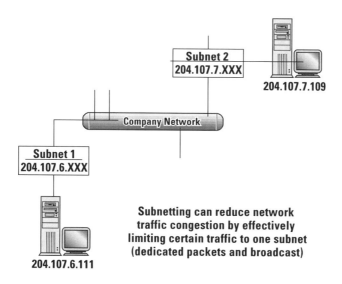

Figure 9-1: Subnetted or smaller networks within the larger network

Bottom line?

Know thy router when designing a network via subnetting. The router will need to be told how to distinguish between the host and network addresses. But more on that in a moment when you get into the details. Remember that subnetting provides planning and design flexibility and integration possibilities in ways you may or may not know today but will most likely appreciate tomorrow.

What Subnetting Isn't

Subnetting is not some elixir that will cure fundamental design errors in your network. In fact, the use of subnetting in a flawed network may only compound problems, forcing you to return to the basics.

OK, so you subnet your network into several smaller networks. What's the downside to that? You've allocated a portion of the bit pattern to the network addresses, thus limiting the quantity of host addresses on each of the smaller networks. There are only so many bit positions, so if some of the bits are used to define network subnets, then (of course) fewer bits are available on each new subnet to define hosts. Surprisingly, this can be a real limitation on real-world enterprise-wide networks.

First, it is essential that you are armed with this dotted decimal notation table for the different subnet mask classes. Why? You will see in a moment that you truly drop down to the bit level as you subnet an enterprise-wide network (see Table 9-1).

Table 9-1   Bit View of Default Subnet Masks for Standard IP Address Classes

Class of Address	Bits	Subnet Mask
Class A	11111111 00000000 00000000 00000000	255.0.0.0
Class B	11111111 11111111 00000000 00000000	255.255.0.0
Class C	11111111 11111111 11111111 00000000	255.255.255.0

Code Breaking 101

So here we go, lower and lower to the bit level. Another view of subnetting is that of code breaking in the military. When breaking a communication code, look for the pattern. Once the patterns are discovered, you can successfully break the code and decode the communication. As you work through the low-level details of subnetting, you are encouraged to keep this perspective.

First, let's look at the simple patterns relating to basic subnets. From Table 9-1, you can see that subnet mask values in each octet position will determine whether the network is operating with a Class A, B, or C license. The subnet mask thus becomes a decoder for the network to use in separating an IP address into the Network ID and the Host ID. For example, a Class C subnet mask of 255.255.255.0 and an IP address of 204.107.7.109 would suggest a Network ID of 204.107.7 and a Host ID of 109. This is known as subnetting along a byte boundary. It is what most people think of when they hear the term subnet or subnetting. In reality, no "subnetting" is really being used.

So far so good. But what if you wanted to take our Class C license and further divide it, that is, engage in "subnetting" along a nonbyte boundary. Then the exercise becomes more complex.

Chapter 9: Advanced TCP/IP Secrets

When subnetting is employed with a Class C scenario, you take advantage of the fourth octet position of the Subnet Mask value to communicate some additional information on the network. As you know, an octet is made up of eight bits or one byte, as shown in Figure 9-2.

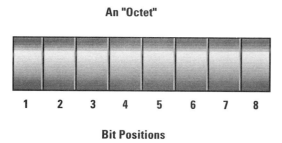

Figure 9-2: An octet position has eight bits.

Now before I go any further, allow me to share Table 9-2, which, based on subnet "size," provides all important decimal to binary bit conversion information. This information is invaluable as you create complex subnetting scenarios.

Table 9-2   Subnet Size, Binary Bit Values, Decimal Values

Subnet Size Measured in Bits	Binary Bit Values	Value in Decimal
1	10000000	128
2	11000000	192
3	11100000	224
4	11110000	240
5	11111000	248
6	11111100	252
7	11111110	254

Let's quickly revisit how binary bit values are really converted to decimal. Remember with binary, you're using a base two counting system (versus the base ten counting system used in the "real world"). You may recall that with the binary system, any value up to 255 can be represented as either a one ("1") or a zero ("0") within a byte or eight bit positions. This phenomenon can be displayed in two ways: as a "Power of 2" table (Table 9-3) or as a simple chart showing the value of each bit position in a byte (Table 9-4).

Table 9-3 Powers of 2

Bit Position within Byte	Power of 2	Decimal Notation Value
00000001	2^0	1
00000010	2^1	2
00000100	2^2	4
00001000	2^3	8
00010000	2^4	16
00100000	2^5	32
01000000	2^6	64
10000000	2^7	128

Table 9-4 Value of Each Bit Position in a Byte

Bit Position	1	2	3	4	5	6	7	8
Decimal Value	128	64	32	16	8	4	2	1

Any questions? Great! Let's move on. Referring back to Table 9-2, you will notice that you can place the decimal value (found in the far right column) in the fourth octet position of the Class C subnet mask value to further subnet your network. Here is what I mean. Remember that the subnet mask communicates to the network which portion of the IP address to mask as the subnet number, and thus by default, the Host number value is the balance. So if I present the following subnet mask to the network, the network will know that the first four bits of the fourth octet are "masked" to communicate subnet number information. This is perhaps better explained in the following table, which shows the "details" for the subnet mask 255.255.255.240. Note that the table only shows the details for the fourth octet position. Octet positions one, two, and three would be fully populated with ones ("1's") to achieve the value 255.

Table 9-5 communicates that the first four bit positions are masked out as part of the subnet number, in that these bit positions are occupied with a binary one value, and most important, this information is being conveyed in the context of the subnet mask value (where it is meaningful).

Table 9-5 Subnetting via "240" in the Fourth Octet Position of Subnet Mask 255.255.255.240

Bit Position	1	2	3	4	5	6	7	8
Decimal Value	128	64	32	16	8	4	2	1
Actual Bit Flags	1	1	1	1	0	0	0	0

Chapter 9: Advanced TCP/IP Secrets

Which leads us to an exercise based on the information presented thus far in the chapter. Given the following information, please determine what the subnet number and the host number are:

Subnet Mask: 255.255.255.240

IP Address: 204.131.7.109

Subnet number: _____

Host number: _____

The solution set is:

1. Understand that subnetting is being used.

2. The fourth octet of the subnet mask has a value of 240. Based on Table 9-5, this can be interpreted to mean that the first four bit positions on the fourth octet position in the IP address relate to the subnet number, and the final four bit position relate to the host number.

3. Because the IP address has a fourth octet position of 109, you need to break the code and determine what explicitly relates to the subnet number. This is accomplished as shown in Table 9-6.

   To assist your efforts, the four bit positions of this fourth octet in the IP address have been shaded so that it's easy to determine that they relate to the subnet number. Now, add the "shaded" value to determine the rest of the subnet number. This is accomplished in Table 9-7.

   Therefore, based on the information in the table, the Subnet number is 96.

4. The host number is now calculated. It is the balance of the bit positions in the fourth octet position of the IP address 204.131.7.96. This is shown in Table 9-8.

Table 9-6 **Bit Breakdown of 109 Value**

Bit Position	1	2	3	4	5	6	7	8
Decimal Value	128	64	32	16	8	4	2	1
Actual Bit Flags	0	1	1	0	1	1	0	1

Table 9-7 **Calculating the Subnet Number (First Four Bit Positions) of the Fourth Octet Position of IP Address 204.131.7.109**

Bit Position	1	2	3	4	
Decimal Value	128	64	32	16	
Actual Bit Flags	0	1	1	0	Subnet number is 96

Table 9-8 Calculating the Host Number (First Four Bit Positions) of the Fourth Octet Position of IP Address 204.131.7.109

Bit Position	5	6	7	8	
Decimal Value	8	4	2	1	
Actual Bit Flags	1	1	0	1	Host number is 13

The solution set is:

Subnet number = 96

Host number = 13

This network can then be depicted graphically as shown in Figure 9-3.

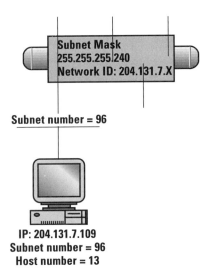

Figure 9-3: A network with a subnet mask of 255.255.255.240

So if you have a basic understanding of the preceding example, you can thus easily interpret the next table, Table 9-9, where the actual bit flags are displayed for each of the possible "subnetting" bit values available for a Class C (255.255.255.*x*) network. Again, referring to Table 9-2 will assist our efforts to better understand subnetting. The bit portion of the fourth octet position that relates to the subnet number is shaded to assist in our comprehension.

Secret

By the way, you may use another technique to convert a decimal value to its binary bit cousin. This method involves a simple use of division and the number two. Because the binary counting system is based on a counting system of "base 2," it is plausible that if you take any number and divide by 2 several times, you'll arrive at the binary equivalent. Isn't it?

Chapter 9: Advanced TCP/IP Secrets 341

Table 9-9 Possible Class C Subnetting Values and Impact on Sample IP Address 204.131.7.109

Description	Bit 1	Bit 2	Bit 3	Bit 4	Bit 5	Bit 6	Bit 7	Bit 8	Comments: Evaluate sample IP address 204.131.7.109 for each subnetting example given.
Subnet Mask: 255.255.255.128	1	0	0	0	0	0	0	0	Subnet number = 0 (INVALID! You can't have zero subnets or a subnet with a value of zero.) Host Number = 109
Subnet Mask: 255.255.255.192	1	1	0	0	0	0	0	0	Subnet number = 64 Host Number = 45
Subnet Mask: 255.255.255.224	1	1	1	0	0	0	0	0	Subnet number = 96 Host Number = 13
Subnet Mask: 255.255.255.240	1	1	1	1	0	0	0	0	Subnet number = 96 Host Number = 13
Subnet Mask: 255.255.255.248	1	1	1	1	1	0	0	0	Subnet number = 104 Host Number = 5
Subnet Mask: 255.255.255.252	1	1	1	1	1	1	0	0	Subnet number = 108 Host Number = 1
Subnet Mask: 255.255.255.254	1	1	1	1	1	1	1	0	Subnet number = INVALID Host Number = INVALID
Decimal Values by Bit Position	128	64	32	16	8	4	2	1	This row is presented to assist in interpreting this table.
Binary Bit Representation of 109 assist in interpreting this table.	0	1	1	0	1	1	0	1	This row is presented to

Let's see how a base-2 scenario works. Take the number 109 again, given that's been your "sample" number.

STEPS:
To convert a decimal value to its binary bit cousin

Step 1. Divide 109 by 2.

109 / 2 = 54 with a remainder of 1

Take the remainder as your first bit value, starting with the far right of the bit listing. Stick with it, as you will see the pattern in a moment.

The cumulative bit order is 1.

Step 2. Divide 54 by 2.

54 / 2 = 27 with a remainder of 0

Thus, the bit value is 0.

The cumulative bit order is 01.

Step 3. Divide 27 by 2.

27 / 2 = 13 with a remainder of 1

Not surprisingly, the bit value is 1.

The cumulative order is 101.

Step 4. Divide 13 by 2.

13 / 2 = 6 with a remainder of 1

The bit value is 1.

The cumulative bit order is 1101.

Step 5. Divide 6 by 2.

6 / 2 = 3 with a remainder of 0

The bit value is 0.

The cumulative bit order is 01101.

Step 6. Divide 3 by 2.

3 / 2 = 1 with a remainder of 1

The bit value is 1.

The cumulative bit order is 101101.

Step 7. Divide 1 by 2.

1 / 2 = 0 with a remainder of 1

The bit value is 1.

The cumulative bit order is 1101101.

Step 8. Because the division is complete, add a zero to the final bit position to "close" the exercise. The resulting bit order is 01101101.

Congratulations! You've just successfully used another tool for converting a base-10 number to a base-2 number.

Secret

You may also use the built-in calculator in Windows NT Server 4.0 for decimal and binary bit conversions (and thus as a tool for subnetting).

The built-in calculator is found under the Accessories area from the Start button (via Programs). After starting the Calculator, perform the following steps.

STEPS:

To use the built-in calculator for decimal and binary bit conversions

Step 1. Launch the Calculator applet. Convert the calculator from Standard view to Scientific view (see Figure 9-4). This is accomplished via the View menu on the Calculator menu bar, resulting in:

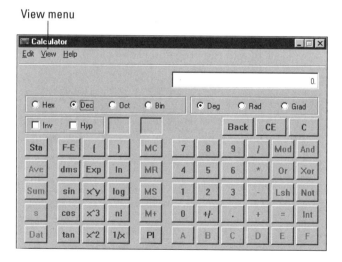

Figure 9-4: The Scientific view

Continued

STEPS

To use the built-in calculator for decimal and binary bit conversions *(continued)*

Step 2. Type in the decimal value. Use 109 for continuity. Make sure the "Dec" or decimal notation radio button is selected, as shown in Figure 9-5.

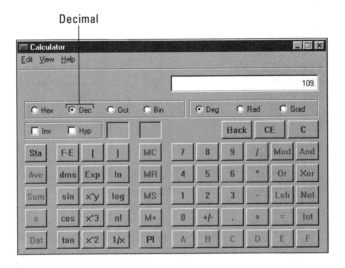

Figure 9-5: Decimal value 109 keyed into the Calculator entry field

Step 3. Select the "Bin" or binary notation button to convert the decimal value to the binary value of 1101101 (see Figure 9-6). Don't forget to add the preceding zero(s) ("0") when only a partial binary value is presented.

Chapter 9: Advanced TCP/IP Secrets 345

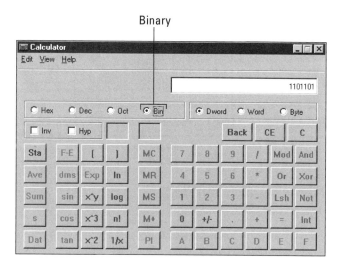

Figure 9-6: The Bin radio button

The Calculator included with Windows NT Server 4.0 is truly a time-saving tool as you implement TCP/IP subnetting on your networks.

A different tact on subnetting is to view it from the MCSE perspective. That is, exam cram! A peer from the industry, John Lambert, shared with readers in *Microsoft Certified Professional Magazine* the following points about mastering subnetting from the practical perspective of just passing the darn TCP/IP certification exam.

Arguably the TCP/IP elective exam in the MCSE track is the most difficult of all. This is the exam for which certification candidates emerge from the testing room looking like ghosts (or at least with a catatonic gaze). Likewise, it can be said with some degree of certainty that you will encounter the advanced areas of TCP/IP during your tenure as a Windows NT Server professional.

But fear not. It's really as simple as 1-2-3. That is, the following two charts will serve as your guide to quickly assessing:

1. What class a TCP/IP address falls into (Table 9-10)
2. What are the possible number of subnet number and host numbers per subnetting scenario (Table 9-11)

Table 9-10 IP Class Chart

Class	First Binary Digits	Decimal Range of First Octet
A	0	1–126
B	10	128–191
C	110	192–223

Two quick questions to test your understanding of advanced TCP/IP concepts. The answers follow:

Questions:

1. Why is the decimal value 127 not included in the third column of Table 9-10?

2. For the Class C row, why are the first binary digits 110 instead of 11?

Answers:

1. The decimal value 127 can't be used for network/host IDs, as it is the IP address area used for loopback testing.

2. It makes the Class C range end at 223. Remember that initial octet values ranging between 224 and 255 are reserved for multicasting, research, and such. They may not be used for network/host IDs.

The next table (Table 9-11) is perhaps the most useful of all. At its core, the table displays the number of subnets and hosts for each subnetting scenario and IP addresses. More important, it draws out specific relationships that will make you a crack code breaker . . . err . . . subnetter in no time.

Table 9-11 Subnet Mask Chart

Bit Split	Subnet Mask	Max. Usable Subnets	# C IPs/Subnet	# B IPs/Subnet	#A IPs/Subnet
2/6	192	2	62	16382	4096K
3/5	224	6	30	8190	2048K
4/4	240	14	14	4094	1024K
5/3	248	30	6	2046	512K
6/2	252	62	2	1022	256K
7/1	254	126	0	510	128K
8/0	255	254	0	254	64K

Here is how you can interpret this chart. First, the bit split is simply the division of bits between the subnet and the host. This is similar to the presentation of such a split in Table 9-9, where shading was used to distinguish between the subnet and host positions.

The Subnet Mask column shows all possible masks. Remember that zero appears in some masks, but a zero octet doesn't mask any bits. As its name implies, the third column refers to the maximum usable subnets for a given scenario. Columns four, five, and six speak toward the number of usable IP addresses for each subnet, given a IP address class.

One of the patterns that is important to see is the tradeoff between the number of subnets and hosts as the subnet-related value in the fourth octet position of the subnet mask increases. Seeing this relationship will enable you to be both a great code breaker and a great subnetter!

Summary

Understanding subnetting is an advanced TCP/IP necessity that will greatly assist you in your effort to manage your larger TCP/IP-based Windows NT Server 4.0 networks. This chapter covered the following:

- Learning what subnetting is
- Learning what subnetting isn't
- Determining subnetting requirements
- Mastering subnet-related calculations

Chapter 10

Internet Secrets

In This Chapter

▶ Learning how to connect to the Internet

▶ Understanding the Point-To-Point Tunneling Protocol (PPTP)

▶ Learning about Internet Explorer 4

▶ Learning about Internet Information Server (IIS)

This chapter could easily be an entire book. In fact, there are many books on the Internet (you can see many of these books listed at www.idgbooks.com). More important, let me set the tone for this chapter so that you will know what to expect. The Internet is necessarily discussed in almost every chapter of this book. So I am using this chapter to answer a few common questions about the Internet that I frequently encounter as a practicing Windows NT Server consultant.

Obviously the history of the Internet has been covered in more texts than you or I care to count, so I'll leave that topic alone. But it is interesting to note that the Internet is creating its own history each day. Its short life to date suggests that there are untold opportunities for you to capitalize on the Internet. But for you to do that, you first need to successfully attach your Windows NT server to the Internet. You have several ways to do this. In this chapter, I'll start with the easiest approach (dial-up) and work toward more complex Internet configurations.

Dial-Up Connection

You will recall that Remote Access Server (RAS) was discussed in Chapter 4 in the context of dial-in users. But did you know that RAS is used to expedite connections to the Internet as well?

A simple dial-up connection to the Internet assumes that you have performed several tasks:

- You have correctly installed a modem via the Modems applet in the Modems Properties applet under the Control Panel (see Figure 10-1).

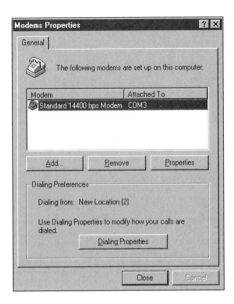

Figure 10-1: Modems Properties

- You have installed the TCP/IP protocol. This was discussed in Chapter 6, "Installing and Configuring TCP/IP."
- You have a valid Internet user account with the Internet service provider (ISP) of your choice. This should be a dial-up account that supports PPP, not SLIP (if possible). Such accounts for individuals with unlimited use average $20 to $25 per month. Business dial-up accounts are more expensive but can easily be found for under $100 per month, with $50 per month being the average.
- You have installed RAS via the Network applet in the Remote Access Setup applet under the Control Panel (see Figure 10-2).

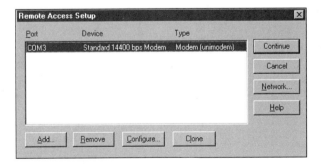

Figure 10-2: RAS Setup

Chapter 10: Internet Secrets 351

Note that RAS must be configured to accommodate dial-out activity. You may elect to have dial-out only or to both dial out and receive calls, as Figure 10-3 shows. As mentioned in Chapter 4, "Implementation," RAS dial-out capabilities apply only to the Windows NT Server machine in which this option is configured. Such a dial-out configuration server does not allow other users on your Windows NT Server network to dial out to the Internet via your Windows NT server. That is, Windows NT Server does not natively provide modem pooling capabilities (the exception being Microsoft Small Business Server, which is discussed in Chapter 20).

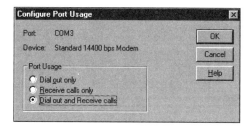

Figure 10-3: Dial-out configuration

Secret

If you have multiple modems attached to your Windows NT server and you are allowed to have multiple dial-up connections to your ISP simultaneously, you may consider implementing multilink functionality. Multilink a feature in Windows NT Server that allows a single RAS session to a remote host (such as an ISP) to take advantage of multiple connection points. In English, you could have two or more modems simultaneously connected to the ISP for a single Internet session, resulting in the combined bandwidth of the modems that are connected. For example, if you invoked multilink and had two 56Kb modems attached to your systems that called the ISP and established an Internet session, the total bandwidth would be close to 2 × 56Kb = 112Kb. That's approaching two-channel ISDN speeds!

To enable multilink, you need to select the Network button in Figure 10-2 and then select the Enable Multilink check box on the Network Configuration dialog box that will appear.

- It is also important that the dial-out RAS capabilities be configured to use the TCP/IP protocol for an Internet connection scenario.

- You have configured Dial-Up Networking. These steps are explained in the text that follows.

Secret

Creating and configuring a dial-up connection to the Internet can be made dramatically easier if you request the setup configuration information from your ISP. By working closely with your ISP, you can save time when configuring your dial-up Internet connection.

Every ISP that I've worked with will provide setup instructions on their Web page to assist you (see Figure 10-4). What information isn't provide on their Web page can usually be obtained with a quick telephone call to the ISP's technical support group. In fact, the ease with which you obtain the configuration information that you need is a leading indicator as to how strong the relationship with the ISP will be.

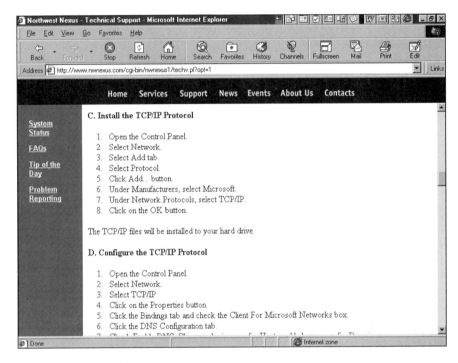

Figure 10-4: An ISP dial-up configuration FAQ

Configuring Dial-Up Networking

Assuming that you've addressed each of the prerequisite points just described, it is now time to configure Dial-Up Networking.

STEPS:
To configure Dial-Up Networking

Step 1. Launch the Dial-Up Networking application. The Dial-Up Networking application is located in an unusual location. As shown in Figure 10-5, select Dial-Up Networking from the Accessories folder in the Programs menu.

Chapter 10: Internet Secrets

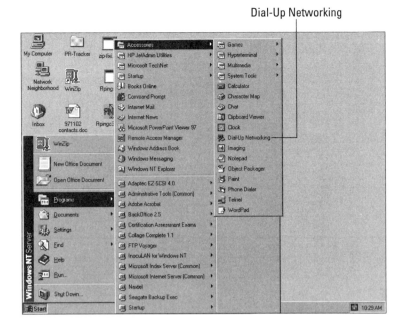

Figure 10-5: The Dial-Up Networking menu option

Step 2. The first time that you launch Dial-Up Networking, the phonebook will be empty. You will be prompted to enter a phonebook entry, as shown in Figure 10-6. Click OK.

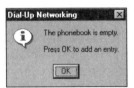

Figure 10-6: An empty phonebook

Step 3. The New Phonebook Entry Wizard appears. Type in the name for the telephone entry. You may select the "know-it-all" check box shown in Figure 10-7 where you proudly declare you know "all about" setting up phonebook entries and do not need the help of the Wizard. Click Next.

Continued

STEPS

To configure Dial-Up Networking *(continued)*

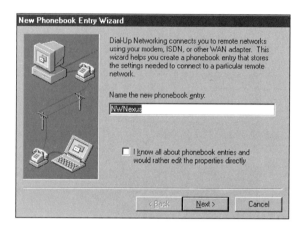

Figure 10-7: The New Phonebook Entry Wizard

Secret

I recommend that you make the phone book entry the same name as your ISP (for example, NWNexus).

Step 4. When the Server dialog box appears, select the I Am Calling the Internet check box on the Server screen, as shown in Figure 10-8. Click Next.

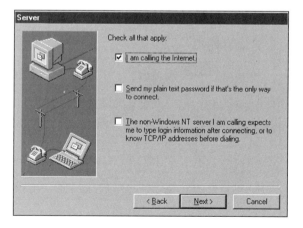

Figure 10-8: The I Am Calling the Internet check box

If you did not properly install RAS to use TCP/IP, you will see the error message in Figure 10-9. You are instructed to fix the problem before continuing.

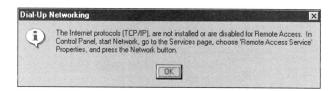

Figure 10-9: A RAS TCP/IP configuration error message

Step 5. Assuming that you have properly configured RAS to use TCP/IP, you will be asked to provide the dial-up telephone number (see Figure 10-10).

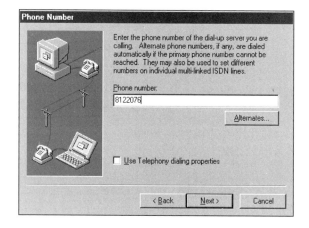

Figure 10-10: A telephone number to dial up the ISP

The Alternates button enables you to enter additional telephone numbers for the Dial-Up Networking configuration to try if attempts to another configured number fail. As you may know, ISPs typically have multiple telephone numbers for dialing in, and indeed some of these numbers work better than others (less busy signals and/or better line speeds). You may want to add these additional numbers in the Phone Numbers dialog box (see Figure 10-11) that appears when you select the Alternates button.

Continued

STEPS

To configure Dial-Up Networking (continued)

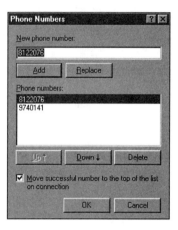

Figure 10-11: Enter alternative telephone numbers.

Secret

Be advised that you may need to enter the full ten-digit telephone number for additional telephone numbers supported by your ISP within the same general geographic area. With the advent of area code redistricting, ten-digit telephone numbers may be needed to place a call within your city (or even same neighborhood!). For example, in Seattle, the metropolitan area now has several area codes, including 206, 425, 360, and 253. You only need to dial the area code and the telephone number to place a call locally; you do not need to precede the area code with a "1" when calling these area codes within the Seattle area.

The global telephony properties discussed in the text that follows and shown in Figure 10-12 do not adequately handle ten-digit telephone numbers (telephony properties were designed to handle 11-digit telephone numbers where a "1" is placed before the area code).

Selecting the Use Telephony Dialing Properties check box will result in global dialing properties being applied to this Dial-Up Networking configuration. Such global configurations might include a set of numbers to disable call waiting (typically *70) and the like.

Also, selecting the Use Telephony Dialing Properties check box will modify the screen in Figure 10-10 to include the country and area code information. This is shown in Figure 10-13.

Chapter 10: Internet Secrets 357

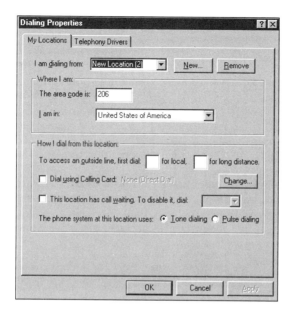

Figure 10-12: Dialing Properties in the Control Panel

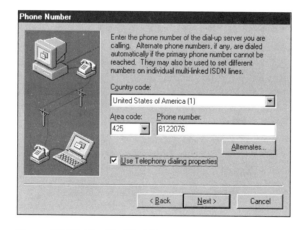

Figure 10-13: The Modified Phone Number dialog box

Continued

STEPS

To configure Dial-Up Networking (continued)

Secret

The other problem is that the global telephone properties will only accommodate one area code for you to select from when configuring a specific Dial-Up Networking connection (such as NWNexus). Thus, given three local ISP dial-in numbers: 425-974-0141; 425-812-2076; 253-735-5646; the telephony properties settings will not be able to "switch out" the proper area code as different telephone numbers are attempted (from the alternative telephone list). So if your first two telephone numbers were entered as seven-digit telephone numbers on the Alternates list in Figure 10-11 and the Use Telephony Properties button was selected, then the telephone number 253-735-5646 would actually be dialed as 425-735-5646. Again, the solution is to enter ten-digit telephone numbers in the New Phone Number field shown in Figure 10-11.

Step 6. After you have completely configured the ISP's telephone numbers, click Next in the Phone Number dialog box.

Step 7. You will be presented with the final screen of the Net Phonebook Entry Wizard. Click Finish. You will be presented with the Dial-Up Networking dialog box (Figure 10-14).

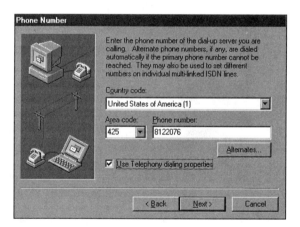

Figure 10-14: Dial-Up Networking

Dial-Up Networking dialog box

Let's take a moment to discuss the Dial-Up Networking dialog box. It has richer feature sets than you might imagine. The New button is for creating additional Dial-Up Networking configuration (different locations, other ISPs, accessing other Windows NT Server networks via RAS). The More button leads to several options of interest, which appear as a drop-down menu that I will discuss next. Note that several remaining configurations need to be made so that you may dial up and connect to your ISP. These configurations are made via the More button.

Edit entry and modem properties

Selected from the More button, Edit Phonebook Entry is a very important dialog box that essentially enables you to complete your Dial-Up Networking configuration for calling an ISP. The Edit Phonebook Entry dialog box has five tab sheets: Basic, Server, Script, Security, and X.25.Basic.

The Basic tab sheet, shown in Figure 10-15, displays information you provided via the New Phonebook Entry Wizard. If you have multiple modems attached to your Windows NT Server, you may select the Use Another Port If Busy check box so that another modem can be used if the first modem selected is busy (say with a dial-in RAS call).

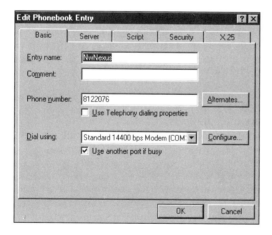

Figure 10-15: Edit Phone Book Entry – Basic tab sheet

Server

In the Dial-up server type drop-down menu shown in Figure 10-16, you may select from three options:

- **PPP: Windows NT, Windows 95, Internet.** This is the most common and preferred method for configuring your dial-in configuration to the

Internet. If you are unsure about which of the three options listed here to select, then retain the default PPP choice.

- **SLIP: Internet.** This is the "old" paradigm for Internet connections. It is rarely used today and is only included for backward compatibility reasons.

- **Windows NT 3.1, Windows for Workgroups.** This option is for older RAS configurations from the Windows NT Advanced Server 3.1 days. In that era, the dial-in model was fundamentally different from Windows NT Server 4.0.

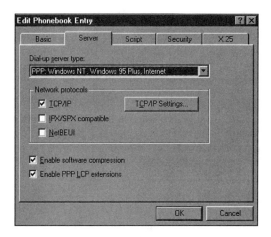

Figure 10-16: Edit Phone Book Entry – Server tab sheet

The Server tab sheet is the most important tab sheet for completing your dial-up connection to the Internet. It is here that you provide critical communication and network protocol information. In fact, did you know that the only Dial-In Networking protocol allowed in the Windows NT Advanced Server 3.1 days was NetBEUI? We've come a long way baby.

For an Internet dial-up connection, you would only need to select the TCP/IP protocol. The two other protocols (IPX/SPX compatible and NetBEUI) are typically selected when you are configuring a RAS scenario.

You will need to select the TCP/IP Setting button to complete your dial-up Internet configuration. Making that selection (assuming you've retained the default PPP communication protocol) results in the dialog box shown in Figure 10-17.

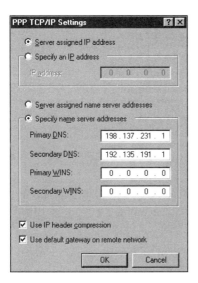

Figure 10-17: PPP TCP/IP settings

The first configuration necessary in Figure 10-17 is deciding whether you want your ISP to assign a dynamic IP address each time that you call in from your Windows NT server or you want to make use of a static IP address. There are different reasons for selecting either course of action, but at a minimum, you need to communicate with your ISP the option you have selected for your Windows NT server (the ISP typically has different user account types to select from depending on whether you want a static or dynamic IP address).

In general, a dynamically assigned IP address is great for browsing with your Internet Explorer web browser. This option, invoked by selecting the Server Assigned IP Address radio button in Figure 10-17, is also appropriate if you have your Internet e-mail stored and managed on the POP3/SMTP mail server at the ISP's site.

Secret

A static IP address, selected via the Specify an IP Address radio button in Figure 10-17, is typically used when you are running Microsoft Exchange and the Internet Mail Service (IMS) on your Windows NT server. The IMS needs a static IP address that serves as a reception point for your incoming Internet e-mail. This static IP address is the IP address that your MX record "points" to. This is, in my experience, the number one reason for having a static IP address with a Dial-Up Networking configuration for an Internet connection.

Note that if you use a static IP address to connect to the Internet, your ISP will provide you with such an IP address.

The next configuration item in Figure 10-17 is the DNS entries. You either select the Server Assigned Name Server Address radio button to have the

DNS information dynamically provided or select the Specify Name Server Addresses radio button to manually enter the DNS addresses. The second option is most common, and your ISP will provide you with the necessary DNS addresses.

You will recall that DNS is discussed in Chapter 8, "DNS, DHCP, WINS." Note that with a Dial-Up Networking connection to the Internet, you will not complete the primary and secondary WINS entries in the PPP TCP/IP Settings dialog box.

Two configuration options remain in the PPP TCP/IP Settings dialog box (Figure 10-17):

- **Use IP Header Compression.** This is selected by default and you typically do not change its value. Technically speaking, the option sets Van Jacobson (VJ) IP header compression at log on and handshake negotiation with the remote PPP server. When selected, Dial-Up Networking will try to use VJ compression. Whether or not that is successful (typically depending on the capabilities of the remote server), the connection attempt will still be attempted. That is, whether the VJ compression works or not, you may still enjoy a successful connection.

- **Use Default Gateway on Remote Network.** This applies only if the Dial-Up Networking client (the machine that you are calling from) is both connected to a LAN (via Dial-Up Networking) and using a network adapter card on another LAN. When this option is selected, packets that are unable to be routed over the local network are passed on to the default gateway of the remote network for resolution.

Secret

With this option, addressing conflicts between the local LAN and the remote LAN are adjudicated in favor of the remote network.

Use Default Gateway on Remote Network is selected by default and is typically not modified when configuring Dial-Up Networking for an Internet connection.

After you complete your configuration in the PPP TCP/IP Settings dialog box, click OK to return to the Server tab sheet of the Edit Phonebook Entry dialog box as shown in Figure 10-16.

Two configuration options, in the form of check boxes, remain to be discussed on the Server tab sheet in Edit Phonebook Entry dialog box.

- **Enable Software Compression.** The default condition is for this is to be selected. It is offered so that you may take advantage of Windows NT Server 4.0's software compression for dial-out RAS-based connections, such as a dial-out connection to the Internet. The thought behind this feature is that whether or not your modem supports hardware compression (typically via the V-standards), you may still benefit from faster transmission speeds if the Windows NT Server operating system manages the compression for you. This option typically remains selected when configuring Dial-Up Networking connections to the Internet, but you are advised to check with your ISP.

- **Enable PPP LCP Extensions.** This option is selected by default and allows your server to take advantage of newer PPP features. The problem is that the servers on the other end of your call must also support newer PPP features. Obviously, there is risk in invoking this feature, and for Dial-Up Networking Internet connections, it is typically left unchecked.

Script

The Script tab sheet for the Edit Phonebook Entry dialog box is shown in Figure 10-18. This Script tab sheet is typically left unconfigured for dial-up connections to the Internet. You would use this configuration for RAS connections to another Windows NT Server network. For example, the Run This Script option might be used to run Kixstart, a logon scripting programming discussed in Chapter 3, "Implementation."

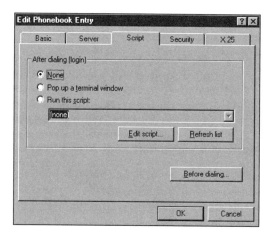

Figure 10-18: Edit Phone Book Entry – Script tab sheet

Security

The Security tab sheet, shown in Figure 10-19, offers three options that provide different levels of password encryption:

- **Accept Any Authentication including Clear Text.** This option means the password will be shared with any authentication authority in the world, including prying eyes that have no business seeing this information.

- **Accept Only Encrypted Authentication.** This is the second-level of password authentication. Call it the middle-of-the-road option between clear text and Microsoft encryption.

- **Accept Only Microsoft Encrypted Authentication.** This is the highest level of encryption security and relates only to Microsoft authentication authorities such as Windows NT Server or LAN Manager.

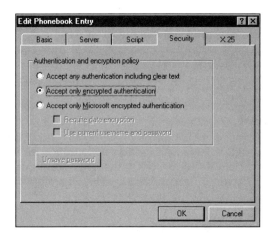

Figure 10-19: Edit Phone Book Entry – Security tab sheet

You will typically select an option suggested by your ISP. The most common setting for a Dial-Up Networking connection to the Internet is the first option: Accept Any Authentication including Clear Text. That is because the server that processes your call when you call your ISP may be a UNIX server. A UNIX server that receives your telephone call will be unable to process the third option (Microsoft encrypted authentication).

Secret

The Unsave Password button on the Security tab sheet is the only place you may gain access to your password entry with Dial-Up Networking if you have selected the Save Password check box when attempting to dial (using your Dial-Up Networking configuration).

Here is what happens: The first time that you attempt to dial out to the Internet, you indeed select the Save Password check box (I discuss this process in several pages in the "Dialing the Internet" section). However, passwords tend to be alphanumeric and mixed case, so it is easy to mistype the password. I've certainly done that. If such is the case, then you would not have the ability to enter the correct password unless you use the Unsave Password button.

X.25

The X.25 tab sheet is rarely used today. This is an older networking solution that I've only seen once. This site was the U.S. Coast Guard. More "modern" networking solutions such as digital lines (ISDN and the like) have replaced X.25. However, I understand that X.25 still has a following overseas in Europe.

User preferences

The option presents the User Preferences dialog box as seen in Figure 10-20. Four tab sheets are presented: Dialing, Callback, Appearance, and Phonebook. User preferences are, of course, very important as it is here that you will configure several important features such as number of redial attempts (important to set to a reasonable number in case the ISP has a busy number) and idle seconds before hangup (this value prevents unintended indefinite connections to your ISP). Beside the Edit Entry and Modem Properties menu options, this is the second most popular menu option from the More menu in Dial-Up Networking.

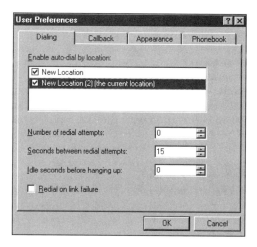

Figure 10-20: User Preferences

Dialing

Here you may configure how autodial works. Autodial is a feature that causes RAS to automatically dial out when an application presents such a request. An example might be the Dial-Up Connection configuration in the IMS in Microsoft Exchange Server. Dialing is also where you elect which location configurations you want to use.

Secret

These location configurations cannot be assigned by application; that is, the elections you make in the Dialing tab sheet are global (or generic) in nature. To assign truly different configurations at the application level, you would need to create multiple Dial-Up Networking configurations with each configuration being assigned to a different application (using the Clone Entry and Modem Properties option discussed later and then modifying the cloned entry appropriately).

The Dialing tab sheet also enables you to specify redial attempts, seconds between redial, and idle seconds before hanging up.

Secret

Note that is wise to set the Idle Seconds before Hanging Up value to some reasonable number such as 600 seconds (10 minutes) so that you don't unnecessarily stay connected to your ISP. Some business Internet access accounts have a monthly limit of connect minutes, so this value is important to set so that you don't unnecessarily use up you monthly allocation of Internet connection minutes (and then perhaps start paying a per-hour fee to the ISP above and beyond your standard agreement). I've made use of this value to protect my Windows NT Server customer's best interest when creating dial-up Internet connections.

Callback

The Callback tab sheet enables you to set a server-based callback feature in RAS. This is where the Windows NT server running RAS would call the remote client back to either create a more secure connection or have the company pay for the telephone call. This is not a meaningful setting when configuring dial-up Internet connections.

Appearance

The Appearance tab sheet enables you to specify how the Windows NT server communicates its connection status to you (Figure 10-21). I would encourage you to experiment with several of these settings so that you know whether you are connected to the Internet and for how long. I discuss this issue more in several pages in connection with the Dial-Up Networking Monitor.

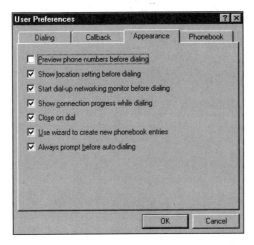

Figure 10-21: The Appearance tab sheet

Phonebook

The Phonebook tab sheet enables you to create personal phonebooks in addition to the system phonebook (which is the default phonebook). This is not a meaningful tab sheet in a dial-up Internet connection scenario.

Note

For the RAS autodial feature to work, it is critical that the Remote Access Autodial Manager service be running. By default, this service is disabled, so you will need to turn it on if you plan to use the RAS autodial capability. I recommend that you configure this service to automatically start via the Services applet in Control Panel.

Logon Preferences

This dialog box has four tab sheets as seen in Figure 10-22. These options apply to the use of Dial-Up Networking when you elect to make a connection to a Windows NT Server network via RAS at the Ctrl-Alt-Del Logon dialog box. These aren't meaningful settings for a dial-up Internet connection.

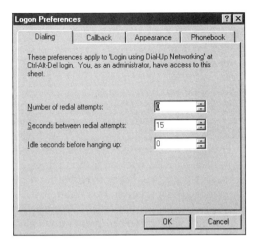

Figure 10-22: Logon Preferences

"More" Dial-Up Networking Settings

There are several other, less frequently used, options on the More menu found on the Dial-Up Networking dialog box. While important, these menu options may be less used than the Edit Entry and Modem Properties and User Preferences options.

- **Clone entry and modem properties.** This enables you to "copy" your Dial-Up Networking settings to save time. This is similar to the Add Users implementation strategy discussed in Chapter 3, "Windows NT Server 4.0 Implementation," where a "model" configuration (a configuration setup just like you want it) is copied to a new name when you are creating new Dial-Up Networking entries.

- **Delete entry.** This option allows you to delete a Dial-Up Networking entry.

- **Create shortcut to entry.** This option places a shortcut for your Dial-Up Networking configuration on the desktop of your Windows NT Server machine.

- **Monitor status.** This launches the Dial-Up Networking Monitor application that I discuss in the text that follows. This monitoring application is very powerful in determining your line speed and managing your modem session.

- **Operator assisted or manual dialing.** This is a selection that allows you to modify the dialing configuration before the telephone number to the

ISP is actually dialed. However, if you have properly configured your Dial-Up Networking connection to your ISP, it is unlikely that you would select this option.

- **Help.** This is the online help system for Dial-Up Networking issues.

Dialing The Internet

It is now time to call your ISP, successfully connect, and start using the Internet. There is no greater test in the eyes of your users than the ability to connect to and use the Internet. In fact, it's unlikely users have much interest in the settings covered in this chapter; they just want to use the Internet. My advice on connecting to the Internet? Be sure to test this feature several times under different conditions and times of day before announcing your new Internet connection. There is nothing more disconcerting than to implement many of the Internet dial-up settings displayed in this chapter only to have your users call and say "I can't get my Internet e-mail." Proper and extensive testing of the dialing the Internet capability will prevent such calls.

Assuming that you have successfully configured your Dial-Up Networking connection, you are now ready to connect to the Internet.

STEPS:
To connect to the Internet via Dial-Up Networking

Step 1. Launch the Dial-Up Networking application from the Accessories program group.

Step 2. The Dial-Up Networking dialog box appears (shown earlier in Figure 10-14). Confirm the Phonebook entry to dial (typically the name of your ISP).

Step 3. Click the Dial button. In Figure 10-23, we are connecting to NwNexus. You will see the Connect To dialog box featuring the ISP in use.

Figure 10-23: Connect To

Secret

In an Internet connection scenario via Dial-Up Networking, it is important that you leave the Domain name blank in Figure 10-23. This field is typically populated in a true RAS scenario when you are calling a Windows NT Server network, not the Internet.

Step 4. After a few moments, you should be successfully connected to the Internet.

You are now ready to browse with your Web browser. You are also ready to monitor your Internet connection via the Dial-Up Networking Monitor, which I discuss next.

Dial-Up Networking Monitor

Often, it is desirable to know whether or not you are still connected to the Internet or to know the speed at which you are connected. Just observing the "dancing" activity light on an external modem is not helpful.

You can monitor your Internet connection activity via the Dial-Up Networking Monitor in Control Panel, as shown in Figure 10-24. I have found Dial-Up Networking Monitor useful for more than confirming my connection, connection speed, and call duration. This application has been invaluable when working with technical support from the ISP to troubleshoot connection problems.

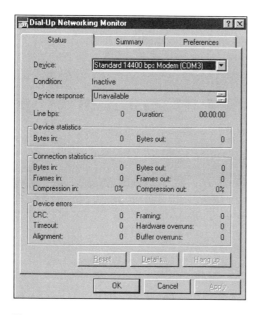

Figure 10-24: Dial-Up Networking Monitor

The Status tab sheet is the most useful of the three presented by Dial-Up Networking Monitor. The most useful fields are, at a glance, Line BPS and Duration. These two fields indicate your connection speed and how long you have been connected (answers to the most common questions relating to dial-up Internet connections).

Secret

The Status tab sheet updates dynamically, so you don't have to hit F5 or open and close it repeatedly for screen refreshes.

The Summary and Preferences tab sheets aren't meaningful in a dial-up Internet connection scenario.

Dial-Up Networking with ISDN modems

Connecting to the Internet via Dial-Up Networking with an ISDN modem is not much different than connecting via an analog modem. Two items must be addressed. First, make sure you have ordered and worked closely with your local telco to ensure that you have a fully functional and tested ISDN line at your location. Second, be sure to correctly install your ISDN modem on your Windows NT server. It will most likely be necessary to use the Windows NT Server 4.0 drivers on the driver disk that ships with your ISDN modem. It is highly unlikely that Windows NT Server 4.0 will natively support your ISDN modem (this is a telecommunications area that is changing much faster than operating systems can keep up).

Note that the preceding discussion applies to ISDN modems, not ISDN routers. ISDN routers are discussed in the text that follows.

Digital and Wide Area Network Internet Connections

Certainly one of the most popular, reliable, and robust ways for Windows NT servers to connect to the Internet is "directly" via a digital network connection. But the term "directly" can mean a lot of different things. I will discuss five Internet/network connection scenarios, but understand that, depending on how you design your Windows NT Server network, there are many different ways to connect to the Internet.

Scenario 1: ISDN Router

An ISDN router (see Figure 10-25) is a low-cost solution for many businesses that allows a robust connection using either one (64Kbps) or two (128Kbps) ISDN channels to connect to your ISP. Typically ISPs offer an ISDN connection solution that may act as dial-on-demand where the ISDN router "calls" the ISP and establishes a connection every time Internet-bound activity is detected by the ISDN router. These ISDN dial-on-demand arrangements usually have a monthly connect hour limit (say 200 hours) after which the business pays something like $10 per hour for each additional connection hour. Such dial-on-demand arrangements can often be found for under $200 per month. Another ISDN router-based solution is a full-time connection to the ISP, which be definition assures unlimited connect hours. This type of arrangement typically starts at $300 per month (but the charges may vary widely between ISPs).

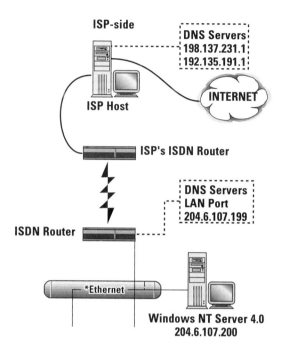

Figure 10-25: An ISDN router connection path to the Internet

This router-based Internet connection solution requires that you make two entries on your Windows NT server for the connection to fully functional. It also requires that your ISDN router be properly programmed to accommodate LAN and real Internet IP addresses and dial the ISP. First, you will need to make sure that the default gateway value on the TCP/IP configuration (via the Network applet in Control Panel, Protocols tab sheet) is populated with the address of the router's LAN port (Figure 10-26).

Part II: TCP/IP

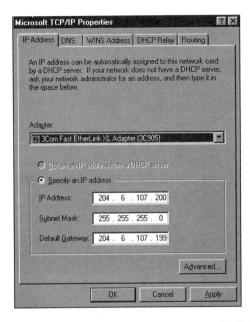

Figure 10-26: An ISDN router IP address as the Default Gateway value

Second, you will need to complete the DNS fields on the DNS tab sheet with the DNS IP address values provided by your ISP (see Figure 10-27).

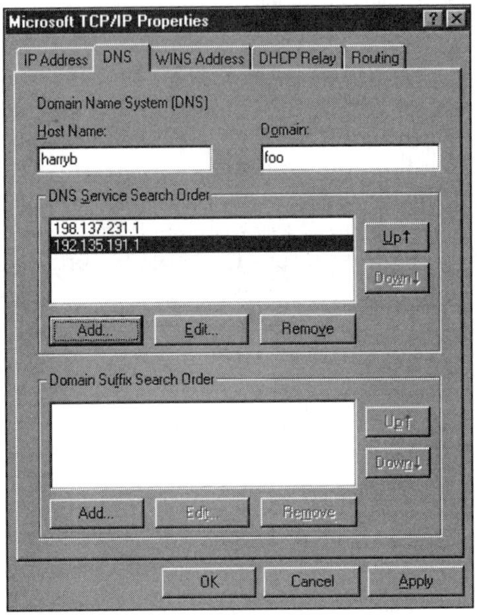

Figure 10-27: DNS IP address values

Note that in the remaining four Internet/network connection scenarios, it will be necessary to populate the default gateway and DNS fields in a similar manner. The key point to remember is that the default gateway field is typically the LAN port of the router (unless you are instructed otherwise such as in a firewall scenario) and the DNS IP address values are the DNS servers used by the ISP.

And in each of these scenarios, significant programming of the routers is required. Don't kid yourself otherwise.

Scenario 2: ISDN and WAN combination

An ISDN connection may be combined with a WAN (see Figure 10-28) by small companies that may have an existing corporate WAN and want the Internet connection to be separate. I've seen this type of implementation in "older" business firms where old-guard CEOs and the like believe a separate Internet connection is the safest connection. And who is to say that they are wrong? Such a scenario also centralizes all Internet traffic through a single point, typically the home office of the company.

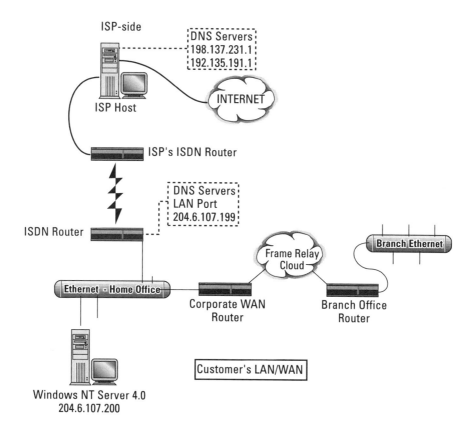

Figure 10-28: An ISDN and WAN connection to the Internet

Scenario 3: Direct Frame Relay Connection

Direct Frame Relay (Figure 10-29) is one of the most popular Windows NT Server Internet connection scenarios. Here, the ISP is connected via a frame relay WAN connection. This is a straightforward solution that allows for different types of communications standards such as fractional T1, full T1, or even faster solutions to be easily implemented.

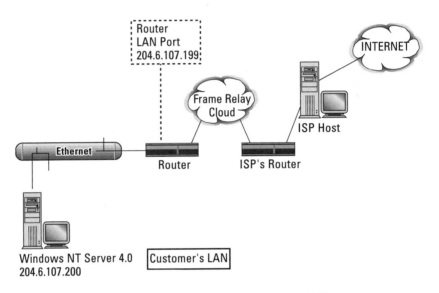

Figure 10-29: A frame relay connection between customer and ISP

Scenario 4: WAN Connection

A WAN connection (Figure 10-30) is another popular Internet connection scenario for Windows NT Server networks. Here the ISP is a node on the company WAN. Simply stated, other nodes such as branch offices connect directly to the ISP without having to route Internet-bound traffic through the home office. With sufficient firewall protection in place, this is a both a viable and desirable solution.

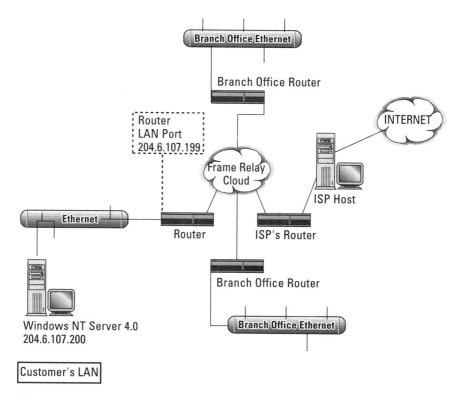

Figure 10-30: An Internet connection via a company WAN

Scenario 5: WAN over Internet (VPN)

A WAN over the Internet is an increasingly popular connection scenario where each company node is also a node on the Internet. That is, the company WAN uses the Internet as its network backbone in a safe and secure manner.

Such a scenario demands that the ISP be reliable, as it plays a central role in this solution. It is not a good idea to shop ISPs by price alone when looking at implementing a virtual private network (VPN) solution (see Figure 10-31).

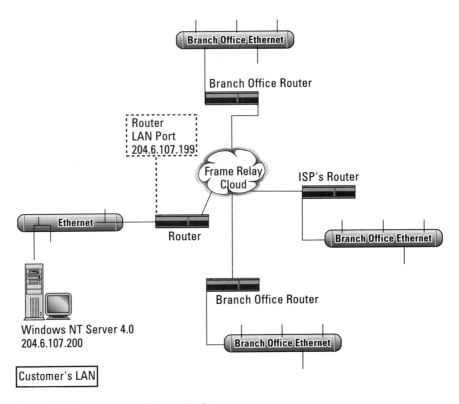

Figure 10-31: A company VPN over the Internet

The good news is that everyone enjoys a robust connection to the ISP and thus the Internet. That will keep the Web surfers happy.

VPNs are further discussed in the next section on the Point-to-Point Tunneling Protocol (PPTP).

Point-To-Point Tunneling Protocol (PPTP)

I'll never forget the day. There I was sitting in the IS Director's office at a leading water cutting tool manufacturer. I was being quizzed relentlessly over the pluses and minuses of Windows NT Server 4.0, which at that time had just been released. The question posed was to name the top new features in Windows NT Server 4.0. After striking out with the obvious answers such as the new Windows 95–like GUI desktop, I gave up. The correct answer, in the eyes of the IS Director, was that the Point-to-Point Tunneling Protocol (PPTP) was the top new feature in Windows NT Server 4.0.

The experience that day spawned a lingering curiosity to learn more about PPTP and to visit sites that have successfully deployed this solution. Interestingly, even as we sit here awaiting the dawn of Windows 2000 Advanced Server, the successful implementations of PPTP are still few and far between. That is expected the change in the near future with the upcoming release of Windows 2000 Advanced Server and greater acceptance of the Internet as a backbone transport for corporate networks.

Defining PPTP

PPTP is really nothing more than a network communications protocol that allows secure transfer of data from a remote site such as a branch office to a host server (typically the main server at the home office). Implementing this solution creates a virtual private network running over TCP/IP-based networks, such as the Internet. PPTP may be implemented over the Internet with dial-up connection or LAN/WAN digital connections as discussed in the previous section. In fact, scenario 5 depicting a VPN shows a typical PPTP implementation.

Security is implemented via encryption. The encryption occurs when the data is prepared for transmission over the Internet "tunnel" and the data packets are encapsulated by PPTP.

Because of this encapsulation, the underlying LAN or network at the ends of the VPN may actually use any of three networking protocols: TCP/IP, NetBEUI, or IXP/SPX. Contrary to popular belief, the VPN clients do not need to use TCP/IP on their internal LANs.

It is also important to understand that your ISP must support PPTP. The list of ISPs that provide such support is growing. When Windows NT Server 4.0 was first released, there was only one ISP in the Seattle area (Microsoft's home town) that provided such support. In fact, the great impediment to the rapid acceptance of PPTP has been ISP support.

The PPTP server must be Windows NT Server 4.0. PPTP clients may be Windows NT Server 4.0, Windows NT Workstation 4.0, or Windows 98/95.

Installing PPTP

This section will describe the steps necessary for installing PPTP on Windows NT Server 4.0 (the server-side installation) and Windows 98 (the client-side installation).

STEPS:

To install PPTP on a Windows NT server

Step 1. Make sure you are logged onto the Windows NT server machine as a member of the Administrators group.

Step 2. Launch the Network applet in Control Panel.

Step 3. Select the Protocols tab sheet. Click Add to display the Select Network Protocols dialog box.

Step 4. Select Point to Point Tunneling Protocol (see Figure 10-32). Click OK.

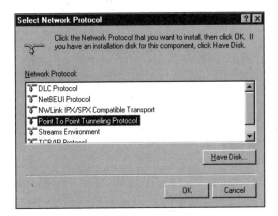

Figure 10-32: Select the PPTP network protocol.

Step 5. Provide the Windows NT Server source file path when requested and click Continue.

Step 6. In the PPTP Configuration dialog box (Figure 10-33), use the drop-down menu to pick the number of VPNs that your server will support. In this case (see Figure 10-33), the selection is 1.

Figure 10-33: Configure the number of VPNs.

Step 7. Approve the setup message that indicates that RAS setup (the Remote Access Setup dialog box shown in Figure 10-2) will launch so that you may configure the PPTP ports. This will enable you to use RAS over PPTP.

Step 8. When the Remote Access Setup dialog box appears, select the Add button. You will then be presented with the opportunity to add a VPN device, as shown in Figure 10-34. Click OK to add the VPN device. Repeat this steps as many times as necessary to add VPN devices.

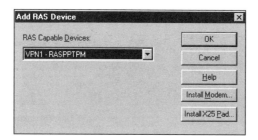

Figure 10-34: Add VPN devices.

Step 9. Configure the VPN device to receive calls only via the Configure button in the Remote Access Setup dialog box.

Step 10. Click Continue Network in the Remote Access Setup dialog box and confirm that only TCP/IP is selected in the Server Setting box. Click OK to return to the Remote Access Setup dialog box.

Step 11. Click Continue.

Step 12. Close Network and restart the computer.

Many resources are available for learning about how to implement PPTP over the Internet. Your ISP will provide you with specific PPTP configuration parameters, such as IP addresses, use of PPTP filtering, and so on. Searching Microsoft support area on its web site (www.microsoft.com) will yield several papers on PPTP configurations.

STEPS:
To install PPTP on a Windows 98 client

Step 1. Launch the Network applet in Control Panel.

Step 2. Select the Add button.

Step 3. Select Adapters. Select Microsoft as the manufacturer and then select the Microsoft Virtual Private Networking Adapter as shown in Figure 10-35. Click OK and, if necessary, provide the path to the Windows 98 source files.

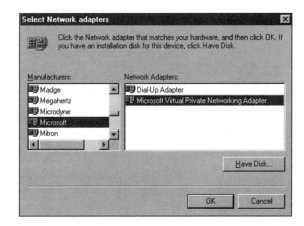

Figure 10-35: The Microsoft Virtual Private Networking Adapter

Step 4. If you have already installed TCP/IP, click OK at the Network dialog box and reboot your Windows 98 machine. If necessary, install the TCP/IP protocol.

Step 5. Your ISP will provide specific settings for connecting to the Internet and create a VPN via its portal (or connection point).

You are now ready to implement a VPN between a PPTP server and a client. Enjoy.

Internet Explorer Secrets

I would be remiss if the Web browser topic wasn't at least addressed in this chapter. On the other hand, it is important not to repeat the work of others that will teach you how to use a browser. Such "browser basic" books are listed at IDG Book's Web site (www.idgbooks.com).

I assume that you know how to use a browser to access information on the Internet. This assumption includes the ability to type an address (or URL) in the address field of Internet Explorer (IE) to get to a Web site on the Internet.

Secret

One important secret is worth sharing. It's an actual experience that I've had at client sites involving IE 4.x. The situation was this: A law firm administrator was responsible for managing the firm's money market account at one of the online stock brokerages (such as e.trade). Like many networks that are connected to the Internet, this firm used a proxy server to protect itself from intruders.

When implementing an Internet connection via a proxy server, it is necessary to configure the Connections setting (Figure 10-36) in IE 4.x so that browsing activity is directed through the proxy server. The configuration sheet is accessed via the Internet Option menu selection on the View menu in IE 4.x.

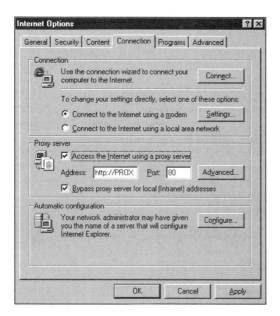

Figure 10-36: The Internet Explorer Configuration sheet

When you are using a proxy server on your network with IE 4.x, the Access the Internet Using a Proxy Server check box will be selected. If you click the Advanced button, you will see the Proxy Setting dialog box displayed in Figure 10-37. Note that the Secure field is blank (a key point to my story).

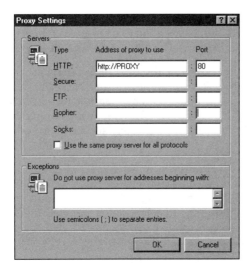

Figure 10-37: Proxy Setting

It is common to only configure the HTTP setting in the Proxy Settings dialog box when using a proxy server on a network with IE 4.x. But many sites use HTTPS, which is the Secure field on the Proxy Settings dialog box. If the Secure field is left blank, you cannot access sites such as online stock brokerages. And that was exactly the problem at the law firm. Once I "fixed" the Secure field to look like Figure 10-38, the legal administrator was once again able to manage the law firm's money. That was an important win for me, the Windows NT Server consultant.

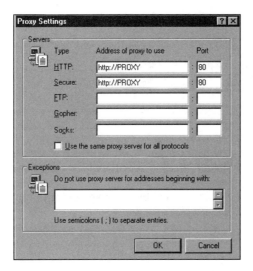

Figure 10-38: Secure field configured to allow access to HTTPS sites

Note

The Proxy client configuration in Microsoft Small Business Server (SBS) leaves the Secure field blank (even though it populates the remaining Type fields in the Proxy Settings dialog box). So if you want to access HTTP sites on an SBS client, you will need to manually configure the Secure setting on your IE browsers (both 3.x and 4.x). SBS is discussed in Chapter 20 of this book.

Internet Information Server

As you now, Internet Information Server (IIS) is a Microsoft BackOffice application that is included in Windows NT Server 4.0. In its raw state, with no service packs applied, IIS 2.0 is the version that ships with Windows NT Server 4.0 (build 1381). When service pack 3.0 is applied to Windows NT Server 4.0, IIS is upgraded to version 3.0. When the Windows NT Server option pack is applied to Windows NT Server, IIS is upgraded to version 4.0. IIS 4.0 is discussed in detail in Chapter 13, "Windows NT 4.0 Options Pack."

Summary

This chapter covered the following:

- Learning how to connect to the Internet
- Understanding Point-to-Point Tunneling Protocol (PPTP)
- Learning about Internet Explorer 4
- Learning about Internet Information Server (IIS)

Part III
Windows NT Server Administration

Chapter 11: The Daily Dozen

Chapter 12: Monthly and Annual Windows NT Server Activities

Chapter 11

The Daily Dozen

In This Chapter

- Using the Windows NT Server 4.0 toolkit and the Administrative Wizards
- Fire fighting — end user support issues
- Troubleshooting
- Performing regularly scheduled tape backups and verifying backups via test restores
- Testing server and desktop virus protection and updating virus data
- Verifying free disk space on your servers
- Keeping tabs on your servers with Event Viewer
- Verifying that all servers, applications, and databases are up and functional
- Verifying LAN and WAN connectivity
- Adding new hardware to your Windows NT server
- Documenting and sharing procedures
- Keeping your users working and happy

At this point, your Windows NT Server network is up and running: Your servers are set up, the applications have been installed, the users are happily working away, and everything's going well. You're the new hero around the office. Now what?

Well, your job isn't getting any easier. Day-to-day administration of your Windows NT network will be every bit as challenging as the initial setup, but it will be just as much fun as well. This chapter will explore the daily tasks every Windows NT administrator should perform to ensure that his or her network stays up and purrs along efficiently. A good network administrator should make it a goal to perform all of these tasks daily, but all of us in the real-life NT administration game know that's not always feasible. Just do your best, and customize these tasks to meet the needs of your network.

Some of the things discussed in this chapter have already been explained in Chapter 3. But this chapter includes a concise 12-step approach to the daily in's and out's of Windows NT Server administration. These are the daily dozen activities a Windows NT Server administrator can expect to perform. Undoubtedly, you will be able to add your own daily activities to this "list" as you see fit.

Step 1: The Windows NT/MCSE Toolkit

As discussed in Chapter 3, every Windows NT administrator has a number of tools he or she uses each day to help keep the network humming along. Most of these tools are supplied with the operating system: User Manager for Domains, Server Manager, Event Viewer, Performance Monitor, and several others. But a few of these tools are physical tools such as "real" hardware tools, CD-ROM guides, books, even emergency telephone numbers. All of these are discussed in this section. Everyone has a different approach to running his or her network, but at least several of these wide-ranging tools are found in just about every admin's list of frequently called-upon utilities and bag of tips, tricks, secrets, and general know-how.

The first step is to gather all of your frequently used programs into one place on your administrative workstation. I have a folder on my Windows NT Workstation's desktop called "Toolkit" (see Figure 11-1). This folder contains all of the programs I use on a daily basis while maintaining my network. I always leave the Toolkit window open, so these programs are within easy reach throughout the day. You'd be surprised how much time this saves over searching through the Start menu.

Figure 11-1: A customized Toolkit folder

User Manager for Domains

User Manager for Domains (see Figure 11-2) is definitely a cornerstone of the Windows NT administrator's toolbox. I covered many uses for User Manager for Domains in Chapter 3, but here is a short list of what you can accomplish using this tool:

- Add and delete users and groups.

- Change user access levels and group memberships.
- Establish trust relationships with other Windows NT domains.
- Establish domain-wide policies governing password characteristics, account lockouts, and other settings.
- Grant or remove specific user and group rights.

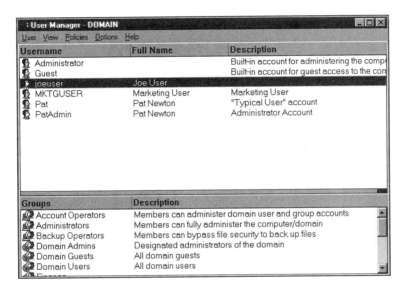

Figure 11-2: User Manager for Domains

I leave User Manager for Domains window open on my desktop through most workdays, and I use it several times a day while maintaining my Windows NT network.

Server Manager

Server Manager (see Figure 11-3) is another key element of running a Windows NT network. With this tool, you can:

- Add and remove computer accounts.
- Administer services.
- Create and delete shares on your servers.
- See who's using resources on servers.
- Disconnect users if necessary.
- Establish alert destinations so that servers can notify you of errors via the NT Messenger Service.
- Set up directory replication between servers.

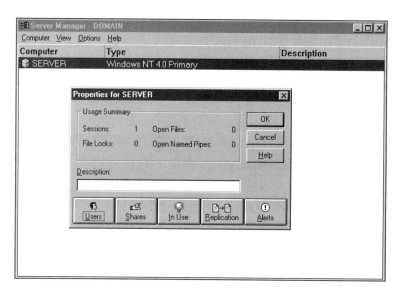

Figure 11-3: Server Manager

Every Windows NT administrator I know uses Server Manager several times daily, so you'll want to keep it handy.

Event Viewer

One of Windows NT's advantages is its logging of all significant system events. I'll cover Event Viewer in more detail later as part of Step 7 in this chapter, but it's worth a mention now as an essential part of the NT admin's toolbox. In the day-to-day grind of running a network, you'll find yourself referring to Event Viewer several times daily.

Secret

One of the best secrets that I can offer you in this entire book is actually one of the simplest; that is, you should check the Event Viewer first thing each day. The Event Viewer, acting as your early warning system, is where you can assess the good and bad activity that has impacted your Windows NT Server overnight.

Performance Monitor

Performance Monitor tips and techniques are explained thoroughly in Chapter 22, "Performance Monitor." Enjoy that chapter, and keep Performance Monitor available for easy access during your workday. Properly used, it's one of the best ways to quickly assess your network's health.

In addition to these daily staples, Windows NT Server comes with other tools you'll use less frequently but should keep available:

- Disk Administrator, for defining disk partitions, expanding drives, setting up fault tolerance, and changing drive letters
- License Manager, to ensure your network is compliant with the licensing scheme you chose during Setup
- Migration Tool for NetWare, if you are moving users from a NetWare environment to NT
- Network Client Administrator, for creating network boot disks so that bare client computers can connect to the network for operating system installation
- System Policy Editor, used to create system policies governing users' access to their computers and the network
- Windows NT Diagnostics, for inspecting hardware and operating system characteristics

Windows NT Server also includes management tools for specialized network services such as Windows Internet Name Service, Dynamic Host Configuration Protocol, Remote Access, and Network Monitor. These tools appear in the Administrative Tools program group as the services are added (see Figure 11-4).

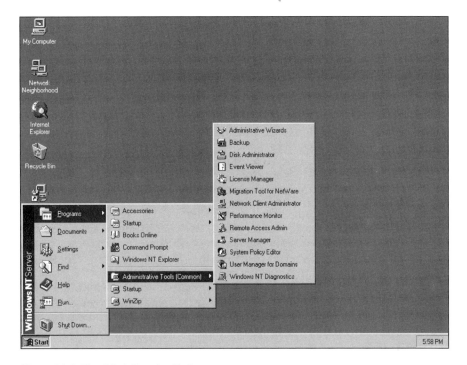

Figure 11-4: The Administrative Tools menu

Administrative Wizards

Windows NT Server's Administrative Wizards utilities are the Rodney Dangerfield of server administration: They don't get no respect. Most experienced administrators scoff at these "cute" wizards, instead choosing to use the appropriate NT Server administration tool or command line utilities. However, the Administrative Wizards (see Figure 11-5) can be very useful, and in fact Microsoft's Small Business Server version of Windows NT Server relies heavily on wizards during setup and for day-to-day administration.

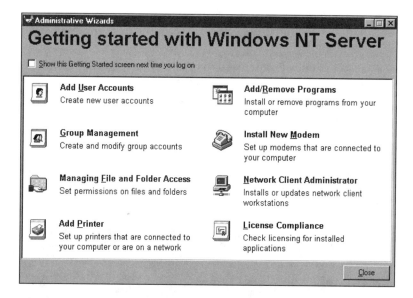

Figure 11-5: Windows NT Server Administrative Wizards

Secret

I have found this tool, Administrative Wizards, to be most useful for sites that have under 100 users. It is here that you find less experienced network administrators who, at least initially, can benefit from the simple Administrative Wizards interface. In fact, it was a peer at a medium-sized firm that brought home this point to me.

The Administrative Wizards make life easier in "regular" versions of Windows NT Server as well, even for seasoned administrators. Although a couple of items in the Wizards window, such as the Add Printer Wizard or the Network Client Administrator, are just shortcuts to NT functions, most of these icons start up actual wizards that simplify common NT Server tasks such as adding users and groups, setting file and directory permissions, and monitoring licensing. Even if you're an experienced NT administrator, give the Administrative Wizards a second look. They might help you accomplish tasks more quickly, and that's one way to work smarter. The different wizard options are:

- **Add User Accounts.** This creates new user accounts.

- **Group Management.** This enables you to create or modify group accounts.
- **Managing File and Folder Access.** This sets permissions on files and folders.
- **Add Printer.** This enables you to set up printers that are connected to your computer or on a network.
- **Add/Remove Programs.** This enables you to install or remove programs from your computer.
- **Install New Modem.** This enables you to set up modems that are connected to your computer.
- **Network Client Administrator.** This installs or updates network client workstations. Note that this is the closest regular Windows NT Server 4.0 (build 1381) comes to having a client installation (or "magic") disk such as that used by Small Business Server (SBS). See Chapter 20 for more discussion on SBS.
- **License Compliance.** This enables you to check the licensing for installed applications.

In many ways, the Administrative Wizards constitute Microsoft's attempt to define and centralize the most common tasks one might perform on a daily basis. In this case, you might call Administrative Wizards the "daily 8" from Microsoft's perspective.

Third-party administration tools

In addition to the tools Microsoft supplies with Windows NT Server, administration utilities are available from several third parties. One that I swear by is Hyena, from Adkins Resource in Adkins, Texas (see Figure 11-6). Hyena makes daily administration a lot easier for myself and my partners at work: It combines all the functionality of User Manager, Server Manager, and Event Viewer into one application, and it includes some Windows Explorer functions as well, such as NTFS permissions management for local and remote servers.

Hyena's tree-based, Windows Explorer-like interface makes viewing domains and servers a snap, and it's been updated every couple of months with major improvements and new functionality. My personal favorite feature about Hyena, and the one that sold my boss on it, was the great improvement in viewing open files on a server. In the Open Files window in Server Manager, you must scroll all the way to the right to see actual filenames, and that can be a real pain when you're searching for a specific file. In Hyena, you can view the open files in a normal-sized, expandable window, which makes for much easier identification of file locks.

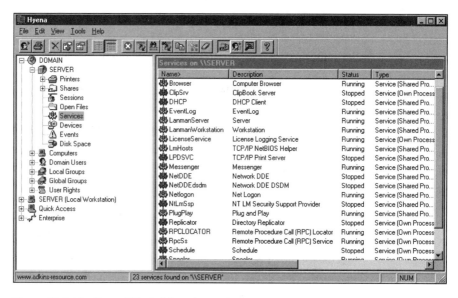

Figure 11-6: The Hyena NT administration tool

The MCSE toolkit

I will now share my MCSE toolkit with you. That is, these are the resources I have found you will most likely be called upon to use in performing your duties as both an MCSE and a Windows NT Server network administrator.

So what's in my toolkit? My toolkit ranges from bona fide tools such as a screwdriver to a list of peers' telephone numbers to a parts catalog. In short, my experience base is reflected in what I carry on my person and in my auto as a day-to-day practicing MCSE. If you haven't already done so, take a moment to look at what you carry or have easy access to as your tools of the trade. Such a self assessment speaks volumes about how you leverage your time and knowledge as a Windows NT Server professional and/or certified professional (such as an MCSE).

Real hardware tools

I carry a limited set of real tools including two Phillips screwdrivers, two flathead screwdrivers, a "Compaq" (Torx) screwdriver that has a star pattern on the end to open older Compaq servers, a chip extractor and static energy discharger wristband. This is the type of kit that may be purchased from national resellers such as PCZone (www.pczon.com, 1-800-258-2088) or Data Comm Warehouse (www.warehouse.com, 1-800-328-2261) for under $50. It's safe to say that this type of toolkit is a necessary and required fixture for any MCSE. I mean, any MCSE has to be at least able to connect a cable or open a workstation! If you're gonna earn the lofty salaries paid to MCSEs, you gotta at least have the basics down.

Because the leather pouch that contains my "real" toolkit has extra room, I carry other invaluable items. These are a "modern" network adapter such as the 3COM 3C9*xx* series with drivers and an "old fashioned" true NE2000 network adapter. The modern network adapter allows me to fix a common point of failure on a workstation or server: layer one of the OSI model (better known as the network adapter). Hey, anyone with the MCSE title should be able to at least replace this component. The NE2000 network adapter shows my age. In the old days when knights were bold and kings owned all the gold, the NE2000 network adapter was fashionable. Today, I carry my remaining NE2000 because it always works. There are some late nights at clients' sites when I've had it up to my neck with PNP and I'm saved by my good old ISA-based NE2000 card! It's a trick worth remembering and adding to your MCSE toolkit.

Oh, two extra items that I added to my toolkit based on my own errors and omissions are a small dental mirror that extends several inches and a pen-sized flashlight. With these tools working in tandem, I can easily see the backside of components and motherboards during surgery. Makes a heck of a difference when you're trying to insert RAM chips into tight slots.

A CD-ROM library

If you were a physical laborer, you would of course enjoy increasing returns and perform your work better if you went to the gym and lifted weights. That activity might enable you to work longer or faster than your peer. As knowledge workers, you and I need to undertake a different type of workout. That work is to increase both our "active" knowledge base (the information we retain in our heads) and our available knowledge resources. For me, that means carrying a meaningful CD-ROM library that contains, within minutes, most of the knowledge I need as an MCSE to complete my work. So here's what I'm carrying in my soft-sided CD-ROM carrier. These selections represent CDs that I frequently need to access and that are current. It is important to make regular additions and subtractions to your CD-ROM library so that it remains germane. Truth be told, not too long ago I had the opportunity to purge my CD-ROM library of "oldies but goodies" such as the complete CPM operating system reference.

- **Microsoft TechNet (the full edition of six CDs including the Technical Information Network, Client Utilities, Microsoft BackOffice Products Evaluation, Service Packs, Server Utilities, Supplemental Drivers, and Patches).** It goes without saying how valuable this collection of CDs is each and every day. Using the term "near" when performing Boolean-type searches in TechNet typically works best. "Near" finds matches within 15 words; it's kind of a fuzzy logic search that works well for us humanoids.

- **Compaq Systems Reference Library version 2.x.** This resource is, of course, invaluable when you are working with Compaq servers and workstations.

- **HP JetAdmin Software for JetDirect Print Servers.** You would be surprised how often you need to implement a new JetDirect card and don't have the correct software. Note the CD version I carry has the drivers for every network known to mankind (from AppleTalk to UNIX).

- **Business Resources Kit and Sales Training Interactive CD.** These CDs were provided by Microsoft as part of our firm's participation in the Microsoft Certified Solution Provider program. Although these CDs are used to fortify my sales efforts, remember that we MCP consultants must hunt before we can eat.

- **Windows NT Server 4.0 Secrets CD-ROM.** This is included at the back of this book. Packed with meaningful utilities, this CD-ROM isn't just a marketing ploy to ship a compact disc. Far from it. To create this CD-ROM, I sought and received the contributions of Windows NT Server professionals from the enterprise level down to the workgroup level.

- **Windows Support Source CD.** This is a CD-ROM subscription service from Cobb, the renowned newsletter publisher, that has an archive of articles that will interest the practicing MCSE.

- **Internet service provider (ISP) CD.** I carry the CD that my ISP issues containing ISP-specific signup information, drivers, and FAQs. This CD is extremely helpful in the field as I implement Internet service on behalf of my clients.

- **Microsoft Evaluation & Migration Planning Kit CD (Part #098-63878).** This CD contains blank templates for creating your BackOffice migration proposal, project schedule, budget, and the like. It saves a lot of time during the "management" of your project.

- **Novell Support Connection CD (monthly).** The rumors aren't true. Big Red isn't dead.

- **Microsoft BackOffice CDs #1 : #4.** How many times are you asked to insert a specific CD to complete the installation of a driver. How many times do you need the BackOffice CD library to install SQL Server Books Online after the fact? How many times have you tried to install client management tools for SMS and found that you didn't have your BackOffice CD library handy?

- **Windows NT Workstation, Windows 95, and Windows 98.** Here again, how many times have you been asked to insert a CD so that a driver will finishing installing. Don't forget that you need to carry at least two versions of these CDs: the original retail version and the upgrade version. Windows 95/98 has a nasty way of knowing whether an operating system was previously installed on the machine; thus it'll ask for one "type" of CD instead of the other.

- **Microsoft Project : BackOffice Deployment Templates CD (Part #098-634461).** More project management templates for your BackOffice engagements. I've found a few extra minutes with this CD saves hours of planning time!

- **Windows NT Workstation and Server Resource Kit CDs.** Yes, you need both CDs. The Server edition contains several more utilities than the Workstation version. These CDs are no substitute for having the hardcopy resource kits, as I shall discuss in a moment.

- **Windows NT 4.0 Service Pack 3 (or higher) CD.** How many times do you go to a site, including perhaps your own, and discover that the Windows NT machines (servers and workstations) don't have the latest service packs installed. Just try getting official Microsoft technical support if that's the unfortunate case.

- **Office 97 (or higher) CD.** Ever been caught flat footed needing the Microsoft Exchange Server resource driver for Outlook 97? I'll bet you discovered that it wasn't on your operating system CD. One of the places it's magically kept is on the Office 97 CD. Just try setting up an Exchange-based mailbox, not personal folders, without this resource (bet you carry this CD after that experience).

- **Network Professional Association Technical Resource CD.** This "goodie" contains cross-platform utilities, product demos, and an article archive. I've found this CD to be of value when I'm working in heterogeneous networking environments (like every day). Check out the NPA at www.npa.org.

- **McAffee VirusScan CD-ROM for Windows 95, 98, NT.** Be careful to honor the licensing agreement (installed on only one machine at a time), but I typically install, run, and deinstall the virus detection program contained on this CD prior to performing surgery on a machine. The reasons are obvious.

More MCSE toolkit items

Finally, my toolkit includes an alphabet soup patchwork of resources I've gathered over the years and still make active use of. It is here, that upon close reflection, I think you will find that you too have gathered goods that you use almost unconsciously in your role as a network professional. I like to think of the following as my network tackle box where I have a special lure for every occasion.

- **Floppies.** Still very much alive, here are a few floppies that I carry in my MCSE toolkit. A good old-fashioned bootable MS-DOS 6.22 disk with EDIT, XCOPY, and a few other invaluables. How many times, for reasons you can't quite explain, do you need to boot from A:> into a "real" DOS environment to get something done? This need always seems to rear its ugly head on Saturday night at 10 p.m. Wonder why that is? Because applications like INSTALL.EXE program contained on 3COM's EtherDisk disk (yes, this is another mandatory floppy to carry) still *only* run under a true MS-DOS environment. And in many cases, this is the *only* way that you will be able to accurately test your 3COM network adapter for failure, configuration settings, and such. It's also not a bad idea to make and carry a copy of the emergency repair disk (ERD) for your favorite Windows NT servers. You never know when you'll need those.

- **Resource kits and other well-tattered books.** Nothing like having a resource kit or two, along with your favorite books, spread in front of you when your performing server surgery.

- **PC Zone catalog, Data Comm Warehouse catalog, and so on.** Like you, I receive the monthly catalog mailings from the national hardware/software resellers. Surprisingly, these catalogs are invaluable when discussing technology solutions with clients (when you literally need to draw a few prices out of thin air).

- **Computer User monthly newspaper.** In Seattle, the January issue of the *Puget Sound Computer User* lists a potpourri of local reseller, consulting, labor, and publishing resources for the technology community to patronize (the "Business Directory" issue). This type of publication, by KFH Publications, Inc., is available in many other North American areas including Colorado (*Rocky Mountain Computer User*). The January issue allows me to refer my clients to competent professionals in technical areas that I don't serve (such as UNIX).

- **Dictaphone, handheld tape recorder to record observations.** Nothing like creating a journal of the steps undertaken to troubleshoot a problem or build a server. An invaluable addition to carry.

- **Laptop computer with ability to call to the Internet and download drivers, search the knowledge base at** www.microsoft.com. If you live in Seattle, the San Francisco Bay Area, or Washington DC, you can use the Ricochet modem (www.ricochet.net) to establish a high-speed connection to the Internet without tying up a fax or voice line.

- **An external modem with modem cable (serial 9 to 25 pinout).** Sometimes the client's modem just won't work correctly and work needs to get done. Because of my experience with SBS, I now carry an external US Robotics 33.6 Sportster modem. It's for "just in case" and it always works!

- **A really long telephone line and an analog telephone.** The really long telephone line is for reaching the telco wall jack that is always across the room. The analog telephone is to plug into that wall jack to thoroughly test the telephone service.

- **Telephone numbers of peers to call for advice.** There's nothing like calling a BackOffice buddy to help you out of a jam.

- **A portable file cabinet to maintain "working" client files that contain office layout drawings, field notes, and billable hour charge sheets.** A well-organized MCSE is a happy MCSE. Trust me.

- **A portable tape deck/radio.** When the cat's away (client or boss), why shouldn't the mice have just a little "play"?

- **Kneepads.** No, these aren't to wear so that you can kneel over and take client or supervisor abuse. I carry them to protect my old skier's knees when I'm fishing cable around a crowded server room.
- **Working suit, pullovers, and tennis shoes.** Many MCSEs face today's formal/casual clothing challenge. One moment you're selling your MCSE services in a glass tower. The next hour you're implementing SBS in a dusty warehouse. Better carry a change of clothes and be prepared to change in the water closet.
- **Peanut butter chocolate chip cookies and granola bars!** Funny how an elevated blood sugar level allows you to accomplish amazing feats.

Step 2: End User Support

Every seasoned NT administrator has experienced this one: You're at your desk, on the verge of solving that server performance problem that's been nagging you for weeks, when the VP of Finance walks up and rather testily informs you that she is unable to print. Read hold everything! It's a fire! Next thing you know, you've spent an hour removing and reinstalling the VP's print drivers, undoing the damage her free online service software did to the PC's network setup, and you can't even remember your fantastic server performance solution.

These "fires" are frustrating sometimes, but it's key for Windows NT administrators and engineers to remember that the end users are our raison d'etre. They are our customers: why we do what we do. Many of "them" also approve our budget. Even if you're lucky enough to be insulated from the end users by a first-tier help desk, chances are that you'll be called upon to provide escalation support at least once a day.

Here are some techniques I've learned that help me dispatch fires as they come up and hopefully prevent new ones.

When a support issue comes up, whether it's bad print drivers or users unable to connect to the network because of a server crash, always jot down a little note to yourself before jumping up from your desk to fight the fire. Five times out of six, before I started doing this, I'd forget what I was working on when I got back to my desk after correcting the problem.

Remember your manners

Even if you're interrupted in the middle of a major breakthrough by what you may consider a minor problem, remember that your minor problem may be a major one for the user. Think back to the days when you were an end user, and how you felt if a technical support person blew you off because they considered your problem inconsequential. Nobody wants to be Dogbert the mean network administrator, and in the real world, brushing off end users' problems can be severely career limiting. Keep your role as "doctor" in mind, and solve the problem quickly and professionally. You'll get back to your breakthrough soon enough.

Educate the user

If possible, explain to the user the steps you're taking to solve their problem. An educated user is a happy user. Obviously some users will not be interested in this level of detail, preferring to be notified "when the darn thing works," but many users will appreciate this extra information. The same goes for first-level tech support people: If they learn how to solve the problem, chances are they won't be escalating it to you next time. Also, many help desk staffers are grateful for the chance to observe more senior administrators. I started my IT career on a help desk, and every chance I got, I went into the server room and watched as the Windows NT administrators solved a problem. This exposure proved very valuable in later years.

Document your solutions

After fighting a fire, it's always a good policy to write an e-mail message or note to yourself explaining the problem and the solution, so you'll have that knowledge available in case the problem crops up again. I can't count the times I've been trying to solve a nagging support issue and got the feeling that I had dealt with the same thing several months before. Had I documented the problem and resolution, I wouldn't have had to reinvent the wheel. If your company has a help desk application or a homegrown solutions database, enter the situation so that the information will be available next time. If the solution was particularly interesting or you think the issue will come up again, share the information with other members of your group, so they'll be "in the know" if they're tapped to solve the problem later.

Like it or not, end user support is a big aspect of any Windows NT Server administration career. If you have the right attitude and follow the proper procedures, you can learn a lot from those day-to-day fires.

Step 3: Server Troubleshooting

Another big part of any Windows NT professional's job is server troubleshooting. Despite what Microsoft would have you believe, NT doesn't run trouble-free at all times, and external influences as well as internal software errors can cause problems with the system. When these issues come up, it's key to remember that you, as the administrator, have many different tools at your disposal. I'll touch on each of these briefly a little later.

Right now, my coworkers and I are trying to narrow down the software villain that's causing our NT server to crash every couple of weeks. A reality of Windows NT networking is that no matter how fault-tolerant you make your server hardware, adding redundant power supplies, RAID arrays, load-balanced network adapters, and so on, there's usually a software bug that can bring all of that crashing down.

When this particular server dies, user impact is very heavy, as the majority of users keep their data on this box. Every two weeks or so, with no regularity or predictability, the server's network response time will begin to slow down, and soon it will quit servicing network users entirely. We'll run into the server room, and the console is unresponsive. There's nothing left to do but perform a dirty reboot. When the server comes back up, we immediately check the NT event logs and the Compaq hardware logs for errors, and yes, you guessed it: nothing. These are the server problems that try administrators' souls and sometimes cause us to question our motives for going into such a crazy business. Luckily, the problem-solving tools are there. Here is how we are applying them on my network.

Documentation

One of the first things to ask when a new server problem crops up is whether anything changed on the server just before the problem began. Windows NT Server can be a fickle system, and even the most innocuous change has the potential to send it into a tailspin, sometimes for unexplained reasons. Keeping a detailed log of any and all changes to each server on your network can save you countless hours of troubleshooting. In my office, we have an Excel spreadsheet with separate sheets for each server, and we record the date, time, and nature of each change to the server, from installing new software to scheduled or unscheduled reboots, adding new drives or other hardware, and so on. These logs have proved very valuable in the past, when a change we made one week caused problems the next. Unfortunately, this technique hasn't helped us with the current challenge, so we moved on to the process of elimination.

Logical deduction and process of elimination

At first glance, my group thought the server might be crashing because of a network problem. However, all the servers reside on a relatively low-usage 100 Mbps Ethernet segment, and none of the other boxes had any problems servicing users: the Exchange server and our main application server were humming along just fine. Also, we weren't seeing an excessive number of collisions on that server's port on the switch. Thus, a broadcast storm or other network problem was eliminated. Since then, we've tried to simplify the server's configuration as much as possible: stopping and disabling nonessential third-party services we've added, moving print services off to another server, and watching closely to see whether these steps make any difference. It's been less than two weeks since our last server crash, so the jury's still out, but we're hopeful that removing some of the load from the server will solve our problem. Then, we'll slowly begin adding the third-party services back in and testing to see which of them might have caused the crashes.

Microsoft TechNet

I guess I can't mention this resource enough. Microsoft TechNet and its online partner Support Online are fantastic resources for Windows NT networking professionals (see Figure 11-7). Chances are if you're having a strange problem with your server, someone else has had the same problem and reported it to Microsoft. When Microsoft identifies a problem, they issue a support article on it, and thousands of those articles are gathered together with white papers and other information on the TechNet CD each month. A TechNet subscription isn't cheap at approximately $300 per year, but it's well worth it: The access to service packs, late-breaking technical information, and upgrades can be priceless.

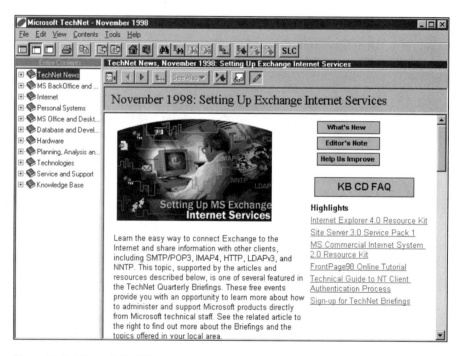

Figure 11-7: Microsoft TechNet

Ironically, one of TechNet's strengths is also one of its weaknesses. There is so much information that it can take most of an afternoon to search through all the articles that may come up on a search. A search for the words "server crash," for example, brings up 710 articles in the November 1998 TechNet. When you are using TechNet or Support Online, the more specific your query, the better.

Support Online can be found at support.microsoft.com/support and offers access to the same Knowledge Base articles as a TechNet subscription does, but without many of TechNet's other features (see Figure 11-8).

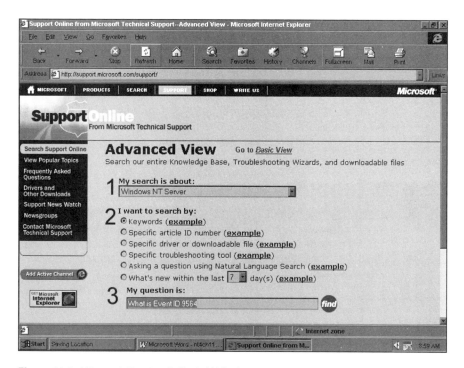

Figure 11-8: Microsoft Support Online's Web site

Internet support groups

In my opinion, the best aspect of the Internet revolution is the ability it has given private citizens to gather together in clubs and user groups to share information and solve problems quickly. Whether it's a car club sharing information about how to go faster at the racetrack or computer types trying to solve a problem, private parties now have much more information at their fingertips than they did just three or four years ago. Rather than waiting for a once-a-month user group meeting, Windows NT professionals have access to many ongoing support discussions, where they can bounce problems off other working administrators. Often, they can get solutions in minutes or hours instead of waiting days or weeks for an answer from Microsoft or another vendor.

This ability to tap into the knowledge of hundreds or thousands of other administrators and ask "Any of you guys ever seen this one before?" has proved priceless on several occasions in my NT administration career. Someone halfway across the world may have solved the same problem you're facing a month ago, or may be able to help you look at the problem in another way that might propel you toward a solution.

Internet support groups come in two flavors: e-mail mailing lists and Web site–based solutions databases. It's worth any NT professional's time to join one of the mailing lists and search these sites for answers.

Windows NT Server troubleshooting is definitely a challenging aspect of any NT administrator's daily task list, but it can be made easier if you take advantage of all the tools that are available.

Step 4: Tape Backups

Back in Chapter 3, I discussed backups as an essential element of any well-run Windows NT network. However, backups are only as good as the media they're recorded on. Even if your network has a bulletproof backup plan in place, you must verify that the proper files were actually backed up and make sure the backups are "good," that the files will be intact should you need to restore them.

Defining a backup schedule

This was touched on in Chapter 3, and I'll review it here. An important part of implementing any backup scheme for your network is defining a schedule and sticking to it. Depending on the size and complexity of your network, and the volatility of your users' data, you may need to do nightly backups, or once a week might be sufficient. Once you determine how often backups will be run, you must ensure that this process happens each day or each week. Most third-party backup solutions have an automatic scheduling facility built in, and Windows NT's native NTBACKUP program can be automated using NT's AT command scheduling utility. Once this task is complete, backing up can become as easy as swapping a few tapes daily. However, even this can have its pitfalls: In my network, we rely on end users in field offices to change tapes each day and send the old tape out for offsite storage. On a couple of occasions, a user assigned that task got busy and forgot to put the new tape in after removing the old one. Luckily the server didn't crash the day after one of these mishaps, as we would have had severe "data exposure," but the incidents made us nervous nonetheless back at the home office.

Checking backup logs

Most backup utilities have logging built in that enables administrators to see which files were backed up, if any backups failed, and why they failed. Good network policy dictates that the administrator checks these logs each day to ensure that backups went the way they planned. This has been a requirement in every network I've worked with and has saved my administrative bacon more than once. If you determine that some files were not backed up, it is sometimes possible to grab a quick online backup, especially if the administrator gets into the office earlier than the users.

Performing test restores

As I mentioned, backup sets are worthless unless the data contained on them is intact. As such, it's a very good idea to restore some test data each day, to make sure that the files were not corrupted during the backup process. It's best to do this with test files that are changed each day, but if you want to test-restore actual user data, restore it to a test server rather than its original location. Users have a funny way of getting annoyed when the Excel spreadsheet they were working on before lunch suddenly becomes yesterday's version.

Secret

When performing a test restore, be sure *not* to select an option that is commonly presented on restore menus. This option is to restore the local Registry. It's an unwise move to say the least. Doing so would overwrite your production Registry with an aged Registry copy. That would of course cause problems on your network.

In my network, we generally restore a few files each day to a test server that we've set up. Once we're convinced that the backup is good, we can send a copy of it to our offsite storage facility. As discussed in Chapter 3, offsite storage is very important to a successful network backup scheme, so don't give it short shrift when budgeting for backups.

Step 5: Virus Protection

As I touched on in Chapter 3, viruses are one of the biggest headaches for Windows NT administrators today. I know I've lived through my share of virus outbreaks, some worse than others, but none pleasant. The company I work for now didn't even have a formal virus protection plan until the CEO's PC got a virus via e-mail. He became understandably upset about this, and within two weeks, every desktop in the organization had some form of virus protection enabled, and the servers soon followed suit.

While installing virus protection was a very important step (you wouldn't believe what we found and cleaned!), testing the protection programs and keeping data files up to date is an ongoing challenge.

Testing your antivirus software

The best way to see if your network is protected is to try and infect it. This is best accomplished in a very controlled environment, such as a test server that's not connected to the network. While this sort of precaution is overkill for the vast majority of viruses out there, there are some real nasties to be found in the wild, and it's much better to be safe than sorry when you're dealing with live production data.

Test documents infected with certain viruses can generally be found on the Internet, so that's a good place to start when you're looking to test your server's safety net. Network Associates' VirusScan product is a popular antivirus solution (see Figure 11-9). Once you have the virus in hand, put the document on a disk, throw it in the server and open it, and see what happens. If your antivirus program is doing its job, it should catch the critter and clean the document. If it doesn't, perhaps you'd better look into updating your software's data files.

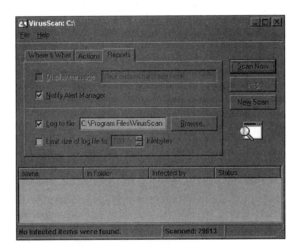

Figure 11-9: Network Associates' VirusScan

Updating data files

Viruses are constantly changing: It seems as though a new one is being written and distributed nearly every week. Antivirus software vendors recognize this and thus update their programs with new "data files" periodically. These files give the antivirus software blueprints for the new viruses, so it is then able to catch and clean them. The real challenge, from a network administrator's point of view, is figuring out how to distribute these updated data files across the network. Even on a 20-user network, visiting each desk is time consuming. In a 3,000-user WAN-connected network, desktop visits are an impossibility. Some vendors offer automatic, built-in data file upgrades with their desktop virus protection products, but you must update the files manually with others.

We're working on this challenge at my workplace right now. We've come up with three solutions:

- Visiting each desktop as new data files come out. This is possible in our network, but we would really prefer to avoid it.

- Distributing the updates via a batch file sent through e-mail. The users run this batch file, and it automatically copies the new data files down from a central network location. This is what we've been doing for a few months: It works, but success depends on the users remembering (or being willing) to run the batch file. As every Windows NT administrator knows, depending on the users to take care of themselves isn't always the wisest option: When that VP's computer becomes infected with a new virus because they forgot to run the batch file, it'll be your hide, not theirs.

- Configuring our network logon script to compare the dates on the users' virus data files to the latest ones on the network, and copy down the latest files if the users' data is out of date. This is a better solution than the one previously described, but it still has some pitfalls. For instance, we have a number of users who work from home offices with telephone lines running at a maximum of 56Kbps. Considering the reality of today's phone lines, this figure is closer to 40–45Kbps. When these users log on after a virus data file update, they will have a pause in their logon script while the data files download, which will almost certainly generate a support call. Even so, we are leaning toward this option; for our network, it's the best solution to the virus data file distribution challenge. Your mileage may vary, as no two networks are the same.

Centralizing virus protection

If most vital data in your organization is kept on the network (and it should be!), then centralized virus protection on your servers is the most effective way to ensure that virus infections do not interrupt your company's business operations. Be sure to install virus protection software on all of your file and application servers, your e-mail or groupware server, and your Internet gateway, if possible, and keep all of these locations updated with the latest data files. This sounds fairly straightforward, but you'd be surprised how many networks I've seen with last year's virus data protecting the servers.

Remember, your network's virus protection is only effective if all workstations and servers have the product installed, and if they are kept up to date with the latest virus data files. It's your job as the Windows NT administrator to ensure these tasks are completed. If you take care in keeping your protection tools healthy, your network can remain virus-free without too much effort.

Step 6: Free Disk Space

In the world of Windows NT Server 4.0, few things can choke a server faster than running out of free disk space. Running low on free space can have all sorts of detrimental effects, ranging from poor performance due to lack of paging space to services actually shutting down for lack of resources. Some products, like Microsoft Exchange Server, will shut themselves down if disk space is getting low, to prevent permanent damage to the application's database. Believe me, you don't want to find out about low disk space when you start getting calls because nobody in the enterprise can get into their e-mail.

In today's environment of cheap storage, there really is no excuse for allowing servers to run low on disk space. As long as you stay on top of the storage situation, you will never be caught with your administrative pants down and end up in a crisis situation.

Successful storage techniques

First, it's very important to "right-size" your drive arrays when a new server is built. Determine approximately how much space the server will need when the network is fully functional, and then add fifty percent to account for future growth. This won't keep you covered for long, though: In a fast-moving business, it might be a good idea to buy double the storage you think you need. Temper this interest with financial sense, however: Depending on your situation, it might be a better idea to hold off on purchasing more drives until you actually need them. You'll likely pay less for the drives a year or two down the road than you'd pay right now.

Second, keep track of your server's disk space on at least a weekly basis. This can be done from the server console, via a batch file that connects network drives and executes DIR commands, or from your desktop with a third-party utility such as Hyena. At this point, it's not necessarily important to note which directories are growing the fastest, although you'll want to map out your directories on at least a monthly basis. More on that in Chapter 12.

Third, it's crucial that you have a plan to add more storage if and when you need it. Don't assume that adding extra hard drives to your existing setup will be easy: Depending on your hardware, you may not be able to accomplish this without destroying the drive partitions and restoring the entire server from backups. It's important to know just what will be involved before it's crunch time and your server is working with less than 100 megabytes of free space while you try to figure out how to add another drive.

Secret

Don't forget that at the enterprise or near-enterprise server environment, ordering a hard disk means that you must order it from your original server manufacturer. With high-end Compaqs, Dells, and the like, it is simply not possible to trot down to your local clone computer shop and purchase appropriate drives on short notice. Thus, you are best advised to keep a supply of hard disks that are known to work on your server in the server room. Just in case!

More detail on weekly disk space monitoring

As I mentioned, you have several ways to monitor your servers' free disk space. The "built-in" way to do this, though not necessarily the most efficient, is to follow this procedure:

1. Go to each server's console.
2. Double-click My Computer, and then right-click the drive in question.
3. Click Properties, and then record the figures given in the server's Properties sheet (see Figure 11-10).

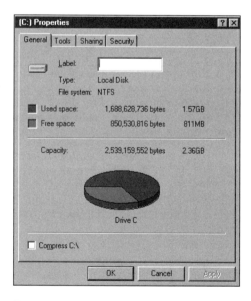

Figure 11-10: A C drive's Properties sheet

An alternative to this is to use a third-party utility. In the Hyena administration tool mentioned earlier, each server has a "Disk Space" object that can be double-clicked and inspected, as seen in Figure 11-11.

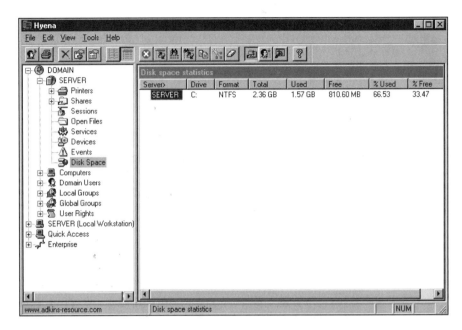

Figure 11-11: The Hyena third-party utility

At my office, one of my coworkers came up with a simple but effective way to monitor all of our servers' disk space using a batch file. The process includes a FOR loop, which calls another batch file for each server listed in a specific text file. The second batch file then connects to the root of each drive on those servers and performs a DIR command, directing the output to another text file that we inspect to get the actual free space readings. It's rather elegant, actually, for a home-grown solution.

Whether you choose to use the built-in NT tools, adopt a third-party solution, or "roll your own" free space utility, definitely keep an eye on your servers' disks, and don't let them fill up. In my career, I've been through a couple of "disk full" situations, and neither of them was very pleasant. Luckily, this type of problem is easily avoided. Each week, spend a few minutes with your hard disks; you'll be glad you did.

Step 7: Event Logs

When Microsoft designed Windows NT, they included a tool that is an essential part of the operating system: event logging. This logging, together with the Event Viewer (see Figure 11-12), which enables administrators to inspect the logs generated, can tell Windows NT professionals exactly what has taken place on their servers. This kind of detail can prove very valuable if the server starts having problems; more often than not, a server problem has a reasonable explanation, and that explanation is often found in the event logs.

Event logging isn't limited to the operating system. Applications that are designed for Windows NT bring with them their own event sources and IDs. Also, security logging takes place when the server is a domain controller or when you have specified that certain actions, such as file accesses, be audited for later inspection.

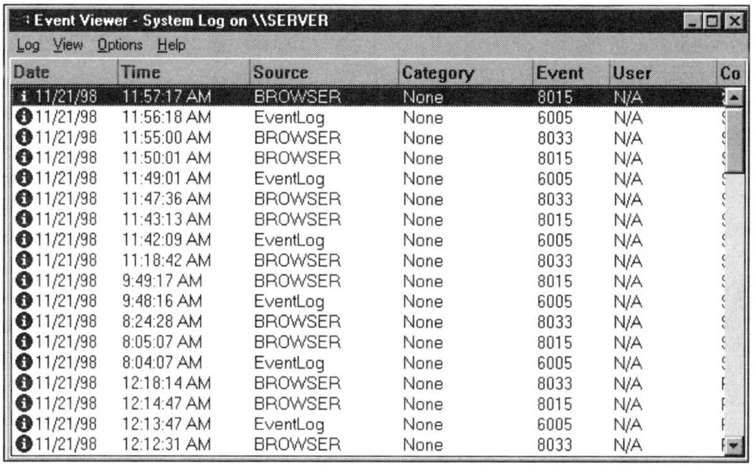

Date	Time	Source	Category	Event	User	Co
11/21/98	11:57:17 AM	BROWSER	None	8015	N/A	
11/21/98	11:56:18 AM	EventLog	None	6005	N/A	
11/21/98	11:55:00 AM	BROWSER	None	8033	N/A	
11/21/98	11:50:01 AM	BROWSER	None	8015	N/A	
11/21/98	11:49:01 AM	EventLog	None	6005	N/A	
11/21/98	11:47:36 AM	BROWSER	None	8033	N/A	
11/21/98	11:43:13 AM	BROWSER	None	8015	N/A	
11/21/98	11:42:09 AM	EventLog	None	6005	N/A	
11/21/98	11:18:42 AM	BROWSER	None	8033	N/A	
11/21/98	9:49:17 AM	BROWSER	None	8015	N/A	
11/21/98	9:48:16 AM	EventLog	None	6005	N/A	
11/21/98	8:24:28 AM	BROWSER	None	8033	N/A	
11/21/98	8:05:07 AM	BROWSER	None	8015	N/A	
11/21/98	8:04:07 AM	EventLog	None	6005	N/A	
11/21/98	12:18:14 AM	BROWSER	None	8033	N/A	
11/21/98	12:14:47 AM	BROWSER	None	8015	N/A	
11/21/98	12:13:47 AM	EventLog	None	6005	N/A	
11/21/98	12:12:31 AM	BROWSER	None	8033	N/A	

Figure 11-12: Windows NT Event Viewer

Before I get too much farther into event logging, a discussion of the types of events and their characteristics is in order.

Windows NT Server events come in five flavors:

- **Information.** These events generally are recorded when a significant but successful event happens on your NT Server; a service starts successfully, for example. You will see several of these events each time a server is booted, as the services start themselves up. Information events are marked in the Event Viewer with a blue circle containing an "I."
- **Warning.** These events are recorded when something happens on the server that may not be significant now but could spell trouble later. Low disk space is a good example of a situation that could cause a Warning event (see Figure 11-13). Warning events are recognized because they appear next to a yellow circle with an exclamation point inside.

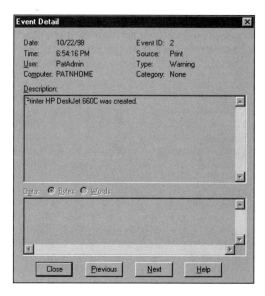

Figure 11-13: A typical Windows NT Warning event

- **Error.** This indicates that a serious problem has occurred on the server that could hamper its performance. Error events are most commonly generated when services fail to start, but they can be associated with such serious events as hard drive failures in a RAID array, or worse. Error events are marked with a red stop sign.
- **Success Audit.** These auditing events are recorded in the Security log when a successful security event takes place, such as a user logging on successfully or gaining access to a file or directory that is marked for auditing. The Success Audit's icon is a yellow key.
- **Failure Audits.** These are generated when a user is unable to log on, or when the user attempts to access a file, directory, or privilege he or she does not have access to. Failure audits are marked with a gray padlock.

Windows NT events also contain several attributes, explained in Table 11-1.

Table 11-1   Windows NT Event Attributes

Attribute	Description
Date	The date the event took place
Time	The time the event took place
Source	The software that generated the event. This can be either an element of Windows NT itself or a third-party application.

Attribute	Description
Type	This describes which of the five event types (described previously) this event belongs to.
Category	A classification of the event, based on information from the source. Many events do not have an associated category.
Event ID	This is a unique number that the source associates with the particular event.
User	The user name of the user whose process or action generated the event
Computer	The computer name the event took place on

At my business, checking event logs is a weekly task, unless something seems to be going wrong with one of the servers. In that case, we go right to the logs to look for information on any possible problems.

One thing that's very important to remember about Event Viewer is that just because a Warning or Error event doesn't sound too serious, or because you don't know what it is, you shouldn't just clear the log and ignore the event. Sometimes these "unknown" events can be precursors to a major system problem. If the error's content or cause isn't clear from the information in the event log, record the Event ID and jump into TechNet or Support Online to query on that ID. Often, these confusing events are caused by bugs in software or the operating system, and eight times out of ten, I've found a solution by searching TechNet and finding references to service packs or hotfixes that correct these strange events. (Service packs and hotfixes are discussed more thoroughly in Chapter 13.) On another occasion, my cohorts and I couldn't identify the cause of a periodic serious error that was recorded in our event logs. After searching TechNet, we were able to determine that is was a precursor to a major SCSI device failure, and we were able to replace the failing device before it took down the server.

In short, Event Viewer is a tremendously powerful tool for Windows NT professionals: The NT event logs are like a continuous record of your server's health, with possible problems recorded in real time throughout the day. By making proper use of Event Viewer, you can prevent server and network problems from rearing their ugly heads. Even if these challenges do get the best of your server, Event Viewer can assist you in diagnosing and correcting the problem.

Step 8: Verification of Servers and Applications

This task should be first and foremost on each administrator's morning checklist. When you get into the office, take a few minutes to check out all the servers, applications, and databases. If they're not working properly, it's a lot better for you to find out about it before too many users get into the office than for your phone to start ringing off the hook while you sit in clueless bliss drinking your coffee. Also, if your schedule allows it, try to get into the office at least a half hour before the majority of the users. This way, if there is a problem, you have a little cushion of time to try to fix it. Even in 7 × 24 shops, most people still work 8 to 5, so getting in at 7:30 or earlier will help lower your stress level if one of your servers decides to go on vacation overnight.

First: Check on the servers and services

Many server hardware products come with Simple Network Management Protocol (SNMP)–based remote management tools that can tell you at a glance which boxes are running and which are not. Although these tools are good for ensuring that the hardware is on and the operating system (networking) is functional, they don't really tell you anything about the services on the server. It is certainly possible for a Primary Domain Controller to be up and running, but if the Netlogon service has stopped, ain't nobody logging on from nowhere. Thus, it's a good idea to look at the actual services on each server using Server Manager or your favorite third-party utility (see Figure 11-14). This process takes a little while, but it definitely pays for itself in the long run. For instance, someday it could save you from having to explain to the boss why you didn't check to make sure the Exchange Information Store was running on your Exchange server because your management tool said the machine was up.

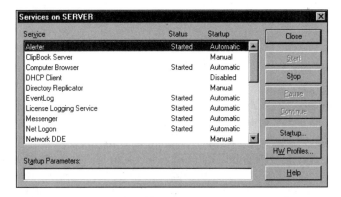

Figure 11-14: Verifying server services using Server Manager

If you do discover a problem during your morning check, now's the time to fix it, before many more users come into the office and start hammering on the systems.

Second: Check applications and databases

After you're convinced that your servers are up and healthy and the services are running, the next step is to actually log onto each application and do some test operations to make sure the apps themselves are working properly.

This operation doesn't have to be elaborate; a simple test query or two will do, but every Windows NT administrator should at least have the access and the know-how to log on and test each application on his or her servers. At my office, we have four main applications that reside on our NT servers, and we try to test them out each morning as soon as we get in. If we find something wrong and it looks like the server itself is up and running, we can report the problem to the appropriate applications group for resolution.

Step 9: Verification of LAN and WAN Connectivity

Once you're satisfied that your servers and applications are running and ready for the users, the next step in a Windows NT administrator's daily checklist is to make sure everybody on the network is talking. This can be accomplished in a couple of ways, depending on the size of your network and the tools at your disposal. If you use an SNMP network management system like HP OpenView, Tivoli NetView, or Computer Associates Unicenter TNG, your SNMP console will tell you in an instant whether network links are up or down. However, if you're in a smaller organization that didn't budget for these rather expensive tools, you can still easily verify whether your network is intact each day. It's a fairly simple task to write a batch file that uses the TCP/IP ping utility to attempt to reach all servers and network devices on your LAN and WAN and then write its results to a text file that's available for your inspection (see Figure 11-15). If you're still using IPX exclusively and do not have TCP/IP running on your networks, you can write a routine that connects to remote machines via RPC calls, such as attempting to map a drive on the remote machine.

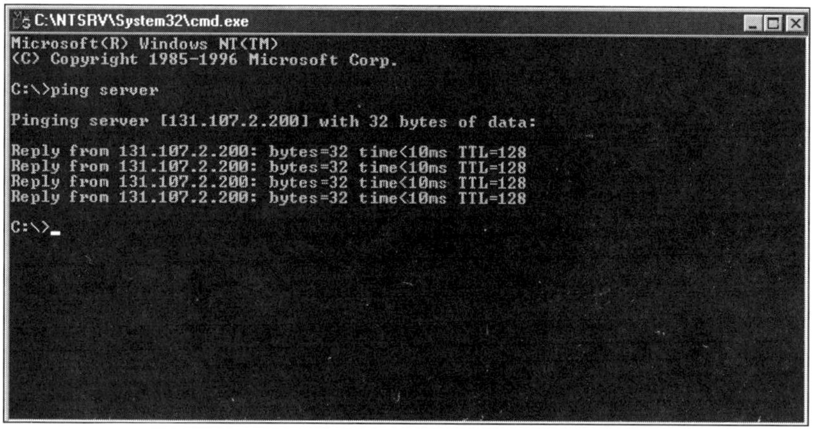

Figure 11-15: Results of a TCP/IP ping command

A TCP/IP ping batch file might look something like this:

```
REM Testing network connectivity on LAN and WAN
ping server1 > conntest.txt
ping server2 > conntest.txt
ping server3 > conntest.txt
ping wan1server2 > conntest.txt
ping wan2server1 > conntest.txt
end
```

Once you have your text file available, you can inspect it and look for ping timeouts and excessive turnaround times that might indicate a problem with your network. In fact, it's a good idea to automate this process with NT's AT command so that you can schedule the connectivity test batch file to run a few minutes before you get into the office. That way, the results will be available when you arrive, and you can take action if necessary.

This method is the way we monitor connectivity at my office, and while it's not as fancy as some of the network management tools, it is effective and gives us what we need and enables us to make sure our users in faraway branch offices stay as connected as the folks in the home office.

Secret

If you need a slightly more sophisticated approach than the "home grown" variety displayed previously, you should consider Ping Plotter, a low-cost shareware application from Richard Ness at Nessoft (www.nessoft.com). Not only does this application test ping connectivity, but it also enables you to observe ping performance across several WAN hops. The hop path is even mapped for you! MCSE consultant-types typically use this tool for testing telco/WAN performance. That is to say that Ping Plotter enables you to test the links and down the food chain on your WAN. This ultimately enables you to answer your questions regarding the subscribed bandwidth the telco sold you and the performance that you are actually enjoying. Important questions indeed to get answers to, might I say, on a daily basis.

Tool like Ping Plotter are also great for keeping a green machine awake. Here is what I mean: Perhaps you've installed Windows NT Server on a truly low-cost workstation. But try as you might, you can't disable the sleep function at the workstation's BIOS level (it's happened to me). To keep the workstation from "sleeping" and crashing Windows NT Server, you can use Ping Plotter to maintain a constant activity level that prevents, shall I say, napping. Problem solved.

Whatever your preferred pinging method is, the bottom line is that you are trying to verify connectivity. On your bad NT days, that becomes an end in itself. Otherwise, this step should just be second nature. And you can always count on your end users to be your connectivity eyes and ears. If they can't connect, you'll know.

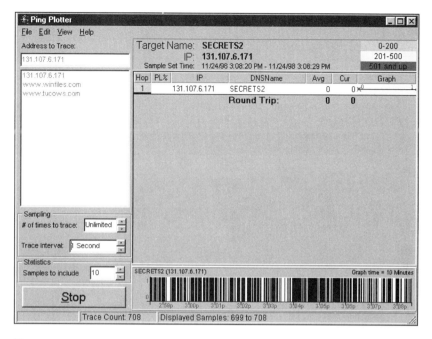

Figure 11-16: Ping Plotter

Step 10: New Hardware

As flaky as it is sometimes, the Plug and Play feature of Windows 95 and 98 is nice to have. Nothing beats buying a Plug and Play–compliant peripheral, throwing it into your PC, and having the operating system detect and set up the new hardware. Easy as pie, as long as you buy compliant hardware.

Windows NT Server doesn't have this feature, at least not yet. Plug and Play functionality is coming in Windows 2000, but unless you're a brave beta tester, you'll have to wait several months or more for that version to hit the streets.

So how the heck do you add new hardware to a Windows NT 4.0 Server? It's actually easier than it seems. When you buy a new piece of hardware for your server, it will come with a Setup disk or CD-ROM that contains drivers for the device. However, using the distribution software in the box should always be your second step; the first step is to check the hardware vendor's Web site. Ninety percent of the time, the drivers on the Web are newer than those in the box, and with very few exceptions, you always want to use the latest driver.

Preparing for installation

Before you set about installing your new hard drive, network adapter, or whatever, you should take stock of the resources currently in use on the system (see Figure 11-17). You can do this by running Windows NT Diagnostics, the NT version of Microsoft's good ol' DOS MSD program. NT Diagnostics will enable you to inspect and print out the list of resources in use on your server, including interrupt request lines (IRQs), memory addresses, I/O ports, and direct memory access (DMA) channels. This way, you can determine where the new hardware will fit in.

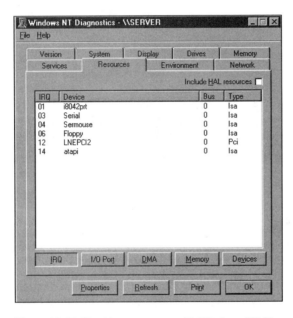

Figure 11-17: Checking resources with Windows NT Diagnostics

In most cases, a device's driver setup program will determine and assign free system resources, so the preceding step is only necessary when the setup program will prompt you to choose resource information.

Installing the hardware

Unless you are installing a "hot-pluggable" device as described in the text that follows, the first step in any hardware installation is to power down the server and disconnect its power source. Also put on some sort of static protection device; in our server room, there are several static control bracelets that can be connected to grounded server parts to prevent static buildup and possible damage to sensitive components.

Once you have opened up the server and identified where the new device will go, install and connect it according to the manufacturer's directions.

Secret

Some servers even allow you to add or replace hard drives while the server is up and running, with no interrruption of service to the end users. These so-called "hot pluggable, hot swappable" drives are invaluable in 7 × 24 operations.

Installing and configuring drivers

After the new hardware is in place, close the server back up and power it on. Take care to properly close all access panels on the computer; some servers have safety switches that prevent them from powering up unless all of these panels are in place.

After the operating system comes up, run the hardware driver setup program and install and configure the hardware, again according to the manufacturer's specifications.

Note

Directions are typically provided on a disk by the manufacturer. This is a key step because you must effectively install new hardware manually under Windows NT Server 4.0 (which only has adequate hardware detection during its setup phase). Windows 95/98 of course have great real-time hardware detection, something you won't see in Windows NT server until Windows 2000 Server.

In many cases, you must reboot the server in order to get Windows NT to recognize and properly utilize the new device, and some device setup programs will even reboot the machine themselves after they're done installing the peripheral. This is usually not the case with "hot-plug" hardware, but if you have a choice, take care to perform these hardware operations after hours, or schedule a bit of downtime, even if you're not sure whether you'll need it.

When all of these operations are complete, your new hardware should be set up and ready for you and your users to use!

Step 11: Documentation and Sharing Procedures

While it's not as "active" a task as some of the others mentioned in this chapter, documentation is very important for the success of any network. There is absolutely no sense in one person being proficient at a network administration or process while his or her coworkers are in the dark. In my mind, this is actually a dangerous situation, especially if the task in question is vital to the health of the network. What if that person were hit by a truck? What would the rest of you do?

Documentation is one thing that's a high priority at my workplace; we are encouraged, in fact required, to document new processes as they are developed and perfected. This isn't just for others' sake, either: Ever get a process down perfectly, only to forget it after a couple of months? Find yourself wishing you had written it down before? I sure have, many times over the years.

In my office, we have a procedures directory on the network that contains more than 100 documents. Some are out of date now, but we keep them around anyway; some of the tasks detailed could crop up again, or the techniques could be adapted for our current network. In addition, we train each other on new procedures as they are written and do "beta testing." When one of us creates a new procedure, such as installing a new application or restoring a Microsoft Exchange mailbox from backups, he will document it thoroughly. The next step is to have another administrator do the "monkey test," where we just follow the procedure step by step, making sure to leave our outside knowledge at the computer room door. When all we have to go on is the procedure before us, it's easy to identify holes or assumptions and correct them. Some of our procedures are so good that any end user could come into the server room and perform the task by following the step-by-step procedure document. Yikes: That's not very good for job security!

If you ever have a bit of downtime between fighting fires and the endless upgrades, think a moment about procedures you use that may not be documented as well as they should be, and address those issues. Good documentation initially makes a Windows NT professional's job *much* easier later on.

Secret

If you are a consultant, performing the documentation task is a great way to find and bill additional hours. Such additional work is great for three reasons. First, it requires virtually no marketing to get. It's easier to sell your existing clients on additional work than it is to sell work to new clients. Second, the work is easy to perform. Third, if help you toward reaching your annual billable hour goal. Be sure to use Visio or some other networking diagramming tool as part of your network documentation approach.

Step 12: Working and Happy Users

This last topic is more a philosophical discussion than a technical one. As a Windows NT professional, it is imperative that you keep the needs of your users in the front of your mind at all times. After all, they are your customers, and despite what your org chart might say, you work for them. After you break out of the front-line support game and earn a position back in the server room, it's sometimes easy to put these thoughts aside, crucial as they may be. I've worked in shops that cover both ends of the spectrum: From a place that would drop the Exchange server in the middle of the day if they deemed it necessary, to my current employer, where one of the IT department's primary goals is to remain invisible, to make sure the users don't even know we're there. I prefer the latter, even if it means quite a bit of after-hours and weekend work. The users' main impression of the company's network is that it just *works*. Your users should feel the same way. To that end, here are some helpful tips I've picked up over the years.

Protect the users

If you have a choice, choose the action that will impact the users least. For example, a few months back we noticed that one of our servers was starting to go downhill; unexplained Server service warning events were showing up in the event logs, response times were increasing slightly, and it was evident that something was wrong. At this point, it was a judgment call for my group: Do we leave the server up in the expectation that it will make it to the end of the day, or do we reboot it now, in the middle of the afternoon? As we evaluated the situation, we noted that the problem likely would not cause any data loss, and we took into account that this was one of the busiest days of the month. We decided to gamble and leave the server up until the end of the business day, and it coasted along fine. Decisions like these are tough, because you obviously don't want the server to come crashing down if you can help it, but we decided that the minimum user impact would be to leave the server up. It was a decision between 10 minutes of *guaranteed* downtime for a reboot, or 10 minutes of *possible* downtime if the server crashed later and had to be rebooted. We did, however, take steps to notify all affected groups about the situation, which brings me to my next point.

Keep the users informed

In my experience, users have an easier time accepting a service interruption if they know it's coming. In the preceding example, my group sent out a company-wide e-mail message advising the users that the server was having problems and might crash, and telling the users to save often. We got positive feedback about this approach; even though the users weren't happy that the server might die in the middle of the day, they appreciated the warning. Had the machine crashed, they would have lost a lot less work than if they hadn't had any warning.

End users do like to know the basic reasons for downtime, but it's also a good practice to keep technical jargon out of end user communications. While you may think it's neato to explain the intricacies of ESEUTIL in an e-mail message informing users that the Exchange server will be down for the weekend, the fact is that most people just don't care. Keep your communications straightforward and to the point, and your message will come across loud and clear. If an end user really is interested in what you're doing with the Exchange box, he or she will reply and ask for more information. For everyone else, a simple note saying "The Exchange server will be down this weekend for database maintenance" will suffice.

Keep the help desk informed

When I worked on an enterprise help desk, it always seemed as if we were the last to know about vital information that would affect the users. Half the time, we gathered this information from the users themselves as they called, which was terribly frustrating and embarrassing. Like every other tech support veteran I know, I swore up and down that once I got to the back of the shop, I'd make help desk communications a priority so that my first-level support would never be without the proper information. Have I made good on this promise? Mostly, although I'm still not as communicative to our help desk as I'd like to be. It's a good goal to have, though; the better informed your first-level support people are, the better the users' impression will be of your department as a cohesive unit where groups communicate among one another.

Strive for 100 percent uptime

Continuous uptime may seem like an obvious goal for anyone who runs a computer system, but keeping it in your mind at all times is a real challenge. Now, everyone who's worked with NT for any length of time knows that NT servers need reboots every so often, but a really good NT administrator should try to minimize this need. Keep your servers simple, assign them only the tasks you need them to perform, and don't clog up the system with additional services or applications unless they're absolutely essential. There's a saying that a person's body is his or her temple; make temples out of your production boxes. Have fun with your test servers, but when you have a spare moment, spend it working to make your Windows NT servers as fault-tolerant as they can be. As I mentioned earlier, many administrators don't have a problem spending hundreds or thousands of dollars to make their hardware bulletproof. Put in the hours necessary to make your operating systems and software just as bulletproof.

Challenge yourself to work smarter each and every day. This might include reading trade journals such as *InfoWorld, PC Week,* and the like. You might read another chapter in this book just for the heck of it. Consider taking an in-classroom or online course. But each and every day, be sure to make a capital investment in yourself so that you work smarter tomorrow than you did today!

Summary

Once your Windows NT Server network is set up, it requires ongoing day-to-day maintenance and improvement. As you can see, a Windows NT professional's workday is a busy one. In this chapter, I shared a dozen daily tasks that a successful Windows NT administrator needs to perform to keep his or her network running smoothly:

- Using the Windows NT Server 4.0 toolkit and the Administrative Wizards
- Fire Fighting: end user support issues
- Troubleshooting
- Performing regularly scheduled tape backups and verifying backups via test restores
- Testing server and desktop virus protection and updating virus data
- Verifying free disk space on your servers
- Keeping tabs on your servers with Event Viewer
- Verifying that all servers, applications, and databases are up and functional
- Verifying LAN and WAN connectivity
- Adding new hardware to your Windows NT server
- Documenting and sharing procedures
- Keeping your users working and happy

Chapter 12

Monthly and Annual Windows NT Server Activities

In This Chapter

- Auditing your network
- Reviewing security
- Performance benchmarking and monitoring
- The monthly reboot
- Mapping disk space on servers
- Disaster recovery simulation
- Implementing operating system service packs and hotfixes
- Creating month-end or quarterly archives
- Implementing network application upgrades
- Annual budgeting for your network
- Having an active technology committee
- Evaluating systems on the horizon
- The annual planning retreat

You're proud of your Windows NT network. You spent a lot of time during planning and setup, configuring every aspect of your systems to your specifications, doing stress testing, developing foolproof daily and weekly maintenance plans, and migrating the users onto the new system. Your network runs smoothly, and the users are happy with its performance. However, even in a network as trouble-free as yours (which most of us could only wish for), certain administrative tasks require attention each month and annually. This chapter will introduce you to many of the tasks I've seen during my time as a Windows NT administrator, and hopefully it will enable you to integrate some of these tasks into your own network. You won't see step-by-step instructions on how to delete users; instead, I'll talk about some good habits to get into that will make your day-to-day job easier and also enable you to more easily train new network administrators as they come on board. After all, you'd like to be sitting in the CIO's leather chair someday, wouldn't you?

Auditing Your Network

In a working day-to-day Windows NT network, new users, directories, and shares are created daily; in a large, growing enterprise, administrators in various locations may create hundreds of these objects in a busy week. How in the world does a Windows NT professional keep track of all this, and more important, how can you assure that users, shares, and such are deleted properly when someone leaves the business? A well thought-out checklist for adding and deleting users is a very good start, but some auditing will always be necessary because steps will be missed and some tasks might fall through the cracks.

Here are the steps we use at my office when deleting a user account:

1. Require an account deletion form. This is useful for two reasons; first, it assures that you have the CYA factor, and second, you can file these forms away for review at the end of the month. If you do not have these forms, it's difficult to remember who you've deleted during the month, especially in a large organization.

2. On the date specified on the deletion form, change the account password and disable the account. Do not delete the account at this point, in case the user's replacement is coming on board soon (in which case you can just rename the original user account to the new account name) or if the user comes back to the organization for some reason. At the same time, inform your end user support group of your action, so they will not accidentally reenable to account if the former employee calls in.

3. Determine if the user's manager needs access to his or her old e-mail. If not, go ahead and delete the e-mail account, if it is not likely that the user will return quickly, as some temporary employees do, for example.

4. If necessary, give the manager permission to access the user's home directory, so he or she may get to documents as needed. Give the managers a set amount of time (usually until the end of the current month) to move any documents they might need before deleting the directory itself.

5. At the end of the month, go through all accounts that have been disabled during the month. If they are still not needed, delete the accounts from the Windows NT domain, and also delete the user's home directory and any network shares specific to that user. If your system logon scripts have references for individual users (and they shouldn't, if you can avoid it) check to see if the deleted accounts were referenced in those scripts. If so, modify the scripts as necessary.

In addition to reviewing user deletions, you also will want to take a look at how your network has changed over the month. For example, let's say a specific application on your network required the creation of several network shares on your main server. During the last month, that application was replaced with a competing vendor's product. As part of your end-of-month audit, you'll want to make sure that the shares created for the old application are deleted; not only will this clean up your users' views in Network Neighborhood, it might improve your NT servers' performance.

Reviewing Security

As I discussed in Chapter 3, documenting your network's security is an essential part of maintaining Windows NT servers. During daily operations, NT File System (NTFS) and network share security settings will be changed, added, and deleted. Without proper monitoring and auditing each month, these settings can get out of control and you won't know which folders and shares have the proper security.

Secret

Consider two alternate ways to test your security, ways that will expose your greatest weaknesses. First, download the SATAN tool from any of the numerous shareware sites (www.winfiles.com, www.shareware.com). SATAN is a tool that you may configure to test the security of your system with respect to outside intruders. It does have a learning curve, so allow yourself a few weeks to master it and achieve the end results you seek: a more secure Windows NT Server!

Second, hire the enemy. Have you ever noticed that successful hackers are often offered jobs by the very firms that they hacked? It is true and probably happens more than the media report. In your case, I'd recommend that you consider hiring a high school or college kid and let the kid take a "controlled" run at your system. Many hackers come from this socioeconomic demographic group, so why not hire the enemy and get 'em on your side?

Establishing and maintaining security settings on your Windows NT network isn't difficult, provided you stay on top of changes as they happen each day, week, or month. Here are three steps that will help you keep your network secure:

1. **Set up and implement a plan.** Implementing an initial security plan is the first step toward a well-maintained network security setup. As mentioned in Chapter 3, every responsible Windows NT professional should create a spreadsheet, database, or other document outlining their network's security setup when the network is installed. Before you turn users loose onto the network, make sure that the actual security on shares, files, and directories is as you intended it, and as you documented it.

2. **Document changes as they occur.** Any security document is a "living document" and must be updated and changed to reflect changes made to the network each day, week, month, or whatever. A security document, be it a database, spreadsheet, or text, must be your security template and reflect the network as it should be.

3. **Audit security regularly.** Once a month, or more often if your environment requires it, compare the security settings in the template with actual security on the network. Are they different? Do you know why they're different? If so, update the security template to reflect the changes, and scold yourself or the administrator responsible for not updating the template when the settings were changed.

If you find inconsistencies or mistakes in your network security, change the permissions back to their intended settings. Make sure that you are satisfied with your audit before moving on to other monthly tasks; security maintenance is one of the most important parts of a Windows NT professional's job. If you doubt this, just wait until the CEO's personal documents are e-mailed throughout the company.

Baselining and Monitoring Performance

Windows NT's Performance Monitor tool is extremely useful in helping you tune your Windows NT network. However, in order for any monitoring data to be useful, you must first generate benchmark measurements so that you have a baseline to compare against. This matter is discussed at length in Part VI, "Optimizing and Troubleshooting Windows NT Server 4.0," but it's worth mentioning again. And it should certainly be on your monthly/annual list of activities!

In a growing network, NT's performance baseline may change significantly each month or every few months, as new users, services, and applications are added to the system. Because of this, that Performance Monitor baseline you took back in February may be far from accurate in August.

In my current network, I usually do a performance benchmark every three months or so, and more often if there is a major user conversion going on. My coworkers and I save these files for future use and refer back to them for comparison when trying to troubleshoot a server problem using Performance Monitor.

Performance baselining and monitoring will be discussed in detail later in the book, but I wanted to mention it in this chapter because accurate baselines are a crucial part of understanding whether your NT network is humming along happily or whether it's heading for a screeching halt.

The Monthly Reboot

All operating systems use and release primary memory, or RAM, as needed. This is normal and occurs constantly. In fact, one way to monitor the RAM usage on your Windows NT Server is to run Task Manager (selected from the taskbar properties from your Windows NT Server desktop). Task Manager is discussed at length in Chapter 24, "Task Manager and Other Neat Tricks!"

The Performance tab on Task Manager enables you to see, at the lower right, the memory consumed over the memory available on you system (see "Mem Usage:"), as seen in Figure 12-1. Another good memory indicator is memory chart in the middle of the Performance tab that shows a memory consumption histogram view on the left and a memory consumption time line or time series at the middle right.

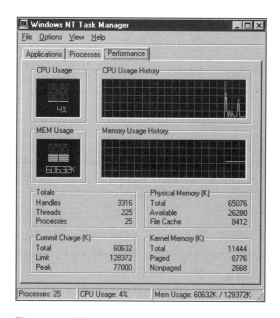

Figure 12-1: The Task Manager Performance tab

Under the best of circumstances, the memory consumption information displayed in Figure 12-1 would increase over the course of a month because Windows NT Server, in the process of using and releasing RAM, will slightly fragment this primary memory. That is, not all of the RAM used will be returned properly and be counted again as unused. In English, Windows NT Server doesn't give back all of the RAM it uses when it is done with it. And I haven't even started to discuss how applications affect RAM yet. It has been my experience that Microsoft Exchange Server can be a poor server citizen when it comes to releasing unused RAM. Microsoft SQL Server can be trained to be a good server citizen because you can specify how much and in what ways SQL Server will use RAM (this is done via the server property sheet in SQL Server's Enterprise Manager).

Third-party applications are what may just cause your Windows NT Server machine fits when it comes to releasing RAM. I've seen lots of offenders (including the backup engine service of a well-known third-party backup application) that not only fail to release all of the RAM used when measured as day-to-day activity but sometimes, in a badly behaved way, cause the

Windows NT Server to consume all available memory. That is, some poorly written applications will cause the memory histogram and time line in Figure 12-1 to "max" at the top of the chart. Perhaps you've experienced this, and you would know that your server slows down so much that it is difficult to launch another application at the server or sometime even move the mouse on the server machine.

Enter the monthly reboot to "reset" and form contiguous RAM space. By rebooting your Windows NT Server, you flush and defragment RAM and get a fresh start. This will certainly solve slowly developing memory consumption creep from the operating system and applications not returning all consumed RAM. To see for yourself, consider the following experiment.

STEPS:
To monitor RAM consumption and defragmentation

Step 1. Launch Task Manager from the taskbar properties of your Windows NT server.

Step 2. Observe and record the Mem Usage value on the lower right of the Performance Tab sheet.

Step 3. Launch one or two server-based applications such as Microsoft Exchange Server or Oracle.

Step 4. Observe and record the Mem Usage value again (similar to Step 2) now that you have launched server-based applications (Step 3).

Step 5. Let both Task Manager and the applications launched previously (Step 3) run for several days. Continue to use your network as usual.

Step 6. Several days later, observe and record the Mem Usage value again and terminate the applications you launched in Step 3.

Step 7. Now observe and record the Mem Usage value with the applications successfully terminated (Step 5).

Step 8. You will now compare the different Mem Usage values over the past few days. Ideally, if there were no RAM leaks, the Mem Usage values in Step 2 and Step 7 would be the same. But most likely these values are not, reflecting the fact that not all RAM was returned to available memory once the applications were terminated. Indeed, the Mem Usage value in Step 7 should be larger than the Mem Usage value in Step 2, all things being equal.

You can also perform the preceding experiment where you simply run Task Manager for several days or weeks without explicitly launching and terminating server-based applications just to observe what level of RAM fragmentation may be attributed to the underlying Windows NT Server operating system. And above all, perform that monthly reboot to flush and reset your RAM to battle this form of memory fragmentation. You might also be interested to know that I like to use the monthly reboot to test the bulletproof nature of my Windows NT server. It is my goal to have networks in place that I can reboot with confidence each month. If I'm afraid to reboot a Windows NT server each month because I'm afraid it won't restart and come back up, I probably have larger, more serious underlying problems with my network than simple RAM fragmentation.

Secret

I'm very comfortable providing the preceding advice regarding the monthly reboot to those of you working on small and medium-sized Windows NT Server networks. However, I reluctant to have you use my advice to override strict and necessary system management policies at the enterprise level. Be sure to check with your Windows NT Server network stakeholders (including your boss) before rebooting your Windows NT Server each month. At the enterprise level, kindly accept my advice as something to consider.

Mapping Disk Space on Servers

In Chapter 11, I mentioned disk space monitoring as an important task for Windows NT professionals to do at least weekly. On a monthly basis, I recommend going one step further and monitoring the growth of individual directories on your servers and running a disk defragmentation utility. A weekly look at total free disk space is fine, but once a month, more granularity is called for. While this seems like (and is) a lot of work, it's also essential; if you don't know which directories are growing out of control, you can't stop a problem before the server runs out of disk space.

The manual method

The most straightforward way to check directory size is by opening up Windows Explorer, right-clicking the directory you want and choosing Properties, and then waiting for the directory size count to stop and recording the size in bytes reflected in the Properties sheet. This method, while it is a nice no-brainer escape from the daily stress of running your network, takes a very, very long time and is quite impractical for larger networks. Even in our medium-sized network of 175 users and several servers, this process can take most of a day.

The "automatic" method

After spending a few months manually recording each folder's size on our NT server, my fellow administrators at work and I decided there must be a better way to determine which directories are growing the fastest. We started looking into third-party utilities and settled on Storage Resource Manager from Highground Systems. While this tool was written as a user space quota utility, it works great for our needs; we can generate database reports indicating which directories on our servers are biggest, and which are growing at alarming rates. Using this information, we can stop any out-of-control growth before it takes out our server's free disk space.

A real-world war story

One client, an online research firm, found that it didn't know exactly where its mission critical data was located on the network. Of course this discovery was made during a hard disk failure when it was time to perform data restoration. From that experience, the table shown in Table 12-1 was devised to better map out how the disk space on the network was being utilized. I've created one example for your benefit (the intent is to have you fill in the blanks with your own information as part of the data location exercise).

Table 12-1   Data Location

Data	Size	Physical Location	Drive Letter-Based Location	UNC Location	ARC Path Location	Comments
Alaska data	12MB	Server1	c:\data\ak	\\server1\ak	multi(0)disk(0)rdisk(1)partition(2)	Is backed up nightly.

Closely related to disk space calculations is the topic of disk fragmentation. Contrary to popular belief, NTFS partitions do indeed suffer fragmentation from the ins and outs of daily Windows NT Server activity. This of course isn't news at the desktop level with FAT and FAT32 in the traditional end user Windows environment. Windows 98 performs disk maintenance activities for you with ease.

But for some reason, many Windows NT Server professionals got it in their minds that NTFS partitions don't suffer from fragmentation, or the best one that I heard was, that NTFS partitions are self-healing when it comes to discontiguous disk space. In fact, if you were to run one of the popular

Windows NT Server disk defragmentation utilities such as Executive Software's DiskKeeper or Symantec's Norton Utilities for Windows NT Server, you would be amazed at the disk maps showing fragmentation. Take my advice and strongly consider purchasing and using one of the disk defragmentation utilities listed previously. Each month, observe the amount of disk fragmentation on your Windows NT Server and consider running the utilities to make your disk space contiguous again.

Secret

Before running a disk utility to "recombine" your fragment secondary storage space, make sure that you've made bona fide and verified tape backups of your data. Just in case!

Recovering from Disaster

First and foremost, update your Emergency Repair Disk (ERD) each and every month, even if you don't believe significant system activity has occurred that might warrant such action. Never underestimate the passing of time and its effects on a Windows NT Server. Sure, you may not have added any users in the past month, but with a default password change duration of 42 days in Windows NT Server 4.0, it's likely that user accounts have been updated in the past month, with or without your knowledge. This immediate example is only one of several "background" system update possibilities that warrant the monthly ERD creation process. The ERD is discussed in more detail in Chapter 25, "Troubleshooting Secrets."

Secret

Because the ERD relies on a floppy disk, I suggest that each month you create a new ERD and save the old one. I'd hate to see you get in the habit of overwriting the ERD each month and ultimately suffer a floppy disk media failure.

You and I both can learn a lot from the mainframers of yesteryear. Specifically, in the area of disaster recovery. The client/server networking community, the community of Windows NT Server, has done a very poor job of addressing disaster recovery. Novell took the lead years ago with its NetWare SFT III specifications, wherein hot "mirrored" servers were kept online some distance away from the main production NetWare servers. Microsoft is, to be quite candid, just arriving at the disaster recovery party with its Windows NT Server–based clustering solution. Look for clustering to become a viable offering in Windows 2000 Advanced Server (today it's just too early to call it truly robust).

So how can you address the disaster recovery matter in Windows NT Server 4.0 today? I've witnessed it being handled several ways.

Third-party solutions

Larger Windows NT Server sites are looking at third-party solutions ranging from robust optical-based backup systems to clustering applications. One notable clustering solution in the Windows NT Server environment is Vinci.

Identical spare servers

Two of my Windows NT Server clients have purchased identical (down to the network adapter card) servers. One acts as the production server. The other is a spare server (see Figure 12-2). The idea is that, if the production server crashes or fails, the hard disks could be moved to the identical spare server and the organization would have its network running again within one business day. An alternative approach is to restore from backup tape to the spare server.

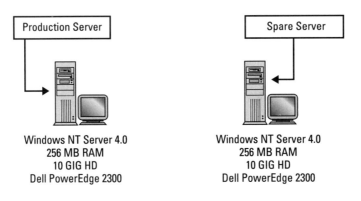

Figure 12-2: Using a spare server

Believe it or not, this spare server approach will actually work in a Windows NT Server environment. I have only performed this in a medium-sized environment, and clearly, at the enterprise level more robust solution such as clustering would be used instead.

Secret

One lesson learned from the spare server approach was how long it took to get back online. Early on I thought I could have an organization back online within one or two hours. Wrong! For whatever reasons (glitches, unexpected issues), the spare server approach takes a full business day to implement. With this fact in view, I can now manage everyone's expectations appropriately.

If you already haven't done so, take a few minutes to assess how you are managing the downtime expectations for the stakeholders on your Windows NT Server network. Have you communicated that server-related downtime might be measured in hours, if not days (but rarely minutes)? If necessary, use this moment to jot down a few ideas on how you might better manage expectations (perhaps an e-mail message to everyone at the office advising people to have alternative work processes in case the server is down for a day).

Secret

Although the spare server solution will work, you must plan for how you will handle the "different" SID value on the backup server, assuming you will use the same server and domain naming conventions. If you are using Windows 95/98, this is not a serious problem, as these desktop operating systems don't bind the SID to their logon process. But if you are using Windows NT Workstation at the desktop, you've got major problems. That is because the spare server's SID numbers (machine and domain) will be different from the original networked environment. In all likelihood, you will need to use a SID changer, an application found in the Windows NT Server 4.0 Resource Kit or at popular shareware sites (www.winfiles.com, www.shareware.com).

Reciprocity agreements/hot sites

Our firm occasionally offers its spare training PCs as potential "rescue" computers for our smaller clients in a crisis. By that I mean that if the property management firm calls with a crashed server, we can trot over with a bare-bones spare Windows NT Server and have the 10 users printing from Microsoft Word by lunch. Not a perfect solution but one that works in a crisis.

Larger enterprises contract with hot sites to address possible failures. These are the airlines, hospitals, and large corporations of the Windows NT Server community. Although this approach is expensive, properly configured, the enterprise customer's network can limit downtime to minutes, not hours or days.

Why bother?

Wouldn't it just be easier to do nothing and wait for the problems at your site to work themselves out inside of following all of the preceding approaches to disaster recovery? Well, you know the answer is of course not, for at least one reason: the cost of downtime. Even small organizations can calculate the cost of downtime in the several thousands of dollars per hour range. Such high costs make a spare server or third-party disaster recovery solution look cheap.

Annual drill

Regrettably, too many of us in the Windows NT Server community aren't performing an annual disaster recovery exercise. The customers I have that do this typically perform this activity in response to some form of EDP audit or at the request of government regulators (if they are in a regulated business).

The annual disaster recovery drill can take many formats. It can be as simple as the CIO pulling a drive out of a RAID array chassis unannounced (after making sure the evening backup tapes were successful — wink wink). My client that runs an online research service performed that exercise, and it was an eye-opener to say the least.

Another disaster recovery exercise is to have your IT consulting firm arrive unannounced, grab last evening's backup tape and several IT staff members, and have said staff perform a complete and successful system restore — within one business day. Again, such an exercise is a real eye-opener.

Implementing Service Packs and Hotfixes

This topic is one of the main focal points of this book and is covered at length in Part IV: "Service Pack 4 and the Windows NT Server Option." However, so that it remains on your radar screen of monthly and annual tasks, allow me to take a few pages to again discuss it here. But starting with the next chapter, you will become immersed in this entire topic.

In every operating system, bugs and shortcomings are bound to appear. Because of this fact, operating system vendors periodically release bug fixes for system administrators to apply to their servers. Microsoft's method for large-scale updates of Windows NT systems involves groups of enhancements and bug fixes they call service packs. While service packs are generally safe, many problems have cropped up as a result of applying them, so it's extremely important for administrators to know exactly what they're doing before attempting to update a production system.

In my experience, it's very important to have the following questions answered before applying any service pack:

1. **Why is this necessary?** Do you have a compelling reason for installing the service pack, or are you just trying to keep your servers up to date? This phenomenon of riding the latest versions or upgrades is often called the "bleeding edge," and with good reason. No matter how much Microsoft or other vendors test their products, some instabilities or incompatibilities will always come up. For example, take Service Pack 4 for Windows NT 4.0. Microsoft put this service pack through months of beta testing, and yet I know of several administrators whose production servers blue-screened and would not boot after they applied it. Remember; if it ain't broke, don't fix it. If the server crashes and you have to restore it from backups, you'd better have a good explanation when the CIO asks you why you were messing with the production environment.

2. **Do you have a backout plan?** What if something does go wrong? While Murphy's Law does not always apply in the world of Windows NT networks, you'd better be ready for anything when doing any sort of

operating system upgrade. In all cases, update your servers' Emergency Repair Disks and use the "Create an Uninstall Directory" option when applying a service pack. Also spend some time planning on what you would do if the server refused to boot after the upgrade; do you have a reliable method for restoring it from "bare metal" if you have to format the drives to correct the problem?

3. **Have you tested the service pack in your environment?** Do you really know how the new files will interact with your production systems? On occasion, third-party or homegrown applications do not respond well to changes made by a service pack and may either refuse to run or behave strangely. Make sure you thoroughly test how the service pack will affect your production environment.

4. **Have you properly researched the upgrade and its possible side effects?** When you're thinking about applying a service pack or performing an application upgrade, Windows NT user groups on the Internet can be invaluable. Before we applied Service Pack 2 to our Microsoft Exchange 5.0 server, I spent a few days out on the net, gathering information from the MS Exchange support forum (www.msexchange.org) and other sources. It's well worth your time to take advantage of these resources and enlighten yourself about the possible consequences of the upgrade.

5. **Have you scheduled an appropriate time window for the work?** Because service pack installations require a server reboot and may require additional downtime, they obviously should not be performed during production hours. In a smaller shop where users work 8 to 5, this is fairly easy; you can schedule the work for any weeknight after everyone has gone home. In a 7 × 24 shop, scheduling downtime is not quite as straightforward. Choose a period of time where the system will be under minimal use, such as the middle of the night. These "O' Dark Thirty" projects may not be fun for you, but this scheduling is necessary to minimize user impact. Also, make sure you give yourself some "cushion" time, in case something goes wrong. Estimate your downtime as accurately as possible, and schedule an hour and a half of downtime, even if you think the work will only take an hour. If you have the system back up and running early, you'll be a hero. If it's late, you'll surely have some explaining to do the next day.

Hotfixes

While service packs replace many files and sometimes add new features, hotfixes are "quick-fix" solutions to urgent problems that come up. Hotfixes replace only a few files at a time and are not as thoroughly tested as service packs are. As with service packs, caution is advised when applying hotfixes; if you are not experiencing the specific problem described in a hotfix Readme file, then don't apply the fix.

Hotfixes are also tricky in that they often must be installed (and removed!) in a specific order, or they won't work properly. As such, it's important that administrators take advantage of all information available about the hotfix they're thinking of installing. Hotfixes also usually require a server reboot, so be sure to schedule some downtime.

Be conservative

The recommendations in this section may sound overly conservative, and this type of caution is definitely not necessary for all environments. However, it is absolutely required in larger enterprises and is a very good idea even in the smallest of shops. If you run your small 25-node, single server network as you would run that of a huge conglomerate, your colleagues and users will respect your professionalism and concern for their interests, and this will pay off later on, believe me.

Upgrading and Removing Applications

Be sure to honor the upgrade cycle of your software vendors. With certainty, you can anticipate upgrading your mission-critical applications every 18 months if not sooner. And many software vendors will release interim upgrades monthly and quarterly. Your challenge as a Windows NT Server professional is to implement these application upgrades in a noninvasive manner. That's a kind way a saying you'll first test each application upgrade on a test server to make sure it works. Then you'll install the application upgrade on the production servers on the weekends when no one is around. Heck, you didn't want to use those weekends for skiing or fishing anyway.

Regarding the "how" of installing an application upgrade, you will most likely perform this via the Add/Remove Software applet in Control Panel or via an application's setup file that most likely launches InstallShield's installation wizard. But did you now that, when uninstalling applications, which may likely be one of your responsibilities, you need to exercise extreme care and be sure to either use the Add/Remove Software applet in Control Panel or the uninstall application that shipped with the application you are trying to remove? By properly uninstalling an application, you've performed your due diligence in clearing Registry entries, removing files and desktop icons, and removing or not removing system files (such as DLLs) as needed.

Creating Backup Archives

In many businesses, it's necessary to create special archives that can be shipped to an offsite storage facility for long-term safekeeping. Some companies are required to do this by governmental regulations, and others keep data as a safety net in case of litigation or other unforeseen circumstances. At my office, we are governed by state regulations and must keep all of our business data for seven years. At the end of each month, we do special data exports from our backup system and ship them off to an offsite storage area. You may not be required to perform this action on your network, but if so, make sure you develop a consistent plan and schedule, and stick to it. It's easy to miss an archive window, especially if the archive is supposed to happen during a busy time, such as the holiday season.

Budgeting for Your Network

Like it or not, a lot of what you accomplish as a Windows NT Server professional centers on the budget you have to work with. Part of your monthly and annual activities include paying attention to the money side of Windows NT Server networking. Here are several approaches to addressing the budget issues, including zero-based budgeting, linear percent growth, percent of revenue, and Windows NT Server on $5 a day.

Zero-based budgeting

This is my favorite. Here, as part of the budgeting exercise, you start with a blank spreadsheet. Each and every expenditure category is critically reviewed. By that I mean each item, down to the network adapter cards you keep on hand, are evaluated for usefulness. Questions to ask are:

- Why do you have so many computer parts in inventory?

- Do you need to add staff? How can you justify such an addition?

- If you're planning to add two more servers, what else would be needed? Here the thought is that adding a server results in other additions such as one printer, one modem. Each of these additions would be listed as line items under the new server as shown Figure 12-3.

Zero-based budgeting is similar to designing a bill of materials (BOM) system in manufacturing. You build up the budget from the lowest levels.

Secret

If you want to learn more about zero-based budgeting, consider learning it the way that I did: from a management consultant. If you have consulting funds available, hire a nontechnical management consultant who specializes in business practices such as zero-based budgeting. After you work closely with such an individual once, in all likelihood, you will be able to create your own zero-based budget in later years.

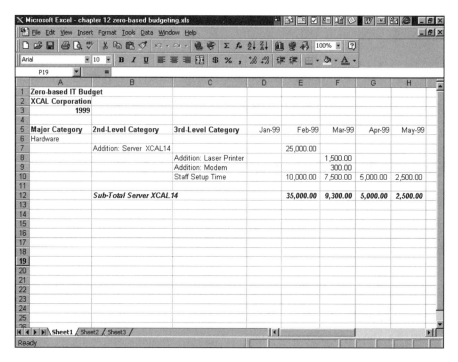

Figure 12-3: A zero-based budgeting example

Linear percent growth

This is the simplest and most popular way to create your IT budget. Here, you simply apply a growth factor to last year's budget. For example, you might say that you'll increase this year's IT budget by five percent across the board. That means that each expense category will simply grow by five percent. Call it overly simplistic, but it works and this method is used extensively.

Percent of revenue

This is how the accountants in your organization think. That is because industry ratios are widely published that compare IT expenses as a percentage of total revenues. For example, many believe that IT as a whole shouldn't exceed two percent of total revenue in the firm.

To use this method, first you would agree on a percent of revenue value. This consensus might be arrived at via the technology committee (I speak of technology committees in the next section) or the board of directors. Once that variable is selected, simply create a spreadsheet similar to Figure 12-4 and enter the Percent of Revenue variable.

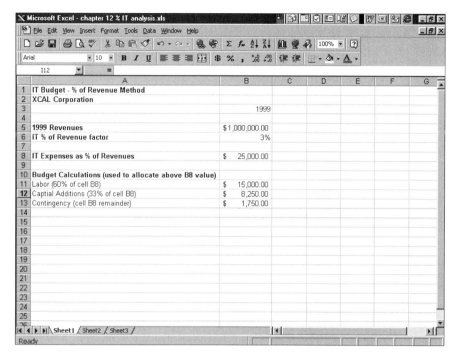

Figure 12-4: Budgeting via Percent of Revenue

Industry ratios that may be useful for your budgeting purposes are indeed widely reported. One of the best sources for this information is *Computerworld*, a weekly trade newspaper. Another great source is *CIO* magazine.

Windows NT Server on $5 a day

Closely related to the Windows NT Server network budgeting process is the "Windows NT Server on $5 a day" or marginal budgeting approach. Believe it or not, it is highly likely that you already understand this approach well. Remember the last time you purchased the car you drive? Did the salesperson attempt to "up sell" you into getting a better car stereo or seat warmers? Was the argument made that these additional features would only cost an additional $1.00 per day over the life of the car? (And wouldn't you enjoy that high-end stereo much more in traffic jams, all for just a $1/day?) The good news is you can apply the same reasoning to your Windows NT Server network!

Let's assume that you plan to amortize or recover the cost of your network software and hardware over 36 months, a reasonable recovery period. This is approximately 1,095 days. Now suppose you are considering the purchase of a Dell PowerEdge server that is dual-processor capable. You are currently unsure whether you intend to add a second processor to the server now or purchase one a few years down the road. You do realize that a second processor would provide immediate and significant benefits to the overall performance of your network. Consider the following.

A second server-class processor is approximately $1,000. And you expect to keep the server for three years (or approximately 1,095 days). This second processor effectively will cost you $1,000 / 1095 days = $0.92 per day (rounded up). That's 92 cents a day to keep everyone happier on your network! Seems like a good investment. And imagine how much more performance and reliability you could add to your network if you were willing to spend an additional (or marginal) $5.00 per day. Depending on your situation, perhaps that extra $5 a day would enable you to have a mirrored RAID array, something that is highly desirable in a production SQL Server environment.

Creating a Technology Committee

Early on in the life of your Windows NT Server network, it is essential that you create a technology committee, populated with key network stakeholders, that meets on a regular basis. I've enjoyed assisting many firms with the process and found a monthly meeting than a quarterly one (this area moves to quickly for a quarterly meeting). Stakeholders that sit on your technology committee include:

- **Executives.** This group, at the C-level (CEO, CIO, CFO, COO), has the ability to make valuable contributions about how technology fits into the mission of the overall organization. They also control the IT budget (something that shouldn't be lost on you).

- **Line managers.** This group is critical. It is from this group that your applications needs will be best identified including new features that would make the organization run more efficiently. Line managers are typically experts at their process, knowing more than you or I what they need out of the computer system.

- **End users.** Another critical group. These technology committee members can offer you insights on how the network is performing on a day-to-day basis. Can they print when they need to? Do they receive prompt attention from you or the help desk when problems occur? Do they trust the network? A great group of people with lots of important feedback for you.

- **Outside IT consultant.** An outside presence is a very meaningful addition to the technology committee. An outsider is typically innocent of the political shenanigans that occur internally in an organization. Outsiders offer that distant view so appreciated by senior management plus expertise gathered at other sites that can benefit you.

- **You.** Don't forget the role you have as the firm's Windows NT Server professional. Welcome to the table!

Secret

Consider having the outside IT consultant serve as the coordinator for the technology committee. When I've seen this process managed by in-house staff, it tends to fade and fall off the radar screen after several months. However, an outside IT consultant brings both the freshness and the motivation to keep the technology alive. The "motivation" I speak of means the billable hours that the outside IT consultant will bill to coordinate and serve on the technology committee. For an IT consultant, there is perhaps no greater motivator than the prospect of billable hours.

Because a picture is worth a thousand words, perhaps Figure 12-5 will enable you to "get it" when speaking of the technology committee. Our roles as Windows NT Server professionals isn't just hardware and software, but communicating with our stakeholders every step of the way.

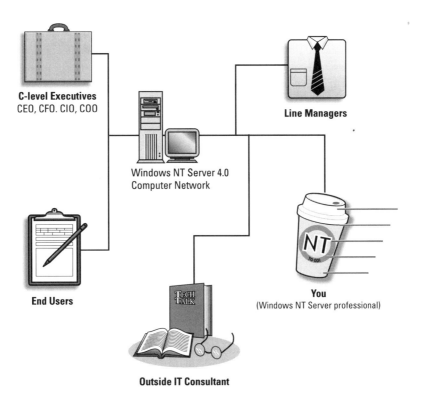

Figure 12-5: Technology committee membership

Issues addressed by the technology committee include, but are not limited, to the following:

- Budget versus actual expenditures
- Implementation schedules
- IT hiring decisions (in-house staff, consultants)
- Vendor selection (services, products, presentations)
- Network performance review (end user satisfaction surveys, network uptime reports, performance monitoring charts and analysis)

Evaluating Systems on the Horizon

One of the biggest frustrations of modern information technology work is the constant barrage of upgrades and enhancements that seem to come down the pike. Talk to anybody at a Windows NT conference, and they'll all say the same thing: Once you finally have that new office suite or e-mail system rolled out to your 10,000-user environment, there's no time to rest before starting work on integrating the product's next version. If you let it get to you, this frantic upgrade schedule can cause untold stress and grief. So what's a frazzled administrator to do?

The answer is simple: Exercise moderation. One of the reasons software vendors hit us with endless upgrades is the incredible competition they face, and the perceived great demand for these new versions. Who generates this perceived demand? Us! So stand up to them; go to your NT conference hotel room window, lean out, and shout, "We're mad as hell, and we're not going to take it anymore!" Seriously, the upgrade frenzy won't stop until the IT world in general learns to relax a bit and capitalize on their current systems. This phenomenon has already started taking root, thankfully, and should continue through the next couple of years.

The case of Windows 2000 Server

Let's take Windows 2000 Server as an example. When first announced, Microsoft projected that Windows 2000 Server would be out early in 1999. That release date has slipped back and slipped back, for two reasons. First, production and development realities at Microsoft have dictated the delay. More important, however, the market has made its desires known: We would rather wait longer and get a stable, advanced operating system than deal with a buggy, feature-poor "beta" release that requires two service packs before it's actually usable in the enterprise.

Given these factors, it is still important to spend time each month, quarter, or year looking at what's coming up, and determining whether you're going to implement it in your business. In some cases, there's no choice; support for older products simply disappears. However, this usually takes a long, long time after a new product comes out. As far as I know, Microsoft is still taking support calls for Windows NT 3.51 and will continue to do so for some time.

Two real-world examples

At my office, we completed a migration from Microsoft Mail to an Exchange Server based e-mail and groupware system several months ago. Our primary reason for doing this was that the text-based and decentralized nature of MS Mail post offices created an administrative nightmare for us, and our users were clamoring for the new features available in Exchange Server. When we began the project, the current version of Exchange Server was 5.0, so that's the system we went with. Now that all the users are on the system and things are running smoothly, we are beginning to evaluate the move to version 5.5. At this point, we haven't seen anything that would really push us over the edge as far as undertaking (and paying for!) an upgrade. Sure, there are many new and useful features in 5.5, plus a better back-end database, but at this point we haven't found any "gotta have it" features that would apply to our network. We also want to see what's coming down the pike in Exchange Server 6; we don't want to be upgrading our e-mail system more than once every couple of years. So we're going to play it cool for a while, keeping our existing Exchange Server 5.0 system on the latest service pack, and enjoying the calm between the migration storms.

At the same time we were doing the Exchange migration, our three-person network administration group was moving our 175 users from nine NetWare 3.12 servers to one central Windows NT 4.0 server. That migration was finished a few months ago as well, and now the users are working along every day, basically oblivious to the system that manages all of their files and printers. After a year of client and server conversions, we're enjoying this lull, believe me. We're also being very conservative about messing with our production systems; we haven't put Service Pack 4 on a single production box yet; we're waiting and watching the Internet forums carefully to see what kinds of problems might await us. We don't have an urgent need to move to SP4, so we're being rather conservative about it and will likely wait for the first round of hotfixes to come out before proceeding. We're also looking at Windows 2000 and what effect that will have on our network. However, we don't have plans to implement that system until at least six months after its release, so that puts us into second quarter 2000. There are plenty of other things to be done sooner, such as optimize our existing NT 4.0 network.

What do these examples have to do with your network? I'm hoping to convey that you don't have to jump on the latest operating system or application upgrade in order to have a successful, well-maintained system. Be aware of what's coming and start thinking about how to integrate it, but don't rush it. Unless the new system is ripe with features your users absolutely can't live without, they won't care what version they're on, as long as they can log on and work each day. Life on the bleeding edge can be fun and exciting, but it can also be painful for you and your users. So be open to the possibility of delaying upgrades a while. Take a few months, optimize your current systems so that they hum along perfectly, and enjoy the silence.

Remembering the Annual Planning Retreat

My favorite! But seriously folks, there are valid reasons for getting away each year for an annual planning retreat. It is critical that this be held off-site so that participants aren't distracted by the telephone, e-mail, pagers, and the like. It is here that budgets are made and better friendships between the business staff and the IT department are cultivated. It is at the annual planning retreat that the strategic vision for technology is cast.

Secret

Use the annual planning retreat to hear from your main technology vendors. Vendors such as Microsoft, Cisco, Oracle, Novell, and others will be happy to send a sales engineer to your retreat, for free, to educate you on their existing and forthcoming solutions. To arrange for such presentations, just call your account representative at the vendor of your choice.

And don't forget that the annual retreat is a chance for you to both show off your successes and receive accolades for a job well done as a Windows NT Server professional.

Summary

In addition to daily administration, Windows NT networks require monthly and annual attention to continue running smoothly and to keep up with the technology that users demand. In this chapter, I covered some of these monthly and yearly tasks:

- Auditing your network
- Reviewing security
- Performance benchmarking and monitoring
- The monthly reboot
- Mapping disk space on servers
- Disaster recovery simulation
- Implementing operating system service packs and hotfixes
- Creating month-end or quarterly archives
- Implementing network application upgrades
- Annual budgeting for your network
- Having an active technology committee
- Evaluating systems on the horizon
- The annual planning retreat

Part IV

Service Pack 4.0 and the Windows NT Server Option Pack

Chapter 13: Windows NT 4.0 Option Pack

Chapter 14: History and Role of Service Packs

Chapter 15: Service Pack 4 Fixes

Chapter 16: Service Pack 4 Additions and Miscellaneous

Chapter 13

Windows NT 4.0 Option Pack

In This Chapter

- Introduction to Windows NT Option Pack
- Installation and troubleshooting
- Internet components
- Administration and management
- Transaction processing
- Miscellaneous components

This chapter introduces the various applications and server components contained in the Windows NT Option Pack. You've probably worked with Microsoft option packs in the past. As you may know, option packs are different from service packs. Service packs often fix bugs and perhaps introduce new features. Option packs introduce new features and functionality. One example of this is at the desktop level. In the Windows 95 days, the release of the Windows 95 operating system in August 1995 was quickly followed by the release of the Windows 95 Option Pack. In this case, Windows 95 introduced additional features oriented to the end user such as screen savers, sounds, and games. Contrast that with Service Pack 1 and various hot fixes for Windows 95, which were bug-fix oriented.

The Windows NT Option Pack is positioned both to offer you additional features extending your use of Windows NT and to atone for Microsoft's sins in being so late with Windows 2000 Server. In other words, the Option Pack, in part, fills that transition from Windows NT Server 4.0 to Windows 2000 Server. That's an important paradigm to keep in mind as your work through this chapter.

Introduction to the Windows NT Option Pack

Microsoft delivered a significant product to the NT world when they released the Windows NT Option Pack. The collection of programs covers numerous topics. Some of them are new to NT, and others are significant upgrades to existing components. They generally fall into three categories: Internet components, administration and management, and transaction processing.

With the release of the software, Microsoft also announced that the Windows NT Option Pack was considered an "official" extension to NT. This means that Microsoft provides full support of the Option Pack and any of its components.

The major components included in the Windows NT 4.0 Option Kit are:

- Internet components
  - Internet Information Server (IIS) 4.0
  - Certificate Server 1.0
  - Index Server 2.0
  - Internet Connections Services for RAS 1.0
- Administration and management components
  - Microsoft Management Console (MMC) 1.0
  - Site Server Express 2.0
  - Windows Scripting Host
- Transaction processing components
  - Microsoft Transaction Server (MTS) 2.0
  - Microsoft Message Queue (MSMQ) Server 1.0
- Miscellaneous components
  - Microsoft Data Access Components (MDAC) 1.5b
  - Microsoft Script Debugger

Installation and Troubleshooting

The Option Kit is available for download from Microsoft as an 80MB file. Installation from the CD version is much easier and much quicker. Obtaining and installing from the CD is recommended.

As tempting as it is to insert the CD into the drive and start installing the software immediately, do yourself a favor and take the time to review the release notes. Make sure that you read the preinstallation requirements very carefully. Some components in the Option Kit contain critical dependencies and require parameters that must be determined before installation time. For example, the Microsoft Message Queue Server requires SQL Server 6.5 prior to installation.

Microsoft has developed checklists for the general requirements of the Option Pack. It is recommended that you follow these checklists carefully. The basic requirements for software are:

- Windows NT Server 4.0 or later
- Service Pack 3 or later
- Internet Explorer 4.01 or later

Many Windows NT Server professionals install onto an NTFS partition. For ease of use and ease of recovery in an emergency, some administrators use FAT partitions for the operating system or boot partition. Others prefer the additional control for security and auditing that NTFS allows. You will recall from Chapter 2, "Planning, Setup, and Installation," that this is a topic of great debate, and I'm sure you have an opinion to weigh in as well. You will be interested to note that the NTFS versus FAT issue is discussed again in Chapter 20, "Windows NT Server — Small Business Server" (where NTFS must be used).

Secret

Always install the IIS root directory on an NTFS-partitioned drive. IIS will attempt to set file and directory security permissions that are only available on NTFS.

It is always a good idea to heed the standard Microsoft warning and stop any applications before installing the software. If an ODBC connection is in use, stop the application that is using it. I always make it a habit to stop both the Index Server and the Certificate Server (if running) before installing any NT Option Pack components. To stop these services, use Services, the Control Panel applet, and select the appropriate services to stop.

To begin installation, insert the CD into the drive and the page shown in Figure 13-1 should appear. If you've met the basic requirements and wish to start the setup program, double-click SETUP.EXE on the CD.

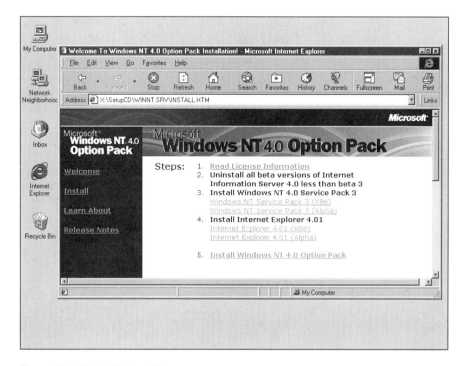

Figure 13-1: The initial installation screen

The NT Option Kit requires Service Pack 3. Install SP3, if necessary. If you've jumped ahead and installed Service Pack 4 (SP4), you'll receive the warning message shown in Figure 13-2. (In fact, you may see it twice!) You can safely ignore this message and click Yes to continue with the installation.

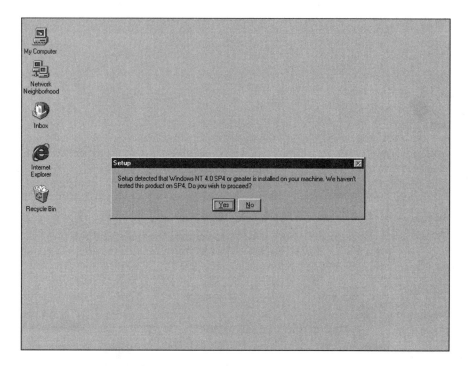

Figure 13-2: Service Pack 4 warning message

Secret

Always remember to reapply the most recent service pack after installing any Option Pack components.

Eventually, the greeting screen in Figure 13-3 appears and you can click Next to continue to the Add/Remove window. The Add/Remove window, plainly speaking, enables you to install all or part of the Windows NT Option Pack, or if you so desire, to remove the Option Pack.

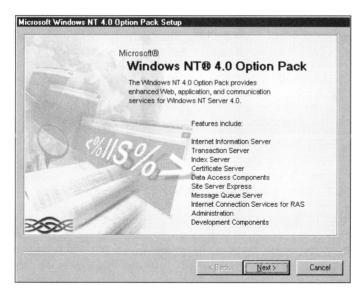

Figure 13-3: Windows NT 4.0 Option Pack Setup

After responding to the Add/Remove dialog box, if you are installing the Option Pack for the first time, you will have the opportunity to choose Upgrade Only or Upgrade Plus. Choose the appropriate option. Next, you will see the Select Components window (see Figure 13-4).

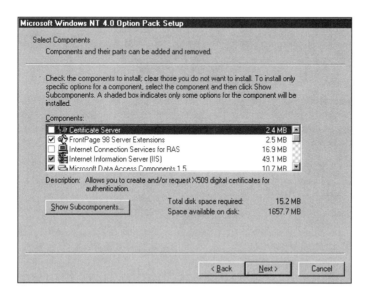

Figure 13-4: Select components

Carefully select the components and subcomponents to install. I prefer to go into each component and select the documentation files to be copied. If the documentation is available somewhere else, this step is not necessary. But on the other hand, if you're worried about not having enough room to install the documentation, then you're probably not a good candidate for installing the Option Pack (with today's low prices on mass storage, installing the documentation should never be a problem). Once the Next button is clicked, the installation application will start copying the files.

Later on, once you're using and enjoying the Option Pack, should you decide to add or remove any Option Pack components, click Start on the desktop taskbar of your Windows NT Server machine, go to Programs ⇨ Microsoft Windows NT Option Pack, and click Option Pack Setup. Select any items that you wish to install and uncheck any items that you wish to remove. Click Remove All to uninstall all the Option Pack components. Some directories and files may remain after the removal. You need to manually delete these files. For a complete list of directories and files that need to be removed manually, refer to the documentation Readme files.

If you are running the setup program from Internet Explorer, you may get an error message that the publisher cannot be determined (see Figure 13-5). This is normal. Setup.exe is a 16-bit program and can't be digitally signed. Note that the reference at the top of the dialog box refers to the source drive for the Option Pack setup files. If you are successful in your setup, you will receive a Finish dialog box (which seems to be in favor these days with developers who are writing setup wizards). Simply click Finish and reboot your Windows NT Server machine.

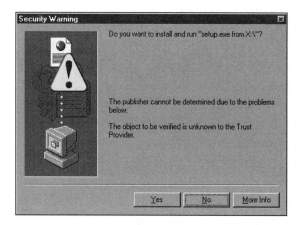

Figure 13-5: Security warning

If you reinstall Service Pack 3 after IIS 4.0 is installed, do not overwrite the newer files that were installed by the IIS installation.

Internet Applications

It would be an understatement to say that Microsoft responded to the Internet threat to Windows NT Server with its Option Pack release. In many respects, that is exactly what happened; the Option Pack makes Windows NT Server more Internet-ready. Thus the huge focus in the Option Pack on the Internet-related applications. This section discusses one of the core applications in Windows NT Server today, Internet Information Server (IIS) 4.0. Other Internet applications including Certificate Server, Index Server 2.0, and Internet Connection Services for RAS are also discussed.

Internet Information Server (IIS) 4.0

IIS 4.0 includes numerous new features, enhancements, and improvements over previous versions. It is HTTP 1.1 compliant, it offers per–Web site bandwidth throttling, it provides configuration backup and replication, and it contains many new features. IIS 4.0 provides new application services such as transactional active server pages using Microsoft Transaction Server and integrated message queuing using Microsoft Message Queue Server. The ability to run scripts within the context of a transaction is very powerful and improves the data handling capability of IIS. Integrated message queuing allows the creation of distributed Web-based applications running under IIS.

IIS 4.0 also features improved Web services. Multiple Web sites can be hosted on a single server, and they can be totally isolated from each other. If a single Web site has problems, the others can continue processing Web requests unhindered.

IIS administrators and developers have been given extensive control over the management of the Web site, security, custom error processing, additional logging options, indexing, and individualized content ratings.

Configuration and Setup

After installation of IIS with the Option Pack, it may be managed via the new Microsoft Management Console (MMC). MMC is the key component in the Microsoft's management strategy and is covered more extensively later in this chapter. You may launch the MMC by typing **MMC** at the command prompt. You would then add in the IIS 4.0 management console window, the result being displayed in Figure 13-6.

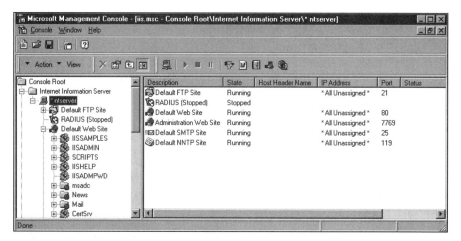

Figure 13-6: IIS Management Console window

While highlighting the server, right-click and select the properties for the server. This is the location for the Master Properties (that is, the default properties) for all sites contained on the server for both Web and FTP services (see Figure 13-7). In addition to the Master Properties parameters, the overall bandwidth throttling setting and default MIME types are configured in this screen.

Figure 13-7: Master Properties window

All Properties sheets work in a hierarchical manner. That is, if you set a property item on a top-level screen, the lower levels will inherit the value.

Web Site tab

When you select the Default Web Site tab sheet and bring up the Properties window, you'll see nine different configuration tabs, as shown in Figure 13-8.

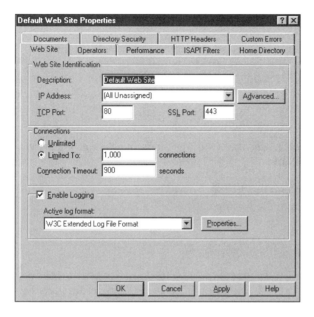

Figure 13-8: Default Web Site Properties

The configuration tabs are:

- **Web Site.** Identification, connections, and logging options
- **Operators.** Granting operator privileges
- **Performance.** Performance tuning and bandwidth throttling
- **ISAPI Filters.** Executable program configuration
- **Home Directory.** Configuration, permissions, and application settings
- **Documents.** Default document settings and footers
- **Directory Security.** Access control settings
- **HTTP Headers.** Content, HTTP headers, and MIME settings
- **Custom Errors.** Custom error handling

The Web Site tab configures the general properties of the Web site. It enables you to enter the Web site identification (descriptive name of the Web site), the IP address, and the TCP port number. If multiple IP addresses are required, they are set by clicking the Advanced button. The number of connections limit and the connection timeout are also enter on this screen. Figure 13-8 shows the default Web site configured for limited connections and with a Secure Sockets Layer (SSL) port enabled.

Secret

The default TCP Port number is 80, but during the installation process, IIS 4.0 will pick a random number for the TCP Port for the "Administration Web Site." When connecting to this Web site, you must supply the TCP port number in the format "http://<server name>:<TCP Port>/iis.asp." This is a security feature that prevents unauthorized users from accessing the administrative portion of your site.

Connections may be unlimited or limited to a specific number of users. I prefer to set the limit based on bandwidth or other conditions, but it is entirely optional. Limiting the number of connections improves your overall system performance from the perspective of the user. You may also modify the connection timeout limit. Fifteen minutes (900 seconds) is the default and is somewhat high in my opinion.

IIS 4.0 allows multiple formats and methods of logging. The following logging options are available:

- Microsoft IIS log file format
- NCSA Common log file format
- ODBC logging
- W3C Extended log file format

Each file method of logging allows the frequency selection of daily, weekly, and monthly, as well as unlimited file size or a maximum file size. The default location for the log files is %SystemRoot%\System32\LogFiles.

The W3C Extended Log File Format additionally allows the selection of various parameters via the Extended Logging Properties tab (see Figure 13-9). Individual page logging can be selectively turned on or off on the General Properties tab sheet in the Extended Logging Properties dialog box. This option reduces the size of the log and makes it easier to track usage.

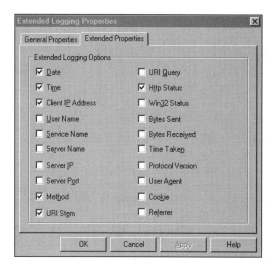

Figure 13-9: Extended Logging Properties

Operators tab

The Operators tab allows entry of additional users, who can be granted operator privileges (see Figure 13-10). The default user is the Administrator.

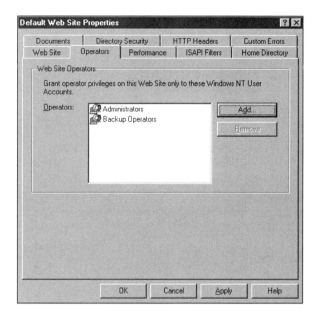

Figure 13-10: Operators tab

Performance tab

The Performance tab includes a tuning option based on expected Web hits per day, bandwidth throttling, and a connection configuration option for enabling keep-alives, all shown in Figure 13-11.

Depending on the setting of the tuning option, Fewer than 10,000, Fewer than 100,000, or More than 100,000, IIS allocates memory for its operation. After monitoring the site and determining the average connections, adjust this parameter for optimum resource usage.

Bandwidth throttling allows IIS traffic to use only a portion of the network connection. This feature is very handy when your network connection is being used for other things besides IIS. If the connection is used for mail traffic, virtual private networking (VPN), or any other applications, make sure that IIS does not consume all available bandwidth.

Always check the HTTP Keep-Alives Enabled option. This allows IIS to keep an HTTP connection for a user and not create a new connection for every client request.

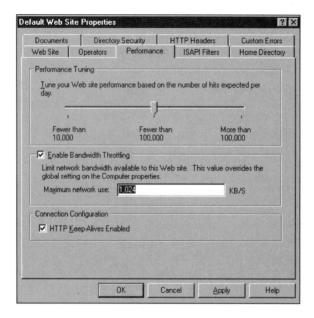

Figure 13-11: Performance tab

ISAPI Filters tab

ISAPI Filters enables entry of programs that will reside in memory and be called when the Web server receives a request (see Figure 13-12). ISAPI Filters can be installed for all sites or just for individual sites. Global ISAPI Filters are set in the Master Properties sheet.

To add a new filter, click Add and browse or enter the program name and physical location of the file.

Secret

The Microsoft IIS Log format and the W3C Extended log format require ISAPI filters for complete log reporting capabilities within the Site Server Express 2.0 component. These DLL filters are not distributed with the Option Pack but must be downloaded from the Microsoft Web site. See the "Site Server Express 2.0" section for how to obtain them.

Home Directory tab

The Home Directory tab enables entry of multiple options concerning the home directory for the Web site. As shown in Figure 13-13, the default location is "C:\InetPub\wwwroot." My preference is to decline the default location and move the directory to another physical drive. When I configure production servers, I keep the operating system files, applications, and data very distinct and separate. This allows me to back up and restore any part of the server more efficiently and quickly. If the Web site is located on a separate drive, I can use a backup server to host the site temporarily, while I rebuild the main server, if needed.

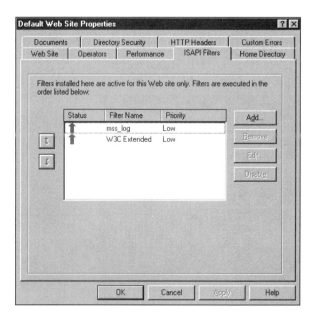

Figure 13-12: ISAPI Filters

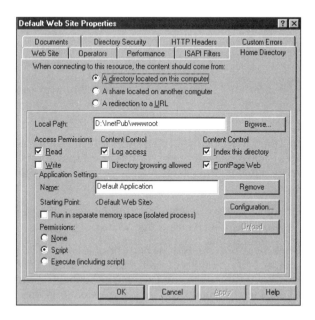

Figure 13-13: Home Directory

The content of the default site can be set to come from a physical directory on the local computer, a remote share point on another computer, or a URL redirection (see Figure 13-14). The subdirectory and the network share option have similar parameters associated with them.

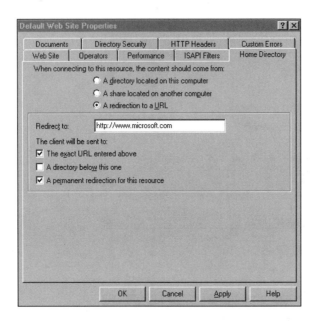

Figure 13-14: URL redirection

The URL option requires entry of the URL address and how the user will be sent to the remote server. The user can be sent to the exact URL, to a subdirectory below the listed URL, or to some permanent redirection.

Back at the Home Directory (Figure 13-13), access permissions and content control for the files located within the home directory may be set. Verify the requirements before allowing the client to write or browse any directory. By enabling these options, you may run a security risk.

Index Server will index the Web site if Index This Directory is set. To create a FrontPage Web for this site, check FrontPage Web.

The Application Settings area is a new and powerful feature of IIS 4.0. An application is a defined group of directories and files within the Web site. By setting the Starting Point directory, you can set the scope of the application. Clicking the Configuration button brings up the Application Configuration window shown in Figure 13-15. Here you can configure the application. The window contains tabs for App Mappings, App Options, and App Debugging.

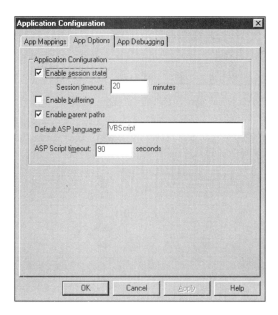

Figure 13-15: Application Configuration

Documents tab

The Documents tab shown in Figure 13-16 enables you to set the default document and to enter a document footer. This may be a copyright or trademark notice or any other information that will be displayed on each page.

Directory Security tab

The Directory Security tab enables you to set up Anonymous Access and Authentication Control, Secure Communications, and IP Address and Domain Name Restrictions. During installation of IIS 4.0, a local anonymous guest user account was created. This account by default is named "IUSR_<computer name>" and is used when anonymous access is allowed.

The Edit button in the Anonymous Access and Authentication Control section enables you to change that account and the password associated with it. Be very careful when changing password or security settings. You may inadvertently modify parameters that adversely affect your users and not allow them into your site.

If anonymous access is not allowed, there are two options. You may use Basic Authentication and Windows NT Challenge/Response. Both use NTFS access controls lists for determining permissions. Basic authentication will send passwords in clear text. This may result in a security risk.

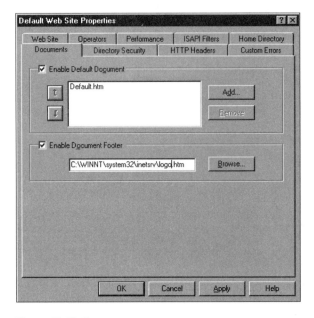

Figure 13-16: Documents

The Secure Communications button brings up the Key Manager. Key Manager is a part of the Certificate Server and will be discussed in another section.

The last option in this tab is the IP Address and Domain Name Restrictions (see Figure 13-17). This powerful option enables you to restrict or allow specific classes of users based on their IP address or domain name.

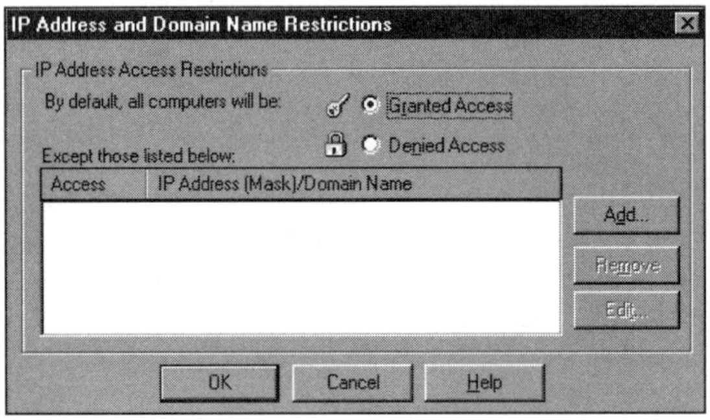

Figure 13-17: IP Address and Domain Name Restrictions

HTTP Headers tab

The HTTP Headers tab sets the values returned to the client in the HTML header. You can add information such as content expiration dates, custom header information, content ratings, or Multipurpose Internet Mail Extensions (MIME) types (see Figure 13-18).

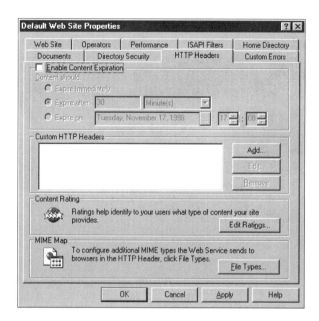

Figure 13-18: HTTP Headers window

The Content Expiration date instructs the browser to compare the current date to the expiration date and if necessary request an updated page from the server.

Custom HTTP headers may be added or the Platform for Internet Content Selection (PICS) rating may be set. This rating system, shown in Figure 13-19, was developed by the Recreational Software Advisory Council (RSAC).

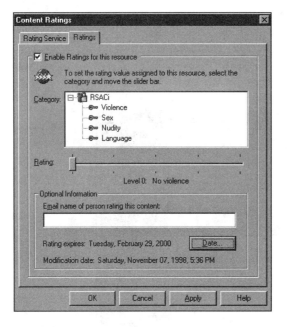

Figure 13-19: Content Ratings

Voluntary ratings for violence, sex, nudity, and language may be set for the Web site as well as each page on the site. Different levels for each category are set. The following levels are available:

- Violence
    - Level 0: No violence
    - Level 1: Fighting
    - Level 2: Killing
    - Level 3: Killing with blood and gore
    - Level 4: Wanton and gratuitous violence
- Sex
    - Level 0: None
    - Level 1: Passionate kissing
    - Level 2: Clothed sexual touching
    - Level 3: Nonexplicit sexual touching
    - Level 4: Explicit sexual activity

- Nudity
  - Level 0: None
  - Level 1: Revealing attire
  - Level 2: Partial nudity
  - Level 3: Frontal nudity
  - Level 4: Provocative frontal nudity
- Language
  - Level 0: None
  - Level 1: Mild expletives
  - Level 2: Moderate expletives
  - Level 3: Obscene gestures
  - Level 4: Explicit or crude language

An optional item is the e-mail address of the person rating this content. For more information, contact the Recreational Software Advisory Council at `www.rsac.org`.

You will also note the MIME Map option on the HTTP Headers dialog box. If your server provides files that are in multiple formats, your IIS server must have a Multipurpose Internet Mail Extension (MIME) mapping for each file type you anticipate working with. If MIME mapping on the server is not set up for a certain file type, Web browsers may be prevented from retrieving the unsupported file.

Custom Errors tab

The final tab, Custom Errors (Figure 13-20), allows entry of custom error handling. Errors returned by the server can be an HTML file or an URL. This powerful feature allows the addition of intelligently processing any user problems or server errors.

IIS Administration

Ongoing administration is a paramount set of duties in a networked environment, and IIS is no exception. Fortunately, IIS offers several tools to make short order of your administration duties. These are backup and restore, a New Web Site Wizard, and a New Virtual Directory Wizard.

Backup and Restore

IIS 4.0 allows the operator to back up and restore any Web site configuration data. Start the Microsoft Management Console and highlight the IIS server. Right-click and select the Backup/Restore Configuration menu choice (see Figure 13-21).

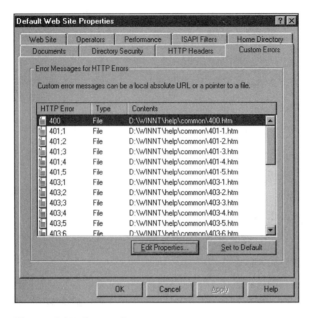

Figure 13-20: Custom Errors

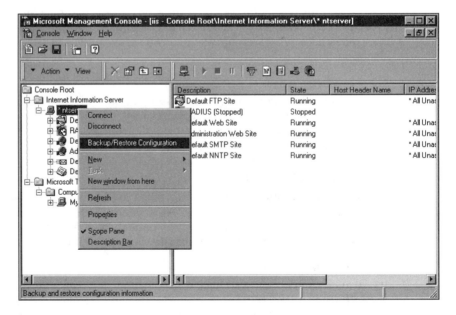

Figure 13-21: Backup/Restore Configuration Selection

This brings up the console window shown in Figure 13-22 to manage previous backups.

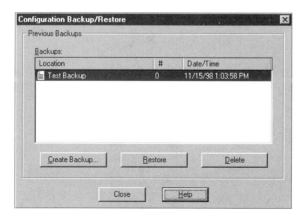

Figure 13-22: Configuration Backup/Restore Console Window

Select Create Backup and enter the name of the backup set. This records the name, the version number, and the date the backup was made. To restore, simply highlight the backup and click Restore.

Note

Restoring configurations requires that all services be stopped and restarted. This may affect all other Web sites on the server.

New Web Site Wizard

The New Web Site Wizard makes it very easy to create a new Web site and to set some of the initial parameters for the site. From the MMC, select the IIS server, right-click, and select New ⇨ Web Site. This brings up the New Web Site Wizard (see Figure 13-23).

Figure 13-23: The New Web Site Wizard

Enter the name for the Web site and click Next. You'll see the Web Site Parameters window shown in Figure 13-24.

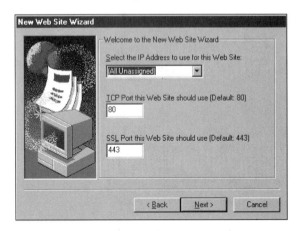

Figure 13-24: Web Site Parameters

Select the IP addresses to use, the TCP port, and the SSL port (if you use SSL) and click Next. The Web Site Home Directory window will appear (see Figure 13-25).

Figure 13-25: Web Site Home Directory

Enter the path name of the Web site and enter a check in the check box to allow anonymous access, or leave it blank. Click Next to see the Access Permissions window shown in Figure 13-26.

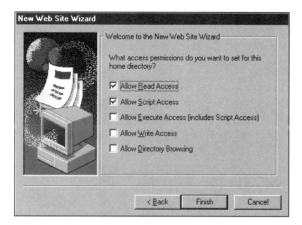

Figure 13-26: Web Site Permissions

After you have assigned user permissions, click Finish and your new Web site is listed in the MMC directory structure. The new Web site will not be running. More than likely, additional parameters will need to be set. If problems exist, you may receive an error message.

Resolve any conflicts, start the Web site, and you've got a brand new site in just minutes.

New Virtual Directory Wizard

The New Virtual Directory Wizard is very similar to the New Web Site Wizard. Enter an alias for the virtual directory. The alias shouldn't contain spaces. It will allow it, but your users will have problems accessing the Web page.

Enter the physical location of the directory with the HTML documents and click Next.

Set the appropriate permissions for read, write, browse, scripts, and execute. Click Finish and you've successfully created a new virtual directory.

FTP Site

The FTP Site server works very similar to the Web Site server. IIS installs a default site during installation. If you start MMC and right-click the Default FTP site, you'll see a configuration window similar to that for the Web Site server (see Figure 13-27).

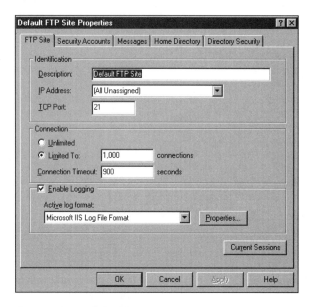

Figure 13-27: FTP Site Properties

The properties may be similar, but the default values are different in some items. For example, the default value is for a limit of 1,000 connections.

The FTP Server also allows multiple formats and methods of logging. The following logging options are available:

- Microsoft IIS log file format
- ODBC logging
- W3C Extended log file format

You may also view the current connections to the FTP Server by clicking the Current Sessions button. This brings up a window listing the connections.

Security Accounts tab

The Security Accounts tab (see Figure 13-28) determines the state of the anonymous user connection. If the option is clicked, anonymous users are allowed under the context of the IUSR_<server name> account.

Figure 13-28: Security Accounts

FTP does not allow any NT authentication methods, and if the anonymous user option is deselected, you will receive a warning message pertaining to clear text passwords (see Figure 13-29).

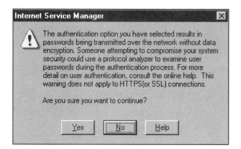

Figure 13-29: Security Warning

If this is acceptable, then click Yes. Back at the Security Accounts tab, the Automatic Password Synchronization check box should remain enabled. If not, problems can arise if this account password should change.

Messages tab

The Messages tab enables you to enter the FTP Greeting Message for your site (see the example in Figure 13-30). Your message should be clear, concise, and instructive for your users. Be careful about giving too much information. FTP greetings may be a security risk when hackers may be looking for user account names, computer names, or general information that may compromise your system.

Figure 13-30: FTP Messages

Home Directory tab

The Home Directory (see Figure 13-31) enables you to specify the physical location of your FTP site or a remote directory. You may also specify whether the files will be presented in UNIX or Microsoft format.

Directory Security tab

The Directory Security tab (Figure 13-32) enables you to grant or exclude specific systems from your FTP site.

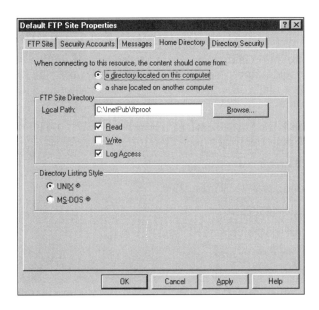

Figure 13-31: FTP Home Directory

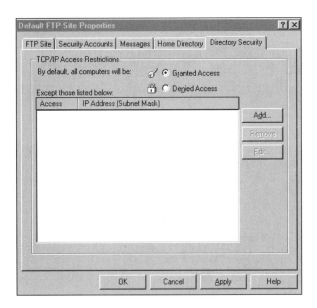

Figure 13-32: Directory Security

Simple Mail Transport Protocol (SMTP) Service

The Microsoft SMTP Service is an outbound mailer for mail-enabled hosts. A common misconception is that the service provides capabilities similar to Microsoft Exchange. It doesn't provide any POP3 or IMAP4 client mailboxes. It does exchange e-mail with other SMTP hosts and accept mail into a single local drop box.

During installation, the SMTP Service creates five directories off the default C:\InetPub\Mailroot directory. Those directories are:

- **Badmail.** All undeliverable mail
- **Drop.** Incoming mail for IIS domains
- **Pickup.** Outgoing messages
- **Queue.** All messages being delivered
- **SortTemp.** Temporary storage

Secret

SMTP Service can upgrade a Microsoft Commercial Internet System (MCIS) Mail Server. You must uninstall the MCIS Mail Server before installing the SMTP Service.

The SMTP Service can be administered in the MMC or via a Web interface. Select the SMTP Host and right-click to select the Properties menu shown in Figure 13-33.

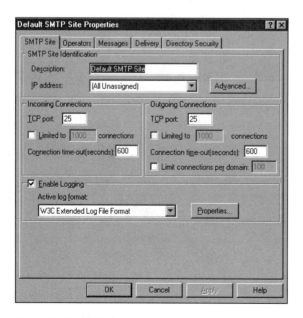

Figure 13-33: SMTP Properties

The SMTP Properties window includes access to tabs for SMTP Site, Operators, Messages, Delivery, and Directory Security:

- The SMTP Site tab contains the description, the IP address, incoming and outgoing TCP ports, connection limits and timeouts, and the logging format.
- The Operator tab allows entry of additional operators for the site.
- The Messages tab sets the message size limit, the maximum number of messages per connection, and the maximum number of recipients per message.

  A copy of a nondelivery report (NDR) may be sent to an e-mail recipient. This is a good administrative item. If it is set up properly, you'll be able to identify problems and solve them rapidly.

  The final entry in this tab is the location of the Badmail directory. The default is C:\InetPub\Mailroot\Badmail.

- The Delivery tab shown in Figure 13-34 controls the local and remote queue retry count and interval and the maximum hop count. The masquerade domain is the name that will be inserted into the FROM field on the user's e-mail interface. The e-mail message will appear to be from this domain. The fully qualified domain name (FQDN) is the name of the server and domain.

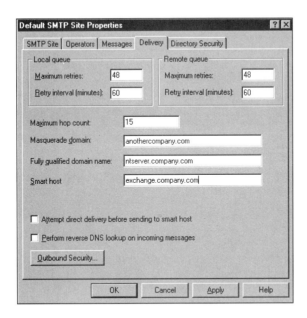

Figure 13-34: The Delivery tab

The Smart Host is another SMTP relay site that can forward e-mail on to the destination. The MS SMTP server may not have a direct connection to the outside world, but the Smart Host does and can provide relay services. Attempt Direct Delivery is akin to a lovesick mate (haven't we all been there?) who doesn't want to communicate through an intermediary but directly with the person of one's affections first. That's what the Attempt Direct Delivery check box is all about. First it tries a direct delivery path, and then it uses a relay site.

The Perform Reverse DNS Lookup option tells the system to try to look up the domain name in the From field in incoming messages and determine if the IP address matches. This security feature causes considerable overhead and should be used only if you are concerned about spoofed mail.

Outbound Security sets the method, type, and account of the SMTP authentication process. The default is no authentication. If you use clear text or Windows NT Challenge/Response, you will have to supply an account and password. You may also enable Transport Layer Security (TLS) encryption.

- The Directory Security tab (see Figure 13-35) is similar to IIS Directory Security with the exception of an extra option for relay restrictions. As with the IIS Directory Security window, it contains options for Anonymous Access and Authentication Control, Secure Communications, and the IP Address and Domain Name Restrictions. The Relay Restrictions screen restricts users from using the SMTP Service as a relay service. This prevents your site from being used by outside e-mail clients in an attempt to disguise the origin of the e-mail. By default, Relay Restrictions are in effect.

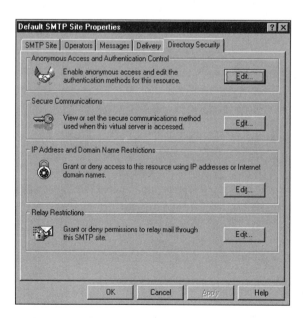

Figure 13-35: Directory Security

Network News Transport Protocol (NNTP) Service

The Microsoft NNTP is a discussion group hosting service for small, single-server installations. It cannot receive or send messages from or to a Usenet group. The internal clients that access the newsgroups may be any NNTP-compliant program such as the Microsoft Internet Mail and News client. Despite the limitations, it is a very handy service.

The NNTP Service is managed by the MMC or via a Web interface. The same methods and processes are used to maintain and administer NNTP as IIS and SMTP. Several tabs are available for configuring the NNTP service:

- The News Site tab (see Figure 13-36) allows for entry of the site description, the path header, the IP address, and TCP/SSL ports. You may also set the number of connections and the logging options.

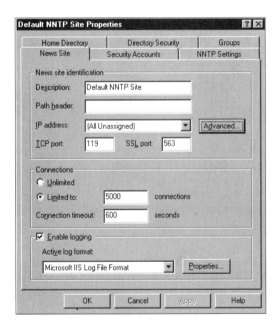

Figure 13-36: News Site

- The Security Accounts tab (Figure 13-37) sets the account used for any anonymous users. By default, it is "IUSR_<server name>." The News Site Operators are also set here.

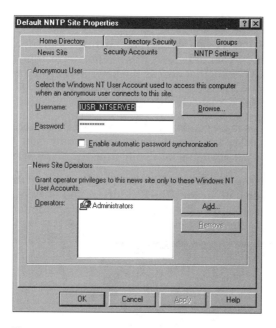

Figure 13-37: Security Accounts

- The NNTP Settings tab (Figure 13-38) controls if and where clients may post messages. It sets limits on post size and connection size. You can enable other servers to pull news articles, allow control messages, set an SMTP server for moderated groups, set the default moderator domain, and set the administrator e-mail.

Secret

The Administrator e-mail account will get all the nondelivery reports (NDRs) for any posting that cannot be delivered. To enable this option, you must create a Registry entry. Create a DWORD value named MailFromHeader in HKEY_LOCAL_MACHINE\SYSTEM\CurrentControlSet\Services\NntpSvc\Parameters\ and assign a value of "1."

- The Home Directory tab, shown in Figure 13-39, sets the default local content path. It also sets access restrictions for posting and newsgroup visibility. I'm not exactly sure of the differences between the Home Directory posting parameter and the similar one in the NNTP Settings tab. I always make sure both are checked.

- The Secure Communications and the Directory Security tab are the very familiar SSL configuration screens. Again, I'm not exactly sure why the Secure Communications button is not located in the Directory Security tab. It would probably make too much sense.

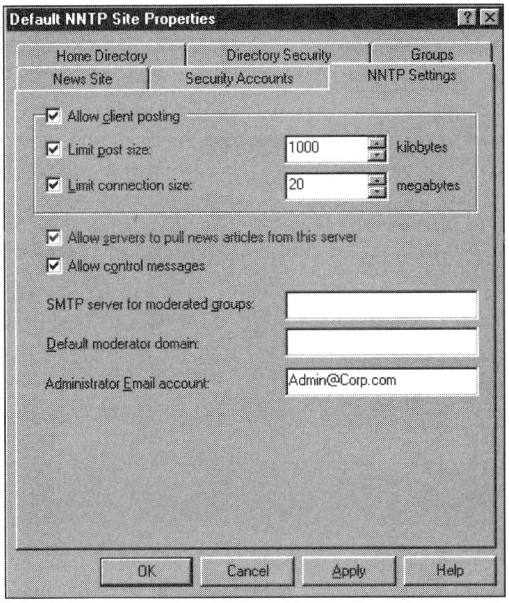

Figure 13-38: NNTP Settings

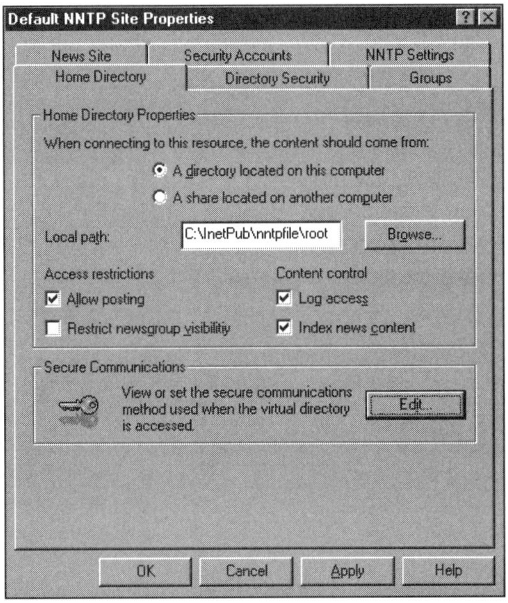

Figure 13-39: Home Directory

- The Groups tab (Figure 13-40) is where you create and manage the newsgroups. Click Create New Newsgroup to bring up the newsgroup screen.

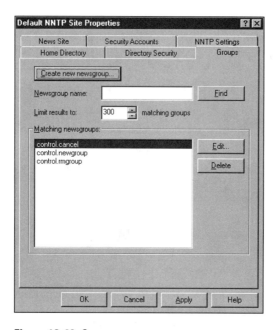

Figure 13-40: Groups

In the newsgroup Properties screen (Figure 13-41), add the newsgroup name in the format that you desire. Then add a description and a "Newgroup prettyname" (the typo is Microsoft's) and whether the newsgroup is read only. Finally, you can set the moderated options.

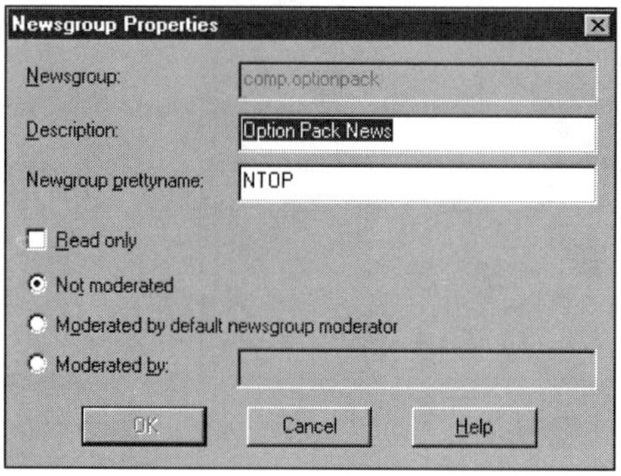

Figure 13-41: Newsgroup Properties

Secret

When using the Newsgroup prettyname feature, some NNTP clients can return Unicode characters. If you support international users, you can include Unicode characters in this field.

After a newsgroup has been defined, a directory for local storage of the messages is required. In the MMC (see Figure 13-6 earlier in this chapter), highlight the Directories item under the Default NNTP Site (found under the default News object in the MMC's left pane) and select New ⇨ Virtual Directory. You'll see the New Virtual Directory Wizard screen shown in Figure 13-42.

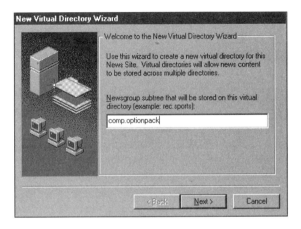

Figure 13-42: NNTP Virtual Directory Wizard

Enter the name of the newsgroup and click Next. The screen shown in Figure 13-43 will appear. Type in the location of the directory and click Finish. A new newsgroup has been defined.

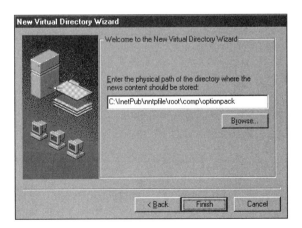

Figure 13-43: NNTP Virtual Directory Path

The final administrative task for the NNTP is setting expiration policies. The New Expiration Policy Wizard, launched by highlighting Expiration Policies and selecting New ⇨ Expiration Policy, enables you to configure the automatic aging of the newsgroups and prevents them from growing unmanageably. The New Expiration Policy Wizard is seen in Figure 13-44.

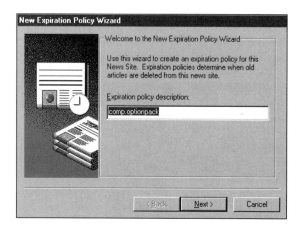

Figure 13-44: Expiration Policy Wizard

Type the name of the new policy and click Next. The screen shown in Figure 13-45 will appear. Choose either All Newsgroups or Only Selected Newsgroups. Click Next.

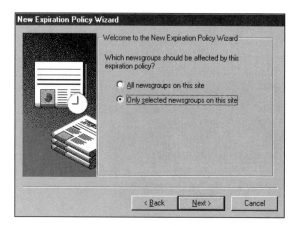

Figure 13-45: Newsgroup policy

When the screen shown in Figure 13-46 appears, define a wildcard entry to select a set of newsgroups. One such wildcard pattern that you could enter might be alt*.* for all of the alternative newsgroups. Remember that wildcards in the computer world are really open-ended queries. Hey — did you already forget from your dearly departed MS-DOS days that *.* meant "everything"?

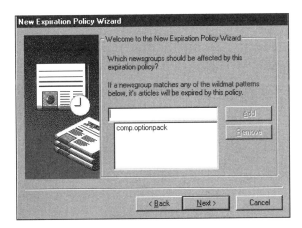

Figure 13-46: Newsgroup wildcard

Finally, select the time and/or the hard drive space quota for the group of newsgroups as seen in Figure 13-47. Click Finish and the policy is added to the NNTP Service. The newly defined newsgroup will run automatically with minimal administrative support.

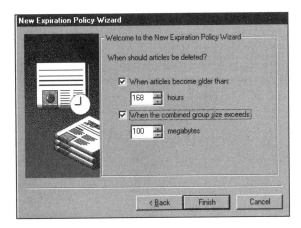

Figure 13-47: Newsgroup aging

Certificate Server 1.0

Certificate Server 1.0 is a server-based application that manages and administers industry-standard X.509 digital certificates. A *digital certificate* is used as a mechanism to prove the identity of users and the authority of servers. An administrator can set up certificate authorities and issue, renew, or revoke certificates to individual users. Those same users can be mapped to a specific NT user account and be allowed access to network resources based on rules that correspond to fields within the digital certificate.

Digital certificates rely on the concept of public and private key encryption. To encrypt any message or text, the sender will use the public key of the recipient and his or her own private key. At the other end, the recipient will decode the message with the public key of the sender and his or her own private key. In this manner, digital certificates act as a method to ensure the identity of the sender by issuing their private key and verifying their public key. The controlling authority for this is the certificate authority (CA).

Certificate processes

The first step in establishing a certificate for your server is requesting it from a certificate authority (CA). The CA takes the request, processes it, and returns it to you for installation on your server. Normally, a CA is a trusted authority like Verisign that has a good reputation. In essence, they are "vouching" for you. Since Certificate Server has the capability to process certificate requests, you can use your own server to vouch for you.

STEPS:

To establish a certificate for your server

Step 1. Start up the Key Manager by clicking the Key Manager icon in the toolbar in the MMC window. This starts the Key Manager session shown in Figure 13-48.

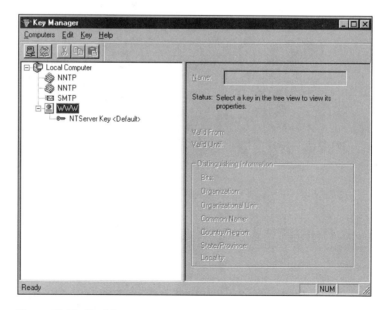

Figure 13-48: Key Manager

Step 2. Right-click the service and select Create New Key to access the Create New Key window shown in Figure 13-49.

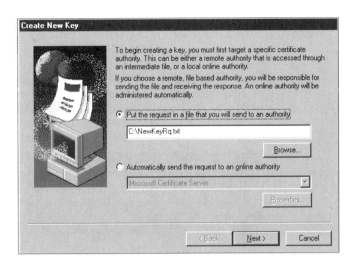

Figure 13-49: Create a new key.

Step 3. For this exercise, you will create a file for the new key request and process it locally. You won't send it online. Key requests can be made to certificate authorities by e-mail, snail mail, or fax. Select the file option and click Next to see the screen shown in Figure 13-50.

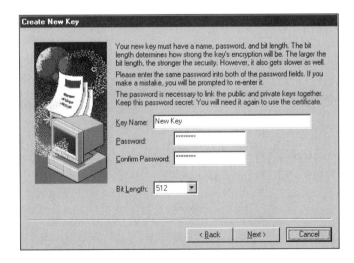

Figure 13-50: Name, password, and bit length

Continued

488 Part IV: Service Pack 4.0 and the Windows NT Server Option Pack

STEPS

To establish a certificate for your server *(continued)*

Step 4. Type a name for the key, a password, and a bit length. It is very important to remember this password. It is required when you want to install the certificate on your server. The bit length of 512K is adequate for most needs. The longer the bit length, the more processing time it takes for each encryption. If you do not have 128-bit encryption installed, 512K is the only option available. Click Next to see the following screen (Figure 13-51).

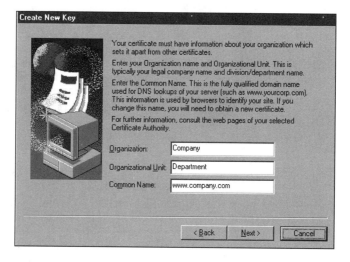

Figure 13-51: Organization, Organizational Unit, and Common Name

Step 5. Enter the names of the organization and organizational unit, as well as the common name. The Organization is the company name. The Organization Unit is the department or division. The Common Name is the fully qualified domain name. These are common X.500 terminology. Click Next to access the screen shown in Figure 13-52.

Step 6. Enter the Country, State, and City. Click Next.

Step 7. Enter your name, e-mail address, and phone number. The last window gives instructions on where the key request file will be made (C:\NewKeyRq.txt) and the next steps. Normally this file would be sent to the CA, but in this case, click Finish to save it. After it has been saved, close Key Manager and start up Internet Explorer.

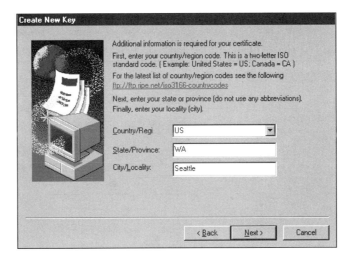

Figure 13-52: Country, State, City

Step 8. Browse to name>/CertSrv to see the Microsoft Certificate Server welcome screen shown in Figure 13-53.

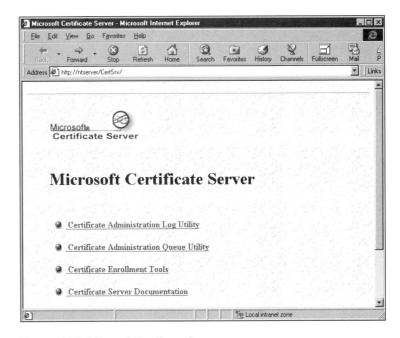

Figure 13-53: Microsoft Certificate Server

Continued

STEPS

To establish a certificate for your server *(continued)*

Step 9. Click Certificate Enrollment Tools to access the window shown in Figure 13-54.

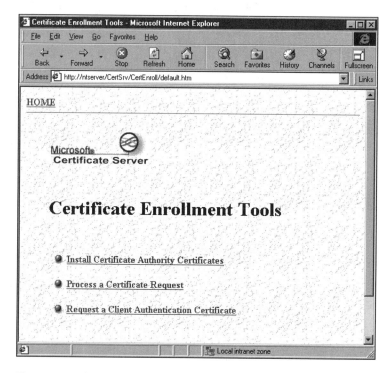

Figure 13-54: Certificate enrollment tools

Step 10. Click Process a Certificate Request.

Step 11. The Web Server Enrollment Page appears as seen in Figure 13-55. But before you work with it, first a side trip. On your Windows NT Server, find and open the text file, NewKeyRq.txt. You may want to use the Find command from the Start menu (accessed from the desktop taskbar on your Windows NT Server machine). Assuming you've double-clicked NewKeyRq.txt, this file will open in Notepad. In Notepad, select the menu option Edit ⇨ Select All to select all the rather odd-looking certificate text (yes I agree, it looks very odd!) and press Ctrl+C to copy the certificate text out of the NewKeyRp.txt file. Open the Web browser window that is currently displaying the Web Server Enrollment Page, place the cursor inside the middle text window, and press Ctrl+V to paste.

Step 12. Click Submit Request. The window shown in Figure 13-56 will appear.

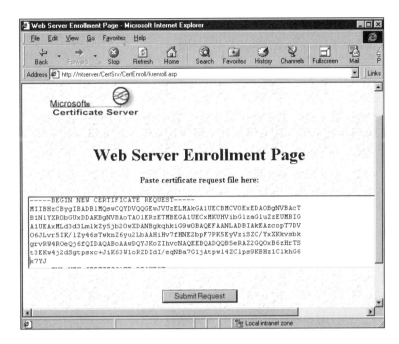

Figure 13-55: The Web Server Enrollment page

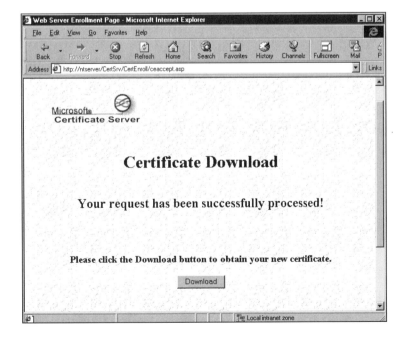

Figure 13-56: Certificate Download

Continued

STEPS

To establish a certificate for your server *(continued)*

Step 13. Click Download and save the file to disk. At this point, go back into Key Manager and highlight the appropriate key. Right-click and select Install Key Certificate. The Bindings window will appear. Select the correct IP address for the bindings and click OK.

After the key is installed, SSL may be configured for any Web site page. Configure the SSL port in the Web Site properties page. By default, it is 443. When accessing a secured Web page, you must use "https://." If you don't, you may see a "HTTP/1.1 403 Access Forbidden (Secure Channel Required)" error.

Certificate administration

The administrative functions for Certificate Server (see Figure 13-57) are done through Web-based modules. The main functions required are to manage, issue, renew, and revoke certificates.

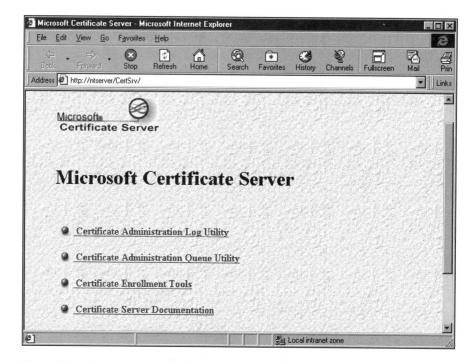

Figure 13-57: Certificate Server administration

When starting the default Certificate Server Web page, you'll have several selections available, as shown in Figure 13-57. These selections are certificate log administration, queue administration, and enrollment tools. A final selection starts the documentation screen.

The Log Administration window enables you to view and browse through all the certificates that have been generated by the server. The certificates can be presented in List view (Figure 13-58) or Form view (Figure 13-59). To revoke a certificate, select a certificate and click the Revoke button shown in the latter figure.

The Queue Administration window enables you to manage requests to the certificate server. Each request can be viewed in List or Form view.

The Enrollment Tools allow the user to:

- Install certificate authority certificates.
- Process a certificate request.
- Request a client authentication certificate.

The install certificate process allows the user to open and install a certificate authority for this particular server to the Web browser. The process certificate request is used to submit the key request file generated by the Key Manager to the Certificate Server. The results of this process is a certificate file. The client authentication request allows a user to request and receive an authentication certificate.

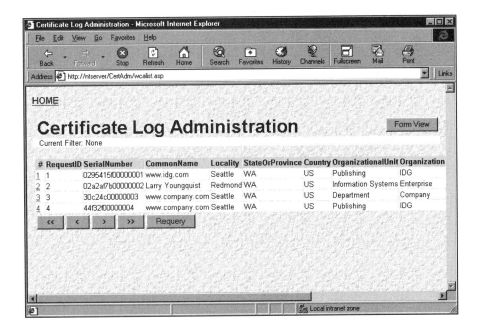

Figure 13-58: Certificate Log Administration — List view

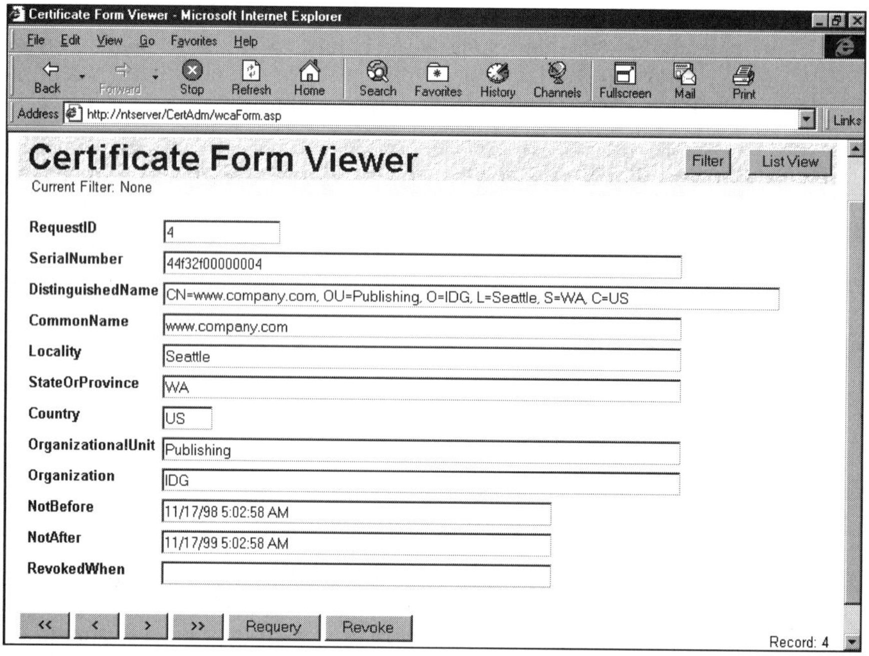

Figure 13-59: Certificate Log Administration — Form view

Index Server 2.0

Index Server 2.0 is a low-maintenance tool for searching or querying the full text of any documents contained within your Web site and in any language. Text files, HTML documents, or Microsoft Office files (Word, Excel, PowerPoint) may be indexed. These files have preinstalled content filters that allow Index Server to process them immediately after installation. Other files may require additional content filters.

Installation

When installing Index Server, one of the most important considerations is the location of the default index file. Index Server creates a master index called CATALOG.WCI. This file is located by default in C:\InetPub and contains the master and "shadow" indexes used by Index Server. This file may grow quite large, depending on the size of the files that are to be indexed. It should be local to the Web server, and it should have adequate space.

STEPS:

To install Index Server

Step 1. Index Server is management by the MMC. Start the MMC in the Start ➪ Programs ➪ Windows NT Option Pack ➪ Microsoft Index Server or add an Index Server snap-in to the MMC window.

Step 2. Type Ctrl+M or use the MMC menu, Console ➪ Add/Remove Snap-In to add a new snap-in.

Through the MMC Index Server snap-in, new catalogs and directories can be added. Make sure that you stop the Index Server and choose Action ➪ New ➪ Catalog. The most common use of Index Server is to have a catalog per Web site. This does provide a limitation since queries cannot use multiple catalogs. Users would only be able to query one Web site at a time.

STEPS:

To add a new directory

Step 1. Right-click Directories and select New ➪ Directory.

Step 2. The directory may be local or remote to the host computer. If the directory is remote, you must give it an account and password to use for indexing.

Sample forms are included with Index Server (example shown in Figure 13-60). The documentation and sample forms provide a way to learn how to use Index Server. In addition, you can copy and modify the sample forms and use them a base for creating your own index forms. Queries support many powerful features, including logical Boolean operands such as AND, OR, or NOT; proximity operators; and wildcards.

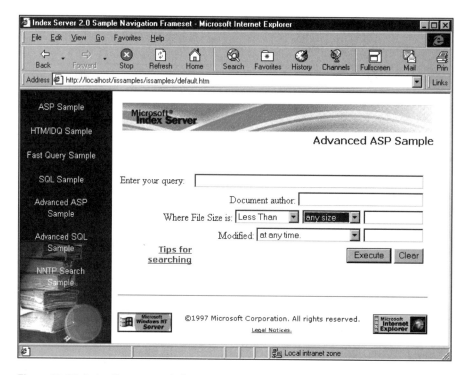

Figure 13-60: Index Server sample form

Administration

Through the MMC or through a browser, you can view statistics or manage certain parameters or actions (see Figure 13-61). The process of merging means to force a combination of the shadow lists to the master catalog. A rescan forces a reindexing of the directories.

From the Index Server Administration Web page (which is selected by double-clicking the Web object in the left pane of the MMC), you may select the Index Statistics on the left side to view the Administration — Index Statistics Web page. As you can see in Figure 13-62, it reports basic traffic and indexing information.

Index Server maintains security on all indexed files based on NTFS permissions. When a user issues a query, Index Server uses the NTFS Access Control List (ACL) to determine the permissions of the user and whether or not to return any or all of the results to the user. If the user is not authenticated or has logged on under the context of the guest account, certain results may not be returned.

Chapter 13: Windows NT 4.0 Option Pack

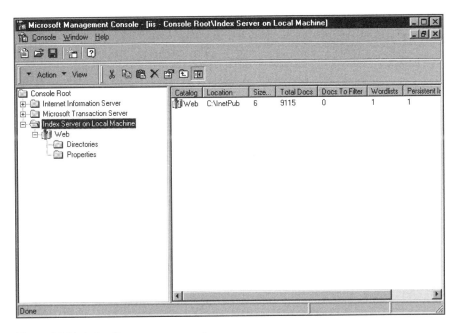

Figure 13-61: Index Server management

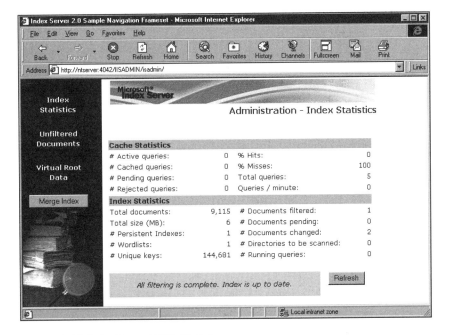

Figure 13-62: Index Server HTML Statistics

Internet Connection Services for RASInternet Connection Services (ICS) is a suite of tools aimed at providing fast, convenient dial-up services for Remote Access Services (RAS) users, whether they are corporate users or Internet service provider (ISP) users. ICS provides a network administrator with the tools to manage remote access to the network over the Internet. Many corporations are turning to Virtual Private Networking (VPN) solutions to allow their users to access the network remotely with all the same services as the local network user. Security and ease of use are the primary concerns.

The ICS suite consists of three modules. Connection Manager Administration Kit (CMAK) is a customizable dialer that simplifies the process of allowing the users to connect to the network. Connection Point Services distributes the phone books that contain information on network access telephone numbers. The Internet Authentication Services (IAS) allows users to authenticate against the NT user database using the Remote Authentication Dial-In User Service (RADIUS) protocol.

Connection Manager Administration Kit (CMAK)

The CMAK Wizard builds custom Connection Manager service profiles that include the exact look and feel and the features that are required by your dial-in users. Connection Manager will automatically configure and use TCP/IP, Dial-Up Networking, Dial-Up Scripting, and a modem if any are not already set up.

STEPS:

To create a service profile

Step 1. The first step is to create a service profile which is a complete, installable package that is distributed to your users using the Connection Manager Administration Kit Wizard. Prior to running the wizard, you'll need to have your dial-in phone numbers, any custom bitmaps, and other additional files.

Step 2. Once you have the necessary items, start the CMAK to access the screen shown in Figure 13-63. Click Next.

Figure 13-63: Connection Manager Administration Kit

Step 3. You'll see the Customize Connection Manager. Choose either to build a new service profile or to edit an existing one (see Figure 13-64). Click Next.

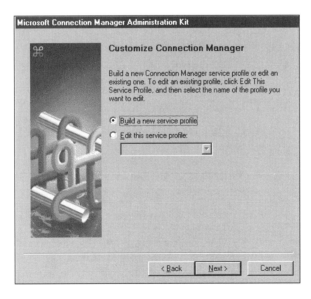

Figure 13-64: CMAK service profile

Continued

> **STEPS**
>
> **To create a service profile** *(continued)*
>
> **Step 4.** The next few screens collect customization information required to build the distribution file. Some of the information is optional.
>
> - Merge other profiles with this profile?
> - Support information
> - Add a realm name prefix or suffix
> - Dial-Up Networking phone numbers
> - Specify if a secure connection and DUN v1.2 required
> - Specify pre- and post-connection actions
> - Set up auto-actions (such as splash screen)
> - Set the custom bitmap (330 × 141)
> - Set the flash animation on connection
> - Customize the Phone Book bitmap (114 × 304)
> - Enter the Phone Book file and "More phone numbers" message
> - Enter the Phone Book download file and Connection Point Server name
> - Customized icons
> - Add, edit, or delete programs in the Connection Manager status area menu
> - Enter the Connection Manager Help file
> - Include the Connection Manager program with the Service Profile?
> - Specify the browser requirements
> - Display a license agreement
> - Add additional files for distribution
> - Specify the Service Profile location

At the end, the CMAK builds a complete distribution file that is compressed. The file I created was approximately 800K in size. This file can be distributed to your users for installation of their dial-up networking application.

Connection Point Services

Connection Point Services (CPS) is a phone book management system. You use it to manage and distribute information about dial-up access numbers for both public and private networks to your users. The Connection Manager uses CPS to automatically provide the correct numbers when the dial-up software is attempting the connection. Phone books can be managed to provide for both public and private numbers and multiple ISPs.

Most network support organizations spend an inordinate amount of time supporting dial-up users. Easy access to network resources is assumed by the user and technological changes have made user mobility a fact of life. This combination has provided a challenge to provide accurate and timely support services to this type of user.

CPS is composed of two modules, the Phone Book Service and the Phone Book Administrator. The Phone Book Service compares users' connection configurations with available files and if necessary, updates the local files. Its job is to synchronize the remote user with the most recent information. The Phone Book Administrator is the tool used to manage and update the Phone Book Service.

The services rely on a WWW and FTP server to distribute updated information to the user when requested. Multiple configurations can be used depending on the requirements and the physical layout of the network. The most basic configuration has both services running on a single server.

An important step in deploying this service is having a complete test environment. You must be able to test and simulate most, if not all, of the scenarios that your users will encounter. I recommend obtaining a call simulator box to use for dial-up connections in your lab. It saves the time and expense of getting an outside telephone line installed. These boxes are readily available via mail order and can be purchased for plain old telephone service (POTS).

Make sure that all other required components are installed and functional. All computers should have TCP/IP installed and be able to communicate with each other. WWW and FTP services should be installed and configured. Internet Connection Services should be installed via the Option Pack setup. To confirm that the Phone Book Service was installed correctly, go into the MMC and select the default FTP site. You should see the PBSData file available, as shown in Figure 13-65.

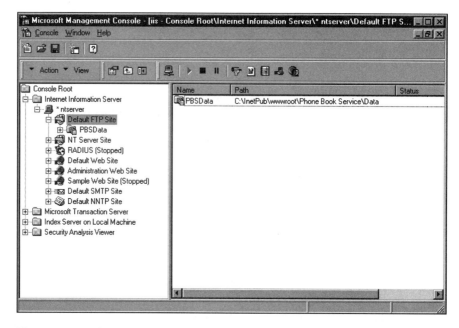

Figure 13-65: PBSData file

The Default Web Site should also contain entries for PBServer (C:\InetPub\wwwroot\Phone Book Service\Bin) and PBSDATA (C:\InetPub\wwwroot\Phone Book Service\Data).

Prior to starting, gather all relevant information pertaining to the dial-up process. Define the name of your phone book that will be used in the CMAK, list all your Point of Presence (POP) numbers, and write any help information that you want to distribute. A good technique is to perform an initial run through the CMAK Wizard and write down all required information. Then create a test phone book and practice.

STEPS:

To create a test phone book

Step 1. Start the Phone Book Administrator (see Figure 13-66).

Chapter 13: Windows NT 4.0 Option Pack

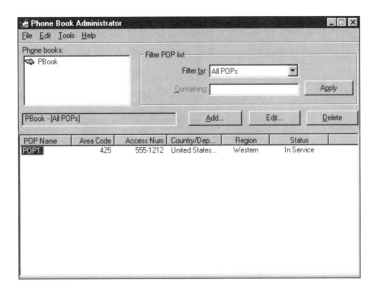

Figure 13-66: Phone Book Administrator

Step 2. Add a test POP number and the access information as shown in Figure 13-67.

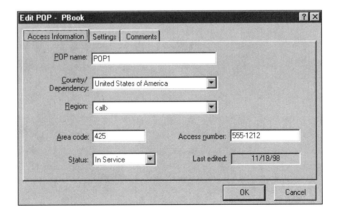

Figure 13-67: POP access information

Step 3. Apply any additional settings to the number by clicking the Settings option. Click the appropriate settings shown in Figure 13-68, and then click OK.

Continued

STEPS

To create a test phone book (continued)

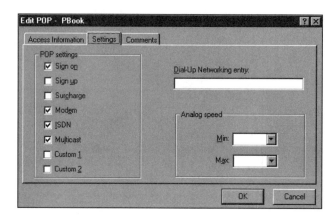

Figure 13-68: POP settings information

Step 4. When all numbers are entered and configured properly, publish the phone book by selecting Tools ➪ Publish Phone Book from the Phone Book Administrator screen shown in Figure 13-68. You'll see the screen shown in Figure 13-69.

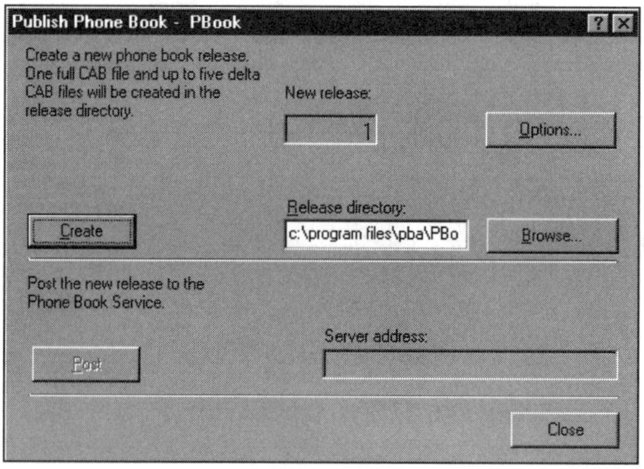

Figure 13-69: Publish Phone Book

Step 5. Click Create. This creates the phone book file, the .cab file, the region file, and version files in the C:\Program Files\PBA directory. Verify that the files have been created. You will use this in the CMAK Wizard when creating your distribution file.

Secret

For your convenience, a sample regions file of the 50 states is supplied. You can import this file and use it for identifying the locations of POPs.

Diagnosing and debugging user connection problems is difficult. The Windows NT Event Log is invaluable in this regard, but the Connection Manager has another tool to assist, the 00000000.tmp file. This file monitors the server and can contain clues about problems in finding the server or finding the phone book.

The file is normally deleted after files are downloaded, but you can set a parameter to prevent that. To view the 00000000.tmp file, edit the .cms file on the client computer and locate the [Connect Actions] section. After the "0=cmdl32.exe %profile%, append the option "/no_delete." This line will only be in the .cms file if the profile was created by the Connection Manager.

Use Notepad to read the 00000000.tmp files for any problems.

Internet Authentication Services

Internet Authentication Services (IAS) provides a method to control access to dial-up services and Internet services. IAS uses the Remote Authentication Dial-In User Service (RADIUS) protocol to authenticate users and audit usage of the services. RADIUS is a standard protocol adopted by the Internet Engineering Task Force (IETF).

IAS works in conjunction with the Connection Manager Administration Kit and the Connection Point Services. The intent of the IAS is to provide a secure, consistent, and user-friendly mechanism to allow the remote user to connect to Internet services, online financial services, databases, or any other information resource.

The RADIUS server is the database that contains information about the user's account and authorized access list (ACL) and that keeps track of accounting information for billing purposes.

The Network Access Server (NAS) receives authentication requests from the remote user, reformats the request into RADIUS protocol, and forwards them to RADIUS servers. The two servers use a "shared secret" that guarantees that the messages were forwarded through two servers that recognized and trusted each other. The NAS and the RADIUS server also provide secure connections to the corporate network via the Internet by using Point-to-Point Tunneling Protocol (PPTP). The communication line is private and secure for the caller.

RADIUS supports multiple PPP authentication protocols. The Password Authentication Protocol (PAP) passes a password as a string from the remote user's computer to the NAS server. PAP is the most flexible protocol available, but also the most vulnerable since the password is passed in clear text to the NAS. All communication between the NAS and RADIUS server is encrypted.

Challenge Handshake Authentication Protocol (CHAP) encrypts the password from the remote user by generating a random number challenge that is then used to encrypt the password. The NAS accepts the encrypted password and passes it to the RADIUS server for validation. A response is generated by the RADIUS server, and if the two match, access is granted.

Microsoft Challenge Handshake Authentication Protocol (MS-CHAP) is closely related to CHAP. Encrypted authentication is possible with a remote user by using a Windows NT primary or backup domain controller that supports MS-CHAP.

An Internet Authentication Services (IAS) server receives authentication requests from NAS servers and makes a comparison to an account password in a Windows NT domain controller. IAS maintains profiles for all files.

Note

Make sure that you back up the database, _Adminui.mdb, after any changes are made to the RADIUS server.

The most common mistake in configuration is not entering the DNS name of the client computer. This will cause an error on starting the program. Also verify that the shared secrets password is correct and the same for each system.

Administration and Management

The Windows NT Option Pack delivers two significant applications for system management. These are the Microsoft Management Console (MMC) and the Site Server Express 2.0. MMC is a key component of Windows 2000, and version 1.0 was first delivered with the Option Pack. In the future, most Windows management processes will be handled through MMC. A third component, Windows Scripting Host, which is discussed at the end of this section, provides you a batch creation tool to run what amount to super batch files.

Microsoft Management Console (MMC) 1.0

Microsoft Management Console, by itself, is nothing more than a framework to accept "snap-ins," folders or links to Web addresses (see Figure 13-70). The snap-ins delivered with each component, such as IIS, Transaction Server, or Index Server, are the specific controls and functions required to manage, monitor, and administer that specific component you wish to manage. Each snap-in may have extensions that are optionally installed. Snap-ins support the Distributed Component Object Model (DCOM) or the Component Object Model (COM).

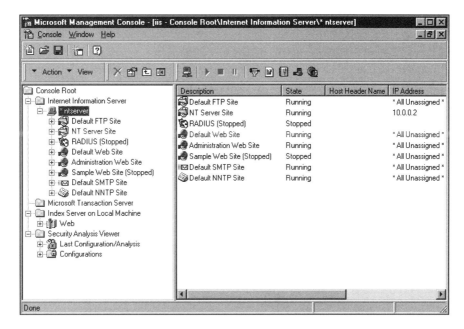

Figure 13-70: Microsoft Management Console 1.0

The console displayed here contains the snap-in for IIS, Transaction Server, Index Server, and the new Security Configuration Editor. All components are accessed on a hierarchical menu and may have elements unique to their specific requirements.

Once a view is configured and customized, it can be saved to a .msc file. A specific console file can then be loaded for individual users or functions unique to the task at hand. These extensible features make MMC a powerful tool for day-to-day management of all your server components.

STEPS:
To create a new snap-in

Step 1. Use the Console menu command to select Add/Remove Snap-In (or press Ctrl+M). This brings up the window to modify your main console window (see Figure 13-71).

Continued

STEPS

To create a new snap-in (continued)

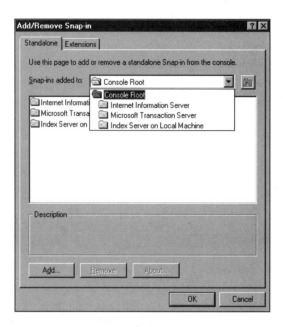

Figure 13-71: Add/Remove Snap-in

Step 2. Pulling down the Console Root item can set the location of the new snap-in. Highlight a folder location and click Add to add the snap-in. This will bring you to the Add Standalone Snap-in window shown in Figure 13-72.

Step 3. Highlight the snap-in desired and press OK. After the snap-in is added, choose the Extension tab to select any available extensions to the snap-in (see Figure 13-73).

Chapter 13: Windows NT 4.0 Option Pack

Figure 13-72: Add standalone snap-in

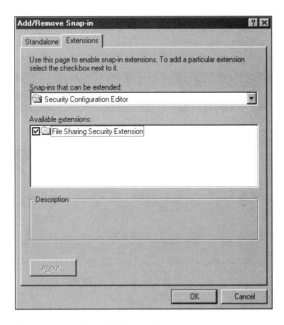

Figure 13-73: Snap-in Extensions

In addition to snap-ins, you may also select folders, URLs, or ActiveX controls for general use or monitoring. This feature will allow the administrator to view performance monitor statistics directly in the MMC window.

Site Server Express 2.0

Initial analysis of Web sites often consisted of a review of the hits on any particular page within the site. This showed the "popularity" of the particular site or particular page. Site Server Express is a tool used to more fully analyze a site using the Content Analyzer, the Usage Import program, and the Report Writer. Content Analyzer creates a visual display of the Web site and tests it. Usage Import loads the log files into a database. Report Writer outputs the database into a number of reports.

Site Server enables you to visually represent your Web site in a form that allows you to view the overall structure. It demonstrates the relationships among the resources of your Web site. The output and format of the Site Server Express modules can be customized and configured to highlight any aspect of the Web site.

Content Analyzer

The Content Analyzer creates a visual map of a Web site in a tree view and a "cyberbolic" view. These views are called a WebMap as you can see front and center in Figure 13-74. The tree view is a normal hierarchical tree structure with which you are accustomed. The cyberbolic view takes a little more effort to understand.

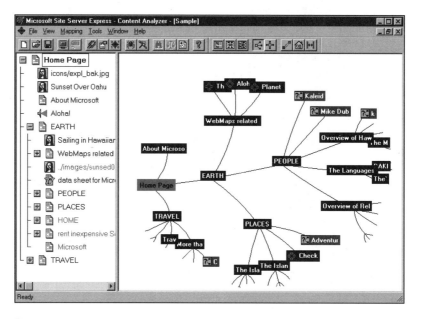

Figure 13-74: Content Analyzer

The tree view lists every component of the Web and identifies their types by use of object icons. Object icons exist for most every type of object, including third-party elements such as Adobe Acrobat files. As you select the object in the tree list, the cyberbolic view changes to display the element. A few minutes trying it and you'll get the idea. Right-click any object, and a menu list will pop up. Select the Properties sheet and view any information about the object. Colors are also significant.

- **Black.** Onsite, main routes
- **Blue.** Offsite objects
- **Green.** Alternate routes
- **Red.** Unavailable object
- **Magenta.** Busiest links
- **Cyan.** Home page

Any children of the off-site links are shown in these normal colors too. When a link is red and not available, it may not be truly "broken." Other reasons include:

- The server is temporarily unavailable.
- The server is busy.
- There are connectivity problems.
- There are security or access problems.

Each object can be explored in detail, and more information is available by viewing the Properties sheet. Right-click the object and bring up the sheet (see Figure 13-75).

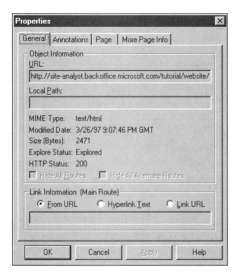

Figure 13-75: The Object Properties sheet

The graphical nature of the WebMap allows the administrator to visualize the overall Web site and to determine bottlenecks, incorrect design, user problems, or other areas. When you drag an object on the map, the overall perspective changes.

The WebMap contains different views to highlight and list certain types of links, such as:

- **Broken Links.** Link not available
- **Home Site Objects.** Objects in the same domain
- **Images Without ALT.** Images without ALT tags
- **Load Size over 32K.** Large Web pages
- **Non-Home Site Objects.** Objects in a different domain
- **Not Found Objects (404).** HTTP 404 errors
- **Unavailable Objects.** All other "not found" objects
- **Unverified Objects.** Objects that have not been searched

For example, select Tools ⇨ Quick Search ⇨ Broken Links to view a list of any broken links that the program has found (see Figure 13-76).

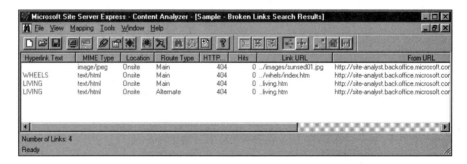

Figure 13-76: Content Analyzer broken links

To generate an HTML report for the site, select Tools ⇨ Generate Site Report, accept the defaults or modify the Generate Site Reports screen, and have the program complete a browser viewable report (see Figure 13-77).

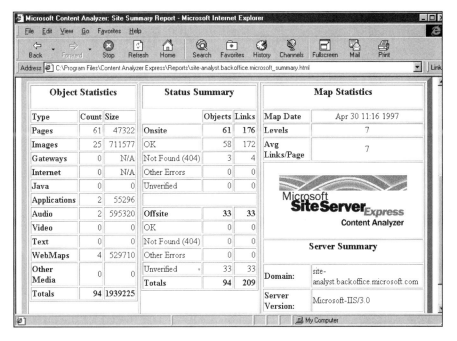

Figure 13-77: Content Analyzer site report

The Report Writer generates more comprehensive reports, but these views are useful snapshots of the Web site. They can be used quite effectively to track down and repair hidden problems within your Web site.

Posting Acceptor

The Microsoft Posting Acceptor is a server-based tool that allows publishing content to IIS using a compatible browser. When used with the Microsoft Content Replication System (CRS), the Posting Acceptor can distribute content to multiple Web servers.

Posting Acceptor is a standardized method of accepting content using HTTP multipart/form-data methods and APIs such as the ActiveX Upload control API 1.5. Since it uses standard APIs, it can provide the same functionality to the Content Replication System input or to content coming through an Internet firewall.

Posting Acceptor runs on NT Server/IIS 3.0, NT Workstation/Peer Web Services 3.0, or Windows 95/Personal Web Server. Content Replication services are only supported on IIS 3.0.

To install the Posting Acceptor 1.01 from the NT Option Kit, make sure that you've selected the subcomponent from the Site Server Express installation screen (see Figure 13-78).

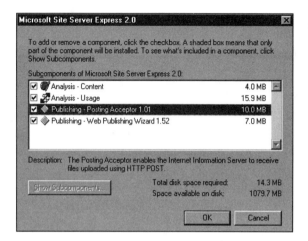

Figure 13-78: Site Server Express components

Secret

Some references appear in the Microsoft documentation to installation via a separate executable program called posting acceptor.exe. This file is not on the NT Option Kit CD, and the program is installed via the normal add/remove method.

There are several known issues with the Posting Acceptor, and the Readme file should be scanned for further details. Details of configuring and programming Posting Acceptor are beyond the scope of this book, but the news groups are a great source of information. You can view news://msnews/microsoft.public.site.posting-acceptor for more information.

Usage Import and Report Writer

The Usage Import and Report Writer programs are extremely useful tools for analyzing the usage of Web sites. The two work in combination to read and import log files into a database and then filter and export the results into nicely formatted reports that may be HTML, Word, or Excel.

The program will optionally use an Internet connection to look up HTML titles, resolve IP addresses to host names, and run WHOIS queries. In order to use these functions, they must be configured properly.

Inference algorithms

A key concept of the logic contained within the Usage Import program is the concept of *inference algorithms*. These algorithms are essentially definitions of what the program will consider hits, requests, visits, users, and organizations.

Hits are a line in a log file that may be requests for content, errors, blank lines, or Internet communications. Hits are not extremely accurate measures of activity. *Requests* are any connections, or hits, that successfully retrieve content. Usage Import reads every hit (that is, every line) in the log file but only copies requests into the database. The HTTP response code in the log must be 200, 302, or 304.

A *visit* is a set of consecutive requests from a user to a site. The Usage Import tool is set to a default of 30 minutes for determining consecutive requests. If a user doesn't make a request for 30 minutes, then that set of requests is considered a visit.

A *user* is anyone who has visited the site at least once. The identity of the user is determined by three different methods. The first method is reading persistent cookie data. If cookie data is found, then the user is considered unique. If no cookie data is found, the Usage Import tool will use a registered user name. If no registered user name is available, then the Internet host name of the user is considered the user name.

An *organization* is the name of the entity that connects users to the Internet. If the IP address can't be resolved, then the address is assumed to be a Class C IP address and is used to represent the organization. If the IP address does resolve correctly, then the full Internet host name is used and the program will parse the descriptor names of the returned name. By using Whois, the program will consolidate all domains registered to a single entity.

Configuring import usage

When the Usage Import program is first started, you will be prompted through a series of steps to create a set of "Log data sources" for the Web servers that you intend to report on (see Figure 13-79). These data sources can be log files in multiple formats, depending on the type of log files that the Web site is producing. Select the appropriate format and click OK.

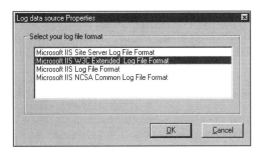

Figure 13-79: Usage Import log file format

If you choose to use the Extended log format, the HYPEREXT_LOG.DLL ISAPI filter may optionally be installed. This filter can be downloaded from the Microsoft Web site. It adds capabilities for logging the User Agent and Referrer to IIS. The Referrer is the URL of the site from which the user came to your site. The User Agent is the browser name, version, and security level of the user. For a description of the extended logging fields, refer to the IIS Properties sheet for W3C Extended Format.

> **STEPS:**
> **To install logging ISAPI filters or the mss_log.dll**
>
> **Step 1.** Download ISAPI filters or the mss_log.dll from:
>
>   http://backoffice.microsoft.com/downloads/sa/mss_log.dll
>
> or
>
>   http://backoffice.microsoft.com/downloads/sa/hyperext_log.dll
>
> **Step 2.** Download these files to the directory where you keep other ISAPI filters.
>
> **Step 3.** Launch the Microsoft Management Console.
>
> **Step 4.** Under Internet Information Server, right-click the server name that you would like to install the filter on and click Properties.
>
> **Step 5.** On the ISAPI Filters tab, click Add, and type the name and executable filename.
>
> **Step 6.** On the Web Site tab, click Active Log Format, and choose either the Microsoft IIS Log File Format for mss_log.dll, or W3C Extended Log File Format for hyperext_log.dll.
>
> **Step 7.** Close the Properties dialog box.
>
> **Step 8.** Close Internet Service Manager.

The next procedure is to configure the properties of the Import Usage server (see Figure 13-80). These parameters are important for correlating and consolidating the information coming from multiple Web sites. The Hosting Facility requires a local time zone and local domain. When reading log files from multiple sites, the Usage Import program will correlate different time zones between the target site and the hosting facility site.

Each target server that you wish to report can be added to the host server element. After adding the server, you can readily direct the Usage Import program to locate the log files and import them into the database. This is done with the Log File Manager shown in Figure 13-81.

Browse the directory where the log files are kept and highlight the files you wish to import. Hit Enter to start the import process. After importing, the program will report any errors or problems encountered.

The database, MSUsage.mdb, is Access-compatible and can be used independently of the Report Writer. Crystal Reports could be used to create production reports that generate printed output directly from MSUsage.mdb.

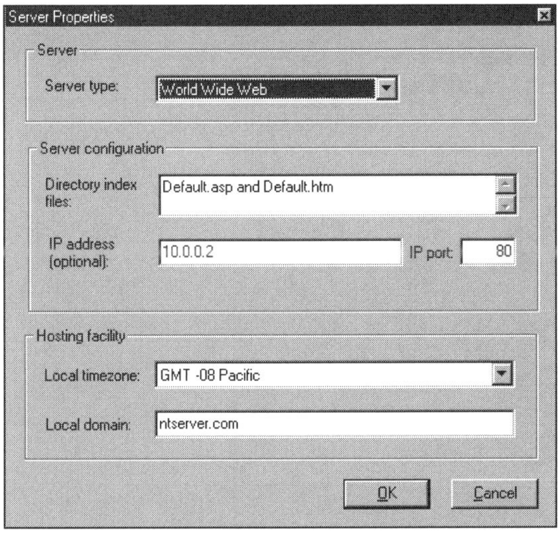

Chapter 13: Windows NT 4.0 Option Pack

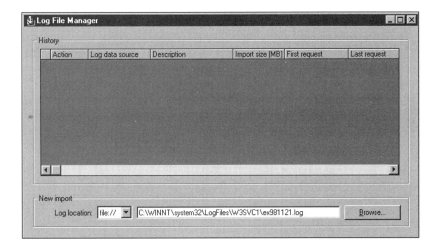

Figure 13-80: Usage Import Server configuration

Figure 13-81: Log File Manager

The Usage Import program (see Figure 13-82) has options for actions to be performed both before and after importing. To improve speed, drop the database indexes. For ease of use, if all of your Web sites are storing their log files in a single location, set the default directory to point to that central directory. Other parameters include using an HTTP proxy, DNS server, spiders, log file rotations, and overlaps, and IP resolution.

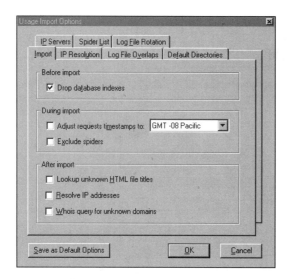

Figure 13-82: Usage Import Options

Importing the log files is a tedious process that should be set up with an automated and scheduled process. Fortunately, the Import Usage and Report Writer programs have an automated scheduling tool that allows "Jobs" to be scheduled. Jobs, by themselves, do nothing. Tasks are defined for every job (see Figure 13-83).

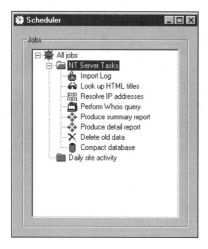

Figure 13-83: Scheduling jobs and tasks

The following actions can be set up as tasks:

- Import log file
- Look up HTML titles

- Resolve IPs
- Run Whois queries
- Run a Summary or Detail report
- Delete requests
- Compact a database

When defining the destination files for any output, the program uses a date replacement macro. These macros are required and need to be carefully defined so that each report or job that produces output is recorded correctly.

The Schedule program produces batch files that can be installed and run using the NT Schedule service. The batch files are run in a silent mode, and any messages are written to a file in the \MESSAGE subdirectory of the executable location.

Importing the log files from a remote server share requires that the scheduler service start with an authorized user of the remote system. Take care in establishing a domain user account that has proper permissions to access the log files.

Report Writer

After the data has been imported into the database properly, the Report Writer module will extract and output the data into HTML, Microsoft Word, or Microsoft Excel files.

Report Writer behaves very much like Usage Import, and some functions overlap. When the Report Writer program is started, you may open a specific report definition or browse multiple default reports in the Report Writer catalog (see Figure 13-84).

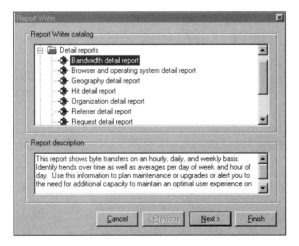

Figure 13-84: The Report Writer catalog

These detail and summary reports may be used, or additional custom reports may be created and added. After a report is selected, the period of the report must be specified. This may be for all data collected, or by a day/month/year, or by a specific date range. Any log values can then be included or excluded from the report by defining specific criteria (see Figure 13-85).

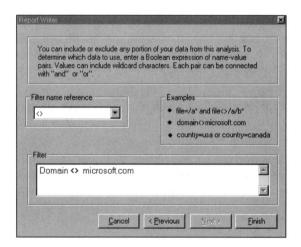

Figure 13-85: Report Writer selection criteria

The Report Writer then creates the report topics, as seen in the Report Content window (see Figure 13-86), before actually generating the report. Any of the titles may be modified or rearranged before output. The Properties sheet for the report provides for modification of the color, fonts, section layout, and such. Attributes for the report objects can also be modified. The Row dimensions can be set to limit the results for a top or bottom amount, a specific sort, and an aggregate (Total, Minimum, Maximum, Average, Median) value. The Measures are predefined to the number of visits and the percentage. The Presentation may be a graph or a table.

Once satisfied, select File ⇨ Create Report Document or press the green triangle. Select the name of the output file, and the report will be generated to the file format specified.

The Scheduler module in the Report Writer is a shared window with the Usage Importer. Any scheduled jobs will show up in either module.

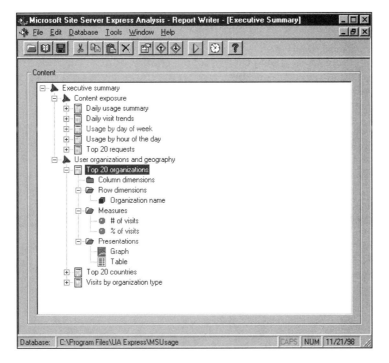

Figure 13-86: Report content

Windows Scripting Host (WSH)

The Windows Scripting Host is a new component that will be standard on Windows 2000. The WSH is an improved version of the tried and true DOS batch language. WSH is based on ActiveX and includes scripting support for VBScript and Jscript while maintaining compatibility with the DOS command line programs. The primary purpose of WSH is to provide administrative support for executing scripts either locally or remotely. Since IIS supports ASP, the Windows Scripting Host allows server-side scripting over the Internet or intranet.

WSH supports two modes and can be run from the Windows desktop via WSCRIPT.EXE or from a command line via CSCRIPT.EXE. Both modes require very little memory overhead and can be used for small, quick tasks.

More information about the WSH can be found in the online documentation or on the Microsoft Web site.

Transaction Processing

The Windows NT Option Pack delivers a powerful distributed transaction processing model using the Microsoft Transaction Server and the Microsoft Message Queue Server. These two technologies give NT Server and IIS the capabilities to offer transaction services for IIS using transactional Active Server Pages and integrated message queuing services using MSMQ.

Distributed transaction processing means simply that a sequence of actions that may be distributed across remote platforms can be considered as one large transaction. The sequence can be either be "committed" when all the actions have happened or "rolled back" when any of the actions fail.

Microsoft Transaction Server (MTS) 2.0

The Microsoft Transaction Server (see Figure 13-87) is the service that defines the application programming model for the distributed application and also is the service that administers and manages the applications that use transaction-based logic. MTS uses the Microsoft Component Object Model (COM) technology as its basis.

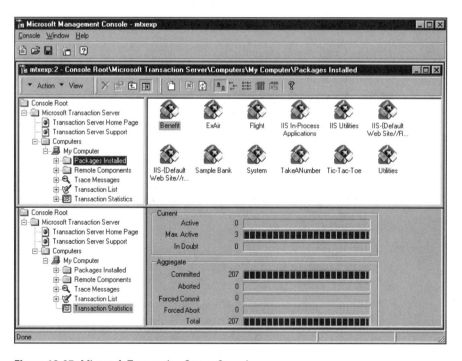

Figure 13-87: Microsoft Transaction Server Console

MTS 2.0 includes transaction connectivity to databases such as Oracle and DB2, integrates with MSMQ 1.0, and provides connectivity to mainframes via

Microsoft SNA Server. MTS allows the application developer to build "three-tier" applications. Three-tier applications simply mean that a server component (such as MTS) operates within an application that may have presentation logic built into the client component (such as a client tier) and application logic built into the database server component (such as a backend tier). MTS provides the "glue" to provide front-end and back-end components to work efficiently and with a maximum of data integrity.

MTS 2.0 supports transactional ODBC 3.0 drivers. This set of drivers allows MTS to work with Oracle and DB2 along with access to SQL Server and MSMQ. MTS will perform connection pooling of Oracle and DBS sessions for improved performance and lower cost.

A few sample applications are distributed with MTS. You can set up and view a banking application or a tic-tac-toe application. When running the client on your system, you can view transaction status while the program executes. The banking application requires the use of SQL Server, which must be loaded and running.

Microsoft Message Queue Server (MSMQ) 1.0

Microsoft Message Queue Server provides a loosely coupled network communications service for interapplication messaging. MSMQ is the message delivery mechanism to exchange information over any interconnected network, including potentially unreliable networks, such as the Internet, and intermittently connected users, such as mobile agents in the field.

Asynchronous versus synchronous messaging

MSMQ provides an asynchronous form of messaging. The common analogy of synchronous versus asynchronous messaging is the difference between a telephone conversation and e-mail. When you call someone, your party either pick up the phone or they don't. While you are on the phone and calling, you don't do anything else. You're listening and waiting for an answer. This procedure is efficient if the called party is ready and available. But if not, it's very inefficient and wasteful of the time that you spend waiting for the answer that never comes. This is synchronous messaging.

E-mail is asynchronous messaging. You write an e-mail message and then send it. You send it to your e-mail host, who may or may not know where the recipient is located. But at a minimum, it knows where to send the message next. After a few hops, the message finally appears in the inbox of the person you are sending it to. The recipient may be sick, on vacation, or busy doing something else at the particular moment the message arrives. Eventually, he or she will pick it up and respond to it. This is asynchronous messaging and is the model used for MSMQ. Just think of the e-mail inbox as the delivery queue location.

The need for robust messaging arises when applications don't need to communicate with another program or process in real time, when reliability of the network or connection isn't assured, and when messages need to be intelligently routed to their final destination. MSMQ answers these requirements and expands functionality for the message delivery process.

MSMQ features and terminology

MSMQ supports store-and-forward message queuing. The application isn't dependent on the network protocol being used by either the sender or receiver. The sender may or may not be able to directly contact the receiver. MSMQ can prioritize urgent messages to guarantee response times for certain applications and the message can be flagged for guaranteed delivery.

MSMQ integrates with MTS to provide transaction-based services for its messages. Messages can be delivered in order, they can be delivered once and only once, and a receipt for message delivery can be requested. If a message is part of a transaction and it fails to be delivered, the entire transaction can be rolled back using an MTS transaction set and a Distributed Transaction Coordinator (DTC) process.

MSMQ supports intelligent routing depending on the physical connection, traffic congestion, and least-cost routing calculations. Security for all messages is maintained by using digital certificates. MSMQ events can be audited using the Windows Event Logging service.

The message queuing services provided by MSMQ are quite easy to understand in principle; the difficulty in learning how MSMQ works is sometimes related to the specific and unique terminology that is used.

A *message* is the basic currency of MSMQ. Messages are sent between computers, and they can be text or binary, database updates or requests, notifications or acknowledgments, or part of an MTS transaction set. The application that sends the message and the receiving applications know how to deal with the message; MSMQ merely delivers it.

Queues are lists or inboxes of messages. MSMQ uses public and private queues to store and forward messages. MSMQ uses multiple queues, which may be public or private, to process messages. These are the journal, dead letter, transactional dead letter, administration, system, and report queues. All MSMQ queues are manipulated with the same MSMQ functions.

MSMQ uses a distributed database called the MSMQ Information Store (MQIS) to keep track of all users, computers, queues, configuration, and other environment information. It doesn't use MQIS to store messages. Messages are stored in queues that may be resident in memory or stored on a hard drive, depending on the type of message delivery requested by the sender. If a message is sent as an express message, it is kept in memory while sent. This approach allows very high-speed message processing, but if a problem occurs, the message may be lost. If a message is sent as a recoverable message, it is stored in a backup file that can be recovered if problems occur. The trade off is safety versus speed.

MSMQ creates its own topology to deal with the messaging environment. The top level configuration is the MSMQ *enterprise*. It contains all the computers and clients for the messaging environment. The enterprise shares a single, common, replicated database called the MQIS. The *primary enterprise controller* (PEC) is defined when the enterprise is created. The PEC maintains the enterprise configuration and also acts as the security manager for all certificates used to authenticate messages.

The MSMQ enterprise is broken up into sites. *Sites* are physically connected networks that have fast and inexpensive connectivity. Sites are connected through *site links*. Site links costs are used to determine the cost of sending messages between sites and then to determine the least-cost routing for a message. A *primary site controller* (PSC) is installed in every site. The PEC is the PSC for its own site. *Backup site controllers* (BSCs) can and should be configured.

Computers communicate over *connected networks* (CNs). A CN is a collection of computers in which any two computers can communicate directly. MSMQ servers can be used as routing servers to control communication between CNs.

In addition to MSMQ servers, MSMQ *clients* also play a role. These clients create and send messages. There are "independent" clients and "dependent" clients. Independent clients are mobile computers that may not be physically connected to the network or to a MSMQ server. These clients will store messages into a local queue and deliver them when they are connected. Dependent clients are physically connected and use a MSMQ server to send messages.

MSMQ and Microsoft Server NT 4.0/Enterprise Edition

MSMQ is a key component of the NT Server—Enterprise Edition (NT Server/E), and some significant differences obtain between the Enterprise version and the Option Pack version. If you intend to implement MSMQ in your production environment, you need to be aware of these limitations. When referencing the Enterprise Edition version, I'll use MSMQ/E as its acronym. (This acronym is not used by Microsoft or in any documentation, but it is used here only for the purpose of distinguishing the features of the two versions.)

SQL Server 6.5

Since MSMQ requires SQL Server 6.5 to store the MQIS, and the Option Pack does not include SQL Server. The evaluation version of SQL Server or the Workstation version of SQL Server must be installed. Both of these versions have limitations. The SQL Server evaluation version has database size limitations, and the SQL Server Workstation version has connectivity limitations.

MSMQ connector support and smart routing

MSMQ/E can communicate with computers using other messaging systems, as IBM's MQSeries. The MSM/Option Pack does not support MSMQ connector servers. MSMQ/E supports "smart routing" based on the physical topology of the network and also supports session concentration. MSMQ/Option Pack supports intermediate store-and-forward routing between sites, but they cannot function as site gates, meaning they can't be "out-routing servers."

Licensing

MSMQ/Option Pack limits MSMQ servers to no more than 25 concurrent sessions with other MSMQ servers and clients. MSMQ requires a client access license (CAL) for sending messages to open queues.

MSMQ Explorer

The MSMQ Explorer is a console for managing and administering all the computers and message queues in a MSMQ enterprise. Unfortunately, it is not an MMC console, yet. Perhaps in Windows 2000 it will be integrated into MMC.

Bring up the MSMQ Explorer shown in Figure 13-88 by selecting Start ➪ Programs ➪ Windows NT 4.0 Option Pack ➪ Microsoft Message Queue ➪ Explorer.

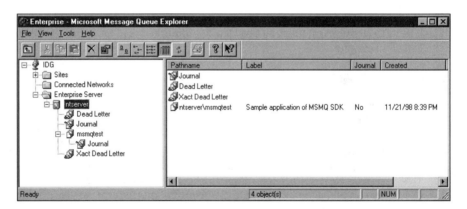

Figure 13-88: MSMQ Explorer

Several sample applications are included in MSMQ. These enable you to see the system in operation and to simulate a complete messaging environment. The samples are:

- **MSMQTest.** Sends messages between computers
- **MQTestOA.** ActiveX version of MSMQTest
- **MQTrans.** Sample banking application
- **Distributed Draw.** Scratchpad application

- **MSMQ API Test.** Test of the API calling procedures

MQTest demonstrates a very basic message-based application. It simply sends messages between two computers (in this case between two programs running on the same computer). The messages are text input into the sending application and displayed on the receiving application.

STEPS:
To run the MQTest application

Step 1. Start two command line sessions and change the directory to the MSMQ location (C:\Program Files\msmq).

Step 2. On one command line session, start MSMQTest as the receiver by typing **msmqtest –r** and start the other command line session as the sender by typing **msmqtest –s**.

Step 3. From the sender session, at the prompt line — "Enter a string:" — type something. In the other session, you should receive the typed text. If you view the MSMQ Explorer, you will not see any messages in the msmqtest queue when the receiving application is running. Stop the receiving application by typing Ctrl+C at "waiting for messages . . ." Now send additional messages by typing text into the sending program.

Step 4. Bring up the MSMQ Explorer and view the msmqtest queue (see Figure 13-89). Hit F5 or Refresh, if necessary.

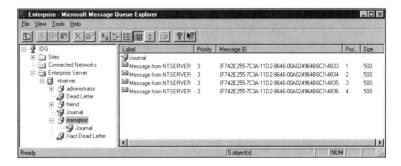

Figure 13-89: MSMQTest queue

Step 5. The messages are stored and waiting in the message queue for deliver. Go back to the receiving application and restart the application by entering **msmqtest –r**. All the stored messages should appear in the order that they were sent. Go back to the MSMQ Explorer and hit F5 to refresh the screen. The messages should not be displayed.

Continued

STEPS

To run the MQTest application (continued)

Step 6. Type **quit** at the prompt line in the sending application. Both instances will halt. If the application is exiting cleanly, the queue will be deleted. If you exit the application by hitting Ctrl+C, the queue will not be removed.

The Distributed Draw test program is very interesting and shows how nontextual information can be sent.

MSMQ configuration

In addition to the MSMQ Explorer, MSMQ uses a Control Panel applet to set various functions. If you start the control panel and click the MS Message Queue icon, you'll see options for storage locations, security settings, and a MSIQ connection option (see Figure 13-90). The Storage and Server tabs are fairly obvious. The Security tab requires some exploration.

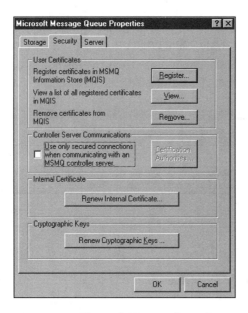

Figure 13-90: Microsoft Message Queue Properties

This panel is used to register user certificates, set secured connections between MSMQ controller servers, renew internal certificates, and renew cryptographic keys.

By clicking the Register button, you can view any user certificates stored and register them in the MQIS. View and Remove enable you to view and remove certificates from the MQIS.

You must use the IIS Key Manager to install digital certificates. If you don't want to install IIS on the PEC, install just the Internet Service Manager from the IIS setup. No services are added to the machine, and you can run Key Manager.

Also make sure that the certificate you install is the same name as the computer name of the MSMQ routing server. If these names don't match, clients can't establish secure communications. IIS supports multiple certificates, but MQIS only supports one certificate. MSMQ lets you know that the certificate was successfully renewed and registered (Figure 13-91).

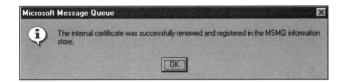

Figure 13-91: An internal certificate renewed

Miscellaneous Components

Microsoft Data Access Components (MDAC)

Microsoft Data Access Components are a group of programs that provide data access services from different sources and through different methods. Applications can use MDAC to access information via a browser interface or through a client/server interface to ODBC data sources. MDAC is a collection of products that include:

- ActiveX Data Objects (ADO) 1.5
- Remote Data Service (RDS) 1.5
- Microsoft OLE DB Provider for ODBC 1.5
- ODBC 3.5

Microsoft Data Access Components 1.5b

Microsoft has definitely made matters somewhat confusing around specific versions of the Microsoft Data Access Components (MDAC). There are five separate versions of MDAC 1.5. The initial version 1.5 was distributed with IE4; then another version was distributed at the Professional Developers Conference; and then 1.5a, 1.5b, and 1.5c were also released.

The version distributed in the NT Option Pack is 1.5b. The latest release, 1.5c, can be downloaded from the Microsoft Web site. The most current version is now 2.0, but you may have some compelling reason to not upgrade immediately, such as conflicts with clients in your organization. Plan your configurations very carefully and watch out for version incompatibilities within the entire suite of database access programs. To determine which version is loaded on any machine, obtain a copy of the KnowledgeBase article Q178840 () and compare the version numbers of the DLL files with the versions given in the article. When dealing with versions of all these programs, change management is very important and critical to a successful deployment.

For the latest information concerning Microsoft's plans on data access components, view their Universal Data Access page. White papers, documentation, download files, and related sites are listed there.

ActiveX Data Objects (ADO) 1.5 and Remote Data Service (RDS)

ActiveX Data Objects (ADO) is an application-level programming interface to data and information. It is a Component Object Model (COM)–based interface that provides for the creation of consistent and high-performance access to data by front-end clients, middleware objects, languages, and browsers. ADO is very efficient and fast, and it requires low memory overhead.

Remote Data Service, the service formerly known as Advanced Database Connector (ADC), is the component that enables applications to access OLE DB providers running on remote machines.

Numerous examples and tutorials are provided for these products in the documentation. If you need a quick test to determine whether or not RDS is operational, enter the following line into your browser, and click Run. If you can read information from the database, then RDS is set up properly. Note the use of the older acronym, ADC, for this test. You may see references to ADC periodically. Figure 13-92 shows the Remote Data Service Query page.

Microsoft Script Debugger

The Microsoft Script Debugger provides a method to test and correct errors in Web scripts. You can debug errors in ASP code, VBScript, Jscript, Java applets, and ActiveX components.

The Script Debugger enables you to find errors in your scripts. Knowing the different types of errors that may occur and how they appear helps you to diagnose and track down elusive problems. Errors can be caused by faulty syntax, run-time errors, or logic errors, and they can be caused by either the client or the server.

In order to debug ASP code executed by the server, you need to enable ASP debugging. Start the MMC and bring up the Properties sheet for the Web site to debug. Click the Home Directory tab and select the Configuration button. The App Debugging tab (see Figure 13-93) allows you to set the parameters for both client- and server-side script debugging.

Chapter 13: Windows NT 4.0 Option Pack

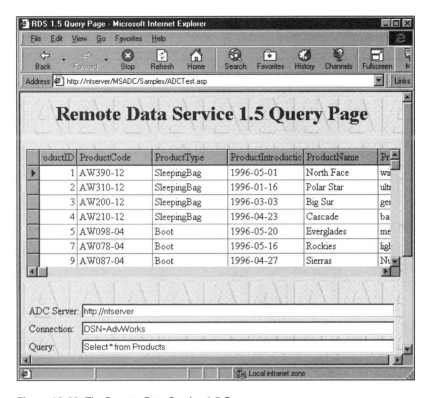

Figure 13-92: The Remote Data Service 1.5 Query page

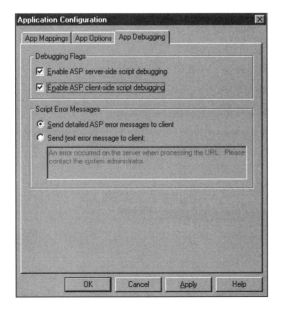

Figure 13-93: Application configuration

Be careful that you can work on the server when you enable script debugging. When it is enabled, all server errors are passed to the debugger. If you are working on a browser that is not running on the server and the error is displayed on the page, then the error is in the server script. If the error is displayed in a dialog box, then it is in the client script.

When debugging, be careful about line numbers. When the error is in the server script, the line number is the line number of the .asp file. If the error is in the client script, then the line number refers to the output of the .asp file (that is, the HTML output) and not the .asp file. To see the line number, view the HTML source file.

Summary

This chapter presented the Windows NT Option Pack from start to finish, covering the following:

- Introduction to Windows NT Option Pack
- Installation and troubleshooting
- Internet components
- Administration and management
- Transaction processing
- Miscellaneous components

Chapter 14

History and Role of Service Packs

In This Chapter

- Introduction to service packs
- The Service Pack 2 fiasco
- Service Pack 3 and hotfixes
- Service Pack 4

This chapter explains the history of service packs for NT and the methods used to upgrade and keep your system current. But more important, this chapter drives home a maxim that I've tried to follow as an MCSE: Never deploy a network operating system on a production server before its time. That time, in my opinion, is measured by service pack release milestones. For example, I didn't implement Windows NT Server 4.0 on anything other than a test server until Service Pack 1 was released. Even then, I know other consultants who won't deploy an operating system in a production environment until several service packs have been released. There are even those who didn't consider Windows NT Server 3.51 to be rock solid until Service Pack 5 was released!

Service Packs and HotFixes

All software companies issue corrections and periodic upgrades to their products. Microsoft is no exception. Microsoft issued DOS updates through a series of major and minor "dot" releases from version 1.0 to the last widely released version of DOS, version 6.22 (some people consider early versions of Windows analogous to DOS v7.0). Some of those DOS versions were more stable than others were, and some versions were used for no more than a few weeks because of serious problems. Microsoft changed their method of applying upgrades with the introduction of Windows NT but continued the tradition of successes and failures for each version.

There is a great deal of debate on what Microsoft should and shouldn't do in regard to their methods of updating their software. I'll leave those questions for another time and place. This chapter will focus on the methods that Microsoft currently uses for upgrades and bug fixes for NT and how to deal with them.

Windows NT relies on a cycle of "service packs" and "hotfixes" to upgrade and fix problems. While service packs are not intended to introduce new features or functions, they may. New features have been introduced and substantial components have found their way into user hands via a service pack. For example, Internet Information Server (IIS) v3.0 and Active Server Pages (ASP) were introduced in Service Pack 3.

Each major release of Windows NT has had multiple service packs that are cumulative in nature and are freely distributed. Microsoft posts them on their public FTP site. "Cumulative" service packs mean that the update needs only to be applied to a fresh copy of Windows NT to bring the system current with the latest versions of the system files, including all previous service packs, hotfixes, new DLLs, and new system programs.

You should always apply the current service pack immediately after making any changes or modifications to your system. Problems or older versions of system components can be introduced during your changes, and various components need to be updated to the latest service pack version.

Because service packs are issued on a six- to twelve-month cycle, emergency fixes called "hotfixes" are issued, as needed, by Microsoft. They are applied to fix or repair explicit situations, and each hotfix deals with a specific problem. Hotfixes are not cumulative, although some fixes are included in later hotfixes. In this case, the earlier hotfix is archived and the later version of the hotfix is applied. You should always refer to the Readme documents that are included with each hotfix for any requirements or instructions.

Hotfixes are not regression tested. This means that the fix has not been fully tested in all scenarios in a production environment. For this reason, it's recommended that you apply hotfixes only for specific problems that you may be experiencing. Some hotfixes are more important than others or may upgrade a specific component that isn't on the system to be upgraded. You should apply a hotfix only after reading the descriptions of the problem and of the hotfix solution itself in the Microsoft Knowledge Base article that accompanies the hotfix.

The Service Pack 2 Fiasco

Microsoft released the Windows NT Service Pack 2 (SP2) directly to users in 1997, and unfortunately, it caused more problems than it corrected. Problems with Remote Access Services (RAS), antivirus programs, CD-ROM autorun, and NTFS were reported immediately. These problems ranged from minor and inconvenient to very serious file partition problems that caused the server to become unusable. Users around the world were not happy, including yours truly.

The furor that SP2 generated caused Microsoft to rethink their processes, and subsequent service packs have been beta-tested by users outside of the company. With the introduction of Service Pack 3 (SP3), Microsoft has beta-tested service packs. Although problems have not been eliminated, they have been minimized.

Secret

Always use the "uninstall" feature when applying any new service packs. By doing so, you can back out any changes and get your system back online in case of problems. This was a new feature of SP2, and I was one of the many who learned this lesson the hard way by overlooking the uninstall feature and not using it. On a positive note, if you don't use the uninstall feature, you'll learn more about the restore capabilities of your backup program. (You did make a backup before you started the service pack installation, right?)

Only after you're very comfortable with the upgrade should you apply the service pack without the uninstall option.

Microsoft addressed the SP2-induced problems with a series of hotfixes that placated most users. The greatest fallout may have been the negative press and user reaction against Microsoft for the flawed release and the problems that it caused. Needless to say, Service Pack 2 had a very short shelf life.

The good news is that Microsoft took ownership of the problem in an honest and sincere way. That point became clear one evening shortly after the release of SP2 when I was attending the bimonthly BackOffice Professional Association (BOPA) meeting in Redmond, WA. The guest speaker was Jim Alchin, a senior Microsoft executive in the Windows NT area. In his words, referring to SP2, "We screwed up!"

Service Pack 3 and Post Hotfixes

Service Pack 3 (SP3) was introduced in 1998 and quickly became a "must-have" upgrade. Most, if not all, software and hardware companies test their products on the latest service pack within a reasonable time frame. If problems are detected, their customers are notified or bulletins are issued. The SP2 fiasco raised the consciousness of all those working with NT, and SP3 was scrutinized very closely. After product testing, most companies recommended that SP3 be applied in order for their software or hardware to work properly. Windows NT 4.0 with SP3 became the standard, common environment for most users.

SP3 installation

You have two ways to obtain SP3. It may be downloaded from the Microsoft FTP site (`ftp.microsoft.com//bussys/winnt/winnt-public/fixes/usa/nt40/ussp3`), or it may be ordered on CD from Microsoft at 800-370-8758.

Versions are available for both Intel (nt4sp3_i.exe, 18MB) and Alpha (nt4sp3_a.exe, 23MB) processors. Symbol files are also available but should only be used if you intend to debug your NT Server. In reality, you will work with the symbol files under the guidance of Microsoft support when you are attempting to discover and trap complex Windows NT Server–related problem. Such was the case when I worked with a medium-sized manufacturer running Windows NT Server 4.0 SP1 on a Compaq server. You may also need to work with symbols files in connection with the required labs and exercises for the MCSE course "Windows NT Server Enterprise Technologies."

The CD version, when inserted into your drive, automatically runs and guides you through the first steps of selecting and starting the installation program for SP3. You can additionally install Active Server Pages 1.0b, Index Server 1.1, NetShow 1.0, FrontPage 97 Server Extensions, and Crystal Reports. The CD also contains FrontPage97 and Internet Explorer 3.02.

The CD version installs the strong 128-bit encryption algorithms for RAS connections, Secure Sockets Layer (SSL) for IIS, and Secure Remote Procedure Calls (RPC). The strong encryption software is also available for download at mssecure.www.conxion.com/cgi-bin.ntitar.pl. This site will determine whether you are located in the United States or Canada and then allow you to download the software after filling out an information form.

Secret

Export restrictions are in effect for any distribution of strong encryption software. The North American (128-bit) version can only be distributed in the United States and Canada. If you have questions or need clarification of the legal restrictions in place, please refer to the U.S. Commerce Department, Bureau of Export Administration (BXA). You may browse their Web site (www.bxa.doc.gov) for more information.

STEPS:

To install SP3

Step 1. Start the SP3 program, either by clicking the link (SPSETUP.BAT) on the CD or by running the compressed file for the processor you are using. You will be presented with the SP3 Welcome screen (see Figure 14-1).

Step 2. Click the Next button and continue the update.

Step 3. After the Welcome screen, you can now call your personnel attorney over to your desk so that both of you can read the Software License Agreement. If your attorney is temporarily unavailable (aren't they always!), you can do what I do and appoint your cubicle mate your "temporary in-house counsel" and have them give their legal blessing. In other words, click Yes to continue.

Chapter 14: History and Role of Service Packs

Figure 14-1: Service Pack 3 Welcome screen

Note

You may also expand the compressed service pack and its files to a subdirectory. This enables you to modify it for your environment (we'll see how later). To do this, expand the file by using the /x parameter (that is, by typing **nt4sp3_I /x**) directly from the command line.

Step 4. If no previous uninstall directory was detected, the update program will present you with only the option to install the service pack. In this case, the second option, Uninstall a Previously Installed Service Pack, will be grayed out and not available (see Figure 14-2). Click Next to continue.

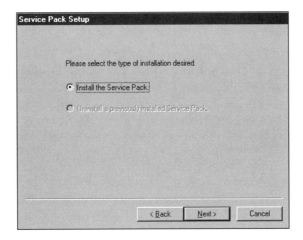

Figure 14-2: Selecting the type of installation

Continued

STEPS

To install SP3 (continued)

Step 5. The next screen allows you to specify if you want to create an Uninstall directory (see Figure 14-3). This is the default and is generally recommended.

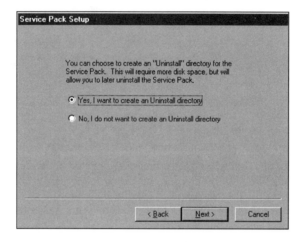

Figure 14-3: Creating an uninstall directory

Secret

Be careful in using this option when SP3 has already been applied to the machine and an Uninstall directory currently exists. You may end up with an uninstall directory of the first SP3 application such that if you "uninstall" after your second SP3 update, you end up with the first SP3 update and not the pre-SP3 version, as you intended. Very confusing, but very important.

Step 6. The next screen (shown in Figure 14-4) is the last step before the update starts copying files. Cancel the update at this point to go back and make modifications to any settings.

Step 7. Click Finish to start. (This is one of those Microsoft Zen-like phrases that only make sense when it's 3:30 A.M. and you're trying to get the last of several servers upgraded by 8 A.M., when the rest of the company comes in to work.)

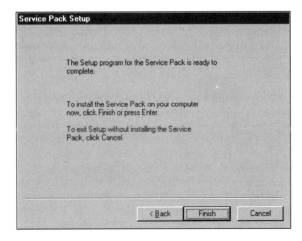

Figure 14-4: Ready to Complete screen

During the update process, you may have been presented with options to overwrite or replace certain files. Typically, these files may be custom drivers or system files from a manufacturer or vendor. Read the screen carefully for your options and review requirements from the vendor. If it is appropriate to your system and you are confident that the file in question requires updating, replace the specified file with the one from the service pack.

If all goes well, you will receive the final screen, telling you that the system must be restarted (see Figure 14-5).

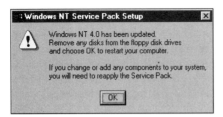

Figure 14-5: The Restart screen

When you reboot the system, you should also see the service pack listed during the boot-up process. If you don't, then reapply the update. After the system has been rebooted and everything looks well, make sure that you update your Emergency Repair Disk.

Secret

To check which service pack is installed on your system without restarting, run the Registry Editor and look for the value of the "CSDVersion" under HKEY_LOCAL_MACHINE\SOFTWARE\Microsoft\Windows NT\Current Version. This will tell you what service pack is installed (or at least, what service pack NT thinks is installed).

If you already haven't done so, now is a good time to verify the service pack version that is running on you machine. You could of course reboot the server to discover this information, or you could check the Registry setting just mentioned.

Secret

The Emergency Repair Disk (ERD) process has been modified in SP3. An updated file, setupdd.sys, should be copied to the second NT installation disk to support the new ERD process. Remove the read-only attribute from the current file on the installation disk (attrib -r a:\setupdd.sys), copy the file, and set the attribute using the "+r" option.

SP3 troubleshooting

If because your system does not reboot correctly or for some other reason, you decide to uninstall the service pack, read this section to learn how. You must be aware of certain changes that have been made to key system files and subtle differences between pre-SP3 and post-SP3 installations.

The first thing to do is stop and assess your situation. I've been in situations where the pressure is on to get a production server back up and running as quickly as possible. You've told the users that this maintenance will only take twenty minutes and that was forty minutes ago. Despite the pressure, you have to plan your actions carefully so that you don't make matters worse.

A great deal of material deals with NT recovery procedures (and you should be aware of all of it!). SP3 adds a few new wrinkles to those procedures especially related to the ERD. The main SP3-related difference is that Microsoft changed the Registry Security Hive. The Samsrv.dll, Samlib.dll, and Winlogon.exe files have all changed. If you repair your system with a pre-SP3 ERD, you may place older versions of these files on your system, and those files cannot access the Windows NT system security information that was updated by SP3. One symptom of this occurring is a "blue screen of death" (BSOD) with a stop code of 0xC00000DF, but there are others. If you manually replace the updated files Samsrv.dll, Samlib.dll, and Winlogon.exe, you do not get BSOD; you do, however, get the following message when you attempt to log on:

```
Logon Message:
! The system can not log you on (C00000DF). Please try again or
consult your system administrator.
```

Chapter 14: History and Role of Service Packs

If the updated file samsrv.dll is missing, you get:

```
lsass.exe - Unable to locate DLL
```

during GUI mode bootup.

If the updated file Samlib.dll is missing, you get the following BSOD:

```
STOP: c000021a {Fatal System Error}
The Windows Logon Process system process terminated unexpectedly
with a status 0xc0000080 (0x00000000 0x00000000).
```

If the updated file Winlogon.exe is missing, you get the following BSOD:

```
STOP: c000021a {Fatal System Error}
The Windows Logon Process system process terminated unexpectedly
with a status 0xc0000034 (0x00000000 0x00000000).
```

If all the updated files Samsrv.dll, Samlib.dll, and Winlogon.exe are missing, you get the following BSOD:

```
STOP: c000021a {Fatal System Error}
The Windows Logon Process system process terminated unexpectedly
with a status 0xc0000034 (0x00000000 0x00000000).
```

While daunting and somewhat disconcerting, at least these errors are fixable, and thus these bothersome error messages can be eliminated.

If your system is not bootable, you may start the recovery process by using the boot NT disks and choosing to repair the system. (Note: Make sure that you have an ERD with the updated version of Setupdd.sys before you begin this process.) If you don't have the original installation disks, make a set using the WINNT /OX command.

Get in the habit of always making fresh copies of the installation disks on a regular basis and for any installation you start.

When I was installing five NT servers for a biotech research firm, I took great care in ordering and properly licensing all the servers for their copy of NT Server. I used the CD media that came with the systems but inadvertently used a set of disks that I had created from an NT Server 120-day trial version CD.

Even though the installation was performed with production NT Server media, all the servers timed out and started crashing on a single Friday afternoon, exactly 120 days later. Again, the bright spot was that I learned more about NT recovery procedures during that single weekend than I had in the previous two years.

STEPS:

To modify the pre-SP3 Emergency Repair Disk

Step 1. Remove the attributes from the Setup.log file (as by entering **attrib -r -h -s a:\SETUP.LOG**).

Step 2. Add the following lines under [Files.WinNt] section:

```
\Winnt\System32\Samsrv.dll="samsrv.dll","30fde","\","nt40 repair
disk","samsrv.dll"
\Winnt\System32\Samlib.dll="samlib.dll","18010","\","nt40 repair
disk","samlib.dll"
\Winnt\System32\Winlogon.exe="winlogon.exe","2d0bb","\","nt40
repair disk","winlogon.exe"
```

Step 3. Copy the SP3 Samsrv.dll, Samlib.dll, and Winlogon.exe files to the root folder of the ERD.

Step 4. Restart your system with the NT boot disks (that you previously created) and select R to repair when prompted.

Step 5. Select Verify Windows NT System Files and continue.

Step 6. If prompted to insert Windows NT setup disk 4, press Esc to continue.

Step 7. After the Samsrv.dll, Samlib.dll, and Winlogon.exe files are replaced, press F3 to exit.

Step 8. Reboot and restart NT.

If this process fails, or you do not have a pre-SP3 Emergency Repair Disk, you must perform an upgrade of Windows NT over the current system. Copy the NT installation files to a network or local drive and then copy the new System Security Files from SP3 to that source directory. Then boot to DOS and run Winnt /B from the source directory to start the installation without requiring the disks.

Post-SP3 hotfixes

Hotfixes are interim fixes to specific problems periodically issued by Microsoft. Standard disclaimers apply to every hotfix. Microsoft recommends that unless you are experiencing the specific problem that the hotfix addresses, you should not apply it and you should wait for the next service pack release. An exception to this rule is when the hotfix is security related.

Microsoft also flatly states that each hotfix is not fully "regression tested." This implies that the hotfix may cause performance problems or may introduce a new problem to your system. Caveat emptor.

I follow this advice, but not for the reasons that Microsoft offers. I have found that keeping my production NT Servers loaded with every hotfix would require an army of technicians, numerous reboots, and an enormous change management system. Instead, I make sure that the most important hotfixes are always applied. The only other ones required are applied on an as-needed basis.

Hotfixes are generally cumulative. A hotfix may contain a newer version of a file that was modified by a previous hotfix. Despite this, you should always take care in applying hotfixes and know what requirements exist for each hotfix and what problem is addressed.

The order in which hotfixes are applied is critical. The POSTSP3.TXT file contains a recommended order of application for each. Follow the recommendations.

You can download hotfixes from the Microsoft FTP site. Make sure you download the correct version for your system (Remember, "i" = Intel, "a" = Alpha) and read the accompanying Readme files for each hotfix.

You can install the hotfix by clicking the executable, or you can copy the file to a directory and expand it by using the /x parameter. The extracted files will contain the updated system files, the Knowledge Base articles concerning the hotfix, a README.TXT file, and a HOTFIX.INF file. At the command line of the extracted directory, install the hotfix by typing **hotfix**.

The installation program will copy the file to your system and add a Registry entry noting that the hotfix has been applied. After the hotfix as been applied, you should reboot your system.

Secret

Multiple hotfixes may be applied simultaneously, and hotfixes may be incorporated into the service pack installation process. In this way, you can consistently apply the hotfixes that you need, in the recommended order. Most important, you can minimize reboot times.

I did not know of this "feature" until I started researching and testing the hotfix program for this book. When I was the IS Director for a broadcasting company, there were many times that knowing the technique for minimizing the reboot times would have paid for the price of multiple NT books. I don't know how many times I stared at a shutdown screen thinking there's got to be a better way. Now there is. (Actually, there always was, I just didn't know it.)

Make a subdirectory and copy the service pack file to it. Expand the service pack using the /x parameter and then make a subdirectory called Hotfix. Copy a single copy of HOTFIX.EXE and the expanded hotfix system files into this directory. *Do not copy the hotfix.inf files at this time.*

You must create a global HOTFIX.INF file that will be used by the installation program to apply the changes you desire. You create this file by merging the separate HOTFIX.INF files using cut and paste.

Most of the sections of HOTFIX.INF are generic and don't change from hotfix to hotfix. Copy any pertinent entries in the [MustReplace.System32.files], [SourceDisksFiles], [Drivers.files], and [Strings] sections to the global HOTFIX.INF file. I create a single comment string describing all the hotfixes included in this single INF file.

Now you can apply these hotfixes from the service pack installation directly or run HOTFIX from the command line in the \Hotfix directory.

One of the challenges enterprise-level Windows NT Server adminstrators have expressed to me is that it is exceeedingly difficult to know and manage exactly what has been applied to each of their servers on the server farm. Some servers have certain hotfixes applied and others don't, all for very important reasons. The Windows NT Server Service Pack Setup dialog box (see Figure 14-6) is one way to help "discover" hotfix version information. Admittedly, it's not perfect, and in fact one of the most frequent requests to the service pack development team at Microsoft has been some type of reporting tool that advises what service packs and hotfixes have been applied to a Windows NT Server machine. I suspect such a reporting tool would operate similar to Oil Change, a desktop application that checks your desktop operating system (such as Windows 98) and applications (Microsoft Office) for outdated files. Oil Change then, via the Internet, retrieves the latest desktop operating system and application upgrades for you to install.

Figure 14-6: Hotfixes have been found.

Secret

Some hotfixes are more essential than others. If you are having specific problems, then you should apply the correct hotfix. But it's been my experience that you don't need to apply all hotfixes just for the sake of applying hotfixes. You will spend a great deal of time that can be better used for other purposes.

If you do not have access to Service Pack 4 or are waiting for some period of time before you apply it, I recommend that you apply a select few critical post-SP3 hotfixes. These are:

- **GetAdmin.** Fixes security issues, Java, double-click issues.
- **Teardrop2.** Fixes UDP issues.
- **SRV.** Fixes denial-of-service issues.
- **PRIV.** Fixes security issues.

Service Pack 4

Service Pack 4 contains many fixes and enhancements to Windows NT. It contains some fixes to NT services and components and also contains some new features for NT.

Preinstallation requirements

The standard philosophy applies; make a backup of your system. You should back up the system, including the Registry files, and you should make a current ERD. Prepare for the worst and hopefully, you won't need it.

You should also have on hand any custom or vendor-supplied drivers. This enables you to quickly correct or supply the installation process files that may be required during the update.

A good idea, but in reality rarely carried out, is to disable nonessential drivers and services. This minimizes any conflicts and aids in copying over updates to files that may be open for use by a running service. Although I know that this is the preferred method and the party line as handed down by Microsoft, my experiences suggest that I introduce problems by not properly reenabling those services. Use your own judgment.

Secret

Internet Explorer (IE) 4.01 should be installed prior to applying SP4 in order to install the Protected Storage service. If IE 4.01 is not installed, an alternative is to run a program included with SP4. Run the command, **pstores -install** to install and register the service. Check the Control Panel Service applet and make sure that Protected Storage is installed and running.

The installation process

The installation process has changed slightly from SP3 to SP4. The initial screen (see Figure 14-7) contains both the option to create an uninstall directory and the legal agreement check box.

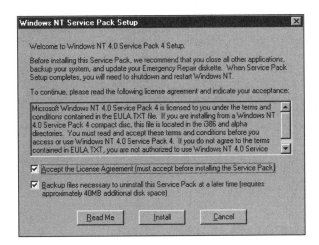

Figure 14-7: Welcome to Windows NT 4.0 Service Pack 4 Setup

If you select the backup option and click Install, you have a chance to stop the update process while the system is backing up your files. Once the process starts the installation process, you shouldn't halt it.

Secret

Again, be very careful about creating an uninstall directory. Only do this on the first time application of the service pack. If you select it after it has already been done once, you may not be able to correctly remove the service pack files and return to your previous state.

You will be able to run the remove process, but the restored files will be SP4 files that you saved during the second application.

40-Bit versus 128-Bit encryption

If the system being updated has "strong encryption" (a.k.a. 128-bit) in place, the screen shown in Figure 14-8 may appear when a 40-bit service pack is being applied.

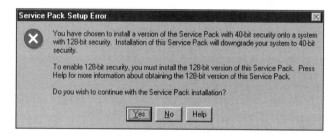

Figure 14-8: A Service Pack Setup error

You must obtain the domestic version of the service pack to continue. If you don't have any requirements for strong encryption at this time, you can ignore the warnings and continue.

As the installation process proceeds and the installation program inspects your system (see Figure 14-9), you have the opportunity to cancel.

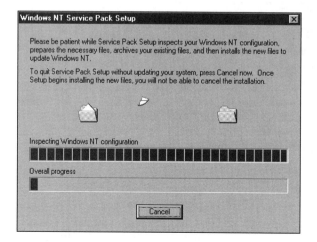

Figure 14-9: Inspecting Windows NT configuration

After this point, when you reach the next screen, you are committed and should wait until the update process finishes. Service Pack Setup updates your system files (see Figure 14-10).

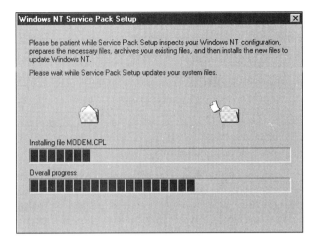

Figure 14-10: Setup updating your system files

If you instructed the program to overwrite your strong encryption files with a 40-bit service pack, you will have the option of not overwriting certain files (see Figure 14-11). You may be asked to copy the files NTLMSSPS.DLL, SCHANNEL.DLL, SECURITY.DLL, and NDISWAN.SYS over the domestic version files.

If your intent is to use strong encryption, then I recommend that you obtain the domestic version of the service pack and not use the older 128-bit files with the newer service pack.

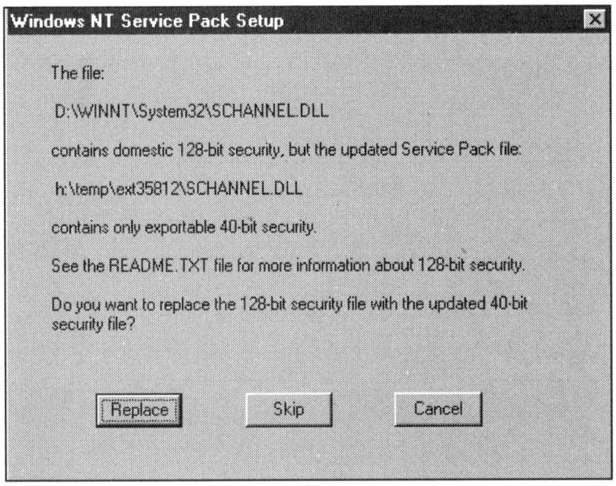

Figure 14-11: Replacing the 128-bit security file

When the update finishes, the system must be rebooted. During the boot phase, you will see the new Service Pack 4 label.

Uninstallation

Earlier service packs allowed you to uninstall by executing the UPDATE program and selecting an option for removal of the service pack. Service Pack 4 changes this and requires you to click the Add/Remove applet in the Control Panel. Open the Add/Remove applet, select Service Pack 4, and click the Add/Remove button. Service Pack 4 will be removed.

If the Service Pack 4 item is not listed in Add/Remove list, look in the \%systemroot%\$NtServicePackUninstall$\spuinst\ directory and execute the program spuninst.exe. This will uninstall Service Pack 4.

Secret

After the first application of a service pack, I always make a copy of the uninstall directory. Use Windows Explorer to highlight the directory, right-click, select copy, and then paste the copy to a safe spot. By doing so, I can be assured that I have a clean copy of the previous files and can always get back to a prior version if I make a mistake on the uninstall process. It may take a little disk space, but it's cheap insurance.

Like SP3, Service Pack 4 modifies the Security Account Manager (SAM) database. When you run the uninstall process, it does not replace the files that access the SAM database, such as Samsrv.dll, Samlib.dll, Lsasrv.dll, Services.exe, Msv1_0.dll, or Winlogon.exe, with their previous versions.

If SP4 is uninstalled and then SP3 is reinstalled, do not replace those files when asked. If you do, you won't be able to log on to the system. When asked to replace any of those files, just say "No."

After uninstalling SP4, to correctly reconfigure the CryptoAPI and Schannel programs, reapply SP3.

Uninstallation may remove the Protected Storage service from your system. If this happens, you will receive numerous event log entries. Simply rerun the PSTORES program to install it.

Summary

This chapter presented the history of service packs, covering the following:

- Introduction to service packs
- The Service Pack 2 fiasco
- Service Pack 3 and hotfixes
- Service Pack 4

Chapter 15

Service Pack 4 Fixes

In This Chapter

- Year 2000 fixes
- Internet Explorer 4.01 Service Pack 1
- Option Pack fixes
- Networking updates

To be honest, Microsoft struggled with Service Pack 4 in several ways. The struggle took the form of not wanting to repeat the Service Pack 2 implementation disaster, so that created a miniboom for Seattle-area temporary agencies providing $15/hour testers to test Service Pack 4 before it went out the door. It took the form of shipping Service Pack 4 later than expected. But the bigger struggle was defining what Service Pack 4 should be. Should it be bug fixes, such as discussed in this chapter, fulfilling the traditional role of service packs? Or should it be an avenue for introduction additional applications, operating system features, and enhancements to the existing functionality Windows NT Server 4.0 (such as are discussed in Chapter 16, "Service Pack 4 Additions and Miscellaneous")? In the end, it was both fixes and additions, reflecting a consensus that may please either everyone or no one, depending on your viewpoint. If you were to guesstimate, Service Pack 4 introduced more applications, features, and functionality than bug fixes.

But don't underestimate the importance of bug fixes. While not as sexy as new features, the bug fixes allow the most conservative among us to implement Windows NT Server as the network operating system (NOS) to run our mission-critical information infrastructure. It is the service pack release value (such as 4) that CIOs and other stakeholders consider when it's time to vote on electing Windows NT Server as the NOS to run their business network. And it has been my experience that these stakeholders aren't interpreting the service pack release number so much as "what new operating system features do I get" as "has Microsoft fixed Windows NT Server yet?" At the stakeholder decision-making level, conservatism prevails.

Part IV: Service Pack 4.0 and the Windows NT Server Option Pack

This chapter explains the fixes that are included with Service Pack 4 for major components of Windows NT Server 4.0. Major and minor updates and fixes are included in Service Pack 4. For detailed information on any of the components, please consult the Microsoft Support Knowledge Base (support.microsoft.com/support) and view article Q150734, "List of Bugs Fixed in Windows NT 4.0 Service Pack 4." You may also refer to Appendix D, "Service Pack 4 Details," of this book for the same information.

Year 2000 (Y2K) Fixes

The Year 2000 problem has been given a great deal of attention by the computer industry and by the general public. In fact, for many MCSE consultants, Y2K has emerged as one of the most lucrative consulting areas in the late 1990s. If only I had bought that stock at $5/share in Data Dimensions (DDIM), a leading Y2K consulting firm that is publicly traded!

Computer operating systems, including NT, have problems in recognizing the proper century, handling four-digit years, and handling a century leap year (any century year that is divisible by 400). If you are interested, you can obtain more information about the Year 2000 problem in numerous books, articles, and Web sites.

Microsoft addressed some of the Y2K issues with NT by releasing the Y2K-fix post-SP3 hotfix during 1998. Service Pack 4 builds on this hotfix and will make Windows NT fully Year 2000 compliant with the installation of the service pack and with an additional program, Y2ksetup.exe.

STEPS:
To run Y2Ksetup.exe

Step 1. Update the system with SP4.

Step 2. Locate and run the Y2ksetup.exe program in the \I386\Update directory for Intel-based systems or the \Alpha\Update directory for Alpha-based systems.

Note

There is no uninstall option for this update. There are two optional switches. The quiet switch, "-q," runs in silent mode, and "-d" runs in display mode. The display mode will not install or update any files and will only display components that may have Year 2000 issues.

When you start the program, you are greeted with the window shown in Figure 15-1. Additional information about the update is in the Y2K.TXT file.

Chapter 15: Service Pack 4 Fixes

Figure 15-1: Initial Year 2000 message

The Y2KSETUP program has a few installation requirements. Service Pack 4, Internet Explorer 4.01 with Service Pack 1, and Microsoft Data Access Components 2.0 with Service Pack 1 are requirements for the Year 2000 update. If your system is lacking any of these components, you are prompted to install them.

Secret

Site Server Express 3.0 is listed in the Readme doc as a requirement for the Y2K update, but not on the initial window listing the requirements. I did not have it installed on my system and all went very well in applying the update. Don't panic if you see this reference and don't have Site Server Express 3.0.

Some of the areas that are fixed with this service pack and Y2K update are:

- User Manager recognizes the year 2000 as a leap century.
- The Date/Time Control Panel applet updates the system clock.
- Find Files support only numeric character recognition in the decades field.
- Word document properties support four-digit years and recognizes 1900 and 2000 as valid centuries.
- Dynamic Host Configuration Protocol (DHCP) supports displaying the years between 2000 and 2009 with two digits.

After updating the system, you're rewarding with the message shown in Figure 15-2.

Figure 15-2: No Y2K issues detected

Internet Explorer 4.01 Service Pack 1 (SP1)

Internet Explorer 4.01 with Service Pack 1 can be installed by expanding the SP4 files and running the Ie4setup.exe program in the Msie401 folder. If the service pack was downloaded from the Microsoft FTP site, you may not have the compressed IE file (ie4setup.exe) on your system. If this is the case, you'll receive the rather ugly error screen shown in Figure 15-3.

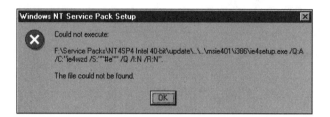

Figure 15-3: Missing IE4SETUP.EXE error message

This installation file is contained on the CD in the \Msie401 directory, or it may be downloaded separately from support/microsoft.com/support/downloads. A similar error message will be displayed for a missing Microsoft Data Access Component (MDAC) installation file.

You must obtain and install the required programs before upgrading the system with Y2KSETUP program.

Option Pack Fixes

Service Pack 4 includes updates and fixes for components that may be installed with the NT Option Pack (NTOP). This includes updates and fixes for Certificate Server, Internet Information Server 4.0, Message Queue (MSMQ) for Windows NT, Microsoft Transaction Server (MTS), Simple Mail Transport Protocol (SMTP), and Network News Transport Protocol (NNTP).

Secret

SP4 should be reinstalled after any NTOP components are added to your system. That is so you keep the most current file versions on board your Windows NT Server system.

Certificate Server

The Certificate Server updates several internal components. They include:

- Teletex encoding
- Serial numbers

- Backup and restore
- Outlook 98 update
- Leap year fix

Internet Information Server 4.0

Internet Information Server (IIS) updates include security enhancements and performance improvements. Several areas that IIS deals with, including memory, scripting, proxy server interaction, and client processing, are fixed.

Message Queue (MSMQ) for Windows NT

The MSMQ has quite a few fixes and enhancements applied in SP4. Here is a list from the SP4 Readme text file of those fixes:

- Performs cleanup of unused message file space every six hours to reduce disk-space usage.
- Clears all obsolete express message files when the MSMQ service starts.
- Enforces case insensitivity with foreign language characters in private queue names.
- Reduces occurrences of duplicate messages in persistent delivery mode.
- Exhibits performance counters for remote queues after a system recovery.
- Correctly shows per-session outgoing message performance counters.
- MSMQ MQIS servers refresh cached information every 12 hours.
- Fixes a problem causing transactional messages to be rejected in some cases.
- Allows specifying external certificates via the MSMQ ActiveX components interface.
- Transactional messages can be read from connector queues after restarting the MSMQ connector application.
- MQSetQueueSecurity for private queue is supported.
- MQCreateQueue for private queues now works on Windows NT Server 4.0 Option Pack installations on Microsoft Cluster Server computers.
- Supports sending Microsoft PowerPoint and Microsoft Word documents using ActiveX components.
- Fails when user attempts the renewal of internal certificates when Primary Enterprise Controller (PEC) is unreachable.

- Machine quota limitation is correctly recomputed after restarting the MSMQ service.
- MSMQ COM objects correctly process asynchronous message arrival events in multithreaded applications.
- Detection and reporting are improved of corrupted message packets in message files that could have resulted in a hung MSMQ service previously.
- Transactional messages sent offline are no longer rejected with a bad message class: MQMSG_CLASS_NACK_BAD_DST_Q. The symptom was that such messages were immediately routed to the sender's exact dead letter queue.
- Supports sending messages to different computers that have the same IP address. This can happen when a server attempts to send messages to two different RAS clients that happen to be assigned the same address one after the other.
- Recovers correctly when sending messages from a server to a client whose address is no longer valid (such as a RAS client that has timed out). Previously, extra message traffic might have been generated.
- Asynchronous messaging now functions correctly on Japanese Windows 95 when using the MSMQ COM objects.
- Fixes a problem in the MSMQ COM objects when referencing the response and admin queue properties of a message for queues not explicitly refreshed from the MQIS.
- In Windows 95, calling MQOpenQueue with a DIRECT format no longer blocks for a long time.
- If the Windows NT 4.0 licensing service isn't running, then MSMQ per-seat licensing is no longer enforced.
- A specific call to MQLocateBegin no longer causes an exception on the MQIS server. This could have occurred previously when the Label restriction was specified with an incorrect vt argument (anything other than VT_LPWSTR).
- MSMQ applications can be run by users logged onto local machine accounts. Note that this used to work anyway for shadowed local accounts—that is, for accounts that had "identical" local accounts (user name/password) on the server machine. The default security for queues created by such users is that everyone is granted full control (in particular, read and delete permissions).
- A new MQIS update/restore utility is supplied that enables administrators to seamlessly recover crashed MQIS servers.

Microsoft Transaction Server (MTS)

MTS is a key component for Microsoft's burgeoning emergence in the electronic commerce area. To say MTS has significant attention devoted to it in the Microsoft BackOffice family is an understatement. MTS is updated with a new Java Context class. If you're building applications using Visual J++, you can use the new Context class instead of IObjectContext. The Context class enables you to do the following using Visual J++:

- Declare that the object's work is complete.

- Prevent a transaction from being processed, either temporarily or permanently.

- Instantiate other MTS objects and include their work within the scope of the current object's transaction.

- Determine whether a caller is in a particular role.

- Determine whether security is enabled.

- Determine whether the object is executing within a transaction. See the Visual J++ section of the *Programmer's Reference* for complete documentation of the new class.

Simple Mail Transport Protocol (SMTP), Network News Transport Protocol (NNTP)

Internet-based e-mail and newsgroups are clearly a strategic area of importance for Microsoft. SMTP now allows multiple virtual servers and an ETRN command for dequeuing mail over dial-up connections. This allows a small SMTP site to transfer e-mail using a very low-cost connection to an Internet service provider (ISP). Using ETRN is the default method for Small Business Server to communicate, via Microsoft Exchange, with ISPs for Internet-based e-mail send and receive communications. NNTP supports newsgroups on your Windows NT Server network.

Networking and OS Fixes

I now know that I have the attention of all the network managers, CIOs, and the like reading this book. Why? Because such readership is extremely interested in what core networking and operating system fixes are contained in SP4. In fact, I'd speculate that for the majority of readers, SP4 is synonymous with networking and OS fixes; it is the reason you would implement SP4. This section will discuss the fixes to core networking services such as IP address assignment (DHCP) and name resolution (DNS,

WINS). You will also read about fixes pertaining to more specialized networking services including Routing Information Protocol (RIP), Routing and Remote Access Service (RRAS), and Point-to-Point Tunneling Protocol (PPTP). This section ends with fixes applied to the Event Log service that most of us can benefit from plus a few miscellaneous operating system fixes.

Dynamic Host Configuration Protocol (DHCP), Domain Name Server (DNS), Windows Internet Naming Service (WINS)

All three of these three key network services received major fixes in Service Pack 4. DHCP, DNS, and WINS are discussed in Chapter 8, "DNS, DHCP, WINS."

Domain Name Server (DNS) had the following problems fixed:

- Non-existent "A" record time-out problem
- Resolving MX records with a recursive query
- BIND incompatibilities
- WriteAuthorityNs Registry key fix
- Zone delegation
- DNS.EXE access violation error fix
- Reduced root server traffic
- Better recursion response times
- Eliminating deadlock conditions
- Local network prioritization of queries
- Adding a WildcardAllTypes Registry flag
- Cache pollution fix
- Non-port 53 operation via the SendOnNonDnsPort Registry key
- No forward of delegations

Dynamic Host Configuration Protocol (DHCP) had the following fixes applied:

- Client failure with multinetted DHCP Server
- Duplicate IP addresses with SP2
- Diskless workstations being unable to find BOOTP Server
- Poor server performance with large numbers of scopes
- Server memory leaks on Alpha version of NT Server
- General performance updates
- Audit logging fixes

Routing Information Protocol (RIP) Listener, Microsoft Routing and Remote Access Service (RRAS), and Point-to-Point Tunneling Protocol (PPTP)

These topics, RIP, RRAS, and PPTP are, to be honest, esoteric and rather far removed from the workaday world of Windows NT Server networks for most of us. But if you are one of the few, you will take great interest in how Microsoft addressed these matters in SP4. Here's how. Service Pack 4 includes the Point-to-Point Tunneling Protocol (PPTP) post-SP3 hotfixes up to and including the PPTP3 fix. Performance has been improved, and other corrections, some involving security issues, have been made.

A new version of Microsoft Challenge and Authentication Protocol (MSCHAP v2) has been implemented for Virtual Private Network (VPN) connections. This new protocol provides mutual authentication, stronger initial data encryption keys, and different encryption keys for the transmit and receive paths. To minimize the risk of password compromise during MSCHAP exchanges, version 2 drops support for the MSCHAP v1 password change and will not transmit the LMHash encoding of the password.

For VPN connection requests, MSCHAP v2 is offered before MSCHAP v1. Dial-up connections are not affected by this change.

A new Registry key, SecureVPN, has been defined to force the use of MSCHAP v2. When set to "1," it causes the server to drop any VPN connections that do not authenticate using MSCHAP v2. If security is a concern, then this method should be used.

To use SecureVPN, modify the Registry key, HKEY_LOCAL_MACHINE\System\CurrentControlSet\Services\RasMan\PPP\SecureVPN, with a DWORD value of 1 to force MSCHAP v2. The default is "0."

Because the SecureVPN Registry key forces the use of MSCHAP v2 for all VPN connections, it should be used on the server. This allows the client to connect to other systems that may not use v2.

The Registry variable UseLmPassword can be set to prevent clients from sending the LM response to an MSCHAP challenge. When this variable is absent, it has a default value of one, allowing use of the LM response. In most circumstances, this variable won't be needed if you use MSCHAP v2.

To prevent this, modify the Registry key, HKEY_LOCAL_MACHINE\System\CurrentControlSet\Services\RasMan\PPP\Chap\UseLmPassword with a DWORD value of 1 to send the LMHash of the password. This is the default. A value of 0 does not allow the LMHash of the password to be sent.

Setting this variable to zero on a server will cause the server to drop any connection that uses the LM response in an MSCHAP exchange. Setting this variable to zero on a client will prevent the client from using LM responses in MSCHAP exchanges. This variable affects both dial-up and VPN connections.

A historyless mode for encryption and compression over PPTP connections has been enabled. This new mode improves performance in high-latency networks, or networks that commonly experience significant packet loss (such as the Internet). In order to negotiate historyless mode, both the PPTP client and the server must use this method. If either client or server refuses the new mode, normal MPPE compression and encryption will be negotiated. A corresponding release, Microsoft Dial-Up Networking 1.3, is available for Windows 95 clients, while the new release of Windows 98 already includes the appropriate client code.

To enable historyless encryption/compression, modify the Registry item HKEY_LOCAL_MACHINE\SYSTEM\CurrentControlSet\Services\NdisWan\Parameters\Historyless with a DWORD value of 1 to enable it and a value of 0 to disable it. The default is enabled.

The following items are noted in the PPTP fix Readme document:

- The default PPTP receive window size was increased to 16.
- The window between the NDISWAN driver and the PPTP driver was increased.
- The PPTP frame size has been set to default to 1,400 bytes to avoid packet fragmentation.
- PPTP server responsiveness has been improved for the time period right after termination of multiple PPTP connections.
- A PPTP server issue of an improperly configured packet header "start session" has been corrected.
- Integrity of session encryption in MPPE has been improved by increasing the randomness of successive packet key management following an encryption or compression reset.
- Corrected a RAS/PPTP user interface design issue that could mislead an administrator regarding the actual configuration of the server.
- Updated MSCHAP to disable sending the LMHash when a client is set to "require" 128-bit encryption.

More information on about MSCHAP v2 may be found in the "Microsoft Windows 98 Dial-Up Networking Security Upgrade Release Notes" included with the client update program on the Strong Encryption site.

Event Log Service

The NT Event Log Service contains three new, useful events. Two new shutdown events and a system version event have been added.

At a broadcasting company, I was responsible for remote NT servers. They were generally unmanned and colocated in the telecommunications room of a vendor connected only by a frame relay circuit. In our case, the servers were running a somewhat buggy version of an interactive voice response (IVR) system developed internally. I used Server Manager to remotely connect to those machines for diagnostic purposes and used remote control software for running programs on the servers.

It was very difficult to diagnose software that had run amok. I often had to guess at the cause of the last shutdown. Was it application related? Did the last person reboot the system and then forget to log it? Did the system crash or lose power? Service Pack 4 would have definitely helped in some of those situations by at least telling me what type of shutdown occurred.

For one thing, SP4 has changed the optional nature of this shutdown/crash debug event for NT Server. (Note: NT Workstation has not changed. It operates the same as always in this regard.) The Event Log now records a shutdown event, no matter how the system may have halted—either gracefully or not so gracefully.

Event ID 6006 records a clean shutdown event. When a user accesses the shutdown screen by issuing a Ctrl+Alt+Delete and pressing the Shutdown/Restart button, by selecting Shutdown/Restart from the Start menu, or by clicking Shutdown/Restart from the logon screen, the system will record this new event.

A "dirty" shutdown event is recorded with an Event ID of 6008. When the system is anything other than a clean shutdown, it is assumed to be a forced shutdown. This can happen when the system is power-cycled or some other catastrophic event happens. (Can you say BSOD? Sure you can.)

While NT is running, it periodically writes a time stamp to the Registry and the system flushes the write to the disk. Additionally, the system writes the clean shutdown event to the Registry. If the clean shutdown flag is not located during reboot, a dirty shutdown event is recorded. The data contained in this event is the last-alive time written to the Registry.

The default last-alive time period is five minutes. This can be changed by changing the Registry field at the following location: HKEY_LOCAL_MACHINE\Software\Microsoft\Windows\CurrentVersion\Reliability\LastAliveStamp. Add a DWORD field named "TimeStampInterval" and enter the value you would like, in minutes. A value of zero prevents any time stamp logging. In this case, only the boot and normal shutdown time stamps will be written.

Other fixes

Many other fixes are described in the 600+ Knowledge Base articles dealing specifically with Service Pack 4. Fixes to problems with Macintosh connectivity, printing, and file sharing are addressed, as are NetWare and IPX issues. I encourage you to look through the list and search for equipment or software components that you run on your system. I'm confident that something relevant will appeal to you.

Summary

This chapter presented specific Service Pack 4 fixes:

- Year 2000 fixes
- Internet Explorer 4.01 Service Pack 1
- Option Pack fixes
- Networking updates

Chapter 16

Service Pack 4 Additions and Miscellaneous

In This Chapter

- Security Configuration Editor
- NetShow Server 3.0
- Site Server Express 3.0
- Miscellaneous SP4 components
- Windows NT Services for UNIX

This chapter describes the new Security Configuration Editor (SCE), the NetShow Server 3.0, Site Server Express 3.0, various SP4 components, and a new package from Microsoft, the Windows NT Services for UNIX. What goes unsaid is that all of these topics will help prepare you for Windows 2000 Server. The additions to Service Pack 4 are among your best guides to what Windows 2000 Server will be like and what it will include.

Security Configuration Editor (SCE)

Microsoft has introduced a very handy security management tool, the Security Configuration Editor (SCE), in SP4. SCE is intended to be a template-based security configuration and analysis tool. It is important that you understand that SCE does not introduce any new security features or capabilities to Windows NT. It simply attempts to consolidate the many configuration settings available for NT. SCE is a first step at change management for NT.

Note

The SCE is sometimes referenced as the Security Configuration Manager or SCM in the documentation and at the Microsoft Web site. The most common reference to it is the "SCE."

Windows NT suffers many complaints from administrators about poor security. You may not be aware that these complaints are well justified. I know I've learned about the importance of security in companies of all sizes.

In fact, I've learned some of my greatest security lessons in small companies where the founder/owner was still active, still saving personal financial information on the network, and still concerned someone would see it who shouldn't. Although numerous programs and utilities are available to modify security settings for the OS and file systems, the time and effort required to plug every hole and stop every gap is monumental. Often those security holes are left after a basic installation and remain for the life of the machine.

In order for a Windows NT server to be secured and still remain usable for its clients, Registry values have to be changed, modifications to the User Manager are required, and Windows Explorer is needed to properly configure permissions on sensitive files. The absence of a unified security program has caused most systems to remain vulnerable because most NT administrators don't take the proper steps in securing their systems. And even if they do, it's very easy to miss a crucial item or two.

In addition to the standard NT utilities, I generally used the C2CONFIG program distributed in the NT Resource Kit. I used it not because it was the only way to set crucial security parameters, but because it was easy to use and convenient. SCE attempts to make the process even easier and more maintainable.

The SCE may not be the end-all NT security manager, nor is it the answer to all of NT's security holes, but it does take a step in the right direction and the price is right—free. In fact, perhaps you, like me, think of computer and network security as an evolving life form. If that is so, SCE is another step in that evolution. SCE is an optional component of SP4 and comes on the CD or can be downloaded from the Microsoft FTP site (ftp://ftp.microsoft.com/bussys/winnt/winnt-public/tools/SCM).

After downloading, the program can be installed with either the GUI front end as a snap-in component for MMC or a command line interface only. The command line interface is very handy when you do not intend to analyze or view the settings locally. The command line program can run and update or analyze the system. The results file can be used back at the console for viewing the results or making setting changes. One of the themes that repeats itself throughout this book is the importance of reporting. The results file serves as your security report.

If set up properly, the Schedule service may be set to run the command line interface on a regular basis for automatic auditing of the system. The resulting log files can e-mailed or copied by for analysis.

Installing SCE

To install SCE, locate the /mssce directory on the CD or extract the downloaded file to a subdirectory, and execute MSSCE.EXE. This installs the proper files and the MMC snap-in that must be configured in the MMC. In

Chapter 16: Service Pack 4 Additions and Miscellaneous

order to install the command line version (see Figure 16-1), execute MSSCE.EXE /C.

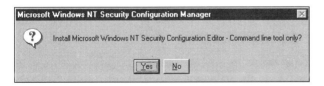

Figure 16-1: SCE command line installation

After finishing the installation, start MMC and install the SCE snap-in. Select Console ⇨ Add/Remove Snap-in and click the Add button. Highlight Security Configuration Editor and click OK. After you have added the component, the main console window should have the SCE tree displayed, as shown in Figure 16-2.

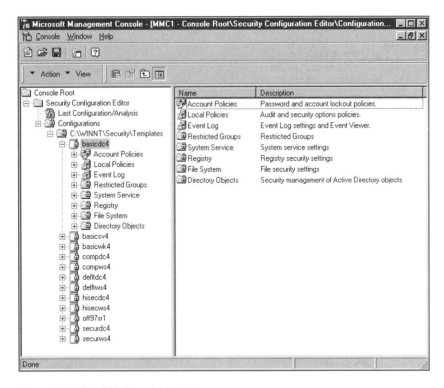

Figure 16-2: The SCE Console directory

At this point, the Last Configuration/Analysis may be empty if a configuration or analysis hasn't been performed. The second directory tree contains 12 predefined configuration templates.

Template components

These predefined templates are intended to provide a starting point for using the SCE, and each contain a specific setting for the intended target machine. Additional security templates may be vendor-supplied configuration templates that must be applied before their application is installed. I would envision firewall vendors using this capability.

The default templates have an .inf extension and are stored in the C:\Winnt\security\templates directory. The predefined templates are:

- **BASICDC4.** Basic Domain Controller 4.0
- **BASICSV4.** Basic Server 4.0
- **BASICWK4.** Basic Workstation 4.0
- **COMPDC4.** Compatible Domain Controller 4.0
- **COMPWS4.** Compatible Workstation 4.0 (and Server 4.0)
- **HISECDC4.** High Security Domain Controller 4.0
- **HISECWS4.** High Security Workstation 4.0 (and Server 4.0)
- **OFF97SR1.** Office 97 SR1
- **SECURDC4.** Secure Domain Controller 4.0
- **SECURWS4.** Secure Workstation 4.0 (and Server 4.0)

Basic

The basic configuration files contain the default Windows NT settings. You may use the basic security settings to reset any modifications you may make using another security file. The only settings that the basic files do not restore are user rights. An application may require special rights such as logging on as a service or acting as part of the operating system.

Compatible

The compatible configuration increases the security settings slightly from the basic configuration. Password and lockout policies are set, and some auditing is established. I would recommend that you start with slight, incremental settings and determine if your users or any of your applications will have problems with increased security settings.

High security

High security configurations are optimum security settings and would not normally be used. Microsoft warns that most applications will not function under this setting level. It is intended to be used as a guide for developing standard security configurations.

MS Office 97 SR1

This configuration is similar to the compatible configuration and should be used when running Office 97. Install Office 97 first, and then set the security levels.

Secure

Secure configurations increase the settings considerably. With this setting level, your applications may have problems.

Always use a copy of the bundled templates. Don't modify them, or if you do, make sure you have made a backup copy of the files on your hard drive.

I've found that the SCE doesn't behave quite the way you expect it to, from an NT Explorer point-of-view. I was unable to single-click on a template name or use F2 to rename it. Instead, I manually changed the filename directly in the Template directory.

When you right-click the template and do a Save As command, the copy of the file with a new name is written to the directory but not reflected in the SCE directory immediately. Right-click the directory in the left pane of the SCE and click Refresh.

The Save As command also doesn't copy comments in the old file to the new file, nor does it allow you to add a description. I manually added two new lines of "[Profile Description] <description>" to the file.

Expand any template and you'll see eight individual items beneath it. These eight categories are account policies, local policies, event log, restricted groups, system service, Registry, file system, and directory objects.

Account policies

Account policies contain information about passwords such as the required complexity, maximum/minimum age, minimum length, and size of a password history. The option to force a user to log on before changing a password is also available (see Figure 16-3).

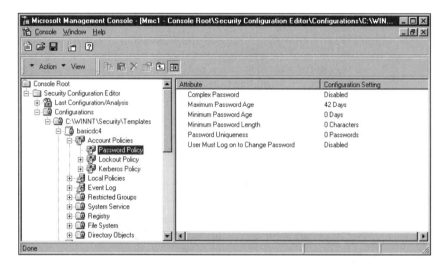

Figure 16-3: Account policies

Policies concerning passwords are probably the most troublesome to users, but also the most important. Many secure systems have been compromised by weak passwords or by lax security surrounding the use of the passwords. This section should not be overlooked in setting the first security configurations. More pragmatically, be sure to strike an appropriate balance between lax and restrictive account policies. If they are too lax, you won't reach your goals of sufficient network security. But if you make your account policies too restrictive, you'll find people remaining logged on nonstop or leaving their passwords on yellow stickies on their workstations.

The account lockout policies determine if, when, and how long to lock out users after invalid logon attempts. A common technique for attempting to break into a system is through brute force and repeated attempts at logging on. This minimizes that possibility.

Kerberos policy refers to a security system that will be deployed with Windows 2000. But if you simply can't wait for Windows 2000 to learn more about Kerberos security, join me up on the Internet. If you type in the term "Kerberos" in any major Internet search engine, you will be overwhelmed with the results.

Local policies

Local policies contain audit policy, user rights assignment, and security options (see Figure 16-4). Audit policies are normally set in the User Manager. Care must be taken when setting audit events. If they are set incorrectly, system performance can suffer if numerous events are being audited. Each audit event requires some overhead. In fact, you must once again exercise caution in the use of audit policies. You can get so excited about knowing when absolutely anything happens on your system that you negatively impact system performance. Imagine this. You know everything that is going on all of the time (literally), but no one can get anything done. Seems kind of backward, doesn't it?

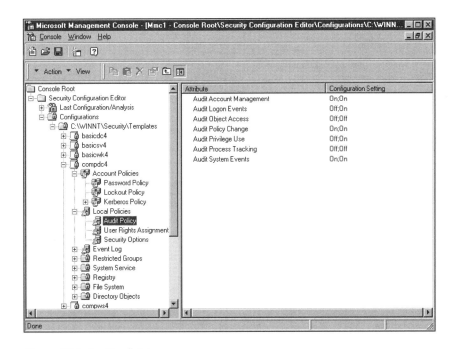

Figure 16-4: Audit policies

User rights assign specific rights to users or groups. Security options contains important settings for overall system use. A key configuration setting allows the change of the default Administrator name and the default Guest name. These easily guessed names should always be changed.

An often overlooked setting is the message text for users attempting to log on. I paid little attention to this until a friend of mine, who was working at a biotech firm at the time, suffered a computer break-in by an outsider. The intruder was caught but successfully defended himself in court because the system greeting said, "Welcome to . . ." The court interpreted this as an open invitation. Make sure you post the "No Trespassing" signs.

Event log

Each log file, application, security, and system, parameter can be set (see Figure 16-5). An additional setting provides the capability to bring the server down when a log file fills up. While a harsh setting, this prevents a hacker from filling the file in order to cover his tracks. The System Administrator must inspect and determine the cause of a full log file before further operation of the system. If the option is used, greater care and attention must be given to each log file.

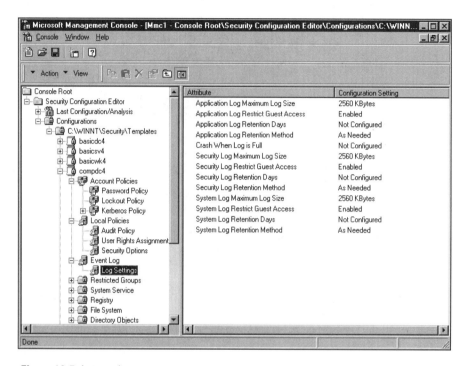

Figure 16-5: Log settings

Restricted groups

Restricted Groups is one of the few new features introduced by SCE. It audits group membership. Members are defined for a group and may be automatically set by the configuration process. If a user is added to the group and the configuration analysis is run, the recently added user will be removed.

While testing this feature, I had some difficulty in getting it to perform as expected. Further exploration and testing of Restricted Groups will be required as SCE is more widely deployed and used.

System service

The System service is an extremely useful tool (see Figure 16-6). I've spent far too much time in the Service Control Panel applet, turning services on and off and from manual to automatic. Then going back in and seeing if I did it correctly. Once the service is set up, it is possible to have many different environments or temporary service configurations for use in unique circumstances. For example, it is preferred to stop all unnecessary services to install certain applications (such as the NT Option Pack). With this tool, the proper configuration could be set, and the system, restarted and ready for the installation process. When the process was finished, the reverse configuration could be run. Very easy and less chance for errors.

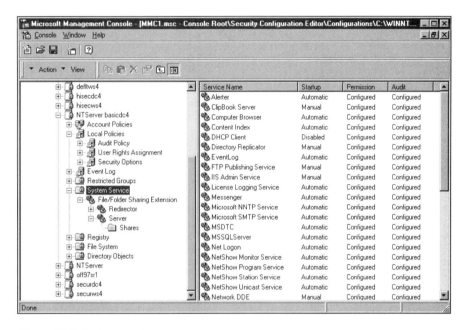

Figure 16-6: System service

If installed, the Folder Sharing Extension can manage security settings on network shares. This also is an extremely handy capability to have when reconfiguring a server after a failure or restore. After a certain amount of time, if proper logs aren't kept, share permissions can become quite messy. They can now be managed and controlled via the SCE.

Registry

SCE facilitates a new capability: Registry change auditing. The Registry component allows security auditing of Registry keys. New keys may be added by right-clicking the Registry header shown in Figure 16-6 and selecting New Key. You'll see the screen shown in Figure 16-7. Key values cannot be set here, just the capability to control and audit security permissions. On a practical level, what does this mean? Perhaps you use a robust client/server accounting application such as Great Plains Dynamics. Such an application requires you to modify the Registry to add keys relating to multiuser conditions (the specifics are provided by the software vendor, Great Plains).

Well, if I'm the battle-hardened and seasoned CIO for a company, I want to be able to see the details on changes that were made to the Windows NT Server machines in my server farm, changes such as those required for Great Plains Dynamics.

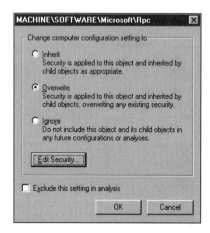

Figure 16-7: Configuration settings

Any of the Registry keys can be set to inherit their security settings from their parent keys, or the security configuration can be overwritten and applied by the SCE. By clicking the Edit Security button, you provide for extensive controls to be set for permissions and auditing (see Figure 16-8). Restrictions can be placed on querying or setting values, creating or enumerating subkeys, and other key values.

The extensive control over Registry keys and the inherent complexity of the key values that affect the overall operation of the system requires that a great deal of thought and testing be done before extensive modifications are made.

File system

The File System component works in the same manner as the Registry. Right-click the header, and you can add files or folders to the preinstalled list. Once inserted, the file or folder can have all of the security permissions set.

The same caveat applies as the Registry. Be careful when setting permissions on critical files. Be aware that someone may change the permissions in the normal manner, but the SCE can set them in unexpected ways.

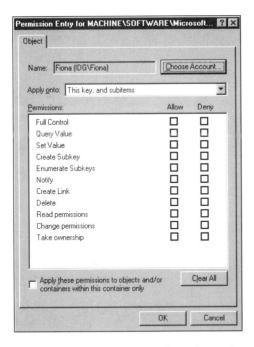

Figure 16-8: Security Audit configuration settings

Configuring and analyzing

Configuring and then later analyzing the system is an easy process. The first step is to assign a configuration template for either configuration or analysis. Highlight Last Configuration/Analysis and right-click to select the Assign Configuration item (see Figure 16-9).

Directory objects

Directory objects are a feature of the Windows 2000 Active Directory and not within the scope of this book.

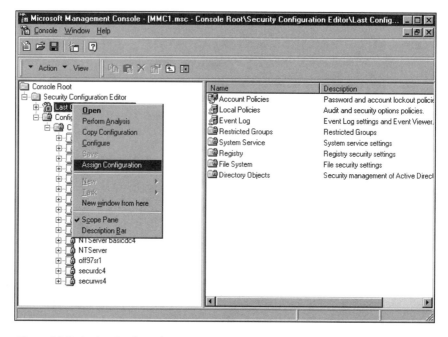

Figure 16-9: Assign Configuration

The File Browse window will open to select the configuration file. Select the one you want to use and click OK. Right-click again and this time select Configure. A window to set the configuration log file appears. Select either the default or a new log file and click OK. The Configuration Status window appears (see Figure 16-10). The process may take some time to complete.

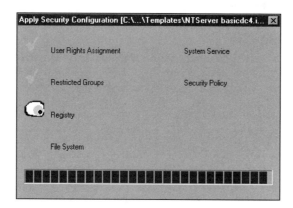

Figure 16-10: Configuration Status window

Chapter 16: Service Pack 4 Additions and Miscellaneous

At this point, you can perform an analysis on the system. Assign a configuration to use and then select Perform Analysis. As shown in Figure 16-11, you are able to see the results of selecting a configuration model.

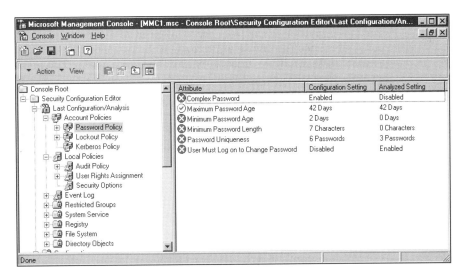

Figure 16-11: Configuration analysis

After the analysis finishes, the results are displayed for review. A green check mark appears beside a setting that is in compliance with the target configuration file. A red circle with an X in it signals a potential problem or deviation from the target configuration file. If there is nothing to the left of the item, the item is not configured and not used in the analysis.

It's a relatively easy task to traverse the tree to spot and correct any problems with any of the items. Once they are modified, reapply the corrected security configuration template on the system.

Command line configuration and analysis

The SCE cannot run on a remote machine. This is a limitation but not a major problem. The command line version of SCE can be installed and run periodically. The resulting log files may be exported back to a console and graphically analyzed.

The secedit.exe file may be run manually or from a batch file. Using the AT command to automatically run it periodically is a very powerful auditing tool. Secedit can configure the system, analyze the system, export a configuration template from a database, or validate a configuration template.

To configure a system, you can use the following command line and parameters:

secedit /configure [/cfg filename] [/areas Areas] [/overwrite] [/db filename] [/log LogPath] [/verbose] [/quiet]

The cfg parameter is the path and configuration file to be used. The areas parameter specifies the security areas to be processed. The default is all areas. If using multiple areas, separate them by a space. The names for the security areas are:

- **SECURITYPOLICY.** Local policy and domain policies
- **GROUP_MGMT.** Restricted group settings
- **USER_RIGHTS.** User logon rights and privilege granting
- **DSOBJECTS.** Security on directory objects
- **REGKEYS.** Security on local Registry keys
- **FILESTORE.** Security on local file storage
- **SERVICES.** Security on defined services

The overwrite parameter specifies that the contents of the database should be overwritten by the contents of the configuration file. The db parameter is the path to database that SCE will use to configure the system. The log parameter is the path to the log file for the process. If not specified, output is to the console window.

Finally, the verbose and quiet parameters control the number of messages in the log file.

The analysis works in a very similar manner to the configuration. The resulting log file can be retrieved by the SCE and analyzed as if it had been run locally.

Conclusion

The SCE is a very powerful tool but is not an absolutely complete security management utility. It has been included in SP4 as a preview to Windows 2000 and likely will be modified by the time that it is distributed with the release of Windows 2000. But it is useful now and a valuable aid in today's environment. It is well worth your while to learn and implement across your network.

NetShow Services 3.0

NetShow Services is a collection of service including a streaming server designed to unicast (one to one) or multicast (one to many) video and audio content over low- and high-bandwidth networks. In addition to the server components, NetShow includes tools for preparing content and also includes the Microsoft Windows Media Player. The Media Player client receives and displays content from the server in the form of Advanced Streaming Format (ASF) files, NetShow Theater Server format, RealNetworks, RealAudio, and RealVideo files.

NetShow will also manage the distribution of multimedia content to other NetShow servers; distribute PowerPoint presentations; make file transfers; and distribute standard wav, avi, or mov files.

NetShow terminology

NetShow introduces several new terms that are crucial to understanding the overall operation of the service.

Streaming

Streaming describes the act of sending and delivering data to a client in a continuous sequence. The client will normally request the data and receive it for display in a client program called the *player*. The streaming player will start decoding the compressed data and immediately display it, without waiting for the full transmission. The RealAudio Player from Progressive Networks and the Microsoft Media Player are both streaming players.

The transmitted data may be of many different content formats such as audio, video, files, presentation files, or any combination. The server and player handle the files and the content contained within them, in the same format. The NetShow Service uses the Advanced Streaming Format (ASF) as its format.

Multicasting or unicasting

The NetShow Service may broadcast the content stream to many different clients. When a single stream of content is broadcast to a single client, this is a *unicast*. When a server broadcasts a stream of content to multiple clients, this is a *multicast*.

The unicast method of broadcasting is done through a publishing point. A *publishing point* is similar to an IIS virtual directory and is simply a folder on the server that holds the content. The multicast method of broadcasting is done through a station. A *station* is a file on the server that contains the locations of the ASF content.

Bandwidth

All streaming servers and clients are sensitive to the bandwidth between them. Clients dialed into the network via a 28.8 modem connection cannot receive the same amount of data in the same amount of time as a user connected through a network interface. NetShow Services takes this into consideration. One of the ways that this is accomplished is through compression of the data. The task of the server is to compress the data, and the task of the client player is to decompress it. The compressor/decompressor, or codec, is the algorithm that performs this task.

Installation

Installation of the NetShow services is very straightforward from the SP4 CD. Start the program from the SP4 opening screen or by executing the nsserver.exe directly to bring up the initial screen, shown in Figure 16-12.

Figure 16-12: The NetShow Service Welcome screen

The next screen specifies the installation requirements. The server components require SP4 to be installed and that the administrator of the system perform the installation. When installing just the administrator components on a Windows 95 system, you must also have installed DCOM 95 and IE 4.01.

The next screen allows you to decide if the full installation will be performed on a Windows NT server or if only the administrator components and the Media Player will be installed. Select one and click Continue.

The next screen allows the selection of the default content directory. The default selection is C:\asfroot. Enter the appropriate directory and continue.

The screen shown in Figure 16-13 offers you the choice whether or not to allow HTTP streaming. If IIS is currently running on your system, then don't choose this option. NetShow will attempt to use port 80, the same one used by IIS, and will not be able to finish the installation. It is possible but not recommended that NetShow Services be installed on the system running IIS. The bandwidth and processor requirements may adversely affect the operation of IIS and the users connecting to it. HTTP streaming is used primarily to extend the delivery of data beyond corporate firewalls. It's assumed that port 80 will already be open and may be used for delivery of streaming data.

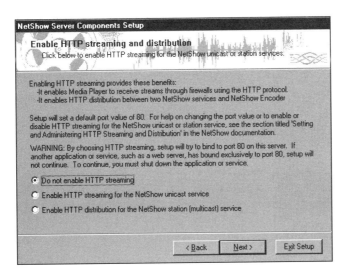

Figure 16-13: HTTP streaming

The next screen allows entry of the NetShow Service account. The system will create a default account to use. Finally, the installation program will stop the IIS services, if running, and finish the installation.

NetShow service administration

At this point, you should be able to bring up the Web-based NetShow Service Administration screen (see Figure 16-14). It is here that you will perform the vast bulk of your NetShow configuration, administration, and troubleshooting. I recommend you take a moment to appreciate this easy Web-based administration tool. Ask yourself, is this the type of tool, from a look and feel perspective, that I might see more of in Windows 2000 Server?

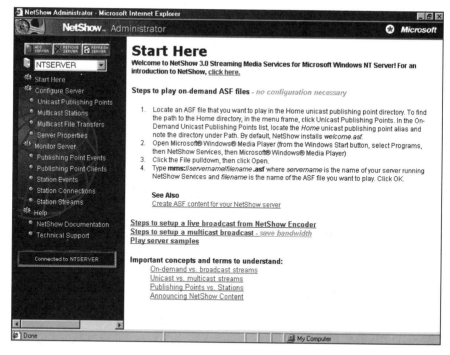

Figure 16-14: NetShow Service Administration

The menu displayed in the left-hand pane enables the complete administration and management of the NetShow Service, including accessing the online documentation. The necessary steps in setting up and configuring a server can be accomplished by working from top to bottom.

Configure Server

The layout of the NetShow Administrator is very easy to follow and extremely helpful (see Figure 16-15). Topics are described, and additional help is found that describes the component and helpful tips in configuration.

Chapter 16: Service Pack 4 Additions and Miscellaneous

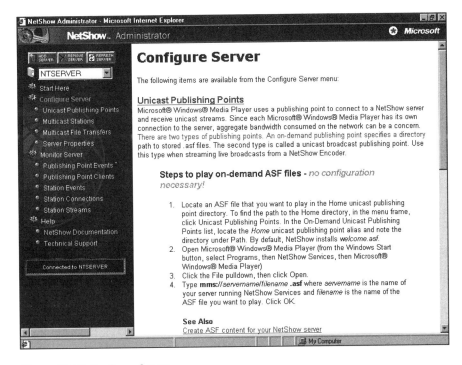

Figure 16-15: Configure Server

NetShow Services installs some demonstration stations that can be used as a guide. To run these samples, click Play Server Samples on the main, Start Here window.

Unicast publishing points

On-demand or broadcast publishing points may be configured (see Figure 16-16). The default on-demand directory is already defined. No broadcast publishing points are created after the initial installation. QuickStart Wizards for both types of publishing points may be used. Check the Wizard box and select New.

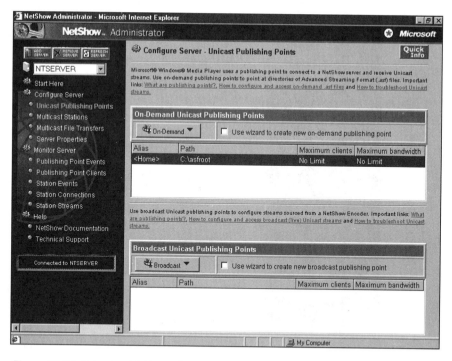

Figure 16-16: Unicast publishing points

You will see the QuickStart Wizard configuring and publishing screen shown in Figure 16-17. Click Next.

Figure 16-17: Unicast On-Demand QuickStart Wizard

You will now see the Unicast On-Demand Wizard. Follow the instructions presented by the wizard (Figure 16-18) and click Next. The key point is that, with Figure 16-18, you are creating a unicast on-demand stream configuration. All combined, these steps result in your creating a publishing point (see Figure 16-19) and entering an alias and a local directory for the content.

Secret

In order to test the publishing point correctly, you must copy the default ASF file into the directory.

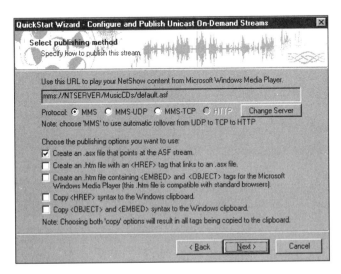

Figure 16-18: Unicast on-demand publishing method

Start the QuickStart Wizard to configure and publish a unicast broadcast stream. Select the source of the broadcast publishing point. It may be a NetShow encoder, a remote station, or a remote publishing point. Then select the alias and path for the publishing point (see Figure 16-19). If a remote station or remote publishing point option is chosen, NetShow Services must be set up on those remote sites.

The final step is to select the properties desired for the publishing point (see Figure 16-20). Remember that the key distinction between unicast and broadcast is the audience. With unicast, you are working with a point-to-point session. With broadcast, you are working with a point-to-multipoint audience. That's the key difference. And you configure NetShow to accommodate both scenarios.

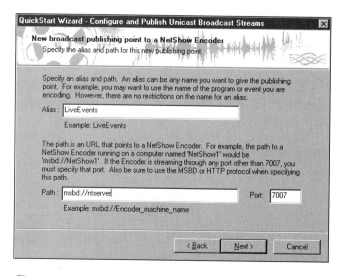

Figure 16-19: A broadcast publishing point alias and path

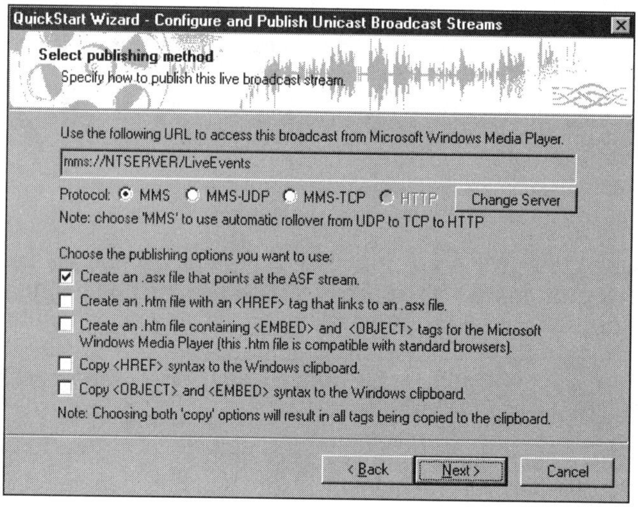

Figure 16-20: Broadcast publishing point properties

Multicast stations

Multicast stations (see Figure 16-21) are similar in concept to a radio station. A "signal" is broadcast and is received by anyone who is specifically listening for a particular broadcast on a particular frequency. In the case of multicast stations, the frequency is the IP address of the station sending the information.

Chapter 16: Service Pack 4 Additions and Miscellaneous

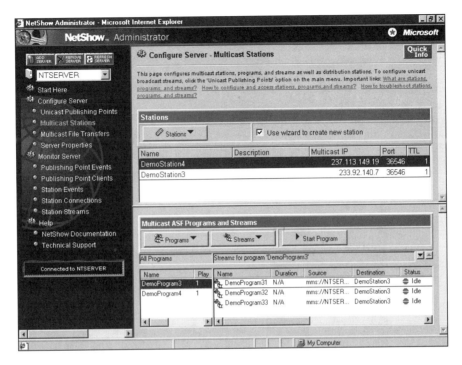

Figure 16-21: Multicast stations

The multicast station feature allows the creation of .nsc files. These hold information about the station and their particular programs that contain .asf content files or streams. The contents of the .nsc file for every station contain contact information as well as technical information such as the multicast IP, the adapter address, the port, the Time-to-Live parameter, and the distribution limit. Stream formats are also contained within the .nsc file. Each station has multiple programs containing multiple streams. Program properties contain some descriptive information and whether to plan a fixed amount of times or to loop continuously. Stream properties also contain descriptive details. In addition the general properties, you may specify source and destination and some advanced property settings.

Multicast file transfers

NetShow Server can multicast file transfers in addition to asf streams (see Figure 16-22). File transfers can be used to distribute graphic files used for presentations or any other type of file needed. The same process is used to configure and set up a file distribution multicast. Rather than programs and streams being defined, the files to be transferred must be defined.

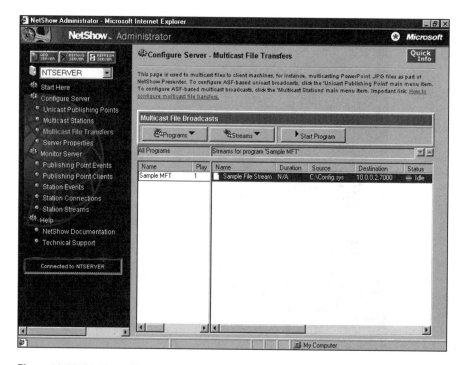

Figure 16-22: Multicast file transfers

Server properties

The NetShow server can be configured with additional properties that affect overall operation. The General tab allows a limitation to be set on clients, bandwidth, and bit rate (see Figure 16-23).

Security may be set for publishing points using multiple methods, including no security (see Figure 16-24).

The available authentication methods are:

- HTTP-BASIC authentication and membership service account
- HTTP-BASIC authentication and NTLM account database
- Microsoft Windows NT LAN Manager authentication and account database
- Access Control List (ACL)

The Distribution Authentication tab enables setting server authentication for distribution of streams to multiple downstream NetShow servers. If a proxy is required for connecting to any of the servers, a user ID and password may be entered.

Chapter 16: Service Pack 4 Additions and Miscellaneous

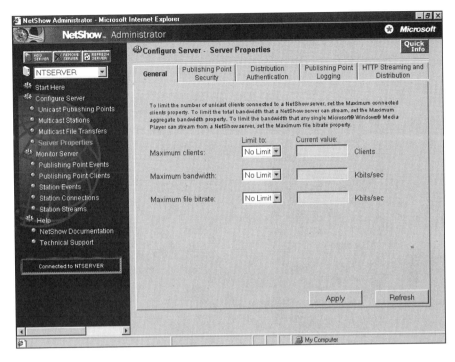

Figure 16-23: General Server properties

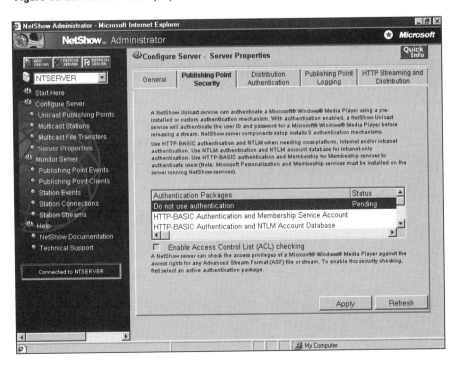

Figure 16-24: Publishing point security

With the Publishing Point Logging tab (see Figure 16-25), logging parameters may be set for daily, weekly, or monthly logging, or logging by file size. The location of the log file directory may be set. The log file contains standard W3C fields and also custom fields.

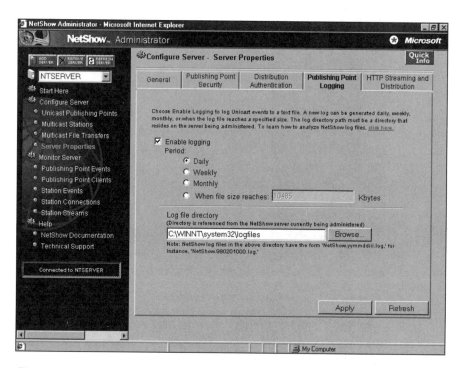

Figure 16-25: Publishing point logging

The final server configuration item, the HTTP Streaming and Distribution tab, allows you to decide whether to stream HTTP (see Figure 16-26). If this option was not set in the installation process, it may be set here. If HTTP streaming is turned on and IIS is running on the same machine, then problems may occur.

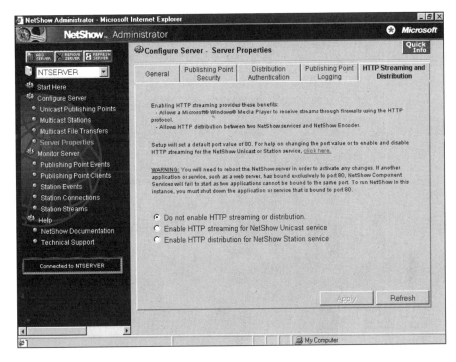

Figure 16-26: HTTP streaming and distribution

Monitor Server

The NetShow Server may be monitored during its operation via the Monitor Server (see Figure 16-27).

The following windows are available for monitoring specific events and clients:

- Publishing point events
- Publishing point clients
- Station events
- Station connections
- Station streams

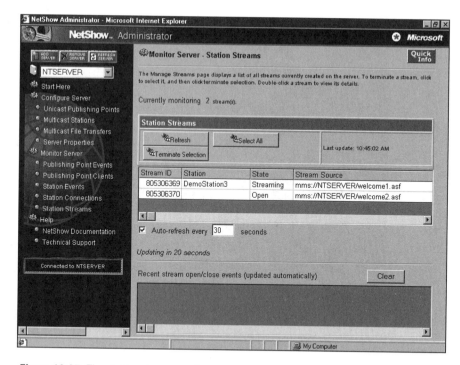

Figure 16-27: The station stream monitor

Site Server Express 3.0

Site Server Express has been upgraded in SP4. The functionality remains the same, but modifications for improved usability have been made to the Usage Import and Report Writer modules, and the documentation has been improved. For more information on Site Server Express, see Chapter 13. The key distinction between the Site Server Express discussed in Chapter 13 and the version discussed here is that SP4 enhances the Site Server Express version delivered in the Option Pack.

When selecting a report from the Report Writer catalog (see Figure 16-28), you will find that the capability to build a data expression has been improved.

Chapter 16: Service Pack 4 Additions and Miscellaneous

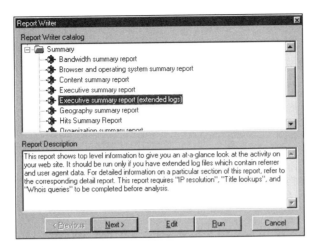

Figure 16-28: The Report Writer catalog

The data dimensions, operands, and values can be selected to build an expression to select the proper data for analysis and display, as shown in Figure 16-29.

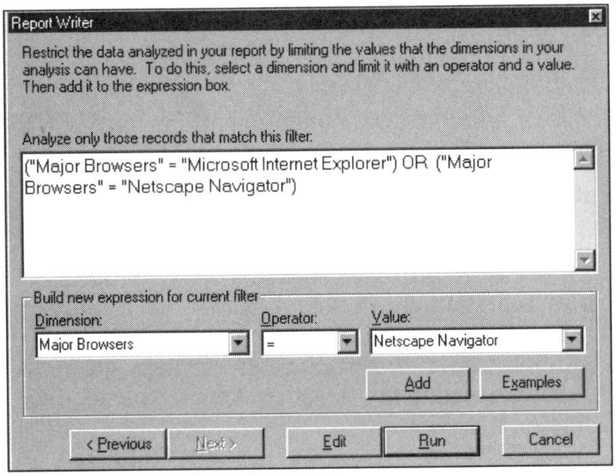

Figure 16-29: Report data selection

Miscellaneous SP4 Components

Various other components are included with SP4. These miscellaneous items are smaller, but significant, programs for specific areas. In some cases, the documentation is minimal and limited to the SP4 Readme file, which can be found on the SP4 media as well as Appendix D, "Service Pack 4 Details." This section describes a variety of SP4 components, including Microsoft Active Accessibility Support, DCOM/HTTP Tunneling, Euro Key Patch, Internet Group Management Protocol (IGMP) v2., Microsoft File and Print Service for NetWare (FPNW) Support for Client 32, Profile Quotas, Remote Winsock (DNS/Port 53), Remote Procedure Calls (RPC) enhancements for Visual Basic (VB), Routing Information Protocol (RIP) Listener, Visual Studio–MICS analyzer events, Compaq Fiber Storage Driver, and Web-Based Enterprise Management(WBEM).

- **Microsoft Active Accessibility Support (MSAA).** MSAA provides a standardized method for interacting with the user interface. Five new APIs are introduced in SP4 that expose all user interface elements and objects. The APIs are:
  - GetGUIThreadInfo
  - GetAncestor
  - RealChildWindowsFromPoint
  - RealGetWindowClassA
  - RealGetWindowClassW

- **DCOM/HTTP Tunneling.** DCOM communications may now use HTTP to tunnel through firewalls using standard protocol ports.

- **Euro Key Patch.** The Euro Key Patch includes the new Euro currency symbol. Arial, Courier New, and Times New Roman are updated as well as the keyboard drivers.

- **Internet Group Management Protocol (IGMP) v2.** IGMP v2 is a router protocol that is useful for multicast environments. Through this protocol, a computer can inform the router that it is leaving a group, and the router may stop forwarding multicast packets to the segment if there are no other clients on it.

- **Microsoft File and Print Service for NetWare (FPNW) Support for Client 32.** Windows NT Server can now support the NetWare Client 32 program for file and printing services. This update is only relevant when FPNW is installed.

- **Profile Quotas.** Proquota is a utility to monitor user profiles and warn the user when file sizes exceed a predefined limit. The user won't be able to log off until the file size is reduced. In other words, this is simply one of the coolest and most requested Windows NT Server features of nearly all time. As you may know, in other environments, such as NetWare, we've had storage space requirements forever. Not so in Windows NT

Chapter 16: Service Pack 4 Additions and Miscellaneous

Server until this implementation in SP4. Not only do we have quotas, but we have an annoying (and great way) to enforce them. You can't end your session properly if you exceed your limits.

1. Start the System Profile Editor and verify that the common.adm and winnt.adm templates are loaded.
2. Create a new profile and open the Default User option.
3. Expand the NT User area and set the profile limit size.

   The default is 30MB, as seen in Figure 16-30 in the Max. Profile size (KB) check box. This may be small in today's environment. Temporary Internet alone may take up 30MB.

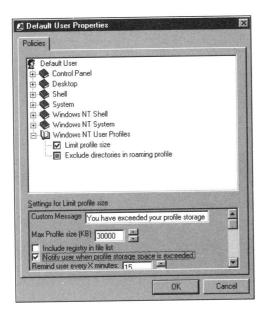

Figure 16-30: Default user properties

Educate and train your users before utilizing this feature. If not, be prepared to handle the support requests for users who cannot get logged off the system properly because of exceeding their profile limits. Nothing like a surprised and angry user discovering your new network features in a negative way. Also, look for greater emphasis and improvement on storage quotas in Windows 2000 Server.

- **Remote Winsock (DNS/Port 53).** Firewalls normally disable the DNS TCP port 53 as a safety precaution. All inbound queries to port 53 are then rejected. SP4 allows the DNS to use different ports for inbound traffic and outbound traffic. Instructions for modifying the Registry are located in the SP4 Readme file.

- **Remote Procedure Calls (RPC) Enhancements for Visual Basic (VB).** New RPC enhancements for VB include a User Data Type (UDT) and new user interfaces.

- **Routing Information Protocol (RIP) Listener.** An update to the RIP routing protocol is included in SP4. Instructions for installing the RIP Listener are included in the SP4 Readme file.

- **Visual Studio–MICS.** Visual Studio Analyzer Events provides a view of high-level system behaviors. The VS Analyzer Events can view event logs, Performance Monitor data, and other system data for analysis.

- **Compaq Fiber Storage Driver.** A new driver for the Compaq Fiber Channel Host Controller for PCI and EISA is included in the \Drvlib subdirectory.

- **Web-Based Enterprise Management (WBEM).** SP4 adds support for WBEM as a standard for representing management information (see Figure 16-31). WBEM is defined and supported by the Desktop Management Task Force (DMTF) as a method of exchanging and consolidating information through well-defined and consistent interfaces.

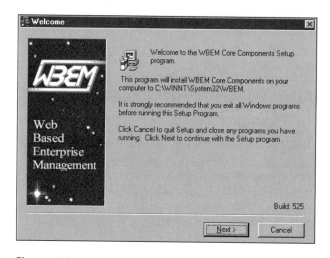

Figure 16-31: WBEM installation screen

More information on WBEM can be read at wbem.freerange.com or msdn.microsoft.com/developer/sdk/wbemskd/default.htm.

Windows NT Services for UNIX

The Microsoft Windows NT Services for UNIX (see Figure 16-32) is an add-on program that provides some very useful information sharing capabilities between NT and UNIX. NT Services for UNIX (SFU) offers Network File System (NFS) volume sharing, NFS client software, a Telnet server, NT-to-UNIX password synchronization, and utilities. You will recall in Part II, "TCP/IP," that a long-standing complaint with the TCP/IP protocol suite in Windows NT Server was the lack of a bona fide NFS client from Microsoft. Usually, to get NFS support, you purchased a third-party NFS application such as WRQ's Reflection series. That has changed with the newly released Windows NT Services for UNIX.

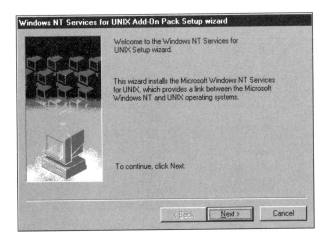

Figure 16-32: Windows NT Services for UNIX

In a traditional Wizard-like setup, you may select which SFU options you want to install. These SFU setup options are shown in Figure 16-33.

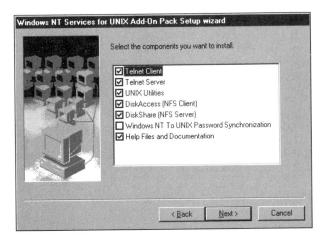

Figure 16-33: SFU components

These options include DiskAccess, DiskShare, robust Telnet capabilities including a Telnet Server (finally) and additional Telnet client functionality, help files, and last but not least, additional UNIX utilities. Here are capsule descriptions of DiskAccess, DiskShare, and Telnet:

- **DiskAccess.** DiskAccess (see Figure 16-34) enables the sharing of files between UNIX and NT by allowing an NT computer to be a client to an NFS server. As an NFS client, the NT system can mount and use NFS shares. DiskAccess uses Remote Procedure Calls (RPCs) common to NFS to provide file access.

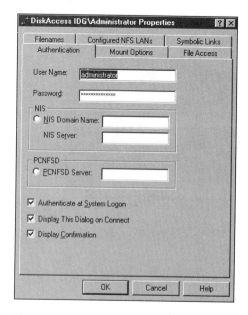

Figure 16-34: DiskAccess properties

Once set up, the NFS client will have an NFS Network entry in the Explorer Network Neighborhood.

- **DiskShare.** DiskShare (see Figure 16-35) allows an NT server or workstation to act as an NFS server. Other NFS clients can access files on the system by mounting them through their NFS client software.

    DiskShare will map users and groups to UNIX users and groups and automatically refresh the lists via a configurable interval.

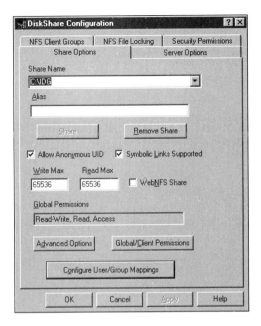

Figure 16-35: DiskShare configuration

- **Telnet.** A Telnet server is installed that allows a Telnet client computer to connect remotely. Once connected, the remote Telnet client can log on and run character-mode applications. Graphical Windows applications can't be run via the Telnet interface.

    The client can connect to the Telnet server via any Telnet client, including the ones included with Windows NT. Administration of the server is via a command line interface, tlntadmn.exe, to set various parameters. The program can list and terminate any user sessions, display and change Registry settings, and start or stop the service.

Summary

This chapter presented the additions to Service Pack 4:

- Security Configuration Editor
- NetShow Server 3.0
- Site Server Express 3.0
- Miscellaneous SP4 components
- Windows NT Services for UNIX

Part V

The Four Flavors of Windows NT Server 4.0

Chapter 17: Regular Windows NT Server

Chapter 18: Windows NT Server — Enterprise Edition

Chapter 19: Windows NT Server — Terminal Edition

Chapter 20: Windows NT Server — Small Business Server

Chapter 17

"Regular" Windows NT Server

In This Chapter

- Rediscovering "plain old Windows NT Server"
- Defining a 32-bit operating system
- Understanding the NT operating system model and architecture
- Defining the features of Windows NT Server 4.0 (build 1381)
- Distinguishing between Windows NT Server and Windows NT Workstation

This chapter talks about the "plain old" retail version you can buy off the proverbial shelf, known in tech circles as "build 1381." Say that and you'll sound cool! I'll try to lay out the key design components of Microsoft's current offering and the strategies behind the company's decisions in the frequently technical war among network operating systems. This will help you in your selection of the correct flavor of NT 4.0.

Windows NT 4.0, both Server and Workstation, is a vast departure from the Old World of their DOS and 16-bit Windows ancestors. There have been significant changes made under the hood from the 3.5 and 3.51 days. In fact, much has changed since the 1996 release of NT 4.0. I will review the key architecture and feature changes in this chapter.

Plain Old Windows NT Server

The key and distinctive features of "plain old" Windows NT 4.0 can best be understood by looking at the engine: the 32-bit NOS. Without belittling "plain old" Windows NT Server 4.0, it is important to understand that this is the baseline build (build 1381) that everyone speaks of. The other versions of Windows NT Server 4.0 covered in the next three chapters as part of the "Four Flavors of Windows NT Server" are hybrids or derivatives of "plain old" Windows NT Server 4.0. That historical context is important as you acquire your baseline Windows NT Server knowledge.

A 32-bit network operating system

Early on in the design of NT, Microsoft's developers were looking for a rock-solid model for an operating system that was both fast and reliable, and that could operate as the central server for an office network. It had to run for days and days without ever missing a beat. It had to serve up files and spool print jobs smoothly and never crash. In short, it had to beat Novell's NetWare at its own game. Furthermore, it had to offer something more; a platform that a company could use to build its network around. File and print services were just the start.

Security and networking subsystems had to perform flawlessly. And the goal was to support as much third-party hardware as possible while keeping the APIs simple, making server applications developers happy to abandon Novell's rather Byzantine NLM requirements. It had to address lots of memory and hard drive space. It had to support at least as many file systems as Novell and, in a most radical departure, run on chips *other* than Intel's.

Secret

In fact, it has been my experience that Windows NT Server sells because it has been well positioned as an application server. That fact is well known. But did you know that the best way to sell Windows NT Server to your bosses is to observe that virtually every major software vendor is directing their development efforts to the Windows NT Sever platform? That is, the applications you depend on (such as accounting software) are increasingly only available on the Windows NT Server platform. Call it being pushed into Windows NT Server whether you want to be or not, but ultimately the applications you use will dictate the platform you will use. It's a case of, to paraphrase a political campaign theme, "It's the applications, stupid!"

Going back to the drawing board, the designers decided to finally abandon the 16-bit DOS/Windows model. Because those operating systems allowed developers full access to the system's memory and hardware, crashes were (and in some cases, still are) frequent. Windows 95 has inherited this problem, as any owner of it can clearly attest. Instead they opted for the better performance of a strict 32-bit user/kernel mode model, making sure to keep lazy programmers away from the coveted memory and hardware.

The NT operating system model

The model chosen was similar to other high-end operating systems already in use in corporate IT centers. This was in no small way related to the guidance of Dave Cutler, who left Digital with the VMS model in his head.

So how to keep the hardware from freaking out? Why not force all execute threads through a mediator — a sort of UN Security Council for the operating system? The NT model in Figure 17-1 shows that mediator, the Executive Services. Along with the Hardware Abstraction Layer, or HAL, these components are referred to as the kernel mode.

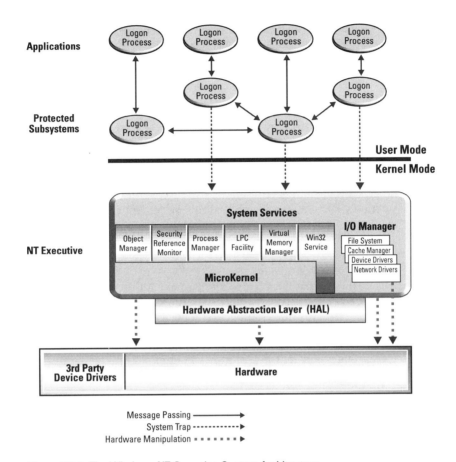

Figure 17-1: The Windows NT Operating System Architecture

The hardware abstraction layer (HAL) shown in Figure 17-1 only provides the common device drivers such as those used by the keyboard, monitor, and mouse. Other devices require that you provide a third-party device driver (typically by inserting a floppy disk). One example of a third-party device requiring a device driver is Iomega's Jaz drive.

Note

Questions regarding HAL have been known to appear on the Windows NT Server MCSE exams.

All applications and protected subsystems (such as file systems) are relegated to the user mode. The kernel mode's job, among other things, is to keep the barbarians at the gate and not let a single instruction hit its own protected memory and hardware. While paying a slight performance hit for this design, NT 4.0 was greatly enhanced in reliability. Microsoft clearly wanted the monkey of a crashing DOS/Windows architecture off its back before touting the software to jittery corporate types concerned about reliability.

Secret

Allow me the opportunity to frame this discussion in the context of NetWare. It is proper to say (loosely), that kernel mode is Ring 0 (zero) and user mode is Ring 3. That's NetWare language but might be helpful as you seek to understand the Windows NT Server architecture.

This means that a badly behaved driver in kernel mode can crash the Windows NT Server operating system (regardless of what anyone tells you). If you worked with Windows NT Server in the past, you've seen this as a blue screen after you've installed a third-party device where the device driver was poorly written and badly behaved.

It also means that a badly behaved application, running in the application subsystem located in user mode, can't crash the Windows NT Server operating system. If you've heard that statement before, it is true.

Be advised that these fine distinctions between user mode and kernel mode have been known to appear on the MCSE exams relating to Windows NT Server.

The beauty of this design also afforded the NT designers a high level of control over security, isolating its routines from the user mode. All the 32-bit applications and subsystems must "check in" at the Executive's gate before going to grab that file, port, memory space, or other system object. Very reliable, very secure. Also, the modularity of its design allowed developers the ease of changing the structure to better suit the demands of the NOS marketplace. The key design goals of the NT team were robustness and extensibility.

Secret

In a dramatic but subtle change from 3.51 to 4.0, the developers saw fit to move parts of the Windows 32-bit graphical device interface subsystem down into the kernel mode. This was done both to simplify the design of the GDI subsystem and also to improve performance and reduce memory requirements by moving certain functions closer to the "metal" in the kernel mode, in short, to open the way for faster and "cheaper" applications that use the Win 32 subsystem. Developers and end users are happy because their apps run faster. The OS is happy because it uses less overhead arbitrating GDI processes. The downside? The cool new Windows 95–like shell ate up a lot of the performance gains.

Features of NT Server 4.0, build 1381

Now that you understand the OS model, it's appropriate to review the functional features of Windows NT Server 4.0, build 1381. It is important to understand that the following points about reliability, performance, scalability, compatibility, security, and services apply to every release of build 1381.

Secret

What? Oh, did I forget to mention that there are several releases of Windows NT Server? Indeed I did. The first version of build 1381 is the retail version that you can purchase from your favorite reseller, the off-the-shelf version if you will. The next version of build 1318 is the developer's version, which has a "soft" logon limit of ten concurrent connections. By "soft" I mean that you may actually have more than ten concurrent connections active on the Windows NT Server machine, but harmless license violation messages are written out to the system event log (which you may view with Event Viewer). Next, the Microsoft MCSE Windows NT Server–related certification courses, known as the Microsoft Official Curriculum (MOC), provide students with a time-bombed version of build 1381 that typically expires in 90 days. Note that you, as an MCSE student, may use this time-bombed release to complete the course and prepare for the applicable certification exams. I have also found that, at the end of 90 days, reinstalling the time-bombed release over itself (that is, to the same directory, such as \winnt) allows you to use this release for another 90 days with your same Registry and SAM (including security, user, and group accounts) settings.

Reliability

As you have seen, the architecture makes this operating system very reliable. Crashes and system restarts have all but completely been eliminated. Not only are disk reads and writes mediated by the Executive's HAL, but writes are also sent to metadata, a sort of ghost copy, for roll-back and recovery purposes should the write fail.

This file write feature makes the OS very stable. Because the main function of a NOS is file sharing, Windows NT shines in all reliability areas related to file I/O.

Don't get me wrong, crashes still occur. You've heard of the dreaded "blue screen of death!" Ninety percent of these crashes are of the access-violation variety. Basically, processes mess with part of the kernel they're not supposed to touch. Normally, the Executive handles this nicely by crashing only the offending application or subsystem. Sometimes, the violation is egregious enough to force the kernel to stop. That's where Dr. Watson comes in. Luckily, Service Pack 4 has fixed over 60 of these annoying little stop errors!

Performance

While some performance hit is taken with the separation of the user and kernel modes, the amount of addressable RAM gives back a huge benefit to running applications. NT 4.0 Server has been tuned from the start as a mission-critical application server. 4GB of RAM can be addressed in a flat, linear fashion, giving application developers more room to move.

NT 4.0 has dramatically improved file I/O performance. Intelligent caching of the file system helps speed up file services, a major component of any good NOS. This is done using a disk cache manager for improving the I/O system. The developers smartly made the manager dynamically sizable as the amount of RAM changes. So if your server is under a heavy I/O load for a backup, for example, and the rest of the RAM is relatively unused, users requesting a large file be opened need not be disappointed, as the disk cache manager readily shifts gears and appropriates more RAM for their I/O. As evidence of the cache manager's success, recent NetBench tests have scored NT Server 4.0 at least 13 percent faster for disk I/O than NetWare 4.1 in identical environments.

Scalability

From the start, Microsoft sought to distinguish its NOS from the small office variety NOS by designing it to scale up to enterprise-sized demands. The Enterprise version, as you'll see in the next chapter, gives you the option to size up to eight-way and higher processor farms. More on this in Chapter 18.

Compatibility

Microsoft took a big leap forward from 3.51 in compatibility. From clients to file systems to protocols, NT embraces a much bigger computing universe. The intention here is, as always, to get you to buy NT even if you have a mixture of computing platforms in your organization.

NT 4.0 comes standard with support for the following clients: MS Windows NT Server and NT Workstation 3.x and 4.0, MS Windows 3.x, MS Windows 95 and 98, MS-DOS, Apple Macintosh, OS/2, and UNIX.

Macintosh support has been in NT since the early 3.5 days. It continues in the latest 4.0 SP4 version with native AppleTalk protocol support, AppleTalk's filing system, and AppleShare printer support. NT 4.0 dropped support for OS/2 HPFS filing system but still supports OS/2's file naming system, FAT, NTFS, and NFS (via a third-party solution).

Standard protocols can be implemented directly to the network adapter. These include, finally, TCP/IP (with a fully RFC-compliant DNS Server!), the standard Windows NetBEUI, IPX/SPX, AppleTalk, OSI (from the SDK), DLC, and DECNet (from Digital).

Security

Probably one of the areas in which NT Server 4.0 shines the most is its tight security model. One of the original design goals was to comply with the U.S. Government's C2-level security guidelines and to make NT Server able to eventually reach the B1 and beyond. Again, this tight level of control owes much to the kernel-user mode design of NT.

The architecture of NT's security database allows single, secure, encrypted logons into not only the local network while in the office but the whole domain, be it local or a WAN spanning the globe. This applies to remote dial-in users as well!

CryptoAPI 2.0 is now available, too. It is an application programming interface that developers can use to facilitate intranet and Internet-based digital key encapsulations within their code. This helps programmers journey into the brave new world of Internet computing with a set of security key tools at their disposal.

The latest service pack includes the latest Common Internet File System's file sharing protocol. This is an SMB (Server Message Block) signing protocol that authenticates by including a digital security signature into each SMB.

With NTFS implemented there is virtually nothing you can't lock down. Using FAT restricts the levels and types of security you can apply to files and directories. With NTFS you can specify the following rights: read, write, execute, delete, change permissions, take ownership, list directory, create files in directory. All of these rights can be audited down to the most intimate detail.

Be careful not to override your individual user account's privileges with your group's privileges. Windows NT considers group privileges to have a higher authority. I found this strange at first. I wanted to grant special rights to a member of a particular group but couldn't without removing them from that group. I guess the planners figured better to be on the safe side, assuming an administrator might forget that the user was a member of the group with lesser rights.

You can access the rights for a drive or directory share through Windows Explorer, the descendant of File Manager. Right-click a directory or a file and select Properties. From the Properties dialog box you click the Sharing tab and then Permissions to get to the access control dialogs, as seen in Figure 17-2.

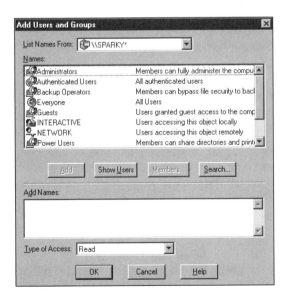

Figure 17-2: Adding users and groups

Services

Given that Microsoft touts NT Server 4.0 as the all-in-one platform for network operating systems, its core service features bear closer review.

File and print

High-availability network print and file systems are included in NT 4.0. This is minimum core for any NOS, but Microsoft really went back to the drawing board after taking it on the chin for 3.51's poor performance relative to NetWare in this area.

NT 4.0's intelligent disk caching and a zippy PCL print spooler have leveled the playing field in this department.

Printing subsystems support a slew of hardware models and now include new drivers for Adobe PostScript compatibility. In fact, you can manage all your NetWare queues from within NT using the File and Print Services for NetWare included in Service Pack 4.

Web

The biggest and hottest service offered standard in NT 4.0 is the capability to build a Web server, everything included! Not only is the server software (IIS 2.0, with free upgrade to 4.0) included, but so are a development and maintenance tool, FrontPage, and a site indexing tool, Site Index Server (free via download).

Microsoft is taking on the UNIX world here. By bundling the Internet/intranet solution right into the server bundle, they're hoping you'll just say, "fine, it's free!" IIS 4.0 is no slouch as a Web server either. Couple its relatively good performance with other tools available from the Options Pack and its integration with NT's security and user management features and you can crank up a high-transaction Web site in relatively little time.

New in NT 4.0's latest offering are the inclusion and support for Active Server Pages, or ASPs. These are just regular HTML pages with scripts on the inside. Web programmers can develop in VB or Java to automate many of the algorithms necessary to build today's highly interactive Web sites. This feature is only available if you've taken the time to upgrade to IIS 3.0.

The much-touted integration with BackOffice and other NT Server applications, including Index Server, Certificate Server, and Site Server Express, makes this an attractive feature for even the smallest companies looking for a platform to launch into cyberspace.

Application

Here is where NT 4.0 shines. As an application server it is clearly outmaneuvering NetWare. As a development platform, NT makes programmers' lives easy, giving them the comfort of knowing that virtual memory and multitasking are taken care of by the operating system. The well-defined and easily recognizable APIs make NT an easy, "cheap," applications development platform for businesses of all sizes.

From a functional point of view, the performance of NT server in running client/server applications has proven to be a great selling tool. Large database server engines do quite well on top of NT, as do DCOM and COM applications that are starting to be de rigueur in corporate computing environments.

Management

The biggest of the visible new features for NT 4.0 are clearly the ease-of-management changes. These include the Win95 interface and a slew of wizards to trim minutes, if not hours, off your corporate IT staff budget.

These management wizards (New User, Add Printer, Add Modem, Network Client Administrator, License, and Group Management) are the basic building blocks to a functional file, print, and communications server. Run these and you'll be hard pressed for excuses for not keeping up with your growing stack of trade publications.

Communications

Remote Access Service is NT's version of the Internet on-ramp. It is also Microsoft's implementation of remote access for dial-in users. This one-stop-shop for communications serving has made administration and configuration of such services very easy. From the Add New Modem wizard to the easy-to-navigate RAS entry dialogs, even the novice sys admin will easily get the server connected to the Internet and answer the boss's home computer when she dials in.

ISDN and multilink PPP support come standard, as does the nifty PPTP, or Point-to-Point Tunneling Protocol, which allows the tunneling of any NT-supported protocols inside an IP packet over a LAN, leased-line, or dial-up connection to the Internet. Furthermore, encryption is supported at logon and at packet build time, giving you the tools for a low-cost virtual private network. I always thought that "private virtual network" sounded more reassuring than the awkward "virtual private," but they never ask me when they are coining those acronyms.

Server versus Workstation: The Right Tool for the Job

In this chapter up to this point, I've discussed Windows NT 4.0 build 1381 generically. Everything mentioned so far relates to both NT Workstation and Server version 4.0 except the Apple file system support that comes with the Services for Macintosh included with Server. So what's the difference? They may seem subtle, but a failure to grasp them could have you looking at the blue screen of death more than you should. Lest you should buy more (or worse, less) than you need, herewith a short comparison of Server and Workstation.

They're both build 1381, you say, aren't they the same? The short answer is yes and no. They are nearly identical by most appearances. In fact, there are only 93 files included with the retail Server version that are not included with Workstation. And no, because they are tuned very differently and are designed to scale to different mountains. The system design for Workstation was to keep the foreground application responsive to the user without too much demand for RAM. The system design for Server is for faster network performance and file I/O. Put another way, NT Workstation is tuned to provide the best possible performance for a single interactive desktop user. NT Server, however, is tuned to provide great performance when used as a server operating system, with lots of users requesting lots of files from the server. As my father always said, buy the right tool for the job.

NT Workstation gives up performance in network file sharing with its peers in favor of faster user interface considerations like screen redraw and application loading. NT Server gives up the UI speed in favor of serving up files and print jobs to users.

A closer look at the following tuning issues makes these design differences more evident.

Tuning issues

You're only as good as your last network in this business. This high bar to success demands that you right-size your clients appropriately. For instance, your clients at a smaller site may believe they could benefit more from the peer-to-peer networking capabilities of Windows NT Workstation than from the client/server networking model of Windows NT Server. Don't laugh. Early on in the history of Windows NT Server, I struggled through this very issue with the small publisher of a Russian political newsletter. With an eye on costs, the client saw the peer-to-peer solution of Windows NT Workstation as a viable replacement for the publisher's existing Windows for Workgroups (WFW) peer-to-peer network. But on closer examination, it became apparent that fundamental architectural-level differences existed between Windows NT Server and Workstation. One difference in particular lay in how to "tune" the Server version for performance vis-à-vis how to tune the Workstation version (for more information on tuning a Windows NT Server–based network, be sure to see Part VI, "Optimizing and Troubleshooting Windows NT Server 4.0").

- **Task scheduling.** NT Workstation uses very short time slices for speed in starting and ending multiple tasks during a session. NT Server uses long time slices, enabling it to focus on serving network requests without interrupting other services that may be running.

- **Memory allocation.** As applications load in Workstation, the OS is typically thrifty with the RAM it gives up. It figures you're just going to use the app a short while and then close it. Not so with Server. Realizing the applications that are loaded generally are for multiple use and generally do not get unloaded that often, the OS in Server grants the maximum requested RAM if it's available.

Chapter 17: "Regular" Windows NT Server

- **I/O throughput.** Network requests coming into the OS over the network card on the Server version are handled with much more grace and alacrity than those coming into Workstation. That is because *multiple* queues and threads are dedicated to this task in Server. Server is even designed to allow sharing network loads among other servers in a cluster. In Workstation, only *one* queue is assigned to dealing with network requests.

- **File cache.** Because NT handles memory in a preemptive multitasking model, memory is prioritized differently on Server and Workstation. In Server, the file cache is given the highest memory priority. In Workstation, it's given a lower priority.

So just how, exactly, do you tune your NT 4.0 Server? Here's one simple way: Giving the foreground application less "boost" provides more boost for the underlying networking services within Windows NT Server. Other ways include many of the methods discussed in Part VI of this book, "Optimizing and Troubleshooting Windows NT Server 4.0." I encourage you to master that part (an advanced topics area) after mastering the basics of your Windows NT Server network. Another of my secret ways of quickly boosting performance is to add RAM in addition to changing the performance setting in the Performance tab shown in Figure 17-3. You'd be amazed how far a little RAM will go when fed to a hungry Windows NT Server.

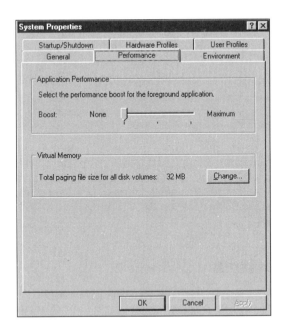

Figure 17-3: The System Properties Performance tab

Processors

Workstation can use only two processors as shipped. If you dig around, you'll hear that it can support up to 32 processors, but you'll need to find a customized Hardware Abstraction Layer (HAL) from Microsoft or your hardware vendor. In any case, it makes little sense to do this with the obvious additional costs given the design benefits already programmed into Server. Server can handle up to four CPUs right out of the box. The latest Enterprise version can use eight. More than that and you'll have to get a customized HAL.

More and more companies are using multiple-processor machines. Even nonprofits. A medium-sized nonprofit in the Boston area just went with a two-processor Compaq/NT 4.0 system to run both its existing Oracle client/server database and its single Intranet application server. They noticed a 40 percent improvement in the Oracle application immediately.

Clustering

Clustering, or using multiple servers to share the network file and application load in a fault-tolerant manner, has traditionally been the buzzword in big-metal IBM and DEC shops. NT Server is designed to support this feature; Workstation is not.

The reason for clustering support? Microsoft is desperate to break into the enterprise computing arena by having lots of "little" Intel (or even Alpha) servers running NT Server on nonproprietary hardware. The goal is to allow a CPU or hard drive to fail and have it be totally transparent to the application and user interface. I'll talk more about this in Chapter 18.

RAS connections

RAS for Workstation is definitely end user driven. While supporting the multilink feature, it still is aimed only at supporting one simultaneous remote access connection per dial in. Any more attempts will be greeted with a busy signal. Workstation's RAS support shines best on dial-out services. Server, on the other hand, is designed to handle up to 256 simultaneous RAS connections, in or out.

Client connections

Client connections of course involve a debate that press types have been flogging to death. To whit: Can a company reliably load up Workstation with more than its maximum of 10 users? No. It doesn't work. Not only is a license limit invoked, causing user 11 to get access denied, but also putting that load on Workstation's background server processes brings it to a crawl. See the earlier tuning discussion for the inside story. Server can handle an unlimited number of simultaneous network client connections. Hard drive and RAM sizes are the only gating factors. Practical concerns suggest, of course, not exceeding 256 connections per server. But Microsoft is working hard with its Windows 2000 Server release to shed this practical concern.

Security

NT Server has a full-domain security model implemented. It can act as both primary and backup domain controllers. Workstation can only authenticate users in the older "Workgroup" model. A Windows NT Server controller is required to authenticate in the domain model.

File system support

Workstation is designed only to operate in peer file sharing mode. Its file system processes are not optimized to serve up large files to even its stated 10-user network client limit. In reality, these clients are viewed as peers. Server meanwhile is geared up to serve files all day long (and often into the night for the Web surfers among us) in a client/server mode. And it's geared to serve them up to all sorts of clients — Macintosh, OS/2, UNIX, and DOS/Windows.

A word about Apple File Sharing. Macintosh file and printer sharing can be loaded into the Server version, not Workstation. This is too bad. I bet many home users would buy Workstation if it could serve up the kids' Macintosh schoolwork files and print jobs over a small LAN. This would save costs in a mixed-node home office environment (you guessed it, mine).

Requirements

NT Workstation 4.0 requires 110MB of hard drive space; Server, 160MB, minimum. For RAM, I wouldn't run Workstation with less than 32MB and Server with less than 64MB, although the minimum stated requirements are a "measly" 12 and 16, respectively. I run my NT Workstation 4.0 laptop with 148MB of RAM, but, hey, that's just me.

Fault tolerance

NT Workstation has no fault tolerance. Sure it can do RAID 0 (basically disk striping), but this isn't a fault tolerant model. Server supports hardware disk mirroring, disk duplexing, and RAID 5 disk striping with parity. Raid 2 (mirroring) is a minimum for even the smallest offices these days.

Internet Server services

NT Workstation 4.0 comes with a nifty Web server called "Peer Web Services" or PWS for short. Basically, this is a scaled-down version of Internet Information Server so that Web administrators can "model" an Internet or intranet site on the local LAN. PWS is a "not ready for prime time" Web server and should not be subjected to the same WAN punishment as IIS. Remember, Workstation has a 10-user connection limit, and this includes your Web server's clients. It has only a 40-bit encryption key model versus IIS's 40- or 128-bit choices. IIS 2.0, included with NT 4.0, is merely a beefier version. It needs to be upgraded to 3.0 or 4.0 (these are free if you have the license for 2.0) before it's ready for prime time in the surf universe.

Using Windows NT Server as a User Workstation

Remember what was said about having the right tool for the job? Well, you may be asking, if this is such a hot multitasking operating system, why do I have to lock it in a closet? Why can't my administrative assistant use it for simple word processing?

Good question. There's a simple answer and a not-so-simple answer. The simple answer is two words "foreground application." When you get to the tuning of Windows NT Server, you'll quickly realize the speed your users see comes from the operating system's management of foreground and background processes. NT Workstation has the foreground processes tuned to provide better local client/server response times. NT Server has the background OS processes tuned to provide better "remote" client/server response times. By "remote," here I mean, "not at the NT server console" — tasks like filing and printing on the local LAN, as well as Proxy services to the WAN. While it may be tempting to use that horsepower for Microsoft Word, you'll be robbing the OS of resources needed for your CEO to surf the Web! Big mistake.

Another simple answer is "oops, I forgot I wasn't supposed to turn it off." That's why I typically put them in closets with locked doors. NT Server was designed not to crash or turn off. If you introduce the "human element" into the equation, you may have a lot of unhappy users trying to reach the server and getting the "file cannot be found" error.

An experience I had led me to never consider using NT Server in a nondedicated mode. Consider the tendency of older, DOS-based or Win16 applications to hang around offices for years. I was installing a network management tool from a router vendor that had been programmed in Win16 days. Needless to say, the setup.exe program ran in DOS mode. When it went into an endless loop, this setup.exe application sucked up all available memory resources from the server to feed the NTVDM process (the virtual DOS machine; remember, no real DOS on NT!). This had the unwanted effect of slowing a mission-critical database to a crawl. Although a reboot solved the problem (killing the NTVDM process would have had the same effect), thirty minutes of prime time during the day were lost. The users were not happy!

Summary

In this chapter, you had the opportunity to understand "regular" Windows NT Server. The following points were covered:

- Rediscovering "plain old Windows NT Server"
- Defining a 32-bit operating system
- Understanding the NT operating system model and architecture
- Defining the features of Windows NT Server 4.0 (build 1381)
- Distinguishing between Windows NT Server and Windows NT Workstation

Chapter 18

Windows NT Server — Enterprise Edition

In This Chapter

- The challenges behind Microsoft's development of Enterprise Edition
- Defining Enterprise Edition
- Key differences between Enterprise Edition and Regular Edition of Windows NT Server
- Defining Enterprise Edition's technologies, including more memory, the eight-processor limit, and Microsoft Message Queue Server
- Understanding the clustering technologies available with Enterprise Edition

Most of us will never work in a production environment with Windows NT Server 4.0 — Enterprise Edition, the topic of this chapter. But for the select few who are ardently implementing Windows NT Server at the enterprise level, this chapter is an invaluable lesson in why the Enterprise Edition exists and how it fits in to the Windows NT Server family.

The rest of us, who are working with medium-sized and smaller organizations, can benefit from reading this chapter on Enterprise Edition. That is because any Windows NT Server professional should seek to understand the full Windows NT Server family as part of being a current and informed service provider. But another reason wasn't apparent to even me until recently: electronic commerce. I've worked with a small Internet-based legal research firm that, on the surface, with their staff of 30 employees, shouldn't have even considered the Enterprise Edition. But a closer look at their business model revealed that, as an information provider, their computing needs were enterprise-level. These needs included 7 × 24 reliability and extreme horsepower. With clustering, which we discuss in a moment, this firm has built the foundation for the 7 × 24 reliability its business model needs. With respect to extreme horsepower, the additional memory and eight-processor limit, both discuss shortly in the "Defining the Enterprise Edition" section, provide the "robustness" so need in the not to distant future for this small company's electronic commerce needs.

Microsoft's Great Challenge — The Enterprise

When Microsoft launched the Enterprise Edition, their intention was to capture more of the IT server NOS budget of larger corporations. They wanted to allow customers to use low-cost hardware technology as a platform for enterprise network application hosting. The challenge was to compete head-to-head with UNIX and RISC minicomputer manufacturers by positioning NT Server Enterprise Edition in the mid- to high-range application development arena. In part, that meant shedding the image that they only provided desktop operating systems and office productivity applications. Their solution was the Enterprise Edition of NT Server, along with some nifty add-on products that CIOs were looking for. In this chapter we will review the technologies Microsoft has developed within and for the Enterprise Edition of Windows NT Server 4.0 and how those technologies address the demands of enterprise-wide applications.

A word of caution at the outset: I have noticed a curious trend as Microsoft tackles the challenge of NT sales in the big corporate IT "glass houses": The higher up the ladder a potential sale goes, the more cryptic become the acronyms Microsoft arms its sales executives with: WLBS, MCS, SMP, MSMQ, MTS, and so on. You should know all of these terms and their suitability for your systems design if you are spec'ing out the hardware and software for a mission-critical application. You should also know that when you add it all up, some of these technologies are a major capital investment.

NT Server 4.0 Enterprise Edition is really a platform for mission-critical application development. Its technologies specifically address the scalability and availability of high-demand applications, whether they be internally focused or externally focused. In terms of the latter, Web e-commerce application hosting is one of the main areas in which Microsoft hopes to win over cautious IT types. Other examples of where Enterprise Edition would be useful are decision support and data mining applications.

In general terms, you can think of both NT Server 4.0 Regular Edition and Enterprise Edition as the bedrock of the BackOffice. This term has been useful in marketing the product, as many corporations are already familiar with the metaphor of Microsoft Office. Like the "front" office metaphor, BackOffice aims to secure the sale of operating systems and tools necessary to host organizations' key operational programs, databases, and Web sites. These "building blocks" provide network services across an organization to get your back office applications running much as the "front" office gets your word processing, spreadsheets, and mini-databases running at your client PCs. Briefly, the BackOffice "applications" consist of corporate groupware and messaging (Exchange), pseudo-firewall and proxy services (Proxy), Web site server management (Site Server and Site Server Commerce Edition), asset control and management (SMS), and a server database engine (SQL Server). Buy it all at once with NT, and it's called "BackOffice Server."

Using these building blocks, corporate and professional developers will find that NT Server 4.0 Enterprise Edition, with its related suite of reliability tools, will be more than adequate to use as a development platform for most mid-range computing tasks. The APIs are all there. The load balancing is there. The multiprocessor support is there. The clustering is there for fail-over and fail-back insurance. The performance is there. The memory is there. With the built-in security and robustness of NT, Enterprise Edition will make a strong dent in the middle- and high-tier server markets.

Let's take a closer look at Enterprise Edition and its associated technologies.

Defining the Enterprise Edition

It is now time to get down to the brass tacks of Windows NT Server 4.0 — Enterprise Edition. This section will first contrast the Enterprise edition to the Regular edition because most Windows NT Server practitioners have the Regular edition as their point of reference. Enterprise-specific features will then be introduced.

Key Differences from "Regular" Edition

There are four key OS differences from the Regular Edition of NT Server 4.0:

- Four-gigabyte memory tuning (4GBT)
- A license allowing the use of up to 8 CPUs in one server (Regular allows up to 4)
- No limit on concurrent users of the Microsoft Message Queue Server product (MSMQ)
- "Wolfpack" or Microsoft Cluster Server (MCS)

Apart from these differences, the Regular Edition is almost identical.

What's in the Option Pack?

If you purchased your copy of NT 4.0 Regular or Enterprise Edition after January 1998, the Option Pack CD is included. Burned onto it are the following products:

- MS Internet Information Server 4.0
- MS Transaction Server 2.0
- MS Index Server 2.0
- MS Message Queue Server 1.0
- MS Certificate Server 1.0

- Internet Connection Services for RAS
- Service Pack 4
- MS Site Server Express 2.0

If you purchased your NT 4.0 Server Regular Edition or Enterprise Edition before January 1998, your license entitles you to a "free" CD options pack. It's really $99.00, but they say that is for the CD costs. You can download the software free from the Microsoft Web site if you don't want to pay the $99.00, but I highly recommend getting the CD.

The Option Pack is covered extensively in Part IV of this book. Specifically, you should refer to Chapter 13.

When to use Enterprise Edition

When should you use Enterprise Edition? My advice is that when you start to consolidate groups of departmental servers of 1,000–2,500 users into the "glass house" for better management and availability, then you should start thinking about Enterprise. If your server's multiple "hats" require increasing numbers of CPU cycles to the detriment of corporate application hosting, this is another reason to go to Enterprise. I would recommend the use of multiple processors in this scenario as well. If your data storage for any SQL database is reaching the multiple gigabyte limit, I would recommend Enterprise, a cluster, and a good RAID solution. And if your are hosting an e-commerce Web site that absolutely can't crash, you need Enterprise Edition.

To give you some benchmarks, during a recent "Scalability Day," vendors demonstrated technologies that achieved the following results: 1 billion transactions per day (MS NT 4.0, MTS 1.0, MS SQL 6.5), a 2-terabyte database (MS NT 4.0 on Tandem hardware), 50,000 e-mail boxes (Alpha server, MS NT 4.0, MS Exchange), and 100 million hits a day (HP LX NetServer, MS NT 4.0, MS IIS). To give you a comparison, Microsoft's Web site, the fourth busiest in the world, gets approximately 70 million hits a day.

Design challenges

Given those numbers, the design challenges of NT Server 4.0 Enterprise Edition are simply for reliability, availability, performance, and security to a degree higher than the Regular Edition. In layman's terms this means: "My Web server has to be up all the time, day and night. It can't fail if a hard drive dies, if a CPU dies, if the power goes off, if a tornado hits the building." It means "My Oracle database cannot go down. It is the data repository of our worldwide sales application. It has to run 24 hours a day, because our sales people are working 24 hours a day somewhere around the globe." In other words: the app must run! Damn the torpedoes!

Microsoft's claim is they can do it for you with NT Server and some cheap hardware! "High performance on Intel servers without crashing?" you say? Regular disclaimers apply: Cheap is a relative term. Check the HCL's! There are many ways Microsoft has covered its marketing muscle with technical "I told you so's" in terms of what hardware is allowed.

To get Microsoft support, your Enterprise Edition is only covered when all your hardware is on the Windows NT Server, Enterprise Edition Hardware Compatibility List. In fact, if you're using other BackOffice products, you should probably cross-reference your hardware off the Microsoft BackOffice Logo list, too. If you are clustering, your configuration must be on the configuration list of the Microsoft Cluster Server Hardware Compatibility List (see Figure 18-1). Check out the following address for the latest approved hardware: www.microsoft.com/isapi/hwtest/hcl.idc.

Figure 18-1: Microsoft's Hardware Compatibility List home page

Technologies

Enterprise Edition employs a host of new technologies for accomplishing design goals of robustness and reliability in a server operating system. Let's dig deeper and review the scalability, availability, reliability, and interoperability of the NT Server 4.0 Enterprise Edition and its related technologies.

Four-gigabyte memory tuning

As a way to make more RAM available to application developers coding mission-critical systems, Enterprise Edition comes with a nice feature that, when enabled in both the operating system and the application, allows the application to use up to three gigabytes of real RAM.

Windows NT has a maximum addressable memory limitation of four gigabytes (4GB). This includes the memory requirements of the core operating system and all the applications running on the server. The Regular Edition has an application memory limitation of two gigabytes (2GB) and a core OS limit of 2GB. Enterprise Edition borrows 1GB from the OS and gives it back to the application, allowing the application a total of 3GB of RAM.

Secret

The 4GB addressable memory limitation of Windows NT is due to the 32-bit nature of the microkernel's memory model. This owes much to the nature of the 32-bit Intel Pentium processors that form the bedrock of NT's sales. Microsoft is working on a very large memory model, or VLM, for 64-bit processors such as the Alpha and the upcoming Intel/HP Merced chip, which will allow up to 32GB RAM to be addressable.

This Enterprise edition feature of addressing large amounts of RAM only makes sense if you have more than 2GB of real RAM and you have a programmer around who can modify your applications source code to take advantage of the feature. You also have to change a system setting. Here's how it works.

To turn on 4GBT, you have to make an entry in your boot.ini file (see Figure 18-2). (Note: all you're really doing is adding the "/3GB" to the end of the entry.)

Figure 18-2: A modified boot.ini file with the 4GBT feature enabled

Secret

You'll need to have your programmer modify the following bit in the header of the application's executable file IMAGE_FILE_LARGE_ADDRESS_AWARE. This can be done using the Imagecfg tool that is included in the Support folder on the Windows NT Server/E compact disc. This allows the application to see the additional memory addresses.

Symmetric multiprocessing (SMP)

Enterprise Edition includes a license for use in servers with up to eight processors. Regular edition allows up to four processors in a single server. This is commonly referred to as *symmetric multiprocessing,* or SMP for short.

In reality, only a handful of hardware vendors actually make servers with more than four processors. In fact, I know of only six or seven.

If you want to go higher than eight processors, you'll have to buy a license from the hardware vendor that makes a system with more than eight CPUs. That is because NT needs a different HAL for addressing more than eight processors. The only vendors that I know of that support more than eight processors are NCR and Sequent.

The advantage of symmetric multiprocessor support is that it affords huge performance gains in both the OS and applications by executing their process threads across all of the CPUs.

Secret

Ninety percent of all servers sold to corporations are of four processors or less. Given Microsoft's tendency to go after the dollars, you can surmise just how much effort they will be putting into higher-processor SMP support. Very little. My guess is that if they can ramp up the four-way performance of NT, they'll do that first. Then they will go after the top 10 percent of the market currently occupied by multiprocessor servers running UNIX variants.

Microsoft Cluster Server (MCS) Wolfpack

Without question, MCS Wolfpack is the best, and most needed, of the features Enterprise Edition offers. It is worth the extra $2,000 just for this feature.

Basically, the Microsoft Cluster Server (formerly code-named "Wolfpack") can automatically recover mission-critical data and applications from many common types of failure by enabling you to set up multiple servers as if they were the same server. Just think, you could swap out a hard drive without taking your server down and not have it affect the users of your application! This works really well for SQL database servers, especially the Enterprise Editions of MS SQL Server and MS Exchange Server (go figure!).

If you need this type of failure protection for your application, you should be familiar with its limitations. Microsoft is currently supporting a clustered server configuration of only two nodes. They plan to support more. Also, this is not a true "load balancing" solution. The technology model in use in MCS is called fail-over and fail-back. Basically, you, the MCS administrator, create a set of resource groups that are essentially a set of NT 4.0 Server services (see Figure 18-3). Then you specify what to do if the "resource" goes south. Generally, you specify a fail-over mode, where node two takes over if resources in node one die. When you get node one's services back online, MCS automatically recognizes the presence of those resources and "fails back" the services running on the original node.

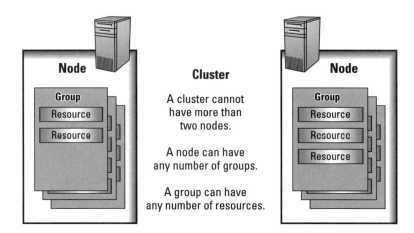

Figure 18-3: The MCS Wolfpack cluster

My explanation is, of course, a vast oversimplification. In reality, there are many ways to set up your cluster. The MCS manual gives you five different models to use as guides in setting up your cluster.

You'll hear the term "shared-nothing" mentioned a lot in the MCS documentation. What it means is that the two nodes in your cluster are really sharing nothing (see Figure 18-4). They each have their own services (or a subset of the "group" of resources or services). Only one node handles a client request for a service shared by the cluster at one time. If that node is not available, the other node takes over automatically. When both nodes are running and a resource is requested by the client that is on the other node, the originating node in the cluster gets the requested information and communicates back to the client.

While the MCS services can generally handle the fail-over and fail-back of most situations within 30 seconds, this may be too much time for today's demanding applications. A set of APIs is in the works for SQL database developers to include this fault tolerance detection in the code.

If you plan to use a RAID array for common storage between your cluster's nodes, before installing MSCS, you must use the SCSI controllers on each node to do the following: Set the SCSI controller ID to a different target ID on each node (for example, **6** on the first node and **7** on the second). Disable the boot-time SCSI reset operation on each controller. (Some SCSI controllers must have the BIOS disabled or they will cause the computer to stop responding at boot.) And make sure you terminate your SCSI bus properly (see Figure 18-5)!

Chapter 18: Windows NT Server — Enterprise Edition

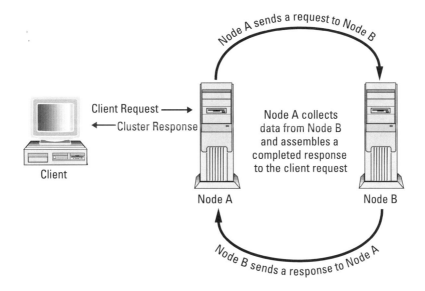

Figure 18-4: The "shared-nothing" cluster model

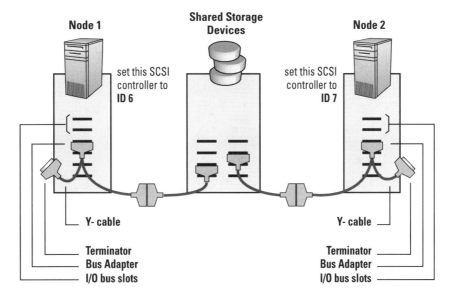

Figure 18-5: A properly terminated SCSI bus for MCS

Be careful when shutting down services in a cluster!

If you use the Services Control Panel to stop a service that is designated as a cluster resource, depending on how that resource is defined in the cluster, the Cluster Administrator may see the stoppage as a failure of the service and move that service with all its related resources to the control of the other server or attempt to restart the server.

If this is not your intention and you subsequently restart the service, it totally confuses the cluster. Only a restart of both systems will get you back to a normal operating state. My advice? Use the Cluster Administrator to start and stop clustered services at the "resource" level (see Figure 18-6).

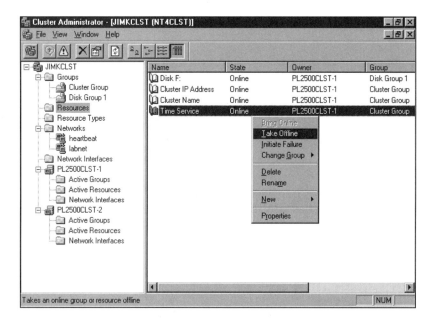

Figure 18-6: The Cluster Administrator

Microsoft's Message Queue (MSMQ) Server

Microsoft's Message Queue Server is available for both the Regular and Enterprise Editions. It comes on the Option Pack CD. This service stores and forwards messages from applications running at different times or that may be offline for a time.

When would you use it? One application of this service that I have heard is at a company that connects doctors who are very distant from one another. This is referred to in medical circles as telemedical communication. This firm has a series of applications to present information to a "medical desktop," be it a PC, laptop, or palm device, and deliver video, case study, expert analysis, and Web services over satellites to places like Alaska, where satellite failures are a given. MSMQ keeps the transmissions between their apps rock-solid reliable.

MSMQ is also helpful in situations where credit information needed to process purchase orders off the Web is delivered via an EDI link. You can use MSMQ when programming your COM application to deliver the information out of and into the appropriate queues, regardless of how much time or how many attempts it takes to access the EDI information.

Secret

You'll need at least one server to be the *primary enterprise controller,* or PEC, to make use of MSMQ. The PEC becomes the message queue "god" with knowledge of all queue, server, and client locations.

Windows Load Balancing Server (WLBS)

An amazing new technology development for enterprise-wide application hosting on NT Server has been added to Enterprise Edition.

Microsoft has just acquired yet another start-up, Main Valance Research. They have licensed their product "Convoy" as the newest feature to the Enterprise Edition. Currently, you have to download or request it separately. The new Microsoft product name is Microsoft Windows Load Balancing Server or WLBS for short.

WLBS enables you to cluster up to 32 servers into a single IP address. This "cluster" is different from the MCS cluster because the clustering is done at the lower network-level layer.

WLBS is basically an incredibly fast IP-level service that loads right into your Network Control Panel. Up to 32 servers can share the same IP address. When one of them goes down, your clients won't even know it.

The initial implementation of this technology is for Web servers. NT Servers running IIS 4.0 can be cloned to multiple machines. When they are all running the Convoy driver, the Web sites on them look like one Web site to the Internet or Intranet browsing clients.

Employing both MCS and WLBS on NT Server 4.0 Enterprise Edition, can make for an awesomely fast and extremely reliable Web-based e-commerce solution. Using a three-tier design, you can scale your Web serving performance using WLBS to meet multiple-hundred million client ("tier one") hits a day on the "middle tier" Web servers of your e-commerce site (see Figure 18-7). On the "back end," where electronic items are stored and purchases are processed, you can use a two-node MCS cluster installed with a huge SQL server database engine and shared RAID array to process billions of transactions a day!

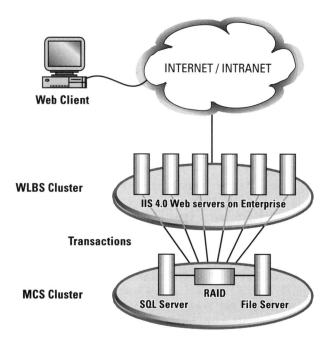

Figure 18-7: A three-tiered model for NT Server Enterprise Edition, MCS, and WLBS technologies

Microsoft Transaction Server (MTS)

Enterprise Edition comes with a powerful application development tool called Microsoft Transaction Server. MTS is a model for developing DCOM-based applications. It has a GUI that helps you easily combining the "plumbing" (what information flows where and when) of your application with the business logic of your application.

A colleague of mine has just used this technology as the transaction engine for a commercial Web site that allows Web clients on the Internet to buy time from a legal resource database. MTS has easy hooks into both IIS's Active Server Pages (ASPs) and popular database engines for rapidly developing e-commerce solutions.

Summary

In this chapter you learned about the Enterprise Edition of Windows NT Server 4.0. The following topics were covered:

▶ Learning the challenges behind Microsoft's development of Enterprise Edition

Chapter 18: Windows NT Server—Enterprise Edition

▶ Reviewing the Enterprise Edition's offerings
▶ Distinguishing between Enterprise Edition and Regular Edition
▶ Reviewing Enterprise Edition's technologies and their real-world uses
▶ Learning the clustering technologies available with Enterprise Edition

Chapter 19

Microsoft NT Server — Terminal Edition

In This Chapter

- Learning the history and environment of Terminal Server
- Comparing and contrasting remote node versus remote control
- Defining the feature of Terminal Server
- Properly implementing Terminal Server on your network
- Learning how to best administer your Terminal Server
- Defining MetaFrame
- Learning how to boost Terminal Server performance

This chapter introduces you to Terminal Server, one of the more interesting ways that Windows NT Server 4.0 has been offered on the market. At the core, Terminal Server is Windows NT Server 4.0 with a modified kernel. For some, Terminal Server is a fancy version of PC Anywhere. For others, Terminal Server is a multisession operating system similar to UNIX where multiple computing sessions can simultaneously run on one machine (this is done via virtual machines). And others see Terminal Server as a management tool, enabling secure and centralized management of the network. Last, there is a Terminal Server constituency that feels they enjoy a lower total cost of ownership (TCO) by using cheap and easy thin clients. To say the least, it's interesting how Terminal Server can mean so many things to so many people. Not only will these points be addressed, but I will compare and contrast Terminal Server to regular Windows NT Server at every opportunity.

History

If there was ever a market-driven software application, Terminal Server is it. In 1994, Microsoft sold some of its kernel code to a company named Citrix, that used its own communications protocol (known as ICA) to build a Windows NT Server operating system mutation named WinFrame, a new kind of computing platform commonly referred to as "remote control" and "thin client." Two years later during the Netscape threat, a programming language named Java surfaced, and suddenly Microsoft was smelling another operating system, based on the Internet and "thin client" hardware. As it turned out, Java was harder to handle than the pundits had first thought, but the thin client threat was gaining momentum.

Continuing this Terminal Server history lesson, in short order industry publications were filled with "the death of the smart client," and the Intel machine was looking for a way to extinguish the idea that thousands of corporate desktops should run on inexpensive CPUs while just a few expensive chips on servers did all the work. Does this story line sound familiar? If you've worked with UNIX and its multisession support for dumb terminals, it would.

Shortly thereafter, in 1997, Microsoft reached for its "embrace and extend" strategy, and six months later Citrix lay bleeding in the street while Microsoft released Microsoft Windows NT Server 4.0, Terminal Server Edition, commonly known as "Terminal Server." The details of Citrix's demise are these: Microsoft purchased a 20 percent stake in Citrix complete with a seat on the board, refused to sell any of the NT 4 kernel code to Citrix, and developed its Remote Desktop Protocol (RDP) to communicate mouse keyboard and video bits from client to server. Presto! Microsoft was fully in the thin client business. Of note is the fact that Terminal Server was originally slated to be a component of the Windows NT Server 5.0 operating system, but with release date slide for Windows NT Server 5.0, and growing thin client popularity, Microsoft modified the Windows NT Server 4.0 code and released Terminal Server as we know it.

Not included with Terminal Server today but expected in Windows NT Server 5.0 is the seamless client experience, including sound, printing, and other local resource access. The seamless client experience speaks toward users being unable to tell whether they are working from smart full-fledged PCs on their desks at work or a via a remote client session on Terminal Server. In fact, at my company, this was the main goal of implementing Terminal Server. The same type of desktop, printers, mapped drives, and so on that you have on your desktop PC at work should be available at play (that is, working from home or remote sites). The computing experience, whether at work or not, should be the same.

Secret

You could think of the Terminal Server environment as the ultimate roving profile. This paradigm benefits both the network administrator and the end user. For the network administrator, this means unprecedented central information technology management. No long will users be able to install pleasure game applications or home accounting and tax preparation software on either the local or network drives of company-owned PCs. Perhaps this example isn't such a big deal to you, but it all translates to this for the network administrator: With Terminal Server, you can control your end user desktops much as if they were dumb terminals. Changes made to a user's commuting environment only need to be made once (at the Terminal Server that manages the user sessions), not at each PC. Users benefit from working in a Terminal Server session-based scenario because they no longer have to worry about breaking something. When it is properly configured, users can't break the session as they can break the PC by deleting files, installing bad applications, and the like. A user less prone to making mistakes is both a more productive and a more satisfied user. And users can count on a consistent desktop each day, whether via a remote connection or at work when Terminal Server is deployed with creating a consistent user computing experience in mind.

Environment

Often, experienced Windows NT Server gurus are perplexed by Terminal Server because they don't really know exactly what it is. These next thoughts should help better introduce Terminal Server so that you at least have a working knowledge of what this product is and does. This section will paint the Terminal Server philosophy for you. In the section that follows this one, specific Terminal Server features will be introduced.

Simply stated, Terminal Server's implementation of Windows NT Server 4.0 allows multiple users to run Windows-based applications on the Terminal Server and control these applications remotely. Terminal Server is terminal emulation of Windows NT Workstation 4.0.

Perhaps the most fundamental principle one needs to understand about Terminal Server is the difference between Remote Control and Remote Access. Terminal Server is a Remote Control operating system that differs from Remote Access Service (RAS) tremendously. Consider a program such as Microsoft Access that is not a client/server application. In a RAS session, where a computer acting as a node on a network running MS Access makes an entry in a table, the entire table is transferred from the server and loaded into memory on the client. On a 33.6K connection, this is an unacceptably slow operation that will cause any user to end the session. This same scenario in a remote control environment on Terminal Server executes at perfectly reasonable speed. The reason is that only mouse, keyboard, and video have been transferred across the wire. None of the application or data crosses the network between the Terminal Server client and the Terminal Server.

The most widely used remote control program is PC Anywhere. If you've experienced PC Anywhere and its benefits, you understand the environment of Terminal Server except for the major difference that PC Anywhere is a single-user product. And that single-user or linear configuration typically makes PC Anywhere an unacceptable solution after five user or more. Why? Because each PC Anywhere session requires its own PC on the host end. Whereas Terminal Server can easily support over five users on one powerful server machine, could you (for example) imagine 20 PCs stacked in a room to support 20 PC Anywhere sessions? Nope!

Secret

Indeed the financial crossover point between PC Anywhere and Terminal Server is after five users. This is based on the assumption that you would have five late model PCs running PC Anywhere in your server room versus one sufficiently powered server running Terminal Server. So below five users, PC Anywhere demands a good look as your solution. Above five users, go with Terminal Server and don't look back.

To better understand remote control versus remote access, look at how the remote session computer runs the Outlook client on the remote computer (see Figure 19-1). The benefits of this are that you can compose e-mail off line and then, once attached to the corporate e-mail system, send the e-mail directly from the Outbox of your remote computer. The drawbacks, aside from the database example just given, is that the logon and synchronization take an amazingly long time over a modem connection, and the reliability of remote sessions via communication applications such as RAS is questionable (you may recall that I've expressed concerns about RAS several times in this book. Sometimes RAS doesn't answer the telephone, doesn't hang up, and so on.). If you are from the NetWare community, you would understand a remote access approach to be NetWare Connect.

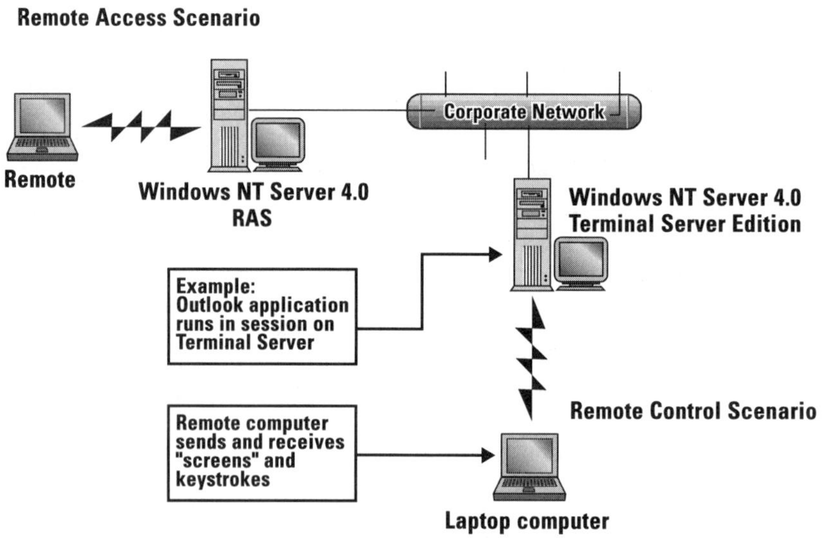

Figure 19-1: Remote access versus remote control

As seen in Figure 19-1, remote control is clearly different from remote access. With a remote control scenario via Terminal Server, the Outlook e-mail program is running on the server. Only the screens and keystrokes are being passed back and forth. This results in a faster and typically more reliable remote computing scenario than I've enjoyed with RAS.

One client, a biotech company, surprised me with its initial preference for RAS over a remote control solution for its remote computing needs. This was a start-up run by a British national who frequently traveled between the United States and Great Britain. Since telephone call charges are high when making overseas calls, he was concerned that a remote control solution would ultimately result in significantly higher telephone bills than a remote access solution. On the surface, he was right. Referring back to Figure 19-1, if you were participating in a remote control scenario and you called in to the corporate e-mail to check your Outlook e-mail, you would typically maintain your remote control session while you read your new e-mail, replied to those messages, and perhaps even composed new messages. The remote control scenario does not provide the opportunity to synchronize your local Outlook application with the server and work offline (cheaply). In fact, remote control sessions are indeed online; there isn't implicitly any offline support.

By electing to use remote access via RAS, this British-born biotech CEO could sit in London and while offline read, answer, and compose e-mail messages via Outlook. Once connected to the company network back in the United States, his Outlook application automatically synchronized with the network server, sending his outgoing e-mail messages and retrieving his new e-mail messages. So far so good, that is, until RAS starting misbehaving. It seemed as if every time he was in London, RAS acted up. It wouldn't answer the telephone reliably, resulting in missed calls. And CEOs don't like missed calls. His staff was driving to the downtown office to reboot the server at odd hours to reinitialize RAS. Finally, he had enough of the poor RAS performance and opted for remote control, recognizing that the additional online time via the telephone would result in higher overall telephone charges.

Secret

A few days after he adopted remote control, I awoke with a thought that might placate the biotech CEO's need for modest telephone bills. The solution? Notepad of course. By composing his e-mail offline with Notepad, he could efficiently copy and paste the text from Notepad to Outlook once he started a remote control session. The result? Less online time via overseas long distance telephone calls and lower telephone bills.

Features

Terminal Server means different things to different people (see Figure 19-2). In fact, that is one of its greatest selling points. You might purchase Terminal Server as a remote control solution for your workers to dial in after hours. I, on the other hand, might be more appreciative of its centralized management capabilities. Perhaps I've been in the technology business too long and have tired of the freedoms of decentralized network environments. At a minimum, Terminal Server is four things:

- A remote control solution for remote users
- A multisession operating system similar to UNIX that allows multiple user sessions
- The advent of centralized management in a networked environment
- A cost savings solution used to lower network TCO

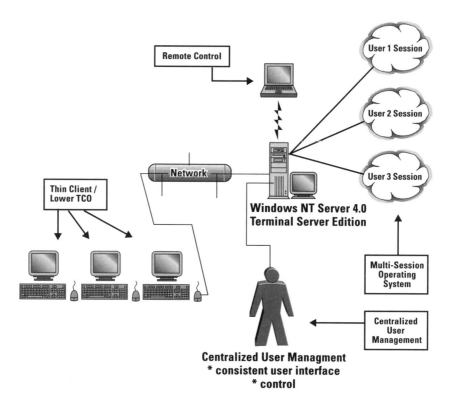

Figure 19-2: Defining Terminal Server

Remote control

Remote control may occur several ways including a direct LAN connection, a secure session over the Internet, and a dial-up connection via a modem. A LAN connection to Terminal Server is often used when the organization wants to take advantage of LAN speeds but likes the centralized administrative control provided by Terminal Server. A Terminal Server session over the Internet is akin to having a quick and dirty virtual private network (VPN). From nearly any workstation running a Web browser, you may attach to the Internet and commence a session with your Terminal Server back at the home office. And the best news is that setting up this across-the-Internet functionality is actually very easy. Our company was able to accomplish the configuration in under 30 minutes. This Internet client connectivity capability is known as the MetaFrame Web Client.

And don't forget the good old modem-based remote control session. In my opinion, this is still on of the most compelling reasons to purchase Terminal Server — to satisfy the end users' desire to work from remote locations.

Secret

The modem you select to implement the remote control capabilities does indeed make a difference. The early feedback from the field, where several of my clients are running terminal server, is that the U.S. Robotics Sportster external modems offer the highest and most reliable performance. My clients have both told and shown me that reliability includes consistent answering and hang-ups, something that is culturally critical when introducing something like remote access to your user base.

Multisession

Terminal Server fools the end user into thinking they, and only they, are enjoying the server's computing resources. In reality, Terminal Server has spawned a virtual machine (VM) for each user, contributing to this illusion. The VM sessions are managed by Terminal Server. This is a great way to leverage your client and server assets more efficiently and effectively if such a strategy fits. For me, this multisession capability was very much like the way SCO UNIX worked when I enjoyed the pleasure of playing with a UNIX network. The fact that many sessions can run simultaneously on the same Terminal Server gave the operating system its beta name Hydra, the many-headed monster in Greek mythology.

Centralized management

Not only can you enforce mandatory logons with Terminal Server, but a network administrator can control the user environment with system policies and other tools to simplify network management. Perhaps the one group that "gets it" when discussing Terminal Server is the mainframe crowd. And if you've struggled to bring control to the decentralized world of network computing, Terminal Server will enable you to prevent users from "screwing up their machines" (an oft-howled resentment amongst network managers).

Lower costs

A cost-saving example is application management. Instead of having to touch each of 100 workstations at your company whenever a new time and billing application upgrade is introduced, Terminal Server enables you to implement this upgrade once at the Terminal Server machine. Future user sessions will reflect this upgrade. This is how using a "fat" server like a properly equipped Terminal Server machine and thin clients (workstations that don't need much power or fuss) can save you time and money.

Components

The Terminal Server software package is made of three components: the operating system, the RDP protocol, and the client software. The modified NT

Server operating system provides all users (sessions) with their own virtual machine; a dedicated connection for mouse, keyboard, and display to travel on; and security for password and data encryption.

Operating system

The OS is in many ways regular Windows NT Server, and in many ways it is not. The similarities include requirements frequently specified for regular Windows NT server 4.0, including the TCP/IP protocol, the use of the NTFS file system, and the way in which Registry entries are created. The is nots include the modified operating system kernel to support a multisession architecture and a slightly different look and feel. Figure 19-3 shows how the Start Menu banner differs from regular Windows NT Server with the term "Terminal Server" used. You will also note the MetaFrame toolbar, something not found on regular Windows NT Server and only found on Terminal Server when MetaFrame is installed. In a few pages, I will also compare and contrast additional features between Terminal Server and regular Windows NT Server.

Secret

At a glance, the only way to quickly tell the difference between regular Windows NT Server 4.0 and Terminal Server is indeed the Terminal Server banner shown in Figure 19-3. Otherwise, it's actually difficult to know what type of Windows NT Server you are logged on to.

Remote Desktop Protocol

The remote control feature set in Terminal Server is based on Microsoft's Remote Desktop Protocol (RDP). RDP is easy to understand, being the mechanism that carries keystrokes and mouse activity from the client workstation to Terminal Server. The results of these keystroke and mouse actions are then returned to the user's workstation as a screen. Stated another way, RDP allows activity and screens to pass to and fro between client and server. RDP is based on the International Telecommunications Union's T.120 protocol, which is optimized for both low- and high-bandwidth networks from dial-up to T1. Encryption and file-level security are fully supported, in addition to the standard NT challenge and response security model.

Terminal Server clients

Since Terminal Server requires very little computing power at the client, organizations do not have to invest in new computers and the latest operating system. With Terminal Server, 386 computers running 16-bit clients like Windows for Workgroups can access the latest versions of 32-bit applications. That's a great way to extend the capabilities of an older client base into the next application cycle in your organization. In addition to supporting 32-bit Windows applications, Terminal Server also supports 16-bit Windows applications, MS-DOS text-mode applications, and client/server network applications such as Great Plains Dynamics accounting software using SQL Server.

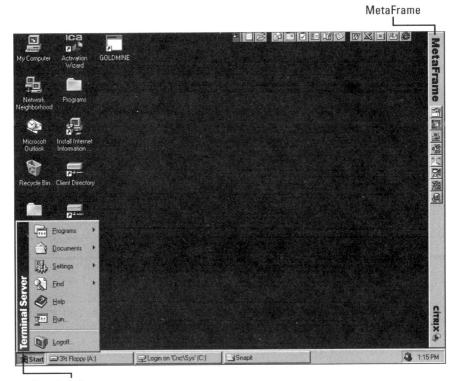

Figure 19-3: Terminal Server desktop differences

At the heart of Terminal Server, as a client, you are running a Windows NT Workstation 4.0 session. This is different from Terminal Server's predecessor, WinFrame, which ran a Windows NT Workstation 3.51 session. The actual workstation client operating systems that may connect to Terminal Server and participate in a session are:

- Windows NT 4.0 Workstation
- Windows 95 and 98
- Windows CE
- Windows for Workgroups 3.11

Note that a new genre of thin client workstation solutions has emerged for the Terminal Server network. These are similar to dumb terminals of days gone by but are known in the Terminal Server community as RDP-based Windows terminals. They are available from such manufacturers like:

- Wyse
- Network Computing Devices (NCD)

- Hewlett-Packard (HP) Windows-based Terminal
- Tektronix

Secret

Be advised that my firm has tested two of these new "thin clients" and decided against purchasing. The reasons were twofold. First, the performance wasn't any different than what we were already obtaining via our traditional workstations in a Terminal Server session (we had been promised better performance). Second, the thin clients ultimately would have cost nearly $800 each. This compares to entry-level Pentium-based workstations at the same price. So the cost savings we had hoped for weren't present. In the end, we simply stayed with our existing Intel-based workstations.

I have observed two ways in which firms benefit from thin clients. First, firms with capital-intensive operations at remote locations greatly benefit from thin clients on a Terminal Server network because these workstations arrive preconfigured and are simply plugged into the network. Nothing like the ability to drop-ship a thin client terminal to your operations in Prudhoe Bay, Alaska, and not have a curious user call to read you a client-side VXD start-up error. For the right companies, getting away from user problems is worth a lot. Other firms like the single application mode found on thin clients. Here, the thin client boots and only runs a single application. Going back to the oil fields of Prudhoe Bay, you probably want those petroleum engineers running the pipeline monitoring application, not games like pinball.

The client software ships in a 16-bit client configuration (for Windows for Workgroups) and a 32-bit client configuration (for Windows 95/98 or Windows NT Workstation 4.0). Microsoft recommends that the workstation running either client have 16MB RAM, but of course you should consider substantially more (such as 48MB RAM). You will need at least 4MB hard disk space for the client-side Terminal Server components.

Implementation

Like any operating system installation, Terminal Server requires planning. Here are a few Terminal Server planning snippets earned the hard way — in the field. Terminal Server should always be installed as a member server. Since sessions are running on the server, users would have the Log on Locally right if a Terminal Server was installed as a domain controller. In large environments, Terminal Server installed as a domain controller may cause authentication problems, because user sessions take priority over user authentication. Also, in large installations, the Security Access Manager (SAM) file may grow too large due to Terminal Server's added configuration options.

Secret

No other BackOffice servers should be installed on a Terminal Server machine. The modified kernel is optimized to support a multiuser environment, not Microsoft BackOffice. In addition, Microsoft's undocumented recommendation is that even Remote Access Service should not be installed on the same machine. These issues make Terminal Server an expensive choice in a small office environment with only one server.

Hardware

Because Terminal Server performs best on multiprocessor systems, a 200 MHz Pentium Pro may be the best choice for Terminal Server. Each processor supports 15 to 25 simultaneous users, and if the number of Terminal Servers needs to be kept to a minimum, four-way processors are in order. Since Pentium IIs don't support more than two processors, the drop in MHz from today's faster machines may be worth the second and third processors.

Terminal Server ups the anti on hardware levels considerably. You will need at least 128MB of hard disk space for the Terminal Server server-side files on the server machine. If you already knew that NT Server is a RAM hog, you may not be surprised to find that Terminal Server is worse. If you haven't experienced NT Server's appetite for RAM, step back, take a deep breath; not only will you want the standard Windows NT Server-level RAM installed on your Terminal Server machine, but you'll need to add at least 16MB RAM to the server for each user session you will support. If possible consider adding 32MB RAM for each user session. It is not uncommon to see Terminal Server machines with over 512MB RAM (that is the amount of RAM memory on the Terminal Server at my company for 100 users). Yes, RAM is inexpensive these days, but as you'll see, $3,000 is a reasonable purchase for high-quality Terminal Server RAM.

Secret

A good friend of mine attended Course 1198B — Supporting Microsoft Windows NT Server 4.0, Terminal Server Edition. One of the in-class exercises was to understand exactly how much memory Terminal Server needs and how it affects machine performance. The drill was simple, using the classroom workstations, each equipped with 32MB RAM. You attached to your partner's machine via a Terminal Server session and launched the pinball game application. Your partner monitored his or her task manager and, once the exercise started, watched the available memory drop and the CPU utilization rate skyrocket and stay at 100 percent. Ouch. Terminal Server requires substantial resources.

Software

Regarding the applications you intend to run on your Terminal Server network, you should (of course) test the applications extensively during the planning phase. Regarding the underlying Windows NT operating system, you are best advised to expand the Registry to 24MB because Terminal Server makes many more Registry entries to accommodate the remote session settings.

Secret

Because the "session" you run via Terminal Server is Windows NT Workstation 4.0, the following comments are germane. I have run many applications on NT Workstation that the manufacturer said couldn't be run. I have also failed to stabilize software that the developers said "should be fine." The only way to be sure is to test. Test all functions, especially printing, and feel free to use an NT Workstation machine running on NT Server, not necessarily Terminal Server. If an app will run on NT Workstation, it will run on Terminal Server.

Another software issue with Terminal Server concerns Microsoft support for regular Windows NT Server versus Terminal Server. The question you must ask yourself when working with hybrid forms of Windows NT Server, such as Terminal Server, is will the standard hot fixes, service packs, and so on for regular Windows NT Server work for Terminal Server. The normal case or basic assumption is no.

Secret

In fact, you cannot use Service Pack 4.0 that was released for "regular" Windows NT Server 4.0 with Terminal Server. You will need to a acquire the Service Pack 4.0 release explicitly for Terminal Server. The difference in the service pack releases reflects the differences in the two products, especially some Registry settings in Terminal Server that relate to sessions.

A Terminal Server Session

It is easy to understand a Terminal Server session. For "regular" personal computers, you start you own machine, and then via the Terminal Server client application, you dial or attach to the Terminal Server and log on. A Terminal Server session is launched.

The process is slightly different for "thin clients" (or dumb terminal-like devices). This approach is akin to the old EPROM days. Remember way back when? I worked with EPROM network adapter cards back in the Novell $2x/3x$ era. Here, the network adapter card contained a special ROM chip (called "EPROM") that, upon booting the personal computer, automatically ran the network client components (IPX protocol and NETX redirector) to initiate an attachment to the NetWare server. Thin clients behave in a similar fashion. Upon startup of the thin client workstation, a Terminal Server connection is automatically initiated.

The five steps range from local user logon to application launch. They are also shown in Figure 19-4:

STEPS:
To log onto and launch Terminal Server

Step 1. At your local workstation, perform a local logon if you are using Windows NT Workstation 4.0. If you are using Windows 98 or Windows 95, bypass the network logon dialog box if you are working remotely and plan to dial into the Terminal Server (this of course assume you are presented with a network logon dialog box). Otherwise, if you are on the network, complete the network logon dialog box as usual.

Step 2. Launch the Terminal Server client application. If you are working remotely and plan to dial into the Terminal Server, this is similar to launching a dial-up networking dialer. Note for a "thin client" such as those just described, Steps 1 and 2 are the same.

Step 3. Observe and verify connection to Terminal Server. The terminal Server session (also known as a VM) is launched.

Step 4. Complete Windows NT Server domain logon.

Step 5. Launch the applications of you choice. Typically, once a Terminal Server session is functional, users launch accounting applications, databases, e-mail programs, or Web browsers.

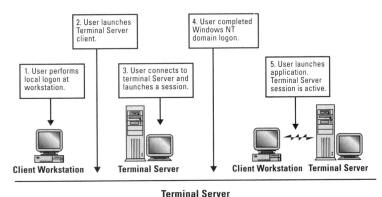

Figure 19-4: User logon steps

MetaFrame

A key component to extending the functionality of Terminal Server is MetaFrame, thin client/server system software available from Citrix (www.citrix.com). You will recall from earlier in the chapter that Citrix developed WinFrame, the predecessor application to Terminal Server. That said, Citrix didn't fade and go away once Terminal Server was released. In fact, Citrix still has their foot in the door with their MetaFrame, which does an excellent job creating a seamless client environment for systems not natively supported by Terminal Server. MetaFrame supports the following clients that aren't supported by Terminal Server:

- Legacy PC environments including MS-DOS, Windows 3.1
- Macintosh
- UNIX
- Java

- OS/2
- Wireless devices

Plainly speaking, the MetaFrame add-on can be viewed as being akin to what Norton Commander does for older Windows environments. That is, additional functionality, via the MetaFrame toolbar, is provided on the server that isn't natively present. This includes additional Terminal Server administrative tools, the capability to run Windows applications on the non-Windows clients just listed (via a terminal emulation session), and additional Terminal Server features such as:

- **Shadowing.** This feature enables you to observe and participate with a user's session.
- **Starting applications.** This is the capability to start an application from or insert an application into Web pages.
- **Application publishing.** This is the capability for applications to be advertised as available for use by other users.
- **Load balancing.** Related to the application just described, this is the capability of clients to connect to and use published applications from several Terminal Servers. The key point here is that the same application may be published from multiple Terminal Servers, in affect balancing the application load across the network.

The Independent Computing Architecture (ICA) protocol is introduced in Terminal Server via the MetaFrame add-on. The ICA protocol is very important in that it provides the support needed for the four features just listed plus client drive mapping, client printer mapping, and client audio support.

Secret

The only way to support Novell NetWare server sessions in your Terminal Server scenario is to deploy MetaFrame and the ICA protocol. Here is what I mean: Many of us work on networks that have multiple servers with different network operating systems. When I call into my office, for example, I need to attach to and map drives to several Windows NT Servers and NetWare 4.*x* servers. If not for MetaFrame and the ICA protocol on our dial-in Terminal Server, I would be unable to use my NetWare server.

Compare and Contrast

Perhaps one of the most interesting ways to learn Terminal Server is to see how it compares to regular Windows NT Server 4.0. The differences, not always apparent at first glance, are striking. These differences include a modified group of Administrative Tools (Common), modified User Properties, and missing menu options.

There are both additions and modifications to the Administrative Tools group. These are shown in Figure 19-5.

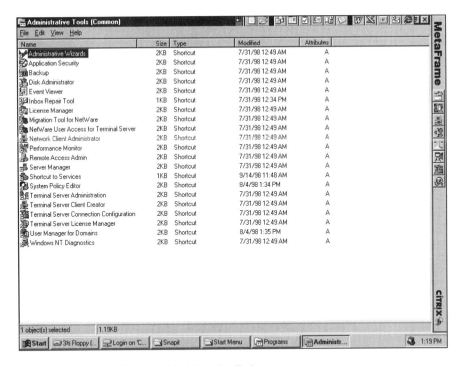

Figure 19-5: Terminal Server's Administrative Tools group

You will note several additions at the lower part of Figure 19-5. These additions are:

- **NetWare User Access for Terminal Server.** If Client Services for NetWare is installed on Terminal Server, then NetWare User Access for Terminal Server will appear. This application can be used to grant NetWare users access to Terminal Server and copy NetWare user and group accounts to Terminal Server.

- **Terminal Server Administration.** This tool is used to manage and monitor users, sessions, and processes (see Figure 19-6)

- **Terminal Server Client Creator.** This tool enables you to create Terminal Server client disks.

- **Terminal Server Connection Configuration.** This tool is used to create and manage the connection between Terminal Server and client. This tool accomplishes numerous tasks including managing the TCP/IP connection settings, setting connection timeout, setting the level of encryption, and allowing reconnections from disconnected clients.

- **Terminal Server License Manager.** This is where you configure the number of client licenses installed for Terminal Server. It is important to note that each client (either Windows-based or terminal machine) must have a valid client license.

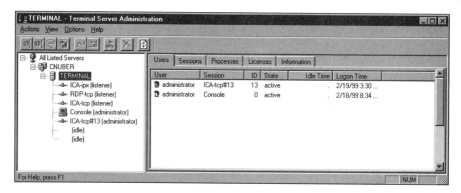

Figure 19-6: Terminal Server Administration

Other modifications occur within existing Administrative Tools applications. For example, Disk Administrator display the local drives on the Terminal Server machine, with the network drive letters you map to these drives. Whereas in Windows NT Server you might look at local drives C: or D:, in Disk Administrator under Terminal Server you would observe drives M:, N:, or whatever network drive you map.

User Manager for Domains has been modified under Terminal Server. Here, the Config button has been added to User Properties as shown in Figure 19-7. The Profile button, though not shown in Figure 19-7, has also been modified.

Selecting the Config button displays the User Configuration dialog box shown in Figure 19-8. User Configuration enables you to configure timeout settings, client devices, the initial program to run, reconnection settings, modem callback settings, and something I'm most concerned about, shadowing settings. I discuss shadowing and ethics at the end of this chapter.

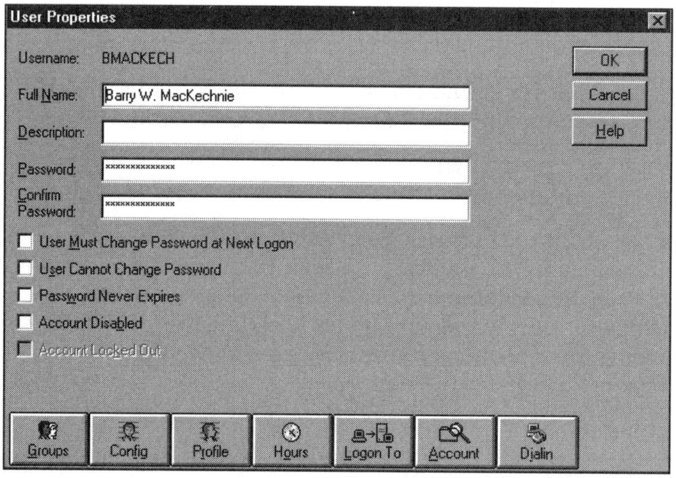

Figure 19-7: Modified User Properties

Chapter 19: Microsoft NT Server — Terminal Edition

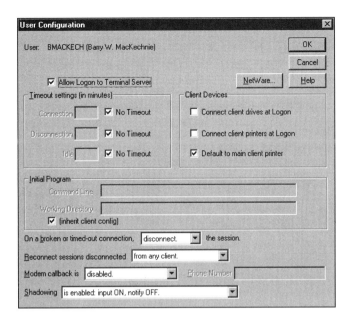

Figure 19-8: User Configuration

The Profile button on User Properties has also been modified. You will note that the Profile dialog box has several additions, as shown in Figure 19-9. These additions include a Terminal Server profile path in addition to the Windows NT Server profile path. There are also settings for specifying a Terminal Server home directory.

Performance Monitor is modified by Terminal Server's addition of the Session object. The Session object enables Terminal Server administrators to track the performance of individual sessions. The counters found under the Session object are akin to the Process object:counters discussed in Chapter 22, "Performance Monitor." But whereas Process object:counters detail a single process, the Session object:counters includes all of the processes within a Terminal Server session. There are three important object:counters to monitor Terminal Server performance with:

- **Session: % Processor Time.** This reports the cumulative elapsed time consumed by all threads used by the processes in the Terminal Server session.

- **Session: Working Set.** This reports the existing number of bytes being using by the Working Set of the processes in a Terminal Server session. The RAM needed and the Working Set value are roughly the same.

- **Session: Working Set Peak.** This reports the highest number of bytes consumed by the Working Set.

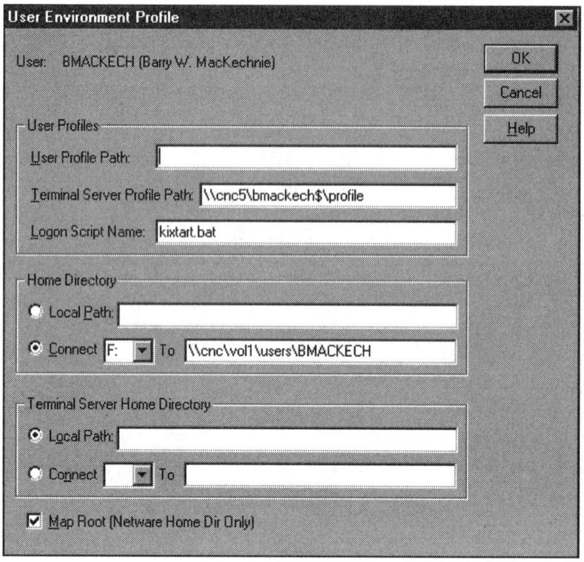

Figure 19-9: User Environmental Profile

Another interesting comparison between Terminal Server and regular Windows NT Server is to observe what's missing. The most notable absence in Terminal Server is the lack of a shutdown button on Terminal Server. Want proof? Just see the lower-left corner of Figure 19-3.

Terminal Server Downfalls

NT Workstation, although more powerful and secure than Windows 95, is behind its cousin in acceptance as a desktop operating system. Because of this, many developers have not written drivers for NT Workstation, and thus their applications will not operate on it. Remember that Terminal Server *is* NT Workstation sessions running on NT Server. This reason alone could prove to be a show stopper in one's choice to implement remote control technology, or it might cause a piece of software to drop from a selection list if Terminal Server is already running.

Long a concern of privacy advocates, managers and users alike, the capability to shadow user activity has been with us for some time. PC Anywhere and the remote control capabilities of Microsoft System Management Server (SMS) have provided this capability for some time. Terminal Server offers this capability as well. Properly used, shadowing is a wonderful tool. I've used it to train users about menu options, keystrokes, and so on. Improperly used, it is a most bothersome tool, allowing the corrupt among us to read the CEO's e-mail and files. And while only the Administrators group may shadow, that creates another problem. The problem is this: I once had the CFO of a large manufacturing concern ask how he might privately terminate his IT Director without the IT Director being aware such an event was looming. The CFO wanted to know that his communications with a head hunting firm would remain private to him. With Terminal Server, shadowing, and the Shadowing configuration variable "notify OFF" as seen in the lower part of Figure 19-7, I was unable to offer the assurance. This is a dangerous Terminal Server area. Be advised to take the ethical high road here.

Summary

In this chapter you were exposed to basic and advanced Terminal Server issues. The following topics were covered:

- Learning the history and environment of Terminal Server
- Comparing and contrasting remote node versus remote control
- Defining the features of Terminal Server
- Properly implementing Terminal Server on your network
- Learning how to best administer your Terminal Server
- Defining MetaFrame
- Learning how boost Terminal Server performance

Chapter 20

Windows NT Server—Small Business Server

In This Chapter

- Defining Small Business Server
- Understanding the small business environment
- Identifying Small Business Server design goals and philosophy
- Planning for your Small Business Server implementation
- Installing Small Business Server
- Using the SBS To Do List
- Installing the Small Business Server - client components
- Performing ongoing administration of Small Business Server
- Troubleshooting Small Business Server
- Comparing and contrasting Small Business Server and "regular" Windows NT Server
- Planning for future releases of SBS

One of the most wonderful things to happen to Windows NT Server 4.0 was the introduction of Small Business Server (SBS) in late 1997. Why? Because Microsoft, by releasing SBS, addressed the underserved small business market. Firms under 25 users, the connection limit for SBS, had historically tried to make regular Windows NT Server and regular Microsoft BackOffice applications fit. And it was a tight fit because small businesses are very different, as I will explain, from larger businesses.

So the arrival of SBS heralded an era of right-sizing a Microsoft solution to meet very different, small business–specific needs. Now, with one piece of software, you can provide a viable and respected networking solution for the long-neglected small business.

This chapter intends to go beyond just introducing SBS to show you how it is set up and operates. At every turn, I intend to compare and contrast SBS with "regular" Windows NT Server 4.0. It has been my experience that many

Windows NT Server gurus are bewildered by SBS because, starting with its initial setup and continuing through the ongoing administration phase, SBS is very different.

Defining Small Business Server

If you were on an elevator and only had 90 seconds to explain SBS to a fellow elevator riders (this is the proverbial 90-second test in life), where might you start? You could of course say that SBS is an alphabet soup mix from Active Server Pages to Windows NT Server 4.0. You might say that it is the Windows NT Server 4.0 operating system, several Microsoft BackOffice components, plus a few additional features thrown in including faxing and modem sharing. Or you might take the approach offered in Table 20-1, which uses a client/server model. On the SBS server side are the operating system and server-based applications. On the SBS client side are client applications such as Internet Explorer; Microsoft Outlook; and SBS redirectors for modems, faxing, and Proxy Server. Have I used up my 90 seconds yet?

First, a short list (Table 20-1) of all SBS components. This is followed by detailed explanations of the SBS server-side components that compose SBS 4.0a. In the table, I've divided the information between server and client components to help you view SBS from a client/server perspective.

Table 20-1: SBS 4.0a Components

Component	Description	Server or Client Component
Windows NT Server 4.0 with Service Pack 3	32-bit network operating system	Server
Microsoft Exchange Server 5.0	E-mail application	Server
Microsoft SQL Server 6.5	Database application	Server
Microsoft Proxy Server	Internet security and firewall	Server gateway application
Microsoft Internet Information Server 3.0	Internet/intranet development and management application	Server
Microsoft Fax Server 1.0	Fax pooling and management application	Server
Microsoft Modem Sharing Server 1.0	Modem pooling and management application	Server

Chapter 20: Windows NT Server — Small Business Server

Component	Description	Server or Client Component
Microsoft Index Server 1.1	Search engine application	Server
Crystal Reports 4.5	Report generation application	Server
Microsoft Active Server Pages Server	Internet development environment for *.asp files	Server
Additional Goodies	HP JetAdmin tools, etc., on SBS CD-ROM	Server
SBS Console	GUI-based management console	Server
Server-based Wizards	SBS Server Setup Wizard, Internet Connection Wizard, device and peripheral management	Server
To Do List	Step-by-step to-do list	Server
Online Guide	Robust online help manual for SBS administrators	Server
Default Intranet Page	Provides extensive SBS information for administrators/users	Client/Server
Internet Explorer 4.01	Internet browser for navigating both the Internet and intranets. Installed on both the SBS server machine and SBS clients	Client/Server
Setup Computer Wizard	Step one creates and registers machine on the SBS server machine. Step two, via the client installation disk, configures and attaches a network-ready workstation to the SBS network.	Client/Server
Client Installation Diskette	A disk that is formatted and created on the SBS server machine. At the client workstation, the setup phase configures the client (TCP/IP protocol, NetBIOS name, user name assigned to machine, etc.). Affectionately known as the "magic disk"	Client/Server
Microsoft Outlook 97	Client-based e-mail, scheduling, and contact management application	Client

Continued

Table 20-1 *(continued)*

Component	Description	Server or Client Component
Microsoft FrontPage 97	Web site creation application	Client
SBS Fax client	Faxing functionality and capabilities	Client
SBS Modem Pool client	Modem pooling functionality (port redirector)	Client
SBS Proxy Client	Client-side Microsoft Proxy Server functionality (WinSock Proxy redirector)	Client
SBS Client	Basic SBS workstationclient application (assists in modifying client configuration)	Client

Before launching you directly into SBS, let's take a few moments to define in painful detail what the SBS product is. As you know, SBS consists of the components that I listed in Table 20-1. But leaving that high-level hooey behind, it's now time to get into the painful details. That said, not only will this section clarify what SBS "is" but I'll compare and contrast those "is-es" to regular Windows NT Server 4.0.

SBS version 4.0a

I assume that you are using SBS version 4.0a, which started shipping in mid-1998. Prior to that, if you purchased SBS, it was most likely version 4.0. To upgrade to version 4.0a from version 4.0, you need to install SBS Service Pack 1. In the Server installation section, I share insights on how to apply SBS Service Pack 1.

Secret

Of course the question that follows is exactly which version of SBS are you running. Suggesting that you can say you are running version 4.0a just because you have Internet Explorer 4.01 on your server's desktop is a fallacy. In fact, the only way to definitively determine which version of SBS you have installed is to check the release notes (see Figure 20-1):

STEPS:

To apply SBS Service Pack 1

Step 1. Launch the SBS Console from the Start menu.
Step 2. Select the Online Guide tab sheet.
Step 3. Select Release Notes in the left pane.
Step 4. Observe the Release Notes for version 4.0a.

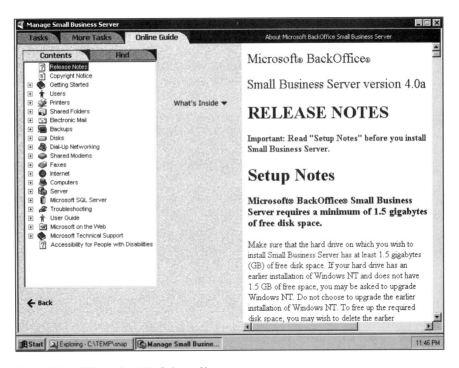

Figure 20-1: SBS version 4.0a Release Notes

Amazingly, you are unable to determine what version of SBS you are using or the SBS Service pack level from three places you would expect to in regular Windows NT Server 4.0:

- **Startup blue screen.** When regular Windows NT Server 4.0 starts, it displays the Windows NT Server 4.0 build number (1381) and the Windows NT Server service pack level (3).

- **System Properties.** Only the regular Window NT Server 4.0 build number (1381) is displayed.

- **WinMSD.** Both the regular Windows NT Server 4.0 build number (1381) and Windows NT Server service pack level (3) are displayed.

SBS Service Pack One not only changed the SBS version number from 4.0 to 4.0a but also fixed bugs and added functionality. I've listed these specifics to enable you to see the difference between SBS 4.0 and 4.0a.

- Internet Explorer 4.01 is installed by default on the server and clients. This was necessary on the server because the SBS Console was redesigned to take advantage of new Internet Explorer 4.x HTML improvements.

- Memory requirements at the SBS client level increased to 12MB RAM (from 8MB) for Windows 95/98 and 24MB for Windows NT Workstation. Clients now need 96MB free hard disk drive space. The increase in RAM requirements was to improve client-side performance and support Internet Explorer 4.01.

- Windows NT Workstation must have Windows NT Service Pack 3 installed to provide appropriate modem and Internet Explorer 4.01 support.

- Internet Mail/News problems were fixed. Internet Mail and News essentially did not work in SBS 4.0. Now, SBS clients are automatically configured so that they can use Mail/News.

- General SBS Console bug fixes include the elimination of script errors and hangs conditions.

- Fixes have been made to Exchange to better report maximum message size errors. I discuss this more in the Microsoft Exchange Server 5.0 detail that follows.

- Bug fixes have been made to the Client License Add Disks.

- You now have the ability to remove the Fax Client from Windows 95/98.

Windows NT Server 4.0

This is, of course, the main point of the entire book. Briefly, Windows NT Server 4.0 is the operating system that supports file and printer sharing, acts as an applications server, supports native remote access capabilities (RAS), manages user accounts and security, and has network protocol support (including TCP/IP).

But now for an SBS perspective. This is and isn't your father's Windows NT Server.

This is your father's NT server

By "is" I mean it is, at a very basic level, the same Windows NT Server 4.0 that you've by now come to love. The Windows NT Server 4.0 that forms the foundation for SBS is good old build 1381 with Service Pack 3 installed. This is what I affectionately refer to as "normal" or "regular" Windows NT Server 4.0.

It is important to understand that SBS indeed ships with "regular" Windows NT Server from a customer's point of view. Given that Windows NT Server 4.0 was entirely acceptable in terms of stability circa Service Pack 3, I've found that customers have a need to know both that SBS ships with Windows NT Server and that said Windows NT Server isn't some type of skinny or light version. I guess that insecurity reflects how many people have felt short-changed by "bundles" where the underlying applications are the "sample" or "skinny" versions. Such is not the case with SBS. It's the real thing.

Based on the discussion contained in this section and Table 20-1, it is critical that you understand SBS includes Windows NT Server. Don't embarrass yourself, and worse yet, lose an attractive SBS engagement, because you incorrectly bid an SBS job like my good friends at Company X (I've changed the names to protect the innocent). Here, the SBS bid included both SBS, Windows NT Server 4.0, and Proxy Server 1.0. Of course the last two items are automatically included with SBS. The two redundant items, Windows NT Server 4.0 and Proxy Server 1.0, were quickly exposed. The representatives from Company X were humiliated.

For details on "regular" Windows NT Server 4.0, you are encouraged to read Chapter 17, "'Regular' Windows NT Server."

This isn't your father's NT server

Now the "isn't" side of the story. Suffice it to say, the Windows NT Server 4.0 operating system contained in SBS is slightly modified from regular Windows NT Server 4.0 in a few ways. First, the addition of the SBS console is clearly an addition. In fact, the only thing that comes close to the SBS console is the Administrative Wizards GUI-based interface in regular Windows NT Server 4.0 (see Figure 20-2).

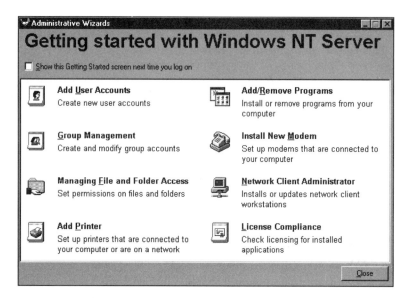

Figure 20-2: "Regular" Windows NT Server 4.0's Administrative Wizards

Note

Both SBS and regular Windows NT Server 4.0 have the Administrative Wizards, which are found under the Administrator Tools program group.

Other ways that the SBS version and regular version of Windows NT Server differ are:

- **Licensing.** Regular Windows NT Server and big BackOffice allow you to select from either per seat or per server licensing. You even have the one-time opportunity to switch between the two. And — here is a life saver in the real world — regular Windows NT Server and big BackOffice do not implicitly lock out users after the license count you defined during setup or via Licensing in Control Panel (for per server mode) or via License Manager in the Administrative Tools program group (for per seat mode). Not that you would break any software licensing agreement, but it's a nice touch to work with the honor system in regular Windows NT Server. Often I'll call my software vendor to purchase more licenses when the number of logons exceeds the license count, but at least staff can work until the "paper" licenses arrive in the mail the next day. The easiest way to discover that you are out of compliance with your licensing is to monitor the System Log in Event Viewer. License Manager will map log entries when either per server or per seat licensing violations have occurred. At that time, it behooves you to order more licenses.

  Licensing for SBS (including Window NT Server 4.0) is on a per server basis and somewhat unique compared to other BackOffice products. The key point regarding SBS licensing is that any user attempting to log on after the maximum licenses have been exceeded will be denied access. No honor system here, rather we're talking hard-core license enforcement.

Secret

Ironically, the user attempting to log on after the number of SBS licenses at the server have has been exceed will appear to be authenticated on the network. That means the logon activity will occur normally where you enter your name and password at the domain logon dialog box. However, the moment that you attempt to map a drive or access a server-based resource such as a printer or e-mail, you will be denied. The denials come in the form of "Error #70," which is undefined except for a reference in Microsoft TechNet.

- **SBS Registry.** The Windows NT Server 4.0 Registry on an SBS machine has additions, restrictions, and modifications that regular Windows NT Server 4.0 doesn't.
    - **Additions.** Additions include Registry entries for unique SBS features such as Microsoft Fax Server and the Modem Sharing Server.
    - **Restrictions.** Restrictions include entries that enforce the SBS client licensing limits and SQL Server 6.5 table size limits.
    - **Modifications.** Many existing Registry keys are treated differently in SBS than other flavors of Windows NT Server and BackOffice. For example, in SBS's CurrrentControlSet key (found via HKEY_LOCAL_MACHINE), you will find the SQL Server Executive server has a start value of 0x3, meaning it is essentially disabled until your turn the service on via Control Panel. In "regular" Windows NT Server with "big" BackOffice, the SQL Server Executive would have a lower start value (0x2) so it automatically starts when Windows NT Server boots.

NT Service Pack 3

SBS ships with Windows NT Server 4.0 Service Pack 3 already applied, so there is no need to undertake this action. However, I'm worried that you might bring forward another regular Windows NT Server behavior that could be very destructive to SBS. As you know from your experience and your MCSE courses, the latest service pack should always be reapplied after major changes to your network operating system have occurred. Changes that qualify include upgrading or reinstalling a BackOffice application, installing a major third-party application on the server such as Oracle, and so on.

Secret

With SBS, it's important that you not perform this type of service pack reinstallation because doing so may cause errors and problems on your SBS machine. I would also caution that whenever a service pack is released, such as Service Pack 4.0 for regular Windows NT Server 4.0, you wait until Microsoft releases either an SBS upgrade wizard to apply the service pack or a statement clarifying that you may apply it just like Windows NT Server.

Under any circumstances, be sure to make at least one verified backup of your SBS machine prior to any upgrade (service pack, application, whatever!).

NT Option Pack

As you may know from Chapter 13, the Option Pack is a way to extend the functionality of Windows NT Server 4.0 in your organization. Historically, the Option Pack was oriented toward the enterprise-level implementations of Windows NT Server 4.0. However, small businesses running SBS may take advantage of Option Pack features.

Secret

Contrary to the words of wisdom in the SBS version 4.0a Release Notes that state "Windows NT 4.0 Option Pack is not compatible with Small Business Server," you can install and utilize the Option Pack. To get the Option Pack and SBS-related instructions, point your Internet Explorer browser to:

www.microsoft.com/backofficesmallbiz/guide/installp.asp

Better news yet! By going to the site mentioned, you will receive the Option Pack for free.

Note both Service Pack 4.0 and the Option Pack are discussed at length in Part IV of this book, "Service Pack 4.0 and the Windows NT Server Option."

Secret

Finally, it is worth repeating that the SBS version of Windows NT Server, while slightly modified, is really just as robust and trustworthy as regular Windows NT Server. That is something you and your SBS customers need to remember.

Microsoft Exchange Server 5.0

By definition, Microsoft Exchange Server 5.0 is a rock-solid and very powerful electronic mail, scheduling, and groupware application. Best known for its e-mail, Microsoft Exchange Server supports:

- **E-mail.** Both internal and external (Internet) e-mail are supported.
- **Server-based Scheduling.** The scheduling function is managed at the server level by the Microsoft Exchange Server engine so that Outlook clients on an SBS network can create appointments and schedule meetings.
- **Groupware.** This is supported by public folders that allow sharing information, applications, corporate contacts, bulletin boards, and the like.
- **Support for Internet newsgroups.** Microsoft Exchange can act as a newsgroup server.
- **Updated communications functionality.** Microsoft Exchange Server replaced Microsoft Mail (thank god!).

Luckily, Microsoft shipped SBS with Microsoft Exchange 5.x instead of the its 4.x predecessor. The improvements are striking, but three stand out:

- **Active Server Page support.** This area, known as *.asp files, has emerged as a big area for additional work in supporting SBS customers after the network is up and running.

- **Web-based Outlook solution.** Properly configured with a robust, full-time connection, this enables you to access your Microsoft Exchange Server–based e-mail from any point of the Internet using a modern WWW browser (Internet Explorer 3.*x* or higher, Netscape Navigator 3.*x* or higher). For example, if your company's Internet domain was `springers.com` and you had correctly implemented this Outlook/Exchange solution, you would point your browser to `exchange.springers.com/exchange` to bring up the Outlook Web client (see Figure 20-3).

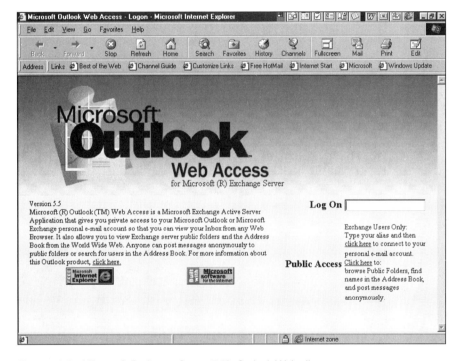

Figure 20-3: Microsoft Exchange Server 5.0's Outlook Web client

- **Internet Mail Service (IMS).** The IMS replaced the older Internet Mail Connector and has significant improvements such as a much more robust and stable ETRN mail retrieval support (see Figure 20-4). ETRN is a popular mail get/retrieve trigger that fires when a periodic dial-up connection is made to your Internet Service Provider. ETRN was dramatically improved with the release of Microsoft Exchange Server 5.0 and is the default mail retrieval method when you implement SB with dial-up networking to an ISP and sign up with the ISP via the Internet Connection Wizard (which I explain later).

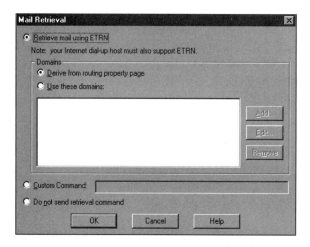

Figure 20-4: Configuring Internet Mail Service for ETRN

If you would like more information on the use of ETRN and configuring the IMS, I highly recommend that you download the Internet Connectivity White Paper (see Figure 20-5) at either of these locations:

www.microsoft.com/directaccess
www.microsoft.com/backofficesmallbiz

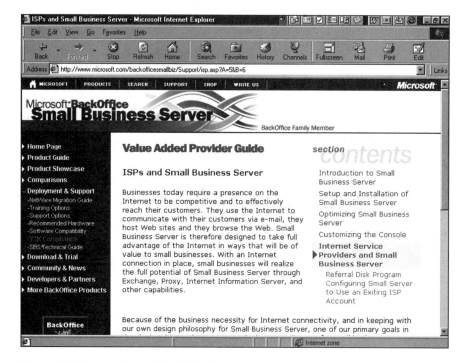

Figure 20-5: Internet Connectivity White Paper

You may also find this information on the Microsoft TechNet CDs.

Microsoft Exchange has been trimmed down to fit inside SBS. At the enterprise level, we commonly place Microsoft Exchange Server on its own server machine (and a very powerful machine at that). With SBS, however, the challenge was to fit Microsoft Exchange Server and other BackOffice applications on the same server. Talk about an engineering accomplishment!

One of the ways that Microsoft Exchange Server "fit" into the SBS family lay in trimming its memory footprint to 8MB RAM, which is dramatically less than the RAM we would allocate at the enterprise level. So not only does Microsoft Exchange Server run slower in SBS than in enterprise-level implementations, but an 800K outbound message size restriction has been implemented. Note that a message size is measured as the actual e-mail composition (typically your typed note) plus all attachments (documents, drawings, spreadsheets).

This outgoing message size restriction has been problematic for several of my SBS customers, but perhaps the most affected has been the landscaping company with its heavy use of the AutoCAD drawing applications (and its associated huge data files).

I've been able to assist the landscaping company overcome this SBS-related outgoing message limitation by modifying the following setting in Microsoft Exchange Server.

STEPS:
To modify message size restrictions in Microsoft Exchange Server

Step 1. Launch the Microsoft Exchange Administrator application (see Figure 20-6) from the Microsoft Exchange (Common) program group (accessed via the Start button ➪ Programs).

Step 2. Expand the Microsoft Exchange Server site icon (it looks like a globe) in the left pane.

Step 3. Click the Recipients icon in the left pane to display all of the recipients in the right pane.

Step 4. Display the properties for a recipient by double-clicking on the recipient's name.

Continued

STEPS

To modify message size restrictions in Microsoft Exchange Server *(continued)*

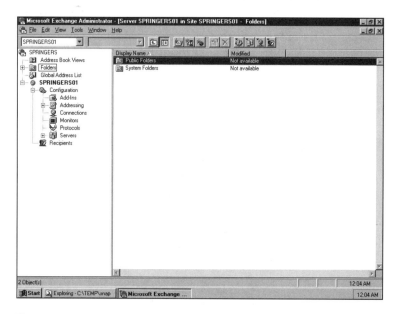

Figure 20-6: Microsoft Exchange Administrator

Step 5. Select the Advanced tab sheet (see Figure 20-7).

Chapter 20: Windows NT Server — Small Business Server

Figure 20-7: Recipient Properties

Step 6. Select No Limit under Outgoing in the Message Size area.

Final Microsoft Exchange Server musings? Be advised that Microsoft Exchange Server 5.0 in SBS ships with Microsoft Exchange Server Service Pack 2 as you consider adding additional features to Microsoft Exchange Server (such as new business applications that hook into this application) or you call Microsoft for technical support. And the SBS version of Microsoft Exchange Server was trimmed to not include directory replication, which is considered an enterprise-level feature.

Secret

Also note that Microsoft Exchange Server is very sensitive to how backups are performed. Just running a normal flat-file backup routine from the SBS built-in backup program is insufficient. You need to run the Exchange-specific backup routine within the SBS tape backup program to ensure that the Information Store and Directory Services (places where the e-mail and user/group information is stored) are properly backed up. More on this topic and the use of third-party SBS backup applications in the "SBS Administration" section of this chapter).

And you can count on the first call from your SBS client, after the network is up and running, to be that e-mail isn't working. Funny how e-mail became the most important thing in the office of the late 1990s.

SQL Server 6.5

A real diamond in the rough in SBS is SQL Server 6.5. It is probably the most powerful application that ships with SBS and frequently one of the most ignored. Most small businesses considering SQL Server don't even know what it is, much less how it might help to better run their businesses.

That ignorance is usually corrected when small businesses look at narrow vertical market applications that run on the SBS network. Great Plains Dynamics — SQL Server version is a great example (as I've previously mentioned). Typically the small business wants to upgrade to the latest accounting software from Great Plains, the SQL Server version. Once that need is identified, SBS sells itself. All the SBS customer knows is that SQL Server is a database engine that drives its accounting system. And that's all they really need to know.

You, on the other hand, are probably interested in more of the "meat" on the bone. Here you go. SQL Server 6.5 that ships with SBS includes SQL Server 6.5 Service Pack 3.0. At its most basic definition, SQL Server 6.5 is a SQL-based server engine, data warehouse, and management tool that "coordinates" the small businesses data. By that I mean SQL Server 6.5 responds to SQL-language queries such as SELECT that are sent by client applications such as Great Plains Dynamics — SQL Server version. Once a SQL query is received by SQL Server 6.5, it is processed and fulfilled, with the results returned to the client applications. SQL Server 6.5 is an extremely powerful relational database application, one that many MCSEs have made great (and profitable) livings from.

Key SQL Server features are:

- **SQL Server performance.** I consider SQL Server to be a rock-solid database application that has the security needed to protect sensitive data.

- **SQL as an open standard.** As stated, applications such as accounting programs can "hook" into SQL Server. This interoperability makes SQL Server a very attractive component of SBS. SQL Server also supports numerous communication avenues such as OLE, OBDC, ActiveX, and integration with the Event Log and e-mail.

- **Internet support.** SQL Server is being used in several ways to extend the reach of the Internet to the small business. One such way lies in its capability to interact with Internet Information Server (IIS), its support for Active Server Pages (ASP), and its role in electronic commerce sites with other Microsoft BackOffice components such as Site Server. The role in electronic commerce is best exemplified by the Great Plains e-commerce module. This electronic commerce accounting software module requires both Site Server and SQL Server to run.

- **Data replication.** The SBS version of SQL Server supports the publish and subscribe metaphor that allows data to be distributed. This feature is key in the area of electronic commerce, where you may have your ISP host your Web pages and transaction information. Under this scenario, the transaction information would be housed on the ISP's SQL server and published to your SQL server periodically. Such support is included right out of the box with SBS's SQL Server.

- **Ease of management.** To the extent a robust database such as SQL Server is easy, you will consider the Microsoft SQL Enterprise Manager (see Figure 20-8), a GUI-based management tool, to demystify SQL Server and make it more manageable by mere mortals.

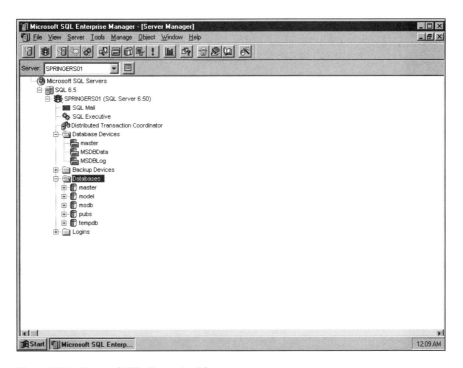

Figure 20-8: Microsoft SQL Enterprise Manager

SQL Server 6.5 was trimmed to fit SBS. The trimming doesn't involve missing SQL commands or support. You basically are using the same SQL Server 6.5 that ships with big BackOffice. However, the cumulative storage limit for data is set to 1.5GB (which includes tables and logs). That's actually a large number, given that much of the data businesses work with today is really plain text in a column/row table format (at least as far as SQL Server 6.5 is concerned). However, if you exceed this storage limit, you can upgrade to the full version of SQL Server 6.5 (I discuss that at the end of the chapter in the section "The Future of SBS").

Microsoft Proxy Server 1.0 and 2.0

Out of the box, SBS provide Microsoft Proxy Server 1.0 (in a moment, I'll discuss a free upgrade path that enables you to install Proxy Server 2.0). Microsoft Proxy Server is best known, in layperson's terms, for its firewall and caching capabilities. Technically, it is a secure gateway to connect a LAN to the Internet with such features as:

- **Single point of connection to the Internet.** Instead of users "doing their own thing" and connecting in an ad hoc manner to the Internet, Microsoft Proxy Server acts as a central connection point or "gateway." This approach enables you to better manage Internet access and activity. Better management alone results in better security.

- **Connection capabilities.** Includes on-demand and scheduled connections. The AutoDial application enables you to set access hours and such in a dial-up Internet connection scenario.

- **Caching.** This allows popular Web pages to be stored locally on your SBS server. This feature reduces frequent connections to the Internet if the requested Web pages are found in local cache. It also speeds user access time for cached pages, as these pages are returned at LAN speed, not Internet connection speeds.

Caching is one of the most popular features of Microsoft Proxy Server.

- **Internet content and access management.** You can allow rich-content Internet sites to be accessed by the browsers on your network. You can also restrict the type of sites your users may visit on the basis of protocol or specific domain name. With the proper configuration, you can also use logging to observe what sites users have visited. I've found such logging to serve as a major deterrent to misbehavior on SBS networks.

- **Full SBS integration.** Microsoft Proxy Server (see Figure 20-9) integrates cleanly with the SBS package. It supports the native TCP/IP protocol (And even IPX/SPX if you like). It is managed via IIS (included with SBS).

Chapter 20: Windows NT Server—Small Business Server

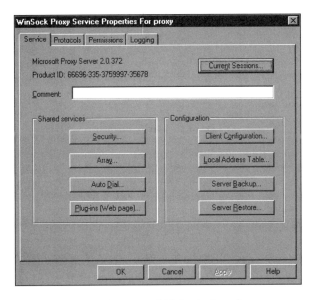

Figure 20-9: Proxy Server 2.0 (WinSock shown)

You may upgrade to Proxy Server 2.0 for free as of October 1998 by calling Microsoft at 1-800-758-1379 for more information. You will need to present proof of purchase information in order to qualify for the free Proxy Server 2.0 upgrade.

Proxy Server 2.0 offers several additional features not found in Proxy Server 1.0, including:

- **Year 2000 compliance.** This is actually one of the main reasons that Microsoft announced the free Proxy Server 2.0 upgrade for SBS sites. Proxy Server 1.0 had Year 2000 issues that are now addressed with this upgrade.

- **Packet layer security with dynamic packet filtering.** Inbound and outbound packet filtering is supported in Proxy Server 2.0.

- **Real-time security alerts.** Immediate notifications that might alert you to intrusions are now available.

- **Reverse proxy.** This allows your Web server, located behind the Proxy Server firewall, to publish to the World Wide Web without security breaches. The benefit of this? In the case of electronic commerce, you can have your Web server communicate with your accounting application server and allow outsiders to legitimately hit the same Web server. In short, the feature helps accommodate electronic commerce.

- **Reverse hosting.** This is as close to clustering as it gets. Here, several Web servers sitting behind your Proxy Server firewall appear as a single virtual directory.

- **Server proxying.** Proxy Server listens for inbound packets destined for other servers, such as an accounting application server. The packets are forwarded to the appropriate server. This feature is great for supporting electronic data interchange (EDI) with your vendors. Properly configured, this feature would allow your vendors to make entries directly into your order entry system.
- **Improved performance.** Proxy Server 2.0 has reported caching performance gains of 40 percent over Proxy Server 1.0.

Secret

You will also need to download the Proxy Server Upgrade Wizard from www.microsoft.com/backofficesmallbiz in order to upgrade from Proxy 1.0 to Proxy 2.0 in SBS. I speak more about this Proxy upgrade process at the end of the chapter (see the "Implementing Proxy 2.0" section).

Key services in Proxy Server 2.0 are:

- **WinSock Proxy.** Supports IPX/SPX, uses Windows NT Challenge/Response (CHAP) authentication, controls inbound and outbound access by port number, protocol, and user or group.
- **Web Proxy.** Is CERN-compatible and supports HTTP, FTP, Gopher. Caches HTTP objects and allows data encryption.

Microsoft Internet Information Server

Microsoft Internet Information Server (IIS) 4.0 (see Figure 20-10) provides an easy way for SBS sites to publish content on the Internet and the firm's internal Intranet. In fact, SBS has a default Intranet page that appears by default when users launch their browsers. But more on that in a moment.

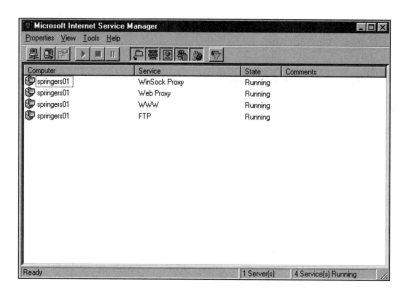

Figure 20-10: Internet Service Manager in IIS 4.0

IIS is integrated with the underlying Windows NT Server 4.0 operating at the service level. IIS is increasingly used by ISVs for application support, an example of this being the reliance on IIS by Great Plains for its new electronic commerce accounting module. IIS is very powerful in its capability to support multiple virtual directories and in its security and performance. Additional support in IIS 4.0 that wasn't present in previous versions includes support for Front Page extensions and Active Server Pages (ASPs). Finally, the ease of use for IIS can't be understated. Its Internet Service Manager allows centralized management of the following IIS services.

The key features of IIS are:

- **WWW Service.** WWW and HTTP hosting service
- **FTP Service.** File Transfer Protocol (FTP) support for transferring files to and from a site

Support for Gopher was dropped in IIS 4.0. SBS 4.0 originally shipped with IIS 3.0, which had Gopher support. When upgrading to SBS 4.0a, you will lose Gopher support.

Microsoft Fax Server 1.0

This application allows users to fax from the desktop using one or more (up to four) fax modems attached to the SBS machine. Faxes may be sent from any program because the fax-related functionality is that of "printing" to the fax modem on the network. Inbound faxes are received at the SBS machine and may be printed, e-mailed to one user who may distribute the faxes over the company Exchange-based e-mail system, or stored to a shared directory on the SBS machine. Security allows the Administrator to determine who may view faxes. Up to four modems, which must provide faxing support, may be attached to an SBS server.

Fax Server is managed via the Fax Server applet in Control Panel. Once launched, you will see the Fax Server Properties dialog box as shown in Figure 20-11.

Ironically, the one feature that many SBS users ask for is surprisingly absent. When faxing, users have an important need to know if the fax arrived at its destination. Up the ante when discussing law firms and their unique faxing needs (law firms typically need a fax confirmation page for legal proceedings). This information is traditionally conveyed to users via a fax confirmation sheet that they receive after the fax has either been successfully sent or failed. This typically occurs in real time with the user standing by the fax machine to grab the fax confirmation report from the fax machine paper tray (on a traditional fax machine).

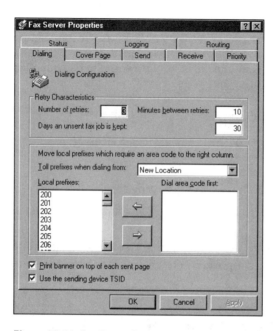

Figure 20-11: Fax Server Properties

The best that Fax Server does in addressing this issue is logging. As Figure 20-12 shows, you may select different logging levels under the Logging tab sheet of the Fax Server Properties dialog box.

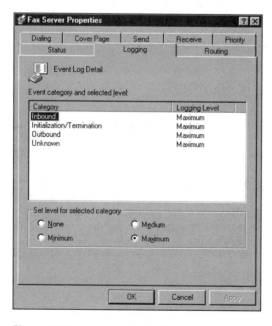

Figure 20-12: Logging with Fax Server

Chapter 20: Windows NT Server — Small Business Server

STEPS:

To display fax logs

Step 1. Launch the SBS Console ("Manage Small Business Server").

Step 2. Select the More Tasks tab sheet.

Step 3. Select the Manage Faxes button.

Step 4. From the Manage Faxes page, select the Generate Fax Reports button (see Figure 20-13).

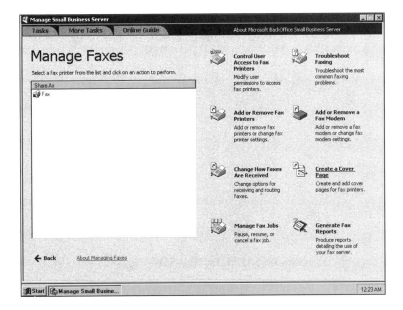

Figure 20-13: Manage faxes

You are next presented with a Crystal Reports–generated "Sent Faxes Report" that presents faxing activity in a batch, not real-time, perspective (see Figure 20-14).

Continued

STEPS

To display fax logs *(continued)*

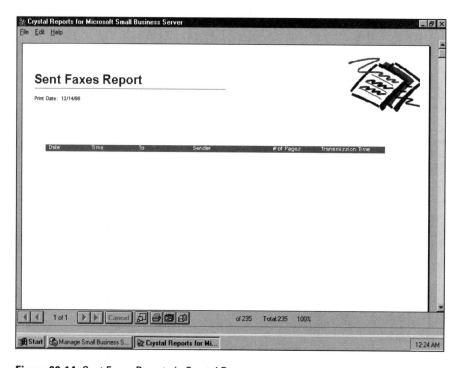

Figure 20-14: Sent Faxes Report via Crystal Reports

Note that Fax Server enables you to send out broadcast faxes from your desktop (send faxes to many recipients). This feature is very popular with small businesses seeking to use SBS as a real marketing tool.

Microsoft Modem Sharing Server 1.0

This is a modem pooling application that is not available either with regular Windows NT Server or big BackOffice. It is also one of the most valuable features for SBS customers that intend to use a dial-up connection to the Internet, take advantage of the capability to dial-in or dial-out via RAS, or use SBS's inbound/outbound faxing capabilities.

Surprisingly, many SBS customers initially plan for great use of the modem polling capabilities, but with the advent of digital full-time Internet connections such as DSL and ISDN, the modem sharing capability is often used in cases where a user needs to dial a BBS, another dial-in site (such as an office building HVAC management system), or secure sites (such as Visa/MasterCard authorization centers or drug testing labs).

Up to four modems may participate in a modem pool. The modem pool is managed via the Modem Sharing applet in Control Panel (see Figure 20-15).

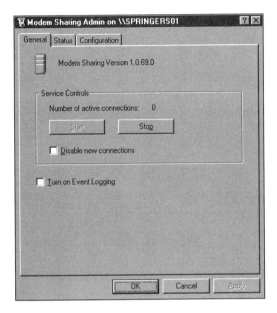

Figure 20-15: Modem Sharing

Note

The modem sharing server interacts with RAS. RAS in SBS is essentially the same RAS that is contained in regular Windows NT Server.

Microsoft Index Server 1.1

This is a more than adequate search engine right out of the SBS box (see Figure 20-16). I've used Index Server for in-class training exercises as part of the MCSE curriculum I deliver as an MCT. An unnamed author who is a good friend of mine has used Index Server to organize newsgroup threads as part of his writing research so that the newsgroup information is readily searchable by keyword.

However, be advised that Index Server has practical limits at the version 1.1 level. By that I mean to say that firms engaged in online electronic commerce and the like don't use this version of Index Server for their "real" online operations. Rather, firms with heavy indexing requirements beyond that capabilities of Index Server 1.1, such as online legal databases, use third-party solutions such as PLS.

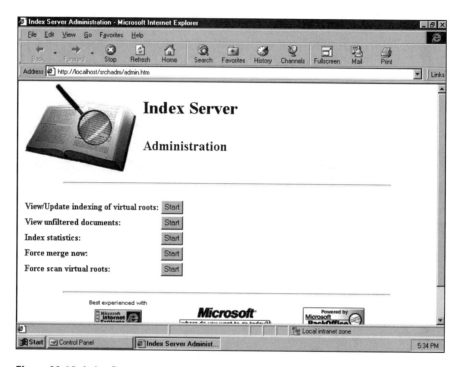

Figure 20-16: Index Server

Secret

To be frank, the best use of Index Server on an SBS network is for indexing and organizing internal company information for use on the firm's intranet. There it shines with its basic query forms and full-text indexing features.

Crystal Reports 4.5

Crystal Reports (see Figure 20-17), a robust report writer, was really included with SBS to provide reporting capabilities from the SBS Console (discussed shortly). But it is interesting to note that often, several months after an SBS network has been installed, someone from the business-side of the SBS customer site discovers that they own Crystal Reports on the SBS server machine. Once that cat is out of the bag, people start using this product to create management reports based on accounting system data, spreadsheets, and such. For example, Crystal Reports may be used to create reports that extract accounting data from Great Plains Dynamics. I've seen it done and it's wonderful. A very positive addition to SBS.

Chapter 20: Windows NT Server — Small Business Server

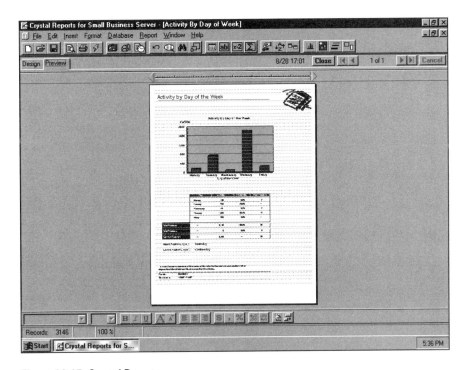

Figure 20-17: Crystal Reports

SBS console

On the server side, it all ends at the SBS Console (see Figure 20-18). This is the primary user interface for managing the SBS server. It is akin to the Administrative Wizards application in "regular" Windows NT Server, found under Administrative Tools (Common), but much more powerful. Microsoft's design goal with the SBS Console was to group the most common tasks on the first page and secondary or less common tasks on the second page.

Secret

The SBS Console is customizable so that you may add your own buttons to it! This is an increasingly popular option for ISVs writing software specifically for SBS (such as tape backup applications). This topic is beyond the scope of this chapter, but you may find more information on it in the Console Customization and Style Guide found at www.microsoft.com/directaccess.

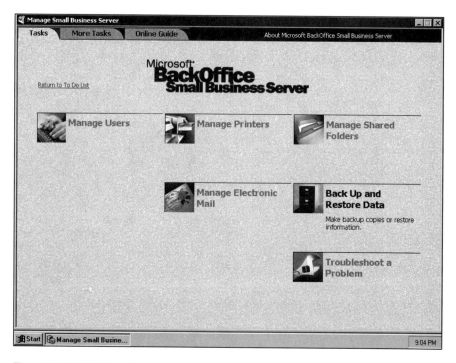

Figure 20-18: SBS Console

Be sure to set your SBS monitor resolution to 800 × 600 so that you may see the entire SBS Console at once without having to scroll around your screen. You might also be interested to know that, if you plan to make screen shots on the SBS server machine to crate a training manual with, the 800 × 600 resolution is necessary for creating the sharpest laser printouts (it's the resolution used to make screenshots for books).

Secret

It is also possible to run the SBS Console on another machine (such as your workstation). This is known as remote console and is similar to running the Windows NT Server 4.0 server tools on your workstation. To implement the SBS remote console, see the online help guide via the SBS Console.

Client-side components

You are already familiar with many of the SBS client-side components such as Internet Explorer (IE) 4.*x* browser and Microsoft Outlook. Other client-side components such as the way in which Proxy Server interacts with the desktop and applications (via the Proxy selection in IE and the WSP applet in Control Panel) are the same as found in via Proxy Server in big BackOffice. So far so good. Not much in the way of differences.

Chapter 20: Windows NT Server—Small Business Server

But two unique client-side components are worth seeing because of their uniqueness to SBS. These are the fax client and the modem sharing client.

The fax client is best seen as an print option that appears in Windows applications after the SBS client setup disk (a.k.a. "Magic Disk") has been run. When it is selected, you essentially "print" to the fax modem on the SBS server machine. You are then prompted for basic fax sending information (see Figure 20-19).

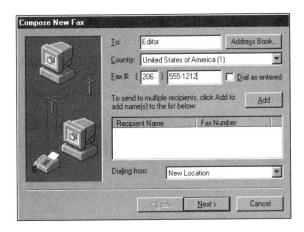

Figure 20-19: Sending a fax via SBS

The other client-side SBS component of note is the modem sharing configuration. When working on a computer that has been properly configured as an SBS client, you have the ability to redirect COM ports from the local machine to the SBS modem pool. This is accomplished by configuring the client's COM ports correctly. On a Windows 98/95 machine, this is accomplished with the following steps.

STEPS:

To configure the client's COM ports

Step 1. Right-click My Computer from the desktop.

Step 2. Select the Properties menu option.

Step 3. Select the Device Manager tab sheet (see Figure 20-20).

Continued

STEPS

To configure the client's COM ports *(continued)*

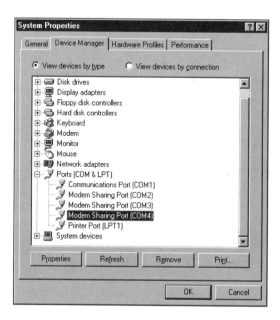

Figure 20-20: Modem sharing port configuration

Step 4. Expand the Ports (COM & LPT) listing.

Step 5. Observe which ports have been automatically redirected. This configuration occurred when you ran the SBS Client Setup disk. Typically COM ports 3 and 4 are automatically redirected.

Step 6. Double-click on the COM port of your choice that you want to redirect to the modem pool. The Modem Sharing Port (COM#) Properties dialog box appears.

Step 7. Select the Model Sharing Settings tab sheet and complete the UNC path to the modem sharing pool on the SBS server.

SBS client-side components are discussed further in this chapter when I show you how to install an SBS workstation.

The Small Business Model

The small business market differs markedly from the medium and large company environment that most of us associate Windows NT Server with. I can think of three ways that this market varies:

- **Affluence.** The small business doesn't have the wealth of the medium- and larger-sized organization. Undoubtedly, you will be asked to make older workstations and printers functional. You'll find yourself cannibalizing older equipment to support the waking wounded.

- **Attitude.** Small businesses can be hostile environments to implement technology. Many of these businesses have gotten along just fine without computers for years. Why should they spend $5,000 to $20,000 or more to implement the SBS solution when perhaps they would rather give out that kind of money as a larger Christmas bonus. This is a tough situation, and I've found that the small business bad attitude toward SBS is often just a cry for more information. Use your skills in educating the SBS customer about when the benefits, such as better information, clearly outweigh the costs.

- **Expertise.** If you've ever wanted to be a big fish in a small pond, become an SBS consultant. It's a great feeling to know an area well and legitimately help the customer. As an SBS consultant, I've found the challenges regarding one's expertise to be far less frequent than at the enterprise-level.

Small business server philosophy

The SBS philosophy is akin to the small business philosophy. That is, we're all seeking the answer to the question "How can I run my business better?" SBS is an answer to that question. I'll show you how via the SBS food chain (see Figure 20-21).

Starting from left to right, you have a small business person trying to run his or her business. To be brutally honest, such a one probably isn't very interested in computers, networks, SBS, and the like. The business person is interested in management reports, accounting reports, and so on.

The desktop computer, again, is considered a tool to accomplish work, such as working with the accounting system. That's an important point. Unlike us MCSE types who view technology as the end-all of everything, small business people tend to view technology as tools to get more important business-related work done.

Moving right across the SBS food chain, the network is only important to the small business person when it doesn't work. Otherwise, it is that silent and forgotten infrastructure that is best left alone.

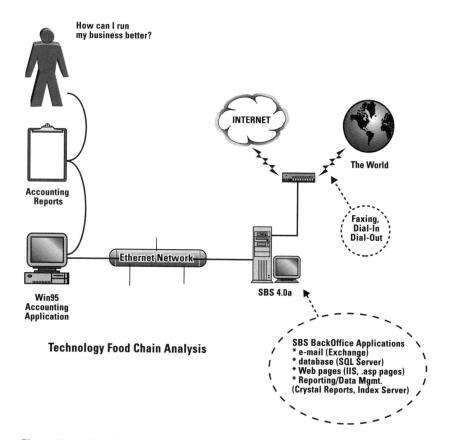

Figure 20-21: The SBS food chain

At the far left of the SBS food chain, there lies the SBS server machine and SBS itself. Here the small business person sees values, for many of the reasons previously stated in this chapter. The ability to send broadcast faxes from the network adds value to the small business's operations. The ability to call in from a remote site and attach to the SBS network adds value. The ability to send and receive e-mail, both internally and externally, adds value. The ability to surf the Web in a secure manner (via Proxy Server) is a great comfort and value to the small business person. Bottom line? The SBS food chain is a value-added process as you move from left to right. And it's the bottom line that clearly matters most to the SBS customer.

Chapter 20: Windows NT Server—Small Business Server

Microsoft extends this paradigm specifically for SBS by adding these design goals:

- **Ease of use/simplicity.** The idea was to Take everything easy, easy, easy. And when compared to the old command line interface of NetWare 3.x (which a surprisingly high number of small businesses are still running, having foregone the opportunity to upgrade to NetWare 4.x or 5.x), you could say that SBS is easier to manage and use. For example, "Dawn," at an athletic club I've counseled, took many years (appropriately so) to master NetWare. When she was confronted with the decision to upgrade to the newly released NetWare 5.0, I lent Dawn a training machine that had SBS installed. One week later, Dawn was confident and had even confirmed that her narrow market vertical applications would run on SBS. Not surprisingly, Dawn and her firm became another SSB success story.

  But easy is in the eye of the beholder. Whereas Dawn was coming from a more complex networking environment, allowing her to enjoy the ease of SBS more decidedly, SBS has fallen short for small businesses that have never been networked. These firms, accustomed to working manually with file cabinets, fax machines, and basic word processing, are often disappointed with SBS initially when they both (a) can't believe installing a network is so difficult and (b) don't understand why it doesn't work perfectly all of the time (witness the blue screens).

  So they take Microsoft's ease-of-use argument with a grain of salt. Such an argument is of course in the eye of the beholder.

  However, if it is usability that you are measuring, then clearly SBS wins when compared to other NOSes such as NetWare. With SBS's Windows 95–type interface, even "users" unaccustomed to managing a network server indeed feel comfortable using the Start button, menus, mouse, and so on. Score one for high usability.

- **Making decisions for the customer.** In the context of having an automated setup and implementation process ("just add water"), SBS (in Microsoft's view) reduces the research, engineering, and guesswork that goes into making the networking decision. More on that in a moment, in the section "Looks can be deceiving." However, Microsoft correctly asserts that users do not have to decide on whether the SBS machine should be a primary domain controller (it should) and whether or not to install DHCP (it is automatically installed).

- **Designing for success.** This point speaks toward the SBS console, which we've previously discussed. The idea is that SBS administrators should enjoy a "simple stupid" networking management experience and not have to really plan what they intend to do. Adding a user is a click away via the Manage Users button in the first sheet of the SBS console. Simple.

Here again, I must interject a few clarifying comments regarding the goals listed. For new users and NetWare administrators coming over to SBS (such as Dawn), I've found the SBS console is great and really aides the learning process. But for good old Windows NT Server gurus with headstrong ways of doing things, the SBS console is more of an enemy. Through pain and agony, these Windows NT Server gurus begrudgingly use the SBS console (but not the first, second, or third time they attempt to perform a task; that would have been too easy!).

Secret

Use the SBS console for everything! Discover why it might not work for you before you resort to the old Windows NT Server way of doing things.

Who are the SBS customers?

The potential SBS customer base is enormous. In the U.S. alone, there are 22-million small businesses. That numbers dwarfs the Fortune 1000, which by definition is limited to the 1,000 largest U.S. enterprises. Approximately $3/4$ of these small businesses own a PC. Just under $1/3$ of these small business are networked, a number that is expected to grow by nearly 50 percent in the next two years. SBS is well positioned to take advantage of this growth.

Looks can be deceiving

On the surface, SBS looks great. Many networking professionals consider SBS to be a small sibling to BackOffice. But here is where we return to our compare and contrast chapter theme. Those who know Windows NT Server well don't necessarily know SBS. Many NT gurus have failed when trying to roll out SBS because they readily drop under the hood and use Windows NT Server tools such as User Manager for Domains instead of the SBS Console. You have been warned. Treat SBS as an entirely new product and you will do fine. In fact, I've observed that NetWare network administrators have more initial success with SBS than the NT guru crowd. Why? Because the NetWare folks are scared to death of SBS and actually read the manual, follow the rules (as by completing the To Do List in SBS Console), and so on. The NT gurus are step skippers, assuming they already know it all.

SBS architecture

A quick look at the SBS architecture (see Figure 20-22): As you have learned, the "official" SBS components sit on top of the Windows NT Server 4.0 Service Pack 3 operating system. The underlying Windows NT Server 4.0 has the same kernel and user mode architecture described in Chapter 17, "Regular Windows NT Server." No difference here. After that, it gets more complex.

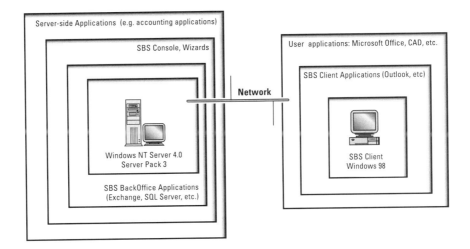

Figure 20-22: SBS architecture

The SBS BackOffice applications reside above the Windows NT Server operating system. Above that you will find SBS tools such as the SBS Console and miscellaneous wizards. Finally, server applications such as client/server accounting packages (Great Plains Dynamics, for instance) run.

On the SBS client side, you start with a workstation operating system such as Windows 98. On top of that, you add the SBS-specific client components such as Outlook, faxing, modem sharing, Proxy Client, and the like. Finally, the user applications such as Microsoft Office run.

SBS server-side setup

The SBS setup process is markedly different from that of Windows NT Server. Before you commence the SBS setup, be sure to read the Readme file on SBS CD-ROM Disc 1 and the Hardware Compatibility List (HCL) in Appendix E of the SBS Start Here manual (it shipped with your SBS software media).

The SBS HCL is dramatically different from the HCL for "regular" Windows NT Server.

In the next several pages, I'll provide each SBS setup step with comments, when appropriate, that compare it to the Windows NT Server setup. In general, SBS setup is much more automated than Windows NT Server setup, which is in keeping with SBS's "just add water" approach.

I've conveniently divided SBS setup into three phases:

- **Phase A.** Windows NT Server character-based setup
- **Phase B.** Windows NT Server GUI-based setup
- **Phase C.** SBS installation and setup

One more pesky task before you actually begin installing SBS: Depending on the media on which you received SBS, you may or may not have the three floppy setup disks in hand. In most cases, you will have the setup disks (perhaps because you purchased SBS via the commercial reseller channel in its retail "box"). If you are "sans" SBS setup disks, however, here are the setup disk creation steps.

Secret

Creating these disks is almost identical to creating the three "regular" Windows NT Server setup disks (something that perhaps you've done hundreds of times). But don't be fooled for a minute! Notice that a later step requires you to copy the winnt.sif file to disk two. The winnt.sif file contains the following line, which automates the SBS setup: ConfirmHardware=no. This single line is what makes the SBS setup experience so different (and automatic) compared to the regular Windows NT Server setup experience.

STEPS:

To create the SBS setup disks

Step 1. Insert SBS Disc 1 into the CD-ROM drive.

Step 2. On the Start menu, point to Programs, and then click Command Prompt.

Step 3. At the Command Prompt, change the drive to your CD-ROM drive letter. If your CD-ROM drive is E:, type **E:** and press Enter.

Step 4. Type **cd i386**.

Step 5. Type **winnt32 /ox**.

Step 6. After the third boot disk is created, copy winnt.sif from *D*:\support directory (replace *D*: with the correct drive letter for your CD-ROM) to boot disk 2.

If you do not copy winnt.sif to boot disk 2, then SBS will not install properly.

Chapter 20: Windows NT Server—Small Business Server

Note

If you wish to run the emergency repair process, you will need three boot disks without winnt.sif on boot disk 2.

Phase A is the phase that will appear most familiar to seasoned Windows NT Server professionals, with a few twists. Phase A is, of course, the character-based portion of the Windows NT Server installation. So far, so good. But use Figure 20-23 in conjunction with the highly detailed comments over the next few pages to see that, indeed, character-based setup is not the same in SBS as in regular Windows NT Server. It's a key point in this whole "compare and contrast" chapter.

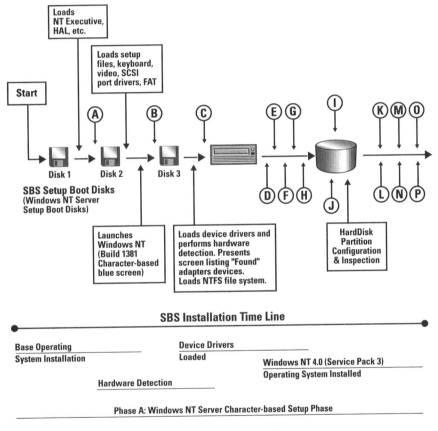

Figure 20-23: Phase A of Windows NT Server character-based setup

STEPS:

To execute Phase A of Windows NT Server Setup

Step 1. Insert the Windows NT Server Setup Boot Disk in floppy drive A: and turn on your computer.

Step 2. When you see the following screen, insert SBS Setup Disk 2 (a.k.a. Windows NT Server Setup Disk #2) and press Enter. This is denoted as (A) on the Figure 20-23.

```
Please insert the disk labeled
Windows NT Server Setup Disk #2
into Drive A:
* Press ENTER when ready.
ENTER=Continue    F3=Exit
```

After inserting Disk 2, you come to where the SBS installation and the "regular" Windows NT Server installation differ. Between Disk 2 and Disk 3, the "regular" Windows NT Server installation would offer a "Welcome" screen that among other things allows you to press R to specify a Windows NT Server repair session. SBS offers no such choice.

If you were installing "regular" Windows NT Server, you would see screens that indicate that setup will now attempt to detect your hardware. The results of the hardware detection would then be displayed. You would also be offered the opportunity, on another setup screen, to specify additional controllers and adapters (via the S key) that might not have been detected. SBS offers no such opportunity by default.

But how would you install SBS on a server machine with unsupported drivers if the SBS automatic installation doesn't stop and allow you to specify additional controllers and so on? Very easily. Simply copy the winnt.sif file on SBS CD-ROM Disc 1 in the \i386 directory down to SBS Setup Disk #2. The winnt.sif file changes from the automatic SBS installation or to the "regular" Windows NT Server manual installation because the following winnt.sif line is changed: ConfirmHardware=yes. You will recall previously that the Confirm Hardware=no statement was "no" from the winnt.sif file contained in the \support\ directory of SBS CD-ROM Disc 1. Now, the \i386\winnt.sif file on SBS CD-ROM Disc 1 forces SBS to perform a "manual" style Windows NT Server installation that allows you to specify additional controllers and so on.

Step 3. When you see the following screen, insert SBS Setup Disk 3 (a.k.a. Windows NT Server Setup Disk 3) and press Enter. This is denoted as (B) in Figure 20-23.

```
Please insert the disk labeled
Windows NT Server Setup Disk #3
into Drive A:
*   Please ENTER when Ready
F3=Exit    ENTER=Continue
```

Chapter 20: Windows NT Server—Small Business Server

Note

If this were a "regular" Windows NT Server setup, you would be offered the opportunity, on another setup screen, to specify additional controllers and adapters (via the S key) that might not have been detected. SBS offers no such opportunity by default.

Step 4. When you see the following screen, insert the SBS CD-ROM Disc 1 (a.k.a. Microsoft BackOffice Small Business Server Disc 1). This is denoted as (C) in the figure. Press Enter.

```
Please insert the compact disc labeled
Microsoft BackOffice Small Business Server Disc 1
into your CD-ROM drive.
*  Press ENTER when ready.
F3=Exit    ENTER=Continue
```

Step 5. When you see the following screen, press Enter if you want to make no changes. Otherwise, make the necessary changes and press Enter. This screen reflects what hardware the Windows NT Server setup program detected on your system. This is denoted as (D) on Figure 20-23.

```
Setup has determined that your computer contains the following
hardware and software components.
Computer:  Standard PC
Display:  Auto Detect
Keyboard:  XT, AT, or Enhanced Keyboard (83-104 keys)
Keyboard Layout:  US
Pointing Device:  Microsoft Serial Mouse
No Changes:  The above list matches my computer.
If you want to change any item in the list, press the UP or DOWN
ARROW key to move the highlight to the item you want to change.
Then press ENTER to see alternatives for that item.
When all the items in the list are correct, move the highlight to
"The above list matches my computer" and press ENTER.
ENTER=Select    F3=Exit
```

Step 6. Assuming you have a new hard disk, you will see the following type of screen. The actual space value (MB) will vary depending on how large of hard disk you have in your computer. In this case, the hard disk is 4GB. This is denoted as (E) on Figure 20-23.

```
The list below shows existing partitions and spaces available for
creating new partitions.
Use UP and DOWN ARROW keys to move the highlight to an item in the
list.
* To install Windows NT on the highlighted partition or
unpartitioned space, press ENTER.
* To create a partition in the unpartitioned space, press C.
* To delete the highlighted partition, press D.
```

Continued

STEPS

To execute Phase A of Windows NT Server Setup *(continued)*

```
| 4119 MB Disk 0 at Id 0 on bus 0 on atapi                          |
|   Unpartitioned space                           4118 MB           |
|                                                                   |
|                                                                   |
|                                                                   |
|                                                                   |
|                                                                   |

ENTER=Install    C=Create Partition    F1=Help   F3=Exit
```

Step 7. You will need to create a partition for Windows NT Server and SBS to install on. Select "C" on your keyboard to create this partition. This partition will range in size from 1.5GB (the minimum system partition size SBS supports) to 2GB (the largest system partition size that SBS supports). In the case of Springer Spaniels Unlimited, enter 2000 (for 2GB) on the following screen (which is displayed after you selected "C").

```
You have asked Setup to create a new partition on 4119 MB Disk 0
at Id 0 on bus 0 on atapi.
*  To create the new partition, enter a size below and press
ENTER.
*  To return to the previous screen without creating the
partition, press ESC.
The minimum size for the new partition is    8 megabytes (MB).
The maximum size for the new partition is 4118 megabytes (MB).
Create partition of size (in MB):  2000
```

For you detail detectives, this is denoted as (F) on Figure 20-23.

Press Enter to return to the screen similar to that shown in Step 6.

Note

It is very frustrating that SBS only allows a system partition between 1.5GB and 2GB. This of course limits the amount of space available on your system partition after SBS is installed. Typically, you format your remaining hard disk space as another partition on which you install your other business applications and save your data. If you specify a partition value greater than 2GB, you will be allowed to continue the SBS setup for several steps until you attempt to format this partition. Once the formatting commences, SBS realizes that the partition size is too large, and you are returned to the screen just shown, where you are asked to select a partition size.

Regular Windows NT Server has no similar partition formatting limitations.

Step 8. Press Enter when you see the screen here to install Windows NT Server and (in several steps) SBS on the newly created 2GB system partition. This is denoted as (G) on Figure 20-23.

Chapter 20: Windows NT Server—Small Business Server

```
The list below shows existing partitions and spaces available for
creating new partitions.
Use UP and DOWN ARROW keys to move the highlight to an item in the
list.
* To install Windows NT on the highlighted partition or
unpartitioned space, press ENTER.
* To create a partition in the unpartitioned space, press C.
* To delete the highlighted partition, press D.

┌─────────────────────────────────────────────────────────────────┐
│ 4119 MB Disk 0 at Id 0 on bus 0 on atapi                        │
│    C:   New (Unformatted)                        2000 MB        │
│    Unpartitioned space                           2118 MB        │
│                                                                 │
│                                                                 │
│                                                                 │
│                                                                 │
└─────────────────────────────────────────────────────────────────┘

ENTER=Install    C=Create Partition    F1=Help    F3=Exit
```

Step 9. When you see the screen that follows, you are being asked to format the C: drive (or system partition). It is essential that you select the NTFS formatting option. Press Enter after making your selection.

Note

NTFS must be used for SBS to properly function. Regular Windows NT Server does not have this same issue (although NTFS is the preferred format).

Returning to the detailed and exact step-by-step analysis, the following screen is shown as (H) on Figure 20-23:

```
The partition you have chosen is newly created and thus
unformatted.  Setup will now format the partition.
Select a file system for the partition from the list below.
Use the UP and DOWN ARROW keys to move the highlight to the file
system you want and then press ENTER.
If you want to select a different partition for Windows NT, press
ESC.
   Format the partition using the FAT file system.
   Format the partition using the NTFS file system.
```

At this point, several activities occur and are displayed on the monitor, as shown on Figure 20-23. At (I), a character-based screen is displayed that communicates "Please wait while Setup formats the partition." At (J), you will see the following: "Please wait while setup examines your hard disks. This may take a few minutes." At (K), you will see the following messages while files are copied to your hard disk: "Please wait while setup copies files to your hard disk."

Step 10. You must now remove SBS Setup Disk 3 from your floppy drive A: even though nothing requests that you do so. This is denoted as (L) on Figure 20-23. After several minutes of file copying from SBS CD-ROM Disc 1, the computer will automatically reboot itself. This is denoted as (M) on Figure 20-23. If SBS Setup Disk 3 is still in drive A:, the machine will not boot properly.

Phase B now commences and represents the Windows NT Server GUI-based setup. What has occurred is that a very bare-bones version of Windows NT Server has been installed in Phase A. Upon the final reboot, you are brought into the GUI-based setup that allows you to use your mouse. Interestingly, the GUI-based setup phase (Phase B) uses the multiprocessor Windows NT Server kernel regardless of whether you have one or more processors. It is after this phase (Phase B) that you will choose either to continue to use the multiprocessor kernel (if you have two or more processors) or the uniprocessor kernel (if you have one processor).

STEPS:

To execute Phase B of Windows NT Server Setup

Step 1. The SBS machine will reboot after several minutes. The boot screen created via BOOT.INI is displayed. This is denoted as (N) in Figure 20-23. After the NTFS partition is completely formatted. This is denoted as (O) in Figure 20-23. Another reboot occurs, denoted as (P) in Figure 20-23, and the boot menu is displayed, denoted as (Q) on Figure 20-24. The GUI-based Windows NT Server phase commences, denoted as (R) in Figure 20-24. You will be presented with the Software License Agreement, denoted as (S) in Figure 20-24. You will also notice that your mouse is now functional. If you select the "I Agree" button, the setup routine will continue. If you select the "I Disagree" button, the setup routine will terminate.

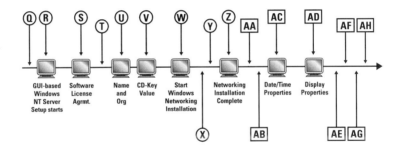

Figure 20-24: Phase B of Windows NT Server GUI-based setup

Note

SBS only allows a fixed installation of Windows NT Server without any setup selections from you. You may recall that regular Windows NT Server only supports a custom setup, where you select which components, such as Internet Information Server, you want to install.

More Windows NT Server–related files will copy from Disc 1 to the hard disk, denoted as (T) on Figure 20-24. A Preparing for Installation dialog box briefly appears and then disappears.

Step 2. You will next be presented with the Name and Organization dialog box. You will be asked to enter the following types of SBS information:

```
Name:
Organization:
Computer Name:
Domain:
```

The name is your name and the organization is your company name. These entries are denoted as (U) on Figure 20-24.

Note

The computer name and domain name will be automatically populated based on the organization name that you enter. You may overwrite the suggested computer and domain names, but if you do, make sure to use unique names for both. Regular Windows NT Server has no such computer or domain autonaming convention.

Continued

STEPS

To execute Phase B of Windows NT Server Setup (continued)

After entering this information, click Next.

Step 3. You will enter CD-KEY value (found in media that shipped with SBS). This is denoted as (V) on Figure 20-24. This is a ten-digit number with a hyphen between the third and fourth digits. Note that you have to tab or mouse click between digit fields. Click Next.

Step 4. Click Next when presented with the dialog box advising you that Setup is now ready to guide you through the setup of Windows NT Networking. This is denoted as (W) on Figure 20-24.

If your network adapter card is not automatically detected, the MS Loopback adapter will be installed by default. Unlike with regular Windows NT Server, you will not be offered the opportunity to select a network adapter card from a list or provide a network adapter card driver on a disk.

The MS Loopback adapter is installed to allow completion of the Windows NT Server networking services and functionality. Once SBS is installed, you will need to properly install your network adapter card via the Network applet in Control Panel.

Note I have also found that SBS will incorrectly detect network adapters. When such is the case, you will need to install the correct network adapter card drivers via the Network applet in Control Panel after SBS has been completely installed.

The adapter is automatically selected, and TCP/IP, the Server and Workstation services, NetBIOS, RPC, and RAS features are installed. Note that the modem is detected here. This process is denoted as (X) on Figure 20-24.

With regular Windows NT Server, you would be allowed to specify additional network protocols and services. SBS setup does not offer you this capability.

The SBS setup process continues and the DHCP Server service is installed, denoted as (Y) on Figure 20-24.

Regular Windows NT Server would present a dialog box regarding the server's use of a dynamically assigned IP address or use of a static IP address. If you elected to use a static IP address, you would be presented with a dialog box to enter an IP address for each network adapter card.

Chapter 20: Windows NT Server—Small Business Server

Step 5. Click Next when presented with the Setup dialog box that informs you that Windows NT Server is ready to start the network—(Z) on Figure 20-24. This signifies that the networking services, adapter, protocol, and other networking components have been installed.

A dialog box displaying the computer and domain name is briefly displayed—(AA) on Figure 20-24. Internet Information Server (IIS) is installed—(AB) on Figure 20-24.

Note

Because regular Windows NT Server only supports a custom setup, you would have the opportunity to elect whether or not to install IIS.

Step 6. Select your time zone when the Date and Time Properties dialog box appears, (AC) on Figure 20-24. Click Close. You would then select the Display Properties (800 × 600 recommended) as shown on (AD) on Figure 20-24.

Step 7. After additional computer files are copied—(AE) on Figure 20-24—initial security setting are invoked—(AF) on Figure 20-24—and temporary files are removed—(AG) on Figure 20-24, the SBS computer will reboot—(AH) on Figure 20-24 and display the following information on its boot screen.

```
OS Loader V4.00
Please select the operating system to start:
    BackOffice Small Business Server
    BackOffice Small Business Server (VGA Mode)
Use   or   to move the highlight to your choice.
Press Enter to choose.
```

This is depicted as (AH) on Figure 20-25. The first selection, BackOffice Small Business Server, will be selected if no key on your keyboard is touched within the 30-second default menu selection time frame. If you want to expedite the process, hit Enter while the BackOffice Small Business Server menu option is selected.

You will briefly see a dialog box that indicates a domain list is being created—(AJ) on Figure 20-25. You do not need to manually log on at this point as an autologon will occur—(AK) on Figure 20-25. A dialog box is displayed that communicates that setup is initializing—(AL) on Figure 20-25.

Continued

STEPS

To execute Phase B of Windows NT Server Setup *(continued)*

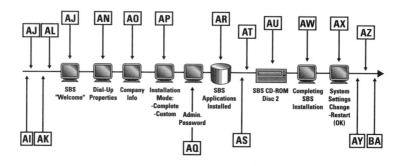

Figure 20-25: Phase C, SBS installation and setup

With the end of Phase B, you now have a functioning Windows NT Server machine, albeit trimmed and otherwise modified to accommodate SBS (these points were raised early when I discussed SBS as and as not your father's Windows NT Server). Interestingly, if you progressed no further with the formal SBS setup, you could run the machine as a functional (I didn't say "fully functional") Windows NT server. That is, users could log on, print, and save files. It is Phase C that really, in most experienced Windows NT Server gurus' eyes, separates SBS from regular Windows NT Server. It is Phase C where you will install the SBS version of Microsoft BackOffice and SBS-specific applications such as modem sharing and fax server capabilities.

STEPS:
To execute Phase C of Windows NT Server Setup

Step 1. The Microsoft Small Business Server Setup "Welcome" dialog box appears (see Figure 20-26). Click Next.

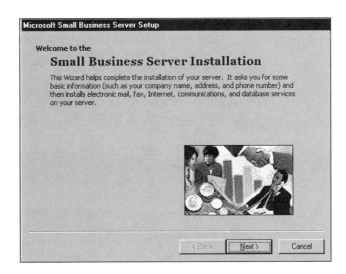

Figure 20-26: Welcome

Step 2. The Microsoft Small Business Server "Dial-Up Properties" dialog box appears. Complete the country, area code, outside line, and tone/pulse options, (AN) on Figure 20-25.

Step 3. When the Company Information dialog box appears, complete each field (address, city, state, zip, country, telephone, and fax). This is depicted as (AO) on Figure 20-25.

Secret

This is meta-information that is used in several other places within SBS, including the SBS client setup process. Be sure to complete as many Company fields as you can.

Step 4. You are now presented with the Installation Mode dialog box, (AP) on Figure 20-25).

The Complete Installation mode option is the most popular selection to use when setting up SBS. However, if you have valid reasons, a partial installation is made by selecting the Custom Installation option.

Step 5. You will now enter a password in the "Set the Password for the Administrator Account" dialog box, (AQ) on Figure 20-25.

Continued

STEPS

To execute Phase C of Windows NT Server Setup *(continued)*

Step 6. The SBS computer will dutifully install the SBS and BackOffice applications you selected. If you selected the Complete Installation option in Step 4, the SBS (modem services, fax services, and so on) and BackOffice applications (Microsoft Exchange, Microsoft Proxy Server, SQL Server, and so on) will be installed. This process may take 15 to 45 minutes depending on the speed of your CD-ROM drive and computer.

A completing installation dialog box is displayed, (AR) on Figure 20-25, and, assuming you elected the complete SBS installation, the following applications are installed and files copied, (AS) on Figure 20-25:

- Modem sharing services
- ASP pages
- Microsoft Exchange Server
- Microsoft Proxy Server
- Microsoft Proxy Client
- Microsoft Fax Services
- Microsoft SQL Server
- Crystal Reports
- Microsoft Internet Explorer
- Microsoft Web Publishing

Secret

If the modem attached to your SBS machine isn't detected, a "standard modem" is installed so that the SBS setup process may continue. You will be asked to either confirm the "standard modem" selection or provide your own modem driver. More important, you must provide this alternative driver within 60 seconds, or else the SBS setup process will continue and then not accept your alternate modem driver.

You may be interested to know that I've had the best luck with the USR Sportster 33.6 external modem from any listed on the SBS HCL.

A completing installation dialog box is displayed, (AT) on Figure 20-25.

Step 7. When requested, insert SBS CD-ROM Disc 2 (a.k.a. Microsoft BackOffice Small Business Server Disc 2). This is (AU) on Figure 20-25.

Chapter 20: Windows NT Server — Small Business Server

At this point, final SBS setup activity will occur, (AV) on Figure 20-25.

Step 8. After approximately five minutes, you will be presented with a Completing the Small Business Server Installation dialog box, (AW) on Figure 20-25.

You will then approve the restart of the SBS computer, (AX) on Figure 20-25. The SBS server machine will reboot and autologon, (AY) on Figure 20-25. Shortcut menus are created, (AZ) on Figure 20-25, and Microsoft Internet Explorer (IE) 4.*x* is set up automatically, (BA) on Figure 20-25.

Finally, the SBS Console is launched and the To Do List is displayed (see Figure 20-27). Typically you would complete each step in the To Do List in order.

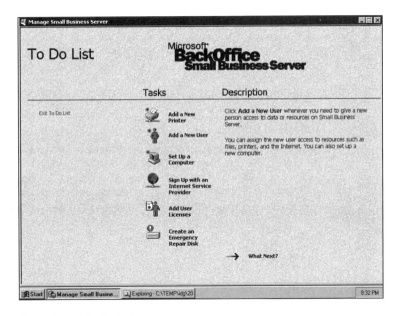

Figure 20-27: To Do List

Secret

I've found that, acknowledging Microsoft's best attempts to create an ordered checklist, the To Do List typically isn't followed step by step. I do recommend that you, at a minimum during the SBS server machine build, complete the Add a New Printer, Add User Licenses, and Create an Emergency Repair Disk options. I've found that the Add a New User and Set Up a Computer options are typically run hours or days later when you are truly ready to add workstations to your SBS network.

`The Internet signup option, in my experience, is best run several days or weeks later when you are truly ready to log onto the Internet. Remember that this option is only used to configure modem-based connections to the Internet. If you plan to have a digital or WAN-like connection to the Internet, you will configure your SBS server machine "manually" just as you would a regular Windows NT Server (that is, using the Protocols tab sheet in the Network applet in Control Panel).

SBS workstation-side setup

A profound difference between regular Windows NT Server and SBS is how client workstations are configured. Unlike regular Windows NT Server, where configuring a network client typically occurs via its Network applet in Control Panel (for Windows 98, Windows 95, and Windows NT Workstation), SBS uses a client installation disk. This is commonly called the "magic disk" amongst SBSers. Its magic is that, based on some basic SBS workstation configuration specifications you elect at the SBS server, the magic disk, in an "autopilot" manner, installs the necessary SBS networking components and applications on the SBS client machine. In fact, using the magic disk is commonly thought of as an "autopilot" approach versus the much more manual approach to configuring workstations to attach to a regular Windows NT Server network.

Add a user

But first things first. Step one is to add a network user, set up the computer, and create the SBS client installation "magic" disk on the SBS server. It is an easy process in which you will decide which SBS components and applications to install on the client. First I will show you how to add an SBS user, and then I'll set up the computer and create the "magic disk."

STEPS:
To add a user

Step 1. Make sure that you are logged onto the SBS server machine as an administrator.

Step 2. Click the Start button at the lower-left side of your screen and select the Return to To Do List option on the Tasks tab (if the To Do List doesn't automatically appear).

Step 3. Select Add a New User. The User Account Wizard launches (see Figure 20-28).

Chapter 20: Windows NT Server—Small Business Server

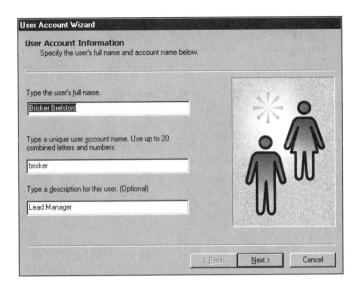

Figure 20-28: User Account Information

Step 4. Complete the User Account Information fields. Click Next.

Step 5. On the Create a Password for (name) screen, elect to have your password automatically created for you or that you will specify a password. Note that I usually specify the password in order to better manage this process. The passwords that are created by SBS tend to be complex mixed-case alphanumeric combinations that no one in a small business can be expected to remember. Furthermore, the users write the "complex" password on yellow stickies (Post-Its) that are typically affixed to the user workstation. I recommend that you pick a simple password for starters such as purple37. Assuming that you made your password election, click Next (see Figure 20-29).

Continued

STEPS

To add a user *(continued)*

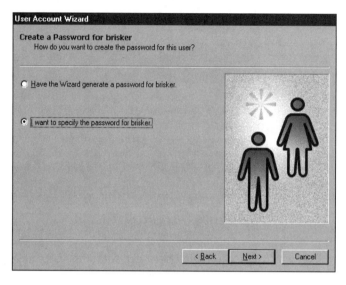

Figure 20-29: Create a Password for. . .

Step 6. On the Password for (user) screen, type the password of your choice (e.g., purple37) and select whether users may or may not change their passwords (see Figure 20-30). Note that most of my SBS sites do not let users change their own passwords.

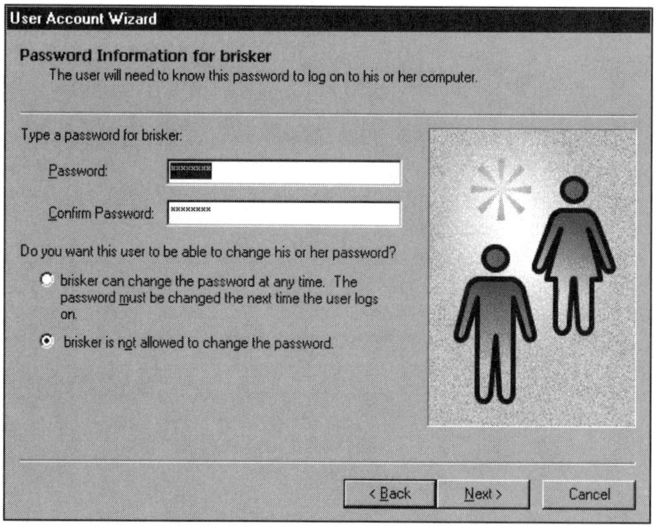

Figure 20-30: Password Information for. . .

Step 7. On the Company Information for (user) screen, provide as much information as possible (see Figure 20-31). To some extent, this is metainformation that is used in several places by SBS, so the more that you can provide, the better. Note I recommend that you populate unused fields with "N/A" for not applicable so that you and others recall this field wasn't inadvertently bypassed, but rather, you lacked relevant information to populate the field with.

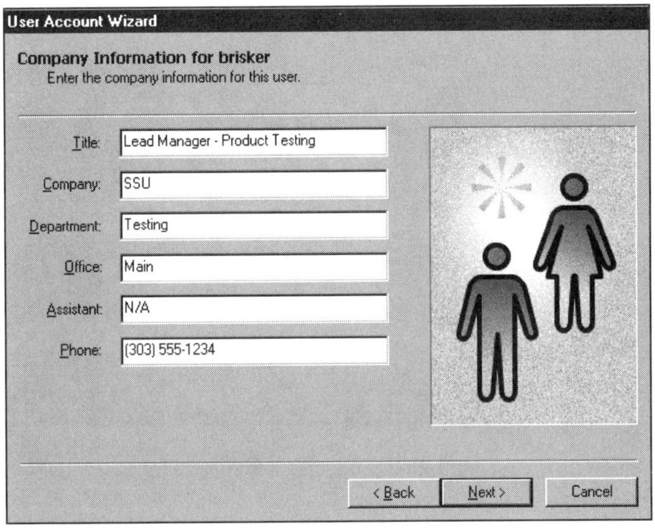

Figure 20-31: Company Information for. . .

Step 8. In the Address Information for (user) screen, complete the Address, City, State, Zip, and Country fields (see Figure 20-32). Click Next.

Continued

STEPS

To add a user *(continued)*

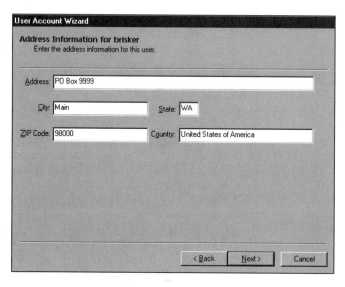

Figure 20-32: Address Information for...

Step 9. In the Communication Information for (user) screen, complete as many fields as possible (see Figure 20-33). These fields are requesting telephone information. Remember to put "N/A" in fields that you don't have legitimate information for. Click Next.

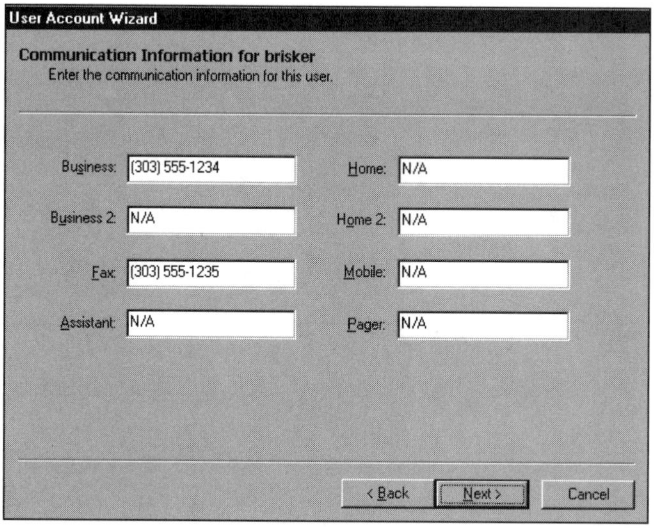

Figure 20-33: Communications Information for...

Chapter 20: Windows NT Server—Small Business Server

Step 10. On the Select the E-mail Distribution Lists for (user), you will note that the default e-mail group for the organization (it is the same as the organization name you created during setup) is automatically selected (see Figure 20-34). Note that this is a Microsoft Exchange group, not a Windows NT Server global or local group. Click Next.

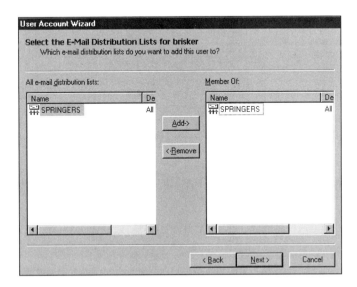

Figure 20-34: E-mail Distribution Lists

Step 11. The Create User Account for (user) screen allows you to finish creating the user account by clicking Finish (see Figure 20-35). Afterward, you will see an information dialog box commenting that the user account was successfully created.

Continued

704   Part V: The Four Flavors of Windows NT Server 4.0

STEPS
To add a user *(continued)*

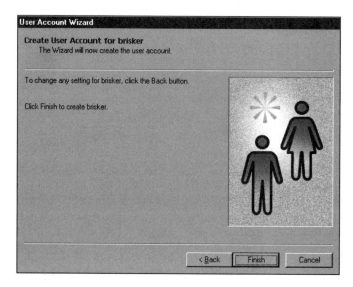

Figure 20-35: Finish creating the user account.

Step 12.   You will then set security for the user. The Select the Shared folders for (user) screen appears, showing the default Read, Edit, and Delete share permission in the upper right and the additional default Read permissions in the lower right (see Figure 20-36). Click Next.

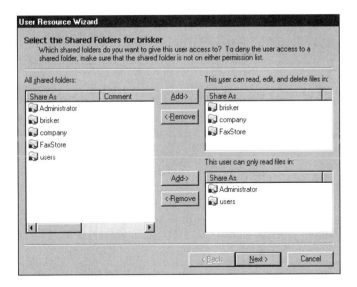

Figure 20-36: SBS shared folder permissions

Secret

It is critical that you carefully configure the screen just described. Notice how the Read permission has, by default, been granted to the Administrator and users shares. This is much too generous for most small business owners, who often need private data storage areas. Remember that small business owners typically commingle personal activity with work. Thus, it is common to see their personal tax returns, stock investment tables, and so on in their personal folders. And for all your opinions about sharing and openness, this is typically too open! So beware that SBS tends to assign too generous security by default.

Step 13. You will now select the printers that the user you have created may use (see Figure 20-37). In this case, the first printer created, an HP Color LaserJet, is selected by default for this user. Click Next.

Continued

STEPS

To add a user *(continued)*

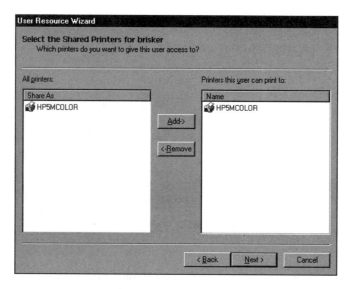

Figure 20-37: Select printers

Step 14. You will now assign the fax printer to the user via the Select the Shared Fax Printers for (user) screen (see Figure 20-38). This is the default fax printer that was automatically created during the SBS installation. Click Next.

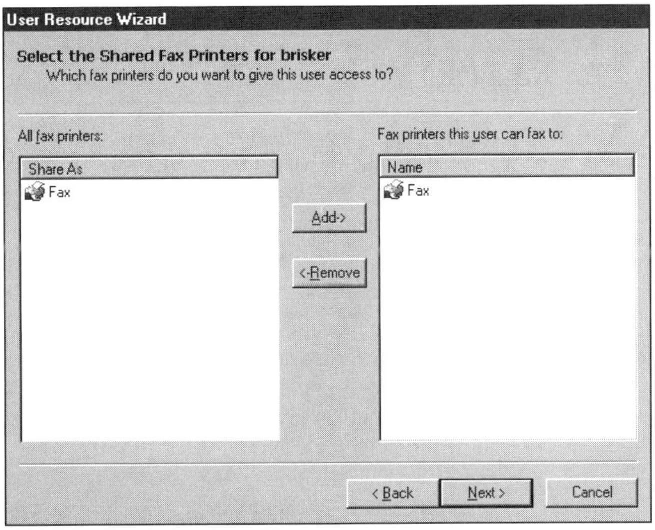

Chapter 20: Windows NT Server — Small Business Server

Figure 20-38: Select fax printer

Step 15. You must now configure additional access rights via the Select Additional Access Rights for (user) screen (see Figure 20-39). The rights you will select include accessing the Internet and accessing the server computer remotely via RAS. Click Next.

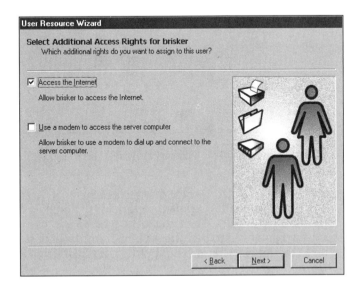

Figure 20-39: Additional access rights

Continued

STEPS

To add a user *(continued)*

Note

The access rights apply to situations wherein a user remotely accesses the SBS server machine and network via RAS. Note that I've found RAS to be a somewhat unreliable and inconsistent performer at my SBS sites and now use third-party remote control solutions such as PC Anywhere running on a networked workstation (not the SBS server machine). If you follow my experience and use a similar third-party remote control solution, then the Access the Server check box is not relevant.

Step 16. Warning! The Administrative Privileges screen appears next and is, of course, very dangerous (see Figure 20-40). Fortunately, the default selection is No. Be careful not to inadvertently change this to Yes. Click Next.

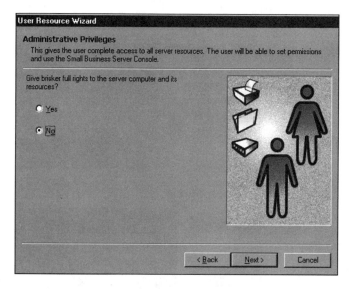

Figure 20-40: Administrative privileges selection

Tip

In fact, if you revisit the best practices of local area network management, you will recall that no regular network user should have administrative rights (including yourself). When you are logged on as a user, you have the rights of a user. If you need to perform Administrator-level duties, than you should log on as the Administrator. Simply stated, it's best if you leave the No radio button selected in all cases on this screen.

Step 17. Click Finish on the Update Resource Permissions for (user) screen to complete the security permissions process (see Figure 20-41). Afterward, an informational dialog box will advise you that the wizard successfully set permissions for your user.

Chapter 20: Windows NT Server — Small Business Server

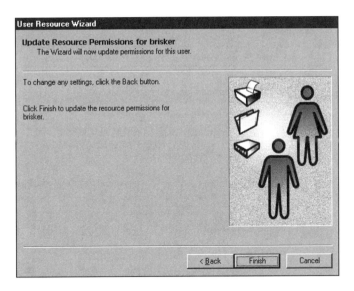

Figure 20-41: Finish the security permissions update

You will next see an informational dialog box asking if you want to set up a computer. This is the process to add an SBS client workstation to the network and to create the client installation disk. If you answer Yes, the Setup Computer Wizard starts. If you select No, the Add User process will appropriately terminate.

Set up a computer

You must now set up the workstation (a.k.a. "computer") for the user to work at. This series of steps will create the SBS client installation (a.k.a. "magic") disk. When run, the "magic" disk installs the necessary Microsoft networking components on the workstation, renames the workstation (the NetBIOS name), and commences the SBS client application installation process.

STEPS:
To setup a computer

Step 1. You will see the Welcome to the Set Up Computer Wizard screen (see Figure 20-42). Click Next.

Continued

STEPS

To setup a computer *(continued)*

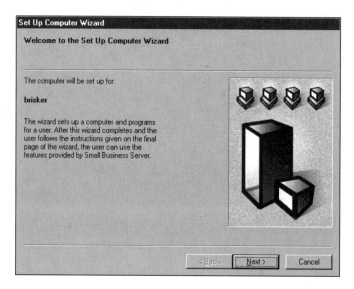

Figure 20-42: Welcome

Step 2. You will see the Set Up Computer Wizard (see Figure 20-43). Select from one of three radio buttons. First, you may add a Windows 95 or Windows NT computer to the SBS network. This option also allows you to add a Windows 98 computer as well (even though that isn't explicitly stated on the dialog box). The second radio button allows you to add another user to a computer that is already set up. This is akin to having a roving Windows NT Server profile and an individual Microsoft Outlook profile. Third, you may add programs to an existing SBS client computer. This allows you to add SBS client-specific applications such as fax, modem, or Proxy Client applications. This is not used for installing business applications such as TimeSlips, FRX Report Writer, and other third-party client applications.

Click Next.

Secret

If you purchased the SBS retail version that also includes Microsoft Office, you will have the opportunity, via the third radio button in the dialog box, to install Microsoft Office applications such as Word and Excel to the SBS client workstation.

Chapter 20: Windows NT Server — Small Business Server

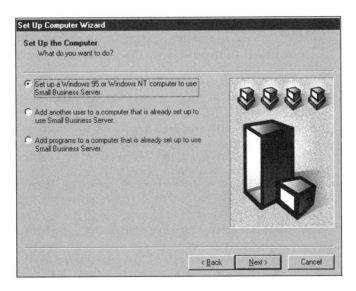

Figure 20-43: Set Up the Computer

Step 3. You will now specify a computer name (see Figure 20-44). By default, the user's name is appended with the underscore character and "01" to create the machine name. Click Next.

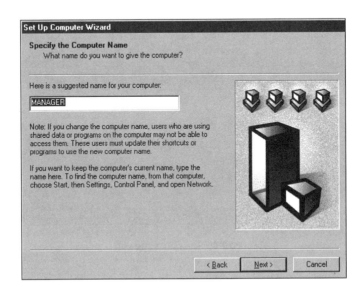

Figure 20-44: Specify the computer name

Continued

STEPS

To setup a computer (continued)

Secret

This is problematic for several reasons. First, the best practices of network management are that machine names typically have a explicit geographic or job title reference. That is, a computer name might be "nw1accountant" for a machine in the Northwest building, first floor, that is used by an accountant. More important, if the user you've created leaves the organization, the next user assigned to this computer doesn't need to work on a machine named for the previous user. I've found this default computer name to be a big problem in small organizations such as a law firm, which given time and turnover, found a new hire Jackie working on CAROL_01. It looked and was silly. Worse yet, Jackie called and asked that I come down to the law firm and fix it (as she was offended to be working on a machine named after her predecessor). Believe me, such problems occur and you may prevent them up front by being smart. You will note on the Figure 20-44 that I named the machine after a job function.

Step 4. You will now identify what operating system is being used (see Figure 20-45). Remember that you would select Windows 95 for a client machine running Windows 98. Click Next.

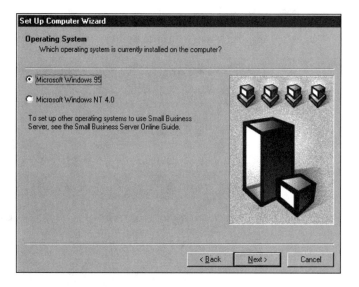

Figure 20-45: Operating system

Step 5. You will now select the SBS-specific client programs to install (see Figure 20-46). By default, all of the SBS-specific client programs are selected. If you had purchased and installed the SBS retail version that ships with Microsoft Office, then a selection for installing Microsoft Office on the client machine would also appear on this dialog box. You will also note that the space required on the client workstation is given. Click Next.

Chapter 20: Windows NT Server — Small Business Server

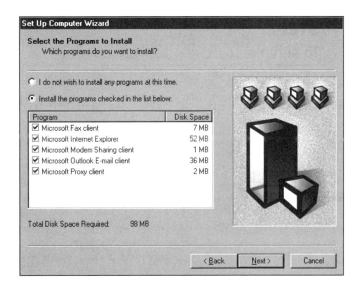

Figure 20-46: Select the program to install.

Step 6. The Create the Setup Disk screen appears (see Figure 20-47). You are advised that you should label a blank floppy disk and insert it in the disk drive now. Perform this step and click Next.

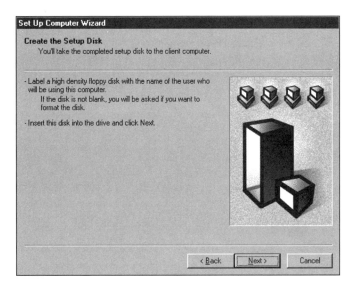

Figure 20-47: Create the Setup Disk

Continued

STEPS

To setup a computer *(continued)*

The Set Up Computer Wizard will then format and copy the necessary files to make the client installation disk (see Figures 20-48 and 20-49).

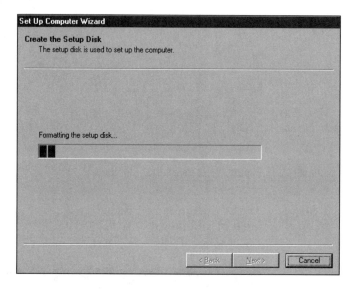

Figure 20-48: Formatting

Chapter 20: Windows NT Server — Small Business Server

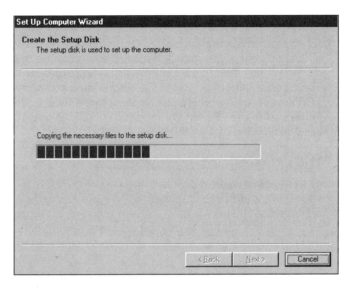

Figure 20-49: Copying necessary files

Step 7. Click Finish on the Completing the Set Up Computer Wizard screen (see Figure 20-50). You have now set up a computer on the SBS network and created the client installation disk.

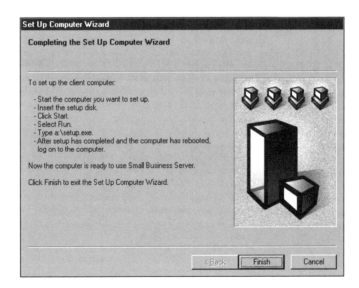

Figure 20-50: Finished!

You are then returned to the To Do List on the SBS Console.

A few more steps remain before your client workstation is a full-fledged citizen on your SBS network. This includes running the client installation disk on the actual client workstation. The client installation disk will rename the client computer according to the information you provided, setting the TCP/IP protocol to receive its address dynamically. After rebooting, an autologon to the SBS network occurs and the applications you selected are downloaded and installed.

Run the client installation

The client installation disk is placed in the floppy drive of the workstation you want to add to the SBS network, representing the end of the setup activities on the server machine and the start of the setup activities on the workstation. That is a significant crossover point, one that is not so distinct and noticeable when you are setting up a regular Windows NT Server.

STEPS:
To run the client installation disk

Step 1. Insert the client installation disk into the disk drive on your client workstation.

Step 2. Run the Setup program on the client installation disk. One way to accomplish this is to click Start ➪ Run and then type **a:\setup** in the Open field.

Step 3. Assuming you have a Windows 98 or 95 machine and followed the preceding steps, the Windows 95 Client Setup screen appears, allowing you to confirm the basic setup information and continue (see Figure 20-51).

Chapter 20: Windows NT Server — Small Business Server 717

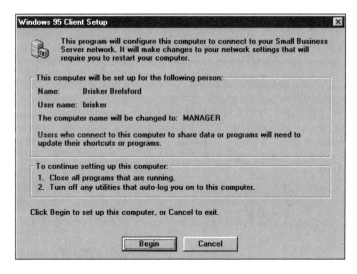

Figure 20-51: Windows 95 Client Setup

Step 4. Click Begin. The computer will reboot, autologon, and install the SBS-specific applications that you previously selected.

The machine will reboot once the SBS-specific applications have been installed. Once you log on with your user name and password, the SBS workstation configuration process is complete.

Secret

An alternative way exists to install the SBS components without using the client installation disk if your clients are running Windows NT Workstation 4.0. This method involves adding the Windows NT Workstation 4.0 computer name to the domain using Server Manager and then using the Add Another User to an Existing Computer option in the Set Up a Computer Wizard.

STEPS:

To carry out this alternative approach

Step 1. Make sure that you are logged on as an administrator on the SBS server machine.

Step 2. Click the Start button, select Programs, select Administrative Tools (Common), and select the Server Manager application.

Step 3. In Server Manager, click the Computer menu and select the Add Computer to Domain menu option (see Figure 20-52).

Step 4. Type in the Windows NT Workstation machine name you want to use. The name will appear in Server Manager after clicking Add. After adding all of the names that you want, click Close.

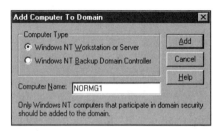

Figure 20-52: Add Computer to Domain

Step 5. Launch the Set Up a Computer Wizard from the SBS Console To Do List (see Figure 20-53).

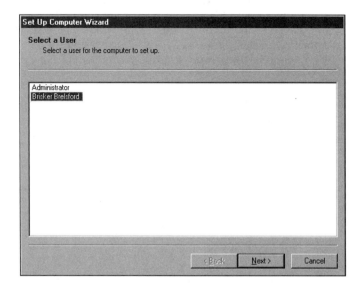

Figure 20-53: Select a user

Chapter 20: Windows NT Server — Small Business Server

Step 6. Select the user you want to add to this SBS workstation and click Next.

Step 7. Select the Add Another User to a Computer That Is Already Set Up to Use Small Business Server radio button on the Set Up the Computer screen (see Figure 20-54).

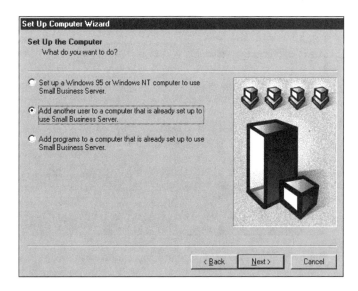

Figure 20-54: Add another user to an existing SBS workstation selection

Complete the rest of the wizard much as you followed the steps under "To set up a computer" presented early in the chapter.

Make sure your Windows NT Workstation has the same computer name that you specified in preceding Step 4 (this is set via the Network applet in Control Panel). When you log on from the Windows NT Workstation 4.0 machine with the selected user name, the SBS applications will automatically install. One of my clients, Xtek in Redmond, WA, used this approach to set up their SBS network with all Windows NT Workstations instead of using the client installation disk. The consensus was that this approach saved a significant amount of time and effort compared to running around with a floppy disk.

SBS Administration

A key contrast between SBS and regular Windows NT Server is the use of the SBS Console to perform most of your SBS-related tasks. This interface is an extension of the Administrative Wizards menu option under Administrative

Tools (Common) in regular Windows NT Server, discussed in Chapter 11 (see Figure 20-55).

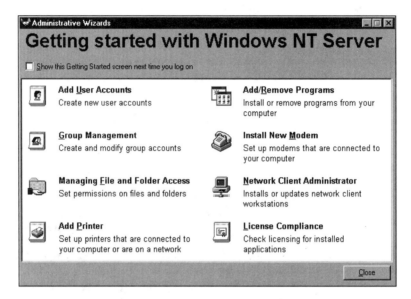

Figure 20-55: Windows NT Server Administrative Wizards

But the SBS Console is much more than a re-release of Administrative Wizards. In fact, it's where you should first try to perform any SBS activity. That's because the many SBS Console options are running complex macros and the like behind the scenes. Adding a user via the SBS Console makes for a much more complete entry than the "old fashioned" way via User Manager for Domains.

The SBS Console was designed to put the most popular tasks on the first Tasks sheet (see Figure 20-56) and secondary tasks on the More Tasks sheet (see Figure 20-57). Each SBS Console option is discussed in Table 20-2, SBS Console Options.

Chapter 20: Windows NT Server — Small Business Server

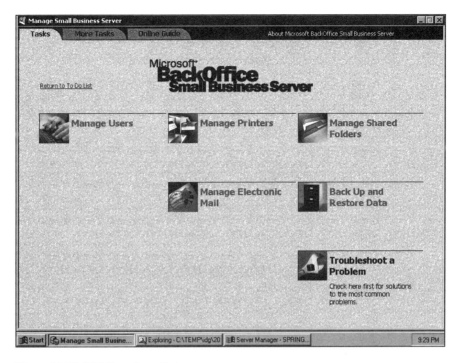

Figure 20-56: SBS Console — Tasks page

Figure 20-57: SBS Console — More Tasks page

Table 20-2 SBS Console Options

Option	Description
Manage Users	This is where basic user management is performed including adding users, changing passwords, and deleting users. It is important that you use this option and not User Manager for Domains.
Manage Printers	This is where you manage printers via the Manage Printers Wizard. It is here you add, change, and control access to printers.
Manage Electronic Mail	This is where you can check the status of your e-mail server.
Manage Shared Folders	This is where you create and control access to shared folders on the SBS computer.
Back Up and Restore Data	This is a series of Help screens that train you on how to use the Backup application. Be advised that most SBS sites elect to use more robust third-party backup solutions such as Seagate's Backup Exec for Small Business Server or ArcServe's Storage Suite for Microsoft SBS.
Troubleshoot a Problem	This is a series of decision-tree Help screens to help you isolate and resolve an SBS-related problem.
Manage E-mail Distribution Lists	This option enables to you to create and edit e-mail distribution lists that consist of internal user e-mail accounts. This option does not allow you to create e-mail distribution lists containing external Internet e-mail address. That said, it isn't a very useful option given the small size of SBS networks and the limited need for many e-mail distribution lists.
Manage Disks	Here you may change disk options and troubleshoot disk problems.
Manage Computers	This is a very popular option that should have been placed on the first page (Tasks) of SBS Console. It is here that you add computers to the SBS network, assign additional users to existing SBS client workstations, and so on. You will use this option a lot.
Manage Internet Access	This option is used to set up dial-in access to the Internet. It is not used to manage your Internet access if you have a digital or WAN connection to your ISP.

Option	Description
Manage Faxes	This option is used to manage fax jobs (delete, review, etc.) and view fax activity reports. It is the only place you may obtain any form of fax confirmation. That is something considered very important to law firms and the like.
Add or Remove Software	This option enables you to add or delete SBS and third-party applications. It is the same as the Add/Remove Programs Properties applet in Control Panel.
Publish on the Internet	This enables you to manage your Web pages from creation to FTP transfer to your ISP.
Manage Modem Pools	This is where you may modify modem pool configuration settings.
Control Panel	This is good old-fashioned Control Panel from Windows NT Server.

Secret

Always try to complete a task first using the SBS Console before going under the hood into regular Windows NT Server. Going under the hood, in my view, means using the traditional Administrative Tools (Common) applications such as User Manager for Domains, Server Manager, and so on. Don't go under the hood unless you can't perform a task from the SBS Console, or you've worked with SBS enough to know how such actions will affect the SBS network. You've been warned!

SBS Troubleshooting

I end this chapter with a just a few lessons learned in working with SBS. Again, the underlying theme is that SBS is so very different from regular Windows NT Server. Honor this above all else.

Do your software vendors support SBS?

If not, then *stop* the SBS project! I've done it twice. In both cases, it involved older releases of business accounting systems that hadn't been approved for SBS. The lesson learned here was that SBS is different. How? Look no further than the SBS subdirectory structure (see Figure 20-58).

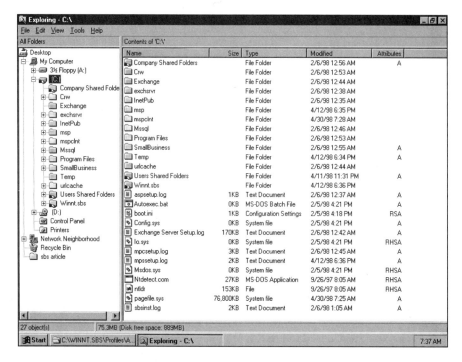

Figure 20-58: Modified Windows NT Server subdirectory names with SBS

As you may be aware, a regular Windows NT Server installation places Windows NT Server in the \WINNT subdirectory by default. SBS is different and places Windows NT Server in the \WINNT.SBS directory, which of course is a modified subdirectory name. This one change can be a point of failure in supporting your older applications. If your older application is approved for Windows NT Server 4.0, it might be expecting the subdirectory path \WINNT and could fail under SBS's modified path.

Modem sharing

The default modem sharing UNC share name is COMPORTS when created/viewed on the server if the modem sharing service is implemented post conversion (see Figure 20-59). If the modem sharing service is implemented during the initial installation, the modem pool is correctly named MODEMS. The clients (Win95, NT4) point to the communication port share name MODEMS by default. So one lesson I've learned is that you need to check the communication port share name being used on the SBS server.

Chapter 20: Windows NT Server — Small Business Server

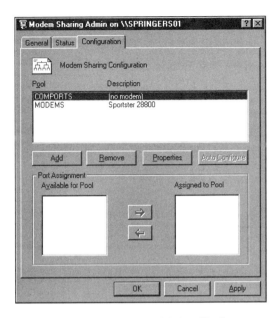

Figure 20-59: Control Panel — Modem Sharing

Then check the communication port share name under your client workstation that has the modem sharing client installed on it. For Windows 98 or 95, you will need to look under the communication ports (COM ports) in Device Manager (see Figure 20-60).

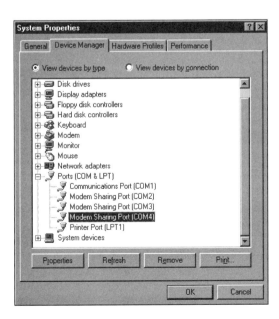

Figure 20-60: Communications ports redirected to the modem share on the SBS server

As you may know, Device Manager is accessed by selecting the property sheet for My Computer (right-click on My Computer and select "Properties" from the secondary menu. Then select the Device Manager tab sheet). When all is said and done, you need to affirm that the communications port share name matches on both the SBS server and clients. If not, you will receive the error message shown in Figure 20-61 when trying to use the modem sharing capabilities.

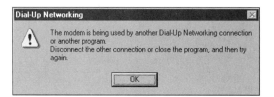

Figure 20-61: Dial-up networking error message

Of course I didn't discover these easy-to-overlook port configuration steps, which are also listed on pages 68–69 of the SBS "Start Here" book, until I had suffered greatly and wasted much time.

HP network printers

A wonderful gift that bailed me out of trouble on a NetWare to SBS conversion was the discovery of HP's JetAdmin tool for SBS on the first SBS CD-ROM disk ("Disc 1"). The client, like many on planet Earth, used HP laser printers that were directly connected to the network via a JetDirect card. Alas, the only HP JetAdmin software on site supported NetWare. Enter SBS's JetAdmin tool and exit problem! Also note that the HP JetAdmin tool installs the HP-related printer monitor so that you can create an HP Jet Direct port and add the printer to the network (see this under the Add Printer Wizard in the Printers folder).

Be careful changing passwords

Changing the Administrators password via User Manager for Domains is a bad thing. Changing it via the SBS Console is a good thing. That is because Administrator is the service account for several services including:

- Microsoft Exchange Directory
- Microsoft Exchange Information Store
- Microsoft Exchange Internet Mail Service
- Microsoft Exchange Message Transport Agent
- Microsoft Exchange System Attendant
- Microsoft Fax Service

When you change the Administrator's password via the Manage User option on the SBS Console, the service account password for the preceding services will automatically be changed.

Note

If you change the same password via User Manager for Domains, you must either change the service account password manually for each service or suffer when you reboot and several of your services fail to start. Your best bet is to use the SBS Console (as always!).

Implementing Proxy 2.0

Early in the chapter, I told you that SBS ships with Proxy Server 1.0 and a free upgrade to Proxy Server 2.0 is possible. However, you will need to use Microsoft's Proxy Server 2.0 Upgrade Wizard to install Proxy Server 2.0 on your SBS server. This must be downloaded from www.microsoft.com/proxy/smallbusiness and installed, or else you will receive the error message shown in Figure 20-62 when you attempt to install Proxy Server 2.0.

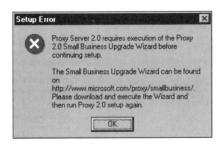

Figure 20-62: Proxy Server setup error message

Harmless event logs errors

Suppose your SBS server uses a direct ISDN connection to the Internet and has no modems attached. Because SBS installs RAS whether you have a modem or not, the Event Viewer will log errors from RAS-related services at startup if you didn't set up any modems. This condition will be displayed as a harmless "A service failed to start" error message upon server startup. Not a big deal but it can freak out novice SBS administrators. To eliminate this situation, disable both the Remote Access Connection Manager and Remote Access Server services.

Revisiting SBS security

Besides standardizing drive mappings for your user populations (say the S: drive for user directories and the T: drive for the company directory), you can better manage the security of your SBS network by following these few steps. This discussion follows my concerns earlier in the chapter in the Add User steps about SBS security being too generous.

As previously mentioned when you added a user, you need to understand that the "default" permission for any SBS user is "read" for any other user's folder (see Figure 20-63).

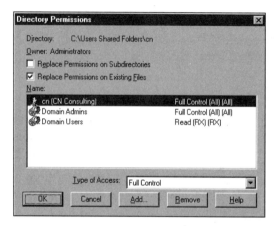

Figure 20-63: The Read right to other users' folders

This is typically unacceptable as small business owners demand confidential storage areas for their work. To fix that, modify the NTFS-based directory permissions to remove the (default) Read right for Domain Users (see Figure 20-64).

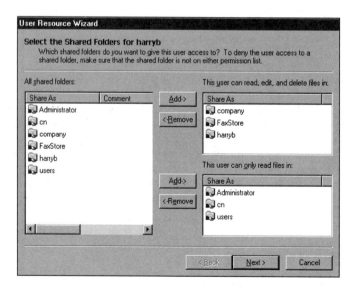

Figure 20-64: Removing the Read permission for Domain Users

Virus detection

Remember that SBS does not have a native virus detection solution. For that you need to consider a robust virus detection solution such as Inoculan (discussed in Chapter 3). You might be interested to know that Computer Associates also offers Inoculan for Small Business Server for $645 suggested retail (see www.cai.com). The Inoculan solution is considered real time because it constantly scans for viruses that may arrive via network file transfers, Internet e-mail and file transfers, floppy disks and so on.

However, there is yet another virus detection alternative in the SBS world. That's Seagate's Backup Exec tape backup application, which has a modified virus detection routine wherein each file to be backed up is scanned for viruses. While not "real time," such regular scanning of files for viruses via a tape backup program is better than what SBS offers you natively out of the box: nothing!

The Future of SBS

In late Spring 1999, it is anticipated Microsoft will release SBS version 4.5. This upgrade is both an application upgrade and a functionality upgrade. The applications that will be upgraded include:

- Windows NT Server 4.0 Option Pack, which will now be automatically installed with Windows NT Server 4.0 (this is not the case with SBS 4.0)
- Microsoft Exchange Server 5.5
- Microsoft Internet Explorer 5.0
- Microsoft Proxy Server 2.0 (in SBS 4.0, you may upgrade to Microsoft Proxy Server 2.0 as discussed in Implementing Proxy 2.0)
- Microsoft SQL Server 7.0
- Microsoft Outlook 2000

The functionality upgrades in SBS 4.5 include a more robust Internet Connection Wizard (ICW) that supports Internet connection approaches beyond simple dial-up (such as ISDN, ADSL, and WAN-based solutions). Troubleshooting will be dramatically improved with the new VAP management tools. The VAP management tools will make use of NetMeeting and facilitate remote administration of the SBS network. And SBS 4.5 will support 50-users, not the 35-users supported today with SBS 4.0!

Summary

In this chapter, Small Business Server was explored and explained, starting with a basic introduction and ending with advanced topics:

- Defining Small Business Server
- Understanding the Small Business environment
- Identifying Small Business Server design goals and philosophy
- Planning for your Small Business Server implementation
- Installing Small Business Server
- Using the SBS To Do List
- Installing the Small Business Server — Client components
- Performing ongoing administration of Small Business Server
- Troubleshooting Small Business Server
- Comparing and contrasting Small Business Server and "regular" Windows NT Server
- Planning for future releases of SBS

Part VI

Optimizing and Troubleshooting Windows NT Server 4.0

Chapter 21: Analyzing and Boosting Performance

Chapter 22: Performance Monitor

Chapter 23: Network Monitor Secrets

Chapter 24: Task Manager and Other Neat Tricks

Chapter 25: Troubleshooting Secrets

Chapter 21

Analyzing and Boosting Performance

In This Chapter

▶ Learning why you should monitor, boost, and forecast Windows NT Server performance

▶ Defining performance analysis

▶ Learning about and distinguishing between quantitative and qualitative tools

▶ Learning the conceptual steps in performance analysis

▶ Learning about troubleshooting via performance analysis

▶ Knowing what the four most important areas to monitor are

▶ Answering questions about why performance declines

Analyzing and boosting performance is a very important part of a Windows NT Server professional's job. You are responsible for getting the most from your implementation of Windows NT Server. Installing, managing, and using Windows NT Server is a big investment on your part in both time and money. By analyzing and boosting performance, you can increase the return on that investment. This chapter will not only define performance analysis from both quantitative and qualitative viewpoints but will also set the foundation for chapters that follow in the Performance Analysis part of this book.

This chapter is for the MBA in all of us. While MBAs spend their days applying linear programming to business scenarios and mastering the inner workings of their Hewlett-Packard (HP) 12C calculators, Windows NT Server engineers have much to learn from our MBA brothers and sisters. That's because the fundamentals of quantitative analysis very much apply to our world of Windows NT Server management. You can apply the quantitative or scientific approach to Windows NT Server performance analysis and add real value to your network and its operations. To do so, consider mastering Performance Monitor, Network Monitor, and Task Manager.

Why? Smart practitioners know that you get what you give to Windows NT Server. If all you do is set up and simply answer several questions posed by the Windows NT Server setup dialog boxes, your signature will be on public display when others follow and look closely at your network. Simple is as simple does. A network setup in a simple fashion will basically perform, but doom lurks. Once your network experiences significant growth either via user count or activity levels, system design and implementation issues often return to wreak havoc. Thus the need to study, master, and implement the performance boosting secrets discussed in this and the next few chapters in the Performance Analysis part. These secrets include third-party products that add to and help you exceed the capabilities of Microsoft's built-in performance analysis tools.

Performance Analysis

In sailing, one wouldn't embark without a plan, a map, and a compass in one's stash of necessities. Everyone likes to know where they are headed, how long it will take, and often, can we get there sooner? Managing Windows NT Server environments is no different. Is our Windows NT Server performance headed in the right direction? Going south on us? Remaining stable or veering sideways? These are the types of questions we ask ourselves in the middle of the night, workaholics that we are in this exciting and demanding field of Windows NT Server network administration and engineering. To answer these questions, we tinker, try again and tinker more, hoping to boost Windows NT Server performance and predict where our environment is headed.

Chant the following mantra: It all starts with the data. While this is a popular refrain among data base administrators (DBAs), it is the data that ultimately matters when analyzing and boosting the performance of your Windows NT Server–based network. Data is at the center of our efforts to analyze Windows NT Server, so we place great importance on the type of data, the quantity of data, and the quality of the data we can obtain from Windows NT Server in our efforts to analyze and boost performance. Fortunately, this data is readily generated by the computer for us. Thank god we don't have to record by hand like door-to-door U.S. government census interviewers of days gone by.

The data we use can be collected as a one-time snapshot of our system health, or it can be systematically collected over time. As quantitative analysts, we desire and seek out large clean data sets that provide enough values for us to perform meaningful analysis and draw wise conclusions.

Tip

Whichever data analysis tool you use to monitor and manage your Windows NT Server network with, you should strive to collect data consistently, frequently, and routinely. We love large data sets as the foundation of our analysis. Statistically, we refer to a large data set as a large sample size.

Built-in performance analysis tools

In Windows NT Server, we typically use five tools to collect and analyze our data: Performance Monitor, Network Monitor, Task Manager, Windows NT Diagnostics, and Event Viewer. Performance Monitor enables us to perform sophisticated analysis via charts, logs, reports, and alerts over time (see Figure 21-1). Performance Monitor is discussed at length in the next chapter, Chapter 22, "Performance Monitor." Network Monitor is truly a gift in Windows NT Server 4.0, enabling basic networking packet analysis without having to spend $5,000 or more on a hardware-based sniffer (see Figure 21-2). Network Monitor is discussed at length in Chapter 23, "Network Monitor Secrets." Task Manager (see Figure 21-3), Windows NT Diagnostics (see Figure 21-4) and Event Viewer (see Figure 21-5) are discussed extensively in Chapter 24, "Task Manager and Other Neat Tricks." You may also read more about Performance Monitor, Network Monitor, and Task Manager in the "Are You Being 'Outperformed'" section of this chapter.

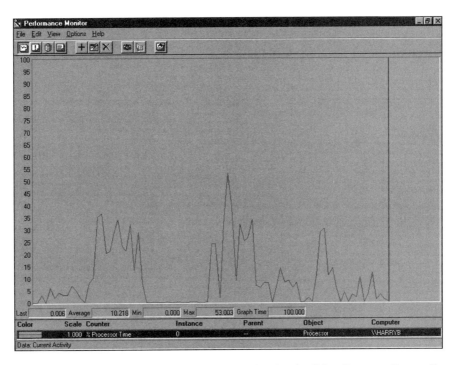

Figure 21-1: Default view of Performance Monitor showing the Object:Processor Counter:% Processor Time

Part VI: Optimizing and Troubleshooting Windows NT Server 4.0

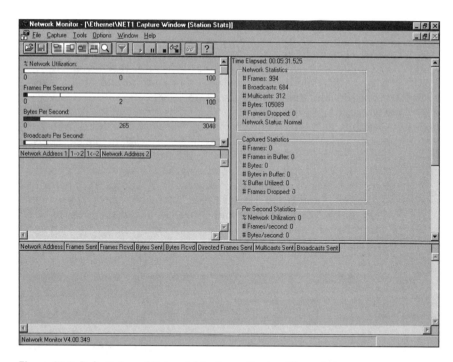

Figure 21-2: Default view of Network Monitor — Capture View window

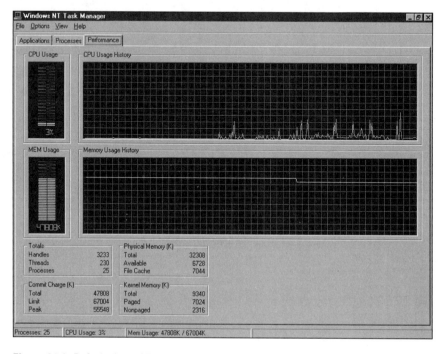

Figure 21-3: Default view of Task Manager — Performance tab sheet

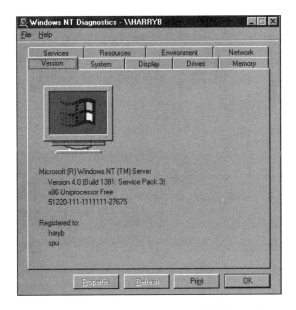

Figure 21-4: Default view of Windows NT Diagnostics — Version tab sheet

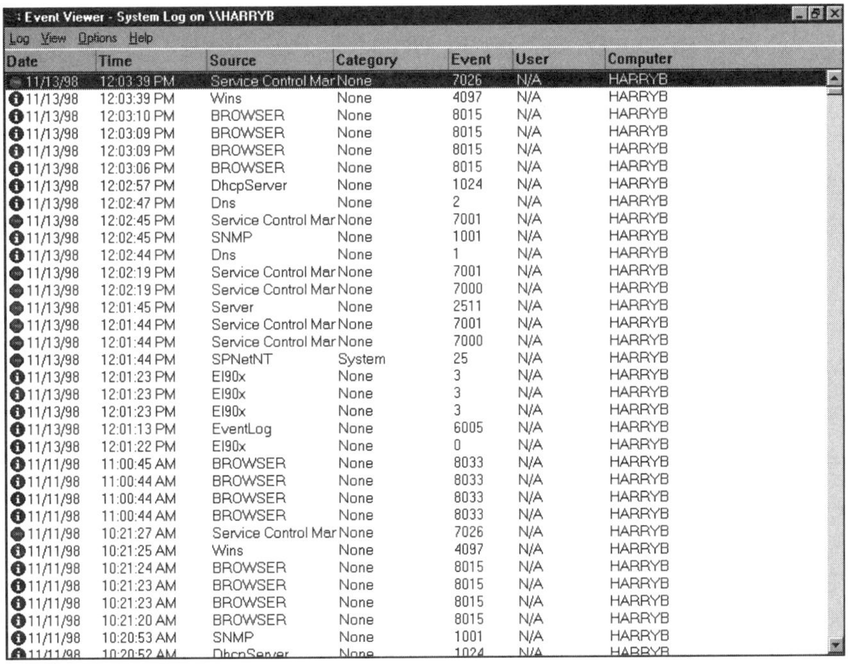

Figure 21-5: Default view of Event Viewer — System Log

Each of these tools will be discussed in the following chapters. It is critical to note that some tools like Performance Monitor work best when analyzing data over time to establish trends. Other tools like Network Monitor are much more "here and now" oriented and typically provide a snapshot of system activity at a point in time. This distinction is critical as you wade through this and the next few chapters.

More quantitative tools

Additional quantitative tools to consider using, beyond those provided with Windows NT Serve, include approaches borrowed from the MBA and quantitative analysis community include manually recording measurements, observing alert conditions in logs, user surveys and basic trend line analysis. Of these, keep in mind that the third item that follows, user surveys, directly involves your users and is therefore perhaps one of the most valuable tools at your disposal.

- Manually record measurements and data points of interest while monitoring Windows NT Server.

- Observe event log error conditions that trigger alerts (a big approach utilized in managing SQL Server).

- Survey users about system performance via e-mail or a paper-based survey. These survey results, when ranked on a scale (say 1 being low performance and 5 being high performance) can be charted and analyzed. It's really fun to deliver the same survey again to your users several months hence and compare the results to your original survey. Feedback from your users is one of the best performance monitoring approaches.

- Carry out trend line analysis, frequency distribution, central tendency, regression, correlation analysis, probability distribution, seasonality, and indexing. Each of these is discussed over the next several pages.

The trend line analysis approach, while extremely powerful, is also the most difficult of the four analysis methods listed. Because it has a high degree of difficulty, I discuss trend line analysis at length over the next several pages. But don't be frightened by this preamble. The trend line analysis that follows may be tried at home, and I didn't hire professionals to complete the stunts.

Trend line analysis

Also known as *time series analysis,* this approach finds the best fit of a trend line applied against a plotted data set. In terms of managing Windows NT Server environments, that means applying the chart view in Performance Monitor to observe data points being charted via a line graph, and then placing a ruler on your screen to create the trend line. The slope of the ruler would be the trend line and represent a line drawn equal distance between each point that has been plotted. Not surprisingly, this is a simple and effective forecasting tool for predicting system performance and is generally known as the freehand method. The mathematicians reading this book know that this is a gross oversimplification, and indeed a trend line is best calculated via the least squares method. See the quantitative methods book of your choice for more in-depth discussion.

Frequency distribution

Imagine you are a network analyst in a large organization deploying Windows NT Servers. You want to know what amount of RAM is found in the client machines. Table 21-1, based on data collected by Microsoft's System Management Server, was created to show a frequency distribution.

Table 21-1 Frequency Distribution Example

RAM	Number of Clients (Frequency)
12MB	150
16MB	200
24MB	100
32MB	50

Simple enough. You have now created the frequency distribution to help plan your technology requirements. Clearly, most of the machines have under 24MB of RAM and may need a memory upgrade in the near future.

Central tendency — the mean, the mode, and the median

Assume you are in a large organization with WAN network traffic management problems. The organization is growing rapidly. You are curious about the nature of the network traffic. Are just a few users creating most of the network traffic? Are all users placing a similar amount of traffic on the wire? Analyzing the mean, mode, and median will accomplish this for you. The mean is simply the mathematical average calculated as the sum of the values divided by the number of observations (ten apples divided by five school children = two apples per child on average). The mode is the most frequently occurring value in a data set (following our apple example, if four school children each took one apple and the fifth school child took six apples, the mode would be one). The median is determined by placing a data set in order from the largest number to the smallest number.

Apples Eaten by School Children
One school child ate one apple
One school child ate two apples
One school child ate three apples
One school child ate four apples

The median would be between two and three apples.

How does this apply to Windows NT Server performance analysis? In the following way. Suppose your network traffic pattern has the characteristics shown in Table 21-2 for eleven users.

Table 21-2 Sample Network Traffic

Central Tendency Measurement	Number of Data Packets
Mean	1,500
Median	225
Mode	200

From this information, we can reliably state that one or more large users generate most of the network traffic as measured by data packets on the wire. How? When your median and mode measurements are smaller than your mean, you can assert that a few users (in this case) are supplying an inordinate amount of data packets. Think about it. If you analyzed the preceding information, you would easily see that the mean (or average) is dramatically larger than the median or mode. The median, being a reflection of the midpoint of the data series when ordered from smallest to largest values, suggests that the data is skewed toward the smaller values. The mode, in this case, confirms this observation in that the most frequently occurring value is much smaller than the average value. Finally, looking at the data set used to create the example (see Table 21-3) proves the argument that a couple of users (Dan and Ellen) are creating most of the network traffic.

Table 21-3 User Network Traffic

User (11)	Network Packets Sent
Adam	225
Betty	100
Carol	50

User (11)	Network Packets Sent
Dan	10,000
Ellen	5,000
Frank	250
Gary	200
Harry	225
Irene	175
Jackie	150
Kia	125
Total 11 Users	16,500 Packets

Regression

This quantitative analysis method, whereby we seek to define the relationship between a dependent variable against an independent variable, can be used as we seek to boost the performance of Windows NT Server. Assume you use Windows NT Server as an Internet server. Suppose you are interested in seeing how Web traffic impacts the processor utilization rate on the server. Perhaps you believe that Web activity ("hits") on your site negatively impact the processor utilization rate by causing that value to grow. You can confirm this belief by charting the dependent variable Processor:% Processor Time (this is an object:counter in Performance Monitor that is described in the Performance Monitor chapter) against the independent variable HTTP Service: Connections/sec. (see Figure 21-6).

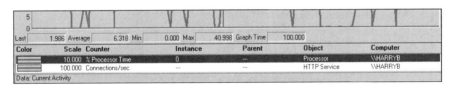

Figure 21-6: Dependent (Processor:%Processor Time) and independent (HTTP Service:Connections/Sec) variables

More hits against our Web site result in a higher processor utilization rate.

Correlation analysis

In the regression example just given, a positive correlation was discovered between Processor:% Processor Time and WWW OBJECT:COUNTER (ADD HERE). A negative correlation between variables in Windows NT Server might exist when comparing two object:counters that seem to move in opposite directions when set side by side on a Performance Monitor chart. At a basic level, the object:counters Memory:Available Bytes and Memory:Pages/sec would have a negative correlations. That is, the less available bytes of memory you have available, more paging activity will occur. These topics are discussed in greater detail in the Performance Monitor chapter.

Secret

A negative correlation isn't necessarily bad. Do not be lulled into the fallacy that a positive correlation is good and a negative correlation is bad. Correlations merely define a relationship, whether that relationship be positive or negative. Another way to think about positive and negative correlations is to view a positive correlation as cyclical and a negative correlation as counter-cyclical.

Probability distribution

Do you work for a manager who worships the bell curve, always wondering where things fit in? Then use this quantitative analysis approach not only to better understand the performance of your Windows NT Server system but to explain technology-related events to your manager. The cool thing about the normal curve is you can easily predict how just over ⅔ (actually 68 percent) of your end users group together when measured against what is called the first standard deviation. A standard deviation measures variability. But let's speak English. The first standard deviation is a very basic measurement and speaks toward behavior of 68 percent of your users on a network. We might say that 68 percent of the users are proficient in mapping drives to another server. Of that 68 percent, some are more proficient than others in mapping drives. A measurement taken to the second standard deviation accounts for 95.4 percent of the user population. Here we'll use the task of being able to log onto the network successfully as our "task" that we believe such a large number of users could complete. However, within that population of 95.4 percent, some may log on without ever having authentication problems, while others may have to repeatedly enter their name and password multiple times to log on (maybe they are poor typists!). Finally, to the third standard deviation, you can account for the behavior of 99.7 percent of the user population. For this group, it might be safe to say that 99.7 percent of the users can turn on their computers. By seeing the underlying trend I've just demonstrated, you can observe that as the bell curve encapsulates more and more of the user population, the activities and behaviors demonstrated by the users become less and less arduous. That only makes sense. To cover the computing behavior of 99.7 percent of your users, you're speaking about some pretty simple tasks that nearly everyone can accomplish.

The normal curve provides a different way of thinking about network performance analysis. What if you believed and measured that 68 percent of your users use three or more applications but 99.7 percent of your users employ at least one application?

Secret

Might you somehow try to group the 68 percent group of users (that is, to the first standard deviation), if we can identify this group easily, into its own separate collision domains? Such is the thought and logic behind switching in network management. So see. This quaint mumbo jumbo really does apply.

Seasonality

Does this really apply? Do Windows NT Servers really have seasons? Maybe so! Doesn't it make sense to remain sensitive to peak system usage when such usage occurs at specific times each year? Take Clark Nuber, the Seattle-based accounting firm that owns the consulting practice where I'm employed. Our network clearly experiences its heaviest loads during tax season (January to April). I can easily document the increased load using the different Windows NT Server performance tools discussed in this chapter, but more important, I can easily predict the increased load on Clark Nuber's network each tax season. Needless to say, we *Clark Nuberites* have learned (sometimes the hard way) not to upset the network with upgrades or enhancements during tax season. On more than one occasion, the network couldn't handle the increased load and crashed!

Create an index

Once you've worked extensively with Windows NT Server and collected large data sets of data, then you can create meaningful measurement indexes. Here's how. Assume you've tracked several sites with Performance Monitor for several months, periodically capturing data to a log file. At this point, you would have a sufficiently large data set. Then you want to know what a fair measure of a user's impact on paging activity is on a typical Windows NT server for your sites. To determine this impact, you would create an index. Suppose you looked at the average Pages/Sec (found under the Memory object) in Performance Monitor and divided that by the average number of users on the system. Note calculating the average Pages/Sec should incorporate readings from different logon periods from different sites so that you can indeed create a generic index. If the average Pages/Sec value were 15.45 and you had 100 users on average, then the index calculation would be 15.45 / 100 = 0.1545. This index value of 0.1545 allows you to predict, on average, what paging file activity might be caused on a per user basis. In effect, an index allows you to predict the load on your system, something that might be very useful when scaling a new system for an upgrade.

Qualitative tools too!

Performance analysis is not only a quantitative exercise. It is also a qualitative endeavor. Whereas we can map and chart Windows NT Server performance until the cows come home, many of us also rely, if not favor, our intuition and other qualitative analysis approaches. Individuals equipped with strong qualitative analysis skill sets may not even need to know the finer points of Performance Monitor and other Windows NT Server performance analysis tools. These people simply "know" when something just isn't correct. Then they set out to troubleshoot the problem and fix it. This is how many CEOs run their organizations. While these leaders might not have a solid grasp of the technologies their firms work with, they do know when something is out of place or not right.

Loosely defined, qualitative approaches to boost Windows NT Server performance include:

- Experience working with Windows NT Server
- Luck
- Intuition
- Luck
- Good judgment
- Luck
- Good advice from peers
- Luck
- Seventh senses
- Luck
- Decision making under uncertainty
- Luck
- ESP
- And finally . . . LUCK!

Several of us long on Windows NT Server work experience rely on our qualitative judgments on a day-to-day basis. We use the quantitative analysis approaches like Performance Monitor logging periodically or during intensive troubleshooting but probably not in our day-to-day world. Those with strong qualitative skills often reap the rewards that accrue to the privileged in this line of work such as higher pay and more work. Why? Because these individuals simply can work more efficiently and "better." Think about that the next time you team with an industry peer to troubleshoot a Windows NT Server problem and find yourself left behind analytically as you marvel at your companion's superior skills. Fear not, however, for the rest of us can be equally successful by employing Windows NT Server's built-in performance analysis tools. Stated another way, when you're short on qualitative tools, you should emphasize the quantitative tools. And of course, even our Windows NT Server companions with ESP can still benefit from the fundamentals of quantitative analysis.

Secret

It takes both the quantitative and qualitative approaches to successfully analyze and boost the performance of your Windows NT Server over the long term! Restated, it takes a combination of the quantitative tools (Performance Monitor, Network Monitor, and Task Manager) plus the qualitative approaches you have at your disposal (experience, intuition, and seventh senses). Both the quantitative and qualitative schools should receive attention if not equal weight. And don't you forget it!

Data = information

The central activity performed in performance analysis is to capture and analyze our Windows NT Server data. In effect, we turn data into information. The information is used to correct Windows NT Server deficiencies, eliminate system bottlenecks, proactively prevent system problems before they occur, troubleshoot problems once they do occur, and plan for system upgrades and enhancements.

Are You Being "Outperformed"?

After you have arrived on the scene as the great net god, whether as consultant or full-time employee, and fixed the obvious problems, your talents often reach a fork in the road. The first fork is that of mediocrity in network management. Many in the network engineering field are content to "coast" once a system is up and running. That's truly what I'd call satisfying behavior; working only hard enough to satisfy management, bosses, clients, and end users. These technology peers are great readers of industry trade journals (on company time!). They also have shoes that are hardly worn because their feet are perched on their desktop while reading those trade journals.

The other fork network professionals take is to exceed everyone's expectations. In the world of Windows NT Server, this is accomplished by mastering tools like Performance Monitor, Network Monitor, and Task Manager. That is when and where you can really master the management your Windows NT Server networked environment. Mastery involves cultivating the ability to identify and mitigate bottlenecks, preventing poor system performance by planning for system additions, and more planning, planning, planning.

Performance Monitor

Mastering Performance Monitor not only enhances your professional standing, but more important, it enables you to provide your end users with a more efficient and stable network for accomplishing their work. And that is how you and your network are ultimately evaluated: by how well your end users do their jobs using computers attached to your Windows NT Server network. By employing the suggestions that follow, you can proactively manage your Windows NT Server networks and provide solutions before encountering problems. In fact, it's been said that preventing problems is the best definition of a superior systems engineer. You don't necessarily have to provide the latest and greatest bells and whistles on your network. You do have to provide an efficient, reliable, and secure Windows NT Server network computing environment that users know they can trust.

Network Monitor

Mastering Network Monitor provides benefits different from Performance Monitor. Network Monitor provides a "snapshot" view of network activity in the form of packet analysis. When working with Microsoft technical support at the senior systems engineer level (read "paid incident level"), it is not uncommon for a Microsoft support engineer to have you install Network Monitor and perform a capture. This capture file is then e-mailed to the engineer for analysis.

Secret

In fact, the way I learned packet analysis was exactly this approach. E-mailing the capture file and then discussing its contents with a Microsoft support engineer provided me the packet analysis fundamentals lacking in many published texts. That is, except Microsoft Official Curriculum course #689: "Windows NT Server 4.0 Enterprise Technologies," which has an excellent Network Monitor section. Realizing that Microsoft periodically updates its course offerings, I suspect the successor courses to course #689 will also teach this important area.

If you have routers in your Windows NT Server network mix, you will be learning and using Network Monitor. And you will inevitably be e-mailing those packet captures to Microsoft for analysis. Count on it!

Task Manager

Task Manager is my buddy. With a deft right-mouse click on the taskbar, I can essentially assess the condition of my Windows NT Server. Task Manager can be thought of as Performance Monitor "light." Task Manager lives for the moment and doesn't really offer any long-term analysis capabilities. But more on that later. First, some thoughts on the conceptual framework of performance analysis.

Conceptual Steps in Performance Analysis

A few basic steps are undertaken to analyze and boost the performance of your Windows NT Server. You can think in terms of four steps:

1. **Develop the model to use.** In Performance Monitor, this means it is critical to pick the correct object:counters as part of your model. For Network Monitor, this step might refer to the duration of your packet capture and from what point on the network you capture packets.

2. **Gather data for input into the model.** This is a collection phase that involves acquiring the data. For Performance Monitor, you log the data to a file for a reasonable amount of time. More important, this step is where we're most concerned about the first two parts of GIGO (garbage in/garbage out). Poor data accumulation results in garbage in, certainly a poor foundation to build the rest of your analysis upon. In fact, this step

is analogous to my recent homebuying experience on Bainbridge Island (near Seattle). As I was writing this book, my family decided to go house shopping. After identifying a house that met our needs, we retained a construction engineer to assess the home's fitness. Unfortunately, he reported the house was built on a wood foundation and it was unacceptable, the rule being that a home's foundation affects everything from that point forward, including resale value. With respect to Windows NT Server: blow this step and suffer for the remainder of your analysis period.

3. **Analyze the results.** Now the fun begins. If steps 1 and 2 went well, you are now ready for step 3: analyzing the results. Success at this stage will truly enable you to boost performance and optimize your Windows NT Server implementation. If you struggle here, see the next section on troubleshooting.

4. **Gather Feedback.** Are we missing the boat with our analysis? Did steps 1, 2, and 3 lead us to optimize the system in such a way that performance was improved, not hampered? Your ability to gather and interpret feedback will make or break your ability to become a superstar system engineer.

Troubleshooting via Performance Analysis

Everything discussed so far is meaningless if the knowledge transfer between us doesn't leave these pages. It is essential that there be a real-world outcome to the intense performance analysis discussion you and I have embarked on. Otherwise this discussion is nothing more than a pleasant academic exercise. The outcome we're both seeking is applying the performance analysis tools and tricks readily available to improve your network's performance. And that obviously includes troubleshooting.

Secret

The performance analysis tools included with Windows NT Server 4.0 are software-based and do a better job of diagnosing virtual problems than truly physical problems. Physical problems like a bad cable run are better diagnosed via a hand-held cable tester.

There is no magic elixir to troubleshooting. Troubleshooting, by most accounts, appears primarily to be a function of on-the-job experience, including long weekends and late nights at work. As an MCT and MCSE instructor, I've seen countless students struggle with the required Networking Essentials exam when their résumés are short and their tenures as Windows NT Server administrators is measured in months, not years. Students with significant industry experience enjoy an easier ride when taking the Networking Essentials exam, and not surprisingly, they have sharper-honed troubleshooting skills. Quite frankly, I'm not sure I can teach you the troubleshooting area. Troubleshooting is something you learn (with lots of on-the-job experience). The performance analysis tools provided with Windows NT Server 4.0 are valuable not only for helping you improve the performance of your network but also for troubleshooting problems more efficiently and effectively.

Secret

Be advised that even the best set of tools in unclean or incompetent hands will usually result in an unfavorable outcome.

Troubleshooting is not only a function of using your Windows NT Server architectural experience but also of your ability to swim comfortably within the Windows NT Server Registry. That's so you can observe and capitalize on driver dependencies and start values, track the Windows NT Server boot process to the point of failure, and understand stop screens. It won't hurt if you've worked with Microsoft support with the "debugger" utilities. But more on that in Chapter 25, "Troubleshooting Secrets."

Secret

Print and review the entire Window NT Server Registry as soon as you install Window NT Server. Learn the location of important information (for example, HKEY_LOCAL_MACHINE is much more important than HKEY_CLASSES_ROOT). By studying and learning the Registry early, you will know where to go to investigate Registry values in an emergency. Don't forget to place this Registry printout in a notebook and update it periodically (quarterly if you make significant changes or install lots of applications). I would highly recommend that you print to file and edit the information in a word processing application such as Microsoft Word. You will shorten the size of the printout considerably and make it more readable. Of course you can always print to file as your only form of storage (and avoiding printing to the printer at all). Either way, whether you print to file or the printer, the Registry information is most valuable.

Misdiagnosing a problem is as bothersome in the world of Windows NT Server 4.0 as it is in the world of medicine. It's obviously not good. Although using Performance Monitor, Network Monitor, and Task Manager will not assure a correct diagnosis, these tools are legitimate ways to eliminate false reads. Furthermore, some third-party performance analysis tools I'll discuss in the next few chapters can be used to supplement Windows NT Server 4.0's built-in tools and dramatically improve your troubleshooting efforts.

The Big Four Areas to Monitor

Quick, name the four resource areas you should monitor in order to boost performance in Windows NT Server 4.0? The four main areas are: memory, processor, disk subsystem. and network subsystem.

Memory

Perhaps the simplest and easiest secret conveyed in this entire book is to add more memory. Adding memory will truly solve many problems in your networked environment. Looking deeper into that reasoning is the idea behind analyzing memory performance. First, you probably have economic and technical constraints that prevent you from adding an infinite amount of memory to your server. Second, simply buying your way out of a problem by purchasing and installing more memory isn't fundamentally sound network engineering. Understanding the reasons for adding memory is what's important. Simply stated, we look at two forms of memory as part of our analysis: RAM and cache memory. RAM is, as we all know, volatile primary storage. Cache memory, also in RAM, is where Windows NT Server 4.0 places files, applications, drivers, and such that are currently being accessed by the users, the operating system, and so forth. In Chapter 22, memory will be discussed in more detail with respect to specific memory object counters used in Performance Monitor.

Processor

My experience with analyzing the processor is that it usually hasn't been the cause of everyone's grief. Many suffer from processor envy, which is no doubt a function of popular advertisements creating wants for the latest and greatest Intel processor. So network engineers and administrators on the front line are often greeted with free advice from users to upgrade the processor. However, in most small and medium-sized organizations, the processor utilization rates are well within acceptable limits. In large networked environments, a strong case can be made for faster, more powerful processors and even implementing multiple processors. These larger enterprises will be interested in learning more about Windows NT Server's multiple processing capabilities using the symmetric multiprocessing model.

Disk subsystem

Another tired adage that's the bane of network engineers and administrators is the often cited "solution" to just buy a faster hard disk. Easier said than done. Again, economic considerations may prevent you from just throwing money at your problems. A more intelligent approach is to analyze your disk subsystem in detail to determine exactly where the bottleneck resides. Issues to consider when analyzing the disk subsystem include:

- What is your disk controller type (ranging from legacy IDE controllers to more modern Fast SCSI-2 and PCI controllers)?

Secret

This technology changes rapidly and new innovations in system buses are introduced frequently. If you do not have a strong hardware orientation, make sure you are reading the hardware ads in popular technology trade journals and occasionally taking your technician/hardware guru buddy to lunch.

- Do your controllers have on-board processors (typically known as "bus master" controllers)?

- Do your controllers cache activity directly on the controller card, thereby bypassing the use of RAM or internal cache memory on the computer to store limited amounts of data?

- Do disk-bound applications and the associated high levels of read and write requests suggest you need to consider the fastest disk subsystem available?

Secret

Current disk device drivers: Are you implementing the latest disk subsystem drivers on your system? While this is an often overlooked duty, using current drivers can go a long way toward boosting your disk subsystem performance (and typically for the low price associated with downloading a driver from the vendor's Internet site).

Hardware-based RAID solutions offer significantly better performance than RAID solutions implemented via software (the software-based RAID capabilities found in Disk Administrator). That's because hardware-based RAID parity calculations are performed independently of the operating system.

Sometimes you just have to reboot! Here's one secret you won't find in any Windows NT Server user manual. For reasons I can't fully explain, sometimes Windows NT Server just freaks out and the hard disks spin excessively. When this happens, you don't even get enough processor time to freely move you mouse. The solution? Just restart the server. This freak-out condition will often disappear upon reboot. Truth be told, this "secret" is one of my best consulting freebies that I offer my clients. Often the best free advice I offer my clients is to reboot and call me in the morning. It's often just what the doctor ordered. I don't know if it is a function of Microsoft products more than other vendor products, but rebooting works wonders! I often say the rebooting Windows NT Server will solve 90 percent of your problems.

Be sure to delay rebooting your Windows NT Server until after work hours if possible. User often take advantage of a reboot condition to call it a day and leave early, causing unexpected traffic jams in the parking lot!

Network subsystem

The network subsystem consists of internal and external network components such as the network adapter type, number of network adapter cards, cabling media, routers and switches, Windows NT Server services, and the types of applications used (SQL Server, Exchange, and other Microsoft BackOffice applications). And don't forget end-users. I consider end-users to be a network component because they can impact the performance of the network with their usage. How you configure Active Directory will also impact the performance of your network. A complex and unwieldy Active Directory structure can hinder rather than help your network. See Chapters 5 and 16 for more information on Active Directory.

In general, network bottlenecks are more difficult to detect and resolve than problems found in the three subsystems just discussed (memory, processor, and disk subsystem). In fact, all of the tools discussed in this and the next several chapters are typically used to resolve network bottlenecks. Additionally, physical tools are readily employed to remedy network subsystem ailments. These physical tools include cable testers and time domain reflectors (TDRs).

In fact, detection of quasi-logical/virtual and quasi-physical problems on your network may present one of your greatest challenges as a Windows

NT Server professional. At a small site, I once fell victim to some tomfoolery placed on the network by a 3COM switch. The device, being used primarily as a media converter between a 100Mbps backbone run to the network adapter on the Windows NT Server and 10Mbps runs to the workstations, decided to both reconfigure itself and downright break one evening when Microsoft Proxy Server 2.0 was introduced. Several hours of sleuthing later, it was determined the 100Mbps downlink port had truly gone down under. That is, the 100Mbps port had lost its configuration. The solution? We quickly implemented a cheap 10Mbps Ethernet concentrator to get everything running again. In fact, the hours spent fussing over the switch clearly eliminated all of the advantages associated with the 100Mbps server backbone. But that's another topic.

Secret

Use 32-bit network adapters. Older 8-bit network adapters transfer up to 400 Kilobytes per second (KBps). Newer (and now standard) 32-bit network adapters transfer up to 1.2 Megabytes per second (MBps). If the network adapter card is too slow, it cannot effectively perform transfers of information from the computer to the network and vice-versa.

Consider installing multiple network adapter cards to boost throughput (see Figure 21-7). A single network adapter card can be a bottleneck in the network subsystem by virtue of its primary role to take 32-bit parallel form data and transfer it to a serial form for placement on the wire. Multiple network cards will boost network subsystem performance.

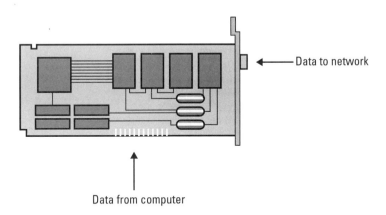

Figure 21-7: A network adapter card performing data transfer

Secret

Bind only one protocol type to each network card if possible. This enables you to perform some load balancing between network adapter cards. For example, if you have a second network cable segment for backing up the servers in your server farm to a backup server, consider binding the fast and efficient NetBEUI protocol to the network adapter cards on this segment (assuming no routing is involved). Binding multiple protocols to each network adapter can result in a performance decline on your network. Reducing excess protocols will reduce network traffic. Some types of network traffic, such as connection requests, are sent over all protocols at the same time. Now that's a traffic jam!

Try and reduce the number of protocols and networking services used on your Windows NT Server. Small is beautiful because overhead is reduced with a smaller networking subsystem footprint.

Secret

Use network adapters from the same manufacturer if possible. Different manufacturers implement drivers against the lower layers of the OSI model differently. Using the same type of card from the same manufacturer results in a consistent implementation of the network subsystem component.

Networking services in Windows NT Server may be installed from the Services tab sheet on the Network Properties sheet. This is found via the Network applet in Control Panel. Select the Network Services you want to install.

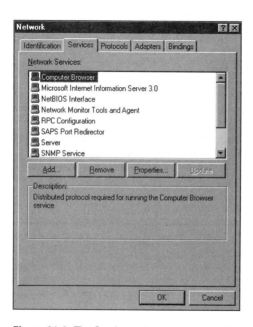

Figure 21-8: The Services tab sheet in on the Network Properties sheet

Table 21-4 is a list and description of possible network-related services that may be installed with Windows NT Server 4.0.

Table 21-4   Windows NT Server 4.0 Networking Services

Service Name	Description
Services for Macintosh	Enables a Windows NT Server to act as an AppleTalk router, allowing PC and Macintosh clients to share files and printers.
Microsoft DHCP Server	Automatically assigns IP addresses to other computers running the DHCP (Dynamic Host Configuration Protocol) Client Service.
Microsoft DNS Server	Maps DNS domain names to IP addresses.

Chapter 21: Analyzing and Boosting Performance

Service Name	Description
Network Monitor Agent and Tools	Captures packets for network analysis. Also provides a point of presence for capturing packets by a Network Monitor tool running on another computer.
Network Monitor Agent	Provides a point of presence for capturing packets by a Network Monitor tool running on another computer.
Simple TCP/IP Services	Client program for simple network protocols, including Character Generator, Daytime, Echo, and Quote of the Day.
Service Name	**Description**
SNMP Service	Enables a Windows NT Server to be administered remotely with an SNMP management tool.
TCP/IP Print Server	Enables Windows NT Server to print on TCP/IP-connected printers or to printers that are physically attached to UNIX computers.
Windows Internet Name Service	Dynamic name registration and resolution service that maps NetBIOS computer names to IP addresses.
SAP Agent	Servers advertise their services and addresses on a network. Clients use SAP to determine what network resources are available.
DHCP Relay Agent	Allows DHCP traffic to occur on multiple subnets. Described in detail in Chapter 6, "Installing and Configuring TCP/IP."
Gateway (and Client) Services for NetWare	Provides client connectivity to NetWare servers and gateway services for Windows NT Server network clients to connect to NetWare servers.
NetBIOS Interface	Provides NetBIOS support.
Remote Access Service	Provides dial-in connectivity for Remote Access Service (RAS) clients.
Remoteboot Service	Starts MS-DOS and Microsoft Windows workstations over the network. Requires DLC protocol.
RIP for Internet Protocol	Routing Information Protocol for IP. This service is necessary to utilize the Routing tab sheet with the TCP/IP Protocol.
RIP for NwLink IPX/SPX compatible transport	Provide routing functionality for NwLink IPX/SPX-based networks.
RPC Configuration	Remote Procedure Call service enables RPC-written programs to perform procedures on multiple computers. Includes the endpoint mapper and other RPC services.
RPC support for Banyan	Provides RPC support for Banyan network nodes.
Server	Installs support for the SMB (Server Message Block) protocol, the core of Microsoft networking.
Workstation	Installs the client for the SMB (Server Message Block) protocol, the core of Microsoft networking.

The bottom line on the network subsystem? You ultimately should be interested in knowing where you are at today in terms of network performance (via Performance Monitor using the Network Segment object and Network Monitor using its statistics pane) plus accurately forecasting where you will be tomorrow.

Why Performance Declines

Several reasons exist for performance declines in Windows NT Server 4.0. Likely suspects include memory leaks, unresolved resource conflicts, physical wear and tear on the system, and system modifications such as installing poorly behaved applications and running poorly configured applications.

The funny thing about operating system patch kits is that previously denied problems such as memory leaks originating from the executive services (like drivers and DLLs) are not only acknowledged but fixed. Memory leaks, which can be monitored by performing specific memory measurements over time, are typically corrected by simply rebooting the server periodically. That's an old trick for those of us who managed NetWare servers in the early days of NetWare 2.*x* and 3.*x* (when a monthly reboot was essential to terminate discontiguous memory).

Unresolved resource conflicts might include the dance of the fighting SCSI cards. I recently had an experience with a new workstation from a well-known hardware manufacturer where the on-board SCSI controller was fighting with the Adaptec SCSI card. Several modifications later the conflict appeared to be resolved (by turning off the SCSI BIOS on the Adaptec card), but I could swear the boot time still remained unacceptably long, suggesting the existence of some lingering difficult-to-detect resource conflict (and yes, the likely causes such as IRQ settings had been checked and resolved).

An example of a poorly configured application might be SQL Server with too much RAM allocated to it, causing a memory shortage for Windows NT Server. That would likely cause Windows NT Server to page excessively, resulting in lower overall system performance. Such a situation not only hurts Windows NT Server but also hurts SQL Server — the application you were trying to help with the original memory optimization scenario. I discuss RAM issues in more detail in Chapter 12, "Monthly and Annual Windows NT Server Activities."

Fragmentation is another source of declining performance in Windows NT Server. All operating systems and secondary storage media are subject to fragmentation. This is where a file can be stored across several areas of the hard disk. That adds to read and write times and user frustration levels. Third-party products such as Executive Software's Diskeeper provide defragmentation services that optimize the secondary storage media and

Chapter 21: Analyzing and Boosting Performance

thus boost performance. I discussed fragmentation in more detail in Chapter 12, "Monthly and Annual Windows NT Server Activities."

Consider running the "error-checking" utility found on the Properties sheet for a drive on the Tools tab (see Figure 21-9) found by right-clicking a hard disk. Error checking automatically checks for system errors and scans for and attempts to recover bad sectors.

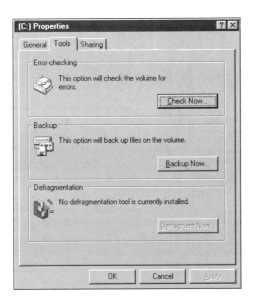

Figure 21-9: The Tools tab sheet for a hard disk (C) Properties sheet

If you have SCSI drives, sector sparing (also known as a hotfix in NetWare) allow your system to essentially self-heal itself, kinda like my old VW Van in my early computing days. That van had a way of healing itself from ailments if I just let it sit for a month or two. Sector sparing works much faster than my mystic VW Van's healing magic by mapping out bad blocks on the secondary storage media and preventing further writes to that bad space.

Secret

When all else fails, you can improve performance by truly manually defragmenting your hard disk using a technique employed during my early Macintosh days. Simply store your data to backup tape (be sure to verify the fitness of your backup by performing a test restore) and reformat your hard disk. No doubt a drastic measure but one that allows you to start fresh!

Additional ways to improve performance after you have suffered declines include:

- Keeping the Recycle Bin empty

- Deleting those pesky temporary files that many applications write to your secondary storage yet don't erase
- Using NTFS for partitions over 400MB in size and FAT for smaller partitions, under 400MB in size. However, be advised that this is a "white paper" recommendation. Many Windows NT Server professionals frown upon the use of FAT partitions because NTFS file and folder-level security isn't available. Other Windows NT Server professionals like to install the operating system on a FAT partition and data and applications on an NTFS partition (see Chapter 3, "Implementation," for more discussion).

Lying with Performance Analysis

A must read for MBA students is *The Honest Truth about Lying with Statistics* (Cooper B. Holmes, ISBN: 0398056730, published 1990), a primer on how to manipulate statistical analysis to meet your needs. To make a long story short, we can apply some of the same principles contained in Holmes book to Windows NT Server performance analysis. For example, changing the vertical scale of data presented in Performance Monitor can radically emphasize or deemphasize performance information, depending on your slant. If you're seeking an generous budget allotment to enhance your Windows NT Server network, perhaps scaling the processor utilization or network utilization counters in Performance Monitor to show dramatic peaks and valleys will "sell" your business decision makers on your argument (see Figure 21-10).

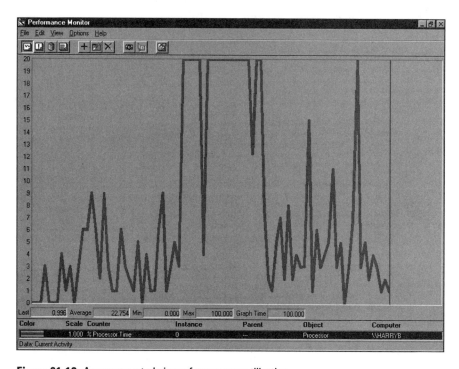

Figure 21-10: An exaggerated view of processor utilization

Performance Benchmarks

Several products exist that enable you to establish performance benchmarks when comparing several servers running Windows NT Server, different applications, or different services and protocols. These tools change frequently, but perhaps your best sources for such benchmarking applications is www.zdnet.com (the Ziff-Davis site). This site has available Socket Test Bench (STB) to test your WinSock-based communications and several other "bench" test applications including ServerBench and Winstone.

ServerBench is a popular client/server benchmarking application that runs on many popular operating systems including Windows NT Server, Novell NetWare, OS/2 Warp Server, and SCO UNIX (see Figure 21-11). The processor, disk, and network subsystems are all exhaustively tested by ServerBench via different tests and load levels placed on the server being tested. The bottom line? Performance is measured in transactions per second for each of the measured subsystems. These transactions reflect the activity between client and server and allow for meaningful comparisons between network operating systems and different makes of computers. The benefits of running a program such as ServerBench are to better evaluate the performance of your Windows NT Servers individually and against other network operating systems you might have at your site.

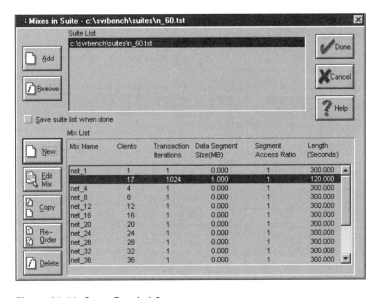

Figure 21-11: ServerBench 4.0

Secret

Be sure to perform the same ServerBench tests periodically so that you can identify any bothersome declines in system performance. Also note that a search of the Internet using popular search engines such as AltaVista will help you identify performance benchmarking applications you can use on your Windows NT Server network.

It's all about positive outcomes. By employing performance analysis methods and approaches to the management of Windows NT Server, you can see trends, observe usage patterns, detect bottlenecks, and plan for the future. You can create meaningful management reports that not only keep the appropriate decision-makers informed but also identify needed equipment acquisitions and facilitate the IT budgeting process. That's a key point! Getting budget approval is the life blood of any Windows NT Server manager. Don't forget it!

Now — onward to Performance Monitor!

Summary

This chapter introduced performance analysis. Specifically, it presented quantitative and qualitative methods to analyze and boost Windows NT Server performance. The following points were covered:

- Learning why you should monitor, boost, and forecast Windows NT Server performance
- Defining performance analysis
- Learning about and distinguishing between quantitative and qualitative tools
- Learning the conceptual steps in performance analysis
- Learning about troubleshooting via performance analysis
- Knowing what the four most important areas to monitor are
- Answering questions about why performance declines

Chapter 22

Performance Monitor

In This Chapter

- Performance Monitor capabilities
- Performance Monitor basics
- Six quick steps to using Performance Monitor
- The four faces of Performance Monitor
- How to collect data
- In depth analysis: memory bottlenecks, disk bottlenecks, network bottlenecks
- Analysis: file and print servers, application server

Nestled away in the Administrative Tools program group you will find Performance Monitor. This unassuming tool holds insights into many of the powers of Windows NT Server 4.0. By the end of this chapter, I think that you will agree that Performance Monitor is a lot stronger than you previously thought.

Here is where the pedal meets the metal. Performance Monitor is a tool to be mastered so that you can optimize and continually improve the performance of your Windows NT Server network. Although Task Manager (discussed in Chapter 24) provides several measurements similar to those presented by Performance Monitor, it is Performance Monitor that enables us to track long-term trends and measurements such as those discussed in the previous chapter (Chapter 21).

The Power of Performance Monitor

One of the best deals about Windows NT Server is the no-cost utilities included out of the box such as Performance Monitor (PERFMON.EXE). While Novell includes its own form of "performance monitor" (MONITOR.NLM) for free with NetWare, I think you will quickly agree that Windows NT Server Performance Monitor, with its many capabilities, is one of the best tools you never had to pay for (see Figure 22-1).

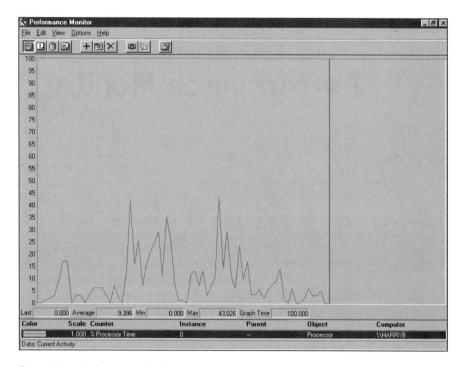

Figure 22-1: Performance Monitor

Here are some features of Performance Monitor:

- Has the capability to log and save historical performance data.
- Can chart data in real time.
- Monitors server-based applications on an individual basis (with its own counters).

Note

This is a huge area with the effective rollout and management of Microsoft SQL Server. In fact, Microsoft has a five-day certification course called "Performance Tuning and Optimization of Microsoft SQL Server 6.5" that addresses this area. Contact Microsoft and ask about Course 665 if you would like more information.

- Provides several real-time and historical views of memory, server, disk, and network performance.
- Enables you to observe the effects of changes to your system.
- Alerts you about system-related problems immediately.
- Has the capability to monitor multiple servers using one session of Performance Monitor.

- Has the capability to run several sessions of Performance Monitor (just try loading multiple instances of MONITOR.NLM on a NetWare server and see what happens).
- Has the capability to save specific analysis configurations via workspaces.
- Has the capability to export data to other applications including Microsoft Excel and Microsoft SQL Server.

Comparing Performance Monitor to NetWare MONITOR.NLM

Let's contrast Windows NT Server Performance Monitor with the NetWare MONITOR.NLM application (see Figure 22-2). MONITOR.NLM provides a real-time, snapshot view of how your network and server are functioning. MONITOR.NLM lives for the moment, but as we know, moments are fleeting. Serious performance analysis demands we view our data both in current snapshots and from a historical perspective. As an old NetWare CNE, I can attest to the value of Windows NT Server Performance Monitor over NetWare MONITOR.NLM. I've recommended and selected Windows NT Server over NetWare in several cases on the basis of Performance Monitor alone. This is truly one of the best-kept secrets about Windows NT Server, one that I'm about to share with you in detail.

Figure 22-2: Novell NetWare MONITOR.NLM

It is essential you employ Performance Monitor for at least bare-bones analysis so that you can monitor the health of your patient (your server and network) over its life from cradle to grave. Rest assured that time spent learning and using Performance Monitor is akin to the time you spend performing system backups: time well spent! Many network professionals have embraced Performance Monitor and employed it to its full extent. Taking full advantage of Performance Monitor, with all of its bells and whistles, is mandatory for larger LANs and WANs. Needless to say, I've found Performance Monitor to be a welcome and wonderful addition to my consulting bag of tricks. That said, welcome to performance analysis via Performance Monitor.

Tip

Performance Monitor is a strong tool for both developers and network engineers. But when you look at that long list of counters associated with numerous objects, please understand that most of the counters don't apply to those of us on the networking side of the aisle. In fact, the mission of this chapter is to present several of the most important Performance Monitor counters that apply to managing your Windows NT Server network. Developers are advised to consult the Windows NT Server 4.0 Software Developer Kit (SDK) for more information about the appropriate use of Performance Monitor counters vis-à-vis application development.

Performance Monitor basics

Most of us know Performance Monitor as an X/Y coordinate graphing application that's kinda fun. But Performance Monitor is much more than that. If all ever you wanted were pretty charts, you can reach that small victory in a variety of Microsoft "front office" applications like Excel, PowerPoint, or even Word. For example, you could use Excel to chart the number of users on your network and possibly dupe your superiors into increasing your networking budget because your chart shows the number of users growing. That might work in the smallest of companies, but serious performance analysis requires serious use of Performance Monitor. But more on that in a moment. First, let's discuss the basics.

Performance Monitor is launched as an application from the Administrative Tools group. It can also be launched from the command line by typing **PERFMON** at the command prompt. Performance Monitor works with objects, counters, and instances (see Figure 22-3). An *object* is a major system area (like Memory or Disk) or an application that reports to Performance Monitor (Microsoft SQL Server, Microsoft Exchange, or the like). A *counter* is a specific subset of an object. Objects typically have many counters. Counters are discrete items that can be measured. For example, the memory counter has over 28 counters ranging from % Committed Bytes in Use to Write Copies/sec. Counters have explanations as shown at the bottom of the dialog box. *Instances* are the occurrence of multiple items. For example, if you have three hard disks, you will have three instances plus a _TOTAL instance that enables you to summarize the three instances (in this example). The syntax of objects, counters, and instances is *object:counter:instance*.

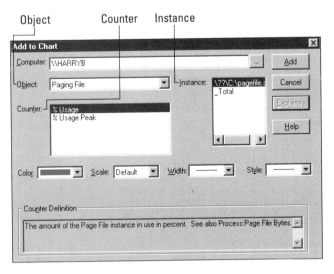

Figure 22-3: Objects, counters, and instances

Secret

Be sure to click the Explain button in the Add to Chart dialog box when adding a counter to a chart. A text field will appear at the bottom of the dialog box that, in sufficient detail, describes each counter. The Microsoft developer who added this feature is a candidate for sainthood in my book!

Six quick steps to using Performance Monitor

Although I assume you are already armed with the user manuals for Windows NT Server 4.0, I'll quickly detail the process for using Performance Monitor. I highly recommend you study the Windows NT Server 4.0 user manuals to better acquaint yourself with basic Performance Monitor feature sets, such as opening and saving files.

Step 1: Select a view

Select the view in Performance Monitor that will work for you. If you are new to Performance Monitor, I'd recommend you start with the Chart view and work up to mastering and using the Log view. In the real world, I haven't found the Alert view or the Report view to be as meaningful.

Step 2: Add objects

Add the appropriate objects, counters, and instances that you want to monitor. When you launch Performance Monitor, you can suffer from what I call the "blank spreadsheet" syndrome. You know the affliction, as you stare at (blank) cell A1 on a spreadsheet and can't think of anything to type. When Performance Monitor starts, the first thing you see is a chart (the default view) with basically nothing but y-axis values from zero to 100. You will need "populate" the Performance Monitor view that you selected. If you are logging, you will select objects. After completing the logging, you will typically chart the individual counters from your selection of logged objects. If you are just charting data, you will select an object followed by one or more counters.

Step 3: Configure

Configure Performance Monitor by setting the time measurement interval, scaling, and so on. Properly configuring Performance Monitor is critical; it is the foundation of your analysis house. A bad foundation could skew your analysis in unfavorable or embarrassing ways.

Setting time intervals

The default time interval for logging is 15 seconds. There are compelling reasons to change this value. Microsoft certification candidates will often change the time interval to one second in order to quickly generate a large data set to complete labs. At large Windows NT Server sites it is common to set the default time interval to 600 seconds because creating a data point every ten minutes is acceptable for analysis purposes. When setting the time interval, just remember it depends on your needs.

Scaling

Given that many of us in the networking profession do not have advanced degrees in operations research and quantitative analysis, the scaling feature for counters in the Chart view can be perplexing. Essentially, you are trying to show a proportional relationship between different object:counters. You typically want to center information on the chart so you can easily detect correlations between the counters you are measuring. If you change a system setting or add another component, you can see how the relationship changes between the counters you are measuring. If these counters are centered on your chart, then sit back and enjoy being spoon fed!

Centering

Suppose you would like to see the relationship between Memory:Available Bytes (Memory is the object, Available Bytes is the counter) and Processor:% Processor Time. And if we assume that you use your Windows NT Server primarily as a file and print server, than we can safely assume that you typically have lots of available bytes of RAM and a low % Processor Time value, as seen in Figure 22-4 (note the default scale is set to 1.0 for the Processor:% Processor Time counter and 0.0000100 for the Memory: Available Bytes counter).

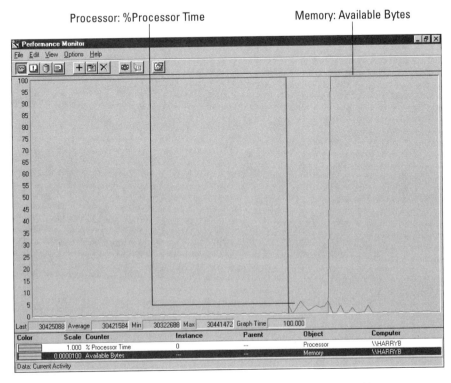

Figure 22-4: Charting Memory:Available Bytes and Processor:% Processor Time

This chart is not super-meaningful from an quantitative analysis perspective because the two counters are charted at different ends of the vertical axis. Now if we modify the scale on Memory:Available Bytes from 0.0000100 to 0.00000100, this counter is charted in the center of the screen, allowing us to extrapolate a much clearer relationship between Memory:Available Bytes and Processor:% Processor Time (see Figure 22-5).

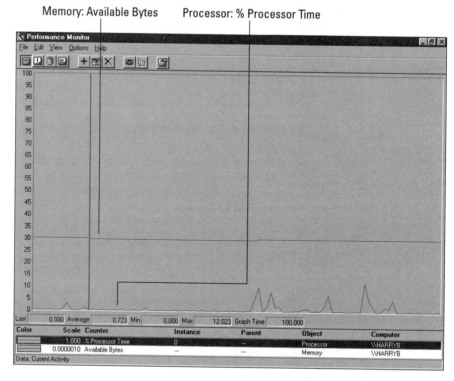

Figure 22-5: Centering the Memory: Available Bytes and Processor:% Processor Time

Learning chart scaling

To learn more about scaling, you can take either of two paths. First, trial and error. Adjust the scaling for different counters to create a chart that is meaningful and easy to interpret. Then freeze these scaling settings for a period of time. Do the relationships look meaningful? Should you change the scaling of one counter to better position it on the chart and demonstrate its relationship to other counters being charted? In a few weeks and after several implementations, you will be a pro at chart scaling.

Secret

The second path to learning more about scaling is to use the Performance Monitor workspaces included with several Microsoft BackOffice applications. The best BackOffice Performance Monitor workspaces I've seen ship with Microsoft Exchange and Microsoft SQL Server. By learning from the Performance Monitor workspaces that Microsoft ships with its BackOffice applications, you are learning directly from the source. And the charts ain't bad lookin' either!

If you have any Microsoft BackOffice applications such as Microsoft Exchange or Microsoft SQL Server, now is a good time to look at the Performance Monitor file created to monitor these respective applications. You may find these files either on the Microsoft BackOffice CD-ROM (by searching on *.pmw with the Windows NT Server 4.0 Find command) or, better yet, if these applications are installed, in the Applications program group (from the desktop Start menu).

Now is also a good time for you to consider saving your Performance Monitor configuration that you have created as a workspace file (*.pmw). That way you can recall this Performance Monitor scenario by simply opening your workspace file.

Step 4: Commence data collection

Next, commence the data collection process so that you can build that data set! In the Chart view, data points are taken as soon as a counter is pasted on the chart. With logging, you will need to start the logging process.

Step 5: Terminate the data collection process

After sufficient data points have been taken, you can terminate the data collection process. This primarily applies to the logging function. We don't want to have our data log file grow forever, so we terminate logging after a set amount of time.

Step 6: Interpret the results

Now the fun really begins. Collecting the data is meaningless unless we interpret it. Thus we spend a great deal of time at this stage, trying to assess where our Windows NT Server–based system is today and where it is headed. Essentially we are looking for trends over time. This topic is covered in much greater detail later in the chapter in the "Collecting Data" and "Making Better Use Of Performance Monitor" sections. You will also recall that trend analysis was discussed in Chapter 21, "Analyzing and Boosting Performance."

The Four Faces of Performance Monitor

Performance Monitor has four views: Chart, Alert, Log, and Report. I discuss each view, but I would be remiss if I didn't share with you that I primarily utilize the Log and Chart views. I have had little real-world need for the Alert and Report views.

Chart

Data is displayed as lines or a histogram. This is what I call the medical view. Whereas medical doctors have EKG machines to closely monitor a patient's heartbeat, we have the Chart view in Performance Monitor to monitor the health, both in real time and when reviewing logged data, of our servers and network. I've always felt really important when viewing these charts, much like a cardiologist looking at EKG reports being generated by a heart attack patient. The Chart view is easily the most interesting view and one that even noncomputer types can get excited about.

Within the Chart view, data points can be displayed as a line graph or a histogram. This election is made in the Chart Option dialog box found via the Chart menu option under the Options drop-down menu. Test the display of your counters to see whether the line graph or histogram best reflects the counter's meaning. You will find many counters are best displayed as a histogram chart (see Figure 22-6), but many Performance Monitor users never invoke that approach on charts, since the line graph is the default.

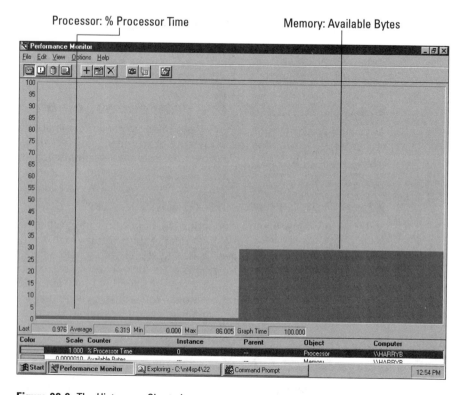

Figure 22-6: The Histogram Chart view

Secret

Always use histogram charting in cases where the data would traditionally be displayed as a pie chart. You will recall that pie charts are drawn to show how individual slices total 100 percent. We can do the same with histograms when comparing the _Total instance of a counter against the individual counters that make up the Total instance (or sum to 100 percent). Note that this why Figure 22-6 is presented as a histogram chart.

Alert

Properly configured, the Alert view enables you to set triggers and conditions that generate alerts when certain boundaries or thresholds are met or surpassed. Alerts can be configured on a per counter (or parameter) basis or more generically.

STEPS:
To configure alerts on an individual or per-counter basis

Step 1. From the View menu, select Alert.

Step 2. From the Edit menu, select Add to Alert (see Figure 22-7).

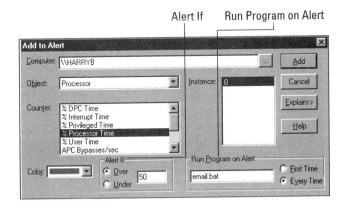

Figure 22-7: Add to Alert

Step 3. Select the appropriate computer, object, and counter for the alert.

Step 4. Select your Alert If condition ("Alert If Over 50%").

Step 5. Complete the Run Program on Alert field and whether such a program should run the First Time or Every Time. Here you might create a batch file that runs when an alert condition is met.

Step 6. To configure Alerts generically, complete the options in the Alert Options dialog box found when selecting the Alert menu item under the Options menu (see Figure 22-8).

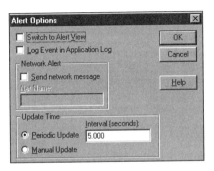

Figure 22-8: Alert Options

Because the Alert options are check boxes, it is possible to select Switch to Alert View, Log Event in Application Log and send a network message to a specific computer based on its NetBIOS name.

Secret

It is not necessary to use traditional Universal Naming Convention (UNC) naming when completing the Net Name field. The NetBIOS name is sufficient.

You can configure the Alert view in Performance Monitor to electronically page you when certain alert conditions occur — such as every time processor utilization exceeds 90 percent. To do this, you would create a batch file that sends e-mail to you when this condition is met. You would then configure your e-mail service to page you when you receive this type of e-mail. I've seen this accomplished with third-party e-mail/pager services such as Message Flash.

Secret

Running Performance Monitor as a service enables you to log data without being logged onto the system. I'd highly recommend you consider running Performance Monitor in this fashion when creating your baseline and logging data (see the "Baseline" discussion later in the chapter). That's because I once found myself trying repeatedly to collect a week of baseline data, via the Performance Monitor logging feature, for a small software developer. I dutifully started logging system data via Performance Monitor on Monday, planning to return the following Monday to review a huge Performance Monitor log.

Upon my return, however, I noticed that Performance Monitor logging had stopped the previous Tuesday evening, a mere 28 hours into a planned full week of logging. What happened? Not knowing exactly at the time, I tried again. A week later I returned, again hoping to see my a large Performance Monitor log. Egads! It happened again. Somehow the logging stopped on the previous Wednesday afternoon, a mere two days into a planned seven-day logging run. Well, it finally dawned on me! Performance Monitor was running as a Windows NT Server application. Performance Monitor stopped when an employee (or "elf" as the client claimed) logged off the current local user of the Windows NT Server machine. As you know, applications terminate when users log off locally from Windows NT Server. Equally important, applications do not automatically restart when users log on locally at the Windows NT Server machine or when Windows NT Server reboots after an unexpected power outage (say one late Sunday evening).

Thankfully, services run whether a user is logged on locally or not. Services start when Windows NT Server boots without requiring a user logon. Sounds like a great way to reliability and securely run Performance Monitor on your Windows NT Server as a service. Here's how you do it.

STEPS:
To run Performance Monitor as a service on your Windows NT server

Step 1. Take two utilities (MONITOR.EXE and DATALOG.EXE) from the Windows NT Resource Kit CD-ROM and place them in the <winroot>\system32 directory. Note the Windows NT Resource Kit CD-ROM contains multiple copies of both utilities under the appropriate directory for each hardware platform (such as Intel and Alpha). Be sure to select the correct platform directory when you copy these tools to your server (believe you me, copying the correct file from the wrong platform directory can wreak total havoc on your Windows NT Server installation). Note that DATALOG.EXE is the Monitor service and MONITOR.EXE is used to configure DATALOG.EXE as a service.

Step 2. Type the following at the command prompt: **monitor setup**. After you execute the command, your screen, as shown on Figure 22-9, will display title, copyright, and version information (Performance Data Logging Service Configuration Tool, Copyright 1994, Microsoft Corporation, Version 1.0 <94.05.04>). At this point you will know that DATALOG has been successfully installed as a service. You may receive the following screen message "Service is set to use the following configuration file: No configuration file." This simply means that you haven't specified a Performance Monitor configuration file (a.k.a. "workspace file" — a file created when you save your workspace settings in Performance Monitor).

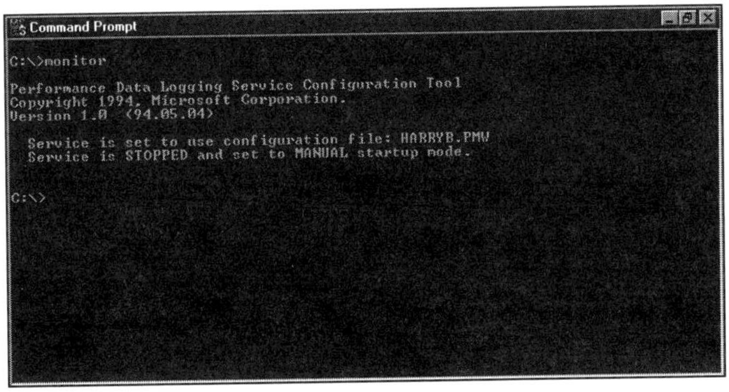

Figure 22-9: The Monitor Setup command

By default, the Monitor service is stopped and set to manual startup mode.

In Table 22-1, I present the possible command line switches you might use with MONITOR.EXE so that this tool ultimately works for you, not vice-versa.

Table 22-1 MONITOR.EXE Command Line Switches

Switch Commands	Description
Setup	The following key is added to the Registry: HKEY_LOCAL_MACHINE\SYSTEM\CurrentControlSet\Services\Monitor. DATALOG.EXE is added as a service.
<filename>	Service is set to use a specific Performance Monitor configuration file (filename.pmw, a Performance Monitor workspace file). Note the value "Setting File" is added to the Monitor Registry key (defined previously). It is a REG_SZ data type.
Start	Starts the service.
Stop	Stops the service.
Pause	Pauses the service and logging is terminated.
Continue	The service is restarted and logging resumes.
Automatic	The service is configured to start automatically at boot time.
Manual	The service must be manually started.
Disable	The service is disabled and monitor-related commands are ignored.

Note all MONITOR commands are preceded with the required term MONITOR and the optional command line term (such as those contained in the preceding table).

You can also manage the Monitor service (and implicitly DATALOG.EXE) via the Services dialog box accessed from Control Panel (see Figure 22-10). I would highly recommend this approach instead of the command line method just described.

The Monitor service would be started, stopped, and configured (automatically or manually) just like any other service. The Monitor service is automatically and dynamically added to the Services dialog box (without having to reboot). Note you would use the Startup Parameters field in the Service dialog box to specify any of the previously described command switches. An example of this might be the a Performance Monitor workspace file titled baseline.pmw. You would enter baseline.pmw in the Startup Parameters field. Be sure to include the full path for the *.pmw file so the service can find it (unless you place it in a directory that is explicitly listed in the search path statement).

Chapter 22: Performance Monitor

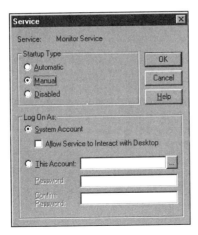

Figure 22-10: Managing the Monitor service via the Service dialog box

To display your directory search path at any time, type **path** at the command line to see which directories are included in the search path (see Figure 22-11). This is just like the old MS-DOS days.

Figure 22-11: The path statement at the command line

The *.pmw file you plan to use with the Monitor service should be configured for logging. It really doesn't make sense to configure such a file for charting real-time data (such activity is not shown on the screen if Performance Monitor is run as a service).

One action that can be performed at the command line and not via the Service dialog box in Control Panel is to start and stop the Monitor service at specific times. To accomplish such a feat, you would use the AT command. This is very handy when logging Performance Monitor data during working hours but not evenings and nights when many Windows NT Server systems experience much less activity. Arguably, the logged Performance Monitor data would be meaningless (plus you would be the proud papa of a huge log file at the end of the week!). Two variations of the AT command under this scenario at your local server are:

```
AT 18:00 "monitor start"
AT 7:00 "monitor stop"
```

The Monitor service would stop at 6:00 P.M., when most users are typically headed home and restart the next morning at 7:00 A.M., when users begin arriving at work.

Log

What appears to be the "driest" aspect of performance monitor, logging, is actually one of the most powerful. It is in the Log view (see Figure 22-12) that you configure Performance Monitor to capture data in a semi-binary/semi-delimited file that can be used for performance analysis. The log files you create and save to disk will enable you to detect bottlenecks and the causes of declining system performance.

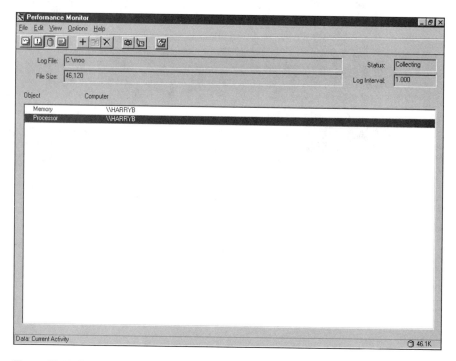

Figure 22-12: Log view

Report

The Report view (see Figure 22-13) displays counters with their current values. Averaged counters display the average value during the time measurement interval (known as the *time window*). Instantaneous counters display ending values that are recorded at the end of the time measurement interval.

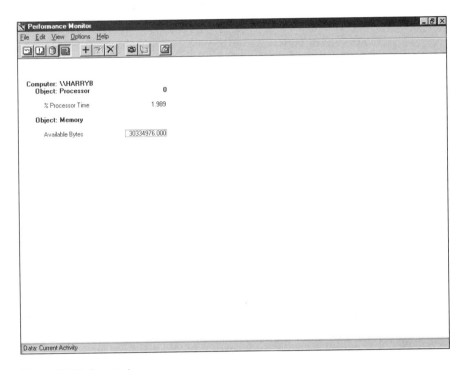

Figure 22-13: Report view

Data Collection and Interpretation

I've heard it expressed the following way by a U.S. Ski Team member who I had the good fortune to know: "Getting out the door is the hardest step; the rest is duck soup." While this individual was referring to cross-country ski training, the same analogy can be applied to using Performance Monitor.

You would be amazed how many of my students from the MOC #689 — "Supporting Microsoft Windows NT 4.0" — Enterprise Technology course learn much about Performance Monitor but then, back at work, don't even launch it. Why is it? I'm not sure, but clearly, launching Performance Monitor from the Administrative Tools (Common) program group is the difficult part; the rest is duck soup.

Collecting data

Collecting data is obviously a critical step that must be performed correctly to ensure valid and meaningful analysis. Here are some suggested steps for you to follow so that your data is collected properly.

Creating a baseline

You might question the value of proactively collecting data when nothing is wrong. You might say, "Don't we already have enough data in this world" and "I'm trying to reduce the data I collect." Well, do a 180-degree turn. Collecting data proactively before system performance issues emerge gives you the easiest, cheapest, and cleanest data you will ever collect. If you start your data collection once system performance problems appear, you are looking at a dance with dirty data. That is because you have no baseline that can be compared against your current predicament. A baseline is created by capturing system-related information early in the life cycle of the system. This baseline is the basis from which all future comparisons are made. It's similar to your dental records. Your early records provide the baseline information that all future dentists will use to track your dental progress. And further, your Performance Monitor baseline and subsequent data can be used by pathologists to help determine your system's cause of death (should it die prematurely).

Secret

Change the default time interval in Performance Monitor from 15 seconds to 600 seconds for your baseline data collection. Observing a data point every ten minutes is sufficient for baseline analysis. Plus longer time intervals will dramatically reduce the size of your baseline data file. Just by collecting the objects I recommend next, you arrange that each data point adds approximately 30K to 50K to the size of your baseline data file. Even with this time interval recommendation, you will have a very large data file at the end of your monitoring period (especially if you perform a 7-day, 24 hours per day baseline capture).

Now is a good time to become familiar with the time interval setting in Performance Monitor. Consider the following exercise: Start one Performance Monitor session and chart the default object: counter (Processor:% Processor Utilization) at the default time interval. Launch a second version of Performance Monitor and, using the same object:counter, set the interval to 600 seconds. Let both of these Performance Monitor sessions run for an hour, and then compare the results. Did the longer interval of 600 seconds help or hinder the "trendline" associated with processor utilization activity? You be the judge.

Tip

I would highly recommend you consider storing your Performance Monitor data files on a removable hard disk. That way you don't use precious secondary storage. Plus, if you are a Windows NT Server consultant, you can take the removable hard drive back to the office and analyze your client's data on your own system. In fact, you can build a library of removable drives that hold client performance data. That's something your clients will appreciate in case of fire or flood. You will directly benefit from building a such a reference library because you can then easily compare the performance of one client site against the performance of another client site.

Suggested baseline objects to capture

You must select objects to create your baseline capture (see Table 22-2). The counters associated with these objects will be viewed at a future point in time using the Chart or Report view. In addition to defining these core objects that should be captured as part of your baseline, I've rated these counters according to whether you are a beginner, power, expert user, or a super-engineer. This rating should help you understand how the object applies to you. Note this is a generic object rating that I've created based on my research and experience. Individual counters within these objects may have significantly different ratings.

Table 22-2   Core Objects to Capture via Performance Monitor Logging

Object	Description	User-Level
Cache	Primary memory area that typically holds such items as recently used documents and file pages, data. This is analogous to cache memory found in NetWare-based servers. Caching file pages dramatically improves access time (no secondary storage activity!).	Power User
Logical Disk	Logical views of disk space including disk partitions. This is how you analyze performance matters relating to contiguous secondary storage. A logical disk is assigned a drive letter.	Beginner
Memory	This object enables you to analyze performance matters relating to real memory. Includes both primary (RAM) and virtual (paging file) memory.	Beginner
Network Segment	This object provides the ability to monitor network activity on the specific cable segment on which the Windows NT Server machine is located. The counters are similar to the measurement tools provide in Network Monitor. This object is added when the Network Monitor Agent service is added to your Windows NT Server.	Beginner
Network Interface	Includes counters that measure bytes and packets sent and received by the network adapter card on a TCP/IP network. This object is added when install the SNMP service on your Windows NT Server (assuming you are using the TCP/IP protocol).	Power User
Objects	Relates to system software objects. Windows NT Server has an object view of the world and sees active system components as objects. Objects have properties and are subject to access control restrictions imposed by Windows NT Server security. Each object steals memory to store basic object information. Therein lies the concern — how much memory are objects stealing?	Beginner

Continued

Table 22-2 *(continued)*

Object	Description	User-Level
Physical Disk	Secondary storage such as hard disks, RAID arrays. Will contain at least one (and likely more) logical partitions.	Beginner
Process	A software object that is an active or running program. A process is created when a user application or a Windows NT Server service is run.	Beginner
Processor	The central processing unit (CPU). Given that Windows NT Server has a scalable architecture, this object can measure multiple CPUs. Multiple CPUs are considered instances when you are viewing a specific counter associated with this object.	Beginner
Redirector	This is the object that manages network connections between your computer and other computers.	Beginner
Server Work Queues	Essentially contain counters used to measure processor congestion on your Windows NT Server. Also used to measure how "busy" your server is in terms of sending and receiving bytes from network clients.	Power User
System	Counters to measure activity on system hardware and software. For example, the System Uptime counter measures (in seconds) the total time that Windows NT Server has been running since the last reboot. This object includes many counters that apply to all of the processor activity on the computer.	Beginner
Thread	Is the basic unit of execution. Every running process contains one or more threads. Multiple threads within a process mean multithreading.	Beginner
Others	This includes specific objects related to applications such as SQL Server and Exchange. Developers are encouraged to write Performance Monitor objects to provide application-specific monitoring capabilities. To analyze the protocols discussed later in this chapter, you need to collect these additional objects: NetBEUI, NWLink IPX, TCP, UDP.	Beginner to Super Engineer

Secret

Be sure to turn on those disk counters at the command line! That's diskperf –y for normal hard disks and diskperf –ye for disk-related fault-tolerant scenarios such as software-based RAID and mirroring. The command diskperf –ye is used when the Ftdisk driver is being used (look at the Device Control Panel to see if this is the case). Note that hardware-based RAID implementations, common on high-end servers from Compaq, HP, and others, would *not* use the diskperf –ye command. That is because hardware-based disk arrays appear as a single contiguous form of secondary storage to Windows NT Server, not an array.

The disk counter diskperf is necessary for the Physical Disk and Logical Disk counters to function. It is interesting to note that Microsoft did not turn on disk counters by default because of the two percent performance decline experienced on older machines (including Intel 386-based machines, the original minimum supported platform for Windows NT Server). On new machines, running diskperf is not a great concern.

Adding to your baseline

Additional data collection activity should occur on a regular basis during the life of your Windows NT Server system. You might collect baseline data weekly if you are a large organization or monthly if you are a smaller organization. There are two ways to collect additional data: log to a new Performance Monitor data file or add to the existing Performance Monitor baseline data file. The choice is yours. By creating a new log file, you discreetly separate the time periods that the data was collected. Plus you can more easily observe the data by tiling the Performance Monitor chart of the updated data against a chart of the baseline data. See my comments near the end of the chapter regarding running two Performance Monitor sessions.

Creating a new baseline

Don't forget to create new baseline measurements when significant additions or subtractions are made to the system. What is the rule for starting a new baseline measurement? Think of it as Economics 101 and the demand curve. Normal activity is reflected by movements up and down the demand curve (such as when product prices are dear, or demand is less). This is analogous to day-to-day system operations. However, in economics, when the fundamental or underlying relationship between consumer and product changes, there is a shift in the demand curve (such as when the introduction of new technology redefines the product). So think of a shift in the demand curve in economics as an event that's analogous to creating a new baseline measurement in Performance Monitor. Such major events might include:

- **A server upgrade to a new, more powerful server.** Obviously your old baseline data, based on the older server, won't be meaningful when compared against system data collected by the newer, more powerful server.

- **Additional servers.** Suppose you keep your existing server that has performed your Performance Monitoring activities for some period of time, but you add new servers to your site to take over certain functions. A great example of this is Microsoft System Management Server (SMS). Small sites often deploy SMS using a primary domain controller (PDC) running both SMS and Microsoft SQL Server. That's a BackOffice combination that's guaranteed to strain servers under the most ideal conditions (see Figure 22-14). Assuming you collected your baseline data under this scenario, and then you acquired another two servers to spread the SMS/SQL Server load, it's now time to create a new Performance Monitor baseline measurement. In an SMS environment, Microsoft recommends that the PDC be used strictly for such activities as authentication and replication. We assume the two new servers would run SMS and SQL Server respectively. The original baseline data is no longer meaningful when compared to any future performance data collected on your PDC. Thus the need to create a new baseline.

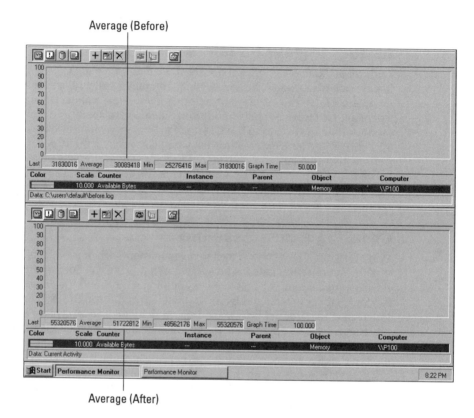

Figure 22-14: Top window: Original Windows NT Server running Microsoft SMS and SQL Server. Bottom window: Same server not running Microsoft SMS or SQL Server

- **Major Capital Additions.** From an accounting view, we might consider creating a new baseline when we make significant capital additions to our network. For example, adding an expensive switch might forever alter (err — improve) the performance of your network. Such an addition might render your original baseline meaningless.

Interpreting your data

Not surprisingly, capturing baseline data via Performance Monitor logging is the easy part. The difficult part is analyzing the data. Therein lie the basics of quantitative analysis. Follow this discussion, you will be a master Windows NT Server analyzer before you know it!

Logged data captured by Performance Monitor isn't very useful alone. You must chart the counters contained within the objects, and in many cases, specific instances within the counters. Plus for really meaningful performance analysis you must have a solid data set, taken as samples over time. When all of these dimensions are in place, you can conduct serious data interpretation. For example, many of the object:counters to be described speak toward adequate system performance as a function of primary memory (RAM). When tracked over time, and when a valid baseline exists, you can easily determine at what point your system's performance took a nosedive (about the time you started using SQL Server for more purposes than serving as a data repository for SMS).

Don't underestimate your simplest, and in many ways, most important data interpreter. I'm speaking about the kind that talks back—end users. While end users will quickly bring system performance matters to your attention, the business manager in all of us knows this is perhaps your most expensive form of system performance analysis: end users not doing their jobs efficiently and complaining about the computer system to you. Isn't it better to proactively manage your system via performance analysis with Performance Monitor than via disgruntled end users?

Table 22-3 depicts a "quick and dirty" guide to analyzing your Performance Monitor log. I recommend you chart these items for the best viewing. Once that is accomplished, you will have a quick view of the health of your Windows NT Server and network.

Table 22-3 Quick and Dirty Analysis

Object	Counter	User Level
Cache	Data Map Hits %	Super-Engineer
Logical Disk	Avg. Disk Queue Length	Beginner
Memory	Pages/sec	Beginner
Network Interface	Bytes Total/sec (for TCP/IP with SNMP counters installed)	Power User
Objects	Processes	Beginner
Physical Disk	Avg. Disk Queue Length	Beginner
Processor	% Processor Time	Beginner
System	% Total Processor Time	Beginner
Redirector	Bytes Total/sec	Beginner
Server	Bytes Total/sec	Beginner

Here is a description (in English to the extent possible) of object:counters.

Cache:Data Map Hits %

This is an advanced counter oriented toward the super-engineers who want to know the percentage of data maps in cache memory that were resolved without calling out to secondary storage to retrieve a page. In simple terms, the system found the page in primary storage. This is a good value to monitor over time, allowing you to determine if your system needs more primary storage (RAM).

Logical Disk:Avg. Disk Queue Length

This reflects the number of requests outstanding over the time measurement interval. Basically this refers to read and write requests awaiting service. This is a great value to track over time and enables you to determine how your hard disk is performing. If this value grows, your hard disk performance is declining. The instance you select is on a drive letter basis (each instance is a partition). Note that the time measurement interval is set under the Option menu in Performance Monitor. Select the Chart Options menu item and change the Interval (seconds) setting in the Update Time portion of the dialog box (see Figure 22-15).

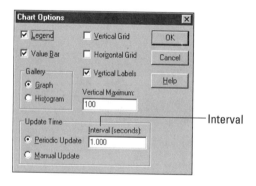

Figure 22-15: Modifying the interval setting

Memory:Pages/sec

Basically this object:counter is used to determine if you have a memory shortage. This is an excellent object:counter to track over time, as you can pinpoint deterioration (as a function of memory problems) in your system's performance if this counter value increases. Technically speaking, this counter measures the number of pages read to or written from secondary storage (disk) when Windows NT Server couldn't find the requested information in primary memory (RAM). This is an important counter to monitor to see if your system is generating too many hard page faults (having to go out and retrieve information from secondary storage). In surfer lingo (ocean surfing, not Web surfing), this counter is used to measure thrashing (excessive memory pressure).

Network Interface:Bytes Total/sec

This refers to the number of bytes per second that were sent and received by the Network Interface. Here we are basically observing activity at layer one of the Open Systems Interconnection (OSI) Model (see Figure 22-16). Layer one of the OSI model is known as the physical layer. In essence, this object:counter measures how busy your network interface card is, and it should be tracked over time. Analyzing this counter would enable you to determine that you need to add extra items such as another NIC card. Note that this value is selected by instance (with the instance being your adapters). Note also that this counter assumes you are using TCP/IP with the SNMP service installed (the SNMP adds several additional TCP/IP-related counters to Performance Monitor).

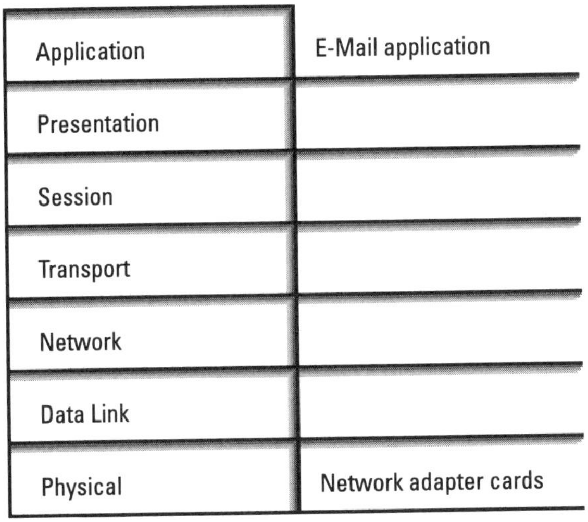

Application	E-Mail application
Presentation	
Session	
Transport	
Network	
Data Link	
Physical	Network adapter cards

Figure 22-16: The OSI model

Objects:Processes

This reflects the number of programs running at the moment the measurement is taken. Technically speaking, it is the number of processes running on the computer when the data was collected. But don't forget that each process is essentially a program.

Secret

This value can also be calculated manually by adding up the "Image Names" in the Process tab sheet in the Task Manager dialog box.

Physical Disk:Avg. Disk Queue Length

This is similar in meaning to the Logical Disk:Avg. Disk Queue Length just described. The primary difference is that the instance category lists your physical disk(s).

Processor:% Processor Time

This object:counter reflects how busy the processor is. This is selected by instance (individual processors). Think of this object:counter as the percentage (or fraction) of time the processor is accomplishing meaningful work. Technically, this counter measures non-Idle threads (threads where meaningful work is being accomplished). Remember that Idle threads are run when no meaningful work awaits the processor (analogous to treading water in swimming!). If this value is over 75 percent on a long-term basis (measured in days and weeks), the processor is a bottleneck and should be upgraded.

If indeed the processor is a bottleneck, you can bank on the following strategies:

- **Application server.** Add multiple processors. Assuming Windows NT Server is being used as an application server, the applications that are running locally on the server are consuming significant processor time. Given Windows NT Servers symmetrical multiprocessing (SMP) architecture, you will directly benefit by adding multiple processors and having the processor load spread over several processors.

- **File and print server.** Those with NetWare backgrounds know that file and print servers typically have lower processor utilization rates than application servers. I've seen many NetWare server with processor utilization rates hovering near zero percent! That is because the file and print server is not doing anything (literally). However, assuming you experience a processor bottleneck, as measured by Processor:% Processor Time when using Windows NT Server as a file and print server, then you need to add a faster processor.

- **Multiple servers.** Windows NT Server 4.0 Enterprise Edition ushers in a new era of clustering technology (see Figure 22-17). Clustering can free up the processor on a single server. Essentially the processor load is distributed over multiple Windows NT Servers. Not ready to implement Windows NT Server–based clustering yet? Then offload some of your processes to other servers (a great BackOffice example is to place Systems Management Server on one server and SQL Server on another server).

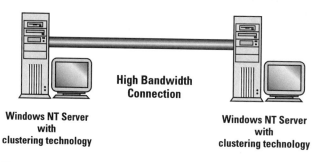

Figure 22-17: Windows NT Server clustering

System:% Total Processor Time

This reflects total time usage over all processors. Obviously, on a single processor machine, this value can't exceed 100 percent. On a multiple-processor machine, this value can easily exceed 100 percent (the mathematics for the maximum counter value on a multiple processor is variable A multiplied by 100 percent, where variable A is the total number of processors).

Redirector:Bytes Total/sec

Found in the middle to lower levels of the OSI model, the Redirector manages network connections between your computer and others on the network. This counter measures the rate that the Redirector is processing bytes. It is a measure of how busy your network-related components are (from the network adapter card up through the protocol stack).

Server:Bytes Total/sec

This relates to the Server service (a process that connects the local computer to network services). This is the rate that the server is sending and receiving bytes from the network. Thus, it is a measure of how busy the server is.

Now that you're armed with a few quick and dirty object counters for analysis at a glance, let's go "under the hood" of Performance Monitor and drill down into the details, by exploring more object:counters and performing analysis in different environments.

Performing In-Depth Analysis

Let's get down to the business of in-depth baseline performance analysis. Six areas are addressed: memory, processor, disk, network, analyzing protocols, and TCP/IP. Note I assume you have or will learn and use all of the counters discussed previously in the "quick and dirty" analysis section. I won't repeat the discussion of those counters here. Don't forget that the counters are best interpreted when analyzed over time, not from the perspective of a single snapshot.

Memory bottlenecks

Sometimes making money as a Windows NT Server consultant is too easy. That's because I often find myself recommending that more RAM be added to the server. Windows NT Server loves RAM, and adding RAM is something of an elixir for what ails your server. Snake oil salespeople aside, just adding more RAM isn't always possible because of budget constraints and possible physical constraints on the computer. Ask yourself — does the server have enough memory slots to add more memory without having to cannibalize your existing memory chips? The object counters that follow can be used to help you justify adding RAM to your server (and if you report to the CFO or Controller in your organization, you will want this type of quantitative analysis provided by Performance Monitor to justify your purchases!).

Secret

Besides just adding RAM to solve your memory bottlenecks, you can increase the size of your paging file if your secondary storage permits. In fact, Windows NT Server allows multiple paging files, but only one paging file can be on a given partition. And don't forget that you can boost overall Windows NT Server performance when you place at least one paging files on (a) partition(s) separate from the partition that the operating system is installed on.

Oh, I almost forgot the third rule of Windows NT Server memory bottleneck consulting (the first two being add more RAM and increase your paging file size). The third rule is to shut down unnecessary services and remove unnecessary protocols and drivers. Take services. On my Windows NT Server test machine, I was running Microsoft Exchange months after I had completed my need for this BackOffice application. However, several Microsoft Exchange services start automatically. Once I disabled the Microsoft Exchange services, I noticed a huge performance gain on my test server and my available memory climbed dramatically.

Trusting applications

Don't overlook the following question. How well do you trust your Windows NT Server applications? Many applications are memory incontinent (a.k.a. leaky apps). Poorly developed applications don't completely close out memory resources upon exit. An example of this would be a user who repeatedly opens and closes files in a word processing application. Soon, not all of the memory is recovered when the file is closed. And you have a leaky application!. The counters presented in the text that follows help you detect leaky apps. Of course once you discover a badly behaved leaky application, you are typically told to notify the appropriate application software developer that they have a leaky application and that it needs to be fixed. Big help that is in the heat of the moment. But at least you know which applications are going to give your system bad gas!

Note that two general trends to look for in detecting memory bottlenecks are how virtual memory is being used and hard page faults. Virtual memory resides on secondary storage and is thus much slower than memory in primary storage. Hard page faults occur when Windows NT Server can't find information in physical memory and has to perform a physical disk read operation.

Guns and butter memory management

Also, be cognizant of how the guns and butter law from economics is applied to Windows NT Server memory management. Guns and butter refers to an economic theorem wherein an economy can produce lots of guns or a lot of butter, but typically not a lot of both without production tradeoffs. In Windows NT Server memory management, this discussion applies to

Windows NT Server applications. We like our Windows NT Server–based applications to be efficient. So simply stated, we like our applications to use as little real memory as possible without having to page out to secondary storage to retrieve data. If an application uses too little real memory, it has to frequently retrieve data from secondary storage (a page out). However, if an application uses too much real memory, it hogs memory from other applications that might enjoy it. Note guns and butter has been renamed to stadiums and school in many cities that are struggling to keep their professional sport franchises and provide adequate educations for school children: Seattle and San Francisco, for example.

Memory:Available Bytes

This instantaneous counter measures the amount of available free memory. The Virtual Memory Manager in Windows NT Server tries to minimize the memory footprint of the operating system and processes so that it can provide the greatest amount of free memory available. Not surprisingly, we like this value to be high and to have a minimum of 8MB free. Anything below that amount and you might suffer excessive paging. In addition to adding RAM to solve problems here, you can attempt to find the process that is hogging all of the memory. See the next two counters to accomplish this.

Process:Working Set

One counter to use in your hunt for memory-hogging applications is the Process:Working Set object:counter for the instance you select (such as NOTEPAD.EXE). When the Working Set counter for NOTEPAD.EXE is high, the Available Bytes counter will be lower (these counters have an inverse relationship).

For a really cool view of the Process:Working Set counter, set the Chart view to histogram and add the _Total instance for this counter in addition to the specific application instances you are monitoring (see Figure 22-18). This view enables you to see how much working set memory the application is hogging relative to all working set memory for all applications and processes.

Note that a process's working set is the amount of physical memory that Windows NT Server has given it.

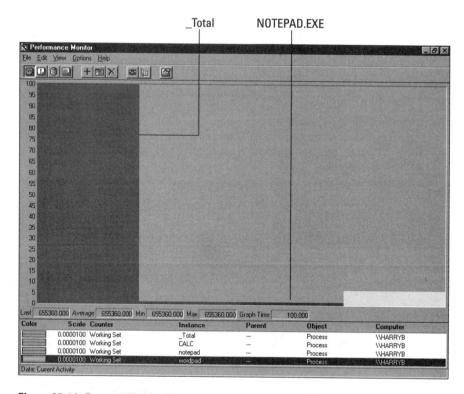

Figure 22-18: Process Working Set

Process:Page Faults/sec

Here is yet another counter used for detecting memory-hogging applications and processes. A bad application that can't get along with Windows NT Server's memory management model might well be causing a high rate of page faults (that is, retrieving data from secondary storage instead of caching frequently accessed data in real memory). To detect such an offender, select this counter and the appropriate instance (such as WORDPAD.EXE). Chart the _TOTAL instance and display this scenario as a histogram chart.

Secret

An easy and informal way to detect your memory-hogging applications is to use Task Manager and view the Processes tab sheet. Visually scan the list for which processes are using the most memory. Take notes and periodically revisit this tab sheet to reevaluate. Be advised that this is a very informal approach that might not meet your needs.

Memory:Committed Bytes

This is an easy definition. This counter refers to the amount of virtual memory that is committed as opposed to reserved. The commitment can be to physical RAM or pagefile space. This memory is unavailable for other purposes. We like to see this counter value remain low.

Memory:Pool Non-paged Bytes

Remember how system-critical activities can't be paged out to virtual memory? Then this is the counter for you! Basically, critical operating system components accomplish their tasks in this memory area. We like this counter value to remain stable.

Process:Page File Bytes

This counter, with the _Total instance selected, enables you to witness the dramatic growth that occurs in page file size when there is a memory shortage. Be sure to chart this as a line in Performance Monitor and watch that positive slope once you hit a severe system memory shortage!

Memory:Pages/sec is a very important counter for this area and was defined early in the "quick and dirty" analysis section.

Now is a good time to launch Performance Monitor and create a chart with the seven counters just listed. Run this session for at least a day and see if you can, at a glance, observe some of the behaviors previously discussed regarding memory consumption. Of course as part of this exercise, I assume that you are using your server for ordinary and necessary activities (that is, generating some form of system activity) to make this exercise meaningful.

Feeling sadistic? Then set the MAXMEM parameter on your friends' Windows NT Server boot.ini file to reduce the amount of available physical memory. Watch people squirm when they can't figure out why performance has dropped so fast since the last reboot. The syntax is /MAXMEM=24 if you want to restrict Windows NT Server to 24MB of RAM. This parameter is placed on the multi() operating system selection line. Ah, this stunt brings back memories of short-sheeting fellow campers in my youth during summer camp in the Texas hill country. Of course use this Secret in good faith. Hey — maybe spring this exercise as an advanced job interview "hands-on" test for a superstar Windows NT Server systems engineer. See if the candidate can detect the cause of the memory shortage.

Processor bottlenecks

Processor bottlenecks are not as common as you think. But that doesn't sell well on Madison Avenue, where ad agencies lead many of us to believe the latest Intel processor will solve all our problems. While this discussion on processor bottlenecks is important, take it with a grain of salt. Looking for a processor bottleneck is where we arrive at in performance analysis, not where we start. In the words of Deepak Chopra, the New Age guru, it is the journey of discovery that is important. The rule is, don't assume you have a processor bottleneck. Discover you have a processor bottleneck.

In fact, the great challenge you face is to recognize a processor bottleneck. Keep in mind when studying the counters that follow that it's critical you run the Performance Monitor logging function during busy times. For larger organizations, you can probably justify 7 × 24 logging periods. For smaller organizations that basically adhere to 40-hour workweeks, consider using the AT command to automatically start and stop your Performance Monitor logging during working hours.

Secret

As a processor bottleneck sleuth, look for the likely suspects. These include CPU-bound applications as well as processes, drivers, and interrupts. CPU-bound applications are processor utilization hogs. You know the ones, like the slide show feature in the Microsoft PowerPoint application. Have you ever been giving a speech to a group using a Microsoft PowerPoint slide show and hotkeyed over to another application to demo (say SQL Server). Were you disappointed with the speed at which the other application ran? Congratulations. You've just met a CPU-bound application and it's taking advantage of your processor. Another problem is excessive interrupts from faulty hardware or a good old fashioned IRQ conflict between hardware devices.

Memory problems have a tricky way of hiding behind high processor use. Add more RAM to your Windows NT Server and you will often see your processor time drop dramatically. That's because page faults are reduced.

Secret

Those dazzling screen savers that ship with Windows NT Server are really adding to your processor load when they run. Please do yourself a favor and don't use screen savers on your server. If you are concerned about your monitor suffering from screen burn, simply turn off the monitor when you aren't viewing it.

Processor: %Processor Time

The previous discussion on Processor:% Processor Time in the "quick and dirty" analysis applies to this discussion on processor bottlenecks. It is interesting to note that one of the great debates among network professionals today is what percentage of processor time is too high. In the Novell CNE program, you are taught that a sustained processor utilization rate in excess of 80 percent over a week (or greater period) suggests a processor bottleneck. Even Microsoft provides conflicting values. In the MCSE curriculum, certification candidates are instructed that a sustained %Processor Time value greater than 75 percent suggests a processor bottleneck. But the Microsoft Windows NT Workstation Resource Kit (for NT version 4.0) states that a frequently observed 90 percent value for the % Processor Time counter is a bottleneck. "Whattaeva" as they say back in Boston! Fact of the matter is that a sustained %Processor Value over 75 percent is going ultimately to be a source of trouble for you. And you guessed it. We like this counter value to stay low.

Processor:% Privileged Time

This is the time spent in Privileged mode running the NT service layer, NT Executive routines, and NT Kernel activity. These are active or nonidle threads. We desire a low counter value here.

Processor:% User Time

This is basically just opposite of the preceding counter. This is a way to view processor time (as a percentage) allocated to applications that are running and subsystem code that is executing. And let me take a moment to remind you that code executing in User mode *cannot* damage device drivers or the Windows NT Executive or Kernel. That's one of the things that makes Windows NT Server so special. We seek a low counter value when tracking Processor:% User Time.

Secret

Here is where you have one up on your NetWare brethren. Remember an NLM (application) running under NetWare can crash the NetWare network operating system. Windows NT Server–based applications cannot crash the Windows NT Server operating system because applications run in a subsystem in User mode.

Processor:Interrupts/sec

Simply stated, the processor is subject to device interrupts. This counter is the number of interrupts per second. This is the type of counter that will be valuable to monitor over time. Hopefully the counter value will remain at a consistent level.

System:Processor Queue Length

According to Microsoft, this is the instantaneous length of the processor queue in units of threads. Translated into English, this refers to queued threads that are waiting to be processed. If you are using a single-processor machine, then only one thread can be processed at a time by the processor. If more than two additional threads are queued, as measured by the object:counter, then you potentially have a processor bottleneck.

Server Work Queues:Queue Length

Requests made to the Windows NT Server are work items. While work items are waiting to be processed, they are queued. This object:counter is the length of that queue. If you observe a value greater than four over a sustained period of time, you are suffering from processor congestion. We want this counter value to remain low.

Process:% Processor Time

This object:counter is the elapsed time, expressed as a percentage (%), that all of the threads of a process used the processor to execute instructions. Note that you would pick a process to measure by selecting from the list of instances. Examples of instances include SQLEXEC (if you are running SQL Server) and NOTEPAD (if you are running the Notepad application). By selecting specific instances and monitoring them over time, you can observe if the process has become an unruly beast or if it is well behaved.

Thread:% Processor Time

This object:counter is the percentage of elapsed time that a thread used the processor to execute its instructions. To effectively use this command, you select one of the threads (in the Instance field in the Add to Chart dialog box in Performance Monitor). Examples of threads you might select would include thread zero if you are running Notepad (a single-threaded application) or any of threads zero to six if your are running the SQLEXEC process. This counter enables us to investigate unruly processes down to the thread level. Of course I would never admit to anyone that's how I spent my summer vacation!

Disk bottlenecks

Admit it, detecting disk bottlenecks was probably one of the first attempts at performance analysis that you undertook. You know the old trick from the Windows for Workgroups (WFW) 3.x days. You tiled two windows in File Manager and copied a large set of files from one hard disk to another. Then you turned on 32-bit disk access, restarted WFW, performed the same file copy exercise, and wowed your audience by showing a dramatic performance increase. It was a simple trick and a simple way to demonstrate disk bottlenecks. Today it's harder to repeat this exact trick because Windows NT Server only uses 32-bit disk access, eliminating a simple bottleneck culprit.

Secret

You can use an old dog for new tricks! Take the preceding example and slightly modify it and apply it to your Windows NT Server computing environment. Here is what you should do: First, add the counters discussed in this section to a Performance Monitor chart. Then perform an enormous file copy operation from one physical disk to another (c: to d: drive, c: to a: drive or even a local drive to a network drive). Monitor the counters that follow and make appropriate observations. Then perform this exercise under the same set of circumstances at a future date (say three months later). How do the charted counters look three months later compared to your original chart? Any declines or improvements in disk-related performance?

Detecting disk bottlenecks is also a function of the different buses on the system, such as I/O and devices. The controller card and the disk access time play into any disk bottleneck scenario. Sometimes the fix is as simple as upgrading your existing controller card or even adding another controller card for a second disk. Other times the solution is more complex, such as upgrading your motherboard so that you can employ the latest system I/O bus architectural standards. Here are some valuable counters for both the Logical and Physical Disk objects to use in your quest to detect and mitigate disk bottlenecks.

LogicalDisk:% Disk Time and PhysicalDisk:% Disk Time

Finally, a very simple definition. This is the percentage of time the disk drive is busy with read and write requests. Note that these two counters are selected on an Instance basis (physical hard disk for PhysicalDisk and partitions for LogicalDisk). It is important this counter value remain low (under 50 percent could be considered an acceptable range).

LogicalDisk:Disk Queue Length and PhysicalDisk:Disk Queue length

This is a snapshot of the number of requests outstanding on the disk. This refers to disk-related requests (for example, read or write). These counters are selected on a per Instance basis. We want to avoid having this counter value exceed two (we want the counter to remain low).

LogicalDisk:Avg. Disk Bytes/Transfer and PhysicalDisk:Avg. Disk Bytes/Transfer

This is an interesting value and speaks to both the performance of your disk and the type of bus used on your computer (such as IDE or SCSI). This is the average number of bytes, during read and write operations, that are transferred to or from the disk. This is a counter value we want to have a high value, as it demonstrates efficient throughput.

LogicalDisk:Disk Bytes/sec. and PhysicalDisk:Disk Bytes/sec

Similar to the preceding counter, this is the rate that the disk bytes are transferred to and from your disk. Not surprisingly, we want this counter value to be high.

Network bottlenecks

A lot of us became network professionals thinking we'd spend a great deal of time troubleshooting network bottlenecks only to find ourselves in the midst of singing the break-fix blues. It's safe to say that when you really start to find and fix network bottlenecks, you have "arrived" as a system engineer. You've earned your wings. Performance Monitor and the counters that follow are a great place to start, but network bottlenecks are typically major problems and require the use of a network analyzer (from Network General or others). You can use the Network Monitor tool that is provided free of charge in Windows NT Server 4.0 to assist you in your troubleshooting efforts.

Server:Bytes Total/sec.

Want to know how "busy" your server really is? This counter measures the number of bytes sent and received from the network wire per second. Although we like this value to be high, if it is too high, consider adding another network adapter card to the server. Monitoring this counter over time will enable you to decide if another network adapter card is warranted.

Server:Logon/sec

This applies to larger environments. It is the rate of all server logons.

Server:Logons Total

With this counter, you can tell how many successful or unsuccessful service, interactive, and network logons have occurred since the last time the machine was rebooted.

Network Segment:% Network Utilization

This counter repeats a value that can be found in Network Monitor: the percentage of network bandwidth in use on this network segment. Remember that with Ethernet, this value will never approach 100 percent because of the silence that is created when packet collisions occur. In fact, we like to see this value remain below 30 percent although it can grow larger on sophisticated networks that employ switches.

Network Interface:Bytes Sent/sec

This one almost defines itself. It is the number of bytes sent via the network adapter per second. Essentially this counter provides the rate at which bytes are being sent. It is a measure of throughput and can be measured on a per network adapter card instance.

The counter Network Interface:Bytes Total/sec, defined in the "quick and dirty" analysis section, applies to this section on network bottlenecks.

Analyzing protocols

The Windows NT Server Network Monitor application or some other network analysis sniffer tool typically handles protocol analysis. However, Performance Monitor enables you to engage in some rough protocol-related analysis. Note that the first three counters are presented for both NetBEUI and NWLink IPX.

NetBEUI:Bytes Total/sec and NWLink IPX:Bytes Total/sec

This is the number of bytes sent to and received from the network and is a throughput measure. This counter is charted by instance (representing the network adapter cards to which this protocol has been bound to).

NetBEUI:Datagrams/sec and NWLink IPX:Datagrams/sec

A datagram is a connectionless packet (meaning delivery is not guaranteed). These counters measure the rate that datagrams are sent and received. It's really reflecting the rate at which datagrams are being processed by the computer.

NetBEUI:Frames/sec and NWLink IPX:Frames/sec

Simply stated, this is the rate at which packets are processed by the computer. We like this value to be high, but not too high. This counter should be measured over time with an eagle eye cast on the trend line when displayed in Performance Monitor Chart view.

TCP:Segments/sec

This basically manages the rate that TCP/IP packets are sent and received. Again, a high value is good but too high is detrimental. You can define "too high" for yourself by measuring and learning about the behavior of this counter over time.

UDP:Datagrams/sec

This is the rate that UDP datagrams (connectionless packets) are sent and received by the computer. UDP packets are typically used in communication scenarios where reliability isn't mission critical, like the streaming of video and sound. Because of its connectionless orientation, UDP packets are faster than TCP-based packets. In fact, UDP packets have a nasty habit of "butting in" and pushing TCP packets out of the way. Yes, the caste system is alive and well in the middle layers of the OSI model.

Network Interface:Output Queue Length

This value represents the backup of outbound packets at layer one of the OSI model (basically the network adapter). This counter value should remain below two.

Analysis in Different Computing Environments

In many ways, Windows NT Server is a "jack of all trades" network operating system. In fact, I have heard it described as the minivan of NOSes, meaning it does a lot of things well and is superior in a few select areas. It competes strongly with NetWare in the file and printer server area (see Figure 22-19). It competes head-on with the AS/400 and UNIX environments as an applications server. Depending on the way that you have implemented Windows NT Server in your organization, you will want to undertake the following analysis for either file and print or application server environments.

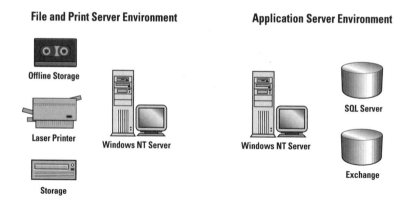

Figure 22-19: File and print server environment versus application server environment

File and print server environment analysis

In a file and print server environment, we are most concerned about server memory and the network subsystem. Our main concern with memory is caching. As always, the more memory the better, so we can cache more files.

With file and print servers, I strongly recommend you add a second network adapter when you have performance concerns in this area. I once worked with a manufacturer that had a large base of AutoCAD users. As you know, AutoCAD files are huge! Needless to say, adding a second network adapter card dramatically improved performance when it came to opening and saving AutoCAD files.

Once again, don't forget we need to track these trends over time (I repeat, an individual snapshot in time just isn't meaningful). When viewing your historical trend data, ask yourself these questions about your file and print server environment (viewing the world this way might just enable you to see the forest and not just the trees).

Here are some questions to ask yourself in a file and print server environment:

- How many users can our Windows NT Server file server support?
- Do users primarily access the file server to open and save data files?
- Do users download applications (as by running network installations of Microsoft Word)?

The Performance Monitor counters in Table 22-4 are specifically oriented to understanding your file and print server environment. These should be tracked in addition to the "quick and dirty" and "in-depth baseline analysis" counters presented earlier.

Table 22-4 File and Print Server Counters

Workload Unit	Performance Monitor counter	Definition
Disk activity	PhysicalDisk: % Disk Time	The time (on a percentage basis) the disk is busy with read and write requests
Average transaction size	PhysicalDisk: Avg. Disk Bytes/Transfer	The average number of bytes transferred during read and write operations
User sessions (concurrent)	Server:Server Sessions	Current server activity expressed by quantifying the number of active sessions on server
Network usage	Network Segment: % Network Utilization	Percentage of network bandwidth in use on a particular cable segment
Files open	Server:Files Open	On the server, the number of files currently open. Is a measure of server activity
Disk activity (reads)	PhysicalDisk: % Disk Read Time	Percentage of time the disk is fulfilling read requests
Disk activity (write)	PhysicalDisk: % Disk Write Time	Percentage of time the disk is fulfilling write requests

Application server environment system performance

By far, our greatest concern is the processor in an application server environment. Application servers (see Table 22-5) typically run robust server-based programs such as SQL Server and other Microsoft BackOffice products. Consequently, the processor is consumed with application threads and can become a bottleneck on your network. An application server can directly benefit from adding multiple processors and distributing the workload. Memory is our second concern because the server will have memory allocated to both the operating system and the server-based applications (and services) that are running.

Table 22-5 Application Server Counters

Workload Unit	Performance Monitor Counter	Definition
Available memory	Memory: Available Bytes	The amount of real memory available
Average disk transaction size	PhysicalDisk: Avg. Disk Bytes/Transfer	The average number of bytes transferred during read and write operations
Average network transaction size	Will vary by protocol, such as NetBEUI: Frame Bytes/sec	The rate that data bytes are processed by the computer
Cache Usage	Cache: Copy Read Hits %	The percentage of Cache Read Requests that find their information in cache memory and don't need to perform a disk read
Disk activity	PhysicalDisk: % Disk Time	The time (on a percentage basis) the disk is busy with read and write requests
Network usage:	Network Segment: % Network Utilization	The percentage of network bandwidth in use on a particular cable segment
Paging	Memory: Pages/sec	The number of pages read from or written to disk per second
Processor Usage	Processor: % Processor Time	The processor utilization rate
User sessions (concurrent)	Server: Server Sessions	The number of current sessions on a server

Making Better Use of Performance Monitor

Now that you have created a baseline and charted the appropriate counters, it's time to discuss several ways to make better use of Performance Monitor.

Relogging

One trick for managing your log files and the mass quantities of stored data is to relog your baseline log file. Relogging enables you to drop objects to create a smaller and more manageable log file. For example, you might capture every counter under the sun as part of your initial baseline logging activity. Then, depending on the analysis you are undertaking, you might relog selected counters to a newly named log file. It's like using your original baseline log file as a master database table and then creating smaller, more manageable tables via relogging.

Secret

Relogging really makes sense if you plan to export log data to a spreadsheet of database program. Correctly done, relogging enables you to export only the objects necessary for your analysis.

Running multiple Performance Monitors

In this section, I share with you reasons that you might consider running multiple copies of Performance Monitor. By doing so, you clearly create the data set you need to perform more detailed analysis, such as comparing and contrasting how different machines behave. Essentially, you gather more information, allowing for more meaningful comparative analysis.

If you run multiple copies of Performance Monitor at the same time, you will most likely want to "tile" the Performance Monitor screens across your desktop so that you can observe the information in a meaningful way. I'd recommend that you tile horizontally, as seen in Figure 22-20, because the Performance Monitor chart fills from left to right. Tiling vertical clearly wouldn't be as meaningful.

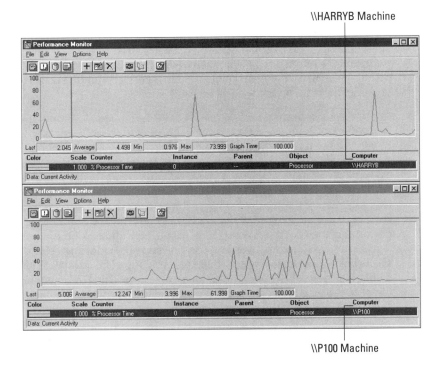

Figure 22-20: Running multiple copies of Performance Monitor

If you are monitoring several machines, create a Performance Monitor Chart window for each machine being monitored. These windows can then be arranged on your desktop in an orderly manner so you can monitor these machines visually from a single desktop. Think of it as creating your own investment trading console. In the trading rooms at investment houses, numerous charts showing different financial trading indicators are displayed simultaneously on one or more CRT monitor screens. In fact, if you manage (and monitor) a large network, you might seriously consider setting up multiple CRT screens to increase the display area (and allow more Performance Monitor charts to be shown at once, as shown in Figure 22-21). Check with video card vendors such as Radius regarding the use of multiple CRTs with Windows NT Server.

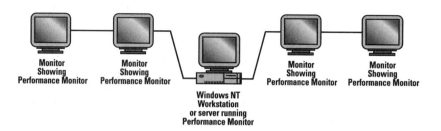

Figure 22-21: Multiple CRTs on a single machine

Don't forget that running multiple copies of Performance Monitor simultaneously on one machine enables you to dedicate that machine to performance monitoring (which is good) and avoid having each monitored machine run its own Performance Monitor session (and having each machine suffer an increased CPU load — which is bad).

Another reason to run multiple copies of Performance Monitor is that one Performance Monitor session can be recording a log while another Performance Monitor session reports current information on the statistics being collected in the log. In effect, you can chart counters of the objects you are logging in "almost" real time. By "almost" I mean that the Performance Monitor session that is doing the charting will only chart up to the point that it has conducted its initial read of the log file being created in the other Performance Monitor session. You would need to "relaunch" the Performance Monitor session that is performing the charting to have it display a later update of the other machine's logging activity. Similarly, you can run one copy of Performance Monitor to display historical logged data while another copy of Performance Monitor displays current charts with data (data you are catching in real time). Don't forget to tile on your desktop by secondary mouse clicking the taskbar and selecting Tile Windows Horizontally.

Consider running multiple copies of Performance Monitor to limit the size of log files during the baseline collection phase. I recently worked with a client that asked for an extensive baseline analysis of its system. The baseline file grew by nearly 50K every 10 minutes. Given a baseline data collection period of seven days, it became apparent we would literally run out of available secondary storage on the first partition. The solution? Breaking the logging activity into two files, via two Performance Monitor logging sessions, allowed the data to be placed on two separate disk partitions.

Removing clutter

Cluttered charts in Performance Monitor are difficult to view and analyze (See Figure 22-22). You can run multiple editions of Performance Monitor to create visually appealing charts.

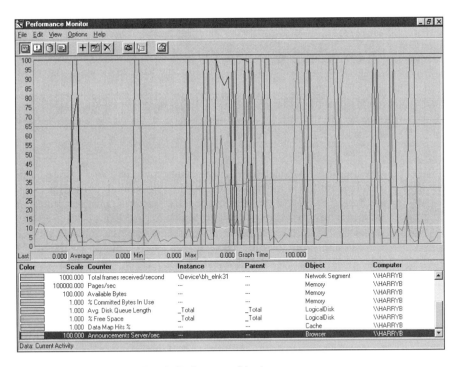

Figure 22-22: A cluttered chart in Performance Monitor

I'd recommend you limit your counters to six or less per chart so that you can easily see the data points being graphed on the chart (see Figure 22-23).

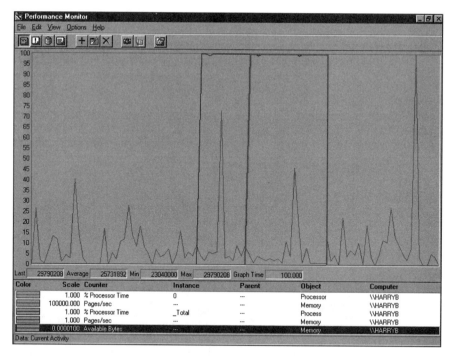

Figure 22-23: A reduced number of counters

Secret

Use the Ctrl+H keystroke when viewing charts in Performance Monitor. Performance Monitor power users know how quickly the Chart view can become cluttered. If you track more than several counters, the relatively limited chart area is impossible to read. Thus the use of Ctrl+H. As seen in the screen that follows, selecting a specific counter and pressing Ctrl+H simultaneously highlights the selected counter line (in bold white). The other lines retain their existing visual properties (thin, colored lines), but the highlighted line stands out dramatically in comparison. Another Ctrl+H tip is to scroll the selected counters via the up-arrow and down-arrow keys in the bottom portion of the Chart window (where the counters are listed). When you perform this scrolling action, the highlighted counter on the chart changes to reflect the counter you've selected from the list that follows. It's a great way to "hop" from counter to counter and view the chart line in bold white.

The key point to highlighting your chart information is to draw attention to specific information over other information (see Figure 22-24). By doing so, you make the chart and the information conveyed more meaningful.

Next steps

Although it is not as important as many topics covered herein, I highly recommend you become functionally familiar with setting a time window and using bookmarks. And don't forget to see Appendix A for full Windows NT Server 4.0 counter definitions.

Chapter 22: Performance Monitor

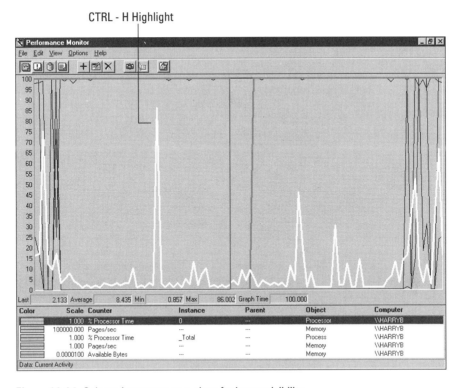

Figure 22-24: Selected counters on a chart for better visibility

Summary

In this chapter, you learned how to apply the Performance Monitor tool on your Windows NT Server network. The following topics were covered:

- Performance Monitor capabilities
- Performance Monitor basics
- Six quick steps to using Performance Monitor
- The four faces of Performance Monitor
- How to collect data
- In-depth analysis: memory bottlenecks, disk bottlenecks, network bottlenecks
- Analysis: file and print servers, application server

Chapter 23

Network Monitor Secrets

In This Chapter

- Initial Network Monitor
- Network Monitor Basics
- Ongoing network monitoring
- Frame capture patterns
- Network analysis timing
- Network Monitor's artificial intelligence features
- Network analysis resources for continued learning
- Windows NT Server Network Monitor versus System Management Server (SMS) Network Monitor

Some areas of the technology industry are still immature. When viewing that statement in the context of Windows NT Server, you will clearly see how it applies to Network Monitor's role in helping you manage your Windows NT Server network. Few network testing standards exist, and even fewer technical texts explain the finer points of packet analysis. Unfortunately, it is still the Wild West when it comes to implementing a sniffer and analyzing frame captures.

This chapter will help you gain a deep understanding of the Network Monitoring tool included with Windows NT Server 4.0. By the end of this chapter, you will be more than adequately equipped to seize the day with your Network Monitor tool. Likewise, I hope your interests will have been piqued to discover more about frame trapping and packet analysis. But you are not left hanging. Several advanced resources, beyond the scope of this book, are listed for you to further study the mysterious world of network analysis via frame trapping and packet analysis.

Initial Network Monitoring

The lesson learned from the Watergate era is that power is corrupting and absolute power is absolutely corrupting. So you want to be very careful with Network Monitor in Windows NT Server. This application is a reasonably powerful sniffer, warts and all. And "sniffer" is another way of spelling trouble on your network, when such a tool is used by unclean hands. Sniffers enable you to analyze network traffic at the packet level, potentially allowing others to trap packets and see unencrypted passwords. Let's just say that, in the wrong hands, Network Monitor is absolutely corrupting.

But on a positive note, Network Monitor is an advanced tool that, while too often used as a last resort in problem solving, can save your bacon big time! Network Monitor is used to provide statistics regarding network utilization and packet traffic as well as capture frames for analysis. The version of Network Monitor included with Windows NT Server is a crippled cousin to the full-featured version included with Microsoft System Management Server (SMS).

For comprehensive network analysis and monitoring, be sure to upgrade to SMS so that you can employ the full version of Network Monitor. In part, the reason for shipping a crippled edition of Network Monitor with Windows NT Server is to prevent unsavory users from trapping packets on a network-wide (actually segment-wide) basis. The crippled version of Network Monitor only allows you to capture frames sent to or from your computer (along with broadcast and multicast frames). At the end of this chapter, you will find a complete comparison between the Windows NT Server 4.0 version of Network Monitor and the SMS version of Network Monitor.

Network Monitor basics

Network Monitor is installed either during the setup of Windows NT Server 4.0 or from the Network applet in Control Panel. Select the Services tab sheet. Previously, in Windows NT Server 3.51, Network Monitor was installed as a service under the Protocols tab sheet on the Networks Properties dialog box. Known officially in Windows NT Server 3.51 as the "Microsoft Network Monitor Tool," this application will consume 4.1MB of hard disk space. In Windows NT Server 3.51, you are only presented with the option to install Network Monitor Tool (it now includes the Network Monitoring Agent in Windows NT Server 4.0). When starting the Network Monitor application in Windows NT Server 4.0 (after you have installed it of course), you select Networking Monitor from the Administrative Tools (Common) program group. You will be presented with Network Monitor's default Capture window (see Figure 23-1).

In Windows NT Server 4.0, you have the option to install just the Network Monitoring Agent or both the Network Monitor Tool and Agent. The new approach makes more sense and eliminates confusion about what each component accomplishes. For the record, the Network Monitor Agent allows for remote monitoring of a distant client's network communications. The Network Monitor Tool is Network Monitor (pictured in Figure 23-1). Figure 23-2 shows you the configuration property sheet that is the interface to Network Monitor Agent. Note that the Network Monitor Agent Driver can be observed on the Protocols tab sheet of the Network Properties sheet.

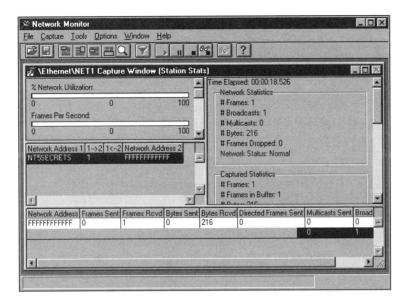

Figure 23-1: Network Monitor Capture Window

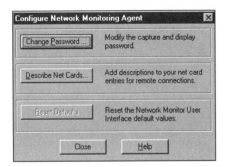

Figure 23-2: Network Monitor Agent configuration property sheet

Capture window components

Network Monitor provides several types of information in the Capture window (the default window at startup). The Capture window is divided into four parts (see Figure 23-3): Graph pane, Total Statistics pane, Session Statistics pane, and Station Statistics pane. Each of these four panes is discussed in the text that follows.

Part VI: Optimizing and Troubleshooting Windows NT Server 4.0

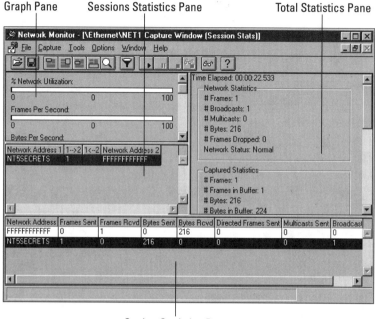

Figure 23-3: Components of the Capture window in Network Monitor

Graph

The upper-left pane is the Graph pane; it depicts current activity occurring on the network in a thermometer bar fashion.

Total statistics

The far upper-right pane is the Total Statistics pane, which displays total network activity detected since the capture process began. In the full-featured Network Monitor included with SMS, the frames depicted in the Total Statistics pane are the frames that are actually trapped, assuming no filtering is occurring (filtering will be discussed in a few pages). In the crippled Network Monitor included with Windows NT Server, the Total Statistics pane presents network statistics for the entire network but only traps the frames shown in the Captured Statistics area of the Total Statistics pane (again, assuming no filtering is occurring).

Session statistics

This pane displays information about individual sessions occurring between two nodes. It is interesting to note that "sessions" means literal sessions wherein Network Address 1 and Network Address 2 (nodes) have negotiated and established a session.

Station statistics

This shows generic statistics about frames sent and received on a per node basis. This pane is useful for determining, at a glance, who your worst offenders are on your network segment in terms of flooding the network with packets.

Capturing frames

Capturing frames is the art and science of trapping packets that will be meaningful to us. Typically this is commenced by clicking the Start Capture button on the Network Monitor tool bar in the Capture window. This button looks very much like the Play button on a typical audio cassette recorder. You may also press the F10 key to commence a frame capture.

Network Monitor will capture frames until system memory is filled. However, you typically capture enough frames to show the condition you are trying to analyze. For example, suppose a workstation cannot successfully log onto the Windows NT Server network. After troubleshooting the obvious causes, such as an unconnected workstation, you decide to trap frames for more analysis. The steps are to basically have the workstation try to log onto the domain while Network Monitor is running on the PDC.

Run the frame capture mode on Network Monitor on the PDC from the moment you power on the workstation you intend to use for logon testing. This workstation will generate client initialization traffic from its startup (just after the power on system test or "POST" phase). For example, client initialization traffic might include renewing the leased IP address from the DHCP server (in most small to medium-sized networks, the PDC is also the DHCP server). *Do not* wait to start capturing frames when the workstation in question is at the "Logon validation" stage (that is, showing the logon dialog box), or you will have missed some very important frame traffic that might help solve your problem.

The logon validation stage follows the acquisition of an IP address (assuming we are using the TCP/IP network protocol suite) and the NetBIOS names have been registered with a WINS server (see Figure 23-4). At this point the user can log on. The frame capturing session we undertake doesn't need to be especially lengthy in this logon validation exercise. The minimum amount of packet traffic generated during logon validation is 24 frames, but traffic can be as high as 44 frames.

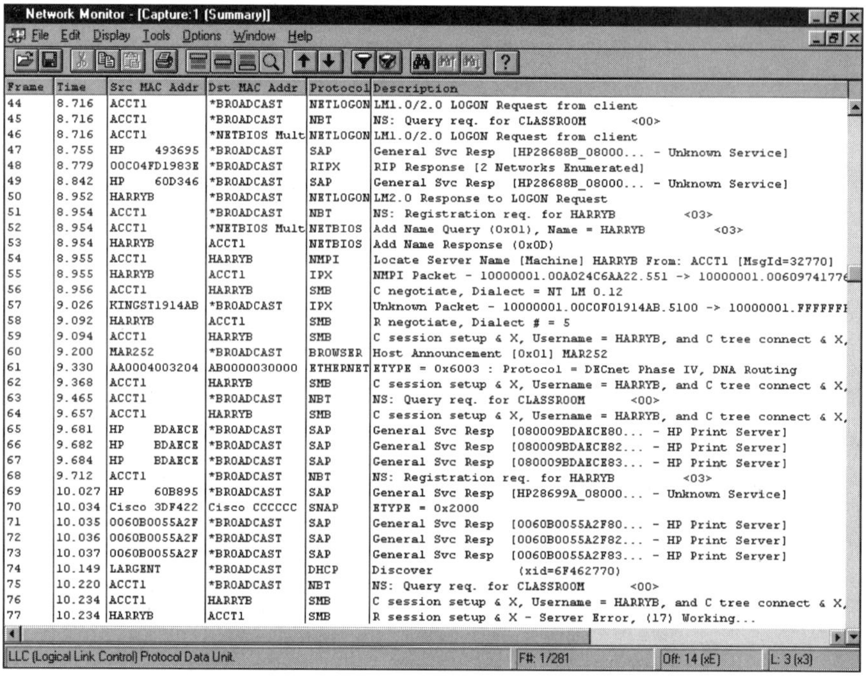

Figure 23-4: Frame capture showing logon validation

Required hardware

To utilize Network Monitor, you must be physically attached to the network. This states only the obvious, but if you are not attached to a network, you will not capture network traffic. To attach to a network, you must have some type of network adapter. This, of course, is typically a network adapter card placed in the computer and connected to the network media or cabling. If you have more than one network adapter card, you may select which network adapter card will be used with your current session of Network Monitor (see Figure 23-5).

Secret

Something that isn't well known is that you may also run multiple editions of Network Monitor simultaneously to monitor multiple network adapter cards. If you run multiple editions of Network Monitor to accommodate multiple network adapter cards, be sure to tile the Network Monitor applications for easy viewing. To tile, right-click the taskbar and select either Tile Horizontally or Tile Vertically.

Secret

Use an NDIS 4.0 driver on your network adapter card. If you have an NDIS 4.0 (or greater) driver installed on your network adapter card, Network Monitor captures in "local mode." This means only packets with the capturing computer's destination address are accepted. Previously, the capturing computer was placed in promiscuous mode, meaning each frame was evaluated whether it was destined for the capturing computer or not. Promiscuous mode increased processor utilization by up to 30 percent. A true bottleneck! This discussion applies to the crippled edition of Network Monitor included in Windows NT Server 4.0. The full-version of Network Monitor contained in SMS supports captures of network-wide traffic. Note that the Hardware Compatibility List contains a list of network adapter cards successfully tested with Network Monitor.

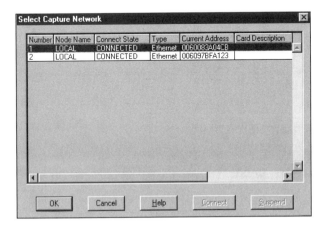

Figure 23-5: Select Capture Network

As we approach the sunset of Windows NT Server 4.0 and the dawn of Windows 2000 Server, most network adapter card manufacturers now provide NDIS drivers without any questions asked. This statement is especially true if you purchase leading network adapter cards from such companies as 3COM and Intel.

Secret

If you have multiple network adapter cards, be sure to use the Network Monitoring Agent option in Control Panel to describe each card. Providing a friendly name facilitates easier identification.

Analysis

Network Monitor presents the information in the Frame Viewer window in such a way that some of the "analysis" has already been completed for you (see Figure 23-6). Assuming you are in the Capture window of Network Monitor, the Frame Viewer window is created by selecting the Stop and View Capture button on the Network Monitor toolbar (the eyeglasses button) or by selecting the Display Captured Data option from the Capture menu (or simply pressing F12).

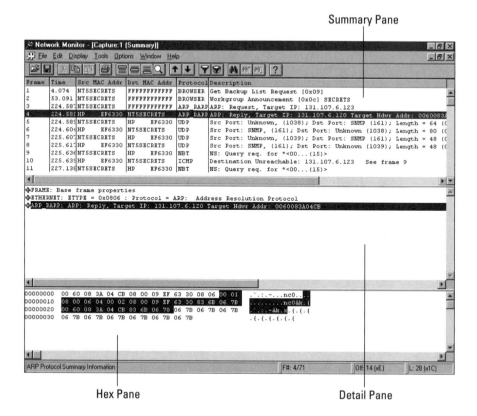

Figure 23-6: The Frame Viewer window in Network Monitor

The window is divided into three sections: Summary pane, Detail pane, and Hex pane.

Summary pane

The Summary pane lists frames captured, the elapsed time since time period zero, source and destination MAC addresses (hardware addresses from layer one and the MAC portion of layer two in the OSI model), the protocol being used, and a very useful text description. Double-clicking one of the frames creates the other two panes for this window.

Detail pane

Here is where Network Monitor really shines. The highlighted frame is presented in greater detail, showing the content of the frame and what protocols sent it, in English to assist your analysis. Even relative novices can educate themselves on the basics of packet analysis, based on the layout in the Detail pane. While it's safe to say the devil is in the details, the Detail pane layout truly enables you to understand the basic structure of a packet

Chapter 23: Network Monitor Secrets

and apply the conceptual knowledge you have of the OSI Model to the real world of network optimization via packet analysis.

Hex pane

This portion of the Capture window, on the far right in Network Monitor, allows you to see the actual data contained in a frame (as ASCII text).

Secret

Where this gets exciting is when clear text passwords are sent over the network and you trap the packets. For instance, you can see for yourself if you are using Windows NT Server on a network that has Macintosh clients that use the Eudora e-mail application. Start the frame capture session using Network Monitor. Walk over to a Macintosh client and force the Eudora e-mail application to check for new mail. Walk back to the Windows NT Server and halt the Network Monitor frame capture session. Press F12 to launch the Capture Viewer window and look at each frame individually. Soon enough, you will see the clear text password displayed as ASCII text in the Hex pane.

Ongoing Network Monitoring

Suppose you want to use Network Monitor to observe the performance of your Windows NT Server network on an ongoing basis. This can be accomplished by running Network Monitor continuously. From this you can observe (as observed via your network adapter card using the crippled Network Monitor in Windows NT Server; or for the entire network using the full-featured Network Monitor in Systems Management Server) the network utilization rate, frame per second, bytes per second, broadcasts per second, and multicasts per second. These are all valuable measurements to observe at a glance. In fact, to see all of these measurements at once, be sure to extend the Graph pane in Network Monitor by clicking and holding the lower Graph pane windows borders and dragging downward.

Secret

Set the Capture Buffer to a small value for continuos network monitoring via Network Monitor. This is accomplished by selecting the Buffer Settings menu option under the Capture menu in Network Monitor. The smallest buffer setting available is 0.5MB, and you are encouraged to use this value for continuous network monitoring. Once the capture buffer is full, the oldest frames are dropped and the newest frames are retained. However, the network statistics values displayed in the Graph pane are still valid as the time sample duration for calculating the statistics displayed in the Graph pane is much shorter than the time required to fill the buffer.

Using the capture trigger

One of the benefits of running a capture is the strategic and wise use of the capture trigger (see Figure 23-7), which provides the capability to "trigger" on conditions ranging from text pattern matches to how much buffer space has been consumed or a combination of these two variables. Interestingly, you can specify that the trigger consider the order of operations when evaluating the pattern match and buffer space variables. You can specify that the pattern match be evaluated before the buffer space variable is considered or vice-versa.

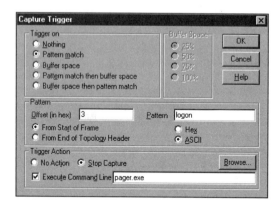

Figure 23-7: The capture trigger

This very similar but much weaker than the Run Program on Alert capability found in Performance Monitor, where you can specify a program that will run or a network message that will be sent to a specific machine. Unfortunately, the trigger action for Network Monitor is restricted to only executing a command line command. It is also unfortunate that you can't launch a program such as SQLALRTR.EXE that runs in Performance Monitor when a SQL Server object:counter is out of whack. As you may know, SQLALRTR.EXE can write an error to the error log and that can generate an e-mail message with important information that is sent to you. Instead, Network Monitor requires you to be a deft batch file programmer to achieve true functionality or have a pager alert e-mail program that perhaps accepts command line variables to really alert you, via pager, to an unacceptable event.

Secret

If you are only interested in monitoring the statistics in the Graph pane, then I highly recommend you consider creating an alert in Performance Monitor using the Network Segment object:counters. The alert capabilities in Performance Monitor are much stronger than those found in Network Monitor. The trigger capabilities of Network Monitor are only oriented toward text strings contained in a packet or the buffer setting value (percent of buffer full). Thus, it isn't possible to use the trigger capabilities in Network Monitor to be alerted of unacceptable network utilization values (such as broadcast storms sending network utilization values through the roof!).

Larger capture sessions

Be sure to consider setting Network Monitor to dedicated capture mode. This is accomplished by selecting the Dedicated Capture Mode option under the Capture menu.

Secret

By selecting dedicated capture mode, you reduce the demands on the microprocessor. Dedicated capture mode allows the computer to "keep up" and drop less frames than might otherwise be the case. Additional screens do not have to be drawn on the computer screen, and more important, the possibility of lost frames is reduced when you run Network Monitor in dedicated capture mode.

Capture buffer size

Don't forget to set the capture buffer to a large value to support your large frame capture sessions. Windows NT Server allows you to set this value as high as 24.5MB using the drop-down menu selection from the Buffer Settings menu option (see Figure 23-8), but it can be overwritten to a much larger value (say 50MB). For the record, the maximum size to which the capture buffer can be set is calculated as total physical RAM less 8MB. Exercise caution with respect to how much RAM you allocate to the capture buffer. We want to ensure that Windows NT Server doesn't perform unnecessary swapping to your hard disk (and dramatically lower overall system performance and lose frames in the capture).

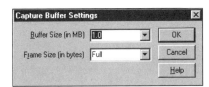

Figure 23-8: The Capture Buffer Settings dialog box

Frame size setting

Capture settings can be modified in another way. The frame size setting enables you to capture just part of the frame. Why might you use this setting? By capturing only part of the frame (the header section), you can still (typically) perform your network analysis without filling your capture buffer unnecessarily with the data portion of the frame. Why waste capture buffer space unless you are really "sniffing" the network to read data?

You cannot reduce the actual size of the frame. That, if possible, would seriously alter the implementation of the different standards (802.2, 802.3, 802.5) on your network, and that's a road you don't even want to travel down. You can determine how much of the frame you want to capture. This is done by setting the Frame Size setting to the size of the header section(s) you want to capture (see Figure 23-9). This setting is in bytes. For an Ethernet frame on a TCP/IP network, this would be approximately 60 bytes, as seen in the middle Detail pane of Network Monitor (see FRAME Base properties).

This is calculated by using Network Monitor to capture this type of frame, and then analyzing the frame with the Capture Viewer window in Network Monitor.

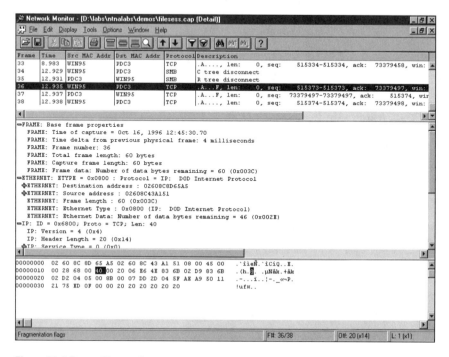

Figure 23-9 Frame Size setting

Capture filters

Capture filters are another way to "cut to the chase" with large captures. The Capture Filter dialog box is found via the Filter option under the Capture menu in the Capture window in Network Monitor (see Figure 23-10). By selecting which network information you want to capture and effectively dictating which information you want to discard, you can capture just a subset of all of the information possible. This is a smart way to perform frame captures, especially large ones. Too many frames in a capture might force you to get lost in the details. However, by selecting just the type of frames you are interested in, you will be much more focused and arrive at your intended results much faster. Experienced network analysts typically perform captures seeking resolution of just one type of problem. The capture filter allows them to select the exact frame traffic necessary. Captures can be filtered by protocol, address, or data patterns.

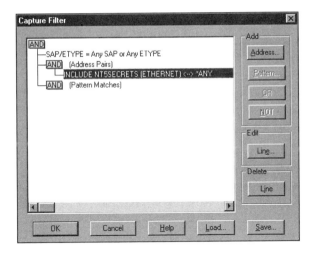

Figure 23-10: The Capture Filter dialog box

Protocols

Here the capture is defined for a set of specific protocols. The default setting for Network Monitor is to capture frames for all protocols supported by your version of Network Monitor. As you will see later in the chapter, the SMS version of Network Monitor supports several more protocols than the abbreviated edition of Network Monitor included with Windows NT Server. The capture settings you designate (see Figure 23-11) can be saved as a capture filter file and reused at a future date and even a different client site when appropriate. Remember that much of our packet analysis occurs on a protocol-by-protocol basis, making this capture capability especially important.

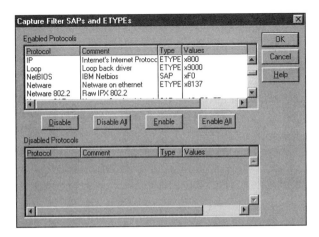

Figure 23-11: Using protocols to define your capture filter

Using capture filters helps you to preserve buffer resources. That will have an impact both on reducing the total amount of frame traffic plus increasing system responsiveness. By using capture filters for a narrowly defined frame capture scenario, you are much less likely to drop frame traffic because the computer can't keep up with the volume of frames.

Addresses

Address settings have major real-world implications for those of us who work in the industry by day (and sometimes night!). How many times has an end user complained that he or she can't connect to the network. Where do you begin to troubleshoot that problem? Start by creating a capture filter that only captures packets between that end user's workstation and the appropriate servers on your network. Why? Because, after you've defined the workstations to capture, the resulting network capture will enable you to view only the traffic between specific network nodes (or "hosts" in the language of TCP/IP, see Figure 23-12).

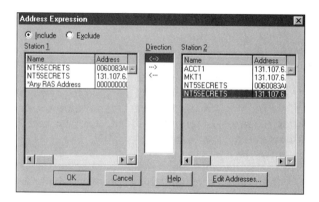

Figure 23-12: A capture will occur for traffic between NT5SEC RETS, ACCT1, and MKT1 as desired

Secret

Note that filtering by address capabilities can be used to specifically include specific addresses or exclude addresses. The exclusion feature is most valuable in situations where you might not be interested in trapping frame traffic generated by the Macintosh computers in the marketing department.

Note that we can define the direction of network traffic to capture. This direction can be one direction or both directions. Also, the computer "address" used by Network Monitor is by default the unique hexadecimal number or MAC address that uniquely defines each computer on the network. The more friendly NetBIOS names are used for those computers for which the NetBIOS name has been autodetected or otherwise registered in Network Monitors address database. Continuing with our previous example with NT5SECRETS, ACCT1, and MKT1, general traffic activity is displayed in Figure 23-13, and detailed frame-by-frame activity is displayed in Figure 23-14.

Chapter 23: Network Monitor Secrets

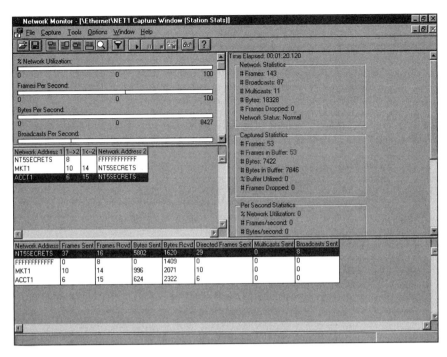

Figure 23-13: Traffic occurring between NT5SECRETS, ACCT1, and MKT1

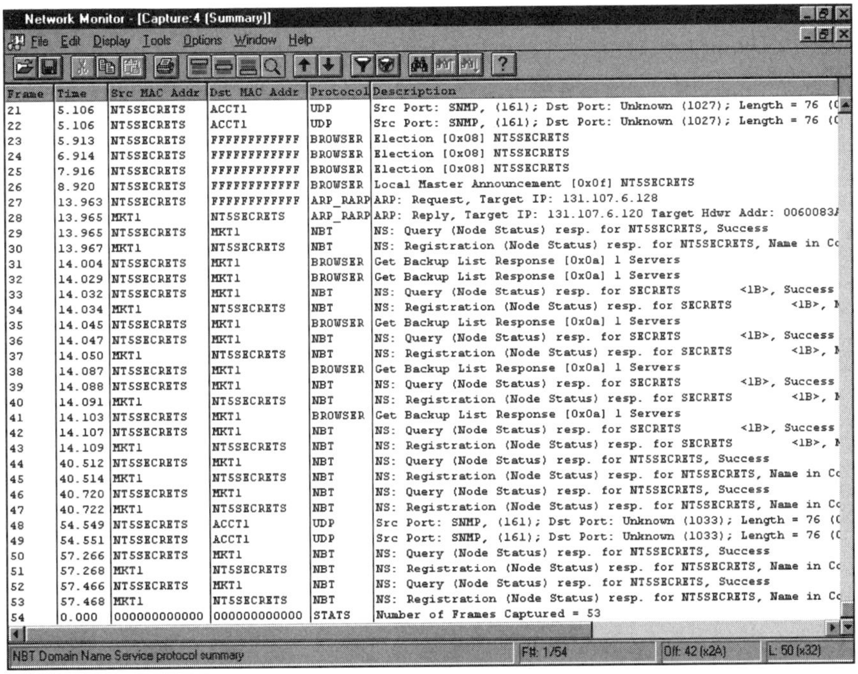

Figure 23-14: Details of the traffic between NT5SECRETS, ACCT1, and MKT1

Data pattern

The data pattern is simply a pattern of data appearing in captured frames. It may be in either ASCII text or hexadecimal form. As will be shown, you must specify how far into the frame the data pattern will occur. This positioning via number of bytes is called an *offset*. This offset value can be specified as a number of bytes from the beginning or end of the frame.

Secret

If you are using either the Ethernet (802.2, 802.3) or Token Ring (802.5) networking standard, you are advised to specify your offset from the end of the frame. Why? These type of frames have a variable-length field in the MAC address field. That will cause fits in your capture if your perform a data pattern capture based on an offset calculation that commences from the start of the frame. You have been warned.

Display filter

Of course, if you blow it during the capture and trap far too many frames, you can always recover via the display filter (see Figure 23-15). Actually it is a very useful tool that fundamentally lets you think a different way about how you capture frames. The thought here is that you could capture an enormous number of frames and save them as a capture file. This capture file could essentially be your baseline frame capture that is representative of network traffic on your Windows NT network at a given point in time. The display filter can, in laypersons' terms, be used to analyze your baseline frame capture for specific features of your network traffic at a later date, even if you didn't define your exact analysis needs at the time of capture.

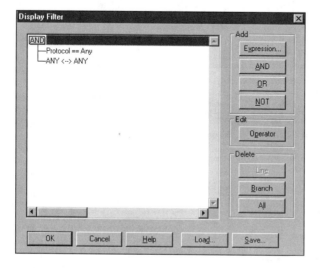

Figure 23-15: The display filter

Likewise, if you capture too many frames by mistake during one session, and you really wanted to analyze a more targeted subset of network activity, then the display filter will (here again) bail you out so that you don't have to undertake another capture session. Think of the display filter, in many respects, as similar to a query executed against SQL Server. By defining this query by address, protocol, or data properties, you can see the specific types of frames you are interested in without having to suffer through analyzing every frame in a large capture. You can extract only the specific frames of interest. As you will see, the way in which we filter frames with the display filter is very similar in nature to the capture filter previously discussed.

Designing a display filter forces you to define your end objectives, that is, what you want your resulting information to be. It's a good process in that you have to decided what you are really trying to accomplish. Of course the good news is that you didn't have to have this sense of definition prior to running the capture; it can arrive post capture.

One example might be all IP packets with a certain protocol stack property such as MERIT Intermodal but not the Locus Address Resolution property (see Figure 23-16).

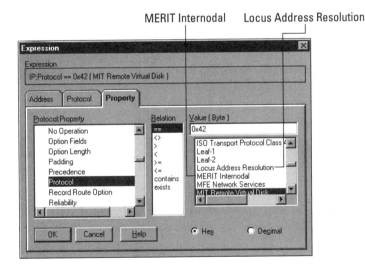

Figure 23-16: Packet activity containing only specific protocols

Another example might be to make sure your DHCP server is sending ACK or acknowledgments. That would be accomplished by selecting the ACK protocol property for DHCP and the "exists" relation (see Figure 23-17).

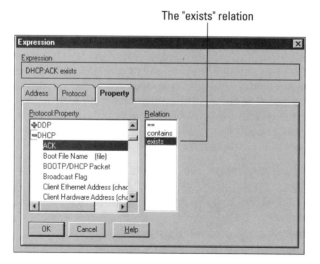

Figure 23-17: The "exists" relation in defining a display filter

To creatively and masterfully design a meaningful display filter, you must first define the problem you are trying to solve. As an example, let's assume you are running the TCP/IP protocol and have great difficulty establishing a session between a workstation and a server. You have run a large frame capture with no capture filtering (that means you capture everything). To better troubleshoot your problem, you create the display filter shown in Figure 23-18, wherein you want to display TCP frames.

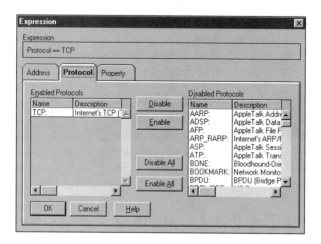

Figure 23-18: TCP as the only enabled protocol in the display filter

Once the display filter is invoked by successively selecting OK on each display filter–related dialog box, you will be presented with only those frames that meet your criterion (see Figure 23-19). Mastering this step, that is, creating a display filter that allows you to cut to the heart of your analysis, will pay enormous dividends when you are trying to solve network traffic problems (usually under somewhat hostile conditions — that is, tense users are asking when the problem will be solved!).

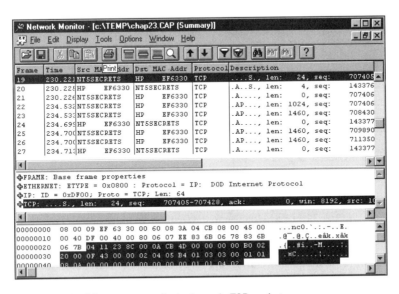

Figure 23-19: A large capture displaying only TCP packets

In this case, we see that a session, at least as far as TCP is concerned, is being established between the workstation and the client. Don't forget that we're very interested in TCP given this scenario. TCP is a connection-oriented upper-level protocol that guarantees delivery in a TCP/IP-based scenario. Clearly, we see that the three-way TCP handshake between client and server has been established, confirming that a session exists. Note that the acknowledgment number of the first frame is zero. That is because it had nothing to acknowledge at this point (this frame initiates the three-way TCP handshake). The second frame, from server back to client, acknowledges the first frame received from the workstation and does so with an interesting acknowledgment number. This acknowledgment number is a function of the sequence number in the prior TCP frame. TCP uses a sequence number as part of its guaranteed delivery promise. Each byte in the frame in a TCP-based scenario is assigned a sequence number. The following return frame, which acknowledges receipt of the TCP frame it received, uses the lowest sequence number of the prior packet plus one as its acknowledgment number. This is normal and can be seen in the frames just described. This same type of acknowledgment algorithm is present for the third frame of the TCP three-way handshake.

Finally, understand that Microsoft presents the Display Capture dialog box, in their words, as a decision tree. Although this is logically correct in that you build up query conditions, there are visual limitations. That is, complex queries aren't especially readable in the Display Capture dialog box.

Secret

You can think of the construction of the query expression as building an out-of-control IF...THEN...ELSE statement. Note that the Display Capture dialog box doesn't present the "decision tree" in the same manner we are familiar with in the Operation Research field. Such a decision tree would make greater use of branches.

You must click the OK button after adding each decision statement to the Display Filter dialog box. To add a second decision statement, once again select Filter under the Display menu in the Capture Viewer window or press F8. It is important to note that multiple decision statements or queries are possible, making this a very powerful and impressive tool.

Differences between capture filter and display filter?

Some fundamental and important differences exist between capture filters and display filters. These difference are:

- Capture filters are for those incredibly organized people who know exactly what they want. Display filters are for the rest of us. The capture filter forces you to define your research parameters in advance. The display filter is much more forgiving. My free advice? Run large unimpeded frame captures when performing network analysis and use a display filter to refine your analysis as you go.

- You can have only three address pairs in the capture filter (see Figure 23-20). Display filters do not have this limitation (see Figure 23-21). Thus, the display filter would be more useful when applied against at-large, general network frame captures if you wanted to analyze lots of sessions among lots of network nodes. I think you would find capture filters to be somewhat limiting if you were trying to undertake the same analysis.

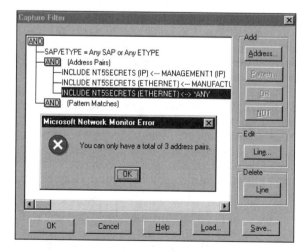

Figure 23-20: Three address pairs in the capture filter

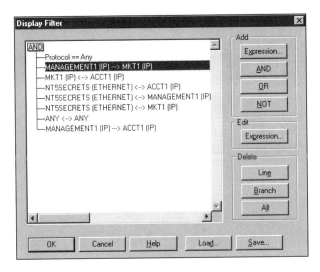

Figure 23-21: Several address pairs in the display filter

- AND, OR, NOT. With the display filter, you have wide open use of these operators in constructing your decision-tree type query (see Figure 23-22).

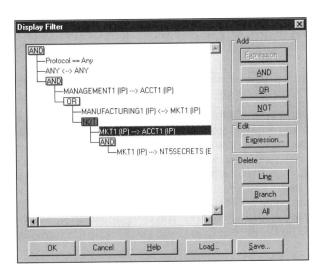

Figure 23-22: Display filter with AND, OR, NOT conditions

- The capture filter allows generous use of the AND operator but does not allow use of the OR and NOT operators in the context of nested pattern search (see Figure 23-23).

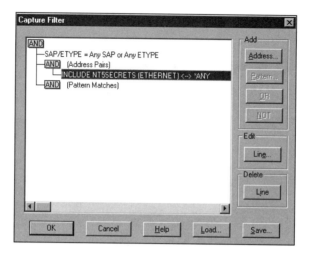

Figure 23-23: Capture filter with only the AND condition

Secret

Don't forget to save your capture session frequently, especially narrowly defined captures that you created via either the capture or display filters, for future use. These saved captures become your capture file library for solving similar problems in the future at the same site and network. In fact, you may capture frames from one site as a benchmark to evaluate captures from other sites. I highly recommend you use both long filenames and the comment field to describe the capture. Properly labeled and stored, these files are akin to medical patient x-ray files saved by a dentist to further his or her knowledge in the future when diagnosing a related problem. A fact worth repeating: Capture files are a great way to learn network analysis.

When you save your capture, notice the Range option in the Save Data As dialog box. This enables you to save all or part of a capture. It is possible to select a tight range of frames for saving in the capture file in order to reduce the overall capture file size and keep the capture file focused on just the area of interest. When you use the range option and only save selected frames, the frames in the capture file will be renumbered starting at one. This renumbering could potentially trip you up in a memo to your boss or in front of a class as an instructor if you have referred to a frame capture via its original numbering but then saved your capture using a defined range.

Password protection

At the beginning of the chapter, I spoke of the corrupting influences of power. One way to reign in the potential for Network Monitor–related abuses is to assign passwords for the Display and Capture modes. Network Monitor–related passwords are entered in the Configure Network Monitoring Agent dialog box found after clicking the Monitoring Agent icon in Control

Panel. Display mode only allows authenticated users to view existing capture files. A capture file is a file of saved capture activity that is encrypted. It cannot be read using an application like Notepad. Capture mode provides the user the keys to the kingdom. The capture password allows a user to both capture and display network activity. Typically you have different passwords for both Display and Capture modes. Once the user supplies the appropriate password for either Display or Capture mode, away they go.

Secret

As with all passwords, be extra careful to create passwords that you can remember. If you forget your password, you can't "remove" the Display and Capture passwords from your Windows NT server.

Watching you watch me

Another mission-critical tool for a Windows NT Server administrator to run is the Identify Network Monitor Users menu selection (under the Tools menu). This tool tells who else is running Network Monitor on your network. Most important, it reports the current state of the other Network Monitor running on the network. Possible current state conditions include "capturing" and "running."

Secret

This tool is your protection from weekend warriors and other computer hobbyists who "acquire" Network Monitor and potentially install it on one of their machines on your network. It is essential that you periodically determine who is "watching" activity on your network.

Once, at a Windows NT Server user group meeting held at the Redmond campus of Microsoft, I saw Network Monitor demonstrated in great detail. When the speaker demonstrated the command to identify network monitor users on the demonstration computer attached directly to the Microsoft corporate network, the screen returned over three dozen instances of Network Monitor running. Now you know what all of those workaholic Microsoft developers do after hours!

The name game

Go to the Addresses menu options under the Capture drop-down menu in Network Monitor. Listed there you will see the NetBIOS name, MAC address, and type of network listed for computers that have contributed frames to the capture. The MAC address field is editable, and the default NetBIOS name can be overwritten as well. It is recommended that you not modify the MAC address but create a street-friendly name for those non–NetBIOS named computers on your network. This street-friendly name will appear in Network Monitor in lieu of MAC addresses (both source and destination) once this street-friendly name has been created in the Address Database. Again, this is extremely useful when working on a network with non–NetBIOS named clients such a Macintosh or Novell NetWare client. Employing the methods discussed here will dramatically simplify your Network Monitor screens and enable you to better focus your attention on core packet analysis and network utilization issues. You will note that a second entry exists for each computer in the Address Database (see Figure 23-24) to reflect its address from layer three (network) of the OSI model. Under the TCP/IP protocol, it is the computer's TCP/IP network address.

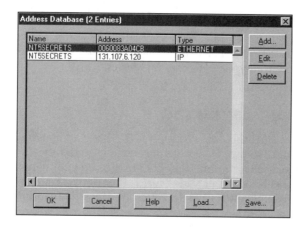

Figure 23-24: Address Database

You may edit the address information in the Address Database by selecting the Edit button. You will then be presented with the Address Information dialog box that enables you to modify the protocol type, computer name, address, and comment field. If you haven't yet done so, click the Edit button now to observe these fields.

To better understand which computers generating traffic are which, you can do two things. First, you can run the Find All Names command found in the Capture menu of Network Monitor when displaying the Capture window (see Figure 23-25). The Find All Names command can also be run from the Display Menu when the View Capture window is displayed. Running this command adds NetBIOS-based computer names to the address database.

Figure 23-25: Find All Names

Another approach to naming computers in Network Monitor is to start at each computer that will run the Network Monitoring agent (including the Windows NT Server with Network Monitor installed). Inside the Network Monitoring Agent, you can edit the MAC address description of the network adapter. So instead of hexadecimal alphanumeric gibberish, you can identify the network card with a meaningful street name. That way, when you observe packets in the Capture view windows, the SRC MAC Addr and the DST MAC Addr (source and destination MAC addresses respectively) will reflect the new names you assigned to the network adapters.

You can find the MAC address for a Windows NT (Server or Workstation) or Windows 95–based PC running the TCP/IP protocol by using the following commands. For a Windows NT Server or Workstation machine running TCP/IP, type **ipconfig /all** at the command line to see the screen shown in Figure 23-26.

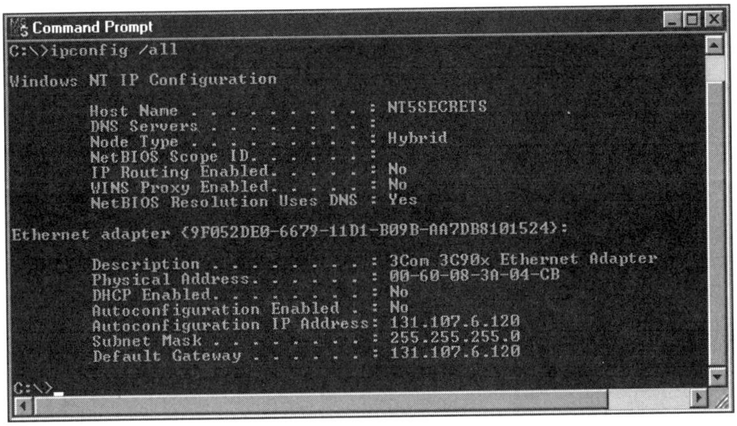

![ipconfig /all command output screen]

Figure 23-26: The ipconfig /all command in Windows NT Server

For a Windows 98 or 95 computer running TCP/IP, type **winipcfg** at the command line. You will see the IP Configuration dialog box that reports MAC address information in addition to the IP address. You may recall that both the ipconfig and the winipcfg commands were discussed at length in Part II, "TCP/IP," earlier in this book.

If you are capturing frames from a network with Macintosh clients or Novell NetWare clients, however, you're potentially in for a world of hurt. But (you ask) "how can I edit the MAC address of the network adapter card for a Macintosh or Novell NetWare client if said computers aren't running the Network Monitor Agent?" Fear not! You will have to get creative and manually populate the Address Database as will be described.

Secret

To "discover" the MAC address on a Novell NetWare client, I recommend that you boot from a DOS-based system disk and then run the utility program on the driver disk that shipped with your network adapter card. These utility programs typically enable you to configure your network adapter card as well as learn more about the card. This includes having the MAC address reported back to you.

For MAC address discovery on 3COM cards, you typically run INSTALL.EXE on the EtherDisk network adapter card utility disk for Ethernet networks (see Figure 23-27).

Figure 23-27: Detecting a MAC address with 3Com's Install program

There is another and possibly easier way to provide a friendly name for the MAC address in Network Monitor. Simply right-click the Session Statistics pane on Network Monitor's Capture window and select the Edit Address option on the context menu shown in Figure 23-28. Highlighting an address affords you the opportunity to edit the address name.

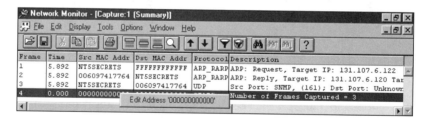

Figure 23-28: The context menu and edit address

To edit the address name, simply overwrite the default entry in the Name field of the Address Information dialog box (see Figure 23-29).

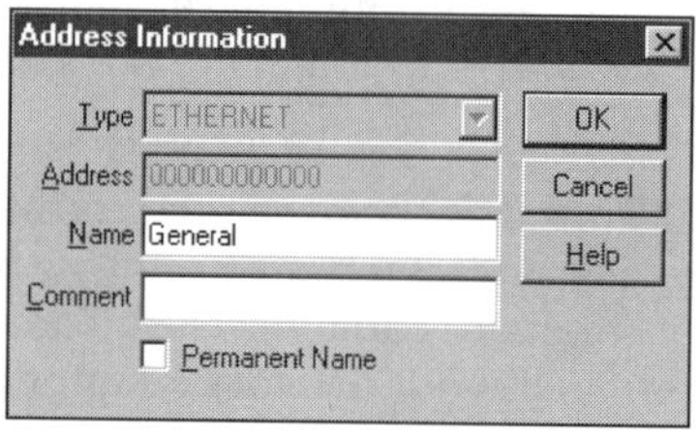

Figure 23-29: The Address Information dialog box in the context menu

You may also right-click the Summary pane of the Display Capture window when your cursor is positioned underneath the SRC MAC Address or DST MAC Address columns. Select the Edit Address context menu option and the Address Information dialog box will appear as in the preceding figure.

Because the Address Database table is automatically populated with the registered friendly or NetBIOS names and addresses (both MAC and TCP/IP) of computers that contributed to the capture session, you do not have to manually make entries to this table. However, you can add computers to this database by simply selecting the Add button in the Address Database dialog box. The benefit here is to create a database that you will use on your network from day one or to add computers that haven't been automatically added to the Address Database for whatever reason. The unique identifier when manually adding a computer is the hexadecimal MAC address or network protocol address (such as IP address). The underlying purpose of adding a computer name to your Address Database is to resolve MAC addresses to street-friendly names that you have created. This capability has a time and a place, but it is most useful when needed.

It's All in the Patterns

Ever watch any one of the outstanding historical documentaries about the beginnings of computers in modern society? An example of such a documentary is "The History of Computers" shown frequently on public television stations. Well guess what! Computers where initially employed to assist the military in World War Two with its wartime efforts. Not a big surprise there. That's because early mathematicians noticed that computers (the machine kind, not the pre-WWII definition of "human" calculators) were exceptionally well equipped to perform complex mathematical tasks such as predicting weapons performance and code breaking. That last point is the important one. Capturing frames and performing network analysis is nothing less than code breaking.

Secret

It is essential you think like a computer when performing network analysis. When you analyze the data in the Capture window of Network Monitor, you must look for the *patterns* that interest you. And herein lies the key to successful network analysis. The patterns tell the whole story of whether or not a particular behavior is correct on your network.

Figure 23-30, for example, shows the TCP/IP session establishment process capture via Network Monitor. Notice the three-way communication pattern, known as a "three-way handshake." In the first frame, the client contacts the PDC in an attempt to establish a session. In the second frame, the PDC replies to the client as an acknowledgment. The third frame represents a return acknowledgment from the client back to the PDC with which the session is established.

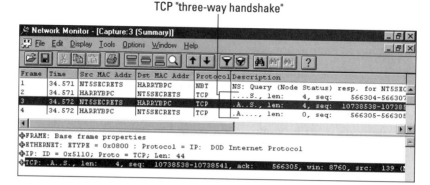

Figure 23-30: TCP/IP packet capture showing session establishment

So what "patterns" can we see from this? Let's take a look:

- **The three-way handshake in a TCP/IP session.** If this pattern is absent, something is amiss on our network. Under the Description column in Figure 23-30, look at the entries for frames 2–4 (three frames). The "S," "A..S," and "A" shown from frame 2 to frame 4 represent the three-way handshake.

- **The "acknowledgment" nature of TCP as our transport-level protocol.** Remember that TCP provides guaranteed, connection-oriented service, thus the acknowledgments.

- **Additional traffic.** These acknowledgment packets, while necessary for the type of guaranteed delivery we insist upon with data transmissions, do add to our overall network traffic.

Secret

The "three way handshake" is further discussed in RFC 793 (section 3.4).

By looking for the patterns and behaviors present in certain types of network communications, you're well on your way to understanding network analysis.

Secret

Although one can research and read about network analysis, the only true way to learn this area is to practice it, and more important, to do it for real in a crisis situation!

Another way to enhance your network analysis is the effective use of color. By selecting the Colors option under the Display menu while in the View Capture window, you can assign a different color to each protocol (see Figure 23-31). Depending on your needs, I recommend you assign a color to just the type of protocol activity you are seeking to observe and analyze to simplify your analysis. For example, you might have IP and IPXCP packets appear in red so that these packets are more visible.

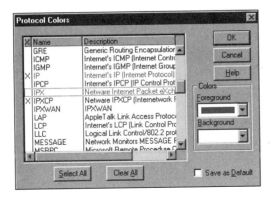

Figure 23-31: Protocol Colors

Timing Is Everything

The standard approach used in network analysis is to measure the frame capture from time period zero, the moment that the frame capture commenced. This is the default setting in Network Monitor and can be modified in the Display Options dialog box found under the Display Menu of the Capture Viewer window. This is conceptually similar to the finance discipline, wherein much financial analysis performed starts at time period zero. For most of us, time period zero is a term used in finance to denote the day that you close the loan on your house. I highly recommend you keep this default setting so that you conform to this generally accepted standard of network analysis.

Artificial Intelligence Arrives in Network Monitor

This is no tabloid headline. It's really about the sixth column of the Summary pane in the Capture Viewer window (titled Description). The default is to show the name of the last protocol for a specific captured frame. By default, the comments in the Description column of the Summary pane in the Capture window "match" the last protocol listed in the packet. In Figure 23-32, frame two is highlighted and the TCP protocol, having been listed last in the Detail pane, is also listed in the Description column of the Summary pane.

I strongly recommend that you select the artificial intelligence option for the Description column. Network Monitor can display the appropriate protocol information it infers you might like to see from the query conditions you have defined in the display filter. Cool! And much more meaningful than defaulting to the last protocol in the frame of interest. Select the Auto radio button in the Display Options dialog box found under the Display menu in the Capture Viewer window (see Figure 23-33) The Auto selection allows Network Monitor to decide what to display in the Description column. Note that you can also select how the Time column is displayed with the Time options.

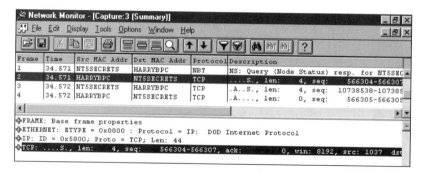

Figure 23-32: Network Monitor's Summary pane

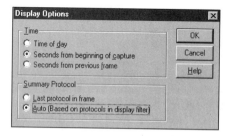

Figure 23-33: The Auto selection

I Want to Learn More!

But how does one really learn the finer points of packet analysis? Unfortunately, few books are on the shelves in the computer section of your neighborhood bookstore that really address this subject well. In many ways, you are on your own in an area where the learning comes in the form of on-the-job (OTJ) training. In the next few pages, I will share with you a few tricks of the trade for performing as a superior Windows NT Server professional and learning more about packet analysis along the way. These tricks include using paid support incidents at Microsoft, joining the Microsoft Solution Provider program, attending official Microsoft certification courses, consulting the Microsoft TechNet CD-ROM library, and conducting Internet-based research. Oh, did I forget to tell you that it is possible to learn more just by using Network Monitor? One way to learn more with Network Monitor is by using the protocol parser definitions, which I describe in a few pages.

Paid support incidents

One of my secrets of success as a Windows NT Server professional has been the use of Microsoft paid support incidents to resolve BackOffice problems and learn a heck of a lot along the way. Before using a paid support incident,

I typically try to solve the problem at hand. But once it is apparent that I'll be unsuccessful, I don't throw in the towel but rather use a paid support incident to be connected to a senior Microsoft support engineer. These guys and gals at Microsoft will stick with you for days until to problem is resolved. More important, they tend to turn you on to better ways to use existing tools, such as Network Monitor.

Secret

It's interesting to note that Microsoft's position on Network Monitor is not what you might think. Microsoft's position is that it will support the "core functionality" of the Network Monitor application (such as its capability to be installed and operate) but that "network-dependent tasks" such as true packet analysis are officially unsupported. However, there is an "undocumented" way to get Microsoft to support your packet analysis efforts. That strategy is to learn packet analysis by purchasing a Microsoft paid support incident ($200). These support incidents are free if you are an MCSE grandfathered into the program back when ten free paid support incidents were granted as part of your MCSE benefits. New MCSEs are not granted any paid support incidents.

Microsoft Solution Provider Program

The Solution Provider program not only provides you with the full BackOffice library via CD-ROM but also provides other benefits such as the TechNet CD-ROM library, low-cost training opportunities, and the right to purchase reduced cost support incidents.

Tip

Use one of these incidents to have a Microsoft Support Engineer walk you through, in great detail, a capture file that you created in Network Monitor.

Official Microsoft Certification Training

As a knowledge worker, you will find that it is in your best interest to continually seek out and attend germane training to further your skill set. One of the most consistent training channels is the Microsoft certified trainer programs. For commercial training centers, you would attend Microsoft Official Curriculum (MOC) courses at authorized technical education centers (ATECs). On the academic side, the same courses are offered at authorized academic training program (AATP) sites.

Tip

Most important, don't overlook Microsoft's certification and training courses for learning packet analysis.

Course #689, "Supporting Windows NT Server 4.0 — Enterprise Technologies," and Course #692, "Microsoft Windows NT Server 4.0 — Network Analysis and Optimization," are highly recommended for learning basic packet analysis in the Windows NT Server environment. Note that Course #689 is a five-day course that covers all (and more) of the material delivered in Course 692 (a two-day class). These courses are delivered at Microsoft ATECs and AATPs (the commercial training and academic training centers authorized by Microsoft). Note that these course names and titles are subject to revision based on new product releases and curriculum enhancements. Check with your Microsoft training provider for the most current version and course number for these classes. For more information on training, see www.microsoft.com/train_cert. I can also suggest that you consider taking one or more of the Instructor-led or self-study courses offered by Cisco (www.cisco.com). In the spirit of the analysis typically undertaken with Network Monitor, you might purchase and complete the "Managing Traffic on Cisco Routers" self-study course sold by Cisco.

In passing, I previously mentioned that frame capture files are a great way to learn network analysis. Not only can you create your own capture files and create a library, but you can use and study the student sample capture files from Microsoft certification Course #689, "Windows NT Server — Enterprise Technologies" (or its successor courses). As a student in the #689 class, you receive a CD-ROM with numerous capture files that show everything from adding a user to a network to observing Windows 95 perform a file copy. Wouldn't that last capture file be a great way to troubleshoot a pesky problem such as when a user complains of not being able to copy a file from a Windows 95 client to a Windows NT Server? You bet! In all, the student CD-ROM for the #689 class provides over 30 meaningful capture files (many with the comment field completed to help you understand at a glance what each capture file is trying to demonstrate). This is truly one of the best ways to master network analysis. The Network Monitor capture files included with Microsoft's "Windows NT Server — Enterprise Technology" class are great for learning packet analysis.

Display Filter Box — protocol definitions

You can learn protocol definitions in the display filter dialog box. Study the basic protocol definitions, conditions, operators, and default values for each element of a protocol. Note that this is a very rich area of Network Monitor and will assist you greatly in trying to learn network analysis. The information conveyed in this rich, multilayered dialog box is, quite frankly, somewhat overwhelming. But the devil is in the details, and if you look closely at the default values for each part of the protocol, you have your road map to understanding and interpreting frame captures. Detailed information about virtually any networking protocol can be obtained via the Property tab sheet in the Expression dialog box selected from display filter (see Figure 23-34).

This is the slow and steady way to go when mastering Network Monitor. To assist and speed your efforts, however, I have listed detailed descriptions of selected protocols supported by the Windows NT Server version of Network Monitor in Appendix B.

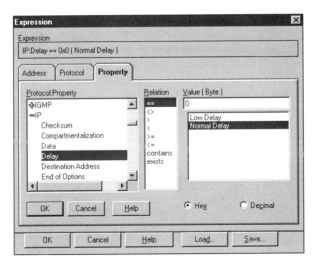

Figure 23-34: Property tab sheet

Microsoft TechNet CD-ROM

A frequently cited tool in *Windows NT Server 4.0 Secrets* (IDG Books Worldwide), Microsoft TechNet, is probably the fastest way to learn about each protocol property by searching on appropriate terms. An annual subscription to TechNet is approximately $300 (U.S.), for which you receive a monthly CD-ROM library. For example, suppose you wanted to learn about the "sequence" value discussed in the TCP portion of the TCP/IP protocol stack. Note that the term "sequence" is shown in Figure 23-31 as "seq" in the Description column for frames 2–4. Here is a recommended sequence of steps to successfully undertake this search.

STEPS:
To search TechNet for information on sequence value

Step 1. First, I would highly recommend you create a subset to narrow your search on Microsoft TechNet. Given our interest in learning about the "sequence" value in the TCP protocol in the context of Windows NT Server 4.0, creating and using the BackOffice (for instance, "BackOffice1") subgroup is a great place to start. Of course, if we were wrong, which we're not, we could expand the scope of the search by creating a broader subgroup or, heck, searching the entire Microsoft TechNet CD-ROM. A subset is easily created via the Define Subset command under the Contents menu in Microsoft TechNet.

Continued

STEPS

To search TechNet for information on sequence value
(continued)

Step 2. Next, create the search query. In the case I'm interested in the term "sequence" in the context of the TCP protocol. Thus, this query is constructed with the term "sequence" near "tcp." Note that the BackOffice1 subset from Step 1 is being used (see Figure 23-35).

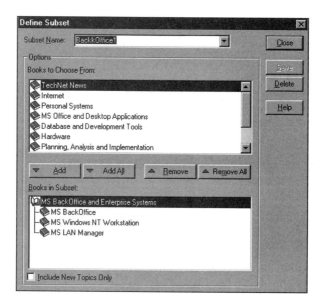

Figure 23-35: The BackOffice Query window

Step 3. The results of this query clearly bear the type of fruit we are seeking. Once you have the results of your query, they will be displayed as shown in Figure 23-36. The challenge you face to is quickly select the article(s) that will provide the knowledge you are seeking.

Secret

Make heavy use of the term "near" when constructing your searches in Microsoft TechNet. The "near" term will look for the requested terms within sixteen words of each other. This search term is much more powerful than the typical Boolean search terms "and" and "or." Take it from a daily user of Microsoft TechNet: The term "near" should be near and dear to your heart.

Step 4. Voila! After selecting the best article (see Figure 23-37), press Ctrl+D to hop quickly down to the appropriate search terms. In this case, Ctrl+D places us in a paragraph that is very descriptive and helpful in our quest to learn about the sequence number in the TCP protocol. The first article we found has a passage that sufficiently defines the term "sequence."

Chapter 23: Network Monitor Secrets 839

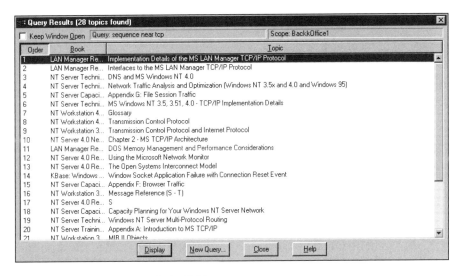

Figure 23-36: The search results in 28 hits

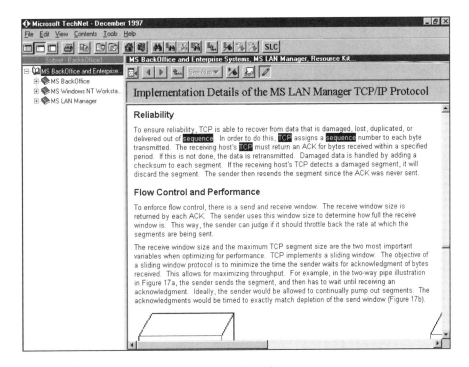

Figure 23-37: A selected article from the search results

Internet-based research

And of course don't overlook the possibilities of the Internet when researching network analysis. Here's a quick example of using it to research network analysis. You can use the Search button on the toolbar of Internet Explorer 4.0 browser and search on the general terms "network analysis" using one of the popular search engines. Using the Search button will take you to the all-in-one search engine page supported by Microsoft.

Secret Consider using Infoseek as your Internet search engine if you think the nature of your queries will be "drill-down." Not to sound biased, but my experience has shown that Infoseek has the strongest drill-down capabilities. Notice that I didn't say Infoseek was the strongest search engine, just that it shines in this one type of structured search. What is "drill-down"? When I recently searched on the word "network" using Infoseek, nearly four million hits were returned. Then I added the term "analysis" to my Infoseek search, and that resulted in under 2,500 hits. Finally, I added the term "packets" to my search, and the results dropped to approximately 126 hits, most of which were germane to my packet analysis educational mission. If you haven't discovered the drill-down nature of Infoseek, I encourage you to repeat the same experiment I've just shared with you. Infoseek may be reached, as previously mentioned, via the Search button on Microsoft Internet Explorer, or at www.infoseek.com.

The other major search engines such as Yahoo! and AltaVista are great for broad general searches, but I've found it is more difficult to drill down into the data I want. For example, the AltaVista search engine has a complex refinement process when I want to append my original search conditions.

While incredibly powerful for general, broad searches, AltaVista presents challenges when trying to refine and drill down into your initial search. Here, on the refine search screen, you must select which terms to include or exclude. Terms are ranked as a percentage of importance. While powerful, this search refinement process is somewhat time consuming and annoying. Feel free to see for yourself by selecting AltaVista after clicking the Search button in Microsoft Internet Explorer or at www.altavista.com.

Surfing directly to major networking vendors' Web sites is, of course, another powerful way to educate yourself on the finer points of network analysis. These Web sites typically host white papers that, while often promoting a specific product, also provide solid technical knowledge. For starters, I can recommend the sites listed in Table 23-1 as good sources of information on network analysis:

Table 23-1   Networking Analysis Resources on the WWW

Vendors	Site	Comments
IBM	www.ibm.com	Yes — IBM. A great site for research relating to network analysis. Yes, it's true. Big Blue has got it right.

Vendors	Site	Comments
3COM	www.3com.com	Search on keywords such as "switches," "routers." Used to have white papers that were truly academic (err, nonsales) in nature.
Shiva	www.shiva.com	This is a long-time player in computer communications including wide area connectivity.
John M. Fluke Company	www.fluke.com	A leading manufacturer of cable testing and network analysis devices. This site has excellent white papers.
Microsoft	www.microsoft.com	Of course!

Hardware devices

You may have arrived in the networking industry via the hardware break/fix and wiring/cabling industry. The experience you bring is worthwhile, and perhaps you've already performed network monitoring using hardware-based analysis tools.

One tool I have used is the Fluke One Touch Network Assistant 10/100. This device provides, in the palm of your hand, many of the same statistics we use Network Monitor to tell us. From the main LCD panel, you can perform the tasks shown in Table 23-2.

Table 23-2   One Touch Network Assistant 10/100 Features

Feature	Description
AutoTest	This option performs discovery. Connectivity tests are performed such that devices are identified on your network. The devices for your cable segment are displayed via NetBIOS names and MAC addresses. I've found the node discovery to be very reliable. Like the full-featured version of Network Monitor in SMS, the Fluke Network Assistant performs router discovery. Servers are listed by type (NetWare, Windows NT Server). Windows NT servers are identified as domain controllers, member servers, and master browsers. Additional information is provided for frame type, protocol, and domain membership.
Network Health	This is very similar to performing a frame capture using the Capture windows in Network Monitor. Tests are performed for utilization, errors, collisions, broadcasts protocols, and individual station statistics. At a glance, I've found the broadcast traffic statistics to be incredibly valuable.

Continued

Table 23-2 *(continued)*

Feature	Description
Cable Tests	Just try this with Network Monitor, my friend. These are the advanced cable testing functions built into the Network Assistant. Tests are included to measure the cable length, the wire pinouts on a cable (this is great for verifying the accuracy of homemade crossover cables), cable quality, and intermittent failures associated with cables.
NIC/Hub Tests	These tests determine if the network adapter card and hub are functioning properly. Here again, with the MCSE Lab where I teach evening classes, this type of test has really helped in troubleshooting those annoying gotchas that students always seem to discover during a lecture. These gotchas include underperforming workstations, dead workstations, no primary domain controller error messages at logon, and other general nonsense.
Ping Station	This is exactly the same as the PING IP test at the C:> prompt in a command prompt window. This capability of the Fluke Network Assistant makes it much more than just another cable tester.

Needless to say, Fluke's Network Assistant has been invaluable in troubleshooting the MCSE lab environments that I teach in and has provided a different view of network analysis. Best of all, you can print out the analysis from the Network Assistant to a printer connected to its printer port. Oh, did I forget to mention that this device is approximately $5,000. That's a little bit more than Network Monitor, which of course is included for free with Windows NT Server.

Books

I've eliminated many of the texts too focused on theoretical hooey. You want results now. These two books deliver and are suggested next steps once you've gained familiarity with Network Monitor.

- Enck, John, and Beckman, Mel. *LAN to WAN Interconnection.* McGraw-Hill, 1995. This book has the appropriate subtitle of "For those who are familiar with one geography and perplexed by the other." Indeed it was this book that enabled me to better understand the world of wide area networking. Better yet, this book provides excellent references to packet construction, so I know my DSOs from my DLCIs. If these two acronyms are foreign to you, it is essential that you read this book on your path to mastering network analysis.

- Buchanan, Robert Jr., *The Art of Testing Network Systems*. Wiley Computer Publishing (John Wiley & Sons, Inc.), 1996. This book provides numerous test methodologies that are directly applicable to structuring your network analysis. Without test methodologies, you may well be tempted to perform your analysis in a willy-nilly fashion, that at a minimum, will take longer to complete. I highly recommend this book.

Secret

For a long list of books that discuss network monitoring from a technical perspective, go to the online Windows NT documentation and select the "book" term in Network Monitoring help area. Look for the chapter titled "Network Monitor Guide to Books on Networking" and you will be presented with over 33 texts to select from. Good luck!

Comparing Network Monitors: SMS versus NT Server 4.0

The basic differences between the crippled version of Network Monitor included with Windows NT Server and the full-featured version of Network Monitor found in SMS are discussed in Table 23-3.

Table 23-3   Network Monitor Comparison

Capability	Network Monitor (crippled version in Windows NT Server)	Network Monitor (full-featured version in SMS)
"Man in the middle" — Editing and resending frames	No	Yes
Remote Capturing based on Network Monitor Agent running on other workstations	No	Yes
Capability to run Network Monitor Agent to allow other workstations running Network Monitor to capture frames at your workstation	Yes	Yes
Determines heaviest user of network resources (bandwidth)	Not built-in. Secret: Can visually determine by observing Station Statistics pane in Network Monitor.	Yes (built-in capability)

Continued

Table 23-3 *(continued)*

Capability	Network Monitor (crippled version in Windows NT Server)	Network Monitor (full-featured version in SMS)
Determining which protocol is using the greatest amount of bandwidth	Not built-in. Secret: Could be determined by capturing all protocols and using the display filter dialog box to display each protocol separately in the Frame Viewer window. This would be a rough "guesstimate" approach at best.	Yes (built-in capability)
Reverse resolution of a device name (NetBIOS name) being resolved to a MAC address	No. The command Resolve Addresses from Name under the Tools menu returns an error message: "Tool Unavailable: This command is available only in the version of Network Monitor provided with Microsoft Systems Management Server."	Yes
I See You and You See Me — determine which machines are running Network Monitor	Yes. Under the Tools menu, select Identify Network Monitor users.	Yes
Capability to find routers	No. Selecting Find Routers under the Tools menu returns an error message: : "Tool Unavailable: This command is available only in the version of Network Monitor provided with Microsoft Systems Management Server."	Yes

Secret

Besides purchasing and installing SMS to obtain the full version of Network Monitor, you can obtain the full-featured version of Network Monitor by attending Microsoft certification course #689, "Supporting Windows NT Server 4.0 — Enterprise Technologies" (or its successor courses). Students are provided the same Network Monitor as found in SMS for training and learning purposes. It is not intended to be used as a tool on your "real" network. However, just having access to the full-feature edition of Network Monitor enables you to learn and exploit its advanced capabilities. At that point, you may decide to purchase SMS and legally obtain the full version of Network Monitor.

Another difference between the Network Monitor contained in Windows NT Server 4.0 and SMS is the support for protocol analysis via "protocol parsing." A dynamic link library (.DLL), a protocol parser identifies a protocol being sent out onto the network. Likewise, this protocol parsing information is used to identify and display frames in the Frame Viewer window. It's a one-to-one relationship with a protocol parser for each protocol that Network Monitor supports. The protocols supported by Network Monitor in either the Windows NT Server 4.0 and SMS edition or both are shown in Table 23-4.

Table 23-4 Protocol Parser Comparison

Protocol	Description	Network Monitor in Windows NT Server	Network Monitor in SMS (version 1.2)
AARP	AppleTalk Address Resolution Protocol	X	X
ADSP	AppleTalk Data Stream Protocol	X	X
AFP	AppleTalk File Protocol	X	X
ARP_RARP	Internet's ARP/RAPR (Address Resolution Protocol/Reverse Address Resolution Protocol	X	X
ASP	AppleTalk Session Protocol	X	X
ATP	AppleTalk Transaction Protocol	X	X
BONE	Bloodhound Oriented Network Entity (BONE) Protocol	X	X
BOOKMARK	Network Monitors BOOKMARK Protocol	X	X
BPDU	Bridge Protocol Data Unit	X	X
BROWSER	MS Browser	X	X
CBCP	Callback Control Protocol	X	X
CCP	Compression Control Protocol	X	X
COMMENT	Network Monitors COMMENT Protocol	X	X
DDP	AppleTalk Datagram Delivery Protocol	X	X
DHCP	Dynamic Host Configuration Protocol	X	X

Continued

Table 23-4 *(continued)*

Protocol	Description	Network Monitor in Windows NT Server	Network Monitor in SMS (version 1.2)
DNS	Domain Name System	X	X
FINGER	Internet's Finger Protocol	X	X
FTP	Internet's File Transfer Protocol	X	X
GENERIC	Network Monitors GENERIC Protocol	X	X
GRE	Generic Routing Encapsulation v2 (GRE)	X	X
HTTP	**Internet's Hypertext Transfer Protocol**		**X**
ICMP	Internet Control Message Protocol	X	X
IGMP	Internet Group Management Protocol	X	X
IP	Internet Protocol	X	X
IPCP	IP Control Protocol	X	X
IPX	NetWare's Internet Packet Exchange Protocol	X	X
IPXCP	Internetwork Packet Exchange Control Protocol	X	X
IPXWAN	IPX over Wide Area Networks	X	X
JAVA	**JAVA Class Format**		**X**
LAP	AppleTalk Link Access Protocol	X	X
LCP	Internet's Link Control Protocol	X	X
LDAP	Lightweight Directory Access Protocol		X
LLC	Logical Link Control/ 802.2 protocol	X	X
MESSAGE	Network Monitors MESSAGE Protocol	X	X

Chapter 23: Network Monitor Secrets

Protocol	Description	Network Monitor in Windows NT Server	Network Monitor in SMS (version 1.2)
MSRPC	Microsoft Remote Procedure Call (RPC)	X	X
NBFCP	NetBIOS Frames Control Protocol	X	X
NBIPX	NetBIOS on IPX protocol	X	X
NBP	AppleTalk Name Binding Protocol	X	X
NBT	Internet's NetBIOS over TP/IP	X	X
NCP	NetWare Core Protocol	X	X
NDR	NetWare Diagnostic Redirector	X	X
NetBIOS	Network Basic Input/Output System protocol	X	X
NETLOGON	MS Netlogon Broadcasts	X	X
NFS	Internet's Network File System	X	X
NMPI	Microsoft Name Management Protocol on IPX	X	X
NNTP	**Network Monitor NNTP Parser**		**X**
NSP	NetWare Serialization Protocol	X	X
NWDP	NetWare WatchDog Protocol	X	X
ODBC	Network Monitors ODBC Protocol	X	X
OSPF	Internet's OSPF (Open Shortest Path First)	X	X
PAP	AppleTalk Printer Access Protocol	X	X

Continued

Table 23-4 (continued)

Protocol	Description	Network Monitor in Windows NT Server	Network Monitor in SMS (version 1.2)
PPP	Internet's Point to Point Protocol	X	X
PPPCHAP	PPP Challenge Handshake Authentication Protocol	X	X
PPPML	PPP Multilink Protocol	X	X
PPPPAP	PPP Password Authentication Protocol	X	X
PPTP	Point to Point Tunneling Protocol (PPTP)	X	X
R_DRSUAPI	Generated RPC parser for interface drsuapi		X
R_INTERNET	Generated RPC parser for interface InternetServer		X
R_LOGON	Generated RPC parser for interface logon		X
R_LSARPC	Generated RPC parser for interface lsarpc		X
R_NSPI	Generated RPC parser for interface nspi		X
R_REMOTEAUTO	Generated RPC parser for interface NetChannel, Remote Automation		X
R_RXDS	Generated RPC parser for interface nxds		X

Protocol	Description	Network Monitor in Windows NT Server	Network Monitor in SMS (version 1.2)
R_SRVSVC	Generated RPC parser for interface srvsvc		X
R_WINSIF	Generated RPC parser for interface winsif		X
R_WINSPOOL	Generated RPC parser for interface winspool		X
RIP	Internet's Routing Information Protocol	X	X
RIPX	NetWare's Routing Information Protocol	X	X
RPC	Internet's Remote Procedure Call	X	X
RPL	Remote Program Load	X	X
RTMP	AppleTalk Routing Table Maintenance Protocol	X	X
SAP	Service Advertising Protocol	X	X
SMB	Server Message Block Protocol	X	X
SMT	FDDI MAC Station Management	X	X
SNAP	Sub-Network Access Protocol	X	X
SPX	NetWare Sequenced Packet Exchange Protocol	X	X
STATS	Network Monitors Capture Statistics Protocol	X	X
TCP	Transmission Control Protocol	X	X

Continued

Table 23-4 *(continued)*

Protocol	Description	Network Monitor in Windows NT Server	Network Monitor in SMS (version 1.2)
TELNET	Inernet's TELNET – remote terminal protocol		X
TMAC	Token Ring MAC layer	X	X
TRAIL	Network Monitors TRAIL Protocol	X	X
UDP	Internet's User Datagram Protocol	X	X
VINES_IP	VINES Internet Protocol	X	X
VINES_TL	VINES Transport Layer Protocol	X	X
XNS	Xerox XNS Protocol	X	X
ZIP	AppleTalk Zone Information Protocol	X	X

Basically, SMS provides more "current" protocol parsers. In addition to marking the SMS column with its unique parsers, I've bolded those rows so you can see at a glance the differences with respect to protocol parsers between the Network Monitors contained in Windows NT Server and SMS respectively.

Note

Notice how SMS is providing additional protocol parsers related to the Internet (HTTP, JAVA, TELNET) that Network Monitor in Windows NT Server does not.

See Appendix B for complete descriptions of selected protocols including specific and detailed properties down to the hex level.

Summary

In this chapter:

- You learned to define Network Monitor.
- You learned the basics of Network Monitor.
- You learned the basics of network analysis.
- Your learned that Network Monitor can be configured for capturing and viewing.

- You learned about resources for learning more about Network Monitor include paid support incidents, Microsoft certification courses, Microsoft TechNet, and specific books on network analysis.
- You learned that, although the products are comparable, there are similar and different features in Windows NT Server Network Monitor and System Management Server (SMS) Network Monitor.

Chapter 24

Task Manager and Other Neat Tricks

In This Chapter

- Defining Task Manager features
- Tuning Task Manager to report the information you need
- Optimizing Windows NT Server via Task Manager
- Defining WinMSD features
- Learning about SQL Trace and ODBCPING
- Learning about the Microsoft Exchange RPING utility
- Viewing and analyzing Event Logs
- Discovering the Microsoft System Information tool

Windows NT Server contains several more performance management tools than just Performance Monitor and Network Monitor to help you manage your system. These tools include Task Manager and WinMSD. Both of these offer a more static view of your system than discussed in the past few chapters.

But don't let the small footprint of Task Manager lull you into complacency. Behind its meek appearance, Task Manager serves a useful purpose. By the end of this chapter, I think you will agree that Task Manager is much larger than you ever imagined. In fact, Task Manager reports some measurements that both Performance Monitor and Network Monitor can only dream about reporting. WinMSD is an old friend and is the reincarnation of MSD from the DOS era. The primary difference between WinMSD and MSD is that WinMSD is GUI-based, stable under Windows NT and reports much more information than its MS-DOS predecessor.

I'll show you the Systems Properties sheet and neat little tools included with SQL Server and Microsoft Exchange to assist with your performance management activities. And don't forget the event logs contained in Event Viewer. You have my personal assurance that you will interact frequently with the event logs as you journey toward the perfectly optimized Windows NT Server configuration.

Secret

One of the best kept secrets is to actually install Microsoft Office on your Windows NT server to dramatically improve the monitoring of your system. That is so that you can use Microsoft System Information contained within Excel. But more on that wonderful trick later.

At the end the chapter, we'll get a house call from our friend, Dr. Watson. Now, let's discuss Task Manager.

Introducing Task Manager

Remember attending college and how important "exact" details seemed? Take the quaint series in the business school. Exact mathematical calculations performed as part of the financial analysis, theoretically, to purchase a stock seemed so doggone necessary. Let me ask you a question several years hence. When you recently met with your life insurance agent, did you perform the same rigorous mathematics as you allocated your retirement fund between high-risk, growth, and conservative investment vehicles? Of course not, even with something as important as your retirement fund. Most likely, you sat on your sofa and barked something like 30 percent to aggressive, 40 percent to high-growth, and 30 percent to conservative. Case closed and investment made.

The preceding example reflects how most of us live in the real world on a day-to-day basis. Intuition, combined with a reasonable amount of information, guides our decisions, including how we manage our Windows NT Server networks. Intuition in the network manager ranks is clearly gained by experience or being blessed with superior intelligence. Efficiently gathering reasonable amounts of information in Windows NT Server is the goal. Thankfully, much of the quick-and-dirty information we need is just a simple right-click away via Task Manager. Let's face it! Task Manager is probably sufficient to provides enough system-based information to meet your casual Windows NT Server decision making needs (see Figure 24-1).

Task Manager is my buddy and I make no bones about it. I use Task Manager on a day-to-day basis as outlined in the text that follows. Access Task Manager by right-clicking while the cursor is on the Windows NT Server taskbar.

- **The Applications tab sheet.** Use the Applications tab sheet (Figure 24-2) to identify which applications are running and what the status of each is. In particular, I'm interested in the not-responding status. It is those applications that are not responding that I deftly annihilate with a swift click on the End Task button.

Chapter 24: Task Manager and Other Neat Tricks 855

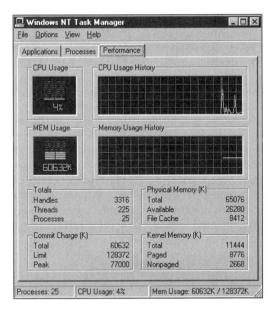

Figure 24-1: Windows NT Task Manager

Figure 24-2: The Applications tab sheet in Task Manager

- **The Performance tab sheet.** The Performance tab sheet is your mini–Performance Monitor (see Figure 24-3). At a glance, you can get a quick view of the CPU usage on your NT Server and a sense of how memory is being used. This tab sheet is most useful when I encounter a badly behaved application or process. Periodically, I know my system is running slow because acceptable response times droops and end users start calling. Looking at the Performance tab sheet typically confirms my beliefs. A war story is in order. Microsoft Exchange is perhaps the one BackOffice application that is still really finding its feet. Exchange-related processes (such as DSX.EXE — a process related to Exchange Directory Services) have a way of freaking out on occasion, resulting in 100 percent processor utilization rates on your server plus no available memory. Not only does the Performance tab sheet confirm this nightmare, but I can terminate this bad dream, as described previously, via the Application tab sheet and the End Task button.

Figure 24-3: The Performance tab sheet in Task Manager

- **The Processes tab sheet.** The Processes tab sheet, while used less frequently, is invaluable when we seek to identify the offending process down to the file name (see Figure 24-4). Take my Microsoft Exchange example. The DSX.EXE process once really did consume the CPU time on my Windows NT server. The solution? I went to the Processes tab sheet, quickly identified the problematic "Image Name" (Microsoft's term for process or application in column one of the Processes tab sheet) and killed it by clicking the End Process button. Yahoo! Problem solved.

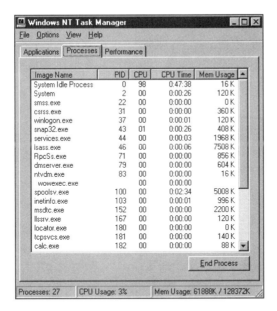

Figure 24-4: The Processes tab sheet in Task Manager

Configuring Task Manager — Applications view

The Applications view is the simplest and most common view found in Task Manager. It is the view that you typically use to determine whether an application is running or not responding. This is typically the screen where you kill your nonrunning applications. Even though the interface for the Applications tab is simple, it underscores a major point about Windows NT Server compared to previous Windows releases. That is, you can kill a crashed application without have to reboot the server. Remember that applications run in a protected memory area separate from the Windows NT Server kernel.

One feature that has been carried over from prior releases of Windows NT Server with respect to the Applications view in Task Manager is the context menu (see Figure 24-5). From the context menu, you may end a task. To access a context menu for an application, simply right-click while an application name has the focus (that is, you have the mouse pointer placed over the application name).

Another possible use for the Applications view in Task Manager is to start a launch another application by selecting the New Task (Run) menu option under the File menu. This same command is available by right-clicking anywhere on an unoccupied area of the Applications tab sheet.

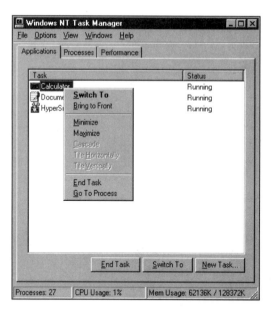

Figure 24-5: A context menu in Task Manager

Configuring Task Manager — Performance view

This is the "heart beat" display in Task Manager. It is, at a glance, perhaps the best view to show a manager. Even basic computer users can understand the two major features of this view: CPU Usage and MEM Usage.

CPU Usage

CPU Usage is similar to two object:counters in Performance Monitor: Processor:% Processor Time and System:% Total Processor Time. Note that CPU Usage doesn't measure Idle threads. To see Idle threads, you would need to view the System Idle Process row on the Processes tab sheet in Task Manager (remember that Windows NT Server uses Idle threads as something of a sleep mode for the CPU).

MEM Usage

MEM Usage not only reflects the kilobytes of virtual memory used but can also be tracked via the Memory:Committed bytes object:counter in Performance Monitor.

Task Manager does something with its Performance view that can only be accomplished in Performance Monitor when two copies of Performance Monitor are running. That special feature is to display the same counter simultaneously as a histogram and a graph (see Figure 24-6).

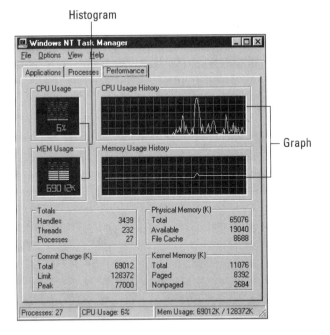

Figure 24-6: The Performance tab sheet histogram, graph, and table formats

Totals

This section refers to several types of system objects including handles, threads, and processes. Because system objects take up space in nonpaged memory that is managed by the operating system, we are indeed concerned about these numbers. Too many active system objects typically results in bottlenecks at the processor or in memory use.

- **Total handles.** Handles essentially refer to system objects such as open files. Technically, it is the object handles present in all active processes.

- **Total threads.** Reflects executing threads or, stated another way, the number of threads running. This measurement is akin to the Process :Thread Count_Total in Performance Monitor.

- **Total processes.** A process, in my eyes, can simply be thought of as an application. This number reflects Idle processes that run basically when the CPU is sleeping.

Physical Memory

This is easy. Total refers to the total RAM installed on the computer running Windows NT Server. It is measured in kilobytes. Not surprisingly, "Available" refers to the available RAM in kilobytes. File Cache refers to the total memory that has been allocated to the file cache.

Commit Charge

This generically refers to memory allocated to the operating system and programs. This is includes both physical RAM and virtual memory. Total refers to the memory (both real and virtual) that is currently in use. Limit refers to the upper limits of all memory combined before the paging file size would have to be increased. Peak refers to highest memory in use during the current session.

Kernel Memory

First, it is important to understand that kernel refers to memory in use by the operating system in kernel mode. Figure 24-7 demonstrates the differences between Kernel mode and User mode in Windows NT Server.

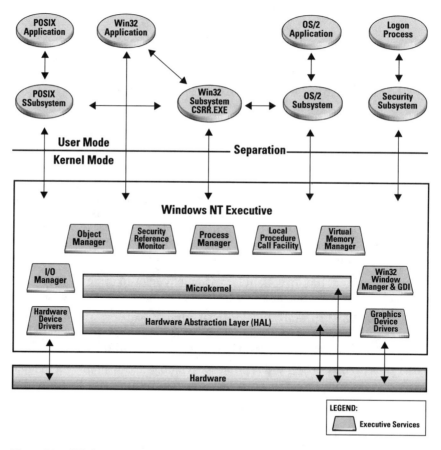

Figure 24-7: Windows NT Server User and Kernel modes

Basically, Windows NT Server Executive-related services run in Kernel mode. Total refers to both the paged and nonpaged memory in use. Pages refers to operating system's page pool. Nonpaged, not surprisingly, refers to the nonpaged memory dedicated to the operating system.

Double-click anywhere on the Performance tab sheet in Windows NT Task Manager and the CPU Usage and MEM Usage real-time charts will expand to fill the entire Task Manager window (see Figure 24-8). This will eliminate the extra descriptions, such as Totals, Physical Memory, Commit Charge, and Kernel Memory, and give you just the charts. You may resize this window to consume the entire screen or just a small portion of it. When this window is resized to cover your desktop, it looks very much like another tool we're familiar with: Performance Monitor (that is, if all we charted on Performance Monitor was the CPU utilization rate).

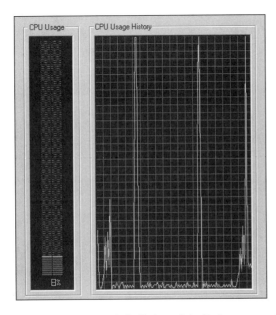

Figure 24-8: An "exploded" view of the Performance tab sheet

Secret

Be sure to select the Show Kernel Times menu option under the View menu. You might think it's the return of Big Red (NetWare) in your Task Manager CPU Usage, but rest easy. This red secondary graph line merely reflects the CPU activity dedicated to the Windows NT Server operating system in Kernel mode. The difference between the green and red CPU utilization chart lines would reflect the CPU activity dedicated to User mode activities such as applications.

Configuring Task Manager — Processes view

Task Manager can be "richly" configured to reflect many different Windows NT Server system conditions. Fully configured, Task Manager in the Processes view would display 16 columns of information and look similar to Figure 24-9.

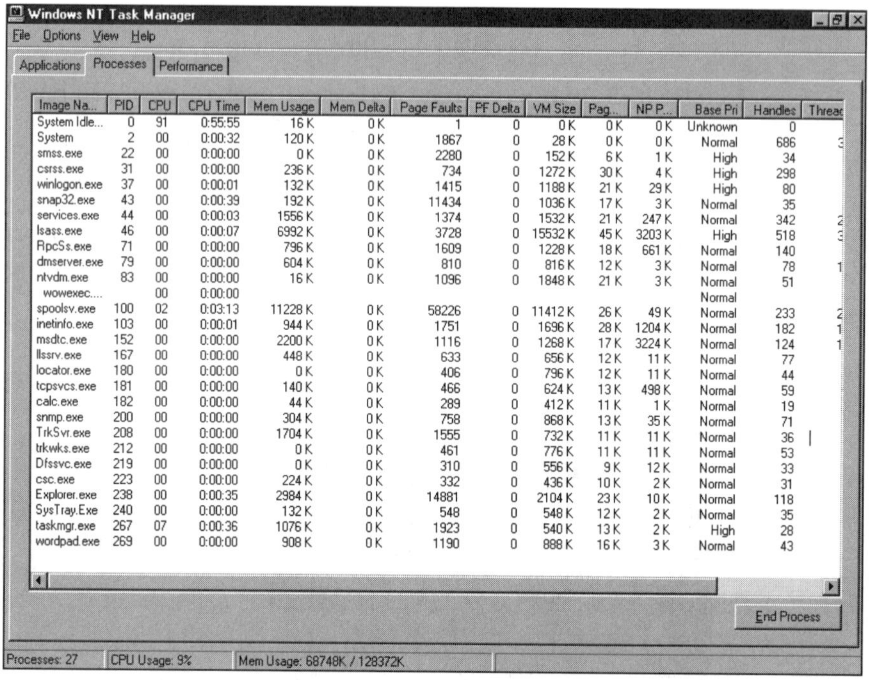

Figure 24-9: Process columns displayed on one screen

Each column reports important system information. When in the Processes view, to add columns, first select the View drop-down menu and click the Select Columns menu option (see Figure 24-10). Then single-click the check box for each column you want to add to the Task Manager Processes view.

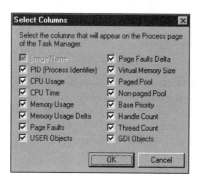

Figure 24-10: The Select Columns dialog box

"So what," you remark. What do all of these columns really do for me? Your answer is in Table 24-1.

Table 24-1 Task Manager Processes Column Definitions

Column	Comments	Relation to Performance Monitor (Process object)
Image Name	This must always be selected and is the process name.	It is similar to selecting one of the instances in the Instances box of Performance Monitor after you have selected a specific Object:Counter.
PID (Process Identifier)	This is the Process ID number that a running process receives. One use of this column is to better understand and "see in action" the nature of processes and threads discussed halfway through Course #687, "WindowsNTServer — Core Technologies" certification course (or its successor).In the certification class, processesare identified in the context of running multiple processes on a single computer or a process being single or multiple threaded. The conceptual discussion also includes priority boosting of processes and threads (we actually handle this vis-à-vis the Set Priority context menu option in a moment). Because the certification exam will hold you responsible for understanding and identifying processes running on Windows NT Server, it is highly recommended that you take a moment to consider the importance of the PID column.	This is the ID Process counter associated with the Process object. Note that Process IDs assigned on a session basis. This ID number will change, for example, the next time you reboot Windows NT Server. Process ID in Performance Monitor maps directly to the PID column in Task Manager. In Performance Monitor, display Process:ID Process in the report format. This value looks silly when plotted in the Performance Monitor Chart view.
CPU Usage (Displayed as CPU)	This is the percentage of processor utilization time since the last update interval. The update interval is discussed later in the chapter.	This is the same as %Processor Time.
CPU Time	Measured in seconds, this is the total CPU time used by a process since its activities commenced.	There is no equivalent measurement in Performance Monitor.
Memory Usage (Mem Usage)	Measured in kilobytes, this is the quantity of main memory used.	This is the same as the Working Set performance counter.

Continued

Table 24-1 *(continued)*

Column	Comments	Relation to Performance Monitor (Process object)
Memory Usage Delta (Mem Delta)	The word "delta" in statistics refers to change, and its usage is no different here. This process measure refers to the memory use change since the last update interval. It is interesting to note that negative values (a decline in memory usage) can be reflected in Task Manager but cannot be reflected in like manner in Performance Monitor.	None.
Page Faults	This is cool. For a given process, this refers to how many times a page fault occurred. That means the data wasn't in memory and had to be retrieved from the hard disk, which of course is much slower. This is a cumulative value from the time the process commenced.	None. You might be tempted to use the Page Faults/sec counter found in the Process object, but that would be misleading and have you effectively comparing apples to oranges. Page Faults/sec is calculated as a rate per second, but Page Faults is, of course, a cumulative value.
Page Faults Delta (PF Delta)	This reflects the difference or change in the number of page faults since the last update interval.	There is no equivalent measure in Performance Monitor.
Virtual Memory in Size (VM Size)	Want to know how much of the paging file your process is consuming? Then this is your measure. Note that the information is reported in kilobytes.	Refer to the counter Page File Bytes under the Process object Performance Monitor for an equivalent measure.
Paged Pool	Reflects how much user memory a process is using. Remember that paged pool memory is the virtual memory that is available and can be paged to disk. It contains user memory (all) and system memory (some). The measurement is in kilobytes.	See the Page File Bytes counter (same as the preceding item).
Nonpaged Pool (NP Pool)	This is the nonpaged pool or system memory used by a process. By definition, this memory is not paged to disk. The measurement is in kilobytes.	See the Pool Nonpaged Bytes counter under the Process object in Performance Monitor.

Column	Comments	Relation to Performance Monitor (Process object)
Base Priority	This measurement ties into the previous discussion about how threads are explained in Windows NT Server Core Technologies course. This value, the base priority, is set by the process itself, not Windows NT Server. The role of Windows NT Server is to adjust the process's threads within a range of the base priority. These ranges are described when setting base priorities via Task Manager is discussed.	Select the Priority Base counter in the Process object.
Handle Count	Reflects the number of object handles in the process's object table. In English, this refers to the process's capability to access an object. When an object is accessed, a handle is created as a token. This identifies who has a connection to the token object. At a very deep level in security auditing in Windows NT Server, we are interested in who is accessing objects. Handles provide the method for monitoring such accesses. An alternative definition of handles is the "the number of system objects."	See the Handle Count counter under the Process object.
Thread Count	This is simple. It is the threads running in a process. Note that 16-bit applications are only going to have one process because 16-bit applications are single-threaded.	See the Thread Count object under the Process object.
USER Objects	Reports information on objects active in user mode.	N/A
GDI Objects	Reports information on graphic display interface related objects.	N/A

See Appendix C for descriptions of common image names displayed in Task Manager.

How to look important with no money down—or how I justified my job using Task Manager! Had enough bulk mail in your e-mail in-box lately promising fantastic returns for little or no effort? Here is one more. Depending on your work situation, you may or may not have a need to justify your existence on occasion. So when those downsizing bean counters are nipping at your paycheck, fight back! Take a Windows NT Server and run Task Manager in the Processes view with all sixteen columns loaded up. Watch the cell values dance as Windows NT Server performs normal operations. This activity gives the illusion of important activity (okay, it is important activity) and makes your role look indispensable! Don't forget the "secret" to magic and sometimes keeping your job is illusion!

Once you have adjusted the Task Manager window to the size you want, it is easy to automatically have the Processes tab sheet display as many of the measurement columns as possible. This is accomplished by using the column autoresize feature in Task Manager. This feature is similar to that found in Excel. Simply place the cursor over the column separator vertical bar along the title line. The cursor will change shapes and look something like a Danforth anchor used in boating (see Figure 24-11). When this Danforth anchor–like symbol is present, double-click while still on the vertical separator bar and the column will automatically adjust to the smallest width possible that still accurately displays the column information. The results are impressive when you do this for the entire set of columns in Task Manager. On a 14" monitor, I was able to get all 13 columns of information to display at once on the Processes tab sheet.

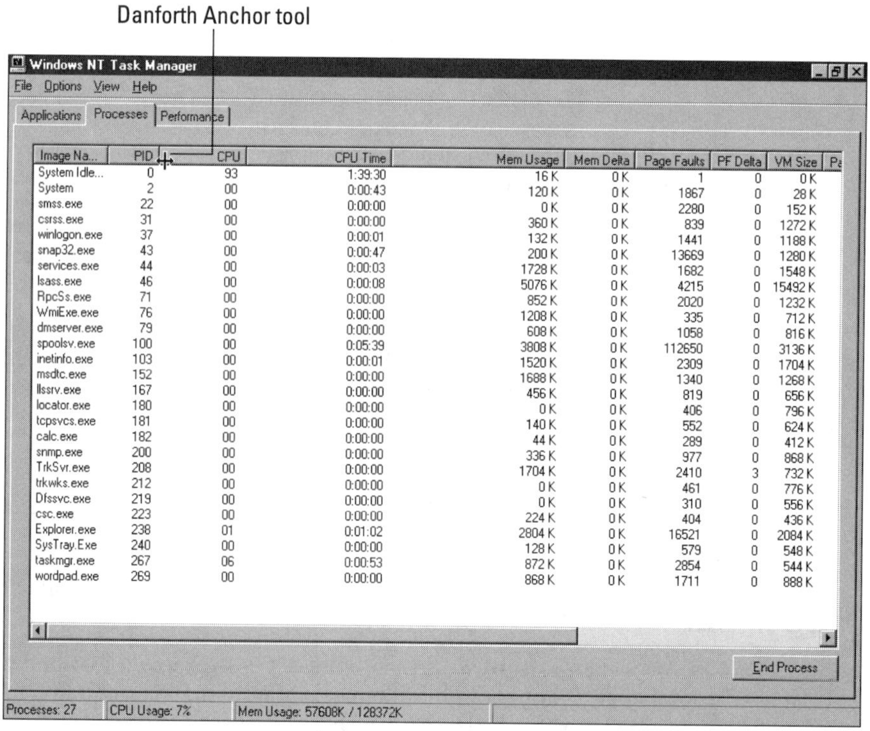

Figure 24-11: Customizing the number of displayed columns

Getting prioritized

Task Manager can be used to set CPU processing priorities for an application or process in Windows NT Server. This is accomplished very easily by selecting a process in the Processes tab sheet in Task Manager and displaying the context menu via a right-click (see Figure 24-12). You can change the base priority of a process to one of several options: Real-time, High, Normal, and Low. These changes are only temporary and last for the current session that the process is running.

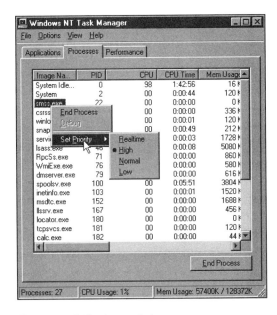

Figure 24-12: Setting a priority

Secret

To change an application's base priority so that the changes are retained each time the application is launched, perform the following: On the properties sheet for an application's executable file (.exe), use the command lines discussed in Table 24-2.

Table 24-2 Setting Application Priority Classes via the Command Line

To Set an Application to This Base Priority Class	Use This Start Command and Switch
Real-time	start /realtime
High	start /high
Normal	start /normal
Low	start /low

For example, if the application is Excel and you want to set a base priority for this application of high, then use this command:

`Start /high excel.exe`

Note that the base priority of applications is normal. In fact, serious system instability can result if an application is set to real-time and competes with operating system–level processes.

But what does this mean?

Windows NT Server uses the microkernel to manage the prioritization threads with respect to processing. So what is the microkernel? It rests atop the hardware abstraction layer (HAL) and is affectionately referred to as the heart and soul of Windows NT Server, as shown in the diagram of the Windows NT Server architecture (see Figure 24-13). You will recall that the Windows NT Server architecture was also discussed in Chapter 17, "Regular Windows NT Server."

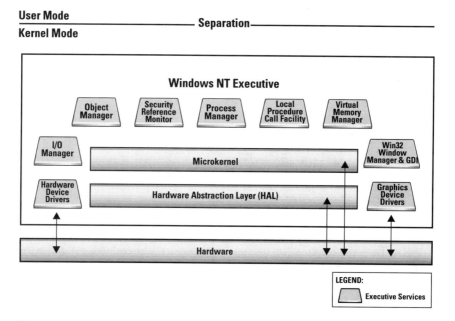

Figure 24-13: Windows NT Server architecture

Threads from an application are scheduled for processor time based upon an assigned priority number from 1 to 31. The priority number assigned can vary within a class, and thus we say threads are scheduled for processing based on their dynamic priority. Huh? Let's break down this concept into simple components.

First, a Windows 32-bit application is a *process* as far as Windows NT Server is concerned. Next, a *thread* is a unit of code that can get a slice of CPU time from the operating system (see Figure 24-14).

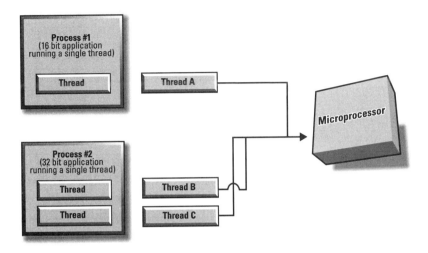

Figure 24-14: Processes and threads

So we see that these threads are scheduled for processor time according to their priority. A priority is determined by a class assignment, which is a range of numbers that are assigned by the application's developers. A process can belong to one of four classes: real-time, high, normal, and idle.

Windows NT Server has four priority classes: Real-time (31–16), High (15–11), Normal (10–6), and Idle (6–1). Notice how these priority classes outlined in Table 24-3 correspond to the options available in Figure 24-12.

Table 24-3 Application Priority Classes

Application Priority Class	Thread Priority	Base
Real-time	Time critical	31
Real-time	Highest	26
Real-time	Above normal	25
Real-time	Normal	24
Real-time	Below normal	23
Real-time	Lowest	22
Real-time	Idle	16

Continued

Table 24-3 *(continued)*

Application Priority Class	Thread Priority	Base
High	Highest	15
High	Above normal	14
High	Normal	13
High	Below normal	12
High	Low	11
Normal	Highest	10
Normal	Above normal	9
Normal	Normal	8
Normal	Below normal	7
Normal	Lowest	6
Idle	Highest	6 (overlaps with Normal-Lowest)
Idle	Above normal	5
Idle	Normal	4
Idle	Below normal	3
Idle	Lowest	2
Idle	Idle	1

Windows NT Server can vary the process's priority within a class. Take normal for example. Normal is a priority class with a range of 6 to 10. The base priority of a process or application in the normal class is 8 (which is the midpoint between the class range of 6 and 10). To efficiently schedule CPU resources, Windows NT Server will "dynamically" boost the priority of a thread within the base class of its process (+/− 2). This is normal and helps balance the competing demands on the processor (see Figure 24-15).

You can, or course, modify the base priority of a process in Windows NT Server. This was shown in Figure 24-12. It can also be accomplished via Windows NT System Properties under the Performance tab when we boost the foreground application priority.

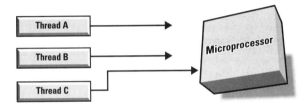

Thread C has been boosted

Figure 24-15: Thread boosting

Converting image names to real names

One of the biggest problems I encountered for *the longest time* was how to identify the application that the process name was associated with. This problem severely limited my effective use of the Processes view of Task Manager. And believe me, I had major needs to effectively use Task Manager, like the time a File and Print Services for NetWare (FPNW) application was being way overpowered in a large client environment. My specific need was to identify the image names or, in lay terms, the process names associated with FPNW. Once so identified, I could experiment with boosting the process's priority so that it was guaranteed more processor time and thus higher performance (but, of course, hopefully without incurring any system instabilities).

Here is how you can identify what image name is associated with what application. The best way is to simply search your drives using the Find command accessed via the Start button in Windows NT Server. Alternative ways to find out more information on a specific image name include searching on the image name with a broad query applied against Microsoft TechNet or one of the powerful search engines on the Internet (see the text that follows).

In this example using the Find command, we will seek to better identify TAPISRV.EXE and demystify what it really is.

STEPS:
To discover the true identity of TAPISRV.EXE

Step 1. Notice the image name TAPISRV.EXE in the Processes tab sheet of Task Manager (see Figure 24-16). You can easily perform these steps to better identify any image name; we are simply using TAPISRV.EXE as an example.

Continued

STEPS

To discover the true identity of TAPISRV.EXE *(continued)*

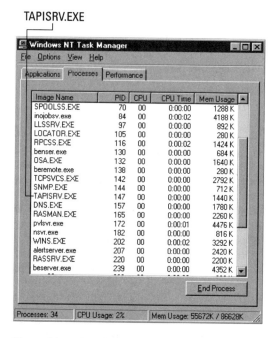

Figure 24-16: The TAPISRV.EXE image name

Step 2. Using the "Find: All Files" dialog box accessed from the Start button, type **TAPISRV.EXE** in the Name field on the Name and Location tab sheet. Then click the Find Now button. Hint: It is recommended that you first search the drive(s) that contain the Windows NT Server operating system and/or related applications. You may either search by specific drive identifier such as [C] for the C drive or search on "My Computer" to search all local drives. It has been my experience that many of the image names I'm interested in are indeed Windows NT Server operating system–related, so by first searching on the drive that contains the operating system, I save search time. The results from our search on TAPISRV.EXE are shown in Figure 24-17.

Step 3. Right-click the file named TAPISRV.EXE (or whatever file you have searched on). Select the Properties menu option on the context menu (see Figure 24-18).

Chapter 24: Task Manager and Other Neat Tricks **873**

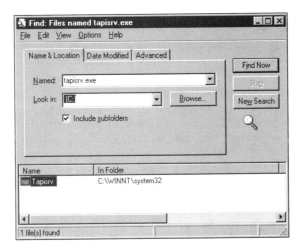

Figure 24-17: Using Find File to "find" TAPISRV.EXE on the computer

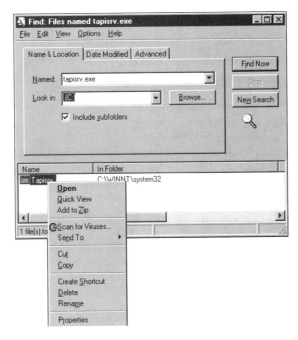

Figure 24-18: Selecting properties for TAPISRV.EXE

Continued

STEPS

To discover the true identity of TAPISRV.EXE *(continued)*

Step 4. Select the Version tab sheet on the Properties dialog box (see Figure 24-19), and you are presented with more information about your image name than you might ever have imagined. This information is most helpful when you are working with third-party drivers and need to know the manufacturer of the file.

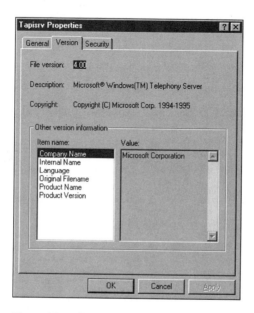

Figure 24-19: Version tab sheet properties for TAPISRV.EXE

Multiple processors

It's just now that one can read a book discussing multiple processors and feel a "real" connection to such a topic. That's because Moore's Law is alive and at work. Moore's Law observes that technology prices will drop and processing power will increase over time (prices will drop by half every 18 months). Compaq workstations with dual Pentium processors can be purchased for under $5,000 as of early 1998 (and of course we'll only see the price drop further in the following years). Today, a computer equipped with multiple processors is still deployed only in server and high-end workstation environments. However, you will see multiple-processor machines at the desktop soon for one simple reason: performance. When I recently installed Windows NT Workstation on a Compaq 6300 Workstation with dual Pentium 266 processors, the installation process took under ten minutes. Now that's performance!

Task Manager was constructed with multiple processors in mind. The Performance tab sheet can display the activity of each processor on separate CPU History windows.

Task Manager enables you to assign which processors may execute which application (or process). To understand the benefit of this feature, you need to understand how Windows NT Server processes threads on a multiple-processor machine. First, Windows NT Server supports up to eight processors. Second, the microkernel in Windows NT Server distributes thread-based activity across the processors (based on the priorities assigned to the threads). Thus, 32-bit applications with multiple threads of execution will have threads processed over more than one processor.

Then there is the matter of Windows NT Server's interpretation of a famous U.S. Supreme Court case, Brown vs. Board of Education, that is, separate but equal. Windows NT Server uses soft affinity to try to equally distribute the processing load over all processors. This is known as symmetric multiprocessing (SMP) and reflects the current design and implementation paradigm in the computing community. This is truly Windows NT Server's way of trying to treat each processor equally. Technically, this is called soft affinity, which assumes all processors are equal and can access the same physical memory.

But back in the days when knights were bold and kings owned all the gold, the computing community used asymmetrical multiprocessing implementations to distribute processes via assignments to specific processors. This approach is known as processor affinity and can be implemented in Windows NT Server via the context menu on the Processes tab sheet in Task Manager (see Figure 24-20).

You can then select which processor(s) this application or process will be executed on. With forethought and planning, you could create a Windows NT Server computing scenario whereby one application had one processor to itself and didn't have to share. However, conventional thinking is such that your entire system will suffer a performance decrease because the other applications will be forced to compete for the limited resources of the remaining processors. And Windows NT Server does such a great job of distributing the load equally over your bed of processors in an SMP scenario — why mess with success? Think of it as an automatic gearbox on an automobile. Real muscle car owners typically prefer automatic transmissions to manual transmissions because the car does a better job than the human driver of shifting under acceleration. Well, that's why you would typically leave well enough alone and allow Window NT Server's soft affinity approach to work unimpeded. It can probably do a better job automatically than you can manually.

WinMSD Is a Winner!

WinMSD is one of the other goodies that I promised to describe for you in addition to Task Manager. It is distinct from Task Manager. WinMSD is a static snapshot of system health with an emphasis on devices. Contrastingly, Task Manager is a dynamic view of processor activity, memory consumption, and currently running applications and processes. In this section, we will review each of the tab sheets in WinMSD: Version, System, Display, Drives, Resources, Environment, Network, Memory, and Services.

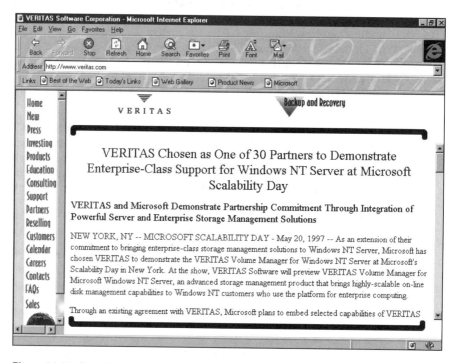

Figure 24-20: Task Manager's Processor Affinity menu

This version of WinMSD is much more accurate and reliable than its distant DOS-based cousin. Perhaps you remember, not too long ago, when MSD was introduced as part of MS-DOS. It was the greatest thing since sliced bread, enabling you not only to troubleshoot interrupt conflicts but also to decide, via the MSD memory map, in what order device drivers should be loaded low or high in your CONFIG.SYS file. Life was great as long as you ran MSD in a strict or true DOS session. But if you launched Windows and then tried to run good old MSD, you not only got a warning screen that the results of MSD may be unreliable, but you were able to witness these unreliable results first hand. Don't believe me? Then just go upstairs to your attic and pull out that old 386-based PC running MS-DOS 5.0 and WFW. Create an interrupt conflict somehow (maybe put in a second sound card). Then, under WFW, launch MSD and attempt to resolve the interrupt conflict. Let's just say I wish you well, my friend.

To launch WinMSD, type the command **WINMSD** in the Run dialog box in Windows NT Server (see Figure 24-21).

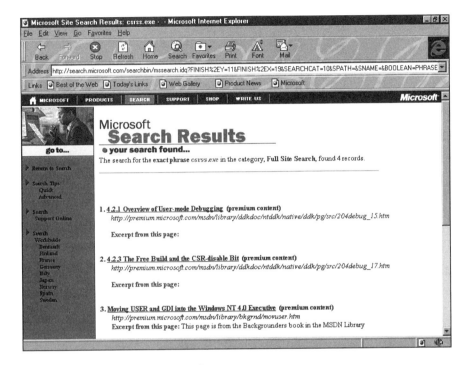

Figure 24-21: The WinMSD command

The WinMSD command actually runs the Windows NT Diagnostics application shown in Figure 24-22. This application has remained virtually unchanged since Windows NT Server 3.5; however, its importance shouldn't be underestimated.

Version tab sheet

At a glance, on the Version tab sheet, you can tell what version of Windows NT Server you are running. This might seem like a silly thing to do, but out on the server farm, it's easy to become confused. Such confusion can be resolved with the Version tab sheet.

Secret

I've made of habit of running Windows NT Diagnostics and looking at the Version tab sheet so that I can tell what service pack has been applied to Windows NT Server. Service Pack version information is shown on the Version tab sheet when you run the Windows NT Diagnostics. Of course service pack information is reported during the startup phase of Windows NT Server at the first blue screen, but who wants to reboot your server just to see that information? It is far easier to run WinMSD.

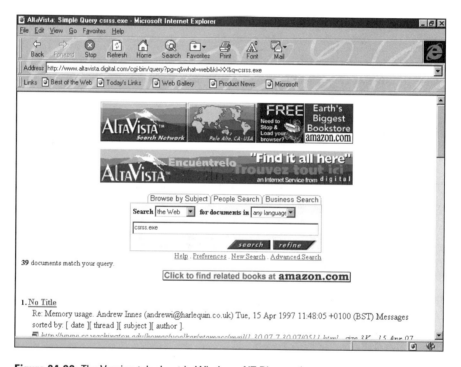

Figure 24-22: The Version tab sheet in Windows NT Diagnostics

System tab sheet

Basically the System tab sheet (see Figure 24-23) reports BIOS and processor information. The BIOS information is useful because, as a Windows NT Server system manager, you need to periodically monitor the Web sites of your BIOS manufacturers and see if a BIOS patch has been released. These patches, usually in the form of downloadable files, are applied as image files to your BIOS chip set. Applying such a file is known as reflashing.

In Figure 24-23, the computer is using Phoenix BIOS version 4.05. A quick glance at the home page for Phoenix at www.phoenix.com reveals different BIOS upgrades that can be downloaded and applied to your existing computers (see Figure 24-24). I have recently downloaded BIOS fixes that allowed my older computer to see hard drives greater than 540MB in size and a newer computer with an Intel chip set to recognize over 64MB of DIMM RAM memory.

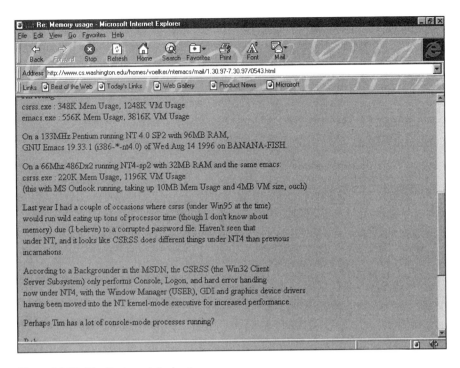

Figure 24-23: The Systems tab sheet

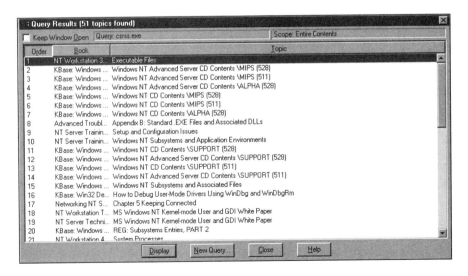

Figure 24-24: BIOS information at www.phoenix.com

Display tab sheet

At a glance, you can see anything and everything you need to know about your video adapter and display with the Display tab sheet (see Figure 24-25). Notice that this is much more meaningful than accessing Display Properties by right-clicking the desktop. I highly recommend you periodically check the home page for your Display BIOS provider. Vendors like S3, Incorporated, periodically provide updated video drivers that repair known incompatibilities with Windows NT Server and, perhaps more important, better optimize the display driver for use in the Windows NT Server environment.

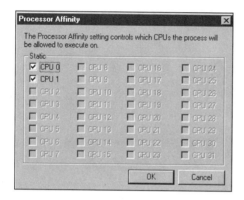

Figure 24-25: The Display tab sheet

Display Properties accessed by right-clicking the desktop reports different information, as shown in Figure 24-26.

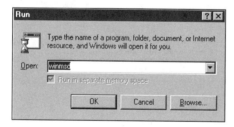

Figure 24-26: The Display Properties menu

Drives tab sheet

You may recall in Chapters 11 and 12 that I discussed the importance of drive space management. The Drives tab sheet in WinMSD is one such area to gather the daily and monthly drive information I suggest.

Chapter 24: Task Manager and Other Neat Tricks 881

Okay, it's only a quick view of your drives and associated properties, but this tab sheet provides access to some important information that is not easily obtained elsewhere. Complete the following steps to see what I mean.

STEPS:
To access information about one of the drives on your Windows NT Server machine from the Drives tab sheet

Step 1. Double-click the drive of your choice on the Drives tab sheet in Windows NT Diagnostics (see Figure 24-27).

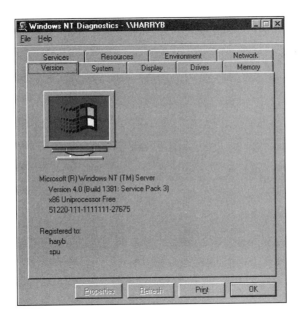

Figure 24-27: The Drives tab sheet

Step 2. The specific drive properties (such as C:> Properties) are displayed (see Figure 24-28). The General tab sheet displays information that is difficult to gather elsewhere: bytes per sector, sectors per cluster, and general clusters information.

Step 3. The File System tab sheet (see Figure 24-29) displays useful flags information that we cannot readily obtain otherwise. For example, notice that Figure 24-29 shows that Unicode characters are allowed in filenames. That means Windows NT Server supports extended and international character sets.

Continued

STEPS

To access information about one of the drives on your Windows NT Server machine from the Drives tab sheet

(continued)

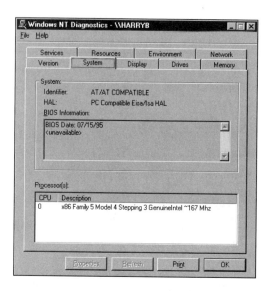

Figure 24-28: General properties for Drive C

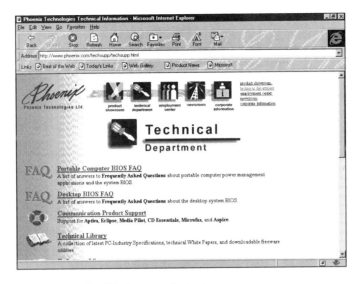

Figure 24-29: The File System tab sheet

Resources tab sheet

The Resources tab sheet, as shown in Figure 24-30, has five different views, each accessed via the five buttons at the bottom of the tab sheet (IRQ, I/O Port, DMA, Memory, Devices) Each provides a wealth of configuration information. However, you will be disappointed to see that the Device column for each tab sheet displays the generic device titles of PNP Manager or PC Compatible EISA/ISA HAL. Unfortunately, that isn't how we refer to devices in the real world.

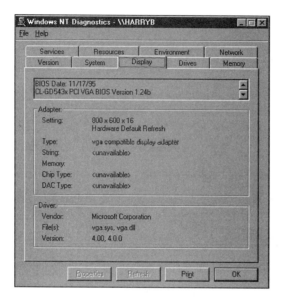

Figure 24-30: The Resources tab sheet

Secret

Be sure to select the Include HAL Resources selection box in the upper-right corner of this tab sheet. Selecting this check box results in much more detailed information being presented.

Environment tab sheet

The Environment tab sheet (see Figure 24-31) displays environmental variables for both the system and the local user in read-only mode. Environmental variables take on more significance as Windows NT Server enters the full-fledged world of corporate computing and starts supporting older, vertical market applications. An example would be the legacy accounting applications. Typically these software applications will force you to, at a minimum, define the temporary (TEMP) directory that it can use. Often you will provde additional environmental information via SET statements.

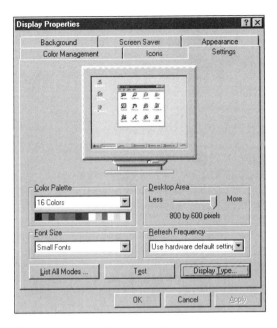

Figure 24-31: The Environment tab sheet

To set environment variables in Windows NT Server, proceed to the Environment tab sheet located on the System Properties dialog box (see Figure 24-32). As you can see, you are provided Variable and Value input fields. It is important to understand that environment variables are typically set in accordance with application specifications relayed by third-party software vendors. Be sure to adhere to these third-party specifications or you risk facing the wrath of Godzilla!

Network tab sheet

NT newbies often learn the importance of gathering, interpreting, and benefiting from core network information the hard way: being shown by a stern, gruff, and unforgiving NT guru. If you're an NT newbie, bless your heart, you are needed in the industry. More important, let's save at least one NT-related embarrassment on the way up. That "embarrassment saver" is the Network tab sheet. The Network tab sheet reports "core" network information with its different views: General, Transport, Settings, Statistics. For now, it's important to know the Network tab sheet exists and serves up the type of information you might be seeking. To actually learn more about some of the advanced information being presented, I can refer you to the Microsoft's MCSE Networking Essentials course, Novell's CNE Networking Basics and Troubleshooting courses, Microsoft TechNet, and the Internet.

Part VI: Optimizing and Troubleshooting Windows NT Server 4.0

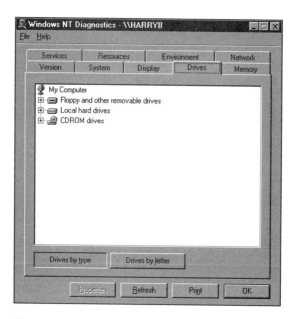

Figure 24-32: The Environment tab sheet in System Properties

Secret

This is one of the most useful tab sheets in Windows NT Diagnostics. It reports networking information at a level of depth unmatched elsewhere in Windows NT Server.

- **General.** Very basic information is reported in the General option of the Network tab sheet (see Figure 24-33). Take it or leave it. Don't worry. The next few tab sheets are much more detailed.

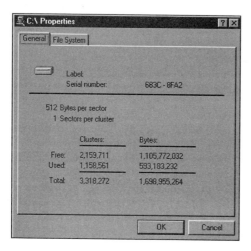

Figure 24-33: The Network tab sheet displaying general information

- **Transports.** The Transports option provides a brief listing of active transport protocols (see Figure 24-34).

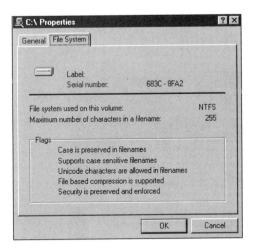

Figure 24-34: The Network tab sheet displaying transport information

- **Settings.** Now the fun begins. The Settings options (Figure 24-35) range from basic to complex. For example, you can determine Session Time Out values via this screen. Note that the information reported on this screen is basically static.

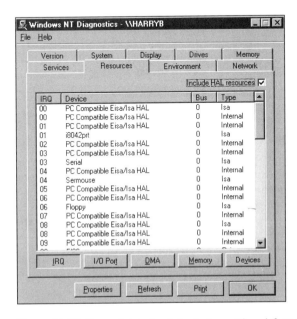

Figure 24-35: Network tab sheet displaying settings information

- **Statistics.** The Statistics screen (see Figure 24-36) reports information, on a dynamic basis when you press the Refresh button, that historically has been difficult to collect in Windows NT Server. This information is akin to the detailed information we can extract from the MONITOR.NLM in NetWare server–based networks. Nice to see this type of information in Windows NT Server!

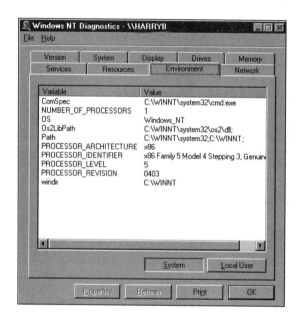

Figure 24-36: Network tab sheet displaying statistics information

Memory and Services tab sheets

Quite frankly, these tab sheets aren't as meaningful and only report basic information that is shown at various locations in the system. For example, the Memory tab sheet displays the same memory information as the Performance tab sheet in Task Manager with the addition of Pagefile Space information (even this is fairly basic info).

The Service tab sheet reports all installed services and devices with their current state, either stopped or running. You can select Services or Device views by clicking the appropriate button. Additional property information may be viewed, but not modified, such as driver file path and name, start type, service account name, error severity, group, and service flags on the General tab. By selecting the Properties Dependencies tab, you may also view Service and Group Dependencies.

Reporting meaningful system information

Time to get back to business basics for a moment. Remember my theme that periodically weaves throughout this book regarding the business use of Windows NT Server with business applications, the business decisions makers you must interact with, and even the business of implementing Windows NT Server in businesses? Well, allow me to add one additional business component: business-style reporting. Anyone in business loves reports, and if you're in the Windows NT Server consulting business, you have the means to provide such reports for both your own system management and client's benefit.

Secret

I've made a good living and kept well-organized system reports by, as a habit, printing out the full report set for all of the system information contained on all tabs found in Windows NT Diagnostics. By completing this exercise for each Windows NT Server at each site that I provide consulting services to, I am able to build detailed and informative client files that are not only great for reference purposes but extremely valuable in an emergency. In fact, I often print two copies of these reports: one printout for my off-site files and another printout to be placed in the system notebook at the client site.

Windows NT Diagnostics doesn't let you down when it comes to creating reports. To create reports in Windows NT Diagnostics, open the Create Report dialog box shown in Figure 24-37 by selecting the Print button on the bottom of the Windows NT Diagnostics dialog box.

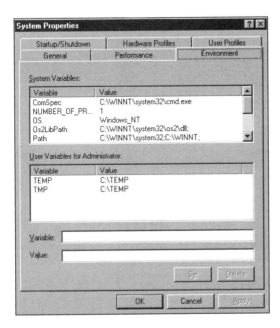

Figure 24-37: The Create Report dialog box

Secret

Be sure to select the All Tabs and Complete radio buttons so that your report is detailed and thus useful.

This information can be printed to a printer, a file, or the clipboard. It is interesting to note that the file created when selecting Print to File is a true ASCII text file that is very readable. I wish I could say the same with respect to how this file print is handled under Windows 95 (under Windows 95 a .PRN file is created that is basically unreadable and useless).

System Properties Sheet

A close cousin to Windows Diagnostics (a.k.a. WinMSD) is the System Properties sheet (see Figure 24-38). The differences between System Properties and Windows Diagnostics are that four different tab sheets are available: Hardware, Performance, Profiles, and Startup/Shutdown. Another minor difference that might win you a round in Windows NT Server trivia is that Windows NT Diagnostics has a minimize button; System Properties does not. System Properties is accessed via the context menu from the My Computer icon on the desktop or via the System icon in Control Panel. I will now discuss each System Properties tab sheet.

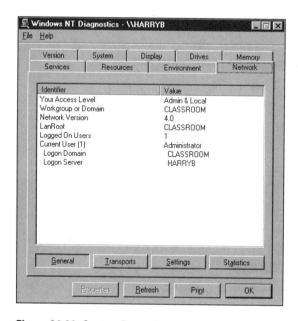

Figure 24-38: System Properties

General

The General tab reports basic system version and registration information. Quite frankly this tab sheet, shown in Figure 24-38, is not too exciting. But, as they say, what you see is what you get.

Performance

We as a species, Windows NT Server professionals, are always seeking ways to boost performance. Here is yet another approach. The Performance tab sheet (Figure 24-39) enables you to set two performance variables: Application Performance and Virtual Memory.

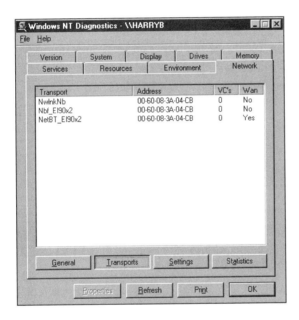

Figure 24-39: The Performance tab sheet

Application performance

This is a more interesting configuration option than it might appear to be at first glance. Remember that one of the niches that Windows NT Server occupies is that of an application server. It is here that Windows NT Server shines and enjoys its acclaim. If such is the case, then it is paramount we get it right at the server when applying performance boosts here and there. The application performance setting allows us to consider which type of performance boost makes the most sense.

Secret

For Windows NT Server, the Boost value should be set to "None." Setting the Boost value to Maximum implies we are running foreground applications that are more important than services. Of course our background services for Microsoft Exchange and SQL Server in the BackOffice world are much more important than giving a boost to a foreground application. An example of a foreground application might be using WordPad to scan a README.DOC file that shipped on a CD-ROM for a server-based application.

Why would we set the boost value to maximum for Windows NT Workstation? Because Windows NT Workstation is traditionally used as a client workstation that is indeed running applications in the foreground. These applications can benefit from such a boost. Note that the foreground application's priority is raised from 7 to 9 and the background priority remains at 7.

The middle position on the Boost slide bar raises the priority of the foreground application by one level, to 8.

Virtual memory

This is where you set the paging file size for *all* disk volumes. Earlier, in Chapter 23, the benefits of having multiple paging files was discussed. Indeed, multiple paging files on multiple volumes is a wonderful way to boost system performance.

Secret

In fact, you are advised to have your paging file(s) on a separate disk than that containing the operating system to boost read/write I/O performance. When it comes to paging file distribution and file size, consider the rule applied to RAM: the more the better.

To actually modify the configuration of your paging file(s), select the Change button under Virtual Memory (see Figure 24-40). This spawns another dialog box titled Virtual Memory. The default paging file size is 12MB plus the total amount of your RAM. If your Windows NT server has 128MB of RAM, the default paging file size would be 140MB.

Tip

Make your paging file size twice the size of the amount of RAM in your system. This will be more than sufficient to cover your primary storage emulation needs (a role filled by paging files) in most cases.

This dialog box enables you to set the paging file size for each paging file and set the maximum size of the Registry. Note that the default Registry size of 5MB is sufficient for 99 percent of us.

Environment

As mentioned earlier in this chapter, the Environment tab sheet is where we can add specific environmental variables of interest including set statements. Remember that you will typically be directed by your software applications vendor to add system or user variables that will allow its program to run. And yes, you will need to reboot Windows NT Server for these changes to kick in.

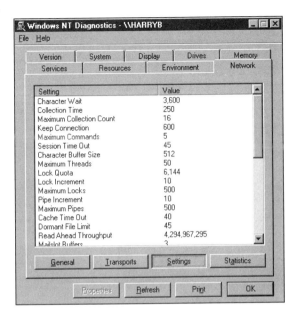

Figure 24-40: Virtual memory

Startup/shutdown

Boring, right? — discussion of startup and shutdowns? Perhaps so on any given day in the life of your Windows NT Server. But that's not really the point of the Startup/Shutdown tab sheet. On any given day with Windows NT Server, you're probably there to manually shut it down in event of error, restart it, and select the BOOT.INI menu option. Heck, you're probably standing there tapping the Enter key to speed past the startup menu timer. But that's not what the Startup/Shutdown tab sheet is about. In my eyes, the Startup/Shutdown tab sheet is about configuring the system for when you're not present. It is here that you will dictate which operating system will start and how soon it will launch at startup. More important, it is here that you will dictate how the Windows NT Server will shut down under different conditions (such as a blue screen crash).

Tip

Here is a great way to edit two variables in your BOOT.INI file without having to use a text editor.

The System Startup section of the Startup/Shutdown tab sheet (see Figure 24-41) enables you to select the default operating system and modify the countdown time value.

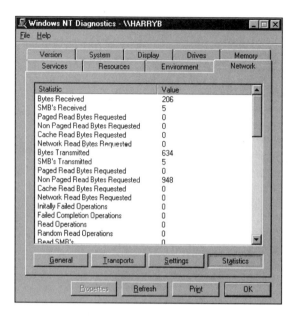

Figure 24-41: The Startup/Shutdown tab sheet

Secret

Booting up in VGA mode might allow you to recycle that older VGA monitor that's been gathering dust and save you some money when you upgrade to Windows NT Server. As you know, a server doesn't need a hot-shot color monitor. It will work just fine with a hand-me-down or older monitor. Those of us from the glory days of Novell NetWare used to procure black-and-white monitors for our NetWare servers to save money. Like a child raised in the Great Depression, I guess it's a habit of thrift not easily lost.

I recently had clients with the best of intentions and a skinny budget who "discovered" they could recycle some older computer components to save money on the systemwide upgrade to Windows NT Server. The client purchased a sufficient system without monitor (you know the ads in the Sunday paper for these deals) and decided to recycle their existing, older VGA monitor. Needless to say Windows NT Server and the video card shipped on the new system were very unhappy. Can you say "narrow horizontal monitor line" (as in that's all you saw on the VGA monitor)? How did I solve the problem? When I set startup to VGA mode (the second Windows NT Server startup option with the /basevideo option), the client's Windows NT Server computer booted into basic VGA mode and ran fine. The net result? The client saved $300 by not purchasing a new monitor, and Windows NT Server performed just fine.

Secret

It is also recommended you set the countdown time value to either zero or one second in the Show List For field. My experience has proven that, unless you have a meaningful need that warrants a longer timer (such as dual-booting between OSes), then you are far better off to set this value to a very low number. At my smaller client sites, I don't want to offer anyone a chance to see or change the startup menu in Windows NT Server. A "zero" value in

Show List For causes my default startup menu selection to essentially start up automatically without delay.

The Recovery section of the Startup/Shutdown dialog box is used to configure what behavior follows a STOP error. A STOP error is a fatal error in Windows NT Server.

As shown in the Figure 24-41, you can:

- Write an event to the system log.

- Send an administrative alert.

- Write debugging information to a dump file. *Important:* This file is typically shared with Microsoft Technical Support as part of the path followed to resolve the problem(s). You will need a debugging utility to interpret the information. Debugging utilities used in the Windows NT Server environment include NTSD (NT Symbolic Debugger), CDB, KD, and WinDBG. These debuggers are discussed at length in the Chapter 25, "Troubleshooting Secrets."

- Automatically reboot.

Hardware profiles

Hardware profiles (Figure 24-42) essentially optimize Windows NT Server on the computer for the current hardware configuration. The typical need for a hardware profile is for laptop or mobile users who may start their computers in different configurations: docked or undocked. In short, the hardware profiles paradigm of computing definitely has a client focus, not a server focus. While hardware profiles have proven essential in managing a fleet of Windows 95/98 clients, in reality, the use of hardware profiles is somewhat limited with Windows NT Server. Depending on your user status, either docked or undocked, Windows NT Server will load the appropriate device drivers.

Hardware profiles essentially manage your Internet and network connection, video, storage, and fonts. This can be seen in the Registry Editor at HKEY_LOCAL_MACHINE\SYSTEM\CurrentControlSet\Hardware Profiles\ as shown in Figure 24-43.

Figure 24-42: Hardware Profiles

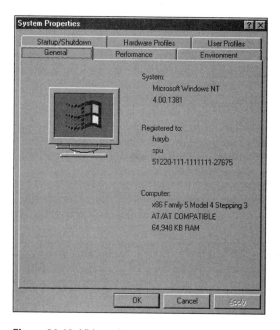

Figure 24-43: Video-related information in the Registry Editor

The concern with hardware profiles is that Windows NT Server typically isn't used on laptops. So who can benefit from multiple hardware profiles in Windows NT Server? Two types of users. First, it is safe to say that hardware profiles are perhaps most useful for training organizations teaching people how to create hardware profiles (and correctly answer such questions on the MCSE exams). However, don't be discouraged! With the advent of removable hard drives, a second type of user can greatly benefit from hardware profiles. This user might use a removable IDE drive at work and have the same type of removable drive arrangement at home. Perhaps you, for instance, by commuting with a removable IDE hard disk drive in hand, can work on Windows NT Server issues at home during off hours. Perhaps you have a "test" Windows NT Server on a removable IDE hard disk that you have been playing with (make that "learning" with). Appropriately using hardware profiles would enable you to use this "test" Windows NT Server removable hard disk by booting from a different hardware profile.

With respect to hardware profiles, user intervention is required to truly optimize your system for different startup configurations. While Windows NT Server does a good job, once the hardware profiles are configured, of letting you select between a docked, undocked, or non–network attached scenario, it does a poor job of automatically adjusting the configuration of the operating system to correctly run. Here is what I mean.

In the Seattle Pacific University MCSE lab where I teach MCSE classes at night, we have employed removable IDE hard disks as our storage solution. At my day job, I maintain another computer that can accommodate these removable IDE drives. The lab computer uses PS/2-style ports for both the mouse and the keyboard. The computer at work uses a serial mouse and an AT-type keyboard. If I take my IDE drive containing Windows NT Server 4.0 from the lab to work, I won't have use of the mouse. Of course I can create profiles that accommodate these different computer systems, but it is essential that I "manually" create these; Windows NT Server will not automatically create these profiles for me.

User profiles

User Profiles are managed via the User Profile tab sheet. User profiles essentially save settings on a per user basis and are largely used at the enterprise level. However, user profiles have also been something of a disappointment in Windows NT Server 4.0 given the lack of true system and user logon script capabilities (at the same high level of performance as Novell NetWare). In fact, the best implementation of user profiles in the world of Windows NT Server 4.0 is under Terminal Server, which I discuss in Chapter 19. The good news, looking forward, is that user profiles are going to get much better in Windows 2000 Server (hint-hint!).

SQL Trace

As we ascend the OSI model, we typically become more interested in application performance, not just OS-level performance. Given that BackOffice is largely responsible for a huge chunk of Windows NT Server's sales, I thought you might like to know about a BackOffice-based tool that can be used for monitoring performance, albeit at the application level. SQL Trace (see Figure 24-44) ships with SQL Server and is a GUI-based utility that tracks SQL Server database activity. How does this apply to Windows NT Server, you ask? In many ways. If your server is being used as an applications server primarily running SQL Server, then you will be very concerned about the interaction of SQL Server, its users, and Windows NT Server. SQL Trace is simply another tool to arm yourself with as you seek the holy grail of eternally optimized Windows NT Server computing environments.

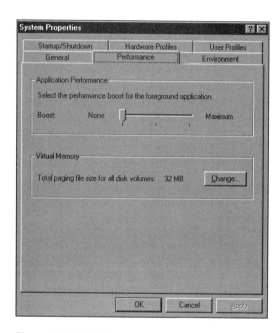

Figure 24-44: SQL Trace

SQL Trace is typically used to monitor connections between users and SQL Server along with SQL statements and RPC activity in SQL Server. These events report a start and end time, CPU utilization, and read and write activity. Believe me, SQL Trace is a tool worth having in your BackOffice back pocket.

SQL Server ODBCPING and Exchange RPING

Another SQL Server tool, ODBCPING (see Figure 24-45) enables you to test ODBC connectivity between nodes. It is intended for use with SQL Server, but it can test ODBC connectivity in a more general sense as well. Typically, this tool is used by software vendors such as Great Plains Accounting to test its Dynamics accounting application's communications with SQL Server via ODBC.

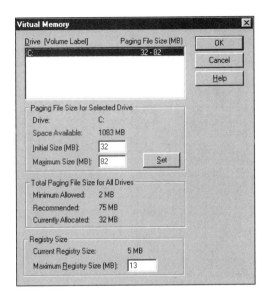

Figure 24-45: Meet ODBCPING.

Another BackOffice buddy is the RPING utility included with Microsoft Exchange (see Figure 24-46). This utility, run on two machines simultaneously, enables you to test the strength and validity of Remote Procedure Calls (RPC) communications. I have used this tool while trying to set up a second Microsoft Exchange Server in an existing Exchange site. In this case, Exchange server setup kept failing when the first Exchange server was trying to perform its directory synchronization with the second Exchange server being set up. RPING was used to verify that we indeed had problems deeper than Microsoft Exchange itself. We proved that the RPC communications were failing between the two servers. Because Microsoft Exchange relies heavily on RPC-based communications for its site communications, our discovery of failing RPC communications proved to be fatal. In fact, the site was ultimately reconfigured to have only one Exchange server, thus eliminating our RPC communication failure problem.

Event Logs

I would be remiss if I didn't discuss event logs in the context of performance. Suffice it to say, event logs are a frequently visited area (FVA) in Windows NT Server as you undertake performance enhancing steps. Often, after you make an adjustment to the system, you will restart the system via a reboot. Often there is no better place to check first than the event logs to see the outcome of your performance enhancing adjustments. More likely, you will be warned via an error message at startup that something somewhere failed to start. You attention will then be directed to Event Viewer. Don't say I didn't tell you — you have now been told.

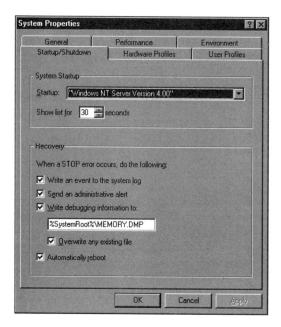

Figure 24-46: The RPING utility

Microsoft Office — Microsoft System Information

Remember at the start of the chapter I suggested the rather oddball idea of installing Microsoft Office on your Windows NT Server machine? Have I forgotten many of the Windows NT Server planning basics I discussed in Chapter 2, where I emphasis that servers should be used as servers, not server/workstations combinations? In other words, am I suggesting that you would type Microsoft Word documents right at your Windows NT Server machine? No, I'm not. It is not my intent to have you actually perform work on the Windows NT Server machine any more than necessary. I'm interested in having you install Microsoft Office so that you're able to access the Microsoft System Information application from any of the major Office applications, such as Microsoft Excel. In fact, I'll use Excel as my sample application to show you Microsoft System Information (a robust system reporting tool).

Secret

This tool, accessed via the About Microsoft Excel menu option under the Help menu in Microsoft Excel, is a little known tool that I keep in my consulting bag of tricks. Hopefully you will too! Note that you can also access this tool via the Help menu in Microsoft Word and PowerPoint.

In the case of Microsoft Excel, you would select the System Info button in the About Microsoft Excel dialog box to launch Microsoft System Information. This is shown in Figure 24-47.

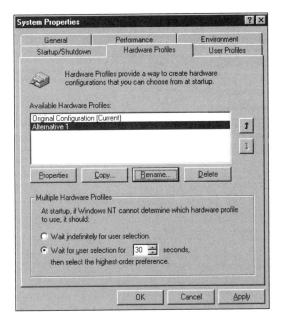

Figure 24-47: About Microsoft Excel

Microsoft System Information is a tool that provides facts pertaining to both user mode operations (applications) and kernel mode operations (Windows NT Server executive). This tool reports on:

- **Microsoft System Information.** Basic system information (see Figure 24-48) such as dynamic swap file settings. This sheet is useful at a glance.

- **System Dynamic Link Libraries (DLLs).** This is the only place in Windows NT Server that you can conveniently observe DLLs installed on your system (see Figure 24-49). It is here that a DLL's version number, creation date, size, build number, and load status are reported. This is an exceedingly important area as you try to optimize your system and implement the latest DLL for the benefit of any application or operating system feature. Needless to say, it is also very important for troubleshooting purposes. Incorrectly managed, an overwritten or missing DLL can bring your system to a crashing halt. For more information about managing DLLs at the application level, see the Windows 95 and Windows 98 Secrets books from my colleague Brian Livingston (IDG Books Worldwide).

- **The Font, Proofing, Graphic Filters, Text Converters, and OLE Registrations.** These relate to how applications are currently configured on your machine and are beyond the scope of this book. The Display, Audio, and Video selections relate to information that is essentially reported via Display and Multimedia Property boxes accessed from the Control Panel.

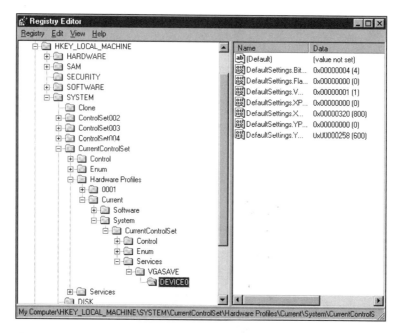

Figure 24-48: Microsoft System Information

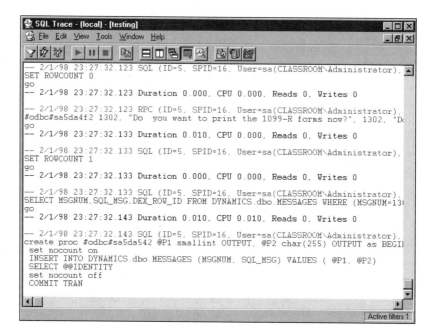

Figure 24-49: The System DLLs view

- **The CD-ROM selection.** This is the only place in Windows NT Server to perform a read/write performance test involving the transfer rate and accuracy of your CD-ROM player. To do this, place a CD-ROM in your CD-ROM player and double-click the CD-ROM selection on the left side of Microsoft System Information. The test can take up to a minute to complete.

    After you double-click the CD-ROM selection in the left pane, the test results will be displayed on the right pane, typically within one minute. These results (see Figure 24-50) display information about the sample transfer file that was used, the total file size, and its transfer rate. This is very useful when measuring the performance of your CD-ROM reader. Note the integrity test that was also performed. This second test essentially verifies the accuracy of the first test by performing tests against another file on the CD-ROM.

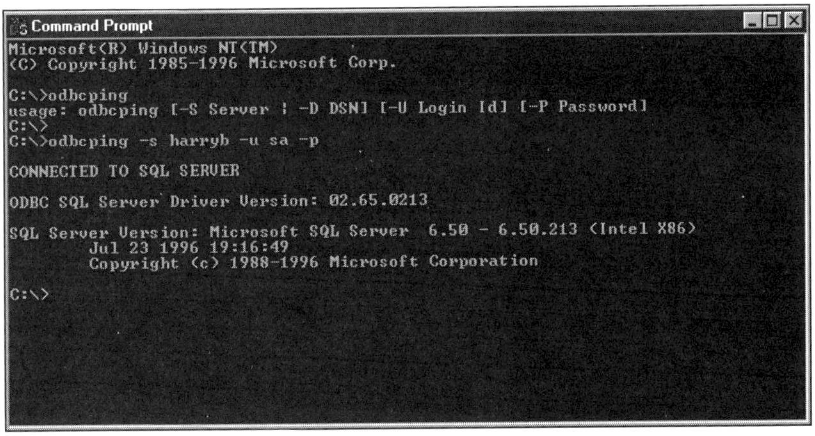

    Figure 24-50: CD-ROM test results

    Windows NT Server Disk Administrator (see Figure 24-51) and CD-ROM properties in My Computer (see Figure 24-52) are proof positive that you cannot run a similar transfer rate test using other common tools in Windows NT Server. Both Disk Administrator and My Computer do not allow for such a test to be performed.

- **Active Modules.** This view in Microsoft System Information (see Figure 24-53) displays information that supplements the Processes view in Task Manager. In fact, it provides more detailed module information than displayed in Task Manager as shown later. However, this information is static and relates to such items as the file build date, file location, size, and whether a module is 16-bit or not. The term "active," while not meaning dynamic, does mean that the modules displayed were active at the time the Active Modules command was executed. Task Manager via the Processes page is designed to report dynamic information such as CPU usage. Active Modules reports different information than the Processes tab sheet in Task Manager (see Figure 24-54).

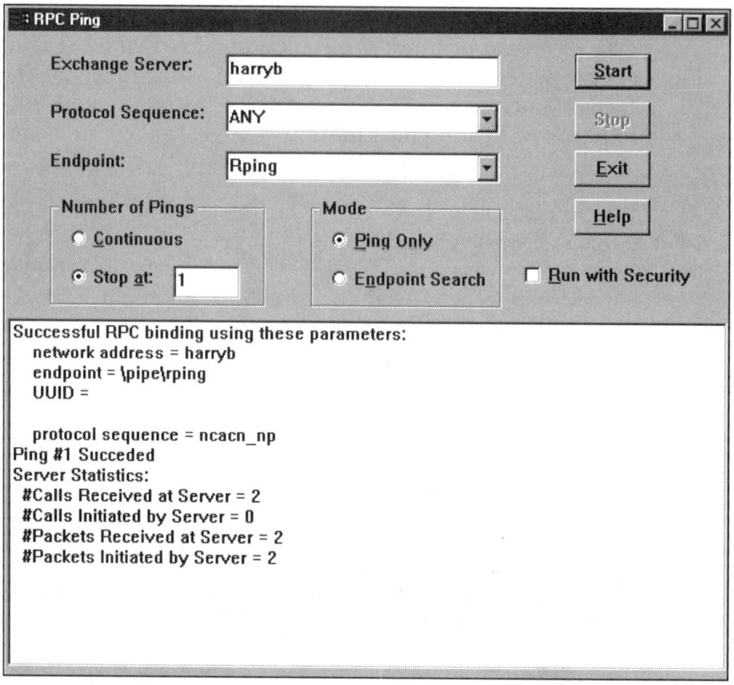

Figure 24-51: Disk Administrator

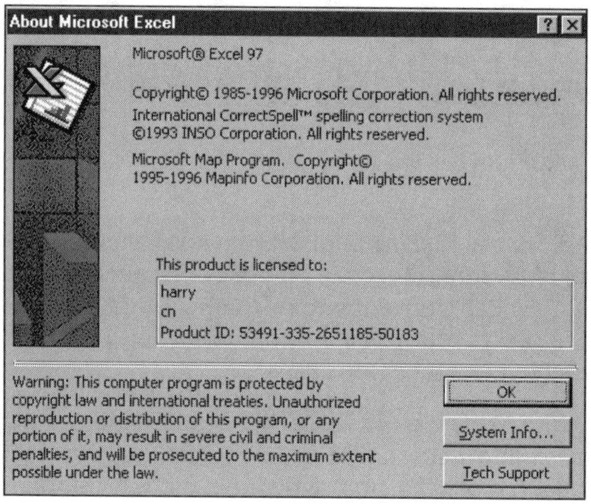

Figure 24-52: CD-ROM Properties

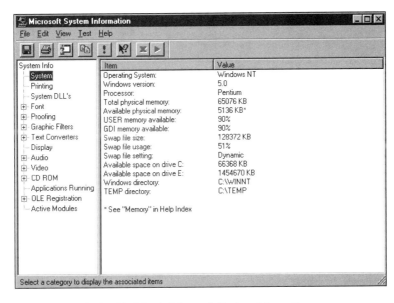

Figure 24-53: Active Modules in Microsoft System Information

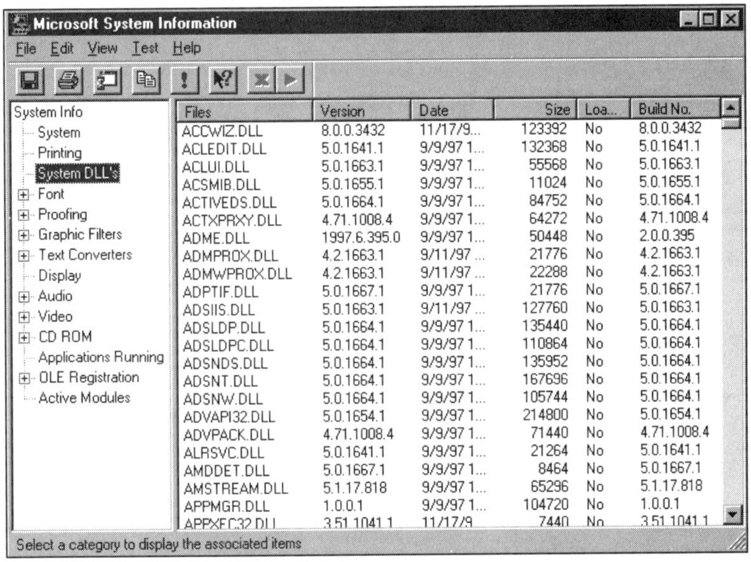

Figure 24-54: The Task Manager Processes tab sheet

Note that it's a nice touch to have the modules' file paths displayed on the far right of the Active Modules window in Microsoft System Information (see Figure 24-55). We can thus quickly get more information on a module by going to the subdirectory containing the module and displaying the properties for that file (see Figure 24-56).

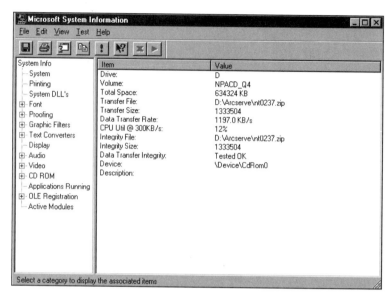

Figure 24-55: The path to SHELL.DLL displayed in the Active Modules view of Microsoft System Information

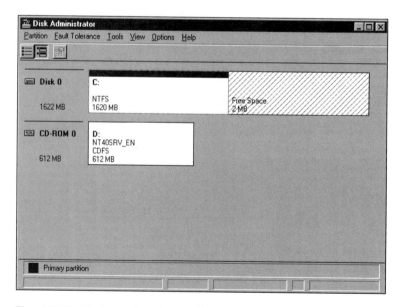

Figure 24-56: The Properties sheet for SHELL.DLL

Secret

Be sure to print out the full system report (select the Print command from the File menu) from Microsoft System Information and place it in the same file in which you store the printout from Windows NT Diagnostics (discussed previously). This report is very different from the Windows NT Diagnostics report, and combined, they provide a nearly exhaustive view of your system.

Last but Not Least — Dr. Watson.

Hey — make a mistake and go to far in your efforts to optimize and boost the performance of Windows NT Server and you'll get a house call from Dr. Watson! Dr. Watson is basically a diagnostic tool that enables you to capture information about the crash (see Figure 24-57). Dr. Watson typically launches when you encounter an application or Windows NT Server executive-layer error. Dr. Watson automatically runs in the background and captures important information when your system crashes. The type of information that Dr. Watson captures includes exception information such as exception number and name. System information is also captured including machine name, OS version, and user name. Finally, a snapshot dump of each thread is captured. This information is given to Microsoft technical support to assist your problem resolution efforts.

While you can turn off Dr. Watson on your Windows NT Server at the following Registry location, there is really no compelling reason to do so: \HKEY _LOCAL _MACHINE\SOFTWARE\Microsoft\Windows NT\CurrentVersion \AeDebug:Auto. (Note you would set the default auto value from 1 to 0. You might recall that, back in the Windows 3.1 days, you had to explicitly turn on Dr. Watson for it to work.)

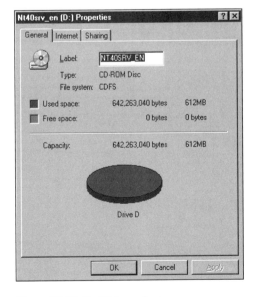

Figure 24-57: Dr. Watson clues

Summary

In this chapter, you:

- Defined Task Manager features.
- Tuned Task Manager to report the information you need.
- Optimized Windows NT Server via Task Manager.
- Defined WinMSD features.
- Learned about SQL Trace and ODBCPING.
- Learned about the Microsoft Exchange RPING utility.
- Analyzed event logs.
- Discovered the Microsoft System Information tool.
- Had a visit from Dr. Watson!

Chapter 25

Troubleshooting Secrets

In This Chapter

▶ Learning formal troubleshooting steps

▶ Listing troubleshooting resources

▶ Defining troubleshooting

▶ Conducting a walkthrough of a troubleshooting example and developing your troubleshooting methodology

▶ Learning and applying the one-hour rule

▶ Calculating the value of downtime

▶ Listing the steps in the Windows NT Server boot process

▶ Mastering the emergency repair process

▶ Analyzing blue screens and debuggers

We finally arrive at the troubleshooting section!

Microsoft reports in Course 689, "Windows NT Server Enterprise Technologies," that over 58 percent of success in troubleshooting is experience-based, whether that prior knowledge derives from general computer systems knowledge or knowledge of the specific problem you are facing. The remaining troubleshooting success factors include luck, research efforts, and your inherent native problem-solving capabilities. Of course, reading and actively using books such as *Windows NT Server 4.0 Secrets* will only increase your odds of success when performing troubleshooting. It's also important to appreciate that developing your troubleshooting skill set is a lifelong journey, not an end that is attained and forgotten.

Secret

Troubleshooting skills, while developed primarily through experience, can be supplemented with outside readings, training, and drawing on your other skill sets. If you are short on experience with Windows NT Server, that doesn't necessarily imply that you will come up short when trying to solve problems. Heck, even that liberal arts degree you hold might just give that angle everyone else is overlooking in a certain Windows NT Server troubleshooting scenario. And while studies can be cited that indicate you need this much experience to successfully perform certain tasks and troubleshoot Windows NT Server, I prefer the Nike advertising slogan — "Just do it." That is, don't let your inexperience necessarily prevent you from gaining more experience.

Troubleshooting Steps

Like performance analysis, troubleshooting involves identifiable steps. These steps are conceptually similar to the steps you take in performance analysis (discussed in the past few chapters). In other words, you will do the "basics" used in solving all problems: identification, assessment, solution planning, testing and verification, and documentation. Consider these troubleshooting steps as the foundation to guide your troubleshooting efforts.

STEPS:
To troubleshoot problems

Step 1. Identify the problem. Can you successfully identify the problem as a software or hardware problem?

Step 2. Perform diagnosis. Separate symptom from cause. Is the system acting out for some underlying fundamental reason? Will addressing the symptoms do nothing for resolving the cause of those symptoms?

Step 3. Develop and implement the solution. Not surprisingly, this step is often repeated again and again.

Step 4. Verify that the solution worked. This is the proverbial feedback loop that assures us of success. Solutions typically need to be tested several times and under different conditions. Fixing a Windows NT Server–specific problem might break a Novell NetWare connection in a mixed server environment.

Step 5. Document the solution. Too often, Windows NT Server professionals (including myself) will successfully implement a wonderful solution only to "forget" the finer problem solving points at a future date when confronting the same scenario. In effect, we have to relearn the solution. Obviously taking a few extra minutes to document each and every solution from our troubleshooting exploits could return huge dividends posthaste!

Microsoft promotes a troubleshooting methodology called D.E.T.E.C.T. (*Windows NT Server 4.0 Enterprise Technologies,* pages 447–448, Microsoft Corporation). This method, created by a group of Microsoft Technical

Support engineers, provides a suggested strategy for systems engineers to pursue when solving Windows NT Server problems. D.E.T.E.C.T. is:

D   Discover the problem

E   Explore the boundaries

T   Track possible approaches

E   Execute the approach

C   Check for success

T   Tie up loose ends

To enlarge on this sequence:

D   Discover the problem. Speak with users at the "user level," not the technical level. Try to find out what software they are using (release versions if possible) and is their hardware on the Hardware Compatibility List (HCL)? What are the symptoms that the problem is displaying?

E   Explore the boundaries. Can you and/or the user identify what changes have occurred since the system was last reported to work correctly? Can you identify what software was running when the problem occurred?

Tip

Here is an important dimension: Is the problem reproducible? Being able to reproduce the problem is an essential step in troubleshooting those tough ones that defy easy explanations and solutions. If you can't reproduce the problem, you are in for a long haul (typically). Can you get lucky and apply a quick fix to the problem?

T   Track possible approaches. This is just the documentation argument in sheep's clothing. You can both learn from this incident and avoid the old inefficient trial-and-error approach by tracking the troubleshooting steps that you undertake.

E   Execute an approach. Aside from managing expectations so that the different parties involved are not bothered if the first resolution attempt fails, you should already be thinking about plan "B" if the first approach fails. Don't forget that critical system and application files should be backed up prior to executing a task (or series of tasks) to solve your problem.

C   Check for success. Assuming you solved the problem, can the user be taught to correct the problem if it should reappear?

T   Tie up loose ends. Share the results with others once the case has been closed.

What is significant about the past several pages is that many different troubleshooting approaches exist, but virtually all follow a simple underlying model, as shown in Figure 25-1.

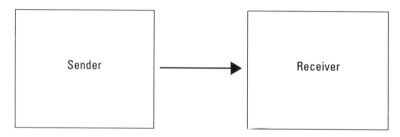

Figure 25-1: Input — Processing — Output model

Having troubleshooting steps to follow methodically is clearly the first step toward successfully troubleshooting your way out of Windows NT Server–related system problems. And don't worry. You're bound to encounter problems along to way with Windows NT Server. The good news is that these problems are what keep us Windows NT Server professionals employed. In fact, I've heard comments from peers that they are hopeful the software industry never figures everything out, lest the resulting layoffs of systems engineers and network administrators would send the industry and leading economic indicators into a tailspin!

Many of the Windows NT Server tools for troubleshooting, such as WinMSD, were discussed in prior chapters. However, you finish this section on performance analysis and troubleshooting by discussing the merits of a structured approach to troubleshooting and what additional tools might benefit you in your quest for a happy and healthy Windows NT server.

Defining Troubleshooting

One definition has troubleshooting as where expensive consultants live. Think about it. Many of us started in the field as $15/hour temps and woke up one day to discover that we were charging a lot more money for our time. We also discovered that the nature of our work had changed dramatically. Whereas a $15/hour temp is allowed to discover the answer via learning, playing, and making mistakes, the $100/hour consultant is called in to troubleshoot problems and know the answers. In fact, a dear friend elected to avoid the stresses and strains of the high-end consulting market and stay at his modest $35/hour rate as a fully qualified MCP so that he might enjoy the journey of life much more. Of course this discussion doesn't just apply to outside consultants. What senior manager doesn't occasionally wax nostalgic for the early carefree career stage of yearning and learning. (Of course it's unlikely this same manager dwells too long on those painful entry-level salaries.)

Secret

The more your charge or make in the technology profession, the more troubleshooting duties you will assume. You'll also have more stress!

Another definition of troubleshooting is those tasks that fall into the pager management category. If you're a network administrator or engineer, you know this all too well. Active pagers equal troubleshooting duties dead ahead. In this section, methodology, the one-hour rule, and downtime value calculations are covered.

A methodology

For many, troubleshooting is a methodology. Here the carpenter's phrase "measure twice, cut once" applies, with a twist. Certainly a Windows NT Server professional should think twice and act once under any circumstances. Perhaps you like me have worked too many Saturdays in your career correcting mistakes on projects you started on late Friday afternoon. Lamenting "if I could only undo that" is a frequent cry for those new to the industry. Unfortunately, Windows NT Server has fewer "undo" capabilities than you might expect. The "Last Known Good" boot option is typically your best "undo" hope. Last Known Good is discussed later in this chapter.

Secret

Save yourself heartache and heartburn by following the golden rule of troubleshooting. That is to change only one variable at a time. Changing only one variable at a time and then testing for success or failure allows you to effectively document your troubleshooting efforts.

An example serves to bring meaning to this issue. In fact, it is recommended you complete portions of this example on a spare Windows NT Server to better understand how to methodically troubleshoot your server environment.

In the world of TCP/IP, it is often necessary to tweak and fine-tune TCP/IP addresses as you implement and manage your network. Suppose you had a TCP/IP configuration on a Windows NT Server running Microsoft Proxy Server, as shown in Figure 25-2.

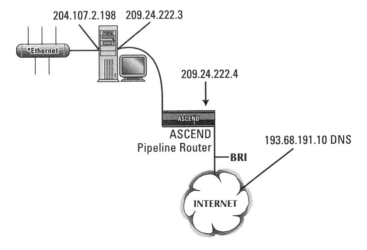

Figure 25-2: A sample network using the TCP/IP protocol and Proxy Server

Users Clint, Teresa, and Diane complain that they can't surf the Internet from their Internet Explorer applications on their Windows 95 workstations. You check the TCP/IP configuration for each network adapter card on Proxy Server and discover the settings shown in Figures 25-3 and 25-4. Note that it is essential to look closely at the IP values in these figures, for they and they alone hold the key to solving our riddle. And don't be concerned if you remain bewildered and befuddled at this point, as I give you the correct answer soon.

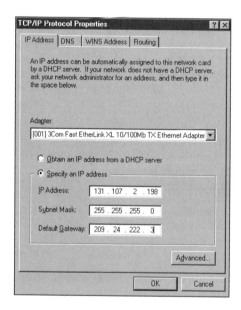

Figure 25-3: The TCP/IP configuration for the internal LAN network adapter card (a.k.a. "first NIC") on the Proxy Server

You now have enough information to solve the problem. Hint: Two TCP/IP configuration problems exist, but only one is causing the users to fail in their efforts to surf the Web via Internet Explorer. The other, noncritical, configuration issue, while it should be corrected, is more of an academic issue as far as Proxy Server is concerned (but it would create problems for your Cisco routers). Now take a few minutes to solve the problem. The challenge is that only one variable needs to be changed to arrive at the solution. By changing one variable and testing the results, you can discover the correct answer, that is, what variable needed to be changed to allow Proxy Server to function correctly.

The solution set is as follows: First, let's evaluate the IP address for the internal network adapter card. This card an IP node address of 131.107.2.198 yet a subnet mask of 255.255.255.0 (which of course suggests a Class C license). The IP node address is out of range for a Class C license because the first octet position has a value of 131. Class C licenses require that node addresses commence with the number 192 or higher in the first octet position. Could this be causing the problem? Change the IP address for the node (and ultimately the IP addresses for all nodes on this subnet) to 204 so that you are within the Class C addressing range (see Figure 25-5).

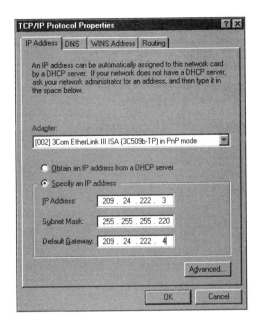

Figure 25-4: The TCP/IP configuration for the external LAN network adapter card (a.k.a. "second NIC") on the Proxy Server

The solution set is as follows: First, let's evaluate the IP address for the internal network adapter card. This card an IP node address of 131.107.2.198 yet a subnet mask of 255.255.255.0 (which of course suggests a Class C license). The IP node address is out of range for a Class C license because the first octet position has a value of 131. Class C licenses require that node addresses commence with the number 192 or higher in the first octet position. Could this be causing the problem? Change the IP address for the node (and ultimately the IP addresses for all nodes on this subnet) to 204 so that you are within the Class C addressing range (see Figure 25-5).

Secret

I highly recommend that you reboot after making troubleshooting modifications to your Windows NT Server. The preceding example is a perfect point. Although it is not officially necessary in Windows NT Server to reboot after changing an IP node address, those of us in the profession know that the dynamic binding capabilities of Windows NT Server demand a reboot to really work right. So the rule is, always reboot after making changes.

Assuming you've rebooted Windows NT Server after making the preceding changes, it is important to test the solution. This first change, while fixing one noncritical problem, doesn't fix the specific problem of external Internet access via Proxy Server. The problem that is fixed by that change affects your "real" routers, such as the Cisco 4500. Routers are typically designed to adhere to the traditional minimum and maximum starting octet values for each IP class (Class A starts at 0, Class B starts at 128, and Class C starts at 192). See Chapter 5, "TCP/IP Implementations," for more information.

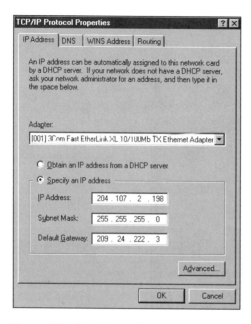

Figure 25-5: Changing the first octet value from 131 to 204

So in the formal troubleshooting approach, we try again. For our second test, we delete the existing default gateway address and leave the field blank on the internal network adapter (see Figure 25-6).

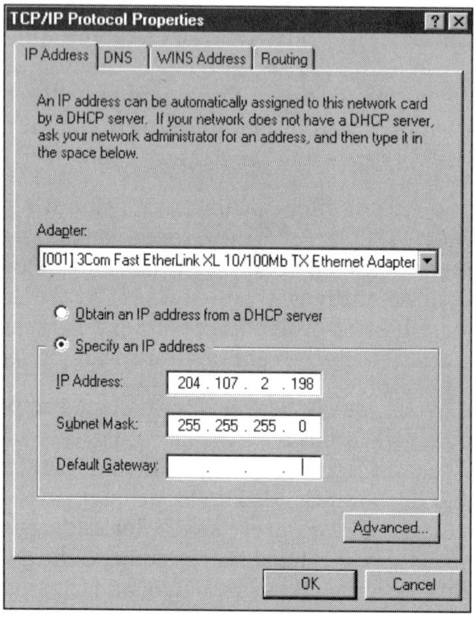

Figure 25-6: Deleting the existing default gateway address

After rebooting, we discover this solution works. Why? Because Proxy Server doesn't require a default gateway field entry for the internal network adapter card. In fact, providing a default gateway value will, as you've discovered in this example, cause Proxy Server to fail.

So what did you learn about methodology from this exercise? When troubleshooting, change one variable at a time and test. Trust me.

The one-hour rule

Experience has shown that our less-experienced brethren have a higher propensity for going "heads down." Heads down occurs when you are troubleshooting a problem and you either get tunnel vision or lose perspective on time. Tunnel vision is the trap of not considering external factors that might be causing your problem. Often external factors are causing your grief. Too often, we look at our Windows NT Server environments from a myopic viewpoint. However, elements beyond our control may well be impacting our situation.

In any case, it is essential to limit your core troubleshooting efforts to just one hour before stepping back from the situation and calling in help and reinforcements. My favorite approach is to get into a Windows NT Server problem for an hour. If I can't solve it or assure myself that I'm reasonably close, then I'm on the telephone with Microsoft Technical Support or at least conferring with another peer in the Windows NT Server community. Be sure to use your fellow professionals from the industry as resources.

Cultivate peer relationships in the Windows NT Server field. Soon you will be on your local Windows NT Server prayer chain providing and receiving advice to help solve Windows NT Server problems. As part of my one-hour rule, I start calling my Windows NT Server prayer chain shortly after I've allowed myself an hour to try and solve a problem. And remember to take a fellow Windows NT Server professional to lunch and develop your troubleshooting resources. It's the best investment you can make in the troubleshooting area.

Another variation on the one-hour rule is that you need to keep in perspective the value of your time relative to the value of the problem you are solving. If you earn $52,000 per year as a Windows NT Server network administrator, then your time could be worth as much as $31.25 per hour ($25 per hour plus 25 percent for benefits). Consider your value when you look up and see you've spent a half day troubleshooting that pesky LPT1 port on your Windows NT Server when a new multifunction I/O card costing under $75.00 would have solved the problem immediately.

So circling back to our earlier discussion, how does this correlate to your experience in the industry? I've observed that newbies tend to take on Windows NT Server troubleshooting as a personal crusade. They have something to prove, and their budding egos sometimes force them to go stupid and heads down. Six hours later, although they may have resolved a TCP/IP configuration problem similar to our exercise earlier in the chapter, it probably could have been solved within one or two hours if outside resources had been consulted. You will find no more (painfully) honest statement in this book.

Area code changes

Many regions are undergoing area code changes to account for the tremendous demand for analog and digital telecommunications services. Pagers, fax devices, cellular telephones, and additional telephone lines at work and home are, as many of you know, rapidly depleting the availability of telephone number within an area code. You might think that this problem only impacts voice telephone lines, but ISDN service is also affected. That is an observation that was learned the hard way when a regional area code was recently split into three new area codes. When that change occurred, my client's Exchange-based e-mail system, and more specifically, the Internet Connector, stopped working. Having battled with Exchange on this particular server recently, that was where I started my troubleshooting efforts. Slowly and methodologically, I worked my way up to the ISDN router. Sure enough, the area code change required a simple modification to the ISDN Router's image file. Problem solved, but I would have rather watched two NFL football games with my Sunday than spend six hours troubleshooting this problem.

Secret

A stronger consideration of external factors would have eliminated hours of unsuccessful troubleshooting. Be sure to monitor scheduled area code changes if you utilize external communication services such as ISDN lines.

Year 2000 issues

Look for Year 2000 issues as a possible source of problems in the near future. Although Windows NT Server doesn't have any implicit Year 2000 issues to confront, you may still be impacted if you are using terminal emulation gateways such as SNA Server from the Microsoft BackOffice family. The legacy machines you attach to may have underlying Year 2000–related problems. Thus those problems become your problems in the Windows NT Server environment. Also, I have seen many clients with heavy metal machines convert to Windows NT Server to avoid having to address their legacy COBOL code. What a nice cop-out!

Workstation side, not server side

Another myopic misdirection is to become so focused on the server side that you forget the entire second half of the equation: the workstation side. I've got war stories galore here, including the construction accounting software package that actually ran fine on the server but had deeply disguised DLL conflicts on the workstation side. One of my tools of choice in troubleshooting workstation-side problems is good old System Editor (sysedit). I realize that this tool, which reports back basic autoexec.bat, config.sys, and *.ini, information isn't as cool as it was in this era of local Registry databases in Windows 95 and Windows 98; however, System Editor helps when an application has installed workstation components and created environment settings in the config.sys file. System Editor will display this file promptly, allowing me to arrive at a better solution.

The point is to think outside of the proverbial box. If you're not getting it fixed on the server side, take a walk over to the workstation side. You may just be surprised to find that's where the problem is!

The value of downtime

Another reality check to consider when troubleshooting is the value of downtime in your organization. By considering this, you might decide to take a markedly different approach to solving your problems. Simply stated, $50 per hour in downtime is different from $5K in downtime per hour or $50K per hour in downtime.

To calculate downtime, use the information in Table 25-1.

Table 25-1	Calculating Downtime	
Number of Employees	Scenario A: Professional Services Firm with $100/hour bill rate (average)	Scenario B: Manufacturing Firm with Annual Sales of $100 million
50	$5,000 per hour of downtime	
1,000		$48,000 per hour of downtime ($100 million divided by 2,080 hours)

Assuming that the lost hours are not absorbed into future work periods, that is, the work can't be made up, these figures are daunting. In Table 25-1, we also assume that Windows NT Server–related downtime prevents people from working. In reality, you might apply a correction factor in your downtime calculations that better reflects Windows NT Server's real role in a organization. For example, with the manufacturing concern I described, perhaps productivity is cut in half when the Windows NT Server fails, and thus the cost of downtime per hour would really be $24,000.

Secret

Don't create such a large correction factor that you underestimate how workers respond to computer downtime. Although your staff cost accountants can accurately determine what processes are negatively impacted by system downtime, our friends from the sociology world will correctly tell us that many workers will use system downtime as an excuse to stop working and perhaps go home. Think about it.

In an office environment, have you ever observed workers taking advantage of computer downtime to return overdue telephone calls? Many workers will simply say the computer system has crashed and they can't work. Another example is using a word processor during downtime. Many organizations have word processing applications such as Microsoft Word installed on a network drive to both save space on local workstation drives and possibly reduce the number of licenses necessary to be purchased. When the system is down under this scenario, Microsoft Word is inaccessible.

Secret

However, WordPad is available and ready for local use if your client workstations are running Windows 95/98 or Windows NT Workstation. WordPad can save its files as *.doc, which is actually Microsoft Word version 6.0. At a later date, your users may indeed use Microsoft Word to edit these WordPad documents.

These two examples, not taking advantage of system downtime or using local applets, are as much a cultural issue as a technical issue. That said, issues such as this need to be managed or you will suffer high system downtime costs.

Given the high cost of system downtime, it is safe to say two things. Those of us in the IT profession are "cheap money," and once you recognize the high cost of downtime, you might now employ more expensive troubleshooting methods than previously considered.

By cheap money, I mean the following. Let's say that you are a Windows NT Server consultant billing at $125 per hour and you have a situation wherein the client is on the cheap (a.k.a. a "nickel and dimer"). Perhaps you have heard that they want to take many of the tasks for a Windows NT Server conversion "in-house," that is, have the staff perform many of the conversion duties without your input and participation. While you might readily agree to such an arrangement, several problems arise here that, while saving money up front, can be very costly later.

The first problem is that you lose control of the project. Windows NT Server tinkering, modifications, and adjustments will occur as in-house activities (well intentioned of course) without your knowledge. Second, suppose the project involves multiple sites over a Windows NT Server WAN. By foregoing the opportunity to learn each site, you risk not having your "head" in the system, that is, not having the Windows NT Server system committed to memory. And this is where matters get expensive when the system goes down. Without your head fully into the system, you have to relearn the system. That takes time and costs money. So truly, you are cheap money as a consultant when you begin to speak of system downtime costs that start at $5,000 per hour for a modest-sized firm and approach $50,000 per hour for a $100 million manufacturer.

System downtime costs will dictate how you approach your troubleshooting. As I have shown, system downtime is surprisingly expensive. Even if you are in a small organization, you can easily calculate system downtime costs that approach hundreds of dollars per hour. So doesn't it make sense to use your best troubleshooting tools sooner rather than later?

The Troubleshooting Quilt

As you know, a quilt results from the combined efforts of many people trying to reach a common end, typically an attractive and functional quilt. Troubleshooting is similar in that it typically requires a variety of people making their own contribution toward reaching a completion: a solution to a problem. In this section, I want to look at some of the patches in the troubleshooting quilt including the troubleshooting map, learning curve analysis, box canyon avoidance, and time management.

A troubleshooting map

Like writing a book, troubleshooting is better performed — and certainly more efficient — if you work from an outline or map. In fact, it's been my experience that you should reserve the conference room and use the mounted whiteboard to create your troubleshooting map. Just getting out of the computer room or server closet is often the dose of troubleshooting elixir that many need to take. I suppose being in a room physically removed from the Windows NT servers allows you to calm down and think with a clear and level head.

Secret

By creating a troubleshooting map on a whiteboard, you can involve the business managers in your efforts. Many business types are accustomed to mapping out scenarios in conference rooms; it's a comfort zone for many. By involving business managers in problem resolution, you not only benefit from some fresh blood — and fresh insights — but you foster positive relations between the technical and business communities in your Windows NT Server environment. That relationship building is especially important when your Windows NT Server troubleshooting efforts take longer than expected.

By creating your troubleshooting map on a whiteboard and perhaps involving the business managers in your efforts, you can "sell" them on the solution(s) and, more important, achieve their buyoff on your strategies. Countless studies and perhaps your own work experience have shown that when you have buyoff from the stakeholders, your likelihood of success is much higher. Do as you like with these suggestions, my friend, but I highly recommend you give 'em a shot.

And don't forget that good relations between the technical and professional staffs and management is worth a lot when your technology budget is reviewed (and hopefully approved) for the next fiscal year. Given the importance of your technology budget in a Windows NT Server environment, perhaps reserving the conference room for some planning on the whiteboard isn't such a bad idea after all. Plus, given that IT is often a cost center in an organization, you can use all the management friends you can get.

Learning curve analysis

Often when confronted with a troubleshooting-related matter in Windows NT Server, you need to confront the limitations of your skill set and honestly assess if you are qualified to remedy the maladies negatively impacting your network. Table 25-2 presents a decision-making model that will enable you to assess when you should attempt to solve the problem and when the skills of outside experts should be employed.

Table 25-2 Defining the Learning Curve

Nature of Problem	Your Skills	Learning Curve	Proposed Solution
Simple	High	Low	Problem solved by you
Occurs often, not difficult	Moderate	Adequate	Problem solved by you after some learning and troubleshooting. Benefits include good use of learning time, because this type of problem occurs often. Once you learn and troubleshoot the solution, it will be much easier to solve again in the future.
Occurs infrequently, problem is "middle of the road" between simple and difficult	Low to Moderate	Medium to High	Perhaps teaming with a Windows NT Server consultant or expert makes sense here. You could have the consultant demonstrate the solution so that perhaps you could solve the problem independently or with telephone support in the future.
Once in a lifetime, incredibly difficult	Nonexistent	Very High	Farm it out. Retain an expert to solve the problem and perhaps try to explain it to you. Don't worry if you can't understand it.

For the first two situations, it is probably a good use of your time to troubleshoot the problem. For the last two, clearly help is needed to minimize system downtime and organization pain associated with Windows NT Server problems that fall into those classes.

Secret

Early on in your troubleshooting efforts, assess the nature of the Windows NT Server problem you are trying to solve and whether you can arrive at the solution individually or should additional help be engaged to fortify your resolution efforts. Make the call as soon as you can.

Avoiding box canyons

How many times in a complex troubleshooting scenario have you started to perform the same steps or action again and again? Kinda like when you lose something at home and you start searching already scoured areas repeatedly. Doesn't seem very rational, does it? Of course not. However, we Windows NT Server engineers do exactly that in the heat of the troubleshooting battle.

One proven way to correct this self-defeating behavior is to dictate into a low-cost micro tape recorder each and every step you have taken from minute one. This record enables you to revisit your approach and determine whether a troubleshooting path has been pursued or not and what the outcome was.

These microcassette tapes can be conveniently transcribed by yourself or a staff secretary so that you can review the steps via a hard copy printout. I recommend dictation over simply handwriting your troubleshooting steps out for one simple reason: burnout. People will often write by hand the troubleshooting steps taken for the first several steps or even the first several hours. But as hours become days, burnout causes a breakdown in this manual system. Steps are missed or skipped altogether. At least dictation is a relatively painless way to document your troubleshooting efforts, and there is hope each and every step will be captured from start to finish.

Secret

Another side benefit from dictation is the document trail you create to resolve billing disputes if you are a consultant. It seems like once per year in my practice a billing is disputed to the extent that all parties resort to their files to seek both truth and resolution. Even though these billing dispute problems occur infrequently, they are monsters when they do. Fortunately, I've been able to prevail more often than not by having extensive documentation of the Windows NT Server system. This documentation included troubleshooting notes that I typically capture via dictation. When you're talking about invoices in the $10,000 to $30,000 range, saying that dictating your troubleshooting steps pays for itself is an understatement.

As an aside, I have found dictation to be an invaluable tool when troubleshooting TCP/IP-related problems due to the sheer details involved in any TCP/IP scenario. Correct me if I'm wrong, but it is easy to get confused when trying to keep multiple subnets clear in your head during the heat of a troubleshooting battle. Sometimes, after many hours at the helm, it's even difficult to communicate verbally about what IP address goes to what router port and what client machine.

So much troubleshooting, so little time

Many of us who are Windows NT Server professionals make a good living by providing services to professionals who are too busy to do it themselves. Here is what I mean. Many technology professionals want to, and given a reasonable amount of time, could troubleshoot and resolve Windows NT Server problems. But given the constraints imposed on each of us by Father Time, we find there simply are not enough hours to do everything we set out to do. Hiring out certain areas such as troubleshooting makes a lot of sense, especially if you consider troubleshooting something of a black hole when it comes to time management. Have you ever been troubleshooting a problem that started on Monday and looked up at the clock to find it was Saturday afternoon? Did you ever notice your other work start to pile up in stacks as your head got into a massive troubleshooting problem?

Secret

Remember that on-the-job success is measured as a whole. Don't get lost in the troubleshooting black hole at the expense of performing poorly in other job areas.

Another "time" issue with respect to troubleshooting involves core competencies. Many want to and even enjoy troubleshooting Windows NT Server problems. But for too many Windows NT Server professionals, the cost is far too high. An example is the professional headhunter I know who also acts as a part-time Windows NT Server administrator at his firm. His role, as a commissioned-based recruiter, is to find and place talent. That's his core competency and greatest contribution to the firm. However, this individual tends to get sucked into Windows NT Server troubleshooting time robbers. At this point he stops performing his job and, I guess, starts performing his hobby. And while he is a competent Windows NT Server administrator, let's just say his talents are more efficiently allocated toward recruiting.

Even if you had stellar Windows NT Server troubleshooting skills, perhaps you were promoted and now run the IT department. Then you had best acknowledge the fact that your role has changed and delegate the Windows NT Server troubleshooting tasks to a more junior, more current, and less expensive staffer. The moral of this discussion? Assess if you are the best person to troubleshoot your Windows NT Server problem from the standpoints of both core competency and use of time.

Hardware versus Software — What a Paradox!

Many nights have been spent debating whether a problem is hardware or software related. And the debate isn't getting any easier with Windows NT Server now performing hardware-like functions such as routing. Viewed from the other side, hardware is also changing. Intel's microprocessors are now assuming more and more software functions such as multimedia management. Even motherboards are contributing to the debate. Is the culprit the on-board video card or the new video driver? Is it harder to troubleshoot an on-board video card than the old-fashioned video adapter cards (which can be readily changed out)?

Secret

If you're strong on one side, let's say software, and you've been diligently troubleshooting a hardware/software problem where the solution escapes you, then the solution is probably emerging from the other side or your weaker half. I know from experience with Windows NT Server that if I try and try to solve a problem from my vantage point (my strengths in software far outweigh my break-fix hardware skill set), then it is usually the other side of the coin causing my grief. More than one bad network adapter card has disguised itself as a software-based network problem in my days. It all depends where you're coming from.

It's worth repeating something from early in the chapter. Be sure to take peers from the industry to lunch occasionally. You can bet several break-fix technicians are on my short list of frequent lunch guests. It's one of my tricks of the trade when troubleshooting hardware and software problems.

Let's Get Technical!

So far, I've spent the first part of this chapter discussing the all-important foundation of troubleshooting. Now let's direct our attention to the more technical aspects of troubleshooting.

The most basic activity to commence the Windows NT Server session is to boot the machine on which Windows NT Server is installed. It is from this point forward that problems might occur. In fact, one of the very first troubleshooting questions you were taught to ask is "can you boot the machine?"

Secret

To see and learn what the boot process is all about, it is recommended that you edit your BOOT.INI file, typically found if the root directory of C:\ drive. Add the /sos command to the "multi" line(s) found underneath the [operating system] section.

The /sos option (see Figure 25-7) displays each driver on your monitor during Window NT Servers Startup phase. Note that the /sos command is automatically appended to the "Windows NT Server Version 4.0 [VGA]" startup menu option. If you don't want to modify your BOOT.INI file, consider selecting the "Windows NT Server Version 4.0 [VGA]" startup menu option.

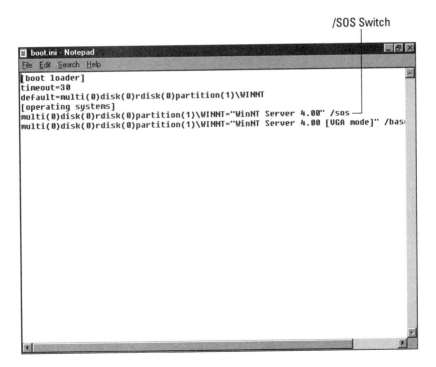

Figure 25-7: BOOT.INI and the /sos option

BOOT.INI switches

Table 25-3 shows the switches that you can append to your [operating system] entries in the BOOT.INI file in Windows NT Server.

Table 25-3 BOOT.INI Switches

Switch	Description
/basevideo	Causes the system to start with standard VGA display driver. Secret: This is a great workaround if you accidentally install an incorrect video driver, reboot, and log on (which removes your last known good configuration workaround option) to find that your video crashes. Basically this option provides you an additional recovery avenue from a badly behaved video adapter.
/baudrate=*nnn*	Sets the baud rate for debugging. This also effectively sets the /DEBUG switch.
/crashdebug	Similar to the System program in Control Panel, this switch turns on the Automatic Recovery and Restart capability.
/debug	Loaded when Windows NT Server starts, the debugger can be started when a host debugger is attached. Reproducible problems are great for troubleshooting with a debugger.
/debugport=com*x*	Defines what COM port is used for debugging (*x* is the specific COM port).
/nodebug	This terminates and disallows debugging.
/maxmem:*n*	Specifies the maximum amount of RAM that Windows can utilize. This is a great switch for troubleshooting RAM memory errors like mismatched memory cards. Be sure never to set this value below 12 for your Windows NT Server environment.
/noserialmice=[COM*x* | COM*x,y,z*]	Used to disable the detection of serial mice on specified COM ports. Can be used to resolve wars between modems and mice. If no COM port is specified, then serial mouse detection is completely disabled.

Four phases of booting

Windows NT Server boots by completing the following four phases: Initial, Boot Loader, Kernel, and Logon.

Initial phase details

The Initial phase includes the power on self test (POST) that a computer runs when it is powered up at the initial startup. The initial startup is where the Master Boot Record and Partition Table are accessed. The job of the Master Boot Record is to search the partition table for the system partition, at which point the operating system boot process commences. In effect, the Master Boot Record serves as a transition layer from the computer system's BIOS to the operating system. The Partition Boot Sector is a function of the file system and underlying operating system. For Windows NT Server on an $x86$-based computer, it is responsible for searching the first physical hard disk for the system partition. In succession, the boot loader (NTLDR) is found, loaded, and executed.

Secret

If Windows NT Server is on a FAT partition, be extra careful not to use an authentic MS-DOS system disk to SYS the hard drive. Doing so will modify the computer such that the Partition Boot Sector no longer launches NTLDR but the bootstrap program in the first sector of the active partition on the disk runs IO.SYS and MSDOS.SYS (followed by CONFIG.SYS and AUTOEXEC.BAT). Note that, under IBM's PC-DOS, the corresponding programs run from the MS-DOS bootstrap program would be IBMBIO.SYS and IBMDOS.SYS. Simply stated, the SYS.COM utility from MS-DOS replaces the Windows NT Server boot sector with an MS-DOS boot sector.

Needless to say, the NTLDR program is mission critical for launching Windows NT Server.

Secret

OK, let's assume that someone evil did indeed use SYS.COM on your hard drive. Are you stuck? No! You may indulge yourself in the emergency repair process and select the Inspect Boot Sector option to "reinstall" the Windows NT Server boot sector. More information on the emergency repair process can be found near the end of this chapter.

In fact if NTLDR is missing, you find yourself bootless. One way to safely create this condition is to make sure your Windows NT Server boots from drive A: at startup. Insert a blank floppy disk that is not bootable. Turn on the computer and observe that the boot process fails because an operating system cannot be found. This is similar condition to a missing NTLDR file on your Windows NT Server.

Secret

If and when you FDISK a FAT partition under Windows NT Server (so you might reinstall everything "fresh" on the computer), it is essential that you refresh the Master Boot Record by running FDISK /MBR, or else you risk inheriting bugaboos when you reuse the hard disk with your next installation. Be very careful when and how you use the /MBR command. Improperly used, the /MBR switch will terminate the dual-boot capability that Windows NT Server enjoys when it is installed on a FAT partition. That is because the Windows NT Server boot sector will be overwritten.

Boot Loader phase details

Here the operating system is selected, the hardware is detected, a configuration is selected if you have multiple hardware profiles, and the Kernel commences loading.

Operating system selection

The operating system is selected from the options made available by BOOT.INI. Prior to your selection menu, NTLDR places the following text in the upper left-hand corner of your screen:

```
OS Loader V4.0
```

Enter NTLDR

Then NTLDR accomplishes the following:

- Places or switches the processor to a 32-bit flat memory mode.
- Starts the appropriate minifile system (FAT or NTFS).
- Reads and displays the operating menu selections found in the BOOT.INI file.

The operating system selection menu appears next. Depending on which operating systems you have installed and any modifications you have made to the BOOT.INI file, the appropriate selections will be displayed on the screen similar to the following:

```
Please select the operating system to start:
Windows NT Server Version 4.0
Windows NT Server Version 4.0 (VGA)
Microsoft Windows
Use ↓ and Ø to move the highlight to your choice.
Press Enter to choose.
```

NTDETECT and hardware detection

The next step in the Boot Loader phase is for NTDETECT to commence and detect the hardware (keyboard, communications ports, bus/adapter type, parallel ports, floppy disks, and mouse/pointing device). This step is displayed on your monitor about halfway down the screen:

```
NTDETECT V4.0 Checking Hardware . . .
```

Post-hardware detection and configuration selection

After Windows NT Server has been selected as the operating system and the hardware information has been collected, this screen is shown:

```
OS Loader V4.0
Press SPACEBAR now to invoke Hardware Profile/Last Known Good menu.
```

After waiting several seconds for you to press the Spacebar, the loading process continues if there is only one hardware profile (the default control set in the Registry is used by the boot loader). If you have more than one hardware profile or you have pressed the Spacebar, the following appears:

Chapter 25: Troubleshooting Secrets

```
Hardware Profile/Configuration Recovery Menu
This menu allows you to select a hardware profile
To be used when Windows NT is started.
If your system is not starting correctly, then you may switch to a
previous
system configuration, which may overcome startup problems.
IMPORTANT: System configuration changes made since the last successful
startup will be discarded.
Original Configuration
Foo (Or the name of another hardware profile)
Use the up and down arrow keys to move the highlight
To the selection you want.  Then press ENTER.
To switch to the Last Known Good configuration, press 'L'.
To Exit this menu and restart your computer, press F3.
```

If you have invoked the /sos option in the BOOT.INI file, several operating system files and drivers will be shown loading before the preceding screen appears. The files that are loaded are:

```
multi(0)disk(0)rdisk(0)partition(1)\WINNT\System32\ntoskrnl.exe
multi(0)disk(0)rdisk(0)partition(1)\WINNT\System32\hal.dll
multi(0)disk(0)rdisk(0)partition(1)\WINNT\System32\config\system
```

Note the addressing references to the disk and partition may vary depending on your system configuration, the number of hard disks and partitions, and whether you are using a SCSI-based architecture. This form of addressing is called the ARC naming convention.

The ntoskrnl.exe file is the operating system kernel for Windows NT Server. The hal.dll file is the hardware abstraction layer dynamic link library. Affectionately know as HAL, it contains the common hardware drivers that allow applications to access hardware devices directly. If your hardware device isn't supported via a common driver with HAL, then the hardware vendor must provide a hardware driver for Windows NT Server on the hardware platform that you are using (such as Intel). Also note that Windows NT Server basically switches out the HAL layer to account for different hardware platforms (Intel, Alpha). The system file is an operating system configuration file that loads the Registry key HKEY_LOCAL_MACHINE\SYSTEM.

If you select F3, you are returned to the operating system selection screen. At that point, you may select another operating system.

Secret

The Last Known Good Configuration option (selected by pressing L at the Hardware Profile/Configuration Recovery Menu) is a true friend indeed. This option has, on numerous occasions, bailed me out of serious trouble when I installed a badly behaved driver that directly accessed the hardware (such as early drivers for Iomega's Jaz drive and the Connectix QuickCam video camera used for CUSEEME). Selecting the Last Known Good configuration, which acts very much like the Undo command in Microsoft Word or Excel, truly undoes the damage I've caused and provides just the built-in recoverability I'm seeking in an operating system.

The Last Known Good Configuration uses the most recent control set that was created at the last successful logon (see Figure 25-8). It is important to know that, once you've successfully logged on to Windows NT Server, the Last Known Good configuration option is updated and you inherited the changes that you made in the last session. Beware.

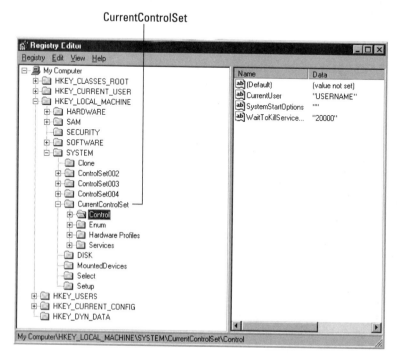

Figure 25-8: Control Sets in the Registry

After you select the hardware profile, the Boot Loader creates the control set used to start the computer. The value contained in HKEY_LOCAL_MACHINE\SYSTEM\Select dictates which control set to use. In fact, unless the Last Known Good menu option is selected, the "default" configuration is used.

Finally, the boot loader scans all of the services in the Registry subkey HKEY_LOCAL_MACHINE\SYSTEM\CurrentControlSet\Services for device drivers that should be loaded but not necessarily initialized. This condition is shown as a Start value as 0X0 (see Figure 25-9). I also share with you a range of possible start values in Table 25-4.

Chapter 25: Troubleshooting Secrets

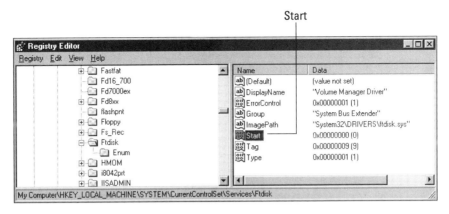

Figure 25-9: The start value of 0X0

Table 25-4 Possible Start Values

Possible Driver Start Values	Description
0	Loaded but not initialized during the Boot Loader phase of the Windows NT Server startup cycle
1	Loaded and initialized during the middle part of the Kernel phase
2	Loaded and initialized at the end of the Kernel phase. Also loaded at the end of the Logon phase when the Service Controller (SCREG.EXE) makes a last pass through the Registry
3	Loaded as required as the drivers initialize

Note that the driver load order shown next may vary slightly depending on the unique configuration of your system and the GroupOrderList subkey (see Figure 25-10) found in HKEY_LOCAL_MACHINE\SYSTEM\CurrentControlSet\Control in the Registry.

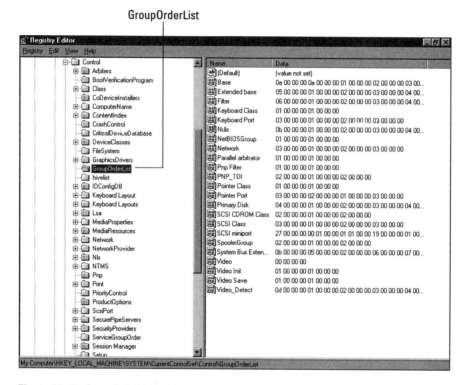

Figure 25-10: GroupOrderList subkey

These drivers that are loaded during the Boot Loader phase indeed have a start value of 0X0. Again, that means the drivers are loaded but not initialized:

```
multi(0)disk(0)rdisk(0)partition(1)\WINNT\System32\c_1252.nls
multi(0)disk(0)rdisk(0)partition(1)\WINNT\System32\c_437.nls
multi(0)disk(0)rdisk(0)partition(1)\WINNT\System32\l_intl.nls
multi(0)disk(0)rdisk(0)partition(1)\WINNT\FONTS\vgaoem.fon
multi(0)disk(0)rdisk(0)partition(1)\WINNT\System32\DRIVERS\pci.sys
multi(0)disk(0)rdisk(0)partition(1)\WINNT\System32\DRIVERS\isapnp.sys
multi(0)disk(0)rdisk(0)partition(1)\WINNT\System32\DRIVERS\intelide.sys
multi(0)disk(0)rdisk(0)partition(1)\WINNT\System32\DRIVERS\PCIIDEX.SYS
multi(0)disk(0)rdisk(0)partition(1)\WINNT\System32\Drivers\MountMgr.sys
multi(0)disk(0)rdisk(0)partition(1)\WINNT\System32\DRIVERS\ftdisk.sys
multi(0)disk(0)rdisk(0)partition(1)\WINNT\System32\Drivers\PartMgr.sys
multi(0)disk(0)rdisk(0)partition(1)\WINNT\System32\DRIVERS\atapi.sys
multi(0)disk(0)rdisk(0)partition(1)\WINNT\System32\DRIVERS\disk.sys
multi(0)disk(0)rdisk(0)partition(1)\WINNT\System32\DRIVERS\CLASSPNP.SYS
multi(0)disk(0)rdisk(0)partition(1)\WINNT\System32\drivers\Dfs.sys
multi(0)disk(0)rdisk(0)partition(1)\WINNT\System32\Drivers\Fastfat.sys
multi(0)disk(0)rdisk(0)partition(1)\WINNT\System32\Drivers\KsecDD.sys
multi(0)disk(0)rdisk(0)partition(1)\WINNT\System32\Drivers\Cnss.sys
multi(0)disk(0)rdisk(0)partition(1)\WINNT\System32\Drivers\NDIS.sys
```

Kernel phase

The Kernel phase commences when control is passed from NTLDR (the Windows NT Server operating system loader) to NTOSKRNL.EXE (the Windows NT Server operating system kernel). The Kernel phase really has three phases:

1. Kernel initialization
2. Loading and initialization device drivers
3. Loading and initializing services

Kernel initialization

```
Microsoft ú Windows NT ← Version 4.0 (Build 1381)
1 System Processor (32 MB Memory)
```

Kernel initialization occurs when the screen turns blue and the preceding text appears. Seeing the preceding screen is your sign that NTOSKRNL.EXE has been successfully initialized. The processor and memory information will vary by machine.

Next, the HKEY_LOCAL_MACHINE\HARDWARE key (Figure 25-11) is created in the Registry on the basis of information provided from the Boot Loader phase. This includes basic interrupt, resource, and system board information.

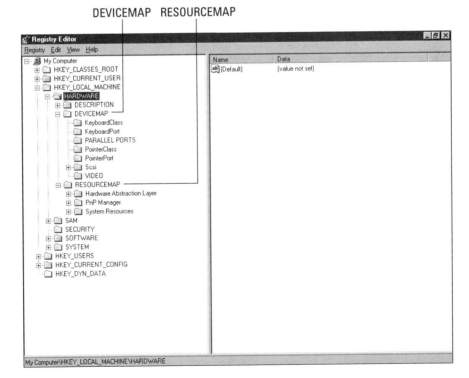

Figure 25-11: HKEY_LOCAL_MACHINE\HARDWARE

The kernel then creates the Clone control set (Figure 25-12) by making a copy of the Current control set. This is simply a backup, as the Clone is not modified.

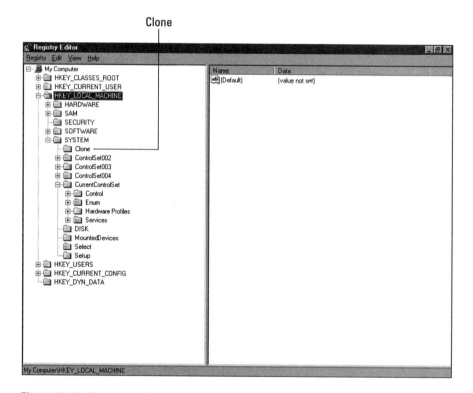

Figure 25-12: Clone control set

Loading and initializing device drivers

At this point, the drivers that were loaded during the Boot Loader are initialized. These are the drivers that were just listed. If any driver initialization errors occur, the error information is written to the HKEY_LOCAL_MACHINE\SYSTEM\CurrentControlSet\Services\DriverName\ErrorControl value (Figure 25-13).

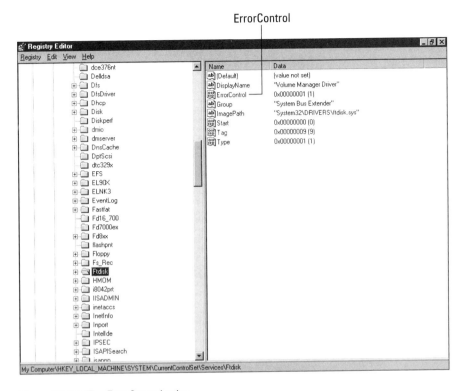

Figure 25-13: The ErrorControl value

The device drivers with a start value of 0X1 are now loaded and initialized.

Loading and initializing services

As the third part of the Kernel phase, the services are loaded and initialized. The Session Manager (SMSS.EXE) is responsible for starting the services and upper-level subsystems. Information need for Session Manager to successfully run is stored in the HKEY_LOCAL_MACHINE\SYSTEM\CurrentControlSet\Control\Session Manager key (see Figure 25-14).

Session Manager executes the instructions contained in the following Registry location situated underneath HKEY_LOCAL_MACHINE\SYSTEM\CurrentControlSet\Control\Session Manager.

Figure 25-14: Session Manager

The BootExecute data item

BootExecute is configured to execute AUTOCHECK.EXE, which is the Windows NT Server version of CHKDSK (the check disk command). The Distributed File System (DFS) is also initialized. Both the BootExecute and the DFS information are shown in Figure 25-15 on the far right side of the Edit Binary Value dialog box.

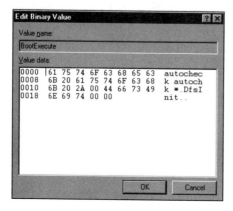

Figure 25-15: BootExecute

The Memory Management key

The Session Manager creates paging information that is necessary and required by Virtual Memory Manager. The screenshot in Figure 25-16 highlights three values that provide paging file configuration information (NonPagedPoolSize, PagedPoolSize, PagingFiles).

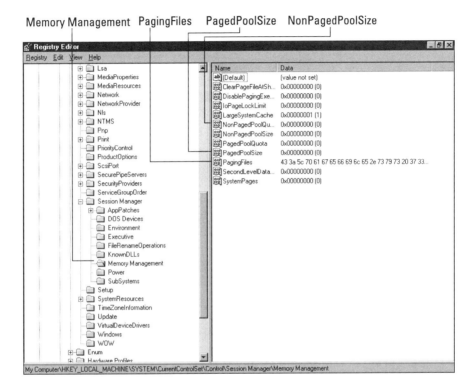

Figure 25-16: Memory Management

The DOS Devices key

Session Manager creates symbolic links that connect specific commands to a correct file system element. Examples include managing LPT1 and COM1.

The Subsystems key

The Windows subsystem (Microsoft Win32) is started. Known by its process name CSRSS.EXE, this subsystem controls all I/O and video screen access by honoring the Windows NT Server architecture's use of messaging to communicate between subsystems. The WinLogon process is then started, which leads to the Logon phase. But before going there, several other important subsystems must be loaded. These include hard disk checks and information from the SOFTWARE hive.

The hard disk checks are completed, and the paging files are created as previously discussed. The paging file configuration information is stored under HKEY_LOCAL_MACHINE\SYSTEM\CurrentControlSet\Control\Session Manager\Memory Management.

Next, the Session Manager loads up the SOFTWARE hive from the Registry. Finally, the required services needed by Windows NT Server are loaded (see Figure 25-17). The information necessary to configure required subsystems is contained in the Required value at HKEY_LOCAL_MACHINE\SYSTEM\CurrentControlSet\Control\Session Manager\SubSystems. Only Win32 is required by default.

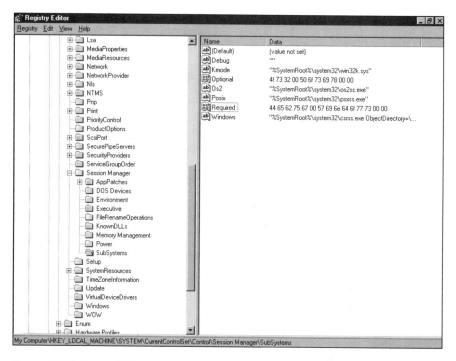

Figure 25-17: Required Value

To end the Kernel phase, SMSS.EXE loads/initializes device drivers with a 0X2 start value. A final note on the Kernel phase: The CHKDSK command will run after an abnormal ending; that is, if Windows NT Server was previously shut down incorrectly, then CHKDSK will run to ensure the integrity of the secondary storage media.

Logon phase

The fourth and final phase to booting Windows NT Server is the Logon phase. As previously mentioned, a logon is not complete (and therefore not successful) until the user successfully logs on.

Chapter 25: Troubleshooting Secrets   **939**

WINLOGON.EXE starts LSASS.EXE (the local security administrator). The Begin Logon dialog box is now made available (this contains the text instructing you to press Ctrl+Alt+Delete to log on). As you may be aware, network device drivers and required services are loading at this point. This last comment underscores a unique feature of Windows NT Server.

You do not need to log on for Windows NT Server to be functional. SCREG.EXE (the Service Controller) executes and takes a last look at the Registry. At this point, the services are loaded that have been marked to autostart and have a start values of 0X2.

One example of the 0X2 value is the Alerter service. This is shown in Figure 25-18 and may be found at HKEY_LOCAL_MACHINE\SYSTEM\CurrentControlSet\Services\Alerter

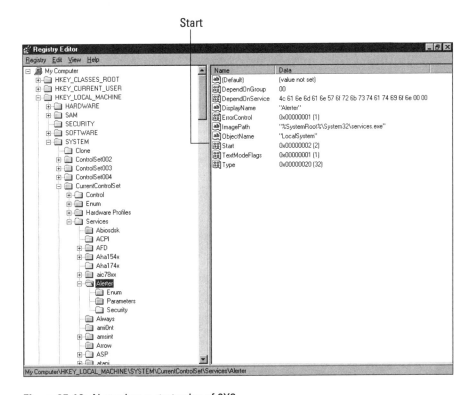

Figure 25-18: Alerter has a start value of 0X2.

At this point, the user may log on. And the Clone control set just discussed is now copied to the LastKnownGood control set.

How to Get Out of Trouble

Some of the most popular books of our time have been "how to" books. You name the topic, and a "how to" book has been published on it. Perhaps the popularity of these books has been their often practical and pragmatic advice for those seeking answers. In that spirit, this section starts to wrap up our excursion of the last few chapters on performance analysis and troubleshooting by offering you sage advice on how to get out of trouble with Windows NT Server. My offerings include replacing files via the EXPAND command, hot wiring via the boot disk, and using the Windows NT Server emergency repair process and the emergency repair disk. Last, I provide advice on how to flee the country if nothing else works.

Expanding your way out of trouble — the case of the missing system files

Although it's unlikely this would be a daily dilemma, there are times (typically when advised by Microsoft Technical Support), when you will replace a corrupt system file from the Windows NT Server CD-ROM. Files on the CD-ROM are stored in a compressed format and need to be expanded. The EXPAND command (see Figure 25-19) is officially known as the Microsoft File Expansion Utility Version 2.50.

The Expand command is used to decompress files on the Windows NT Server CD-ROM so that you may replace an already installed file. The -r switch is necessary as compressed files typically have a shortened file extension on the CD-ROM (the file *.sys would be stored as *.sy_).

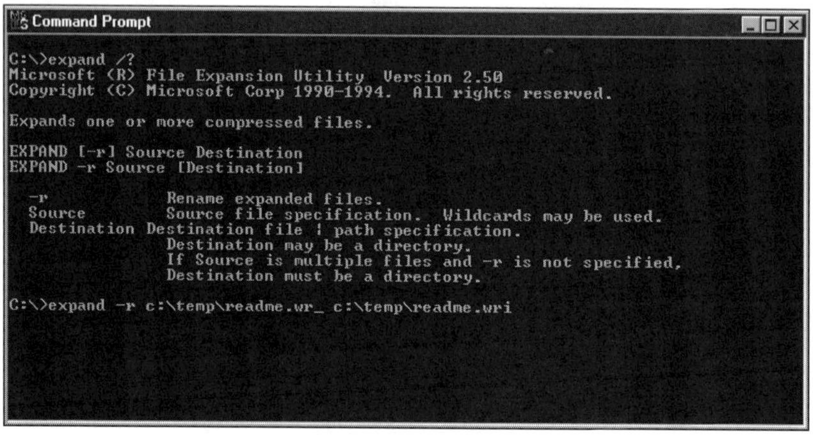

Figure 25-19: The EXPAND command

Did you know that system files and drivers may be replaced even while they are in use? How? you ask. Simple. Once such files are loaded in memory, it is possible to rename the driver in question and then replace it with a fresh copy from the Windows NT Server CD-ROM. Here is how you would accomplish that.

STEPS:
To rename and replace a driver

Step 1. Let's assume the corrupted file is winmsd.exe, which is Microsoft Windows NT Diagnostics (version 4.00) that ships with Windows NT Server 4.0. This file needs to be replaced in its existing subdirectory: \WINNT\system32. The file is currently loaded and in use.

Step 2. Rename the file to winmsd.foo (see Figure 25-20).

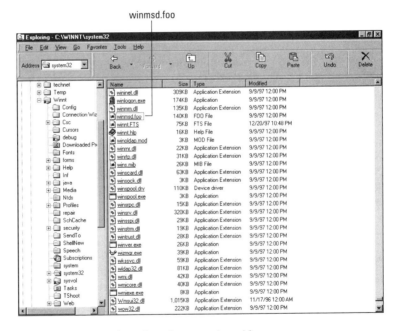

Figure 25-20: Renaming winmsd.exe to winmsd.foo

Step 3. Copy the file winmsd.ex_ from the Windows NT CD-ROM (this file is located in the I386 subdirectory). Place the file in the same subdirectory as the original winmsd.exe file: \WINNT\system32.

Step 4. Use the EXPAND command to decompress the file (see Figure 25-21).

Continued

STEPS
To rename and replace a driver (continued)

Figure 25-21: The EXPAND command

Step 5. You are done. Restart the computer so that the changes may take effect. You may now "trash" (oops, recycle) the old file that was corrupted.

Note that it has been my experience that the preceding steps are typically performed in conjunction with recommendations from Microsoft Technical Support. If you are performing preceding Steps 1–5, you should have very specific reasons for doing so. It is not recommend that you attempt these steps just for the fun of it. In advertising lingo, do not try this at home.

Secret

An expanded file reports much more property information than a compressed file. In fact, a compressed file doesn't report its File Version, Description, Copyright, and specific Item Name information — the type of information contained on the Version tab sheet (that's because compressed files don't have Version tab sheets). This type of detailed information is especially important when you are working with Microsoft Technical Support to resolve a problem.

If you haven't used the EXPAND command before, now is a good time to try it. I would recommend that you expand a relatively safe file such as a Readme file from an application CD-ROM disc such as Microsoft Office to your Windows NT Server. In fact, if you have a "test" Windows NT Server that you are using to practice with as you earn your MCSE, all the better.

Secret

So far everything discussed with respect to the EXPAND -R command assumes that the system is running and you can get to the corrupted file in question. However, if the system is not running and you encounter a corrupted file or driver that prevents you from logging on successfully, you might again be thinking it's time to update your résumé and run for the nearest exit. But first try one more thing, assuming you have an NTFS partition. Install a fresh copy of Windows NT Server to another subdirectory on your NTFS partition and then replace the corrupted file or driver in the location of the original Windows NT Server installation. Also see my hot-wired method in the next paragraph. If you have a FAT partition, you could boot from a system disk and simply copy over the necessary files.

Hot-wiring NT so the it will start: The NT boot disk

Yet another angle on gaining access to an NTFS partition is the hot-wire method. Like the respected preacher I know (no names please) who grew up as a greaser in the 1950s with a propensity for hot-wiring cars, you can hot-wire Windows NT Server when you lose the keys (so to speak — the system won't start as normal). This method is to create an NT Boot Disk. Quite frankly, the boot disk has limited usefulness, but it can get you going if the primary startup files such as NTLDR or NTDETECT.COM are corrupted. It's just another troubleshooting tool that you might find useful.

Windows NT Server uses the files presented in Table 25-5 to boot.

Table 25-5   Windows NT Server Boot Files

Windows NT Server Boot Files	File Size in Windows NT Server 4.0	Description
NTLDR	151KB	Operating system loader that must be in the root directory
BOOTSEC.DOS	1KB	Hidden system file for launching alternate operating systems such as MS-DOS
BOOT.INI	1KB (est.)	Builds the Operating System Selection menu.
NTDETECT.COM	27KB	Detects and shares hardware information with NTOSKRNL.EXE.
NTOSKRNL.EXE	1.03MB	Windows NT Server operating system kernel
NTBOOTDD.SYS	25KB	Device driver found in SCSI-based systems to access a SCSI hard disk with BIOS disabled on SCSI card
SYSTEM	1.49MB	The system hive located at HKEY_LOCAL_MACHINE\SYSTEM

As you can see in the size column, it is not possible to place all of the standard startup files on a single 1.44MB floppy. However, you don't need to. Here is how you create an NT boot disk.

STEPS:
To create an NT book disk

Step 1. Format a floppy disk via Windows NT Explorer. It is not possible to format the floppy disk using the FORMAT command under MS-DOS because that floppy disk isn't bootable under a Windows NT scenario (see the boot sector discussion early in the chapter).

Under Windows NT Server, you may type **format a:** at the command prompt, assuming the disk is in Drive A. You may also format a disk using Windows Explorer.

Step 2. Copy these boot files to the floppy disk from the Windows NT Server root directory.

NTLDR

NTDETECT.COM

BOOT.INI

NTBOOTDD.SYS (only needed if you have a SCSI card with the SCSI BIOS disabled)

Step 3. Restart Windows NT Server with this NT Boot Disk in Drive A. Make sure your machine's BIOS has been set to boot from Drive A before trying to boot from Drive C.

And there is yet another way to replace corrupted files! The emergency repair process that is detailed next has an option to "Verify Windows NT System Files."

911 — The emergency repair process

The emergency repair process is a life saver for not only recovering a corrupt installation of Windows NT Server but also narrowing the search and remedy to corrupt files and drivers. Here is how to invoke the emergency repair process.

STEPS:

To invoke the emergency repair process

Step 1. Insert the Microsoft Windows NT Server version 4.0 Setup Boot Disk (a.k.a. Setup Disk 1) in the floppy drive and power on your computer.

Step 2. When requested, insert Disk 2.

Step 3. When requested, insert Disk 3.

Step 4. When you see the Windows NT Setup Welcome Screen, select "R" for the repair option. The Welcome Screen appears as:

```
Windows NT Server Setup
=====================
Welcome to Setup.
The Setup program for the Microsoft ú Windows NT ← operating system
version 4.0 prepares Windows NT to run on your computer.
*To learn more about Windows NT Setup before continuing, press F1.
*To set up Windows NT now, press ENTER.
*To repair a damaged Windows NT version 4.0 installation, press R.
*To quit Setup without installing Windows NT, press F3.
```

Step 5. Next, select the appropriate actions from the Repair screen.

```
Windows NT Server Setup
=====================
As part of the repair process, Setup will perform each optional task
shown below with an 'X' in its check box.

To perform the selected tasks, press ENTER to indicate "Continue."
If you want to select or deselect any item in the list, press the UP
or DOWN ARROW key to move the highlighted to the item you want to
change. Then press ENTER.

[X] Inspect registry file
[X] Inspect startup environment
[X] Verify Windows NT system files
[X] Inspect boot sector
 Continue (perform selected tasks)
```

Note that each option has been selected (as denoted by the "X"). Table 25-6 provides an explanation of each emergency repair option.

Table 25-6   Emergency Repair Options

Emergency Repairs Option	Description
Inspect registry files	This option will restore your Registry files. This process enables you to select which files in the Registry you want to replace (which effectively repairs these files). Changes that you have made since the system was originally installed or your last update to the ERD will be lost.
Inspect startup environment	Used when you know you have Windows NT Server 4.0 installed on your system but there is no startup menu option to select it. Basically modifies the BOOT.INI file. Will request that you insert the Emergency Repair Disk you created when you installed Windows NT Server (and have hopefully updated periodically).
Verify Windows NT system files	Simply stated, this option verifies the existence and integrity of all Windows NT system files. If you provide the confirmation, damaged files will be replaced on a case-by-case basis. You can even have all damaged files replaced automatically without having a confirmation required for each file.
Inspect boot sector	A new boot sector is copied to your disk. This is a good option to use if the Windows NT Server boot sector has been damaged by errant use of the MS-DOS sys.com command. Dual-boot capabilities are preserved by running this command.

You will be prompted to insert the Emergency Repair Disk (ERD) depending on the options that you have selected. For example, with the "Inspect registry files" option, you will be prompted to elect which portions of the Registry you want to replace. This replacement Registry information is taken from the ERD.

Secret

Be sure to verify the security on the files and directories that the repair process just described may affect. The repair process will set the security on impacted files and subdirectories back to a default installation state. That may or may not be how you maintained your system prior to running the repair processes.

If you already haven't done so, take a moment to observe the security settings on files and folders contained in the \\%SYSTEMROOT\WINNT directory. This is accomplished by selecting the folder or file you seek to observe security information on and then selecting the secondary menu (via a right-click). Next, select either Sharing or Properties, and then the Security option. You will then be able to observe the security that is currently applied to that file or folder.

Secret

After making systemic or significant changes to your Windows NT Server environment, such as running the emergency repair process and having files replaced, it is essential you reapply the appropriate Windows NT Server service packs. I say "appropriate" because Microsoft has been somewhat inconsistent with respect to its service packs. Some service pack life cycles have been inclusive; that is, you only needed to apply the latest service pack and all prior or predecessor patches and fixes were brought forward. However, some service pack histories have been more bothersome. For example, with Microsoft Exchange 4.*x*, it was necessary to apply Service Pack 2 prior to applying Service Pack 4. So not only should you reapply the service packs as needed, but be darn sure to do so in the correct order.

Double 911 — Keep a current emergency repair disk

Even if you didn't create an ERD while installing Windows NT Server, you may do so at any time by running the RDISK command at the command prompt or Run dialog window (see Figure 25-22).

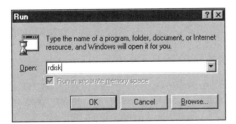

Figure 25-22: Running the RDISK command

RDISK can be used to either create or update your ERD. It essentially copies the updated system information found in the \\WINNT\REPAIR directory (see Figure 25-23).

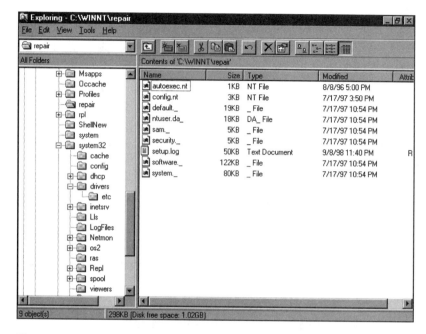

Figure 25-23: The WINNT\Repair directory

It is essential that you periodically update your ERD so that it maintains current system-related information in the event that you should suffer problems with your Windows NT Server installation. I typically update the ERD for my clients when I make my "house call" visits to inspect their networks. At a minimum, I try to perform this ERD update once per month. Major updates such as adding a service pack to your Windows NT Server or new drivers would justify an update to your ERD via RDISK regardless of when the last backup occurred.

If you don't update your ERD periodically and it is used to recover from a Windows NT Server dilemma, you face to prospect of going two steps backward. That's because the ERD will reapply historical system information such as for the Security Account Manager (SAM) that may or may not contain the last users added to your system.

Secret

After major system changes to your Windows NT Server, be sure to do at least one of following two things before you update your ERD. First, reboot and test the new configuration. Can you successfully log on? Does the new configuration on your Windows NT Server operate at a level you are satisfied with? If so, then go ahead and update your existing ERD. What you are trying to avoid is overwriting a good ERD with potentially flawed information. Second, I have a better idea. Why not just create a new ERD using RDISK and archive your existing ERD? That way you have an ERD update history archived on successive floppies, plus you address a really weak link in the entire Windows NT Server recovery chain: the reliance on floppy disk–based media. Don't forget that floppy disks periodically fail due to moisture, destruction, and other acts of God. Given that your Windows NT Server network is only as strong as its weakest link, do you really want this weak link to be an old floppy disk? No!

However, with this multifloppy scenario, be sure to limit the number of floppies in your rotation. Perhaps three floppies would work, giving you child, parent, and grandparent versions of the ERD. And of course be sure to clearly label each floppy with the ERD creation date. For a real good time, you can ship an ERD floppy copy to underground former salt mines located in the Midwest U.S., where large petroleum companies and other major corporations store their magnetic media. Old salt mines have a wonderful way of dramatically preserving and extending the life of floppies!

Each Windows NT Server must have its own ERD. These disks are not interchangeable between machines because of the machine-specific information contained on the ERD.

Finally, I promised to share with you the ultimate way to get out of trouble: keep an updated passport. You laugh now at such a suggestion, but wait until we meet offshore from the Florida Keys under the palm trees one day, my friend!

Examining Stop Screens

The dreaded ARGGH! The infamous "blue screen." It's Revenge of the Nerds, Part Three. All are appropriate descriptions of the fatal error stop screen. And stop means stop. You ain't goin' no further, my friend, when Windows NT Server generates one of these babies.

Stop screens can be created a variety of ways. By far the easiest way is to have a badly behaved device driver *not* make your day. I've been there and done that. To this day, I can crash Windows NT Server by installing one of a handful of known bad drivers that I've collected. Boom. Stop screen generated at startup. The technical reasons for this are that said drivers are supporting devices that aren't natively supported by HAL. Well, if you leave it up to third-party ISVs to write the perfect driver to run under Windows NT Server, you're bound to have an occasional stop screen.

The most common cause of stop screens is hardware-related errors. That's because these drivers are granted access by the Windows NT Server kernel to "touch" the hardware. And it is possible for bad things to happen when the hardware is touched by dirty hands . . . err, drivers. Other specific causes of stop screens include corrupted system files and/or a corrupted file system.

So just what are stop screens really? They are really divided into three sections: top, middle, and lower (see Figure 25-24).

Figure 25-24: Blue Screen

1. The top portion of the screen provides error code and related parameter information. First you naturally see the word STOP. Next you see the error code, which is also known as the bug check code.

2. The middle portion of the screen displays loaded and initialized device drivers and processes (applications). This information is displayed in three columns. Column one displays the memory address in which the driver or process was loaded. The second column displays the creation date for the driver or process. The third column displays the given name of the driver or process.

3. Modules that were in the stack at the time of the error are listed. First the kernel build number is displayed, followed by memory stack addresses that are valuable in your troubleshooting efforts if you are armed with a debugger. The stack is a memory area that basically tracks recently used data.

Secret

Although stop screens seem to convey lots of information that might be overwhelming to the uninitiated, fear not. Only the first four lines or so are the most meaningful in your troubleshooting journey. Not surprisingly, the next step is to run, not walk, to the nearest telephone and recite these lines of information to Microsoft Technical Support. Rest assured, the good guys and gals in tech support will get it from there, with your hands-on assistance of course.

Here are a few common stop screens that you are likely to encounter as a Windows NT Server Professional:

- **0x0000001E.** It's likely the file system is causing this untrapped kernel exception error. The bottom of the stop screen may list a resource, such as the network redirector (RDR.SYS), that may be the leading suspect. Run the check disk program (CHKDSK.EXE) with the fix switch (/F) if you see any mention of the file systems (FASTFAT.SYS or NTFS.SYS).

- **0x00000067 or 0x00000069.** Here the likely problem is a hard disk controller error. A few possible solutions exist. You may need to reconfigure the DIP switches on your hard drive to slow down the DMA transfer rate. Check to see that you don't have an unterminated SCSI connection on either end of a SCSI cable run (be sure to account for self-termination SCSI scenarios). Be sure to double-check that you are interrupt (IRQ) and memory address conflict free. Download and apply the latest hard disk controller driver if possible (perhaps you are inadvertently using an unsupported controller driver). And then consider some of the usual suspects as by making sure no Windows NT Server system or boot files are missing.

- **0x0000000A.** This most likely indicates a IRQ, I/O, or DMA conflict. These types of conflicts aren't much different from the "old" days of computing, when, for example, an IRQ conflict made your system inoperable. That's another way of saying that, with this specific error message, you are on more solid ground than you might believe. Just resolve the conflict as you did in the "old" days.

- **0x0000007B.** Here your boot drive isn't accessible. Somehow the boot drive has been trashed. Possibilities include mechanical failure, an unsupported compression scheme being run, or an unsupported format (such as HPFS or NetWare). Don't overlook the possibility that you have a boot sector virus.

- **F002.** This typically relates to a parity error or nonmaskable interrupt conflict. Bottom line? This error is probably memory-related. Believe it or not, I've seen this error before, and the cause was failed server RAM. You might also consider reseating each memory chip just in case the server has been bumped or the memory connection has become fouled.

- **NMI.** This is a hardware error that is typically related to server memory. One possible suspect is RAM that has a speed or type mismatch with the server motherboard.

You may find additional stop screen information on Microsoft TechNet or Volume 3, "Windows NT Messages," of the Windows NT Resource Kit.

So what to do with stop screens?

The next step is to jump into system debugging, also known as the art of searching for and eliminating fatal errors. The following discussion is intended to introduce you to debugging terms and tools. After that, you'll be armed and ready for action.

Important debugging terms

Let's set aside our engineering hats and put on our developer hats. These terms are important to understanding how debugging devices work.

Symbol file

Developers build code. This code comes in two flavors: checked and free. Checked code contains debugging code that helps the developers, but alas, it runs slower. Free code is speedy and dangerous. It doesn't contain the necessary debugging code to help developers debug their coding efforts. However, with less overhead to deal with, free code–based applications run much faster. Windows NT Server, when viewed from a code perspective (that is, the many millions of lines of code) brings the best of both worlds by combining speed, debugging capabilities, and less overhead. In effect, the source code for Windows NT Server tastes great and is less filling; it is a combination of checked and free versions. Important: You would know the symbol files in one of two ways. The first way is through the Symbols subdirectory underneath the I386 directory on the Windows NT Server CD-ROM. The second way that you are probably familiar with symbols is the way in which service packs have historically been applied to Windows NT Server. Remember those extra steps described in the readme.txt file of a service pack release that detail how to install the symbols? In a service pack, installing the updated symbols files is for the benefit of your debugging efforts.

Structured exception handling

Active at all times in Windows NT Server, this provides the capabilities to trap exceptions for possible later manipulation. If the exception is "handled" via structured exception handling, the application may continue unimpeded.

Local debugging

Using a null-modem cable, the host computer is connected to a target computer.

Remote debugging

Via Remote Access Services (RAS), you can set up a debugging session with Microsoft Technical Support. This would be considered deep diagnostics.

Debuggers du jour

We basically are concerned with four types of debuggers, as shown in Table 25-7. It is interesting to note that these debuggers run in different processing modes.

Table 25-7 Debuggers

Debugger Name	Description
CDB	Running in User mode, this is known as the Windows NT Console Debugger. It is similar to NTSD (but without the console window). The file, CDB.EXE, is located in the \SUPPORT\DEBUG\I386 or (\ALPHA) subdirectory.
KD	This is a command line kernel debugger with modem support features. The file I386KD.EXE supports the Intel platform. The file ALPHAKD.EXE supports the Alpha platform. Both files are located in the \SUPPORT\DEBUG subdirectory under either \INTEL or \ALPHA depending on your platform of choice. Runs in Kernel mode.
NT Symbolic Debugger	Windows NT Symbolic Debugger, when launched, creates a character-based MS-DOS console window that passes user-input debugging arguments. The output can be directed to a kernel debugging port. This debugger runs in User mode.
WinDBG	Running in both User and Kernel mode, this tool is typically employed by developers to remotely debug a Windows 32 application. This debugger is located in the Windows NT System Developers Kit.

Kernel debugger

Here's what you need to know with respect to the Kernel Debugger. The host and target computers are connected via a null modem cable (or "regular" modem for remote support). The host Windows NT Server computer runs the Kernel Debugger (KD), shown in Figure 25-25. The target Windows NT Server computer, the computer to be debugged, runs under a debugging environment created by the /debug switch in the BOOT.INI file. Symbols (the symbols files) must be available on the host computer. For more information, consult Microsoft TechNet or www.microsoft.com on the Internet.

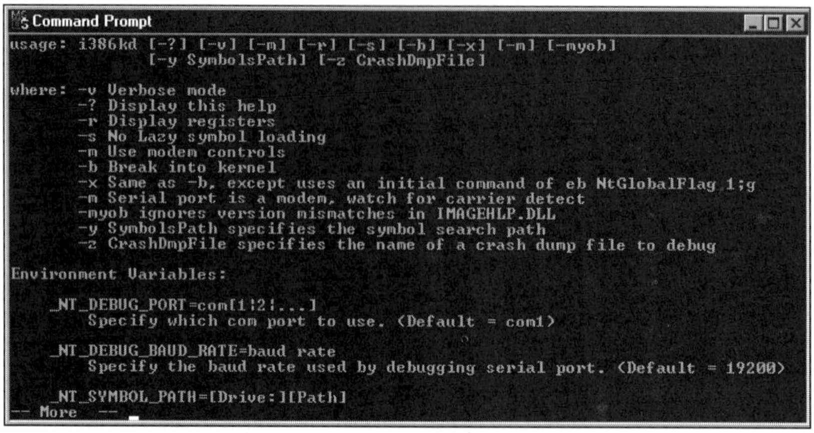

Figure 25-25: The KD debugger for the Intel platform

CrashDump

This was created primarily for the benefit of Microsoft Technical Support when working with you on troubleshooting a problem. The CrashDump capabilities are set on the Startup/Shutdown tab sheet in the System Properties dialog box. The check box "Write debugging information to:" is where you configure the CrashDump file (see Figure 25-26).

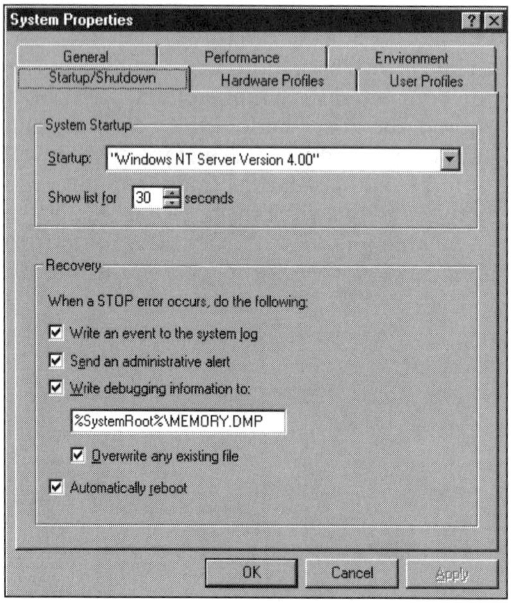

Figure 25-26: The check box "Write debugging information to"

Assuming you have configured everything correctly with respect to CrashDump, when a stop error occurs, the following events happen:

1. RAM contents are dumped to a pagefile by the system.
2. The computer automatically restarts.
3. Pagefile contents in step 1 are written to the Memory.dmp file.

Interpreting dump files

Three files located on the Windows NT Server 4.0 CD-ROM in the \SUPPORT\DEBUG\I386 or \SUPPORT\DEBUG\ALPHA subdirectories (depending on your platform) assist you in your efforts to groom and analyze your dump data. The three files are: DUMPCHK.EXE, DUMPEXAM.EXE, and DUMPFLOP.EXE.

DUMPCHK.EXE ensures that your files may be read by a debugger.

DUMPEXAM.EXE basically creates a text file that contains pertinent information from the Memory.dmp (crash dump) file.

DUMPFLOP.EXE is, as the name implies, a utility that you can use to write a dump file in segments to the floppy disk. This utility compresses the information so that it may be placed on as few floppy disks as possible. Access to symbols is not required.

Troubleshooting via the Registry

Of course, during your career as a Windows NT professional, it will be essential to master the Registry. Not surprisingly, the Registry is a huge area. Typically troubleshooting via the Registry is performed under the guidance and watchful eye of Microsoft Technical Support. However, there are other ways to learn the Registry.

Tip

I've learned to swim around the Registry by drawing on the tips and experience of highly qualified Microsoft Certified Trainers during my days as an MCSE candidate. Another approach I've employed is to draw on tips from the Microsoft newsgroups found at www.microsoft.com. Although some of the information on these newsgroups is suspect, pay close attention to the offerings from the "Most Valuable Players" (MVPs).

Troubleshooting Resources

Remember that troubleshooting is part method, part luck, and part research. Strong research demands great resources. A world of tools is available to help you troubleshoot including the Internet, books, Microsoft TechNet, journals, newspapers, training, and other professional resources such as trade associations.

The Internet: The Web and Newsgroups

Here we sit, turning the corner on a new century and millennium for that matter, and we're equipped with a research tool that was simply unimaginable even a few years ago, back in the early networking days (the LAN Manager and NetWare 1.x days). That tool of course is the Internet. You will recall that in Chapter 10, "Internet Secrets," I discuss configuring Windows NT Server to connect to the Internet. Here, the context of the Internet discussion is slightly different and relates to research.

Secret

Using the World Wide Web, newsgroups, e-mail, and the powerful search engines, you can often resolve your problems for little or no cost. The only investment you must make is time. But many feel that time spent researching a solution to a problem is time well spent.

The Microsoft site at www.microsoft.com provides the Windows NT Server fan a wealth of information (see Figure 25-27). The search engine dedicated strictly to searching the Microsoft site enables you to tap into the online knowledge base (which contains some information separate from the CD-ROM version discussed later as part of the Microsoft TechNet discussion).

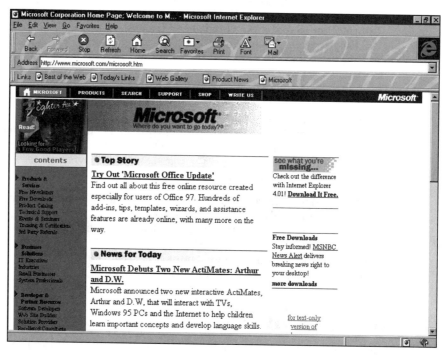

Figure 25-27: Microsoft's Web site (www.microsoft.com)

The newsgroups supported at www.microsoft.com provide an abundance of information plus offer you the opportunity to contribute your own expertise (see Figure 25-28). As when investing, however, you are warned to exercise care when disseminating information obtained from public newsgroups. The information is often worth exactly what you paid for it (nothing). Let the buyer beware! Also — the newsgroups sometimes are dominated by anti-Microsoft postings. While occasionally amusing, these irrelevant postings are severe time wasters.

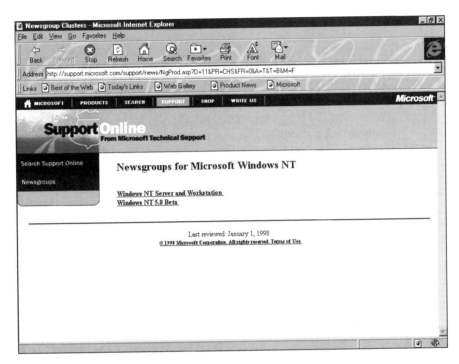

Figure 25-28: Windows NT Server newsgroups at www.microsoft.com

Books to help you

Of course this book was written with you in mind, so it is hoped that *Windows NT Server 4.0 Secrets* will be a well-worn, doodled, and tattered companion residing atop your Windows NT Server. But don't overlook the Windows NT Resource Kits. You will want to purchase both the server and workstation editions, as both kits contain relevant information that pertains to both the server and workstation environments.

Secret

It is highly recommended you keep the resource kits from previous versions of Windows NT Server for two reasons. First, the older books often contains useful subject matter that has been deleted from updated releases. Second, the resource kits enable you to successfully administer older sites you are bound to see as a Windows NT Server professional. What I wouldn't give for a copy of the original Window 3.1 Resource Kit (yes, that old Windows circa 1991).

In fact, this book you are reading assumes that you own and frequently refer to the Windows NT Resource Kits (Workstation and Server). Combined together, you've armed yourself with the referral resources necessary to enjoy success as a Windows NT Server professional. Another classic to consider is Helen Custer's *Inside the Windows NT File System* — a book that set the standard for understanding the Windows NT architecture (it is reportedly out of print, but you often see it on the bookshelves of seasoned network professionals).

Microsoft TechNet

Be sure to use Microsoft TechNet. This is a monthly CD-ROM subscription service that contains countless articles on Microsoft products including Windows NT Server, the Knowledge Base with extensive references to Windows NT Server, articles and presentations, and resource kits and training materials for Windows NT Server and other Microsoft products. It costs approximately $300/annually.

Secret

Keep old versions of TechNet on your shelf (see Figure 25-29). TechNet is updated each month, so older drivers and articles are removed to make room for new entries. By keeping your old TechNet releases, you can keep a surprisingly valuable library at your fingertips.

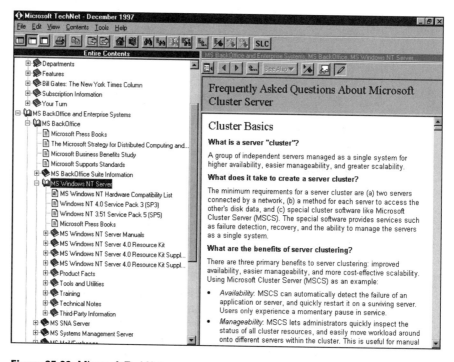

Figure 25-29: Microsoft TechNet

And speaking of articles and the like, don't forget the weekly trade rags. Publications such as *InfoWorld* offer a wealth of advice. Make these publications a regular part of your weekend reading.

Training and education

Because you are a knowledge worker, clearly one of your best avenues to develop strong troubleshooting skills is to increase your knowledge. Knowledge, obviously, is multidimensional. Many acquire knowledge via experience (a.k.a. the "School of Hard Knocks"). Others prefer a mix of education in the knowledge equation. Therein lies another resource for you to consider: education. If you put on your manager hat, perhaps you will be able to step back and develop your own sense of how important additional education is in developing your technical skills and troubleshooting talents.

Education comes in many forms, ranging from instructor-led to self-study. To discover formal training avenues authorized by Microsoft, visit `www.microsoft.com/services`. To see an example of an online training opportunity, you may surf to `www.spu.edu/depts/dcs` and learn about the program that I am an instructor for.

When selecting an educational avenue to hone our troubleshooting skills, it is highly recommended that you consider three things to maximize your return, considering the time and money you will be asked to invest:

- **Attend a sample class session if possible.** Do you and the instructor get along? Can you learn from this instructor? Are there style differences that might negatively impact your learning experience?

- ***Read* the objectives.** Are your expectations in alignment with the objectives of the class? There is nothing worse than a dissatisfied student who discovered the course wasn't his or her cup of tea (after investing lots of time and money to attend).

- **Shop around and look at the alternatives.** Perhaps self-study doesn't look so bad after you have shopped and sampled the instructor-led and online education alternatives. Are the unauthorized training centers a better fit for you and your pocketbook? Does the training center have any tools to screen students with behavioral problems, or can anyone and everyone attend the classes?

Professional resources

Aside from the peer relationships that you may have developed as a Windows NT Server professional, professional resources are available to help you troubleshoot your problems.

Microsoft Solutions Providers

Consider engaging the services of a Microsoft Solution Provider. Calling the Solution Provider program at 1-800-SOLPROV will enable you to communicate your needs, location, and budget to the representative, who will then forward your request as a lead to three or four qualified Solution Providers in your area. While not a perfect avenue for finding and engaging competent professionals, the Microsoft Solution Provider program does provide you a better approach than just using the Yellow Pages. Solution Providers receive the latest Microsoft software for learning and testing purposes. Solution Providers are also required to employ a minimum number of Microsoft Certified Professionals. Again, not a perfect approach, but the Solution Provider program does create a base standard that its members must adhere to.

Microsoft Consulting Services

Some clients implementing Windows NT Server want to go right to the source. Microsoft Consulting Services, with billing rates comparable to the Big Six accounting firms, dispatches Microsoft employees to work with you. While this approach is an expensive option to say the least, it is the best option for many organizations (typically larger organizations). There is nothing like having a representative from the software company that developed Windows NT Server side by side with you solving complex implementation problems. Kinda makes you feel as if you're feeding Microsoft a bowl of its own dog food. Contact Microsoft Consulting Services at 425-882-8080. Telephone support is available starting at $195/hour.

BackOffice Professional Association (BOPA), Network Professional Association (NPA)

These two trade organizations rate one and two respectively in providing and connecting you with the professional resources necessary to solve your Windows NT Server problems. The BOPA may be contacted at www.bopa.org. The NPA may be contacted at www.npa.org.

Tip

Be sure to save those business cards from peers and sales engineers that you meet at conferences and trade shows. Often the sales engineer from a specific vendor will provide a certain amount of free support (a.k.a. "presales engineering") if you call so that they can earn your approval and goodwill.

Microsoft paid support incidents

And don't overlook the easiest path to escalated Windows NT Server support: paid incident premium support. It is $200 well spent (and for consultants, more often than not, the incident fee is billable to your clients).

From the Backroom to the Boardroom

Mind if I borrow from the Grateful Dead for a moment? What a long, strange, and interesting trip it's been to be a technology professional in the 1990s. From the rise and fall of NetWare to the current dominance of Windows NT Server, it's been quite a ride. But some things have remained constant throughout, including the need for top-notch troubleshooting skills. With the release of Windows NT Server 4.0, it is even more apparent that these skills are needed, watched for, and utilized. That's because the technology professional standing behind each Windows NT Server deployed is no longer viewed as a backroom technician. The fact of the matter is that Windows NT Server professionals now have the full attention of the executive staff, if only for the reasons this chapter has pointed out. One point would be the staggering cost of downtime. Even nontechnical executives understand that. And as more and more Windows NT Servers are deployed in mission-critical enterprise-wide roles, more boardroom executives are relying on your superior troubleshooting skills to keep these things up and running!

Summary

In this chapter, you:

- Learned formal troubleshooting steps.
- Listed troubleshooting resources.
- Defined troubleshooting.
- Completed a troubleshooting example and developed your troubleshooting methodology.
- Learned and applied the one-hour rule.
- Calculated the value of downtime.
- Listed the steps in the Windows NT Server boot process.
- Mastered the emergency repair process.
- Analyzed blue screens and debuggers.

Part VII
Preparing for Windows 2000

Chapter 26: Defining and Planning for Windows 2000 Server

Chapter 26

Defining and Planning for Windows 2000 Server

In This Chapter

- Understanding the importance of the forthcoming Windows 2000 Server release
- Identifying key feature areas and functional classes
- Identifying key features found in Windows 2000 Server
- Planning for migrating Windows 2000 Server in your organization
- Understanding Windows NT server 4.0 to Windows 2000 Server migration issues

The most popular questions while walking the urban streets in Microsoft's home town of Seattle have been not only do you have any change to spare? but when will Windows 2000 Server ship? Such has been the wait for Windows NT professionals. And such have been the expectations for Windows 2000 Server's arrival. Given the hype in the media, the release of Windows 2000 Server is perhaps the second best known "noun" associated with Microsoft. The first would obviously have to be Microsoft's ongoing antitrust legal tangles with the Department of Justice.

For me, Windows 2000 Server, all technical discussions aside, means one thing: better access to information. Ultimately, in business computing, we're seeking more efficient ways gather data and convert it into information. It is the information that holds the value, and the data-to-information conversion process is the value-added step. So given that paradigm, how does Windows 2000 Server stack up? Very nicely, thank you. For many of us, this better information takes the form of the Active Directory and its object management orientation. For others, it's tighter integration with the Internet (the ultimate data warehouse). Note that such integration may include a more stable, secure, and bandwidth-managed connection to the Internet (more on that in a moment). Finally, "better information" should be considered from an end user's perspective. One example of this is the more powerful Find tool (from the desktop) that enables you to easily find resources on your computer, your network, and the Internet with keywords. Throw in, at long last, hardware Plug and Play capabilities and . . . you get the picture. Read on.

The Transition Chapter

As we come to the final chapter in perhaps the last book published on Windows NT Server 4.0, it is important to revisit the mission of this book. One of the underlying purposes of this book was to serve as a transition from your tried-and-true Windows NT Server 4.0 networks to the new world of Windows 2000 Server via the Option Pack and SP4. Indeed, the Option Pack is a transitional product in that you are introduced to features that will be assumed in Windows 2000 Server. And it is this chapter, providing an early look at the features, planning, and migration issues surrounding Windows 2000 Server that you will use to make the transition.

Expectation Management

The greatest concern among long-time Windows NT Server professionals, with regard to the forthcoming arrival of Windows 2000 Server, is expectation management. Expectation management is that part of our job as Windows NT professionals that we often find to be exceedingly difficult. It is the need to communicate, deliver, and not over-promise or over-commit our technology to our stakeholders. For example, in a few pages I discuss a bandwidth control feature called Admission Control Service (ACS). It's a wonderful tool for managing the bandwidth on LANs and WANs under Windows 2000 Server. However, some expectation management is necessary in presenting this feature to my stakeholders. By itself, ACS isn't going to solve bandwidth problems overnight. In fact, applications will need to be ACS compliant to fully exploit the ACS feature. That's something I must communicate today so that I don't over-promise and under-deliver with Windows 2000 Server. This Windows 2000 Server expectation management issue is multidimensional and includes the timing for your purchase and installation, promised and delivered features, and early operating system stability.

Buy today/install today

Either you will feel this one yourself, or you will have managers placing undue influence upon you to buy Windows 2000 Server on or near the release date and install it shortly thereafter in a production environment. A recurring theme that I've emphasized throughout this book has been this: The early days of Windows 2000 Server will undoubtedly be a period for:

- Ascending the Windows 2000 Server learning curve (training, mistakes, and lessons learned)
- Running Windows 2000 Server on a test network
- Both testing and waiting for your applications to become Windows 2000 Server compatible
- Continuing to run Windows NT Server 4.0 SP4 as the backbone of your existing network

Let's face it. You may well purchase Windows 2000 Server on day one. But that's about all you will do with it. On day two, you'll probably install it on a powerful yet noncritical server. And maybe around day 400, 500, or 600 you will be running it as the backbone network operating system in your organization.

In fact, that "production delay" experienced when implementing any new NOS, including Windows 2000 Server, is one of the main reasons for this book. By better using Windows NT Server 4.0 with its Option Pack and SP4, you can better implement Windows 2000 Server when that crossover date ultimately arrives.

Feature short

In its push to ship Windows 2000 Server, it will be necessary for Microsoft to ultimately cut planned features and functionality. That is normal in the software development business. If such weren't the case, you would never ship any products, always hoping to perfect features down to the minute details. And we would all suffer.

So be cautious with your expectations regarding what Windows 2000 Server will actually be able to accomplish. Depending on the pressures put upon Microsoft by itself, the marketplace, and most important, Windows 2000 Server beta testers, the product may look very different from what you are reading about in the popular trade journals today. Be cautious by expecting less and receiving more than you expected in the first release of Windows 2000 Server.

Unstable

Finally, perhaps the best reason for casting a cautious eye on the initial shipping version of Windows 2000 Server is your experiences with unstable operating systems. Remember early in the book, in Chapter 1, when I mentioned that there were those in the Windows NT Server community who felt Windows NT Server 3.51 wasn't ready for prime time until SP5 came along? And this is the same group that, with the release of SP4, are now enthusiastically embracing Windows NT Server 4.0. So you can easily imagine that these people will undoubtedly be cautious about the first release of Windows 2000 Server.

Perhaps their fears are well founded. You, as a Windows NT Server professional, will receive no quicker call than that of the blue screen. And yes, you can anticipate blue screens in the early releases of Windows 2000 Server. So we'll all keep high hopes and assume that Windows 2000 Server will achieve its stability like a fine wine — over time.

Microsoft's Position on Windows 2000 Server

Look beneath Microsoft's high-level "vision" of quality, value, delivery, and teamwork when speaking about the Windows 2000 Server development team, and you can see what the "goals" are. The goals for Windows 2000 Server are to provide a great network server operating system that provides file/print/Web services, application services, robust infrastructure services, and communications services. A key tenet to achieving these goals is to have the highest reliability ever.

File servers

With basic file server activity, it will be easier to locate information via Active Directory (which is discussed more in a moment). Storage management has dramatically improved with disk quotas, hierarchical storage management, and dynamic volume management. If you're from the NetWare community, perhaps you've already used disk quotas (and were somewhat dismayed that earlier versions of Windows NT Server had no such feature). Windows 2000 Server clearly bring performance improvement over its predecessors, with Microsoft reporting 20 percent faster file access.

Print servers

Printers are now objects in Active Directory to allow more robust management from anywhere on the network. Printers will also be available over the Internet via the Internet printing protocol. Bottom line? Faster printing, more efficient queue management, and dramatic network printing driver improvements.

Web servers

Web servers are a key focus of Windows 2000 Server. Clearly, the emphasis is on higher performance, and there is support for HTTP compression.

Applications servers

This is where Windows 2000 Server shines. A few improvements here include better scaling, fewer reboots, improved clustering services, and the autostart of failed services. Application management has been improved with the introduction of terminal services, via Terminal Server, at the desktop. That is because you may deploy terminals at the desktop, dramatically simplifying the deployment of applications.

Infrastructure servers

With Windows 2000 Server, you will see two main improvements. First, Active Directory will dramatically change the way the networking infrastructure is managed (as a distributed object database). The other huge feature is improved security services based on Kerberos and public key infrastructure. You will also benefit from the Security Configuration Editor.

Communications servers

Three areas of improvement. There is a stronger emphasis on policy-based networking. An example of this is quality of service (QoS). I discuss this more in this chapter, but basically QoS enables you to set a policy on how much bandwidth may be used by a multimedia application or Web browsing and the like.

Microsoft concludes that Windows 2000 Server will provide the power that customers demand with such features as Internet Explorer 5.0, automatic network setup, exploitation of advanced hardware, and fitness for world-wide use (including multilingual support). Customers benefit from the robust nature of Windows 2000 Server including fewer reboots. Finally, customers will be able to leverage existing assets. Here the goal is broad application compatibility plus better hardware compatibility.

Introducing Windows 2000 Server

Known by its present name for most of its development cycle, Windows 2000 Server is clearly the next generation of network operating system from Microsoft. It is a major release with substantial rework. It is clearly not a minor upgrade (as was Windows NT Server 3.5 to 3.51).

So what is Windows 2000 Server? Here we go. I have divided this discussion into key areas that reflect the areas of improvement in Windows NT Server.

General

From fewer reboots to an improved user interface, I share with you the general improvements to Windows 2000 Server that I consider to be my favorites.

Fewer reboots

Fewer reboots is clearly one of my favorites and the favorite of many long-time Windows NT Server professionals. Microsoft claims to have eliminated over 60 reboot conditions that previously have wreaked havoc on critical workday operations. In fact, at the enterprise level, it has been difficult to take Windows NT Server seriously in the past because of the pervasive need to reboot. Rebooting during daytime hours is of course not practical.

Device Manager

In Chapter 11 of this book, adding new hardware to Windows NT Server 4.0 is discussed and cursed. That has changed in Windows 2000 Server with its Windows 98–like Device Manager. In fact, upon booting, Windows 2000 Server performs a robust hardware detection routine.

I consider Device Manager to be one of the best improvements in Windows 2000 Server, at least from a network administration point of view.

Note

Understand that one of the things that makes Device Manager possible is Plug and Play (PnP) support. Yes, it's finally here, making it easy to install and troubleshoot new hardware.

Improved user interface — Active Desktop

Similar to Windows 98 with its Web orientation, the Active Desktop is both an improvement in user interface design and functionality over Windows NT Server 4.0. One feature of the Active Desktop is the ability to launch applications and documents via a single click.

Microsoft Management Console

Another usability and functionality enhancement is the Microsoft Management Console (MMC). The idea behind the MMC is simple. Present the user a consistent interface regardless of the server tool or application being used. This is huge improvement over the varied looks of Event Viewer, Server Manager, and User Manager for Domains in Windows NT Server 4.0. In Windows 2000 Server, each of these tools is now presented via a MMC.

Another cool thing about the MMC concept is that it accepts snap-ins. That's another way of saying the MMC is extensible and customizable. A developer could write to the MMC to create a custom snap-in. I can only imagine the improvements in application management that will result from this approach. Such improvements might include the ability to configure your accounting application from an MMC snap-in.

Secret

It is likely that, in your early experience with Windows 2000 Server, you will instinctively go to Control Panel to perform many configuration actions on your server. I know I did. However, much of the Control Panel has been moved to the MMC format. After a few days, you will get used to that change. You will be interested to know that the MMC is now available to you in Windows NT Server 4.0 via the Option Pack. This is discussed in Part IV of this book.

Improved wizards

Windows 2000 Server, as you would expect, has made great strides in the usability arena by introducing new wizards such as the Disk Cleanup Wizard, the Driver Update Wizard, and so on.

New tools

Windows 2000 Server includes a host of new and powerful tools that not only improve the core network operating system and its use but improve the way that we as humans interact with information (again, one of the ultimate goals of computing).

Strong finds

The Find option via the Start menu has been renamed "Search" to reflect its broader search capabilities to include the Internet. Know, when you select Search, you will see an option for finding information on the Internet. You may also find people via you local Windows Address Book and Web-based directory services. This is similar in functionality to that enjoyed by Windows 98 users (with their Find command).

Power management

Let it be said that Microsoft didn't hold back on the bells and whistles in Windows 2000 Server. The Power Management Properties in Control Panel enable you conserve machine energy by offering sleep and hibernation functions.

The power management features are intended for Windows 2000 Professional, Microsoft's workstation operating system. You would be ill-advised to use such power management functions on a true server.

Task Scheduler

This is one of the most practical improvements in Windows 2000 Server. With Windows NT Server 4.0 and before, it is necessary to use the AT command at the command prompt to enjoy any real form of scheduling. The AT command is mentioned in the context of tape backups in Chapter 3 of this book. Task Scheduler is similar to the WinAT application found on the Windows NT Server 4.0 Resource Kit CD-ROM. Using the Add Scheduled Task Wizard, you may easily add tasks, such as backup, that you want automated. New to Windows 2000 Server is the capability to run tasks when the computer starts or your logon (these features weren't available via the AT command).

Storage/file system management

Another favorite, storage quotas now enable you to realistically manage storage space on a per user basis. This is a feature that NetWare has had for some time. You will enjoy this tremendously. Windows 2000 Server will have backward support for FAT32, which means there will be direct compatibility with Windows 95 OSR2 and later. Major NTFS enhancements include the ability to add storage space without rebooting. The Encrypting File System provides transparent on-disk file encryption for NTFS files using Public Key technology. Universal Disk Format (UDF) has been added, which is a new file system to support DVD and CD media.

Even the old-fashioned backup program, NTBackup, has been upgraded to allow for a Windows Explorer–like look and feel.

Printing

Needless to say, printing performance and functionality continues to evolve. First and foremost is the support for printing to an Internet-based printer via the URL address. My favorite feature is that printers are now an object in the Active Directory, allowing users to easily locate and use a printer in the enterprise.

Networking

You won't be let down here. Microsoft is providing a host of networking-related improvements in Windows 2000 Server.

Large Ethernet frames

Large Ethernet frames are something that NetWare has had for some time and are now finally available in Windows 2000 Server. This feature allows the network to transfer information efficiently by effectively cutting down on the number of acknowledgment packets.

Dynamic DNS

Dynamic DNS, discussed in passing in Chapter 8, "DNS, DHCP, WINS," is the next generation of DNS that eliminates its historical weakness of being too static. In fact, Dynamic DNS is similar to merging old WINS and old DNS, making a best-of-breed name resolution service.

With Dynamic DNS, updates in distributed DNS records are made and propagated automatically to all affected DNS name servers throughout your network. This effectively decreases DNS-related administration expenses because manual edits of DNS databases are eliminated.

Distributed File System (DFS)

This feature provides a single namespace for disparate file system resources at a site. DFS is organized into a hierarchical structure of logical volumes completely independent of the resource's physical location. You may have already worked with DFS, version 4.1 of which is shipping with Windows NT Server 4.0.

IP security management

This feature ensures end-to-end secure communications. This is implemented by your configuring what IP addresses are valid to establish a session with, something I've done and is very simple.

Microsoft Directory Service Migration tool

Great improvements have been made here for those of us who are migrating from a NetWare network or need to coexist with a NetWare network. The

Directory Service Migration Tool now has NDS support! You will recall that the migration tool used in Windows NT Server 4.0 used bindery emulation, an approach with practical limitations. The Directory Service Migration Tool provides for the discovery of any NetWare user and group properties and then exports these properties to the Active Directory.

Note that it is commonly believed that Windows 2000 Server will only provide support for migrations from NDS trees. It is not expected that you will actually be able to synchronize the Active Directory with NDS resources on a network.

Robust routing and clustering support

Windows 2000 Server has robust routing via the "steelhead" technology, which improves upon the simple subnet routing in Windows NT Server 4.0. Windows 2000 Server also has clustering support. It s here that I suggest you not only learn the technology area but expect this to improve in future Windows 2000 Server releases. Clustering is the next battleground for Microsoft in its fight for success at the enterprise level. It is here that UNIX and other seasoned operating systems are formidable opponents.

Admission Control Services

A new feature in Windows 2000 Server, Admission Control Services will be conceptually familiar to those of us who have worked with and optimized Microsoft Proxy Server. How? Two words. Bandwidth Control. Whereas Proxy Server allows the management of WAN bandwidth dedicated to Internet browsing and the like, Admission Control Services (ACS) essentially do the same on a subnet-by-subnet basis. This is accomplished by managing the bandwidth on the subnet, and more particularly, by preventing the consumption of too much bandwidth by applications. But how is this done? It is accomplished by invoking the Quality of Service (QoS) standards discussed in numerous Internet drafts.

I for one am extremely excited about the new Admission Control Service and will dedicate the next several pages to this topic.

Secret

It is also important to understand that ACS is how we can manage multimedia and other network resource hogs on our Windows 2000 Advanced Server networks.

Quality of Service

QoS is officially defined in an Internet Draft as a set of service requirements to be met by the network while transporting a flow. A more practical definition is the service expectations and requirements that a network must satisfy when transmitting a flow or stream of data. QoS is here today in Windows 2000 Server because of these three underlying issues:

1. QoS is necessary because the existing best-effort IP service isn't good enough for audio-visual real-time traffic where packet loss conditions from congestion exist and applications and systems may suffer from variable delay.

2. Network managers need to be able to manage their resources. Mission-critical applications such as distributed databases need bandwidth protection. Real-time audio-visual applications require bandwidth commitment.

3. QoS in Windows 2000 Server interoperates with the current infrastructures of Ethernet, current generation IPv4, ISP-based WANs, and so on.

It helps to observe the history of QoS to better understand its role in Windows 2000 Server. Table 26-1 presents the QoS Life Cycle.

Table 26-1 **The QoS Life Cycle**

Component	1997	1998–1999
Routers	Low to medium data rate support for RSVP and precedence queuing	RSVP support in border routers, IP switching with precedence queuing
Hosts	No RSVP signaling	RSVP signaling, precedence bits in IP and Ethernet. Traffic control
Ethernet Switches	High-end switches supporting 802.1p precedence queuing	802.1p support in most switches and hubs with Admission Control (Subnet Bandwidth Manager)
ISPs	Trial deployment of precedence-based services based on Static Classes (VPNs)	Edge routers mapping RSVP-signaled traffic into precedence classes. First Tier ISPs interconnect

Still seeking understanding? How about this angle: QoS services and protocols provide a connection-oriented, point-to-point delivery system for IP traffic. This is interesting because this set of rules, which is governing the guaranteed delivery of packets, is so different (and so much better) from the rule set we historically used for multimedia transmissions in the past. Back in the days when knights were bold and kings owned the gold, UDP was utilized to transmit multimedia traffic such as video and sound. Under Windows 2000 Server, as we shall see, ACS can help us better manage this process.

In short, we're talking about how much subnet bandwidth will be allocated to specific QoS-aware applications and how it will be allocated. That is the name of the Microsoft ACS implementation game. So if you understand that, then it's easy to conceptualize the fact that applications adhering to QoS can make a reservation for a certain amount of bandwidth on a subnet and establish priority for data transmission. That last point is especially important for those who have worked with HP's 100VG-AnyLAN implementation with its demand priority access method (where two priority levels could be established: low and high). The demand priority access method is conceptually similar to the QoS-related ability to establish data transmission priorities.

ACS benefits

As alluded to previously, certain application types can benefit from higher network bandwidth allocations or the ability to enjoy higher network utilization rates. Initially, these applications include some of the worst bandwidth consumers including multimedia, video, and audio applications. Look for the benefits of ACS to be extended to a greater range of applications as Windows 2000 Server matures.

- **Multimedia.** Of course multimedia with the "streaming" nature of video and audio are easily identified candidates that can benefit from ACS in Windows 2000 Server.

- **Video.** Historically, using the UDP protocol resulted in video such as CUSEEME being delivered via a "best effort" but no guaranteed transmission method. That meant video frames were dropped during a video session, resulting in "choppy" video.

- **Audio.** Audiophiles, those of us who are audio experts, know computers are increasingly assuming more important roles in the delivery of high-fidelity sound. Not that we completely agree with this macro trend. That's because the true audiophile still relishes the analog-based inherit wave delivery of sound. Computers, being digital, deliver sound via sampling or sample rates. This is a major point of contention with audiophiles. Digital sampling can't approximate the quality of analog wave-based sound.

  When we were delivering sound via UDP, not only were we still subject to the inherent digital sampling deficiencies, but we also suffered from dropped packets given UDPs best-effort delivery commitment. Well that certainly wasn't entirely acceptable to the audiophile community. Of course the "fast" delivery via UDP was desirable, but the lower overall service level because of dropped packets wasn't.

  However, the delivery of sound under Windows 2000 Server via ACS is closer to perfection but of course still not perfect. At least under ACS we can institute a basic service-level commitment wherein sound information will be received with more reliability than was possible with UDP via older versions of Windows NT Server.

- **Manufacturing.** Real-time and reliable transport systems are essential in manufacturing for such critical applications as inventory control systems and computer aided manufacturing (CAM). A little history is necessary to set the stage. Back in the old days of networking, ArcNet was popular in the manufacturing community for its "deterministic" delivery method. As you know from courses such as Networking Essentials and your own experience, deterministic networks enable us to, within reason, control what nanosecond a packet will arrive at a node. Obviously, in CAM environments, this is "critical" to the success of the production line. Why? We need to have the specific manufacturing equipment make the punch in the sheet metal at the exact right moment. Important? You bet. Just think about it next time you fly on a Boeing jet. By the way, for the sake of comparison, Ethernet, a widely used networking standard, is considered "opportunistic" for its contention method of listening to silence on the network.

So that leads us to how ACS impacts manufacturing applications or environments such as CAM. Think of it as adding some deterministic behavior back into an opportunistic network such as Ethernet. How? By devoting a certain commitment of bandwidth, we effectively address the top issues negatively impacting real-time applications and environments: packet delay and bandwidth. Another view is this: If the CAM-related command is delivered late, it is useless and might well be the source of rework further down the manufacturing line.

Practical ACS applications

Look for ACS to be one of the more practical built-in solutions at your disposal in Windows 2000 Server. Here I mean that business software vendors such as database developers will see the benefit of ACS compliance. The ACS capabilities of Windows 2000 Server should also expose additional opportunities for third-party software developers such as security monitoring (for instance, restricting which users get bandwidth to run Web browsers).

Secret

ACS will yield high dividends for you on your WAN when facing a common issue that is negatively impacting organizations today. That is the appropriate use of Internet browsers such as Microsoft Internet Explorer or Netscape's Navigator. The issue is this: Organizations are attempting to implement robust client/server-based solutions such as business databases over multiple sites using WAN links as "skinny" as possible to save monthly telco charges. Can't blame 'em. So whereas a 56K single-channel Frame Relay link may allow for adequate business database performance in a natural state, those assumptions can be dramatically altered for the worse when you, in an untimely manner, discover that the staff is also using browsers from the desktop. Oops. Now the business database traffic is being severely crowded out by the often frivolous browser traffic.

Enter ACS and the ability to assign bandwidth and a high priority to the important business database traffic. Some of us in the technology profession believe that the Internet surfers can suffer a little when it comes to business networks.

The Windows QoS program

Microsoft's first step in implementing the QoS is via its Admission Control Service. ACS allows QoS-aware applications running on a Windows NT Server network to reserve subnet bandwidth and establish transmission priority while preventing the overcommitment of network bandwidth. This is accomplished by the new QoS API under WinSock 2.0. As discussed in Chapter 4, "TCP/IP Secrets," WinSock 2.0 was a new networking API originally introduced in the later life cycle of Windows NT 4.0 and made widely available in Windows NT 5.0 and Windows 98. WinSock 2.0 supported QoS and layered service providers such as remote WinSock for proxy. Additional QoS features that will be defined over the next several pages include:

- **Native stack support for QoS.** This includes traffic control via Queue Management, signaling via RSVP and precedence bits in the IP header, and, of course, admission control via ACS.
- **Shared media admission control service.** This includes the subnet bandwidth manager (SBM), IETF RSVP effort with Intel, Cisco, 3Com, Extreme, and Sun vendor support.
- **Network resource management.** This includes end system management of traffic control and hop-by-hop bandwidth management.

QoS host architecture

QoS service providers in Windows 2000 Server are open and extensible with RSVP support built in. These upper OSI layer service providers rely on the packet classifier and the packet scheduler, both located at the lower area of the OSI model as seen in Figure 26-1. The packet classifier directs traffic to queues maintained by the packet scheduler. The packet scheduler delivers queued packets to the network.

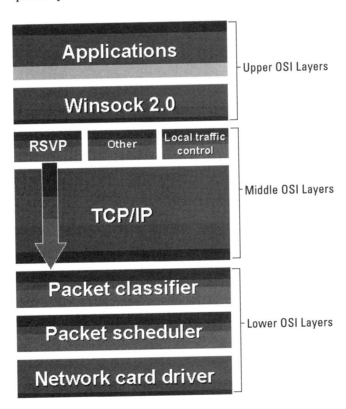

Figure 26-1: QoS host architecture

Relating QoS to ACS

Under Windows 2000 Server, ACS handles the bandwidth and packet delay issues. This is done by ACS implementing its "rules" in accordance with the QoS service requirements. Specifically, Windows 2000 Server implements QoS capabilities via the following functions, protocols, services, and behaviors:

- ACS, which allows resource usage control. This is accomplished by routing all QoS reservations on a subnet via the ACS server.

- Assured or guaranteed service levels for real-time applications

- Independent functionality without respect to network media: LAN, WAN, ATM. This refers to the ability to mix media.

- Support for multicasting over LANs and WANs

- Multimedia queuing that is considered "friendly"

- Enhanced connectivity capabilities

- Users seeing QoS transparently

- Data transportation with end-to-end reliability

- Subnet Broadcast Management (SBM). This is the primary service that manages network resources on a subnet. Herein also lies one of the important management functions: preventing a subnet from becoming overwhelmed with requests. This is accomplished by SBM asserting itself along the path between the hosts and the routers. SBM is configured within ACS under Windows NT Server.

- Resource Reservation Protocol (RSVP). Perhaps you could think of this as a facilitator. Here is what I mean: RSVP facilitates the communication session by constructing a QoS highway between the sender and the receiver. The RSVP packet is responsible for carrying the reservation request to the routers and switches between the hosts (both senders and receivers). The catalyst for this function is the ACS server. The RSVP-based communication occurs periodically so that the QoS-based reservations are maintained.

  Note that the reservation process facilitated by RSVP is designed to occur at each router and/or switch to fully adhere to the QoS implementation. RSVP, as defined by the Internet Engineering Task Force, is designed to process multicast IP packet traffic.

- Traffic Control. Akin to traffic management in the physical world, QoS-based traffic control refers to the "lane" that packet traffic will travel across. Two components are at work: the packet classifier and the packet scheduler.

    - The packet classifier divides packets into waiting queues based upon an algorithm that takes into account the packet's priority. This component also tells the packet scheduler at what rate to empty these queues.

Chapter 26: Defining and Planning for Windows 2000 Server

- The packet scheduler provides management for those queues set up by the packet classifier. This component not only retrieves packets from the queues but sends those packets across the QoS reserved communication channel discussed previously.

■ Ease of administration

ACS specifics

So how does ACS actually work? Given that we know that ACS handles bandwidth resources for networks, it is important to note that a network using ACS may consist of several subnets (see Figure 26-2). The clients and Windows NT Servers are able to utilize the shared bandwidth found on that subnet. On the subnet, an ACS server evaluates each bandwidth reservation request prior to forwarding it to a router or switch. By performing this function, the ACS server effectively reduces the stress and strain on the network.

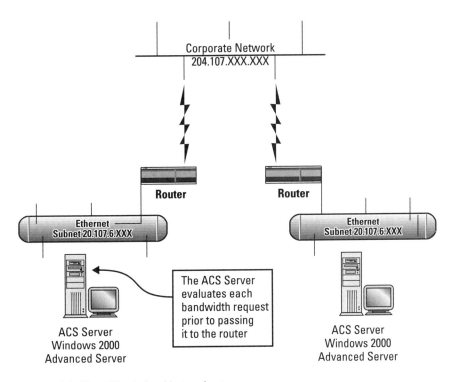

Figure 26-2: The ACS relationship to subnets

Working our way down to the detail level, observe that each sender, perhaps a multimedia server handling audio and video, sends its QoS reservation message to the ACS server (see Figure 26-3). The ACS server then determines whether the bandwidth level request is allowed. If so, a reservation logically blocks out that bandwidth for the sender (a multimedia server in this example) to utilize. The ACS server then forwards a request to the router, where a physical bandwidth commitment is made.

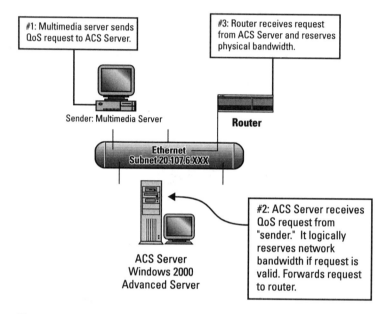

Figure 26-3: The basic ACS Server and sender relationship

Because of its subnet-centric orientation, an ACS server is also known as a subnet monitor. Also, it is important to understand that an ACS server may serve as an adjudicator or authority to allocate a subnet's bandwidth among several QoS-compliant senders. For example, if you had several multimedia servers on one subnet, the ACS server would assert itself by sending out beacon packets (the ACS server broadcasts its service) and allocating the network bandwidth among those senders. Thus, an ACS server is a badly needed central point of administration when it comes to management of network resources.

The ACS server running on a Windows NT Server enables network administrators to manage network bandwidth on a subnet-by-subnet basis. That means an .AVI file on a intranet page located on a the local subnet may receive sufficient bandwidth to be downloaded and played properly. However, a request to the Internet for an .AVI file may result in a denial or less bandwidth on the network. This last part happens when the ACS server managing the backbone or subnet connected to the Internet rejects the bandwidth request for the Internet-based multimedia .AVI file.

What occurs if there are multiple ACS servers on a single subnet? This is certainly a possibility, and before answering, consider how Windows NT Server handles multiple servers in general: One typically leads and the others follow. Such is the case with multiple ACS servers on one subnet. One ACS server assumes the role of primary ACS server that actually provides the ACS-related service. The other ACS servers are, of course, backups. If and when the primary ACS server fails, then one of the other ACS servers will be promoted to serve as the primary ACS server. This election is determined by the ACS Election Priority setting.

ACS and routers

An advanced example shown in Figure 26-4 underscores several points about ACS and routers. The PATH message sent from the sender to the receiver installs an RSVP condition at each router. This effectively creates the roadmap that should be followed. The returning RESV message reserves the necessary resources. RESV messages are processed by the ACS servers, and then the traffic is allowed to travel through router. The router accepts RESV reservations, and based on its traffic control service that configures the proper QoS, the RESV message is passed to the next router. When a non-RSVP compliant router is encountered, it is passed on to the next router, all the while hoping to find an RSVP-compliant router in its travels.

One point of failure in the RSVP/RESV process occurs when the router rejects the reservation. When that occurs, a ResvErr transmission is sent from the router back to the receiver.

Two additional points about ACS and routers: First, it is important to note that not all routers are compliant with ACS under Windows 2000 Server. Second, like a user suffering from attention deficit disorder, this process requires constant attention. Known as a soft-state protocol, RSVP induces the receiver to continuously issue RESV messages.

RFCs and ACS

In computer networking, RFCs are both the judge and jury; RFCs are the laws of the LAN (and WAN and Internet). Not only are RFCs a great place to educate yourself on the finer points of networking, but you can also observe which computer hardware and software vendors are just staying within the rules of the RFC laws. That is, vendors implement RFCs with varying degrees of compliance.

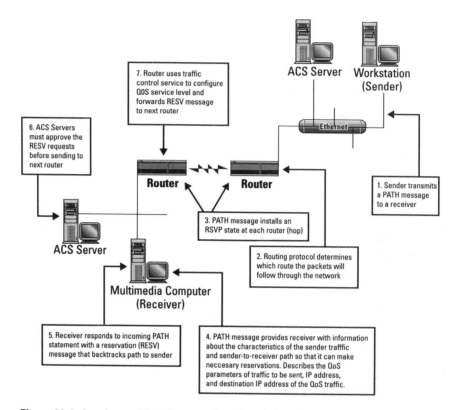

Figure 26-4: An advanced ACS Server and sender relationship

Secret

To really learn about the nuts and bolts of ACS, I highly recommend that you acquire the related RFCs. For example, one RFC (draft-ietf-issll-is802-sbm-06.txt) provides an understanding of the ACS area that is, quite frankly, beyond the scope of this book. Specifically, RFC draft-ietf-issll-is802-sbm-06.txt draws out a valuable discussion that compares modern switching mechanisms or switched networks with legacy networks using bandwidth control mechanisms such as ACS. Very interesting and highly recommended.

Another RFC, draft-ietf-qosr-framework-05.txt, is worthy for its description of QoS. I'd rate this RFC as educational in nature.

ATM

Windows 2000 Server provides new and improved support for hardware and software that uses Asynchronous Transfer Mode (ATM). New user- and kernel-mode APIs enable applications and drivers to create and manage ATM virtual circuits (VCs). In fact, these APIs can be used to determine the QoS and stream multiple information types (video, data, voice) through each VC. There is an ATM LAN emulation client module to enable your existing network applications and protocols to use Ethernet or Token Ring to run well over an ATM network. Windows 2000 Server has an ATM Call Manager that conforms to the ATM Forum UNI specification for signaling over ATM. There is integrated ATM support for allowing Windows 32-bit (Win32) TAPI applications to create and manage virtual circuits over ATM. Finally, there is integrated ATM support for WinSock2.

Internet

Basic Internet support in Windows 2000 Server is provided via Internet Information Server 5.0 (which will be installed as part of the core Windows 2000 Server setup). The goal of IIS 5.0 is to reduce the total cost of ownership and increase reliability and performance. Pretty standard stuff. This will be accomplished by extensive use of wizards and MMC.

The IIS application environment will enjoy ASP enhancements and security improvements. These security improvements include Kerberos integration for delegation support and certificate storage in Windows NT Directory.

Secret

To prepare for Windows 2000 Server's Internet features, you are strongly encouraged to develop Web applications today with the Windows NT Server 4.0 Option Pack.

Active Directory

Active Directory is a huge area and has already garnered excessive attention in the popular media. This is a volatile feature set that as of this writing is still not feature complete. In fact, it is generally assumed that Microsoft's attempts to fortify Active Directory have resulted in the delays associated with Windows 2000 Server. Note the popular perception is that domains have disappeared with Active Directory. That is actually not true. Domains are now an object in the Active Directory tree.

Active Directory with its Directory Services (DS) replaces the Registry-based Security Account Manager (SAM). Yet it retains 100 percent backward compatibility to Windows NT Server 4.0's SAM. DS is replicated across the Active Directory to provide for load balancing and redundancy.

Here are three angles in discussing Active Directory.

First

Active Directory is the functional equivalent of NDS from the NetWare community, so if you have already worked with NetWare 4.x or higher, you already have a leg up on mastering Active Directory.

Secret

One thing you can do today to prepare for Windows 2000 Server is to learn NDS on a NetWare server. True Story. Take a few days to learn NDS, and Active Directory will seem very familiar to you when Windows 2000 Server ships. I am most concerned about those who have only worked with Windows NT Server 4.0 with its domain model, for these people will undergo a major paradigm shift when they encounter Active Directory.

Second

Here is a practical view: Think of Active Directory as a more intelligent way to manage information. Remember my early comments that a goal of Windows 2000 Server is to better manage our information. Active Directory, with its object orientation, is a step in the path toward removing metadata redundancies in a Windows network. An example of this is how separate and very different user information is stored in Microsoft SQL Server, SMS, Windows 2000 Server, and Microsoft Exchange Server. Only the operating system, Microsoft Exchange, and to some extent (depending on the security model invoked) Microsoft SQL Server share common information about users. In the future, Active Directory will enable you to enter user information once and have this information seamlessly used in other parts of the network, such as BackOffice applications.

Third

A quick view of Microsoft's public position on Active Directory: It is considered to be a new directory service that stores information about all objects on the computer network and makes this information easy for administrators to find and use. Active Directory provides a single network logon, a single point of administration for all network objects, and full query ability for any attribute of any object. Active Directory is replicated, partitioned, hierarchical, and extensible.

Change and configuration management

Several improvements have been made to configuring the machine's and user's environments.

Scripts

Scripts may now be executed via the Windows Scripting Host (WSH). WSH is a scripting host for Windows 2000 Server that includes Visual Basic Scripting (VBScript) and Jscript capabilities. This is a vast improvement over the previous restrictions in the Windows NT Server environment, where absent a third-party scripting solution, you were stuck with the MS-DOS command language. With Windows 2000 Server and smart hands at the console, you could say that true logon scripts now exist.

Group Policy Editor

The Group Policy Editor is an MMC snap-in that is responsible for managing the settings for Group Policy as it is applied to a given site, domain, or organizational unit.

Zero Administration Windows

This is a method for reducing the total cost of ownership (TCO) by assisting with the setup and management of applications.

Security

Security improvements in Windows 2000 Server are numerous. The two greatest and best-known improvements are the use of Kerberos and Public Key. These are two well-documented security models, the details of which are easily searchable by typing these key words on any Internet engine. For example, typing Kerberos in Infoseek at www.infoseek.com resulted in over 10,000 hits (see Figure 26-5).

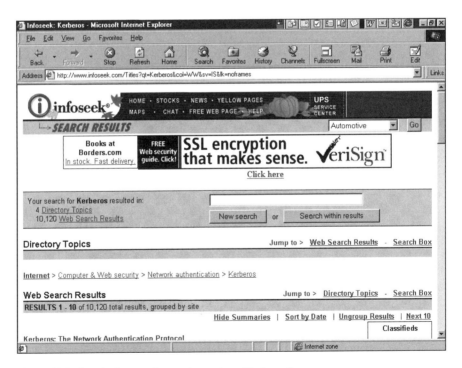

Figure 26-5: Results from an Internet search on "Kerberos"

Note that the Windows 2000 Server security topic will be discussed extensively in the forthcoming *Windows 2000 Server Secrets* title from IDG Books Worldwide.

Planning for Windows 2000 Server

The good news is that there are activities you can undertake today in the sunset of Windows NT Server 4.0 to prepare you for the dawn of Windows 2000 Server. Here are the top ten things you can do today to prepare for Windows 2000 Server:

1. Leverage your Windows NT Server 4.0 architectural knowledge in the domain architecture and name resolution services (DNS, WINS) to your advantage in implementing Windows 2000 Server.

2. Understand the basic concepts of Active Directory. The best way today, as previously mentioned, to gain this understanding, is to learn NetWare's NDS tree.

3. Gain a deeper understanding of network security. Consider my advice earlier in the chapter to search the Internet on terms such as "Kerberos" to gain a better understanding of advanced network security models.

4. Have fewer and larger domains today. Such a strategy will dramatically simplify your migration to Windows 2000 Server. That is because domain deletion has a high tax associated with it in the world of Active Directory. Note that Active Directory prefers a shallow tree over a deep tree. Thus, advice I gave in Chapter 2 regarding planning and Chapter 3 regarding implementation rings true here in Chapter 26: Keep your domain structure simple.

5. Keep trust relationships between domains simple (today) to simplify your migration tomorrow.

6. Avoid domain names that violate DNS RFCs and BackOffice applications. Remember that SQL Server doesn't appreciate the hyphen (-) or dash character in a domain name. Other problematic characters in domain names include the underscore and period.

7. Assess your vendor preparedness. Are your vendors porting their applications to the Windows 2000 Server environment? Are they knowledgeable when it comes to Active Directory? Pay close attention to server-based applications that will rely heavily on core Windows 2000 Server services and Active Directory. Be sure to encourage these vendors to create migration DLLs. Speak to your vendors. Ask the tough Windows 2000 Server questions of your vendors today to avoid failures tomorrow.

8. Plan your DS schema today. The key point is that everyone must agree on the schema. Schemas in networking are the equivalent of the chart of accounts in accounting: critical infrastructure.

9. Stay current on Windows 2000 Server trends by monitoring industry trade journals (*InfoWorld*), monitoring Microsoft's Web site (www.microsoft.com), and monitoring important third-party information provider Web sites (www.winntmag.com, www.mcpmag.com).

10. Above all, install Windows NT Server 4.0 with SP4 and the Option Pack to simplify your migration to Windows 2000 Server.

So enjoy Windows NT Server 4.0 with SP4 and the Option Pack today. And get ready for Windows 2000 Server!

Summary

Here are the key points to retain from this concluding chapter:

- Understand the importance of the forthcoming Windows 2000 Server release.
- Identify key feature areas and functional classes.
- Identify key features found in Windows 2000 Server.
- Plan for migrating Windows 2000 Server in your organization.
- Understand Windows NT server 4.0–to–Windows 2000 Server migration issues.

Appendix A

Performance Monitor Objects

As discussed in Chapter 22, this appendix provides you with selected object:counter definitions. I've only provided the "core" object:counters here in the interest of time and space but also of importance. To be honest, most of object:counters omitted are not used by Windows NT Server administrators and engineers. What I've attempted to do is only list the definitions and explanations for the object:counters you are likely to use in the management of your Windows NT Server network. However, exceptions and additions exist.

Third-party ISVs have long taken advantage of Performance Monitor in several ways. First, during the software application development cycle, ISVs use Performance Monitor to monitor the health and performance of the Windows NT Server machine and network. This not only allows them to see that their development environment is either running optimally or in a state similar to that of their customers, but it allows them to see how their software applications are impacting the system. Second, the ISVs typically write object:counters that are unique to their software application, which they run as part of Performance Monitor. Here again, this allows them to monitor and optimize their software application during the development cycle. But perhaps most important, by creating application-specific object:counters, ISVs expose a wealth of monitoring and optimization possibilities for you, the customer. For example, when you purchase and install Microsoft SQL Server, several object:counters specific to this application are added to Performance Monitor. When using and developing with SQL Server, you benefit greatly from these SQL Server–specific object:counters in the management of your database applications and your network.

For descriptions of object:counters not listed here, simply click the explain button for the object:counter of your choice in the Add To Chart dialog box.

Table A-1 Performance Monitor Object Types

Object	Object Counter	Description
Cache	Async Copy Reads/sec	Measures the frequency of reads from cache pages involving a memory copy of the data from the cache to the application's buffer. Application will regain control immediately even if the disk must be accessed to retrieve the page.
Cache	Async Data Maps/sec	Measures the frequency that an application using a file system such as NTFS or HPFS to map a page of a file into the cache reads the page and does not wait for the cache to retrieve the page if not found in main memory.
Cache	Async Fast Reads/sec	Measures the frequency of reads from cache pages that bypass the installed file system and retrieve the data directly from the cache. Typically, the file I/O requests will invoke the appropriate file system to retrieve data from a file, but this path permits direct retrieval of cache data without file system involvement if the data is in the cache. Even if the data is not in the cache, one invocation of the file system is avoided. If the data is not in the cache, the request (application program call) will not wait until the data has been retrieved from disk but will get control immediately.
Cache	Async MDL Reads/sec	Measures the frequency of reads from cache pages using a Memory Descriptor List (MDL) to access the pages. Note the MDL contains the physical address of each page in the transfer, thus permitting direct memory access (DMA) of the pages. If the accessed page(s) are not found in main memory, the calling application program will *not* wait for the pages to fault in from disk.
Cache	Async Pin Reads/sec	This measures the frequency of reading data into the cache preparatory to writing the data back to disk. Pages read in this fashion are pinned in memory at the completion of the read. File system regains control immediately even if the disk must be accessed to retrieve the page. A page's physical address will not be altered while pinned.

Object	Object Counter	Description
Cache	Copy Read Hits %	Displays the percentage of cache Copy Read requests that hit the cache. Stated another way, did not require a disk read in order to provide access to the page in the cache. Copy Read is a file read operation that is satisfied by a memory copy from a cache page to the application's buffer. The LAN redirector and disk file systems use this method for retrieving cache information, as does the LAN server for small transfers.
Cache	Copy Reads/sec	Measures the frequency of reads from cache pages that involve a memory copy of the data from the cache to the application's buffer. The LAN redirector uses this method for retrieving cache information, as does the LAN server for small transfers.
Cache	Data Flush Pages/sec	Number of pages that the cache has flushed to disk as a result of a request to flush or to satisfy a write-through file write request. More than one page can be transferred on each flush operation.
Cache	Data Flushes/sec	This is the frequency that the cache has flushed its contents to disk as the result of a request to flush or to satisfy a write-through file write request. One page or more can be transferred on each flush operation.
Cache	Data Map Hits %	This is the percentage of data maps in the cache that could be resolved without having to retrieve a page from the disk, that is, the page was already in physical memory.
Cache	Data Map Pins/sec	This is the frequency of data maps in the cache that resulted in pinning a page in main memory, an action usually preparatory to writing to the file on disk. A page's physical address in main memory and virtual address in the cache will not be altered while pinned.
Cache	Data Maps/sec	This is the frequency that a file system such as NTFS or HPFS maps a file page into the cache to read the page.
Cache	Fast Read Not Possible/sec	This is the frequency of attempts by an Application Program Interface (API) function call to bypass the file system to get at cache data that could not be honored without invoking the file system after all.

Continued

Table A-1 *(continued)*

Object	Object Counter	Description
Cache	Fast Read Resource Misses/sec	This is the frequency of cache misses necessitated by the lack of available resources to satisfy the request.
Cache	Fast Reads/sec	This is the frequency of reads from cache pages that bypass the installed file system and retrieve the data directly from the cache. Typically, file I/O requests invoke the appropriate file system to retrieve data from a file, but this path permits direct retrieval of cache data without file system involvement if the data is in the cache.
Cache	Lazy Write Flushes/sec	Lazy writing is the process of updating the disk after the page has been changed in memory, so that the application making the change to the file does not have to wait for the disk write to complete before proceeding. It is possible for more than one page can be transferred on each write operation.
Cache	Lazy Write Pages/sec	This is the frequency with which the cache's lazy write thread has written to disk. Lazy writing is the process of updating the disk after the page has been changed in memory, so that the application making the change to the file does not have to wait for the disk write to complete before proceeding. It is possible for more than one page can be transferred on a single disk write operation.
Cache	MDL Read Hits %	This is the percentage of cache memory descriptor list (MDL) read requests that have hit the cache, that is, did not require disk accesses in order to provide memory access to the page(s) in the cache.
Cache	MDL Reads/sec	This is the frequency of reads from cache pages that use a memory descriptor list (MDL) to access the data. The MDL contains the physical address of each page involved in the transfer and thus can employ a hardware direct memory access (DMA) device to effect the copy. Note that a LAN server uses this method for large transfers out of the server.

Object	Object Counter	Description
Cache	Pin Read Hits %	This is the percentage of cache Pin Read requests that have hit the cache, that is, did not require a disk read in order to provide access to the page in the cache. A page's physical address in the cache will not be altered while pinned. Note that a LAN redirector uses this method for retrieving cache information, as does the LAN server for small transfers, and as do disk file systems.
Cache	Pin Reads/sec	This is the frequency of reading data into the cache preparatory to writing the data back to disk. Pages read in this fashion are pinned in memory at the completion of the read. A page's physical address in the cache will not be altered while it is pinned.
Cache	Sync Copy Reads/sec	This is the frequency of reads from cache pages that involve a memory copy of the data from the cache to the application's buffer. A file system will not regain control until the copy operation is complete, even if the disk must be accessed to retrieve the page.
Cache	Sync Data Maps/sec	This is the frequency that a file system such as NTFS or HPFS maps a page of a file into the cache to read the page and requests to wait for the cache to retrieve the page if it is not in main memory.
Cache	Sync Fast Reads/sec	This is the frequency of reads from cache pages that bypass the installed file system and retrieve the data directly from the cache. Typically, file I/O requests invoke the appropriate file system to retrieve data from a file, but this path permits direct retrieval of cache data without file system involvement if the data is in the cache. Whether or not data is in the cache, one invocation of the file system is avoided. If the data is not in the cache, the request (application program call) will wait until the data has been retrieved from disk.

Continued

Table A-1 (continued)

Object	Object Counter	Description
Cache	Sync MDL Reads/sec	This is the frequency of reads from cache pages that use a memory descriptor list (MDL) to access the pages. The MDL contains the physical address of each page in the transfer, thus permitting direct memory access (DMA) of the pages. If accessed page(s) are not in main memory, then the caller will wait for the pages to fault in from the disk.
Cache	Sync Pin Reads/sec	This is the frequency of reading data into the cache preparatory to writing the data back to disk. Pages read in this fashion are pinned in memory at read completion. The file system will not regain control until the page is pinned in the cache, in particular, if the disk must be accessed to retrieve the page. While pinned, a page's physical address in the cache will not be altered.
LogicalDisk	% Disk Read Time	This is the percentage of elapsed time the selected disk drive is busy servicing read requests.
LogicalDisk	% Disk Time	This is the percentage of elapsed time the selected disk drive is busy servicing read or write requests.
LogicalDisk	% Disk Write Time	This is the percentage of elapsed time the selected disk drive is busy servicing write requests.
LogicalDisk	% Free Space	This is the ratio of the free space available on the logical disk unit to the total usable space provided by the selected logical disk drive.
LogicalDisk	Avg. Disk Bytes/Read	This is the average number of bytes transferred from the disk during read operations.
LogicalDisk	Avg. Disk Bytes/Transfer	This is the average number of bytes transferred to or from the disk during write or read operations.
LogicalDisk	Avg. Disk Bytes/Write	This is the average number of bytes transferred to the disk during write operations.
LogicalDisk	Avg. Disk sec/Read	This is the average time in seconds of a read of data from the disk.

Appendix A: Performance Monitor Objects

Object	Object Counter	Description
LogicalDisk	Avg. Disk sec/Transfer	This is the average time in seconds of the disk transfer.
LogicalDisk	Avg. Disk sec/Write	This is the average time in seconds of a write of data to the disk.
LogicalDisk	Disk Bytes/sec	This is the rate at which bytes are transferred to or from the disk during write or read operations.
LogicalDisk	Current Disk Queue Length	This is the number of outstanding requests on the disk at the time the performance data is collected, including requests in service at the time of the snapshot. It is one instantaneous length, not an average over the time interval. Multispindle disk devices can have multiple requests active at one time, but other concurrent requests are awaiting service. This counter reflects a transitory high or low queue length, but if there is a sustained load on the disk drive, it is likely that this will be consistently high. Requests experience delays proportional to the length of this queue minus the number of spindles on the disks. Look for a difference averaging less than 2 for good performance.
LogicalDisk	Disk Read Bytes/sec	This is the rate at which bytes are transferred from the disk during read operations.
LogicalDisk	Disk Reads/sec	This is the rate of read operations on the disk.
LogicalDisk	Disk Transfers/sec	This is the rate of read and write operations on the disk.
LogicalDisk	Disk Write Bytes/sec	This is the rate at which bytes are transferred to the disk during write operations.
LogicalDisk	Disk Writes/sec	This is the rate of write operations on the disk.
LogicalDisk	Free Megabytes	This displays the unallocated space on the disk drive in megabytes. (One megabyte equals 1,048,576 bytes.)
Memory	Available Bytes	This displays the size of the virtual memory currently on the Zeroed, Free, and Standby lists. Zeroed and Free memory is ready for use, with Zeroed memory cleared to zeros. Standby memory is memory removed from a process's working set but still available. Notice that this is an instantaneous count, not an average over the time interval.

Continued

Table A-1 (continued)

Object	Object Counter	Description
Memory	Cache Bytes	This measures the number of bytes currently in use by the system cache. The system cache is used to buffer data retrieved from disk or LAN. The system cache uses memory not in use by active processes in the computer.
Memory	Cache Bytes Peak	This measures the maximum number of bytes used by the system cache. The system cache is used to buffer data retrieved from disk or LAN. The system cache uses memory not in use by active processes in the computer.
Memory	Cache Faults/sec	This occurs whenever the cache manager does not find a file's page in the immediate cache and must ask the memory manager to locate the page elsewhere in memory or on the disk so that it can be loaded into the immediate cache.
Memory	Commit Limit	This is the size (in bytes) of virtual memory that can be committed without having to extend the paging file(s). If the paging file(s) can be extended, this is a soft limit.
Memory	Committed Bytes	This displays the size of virtual memory (in bytes) that has been committed (as opposed to simply reserved). Committed memory must have backing (disk) storage available or must be assured never to need disk storage (because main memory is large enough to hold it). This is an instantaneous count, not an average over the time interval.
Memory	Demand Zero Faults/sec	This is the number of page faults for pages that must be filled with zeros before the fault is satisfied. If the Zeroed list is not empty, the fault can be resolved by removing a page from the Zeroed list.
Memory	Free System Page Table Entries	This is the number of Page Table Entries not currently in use by the system.

Object	Object Counter	Description
Memory	Page Faults/sec	This is the number of page faults in the processor. A page fault occurs when a process refers to a virtual memory page that is not in its Working Set in main memory. A page fault will not cause the page to be fetched from disk if that page is on the standby list, and hence already in main memory, or if it is in use by another process with which the page is shared.
Memory	Page Reads/sec	This is the number of times the disk was read to retrieve pages of virtual memory necessary to resolve page faults. Multiple pages can be read during a disk read operation.
Memory	Page Writes/sec	This is the number of times that pages have been written to the disk because they were changed since last retrieved. Each such write operation may transfer a number of pages.
Memory	Pages Input/sec	This is the number of pages read from the disk to resolve memory references to pages that were not in memory at the time of the reference. This counter includes paging traffic on behalf of the system cache to access file data for applications. This is an important counter to observe if you are concerned about excessive memory pressure (that is, thrashing) and the excessive paging that may result.
Memory	Pages Output/sec	This is the number of pages that are written to disk because the pages have been modified in main memory.
Memory	Pages/sec	This is the number of pages read from the disk or written to the disk to resolve memory references to pages that were not in memory at the time of the reference. This is the sum of Pages Input/sec and Pages Output/sec. This counter includes paging traffic on behalf of the system cache to access file data for applications. This is the primary counter to observe if you are concerned about excessive memory pressure (that is, thrashing) and the excessive paging that may result.

Continued

Table A-1 *(continued)*

Object	Object Counter	Description
Memory	Pool Nonpaged Allocs	This is the number of calls to allocate space in the system Nonpaged Pool. Nonpaged Pool is a system memory area where space is acquired by operating system components as they accomplish their appointed tasks. Nonpaged Pool pages cannot be paged out to the paging file but instead remain in main memory as long as they are allocated.
Memory	Pool Nonpaged Bytes	This is the number of bytes in the Nonpaged Pool, which is a system memory area where space is acquired by operating system components as they accomplish their appointed tasks. Nonpaged Pool pages cannot be paged out to the paging file but instead remain in main memory as long as they are allocated.
Memory	Pool Paged Allocs	This is the number of calls to allocate space in the system Paged Pool. Paged Pool is a system memory area where space is acquired by operating system components as they accomplish their appointed tasks. Paged Pool pages can be paged out to the paging file when not accessed by the system for sustained periods of time.
Memory	Pool Paged Bytes	This is the number of bytes in the Paged Pool, which is a system memory area where space is acquired by operating system components as they accomplish their appointed tasks. Paged Pool pages can be paged out to the paging file when not accessed by the system for sustained periods of time.
Memory	Pool Paged Resident Bytes	This is the size of Paged Pool resident in core memory. This is the actual cost of the Paged Pool allocation, because this is actively in use and using real physical memory.
Memory	System Cache Resident Bytes	This is the number of bytes currently resident in the global disk cache.
Memory	System Code Resident Bytes	This is the number of bytes of System Code Total Bytes currently resident in core memory. This is the code working set of the pageable executive. In addition, there are another ~300K bytes of nonpaged kernel code.

Appendix A: Performance Monitor Objects

Object	Object Counter	Description
Memory	System Code Total Bytes	This is the number of bytes of pageable pages in NTOSKRNL.EXE, HAL.DLL, and the boot drivers and file systems loaded by NTLDR/OSLOADER.
Memory	System Driver Resident Bytes	This is the number of System Driver Total Bytes currently resident in core memory. This number is the code working set of the pageable drivers. In addition to this, there are another ~700K bytes of nonpaged driver code.
Memory	System Driver Total Bytes	This is the number of bytes of pageable pages in all other loaded device drivers.
Memory	Transition Faults/sec	This is the number of page faults resolved by recovering pages that were in transition, that is, being written to disk at the time of the page fault. The pages were recovered without additional disk activity.
Memory	Write Copies/sec	This is the number of page faults that have been satisfied by making a copy of a page when an attempt to write to the page is made. This is an economical way of sharing data because the copy of the page is only made on an attempt to write to the page; otherwise, the page is shared.
Network Interface	Bytes Received/sec	This is the rate at which bytes are received on the interface, including framing characters.
Network Interface	Bytes Sent/sec	This is the rate at which bytes are sent on the interface, including framing characters.
Network Interface	Bytes Total/sec	This is the rate at which bytes are sent and received on the interface, including framing characters.
Network Interface	Current Bandwidth	This is an estimate of the interface's current bandwidth in bits per second (bps). For interfaces that do not vary in bandwidth or for those where no accurate estimate can be made, this value is the nominal bandwidth.
Network Interface	Output Queue Length	This is the length of the output packet queue (in packets.) If this is longer than 2, delays are being experienced, and the bottleneck should be found and eliminated if possible. Because the requests are queued by NDIS in this implementation, this will always be 0.

Continued

Table A-1 *(continued)*

Object	Object Counter	Description
Network Interface	Packets Outbound Discarded	This is the number of outbound packets that were discarded — even though no errors had been detected — to prevent their being transmitted. One possible reason for discarding such a packet could be to free up buffer space.
Network Interface	Packets Outbound	This is the number of outbound packets that could not be transmitted because of errors.
Network Interface	Packets Received Discarded	This is the number of inbound packets that were discarded — even though no errors had been detected — to prevent their being delivered to a higher-layer protocol. One possible reason for discarding such a packet could be to free up buffer space.
Network Interface	Packets Received Errors	This is the number of inbound packets that contained errors preventing them from being delivered to a higher-layer protocol.
Network Interface	Packets Received Non-Unicast/sec	This is the rate at which non-unicast (that is, subnet broadcast or subnet multicast) packets are delivered to a higher-layer protocol.
Network Interface	Packets Received Unicast/sec	This is the rate at which unicast (subnet) packets are delivered to a higher-layer protocol.
Network Interface	Packets Received Unknown	This is the number of packets received via the interface that were discarded because of an unknown or unsupported protocol.
Network Interface	Packets Received/sec	This is the rate at which packets are received on the network interface.
Network Interface	Packets Sent Non-Unicast/sec	This is the rate at which packets are requested to be transmitted to non-unicast (that is, subnet broadcast or subnet multicast) addresses by higher-level protocols. The rate includes the packets that were discarded or not sent.
Network Interface	Packets Sent Unicast/sec	This is the rate at which packets are requested to be transmitted to subnet-unicast addresses by higher-level protocols. The rate includes the packets that were discarded or not sent.

Appendix A: Performance Monitor Objects

Object	Object Counter	Description
Network Interface	Packets Sent/sec	This is the rate at which packets are sent on the network interface.
Network Interface	Packets/sec	This is the rate at which packets are sent and received on the network interface.
Network Segment	% Broadcast Frames	This is the percentage of network bandwidth that is made up of broadcast traffic on this network segment.
Network Segment	% Multicast Frames	This is the percentage of network bandwidth that is made up of multicast traffic on this network segment.
Network Segment	% Network Utilization	This is the percentage of network bandwidth in use on this network segment.
Network Segment	Broadcast Frames Received/sec	This is the number of broadcast frames received per second on this network segment.
Network Segment	Multicast Frames Received/sec	This is the number of multicast frames received per second on this network segment.
Network Segment	Total Bytes Received/sec	This is the number of bytes received per second on this network segment.
Network Segment	Total Frames Received/sec	This is the total number of frames received per second on this network segment.
Objects	Events	This is the number of events in the computer at the time of data collection. This is an instantaneous count, not an average over the time interval. An event is used when two or more threads have to synchronize execution.
Objects	Mutexes	This counts the number of mutexes in the computer at the time of data collection. This is an instantaneous count, not an average over the time interval. Mutexes are used by threads to ensure that only one thread is executing some section of code.
Objects	Processes	This is the number of processes in the computer at the time of data collection. It is an instantaneous count, not an average over the time interval. Each process represents the running of a program.

Continued

Table A-1 (continued)

Object	Object Counter	Description
Objects	Sections	This is the number of sections in the computer at the time of data collection. This is an instantaneous count, not an average over the time interval. A section is a portion of virtual memory created by a process for storing data. A process may share sections with other processes.
Objects	Semaphores	This is the number of semaphores in the computer at the time of data collection. This is an instantaneous count, not an average over the time interval. Threads use semaphores to obtain exclusive access to data structures they share with other threads.
Objects	Threads	This is the number of threads in the computer at the time of data collection. This is an instantaneous count, not an average over the time interval. A thread is the basic executable entity that can execute instructions in a processor.
PhysicalDisk	% Disk Read Time	This is the percentage of elapsed time that the selected disk drive is servicing read requests.
PhysicalDisk	% Disk Time	This is the percentage of elapsed time that the selected disk drive is servicing read or write requests.
PhysicalDisk	% Disk Write Time	This is the percentage of elapsed time that the selected disk drive is servicing write requests.
PhysicalDisk	Avg. Disk Bytes/Read	This is the average number of bytes transferred from the disk during read operations.
PhysicalDisk	Avg. Disk Bytes/Transfer	This is the average number of bytes transferred to or from the disk during write or read operations.
PhysicalDisk	Avg. Disk Bytes/Write	This is the average number of bytes transferred to the disk during write operations.

Object	Object Counter	Description
PhysicalDisk	Avg. Disk sec/Read	This is the average time in seconds of a read of data from the disk.
PhysicalDisk	Avg. Disk sec/Transfer	This is the time in seconds of the average disk transfer.
Object	**Object Counter**	**Description**
PhysicalDisk	Avg. Disk sec/Write	This is the average time in seconds of a write of data to the disk.
PhysicalDisk	Disk Bytes/sec	This is the rate bytes are transferred to or from the disk during write or read operations.
PhysicalDisk	Current Disk Queue Length	This is the number of requests outstanding on the disk at the time the performance data is collected. It includes requests in service at the time of the snapshot. It is an instantaneous length, not an average over the time interval. Multispindle disk devices can have multiple requests active at one time, but other concurrent requests are awaiting service. Note that this counter may reflect a transitory high or low queue length, but if there is a sustained load on the disk drive, it is likely that this will be consistently high. Requests are experiencing delays proportional to the length of this queue minus the number of spindles on the disks. For good performance, this difference should average less than 2.
PhysicalDisk	Disk Read Bytes/sec	This is the rate at which bytes are transferred from the disk during read operations.
PhysicalDisk	Disk Reads/sec	This is the rate of read operations on the disk.
PhysicalDisk	Disk Transfers/sec	This is the rate of read and write operations on the disk.
PhysicalDisk	Disk Write Bytes/sec	This is the rate at which bytes are transferred to the disk during write operations.
PhysicalDisk	Disk Writes/sec	This is the rate of write operations on the disk.

Continued

Table A-1 *(continued)*

Object	Object Counter	Description
Process	% Privileged Time	This is the percentage of elapsed time that this process's threads have spent executing code in Privileged mode. If a Windows NT system service is called, the service will often run in Privileged mode to gain access to system-private data. Such data is protected from access by threads executing in User mode. Calls to the system may be explicit, or they may be implicit such as when a page fault or an interrupt occurs. Note that Windows NT, unlike earlier operating systems, uses process boundaries for subsystem protection in addition to the traditional protection of User and Privileged modes. Therefore, some work done by Windows NT on behalf of your application may appear in other subsystem processes in addition to the Privileged Time in your process.
Process	% Processor Time	This is the percentage of elapsed time that all of the threads of this process used the processor to execute instructions. An instruction is the basic unit of execution in a computer, a thread is the object that executes instructions, and a process is the object created when a program is run. Code executed to handle certain hardware interrupts or trap conditions may be counted for this process.
Process	% User Time	This is the percentage of elapsed time that this process's threads have spent executing code in User mode. Applications execute in User mode, as do subsystems like the window manager and the graphics engine. Code executing in User mode cannot damage the integrity of the Windows NT Executive, Kernel, and device drivers. Windows NT uses process boundaries for subsystem protection in addition to the traditional protection of User and Privileged modes (unlike some early operating systems). Therefore, some work done by Windows NT on behalf of your application may appear in other subsystem processes in addition to the Privileged Time in your process.

Object	Object Counter	Description
Process	Elapsed Time	This is the total elapsed time (in seconds) that this process has been running.
Process	Handle Count	This is the total number of handles currently open by this process. This number is the sum of the handles currently open by each thread in this process.
Process	ID Process	Simply stated, this is the unique identifier of this process. ID Process numbers are reused, so they only identify a process for the lifetime of that process.
Process	Page Faults/sec	This is the rate of page faults by the threads executing in this process. A page fault occurs when a thread refers to a virtual memory page that is not in its working set in main memory. This won't cause the page to be fetched from disk if it is on the standby list and hence already in main memory, or if it is in use by another process with which the page is shared.
Process	Page File Bytes	This is the current number of bytes that this process has used in the paging file(s). Note that paging files are used to store pages of memory used by the process that are not contained in other files. Paging files are shared by all processes, and lack of space in paging files can prevent other processes from allocating memory.
Process	Page File Bytes Peak	This is the maximum number of bytes that this process has used in the paging file(s). Paging files are used to store pages of memory used by the process that are not contained in other files. Paging files are shared by all processes, and lack of space in paging files can prevent other processes from allocating memory.
Process	Pool Nonpaged Bytes	This is the number of bytes in the Nonpaged Pool, which is a system memory area where space is acquired by operating system components as they accomplish their appointed tasks. Nonpaged Pool pages cannot be paged out to the paging file but instead remain in main memory as long as they are allocated.

Continued

Table A-1 *(continued)*

Object	Object Counter	Description
Process	Pool Paged Bytes	This is the number of bytes in the Paged Pool, which is a system memory area where space is acquired by operating system components as they accomplish their appointed tasks. Paged Pool pages can be paged out to the paging file when not accessed by the system for sustained periods of time.
Process	Priority Base	This is the current base priority of this process. Threads within a process can raise and lower their own base priority relative to the process's base priority.
Process	Private Bytes	This is the current number of bytes that this process has allocated that cannot be shared with other processes.
Process	Thread Count	This is the number of threads currently active in this process. An instruction is the basic unit of execution in a processor, and a thread is the object that executes instructions. Every running process has at least one thread.
Process	Virtual Bytes	This is the current size in bytes of the virtual address space that the process is using. Use of virtual address space does not necessarily imply corresponding use of either disk or main memory pages. Virtual space is finite, and by using too much, the process may limit its ability to load libraries.
Process	Virtual Bytes Peak	This is the maximum number of bytes of virtual address space that the process has used at any one time. Use of virtual address space does not necessarily imply corresponding use of either disk or main memory pages. Virtual space is finite, and by using too much, the process may limit its ability to load libraries.
Process	Working Set	This is the current number of bytes in the Working Set of this process. The Working Set is the set of memory pages touched recently by the threads in the process. If free memory in the computer is above a threshold, pages are left in the Working Set of a process even if they are not in use. When free memory falls below a threshold, pages are trimmed from Working Sets. If they are needed, they will then be soft-faulted back into the Working Set before they leave main memory.

Object	Object Counter	Description
Process	Working Set Peak	This is the maximum number of bytes in the Working Set of this process at any point in time. The Working Set is the set of memory pages touched recently by the threads in the process. If free memory in the computer is above a threshold, pages are left in the Working Set of a process even if they are not in use. When free memory falls below a threshold, pages are trimmed from Working Sets. If they are needed they will then be soft-faulted back into the Working Set before they leave main memory.
Processor	% DPC Time	This is the percentage of elapsed time that the processor spent in Deferred Procedure Calls. When a hardware device interrupts the processor, the Interrupt Handler may elect to execute the majority of its work in a DPC. DPCs run at lower priority than interrupts and so permit interrupts to occur while DPC is being executed. Deferred Procedure Calls are executed in Privileged mode, so this is a component of Processor: % Privileged Time. This counter can help determine the source of excessive time being spent in Privileged mode.
Processor	% Interrupt Time	This is the percentage of elapsed time that the processor spent handling hardware interrupts. When a hardware device interrupts the processor, the Interrupt Handler will execute to handle the condition, usually by signaling I/O completion and possibly issuing another pending I/O request. Some of this work may be done in a Deferred Procedure Call (see % DPC Time). However, time spent in DPCs is not counted as time in interrupts. Interrupts are executed in Privileged mode, so this is a component of Processor: % Privileged Time. This counter can help determine the source of excessive time being spent in Privileged mode.

Continued

Table A-1 *(continued)*

Object	Object Counter	Description
Processor	% Privileged Time	This is the percentage of processor time spent in Privileged mode in non-Idle threads. The Windows NT service layer, the Executive routines, and the Windows NT Kernel execute in Privileged mode. Device drivers for most devices other than graphics adapters and printers also execute in Privileged mode. Windows NT uses process boundaries for subsystem protection in addition to the traditional protection of User and Privileged modes (unlike some early operating systems). Thus, some work accomplished by Windows NT on your application's behalf may appear in other subsystem processes in addition to the Privileged Time in your process.
Processor	% Processor Time	This is the percentage of the elapsed time that a processor is busy executing a non-Idle thread. It can be viewed as the fraction of the time spent doing useful work. Each processor is assigned an Idle thread in the Idle process which consumes those unproductive processor cycles not used by any other threads.
Processor	% User Time	This is the percentage of processor time spent in User mode in non-Idle threads. All application code and subsystem code executes in User mode. The graphics engine, graphics device drivers, printer device drivers, and window manager also execute in User mode. Code executing in User mode cannot damage the integrity of the Windows NT Executive, Kernel, and device drivers. Unlike some early operating systems, Windows NT uses process boundaries for subsystem protection in addition to the traditional protection of User and Privileged modes. Therefore, some work done by Windows NT on behalf of your application may appear in other subsystem processes in addition to the Privileged Time in your process.
Processor	APC Bypasses/sec	This is the rate at which kernel APC interrupts were short-circuited.

Appendix A: Performance Monitor Objects

Object	Object Counter	Description
Processor	DPC Bypasses/sec	This is the rate at which Dispatch interrupts were short-circuited.
Processor	DPC Rate	This is the average rate at which DPC objects are queued to this processor's DPC queue per clock tick.
Processor	DPCs Queued/sec	This is the rate at which DPC objects are queued to this processor's DPC queue.
Processor	Interrupts/sec	This is the number of device interrupts that the processor is experiencing. A device interrupts the processor when it has completed a task or when it otherwise requires attention. Normal thread execution is suspended during interrupts. An interrupt may cause the processor to switch to another, higher-priority thread. Clock interrupts are frequent and periodic and create a background of interrupt activity.
Redirector	Bytes Received/sec	This is the rate of bytes coming in to the redirector from the network. It includes all application data as well as network protocol information (such as packet headers).
Redirector	Bytes Total/sec	This is the rate at which the redirector is processing data bytes. This includes all application and file data in addition to protocol information (such as packet headers).
Redirector	Bytes Transmitted/sec	This is the rate at which bytes are leaving the redirector to the network. It includes all application data as well as network protocol information (such as packet headers and the like).
Redirector	Connects Core	This is the number of connections to servers running the original MS-Net SMB protocol, including MS-Net itself, Xenix, and Vax.
Redirector	Connects Lan Manager 2.0	This is the number of connections to Lan Manager 2.0 servers, including LMX servers.
Redirector	Connects Lan Manager 2.1	This is the number of connections to Lan Manager 2.1 servers, including LMX servers.
Redirector	Connects Windows NT	This is the number of connections to Windows NT computers.

Continued

Table A-1 *(continued)*

Object	Object Counter	Description
Redirector	Current Commands	This is the number of requests to the redirector that are currently queued for service. If this number is much larger than the number of installed network adapter cards, the network(s) and/or server(s) being accessed will be seriously bottlenecked.
Redirector	File Data Operations/sec	This is the rate at which the redirector processes data operations. One operation includes (hopefully) many bytes. I say "hopefully" here because each operation has overhead. This allows you to determine the efficiency of this path by dividing the Bytes/sec by this counter to determine the average number of bytes transferred per operation.
Redirector	File Read Operations/sec	This is the rate at which applications ask the redirector for data. Each call to a file system or similar Application Program Interface (API) call counts as one operation.
Redirector	File Write Operations/sec	This is the rate at which applications send data to the redirector. Each call to a file system or similar Application Program Interface (API) call counts as one operation.
Redirector	Network Errors/sec	This is the number of serious unexpected errors, which generally indicate that the redirector and one or more servers are having serious communication difficulties. For example, an SMB (server manager block) protocol error will generate a Network Error. These errors result in an entry in the system Event Log, so look there for details.
Redirector	Packets Received/sec	This is the rate at which the redirector is receiving packets (also called SMBs or server message blocks). Network transmissions are divided into packets. It is the average number of bytes received in a packet can be obtained by dividing Bytes Received/sec by this counter. Some packets received may not contain incoming data; for example, an acknowledgment to a write made by the redirector would count as an incoming packet.

Object	Object Counter	Description
Redirector	Packets Transmitted/sec	This is the rate at which the redirector is sending packets (also called SMBs or server message blocks). Network transmissions are divided into packets. It is the average number of bytes transmitted in a packet can be obtained by dividing Bytes Transmitted/sec by this counter.
Redirector	Packets/sec	This is the rate at which the redirector is processing data packets. One packet typically includes many bytes. You may determine the efficiency of this path by dividing the Bytes/sec by this counter to determine the average number of bytes transferred per packet, you may divide this counter by Operations/sec to determine the average number of packets per operation.
Redirector	Read Bytes Cache/sec	This is the rate at which applications on your computer are accessing the cache using the redirector. Many data requests may be satisfied by merely retrieving the data from the system cache on your own computer if it happened to have been used recently and there was room to keep it in the cache. Requests that miss the cache will cause a page fault (see Read Bytes Paging/sec).
Redirector	Read Bytes Network/sec	It is the rate at which applications are reading data across the network. For some reason, the data was not in the system cache, and these bytes actually came across the network. Dividing this number by Bytes Received/sec will indicate the efficiency of data coming in from the network, because all of these bytes are real application data (see Bytes Received/sec).
Redirector	Read Bytes Non-Paging/sec	This is the bytes read by the redirector in response to normal file requests by an application when those bytes are redirected to come from another computer. In addition to file requests, this counter includes other methods of reading across the network such as Named Pipes and Transactions. This counter doesn't count network protocol information, it counts application data.

Continued

Table A-1 *(continued)*

Object	Object Counter	Description
Redirector	Read Bytes Paging/sec	This is the rate at which the redirector is attempting to read bytes in response to page faults. Page faults are caused by loading of modules (such as programs and libraries), by a miss in the cache (see Read Bytes Cache/sec), or by files directly mapped into the address space of applications (a high-performance feature of Windows NT).
Redirector	Read Operations Random/sec	This is the rate at which, on a file-by-file basis, reads are made that are not sequential. If a read is made using a particular file handle and then is followed by another read that is not contiguous, this counter increases by one increment.
Redirector	Read Packets Small/sec	This is the rate at which reads less than one-fourth of the server's negotiated buffer size are made by applications. Too many of these could indicate a waste of buffers on the server. This counter is increased by one increment for each read, but packets are not counted.
Redirector	Read Packets/sec	This is the rate at which read packets are being placed on the network. Each time a single packet is sent with a request to read data remotely, this counter is increased by one increment.
Redirector	Reads Denied/sec	This is the rate at which the server is unable to accommodate requests for Raw Reads. When a read is much larger than the server's negotiated buffer size, the redirector requests a Raw Read which, if granted, permits the transfer of the data without a lot of protocol overhead on each packet. Consequently, the server must lock out other requests, so the request is denied if the server is really busy.
Redirector	Reads Large/sec	This is the rate at which reads over twice the server's negotiated buffer size are made by applications. Too many of these could place a strain on server resources. This counter increases by one increment for each read. It does not count packets.
Redirector	Server Disconnects	This is the number of times that a server has disconnected your redirector. See also Server Reconnects.

Object	Object Counter	Description
Redirector	Server Reconnects	This is the number of times that your redirector has had to reconnect to a server in order to complete a new active request. You may be disconnected by the server if you remain inactive for too long. Locally even if all your remote files are closed, the redirector will keep your connections intact for (nominally) ten minutes. Inactive connections are called Dormant Connections. Reconnecting is expensive in terms of time.
Redirector	Server Sessions	This is the number of active security objects that the redirector is managing. For example, a logon to a server followed by a network access to the same server will establish one connection, but two sessions.
Redirector	Server Sessions Hung	This is the number of active sessions that are timed out and unable to proceed due to a lack of response from the remote server.
Redirector	Write Bytes Cache/sec	This is the rate at which applications on your computer are writing to the cache using the redirector. The data may be retained at your computer in the cache for further modification before being written to the network. This saves network traffic. Each write of a byte into the cache is counted here.
Redirector	Write Bytes Network/sec	This is the rate at which your applications are writing data across the network. Either the system cache was bypassed, as for Named Pipes or Transactions, or else the cache wrote the bytes to make room for other data. Dividing this counter by Bytes Transmitted/sec will indicate the efficiency of data written to the network, because all of these bytes are real application data (see Bytes Transmitted/sec).
Redirector	Write Bytes Non-Paging/sec	This is the rate of the bytes that are written by the redirector in response to normal file outputs by an application when they are redirected to go to another computer. In addition to file requests, this counter includes other methods of writing across the network such as Named Pipes and Transactions. This counter counts application data, not network protocol information.

Continued

Table A-1 (continued)

Object	Object Counter	Description
Redirector	Write Bytes Paging/sec	This is the rate at which the redirector is attempting to write bytes changed in the pages being used by applications. The program data changed by modules (such as programs and libraries) that were loaded over the network are "paged out" when no longer needed. Other output pages come from the cache (see Write Bytes Cache/sec).
Redirector	Write Operations Random/sec	This is the rate at which, on a file-by-file basis, writes are made that are not sequential. If a write is made using a particular file handle and then is followed by another write that is not contiguous, this counter is increased by one increment.
Redirector	Write Packets Small/sec	This is the rate at which writes are made by applications that are less than one-fourth of the server's negotiated buffer size. Many of these writes could indicate a waste of buffers on the server. This counter is increased by one for each write, not packets.
Redirector	Write Packets/sec	This is the rate at which writes are being sent to the network. Every time that a single packet is sent with a request to write remote data, this counter is increased by one increment.
Redirector	Writes Denied/sec	This is the rate at which the server is unable to accommodate requests for Raw Writes. When a write is much larger than the server's negotiated buffer size, the redirector requests a Raw Write which, if granted, would permit the transfer of the data without a lot of protocol overhead on each packet. The server must lock out other requests, so the request is denied if the server is really busy.
Redirector	Writes Large/sec	This is the rate at which writes are made by applications that are over twice the server's negotiated buffer size. Many of these writes could place a strain on server resources. This counter is increased by one increment for each write, not packets.

Object	Object Counter	Description
Server Work Queues	Active Threads	This is the number of threads presently working on a request for a CPU. The operating system keeps this number as low as possible to minimize unnecessary context switching. This is an instantaneous count for the CPU, not an average over time.
Server Work Queues	Available Threads	This is the number of server threads the CPU currently is not working on. The server dynamically adjusts the number of threads to maximize server performance.
Server Work Queues	Available Work Items	Every request from a client is represented in the server as a work item, and the server maintains a pool of available work items per CPU to speed processing. This is the instantaneous number of available work items for this CPU. A sustained near-zero value indicates the need to increase the MinFreeWorkItems Registry value for the server service. This value will always be 0 in the Blocking Queue instance.
Server Work Queues	Borrowed Work Items	Every request from a client is represented in the server as a work item, and the server maintains a pool of available work items per CPU to speed processing. When a CPU runs out of work items, it borrows a free work item from another CPU. An increasing value of this running counter may indicate the need to increase the MaxWorkItems or MinFreeWorkItems Registry values for the server service. This value will always be 0 in the Blocking Queue instance.
Server Work Queues	Bytes Received/sec	This is the rate at which the server is receiving bytes from the network clients on this CPU. This value is a measure of how busy the server is.
Server Work Queues	Bytes Sent/sec	This is the rate at which the server is sending bytes on the network to clients, measured by CPU. This value is a measure of how busy the server is.
Server Work Queues	Bytes Transferred/sec	This is the rate at which the server is sending and receiving bytes with the network clients on this CPU. This value is a measure of how busy the server is.

Continued

Table A-1 (continued)

Object	Object Counter	Description
Server Work Queues	Context Blocks Queued/sec	This is the rate at which work context blocks had to be placed on the server's FSP queue to await server action.
Server Work Queues	Current Clients	It is the instantaneous count of the clients being serviced by this CPU. The server actively balances the client load across all of the CPUs in the system. This value will always be 0 in the Blocking Queue instance.
Server Work Queues	Queue Length	This is the current length of the server work queue for this CPU. A sustained queue length greater than four may indicate processor congestion. This is an instantaneous count, not an average over time.
Server Work Queues	Read Bytes/sec	This is the rate at which the server is reading data from files for the clients on this CPU. This value is a measure of how busy the server is.
Server Work Queues	Read Operations/sec	This is the rate the server is performing file read operations and is a measure of how busy the server is. This value will always be 0 in the Blocking Queue instance.
Server Work Queues	Total Bytes/sec	This is the rate at which the server is reading and writing data to and from the files for the clients on this CPU. This value is a measure of how busy the server is.
Server Work Queues	Total Operations/sec	This is the rate at which the server is performing file read and file write operations for the clients on this CPU. This value is a measure of how busy the server is. This value will always be 0 in the Blocking Queue instance.
Server Work Queues	Work Item Shortages	Every request from a client is represented in the server as a work item, and the server maintains a pool of available work items per CPU to speed processing. A sustained value greater than zero indicates the need to increase the MaxWorkItems Registry value for the Server service. This value will always be 0 in the Blocking Queue instance.
Server Work Queues	Write Bytes/sec	This is the rate at which the server is writing data to files for the clients on this CPU. This value is a measure of how busy the server is.

Object	Object Counter	Description
Server Work Queues	Write Operations/sec	This is the rate at which the server is performing file write operations for the clients on this CPU. This value is a measure of how busy the server is. This value will always be 0 in the Blocking Queue instance.
System	% Total DPC Time	This is the sum of % DPC Time of all processors divided by the number of processors in the system. (See Processor: % DPC Time for details.)
System	% Total Interrupt Time	This is the sum of % Interrupt Time of all processors divided by the number of processors in the system. (See Processor: % Interrupt Time for details.)
System	% Total Privileged Time	This is the average percentage of time spent in Privileged mode by all processors. On a multiprocessor system, if all processors are always in Privileged mode, this is 100%; if one-fourth of the processors are in Privileged mode, this is 25%. When a Windows NT system service is called, the service will often run in Privileged mode in order to gain access to system-private data. Such data is protected from access by threads executing in User mode. Calls to the system may be explicit, or they may be implicit such as when a page fault or an interrupt occurs. Windows NT uses process boundaries for subsystem protection in addition to the traditional protection of User and Privileged modes (unlike some early operating systems). Thus, some work done by Windows NT on behalf of an application may appear in other subsystem processes in addition to the Privileged Time in the application process.
System	% Total Processor	This is the average percentage of time that all of the processors on the system are busy executing non-Idle threads. On a multiprocessor system, if all of the processors are always busy, this is 100%; if all of the processors are busy half the time, this is 50%; and if all processors are busy one-fourth of the time, this is 25%. This number can be viewed as the fraction of the time spent doing useful work. Each processor is assigned an Idle thread in the Idle process which consumes those unproductive processor cycles not used by any other threads.

Continued

Table A-1 *(continued)*

Object	Object Counter	Description
System	% Total User Time	This is the average percentage of time spent in User mode by all processors. On a multiprocessor system, if all processors are always in User mode, this is 100%; if all processors are in User mode half the time, this is 50%; and if all the processors are in User mode one-fourth the time, this is 25%. Applications execute in User mode, as do subsystems like the window manager and the graphics engine. Code executing in User mode cannot damage the integrity of the Windows NT Executive, Kernel, and device drivers. Unlike some early operating systems, Windows NT uses process boundaries for subsystem protection in addition to the traditional protection of User and Privileged modes. Therefore, some work done by Windows NT on behalf of an application may appear in other subsystem processes in addition to the Privileged Time in the application process.
System	Alignment Fixups/sec	This is the rate of alignment faults fixed by the system.
System	Context Switches/sec	This is the rate of switches from one thread to another. Thread switches can occur either inside of a single process or across processes. A thread switch may be caused either by one thread asking another for information, or by a thread being preempted by another, higher-priority thread becoming ready to run. Unlike some early operating systems, Windows NT uses process boundaries for subsystem protection in addition to the traditional protection of User and Privileged modes. Therefore, some work done by Windows NT on behalf of an application may appear in other subsystem processes in addition to the Privileged Time in the application. Switching to the subsystem process causes one Context Switch in the application thread. Switching back causes another Context Switch in the subsystem thread.
System	Exception Dispatches/sec	This is the rate of exceptions dispatched by the system.

Object	Object Counter	Description
System	File Control Bytes/sec	This is the aggregate of bytes transferred for all file system operations that are neither reads nor writes. These operations usually include file system control requests or requests for information about device characteristics or status.
System	File Control Operations/sec	This is the aggregate of all file system operations that are neither reads nor writes. These operations Operations/sec usually include file system control requests or requests for information about device characteristics or status.
System	File Data Operations/sec	This is the rate at which the computer is issuing read and write operations to file system devices. It does not include file control operations.
System	File Read Bytes/sec	This is the aggregate of the bytes transferred for all of the file system read operations on the computer.
System	File Read Operations/sec	This is the aggregate of all of the file system read operations on the computer.
System	File Write Bytes/sec	This is the aggregate of the bytes transferred for all of the file system write operations on the computer.
System	File Write Operations/sec	This is the aggregate of all of the file system write operations on the computer.
System	Floating Emulations/sec	This is the rate of floating emulations performed by the system.
System	Processor Queue Length	It is the instantaneous length of the processor queue in units of threads. This counter is always 0 unless you are also monitoring a thread counter. All processors use a single queue in which threads wait for processor cycles. This length does not include the threads that are currently executing. A sustained processor queue length greater than 2 generally indicates processor congestion. This is an instantaneous count, not an average over the time interval.

Continued

Table A-1 *(continued)*

Object	Object Counter	Description
System	System Calls	This is the frequency of calls to Windows NT system service routines. These routines perform all of the basic scheduling and synchronization of activities on the computer and provide access to nongraphical devices, memory management, and name space management.
System	System Up Time	This is the total time (in seconds) that the computer has been operational since it was last started.
System	Total Interrupts/sec	This is the rate at which the computer is receiving and servicing hardware interrupts. Some devices that may generate interrupts are the system timer, the mouse, data communication lines, and network interface cards. This counter indicates how busy these devices are on a computer-wide basis. See also Processor: Interrupts/sec.
Thread	% Privileged Time	This is the percentage of elapsed time that this thread has spent executing code in Privileged mode. When a Windows NT system service is called, the service will often run in Privileged mode in order to gain access to system-private data. Such data is protected from access by threads executing in User mode. Calls to the system may be explicit, or they may be implicit such as when a page fault or an interrupt occurs. Windows NT uses process boundaries for subsystem protection in addition to the traditional protection of User and Privileged modes (unlike some early operating systems). Therefore, some work performed by Windows NT on behalf of your application may appear in other subsystem processes in addition to the Privileged Time in your process.

Object	Object Counter	Description
Thread	% Processor Time	This is the percentage of elapsed time that this thread used the processor to execute instructions. An instruction is the basic unit of execution in a processor, and a thread is the object that executes instructions. Code executed to handle certain hardware interrupts or trap conditions may be counted for this thread.
Thread	% User Time	This is the percentage of elapsed time that this thread has spent executing code in User mode. Applications execute in User mode, as do subsystems like the window manager and the graphics engine. Code executing in User mode cannot damage the integrity of the Windows NT Executive, Kernel, and device drivers. Unlike some early operating systems, Windows NT uses process boundaries for subsystem protection in addition to the traditional protection of User and Privileged modes. Therefore, some work done by Windows NT on behalf of your application may appear in other subsystem processes in addition to the Privileged Time in your process.
Thread	Context Switches/sec	This is the rate of switches from one thread to another. Thread switches can occur either inside of a single process or across processes. A thread switch may be caused either by one thread asking another for information, or by a thread being preempted by another, higher-priority thread becoming ready to run. Unlike some early operating systems, Windows NT uses process boundaries for subsystem protection in addition to the traditional protection of User and Privileged modes. Therefore, some work done by Windows NT on behalf of an application may appear in other subsystem processes in addition to the Privileged Time in the application. Switching to the subsystem process causes one Context Switch in the application thread. Switching back causes another Context Switch in the subsystem thread.
Thread	Elapsed Time	This is the total elapsed time (in seconds) that this thread has been running.

Continued

Table A-1 (continued)

Object	Object Counter	Description
Thread	ID Process	This is a unique identifier of this process. ID Process numbers are reused, so they only identify a process for the lifetime of that process.
Thread	ID Thread	This is a unique identifier of this thread. ID Thread numbers are reused, so they only identify a thread for the lifetime of that thread.
Thread	Priority Base	This is the current base priority of this thread. The system may raise the thread's dynamic priority above the base priority if the thread is handling user input, or the system may lower it toward the base priority if the thread becomes computer bound.
Thread	Priority Current	This is the current dynamic priority of this thread. The system may raise the thread's dynamic priority above the base priority if the thread is handling user input, or the system may lower it toward the base priority if the thread becomes computer bound.
Thread	Start Address	This is the starting virtual address for this thread.
Thread	Thread State	This is the current state of the thread. It is 0 for Initialized, 1 for Ready, 2 for Running, 3 for Standby, 4 for Terminated, 5 for Wait, 6 for Transition, 7 for Unknown. A Running thread is using a processor; a Standby thread is about to use one. A Ready thread wants to use a processor but is waiting for a processor because none are free. A thread in Transition is waiting for a resource in order to execute, such as waiting for its execution stack to be paged in from disk. A Waiting thread has no use for the processor because it is waiting for a peripheral operation to complete or a resource to become free.

Object	Object Counter	Description
Thread	Thread Wait Reason	This is only applicable when the thread is in the Wait state (see Thread State). It is 0 or 7 when the thread is waiting for the Executive, 1 or 8 for a Free Page, 2 or 9 for a Page In, 3 or 10 for a Pool Allocation, 4 or 11 for an Execution Delay, 5 or 12 for a Suspended condition, 6 or 13 for a User Request, 14 for an Event Pair High, 15 for an Event Pair Low, 16 for an LPC Receive, 17 for an LPC Reply, 18 for Virtual Memory, 19 for a Page Out; 20 and higher have not been assigned at the time of this writing. Event Pairs are used to communicate with protected subsystems (see Context Switches).

Appendix B
Protocol Definitions

These selected protocol definitions are extremely helpful in learning the finer protocols points about network protocols. This information is exposed under Network Monitor's Display Capture dialog box. While only selected protocols are displayed here in the interest of space, you may be interested using Network Monitor and learning more about definitions not presented here.

Data Type	Legend
●	Byte
○	Array of Bytes
■	Word
▢	Array of Words
▲	Dword
✔	Array of DWords
✕	Large Integer
▶	Date & Time
✚	Address
◆	No Value

Protocol Name/Properties	Relations								
	$\genfrac{}{}{0pt}{}{=}{=}$	$\genfrac{}{}{0pt}{}{>}{<}$	$>$	$<$	$\genfrac{}{}{0pt}{}{=}{>}$	$\genfrac{}{}{0pt}{}{=}{<}$	Contains	Exists	Includes
ARP_RARP (Address Resolution Protocol\Reverse Address Resolution Protocol)	○	○							
ARP	○						○	◆	
Frame Padding							○	◆	
Hardware Address length	●	●	●	●	●	●	○	◆	
Hardware Address Space	■	■	■	■	■	■	○	◆	
Opcode	■	■	■	■	■	■	○	◆	
Protocol Address Length	●	●	●	●	●	●	○	◆	
Protocol Address Space	■	■	■	■	■	■	○	◆	
RARP Protocol	○						○	◆	
Sender's Hardware Address	✚						○	◆	
Sender's Protocol Address	✚						○	◆	
Target's Hardware Address	✚						○	◆	
Target's Protocol Address	✚						○	◆	
IP (Internet Protocol)	○	○							
Checksum	■	■	■	■	■	■	○	◆	
Compartmentalization	■	■	■	■	■	■	○	◆	
Data							○	◆	
Delay	●	●	●	●	●	●	○	◆	
Destination Address	✚						○	◆	
End of Options	●	●	●	●	●	●	○	◆	
Flags							○	◆	●
Flags Summary	●	●	●	●	●	●	○	◆	
Fragment Offset	■	■	■	■	■	■	○	◆	
Fragmented Datagram Data							○	◆	
Gateway	✚						○	◆	
Handling Restrictions	○						○	◆	
Header Length	●	●	●	●	●	●	○	◆	

Appendix B: Protocol Definitions

Protocol Name/Properties	= =	< >	<	>	= <	= >	Contains	Exists	Includes
Identification	■	■	■	■	■	■	○	◆	
Internet Timestamp Option	●	●	●	●	●	●	○	◆	
Invalid Option	●	●	●	●	●	●	○	◆	
Loose Source Routing Option	●	●	●	●	●	●	○	◆	
Missed Stations	●	●	●	●	●	●	○	◆	
Next Slot Pointer	●	●	●	●	●	●	○	◆	
No Operation	●	●	●	●	●	●	○	◆	
Option Fields									
Option Length	●	●	●	●	●	●	○	◆	
Padding							○	◆	
Precedence	●	●	●	●	●	●	○	◆	
Protocol	●	●	●	●	●	●	○	◆	
Record Route Option	●	●	●	●	●	●	○	◆	
Reliability	●	●	●	●	●	●	○	◆	
Reserved Bytes	●	●	●	●	●	●	○	◆	
Route To Go	●	●	●	●	●	●	○	◆	
Route Traveled	●	●	●	●	●	●	○	◆	
Routing Pointer	●	●	●	●	●	●	○	◆	
Security Level	■	■	■	■	■		○	◆	
Security Option	●	●	●	●	●	●	○	◆	
Service Type	●	●	●	●	●	●	○	◆	
Source Address	✚						○	◆	
Stream Identifier	■	■	■	■	■		○	◆	
Stream Option	●	●	●	●	●	●	○	◆	
Strict Source Routing Option	●	●	●	●	●	●	○	◆	
Summary	○						○	◆	
Throughput	●	●	●	●	●		○	◆	
Time Options	●	●	●	●	●	●	○	◆	

Continued

Protocol Name/Properties	==	<>	<	>	=<	=>	Contains	Exists	Includes
Time Point	▲	▲	▲	▲	▲	▲	○	◆	
Time Pointer	●	●	●	●	●	●	○	◆	
Time Route	▲	▲	▲	▲	▲	▲	○	◆	
Time to Live	●	●	●	●	●	●	○	◆	
Total Length	■	■	■	■	■	■	○	◆	
Transmission Control Code	●	●	●	●	●	●	○	◆	
Version	●	●	●	●	●	●	○	◆	
NBT (NetBIOS over TCP/IP)	○	○							
Adapter Address	✚						○	◆	
Additional Record Count	■	■	■	■	■	■	○	◆	
Answer Count	■	■	■	■	■	■	○	◆	
ASCII Name	○						○	◆	
Called Name	○						○	◆	
Calling Name	○						○	◆	
Datagram Flags	●	●	●	●	●	●	○	◆	
Datagram ID	■	■	■	■	■	■	○	◆	
Datagram Length	■	■	■	■	■	■	○	◆	
Datagram Packet Type	●	●	●	●	●	●	○	◆	
Destination Name							○	◆	
DS	○						○	◆	
DS Data							○	◆	
DS First/More Packet Flags							○	◆	●
Duration	■	■	■	■	■	■	○	◆	
Error Code	●	●	●	●	●	●	○	◆	
Flags Summary	■	■	■	■	■	■	○	◆	
Frame Padding							○	◆	
Free NCBS	■	■	■	■	■	■	○	◆	
FRMRs Received	■	■	■	■	■	■	○	◆	
FRMRS Transmitted	■	■	■	■	■	■	○	◆	

Appendix B: Protocol Definitions

Protocol Name/Properties	=	≠	<	>	≤	≥	Contains	Exists	Includes
Group Name Flag							○	◆	■
Iframe Receive Errors	■	■	■	■	■	■	○	◆	
Iframe Transmit Errors	■	■	■	■	■	■	○	◆	
Lanman Destination Name							○	◆	
Lanman Source Name							○	◆	
Length Extensions							○	◆	●
Max Config Sessions	■	■	■	■	■	■	○	◆	
Max Datagram	■	■	■	■	■	■	○	◆	
Max NCBS	■	■	■	■	■	■	○	◆	
Max Sessions	■	■	■	■	■	■	○	◆	
Name Flags							○	◆	■
Name Service Count	■	■	■	■	■	■	○	◆	
Name Service Flags							○	◆	■
NBT Summary	○						○	◆	
NCBS	■	■	■	■	■	■	○	◆	
No Receive Buffers	■	■	■	■	■	■	○	◆	
No Transmit Buffers	■	■	■	■	■	■	○	◆	
NS	○						○	◆	
Number of Names	●	●	●	●	●	●	○	◆	
Opcode	■	■	■	■	■	■	○	◆	
Opcode Reply Flag							○	◆	■
Owner IP Address	+						○	◆	
Owner Node Type	■	■	■	■	■	■	○	◆	
Packet Flags	●	●	●	●	●	●	○	◆	
Packet Length	■	■	■	■	■	■	○	◆	
Packet Offset	■	■	■	■	■	■	○	◆	
Packet Size	■	■	■	■	■	■	○	◆	
Packet Type	●	●	●	●	●	●	○	◆	

Continued

Protocol Name/Properties	Relations (continued)						Contains	Exists	Includes
	= =	< >	<	>	= >	= <			
Pending Sessions	■	■	■	■	■	■	○	◆	
Question Class	■	■	■	■	■	■	○	◆	
Question Count	■	■	■	■	■	■	○	◆	
Question Name							○	◆	
Question Type	■	■	■	■	■	■	○	◆	
RDATA Length	■	■	■	■	■	■	○	◆	
Received	▲	▲	▲	▲	▲	▲	○	◆	
Reserved	■	■	■	■	■	■	○	◆	
Reserved Flags	●	●	●	●	●	●	○	◆	
Reserved Packet Flags	●	●	●	●	●	●	○	◆	
Reserved Record Class	●	●	●	●	●	●	○	◆	
Resource Record Flags	■	■	■	■	■	■	○	◆	
Resource Record Name							○	◆	
Resource Record Type	■	■	■	■	■	■	○	◆	
Result Code	■	■	■	■	■	■	○	◆	
Retarget IP Address	✚						○	◆	
Retarget Port	■	■	■	■	■	■	○	◆	
Session Service Error Code	●	●	●	●	●	●	○	◆	
Source End-Node Type	●	●	●	●	●	●	○	◆	
Source IP Address	✚						○	◆	
Source Name							○	◆	
Source Port	■	■	■	■	■	■	○	◆	
SS	○						○	◆	
SS Data							○	◆	
SS: Session Message Cont.	○						○	◆	
T1 Timeouts	■	■	■	■	■	■	○	◆	
Ti Timeouts	■	■	■	■	■	■	○	◆	
Time to Live	▲	▲	▲	▲	▲	▲	○	◆	
Transmitted	▲	▲	▲	▲	▲	▲	○	◆	

Appendix B: Protocol Definitions

Protocol Name/Properties	Relations						Contains	Exists	Includes
	==	^ v	^	v	=^	=v			
Transaction ID	■	■	■	■	■	■	○	◆	
Transmit Aborts	■	■	■	■	■	■	○	◆	
Version Major	●	●	●	●	●	●	○	◆	
Version Minor	●	●	●	●	●	●	○	◆	
Netlogon (MS Netlogon Broadcasts)	○	○							
Allowable Account Control Bit							○	◆	▲
Allowable Account Control Bits Summary							○	◆	▲
Computer Name							○	◆	
Database Index	▲	▲	▲	▲	▲	▲	○	◆	
Date and Time	▲	▲	▲	▲	▲	▲	○	◆	
DB Change Info Summary	○						○	◆	
DB Count	▲	▲	▲	▲	▲	▲	○	◆	
Domain Name							○	◆	
Domain SID	○						○	◆	
Domain SID Size	▲	▲	▲	▲	▲	▲	○	◆	
Large Serial Number	×	×	×	×	×	×	○	◆	
LM20 Token	■	■	■	■	■	■	○	◆	
LMNT Token	■	■	■	■	■	■	○	◆	
Logon Server Name							○	◆	
Low Serial Number	▲	▲	▲	▲	▲	▲	○	◆	
Mailslot Name							○	◆	
NT Date and Time	×	×	×	×	×	×	○	◆	
NT Version	▲	▲	▲	▲	▲	▲	○	◆	
Opcode	■	■	■	■	■	■	○	◆	
Pad	●	●	●	●	●	●	○	◆	
Primary DC Name							○	◆	
Pulse	▲	▲	▲	▲	▲	▲	○	◆	

Continued

Protocol Name/Properties	= =	^ v	^	v	= ^	= v	Contains	Exists	Includes
Random	▲	▲	▲	▲	▲	▲	○	◆	
Request Count	■	■	■	■	■	■	○	◆	
Script Name							○	◆	
Signature	■	■	■	■	■	■	○	◆	
Summary	○						○	◆	
Unicode Computer Name							○	◆	
Unicode Domain Name							○	◆	
Unicode Logon Server							○	◆	
Unicode Primary DC Name							○	◆	
Unicode User Name							○	◆	
Update Type	■	■	■	■	■	■	○	◆	
Use Name							○	◆	
User Name							○	◆	
Workstation Major Version	●	●	●	●	●	●	○	◆	
Workstation Minor Version	●	●	●	●	●	●	○	◆	
Workstation OS version	●	●	●	●	●	●	○	◆	
SMB (Server Message Block Protocol)	○	○							
Access Mask Standard Flags							○	◆	▲
Access Mask Summary	▲	▲	▲	▲	▲	▲	○	◆	
Access Mask Token Specific Flag							○	◆	▲
Access Mode	■	■	■	■	■	■	○	◆	
Account Name							○	◆	
ACE							○	◆	
ACE Count	■	■	■	■	■	■	○	◆	
ACE Flags							○	◆	●
ACE Flags Summary	●	●	●	●	●	●	○	◆	
ACE Size	■	■	■	■	■	■	○	◆	
ACE Type	●	●	●	●	●	●	○	◆	
ACL Size	■	■	■	■	■	■	○	◆	

Appendix B: Protocol Definitions

Protocol Name/Properties	= / =	∧/∨	∧	∨	=/∧	=/∨	Contains	Exists	Includes
Action Taken	■	■	■	■	■	■	○	◆	
Action Taken Flags	■	■	■	■	■	■	○	◆	
Allocation	▲	▲	▲	▲	▲	▲	○	◆	
Available Allocation Units (NT)	×	×	×	×	×	×	○	◆	
Bad SMB Error Code	■	■	■	■	■	■	○	◆	
Block Mode	■	■	■	■	■	■	○	◆	
Block Mode Flags							○	◆	■
Blocking	●	●	●	●	●	●	○	◆	
Blocks Per Unit	▲	▲	▲	▲	▲	▲	○	◆	
Blocks Per Unit (WORD)	■	■	■	■	■	■	○	◆	
Boolean Is Directory	●	●	●	●	●	●	○	◆	
Boolean Volume Supports Object	●	●	●	●	●	●	○	◆	
Buffer Length	▲	▲	▲	▲	▲	▲	○	◆	
Byte Count	■	■	■	■	■	■	○	◆	
Byter Parameters							○	◆	
Bytes Left	■	■	■	■	■	■	○	◆	
Bytes Per Block	■	■	■	■	■	■	○	◆	
Bytes Per Block (NT)	▲	▲	▲	▲	▲	▲	○	◆	
Bytes Remaining in Message	■	■	■	■	■	■	○	◆	
Bytes Remaining in Pipe	■	■	■	■	■	■	○	◆	
Caching Mode	■	■	■	■	■	■	○	◆	
Capabilities	▲	▲	▲	▲	▲	▲	○	◆	
Capabilities Flags							○	◆	▲
Change Count	■	■	■	■	■	■	○	◆	
Change Time	▶	▶	▶	▶	▶	▶	○	◆	
Command	●	●	●	●	●	●	○	◆	
Common Header	○						○	◆	
Computer Name	○						○	◆	

Continued

Protocol Name/Properties	= =	∧ ∨	∧	∨	= ∧	= ∨	Contains	Exists	Includes
Copy Flags	■	■	■	■	■	■	○	◆	
Create Action	▲	▲	▲	▲	▲	▲	○	◆	
Create Disposition	▲	▲	▲	▲	▲	▲	○	◆	
Create Flags Dword	▲	▲	▲	▲	▲	▲	○	◆	
Create Flags flags							○	◆	▲
Create Options	▲	▲	▲	▲	▲	▲	○	◆	
Create Option Bits							○	◆	▲
Creation Time	◗	◗	◗	◗	◗	◗	○	◆	
Data							○	◆	
Data Bytes	■	■	■	■	■	■	○	◆	
Data Count	▲	▲	▲	▲	▲	▲	○	◆	
Data Displacement	■	■	■	■	■	■	○	◆	
Data Displacement (NT)	▲	▲	▲	▲	▲	▲	○	◆	
Data Length	■	■	■	■	■	■	○	◆	
Data Offset	▲	▲	▲	▲	▲	▲	○	◆	
Data offset	■	■	■	■	■	■	○	◆	
Desired Access	▲	▲	▲	▲	▲	▲	○	◆	
Desired Access Flags							○	◆	▲
Destination Mode	■	■	■	■	■	■	○	◆	
Destination Name	○						○	◆	
Destination Tree ID (TID2)	■	■	■	■	■	■	○	◆	
Destination Type	■	■	■	■	■	■	○	◆	
Device State	■	■	■	■	■	■	○	◆	
DFS 8.3 Filename							○	◆	
DFS Filename							○	◆	
DFS Max Referral Level	■	■	■	■	■	■	○	◆	
DFS Number of Referrals	■	■	■	■	■	■	○	◆	
DFS Path Consumed	■	■	■	■	■	■	○	◆	
DFS Proximity	▲	▲	▲	▲	▲	▲	○	◆	

Appendix B: Protocol Definitions

Protocol Name/Properties	Relations							Contains	Exists	Includes
	=,=	<,>	<	>	=,>	=,<			
DFS Request Filename							○	◆	
DFS Server Function	▲	▲	▲	▲	▲	▲	○	◆	
DFS Server Function Flags							○	◆	▲
DFS Server Type	■	■	■	■	■	■	○	◆	
DFS Sharename							○	◆	
DFS Strip Path	■	■	■	■	■	■	○	◆	
DFS Time ToLive	■	■	■	■	■	■	○	◆	
DFS Version 1 Referral							○	◆	
DFS Version 2 Referral							○	◆	
DFS Version Number	■	■	■	■	■	■	○	◆	
Dialect String	○						○	◆	
Dialect Strings Understood	○						○	◆	
Directory Entry	○						○	◆	
Disconnect Flag	■	■	■	■	■	■	○	◆	
Discretionary ACL (DACL)							○	◆	
Domain Name							○	◆	
DOS Error Code	■	■	■	■	■	■	○	◆	
EA Offset Error	■	■	■	■	■	■	○	◆	
EA Size	▲	▲	▲	▲	▲	▲	○	◆	
Echo Reverb	■	■	■	■	■	■	○	◆	
Echo Sequence	■	■	■	■	■	■	○	◆	
Encrypted Password	○						○	◆	
Encryption Key	●	●	●	●	●	●	○	◆	
Encryption Key Length	●	●	●	●	●	●	○	◆	
Encryption Key Offset	■	■	■	■	■	■	○	◆	
End of File	×	×	×	×	×	×	○	◆	
End of Search	■	■	■	■	■	■	○	◆	
Error Class	●	●	●	●	●	●	○	◆	

Continued

Protocol Name/Properties	Relations (continued)						Contains	Exists	Includes
	=/=	<;>	<	>	=/>	=/<			
Error Code	■	■	■	■	■	■	○	◆	
Errored Path							○	◆	
Exist Action	■	■	■	■	■	■	○	◆	
Extended Attribute List	■	■	■	■	■	■	○	◆	
Extended Attributes	■	■	■	■	■	■	○	◆	
Extended OS Error Code	■	■	■	■	■	■	○	◆	
File Allocation Size	×	×	×	×	×	×	○	◆	
File Attribute Flags							○	◆	▲
File Attributes							○	◆	▲
File Attributes	■	■	■	■	■	■	○	◆	
File Creation Time	▶	▶	▶	▶	▶	▶	○	◆	
File Creation Time (sec)	▶	▶	▶	▶	▶	▶	○	◆	
File ID (FID)	■	■	■	■	■	■	○	◆	
File Index	▲	▲	▲	▲	▲	▲	○	◆	
File Name							○	◆	
File Name Length	▲	▲	▲	▲	▲	▲	○	◆	
File Offset	▲	▲	▲	▲	▲	▲	○	◆	
File Offset (NT)	×	×	×	×	×	×	○	◆	
File Offset, High	▲	▲	▲	▲	▲	▲	○	◆	
File Share Access	▲	▲	▲	▲	▲	▲	○	◆	
File Size	▲	▲	▲	▲	▲	▲	○	◆	
File System Info							○	◆	▲
File System Info Summary	▲	▲	▲	▲	▲	▲	○	◆	
File Type	■	■	■	■	■	■	○	◆	
Files Copied	▲	▲	▲	▲	▲	▲	○	◆	
Find Count	■	■	■	■	■	■	○	◆	
Find Entry	▲	▲	▲	▲	▲	▲	○	◆	
Find Flags	■	■	■	■	■	■	○	◆	
Find Flags Detail							○	◆	■

Protocol Name/Properties	= / =	^ / v	^	v	= / ^	= / v	Contains	Exists	Includes
Find Handle	■	■	■	■	■	■	○	◆	
Find Key	○						○	◆	
Find Key (client)	○						○	◆	
Find Key (server)	○						○	◆	
Find Key ID	●	●	●	●	●	●	○	◆	
Find Key Length	■	■	■	■	■	■	○	◆	
Find Resume Key	▲	▲	▲	▲	▲	▲	○	◆	
Flags							○	◆	●
Flags Summary	●	●	●	●	●	●	○	◆	
flags2							○	◆	■
flags2 Summary	■	■	■	■	■	■	○	◆	
Free Allocation Units	▲	▲	▲	▲	▲	▲	○	◆	
Free Units (WORD)	■	■	■	■	■	■	○	◆	
FSCTL function	■	■	■	■	■	■	○	◆	
FSCTL method	■	■	■	■	■	■	○	◆	
Group ID	■	■	■	■	■	■	○	◆	
Group SID							○	◆	
Guest logon	■	■	■	■	■	■	○	◆	
Hard Error Code	■	■	■	■	■	■	○	◆	
I/O Bytes	■	■	■	■	■	■	○	◆	
Impersonation Level	▲	▲	▲	▲	▲	▲	○	◆	
Info Level	■	■	■	■	■	■	○	◆	
Instance Count	●	●	●	●	●	●	○	◆	
IOCTL Category	■	■	■	■	■	■	○	◆	
IOCTL Data	●	●	●	●	●	●	○	◆	
IOCTL Function	■	■	■	■	■	■	○	◆	
IOCTL Parameters	●	●	●	●	●	●	○	◆	
IPX Group ID	■	■	■	■	■	■	○	◆	

Continued

Protocol Name/Properties	==	<>	<	>	=<	=>	Contains	Exists	Includes
IPX Key	▲	▲	▲	▲	▲	▲	○	◆	
IPX Sequence Num	■	■	■	■	■	■	○	◆	
IPX Session ID	■	■	■	■	■	■	○	◆	
Kerberos Ticket	○						○	◆	
Lanman Destination Name							○	◆	
Lanman Source Name							○	◆	
Last Access Time	◗	◗	◗	◗	◗	◗	○	◆	
Last Access Time (sec)	◗	◗	◗	◗	◗	◗	○	◆	
Last Modify Time	◗	◗	◗	◗	◗	◗	○	◆	
Last Modify Time (sec)	◗	◗	◗	◗	◗	◗	○	◆	
Last Name	■	■	■	■	■	■	○	◆	
Last Write Time	◗	◗	◗	◗	◗	◗	○	◆	
Locality	■	■	■	■	■	■	○	◆	
Lock Bytes	▲	▲	▲	▲	▲	▲	○	◆	
Lock Length	▲	▲	▲	▲	▲	▲	○	◆	
Lock Length (NT)	×	×	×	×	×	×	○	◆	
Lock Range	○						○	◆	
Lock Status	■	■	■	■	■	■	○	◆	
Lock Type	■	■	■	■	■	■	○	◆	
Lock Type Flags							○	◆	■
Mailslot Class	■	■	■	■	■	■	○	◆	
Mailslot Opcode	■	■	■	■	■	■	○	◆	
Major Version	●	●	●	●	●	●	○	◆	
Max Buffer Size	■	■	■	■	■	■	○	◆	
Max Component Name Length	▲	▲	▲	▲	▲	▲	○	◆	
Max Count	■	■	■	■	■	■	○	◆	
Max Data Bytes	■	■	■	■	■	■	○	◆	
Max Data Count	▲	▲	▲	▲	▲	▲	○	◆	
Max MPX Requests	■	■	■	■	■	■	○	◆	

Relations (continued)

Protocol Name/Properties	=/=	^/v	^	v	=/^	=/v	Contains	Exists	Includes
Max Parameter Count	▲	▲	▲	▲	▲	▲	○	◆	
Max Parm Bytes	■	■	■	■	■	■	○	◆	
Max Print Jobs	■	■	■	■	■	■	○	◆	
Max Raw Size	▲	▲	▲	▲	▲	▲	○	◆	
Max Setup Words	●	●	●	●	●	●	○	◆	
Max Setup Words	■	■	■	■	■	■	○	◆	
Max Transmit Size	■	■	■	■	■	■	○	◆	
Max VCs	■	■	■	■	■	■	○	◆	
Min Count	■	■	■	■	■	■	○	◆	
Minor Version	●	●	●	●	●	●	○	◆	
Multiplex ID (MID)	■	■	■	■	■	■	○	◆	
Name Length	●	●	●	●	●	●	○	◆	
Name Length (NT)	■	■	■	■	■	■	○	◆	
Native FS	●	●	●	●	●	●	○	◆	
Native Lanman							○	◆	
Native OS							○	◆	
Negotiate Encryption Key	○						○	◆	
New Path							○	◆	
Next Offset	■	■	■	■	■	■	○	◆	
No-exist action	■	■	■	■	■	■	○	◆	
Notify Completion Filter	▲	▲	▲	▲	▲	▲	○	◆	
Notify Completion Filter Flags							○	◆	▲
Notify Watch Tree	●	●	●	●	●	●	○	◆	
NT File Attributes	▲	▲	▲	▲	▲	▲	○	◆	
NT IOCTL Function Code	▲	▲	▲	▲	▲	▲	○	◆	
NT Last Access Time	◗	◗	◗	◗	◗	◗	○	◆	
NT Max Buffer Size	▲	▲	▲	▲	▲	▲	○	◆	
NT Status Code	▲	▲	▲	▲	▲	▲	○	◆	

Continued

Protocol Name/Properties	Relations (continued)						Contains	Exists	Includes
	= =	< >	<	>	= >	= <			
NT Status Code System Error	■	■	■	■	■	■	○	◆	
NT Status Code System Information	■	■	■	■	■	■	○	◆	
NT Status Code System Success	■	■	■	■	■	■	○	◆	
NT Status Code System Warning	■	■	■	■	■	■	○	◆	
NT Status Customer Code	●	●	●	●	●	●	○	◆	
NT Status Facility	■	■	■	■	■	■	○	◆	
NT Status Reserved Bit	●	●	●	●	●	●	○	◆	
NT Status Severity Code	●	●	●	●	●	●	○	◆	
NT Transact Flags	■	■	■	■	■	■	○	◆	
Number of Locks	■	■	■	■	■	■	○	◆	
Number of Print Jobs	■	■	■	■	■	■	○	◆	
Number of Unlocks	■	■	■	■	■	■	○	◆	
Open Flags							○	◆	■
Open Flags Summary	■	■	■	■	■	■	○	◆	
Open Function	■	■	■	■	■	■	○	◆	
Open Mode	■	■	■	■	■	■	○	◆	
Open Mode FCB Open	■	■	■	■	■	■	○	◆	
Open Mode File Access							○	◆	■
Open Mode Files Sharing	■	■	■	■	■	■	○	◆	
Open Timeout	▲	▲	▲	▲	▲	▲	○	◆	
Oplock Level	●	●	●	●	●	●	○	◆	
Optional Support	■	■	■	■	■	■	○	◆	
Optional Support Flags							○	◆	■
Originator Name	○						○	◆	
Owner SID							○	◆	
Parameter Bytes	■	■	■	■	■	■	○	◆	
Parameter Count	▲	▲	▲	▲	▲	▲	○	◆	
Parameter Displacement	▲	▲	▲	▲	▲	▲	○	◆	
Parameter Displacement	■	■	■	■	■	■	○	◆	

Appendix B: Protocol Definitions

Protocol Name/Properties	=	<>	<	>	=>	=<	Contains	Exists	Includes
Parameter Offset	▲	▲	▲	▲	▲	▲	○	◆	
Parameter offset	■	■	■	■	■	■	○	◆	
Password	●	●	●	●	●	●	○	◆	
Password Length	■	■	■	■	■	■	○	◆	
Path nameX	○						○	◆	
Pipe Endpoint	●	●	●	●	●	●	○	◆	
Pipe Function	■	■	■	■	■	■	○	◆	
Pipe Status	■	■	■	■	■	■	○	◆	
Pipe Type	●	●	●	●	●	●	○	◆	
Print Job Info	●	●	●	●	●	●	○	◆	
Print Job Status	●	●	●	●	●	●	○	◆	
Print Job Time	■	■	■	■	■	■	○	◆	
Process High ID	■	■	■	■	■	■	○	◆	
Process ID (PID)	■	■	■	■	■	■	○	◆	
Protocol Index	■	■	■	■	■	■	○	◆	
QFS Info Level	■	■	■	■	■	■	○	◆	
Query Mode							○	◆	■
Query mode	■	■	■	■	■	■	○	◆	
Read Mode	●	●	●	●	●	●	○	◆	
Read-ahead	■	■	■	■	■	■	○	◆	
Recognized as FSCTL	●	●	●	●	●	●	○	◆	
Rename Flags	■	■	■	■	■	■	○	◆	
Rename Flags Flags							○	◆	■
Reserved Byte	●	●	●	●	●	●	○	◆	
Reserved Dword	▲	▲	▲	▲	▲	▲	○	◆	
Reserved Word	□						○	◆	
RMX Error Code	■	■	■	■	■	■	○	◆	
Root Dir FID	▲	▲	▲	▲	▲	▲	○	◆	

Continued

Protocol Name/Properties	=	≠	>	<	≥	≤	Contains	Exists	Includes
Search Attributes	■	■	■	■	■	■	○	◆	
Search Count	■	■	■	■	■	■	○	◆	
Search Path							○	◆	
Security Descriptor Control Summary							○	◆	■
Security Descriptor Control Summary	■	■	■	■	■	■	○	◆	
Security Flag Bits							○	◆	●
Security Flags	●	●	●	●	●	●	○	◆	
Security Identifier Authority	○						○	◆	
Security Identifier Offset to the Group SID	▲	▲	▲	▲	▲	▲	○	◆	
Security Identifier Offset to the Owner SID	▲	▲	▲	▲	▲	▲	○	◆	
Security Identifier Sub Authority	✓						○	◆	
Security Identifier Sub Authority Count	●	●	●	●	●	●	○	◆	
Security Information	■	■	■	■	■	■	○	◆	
Security Information Flags							○	◆	■
Security Mode							○	◆	●
Security Mode Summary (NT)	●	●	●	●	●	●	○	◆	
Security Mode Summary (WORD)	■	■	■	■	■	■	○	◆	
Security Object Revision	○						○	◆	
Seek Mode	■	■	■	■	■	■	○	◆	
Server Announce Opcode	■	■	■	■	■	■	○	◆	
Server Announce Rate	■	■	■	■	■	■	○	◆	
Server Comment	○						○	◆	
Server Error Code	■	■	■	■	■	■	○	◆	
Server Time	▶	▶	▶	▶	▶	▶	○	◆	
Server Time	■	■	■	■	■	■	○	◆	
Server Time Zone	■	■	■	■	■	■	○	◆	
Service Flags							○	◆	▲

Relations *(continued)*

Appendix B: Protocol Definitions

Protocol Name/Properties	Relations						Contains	Exists	Includes
	= =	∧ ∨	∧	∨	= ∧	= ∨			
Service Flags Summary	▲	▲	▲	▲	▲	▲	○	◆	
Service Name	○						○	◆	
Session Key	▲	▲	▲	▲	▲	▲	○	◆	
Set File Info Level	■	■	■	■	■	■	○	◆	
Setup Action	■	■	■	■	■	■	○	◆	
Setup Count	●	●	●	●	●	●	○	◆	
Setup Words	○						○	◆	
Sharing Bits							○	◆	▲
Short File Name							○	◆	
Short Name Length	●	●	●	●	●	●	○	◆	
Signature	▲	▲	▲	▲	▲	▲	○	◆	
SMB Status	▲	▲	▲	▲	▲	▲	○	◆	
Source Mode	■	■	■	■	■	■	○	◆	
Spool Header Size	■	■	■	■	■	■	○	◆	
Spool Mode	■	■	■	■	■	■	○	◆	
Spool Restart Index	■	■	■	■	■	■	○	◆	
Spool Start Index	■	■	■	■	■	■	○	◆	
Summary	○						○	◆	
Supported Services	■	■	■	■	■	■	○	◆	
System ACL (SACL)	▲	▲	▲	▲	▲	▲	○	◆	
T2 I/O Flags							○	◆	■
T2 I/O Flags Summary	■	■	■	■	■	■	○	◆	
Total Allocation Units	▲	▲	▲	▲	▲	▲	○	◆	
Total Allocation Units (NT)	×	×	×	×	×	×	○	◆	
Total Data Bytes	■	■	■	■	■	■	○	◆	
Total Data Count	▲	▲	▲	▲	▲	▲	○	◆	
Total Parameter Count	▲	▲	▲	▲	▲	▲	○	◆	
Total Parm Bytes	■	■	■	■	■	■	○	◆	

Continued

Appendixes

Protocol Name/Properties	Relations (continued)						Contains	Exists	Includes
	=/=	∧/∨	∧	∨	=/∧	=/∨			
Total Units (WORD)	■	■	■	■	■	■	○	◆	
Transact Flags Summary							○	◆	■
Transact Flags Summary	■	■	■	■	■	■	○	◆	
Transact Function	■	■	■	■	■	■	○	◆	
Transact Timeout	▲	▲	▲	▲	▲	▲	○	◆	
Transact2 Function	■	■	■	■	■	■	○	◆	
Transaction Data	○						○	◆	
Transaction Parameters	○						○	◆	
Transaction Priority	■	■	■	■	■	■	○	◆	
Tree Copy	■	■	■	■	■	■	○	◆	
Tree ID (TID)	■	■	■	■	■	■	○	◆	
Unicode Password Length	■	■	■	■	■	■	○	◆	
Unique File ID	▲	▲	▲	▲	▲	▲	○	◆	
Unlock Range	○						○	◆	
User ID (UID)	■	■	■	■	■	■	○	◆	
VC Number	■	■	■	■	■	■	○	◆	
VC Number	■	■	■	■	■	■	○	◆	
Verify	■	■	■	■	■	■	○	◆	
Volume Creation Time	▶	▶	▶	▶	▶	▶	○	◆	
Volume Name							○	◆	
Volume Name Size	■	■	■	■	■	■	○	◆	
Volume Serial Number	▲	▲	▲	▲	▲	▲	○	◆	
Volume Time	▶	▶	▶	▶	▶	▶	○	◆	
Word Count	●	●	●	●	●	●	○	◆	
Word count	●	●	●	●	●	●	○	◆	
Word Parameters	□						○	◆	
Write Mode	■	■	■	■	■	■	○	◆	
Write Mode Flags							○	◆	■
TCP (Transmission Control Protocol)	○	○							

Protocol Name/Properties	==	<> ∨	∧	∨	|| ∧	|| ∨	Contains	Exists	Includes
Acknowledgement Number	▲	▲	▲	▲	▲	▲	○	♦	
Checksum	■	■	■	■	■	■	○	♦	
Data							○	♦	
Data Offset	●	●	●	●	●	●	○	♦	
Destination Port	■	■	■	■	■	■	○	♦	
Flags	●	●	●	●	●	●	○	♦	
Frame Padding							○	♦	
Invalid Option	■	■	■	■	■	■	○	♦	
Option End	■	■	■	■	■	■	○	♦	
Option Kind (Maximum Segment Size)	●	●	●	●	●	●	○	♦	
Option Length	●	●	●	●	●	●	○	♦	
Option MaxSegSize	●	●	●	●	●	●	○	♦	
Option Nop	●	●	●	●	●	●	○	♦	
Option Value	■	■	■	■	■	■	○	♦	
Options							○	♦	
Padding	■	■	■	■	■	■	○	♦	
Reserved	■	■	■	■	■	■	○	♦	
Sequence Number	▲	▲	▲	▲	▲	▲	○	♦	
Source Port	■	■	■	■	■	■	○	♦	
Summary	○						○	♦	
TCP Flags							○	♦	●
Unknown Option							○	♦	
Urgent Pointer	■	■	■	■	■	■	○	♦	
Window	■	■	■	■	■	■	○	♦	

Appendix C

Common Image Names in Task Manager

This appendix provides the descriptions of common image names displayed when you select the Processes tab sheet in Task Manager (see Table C-1). These descriptions allow you to better understand what the files does. More important, knowing the description of the Task Manager image name would allow you to conduct more research on that image name on the Web or Microsoft TechNet.

Table C-1 Task Manager Image Names

Image Name (Original Name)	Real Name (Description)	Vendor (Company Name)	Location (In Folder)
Smss.exe	Windows NT Session Manager	Microsoft	\WINNT\system32
CSRSS.Exe	Client Server Runtime Process	Microsoft	\WINNT\system32
WINLOGON.EXE	Windows NT Logon Application	Microsoft	\WINNT\system32
Services.exe	Services and Controller app	Microsoft	\WINNT\system32
lsass.exe	LSA Executable and Server DLL	Microsoft	\WINNT\system32
RpcSs.exe	Distribute COM Services	Microsoft	\WINNT\system32
Spoolss.exe	Spooler SubSystem App	Microsoft	\WINNT\system32
Tcpsvcs.exe	TCP/IP Services Application	Microsoft	\WINNT\system32
Llssrv.exe	Microsoft License Server	Microsoft	\WINNT\system32
Wins.exe	WINS SERVER	Microsoft	\WINNT\system32
Snmp.exe	SNMP Service	Microsoft	\WINNT\system32
Locator.exe	Rpc Locator	Microsoft	\WINNT\system32
Taskmgr.exe	Windows TaskManager	Microsoft	\WINNT\system32
Dns.exe	Domain Name Server (DNS) Service	Microsoft	\WINNT\system32
Explorer.exe	Windows Explorer	Microsoft	\WINNT
Systray.exe	System Tray Applet	Microsoft	\WINNT\system32

Appendix D

Details of Service Pack 4.0: Fixes/Enhancements/Additions

Service Pack 4 is composed of both operating system additions and bug fixes. This appendix provides the Service Pack 4 details you will need to accurately assess how or if Service Pack 4 is the right upgrade for you. This appendix covers everything in SP4 from active accessibility support to DNS enhancements.

Active Accessibility Support

Microsoft Active Accessibility (MSAA) is a COM-based standard method by which a utility program interacts with an application's user interface (UI). Using MSAA applications can expose all UI elements and objects with standard properties and methods. SP4 includes five new application programming interfaces (APIs). These new APIs include:

- GetGUIThreadInfo
- GetAncestor
- RealChildWindowsFromPoint
- RealGetWindowClassA
- RealGetWindowClassW

DCOM/HTTP Tunneling

This update allows DCOM client/server communication to cross firewalls over the HTTP protocol port. The new protocol "Tunneling TCP" is used like other DCOM protocols. The new moniker type OBJREF is passed in HTML to the client. The benefits of Tunneling TCP include high performance, use of existing open ports in the firewall, and control of client access for proxy administrators. For more information, see www.microsoft.com/com.

Euro Key Patch

The Euro Key Patch is an update to include the new European "euro" currency symbol. The update supplies the core fonts (Arial, Courier New, and Times New Roman) and the keyboard drivers.

InternetGroup Management Protocol (IGMP) v2

IGMP v2 allows a computer to inform the router that it's leaving a group. This update enables the router to determine if there are no more members in a group and then executes a command to stop forwarding multicast packets on to the link. This update is useful when users are frequently joining and leaving groups.

Microsoft File and Print Service for NetWare (FPNW) Support for Client 32

Microsoft File and Print Services for NetWare permits the Windows NT 4.0 Server to act as a NetWare 3.*x* Server and is able to process file and print requests from NetWare clients without changing or updating the NetWare client software. This Service Pack provides an update that allows Windows NT 4.0 to support NetWare's Client 32. This update installs only on those computers that have the FPNW service already installed.

Proquota.exe

Proquota.exe is a utility that can be set up to monitor the size of users' profiles. If an individual user's profile exceeds the predetermined file limit, the user won't be able to log off the computer until the user reduces the size of the file.

Remote WinSock (DNS/Port 53)

Proxies or firewalls will often disable the Domain Name System (DNS) port number 53 in order to deter external sites from querying the internal DNS structure. As a result, inbound response packets sent on port 53 can't be received. SP4 provides a solution to change the Windows NT DNS server port number and configure it to use a different port number when connecting outbound.

To enable this feature, a registry value "DWORD" is created. Locate \services\dns\parameters\SendOnNonDnsPort and set it to a nonzero value to go off port 53. If the value is < 1024, the server can use any port number. If the value is > 1024, the server will use the port number specified.

Remote Procedure Calls (RPC) Enhancements for Visual Basic (VB)

RPC enhancements for VB have been provided in this release. In VB, a "User Data Type (UDT)" is added allowing the TypeLib arrangement of structures. These new user interfaces, IRecordInfo, provide UDT information and a UDT field for the Access Database.

Routing Information Protocol (RIP) Listener

If you utilize RIP Listener on a computer running Windows NT 4.0, you can use SP4 to update this component. If you want to install RIP Listener after you apply SP4, use the following procedure.

STEPS:
To install the RIP Listener

Step 1. Insert the SP4 CD into the disc drive, and change the folder to \I386 (or \Alpha).

Step 2. Copy Oemnsvir.wks to D:\<winntsystemroot>\system32\oemnsvir.inf.

Step 3. Click Start, point to Settings, and click Control Panel. Double-click Network, and on the Services tab, click Add.

Step 4. In Network Service, select RIP for Internet Protocol, and then click OK.

Step 5. In the Windows NT Setup dialog box, type the path for the location of the SP4 files and click OK.

Visual Studio-MICS

This Service Pack includes an update to Visual Studio called Visual Studio Analyzer Events. Visual Studio Analyzer Events provides a graphical representation of high-level behaviors and their solutions. Use Visual Studio Analyzer Events to view graphically simple tables of event logs, the system's performance, and Windows NT Performance Monitor (NT PerfMon), as well as other system data.

Year 2000 (Y2K) Fixes

This Service Pack contains fixes for known Year 2000 issues for Windows NT 4.0, including these:

- The User Manager and User Manager for Domains recognize the year 2000 as a leap year.
- The Date/Time Control Panel applet can update the system clock.
- Find Files supports only numeric character recognition in the decades field.
- Word document properties recognize both 1900 and 2000 as valid centuries and support four-digit years.
- The Dynamic Host Configuration Protocol (DHCP) administrators program supports displaying the years between 2000–2009 with a minimum of two digits. For more information, see section 2.4, "Year 2000 Service Pack Installation."

Compaq Fiber Storage Driver

This driver and .Inf are located in the \Drvlib folder. When installed, the Compaq fiber storage driver along with the .Inf provides support for Compaq fiber storage devices. The certified devices are:

- Compaq Fiber Channel Host Controller/P for PCI
- Compaq Fiber Channel Host Controller/E for EISA

Internet Explorer 4.01 Service Pack 1

Internet Explorer 4.01 Service Pack 1 is located in SP4 in the \Msie401 folder. Run Ie4setup.exe to install this version of Internet Explorer on your computer.

Message Queue (MSMQ) for Windows 95 Client

This Service Pack also includes MSMQ Windows 95 Client fixes, located in the \Support\Msmq.95 folder. Most problems that are mentioned in section 3.10, "Message Queue (MSMQ) Notes," also apply to Windows 95. In addition, the Windows 95 MSMQ update fixes a problem causing long delays with MQOpenQueue() and MQIS operations on offline computers. This MSMQ Windows 95 update doesn't have an uninstall option.

Option Pack Fixes

This Service Pack release includes Option Pack fixes and enhancements. If you have the Internet Information Server version 4.0 Option Pack installed, the Service Pack 4 update program will automatically update the Option Pack components installed on your computer.

When beginning the installation of the Windows NT Option Pack 4.0 on a server with Windows NT SP 4.0 and Internet Information Server 3.0, the following message may appear:

"Setup detected that Windows NT 4.0 SP4 or greater is installed on your machine. We haven't tested this product on SP4. Do you wish to proceed?"

The Windows NT Option Pack 4.0 is fully tested and supported to run on servers with the Windows NT Service Pack 4.0. Click Yes to continue Setup.

It's recommended that you reinstall SP4 after you install Windows NT Option Pack 4.0. Otherwise, an MSMQ MQIS Controller installation won't work until the Windows NT Service Pack 4.0 is reinstalled.

Certificate Server

The Microsoft Certificate Server is a standards-based, highly customizable server application for managing the creation, issuance, and renewal of digital certificates. Certificate Server generates certificates in standard X.509 format. These certificates are used for a number of public-key security and authentication applications including, but not limited to, server and client authentication under the Secure Sockets Layer (SSL) protocol and secure e-mail using Secure/Multipurpose Internet Mail.

The update to Certificate Server includes:

- **Teletex encoding.** Data encoded as teletex in a certificate request will be encoded as teletex data in the certificate issued. Formerly, this data would have been encoded as Unicode in the certificate issued.

- **Serial number.** Serial numbers are generated according to X.509 standards. These serial numbers are automatically generated, unique, and always positive. This is to accommodate restrictive mail clients.

- **Backup/restore.** Specific backup requests are supported, including backing up keys and certificates.

- **An update to the default policy module** so that mail certificates issued are usable by Outlook 98.

- **An update to Certificate Server** to fix a problem with certificates issued on February 29 of a leap year. Previously, the validity period would have the NotBefore and NotAfter dates set to the same date. With this update, NotBefore and NotAfter are now set correctly in the context of the CA validity for certificates issued on February 29 of a leap year.

For information on how to use the keys and certificate backup/restore utility, go to the Knowledge Base at support.microsoft.com/support/ and search for KB article Q185195.

This release of Certificate Server doesn't support certificate hierarchies. However, a limited subset of the functions of certificate hierarchies work specifically with Exchange. You can get additional information on this from a white paper titled "Creating Certificate Hierarchies with Microsoft Certificate Server Version 1.0." This is available as a self-extracting .exe file (Hier3.exe) on the Microsoft Web site at support.microsoft.com/support/downloads/LNP279.asp.

Index Server

Index Server is a content indexing engine that provides full text retrieval for Web sites. Index Server requires that Internet Information Server be installed.

Internet Information Server (IIS)

The following Internet Information Server version 4.0 Option Pack components are installed on your computer:

1. **Security enhancements.** Support for long filenames for access restrictions on a file or a folder

2. **Performance.** Improvements on the logging and caching of information. These improvements include, but aren't limited to:

   - IIS 4.0 performance on extension mapping
   - IIS 4.0 memory performance for mapping log files
   - IIS 4.0 performance in mapping unmapped data files if memory configuration is low or stressed

Message Queue (MSMQ) for Windows NT

This update to MSMQ includes these features:

- Performs cleanup of unused message file space every six hours to reduce disk-space usage.

Note

This schedule may be configured via the <MessageCleanupInterval> MSMQ Registry key (in milliseconds).

- Clears all obsolete express message files when the MSMQ service starts.
- Enforces case insensitivity with foreign language characters in private queue names.
- Reduces occurrences of duplicate messages in persistent delivery mode.
- Exhibits performance counters for remote queues after a system recovery.

Appendix D: Details of Service Pack 4.0

- Correctly shows per-session outgoing messages performance counters.
- MSMQ MQIS servers refresh cached information every 12 hours.
- Fixes a problem causing transactional messages to be rejected in some cases.
- Allows specifying external certificates via the MSMQ ActiveX components interface.
- Transactional messages can be read from connector queues after restarting the MSMQ connector application.
- MQSetQueueSecurity for private queue is supported.
- MQCreateQueue for private queues now works on Windows NT Server 4.0 Option Pack installations on Microsoft Cluster Server computers.
- Supports sending Microsoft PowerPoint and Microsoft Word documents using ActiveX components.
- Fails when user attempts to renew internal certificates when the Primary Enterprise Controller (PEC) is unreachable.
- The machine quota limitation is correctly recomputed after restarting the MSMQ service.
- MSMQ COM objects correctly process asynchronous message arrival events in multithreaded applications.
- Detection and reporting is improved of corrupted message packets in message files that could have resulted in a hung MSMQ service previously.
- Transactional messages sent offline are no longer rejected with a bad message class: MQMSG_CLASS_NACK_BAD_DST_Q. The symptom was that such messages were immediately routed to the sender's exact dead letter queue.
- Supports sending messages to different computers that have the same IP address. This can happen when a server attempts to send messages to two different RAS clients that happen to be assigned the same address one after the other.
- Recovers correctly when sending messages from a server to a client whose address is no longer valid (such as a RAS client that has timed out). Previously, extra message traffic might have been generated.
- Asynchronous messaging now functions correctly on Japanese Windows 95 when using the MSMQ COM objects.
- Fixes a problem in the MSMQ COM objects when referencing the response and admin queue properties of a message for queues not explicitly refreshed from the MQIS.
- In Windows 95, calling MQOpenQueue with a DIRECT format no longer blocks for a long time.
- If the Windows NT 4.0 licensing service isn't running, then MSMQ per-seat licensing is no longer enforced.

- A specific call to MQLocateBegin no longer causes an exception on the MQIS server. This could have occurred previously when the Label restriction specified with an incorrect vt argument (anything other than VT_LPWSTR).

- MSMQ applications can be run by users logged onto local machine accounts. Note that this used to work anyway for shadowed local accounts — that is, for accounts that had "identical" local accounts (user name/password) on the server machine. The default security for queues created by such users is that everyone is granted full control (in particular, read and delete permissions).

- A new MQIS update/restore utility is supplied that enables administrators to seamlessly recover crashed MQIS servers. See support\msmq.nt\MQISwizard.doc for more information.

Microsoft Transaction Server (MTS)

MTS is updated with a new Java Context class. If you're building applications using Visual J++, you can use the new Context class instead of IObjectContext. The Context class allows you to do the following using Visual J++:

- Declare that the object's work is complete.

- Prevent a transaction from being processed, either temporarily or permanently.

- Instantiate other MTS objects and include their work within the scope of the current object's transaction.

- Determine whether a caller is in a particular role.

- Determine whether security is enabled.

- Determine whether the object is executing within a transaction.

See the Visual J++ section of the Programmer's Reference for complete documentation of the new class.

SMTP, NNTP

Simple Mail Transport Protocol (SMTP), Network News Transport Protocol (NNTP) enhancements are available in this Service Pack. SMTP now supports the following services:

- Multiple virtual servers, or sites

- ETRN command for dequeuing mail over dial-up connections

STEPS:
To enable this functionality

Step 1. Create a text file with the following text:
```
set obj = GetObject ( "IIS://localhost/smtpsvc" )
    obj.Put "SmtpServiceVersion", 2
    obj.SetInfo
```

Note

This is an Active Directory Service Interface (ADSI) script that will update a value in the metabase.

Step 2. Save this file as Enable.vbs.

Step 3. From a command prompt, type the following and press Enter:
```
cscript enable.vbs
```

For more information, go to the Knowledge Base at `support.microsoft.com/support/` and search for KB article Q183476. You can also point to specific KB articles using the following example: `support.microsoft.com/support/kb/articles/Q151/8/60.asp`.

Security Configuration Manager (SCM)

Security Configuration Manager (SCM) is an integrated security system that gives administrators the ability to define and apply security configurations for Windows NT Workstation and Windows NT Server installations. SCM also has the capability to perform inspections of the installed systems to locate any degradation in the system's security. For further information on SCM, including installation and usage instructions, refer to Readme.txt in the \Mssce folder.

Web-Based Enterprise Management (WBEM)

WBEM/WMI is Microsoft's implementation of Web-Based Enterprise Management (WBEM), the new standard for representation of management information as supported by the Desktop Management Task Force. It surfaces important management data from Windows NT and makes it freely available to any management tool through a number of well-defined interfaces so that management of Windows NT becomes much easier (included on CD-ROM only). For more information on WMI, see `www.microsoft.com/management/wbem`.

WBEM consolidates and unifies the data provided by existing management technologies. WBEM focuses on solving real enterprise issues by tracking problem areas from the user/application level through the systems and network layers to remote service/server instances. For more information, see `wbem.freerange.com/`.

You can download the Web-Based Enterprise Management Software Developer's Kit (SDK) at `msdn.microsoft.com/developer/sdk/wbemsdk/default.htm`.

Microsoft Windows NT Server NetShow Services

SP4 contains an updated version of NetShow Services, located on this CD in the \NetShow folder. NetShow Services enables Internet service providers (ISPs) and organizations to deliver the highest-quality audio and video at every bandwidth across the Internet or enterprise networks.

This release of NetShow Services features greatly enhanced audio and video that delivers the best user experience. Simplified setup, configuration, and administration of the NetShow server components and tools give ISPs a reliable and cost-effective platform for hosting large amounts of content.

Consult the NetShow Services information page (\NetShow\ntsp4-ns.htm) for details on installing and configuring this product. Before installing this product, you should also carefully review the NetShow Services release notes at \NetShow\ns-readme.htm.

Microsoft Windows Media Player

Microsoft Windows Media Player replaces Microsoft ActiveMovie as well as the Microsoft NetShow Player. Windows Media Player has all the features found in both of the other multimedia players, plus many more. It also upgrades existing Windows Media Player and ActiveMovie support to provide convenient access to new Windows Media content. Windows Media Player supports most local and streaming multimedia file types including WAV, AVI, QuickTime, RealAudio 4.0, and RealVideo 4.0. The new player takes over the class IDs of the previous players. After you install the new player, programs that used the old class IDs will function as usual. Windows Media Player is located in the \Mplayer2 folder on the compact disc.

Security Privilege Must Be Enabled to View Security Event Log

SP4 includes a bug fix in the Event Log service that requires that the SE_SECURITY_NAME privilege, also known as the Security privilege, be enabled in order to view and manage the security event log. By default, Windows NT grants the privilege to administrators and the local System. In order to take effect however, the privilege must also be enabled in the program accessing the security event log.

Prior to this change, members of the Administrators group and services running as local System could open the security log for read or change access without enabling the Security privilege. If the privilege was removed from the Administrators group, members of the Administrators group could still manage the security log. This change enforces the security model that administrators need to be granted the privilege to manage the security log; they won't be able to manage the log simply because they are members of the Administrators group. Administrators can always grant themselves the Security privilege to manage the security log, however, although this event can be audited.

For more information, consult the Knowledge Base at `support.microsoft.com/support/` and search for KB article Q188855.

Dynamic Host Configuration Protocol (DHCP)

This Service Pack includes several quality improvement fixes to correct known Dynamic Host Configuration Protocol (DHCP) issues reported for Microsoft DHCP Server, the DHCP Manager administration tool, and for Microsoft DHCP-enabled clients running under earlier released versions of Windows NT 4.0.

These fixes address specific problems fully described in article Q184693, "DHCP/WINS Release Notes for Windows NT 4.0 SP4 Update," in the Knowledge Base.

You can obtain the specific article from Microsoft Support Online at `support.microsoft.com/support`.

Windows Internet Naming Service (WINS)

Windows NT Server includes the following new Windows Internet Naming Service (WINS) and WINS Manager features:

- Manual removal of dynamic WINS database records
- Multiselect operations for WINS database records
- Burst mode handling for WINS servers

Microsoft Routing and Remote Access Service (RRAS)

SP4 can now be installed on a Windows NT 4.0 system running Routing and Remote Access Service (RRAS). SP4 will update your RRAS system to RRAS Hotfix 3.0 components automatically. If you install RRAS after installing SP4, you must reinstall SP4 to get the updated RRAS files to ensure RRAS will work properly. For more information on RRAS Hotfix 3.0, see `support.microsoft.com/support/kb/articles/Q189/5/94.asp`.

PPTP Performance and Security Update

SP4 now includes new performance and security updates to PPTP that greatly increase data transfer speeds and enhance security. The PPTP client and server system must both be running the updated files to get the new benefits. For more information, see `support.microsoft.com/support/kb/articles/q189/5/95.asp`.

NTLM v2 Security

SP4 contains an enhancement to NTLM security protocols called NTLM v2, which significantly improves both the authentication and session security mechanisms of NTLM. For more information, see `support.microsoft.com/support/kb/articles/q147/7/06.asp`.

Secure Channel Enhancements

SP4 contains an enhancement to the secure channel protocols used by member workstations and servers to communicate with their domain controllers and by domain controllers to communicate with other domain controllers. In addition to authentication, you can now encrypt and check the integrity of these communications. For more information, see `support.microsoft.com/support/kb/articles/q183/8/59.asp`.

IP Helper API (IPHLPAPI)

The IP Helper API provides Windows network configuration and statistics information to Win32 applications. The public API is available on Windows NT 4.0 and above, and Windows 95 and above. SP4 updates the API with a new .dll so that applications can communicate to a TCP/IP stack.

Event Log Service

This Service Pack contains new features in the Event Log Service to assist how administrators measure the reliability and availability of Windows NT.

The SP4 Event Log Service records three new events in the system event log that are useful in measuring operating system availability:

- Clean Shutdown Event (Event ID: 6006)
- Dirty Shutdown Event (Event ID: 6008)
- System Version Event (Event ID: 6009)

Domain Name Server (DNS) Service

This Service Pack includes several quality improvement fixes to correct known Domain Name Server (DNS) issues reported for Microsoft DNS Server and the DNS Manager administration tool. These fixes address specific problems described in the Q184693, "DNS/DHCP/WINS Release Notes for Windows NT 4.0 SP4 Update." This article is available via Microsoft TechNet.

Appendix E
About the CD-ROM

CD-ROM Contents

The CD-ROM included with this book contains the following materials:

- Adobe Acrobat Reader
- An electronic version of this book, *Microsoft Windows NT Secrets, Option Pack Edition,* in .pdf format
- European Centere for NT Development's WAIS, Gopher, HTTP software
- Executive Software's Diskeeper Lite 4.0
- Executive Software's UnDelete for NT
- HotFix Control
- PingPlotter
- Remote Task Manager
- WinZip 7.0
- Microsoft Windows NT Server 4.0 (120-day evaluation edition)
- Microsoft Windows NT 4.0 Option Pack
- Microsoft Windows NT Service Pack 4

Installing and Using Items on the CD-ROM

The following sections describe each product and include detailed instructions for installation and use.

The Adobe Acrobat Reader Version of NT Secrets, Option Pack Edition

Adobe's Acrobat Reader is a helpful program that will enable you to view the electronic version of this book in the same page format as the actual book.

To install and run Adobe's Acrobat Reader and view the electronic version of this book, follow these steps:

1. Start Windows Explorer (if you're using Windows 95/98) or Windows NT Explorer (if you're using Windows NT), and then open the `Acrobat` folder on the CD-ROM.

2. In the `Acrobat` folder, double-click `ar32e30.exe` and follow the instructions presented onscreen for installing Adobe Acrobat Reader.

3. To view the electronic version of this book after you have installed Adobe's Acrobat Reader, start Windows Explorer (if you're using Windows 95) or Windows NT Explorer (if you're using Windows NT), and then open the `NTSecrets PDF` folder on the CD-ROM.

4. In the `NTSecrets PDF` folder, double-click the chapter or appendix file you want to view. All documents in this folder end with a `.pdf` extension.

European Centere for NT Development's Wais, Gopher, Http

The European Centere for NT Development's Wais, Gopher and Http software applications represent an alternative to Microsoft Internet Information Server.

To install and run Wais, follow these steps:

1. Log into your Windows NT system.

2. Copy the `\European Centere for NT Development\Wais\ti386` (for Intel-based processors) or `\European Centere for NT Development\Wais\talpha` (for DEC Alpha-based processors) folder on the CD-ROM to your machine's hard disk.

3. You should have the following files:

    ```
    WAISINDX.EXE    The WAISINDEX program.
    WAISLOOK.EXE    The searching program.
    WAISSERV.EXE    The Z39.50 searching program.
    WAISTOOL.DOC    This manual in Word for Windows format.
    WAISTOOL.WRI    This manual in Windows Write format.
    WAISTOOL.PS     This manual, in postscript ready for printing.
    READ.ME         Summary of new features, etc.
    ```

4. If you have installed a previous version of the toolkit, remove it by deleting the old files, or by moving them to another directory (off the PATH) for deletion once you have validated that the new version works correctly.

5. Decide which directory you are going to put the tools in, and move the .EXE programs there. Ensure that the directory is on the PATH so that the commands may be executed from the command line. If you plan to use the WAIS Toolkit with the WAIS, Gopher or HTTP servers, you should put the .EXE programs into the `\WINNT\SYSTEM32` directory do that the servers can find them.

Appendix E: About the CD-ROM

6. If you are using NTFS for the volume on which the tools are stored, you should rename the `WAISINDX.EXE` program to `WAISINDEX.EXE`. (It is not distributed with that name, because of problems when extracting the file to a FAT volume.) The remainder of this manual assumes you have done this.

7. Determine which version of the toolkit you have. To do this, at the Windows NT Command Prompt, type the commands:

   ```
   waisindex -v
   waislook -v
   waisserv -v
   ```

   and the version number for each program will be displayed. (In fact, two version numbers will be shown for `WAISINDEX` and `WAISSERV` - the first refers to the version of the freeWAIS code from which the programs were ported, the second is the number of the Windows NT version.) These instructions cover WAIS code version 7.0. If the programs report a later version number, you will find a corresponding later manual in the files you unpacked from the ZIP archive.

To install and run Gopher, follow these steps:

1. Log into your Windows NT system as a user with administrative privileges.

2. The Gopher Server is distributed in three versions, for the Intel, MIPS and DEC Alpha architectures. Select the appropriate folder for your processor from the `\European Centere for NT Development\Gopher` folder on the CD-ROM. The folder choices are alpha, i386 and mips.

3. Unzip the file. You should have the following files:

   ```
   GOPHERS.EXE     The Gopher Server itself.
   GOPHERS.CPL     The Control Panel applet.
   GOPHERS.HLP     The Control Panel applet help file.
   GOPHERS.DOC     This manual in Word for Windows format.
   GOPHERS.WRI     This manual in Windows Write format.
   GOPHERS.PS      This manual, in postscript ready for printing.
   COPYRITE.TXT    The copyright statement for this product.
   READ.ME         Summary of new features, etc.
   ```

4. Decide which directory you are going to put `GOPHERS.EXE` in, and move it there. A good choice is the `\WINNT\SYSTEM32` directory, which is where many other services live. Using the SecurityPermissions menu option in the File Manager, ensure that the SYSTEM user has read permission for the file.

5. Move `GOPHERS.CPL` and `GOPHERS.HLP` to the `\WINNT\SYSTEM32` directory. Start the Control Panel from the Program Manager to verify that the Gopher Server applet is represented as an icon in the Control Panel.

6. Determine which version of gophers you have. To do this, at the Windows NT Command Prompt, type:

   ```
   gophers -version
   ```

   and the version number will be displayed. (If the program reports a later version number, you will find a corresponding later manual in the files you unpacked from the ZIP archive.) You should also check the IP address of your machine using the command:

   ```
   gophers -ipaddress
   ```

   This will display the name of your machine (*eg* emwac.ed.ac.uk) and its IP address(es) as reported by the Windows Sockets API. If this information is incorrect, you need to reconfigure the TCP/IP software on your machine. The Gopher Server will not work if this address (or list of addresses if your machine has more than one network interface) is wrong.

7. If you have installed a previous version of the Gopher Server, you must remove it by typing:

   ```
   gophers -remove
   ```

   See section 2.4 for further information. You can use either the old or the new version of GOPHERS.EXE to perform this remove operation. Note that this will delete your existing Gopher Server configuration information from the Registry.

Caution

If you are replacing version 0.7 or earlier with version 0.8 or later, read the note at the end of this section.

8. Install gophers into the table of Windows NT Services (and simultaneously register it with the Event Logger) by running the program from the Windows NT command line, specifying the -install flag. (Note: It is vital that you execute this command using the copy of GOPHERS.EXE which you placed in the \WINNT\SYSTEM32 directory, and not using some other copy which you plan subsequently to delete.) For instance:

   ```
   gophers -install
   ```

   The program will register itself and its location with the Service Manager and with the Event Logger, and will report success or failure. In the case of failure, see the section on Installation Problems below.

9. To verify that the installation has succeeded, start the Windows NT Control Panel and double-click on the Services icon. The resulting dialog should list Gopher Server as one of the installed services. If so, see the Configuration section for further instructions.

10. If you plan to use the WAIS index searching capabilities of the Gopher Server, you should obtain and install the WAIS toolkit for Windows NT, available from the same place you obtained this software. Ensure that you place the WAISLOOK program in a directory where the Gopher Server can find it - \WINNT\SYSTEM32 is a good choice.

To install and run Http, follow these steps:

1. Log into your Windows NT system as a user with administrative privileges.

2. The HTTP Server is distributed in four versions, for the Intel, MIPS, Power PC and DEC Alpha architectures. Select the appropriate folder for your processor from the \European Centere for NT Development\ Gopher folder on the CD-ROM. The folder choices are alpha, i386 and mips.

3. Unzip the file. You should have the following files:

   ```
   HTTPS.EXE      The HTTP Server itself.
   HTTPS.CPL      The Control Panel applet.
   HTTPS.HLP      The Control Panel applet help file.
   HTTPS.DOC      This manual in Word for Windows format.
   HTTPS.PS       This manual, in postscript ready for printing.
   HTTPS.WRI      This manual in Windows Write format.
   EGSCRIPT.ZIP   Sample CGI script programs.
   COPYRITE.TXT   The copyright statement for the software.
   READ.ME        Summary of new features, etc.
   ```

4. Decide which directory you are going to put HTTPS.EXE in, and move it there. A good choice is the \WINNT\SYSTEM32 directory, which is where many other services live. Using the SecurityPermissions menu option in the File Manager, verify that the SYSTEM user has read permission for the file.

5. Move HTTPS.CPL and HTTPS.HLP to the \WINNT\SYSTEM32 directory. Start the Control Panel from the Program Manager to verify that the HTTP Server applet is represented as an icon in the Control Panel.

6. Determine which version of https you have. To do this, at the Windows NT Command Prompt, type:

   ```
   https -version
   ```

   and the version number will be displayed. (If the program reports a later version number, you will find a corresponding later manual in the files you unpacked from the ZIP archive.) You should also check the IP address of your machine using the command:

   ```
   https -ipaddress
   ```

   This will display the name of your machine (for example, emwac.ed.ac.uk) and its IP address(es) as reported by the Windows Sockets API. If this information is incorrect, you need to reconfigure the TCP/IP software on your machine. The HTTP Server will not work if this address (or list of addresses if your machine has more than one network interface) is wrong.

7. If you have installed a previous version of the HTTP Server, you must remove it by typing:

   ```
   https -remove
   ```

See section 2.4 for further information. You can use either the old or the new version of HTTPS.EXE to perform this remove operation.

Caution

If you are replacing version 0.7 or earlier with version 0.8 or later, read the note at the end of this section.

8. Install https into the table of Windows NT Services (and simultaneously register it with the Event Logger) by running the program from the Windows NT command line, specifying the -install flag. (Note: It is vital that you execute this command using the copy of HTTPS.EXE which you placed in the \WINNT\SYSTEM32 directory, and not using some other copy which you plan subsequently to delete.) For instance:

```
https -install
```

The program will register itself with the Service Manager and with the Event Logger, and will report success or failure. In the case of failure, see the section on Installation Problems below.

9. To verify that the installation has succeeded, start the Windows NT Control Panel and double-click on the Services icon. The resulting dialog should list HTTP Server as one of the installed services. If so, see the Configuration section of this manual for further instructions.

Executive Software's Diskeeper Lite 4.0

Executive Software's Diskeeper Lite 4.0 is a hard disk defragmentation program. Hard disk defragmentation is not a feature natively supported in Microsoft Windows NT Server 4.0.

To install and run Diskeeper Lite 4.0, follow these steps:

1. Log into your Windows NT system as a user with administrative privileges.

2. Copy the us_dksrtr_i.exe program from the CD-ROM's \Executive Software\DiskKeeper Lite 4.0 folder to your computer's hard disk.

   Double-click the us_dksrtr_i.exe file you just copied to launch the installation wizard.

   Click Finish on the Diskeeper Trailware – Welcome dialog box. Complete the remaining setup steps.

Executive Software's UnDelete for NT

Executive Software's UnDelete for NT is an undelete utility for Microsoft Windows NT Server. The undelete feature is not natively supported by Microsoft Windows NT Server.

To install and access the Executive Software's UnDelete for NT, follow these steps:

1. Log into your Windows NT system as a user with administrative privileges.
2. Double-click the `Setup.exe` file in the `\Executive Software\UnDelete` folder on your CD-ROM.

   Click Next in the setup wizard's Welcome dialog box. Complete the remaining setup steps.

   After completing the installation, reboot you machine.

HotFix Control

HotFix Control is an application that allows you to track which hot fixes and service packs have been applied to a Windows NT Server machine. This functionality is not natively provided by Microsoft Windows NT Server 4.0.

To install HotFix Control, follow these steps:

1. Log into your Windows NT system as a user with administrative privileges.
2. Copy the contents of the `\HotFix Control` folder on the CD-ROM to a folder on your hard disk.

   Double-click the `hotfxctl.exe` file to run HotFix Control.

PingPlotter

PingPlotter is an application that traces packet paths across the LAN, WANs by identifying each hop taken by the packet. It is also useful for maintain WAN connections by periodically sending out packets via the Ping command.

To install PingPlotter, follow these steps:

1. Log into your Windows NT system as a user with administrative privileges.
2. Copy the `pngplt_2.exe` file from the `\Ping Plotter` folder on the CD-ROM to your hard disk.
3. Double-click the `pngplt_2.exe` file.
4. Complete the steps in the setup wizard.

Remote Task Manager

Remote Task Manager (RTM) is an easy to use tool that allows you to manage tasks, processes and services on remote computers. It is similar to Task Manager with remote control functionality added.

To install Remote Task Manager, follow these steps:

1. Log into your Windows NT system as a user with administrative privileges.
2. Double-click the `rtm.exe` file in the `\Remote Task Manager` folder on your CD-ROM.
3. Complete the steps in the setup wizard.

WinZip 7.0

WinZip 7.0, by Nico Mak Computing, Inc., is a popular file/folder ompression and decompression application. It is typically used to transfer large files as e-mail attachments or on a floppy disk.

To install WinZip 7.0, follow these steps:

1. Log into your Windows NT system as a user with administrative privileges.
2. Double-click the `winzip70.exe` file in the `\WinZip 7.0` folder on your CD-ROM.
3. Complete the steps in the setup wizard.

Microsoft Windows NT Server 4.0 (120-day Evaluation Edition)

Windows NT Server 4.0 is an operating system intended for use in networked environments. It is more fully described in Chapter 17, "Regular Windows NT Server" of this book. An evaluation edition of Windows NT Server 4.0 is included with this book for your benefit.

Basic Windows NT Server 4.0 installation requirements include:

- 32-bit x86-based microprocessor (such as Intel 80486/25 or higher), Intel Pentium, or supported RISC-based microprocessor such as the MIPS R4x00, Digital Alpha Systems, or PowerPC
- VGA, or higher resolution, monitor
- One or more hard disks, with 124MB minimum free disk space on the partition that will contain the Windows NT Server system files (158MB minimum for RISC-based computers)

- For x86-based computers, a high density 3.5-inch disk drive plus a CD-ROM drive (for computers with only a 5.25-inch drive, you can only install Windows NT Server over the network)
- For any computer not installing over a network, a CD-ROM drive
- Memory: 12MB RAM minimum for x86-based systems; 16MB recommended, 16MB RAM minimum for RISC-based systems

Optional components include:

- Mouse or other pointing device
- One or more network adapter cards, if you want to use Windows NT Server with a network
- Windows NT Server supports computers with up to four microprocessors. Support for additional microprocessors is available from your computer manufacturer.

To install Windows NT Server 4.0, follow these steps:

1. From your existing operating system environment (e.g., Windows 98), run the following command (assuming your CD-ROM drive is D:) from the Run dialog box (accessed via the Start menu): d:\i386\winnt.exe /ox

   This command will run the winnt.exe program from the i386 directory contained on the CD-ROM included with this book. The /ox switch will create the Windows NT Server 4.0 setup floppy disks (you will need three blank floppy diskettes).

2. After the three Windows NT Server 4.0 setup diskettes have been created, place setup disk #1 in drive A: and reboot the computer.

3. Complete the installation of Windows NT Server according to the steps presented in Chapter 2, "Planning, Setup, and Installation" of this book.

Microsoft Windows NT Server 4.0 Option Pack

The Option Pack greatly extends the reach of Windows NT Server 4.0 by providing additional features and functionality. These additions include:

- Internet Information Server (IIS) 4.0
- Microsoft Transaction Server (MTS) 2.0
- Index Server 2.0
- Certificate Server 1.0
- Data Access Components 1.5
- Site Server Express 2.0

- Microsoft Message Queue (MSMQ) 1.0
- Internet Connections Services for RAS 1.0
- Windows Scripting Host
- Microsoft Management Console (MMC) 1.0

To install the Option Pack, complete the following steps:

1. Verify that you have installed Service Pack 4. Option Pack requires at least Service Pack 3, but for best performance, install Service Pack 4 prior to installing the Option Pack. To verify which Service Pack is installed on your Windows NT Server, select the Run command from the Start menu and type **winmsd**. The Windows NT Diagnostics application will launch. View the text on the General tab sheet and observe which Service Pack is installed.

2. Using the Run command from the Start menu, run setup.exe from the \Option Pack folder on the CD-ROM that accompanies this book.

3. Complete the Option Pack setup based on the steps discussed in Chapter 13, "Windows NT Server Option Pack" of this book.

Microsoft Windows NT Server Service Pack 4

Service Pack 4 provides both bug fixes and additional features for Windows NT Server 4.0. It is discussed at length in Chapters 14, 15, and 16 of this book.

To install Service Pack 4, follow these steps:

1. From the Run command accessed from the Start menu, select update.exe from the SP4 folder on the CD-ROM that accompanies this book.

2. Complete the installation of Service Pack by electing whether or not to create an uninstall directory.

3. Reboot after the installation of Service Pack 4.

Index

Numbers
100MB PCI cards, hidden cost concerns, 18
32-bit NOS (network operating system), described, 600

A
Access Through Share Permissions dialog box, share permissions, 75
account policies, SCE (Security Configuration Editor), 565–566
accounts
  local versus global groups, 62
  renaming uses, 59
  templates, 58
Acknowledgement Number field, TCP/IP packet element, 134
Active desktop, Windows 2000 Server, 970
Active Directory, Windows 2000 Server, 983–984
Active Leases dialog box, client lease information, 315
adapter cards
  drivers, 810
  TCP/IP configuration, 914–915
Add DHCP Server to Server List dialog box, DHCP, DHCP server connection, 303
Add Printer Wizard
  described, 393
  local port printer connection, 64
  printer installation/sharing options, 66–68
Add Reserved Clients dialog box, client reservations, 317
Add to Chart dialog box, Explain button uses, 763
Add User Accounts wizard, described, 392
Add/Remove dialog box, Windows NT 4.0 Option Pack, 453
Add/Remove Programs Wizard, described, 393
address caching, ARP, 224
Address Database
  computer names, 828, 831
  edit address information, 828, 831
addresses, Network Monitor, 818–819
Adkins Resources, Hyena program, 393–394
Administration tool, Terminal Server, 643–644
Administrative Wizards, described, 392–393
administrator accounts
  delegating, 59
  setup guidelines, 56
administrators
  password conventions, 33
  run Identify Network Monitor Users menu selection, 827
  subnetting, 334
  technology committee members, 443
Admission Control Services
  ATM, 982–983
  benefits, 975–976
  practical applications, 976
  QoS host architecture, 977
  quality of service, 973–974
  relating QoS, 978–979
  RFCs, 981–982
  routers, 981
  specifics, 979–981
  Windows 2000 Server, 973–982
  Windows QoS program, 976–977
ADO (ActiveX Data Objects) 1.5, described, 530
Advanced IP Addressing dialog box, TCP/IP configuration, 182–183
Advanced IP Addressing property sheet, multiple gateways, 157–161
Agent dialog box, SNMP agent configuration, 203–204
Alert view
  paging configuration, 770
  Performance Monitor, 763, 768–774
alerts, real-time, 667
algorithms, encryption, 536
Alpha processors, Service Pack 3 support, 536
analog telephone, MCSE toolkit component, 398
AND operator, capture filter, 825–826

1074 Index

annual planning retreat, described, 446
annual server activities, disaster recovery drill, 435–436
antivirus software, testing, 406
application layer, DOD model versus OSI model, 112–113
application performance option, Performance tab sheet, 892
application servers
  Performance Monitor environment system performance, 797
  Windows 2000 Server, 968
application services, build 1381 version issues, 606–607
Applications tab sheet, Task Manager, 854–855
applications view, Task Manager, 857
applications
  day-to-day administration tasks, 413–415
  legacy issues, 37
  removing, 438
  upgrading, 438
  Windows NT 4.0 Option Pack Internet components, 455–506
ARC naming conventions, described, 51
archives, backups, 438–439
ARCServe program, described, 90
area codes, changing, 918
ARP (Address Resolution Protocol)
  address caching, 224
  broadcasting, 224–225
  described, 119–121
  MAC address to IP address resolution, 124
  Microsoft, 226
  physical address, 223
  related problems, 225–226
  TCP/IP troubleshooting tools, 223–226
ARPANET, TCP/IP development history, 108
ArpCacheLife, TCP/IP values, 128
artificial intelligence option, Network Monitor, 833–834
as-built drawing, physical site planning, 12–13
ASF (Advanced Streaming Format) files, NetShow Services 3.0, 575
asynchronous messaging, described, 523–524
ATM (Asynchronous Transfer Mode), Admission Control Services, 982–983
ATTRIB command, changing file attributes, 47
attributes
  events, 412–413
  read-only, 47
auditing, monthly server activities, 426–427

B

BackOffice Query window, 838
Backup Exec program
  described, 89
  virus detection routine, 729
backup logs, day-to-day administration task, 405
backups
  archive creation, 438–439
  Cheyenne ARCServe program, 90
  day-to-day administration tasks, 404–405
  described, 85–86
  Exchange Server issues, 663
  IBM ADSTAR Distributed Storage Manager, 90
  IIS, 467–469
  NTBACKUP program, 86–89, 404
  off-site storage, 90–91
  scheduling, 404
  Seagate Software BackupExec program, 89
  strategies, 86–91
  test restores, 405
  timed, 87–89
Badmail directory, SMTP, 476
bandwidth
  multilink modems, 351
  NetShow Services 3.0, 575–576
bandwidth control, 966, 973–982
bandwidth throttling, IIS settings, 459–460
baselines
  additional data collection methods, 779
  creating, 779–780
  data collection creation, 776
  object capturing guidelines, 777–779
  when to create, 779–780
baselining, described, 428
BDC (Backup Domain Controller)
  administrator password issues, 33
  described, 29–30
benchmarks, performance, 757–758
benefits, Admission Control Services, 975–976
Berkeley Sockets Interface, TCP/IP support, 108–109
beta-testing, service packs, 535
binary bit values, decimal values, 337
bindings, DHCP, 299

BIOS monitoring, system tab sheet, 878
BIOS, updating, 878
blue screen (text-based) setup stage, described, 34–38
Boeing fix, computer naming conventions, 31
books
  keep older versions, 957
  networking analysis resource, 842–843
  troubleshooting resource, 957–958
boot disk
  creating, 944
  tart NT, 943–944
boot files
  copying to the boot partition, 50–51
  described, 269
  viewing, 925
  Windows NT Server, 943
Boot Loader phase
  Last Known Good Configuration option, 929–930
  NTDETECT, 928
  NTLDR, 928
  operating system selection, 928
  post-hardware detection/configuration selection, 928–932
  start values, 931
boot partition
  advantages, 37
  boot.ini file editing, 50–51
  copying boot files to, 50–51
  creating, 48–51
  FAT formatting process, 49–50
boot process, described, 49
BOOT.INI file
  boot partition component, 37
  boot partition number editing, 50–51
  boot processing, 49
  editing, 893, 925
  OS startup delay shortening, 46–48
  read-only attribute, 47
bootable floppy disks, MCSE toolkit component, 397–398
BootExecute data item, Kernel, 936
booting
  Boot Loader phase, 928–933
  Initial phase, 927
  Kernel phase, 933–938
  Logon phase, 938–939
  MS-DOS system disk, 927
  Win32, 937–938
BOOTP (Bootstrap protocol)
  DHCP development history, 289
  DHCP similarities, 195
BOOTSECT.DOS file
  boot partition component, 37
  dual-boot system setup, 44
BPOA (BackOffice Professional Association), troubleshooting resource, 960
breeder networks, described, 137
broadcasting, ARP, 224–225
browsers, Internet Explorer, 380–383
BSC (backup site controller), MSMQ, 525
buffers, Capture size, 815
bug fixes, importance of, 549
build 1381 version
  compatibility issues, 604
  described, 602–603
  features, 602–607
  performance issues, 603–604
  reliability, 603
  scalability issues, 604
  security issues, 604–605
  services, 606–607
  server versus workstations, 607–612
Business Resources Kit and Sales Training Interactive CD, CD-ROM library, 396

C

CA (certificate authority), described, 486
cable testers, network bottleneck detection, 750
cables, external modems, 398
cabling
  physical site planning/testing, 12
  planning guidelines, 22
cache files, described, 268
Cache:Data Map Hits% counter, Performance Monitor, 782
caching
  name resolution element, 272
  Proxy Server 1.0/2.0, 666
caching-only servers, described, 270
CAL (Client Access Licenses), purchasing guidelines, 31
calculator
  bin radio button, 345
  decimal and binary bit conversions, 343–344
  scientific view, 343
capture buffer
  ongoing network monitoring, 813
  size in Network Monitor, 815

Capture Buffer Setting dialog box, 815–816
capture filter
   address pairs, 824
   addresses, 818–819
   AND operator, 825–826
   data pattern, 820
   Network Monitor, 816–817
   protocols, 817–818
   traffic details, 819
   versus display, filter, 824–826
Capture Filter dialog box, Network Monitor, 816–817
capture session, save frequently, 826
capture trigger, Network Monitor, 813–814
Capture Viewer window, Summary pane, Description column, 833–834
Capture window
   Graph pane, 808
   Session Statistics pane, 808–809
   Station statistics, 808
   Total Statistics pane, 808
CATALOG.WCI file, Index Server 2.0, 494
catalogs
   Data Comm Warehouse, 398
   PC Zone, 398
   Report Writer, 519
CD-ROM library, MCSE toolkit components, 395–397
centering, Performance Monitor, 764–766
central tendency, quantitative analysis method, 739–741
Certificate Server 1.0
   CA (certificate authority) request, 486
   digital certificate creation process, 485–492
   enrollment, 489–492
   hotfixes, 552–553
   Key Manager, 486–488
   Web-based module administration, 492–494
certification exam, TCP/IP, 345
Chameleon UNIX Link97 program, TCP/IP protocol support, 139
change and configuration management, Windows 2000 Server, 984–985
CHAP (Challenge Handshake Authentication Protocol), Index Server 2.0, 506
Character Generator, TCP/IP support, 125
charge per hour, troubleshooting, 912
chart scaling, Performance Monitor, 766–767
Chart view, Performance Monitor, 763, 767–768
charts
   adding counters to, 763
   Performance Monitor clutter avoidance, 801–802
   scaling with Performance Monitor, 766–767
Checksum field, TCP/IP packet element, 135
Cheyenne
   ARCServe program, 90
   InocuLAN for Windows NT program, 93–94
chip extractor, MCSE toolkit component, 394
Citrix
   MetaFrame, 641–642
   Terminal Server development history, 629–631
Class A network, IP address assignment, 151
Class B network, IP address assignment, 152
Class C network, IP address assignment, 152
clear-text passwords, 215
client connections, servers versus workstations, 610–611
Client Creator tool, Terminal Server, 643
client leases, DHCP Manager, 314–316
client PC, logon script time settings, 83
Client Properties dialog box, client lease information, 316
client reservations, DHCP Manager, 316–318
clients
   DHCP, 288–289
   Media Player, 575
   MSMQ, 525
   Small Business Server installation process, 716–719
   Terminal Server, 636–638
   WINS, 321
   WINS configuration, 326–327
clones, versus name brand system components, 20–21
clothing, MCSE toolkit component, 399
clustering/routing support, Windows 2000 Server, 973
clustering, servers versus workstations, 610
CMAK (Connection Manager Administration Kit), Index Server 2.0, 498–500
CMAK Wizard, described, 498–500
CNs (connected networks), MSMQ, 525
code, subnetting, 336
cold-reboot, TCP/IP troubleshooting, 213
colors, used in network analysis, 832
COM (Component Object Model), snap-ins support, 506
COM ports, Small Business Server client configuration, 677–678

Index **1077**

command line
  disk counter activation, 778–779
  launching Performance Monitor from, 762
  MONITOR.EXE switches, 772
  net config workstation command, 318
  SCE configuration/analysis parameters, 573–574
  WINNT.EXE options, 42
  WINNT32.EXE options, 42
command line switches
  /?, ping command, 219
  IPConfig, 217
commands
  ATTRIB, 47
  DHCP server command line, 300
  EXPAND, 940–942
  Find All Names, 828
  FTP session, 232–233
  ipconfig /all, 829
  MMC (Microsoft Management Console), 455
  net confide workstation, 318
  NET TIME, 83
  netstat 229–231
  PERFMON, 762
  Policies⇨Trust Relationships, 60
  RDISK, 947
  redirecting, 216
  ROUTE ADD, 155–157
  TCP/IP connectivity, 215
  TCP/IP diagnostic, 215
  TFTP, 234–235
  Tools⇨Format, 50
  Tools⇨Map Network Drive, 69
  User⇨New User, 54
  View⇨Options, 50
  whois, 214–215, 236–237
  winipcfg, 219
  WINMSD, 877
  XCOPY, 45
commit charge, performance view, 860
communication servers, Windows 2000 Server, 969
communication services, build 1381 version issues, 607
communications, Exchange Server functionality improvements, 658
Compaq Fiber Storage Driver, SP4, 592
Compaq Systems Reference Library version 2.x, MCSE toolkit component, 395
compatibility, build 1381 version issues, 604
complete trust domain trust model, described, 61

components
  network system, 14–23
  Option Pack and Service Pack 4, 7
  Terminal Server, 635–638
  Windows NT 4.0 Option Pack selection process, 453–454
Computer Associates, Inoculan for Small Business Server, 729
Computer User newspaper, MCSE toolkit component, 398
computers
  naming conventions, 30–31, 254, 828–829
  Small Business Server setup, 709–716
concepts, TCP/IP, 346
CONFIG.SYS file, WinMSD, 876
Configure Network Monitoring Agent dialog box, passwords, 826
Configure Port Usage dialog box, dial-out configuration, 351
Configure Server
  multicast file transfers, 583–584
  NetShow Services 3.0, 578–587
  server properties, 584–587
  Unicast On-Demand Wizard, 581
  unicast publishing points, 579–582
Connection Configuration tool, Terminal Server, 643
connections, dial-up, 349–370
consultants, planning guidelines, 22
Content Analyzer, Site Server Express 2.0 WebMap views, 510–513
Control Panel, changes made in Windows 2000 Server, 970
controllers
  IDE (Integrated Drive Electronics), 28
  pre-setup information gathering, 28
  SCSI (Small Computer System Interface), 28
  setup detection process/decisions, 35–36
CONVERT.EXE utility
  FAT/NTFS conversion issues, 32
  setup partition decisions, 37
converting image names to real names, processes view, 871–874
correlation analysis, quantitative analysis method, 741–742
cost-effective, TCP/IP troubleshooting 211
counters
  adding to charts, 763
  application server, 798
  Cache: Data Map Hits%, 782
  file servers, 797
  Logical Disk:Avg.Disk Queue Length, 782

continued

counters *(continued)*
   LogicalDisk:% Disk Time, 792
   LogicalDisk:Avg. Disk Bytes/Transfer, 793
   LogicalDisk:Disk Bytes/sec, 793
   LogicalDisk:Disk Queue Length, 793
   Memory:Available Bytes, 787
   Memory:Committed Bytes, 788
   Memory:Pages/sec, 782
   Memory:Pool Non-paged Bytes, 789
   NetBEUI:Bytes Total/sec, 794
   NetBEUI:Datagrams/sec, 794
   NetBEUI:Frames/sec, 795
   Network Interface:Bytes Sent/sec, 794
   Network Interface:Bytes Total/sec, 783
   Network Interface:Output Queue Length, 795
   Network Segment:% Network Utilization, 794
   NWLink IPX:Bytes Total/sec, 794
   NWLink IPX:Datagrams/sec, 794
   NWLink IPX:Frames/sec, 795
   Object:Processes, 783
   Performance Monitor, 762–763
   Physical Disk:Avg. Disk Queue Length, 783
   PhysicalDisk: Disk Time, 792
   PhysicalDisk:Avg. Disk Bytes/Transfer, 793
   PhysicalDIsk:Disk Bytes/sec, 793
   PhysicalDisk:Disk Queue Length, 793
   print servers, 797
   Process:% Processor Time, 791
   Process:Page Faults/sec, 788
   Process:Page File Bytes, 789
   Process:Working Set, 787
   Processor:% Privileged Time, 790
   Processor:% Processor Time, 784, 790
   Processor:% User Time, 791
   Processor:Interrupts/sec, 791
   Redirector:Bytes Total/sec, 785
   Server Work Queues:Queue Length, 791
   Server:Bytes Total/sec, 785, 793
   Server:Logon/sec, 793
   Server:Logons Total, 793
   System:% Total Processor Time, 785
   System:Processor Queue Length, 791
   TCP:Segments/sec, 795
   Thread:% Processor Time, 792
   UDP:Datagrams/sec, 795
CPS (Connection Point Services), Index Server 2.0, 501–505
CPU usage, performance view, 858
CrashDump debugger, 954–955
Create Report dialog box, 889
CRS (Content Replication System), Posting Acceptor support, 513
Crystal Reports 4.5, Small Business Server, 674–675

D

D.E.T.E.C.T., troubleshooting methodology, 910–913
data, backup strategies, 85–91
data = information, qualitative analysis method, 745
data collection
   baseline creation, 776, 779–780
   Performance Monitor, 767, 775–780
Data Comm Warehouse, MCSE toolkit catalog, 394, 398
data files
   logon script automatic updating, 82
   storage issues, 776
   updating for virus protection, 406–407
data interpretation
   Cache:Data Map Hits % counter, 782
   described, 780–781
   Logical Disk:Avg.Disk Queue Length counter, 782
   LogicalDisk:% Disk Time counter, 792
   LogicalDisk:Avg. Disk Bytes/Transfer counter, 793
   LogicalDisk:Disk Bytes/sec counter, 793
   LogicalDisk:Disk Queue Length counter, 793
   Memory:Available Bytes counter, 787
   Memory:Committed Bytes counter, 788
   Memory:Pages/sec counter, 782
   Memory:Pool Non-paged Bytes counter, 789
   NetBEUI:Bytes Total/sec counter, 794
   NetBEUI:Datagrams/sec counter, 794
   NetBEUI:Frames/sec counter, 795
   Network Interface:Bytes Sent/sec counter, 794
   Network Interface:Bytes Total/sec counter, 783
   Network Interface:Output Queue Length counter, 795
   Network Segment:% Network Utilization counter, 794
   NWLink IPX:Bytes Total/sec counter, 794
   NWLink IPX:Datagrams/sec counter, 794
   NWLink IPX:Frames/sec counter, 795
   Object:Processes counter, 783

Index

Performance Monitor, 780–785
Physical Disk:Avg. Disk Queue Length counter, 783
PhysicalDisk: Disk Time counter, 792
PhysicalDisk:Avg. Disk Bytes/Transfer counter, 793
PhysicalDIsk:Disk Bytes/sec counter, 793
PhysicalDisk:Disk Queue Length counter, 793
Process:% Processor Time counter, 791
Process:Page Faults/sec counter, 788
Process:Page File Bytes counter, 789
Process:Working Set counter, 787
Processor:% Privileged Time counter, 790
Processor:% Processor Time counter, 784, 790
Processor:% User Time counter, 791
Processor:Interrupts/sec counter, 791
quick and dirty analysis example, 781
Redirector:Bytes Total/sec counter, 785
Server Work Queues:Queue Length counter, 791
Server:Bytes Total/sec counter, 785, 793
Server:Logon/sec counter, 793
Server:Logons Total counter, 793
System:% Total Processor Time counter, 785
System:Processor Queue Length counter, 791
TCP:Segments/sec counter, 795
Thread:% Processor Time counter, 792
UDP:Datagrams/sec counter, 795
data location table, server disk space mapping, 432–433
Data Offset field, TCP/IP packet element, 134
data pattern, capture filter, 820
database files
  DHCP management, 319
  TCP/IP troubleshooting, 240–247
DataBasePath, TCP/IP values, 127
databases, daily verification, 414–415
dates, setup settings, 40–41
Daytime, TCP/IP support, 125
day-to-day administration
  documentation/sharing procedures, 419–420
  end user support, 399–400
  end user tasks, 420–422
  event logs, 410–413
  free disk space techniques, 408–410
  LAN connectivity verification, 415–417
  new hardware installation, 417–419
  server troubleshooting, 400–404
  server/application verification, 413–415
  telephonee backups, 404–405
  test restores, 405
  virus protection, 405–408
  WAN connectivity verfication, 415–417
  Windows NT/MCSE toolkit, 388–399
DCOM (Distributed Component Object Model), snap-ins support, 506
DCOM/HTTP Tunneling, SP4, 590
DDIM (Data Dimensions), Y2K consulting firm, 550
debuggers
  CrashDump, 954–955
  Kernel, 953–954
debugging, terms, 952
decimal and binary bit conversions, calculator, 343–344
decimal value converted to binary bit, 340, 342–343
decimal values, binary bit values, 337
Dedicated Capture Mode, Network Monitor, 815
default computer, system policy setup, 79
default gateway address, 915–916
default gateways
  See also gateways
  described, 152–154
  gateway address, 155
  interface address, 155
  multiple uses, 157–161
  netmask, 154
  network address, 154
  remote network enabling, 362
  ROUTE ADD command, 155–157
default subnet masks, subnetting, 336
default user, system policy setup, 79–80
Default Web Site Properties tab, Windows NT 4.0 Option Pack, 457–458
DefaultTTL, TCP/IP values, 128
delegate administrators, access guidelines, 59
dental mirror, MCSE toolkit component, 394
desktops, system policy customization uses, 78
Destination Address field, TCP/IP packet element, 133
Destination field, TCP/IP packet element, 133
Detail pane, Network Monitor Frame Viewer window, 812–813
Detailed Information dialog box, WINS server information, 328–329

device drivers, loading/initializing in booting up, 934–935
Device Manager, Windows 2000 Server, 970
devices, naming conventions, 30–31
DFS (Distributed File system), Windows 2000 Server, 972
DHCP (Dynamic Host Configuration Protocol)
  benefits, 287–289
  BOOTP (Bootstrap Protocol) roots, 289
  clients, 288–289
  command line commands, 300
  database file management, 319
  described, 287–289
  DHCP Manager, 302–318
  DHCPACK message, 292
  DHCPDECLINE message, 293
  DHCPDISCOVER message, 290
  DHCPNAK message, 293
  DHCPOFFER message, 290–291
  DHCPRELEASE message, 293
  DHCPREQUEST message, 291–292
  disabling bindings, 299
  error conditions, 320
  installation, 297–300
  IP address leasing, 289–293
  IP lease renewal process, 292–293
  Microsoft Access (mdb) file format, 290
  modifying scope properties, 306
  pausing, 300
  removing scopes, 306
  RFCs, 287
  scope creation, 300–301, 304–306
  server connection/disconnection, 303–304
  server planning, 294
  servers, 287–288
  small LAN server implementation, 295
  SP4 hotfix, 556
  TCP/IP relay configuration, 195–197
  TCP/IP support, 125
  troubleshooting, 319–320
  versus DNS, 318–319
DHCP clients, described, 288–289
DHCP Manager
  adding/removing scopes, l306
  category configurations, 314
  client configuration options, 309–314
  client lease management, 314–316
  client reservations, 316–318
  configuration options, 306–314
  modifying scope properties, 306
  startup process, 302–303
  uses, 302–306

DHCP Options: Global dialog box, described, 307–308
DHCP servers
  described, 287–288
  command line commands, 300
  connection/disconnection, 303–304
  large LAN implementation, 295–297
  small LAN implementation, 295
  troubleshooting, 319–320
DHCP.MDB file, described, 319
DHCP.TMP file, described, 319
DHCPACK message, described, 292
DHCPDECLINE message, described, 293
DHCPDISCOVER message, described, 290
DHCPNAK message, described, 293
DHCPOFFER message, described, 290–291
DHCPRELEASE message, described, 293
DHCPREQUEST message, described, 291–292
Dialing Properties dialog box, Dial-Up Networking configuration, 357
dial-up connections
  Dial-Up Networking configuration, 352–358
  Dial-Up Networking dialing process, 368–369
  Dial-Up Networking dialog box properties, 359–368
  hardware requirements, 349–350
  ISP (Internet Service Provider) requirements, 350
  multilink enabling, 351
  PPP versus SLIP, 350
  RAS (Remote Access Services) setup, 350–351
  TCP/IP requirements, 350
Dial-Up Networking
  configuration process, 352–358
  Dial-Up Networking Monitor, 369–370
  Internet dialing process, 368–369
  ISDN modem issues, 370
  ISP telephone number configuration, 355–358
Dial-Up Networking dialog box
  Edit Phonebook Entry properties, 359–364
  Logon Preference properties, 366–367
  More menu options, 367–368
  property settings, 359–368
  User Preference properties, 364–366
Dial-Up Networking Monitor, described, 369–370
dictaphone, MCSE toolkit component, 398
digital certificates
  CA (certificate authority) request, 486
  creation process, 485–492

described, 485–486
Key Manager, 486–488
Microsoft Certificate Server enrollment, 489–492
Web-based module administration, 492–494
digital network, Internet connection scenarios, 370–376
Direct Frame Relay, Internet connection scenario, 374
directories, SMTP, 476
Directory Permissions dialog box, NTFS permissions, 73–74
directory security
  FTP Site server settings, 474–475
  IIS settings, 463–464
disaster recovery
  annual drill, 435–436
  described, 433–436
  ERD (Emergency Repair Disk), 433
  hot sites, 435
  identical spare servers, 434–435
  reciprocity agreements, 435
  third-party solutions, 433
Discard, TCP/IP support, 125
Disk Administrator
  copying boot files to the boot partition, 50–51
  FAT file system boot partition formatting, 49–50
  hiding/displaying files, 50
  NTFS partition deletion cautions, 36
disk controllers, setup detection process/decisions, 35–36
disk defragmentation, monthly server activities, 432–433
disk storage
  adequate design solutions, 19–20
  planning guidelines, 19–20
  poor design forms, 19
  RAID-based solutions, 20
  superior design solutions, 20
disk subsystem, performance analysis, 749–750
DiskAccess, Windows NT Services for UNIX, 594
DiskKeeper program, disk defragmentation, 433, 754
disks, bottleneck analysis, 792–793
DiskShare, Windows NT Services for UNIX, 594
display adapters, default setup settings, 40–41

Display Capture dialog box, 823–824
display filter
  address pairs, 825
  Capture Viewer window, 824
  creating, 822
  enabled protocol, 822
  exists relation, 822
  Network Monitor, 820–827
  operators, 825
  query expression construction, 824
  TCP packets, 823
  versus capture filter, 824–826
display filter box, protocol definitions, 836–837
Display Filter dialog box, 824
Display Options dialog box, 833
Display tab sheet, WinMSD, 880
DNS (Domain Name System)
  benefits, 262
  boot files, 269
  cache files, 268
  configuration, 273–285
  described, 257–261
  DNS Manager, 273–285
  domain name evaluation process, 266–267
  domain name resolution process, 262
  domain name space, 262
  domain types, 263–266
  dual DNS server requirements, 259
  forwarders, 270
  installation, 273
  InterNIC registration, 258
  name resolution process, 271–272
  name server types, 269–270
  resolvers, 271
  reverse lookup files, 268
  revisions, 285–286
  RFC standards, 285–286
  server statistics, 286–287
  services configuration, 275–276
  slaves, 270
  SP4 hotfix, 556
  TCP/IP configuration, 188–192
  TCP/IP support, 125
  versus DHCP, 318–319
  WINS integration, 330
  zone transfers, 272–273
  zones, 267–268
DNS Manager
  described, 273
  DNS configuration, 273–285
  object configurations, 274

continued

DNS Manager *(continued)*
  zone menu options, 280–285
  zone record definitions, 277–279
DNS Manager Preferences dialog box, DNS configuration, 285
documentation
  day-to-day administration tasks, 419–420
  network security, 72
  server troubleshooting, 401
documents
  end user solutions, 400
  IIS settings, 463
DOD (Department of Defense) model, TCP/IP layers, 112–114
Dogpile, name resolution uses, 261
dollar sign ($) character, hidden shares, 69
domain name space, described, 262
domain names
  evaluating, 266–267
  IIS restrictions, 464
  InterNIC registration, 258
  IP address reassignment, 147–148
  naming conventions, 31
  second-level, 264
  setup decisions, 40
  third-level (subdomains), 264–265
  top-level, 263
domain root, described, 263
domains
  described, 59, 263–266
  host names, 266
  second-level, 264
  TCP/IP values, 127
  top-level, 263
  trust relationships, 59–61
DOS, upgrading to NT Server 4.0, 43
downtime
  calculating, 919
  troubleshooting, 919–920
drawings, as-built computer network, 12–13
drive mappings, advance planning, 23
drive space management, 880–883
drivers
  adapter cards, 810–811
  built-in disk controller setup, 35–36
  installation/configuration, 419
  rename/replace, 941–943
Drivers tab sheet, access information about drives, 881–882
drives, hot pluggable, 419
Drives tab sheet, WinMSD, 880–883
Drop directory, SMTP, 476
dual-boot systems, setup process, 44
dual-processor motherboards, server advantages, 17
dump files, interpreting, 955
duplexing, described, 19
Dynamic DNS, described, 330–331
dynamic IP address, described, 361
dynamic packet filtering, Proxy Server 1.0/2.0, 667

E
Echo, TCP/IP support, 125
Edit Phonebook Entry dialog box, Dial-Up Networking properties, 359–364
elective exam, TCP/IP, 345,
e-mail
  Exchange Server support, 658
  Microsoft Mail program, 98–102
  remote access, 236
  virus infection point, 91
emergency repair process, invoking, 945
employees, troubleshooting downtime, 919–920
EnableSecurityFilters, TCP/IP values, 127
encrypted password-based security, 215
encryption
  40-bit versus 128-bit, 546–548
  password options, 363–364
encryption algorithms, export restrictions, 536
end user support, day-to-day administration tasks, 399–400
end users, technology committee members, 442
Enterprise Edition
  BackOffice application building blocks, 616–617
  design challenges, 618–619
  four-gigabyte memory tuning, 619–620
  MCS (Microsoft Cluster Server) Wolfpack, 617, 621–624
  Microsoft challenges/intentions, 616–617
  mission-critical application development, 616
  MSMQ (Microsoft Message Queue) Server, 525, 624–625
  MSMQ unlimited concurrent users, 617
  MTS (Microsoft Transaction Server), 626
  Option Pack CD components, 617–618
  SMP (symmetric multiprocessing), 621
  technologies, 619–626

versus NT Server 4.0 regular edition, 617
when to use, 618
Windows NT Server 4.0 variation, 5
WLBS (Windows Load Balancing Server), 625–626
Environment tab
System Properties dialog box, 886
WinMSD, 884–885
environment variables, 82, 284
ERD (Emergency Repair Disk)
creating, 38
disaster recovery, 433
installation repair, 35
monthly updating, 433
Service Pack 3 modifications, 540–542
troubleshooting use, 946–949
error events, described, 412
error handling, IIS, 467
error messages
duplicate IP address, 177
host name resolution failure, 257
IE/Windows NT 4.0 Option Pack security, 454
IP address conflict, 146
RAS TCP/IP configuration, 355
second host IP address, 146
Ethernet, subnetting, 334
Ethernet 10BaseT networks, network startup troubleshooting, 40
Ethernet frames, Windows 2000 Server, 972
ETRN, described, 659–660
Euro Key Patch, SP4, 590
Event Log Service, SP4 hotfix, 559
event logs
day-to-day administration tasks, 410–413
SCE (Security Configuration Editor), 567–568
Small Business Server harmless errors, 727
Event Viewer, day-to-day administration tasks, 390, 411–413
events
attributes, 412–413
types, 411–413
Exchange Server
active server page support, 658
backup issues, 663
ETRN, 659–660
IMS (Internet Mail Service), 659
memory footprint, 661
message size restriction modification, 661–663
migrating from MS Mail, 445

Service Pack 2, 663
supported services, 658
version 5.0 improvements over version 4.0, 658–659
Web-based Outlook solution, 659
Executive Software, DiskKeeper, 433, 754
executives, technology committee members, 442
exists relation, display, filter, 822
EXPAND command, 940–942
expectation management
buy today/install today, 966–967
instability issues, 967
lack of features, 967
experience, TCP/IP troubleshooting, 211–212
external modems, MCSE toolkit component, 398

F

failure audit events, described, 412
FAT (file allocation table)
boot partition formatting, 49–50
CONVERT.EXE utility issues, 32
setup advantages/disadvantages, 32
fatal error stop screen, 949
fault tolerance, servers versus workstations, 611
fax logs, Fax Server 1.0, 670–672
Fax Server 1.0, Small Business Server, 669–672
faxes, Microsoft Fax Server 1.0, 669–672
FDISK utility, partition deletion cautions, 36
fields, TCP/IP packet elements, 129–136
file cache, servers versus workstations, 609
file servers
Performance Monitor environment analysis, 796–797
second NIC advantages, 18
Windows 2000 Server, 968
build 1381 version issues, 606
file sharing
dollar sign ($) character with hidden shares, 69
folder selections, 68–69
share setup, 68–69
user connections, 69
file system management, Windows 2000 Server, 971
File System tab sheet, WinMSD, 883

file systems
    FAT (file allocation table)
        advantages/disadvantages, 32, 49–51
    HPFS (High Performance File System) non-support, 32–33
    NTFS (NT file system)
        advantages/disadvantages, 32
    SCE (Security Configuration Editor), 570–571
    servers versus workstations, 611
    setup decisions, 32–33, 37
files
    ASF (Advanced Streaming Format), 575
    boot, 269, 925
    boot partition, 37, 48–51
    boot.ini, 37, 46–51
    BOOTSECT.DOS, 37, 44
    cache, 268
    CATALOG.WCI, 494
    decompressing, 940
    DHCP database, 319
    DHCP.MDB, 319
    DHCP.TMP, 319
    expanding, 942–943
    hiding/displaying, 50
    HOTFIX.INF, 543
    JET.LOG, 319
    lmhosts, 243
    missing system, 940–949
    NT boot process order, 49
    NTBOOTDD.SYS, 37, 49
    NTDETECT.COM, 37, 49
    NTLDR, 37, 49
    replacing corrupted, 944
    reverse lookup, 268
    SETUP.EXE, 451
    SHOWACLS.EXE, 72
    symbol, 536
    SYSTEM.MDB, 319
    WINLOGON.EXE, 939
    WINNT.EXE, 42
    WINNT32.EXE, 42
    zone, 267–268
filtering, address capabilities, 818–819
filters, ISAPI, 460, 516
Find All Names command, 828
finds, Windows 2000 Server, 971
Finger command, TCP/IP troubleshooting tools, 239
FINGER, TCP/IP support, 124
first octet value, changing, 916
flags
    TCP Control Bits, 134–135
    TCP/IP packet element, 132
flashlight, MCSE toolkit component, 394
flathead screwdrivers, MCSE toolkit component, 394
floppy disks
    ERD (Emergency Repair Disk), 433
    MCSE toolkit component, 397–398
    virus infection point, 92
Fluke One Touch Network Assistant 10/100, 841–842
folders, share setup, 68–69
foods, MCSE toolkit components, 399
forms, Index Server 2.0, 495–496
forums, MS Exchange support, 437
ForwardBroadcasts, TCP/IP values, 127
forwarders, DNS, 270
four-gigabyte memory tuning, Enterprise Edition, 619–620
fourth octet position, subnet mask, 338
FPNW (File and Print Service for NetWare), SP4, 26, 590
Fragment Offset, TCP/IP packet element, 132
fragmentation, declining performance reason, 754–755
Frame Viewer window
    Detail pane, 812–813
    Hex pane, 813
    Network Monitor, 811
    Summary pane, 812
frames
    capturing, 809–810
    setting size, 815–816
    variable length, 820
frequency distribution, quantitative analysis method, 739
FTP (File Transport Protocol)
    return codes, 233
    secure server site, 234
    TCP/IP support, 124
    TCP/IP troubleshooting tools, 232–234
FTP command, 232
FTP session command, 233
FTP Site server
    configuration, 471–476
    directory security settings, 474–475
    greeting message, 474
    home directory settings, 474
    security accounts settings, 472–473
FTP sites
    InterNIC cache files, 268
    RFCs (Requests for Comments), 111
    SCE (Security Configuration Editor), 562
    Service Pack 3 download, 535

functions, logon scripts, 82–83

G
gateway address, default gateway, 155
gateways
   See also default gateways
   described, 152–154
   TCP/IP configuration, 186–188
General option, Network tab sheet, 886
General tab sheet, System Properties sheet, 891
GetAdmin hotfix, Service Pack 3, 544
getting prioritized
   processes view, 867–871
   thread boosting, 870–871
global groups, described, 62
goals, Windows 2000 Server968
Gopher, IIS non-support, 669
Graph pane, Network Monitor Capture window, 808
graphical setup stage, described, 38–41
Great Plains Dynamics, dual-processor advantages, 17
greeting message, FTP Site server, 474
Group Management Wizard, described, 393
Group Policy Editor, Windows 2000 Server, 985
GroupOrderList subkey, 932
groups
  adding users to, 55–56
  global versus local, 62
  logon script membership determination, 84–85
groupware, Exchange Server support, 658
GSNW (Gateway Services for NetWare), described, 25

H
hackers, security testing, 427
hard drives
  bottleneck analysis, 792–793
  controller types, 28
  defragmenting for performance boost, 754–755
  duplexing, 19
  free disk space techniques, 408–410
  mirroring, 19
  partition decisions, 36–37
  performance analysis, 749–750
  planning guidelines, 19–20
  RAID-based, 20
  source file storage advantages, 44
  successful storage techniques, 408–409
  weekly disk space monitoring, 409–410
hardware
  hot pluggable drives, 419
  installing, 417–419
  MCSE toolkit tool elements, 394–395
  Network Monitor, 810–811
  NT Diagnostics program, 418
  stop screens, 949
hardware detection, NTDETECT, 928
hardware profiles, WinMSD, 895
hardware requirements, Terminal Server, 639
hardware/software resellers, planning guidelines, 22
HCL (Hardware Compatibility List)
  described, 29
  hard drive controller concerns, 28
  Small Business Server issues, 683
Header Checksum field, TCP/IP packet element, 133
help desk
  disabling versus deleting user concerns, 57
  keeping informed of server status, 421
heterogeneous networks, described, 137–138
Hex pane, Network Monitor Frame Viewer window, 813
hidden files, displaying in Disk Administrator, 50
hidden shares, dollar sign ($) character, 69
Highground Systems, Storage Resource Manager, 432
hits, described, 514
HKEY_CURRENT_USER key, system policies, 78
HKEY_LOCAL_MACHINE key, system policies, 78
home directory
  FTP Site server settings, 474
  IIS settings, 460–463
  NNTP, 480
hop count, default gateways, 155–157
host addresses, described, 150–151
host number, determination, 339–340
hostnames
  changing, 232

continued

hostnames *(continued)*
  described, 266
  resolution, 255–257
  TCP/IP troubleshooting tools, 232
  TCP/IP values, 128
hostname command, 232
hot pluggable drives, described, 419
hot sites, disaster recovery, 435
HOTFIX.INF file, when to copy, 543
hotfixes
  application order, 543
  Certificate Server, 552–553
  described, 437–438, 533–534, 542
  DHCP, 556
  DNS, 556
  Event Log Service, 559
  GetAdmin, 544
  HOTFIX.INF file, 543
  IE 4.01 Service Pack 1, 552
  IIS 4.0, 553
  installation, 543
  MSMQ for Windows NT, 553–555
  MTS, 555
  networking, 555–559
  NNTP, 555
  operating systems, 555–559
  PPTP, 557–558
  PRIV, 544
  regression testing shortcomings, 542
  RIP, 557–558
  RRAS, 557–558
  Service Pack 2, 535
  Service Pack 3, 542–544
  Service Pack 4, 549–560
  SMTP, 555
  SRV, 544
  Teardrop2, 544
  version information display, 544
  WINS, 556
  Y2K (Year 2000), 550–551
HP JetAdmin Software for JetDirect Print Servers, CD-ROM library, 396
HP JetDirect-connected printers, port installation, 64–66
HP network printers, Small Business Server issues, 726
HPFS (High Performance File System), NT 4.0 non-support, 32–33
HTTP at Port 80, lack of registration, 247
HTTP header, IIS settings, 465–467
Hyena program
  disk space monitoring, 409–410
  NT administration, 393–394

hyphen (-) character, computer naming convention cautions, 30–31

I

I/O throughput, servers versus workstations, 609
IAB (Internet Activities Board), RFCs management, 109–111
IAS (Internet Authentication Services), Index Server 2.0, 505–506
IBM ADSTAR Distributed Storage Manager program, described, 90
ICA (Independent Computing Architecture) protocol, Terminal Server, 642
ICMP (Internet Control Message Protocol), described, 121
IDE (Integrated Drive Electronics), pre-setup information gathering, 28
identical spare servers, disaster recovery techniques, 434–435
Identification field, TCP/IP packet element, 132
IE 4.01 Service Pack 1 hotfix, Service Pack 4, 552
IETF (Internet Engineering Task Force)
  Internet problems/solutions, 109
  RADIUS protocol standard developer, 505
IGMP (Internet Group Management Protocol) v2
  described, 121–122
  SP4, 590
  TCP/IP support, 126
IHL (Internet Header Length) field, TCP/IP packet element, 130
IIS (Internet Information Server) 4.0
  administration tasks, 467–471
  bandwidth throttling, 459–460
  configuration options, 455–467
  custom error handling, 467
  described, 234, 383, 455
  directory security settings, 463–464
  document settings, 463
  FTP Site server configuration, 471–476
  Gopher non-support, 669
  home directory settings, 460–463
  hotfixes, 553
  HTTP header settings, 465–467
  IP address and domain name restrictions, 464
  ISAPI filters, 460

Index **1087**

keep-alives, 459–460
logging options, 458
Microsoft IIS log file format, 458
MMC (Microsoft Management Console) management, 455–467
NCSA Common log file format, 458
New Virtual Directory Wizard, 471
New Web Site Wizard, 469–471
NNTP (Network Transport Protocol) Service, 479–485
NTFS-partitioned drive advantages, 451
ODBC logging, 458
operator privilege settings, 459
performance settings, 459–460
PICS (Platform for Internet Content Selection) ratings, 465–467
Small Business Server, 668–669
SMTP Service, 476–478
TCP Port 80, 458
TCP/IP support, 125
W3C Extended log file format, 458
Web site data backup/restore, 467–469
improved security, subnetting, 334–335
IMS (Internet Mail Service)
  described, 659
  ETRN configuration, 659–660
  static IP address, 361
Index Server 1.1, Small Business Server, 673–674
Index Server 2.0
  CATALOG.WCI file, 494
  CHAP (Challenge Handshake Authentication Protocol), 506
  CMAK (Connection Manager Administration Kit), 498–500
  CMAK Wizard, 498–500
  CPS (Connection Point Services), 501–505
  described, 494
  IAS (Internet Authentication Services), 505–506
  installation, 494–496
  MMC administration, 496–498
  sample forms, 495–496
  service profile creation, 498–500
  snap-in creation, 507–510
indexes, quantitative analysis method, 743
inductive reasoning, TCP/IP troubleshooting, 212
inference algorithms, described, 514
information events, described, 411
Infoseek, name resolution uses, 260–261
infrastructure elements, physical site planning, 13–14

infrastructure servers, Windows 2000 Server, 969
in-house help, TCP/IP troubleshooting, 212
Inoculan for Small Business Server program, described, 729
Install New Modem Wizard, described, 393
installation, TCP/IP, 247–249
instances, Performance Monitor, 762–763
Intel processors, Service Pack 3 support, 536
interface address, default gateways, 155
interface cards
  See also NICs (Network Interface Cards)
  reseating when building the server, 24
Internet
  ARPANET roots, 108
  dialing process, 368–369
  dial-up connections, 349–370
  digital network connection scenarios, 370–376
  lowercase when referring to private wide area network, 108
  paradigm shift, 7
  research, 840–841
  TCP/IP support features, 125
  troubleshooting resource, 956–957
  uppercase when referring to global Internet, 108
  Windows 2000 Server, 983
  Windows NT 4.0 Option Pack applications, 455–506
Internet access management, Proxy Server 1.0/2.0, 666
Internet addressing
  default gateways, 152–161
  described, 143
  IP address components, 144–148
  TCP/IP address components, 143–161
Internet content management, Proxy Server 1.0/2.0, 666
Internet domain name registration information, 237
Internet Explorer 4.0
  configuration, 381–383
  described, 380–383
  Service Pack 4 preinstallation requirement, 545
  Windows NT 4.0 Option Pack security error message, 454
Internet layer, DOD model versus OSI model, 113
Internet support groups, server troubleshooting resource, 403–404

Internetworking
  breeder networks, 137
  heterogeneous networks, 137–138
  simple routing, 140–141
  TCP/IP uses, 136–141
  third party TCP/IP software support, 138–140
  Windows Sockets, 138
InterNIC (Internet Network Information Center), IP address registration, 147
IP (Internet Protocol)
  described, 118–119
  TCP/IP packet element, 130
IP address conservation, subnetting, 334
IP addresses
  binary to decimal conversion table, 145
  binary to IP address conversions, 145
  binary value translations, 145
  classes, 151–152
  components, 144–148
  DHCP lease renewal process, 292–293
  DHCP leasing, 289–293
  domain name reassignment, 147–148
  duplicate, 218
  dynamic versus static, 361
  host addresses, 150–151
  IIS restrictions, 464
  Microsoft Proxy Server "phony" addresses, 147
  subnet masks, 148–150
  TCP/IP configuration, 182–186
  valid host portion addresses, 151
  valid private Internet network address ranges, 150
IP Configuration dialog box
  adapter (MAC) address display, 317
  DHCP configuration, 293
IP Header Compression, enabling, 362
IP network, subnetting, 334
IP routing
  described, 161–163
  multihomed, 140–141
IP security management, Windows 2000 Server, 972
IPConfig command
  /all switch, 217–218, 829
  command line switches, 217, 219
  interpreting output, 218
  TCP/IP shortcomings, 124
  TCP/IP troubleshooting tools, 216–219
  use of, 221
IPEnableRouter, TCP/IP values, 128
IRTF (Internet Research Task Force), TCP/IP research projects, 109
ISAPI filters
  IIS settings, 460
  Usage Import installation, 516
ISDN, WAN combination scenario, 373
ISDN modems, Dial-Up Networking issues, 370
ISDN router, described, 370–373
ISP (Internet service providers)
  planning guidelines, 22
  dial-up connection requirements, 350
  Dial-Up Networking telephone number configuration, 355–358
ISP (Internet Service Provider) CD, MCSE toolkit component, 396
ISVs, needs planning, 23
IT consultant, technology committee member, 442–443
iteration, name resolution element, 271–272

J

JET.LOG file, described, 319

K

KeepAliveInterval, TCP/IP values, 129
keep-alives, IIS, 459–460
KeepAliveTime, TCP/IP values, 129
Kernel debugger, 953–954
kernel memory, performance view, 860–861
Kernel phase
  BootExecute data item, 936
  Clone Control set, 934
  DOS Devices key, 937
  Error Control values, 935
  initialization, 933–934
  loading/initializing device drivers, 934–935
  loading/initializing services, 935
  Memory Management key, 937
  Session Manager, 935
key contact list, planning guidelines, 23
Key Manager, Certificate Server 1.0, 486–488
keys
  DOS devices, 937
  Memory Management, 937
  Subsystems, 937–938
KFH Publications, Inc., Computer User monthly newspapers, 398
KISS (keep it simple starting)

Index **1089**

domain trust relationships, 61
NTFS permission designing, 71–72
system planning, 24
Kixtart program, logon script interpreter, 84
kneepads, MCSE toolkit component, 399

L
LANs (Local Area Networks)
   day-to-day administration connectivity verification, 415–417
   default gateway on remote network enabling, 362
   DHCP implementation, 295–297
   external adapter card configuration, 915
laptop computers, MCSE toolkit component, 398
large LAN, DHCP implementation, 295–297
Last Known Good Configuration option, 929–930
learning curve analysis, troubleshooting, 921–922
learning curve, defining, 922
License Compliance Wizard, described, 393
License Manager, Terminal Server, 643
licensing
   Enterprise Edition limitations, 617
   SBS (Small Business Server) requirements, 656–657
licensing modes, types, 31–32
line managers, technology committee members, 442
linear percent growth, network budgeting, 40
lmhosts.sam file, converting for use, 243
local debugging, described, 952
local groups, described, 62
local name cache, 228
local policies, SCE (Security Configuration Editor), 566–567
local port, printer connection, 64
log files, IIS formats, 458
Log view, Performance Monitor, 763, 774
logical deduction, server troubleshooting steps, 401
LogicalDisk:% Disk Time counter, Performance Monitor, 792
LogicalDisk:Avg. Disk Bytes/Transfer counter, Performance Monitor, 793
LogicalDisk:Disk Bytes/sec counter, Performance Monitor, 793
LogicalDisk:Disk Queue Length counter, Performance Monitor, 793
Logon phase, 938–939
Logon Preferences dialog box, Dial-Up Networking options, 366–367
logon scripts
   client PC time setting, 83
   data file automatic updating, 82
   described, 81–82
   environment variable settings, 82
   functions, 82–83
   group membership determination, 84–85
   Kixtart interpreter, 84
   naming conventions, 83
   network printer connections, 82
   network share connections, 82
   PUTINENV utility, 84
   requirements, 83
   software updating, 82
logon security, described, 70–71
Logon validation stage, frame capture, 809–810
logs
   backup, 405
   event, 410–413
   Fax Server 1.0, 670–672
lpq (print queue status), TCP/IP support, 124
LPR printing, TCP/IP support, 124

M
MAC address
   3COM cards, 829–831
   Network Monitor, 826–831
Macintosh
   introducing Windows NT Server 4.0 to existing network, 25
   Windows NT Server 4.0 support issues, 27
mailing lists, Internet support groups, 404
management services, build 1381 version issues, 607
Managing File and Folder Access Wizard, described, 393
mandatory profiles, described, 77
manners, end user support, 399
Map Network Drive dialog box, described, 69
mapping, server disk space, 431–433
Master Boot Record, refreshing, 927
McAfee VirusScan program, NT Server 4.0 issues, 92–93

McAffee VirusScan CD-ROM for Windows 95/98/NT, MCSE toolkit component, 397
MCIS (Microsoft Commercial Internet System), SMTP upgrading, 476
MCS (Microsoft Cluster Server) Wolfpack, Enterprise Edition, 617, 621–624
MCSE (Microsoft Certified Systems Engineer), described, 8
MCSE toolkit
　bootable floppy disks, 397–398
　CD-ROM library components, 395–397
　clothing, 399
　Computer User newspaper, 398
　Data Comm Warehouse catalog, 398
　external modems/cable, 398
　foodstuffs, 399
　hardware tools, 394–395
　kneepads, 399
　laptop computer w/Internet capability, 398
　PC Zone catalog, 398
　portable file cabinet, 398
　resource kits, 398
　tape deck/radio, 398
　tape recorder/dictaphone, 398
　telephone line/analog telpehone, 398
　telephone numbers, 398
MDAC (Microsoft Data Access Component), described, 529–530
mean, quantitative analysis method, 739–741
Media Player, NetShow Services 3.0 client, 575
median, quantitative analysis method, 739–741
MEM usage, performance view, 858–859
member servers, described, 30
memory allocation, servers versus workstations, 608
memory leaks, declining performance reason, 754
memory
　See also RAM
　bottleneck analysis, 785–786
　described, 18
　Exchange Server footprint, 661
　mail order purchasing cautions, 18
　monitoring, 748–749
　monitoring with Task Manager, 428–431
　one-to-one performance return for each dollar spent, 18
　planning guidelines, 18
Memory tab sheet, WinMSD, 888
Memory:Available Bytes counter, Performance Monitor, 787
Memory:Committed Bytes counter, Performance Monitor, 788
Memory:Pages/sec counter, Performance Monitor, 782
Memory:Pool Non-paged Bytes counter, Performance Monitor, 789
messages, MSMQ, 524
messaging, asynchronous versus synchronous, 523–524
MetaFrame, Terminal Server, 641–642
Microsoft BackOffice CDs #1 and #4, MCSE toolkit component, 396
Microsoft Certificate Server, digital certificate enrollment, 489–492
Microsoft Certification Training, 835–836
Microsoft Consulting Service, troubleshooting resource, 960
Microsoft Directory Service Migration tool, 972–973
Microsoft evaluation & Migration Planning Kit CD, CD-ROM library, 396
Microsoft File Expansion Utility 2.50, 940
Microsoft IIS log file format
　FTP Site server support, 472
　IIS support, 458
Microsoft Internet Explorer, TCP/IP troubleshooting tools, 239–240
Microsoft Mail
　configuration, 99–101
　described, 98
　installation, 98–99
　user addition, 101–102
Microsoft, Network Monitor support position, 835
Microsoft paid support incidents, troubleshooting resource, 960
Microsoft Project: BackOffice Deployment Templates CD, MCSE toolkit, 396
Microsoft Proxy Server, "phony" IP addresses, 147
Microsoft Script Debugger, described, 530–532
Microsoft Solution Provider
　described, 835
　troubleshooting resource, 960
Microsoft TechNet
　BackOffice Query window, 838
　CD-ROM, MCSE toolkit component, 395
　described, 402–403
　information on sequence value, 837–839
　troubleshooting resources, 958–959
　use of near in searches, 838

Migration Tool for Netware, described, 26
mirroring, described, 19
MMC (Microsoft Management Console) 1.0
  described, 506–510
  backups/restores, 467–469
  bandwidth throttling, 459–460
  custom error handling, 467
  default Web Site properties, 457–458
  described, 455
  directory security settings, 463–464
  document settings, 463
  FTP Site server configuration, 471–476
  home directory settings, 460–463
  HTTP header settings, 465–467
  IIS management, 455–467
  Index Server 2.0 management, 494–506
  IP address and domain name restrictions, 464
  ISAPI filters, 460
  keep-alives, 459–460
  launching from the command prompt, 455
  New Virtual Directory Wizard, 471
  New Web Site Wizard, 469–471
  NNTP administration, 479–485
  operator privilege settings, 459
  performance settings, 459–460
  PICS (Platform for Internet Content Selection) ratings, 465–467
  SCE snap-in installation, 563
  server properties, 456–467
  SMPT administration, 476–478
  snap-ins support, 506–507
  window elements, 456
  Windows 2000 Server, 970
MMC (Microsoft Management Console) command, 455
mode, quantitative analysis method, 739–741
Modem Sharing Server 1.0, Small Business Server, 672–673
Modems Properties dialog box, described, 350
modems
  dial-up connection requirements, 349–350
  dial-up server setup, 38
  ISDN/Dial-Up Networking issues, 370
  Modem Sharing Server 1.0, 672–673
  multilink capability, 351
  sharing, Small Business Server issues, 724–726
Modified Phone Number dialog box, Dial-Up Networking configuration, 357

Monitor Server, NetShow Services 3.0, 587–588
MONITOR.EXE, command line switches, 772
monitors
  default display settings, 40–41
  VGA mode, 894
monthly server activities
  backup archive creation, 438–439
  baselining, 428
  disaster recovery methods, 433–436
  disk defragmentation, 432–433
  ERD (Emergency Repair Disk) updating, 433
  network auditing, 426–427
  performance monitoring, 428
  security review, 427–428
  server disk space mapping, 431–433
  software upgrading, 438
  system reboot, 428–431
More menu, Dial-Up Networking dialog box options, 367–368
motherboards, dual-processor, 17
MS Mail, Exchange Server migration process, 445
MSAA (Microsoft Active Assebility Support), SP4, 590
MS-CHAP (Microsoft Challenge Handshake Authentication Protocol), 506
MS-DOS system disk, disadvantages of booting from, 927
MSMQ (Microsoft Message Queue) 1.0
  asynchronous versus synchronous messaging, 523–524
  BSC (backup site controller), 525
  clients, 525
  CNs (connected networks), 525
  configuration, 528–529
  connector support, 526
  described, 523–529
  enterprise, 525
  Enterprise Edition components, 525–526
  Enterprise Edition unlimited concurrent users, 617
  hotfixes, 553–555
  licensing limitations, 526
  message, 524
  MQTest application, 527–528
  MSMQ Explorer, 526–528
  MTS integration, 524
  PEC (primary enterprise controller), 525
  PSC (primary site controller), 525
  queues, 524

continued

1092 Index

MSMQ (Microsoft Message Queue) 1.0
   (continued)
   smart routing, 526
   SQL Server 6.5 requirements, 525
   store-and-forward message queuing, 524
MSMQ (Microsoft Message Queue) Server,
      Enterprise Edition, 624–625
MSMQ Explorer, described, 526–528
MTA (Messaging Transfer Agents), hop
      count similarities, 155
MTS (Microsoft Transaction Server) 2.0
   described, 522–523
   hotfix, 555
   MSMQ integration, 524
MTS (Microsoft Transaction Server),
      Enterprise Edition, 626
multicast file transfers, NetShow Services
      3.0, 583–584
multicast stations, NetShow Services 3.0,
      582–583
multicasting, NetShow Services 3.0, 575
multihomed, described, 140–141
multilink, described, 351
multiple gateways, uses, 157–161
multiple master domain trust model,
      described, 61
multiple processors, 874–875
multisession, Terminal Server features, 635

N

name brand system components, versus
      clones, 20–21
name resolution
   caching, 272
   described, 253–254
   hosts, 255–257
   iteration, 271–272
   NetBIOS, 254–255
   recursion, 271
   reverse lookup, 272
   search engine uses, 260–261
   WINS process, 322
name servers, described, 269–270
NameServer, TCP/IP values, 128
naming conventions
   administrator passwords, 33
   advance planning, 24
   ARC, 51
   Boeing fix, 31
   computers, 254

   domain names, 31
   hyphen (-) character cautions, 30–31
   logon scripts, 83
   non-NetBios computers, 828
   setup process, 30–31
   shared file/folders, 69
   shared printers, 68
   Small Business Server computers, 712
nbstat command
   local name cache, 228
   -r switch, 228
   TCP/IP support, 124
   TCP/IP troubleshooting tools, 226–228
NCSA Common log file format, IIS support,
      458
NDR (nondelivery report)
   SMTP, 477
   NNTP, 480
near, term used in searches using Microsoft
      TechNet, 838
net confide workstation command, 318
net config workstation command, MAC
      address display, 318
NET TIME command, 83
NetBEUI protocol, setup option, 39
NetBEUI:Bytes Total/sec counter,
      Performance Monitor, 794
NetBEUI:Datagrams/sec counter,
      Performance Monitor, 794
NetBEUI:Frames/sec counter, Performance
      Monitor, 795
NetBIOS name resolution, described,
      254–255
NetManage, Chameleon Link97 program, 139
netmasks, default gateways, 154
NetShow Services 3.0
   administration tasks, 577–588
   ASF (Advanced Streaming Format) files,
      575
   authentication methods, 584
   bandwidth, 575–576
   Configure Server, 578–587
   described, 574–575
   installation, 576–577
   Media Player client, 575
   Monitor Server, 587–588
   multicast file transfers, 583–584
   multicast stations, 582–583
   multicasting, 575
   publishing point, 575
   QuickStart Wizard, 579–582
   server configuration, 578–588
   server properties, 584–587

Service Administration screen elements, 577–578
station, 575
streaming, 575
Unicast On-Demand Wizard, 581
unicast publishing points, 579–582
unicasting, 575
netstat command, 229–231
-a switch, 229–230
-e switch, 229
ICMP statistics, 231
-r switch, 230
-s switch, 230–231
TCP statistics, 231
TCP/IP session information, 124
TCP/IP troubleshooting tools, 228–231
UDP statistics, 231
NetWare, migrating to Windows NT Server 4.0, 26–27
NetWare MONITOR.NLM, versus Performance Monitor, 761–762
NetWare User access for Terminal Server, Terminal Server, 643
network adapters
See also NICs
MCSE toolkit component, 394
multiple, 811
performance analysis, 751
network address, default gateways, 154
network analysis
colors, 832
Internet resources, 840–841
Network Monitor, 832
timing, 833
Network Associates, VirusScan program, 406
network auditing, monthly server activities, 426–427
Network Bindings dialog box, DHCP disabling, 299
network budgeting
linear percent growth, 440
percent of revenue, 440–441
Windows NT Server on $5 a day approach, 441–442
zero-based, 439–440
Network Client Administrator Wizard, described, 393
network interface layer, DOD model versus OSI model, 113
Network Interface:Bytes Sent/sec counter, Performance Monitor, 794
Network Interface:Bytes Total/sec counter, Performance Monitor, 783

Network Interface:Output Queue Length counter, Performance Monitor, 795
Network Monitor
Address Information dialog box, 830
addresses, 818–819
analysis, 811–812
artificial intelligence option, 833–834
basics, 806–807
benefits, 746
Capture Filter dialog box, 816–817
capture filters, 816–817
Capture menu, 814–815
capture sessions, 814–815
capture trigger, 813–814
Capture window components, 807–809
capturing frames, 809–810
cature buffer size, 815
creating street friendly names for files, 827–831
data patterns, 820
display filter, 820–827
Display Options dialog box, 833
Find All Names command, 828
frame capture mode, 809
frame size settings, 815–816
hardware required, 810–811
Identify Network Monitor Users menu selection, 827
learning more, 834–851
MAC addresses, 826–831
naming computers, 828–831
network analysis, 832
obtaining full version, 844
password protection, 826–827
patterns, 831–833
protocols 817
running continuously, 813
session establishment, 832
SMS versus NT Server 4.0, 843–851
Summary pane, 834
three-way handshake, 832
tiling for easy viewing 810
timing, 832
Network Monitor Agent configuration property sheet, 807
Network Monitor Capture Window, 807
Network Monitor Tool, installation, 806
network monitoring
initializing, 805–831
ongoing, 813–831
network printers, logon script uses, 82
Network Professional Association Technical Resource CD, MCSE toolkit, 397

network professionals, widespread Windows NT Server support, 3–4
Network Segment:% Network Utilization counter, Performance Monitor, 794
Network Services dialog box, DHCP installation, 298–299
network services, setup options, 39–40
network shares
  logon script uses, 82
  Windows NT Server 4.0 installation, 41–43
network subsystem
  bottleneck detection tools, 750
  described, 750
  performance analysis, 750–754
  planning guidelines, 18
Network tab sheet
  core network information, 885
  General option, 886
  Settings option, 887
  Statistics option, 888
  Transports option, 887
network wide captures, 811
networking, Service Pack 4 fixes, 555–559
networking improvements
  Active Directory, Windows 2000 Server, 983–984
  Admission Control Services, Windows 2000 Server, 973–982
  change/configuration management, Windows 2000 Server, 984–985
  Distributed File system, Windows 2000 Server, 972
  Dynamic DNS, Windows 2000 Server, 972
  Internet, Windows 2000 Server, 983
  IP security management, Windows 2000 Server, 972
  large Ethernet frames, 972
  MSoft Directory Service Migration tool, 972–973
  routing/clustering support, Windows 2000 Server, 973
  security, Windows 2000 Server, 985–986
networking services, listing, 752–753
networks
  bottleneck analysis, 793–794
  breeder, 137
  data storage versus individual PC hard disk, 71
  heterogeneous, 137–138
  IP address class assignments, 151–152
  security settings, 69–81
  setup startup process, 40
  Windows NT Server 4.0 introduction to existing, 25
  zero-based budgeting, 439–440
New Domain dialog box, DNS configuration, 282
New Expiration Policy Wizard, NNTP expiration policies, 484–485
New Host dialog box, DNS configuration, 280
New Phonebook Entry Wizard, Dial-Up Networking phonebooks, 353–354
New Resource Record dialog box, DNS configuration, 281–282
New User dialog box, new user creation, 54–56
New Virtual Directory Wizard, described, 471
New Web Site Wizard, described, 469–471
newsgroups
  Exchange Server support, 658
  NNTP settings, 482–483
  troubleshooting resource, 956–957
newspapers, Computer User, 398
NIC (network interface card)
  100MB PCI advantages, 18
  performance analysis, 751
  reseating when building the server, 24
  second card file server advantages, 18
  setup detection, 38–39
  setup information gathering, 29
NNTP (Network Transport Protocol)
  configuration, 479–485
  described, 479
  expiration policies, 484–485
  home directory, 480
  hotfix, 555
  IIS configuration, 479–485
  NDR (nondelivery reports), 480
  New Expiration Policy Wizard, 484–485
  newsgroup properties, 482–483
Norton Utilities, disk defragmentation, 433
NOS (network operating system)
  32-bit, 600
  early release mistrust, 3–4
Novel Support Connection CD, MCSE toolkit component, 396
NPA (Network Professional Association), troubleshooting resource, 960
NT. *See* Windows NT Server 4.0
NT boot disk, 943–944
NT Diagnostics program, new hardware installation checking, 418
NT operating system model, described, 600–602

NT Server CD, setup process, 34–35
NT Server Client Access Licenses, purchasing guidelines, 31
NT Workstation
 client connection issues, 610–611
 clustering non-support, 610
 fault tolerance non-support, 611
 file system support issues, 611
 processor support, 610
 PWS (Peer Web Services), 612
 RAS connection issues, 610
 security issues, 611
 system requirements, 611
 tuning issues, 608–609
 versus Windows NT Server 4.0, 607–612
NTBACKUP program
 daily backups, 404
 timed backups, 87–89
NTBOOTDD.SYS file
 boot partition component, 37
 boot processing, 49
NTDETECT.COM file
 boot partition component, 37
 boot processing, 49
NTFS (NT file system)
 access types/associated rights, 74
 CONVERT.EXE utility issues, 32
 designing permissions, 71–72
 implementing permissions, 72–74
 limiting partition size to improve performance, 756
 network security documentation, 72
 permissions, 71–74
 planning permissions, 71
 setup advantages/disadvantages, 32
NTFS partitions
 deleting, 36
 Windows NT 4.0 Option Pack advantages, 451
NTLDR file, boot processing, 37, 49
NTLDR program, affected by DOS boot disk, 927
NWLink IPX/SPX Compatible Protocol, setup option, 39
NWLink IPX:Bytes Total/sec counter, Performance Monitor, 794
NWLink IPX:Datagrams/sec counter, Performance Monitor, 794
NWLink IPX:Frames/sec counter, Performance Monitor, 795

O

Object:Processes counter, Performance Monitor, 783
objects
 adding to Performance Monitor, 764
 baseline capturing guidelines, 777–779
 DNS configuration, 274
 Performance Monitor, 762–763
octet, subnetting, 337
ODBC logging
 FTP Site server support, 472
 IIS support, 458
Office 97 CD, MCSE toolkit component, 397
One Touch Network Assisstant 10/100, 841–842
one-hour rule, troubleshooting, 917
one-way trust relationship, described, 60–61
operating system ring model, TCP/IP, 114–115
operating systems
 dual-boot system setup, 44
 installing NT Server 4.0 over, 43
 SBS modifications, 655–656
 Service Pack 4 fixes, 555–559
 TCP/IP comparisons, 114
 Terminal Server supported types, 637
 unstable, 967
operators, display, filter, 825
Option Pack and Service Pack 4, components, 7
options: variable field
 TCP header element, 135–136
 TCP/IP packet element, 133
organization, described, 515
OSI model, versus TCP/IP DOD model, 112–113
outside IT consultant, technology committee members, 442–443

P

packet layers, Proxy Server 1.0/2.0 security, 667
packets, TCP/IP components, 129–136
Padding: variable field
 TCP header element, 136
 TCP/IP packet element, 133
pager management, troubleshooting, 912–913
paid support incidents, troubleshooting resource, 960

parity zone, RAID calculations, 20
partitions
   boot, 37, 48–51
   NTFS deletion, 36
   planning guidelines, 24
   setup decisions, 36–37
password encryption, security options, 363–364
passwords
   administrator conventions, 33
   Network Monitor, 826–827
   Small Business Server cautions, 726–727
patches, BIOS, 878
Path MTU Discovery, TCP/IP support, 126
patterns, Network Monitor, 831–833
PC Anywhere, versus Terminal Server, 631
PC Zone, MCSE toolkit catalog, 394, 398
PCAnywhere program, described, 97
PDC (Primary Domain Controller)
   administrator password issues, 33
   described, 29
   SAM database, 29
PEC (primary enterprise controller)
   Enterprise Edition, 625
   MSMQ, 525
PEFMON command, launching Performance Monitor, 762
people, planning guidelines, 22–23
Per Seat licensing mode, described, 31
Per Server licensing mode, described, 31
percent of revenue, network budgeting 440–441
PERFMON command, 762
performance, build 1381 issues, 603–604
performance analysis
   built-in tools, 735–738
   central tendency, 739–741
   conceptual steps, 746–747
   correlation analysis, 741–742
   described, 734
   disk subsystem, 749–750
   Event Viewer, 735, 737
   frequency distribution, 739
   index creation, 743
   mean, 739–741
   median, 739–741
   memory monitoring, 748–749
   mode, 739–741
   network adapters, 751
   Network Monitor, 735–736, 746
   network services listing, 752–753
   network subsystem, 750–754
   Performance Monitor, 735, 745, 759–804
   probability distribution, 742
   processors, 749
   protocol limiting advantages, 752
   qualitative tools, 743–745
   quantitative tools, 738–743
   reasons for declining performance, 754–756
   regression, 741
   seasonality, 743
   statistical manipulation, 756
   Task Manager, 735–736, 746
   trend line analysis, 738–739
   troubleshooting processes, 747–748
   Windows NT Diagnostics, 735, 737
performance benchmarks, described, 757–758
Performance Monitor
   adding counters to a chart, 763
   Alert view, 763, 768–774
   application server environment system performance, 797
   baseline creation, 776, 779–780
   baseline object capturing guidelines, 777–779
   benefits, 745
   capabilities, 759–762
   centering, 764–766
   chart scaling, 766–767
   Chart view, 763, 767–768
   cluttered chart workarounds, 801–802
   configuration settings, 764–767
   counters, 762–763
   data collection, 767, 775–780
   data file storage issues, 776
   data interpretation, 780–785
   day-to-day administration, 390–391
   default time interval setting for data collection, 776
   disk bottlenecks, 792–793
   environment analysis, 795–798
   features, 760–761
   file server counters, 797
   file/print server environment analysis, 796–797
   in-depth analysis process, 785–795
   instances, 762–763
   launching, 762
   Log view, 763, 774
   Logical Disk:Avg.Disk Queue Length counter, 782
   LogicalDisk:% Disk Time counter, 792
   LogicalDisk:Avg. Disk Bytes/Transfer counter, 793

LogicalDisk:Disk Bytes/sec counter, 793
LogicalDisk:Disk Queue Length counter, 793
memory bottlenecks, 785–786
memory management, 786–787
memory monitoring, 748–749
Memory:Available Bytes counter, 787
Memory:Committed Bytes counter, 788
Memory:Pages/sec counter, 782
Memory:Pool Non-paged Bytes counter, 789
MONITOR.EXE command line switches, 772
monthly server activities, 428
NetBEUI:Bytes Total/sec counter, 794
NetBEUI:Datagrams/sec counter, 794
NetBEUI:Frames/sec counter, 795
network bottlenecks, 793–794
Network Interface:Bytes Sent/sec counter, 794
Network Interface:Bytes Total/sec counter, 783
Network Interface:Output Queue Length counter, 795
Network Segment:% Network Utilization counter, 794
NWLink IPX:Bytes Total/sec counter, 794
NWLink IPX:Datagrams/sec counter, 794
NWLink IPX:Frames/sec counter, 795
object addition, 764
Object:Processes counter, 783
objects, 762–763
Physical Disk:Avg. Disk Queue Length counter, 783
PhysicalDisk: Disk Time counter, 792
PhysicalDisk:Avg. Disk Bytes/Transfer counter, 793
PhysicalDIsk:Disk Bytes/sec counter, 793
PhysicalDisk:Disk Queue Length counter, 793
pmw file logging configuration, 773
print server counters, 797
Process:% Processor Time counter, 791
Process:Page Faults/sec counter, 788
Process:Page File Bytes counter, 789
Process:Working Set counter, 787
processor bottlenecks, 789–792
Processor:% Privileged Time counter, 790
Processor:% Processor Time counter, 784, 790
Processor:% User Time counter, 791
Processor:Interrupts/sec counter, 791
protocol analyzing, 794–795
Redirector:Bytes Total/sec counter, 785
relogging, 798–799
Report view, 763, 775
results interpretation, 767
running as a service, 770–774
running multiple copies, 799–801
scaling, 764
Server Work Queues:Queue Length counter, 791
Server:Bytes Total/sec counter, 785, 793
Server:Logon/sec counter, 793
Server:Logons Total counter, 793
Service dialog box, 773
statistical manipulation, 756
System:% Total Processor Time counter, 785
System:Processor Queue Length counter, 791
TCP:Segments/sec counter, 795
Terminal Server modifications, 645–646
Thread:% Processor Time counter, 792
time intervals, 764
trusting applications, 786
UDP:Datagrams/sec counter, 795
versus NetWare MONITOR.NLM, 761–762
view selection, 763
performance monitoring, described, 428
Performance tab sheet
  Application performance option, 891–892
  System Properties sheet, 891–892
  Task Manager, 856
  virtual memory, 892–893
performance view
  commit charge, 860
  CPU usage, 858
  kernel memory, 860–861
  MEM usage, 858–859
  physical memory, 859
  total handles, 859
  total processes, 859
  total threads, 859
  totals, 859
period (.) character, domain level separator, 262
permissions
  NTFS (NT File System), 71–74
  share, 74–76
Phillips screwdrivers, MCSE toolkit component, 394
Phoenix, BIOS upgrades, 879
Phone Book Administrator, CPS, 501–505
Phone Book Service, CPS, 501–505

phone books
  CPS (Connection Point Services) management, 501–505
  New Phonebook Entry Wizard, 353–354
Phone Number dialog box, ISP/Dial-Up Networking configuration, 355–356
physical address, ARP, 223
physical memory,, performance view, 859
physical security, described, 70
physical site
  as-built drawing, 12–13
  cable planning/testing, 12
  infrastructure elements, 13–14
  media infrastructure, 12
  planning guidelines, 11–14
physical wear, declining performance reason, 754
PhysicalDisk: Disk Time counter, Performance Monitor, 792
PhysicalDisk:Avg. Disk Bytes/Transfer counter, Performance Monitor, 793
PhysicalDisk:Avg. Disk Queue Length counter, Performance Monitor, 783
PhysicalDisk:Disk Bytes/sec counter, Performance Monitor, 793
PhysicalDisk:Disk Queue Length counter, Performance Monitor, 793
Pickup directory, SMTP, 476
PICS (Platform for Internet Content Selection) ratings, IIS, 465–467
ping
  LAN/WAN connectivity verification, 415–417
  TCP/IP connectivity testing, 124
  TCP/IP troubleshooting tools, 219–223
ping command
  /? command line switch, 219
  general steps, 222–223
  testing IP security, 221–222
  use of, 221
Ping Plotter program, described, 416–417
planning guidelines
  drive mappings, 23
  existing networks, 25
  GSNW (Gateway Services for NetWare), 25
  key contact list, 23
  KISS (keep it simple starting), 24
  naming conventions, 24
  partition guidelines, 24
  people, 22–23
  physical site, 11–14
  reseating interface cards, 24
  service providers, 22

software, 21–22
system components, 14–23
user security, 23
utility partition building, 24
Plug and Play, Windows 2000 Server, 970
policies, SCE (Security Configuration Editor), 565–567
Policies⇨Trust Relationships command, 60
portable file cabinet, MCSE toolkit component, 398
ports, HP JetDirect-connected printers, 64–66
POST (power on system test), 809
post-hardware detection, configuration selection, 928–932
Posting Acceptor, Site Server Express 2.0 component, 513–514
power management, Windows 2000 Server, 971
power outlets, physical site planning, 14
PPP (Point-to-Point Protocol)
  LCP extensions, 363
  versus SLIP dial-up connections, 350
PPP TCP/IP Settings dialog box, described, 361–362
PPTP (Point-to-Point Tunneling Protocol)
  described, 376–377
  installation, 377–380
  SP4 hotfix, 557–558
  TCP/IP configuration, 188
Precedence field, TCP/IP packet element values, 131
primary servers, described, 270
print servers
  Performance Monitor environment analysis, 796–797
  Windows 2000 Server, 968
print services, build 1381 version issues, 606
printers
  HP JetDirect-connected, 64–66
  HP network, 726
  local port connection, 64
  naming conventions, 68
  server addition, 63–68
  share options, 66–68
printing
  TCP/IP features, 125
  Windows 2000 Server, 972
PRIV hotfix, Service Pack 3, 544
probability distribution, quantitative analysis method, 742
problem solving methodology, 913–917

process of elimination, server
    troubleshooting steps, 401
Process:% Processor Time counter,
    Performance Monitor, 791
Process:Page Faults/sec counter,
    Performance Monitor, 788
Process:Page File Bytes counter,
    Performance Monitor, 789
Process:Working Set counter, Performance
    Monitor, 787
processes view
  converting image names to real names,
    871–874
  getting prioritized, 867–871
  Task Manager, 861
Processor:% Privileged Time counter,
    Performance Monitor, 790
Processor:% Processor Time counter,
    Performance Monitor, 784, 790
Processor:% User Time counter,
    Performance Monitor, 791
Processor:Interrupts/sec counter,
    Performance Monitor, 791
processors
  bottleneck analysis, 789–792
  dual-processor motherboard advantages,
    17
  multiple, 674–675
  performance analysis, 749
  planning guidelines, 15–17
  purchasing guidelines, 15–17
  servers versus workstations, 610
  Service Pack 3 supported types, 536
  statistical manipulation, 756
  utilization test, 15–17
professional resources, 959–960
profile quotas, SP4, 590–591
profiles
  mandatory, 77
  new user settings, 55–56
  roaming, 76–77
  user, 76–77
programs
  See also utilities
  ARCServe, 90
  Backup Exec, 89, 729
  Chameleon UNIX Link97, 139
  Cheyenne's InocuLAN for Windows NT,
    93–94
  DiskKeeper, 433, 754
  Hyena, 393–394, 409–410
  IBM ADSTAR Distributed Storage Manager,
    90

Inoculan for Small Business Server, 729
McAffee VirusScan, 92–93
MetaFrame, 641–642
Microsoft Mail, 98–102
Norton Utilities, 433
NT Diagnostics, 418
NTBACKUP, 86–89, 404
PCAnywhere, 97, 631
Ping Plotter, 416–417
Reflection NFS Connection, 140
SATAN, 427
ServerBench, 757
STB (Socket Test Bench), 757
Storage Resource Manager, 432
Vinci, 433
VirusScan, 406
WinSock 2, 138
protocol definitions, display filter box,
    836–837
Protocol field, TCP/IP, 132
protocols
  ARP (Address Resolution Protocol),
    119–121
  BOOTP (Bootstrap protocol), 195
  CHAP (Challenge Handshake
    Authentication Protocol), 506
  define filter, 817–818
  enabled, 822
  ICA (Independent Computing
    Architecture), 642
  ICMP (Internet Control Message Protocol),
    121
  IGMP (Internet Group Management
    Protocol), 121–122, 126
  IP (Internet Protocol), 118–119
  MS-CHAP (Microsoft Challenge Handshake
    Authentication), 506
  Network Monitor, 817
  packet activity, 821
  performance analysis, 752
  PPTP (Point-to-Point Tunneling Protocol),
    376–380
  RADIUS (Remote Authentication Dial-In
    User Service), 505
  RCP (Remote Copy Protocol), 124
  RDP (Remote Desktop Protocol), 636
  setup options, 39–40
  SNMP (Simple Network Management
    Protocol), 123
  TCP (Transmission Control Protocol),
    116
  TCP/IP, 107–142, 143–210
  UDP (User Datagram Protocol), 117

Proxy Server 1.0/2.0
　described, 666–668
　Proxy Server Upgrade Wizard, 668
　SBS implementation troubleshooting, 727
Proxy Server Upgrade Wizard, downloading, 668
proxy servers, Internet Explorer configuration, 381–383
PSC (primary site controller), MSMQ, 525
publishing point, NetShow Services 3.0, 575
publications
　Art of Testing Network systems, The, 843
　CIO magazine, 441
　Computerworld, 441
　Honest Truth about Lying with Statistics, The, 756
　InfoWorld, 422
　Internet Connectivity White Paper, 660
　LAN to WAN Interconnection, 842
　Microsoft Certified Professional Magazine, 345
　Network Essentials, 162
　Networking Essentials MCSE Study Guide, 19
　PC Week, 422
　Puget Sound Computer User, 398
　Rocky Mountain Computer User, 398
PUTINENV utility, described, 84
PWS (Peer Web Services), NT Workstation, 612

Q

QoS (Quality of Service)
　Admission Control Services, 973–974
　relating to Admission Control Services, 978–979
QoS host architecture, Admission Control Services, 977
qualitative tools, performance analysis, 743–745
quantitative tools, performance analysis, 738–743
Queue directory, SMTP, 476
queues, MSMQ, 524
QuickStart Wizards, unicast publishing points, 579–582
Quote of the Day, TCP/IP support, 125

R

radio, MCSE toolkit component, 398
RADIUS (Remote Authentication Dial-In User Service) protocol, 505
RAID (redundant array of inexpensive disks)
　described, 20
　parity zone space calculations, 20
RAID 5, described, 20
RAM
　See also memory
　described, 18
　monitoring with Task Manager, 428–431
　one-to-one performance return for each dollar spent, 18
RAS (Remote Access Service)
　128-bit encryption algorithms, 536
　described, 95
　dial-out configuration, 351
　installation, 96–97
　multilink capability, 351
　Terminal Server support, 6
RAS connections, servers versus workstations, 610
RCP (Remote Copy Protocol) command, TCP/IP troubleshooting tools, 238
RDISK command, 947
RDP (Remote Desktop Protocol), Terminal Server, 636
RDP-based Window terminal, manufacturers, 637–638
RDS (Remote Data Service), described, 530
read-only attribute, changing, 47
real-time security alerts, Proxy Server 1.0/2.0, 667
reboots
　after modifications, 915
　fewer with Windows 2000 Server, 969
　monthly server activities, 428–431
　TCP/IP troubleshooting, 212
reciprocity agreements, disaster recovery, 435
record class, zone files, 267
record type, zone files, 267
Recovery section, Startup/Shutdown tab sheet, 895
recusion, name resolution element, 271
Recycle Bin, emptying to improve performance, 755
redirecting commands, 216
Redirector:Bytes Total/sec counter, Performance Monitor, 785
reflashing, described, 878

Reflection NFS Connection program, TCP/IP
    protocol support, 140
Registry
    change auditing with SCE, 569–570
    hard drive source file path, 45–46
    removing TCP/IP files, 249
    SBS (Small Business Server) issues, 657
    SOFTWARE hive, 937–938
    TCP/IP Parameters subkey settings,
        126–129
    troubleshooting via, 955
Registry Editor, service pack version
    number display, 540
regression, quantitative analysis method,
    741
relationships, domain trusts, 59–61
reliability, build 1381 issues, 603
relogging, Performance Monitor, 798–799
remote access
    PCAnywhere program, 97
    RAS (Remote Access Service), 96–97
    versus remote control, 631–633
Remote Access Setup dialog box, dial-up
    connections, 350–351
remote computer, file transfer, 234
remote control
    Terminal Server features, 634–635
    versus remote access, 631–633
remote networks, default gateways, 362
Remote Winsock (DNS/Port 53), SP4, 591
removable hard disks, data file storage, 776
repair process, 944–947
Report view, Performance Monitor, 763, 775
Report Writer
    catalog, 519
    selection criteria, 520
    Site Server Express 2.0, 514–521
    topics creation, 520–521
reports, WinMSD, 889
reproducing problems, troubleshooting, 911
requests, described, 514
Reserved field, TCP/IP packet element, 134
resolution problems, TCP/IP
    troubleshooting, 243
resolvers, DNS, 271
resource conflicts, declining performance
    reason, 754
resource kits, MCSE toolkit component, 398
resources
    books, 842–843, 957–958
    display filter box, protocol definitions,
        836–837
    hardware devices, 841–842
    Internet research, 840–841, 956–957
    Microsoft Solution Provider program, 835
    Microsoft TechNet, 837–839, 958–959
    newsgroups, 956
    Official Microsoft certification training,
        835–836
    paid support incidents, 834–835
    professional, 959–960
    TCP/IP troubleshooting, 251
    training and education, 959
    Web, 956–957
Resources tab sheet, 883–884
restores
    day-to-day administration testing, 405
    IIS, 467–469
restricted groups, SCE (Security
    Configuration Editor), 568
reverse hosting, Proxy Server 1.0/2.0, 667
reverse lookup, name resolution element,
    272
reverse lookup files, described, 268
reverse proxy, Proxy Server 1.0/2.0, 667
REXE (Remote Execution), TCP/IP support,
    124
REXEC command, TCP/IP troubleshooting
    tools, 239
RFCs (Requests for Comments)
    Admission Control Services, 982
    described, 109–111
    DHCP, 287
    DNS standards/revisions, 285–286
RIP (Routing Information Protocol), SP4
    hotfix, 557–558
RIP (Routing Information Protocol) Listener,
    SP4, 592
roaming profiles, described, 76–77
ROUTE ADD command, default gateways,
    155–157
route command, options, 228
route
    TCP/IP routing table modification, 124–125
    TCP/IP troubleshooting tools, 228
routers, Admission Control Services, 981
routing tables, described, 163–166
routing, TCP/IP configuration, 197–198
routing/clustering support, Windows 2000
    Server, 973
roving users, TCP/IP support, 198–199
RPC (Remote Procedure Calls)
    enhancements for VB, SP4, 592
RRAS, SP4 hotfix, 557–558
RSAC (Recreational Software Advisory
    Council), rating systems, 465–467

RSH (Remote Shell), TCP/IP support, 124
RSH command, TCP/IP troubleshooting tools, 239
Run dialog box, 877, 947

S

SAM database
   administrator password issues, 33
   PDC (Primary Domain Controllers), 29
SATAN program, security testing, 427
saving, captures, 826
SBM (Subnet Broadcast Management), 978
SBS (Small Business Server)
   administration, 719–723
   Administrator Read permission, 705
   architecture, 682–683
   attitude differences, 679
   client COM port configuration, 677–678
   client installation, 716–719
   client-side components, 676–678
   component list, 650–652
   computer naming conventions, 712
   computer setup, 709–716
   Console, 675–676
   Crystal Reports 4.5, 674–675
   customer base, 682
   described, 650
   design goals, 681–682
   event log errors, 727
   expertise advantages, 679
   fax client, 677
   Fax Server 1.0, 669–672
   future development issues, 729
   Hardware Compatibility List issues, 683
   HP network printer issues, 726
   IIS (Internet Information Server), 668–669
   Index Server 1.1, 673–674
   licensing requirements, 656–657
   market affluence, 679
   Microsoft Exchange Server 5.0, 658–663
   Microsoft Proxy Server 1.0/2.0, 666–668
   modem sharing, 724–726
   modem sharing client, 677–678
   Modem Sharing Server 1.0, 672–673
   MS Office applications installation, 710
   NT Option Pack utilization, 658
   NT Service Pack 3 issues, 657
   operating system modifications, 655–656
   password cautions, 726–727
   Phase A character-based setup, 685–690
   Phase B Windows NT Server GUI-based setup, 690–694
   Phase C Windows NT Server setup, 695–698
   philosophy, 679–682
   Proxy Server 2.0 implementation troubleshooting, 727
   Registry issues, 657
   release notes, 652–653
   release version differences, 654
   security troubleshooting, 727–728
   server-side setup process, 683–698
   Service Pack 1 application process, 653–654
   setup disk creation process, 684
   small business model, 679–719
   software vendor support issues, 723–724
   SQL Server 6.5, 664–665
   troubleshooting, 723–729
   user access rights, 708
   user addition, 698–709
   versus Windows NT Server 4.0, 655–658
   virus detection issues, 729
   Windows NT Server 4.0 variation, 6
   workstation-side setup, 698–719
SBS Console
   described, 675–676, 719–720
   More Tasks sheet, 720–721
   option listing, 722–723
   password changing issues, 726–727
   Small Business Server administration tool, 719–723
   Tasks sheet, 720–721
scaling
   BackOffice application Performance Monitor workspaces, 766–767
   build 1381 version issues, 604
   charts, 766–767
   Performance Monitor, 764
SCE (Security Configuration Editor)
   account policies, 565–566
   analyzing, 571–573
   basic configuration files, 564
   command line configuration/analysis parameters, 573–574
   compatible configuration versus basic configuration, 564
   configuration, 571–573
   described, 561–562
   directory objects, 571
   event log, 567–568
   file system component, 570–571
   high security configuration issues, 565

installation, 562–564
local policies, 566–567
MS Office 97 SR1 configuration issues, 564
Registry change auditing, 569–570
restricted groups, 568
secure configuration issues, 565
system service, 568–569
template components, 564–571
Scope Properties dialog box, DHCP, 304–306
scopes
  creating, 304–306
  DHCP, 300–301
  modifying properties, 306
  removing, 306
screwdrivers, MCSE toolkit component, 394
scripts
  Edit Phonebook Entry dialog box options, 363
  logon, 81–85
  Microsoft Script Debugger, 530–532
  Windows 2000 Server, 984
SCSI (Small Computer System Interface), pre-setup information gathering, 28
SCSI drives, sector sparing, 755
Seagate, Backup Exec, 89, 729
search engines, name resolution uses, 260–261
SearchList, TCP/IP values, 128
seasonality, quantitative analysis method, 743
secondary servers, described, 270
second-level domains, described, 264
sector sparing, SCSI drives, 755
security
  administrator password conventions, 33
  backups, 85–91
  balance issues, 69–70
  build 1381 version issues, 604–605
  documentation, 72
  Edit Phonebook Entry dialog box options, 363–364
  forms, 70
  FTP server site, 234
  FTP Site server account settings, 472–473
  FTP Site server settings, 474–475
  hackers, 427
  IIS directory settings, 463–464
  logon, 70–71
  logon scripts, 81–85
  NTFS access types/associated rights, 74
  NTFS permissions, 71–74
  password protection, Network Monitor, 826–827

  physical, 70
  Proxy Server 1.0/2.0 packet layers, 667
  RSAC (Recreational Software Advisory Council), 465–467
  run Identify Network Monitor Users menu selection, 827
  SATAN program testing, 427
  servers versus workstations, 611
  share permissions, 74–76
  SIDs (security identifiers), 62
  Small Business Server troubleshooting, 727–728
  SNMP configuration, 206–208
  system policies, 78–81
  TCP/IP configuration, 188–189
  testing activities, 427–428
  user planning, 23
  user profiles, 76–77
  verify after repairs, 946
  virus protection schemes, 91–94
  Windows 2000 Server, 985–986
security alerts, Proxy Server 1.0/2.0 real-time, 667
Select Network Service dialog box, SNMP installation, 201–202
Sequence Number field, TCP/IP packet element, 133
sequence value, searching for, 837–839
Server dialog box, Dial-Up Networking setup, 354–355
server internals, planning guidelines, 19
Server Manager
  day-to-day administration, 389–390
  server services verification, 414
server proxying, Proxy Server 1.0/2.0, 668
Server Work Queues:Queue Length counter, Performance Monitor, 791
Server:Bytes Total/sec counter, Performance Monitor, 785, 793
Server:Logon/sec counter, Performance Monitor, 793
Server:Logons Total counter, Performance Monitor, 793
server-based scheduling, Exchange Server support, 658
ServerBench program, performance benchmarks, 757
servers
  100 percent uptime goal, 422
  BDC (Backup Domain Controller), 29–30
  boot.ini file timeout parameter editing, 46–48

continued

servers *(continued)*
  caching-only, 270
  daily application verification, 413–415
  DHCP, 287–288, 295–297
  DHCP planning, 294
  disaster recovery, 433–436
  disk space mapping, 431–433
  dual-processor motherboard advantages, 17
  Edit Phonebook Entry dialog box options, 359–363
  FTP Site, 471–476
  identical spares, 434–435
  member, 30
  MMC property settings, 456–467
  name, 269–270
  NetShow Services 3.0 configuration, 578–588
  PDC (Primary Domain Controllers), 29
  physical security issues, 70
  primary, 270
  printer addition, 63–68
  proxy, 381–383
  secondary, 270
  Small Business Server philosophy, 679–682
  source file hard disk storage advantages, 44
  stand-alone, 30
  troubleshooting, 400–404
  versus workstations, 607–612
  WINS configuration, 321–326
server-side, Small Business Server setup process, 683–698
Service dialog box, Performance Monitor, 773
Service Pack 2, problems, 534–535
Service Pack 3
  CD version advantages, 536
  download FTP site, 535
  ERD (Emergency Repair Disk) modifications, 540–542
  expanding to a subdirectory, 537
  hotfixes, 542–544
  installation, 535–540
  installation troubleshooting, 540–542
  NT server debug symbol files, 536
  overwriting existing files/driver concerns, 539
  SBS (Small Business Server) issues, 657
  uninstall directory issues, 538
Service Pack 4
  40-bit versus 128-bit encryption, 546–548
  Certificate Server fix, 552–553
  Compaq Fiber Storage Driver, 592
  DCOM/HTTP Tunneling, 590
  DHCP fix, 556
  DNS fix, 556
  Euro Key Patch, 590
  Event Log Service fix, 559
  FPNW (File and Print Service for NetWare), 590
  IE 4.01 Service Pack 1 fix, 552
  IGMP (Internet Group Management Protocol) v2, 590
  IIS 4.0 fix, 553
  installation process, 545–546
  Internet Explorer 4.0 preinstallation advantages, 545
  MSAA (Microsoft Active Accessibility Support), 590
  MSMQ for Windows NT fix, 553–555
  MTS fix, 555
  multicast stations, 582–583
  NetShow Services 3.0, 574–588
  networking fixes, 555–559
  NNTP fix, 555
  option pack fixes, 552–555
  OS (operating system) fixes, 555–559
  PPTP fix, 557–558
  preinstallation requirements, 545
  profile quotas, 590–591
  Remote Winsock (DNS/Port 53), 591
  RIP (Routing Information Protocol) Listener, 592
  RIP fix, 557–558
  RPC (Remote Procedure Calls) enhancements for VB, 592
  RRAS fix, 557–558
  SCE (Security Configuration Editor), 561–574
  Site Server Express 3.0, 588–589
  SMTP fix, 555
  uninstallation, 548
  Visual Studio-MICS, 592
  WBEM (Web-Based Enterprise Management), 592
  Windows NT Services for UNIX, 592–595
  WINS fix, 556
  Year 2000 (Y2K) fix, 550–551
service packs
  beta-testing, 535
  described, 436–437, 533–534
  reapplying after repairs, 947
  SBS Service Pack 1, 653–654
  Service Pack 2 problems, 534–535

Service Pack 3, 535–544
Service Pack 4, 544–548, 561–596
uninstall feature, 535
version number display, 540
service profiles, Index Server 2.0 creation, 498–500
services
 build 1381 version, 606–607
 loading/initializing at boot up, 935
 running Performance Monitor as, 770–774
Services for NetWare, described, 26
Services tab, WinMSD, 888
session establishment, Network Monitor, 832
Session Manager
 DOS Devices key, 937
 Kernel phase of booting, 935
 Memory Management key, 937
Session Statistics pane, Network Monitor Capture window, 808–809
SET statements, Environment tab sheet, 884
Settings option, Network tab sheet, 887
setup
 administrator password issues, 33
 alternate methods, 41–44
 boot partition advantages, 37
 date/time settings, 40–41
 default display settings, 40–41
 dial-up versus wired server options, 38
 disk controller detection, 35–36
 domain names, 31
 dual-boot systems, 44
 ERD (Emergency Repair Disk) installation repair, 35, 38
 file copying process, 38
 file system decisions, 32–33, 37
 freezes on startup, 40
 graphical setup stage, 38–41
 hard drive controller recognition information gathering, 28
 HCL (Hardware Compatibility List), 29
 information gathering, 38
 installing NT Server 4.0 from a network share, 41–43
 installing NT Server 4.0 over other operating systems, 43
 legacy application issues, 37
 licensing modes, 31–32
 network services, 39–40
 network startup process, 40
 NIC detection, 38–39
 NIC recognition information gathering, 29
 NTFS partition deletion, 36
 partition creation, 36–37

Per Seat licensing mode, 31
Per Server licensing mode, 31
pre-installation information gathering, 28–33
protocol options, 39–40
searching for previous NT version options, 36
server roles, 29–30
system boot process, 34–35
TCP/IP installation issues, 170
text-based (blue screen) stage, 34–38
two-stage process, 34
WINNT directory, 37
SETUP.EXE file, Windows NT 4.0 Option Pack, 451
share permissions
 described, 74–75
 versus NTFS permission, 75
shared printers, naming conventions, 68
shares
 file sharing setup, 68–69
 logon script uses, 82
sharing, day-to-day administration procedures, 419–420
SHOWACLS.EXE file, security configuration documentation source, 72
SIDs (security identifiers), described, 62
simple protocols, TCP/IP, 125
simple routing, described, 140–141
single domain trust model, described, 61
single hard drives, disk storage poor design example, 19
single master domain trust model, described, 61
single-point Internet connection, Proxy Server 1.0/2.0, 666
Site Server Express 2.0
 Content Analyzer, 510–513
 described, 510
 Posting Acceptor, 513–514
 Report Writer, 514–521
 Usage Import, 514–521
Site Server Express 3.0, Service Pack 4, 588–589
slaves, DNS, 270
SLIP, versus PPP dial-up connections, 350
small LAN, DHCP server implementation, 295
smart routing, MSMQ/E, 526
SMP (symmetric multiprocessing), Enterprise Edition, 621
SMS (System Management Server), described, 200, 806

SMS Network Monitor versus Windows NT
    Server 4, 844–851
SMTP (Simple Mail Transport Protocol)
  described, 476
  directories, 476
  hotfix, 555
  IIS configuration, 476–478
  MCIS (Microsoft Commercial Internet
      System) upgrading, 476
  NDR (nondelivery report), 477
  property settings, 476–478
snap-ins
  COM (Component Object Model) support,
      506
  creating, 507–510
  DCOM (Distributed Component Object
      Model) support, 506
  described, 506
  SCE (Security Configuration Editor),
      561–574
SNMP (Simple Network Management
    Protocol)
  agent configuration, 202–204
  communities configuration, 204–206
  described, 123, 199–200
  TCP/IP agent, 125
  TCP/IP configuration, 199–208
  installation planning/process, 200–202
  security configuration, 206–207
  traps, 204–206
software
  logon script automatic updating, 82
  planning guidelines, 21–22
  Terminal Server requirements, 639–640
software compression, enabling, 362
SOFTWARE hive, 937–938
software vendors
  application upgrading, 438
  Small Business Server support issues,
      723–724
SortTemp directory, SMTP, 476
Source Address field, TCP/IP packet
    element, 133
source files
  hard drive path Registry editing, 45–46
  storing on server's hard disk, 44
Source Port field, TCP/IP packet element,
    133
spanned hard drives, disk storage poor
    design example, 19
spare servers, disaster recovery techniques,
    434–435
SQL Server 6.5
  described, 664
  key features, 664–665
  MSMQ requirements, 525
  SBS (Small Business Server), 664–665
SRV hotfix, Service Pack 3, 544
stand-alone servers, described, 30
start values, Boot Loader phase, 931
Startup/Shutdown tab sheet
  BOOT.INI file, 894
  countdown value, 894–895
  Recovery section, 895
  VGA mode, 894–895
  WinMSD, 893–895
static energy discharge wristband, MCSE
    toolkit component, 394
static IP address, described, 361
static route, described, 125
Station statistics, Network Monitor Capture
    window, 808
station, NetShow Services 3.0, 575
statistics option, Network tab sheet, 888
statistics, WINS Manager view, 327–329
STB (Socket Test Bench) program,
    performance benchmarks, 757
steelhead technology, Windows 2000 Server,
    973
stop screens
  debuggers, 952–955
  debugging terms, 952
  described, 950–951
  hardware related errors, 949
  troubleshooting, 949–955
  using, 951
storage of files, Windows 2000 Server, 972
Storage Resource Manager program,
    described, 432
streaming, described, 575
structured exception handling, described,
    952
subdomains, described, 264–265
subkeys, GroupOrderList, 932
subnet mask
  described, 148–150
  Fourth Octet Position, 338
subnet mask value, position, 337
subnet number, determination, 339–340
subnet size
  binary bit values, 337
  decimal values, 337
subnetting
  administration advantages, 334
  binary bit values converted to decimal,
      337, 342–343

bottom line, 335
calculator, 343
Code, 336
default subnet masks, 336
described, 333–334
Ethernet, 334
host number, 339–340
improved security, 334–335
IP address conservation, 334
IP network, 334
LANs, 334
license class, 336
limitations, 336
octet, 337
powers of 2, 338
routers Versus switches, 335
subnet mask chart, 346
subnet number, 339–340
switching, 335
Token Ring, 334
success audit events, described, 412
Summary pane, Network Monitor Frame Viewer window, 812
surface space, physical site planning, 13–14
switches
/?, ping command, 219
/all, 217–218
BOOT.INI file, 926
IPConfig, 217
switching, subnetting, 335
Symantec
Norton Utilities, 433
PCAnywhere program, 97
symbol file
described, 952
Service Pack 3 NT server debugging, 536
symmetric multiprocessing, Enterprise Edition, 621
synchronous messaging, described, 523–524
system boot, setup process, 34–35
system components
disk storage, 19–20
memory, 18
name brands versus clones, 20–21
network subsystem, 18
processor type, 15–17
server internals, 19
system date/time, setup settings, 40–41
System Editor, troubleshooting, 918–919
system files, missing, 940–949
system information reports, 889–890

system modifications, declining performance reason, 754
system partition, copying installation files to, 44–45
system policies
default computer settings, 79
default user settings, 79–80
described, 78
setup process, 79–81
uses, 78–79
System Policy Editor, system policy setup, 79–81
System Properties dialog box
environment tab, 886
Startup/Shutdown tab sheet, 954
System Properties sheet
General tab sheet, 891
OS startup delay parameter editing, 46–47
Performance tab sheet, 891–892
system reboot, monthly server activities, 428–431
system requirements
servers versus workstations, 611
Terminal Server, 639–640
system service, SCE (Security Configuration Editor), 568–569
System tab sheet
BIOS monitoring, 878
WinMSD, 878–879
SYSTEM.MDB file, described, 319
System:% Total Processor Time counter, Performance Monitor, 785
System:Processor Queue Length counter, Performance Monitor, 791

T

tables, data location, 432–433
tape backups, day-to-day administration tasks, 404–405
tape deck, MCSE toolkit component, 398
tape recorders, MCSE toolkit component, 398
Task Manager
Applications tab sheet, 854–855
benefits, 746
introduction, 854
multiple processors, 874–875
Performance tab sheet, 856
Processes tab sheet, 856–857
processor utilization test, 15–17
RAM monitoring, 428–431

Task Manager configuration
  applications view, 857
  performance view, 858–861
  processes column definitions, 863–866
  processes view, 861–874
Task Manager's Processor affinity menu, 876
Task Scheduler, Windows 2000 Server, 971
task scheduling, servers versus workstations, 608
TCP (Transmission Control Protocol), 116
TCP packets, captured with Display, filter, 823
TCP Port 80, IIS default setting, 458
TCP/IP (Transmission Control Protocol/Internet)
  advanced configurations, 182–188
  ARP (Address Resolution Protocol), 119–121, 124
  Berkeley Sockets interface support, 108–109
  BOOTP (Bootstrap protocol), 195
  breeder networks, 137
  certification exam, 345
  concepts, 346
  configuration settings, 177–182
  connectivity commands, 215
  connectivity utilities, 124
  core TCP/IP support, 123
  cross-platform client/server framework, 109
  database files, 240
  default gateways, 152–161
  default installation protocol history, 169
  default setup option, 39
  described, 107–108
  development history, 107–114
  DHCP (Dynamic Host Configuration Protocol) support, 125
  DHCP relay configuration, 195–197
  diagnostic commands, 215
  diagnostic utilities, 124
  dial-up connection requirements, 350
  DNS (Domain Name System) support, 125
  DNS configuration, 188–192
  DOD (Department of Defense) model layers, 112–114
  elective exam, 345
  existing Windows NT Server installation process, 171–176
  FINGER support, 124
  FTP support, 124
  heterogeneous networks, 137–138
  host addresses, 150–151
  hostname authentication, 124
  HP Jet-Direct device issues, 66
  IAB Official Protocol Standard, 111
  ICMP (Internet Control Message Protocol), 121
  IGMP (Internet Group Management Protocol), 121–122, 126
  installation preparations, 167–169
  installation process, 169–176
  Internet addressing components, 143–161
  Internet Information Server, 125
  Internet support features, 125
  Internetworking uses, 136–141
  IP (Internet Protocol), 118–119
  IP address classes, 151–152
  IP addresses, 144–148, 182–186
  IP routing, 161–163
  Ipconfig shortcomings, 124
  lpq (print queue status), 124
  LPR printing, 124
  manual configuration settings, 177–182
  multiple address assignments, 182–186
  multiple gateway configuration, 186–188
  nbstat (NetBIOS computer name listing), 124
  netstat session information, 124
  network programming support, 123
  NT Server 4.0 features, 123–129
  operating system comparisons, 114
  operating system ring model, 114–115
  packet implementation process, 129–136
  paradigm shift, 6
  Path MTU Discovery capability, 126
  ping connectivity testing, 124
  PPTP (Point-to-Point Tunneling Protocol) configuration, 188
  printing features, 125
  protocol suite versus protocol, 112–114
  Q & A, 249–251
  RCP (Remote Copy Protocol), 124
  Registry Parameters subkey settings, 126–129
  reinstalling, 247–249
  related services, 208–209
  researching, 142
  REXE (Remote Execution), 124
  RFCs (Requests for Comments), 109–111
  route routing table modification, 124–125
  routing configuration, 197–198
  routing tables, 163–166
  roving user support, 198–199
  RSH (Remote Shell), 124
  security configuration, 188–189

simple protocols, 125
simple routing, 140–141
small network configuration map, 168–169
SNMP (Simple Network Management
    Protocol), 123, 125, 199–208
subnet masks, 148–150, 181
subnetting, 333
TCP (Transmission Control Protocol), 116
Telnet support, 124
Tftp bidirectional file transfer support,
    124
third party software support, 138–140
tracert packet path display, 125
troubleshooting, 211–252
UDP (User Datagram Protocol), 117
Windows NT Server setup issues, 170
Windows Sockets, 108, 138
WINS (Windows Internet Naming Service)
    support, 125
WINS address configuration, 192–195
TCP/IP connectivity commands, 215
TCP/IP diagnostic commands, 215
TCP/IP installation
    connectivity utilities, 248
    DHCP server service, 248
    network printing support, 248
    SNMP services, 248
    WINS server service, 249
TCP/IP Protocol Properties dialog box
    default gateway values, 153
    enabling IP forwarding, 141
TCP/IP troubleshooting
    basics, 211–213
    database files, 240–247
    DNS server service, 249
    Q & A, 249–251
    questions, 213
    reinstalling TCP/IP, 247–249
    resolution problems, 243
    resources, 251
    timeout conditions, 243
    tool definition, 213–215
    tools use of, 215–240
TCP/IP troubleshooting tools
    ARP, 223–226
    Finger command, 239
    FTP, 232–234
    hostname, 232
    IPConfig, 216–219
    Microsoft Internet Explorer, 239–240
    nbstat, 226–228
    netstat, 228–231
    ping, 219–223

RCP command, 238
REXEC command, 239
route, 228
RSH command, 239
Telnet, 235–238
TFTP commands, 234
tracert, 231–232
TCP:Segments/sec counter, Performance
    Monitor, 795
TcpMaxConnectReTransmissions, TCP/IP
    values, 129
TcpMaxDataRetransmissions, TCP/IP values,
    129
TcpNumConnections, TCP/IP values, 129
TcpTimeWaitDelay, TCP/IP values, 129
TcpUseRFC1122UrgentPointer, TCP/IP
    values, 129
TDRs (time domain reflectors), network
    bottleneck detection, 750
Teardrop2 hotfix, Service Pack 3, 544
technology committee, described, 442–444
technology professionals, charges, 912
telco, line planning guidelines, 22
telephone jacks, physical site planning, 14
telephone line, MCSE toolkit component, 398
telephone numbers
    ISP/Dial-Up Networking configuration,
        355–358
    MCSE toolkit, 398
telephones, MCSE toolkit component, 398
Telnet command
    remote access of e-mail, 236
    TCP/IP support, 124
    TCP/IP troubleshooting tools, 235–238
    Windows NT Services for UNIX, 595
Telnet screens, 237–238
TEMP (temporary) directory, 884
template accounts, described, 58
templates, SCE (Security Configuration
    Editor), 564–571
temporary files, deleting to improve
    performance, 756
Terminal Server
    Administration tool, 643–644
    centralized management advantages, 635
    Client Creator tool, 643
    clients, 636–638
    components, 635–638
    Connection Configuration tool, 643
    cost lowering advantages, 635
    development history, 629–631
    environment, 631–633

continued

Terminal Server *(continued)*
  features, 633–635
  hardware requirements, 639
  ICA (Independent Computing Architecture), 642
  implementation processes, 638–640
  License Manager, 643
  MetaFrame component, 641–642
  multisession features, 635
  NetWare User access for Terminal Server, 643
  Novell NetWare server session support issues, 642
  operating system component, 636
  Performance Monitor modifications, 645–646
  RAS (Remote Access Services) support, 6
  RDP (Remote Desktop Protocol), 636
  RDP-based Window terminal manufacturers, 637–638
  remote control features, 634–635
  remote control versus remote access, 631–633
  sample session, 640–641
  shortcomings, 646–647
  supported operating systems, 637
  User Configuration dialog box, 644–645
  versus PC Anywhere, 631
  versus Windows NT Server 4.0, 642–646
  VM (virtual machine) sessions, 635
  Windows NT Server 4.0 variation, 6
test restores, described, 405
text-based (blue screen) setup stage, described, 34–38
TFTP (Trivial File Transfer Protocol), 234–235
Tftp bi-directional file transfer, TCP/IP support, 124
TFTP command, 234–235
thin clients, manufacturers, 637–638
third-level domains
  described, 264–265
  evaluating, 266–267
third-party tools, TCP/IP troubleshooting, 212
thread boosting, getting prioritized, 870–871
Thread:% Processor Time counter, Performance Monitor, 792
three setup boot disks, setup process, 34–35
three-way handshake, Network Monitor, 932
time interval, Performance Monitor settings, 764, 776

time series analysis, quantitative analysis method, 738–739
time zones, NET TIME command concerns, 83
timed backups, NTBACKUP program, 87–89
timeout conditions, TCP/IP troubleshooting, 243
timeout parameters, boot.ini file, 46–48
times
  client PC logon script setting, 83
  setup settings, 40–41
timing, network analysis, 833
Token Ring, subnetting, 334
Tools⇨Format command, 50
Tools⇨Map Network Drive command, 69
tools, new in Windows 2000 Server, 971–972
top-level domain, described, 263
Torx screwdrivers, MCSE toolkit component, 394
total handles, performance view, 859
Total Length field, TCP/IP packet element, 132
total processes, performance view, 859
Total Statistics pane, Network Monitor Capture window, 808
total threads, performance view, 859
totals, performance view, 859
tracert command, 231–232
  TCP/IP packet path display, 125
  TCP/IP troubleshooting tools, 231–232
traffic details, Network Monitor, 819
training and education, troubleshooting resource, 959
training, Microsoft certification, 835–836
transaction processing
  MSMQ (Microsoft Message Queue) 1.0, 523–529
  MTS (Microsoft Transaction Server) 2.0, 522–523
  Windows NT 4.0 Option Pack components, 522–529
transport layer, DOD model versus OSI model, 112–113
Transports option, Network tab sheet, 887
trapping packets, 809
Traps dialog box, SNMP configuration, 205–206
traps, SNMP configuration, 204–206
trend line analysis, quantitative analysis method, 738–739
troubleshooting
  area code changes, 918
  avoid shotgun theory, 913

boot files, 925–939
charge per hour, 912
debuggers, 952–955
debugging terms, 952–955
described, 912–913
DHCP servers, 319–320
disaster recovery, 433–436
display filter box, protocol definitions, 836–837
emergency repair process, 944–947
ERD (Emergency Repair Disk), 946–949
examine stop screens, 949–955
external factors, 918
first octet value, 916
getting out of trouble, 940–949
hardware versus software, 924–925
Input-Processing-Output model, 912
interpreting dump files, 955
Internet support groups, 403–404
lack of experience, 910
Last Good Boot option, 913
learning curve analysis, 921–922
map, 921
methodology, 910–913
Microsoft Solution Provider program, 835
Microsoft TechNet, 402–403
Microsoft TechNet CD-ROM, 837–839
missing system files, 940–943
network freezes on setup startup, 40
Official Microsoft certification training, 835–836
one-hour rule, 917
organization, 920–924
pager management, 912–913
paid support incidents, 834–835
performance analysis, 747–748
reapply service packs, 947
reboot after modifications, 915
record you actions/steps, 924
refresh Master Boot Record, 927
rename/replace a driver, 941–943
repair options, 946–947
reproducible problems, 911
resources, 955–961
separate ERD per machine, 949
servers, 400–404
Service Pack 3 installation, 540–542
Small Business Server, 723–729
starting NT with boot disk, 943–944
System Editor, 918–919
TCP/IP, 211–252
TCP/IP addresses, 913
technical aspects, 925
using hardware devices, 841–842
value of downtime, 919–920
verify security, 946
via Registry, 955
Windows NT 4.0 boot files, 943
Windows NT 4.0 Option Pack installation, 450–454
workstation side versus server side, 918–919
Year 2000 issues, 918
troubleshooting methodology, 913–917
trust models, described, 61
trust relationships
    described, 59–60
    one-way versus two-way, 60–61
    trust models, 61
Trust Relationships dialog box, described, 60
trusted domain, described, 60
trusting domain, described, 60
TTL (Time to Live) field, TCP/IP packet element, 132
two-way trust relationship, described, 60–61
Type of Service field, TCP/IP packet element, 130–131

U

UDP (User Datagrapm Protocol), described, 117
UDP:Datagrams/sec counter, Performance Monitor, 795
UGLR (users, global, local, rights), described, 62–63
undo capabilities, 913
Unicast On-Demand Wizard, unicast publishing points, 581
unicast publishing points, NetShow Services 3.0, 579–582
unicasting, NetShow Services 3.0, 575
uninstall directory
    Service Pack 4 issues, 548
    service pack feature, 535
UNIX
    introducing Windows NT Server 4.0 to existing network, 25
    RSH command, 239
    Windows NT Server 4.0 support issues, 27
UNIX-style database files, 240
updates, BIOS, 878

Urgent Pointer field, TCP/IP packet element, 135
Usage Import
  configuring import usage, 515–519
  hits, 514
  inference algorithms, 514–515
  ISAPI logging filter installation, 516
  organization, 515
  requests, 514
  Site Server Express 2.0, 514–521
  task setup, 518–519
  users, 515
  visits, 515
User⇨New User command, 54
user accounts, deleting, 426–427
User Configuration dialog box, Terminal Server, 644–645
User Environment Profile dialog box
  logon script naming, 83
  roaming profiles, 77
user interface, Windows 2000 Server, 970
User Manager for Domains
  account management tasks, 57–59
  day-to-day administration, 388–389
  delegate administrator access guidelines, 59
  deleting users, 56–57
  described, 54
  disabling versus deleting users, 57
  domain trust relationships, 59–61
  new user creation, 54–56
  renaming user accounts, 59
  roaming profiles, 76–77
  template account creation, 58
  user domain authentication, 59
  user profile settings, 55–56
User Preferences dialog box, Dial-Up Networking properties, 364–366
user profiles, described, 76–77
user security, needs planning, 23
user services
  adding printers to your server, 63–68
  file sharing, 68–69
UserData Properties dialog box
  file sharing setup, 68–69
  NTFS permissions, 73
users
  adding to groups, 55–56
  adding to Microsoft Mail, 101–102
  beta-testing service packs, 535
  creating, 54–56
  deleting, 56–57
  described, 515
  disabling versus deleting account advantages, 57
  domain authentication, 59
  education process, 400
  file sharing connection, 69
  global versus local group accounts, 62
  keeping informed of server status, 421
  mandatory profiles, 77
  NTFS access types/associated rights, 74
  profile settings, 55–56
  protecting, 421
  renaming, 59
  roaming profiles, 76–77
  roving TCP/IP support, 198–199
  share permissions, 74–76
  SIDs (security identifiers), 62
  Small Business Server addition, 698–709
  template accounts, 58
utilities
  See also programs
  ARP, 223–226
  FTP, 232–234
  hostname, 232
  IPConfig, 216–219
  nbstat, 226–228
  netstat, 228–231
  ping, 219–223
  RCP (Remote Copy Protocol), 238
  REXEC, 239
  RSH, 239
  Telnet, 235–238
  tracert, 231–232
utility partition, creating, 24

V

variables, troubleshooting, 913
ventilation, physical site planning, 14
Verisign, CA (certificate authority), 486
Version tab sheet, WinMSD, 877–878
video adapters, default setup settings, 40–41
View⇨Options command, 50
Vinci, clustering application, 433
virtual memory, Performance tab sheet, 892–893
viruses
  antivirus software testing, 406
  centralizing protection, 407
  Cheyenne's InocuLAN for Windows NT program, 93–94
  data file updating, 406–407

Index **1113**

day-to-day administration protection
    tasks, 405–408
e-mail concerns, 91
floppy disk concerns, 92
infection points, 91–92
McAffee VirusScan program, 92–93
Small Business Server detection solution
    issues, 729
VirusScan program, 406
virus-warning virus, 92
Web browser concerns, 91–92
VirusScan program, described, 406
visits, described, 515
Visual Studio-MICS, SP4, 592
VM (virtual machine), Terminal Server
    sessions, 635
VPN (virtual private network) WAN over
    Internet connection, 375–376

W

W3C Extended log file format
    FTP Site server support, 472
    IIS support, 458
WAN (Wide Area Network)
    Admission Control Services, 976
    day-to-day administration connectivity
        verification, 415–417
    Internet connection scenarios, 370–376
    ISDN combination scenario, 373
warning events, described, 411
WBEM (Web-Based Enterprise Management),
    SP4, 592
Web, troubleshooting resource, 956–957
Web browsers, virus infection point, 91–92
Web publications, develop for Windows
    2000 Server, 983
Web scripts, Microsoft Script Debugger,
    530–532
Web servers, Windows 2000 Server, 968
Web services, build 1381 version issues, 606
Web sites
    Alta Vista, 260
    Cisco, 836
    Citrix, 641
    Data Comm Warehouse, 394
    Dogpile, 261
    HCL (Hardware Compatibility List), 29
    IAB (Internet Activities Board), 111
    IDG Books, 380
    Infoseek, 260
    Inoculan for Small Business Server, 729
    InterNIC (Internet Network Information
        Center), 147, 258
    Microsoft, 168, 956, 987
    Microsoft Developer's Resource Group,
        200
    Microsoft Hardware Compatibility List,
        619
    Microsoft Support Knowledge Base, 251,
        550
    Microsoft Support Online, 403
    Microsoft TechNet, 953
    Microsoft training, 836
    MS Exchange support forum, 437
    network analysis, 840–841
    NPA (Network Professional Association
        Technical Resource CD, 397
    Option Pack/SBS-related instructions, 658
    PCZone, 394
    Phoenix, 878–879
    Ping Plotter, 416
    RAS 128-bit encryption algorithms, 536
    Ricochet modem, 398
    RSAC (Recreational Software Advisory
        Council), 467
    SATAN tool, 427
    SBS Console Customization and Style
        Guide, 675
    SID changer, 435
    U.S. Commerce Department Bureau of
        Export Administration, 536
    Yahoo!, 260
    Ziff-Davis, 757
WebMap views, Content Analyzer, 510–513
whiteboard, security map creation, 23
whois command, 214–215, 236–237
Window field, TCP/IP packet element, 135
Windows 2000 Server
    Active desktop, 970
    Active Directory, 983–984
    Admission Control Services, 973–982
    applications server, 968
    communication servers, 969
    described, 8, 444–445
    Device Manager, 970
    Distributed File system, 972
    Dynamic DNS, 972
    expectation management, 966–967
    features cut due to timeframes, 967
    fewer reboots, 969
    file servers, 968
    Group Policy Editor, 985

continued

Windows 2000 Server *(continued)*
  improved wizards, 970
  infrastructure servers, 969
  Internet, 983
  IP security management, 972
  large Ethernet frames, 972
  Microsoft Management Console, 970
  Microsoft's position, 968–969
  networking improvement, 972–983
  new tools, 971–972
  planning for, 986–987
  Plug and Play, 970
  print servers, 968
  reality of purchase/use timeframe, 967
  routing/clustering support, 973
  scripts, 984
  security, 985–986
  Web server, 968
Windows 95 CD, MCSE toolkit component, 396
Windows 95/98, upgrading to NT Server 4.0, 43
Windows 98 CD, MCSE toolkit component, 396
Windows Explorer, server disk space mapping, 431
Windows NT 4.0 Option Pack
  Add/Remove dialog box, 453
  ADO (ActiveX Data Objects) 1.5, 530
  Certificate Server 1.0, 485–494
  component listing, 450
  component selection process, 453–454
  default Web Site properties, 457–458
  IIS (Internet Information Server) 4.0, 455–485
  Index Server 2.0, 494–506
  installation, 450–454
  Internet applications, 455–506
  introduction, 449–450
  MDAC (Microsoft Data Access Component), 529–530
  Microsoft Script Debugger, 530–532
  MMC (Microsoft Management Console), 506–510
  MSMQ (Microsoft Message Queue) 1.0, 523–529
  MTS (Microsoft Transaction Server) 2.0, 522–523
  NTFS partition advantages, 451
  pre-installation checklist, 450–452
  RDS (Remote Data Service), 530
  SBS (Small Business Server) utilization, 658

SETUP.EXE file, 451
Site Server Express 2.0, 510–521
software requirements, 450
SP3 warning message, 452
stopping applications before installation, 451
transaction processing components, 522–529
troubleshooting, 450–454
WSH (Windows Scripting Host), 521
Windows NT 4.0 Service Pack 3 CD, MCSE toolkit component, 397
Windows NT Diagnostics dialog box, 889
Windows NT Diagnostics. *See* WinMSD
Windows NT Server 4.0
  32-bit NOS, 600
  build 1381 features, 602–607
  client connection issues, 610–611
  clustering support, 610
  described, 4–6
  Enterprise Edition, 5, 615–628
  Enterprise Edition variation, 5
  Macintosh support issues, 27
  Migration Tool for NetWare, 26
  Network Monitor, versus SMS Network Monitor 844–851
  operating system model, 600–602
  Option Pack and Service Pack 4, 7
  planning guidelines, 11–27
  processor support issues, 610
  RAS connection issues, 610
  release versions, 603
  server versus workstations, 607–612
  Services for NetWare, 26
  setup process, 27–44
  Small Business Server, 6, 649–730
  TCP/IP paradigm shift, 6
  Terminal Server Edition, 6, 629–648
  tuning issues, 608–609
  UNIX support issues, 27
  upgrading from a previous version, 43
  using as a user workstation, 612–613
  versus NT Workstation, 607–612
  versus Terminal Server Edition, 642–646
  widespread network professional support, 3–4
Windows NT Server 4.0 Secrets CD-ROM, CD-ROM library, 396
Windows NT Server domains, adding Windows NT Server 4.0 to, 25
Windows NT Server improvements, 969–986
Windows NT Service Pack Setup dialog box, hotfix version display, 544

Windows NT Services for UNIX, Service Pack
    4 add-on, 592–595
Windows NT Workstation and Server
    Resource Kit CDs, MCSE toolkit, 397
Windows NT Workstation CD, MCSE toolkit
    component, 396
Windows NT/MCSE toolkit
  Administrative Wizards, 392–393
  Event Viewer, 390
  Performance Monitor, 390–391
  Server Manager, 389–390
  third-party administration tools, 393–394
  User Manager for Domains, 388–389
Windows Qos program, 976–977
Windows Sockets
  described, 138
  TCP/IP interface support, 108
Windows subsystem (Microsoft Win32),
    937–938
Windows Support CD, MCSE toolkit
    component, 396
winipcfg command, 219
WINLOGON.EXE file, 939
WinMSD
  CONFIG.SYS file, 876
  Display tab sheet, 880
  Drives tab sheet, 880–883
  Environment tab sheet, 884–885, 892–893
  File System tab sheet, 883
  hardware profiles, 895
  Memory tab sheet, 888
  Network tab sheet, 885–888
  Resource tab sheet, 883–884
  Services tab, 888
  Startup/Shutdown tab sheet, 893–895
  system information reports, 889–890
  System tab sheet, 878–879
  Version tab sheet, 877–878
WINMSD command, 877
WINNT directory
  default setup directory, 37
  legacy application issues, 37
WINNT.EXE file, command line options, 42
WINNT32.EXE file, command line options, 42
WINS (Windows Internet Naming Service)
  benefits, 320–321
  client configuration, 326–327
  client/server components, 321
  DNS integration, 330
  installation, 322–323
  name resolution process, 322
  server configuration, 323–326
  SP4 hotfix, 556

TCP/IP support, 125
WINS addresses, TCP/IP configuration,
    192–195
WINS clients, described, 321
WINS Manager
  client configuration, 326–327
  server configuration, 323–326
  statistics view, 327–329
WINS servers
  configuration, 323–326
  described, 321
WinSock 2 program, described, 138
wizards
  Add Printer, 393, 64–68
  Add User accounts, 392
  Add/Remove Programs, 393
  Administrative, 392–393
  CMAK, 498–500
  Group Management, 393
  Install New Modem, 393
  License Compliance, 393
  Managing File and Folder Access, 393
  Network Client Administrator, 393
  New Expiration Policy, 484–485
  New Phonebook Entry Wizard, 353–354
  New Virtual Directory, 471
  New Web Site, 469–471
  Proxy Server Upgrade, 668
  QuickStart, 579–582
  Unicast On-Demand, 581
  Windows 2000 Server, 970
WLBS (Windows Load Balancing Server),
    Enterprise Edition, 625–626
workstations
  using Windows NT Server 4.0 as, 612–613
  versus servers, 607–612
workstation-side, Small Business Server
    setup, 698–719
wristbands, MCSE toolkit component, 394
WRQ, Reflection NFS Connection program,
    140
WSH (Windows Scripting Host), described,
    521

X
X.25, described, 364
X.509 digital certificates, Certificate Server
    1.0, 485–492
XCOPY commands, copying installation files
    to a system partition, 45

Y

Y2K (Year 2000) hotfix, Service Pack 4, 550–551
Yahoo!, name resolution uses, 260
Year 2000 issues
    Proxy Server 1.0/2.0 compliance, 667
    troubleshooting, 918

Z

Zero Administration windows, Windows 2000 Server, 985
zero-based budgeting, described, 439–440

zone files
    described, 267–268
    record class, 267
    record type, 267
Zone Properties dialog box, DNS configuration, 283–284
zone transfers, described, 272–273
zones
    DNS (Domain Name Service), 267–268
    DNS Manager record definitions, 277–279
    DNS Manager secondary menu options, 280–285

IDG BOOKS WORLDWIDE, INC. END-USER LICENSE AGREEMENT

READ THIS. You should carefully read these terms and conditions before opening the software packet(s) included with this book ("Book"). This is a license agreement ("Agreement") between you and IDG Books Worldwide, Inc. ("IDGB"). By opening the accompanying software packet(s), you acknowledge that you have read and accept the following terms and conditions. If you do not agree and do not want to be bound by such terms and conditions, promptly return the Book and the unopened software packet(s) to the place you obtained them for a full refund.

1. **License Grant.** IDGB grants to you (either an individual or entity) a nonexclusive license to use one copy of the enclosed software program(s) (collectively, the "Software") solely for your own personal or business purposes on a single computer (whether a standard computer or a workstation component of a multiuser network). The Software is in use on a computer when it is loaded into temporary memory (RAM) or installed into permanent memory (hard disk, CD-ROM, or other storage device). IDGB reserves all rights not expressly granted herein.

2. **Ownership.** IDGB is the owner of all right, title, and interest, including copyright, in and to the compilation of the Software recorded on the disk(s) or CD-ROM ("Software Media"). Copyright to the individual programs recorded on the Software Media is owned by the author or other authorized copyright owner of each program. Ownership of the Software and all proprietary rights relating thereto remain with IDGB and its licensers.

3. **Restrictions On Use and Transfer.**

    (a) You may only (i) make one copy of the Software for backup or archival purposes, or (ii) transfer the Software to a single hard disk, provided that you keep the original for backup or archival purposes. You may not (i) rent or lease the Software, (ii) copy or reproduce the Software through a LAN or other network system or through any computer subscriber system or bulletin-board system, or (iii) modify, adapt, or create derivative works based on the Software.

    (b) You may not reverse engineer, decompile, or disassemble the Software. You may transfer the Software and user documentation on a permanent basis, provided that the transferee agrees to accept the terms and conditions of this Agreement and you retain no copies. If the Software is an update or has been updated, any transfer must include the most recent update and all prior versions.

4. **Restrictions On Use of Individual Programs.** You must follow the individual requirements and restrictions detailed for each individual program in the "About the CD-ROM" appendix of this Book. These limitations are also contained in the individual license agreements recorded on the Software Media. These limitations may include a requirement that after using the program for a specified period of time, the user must pay a registration fee or discontinue use. By opening the

Software packet(s), you will be agreeing to abide by the licenses and restrictions for these individual programs that are detailed in the "About the CD-ROM" section and on the Software Media. None of the material on this Software Media or listed in this Book may ever be redistributed, in original or modified form, for commercial purposes.

5. **<u>Limited Warranty</u>.**

   (a) IDGB warrants that the Software and Software Media are free from defects in materials and workmanship under normal use for a period of sixty (60) days from the date of purchase of this Book. If IDGB receives notification within the warranty period of defects in materials or workmanship, IDGB will replace the defective Software Media.

   (b) IDGB AND THE AUTHOR OF THE BOOK DISCLAIM ALL OTHER WARRANTIES, EXPRESS OR IMPLIED, INCLUDING WITHOUT LIMITATION IMPLIED WARRANTIES OF MERCHANTABILITY AND FITNESS FOR A PARTICULAR PURPOSE, WITH RESPECT TO THE SOFTWARE, THE PROGRAMS, THE SOURCE CODE CONTAINED THEREIN, AND/OR THE TECHNIQUES DESCRIBED IN THIS BOOK. IDGB DOES NOT WARRANT THAT THE FUNCTIONS CONTAINED IN THE SOFTWARE WILL MEET YOUR REQUIREMENTS OR THAT THE OPERATION OF THE SOFTWARE WILL BE ERROR FREE.

   (c) This limited warranty gives you specific legal rights, and you may have other rights that vary from jurisdiction to jurisdiction.

6. **<u>Remedies</u>.**

   (a) IDGB's entire liability and your exclusive remedy for defects in materials and workmanship shall be limited to replacement of the Software Media, which may be returned to IDGB with a copy of your receipt at the following address: Software Media Fulfillment Department, Attn.: *Microsoft Windows NT Secrets, Option Pack Edition*, IDG Books Worldwide, Inc., 7260 Shadeland Station, Ste. 100, Indianapolis, IN 46256, or call 1-800-762-2974. Please allow three to four weeks for delivery. This Limited Warranty is void if failure of the Software Media has resulted from accident, abuse, or misapplication. Any replacement Software Media will be warranted for the remainder of the original warranty period or thirty (30) days, whichever is longer.

   (b) In no event shall IDGB or the author be liable for any damages whatsoever (including without limitation damages for loss of business profits, business interruption, loss of business information, or any other pecuniary loss) arising from the use of or inability to use the Book or the Software, even if IDGB has been advised of the possibility of such damages.

(c) Because some jurisdictions do not allow the exclusion or limitation of liability for consequential or incidental damages, the above limitation or exclusion may not apply to you.

7. **U.S. Government Restricted Rights.** Use, duplication, or disclosure of the Software by the U.S. Government is subject to restrictions stated in paragraph (c)(1)(ii) of the Rights in Technical Data and Computer Software clause of DFARS 252.227-7013, and in subparagraphs (a) through (d) of the Commercial Computer — Restricted Rights clause at FAR 52.227-19, and in similar clauses in the NASA FAR supplement, when applicable.

8. **General.** This Agreement constitutes the entire understanding of the parties and revokes and supersedes all prior agreements, oral or written, between them and may not be modified or amended except in a writing signed by both parties hereto that specifically refers to this Agreement. This Agreement shall take precedence over any other documents that may be in conflict herewith. If any one or more provisions contained in this Agreement are held by any court or tribunal to be invalid, illegal, or otherwise unenforceable, each and every other provision shall remain in full force and effect.

my2cents.idgbooks.com

Register This Book — And Win!

Visit **http://my2cents.idgbooks.com** to register this book and we'll automatically enter you in our fantastic monthly prize giveaway. It's also your opportunity to give us feedback: let us know what you thought of this book and how you would like to see other topics covered.

Discover IDG Books Online!

The IDG Books Online Web site is your online resource for tackling technology — at home and at the office. Frequently updated, the IDG Books Online Web site features exclusive software, insider information, online books, and live events!

10 Productive & Career-Enhancing Things You Can Do at www.idgbooks.com

- Nab source code for your own programming projects.
- Download software.
- Read Web exclusives: special articles and book excerpts by IDG Books Worldwide authors.
- Take advantage of resources to help you advance your career as a Novell or Microsoft professional.
- Buy IDG Books Worldwide titles or find a convenient bookstore that carries them.
- Register your book and win a prize.
- Chat live online with authors.
- Sign up for regular e-mail updates about our latest books.
- Suggest a book you'd like to read or write.
- Give us your 2¢ about our books and about our Web site.

You say you're not on the Web yet? It's easy to get started with IDG Books' *Discover the Internet,* available at local retailers everywhere.

CD-ROM Installation Instructions

Each software item on the *Microsoft Windows* NT Secrets, Option Pack Edition CD-ROM is located in its own folder. To install a particular piece of software, open its folder with My Computer or Internet Explorer. What you do next depends on what you find in the software's folder:

1. First, look for a ReadMe.txt file or a .doc or .htm document. If this is present, it should contain installation instructions and other useful information.

2. If the folder contains an executable (.exe) file, this is usually an installation program. Often it will be called Setup.exe or Install.exe, but in some cases the filename reflects an abbreviated version of the software's name and version number. Run the .exe file to start the installation process.

3. In the case of some simple software, the .exe file probably is the software — no real installation step is required. You can run the software from the CD to try it out. If you like it, copy it to your hard disk and create a Start menu shortcut for it.

The ReadMe.txt file in the CD-ROM's root directory may contain additional installation information, so be sure to check it.

For a listing of the software on the CD-ROM, see Appendix E.

Microsoft Product Warranty and Support Disclaimer

The Microsoft program was reproduced by IDG Books Worldwide, Inc. under a special arrangement with Microsoft Corporation. For this reason, IDG Books Worldwide, Inc. is responsible for the product warranty and for support. If your CD-ROM is defective, please return it to IDG Books Worldwide, Inc. which will arrange for its replacement. PLEASE DO NOT RETURN IT TO MICROSOFT CORPORATION. Any product support will be provided, if at all, by IDG Books Worldwide, Inc. PLEASE DO NOT CONTACT MICROSOFT CORPORATION FOR PRODUCT SUPPORT. End users of this Microsoft program shall not be considered "registered owners" of a Microsoft product and therefore shall not be eligible for upgrades, promotions, or other benefits available to "registered owners" of Microsoft products.